POLITICAL PROFILES

☆ ☆ ☆

The Kennedy Years

POLITICAL PROFILES

The Kennedy Years

EDITOR:

Nelson Lichtenstein, Ph.D., University of California, Berkeley

ASSOCIATE EDITOR:

Eleanora W. Schoenebaum, Ph.D., Columbia University

Facts On File, Inc.
119 West 57th Street, New York, N.Y 10019

POLITICAL PROFILES
The Kennedy Years

Library of Congress Catalog Card No. 76-20897
ISBN 0-87196-450-3
9 8 7 6 5 4 3 2 1

PRINTED IN THE UNITED STATES OF AMERICA

Contents

Preface

The Kennedy Years is one volume in the *Political Profiles* reference series. This volume contains the biographies of 502 individuals who played an important role in American politics in the early 1960s. When complete the entire *Political Profiles* series will consist of six volumes including biographies of more than 2,500 men and women who dominated American politics in the years since the end of World War II. Each volume in the series covers the period of a single presidential administration and profiles the several hundred figures who were most influential in shaping public life during that period.

Each entry is a detailed account of an individual's career, including his social and political background, or his major accomplishments and activities, and an assessment of his impact on politics, international affairs, social thought or political ideology. Individuals with long public careers, like Walter Reuther, Lyndon Johnson and Clark Clifford, appear in two or more volumes in the series. In such cases, each volume's profile briefly summarizes the individual's entire career but focuses on his activity during the years of the presidential administration covered by that volume. For example, John Connally's profile in *The Kennedy Years* records his role as Secretary of the Navy and his early record as governor of Texas. His entry in *The Johnson Years* focuses on his governorship, his recurring feuds with Texas liberals and the Mexican-American community and his close relationship with the President. Connally's longest entry, in the volume covering the Nixon Administration, provides a full account of his tenure as Secretary of the Treasury, White House adviser and an influential figure in the business community and the Republican Party.

This unique organizational structure enables the *Political Profiles* series to be continuously updated and provides a richness of personal detail, political context and historical perspective unavailable in any other biographical reference work. Readers can trace the career of an important figure systematically through several volumes or can compare the interaction of many individuals using just a single volume.

Each profile begins with the name of the individual, his or her date and place of birth, and the date and place of death. This headnote continues with the name of the most important office or offices he or she held, or the activity or occupation for which the subject was most noted during the period covered by the volume. In the case of those holding important political office, the years—and where relevant, the months—at which they began and ended service are also given. Thus, Robert McNamara is listed in this volume as "Secretary of Defense, January 1961—February 1968." Norman Mailer, however, is recorded simply as "Novelist, journalist."

The body of the profile then follows, its length roughly commensurate with the significance of the individual during the years covered by the volume. If the figure has another profile in a preceding or succeeding volume this is indicated by a bracketed notation in the text. The notation [*q.v.*] (i.e. *quod vide*) follows the names of other individuals whose profiles appear in the same volume. We have not given this notation following the names of presidents to avoid unnecessary repetition. Each profile ends with the initials of its author. Many also include brief suggestions referring the reader to the most readily available books or articles where additional information on the subject can be found.

One of the most critical tasks in the preparation of a biographical reference work is the selection of those to be included. Although a substantial portion, probably a majority of the choices, are self-evident, many individuals should be included who are significant and interesting but who are not of immediate and obvious importance. In choosing, we were guided by two questions: Did the individual under consideration have an important, measurable impact on American politics as defined in its commonly accepted and broadest sense? And second, even if the potential subject was not of lasting political importance, did he or she achieve such fame or notoriety that, for a moment, the person captured the political attention of the nation? We have included, therefore, not only elected and appointed officeholders but also influential journalists and intellectuals, business and labor leaders, civil rights and peace activists, leaders of left and right-wing movements and cultural and social trendsetters.

In some cases our selections were made ex officio: the president and vice president, all Supreme Court justices and cabinet officers and almost all congressional committee chairmen are included in each volume of the series. Beyond these categories, we were more selective. Because of the importance of the executive branch in the postwar era we have included the president's influential aides and advisers. *The Kennedy Years* also includes biographies of the most important figures from the Central Intelligence Agency, the Federal Bureau of Investigation, the military services and the Departments of Defense, State and Treasury. The importance of many of these individuals has only recently become apparent with the publication of the *Pentagon Papers* and congressional probes of intelligence activities.

Because of the traditional and prominent role in national politics played by almost every member of the U.S. Senate, we have included profiles of nearly the entire membership of that chamber. Given the larger membership and shorter terms in the House of Representatives, individual congressmen tend to hold less influence and are often more parochial in their interests than senators. Therefore, we have been more selective in choosing representatives to be profiled. The volume also contains profiles of governors and mayors who had an impact on national politics. Because of the importance of the civil rights struggle in the early 1960s, individuals from the American South are well represented. Among them are a number of local figures who under normal circumstances would not have appeared in a reference work of this sort. These include such men as Eugene "Bull" Connor, Birmingham, Ala., public safety director, and Leander Perez, justice of the peace in Plaquemines Parish, La. Also included are some 20 prominent civil rights activists.

Some of the more difficult selections we had to make involved choosing among those intellectuals, journalists and leaders of social movements whose influence was hard to measure. We chose, among others, Hannah Arendt, C. Wright Mills, Daniel Bell, William F. Buckley and Paul Goodman because of their roles as creative spokesmen for a particular intellectual trend or ideology. Left out of our list were many academic figures whose influence, though great within their disciplines, failed to touch a responsive chord in the larger body politic. Finally, we chose a number of figures who enjoyed a brief moment of national political recognition. Among these were Edwin Walker, the right-wing general, Francis Gary Powers, the U-2 spy plane pilot, and Lee Harvey Oswald, the probable assassin of the President.

One final point should be made about our selection process: We have sought to include those persons who collectively dominated the visible surface of public affairs in the early 1960s. The list of those included in *The Kennedy Years* contains no quotas. No attempt was made to provide an even geographical, political or ethnic balance. There are few women and no American Indians. Most of those profiled in the book are white males, many educated in Ivy League colleges and living in Washington, D.C., New York or a handful of other cities. Such, while we might have preferred otherwise, reflects the political realities of the early 1960s. Our volume, on the other hand, does not purport to be a collective biography of the American political and economic elite. For example, while two members of the politically active Rockefeller family are included, there are no representatives of the Mellon or DuPont dynasties.

Naturally, the selection of individuals included in each volume of the series is governed by the changing nature of national politics under each President. *The Truman Years*, for example, will have a larger number of trade union figures than does the present collection. The volume covering the Nixon Administration will contain more radicals, more women and minority group representatives than *The Eisenhower Years*.

Almost all of the profiles in this volume were written by trained historians, either advanced graduate students or Ph.Ds. Edward W. Knappman, the executive editor of Facts On File, conceived the *Political Profiles* series, worked closely with the editors in its completion and reviewed all profiles included in the volume. Judith Buncher, Howard Langer and Allen E. Schechter provided valuable assistance on many of the profiles. Martin Goldberg took on the arduous task of compiling the index. A distinguished editorial board of historians, social scientists and journalists assisted us in the selection of those to be profiled and reviewed many of the entries. In all cases, however, responsibility for the selection of subjects and for their content rests solely with Mr. Knappman and the editors.

The Kennedy Years contains several useful appendixes. It has a complete chronology of the period, the membership role of the entire 87th and 88th Congresses, a list of the Kennedy cabinet, the Supreme Court and the membership of the most important regulatory agencies. The volume also contains an extensive bibliography covering Kennedy era politics.

We thought it useful to include a career index among the appendixes for the convenience of those seeking information about related groups of individuals. Of course, the volume also contains an extensive combined name and subject index.

New York City   Nelson Lichtenstein

The Kennedy Years:
An Introduction

By the time John F. Kennedy was inaugurated 35th President of the United States, America's highest office held a political and imaginative influence unsurpassed in its history. Still unsullied by Vietnam and Watergate, the American presidency was regarded by most as a center of moral and intellectual guidance, as well as of political leadership. Fear of nuclear holocaust, belief in the permanency of the Cold War, and a post-New Deal sense that the federal government was directly responsible for the economic and social well-being of the nation had brought about an unprecedented centralization of authority in the White House. Kennedy assumed the presidency determined to give the office the activist orientation he and many other liberals thought it had lacked under President Eisenhower. The chief executive, Kennedy had declared in his campaign, "must be prepared to exercise the fullest powers of his office—all that are specified and some that are not." His ambition was to shape a new political rhetoric and intellectual style, not only for the government, but for the society as a whole. As journalist Henry Fairlie put it, Kennedy offered the American people "an elevated sense of national purpose," a "politics of expectation." Even flinty New England poet Robert Frost was extravagant at the inaugural. He foretold a "golden age of poetry and power/Of which this noonday's the beginning hour."

"The torch has been passed to a new generation of Americans," Kennedy assured the nation, "born in this century, tempered by war, disciplined by a hard and bitter peace. . . ." Like the 43-year-old President, the new men of his Administration represented the first truly postwar generation of American political leadership. They were almost two decades younger and had had a substantially different life experience than their predecessors under Eisenhower. Most had gone to college in the 1930's, and their liberalism and internationalism had been shaped by the social and political ferment of that era. Service in World War II abruptly shifted the course of many of their careers, but it gave to the future New Frontiersmen much of their sense of administrative self-confidence and intellectual elan. Some, among them the President, had been genuine combat heroes, but their most characteristic experience had been the opportunity to exercise great responsibility at an unusually early age. Robert McNamara and McGeorge Bundy were staff officers during the war who applied their formidable intelligence to the manipulation of the vast and complicated array of men and arms that modern war required. Walter Heller, John Kenneth Galbraith, Charles Hitch, Kermit Gordon, David Bell and other economists in the Kennedy Administration owe much of their faith in Keynesian central planning as young administrators at the Treasury Department, the Office of Price Administration and on the War Labor Board. An even more common experience was service in what was undoubtedly the Ivy League's favorite wartime agency, the Office of Strategic Services (OSS), later reconstituted as the Central Intelligence Agency (CIA). Roger Hilsman, Walt W. Rostow, Arthur Goldberg, Carl

Kaysen, Stewart Alsop, William Bundy and Arthur Schlesinger, Jr., had all sharpened their analytic skills in either the OSS or the CIA.

After the war few began careers in business or opted for elective office. Many stayed with the government until the end of the Truman Administration as mid-level policymakers and then began successful careers with Washington-oriented law firms. A remarkable number took advantage of expanding postwar opportunities in universities, foundations and defense-related research institutes. A 1962 survey of the top 200 officeholders in the Kennedy Administration showed that three times as many had come from academia as under President Eisenhower (18% vs. 6%), while only a fraction as many had business backgrounds (6% vs. 42%).

The new generation of officeholders with which Kennedy filled his top Administration posts was representative of America's cultural and political elite. These new men and women were members of the Establishment, a British term that gained currency in the U.S. during the first year of the Kennedy Administration. The academics were typically from Harvard, Yale and Columbia; the lawyers were from firms like Covington and Burling in Washington and Cravath, Swaine and Moore in New York. Many of the diplomats moved easily between investment banking or corporate law practice and government service. This group included Arthur Dean, Robert Bruce, W. Averell Harriman, Eugene Black, Adrian Fisher and George Ball, all of whom took regular posts in the new Administration. Equally important were those quintessential Establishment figures, like Robert Lovett, Clark Clifford, Lucius Clay, John McCloy and Dean Acheson, who remained for the most part in private life but who exercised great influence over Administration policy in times of confusion or crisis.

Trusting their own brilliance and eager to exercise the power they now controlled, the New Frontiersmen radiated self-assurance. They saw themselves as vigorous and hardworking technocrats, skillful administrators who through the intelligent manipulation of the political and economic equation could solve the nation's—and by extension the world's—problems. Therefore, decision-making in the White House would be "tough-minded" and "pragmatic," unswayed by sentiments, ideology and the usual pull of interest and faction. Arthur Schlesinger, Jr., later recalled a sense of "auto-intoxication" in the first few weeks of 1961 when it seemed that "intelligence was at last being applied to public affairs, euphoria reigned: we thought for a moment that the world was plastic and the future unlimited." Youthful and versatile, Robert Kennedy, Richard Goodwin and McGeorge Bundy exemplified the New Frontier ideal. Adlai Stevenson and Chester Bowles, considered soft and sentimentally liberal, did not, and their influence rapidly declined in high administration circles.

The glamour and drive that characterized the New Frontier "style" won the Kennedy presidency enormous popularity both at home and abroad. These action-oriented intellectuals, so many thought, would finally resolve intractable problems and get America moving again. Influential political scientists like James MacGregor Burns and Richard Neustadt applauded their crisp sense of administrative elan and centralization of decision-making as necessary for effective statesmanship in a complicated and dangerous world.

Within a decade historians and journalists would begin to view these New Frontiersmen in a less flattering light. By the early 1970's their self-confidence seemed to have been arrogant and elitist. They may have been the best and the brightest," as David Halberstam called them, but they often seemed blinded by the surface glare of their own brilliance. Seventy-eight-year-old Speaker of the House Sam Rayburn caught the measure of their weakness. "They may be every bit as intelligent as you say," he told Lyndon Johnson, the new Vice President, "but I'd feel a whole lot better about them if just one of them had run for sheriff once."

Kennedy considered the conduct of foreign affairs his Administration's most important responsibility and his own most difficult challenge. In an inaugural address devoted almost exclusively to world affairs, he pledged the nation "to pay any price, bear any burden, meet any hardship, support any friend, oppose any foe, to assure the survival and success of liberty." In the increasingly complex conflict with world Communism, New Frontiersmen like Gens. Maxwell Taylor and James Gavin and strategists Walt and Eugene Rostow were highly critical of Eisenhower-era policymakers. They thought their predecessors rigid and unimaginative, trapped by a dangerous and ultimately ineffective overreliance upon the massive nuclear deterrent and upon an ideology of unsophisticated anti-Communism. Instead, they sought a more "flexible response" to the Communists, one that would meet the new challenge posed by local insurgencies and wars of national liberation and allow the American government a wide range of policy options to meet any threat.

At its most constructive the new approach called for American encouragement of progressive democracy in the underdeveloped world and an extensive program of economic assistance. The Alliance for Progress and the Peace Corps were notable programs advancing this aim. Administration liberals like Aldolph Berle, George McGovern, G. Mennen Williams, Roger Hilsman, Sargent Shriver and Teodoro Moscoso were closely identified with this policy.

But new counterinsurgency efforts were also part of a sophisticated strategy of graduated response to Communist military and political advances. Kennedy took personal pride in the Green Berets, whose esprit de corps he thought typified the New Frontier's sense of determination and adventure. Backed by a growing conventional warfare capability, the Green Berets and other special forces were to provide the muscle to express the new theories of limited war that gained favor in the McNamara-era Pentagon. White House special assistant Theodore Sorenson explained, "It was necessary to build our own non-nuclear forces to the point where any aggressor would be confronted with the same poor choice Kennedy wanted to avoid: humiliation or escalation. A limited Communist conventional action, in short, could best be deterred by a capacity to respond effectively in kind."

The capacity to wage limited warfare opened to American leaders an arena in which to demonstrate the credibility of the national "resolve" far below the dangerous threshold of nuclear confrontation. The outcome of each conflict was seen as important for its long-term psychological impact on Russian policymakers as much as for its immediate tangible objectives.

Such a strategic viewpoint tended to transform minor difficulties in remote places into major foreign policy crises.

Except for the routine day-to-day conduct of foreign policy, Kennedy Administration strategists ignored the State Department's bureaucracy and, after the Bay of Pigs fiasco, devalued the advice of the Central Intelligence Agency and the Joint Chiefs of Staff as well. Even relatively minor decisions were usually made by an informal group of top White House aides who were advised, when it was felt necessary, by important non-governmental figures like Acheson, McCloy and Clifford. Policy decisions were often reached in a breathless and hurried atmosphere. Laos, Cuba, Berlin and Vietnam all produced issues that were considered important military-diplomatic confrontations and tests of American resolve that demanded immediate action and a firm response.

The pattern for "crisis management" was most perfectly executed in October 1962, when nuclear-armed missiles supplied by the Soviet Union were reported on the island of Cuba. Kennedy convened a special meeting of the Executive Committee of the National Security Council (Excom). The group met almost continuously for more than a week. Policy options were discussed, discarded and discussed again. A "quarantine" of the island, the first of a prepared series of rapidly escalating measures, was finally decided upon. Only after the decision for the blockade was made were American allies, the bulk of Congress and the American people informed. Fortunately, the leaders of the Soviet Union were convinced by the show of American resolve. They ordered their ships to respect the blockade; a potential nuclear confrontation was narrowly avoided.

Kennedy Administration policymakers also sought to "manage" the U.S. commitment to Vietnam, but there the conflict was far more protracted and multifaceted than in Cuba. With the erosion of popular support for the regime of Ngo Dinh Diem and the growth of the Communist insurgency, Kennedy and his close circle of advisers found themselves facing progressively more difficult choices. While the President was not as much of a "hawk" as Taylor, Rostow, McNamara and Rusk, he was nevertheless determined to avoid a defeat and preserve American options there. Ironically, each escalation of the American commitment in Vietnam narrowed the freedom of choice with which American policymakers could approach the next crisis. As George Ball put it 15 years later, "Time relentlessly destroys unexercised options." By the time of Kennedy's death, a major reversal in policy would have been necessary for the U.S. to avoid further escalation of the war.

The problem of domestic economic growth was intimately linked by the rhetoric of New Frontiersmen to American success or failure in the Cold War. In his campaign for the presidency, Kennedy pledged to "get the country moving again." Although the phrase was often used in a vague and symbolic sense, its specific meaning centered on what most economists considered the disappointing rate of growth in America's postwar Gross National Product (GNP). Administration economists particularly hoped to increase the GNP growth rate from 2% to 3% under Eisenhower to the level the Soviets then claimed, 4% to 6%. Such an increase would help fulfill traditional Democratic Party commitments to a high level of employment and a larger level of federal social welfare expenditure, but it would also assure future American parity with the USSR in the arms race and demonstrate to the underdeveloped world Western capitalism's continuous vitality.

Three schools of thought vied for influence in the economic decision-making councils of the new Administration. The first was that of fiscal orthodoxy, represented by Secretary of the Treasury C. Douglas Dillon and by Federal Reserve Board Chairman William McChesney Martin. Dillon and Martin thought that the balance of payments deficit was the most important economic issue, feared that inflation threatened the standard of living and argued that business confidence was a vital key to economic growth. Kennedy's inaugural call for sacrifice and dedication placed him temperamentally, if not intellectually, among the fiscal conservatives.

Counterposed to Dillon and Martin were the "new economists," the American followers of John Maynard Keynes, including John Kenneth Galbraith, Paul Samuelson and Walter Heller, chairman of the Council of Economic Advisers (CEA). They favored the direct use of government fiscal and monetary policy as a tool to maintain full employment and increase the rate of economic growth. According to Keynesian theory, in a period of recession a planned budget deficit would have the effect of increasing aggregate demand within the economy, thus spurring the private sector and, ultimately, increasing tax revenues sufficient to balance the federal budget once again. The inflationary threat inherent in such a policy, so the argument ran, could be stemmed by the use of budget surpluses when the economy became overheated. By the mid-1960's such decisions over the size and timing of budget surpluses and deficits would be called "fine-tuning" the economy.

The Keynesians were themselves divided into two groups. A group led by Galbraith, and backed in the Congress by such liberals as Paul Douglas (D, Ill.) and Albert Gore (D, Tenn.), strongly urged a substantial expansion of public spending to improve public services and rectify what they claimed was an imbalance between public and private spending. A second group of Keynesians, closely associated with the Council of Economic Advisers, proposed to increase aggregate demand by a massive tax reduction rather than an increase in government spending. Heller proposed a $13 billion package of tax reductions and tax reforms. Such a program would have had the effect of putting investment and spending decisions in the hands of individuals and corporations. Politically, it was more acceptable than a massive increase in government spending to moderates and conservatives in both the Administration and Congress.

By mid-1962 Kennedy had been convinced that the orthodox policy pursued by Dillon and Martin had failed and that the tax cut outlined by the CEA was necessary to stimulate faster economic growth. Although the tax reduction decision had profound social and political consequences, Kennedy and Heller saw the idea in administrative and technical terms. Nothing better exemplified the spirit of the New Frontier than Kennedy's argument for a policy of fiscal innovation before a Yale audience in June

1962. Attacking the economic "myths"—chiefly the belief in a balanced budget at all times—that he thought retarded congressional action and darkened public understanding, he went on to assert, "Most of the problems. . .that we now face are technical problems. They are very sophisticated judgments which did not lend themselves to the great sort of 'passionate movements' which have stirred this country so often in the past." The Kennedy tax cut, ultimately totaling about $11.5 billion, was finally passed in February 1964. Combined with the 7% investment tax credit of 1962, a liberalization of the depreciation allowance on new plant and equipment and increased federal expenditures on space and the military, the Kennedy-Johnson fiscal program inaugurated the longest period of sustained economic growth since the Depression. The boom lifted the real income of rich and poor and helped pay for the expanded social programs begun under the Administration of Lyndon Johnson.

Although he was hailed as the first Keynesian in the White House, Kennedy's application of the "new economics" left the basic shape of the American economy little changed. Most of the reform provisions of the original Kennedy tax-cut bill were dropped by the Administration to win support of congressional conservatives, and the final tax legislation was mildly regressive. The Kennedy fiscal program did not attempt central planning for the economy. Economist Robert Lekachman labeled the new policy "commercial Keynesianism" because crucial investment decisions were still left in the hands of banks and corporations.

The Kennedy Administration had adequate support to carry out its new fiscal and foreign policy programs, but the President met frustration and disappointment when he put the rest of his legislative program before Congress. At first glance the President would seem to have few obstacles in the national legislature. In 1958 the Democratic Party had won major victories in the off-year elections. Attractive new liberals like Philip Hart (D, Mich), Eugene McCarthy (D, Minn.) and Edmund Muskie (D, Me.) added luster to the almost two-thirds majorities the Party held in each House of Congress. In 1960 the Party lost a few seats in the House, but in 1962 it did surprisingly well by avoiding the reverses the president's party usually suffers in an off-year election.

Unfortunately for the President, the vast majorities the Democrats held in the 87th Congress (262-174 in the House; 65-35 in the Senate) were calculated on the basis of party label rather than on grounds of political philosophy. The real division in both chambers took place not between Democrats and Republicans but between a conservative coalition of Southern Democrats and Republicans and a shifting alliance of liberals and moderates, chiefly Democrats, but aided on occasion by a few liberal Republicans from the Northeast and Northwest. The conservative coalition held a slight majority in the House; the liberals and moderates were somewhat ahead in the Senate. But in fact the conservative coalition dominated both by virtue of its control of the committee system, the weakness and disorganization of the opposition and the conservative bias of the Senate rules, which permitted use of the powerful filibuster tactic.

About three-quarters of all seats in the House and about half in the Senate were "safe" seats, which did not change hands except upon the death or retirement of the incumbent. Such seats were frequently rural, and usually conservative. Many were located in the South or Midwest, bastions of the conservative coalition. Representing these seats and building up long years of seniority, Southern Democrats came to command a majority of the powerful committee chairmanships: 14 of 21 in the House, 10 of 16 in the Senate. Many of these chairmen had first been elected to Congress before World War II, some even before the vast social and political changes inaugurated by the Depression and the New Deal. On the House side there was Carl Vinson (D, Ga.), chairman of the Armed Services Committee, who had first entered Congress in 1914. With only a few years less seniority, there was Clarence Cannon (D, Mo.), elected in 1923, who chaired the Appropriations Committee, followed by Wright Patman (D, Tex.), the populist chairman of the Banking and Currency Committee who was first elected to the House in 1929. Rep. Howard W. Smith (D, Va.), powerful chairman of the Rules Committee and a pillar of the ultra-conservative Byrd machine in Virginia, had held House office for three decades. A relative newcomer, but one of the most powerful and knowledgeable men in the lower chamber, was Wilbur Mills (D, Ark.), chairman of the Ways and Means Committee. In 1961 he was only 55 and had been a member of the House since 1939.

In the Senate seniority was neither as great nor as significant as it was in the House. Although the average senator was six years older than the average representative (59 vs. 53), many members of the upper chamber had held careers in state politics, business and in the House itself before arriving in the Senate. Many of the most powerful senators had first been elected in the 1940's, including wealthy Robert S. Kerr (D, Okla.), chairman of the Aeronautical and Space Sciences Committee, and the dean of the Southerners, Richard Russell (D, Ga.) of the Armed Services Committee. A. Willis Robertson (D, Va.) of Banking and Currency and Harry F. Byrd (D, Va.) of Finance, products of the Byrd organization, were champions of frugal government. At the Judiciary Committee, James O. Eastland (D, Miss.) held a strategic chairmanship in which he could bottle up civil rights legislation. Everett M. Dirksen (R, Ill.), the Republican minority leader, frequently cooperated with the Southern Democrats to resist Kennedy Administration social welfare legislation, but he broke with the Southerners during the climactic debates over civil rights in 1963 and 1964.

Liberals and moderates in Congress could marshall neither the power nor the parliamentary skill of the conservative coalition. In one of their rare victories, they defeated the conservatives in January 1961, when both Kennedy and Speaker Sam Rayburn (D, Tex.) put their prestige behind a move to expand and liberalize the House Rules Committee. By the narrowest of margins, 217-213, they won. Thereafter Kennedy was considerably less successful; his aid-to-education, medicare and minimum-wage bills were either defeated or greatly diluted. By the end of the summer of 1961, Tom Wicker reported, "Kennedy has lost Congress."

One reason for these defeats was the lack of effective and forceful leadership in Congress. Although neither Lyndon Johnson nor Sam Rayburn were liberals, they had in the late 1950s provided the congressional Democrats with strong leadership on national issues. More importantly, the two Texans had disciplined to some degree the conservative committee chairmen. But by the middle of 1961 Johnson was vice president, and Rayburn was dying of cancer. Their replacements, Sen. Mike Mansfield (D, Mont.) and Rep. John McCormack (D, Mass.) were more liberal, but neither man had the political stature of his predecessor. As a result, power in the Congress was even more fragmented, falling naturally into the hands of the strategically placed conservatives. Most rank-and-file liberals exhibited neither the aptitude nor the appetite to master and apply the intricate legislative techniques necessary to have influence in the Congress. As a consequence, they were unable to make their sizeable numerical voice heard.

Furthermore, many liberals came from marginal districts in the North and Far West. A few urban liberals with strong ethnic constituencies did achieve important committee chairmanships. Two of these were Emanuel Celler (D, N.Y.) at the Judiciary Committee and Adam Clayton Powell (D, N.Y.) at the Education and Labor Committee. But many liberals failed to achieve long seniority. In the House liberals frequently used their seats to run for statewide office or move up to the Senate. Some, like George McGovern (D, S.D.) and Chester Bowles (D, Conn.), joined the new Administration. Others, especially several in the Senate, Spoke for a national liberal constituency, sometimes at odds with President Kennedy and his pragmatic approach to domestic legislative policies. Sens. Wayne Morse, (D, Ore.), Estes Kefauver (D, Tenn.), Ernest Gruening (D, Alaska), William Proxmire (D, Wisc.), Joseph Clark (D, Pa.) and Paul Douglas (D, Ill.) were members of this outspoken but often isolated group. They were issue-oriented political leaders, strong civil rights and civil liberties advocates, and vigorous opponents of the conservative coalition. These liberals were often suspicious of Kennedy for his willingness to compromise with the congressional conservatives. In August 1962 they staged a revolt against the Administration over the President's proposal to put the new Communications Satellite Corporation under substantial private control. Ten Senate liberals began a filibuster against the bill. They were defeated when Southern Democrats joined Administration loyalists in a successful vote, the first since 1927, to end debate by invoking cloture on the bill.

The great influence of the conservative coalition in Congress had long thwarted liberal efforts to pass effective civil rights legislation. In 1961 President Kennedy seemed to accept continued defeat on this issue when he failed to include a civil rights measure in his initial legislative program sent to Congress shortly after his inauguration. However, the national stalemate over civil rights was broken in the early 1960s and in a way even many civil rights advocates had never expected. Beginning with the Montgomery bus boycott of 1955, traditionally voiceless and powerless Southern blacks formed a mass movement that soon had an immense impact throughout the entire body politic. Because of the political resistance encountered, especially in the South, but also in Washington, the movement adopted an ever more militant strategy and made an increasingly radical critique of American society.

For several decades before 1960 the NAACP had waged a methodical, largely successful effort in the federal courts to end de jure segregation. Skilled lawyers such as Jack Greenberg and Thurgood Marshall had moved case after case to the Supreme Court, where liberal justices like William O. Douglas, Hugo Black and Chief Justice Earl Warren had led the Court in its increasingly favorable interpretations of the law. Although the Warren Court would continue to hand down landmark civil rights and civil liberties decisions throughout the 1960s, the main problem facing civil rights activists at the turn of the decade was enforcement of existing law. The white South had embarked on a program of massive resistance, while in Washington both Presidents Eisenhower and Kennedy were reluctant to confront the politically powerful region on this explosive issue.

This stalemate was shattered by the mobilization of Southern blacks on a scale not seen since Reconstruction and by the emergence of two distinct but complementary generations of black leadership. The first leadership group came out of the Southern Baptist ministry. Its preeminent representative and the clear moral leader of the entire civil rights movement for over a decade was Martin Luther King, Jr. As a 26-year-old minister newly arrived in Montgomery, Ala., King had won national recognition as the leader of the citywide bus boycott there in 1955. He brought to the civil rights movement two principles that would guide it through the early 1960s, the philosophy of nonviolent direct action and the tactic of massive civil disobedience. King worked through the Southern Christian Leadership Conference (SCLC), which he had organized in 1957. Based solidly on the black church, the SCLC provided the link between more traditional civil rights groups like the NAACP and an increasingly radical generation of student activists both in the North and South. Among the most important SCLC leaders in the early 1960s were Fred Shuttlesworth, Wyatt T. Walker and Ralph Abernathy, King's closest associate.

On Feb. 1, 1960 four black North Carolina college students sat down at a segregated Woolworth lunch counter in Raleigh to demand service. Their nonviolent sit-in captured the imagination of black college students and awakened a new generation of young activists who soon assumed leadership positions in the sit-in movement as it swept through the entire South. With the SCLC's encouragement, many of these students formed the Student Nonviolent Coordinating Committee (SNCC) in April 1960. SNCC activists soon became the shock troops of the civil rights revolution. By 1961 and 1962 young SNCC workers like Robert Moses, John Lewis and James Forman were conducting voter registration projects in the most remote and virulently racist counties of the Mississippi and Alabama black belts. They were the most insistent that the poorest Southern blacks be involved in the civil rights struggle, and they were the first to recognize the radical implications of the movement, not only for the South but for the North as well.

By exposing and resisting local Southern patterns of discrimination, movement activists sought to mobilize the black community, arouse Northern public opinion and prod the federal government to corrective action. In May 1961, for example, the Congress of Racial Equality, a predominantly Northern civil rights group with ties to the peace movement, began a Freedom Ride throughout the South to "test" a recent Supreme Court decision banning segregation in interstate transportation. Led by James Farmer, the riders encountered white violence in North Carolina, Alabama and Mississippi. The destruction of a bus in Alabama and the repeated beatings suffered by the freedom riders shocked Northern public opinion. A reluctant Kennedy Administration now put pressure on Southern governors to protect the riders, and in September 1961 the Interstate Commerce Commission finally issued an order desegregating all interstate transportation facilities. "Our intention," Farmer later explained, "was to provoke the Southern authorities into arresting us and thereby prod the Justice Department into enforcing the law. . . ."

The Freedom Rides also exemplified the response of the Kennedy Administration to the civil rights movement itself. Most members of the new Administration, especially in the Justice Department, were personally sympathetic to integrationist demands, but both Attorney General Robert Kennedy and his brother were reluctant to act against the white South except in response to a major crisis. Only when civil rights activists raised the pitch of their activity to an embarrassingly high level did the Administration begin to put its weight firmly behind the movement. "We put on pressure and create a crisis and then they react," was the way Farmer described the situation.

This pattern was played out on a grand scale in Birmingham, Ala., in the spring of 1963. Under SCLC direction massive demonstrations were organized in April and May 1963 to protest widespread discrimination practiced by the Birmingham business community and by the city government. Although Robert Kennedy and his representative, Burke Marshall, urged King and Shuttlesworth to "cool off" the protests, the demonstrations continued. While television cameras transmitted the scene across the nation, intransigent city officials used fire hoses and police dogs against the demonstrators and filled the city jails with school-age marchers. The demonstrations failed to win more than a compromise desegregation plan in Birmingham, but they were decisive in sparking a wave of some 700 other protests across the South in the summer of 1963, in winning Northern public opinion strongly to the side of the civil rights movement and in forcing the Kennedy Administration to finally make its own commitment to the passage of substantial civil rights legislation. The historic 1963 March on Washington, organized by Bayard Rustin and A. Philip Randolph, symbolized the power and achievement of this new force in American politics.

The civil rights movement was the most dramatic new social movement of the early 1960s, but the revival of political controversy after the quiescence of the 1950s also generated a new burst of activity on the right. An aggressive brand of American conservatism enjoyed a considerable revival during the Kennedy Administration. Some social scientists called the new politics "pseudo-conservatism" and explained its rise in terms of the "status anxiety" of newly affluent groups in a pluralist society. The burst of ultra-conservative activity during the Kennedy years was in responde to what many considered the dangers to older values posed by the sophisticated and youthful Democratic President. In addition, the "fall" of Cuba and the continued unresolved tension of the Cold War created a milieu in which an extreme form of anti-Communism could flourish.

The most important radical-right organization in the early 1960s was Robert Welch's John Birch Society, which counted a membership of between 60,000 and 100,000 in 1963. Another well-publicized group was the Christian Anti-Communist Crusade, led by Fred C. Schwarz, which held numerous mass rallies and won the support of important congressional figures like Rep. Walter Judd (R, Minn.) and Sen. Thomas Dodd (D, Conn.). Right-wing oil billionaire H.L. Hunt spent an estimated $1 million on radical right causes; his radio program was carried by 212 stations. A revived spirit of militant anti-Communism also infected the military. Gens. Edwin C. Walker and Curtis LeMay came into public conflict with the Administration due to their outspoken comments on diplomatic and defense policies toward the Communist nations. The growth of the new conservatism was also reflected in the influence of William F. Buckley's *National Review* and, more importantly, in the rising stature enjoyed by Sen. Barry Goldwater (R, Ariz.) and other anti-Establishment conservatives in the Republican Party.

"The politics of our country have grown dangerously lop-sided," wrote I.F. Stone in early 1962. "There is a vocal extreme right. There is a center, which Mr. Kennedy had preempted. There is no longer a liberal opposition." Indeed, by the early 1960s the radical impulse, which had motivated so many trade unionists and intellectuals in the 1930s, seemed to have exhausted itself. Under the conservative leadership of George Meany, the newly merged American Federation of Labor-Congress of Industrial Organizations was at a standstill, with its membership stagnant and its political influence declining. More liberal, activist unionists like Walter Reuther, James Carey and A. Philip Randolph found themselves frustrated and isolated within the AFL-CIO.

Like the labor movement upon which they had once placed so much hope, most left-wing intellectuals had also grown reconciled to the liberal capitalism and pluralist democracy of postwar America. Repelled by the rise of communist and fascist movements in Europe and Asia, many American leftists had become skeptical about the democratic potential of mass politics and the efficacy of socialist ideology. In his *End of Ideology*, published in 1960, Daniel Bell spoke for this generation of ex-radical intellectuals. "There is today," wrote Bell, "a rough consensus among intellectuals on political issues: the acceptance of a welfare state, the desirability of decentralized power, a system of mixed economy and of political pluralism. . . . The ideological age has ended."

Bell's rough consensus framed much of the social and political thought of the era, but it was challenged, at first timidly, by a few scattered individuals and groups who would soon have a great impact on American society. The peace issue was one of the first questions to revive political controversy. By the late 1950s an older generation of socialists and pacifists led by Norman Thomas and A.J. Muste were joined by liberals such as Norman Cousins, Eleanor Roosevelt and Linus Pauling in a campaign for an end to the testing of nuclear weapons and a reduction in the arms race. SANE (Committee for a Sane Nuclear Policy) was the most prominent organization in this new movement. Peace groups were spurred to greater activity in 1961, when both the U.S. and the USSR resumed nuclear testing after a three-year moratorium. In 1963 several demonstrations were held and peace candidates were entered in several elections. Radical intellectuals like H. Stuart Hughes and I.F. Stone won a larger and more respectful audience. After the signing of a limited nuclear test ban treaty between the U.S. and the USSR, the peace movement shifted much of its attention from the specific issues of atmospheric nuclear testing to the growing U.S. involvement in Southeast Asia and broader aspects of American foreign policy.

The peace movement attracted many young people to its ranks, but its leadership came from a generation already adult when the atomic age began. What came to be known as the New Left was in the early 1960s almost exclusively a college-age phenomenon. As an organized movement it hardly existed, but the ideas that would characterize the New Left were virtually all in place by the end of the Kennedy years. There was a sense that the cultural and political sterility of the previous decade was lifting and that the new generation could have an impact on the larger society. The activism of the civil rights movement inspired many Northern white students, as did the seeming idealism of the new and youthful President. At its 1962 Port Huron convention the newly formed Students for a Democratic Society emphasized the alienation of contemporary life and declared that "politics has the function of bringing people out of isolation and into community."

Three American intellectuals had a special impact on the new generation of politically-minded young people. Paul Goodman provided a cultural and social critique of American capitalism and called for decentralized and democratic decision-making throughout the society, an idea the New Left later adopted as "participatory democracy." Michael Harrington demonstrated the extent of poverty amid affluence in his *The Other America*, a book that had an extraordinary impact on both high government policymakers and young college students when it was published in 1962. Finally, C. Wright Mills made an impassioned attack upon the American "power elite" in a series of books and articles published in the late 1950s and early 1960s. He argued that it was the "young intelligentsia," both in America and the third world, who were to be the main agency of social change.

Even in their most apocalyptic visions, few political or social commentators of either the left or the right could have foreseen the social turmoil and political division of the years after 1963. For all the controversy over civil rights and Cuba, for all the stirring words of the New Frontier, the Kennedy era was a stable period. The young President failed to break the 20-year stalemate over domestic social legislation; he presided over a continued—if somewhat more sophisticated—Cold War concensus on foreign policy issues; his innovations in economic policy were more notable in theory than in practice. Yet, Kennedy's attractive personality and his faculty for generating a strong emotional response among the American people tapped widespread feelings of hope and idealism, despite the New Frontier's own mistrust of enthusiasm and passion in politics.

Ironically, it was Kennedy's assassination that seemed to shatter the unquestioning self-confidence in the nations's future, especially among the young. The assassination, wrote Christopher Lasch, "helped to dispel the illusion that the United States was somehow exempt from history, a nation uniquely favored and destined . . . to be spared the turmoil and conflict which had always characterized the politics of other countries."

POLITICAL PROFILES
The Kennedy Years

ABERNATHY, RALPH D(AVID)
b. March 11, 1926; Linden, Ala.
Secretary-Treasurer, Southern Christian Leadership Conference, 1957-65; Vice President, 1965-68; President, 1968- .

The tenth of 12 children, Abernathy was born and raised on his parents' 500-acre farm in Morengo County, Ala. Ordained a Baptist minister in 1948, he received a B.S. from Alabama State University in Montgomery in 1950 and an M.A. in sociology from Atlanta University the next year.

Abernathy was appointed pastor of the First Baptist Church in Montgomery, Ala., in 1951 and when Martin Luther King, Jr. [q.v.], became pastor at the city's Dexter Avenue Baptist Church in 1954, the two young ministers soon became close friends. In December 1955 King was chosen by the local black community to lead the historic Montgomery bus boycott. Throughout the protest, King later wrote, Abernathy was his "closest associate and most trusted friend," aiding King in organization and strategy-making and taking charge of the boycott when King was out of Montgomery. In January 1957, shortly after the boycott's end, Abernathy's home and church were bombed. He helped found the Southern Christian Leadership Conference (SCLC) in 1957 and was elected secretary-treasurer at the same time that King was elected the organization's president. [See EISENHOWER Volume]

With their deep friendship and shared commitment to nonviolence, Abernathy became King's top aide in the SCLC. A short, stocky man, Abernathy was less intellectual and more informal in his preaching than King and had, as King once said, "the gift of laughing people into positive action." He was King's constant companion during major protests. In 1961, at King's urging, Abernathy moved to Atlanta, site of the SCLC's headquarters, and became pastor of the West Hunter Street Baptist Church there.

During the 1961 Freedom Rides, Abernathy, then still in Montgomery, opened his church to the interstate riders and was arrested on May 25 when he accompanied other ministers in a protest at Montgomery's segregated bus terminal. In December 1961 Abernathy joined King in aiding a desegregation campaign in Albany, Ga. The two were arrested for leading a march there in December, found guilty of the charges stemming from that arrest in February 1962 and began serving their 45-day jail sentence together in July. They were soon released from jail when someone anonymously paid their fines. At Abernathy's urging the SCLC stepped up demonstrations in Albany, and he and King were again arrested. Both were given suspended sentences, and the Albany campaign ended inconclusively soon after.

The SCLC decided to mount a major desegregation drive in Birmingham, Ala., in 1963. With King and SCLC Executive Director Wyatt Tee Walker [q.v.], Abernathy went to Birmingham in January 1963 to plan the demonstrations and to build support for the protest among local black leaders. The massive campaign began on April 3 and on April 12, Good Friday, King, Abernathy and the Rev. Fred Shuttlesworth

1

[*q.v.*], the key local leader of the protest, headed a march to city hall in defiance of a court injunction prohibiting further demonstrations. They were arrested and King and Abernathy remained in jail until April 20. Abernathy participated in negotiations with the city's white leadership early in May; on May 10 he joined King and Shuttlesworth in announcing that an agreement had been reached ending the dramatic Birmingham campaign. Abernathy then aided a desegregation effort in Danville, Va., in the summer of 1963. After a bomb exploded at a black church in Birmingham on Sept. 15, 1963, killing four young black girls, Abernathy was one of seven black leaders who met with President Kennedy on Sept. 19 to discuss the Birmingham situation.

Abernathy participated in an SCLC-aided desegregation campaign in St. Augustine, Fla., in 1964 and the Selma, Ala., protests and march in 1965. He helped King plan the Poor People's Campaign to protest poverty and unemployment which was scheduled for the spring of 1968. Abernathy was with King when he was assassinated in Memphis, Tenn. on April 4, 1968 and was immediately named King's successor as president of the SCLC. Under Abernathy's leadership the SCLC remained committed to King's principles of nonviolence and interracial cooperation and went forward with the planned Poor People's Campaign in the spring and summer of 1968. [See JOHNSON Volume]

[CAB]

ACHESON, DEAN G(OODERHAM)
b. April 11, 1893; Middletown, Conn.
d. Oct. 12, 1971; Silver Spring, Md.
Foreign policy adviser.

After graduating from Harvard Law School in 1918, Acheson served as private secretary to Supreme Court Justice Louis Brandeis and then entered private law practice with the Washington firm of Covington and Burling. With the exception of a few months spent as undersecretary of the treasury in 1933, Acheson remained out of government until he was appointed assistant secretary of state in 1941. Four years later he became undersecretary of state. In this post Acheson helped plan the United Nations and formulate both the Truman Doctrine and the Marshall Plan.

Acheson left the State Department to return to his law practice in 1947 but was recalled to become Secretary of State in 1949. As Secretary he put into effect the policy of containment of the Soviet Union that shaped the American response in the early stages of the Cold War. Assuming that Russia was bent on world conquest and consequently that negotiations would be useless, he concluded that Communist expansion could only be deterred by overwhelming economic, political and arms aid to countries on the perimeter of the Communist bloc, particularly Germany. Before and after Acheson retired from office in 1953, he was attacked by Republicans for "losing" China, pursuing a "no-win" policy in Korea and "coddling" Communists in government. [See TRUMAN, EISENHOWER Volumes]

Although formally out of government, Acheson served as a foreign policy adviser during the Kennedy Administration. In March 1961 Kennedy invited him to undertake a special study of German problems, including those posed by the Russian threat to sign a peace treaty with East Germany and make Berlin a "free city" theoretically independent of Eastern or Western control.

Acheson's analysis and his recommendations reflected his view of Communism and the pivotal role Germany should play in American strategy. He saw the confrontation over Berlin as a Russian pretext for testing the general American resolve to resist a Soviet challenge. Because the U.S. was engaged in a conflict of wills over a strategically important area, America had no choice but to show the Soviet Union that it would risk nuclear war rather than abandon the status quo in Germany. In Acheson's view negotiations would only be a sign of weakness. Consequently, he recommended that America build up both its conventional and nuclear forces in preparation for an "inevitable" armed confrontation with the Soviet Union. However Kennedy, seeking a more flexible approach to the conduct of the Cold War, rejected Acheson's advice and in July 1961 announced a policy of negotiation combined with continued military buildup.

Acheson was again called to advise the President in October 1962 after Kennedy learned of the presence of Soviet missiles in Cuba. Believing that the missiles not only threatened America's security but also its position as leader of the Western world, Acheson advocated bombing of the missile sites to show U.S. resolve against this new Soviet challenge. He opposed Attorney General Robert Kennedy's [q.v.] suggested blockade, believing that any delay in attacking would increase Soviet missile strength and eventually necessitate a larger American counter-strike, thus increasing the chances of nuclear war. Again rejecting Acheson's advice, Kennedy announced a "quarantine" of the island and demanded the removal of the missiles on Oct. 22.

Acheson remained a foreign affairs consultant throughout the Johnson Administration. Although an early supporter of a policy of military victory in Vietnam, he recommended de-escalation of the conflict in March 1968 after making an independent study of the situation at the request of the President. Acheson died of a heart attack while working at his home on Oct. 12, 1971. [See JOHNSON Volume]

[EWS]

AIKEN, GEORGE D(AVID)
b. Aug. 30, 1892; Dummerston, Vt.
Republican Senator, Vt., 1941-74.

Aiken was raised on a farm near Brattleboro, Vt. After graduating from high school he entered the nursery business and became one of the nation's leading experts in the commercial cultivation of wild flowers. In 1930 he was elected to the Vermont House of Representatives, and he became its speaker in 1933. Two years later Aiken was elected lieutenant governor; in 1937 he won the governorship.

During the 1930s Aiken won national attention when he advised Republicans to abandon their "hate Roosevelt" campaign in favor of more constructive opposition. He was elected to the Senate from Vermont in 1940 and over the next 34 years had little difficulty winning reelection. Aiken, unlike more conservative Republicans, favored low rather than high tariffs; he also was a strong proponent of federal flood control projects and became a leading advocate of the construction of the St. Lawrence Seaway. The Senator also favored a revival of the Depression-era food stamp program to permit poor families to purchase food at reduced prices. In 1954 he sponsored the Water Facilities Act, which provided federal aid to rural communities seeking to develop an adequate water supply. Aiken considered this bill critical for the development of rural America and believed it was one of the most important bills he ever sponsored. [See TRUMAN, EISENHOWER Volumes]

During the Kennedy years Aiken was the ranking Republican on the Senate Agriculture and Forestry Committee. He also served on the Senate Foreign Relations Committee and on the Joint Atomic Energy Committee. Aiken was generally associated with the moderate wing of the Republican Party although his voting behavior was difficult to categorize. For example, the liberal Americans for Democratic Action gave him a 50% rating in 1961, a 25% rating in 1962 and a 62% rating in 1963. He voted for the Administration's 1961 minimum wage bill and its school aid proposal. He broke ranks with the conservative majority on the Agriculture Committee to support an amendment requiring U.S. farmers to pay Mexican "bracero" farm workers the same wages as U.S. workers. In July 1962 he voted against the Administration's medicare bill but reversed himself in 1965 to vote in favor of a similar health care bill, which became law in July.

As a member of the Senate Agriculture Committee, Aiken voted against the Administration's 1962 farm bill. He was particularly concerned with legislation affecting dairy farmers, whose livelihood was important to Vermont's economy. In 1963 the Senator opposed the Administration's efforts to reduce the federal government's massive stockpile of surplus dairy goods through a voluntary milk production allotment program. Such a measure, he argued, would increase milk costs to the consumer and would be of little benefit to dairy farmers. In 1963 Aiken also opposed an Administration measure modifying and extending for two years a voluntary feed-grain diversion program. He suggested that the bill would give to the Secretary of Agriculture unprecedented authority over the subsidy program.

During the Johnson years Aiken won national attention as a leading Republican critic of the Administration's Vietnam war policy. Although Aiken spoke out against U.S. involvement in Vietnam as early as 1965, he continued to vote for bills funding the war effort. To vote against funding, he argued, would effectively disarm our troops in the field. In 1970 he voted for the Cooper-Church amendment barring the President from spending funds to maintain troops in Cambodia. [See JOHNSON, NIXON Volumes]

When Aiken retired from the Senate in 1974 he was 82 and the chamber's oldest member.

[JLW]

ALBERT, CARL (BERT)
b. May 10, 1908; McAlaster, Okla.
Democratic Representative, Okla.,
1947-   ; House Majority Whip, 1955-
62; House Majority Leader, 1962-71.

Albert was the son of a poor cotton farmer and coal miner. Demonstrating considerable scholastic aptitude, he graduated Phi Beta Kappa from the University of Oklahoma in 1931 and received a Rhodes Scholarship to study at Oxford University, where he earned two law degrees. After practicing law and serving in the Army, in 1946 Albert won a seat in the U.S. House of Representatives from Oklahoma's impoverished third district.

In Congress Albert consistently backed liberal measures but also voted for legislation favored by oil companies, which formed a major interest group in his state.

Albert uniformly supported the lower chamber's Democratic leadership. From his earliest days as a representative, the Congressman later recalled, he carefully observed the operations of the House to familiarize himself with its procedures and with the voting patterns of its members. Impressed by Albert's loyalty and diligence, Speaker Sam Rayburn (D, Tex.) [q.v.] and Majority Leader John W. McCormack (D, Mass.) [q.v.] tapped him to serve as majority whip in 1955. [See EISENHOWER Volume]

As whip Albert helped the House majority leadership pass bills by keeping track of the sentiments of the Democratic members, convincing wavering representatives to vote as the leadership wished and making sure that members were on the floor for crucial votes. Known as a quiet, scholarly and modest man, Albert worked behind the scenes and shunned publicity. He was a conciliator and compromiser who preferred winning votes by persuasion rather than by threats. Albert believed that the excessive use of pressure might secure short-term support but would create antagonism towards the leadership in the long run.

When President Kennedy took office in 1961, Albert assumed the additional function of advising the White House on the congressional reception of the Administration's programs. He soon proved his acute sensitivity to House opinion. When the White House was considering modifications of its 1961 depressed areas bill to win additional support, Albert reported that the measure could pass unchanged, and his judgment proved to be correct. He warned Agriculture Secretary Orville A. Freeman [q.v.] that the Administration's farm program of the same year would not pass the House without alterations. The advice was ignored, and the program was defeated in the lower chamber.

Shortly after the death of Rayburn in October 1961, Albert, assuming that Majority Leader McCormack would be elected to the speakership, began to seek backing for McCormack's post. He was opposed by Rep. Richard W. Bolling (D, Mo.) [q.v.], a more ideological and outspoken liberal, who lined up the support of outside forces such as labor unions, academic groups and the press. As a House insider with extensive contacts among his colleagues, Albert campaigned within Congress, calling all of the Democratic representatives and asking each for his support. Bolling withdrew from the contest early in January 1962, and Albert was chosen by the Democratic caucus later in the month.

As majority leader, Albert's functions included devising Democratic floor strategy and speaking on behalf of Administration programs. In January 1963 he helped secure the permanent expansion of the Rules Committee. It had originally been enlarged in 1961 to create a liberal majority and thereby prevent the panel from blocking Administration bills. In seeking support for the President's programs, he retained his low-key, conciliatory approach. A hard worker, Albert continued performing some of the functions of the whip and tried to maintain contact with all Democratic representatives.

Albert was a strong supporter of Johnson Administration policies, including the Vietnam war. In 1968 he was criticized by anti-war Democrats for being excessively partisan in his role as chairman of the Democratic National Convention. In 1971 he succeeded McCormack as speaker. During the early and mid-1970s Albert came under increasing attack from liberal Democrats for not articulating coherent policy alternatives to the programs of the Republican-controlled White House and for being insufficiently aggressive in his efforts to secure the support of conservative Democrats for progressive measures. [See JOHNSON, NIXON Volumes]

[MLL]

ALEXANDER, DONALD W(ILLIAM)

b. Sept. 30, 1904; Des Plaines, Ill.
Maritime Administrator, September 1961-September 1963.

Donald W. Alexander was a 1926 graduate of the U.S. Naval Academy. Although he attained the rank of captain in the Naval Reserve during World War II, most of his career was spent in industry, where he won a reputation for expertise as a production manager. From 1951 to 1959 he served as a vice president for operations of the Whirlpool Corporation.

Kennedy named Alexander as Maritime Administrator in September 1961, and he was confirmed by Congress the following April. The Maritime Administration was the division of the Commerce Department that controlled subsidies for the operation and construction of merchant ships. It was generally conceded that without these subsidies, American shipping lines, beset with high labor and operating costs, could not stay in business against foreign competition. The U.S. subsidized its merchant fleet to ensure that in time of war the nation would not be forced to rely on foreign shipping. As a result of government support, however, the industry had little incentive to increase efficiency. In August 1962 in a prepared address delivered in Los Angeles, Alexander urged the use of new technology to ensure that the U.S. would in the future be able to compete with foreign carriers. He warned that shippers could not expect to rely on the subsidies indefinitely.

In November 1962 the Maritime Administration sponsored a conference on automation procedures. The conference was considered a failure, however, because maritime union leaders, fearing that automation and containerization would spell a loss of jobs, refused to attend. A month earlier the House Rules Committee, under pressure from the maritime unions, had cut $1.95 million in funds earmarked in the Maritime Administration budget for automation research.

Although the Secretary of Labor and the President had assumed responsibility for settling major maritime labor disputes, Alexander was responsible for carrying out studies of overall labor-management relations within the industry. He pointed out that wage pacts signed by 15 subsidized shipping lines in 1962 had cost the government $9.5 million in additional subsidies. He implied that management had been willing to settle for excessive wage increases because the costs could be passed on to the government and warned that his office would closely scrutinize all future negotiations.

Alexander made no progress in scaling down subsidies and, because of the great influence of maritime unions and management, was under persistent pressure to maintain or increase them. Indeed, when Congress in July 1962 increased subsidies for ship reconstruction by 5%, the Administration found it expedient to go along with the measure.

Alexander resigned his post in September 1963 to become head of the Far Eastern Consulting Corporation.

[JLW]

ALGER, BRUCE
b. June 12, 1918; Dallas, Tex.
Republican Representative,
Tex., 1955-65.

When Alger won election to Congress in 1954 from Dallas County, he became the first Texas Republican since 1930 to be chosen for a full term in the U.S. House of Representatives. An ideological conservative to the right of the Eisenhower Administration, Alger declared his support in 1954 for the general outline of Administration policy but criticized Eisenhower-supported federal housing programs as socialistic. In November 1960 he gained national attention as a result of his participation in a Dallas demonstration against Democratic vice presidential nominee Lyndon B. Johnson [q.v.], which culminated in the jostling of the candidate.

Alger was a consistent opponent of Kennedy Administration measures, particularly in the area of social welfare legislation. In 1962, according to Congressional Quarterly, he voted against 88% of the major bills supported by the President, a higher percentage than was compiled by any other Republican representative. During February 1961 Alger opposed an Administration aid-to-dependent-children bill, contending that such a program should be carried out by state and local governments "without federal intervention." Two months later he spoke out against an appropriations bill for the Departments of Labor and Health,

Education and Welfare because, he said, the sums "should and could be considerably less."

In May 1963 he opposed a bill extending most existing corporate and excise taxes on the ground that it asked Americans "to pick up the tab for the unnecessary compulsive spending" of the Kennedy Administration. On the other hand, in October 1963 he was among only three members of the House to vote against a bill which reduced the President's requested military budget.

Alger supported Sen. Barry Goldwater's (R, Ariz.) [q.v.] drive for the Republican presidential nomination in 1964. He lost his House seat in the Johnson landslide of that year.

[MLL]

ALLEN, IVAN, JR.
b. March 15, 1911; Atlanta, Ga.
Mayor, Atlanta, Ga., 1961-69.

After graduating from the Georgia Institute of Technology in 1933, Allen entered his father's office equipment supply company in Atlanta. An aggressive entrepreneur, he skillfully compounded the success of the firm and became a millionaire. He played an active role in the affairs of the business community, which culminated in his election to the presidency of the city's Chamber of Commerce in 1960. He served as executive secretary to liberal Georgia Gov. Ellis Arnall shortly after World War II. In 1954 he briefly entered the race for governor of Georgia but withdrew after failing to attract enough support to mount an effective campaign. During a speech-making tour associated with this abortive gubernatorial effort, Allen took the conventional white Southern view on segregation, defending it as a part of the region's way of life.

Allen altered his position on segregation during the next decade. He was a member of a dynamic, powerful and politically active local business community, which was more interested in promoting the economic growth of Atlanta than in defending traditional Southern social mores. Furthermore, over 28% of Atlanta's registered voters were black, and Mayor William B. Hartsdale, who retired from office in 1961, had built his political power upon a moderate white-Negro coalition. According to his associates, Allen also had genuinely changed his views on racial questions since the 1950s. Therefore, after deciding to run in the 1961 Democratic mayoral primary against arch-segregationist Lester Maddox [q.v.], Allen declared his support for racial integration. He received slightly less than half of the white ballots in the primary, winning the contest by an almost 2-to-1 margin by drawing almost all of the Negro vote. No other candidate appeared on the ballot in the general election.

Atlanta's mayor had little patronage power, and the city's department heads were responsible not to him but to the Board of Aldermen. However, during his initial term Allen employed his influence to integrate many of Atlanta's public facilities, particularly after black and white college students staged anti-segregation sit-ins in restaurants and hotels during the spring of 1963. In July of that year Allen, testifying before the Senate Commerce Committee, supported the Kennedy Administration's bill to desegregate public accommodations. The only major white Southern political figure to favor the bill, he declared, "I am firmly convinced that the Supreme Court insists that the same fundamental rights must be held by every American citizen." A year later Allen again demonstrated his uniqueness in the South when he congratulated Martin Luther King [q.v.] for winning the Nobel Peace Prize and praised him for furnishing "the leadership that a white leader would have given his race should it have been a minority seeking equal rights and full citizenship."

Allen's concern with advancing the development of Atlanta, which was already an economic and social center of the South, aroused some opposition among the city's black population during his first term. He promoted a number of large-scale municipal construction projects such as a downtown expressway, a convention center and an $18 million sports stadium that was built on the site of a black ghetto. Many Atlanta blacks contended that the city was devoting excessive attention to highly visible downtown construction while giving insufficient weight to the building of low-income housing for black slum dwellers.

Allen was reelected mayor in 1965, but tension between the city administration and the black community increased during his second term. Problems involving the high level of minority unemployment and of segregated housing continued. Riots flared in 1966 and 1967, and Allen denounced leaders of the Student Nonviolent Coordinating Committee as the instigators of the disturbances. But he also acknowledged that poverty was the ultimate cause of the riots and urged the federal government to provide massive aid to the cities to resolve the crisis. Although expected to easily win reelection for a third term, in January 1969 the Mayor announced that he would not seek office again for personal reasons. [See JOHNSON Volume]

[MLL]

ALLEN, JAMES E(DWARD), JR.
b. April 25, 1911; Elkins, W. Va.
d. Oct. 16, 1971; Peace Springs, Ariz.
Commissioner of Education, N.Y., 1955-69.

A Presbyterian minister's son, James E. Allen, Jr., received his B.A. from Elkins College in 1932 and worked for six years in the West Virginia State Department of Education. Leaving his native state to study educational administration, he earned a Ph.D. from Harvard in 1945. Allen joined the staff of the Commissioner of the New York State Department of Education in 1947. Eight years later he became commissioner, an office of broad powers in the administration and planning of the state's local school systems and universities. He established a liberal record. In January 1961 Allen claimed to have refused President Kennedy's offer of appointment as U.S. Commissioner of Education.

In June 1962 the Supreme Court banned a public school prayer approved by the New York State Board of Regents. In sympathy with the Court's decision and acting against the wishes of several local boards, Allen dutifully ordered all school boards in the state to obey the high court's controversial ruling.

Although he had initially wavered on the issue, by 1960 Allen had come out against the existence of school district boundaries that systematically separated black and white student populations. In June 1962 Allen ordered the Malverne school board to redraw a de facto segregated elementary school district. When local officials delayed implementation of Allen's command, local black leaders held a sit-in at the contested facility in September. Similar protests took place at Amityville and Mineola. The following summer Allen directed systems with districts having black enrollments of more than 50% to submit plans designed to reduce racial imbalances. Most districts immediately complied with the ruling. The Allen plan also called for improvement of educational opportunities in New York City districts with high Negro or Puerto Rican populations.

Allen remained state commissioner of education until 1969. He superintended the revitalization of the state university but encountered a host of troubles in the desegregation and decentralization of New York City's mammoth school system. Appointed U.S. Commissioner of Education by President Richard M. Nixon in February 1969, Allen antagonized the President's Southern and conservative supporters by his vigorous support of school desegregation. Nixon dismissed him in June 1970. Allen and his wife died in a private plane crash in October 1971. [See JOHNSON, NIXON Volumes]

[JLB]

ALLOTT, GORDON (LLEWELLYN)
b. Jan. 2, 1907; Pueblo, Colo.
Republican Senator, Colo., 1955-73.

A graduate of the University of Colorado Law School and a World War II veteran, Gordon L. Allott won election as lieutenant governor of Colorado in 1950. Four years later he upset a popular Democrat in the contest for the U.S. Senate and easily won reelection in 1960. [See EISENHOWER Volume]

Allott proved to be a conservative foe of most Kennedy Administration legislation. He cast the only vote against the President's nomination of Robert F. Kennedy [q.v.] as Attorney General, declaring that the younger Kennedy lacked "the legal experience to qualify him" for the post. In June 1961 he opposed the President's pledge to place an American on the moon as a "useless contest with the Russians." The only Senator to vote against the National Aeronautics and Space Administration's request of $1.8 billion for fiscal 1962, Allott warned of the probable costs of the moon mission, which he estimated at between $20 billion and $30 billion. Instead he urged the government to concentrate its space efforts on orbital missions, including weapon-carrying space vehicles. Allott cosponsored a resolution introduced by Sen. Thomas Dodd (D, Conn.) [q.v.] in August 1961 requesting the President to resume the testing of nuclear weapons. In September 1963, however, he voted with the Administration in favor of the nuclear test ban treaty.

Twice Allott fought the Administration's wilderness preservation legislation. As the bill's principal opponent during the Senate's 1961 debate, Allott sought unsuccessfully to amend the proposal's grant of authority to the President to exclude about 52 million acres of federal land from commercial and recreational use. His amendments won the support of the U.S. Chamber of Commerce, the Farm Bureau Federation and mining and cattle industry interests. Although the Administration measure passed the Senate, it failed to reach the House floor, due in large part to the opposition of Rep. Wayne Aspinall (D, Colo.) [q.v.], chairman of the House Interior and Insular Affairs Committee. The White House resubmitted a similar bill in April 1963. Allott criticized its ban on roadways and commercial development in designated areas, remarking that the proposed law "would give to a very few people in the United States the unbridled use of [wilderness] land to the detriment of every other public use, whether it be mining, grazing, forestry or plain recreation." Senate colleagues again frustrated Allott's efforts to weaken the Administration's request, which passed the Senate in April 1963. Aspinall's continued resistance to the bill, however, forced the White House to compromise, and the final Wilderness Act of 1964 incorporated many of the amendments Allott had fought for in the Senate. [See JOHNSON, NIXON Volumes]

[JLB]

ALSOP, JOSEPH W(RIGHT), JR.
b. October 11, 1910; Avon, Conn.
Journalist, author.

Joseph Alsop, the son of socially prominent parents, grew up in Avon, Conn. His mother was a distant relative of Franklin Roosevelt. Alsop attended Groton School and graduated from Harvard University in 1932. Through family connections he joined the staff of the *New York Herald Tribune* and in 1937 became coauthor of his first newspaper column. During World War II Alsop joined Claire Chennault's American Volunteer Group in China, where his skill at public relations helped popularize the air group in the United States.

After the war Alsop teamed with his brother Stewart [q.v.] on another syndicated column for the *Tribune*. In 1958 the partnership ended amicably, and Joseph Alsop continued the column, this time syndicated through the *Los Angeles Times*.

Prominent on the Washington social and political scene throughout his career, Joseph Alsop was one of a select group of journalists who were close friends of John F. Kennedy. Alsop urged the nomination of Lyndon B. Johnson [q.v.] for vice president in 1960, recommended that Republican C. Douglas Dillon [q.v.] be appointed Secretary of the Treasury and vigorously but unsuccessfully advocated that David Bruce [q.v.] be named Secretary of State in the Kennedy cabinet. In 1963 Alsop was among the first to recommend that a blue-ribbon panel be set up to investigate the circumstances surrounding the Kennedy assassination.

Alsop's attitude in both domestic and foreign affairs was often described as "hard-line." According to Richard J. Walton's *Cold War and Counter-Revolution*, it was in 1961 that Joseph Alsop "began to establish his incontestable claim to the eminence of 'superhawk.' " He remained among the staunchest defenders of American policy in Southeast Asia throughout the decade. Alsop denounced young Vietnam war correspondents David Halberstam [q.v.], Malcolm Browne and Neil Sheehan and compared them to those newspapermen of an earlier generation who had called the Chinese Communists "agrarian reformers." He accused them of painting a "dark indignant picture" of the developing situation in South Vietnam.

In 1962, when a flood of Communist Chinese refugees into Hong Kong led to speculation of widespread famine, Supreme Court Justice William O. Douglas [q.v.] suggested sending aid to the mainland. Alsop replied scathingly, "Sentimentalists are beginning to talk of feeding starving China, which would simply mean getting Mao Tse-tung off his self-created hook." In a 1965 column Alsop lamented the "unhappy secret" that Communists had infiltrated the civil rights movement and were stirring up racial strife. During Johnson's tenure in office he defended the President's Vietnam policy while he criticized the man. "[Johnson] is not forthright, either with the country, or with his associates, or even, one suspects, with his nearest or dearest," Alsop once wrote. In 1973 Alsop retired from the routine of his syndicated column to devote himself to studies of Greek antiquities.

[FHM]

ALSOP, STEWART J(OHONNOT) (OLIVER)
b. May 17, 1914, Avon, Conn.
d. May 26, 1974, Washington, D.C.
Journalist, author.

Born to wealth and a Rooseveltian sense of social responsibility, Stewart Alsop was educated at the Groton School and at Yale University, from which he graduated in 1936. After a few years with the publishing firm of Doubleday Doran in New York, he served in World War II with the Office of

Strategic Services (OSS) and parachuted into occupied France shortly after D-day. Out of his experiences with the OSS came Alsop's first book, *Sub Rosa: the OSS and American Espionage*, written in collaboration with reporter Thomas Braden.

In 1945 Alsop teamed with his brother Joseph on a column syndicated through the *New York Herald Tribune*. Both men became renowned for their painstaking research, indefatigable legwork and regular trips to foreign capitals. In November 1949 the Alsop brothers were denounced before the U.N. General Assembly by Soviet Foreign Minister Andrei I. Vishinsky because they had advocated the creation of new air bases in India, the Middle East and North Africa.

From 1958 to 1968 Alsop served as a contributing editor of the *Saturday Evening Post*. A 1962 article, written in collaboration with Kennedy confidant Charles Bartlett, caused a furor when Alsop asserted that Adlai Stevenson [*q.v.*], then U.S. ambassador to the United Nations, had "dissented" strongly from the Kennedy Administration's decision to impose a naval blockade of Cuba. Kennedy, Stevenson and various Kennedy aides vigorously denied that any such dissension had taken place, but Alsop and Bartlett maintained their story was accurate. Stevenson accused the reporters of being "character assassins," and said, "I am used to assassins. I remember [the late Sen. Joseph] McCarthy very well." In a Jan. 26, 1963 article for the *Post*, Alsop wrote that his principal source for the story had been Clayton Fritchey, Stevenson's U.N. spokesman. While the Stevenson-Alsop dispute remained unresolved in the 1960s, Graham T. Allison, in his scholarly 1973 assessment of the Cuban missile crisis, *Essence of Decision*, wrote that the Ambassador always exercised a cautionary role during high-level deliberations. Allison further speculated "that Kennedy had in fact sacrificed the Ambassador to the hawks in order to allow himself to choose the moderate, golden mean."

In 1968 Alsop joined *Newsweek* magazine as a political columnist. He defended the Vietnam war through much of the Johnson Administration. Alsop's 1968 book *The*

Center denounced academics and "liberal intellectual" critics of Administration policy.

Stewart Alsop's last work, *Stay of Execution* (1973), described the advances and remissions of his own terminal cancer in a book characterized by good will, clarity and even humor in the face of death.

[FHM]

ANDERSON, CLINTON P(RESBA)
b. Oct. 23, 1895; Centerville, S.D.
d. Nov. 11, 1975; Albuquerque, N.M.
Democratic Senator, N.M., 1949-1972.
Chairman, Interior and Insular Affairs Committee, 1961-1963; Chairman, Aeronautical and Space Sciences Committee, 1963-72.

During the 1960s Clinton P. Anderson was among the most influential members of the Senate. Anderson was raised in rural South Dakota and attended Dakota Wesleyan University and the University of Michigan. Rejected for service in World War I because he was suffering from tuberculosis, he settled in New Mexico where the climate helped him recuperate. He worked from 1918 to 1922 as a reporter for the *Albuquerque Journal* and helped uncover evidence relating to the Teapot Dome scandal. In the mid-1920s he made his fortune as head of his own insurance agency, the Mountain States Casualty Company.

Anderson's political career began in 1933 when the governor of New Mexico appointed him to fill the post of state treasurer. He later helped administer New Deal relief and unemployment compensation programs in New Mexico. He was elected to Congress in 1940 and served for three terms. Early in 1945 he headed a congressional probe into food shortages and blackmarketing in the distribution of meat. Anderson's report so impressed Harry S Truman that the President appointed him Secretary of Agriculture in the spring of 1945. Anderson held the post for three years. In 1948 he won election to the Senate where, he served for the next 23 years. [See TRUMAN, EISENHOWER Volumes]

Anderson was generally regarded as one of the more liberal members of a powerful group of Democratic senators that set the pace of upper house business. During the 1960s Anderson's influence was based on his long seniority, chairmanship of several important committees and close ties to the Kennedy and Johnson Administrations.

Beginning in 1959 Anderson attempted to limit the use of the filibuster by Southern senators to thwart the passage of civil rights and social welfare legislation. When Senate rules were adopted at the start of each new Congress, Anderson proposed that the rule governing Senate debate—Rule 22—be changed so that three-fifths rather than two-thirds of the senators present and voting could terminate unlimited debate. Throughout the 1960s, however, Anderson failed to overcome the resistance of Southern Democrats and some conservative Republicans who used the filibuster itself to prevent a change in the Senate rules.

As chairman of the Interior and Insular Affairs Committee from 1961 to 1963, Anderson was closely involved in shaping water resources legislation, a subject of vital interest to arid New Mexico. He also served as floor manager for a number of successful water reclamation project bills, including the Navaho-San Juan water storage project, which irrigated a considerable expanse of New Mexico's land by diverting Colorado River water into the Rio Grande Valley.

During the Kennedy Administration Anderson and Rep. Cecil R. King (D, Calif.) [q.v.] sponsored legislation that mandated raises in Social Security taxes to provide hospital care for old age assistance beneficiaries. The King-Anderson medicare bill, strongly backed by the Administration, was defeated every year between 1961 and 1964 because of the stiff opposition of the American Medical Association and Rep. Wilbur Mills (D, Ark.) [q.v.], the powerful chairman of the House Ways and Means Committee. In the summer of 1965 a version of the bill became law, thanks in part to a change of attitude by Rep. Mills and a sweeping congressional victory for medicare advocates in the 1964 elections.

In January 1963 Anderson became chairman of the Senate Aeronautical and Space Sciences Committee, a post he held for the next nine years. Anderson headed this Committee during the boom years of the American space program, which he supported enthusiastically. Led by Anderson, the Aeronautics Committee was generous in handling National Aeronautics and Space Administration requests for funds.

During the Johnson years Anderson supported the Administration on key domestic legislation. However, because he backed the Administration's Vietnam policy, supported large-scale military appropriations and opposed strict gun control legislation, he began to lose his standing with liberal elements of the Democratic Party. [See JOHNSON Volume]

Anderson, in ill health, retired from the Senate in 1972. He died three years later at the age of 80.

[JLW]

ANDERSON, GEORGE W(HELAN), JR.
b. Dec. 15, 1906; New York, N.Y.
Chief of Naval Operations, August 1961-July 1963; Ambassador to Portugal, August 1963-March 1966.

George W. Anderson, Jr., a career naval officer who served in the Pacific during World War II, rose through the ranks and in 1959 became commander of the Sixth Fleet in the Mediterranean. In June 1961 Secretary of the Navy John Connally [q.v.] passed over ten admirals senior to Anderson to name him successor to Adm. Arleigh A. Burke [q.v.] as chief of naval operations.

As chief command officer for the Navy, Anderson assumed responsibility in October 1962 for setting up the "quarantine" to prevent the Soviet Union from continuing to deliver missiles to Cuba. On Sunday afternoon Oct. 21, President John F. Kennedy met with Anderson and asked him to outline procedures for dealing with the approaching Russian vessels. According to Theodore Sorensen [q.v.], the President's special counsel, the Admiral reported that each approaching ship would first be signaled to stop for boarding and inspection; if the ship did not respond a shot would be fired across her bow and if there were still no satisfactory response, a shot would be fired into the rudder to cripple but not sink her. "You're certain that can be done?" asked the President. "Yes, sir!" replied Adm. Anderson.

On Oct. 24 Anderson met with Secretary of Defense Robert S. McNamara [q.v.], who was responsible for the overall planning and supervision of the action. McNamara stressed that the quarantine had been ordered not to humiliate the Russians but to prevent further arming of their missile bases in Cuba. Fearing that the Navy might commit some blunder that could touch off nuclear war, the Secretary pressed Anderson on matters of tactics. Which ship would make the first interception? Were Russian-speaking officers on board? How would Russian submarines be dealt with? What would be done if a Soviet captain refused to answer questions about cargo?

Anderson then picked up a copy of the Manual of Naval Regulations and shouted "It's all in there." "I don't give a damn what John Paul Jones would have done,", McNamara answered back, "I want to know what you are going to do, now." Anderson advised McNamara to return to his office and let the Navy handle the problem. McNamara obliged, but according to his biographer, Henry L. Trewhitt, it had become apparent that "the two men could never again have a sound working relationship."

Relations between the Admiral and the Defense Secretary were further strained when Anderson, appearing before the Senate Permanent Investigations Subcommittee in April 1963, testified that the Defense Department's choice of General Dynamics as the prime contractor for the new TFX jet fighter would result in the construction of an aircraft far too heavy for the majority of carriers. McNamara, in turn, challenged Anderson's recommendation that new surface ships utilize nuclear power, charging that nuclear powered ships were too costly.

Anderson later deplored the "lack of trust and confidence between military and civilian echelons."

"Any President," said John F. Kennedy in the spring of 1963, "should have the right to choose carefully his military advisers." Kennedy then broke with precedent and refused to appoint Anderson to a second term as chief of naval operations. To placate Anderson's many supporters on Capitol Hill, Kennedy named Anderson ambassador to Portugal. He held the post until March 1966. In March 1969 he was appointed to the President's Foreign Intelligence Advisory Board. Anderson also served as director of several corporations, including National Airlines and Value Line Funds.

[JLW]

ANNIS, EDWARD R.
b. March 27, 1913; Detroit, Mich.
President, American Medical Association, June 1963-June 1964.

During the early 1960s Dr. Edward R. Annis, president of the American Medical Association (AMA), became the most conspicuous opponent of the Kennedy Administration's proposed medicare legislation. Annis grew up in Detroit. As a student at Annunciation High School and the University of Detroit, he earned a reputation as a formidable debater in interscholastic forensic competition. His skill in public speaking later proved to be a key element in his rise to the AMA presidency.

Annis earned his M.D. from the Marquette University School of Medicine in 1938. He later studied at the Cook County Graduate School of Surgery. During the early 1940s he practiced in Tallahassee, Fla. and then moved to Miami, where he became chief of surgery at Mercy Hospital in 1953.

In December 1959 Annis joined the AMA speakers bureau, a post which offered him the opportunity to lecture throughout the country on key public health and medical issues. None was more important than medicare.

From January 1961 to June 1962 Annis delivered some 500 speeches in 100 cities against key legislation that had been introduced by Rep. Cecil R. King (D, Calif.) [q.v.] and Sen. Clinton P. Anderson (D, N.M.) [q.v.]. The King-Anderson bill, which had the strong support of the Administration, authorized raises in Social Security payroll taxes to provide hospital care for old age assistance beneficiaries. In televised debates with Sen. Hubert H. Humphrey (D, Minn.) [q.v.] and United Auto Workers President Walter P. Reuther [q.v.], Annis denounced the use of the Social Security system to finance medical care for the aged.

He argued that the King-Anderson bill was a "cruel hoax and delusion," which would offer no benefit to the three million elderly Americans not enrolled in the Social Security system. He pointed out that for a patient to qualify for more than 30 days hospitalization under medicare he or she would need approval of a special "utilization board." These boards, he suggested, would destroy personal doctor-patient relationships. Further, Annis claimed the King-Anderson bill might bankrupt the Social Security system, destroy useful voluntary health insurance schemes like Blue Cross and ultimately pave the way for socialized medicine.

Annis stressed that the AMA was not opposed to all federally financed health programs. It had supported the legislation introduced by Rep. Wilbur Mills (D, Ark.) [q.v.] and Sen. Robert S. Kerr (D, Okla.) [q.v.] that became law in October 1960. This measure permitted states wishing to broaden the scope of medical programs for the aged to apply for federal matching grants. (Critics of state programs established under the Kerr-Mills Act contended that only a relatively small percentage of the elderly benefited.)

On May 20, 1962 President Kennedy spoke on behalf of the King-Anderson bill before a mass rally at Madison Square Garden in New York City. Dr. Leonard W. Larson [q.v.], AMA president, demanded that the television networks provide the AMA equal time to rebut the President's remarks. The networks refused, and the AMA then rented Madison Square Garden

and a half hour of prime television time to permit Larson and Annis, then head of the AMA speakers bureau, to present organized medicine's case. On May 21, Annis dramatically stood before 18,000 empty seats as an announcer explained to television viewers that "these seats are yours. There will be no pageant. But there will be an appeal to you from the physicians of America."

Annis was generally credited with having successfully defended the AMA position in the broadcast. A union official, sympathetic to medicare, admitted that Annis's "distortions were simply more credible than Kennedy's truths." The AMA proved effective in preventing passage of the King-Anderson bill, which died in the House Ways and Means Committee in 1962 and 1963.

In June 1962 Annis ran for president of the AMA, disregarding the tradition that dictated that an AMA president first serve on the organization's executive board. His victory demonstrated that he had become a well-known figure as a result of the anti-medicare campaign.

Annis officially assumed office in June 1963. He had previously called for a stepped up "educational" campaign against medicare, and during his year-long term local AMA branches were active in campaigning against the King-Anderson bill. Several journalists estimated that the AMA spent several million dollars in its campaign against medicare during this period.

In January 1964 U.S. Surgeon General Luther L. Terry [q.v.] issued the first government report which linked cigarette smoking to cancer. Annis suggested that the Surgeon General's report was far from conclusive. "The AMA is not opposed to smoking and tobacco," he said, "but it is opposed to disease."

When the Federal Trade Commission in June 1964 announced that it would attempt to compel cigarette manufacturers to print a warning announcement concerning the hazards of smoking on cigarette packs and advertisements, the AMA opposed the order. In a letter to the Commission, the AMA argued that the order was unnecessary because the hazards of smoking were well-known to the public. Moreover, it noted that a decline in smoking by the American public would seriously damage an industry—tobacco—that was important to the American economy. Critics of the AMA charged that it had made a deal with the tobacco industry to ensure that tobacco-state congressmen would vote against medicare. These charges were denied by the organization.

Annis was succeeded by Dr. Donovon Ward as AMA president in June 1964. He remained, nonetheless, an influential voice within the organization.

With the aid of Rep. Mills and a massive congressional victory in 1964, the Johnson Administration won passage of a medicare bill in the summer of 1965. Amid widespread rumors of a boycott, Dr. Annis predicted that 90% of physicians would have nothing to do with the program. However, at a special session of the AMA's House of Delegates in 1965, Annis argued against such a boycott. His influence was called decisive in convincing the AMA to cooperate with the new program.

[JLW]

For further information:
Richard Harris, *A Sacred Trust* (New York, 1966).

ARENDS, LESLIE C(ORNELIUS)
b. Sept. 27, 1895; Melvin, Ill.
Republican Representative, Ill., 1935-75.

Leslie C. Arends represented a prosperous farming district south of Chicago for 39 years. He became House Republican whip in 1943 and remained so until his retirement in 1975. His primary function as whip was to bring out the Republican vote on issues where the Party position had been determined by the Republican Policy Committee.

During the Kennedy years Arends, like fellow conservatives, generally opposed the Administration's key housing, labor, education and agriculture bills. As the ranking Republican member of the House Armed Services Committee, Arends maintained close, cordial relations with its Democratic chairman, L. Mendel Rivers (D, S.C.)

[*q.v.*]. Arends, like Rivers, consistently voted for increased military appropriations and generally sided with the Pentagon in its disputes with Secretary of Defense Robert S. McNamara [*q.v.*]. For example in March 1963 he criticized McNamara for his opposition to the funding of the RS-70, a manned supersonic bomber favored by the Air Force. Congress, he said, "never for a moment thought that civilian control would become civilian dictation of military planning . . . 'I-got-all-the-answers-McNamara' is not the last word in military strategy."

Arends opposed much of the Johnson Administration's domestic social legislation. However, he voted for the 1964 Civil Rights Act and was a staunch supporter of the Administration's Vietnam war policy. [See JOHNSON, NIXON Volumes]

[JLW]

ARENDT, HANNAH
b. Oct. 14, 1906; Hanover, Germany
d. Dec. 4, 1975; New York, N.Y.
Philosopher, political scientist.

Hannah Arendt was born the only child of middle class German-Jewish parents. She studied at Marburg and Freiburg and took a doctorate in philosophy under Karl Jaspers at Heidelberg in 1928. With the rise of the Nazi regime in 1933, Arendt left Germany for Paris, where she continued to study and for four years did social work with Jewish orphans. She fled to the United States in 1940 where she again worked with Jewish cultural and social organizations. In the late 1940s she was an editor of Schocken Books.

Arendt won wide recognition in academic and intellectual circles with her first major book, *Origins of Totalitarianism*, published in 1951. The work traced the roots of modern totalitarianism, particularly Nazism and Stalinism, back to the imperialism and anti-Semitism of the 19th century. *The Human Condition* (1958) and *On Revolution* (1963) extended her reputation as a pessimistic critic of contemporary society. She feared the erosion of individual freedom under the conditions created by modern industrial life and thought the potential for totalitarianism inherent in the frustrations of mass democracy.

In 1962 Arendt covered the trial of Nazi war criminal Adolf Eichmann in Jerusalem for the *New Yorker*. Her account of the trial, *Eichmann in Jerusalem, a Report on the Banality of Evil*, was published as a book in the spring of 1963. A highly controversial work, her book met with both acclaim and a wave of criticism. Arendt startled many by offering an interpretation of Eichmann as a banal functionary of mass murder, a personally inoffensive bureaucrat whose unreflective role in the Nazi system made him a moral monster. She also argued that the Nazi destruction of European Jewry would have been much more difficult, perhaps impossible, had not the Jewish community passively cooperated with its oppressors in a series of small but ultimately self-destructive acts. Arendt's ideas had great impact in the 1960s. Although unsympathetic to the emerging New Left, her analysis of modern state bureaucracies and the symbiotic relationship between oppressors and victims did much to shape the New Left critique of modern liberal society.

Arendt taught philosophy and political science at several universities before joining the faculty of the New School for Social Research in 1967. A prolific author and lecturer she also published *Men in Dark Times* (1968), *On Violence* (1970) and *Crises of the Republic* (1972). She died of a heart attack in New York in December 1975.

[NNL]

ASPINALL, WAYNE N(ORVIEL)

b. April 3, 1896, Middleburg, Ohio.
Democratic Representative, Colo., 1949-73; Chairman, Interior and Insular Affairs Committee, 1959-73.

After several years as a fruit grower, lawyer and leading figure in the Colorado legislature, Aspinall was elected to the House of Representatives in 1948. Representing a western Colorado district heavily dependent upon agriculture, timber and mining, Aspinall was immediately assigned to the Public Lands Committee (later renamed Interior and Insular Affairs). He became a leader in sponsoring water reclamation legislation for Colorado and the West. During the 1950s Aspinall favored a "multiple-use" conservation policy to open the government's extensive Western wilderness holdings to both commercial and recreational development. This approach was generally backed by the forest products, cattle and mining industries.

As chairman of the Interior and Insular Affairs Committee during the Kennedy years, Aspinall played a decisive role in first defeating and then substantially reshaping wilderness preservation legislation. For several years conservationist groups had unsuccessfully pressed for a law that would protect wilderness lands under Forest Service jurisdiction against commercial exploitation. The Senate finally approved a strong conservation bill in September 1961. The proposed legislation gave the President authority to include new lands in the wilderness system unless Congress vetoed the additions within a specified time. Under Aspinall's direction the House Interior Committee effectively rewrote the bill to allow public lands to be declared wilderness only by an express vote of Congress itself. Backed by conservation groups President Kennedy and Interior Secretary Stewart Udall [*q. v.*] opposed Aspinall's proposed revisions and the bill died in committee. At the time Aspinall commented, "[Conservationist] extremists . . . have created an atmosphere which makes impossible the enactment of any wilderness legislation during this Congress."

The Senate passed another Kennedy-backed wilderness bill on April 9, 1963. Aspinall delayed the measure in the Interior Committee. On Nov. 20 he met with President Kennedy and agreed to report a modified wilderness bill out of committee in return for Administration support of an Aspinall-controlled commission to make a general review of public land-management policies. The Wilderness Act, signed by President Johnson Sept. 3, 1964, protected mining and grazing rights in the new wilderness areas until 1984 and required Congress to act before additional lands could be placed in the wilderness system beyond an initial 9.1 million acres. The final law was considered a defeat for the growing wilderness preservation movement. [See JOHNSON Volume]

[NNL]

BADEAU, JOHN S(TOTHOFF)
b. Feb. 24, 1903; Pittsburgh, Pa.
Ambassador to the United Arab Republic, May 1961-May 1964.

A theology student at Union College, Rutgers and Union Theological Seminary, Badeau was ordained a minister of the Reformed Church of America in 1928. In the same year he went to Iraq as a civil and sanitary engineer for the United Mission in Mesopotamia. Between 1936 and 1953 Badeau was associated with the American University in Cairo, first as a professor of religion and philosophy and, for the final eight years, as its president. He was president of the Near East Foundation in New York in May 1961 when Kennedy appointed him ambassador to the United Arab Republic (UAR).

A number of factors played a role in Kennedy's choice of Badeau. In picking the New Yorker Kennedy bypassed the New York State Democratic organization of Michael H. Prendergast and Carmine G. DeSapio [q.v.]. This was one of the many moves by which Kennedy hoped to break the power of the New York machine. Secondly, the choice of Badeau illustrated Kennedy's desire to appoint scholars and experts as ambassadors instead of career foreign service officers and political figures. Most importantly, Badeau was well liked in Egypt. Because U.S.-Egyptian relations had been strained since the Suez crisis of 1956, Kennedy wanted to establish a friendly relationship with President Gamal Abdel Nasser, head of the most powerful state in the Arab world.

The 1963 civil war in Yemen strained relations between the U.S. and UAR still further and threatened the precarious political balance in the Middle East. While Jordan and Saudi Arabia backed the royalist forces, the Egyptians and the U.S. supported the Yemeni republicans. The Kennedy Administration believed that a republican Yemen constituted the best chance for maintaining political stability in the area. The decision was also consistent with Kennedy's avowed policy of backing the forces of change in international conflicts, as long as these forces were anti-Communist. Although the U.S. and Egyptian positions were ostensibly identical, the U.S. opposition to UAR military attacks on Saudi territory, generated by the Administration's desire to preserve Saudi political stability and maintain Saudi oil supplies, hindered Badeau's attempt at a rapprochement with Cairo.

Badeau's own position was further undermined by Kennedy's penchant for personal diplomacy—in this case carried on in an exchange of letters with Nasser in the early 1960s. The President's use of such special envoys as Ellsworth Bunker [q.v.], whom he sent to confer with Nasser in April 1963, also undercut Badeau's position. At the time of Kennedy's assassination, Cairo was moving closer to the Communist bloc. This trend was underscored by Chou En-lai's visit to Cairo in December 1963.

Badeau wrote later that the "Johnson Administration did not display as much patience toward Arab affairs as President Kennedy had," making rapprochement with Nasser much more difficult. Furthermore, economic aid, which was the cornerstone of the Kennedy policy of conciliation toward the UAR, was drastically reduced, partly because of American involvement in Vietnam.

Badeau resigned as ambassador in May 1964 to become head of the Middle East Institute at Columbia University. He remained there until his retirement in 1971.

[JCH]

For further information:
John Badeau, *The American Approach to the Arab World* (New York, 1968).

BAILEY, JOHN M(ORAN)
b. Nov. 23, 1904; Hartford, Conn.
d. April 10, 1975; Hartford, Conn.
Chairman, Connecticut State Democratic Committee, 1946-75; Chairman, Democratic National Committee, January 1961-August 1968.

John M. Bailey grew up in Hartford and received a B.S. degree from Catholic University in 1926 and an LL.B degree from Harvard Law School in 1929. Following his admission to the bar, Bailey quickly immersed himself in local Democratic politics. In 1932 he became a member of the Democratic State Committee and in 1946 won the chairmanship. Allying himself with Rep. Abraham A. Ribicoff (D, Conn.) [q.v.], Bailey created a powerful Democratic organization, gaining the governor's chair for Ribicoff in 1954 and a U.S. Senate seat for Thomas Dodd [q.v.] in 1958.

In national politics Bailey proved a steadfast supporter of Sen. John F. Kennedy. At the 1956 Democratic National Convention, he worked for Kennedy's nomination as vice president. Under his name Kennedy strategists released "the Bailey Memorandum," which claimed that the Senator, as a Roman Catholic, would add enormous strength among Catholic voters to the Party's presidential campaign. Although Kennedy's race for second place on the 1956 ticket failed, his managers again utilized the memorandum during the Senator's drive for the presidential nomination four years later.

With Congressman Eugene J. Keogh (D, N.Y.) [q.v.], Bailey led efforts in 1960 to round up Convention support for Kennedy among New England and New York delegates. All 114 New England votes and 104½ of New York's 114 votes were cast for Kennedy, who won on the first ballot. Following Kennedy's nomination, Bailey strongly endorsed the selection of Sen. Lyndon B. Johnson (D, Tex.) [q.v.] for vice president. Between the Convention and general election, Bailey worked primarily as a liaison with other state Party leaders, while successfully directing the Connecticut Kennedy-Johnson campaign.

Kennedy named Bailey as chairman of the Democratic National Committee in January 1961 and gave him a major voice in the distribution of Party patronage. Beginning in October 1961 the President assigned to Bailey, normally regarded as a political technician rather than a spokesman, the task of defending the Administration against criticisms made by the Republican National Committee Chairman, Rep. William E. Miller (R, N.Y.) [q.v.]. In what Kennedy termed "the battle of the mimeograph," Bailey accused New York Gov. Nelson A. Rockefeller [q.v.] of "political larceny in the robber baron tradition" in November 1961, and a month later warned voters of a "curious union of Republicans and right-wing fanatics."

As national committee chairman, Bailey's main task was to maintain Democratic majorities in Congress. In the 1962 elections the Democratic Party avoided the usual off-year losses for the party occupying the White House. The Democrats gained four Senate seats while losing only four in the House. The number of Democratic governors remained unchanged at 34, although the GOP captured state houses in several large, industrial states. In Connecticut, where Bailey continued as state chairman, the Democrats retained the governorship and elected Ribicoff to the U. S. Senate.

On Nov. 12, 1963 President Kennedy and his aides met with Bailey to plan the 1964 Presidential campaign. Kennedy designated Stephen Smith, his brother-in-law, and Bailey as co-directors of the effort. Although he remained party chairman after Kennedy's death 10 days later, Bailey played a limited role in the presidential campaign of Lyndon Johnson. [See JOHNSON Volume]

[JLB]

BAKER, BOBBY (ROBERT GENE)
b. 1928; Pickens, S.C.
Secretary to the Senate Majority
January 1955-October 1963.

Bobby Baker came to Washington in 1943 at the age of 15 to be a Senate page. He held a succession of minor positions over the decade, accumulating a valuable fund of knowledge about the Senate and impressing senators with his energy and ability. Simultaneously he earned a college degree from George Washington University and then attended night law classes at American University. After 1949 Sen. Lyndon Johnson (D, Tex.) and Sen. Robert Kerr (D, Okla.) [q.v.] became Baker's most powerful patrons. Appointed assistant secretary to the Democratic minority in 1953, Baker, dubbed "Lyndon Junior" by Sen. Alan Bible (D, Nev.) [q.v.], became secretary to the majority in 1955 when Johnson became Senate majority leader.

With a sophisticated understanding of the traditions and procedures of the Senate and a shrewd knowledge of individual senators, Baker helped Johnson run the upper house. "Bobby Baker is my strong right arm," Johnson said in 1960. "He is the last person I see at night and the first person I see in the morning." It was Baker's task to round up senators behind measures favored by the leadership. The precision of his preliminary "head counts" was celebrated. Baker's ability to perform numerous favors for senators and others won him power and prestige in the Capitol. His position as secretary-treasurer of the Senate Democratic Campaign Committee from 1957 to 1960 enhanced his influence.

When Johnson left the Senate to assume the vice presidency in 1961, the new majority leader, Sen. Mike Mansfield (D, Mont.) [q.v.], asked Baker to remain as secretary. Baker stayed on, but during the Kennedy Administration he worked more closely with his wealthy conservative sponsor, Kerr, than with his ostensible superior, Mansfield. Baker helped Kerr engineer the narrow defeat of the Administration's medicare bill in July 1962. "On any given issue, I have ten senators in the palm of my hand," Baker told the Chicago Daily News.

In January 1963 President Kennedy was contemplating an enlargement of the Senate Finance Committee, whose conservative majority had the potential to block his legislative program. Kennedy dropped the idea after Baker advised him that there were not enough votes to pass such a reform, but Sen. Joseph Clark (D, Pa.) [q.v.] believed that the Administration was "naive" to rely on Baker's estimate. Clark and other senators outside the Senate establishment

resented the power of Baker, whom Clark identified as a "protagonist of the conservative coalition" in his Congress: The Sapless Branch. Liberal Sens. Stephen Young (D, Ohio) [q.v.] and Quentin Burdick (D, N.D.) [q.v.] claimed that Baker had maneuvered to deny them requested committee assignments.

Relatively unknown outside Washington circles, Baker won national notoriety during the fall of 1963 when it was discovered that he had used his official position to enrich himself. Baker's salary in 1963 was $19,600; yet his net worth was $1.7 million. His downfall began in September 1963 with the filing of a civil suit against him by a business associate, Ralph Hill, president of the Capitol Vending Company. Charging Baker with "influence peddling," Hill said that Baker had accepted $5,600 from him for getting his company a vending franchise at the plant of a government contractor. After failing in an attempt to purchase Capitol Vending, Baker "conspired maliciously," according to the suit, to have the contract canceled and placed with his own vending company, the Serv-U Corp. Amid rumors about his other business activities, Baker resigned as secretary to the majority in October.

The Capitol Vending suit represented only the tip of the iceberg as far as Baker's improper business activities were concerned. An investigation by the Senate Rules and Administration Committee in 1964 and 1965 revealed the greater portion, which included accepting payments for backing an ocean freight forwarders' licensing bill, helping to win favorable tax rulings for banks and the Mortgage Guarantee Insurance Corp. and arranging for a builder to get the contract for construction of the District of Columbia Stadium. The investigation also disclosed Baker's acquisition of lucrative vending contracts for his Serv-U Corp. from aerospace firms working for the government.

The Bobby Baker case was a major campaign issue in the elections of 1964. Republicans accused the Rules Committee's Democratic majority of overlooking Baker's alleged use of "party girls" for political and business purposes. While President

Johnson said little in public about the Baker case and tried to dissociate himself from his former aide, Republican presidential candidate Sen. Barry Goldwater (R, Ariz.) [q.v.] repeatedly held up the scandal as symptomatic of the ethics of Johnson's Washington.

In August 1964 the Rules Committee report found Baker "guilty of many gross improprieties." In January 1967 a U.S. District Court in Washington convicted Baker of income tax evasion, theft and conspiracy to defraud the government. Baker started serving a one-to-three-year prison sentence in January 1971 and was paroled in June 1972. [See Johnson Volume]

[TO]

For further information:
Robert Rowe, *The Bobby Baker Story* (New York, 1967).

BALDWIN, JAMES A(RTHUR)
b. Aug. 12, 1924; New York, N.Y.
Author.

The son of a minister, Baldwin described his Harlem childhood as a "bleak fantasy." As an adolescent he tried preaching but gave up at age 17 and left home shortly thereafter. Taking odd jobs to support himself, Baldwin worked on a novel, won two fellowships and at the age of 24 went to live in France. There, in 1953, he finished *Go Tell It On the Mountain*, his highly praised novel of religious experience in Harlem. Baldwin's most widely acclaimed work during the 1950s was *Notes of a Native Son*, a collection of personal essays that probed what one reviewer called "the peculiar dilemma of Northern Negro intellectuals who can claim neither Western nor African heritage as their own."

During the 1960s Baldwin was probably the most successful black writer in America. His novel *Another Country* and a collection of essays, *Nobody Knows My Name*, were among the leading paperback best-sellers in 1963. Baldwin's literary skills and large audience also made him a major presence in the early civil rights movement. In *The Crisis of the Negro Intellectual* Harold Cruse described Baldwin as "the chief spokesman for the Negro among the intellectual class" during the Kennedy years.

Shortly after the January 1963 publication of *The Fire Next Time*, two essays by Baldwin on the imminent escalation of America's racial crisis, Assistant Attorney General Burke Marshall [q.v.] arranged a private breakfast meeting between Baldwin and Attorney General Robert Kennedy [q.v.], who was then concerned about rising black protest against discrimination.

Baldwin later arranged for Kennedy to meet with a dozen prominent black leaders including singer Lena Horne, playwright Lorraine Hansberry and Dr. Kenneth Clark, the distinguished psychologist, in New York on May 24. According to David Lewis, a biographer of Dr. Martin Luther King, Jr. [q.v.], the well publicized meeting was an "unmitigated failure." Robert Kennedy was upset that Baldwin had selected mostly artists and entertainers for the meeting and was incensed at their disrespect for the Administration's civil rights accomplishments. After the meeting Baldwin stated that the group felt it had failed to impress Kennedy "with the extremity of the racial situation" in the North and their view that the Administration's civil rights activity was not sufficient to avert a deepening crisis.

A week before the Aug. 28, 1963 March on Washington, Baldwin led a group of 80 American artists in Paris who presented a petition to the U.S. embassy supporting the Washington demonstration. Later, Baldwin flew to Washington to deliver an address to the marchers.

Baldwin was also among the speakers at a Sept. 22, 1963 rally at New York's Foley Square, where 10,000 people gathered to protest the Sept. 15 Birmingham, Ala., church bombing, which killed four black children. At the rally Baldwin called for a nationwide campaign to boycott Christmas shopping as a protest against the bombing. On Oct. 7 Baldwin addressed a Student Nonviolent Coordinating Committee (SNCC) voter registration rally in Selma, Ala. A week after President Kennedy was assassinated, Baldwin gave the keynote address at SNCC's annual conference and lauded the late President for breaking the traditional compact between the South and North that had let Southern whites do as they wished with "their niggers." Though he lived abroad for most of the 1960s, Baldwin continued to lend his prestige to the civil rights movement in America and flew in from Paris for the last leg of the 1965 Selma march. [See JOHNSON Volume]

[DKR]

For further information:
James Baldwin, *Nobody Knows My Name* (New York, 1961).
———, *The Fire Next Time* (New York, 1963).

BALL, GEORGE W(ILDMAN)
b. Dec. 21, 1909; Des Moines, Iowa.
Undersecretary of State for Economic Affairs, January 1961-November 1961; Undersecretary of State, November 1961-September 1966.

Following his graduation from Northwestern University Law School in 1933, Ball worked for the Farm Credit Administration and Treasury Department. In 1935 he returned to Illinois and joined a Chicago law firm where Adlai Stevenson [q.v.] was one of his colleagues. Ball reentered government service in 1942 in the Office of Lend-Lease Administration and in 1944 was appointed director of the U.S. Strategic Bombing Survey.

After the war he resumed private law practice and became a specialist on international trade. Ball worked closely with Jean Monnet on plans for the new European Coal and Steel Community. He later represented it and several other Common Market agencies in the U.S. In 1952 and 1956 Ball played an important role in Stevenson's presidential campaign and in 1960 served as Stevenson's manager at the Los Angeles convention. Despite Ball's support of Stevenson, President Kennedy, impressed with a report on economic and commercial policy that the lawyer had written, designated Ball as undersecretary of

state for economic affairs in January 1961. [See EISENHOWER Volume]

During the early months of the Kennedy Administration, Ball was primarily involved in the formation of U.S. trade policy. Concerned with America's continued adverse balance of payments and anticipating increased problems after Britain's expected entrance into the Common Market, Ball advocated a complete revision of U.S. trade policy to bring down tariff levels and give the President flexibility to meet new conditions. These proposals were embodied in the Trade Expansion Act of 1962, which Ball helped draft. This measure cut tariffs by 50% to 100% on many foreign goods and gave the President wide discriminatory powers to retaliate against foreign import restrictions.

In addition to his activities as economic adviser, Ball was concerned with U.S. policy toward the Congo, where the secession of mineral-rich Katanga province shortly after Belgium had granted independence in June 1960 threatened the viability of the central government. Despite his close connection with Western Europe and sympathy for the plight of the Belgians, Ball supported the policy of the State Department's "New Africa" group, led by men such as Harlan Cleveland [q.v.], which advocated the use of force against Katanga if necessary to achieve reunification. Ball lobbied behind the scenes at the U.N. and within the Administration for the adoption of this policy. Reunification was achieved in January 1963 through the use of U.N. troops backed by American military support.

In November 1961 Ball replaced Chester Bowles [q.v.] as undersecretary of state, the second-ranking position in the State Department. The change was made because of Kennedy's desire to place trusted aides in the State Department, which he felt had not performed effectively, and because of continual clashes between Bowles and Kennedy advisers, particularly Attorney General Robert Kennedy [q.v.].

During the Cuban missile crisis of October 1962, Ball served as a member of Excom, the committee of high-ranking advisers formed to counsel the President after the discovery of Soviet offensive missiles in Cuba. After Kennedy proclaimed a "quarantine" of Cuba on Oct. 22, Ball directed the arrangement of a program to inform the allies of the U.S. decision and to write a legal justification of the action.

During the early 1960s Ball became increasingly involved with the growing war in Vietnam. In 1961 when the Administration was discussing policy options in Vietnam, Ball opposed the recommendation of Maxwell Taylor [q.v.] and W. W. Rostow [q.v.] to introduce combat forces into that country because he felt it would lead to an ever-increasing involvement. The recommendation was not approved.

Ball strongly opposed the regime of South Vietnamese President Ngo Dinh Diem and his brother Ngo Dinh Nhu. In August 1963 he urged that American support of the government be withdrawn to force either a change of policy or a coup. Following the August 1963 attack of Nhu's secret police on Buddhist dissidents, Ball, in conjunction with Michael Forrestal [q.v.], Averell Harriman [q.v.] and Roger Hilsman [q.v.], drafted the "August 24 Cable" sent to Henry Cabot Lodge [q.v.], the new U.S. ambassador to Vietnam. The message stated that the U.S. could not accept Nhu's crackdown. It also informed Lodge that "Diem must be given [a] chance to rid himself of Nhu" but cautioned that if Diem did not take that step the U.S. "must face the possibility that Diem himself cannot be preserved." Lodge was also instructed to privately inform South Vietnamese generals contemplating a coup that if Nhu remained, the U.S. would "give them direct support in any interim period of breakdown [of the] central government mechanism." The coup failed to take place immediately because of the generals' inability to achieve a favorable balance of forces in the Saigon area and because of doubts about the firmness of U.S. commitments to Diem's overthrow. However, a coup, staged by different military leaders, was eventually carried out in November 1963.

During the Johnson Administration Ball objected to the large-scale troop commitments and intensive bombing raids against North Vietnam ordered by the President.

Convinced that he could not change American policy, he left office in September 1966 to return to his law firm and to investment banking. A quiet man who remained personally loyal to Johnson and Secretary of State Dean Rusk [q.v.], his determined opposition to the war only became widely known after the publication of the *Pentagon Papers* in 1971. [See JOHNSON Volume]

[EWS]

For further information:
David Halberstam, *The Best and the Brightest* (New York, 1972).

BARGHOORN, FREDERICK C(HARLES)

b. July 4, 1911; New York, N.Y.
Political scientist.

Barghoorn, an historian who specialized in Soviet affairs, became an attache at the American embassy in Moscow following the receipt of his Ph.D. from Harvard in 1941. In 1947 he joined the faculty of Yale University and became a professor of political science in 1957.

At the end of a research trip to the Soviet Union in November 1963, Barghoorn was arrested on charges of spying for the U.S. during his service with the embassy and during each of his six visits to the USSR since 1947. Barghoorn denied the Soviet charges.

In reaction to the arrest President Kennedy issued an unusual personal demand for Barghoorn's release. Kennedy also ordered the postponement of scheduled U.S.-Soviet talks on a cultural exchange agreement and hinted that the arrest might affect American attitudes about the Soviet purchase of U.S. wheat then under discussion.

Barghoorn was freed after 16 days in solitary confinement. According to Soviet Foreign Minister Andrei A. Gromyko, he was released "in view of the personal concern expressed by President Kennedy." The charges against him were never dropped.

[EWS]

BARNETT, ROSS R(OBERT)
b. Jan. 22, 1898; Standing Pine, Miss.
Governor, Miss., 1960-64.

The youngest son of a Confederate veteran, Barnett worked his way through Mississippi College and the University of Mississippi Law School, receiving his law degree in 1926. He then began private practice in Jackson, served as president of the State Bar Association in 1943 and 1944 and made two unsuccessful attempts for the governorship in 1951 and 1955. He tried again in 1959, this time placing first in the Aug. 5 Democratic primary and winning the Aug. 25 runoff by a wide margin. A member of the segregationist Citizens Councils, Barnett preached white supremacy during his campaign with what one observer called a "Bible-pounding evangelistic fervor." Repeatedly promising he would "rot in jail" before he would "let one Negro ever darken the sacred threshold of our white schools," Barnett won the November election easily and was inaugurated on Jan. 19, 1960.

In Barnett's first 10 weeks in office, 24 new segregation bills were introduced in the state legislature and circuit clerks were ordered not to give the Justice Department any voter registration figures. As chairman of the State Sovereignty Commission, Barnett subsidized the Mississippi Association of Citizens Councils throughout his term, awarding it over $100,000 in state grants in 1962 alone. Labeling the civil rights plank adopted at the Democratic National Convention in 1960 "repulsive," Barnett tried to organize a third party movement comparable to the Dixiecrats of 1948 but won little support from other Southern governors. Barnett then put forward a slate of unpledged Democratic electors, which defeated the Mississippi slate pledged to support Kennedy in November. They ultimately cast the state's eight electoral votes for Sen. Harry F. Byrd (D, Va.) [q.v.].

All these events were a prelude to Barnett's defiance of federal court orders mandating the admission of James Meredith [q.v.] to the University of Mississippi in September 1962. There had been no desegregation in any of the state's public schools until then, and shortly after the final court order for Meredith's admission was handed down on Sept. 10, Barnett promised to oppose it, declaring, "We

will not surrender to the evil and illegal forces of tyranny." Appointed special registrar for Meredith by the University's Board of Trustees, Barnett met Meredith in Oxford when he came to register on Sept. 20 and read him and accompanying federal officials a lengthy proclamation denying Meredith entry. On Sept. 25 the Fifth Circuit Court issued an injunction prohibiting Barnett from interfering with Meredith's enrollment, but when Meredith tried to register at the trustees' office in Jackson that day, Barnett refused to accept a copy of the injunction and once again denied Meredith admission. Acting under Barnett's orders, Lt. Gov. Paul B. Johnson [q.v.] blocked Meredith's third registration attempt in Oxford on Sept. 26. Two days later the Fifth Circuit Court found Barnett guilty of civil contempt and required him to comply with court orders by Oct. 2 or face a $10,000 per day fine.

Beginning Sept. 15 Attorney General Robert F. Kennedy [q.v.] negotiated with Barnett in a series of phone conversations, hoping to persuade the Governor to comply with the court orders and thus obviate the need to call in federal troops. Barnett did work out a plan with the Justice Department on Sept. 27 in which the Governor would physically block Meredith and a force of U.S. marshals when they came on the campus that day, but would step aside when the marshals drew guns. This plan was canceled, however, when a gathering crowd in Oxford made Barnett and federal officials fearful that violence would result. President Kennedy entered the behind-the-scenes negotiations on Sept. 29 and, in three phone conversations with Barnett, worked out a new arrangement in which Barnett would go to Oxford on Oct. 1, ostensibly planning to deny Meredith admission again, while Meredith would quietly register in Jackson. Late that evening Barnett canceled the deal and on Sept. 30, after President Kennedy had federalized the Mississippi National Guard, Barnett suggested staging a dramatic show of force at Oxford in which state forces would give way to the U.S. Army. The Attorney General dismissed the idea as, "foolish and dangerous" and added that the President, in a television address that night, intended to reveal the plans Barnett had agreed to on the 29th and announce that the Governor had gone back on his word. In response Barnett now suggested that Meredith be taken quietly onto campus that day before the President's address. Barnett promised that state police would aid federal marshals in protecting Meredith and maintaining order, and it was agreed he would issue a statement saying he was yielding to force but condemning any talk of violence.

Federal marshals and state police entered the campus late that afternoon, while Meredith was flown in from Memphis and taken to his dormitory room around 6 p.m. At 9 p.m. Barnett issued a statement declaring that the state was "surrounded by armed forces" and "physically overpowered" but calling on Mississippians to "preserve the peace and avoid bloodshed." A riot had already erupted on the campus, however, and at a crucial point the state police were suddenly ordered away from the University. It was never clear who gave the order, but the troopers returned after the Kennedys urged Barnett to get them back onto the campus. Shortly before midnight Barnett issued a second statement accusing the federal government of "trampling on the sovereignty of this great state" and asserting that Mississippi "will never surrender." The riot lasted into the early morning hours and ended only after President Kennedy called in both the National Guard and the Army. Two men died during the night of violence and over 350 were injured. At 8 a.m. on Oct. 1, Meredith finally registered at the University.

In the aftermath of what was termed the most serious clash between federal and state authority since the Civil War, Barnett blamed the riot on "inexperienced, nervous and trigger-happy federal marshals" and said Mississippians were "enraged, incensed—and rightly so" by federal intervention. Although Meredith had at last enrolled, the Fifth Circuit Court refused to drop the contempt charges against Barnett. Late in 1962, at the explicit request of the Court, the Justice Department added criminal contempt-of-court charges to the pending civil contempt action against the Governor. The Kennedys were reportedly averse to prosecuting Barnett once the September crisis was past and did not want him arrested and imprisoned for fear of touching off another confrontation. The case remained in court until May 1965 when the Fifth Circuit, in a 4-3 ruling, dismissed the contempt charges against Barnett.

Barnett meanwhile denounced civil rights workers in Mississippi as "alien agitators, provocateurs and mercenaries," testified in Senate hearings against the 1964 Civil Rights Act and called for continuation of voter literacy tests and poll taxes so that there would not be "a government of the ignorant, by the ignorant, and for the ignorant." He acquiesced in the enrollment of a second black student at the University of Mississippi in June 1963 only because it was forced on him, he said, by "the armed might of the federal government."

Aside from his defense of Southern segregation policy, Barnett made an all-out drive during his administration to bring new industry into the state. He lowered the state income tax, offered special tax exemptions to new plants and emphasized the low level of wages in Mississippi. Total state income grew 9% in 1962, the fourth highest increase of any state, but Mississippi still had the lowest per capita income level in the nation in 1963. When his term ended in January 1964, Barnett returned to his private law practice. He entered a 1967 Democratic gubernatorial primary but polled only 11% of the vote and did not qualify for the runoff.

[CAB]

For further information:
Walter Lord, *The Past That Would Not Die* (New York, 1965).
Victor S. Navasky, *Kennedy Justice* (New York, 1971).

BARTLETT, E(DWARD) L(EWIS)
b. April 20, 1904; Seattle, Wash.
d. Dec. 11, 1968; Washington, D.C.
Democratic Senator, Alaska, 1959-68.

E. L. "Bob" Bartlett grew up in Fairbanks, Alaska, attended the University of Washington and the University of Alaska and worked as a reporter for the *Fairbanks Daily News-Miner*. President Franklin D. Roosevelt appointed him secretary of the Alaska Territory (equivalent to state lieutenant governor) in 1939. From 1945 to

1959 he represented the territory in Congress as a non-voting delegate. Bartlett served on a number of congressional committees, introduced bills to benefit his constituents and lobbied effectively for Alaskan statehood, finally attained in 1959. That year Bartlett and Ernest Gruening (D, Alaska) [q.v.] were chosen as the state's first U.S. senators. A flip of a silver dollar determined that Bartlett rather than Gruening would be designated as the senior senator.

During the Kennedy years, Bartlett voted for much of the Administration's legislative program, including area redevelopment, school aid and medicare. He also voted for the 1963 nuclear test ban treaty. Bartlett, however, opposed efforts by the Administration to establish a privately owned Communications Satellite Corporation. Along with other liberals he argued that communications satellites should remain under government control. In August 1962 Bartlett, in conjunction with Sens. Wayne Morse (D, Ore.) [q.v.], Maurine Neuberger (D, Ore.) [q.v.], Estes Kefauver (D, Tenn.) [q.v.] and others, staged a filibuster, but the tactic failed and the Administration's communications satellite bill became law.

As a member of the Senate Commerce Committee, Bartlett advocated federal appropriations for the fishing and maritime industries, which were important to the economy of his state. He sponsored legislation promoting commercial fishery research and development and also proposed that foreigners fishing within U.S. territorial waters be subject to criminal penalties. (Alaskan fishermen had been hard hit by competition from Japanese fishing vessels.) Bartlett also attained prominence on the Commerce Committee for his efforts to establish stricter federal regulations to reduce the levels of permissible radiation from medical and dental equipment and from home color television sets.

During the Johnson years Bartlett gained the chairmanship of the Merchant Marine and Fisheries Subcommittee of the Senate Commerce Committee and won enactment of a number of bills favorable to the maritime industry. He also earned a reputation as an outspoken critic of the Johnson Administration's Vietnam policies. [See JOHNSON Volume]

[JLW]

BAYH, BIRCH E(VANS)
b. Jan. 22, 1928; Terre Haute, Ind.
Democratic Senator, Ind., 1963- .

After graduating from Purdue University's School of Agriculture, Birch Bayh settled on a 340-acre farm outside Terre Haute in 1951. He won election as a Democrat to the largely Republican Indiana House of Representatives in 1954. Following the elections of 1958 a new Democratic majority in the state legislature elected the 30-year-old Bayh speaker of the House for the 1959-1960 session. Simultaneously, Bayh studied law at the Indiana University School of Law, receiving his degree in 1960. In 1962 he challenged Sen. Homer E. Capehart (R, Ind.) [q.v.] for a seat in the U.S. Senate.

Capehart, a conservative Republican, was generally considered unbeatable. His harsh criticism of the Kennedy Administration's handling of the Cuban question throughout most of 1962 seemed to find greater favor among the Indiana electorate than Bayh's identification with President Kennedy, who in the fall decried Capehart's "19th century voting record." Nevertheless, aided by Capehart's overconfidence, the strong support of the state AFL-CIO and a saturation television campaign, Bayh upset the incumbent with 50.3% of the vote.

In his first year in the Senate, Bayh supported most of the Administration's legislative program. He voted for the Youth Employment Act in April 1963 and, in his maiden speech in October, proposed an amendment increasing the appropriation for vocational education by $224 million over a three-year period. He withdrew the amendment at the request of Sen. Wayne Morse (D, Ore.) [q.v.]. Bayh was one of 46 senators who co-sponsored the Administration's civil rights bill in June 1963. He also backed Kennedy forces in August in defeating, 37-32, an amendment to reduce funds for the National Aeronautics and

Space Administration. Bayh opposed the Administration-backed Mass Transportation Act, however, which authorized federal aid to urban transportation systems.

Bayh held seats on the Senate's Judiciary and Public Works Committees. When the chairmanship of the Judiciary Committee's Subcommittee on Constitutional Amendments became vacant in August 1963 and no other senator volunteered for it, Bayh took the obscure post. The position became unexpectedly prominent when the death of President Kennedy and the accession of Vice President Lyndon Johnson to the presidency left the country without a vice president. Bayh sponsored the 25th Amendment which provided for the selection of a new vice president and the replacement of the president in case of disability. [See JOHNSON, NIXON Volumes]

[TO]

BEIRNE, JOSEPH A(NTHONY)
b. Feb. 16, 1911; Jersey City, N.J.
d. Sept. 2, 1974; Washington, D.C.
President, Communications Workers of America, 1947-74.

Beirne began working for Western Electric in 1928 and became an important leader of its employes association during the 1930s. Initially resisting Congress of Industrial Organization (CIO) efforts to organize telephone workers, Beirne was elected president of the independent National Federation of Telephone Workers in 1943. He negotiated the first national contract with the American Telephone and Telegraph Company in 1946. Following the first nationwide telephone strike the next year he became president of the reorganized Communications Workers of America (CWA) which affiliated with the CIO in 1949. Beirne became a CIO vice president and, after the AFL-CIO merger in 1955, a vice president of that organization. [See TRUMAN Volume]

During the early 1960s the CWA suffered a loss of membership when the International Brotherhood of Teamsters, a union Beirne had helped to expel from the AFL-CIO in 1957, began to raid the tele-

phone workers' union. Although the CWA leadership at Western Electric was expelled in August 1961 for conspiring to sway the allegiance of CWA members to the Teamsters, the CWA emerged the victor in two critical jurisdictional elections. In December 1962 they defeated the Teamsters in a National Labor Relations Board election to represent telephone equipment installers at Western Electric, and in February 1964 the CWA outpolled the Teamsters in the union's New York Telephone local.

In the 1950s the CWA had developed training programs in American-style unionism for Latin American communications workers. In 1960 Beirne, a Democrat and a strong supporter of Kennedy in the 1960 presidential election, urged the AFL-CIO to establish a broader program to promote a pro-U.S. labor movement in Latin America. With enthusiastic support from Kennedy the American Institute for Free Labor Development was launched in 1961, sponsored by the AFL-CIO, the U.S. government and private corporations. Beirne also served on several presidential commissions and panels, including the Peace Corps "career planning board" designed to aid returning Peace Corpsmen in finding jobs. He later served on several other presidential commissions and panels. He was also a member of the Citizens Committee for a Free Cuba, a group formed in 1963 which warned of "growing Castro-Communist infiltration of Latin America."

An influential AFL-CIO leader, Beirne broke with President George Meany's [q.v.] leadership and became a secretary-treasurer of a national labor committee supporting Sen. George McGovern (D, S.D.) [q.v.] for president in 1972. He remained president of the CWA until his death in 1974. [See JOHNSON, NIXON Volumes]

[MDB]

For further information:
Jack Barbash, *Unions and Telephones: The Story of the Communications Workers of America* (New York, 1952).

BELL, DANIEL
b. May 10, 1919; New York, N.Y.
Sociologist.

Daniel Bell, an influential American sociologist of the 1950s and 1960s, was born into a family of Polish-Jewish garment workers on New York's Lower East Side. A precocious student, Bell was soon attracted to the socialist movement. By the time he graduated from the City College of New York in 1938, he was a politically knowledgeable member of the Young People's Socialist League. He edited the social democratic *New Leader* during the war, then taught at the University of Chicago and in 1948 began a decade-long association with *Fortune* as its labor editor.

During the 1950s Bell was an articulate spokesman for the growing centrist mood among postwar intellectuals. In a series of articles and essays he celebrated the pluralist and interest group politics of contemporary America. Bell reinterpreted the mass social movements of the early 20th century as dangerously utopian and chiliastic. In 1954 Bell edited *The New American Right*, an influential collection of essays by several scholars which popularized the view that McCarthyism was the heir to the radical populist and agrarian agitation of an earlier era. Bell resigned from the staff of *Fortune* in 1958 and spent a year at Stanford University before joining the sociology department at Columbia University.

In mid-1960 Bell republished several of his most important sociological and political essays in a collection entitled *The End of Ideology: On the Exhaustion of Political Ideas in the Fifties*. The work was soon acclaimed a classic; for a great number of liberal intellectuals it summed up the political consensus of the era. Bell argued that the experience of Stalinism and Fascism had destroyed the radical faith in ideological mass movements for social change. Meanwhile, the emergence of the postwar welfare state had muted and ameliorated class and social conflict. "In the West, among intellectuals," wrote Bell, "the old passions are spent." Bell urged upon intellectuals both the responsibility and self-discipline necessary to work for limited and empirical social goals: "A utopia has to specify *where* one wants to go, *how* to get there, the costs of the enterprise, and some realization of, and justification for the determination of *who* is to pay."

Bell revised and updated his earlier work on American conservatism in 1963 and republished it as *The Radical Right*. With the other intellectuals whose essays were collected in the book, Bell argued that an authentic American conservatism hardly existed and that much of the support won in the early 1960s by extreme anti-Communist groups stemmed from the "status anxieties" of newly wealthy but socially insecure elements in the fast-moving postwar American society.

In the mid and late 1960s, Bell turned to the use of sociology as a tool for social prediction and the making of public policy. He was a co-founder of the journal *Public Interest* in 1965 and an editor of a collective study, *Toward the Year 2000*, published three years later. With like-minded intellectuals, Daniel Moynihan, Robert Nisbet, Irving Kristol and others, Bell grew increasingly pessimistic in the late 1960s and early 1970s about the possibility that government action could produce significant and beneficial social change. In 1969 Bell left Columbia's sociology department for Harvard's.

[NNL]

For further information:
Daniel Bell, *The End of Ideology* (New York, 1960, 1961).
———— ed., *The Radical Right* (New York, 1963).
"Daniel Bell," *Current Biography Yearbook 1973* (New York, 1974), pp. 40-42.

BELL, DAVID E(LLIOTT)
b. Jan. 20, 1919; Jamestown, N.D.
Director, Bureau of the Budget, January 1961-November 1962; Administrator of the Agency for International Development, January 1963-July 1966.

Raised in an academic atmosphere in Palo Alto, Calif., David Bell studied economics at Pomona College and Harvard. He joined the Bureau of the Budget in

1942, served in the Marine Corps and then returned to the Bureau in 1945. Between 1947 and 1953 Bell alternated between the Budget Bureau and the White House, specializing in drafting presidential budget messages and speeches on economic affairs. After helping with Adlai Stevenson's [q.v.] presidential campaign, Bell returned to Harvard. From 1954 to 1957, as a member of a Harvard-Ford Foundation team, he assisted the government of Pakistan in formulating fiscal policies, becoming a recognized authority on the economic problems of underdeveloped countries. [See TRUMAN Volume]

Although Bell did not work for Kennedy's election, Clark Clifford [q.v.] recommended him to Kennedy for the post of budget director. Kennedy announced the appointment on Dec. 2, 1960, citing Bell's experience in working with both the Bureau and the White House and his experience in the area of foreign aid.

The post of budget director had become more critical since Franklin Roosevelt's time as the government's role in the economy expanded. The Bureau of the Budget not only made the final judgment on allocations to federal programs, but it also made policy by sponsoring legislation, encouraging certain programs and discouraging others. More than most agencies, it worked closely with Congress.

Kennedy publicly stated that he wanted a balanced budget, but he felt that the economic recession and high unemployment rate inherited from the Eisenhower years constituted a higher priority. Working with the fiscal 1962 budget which had been prepared by the Eisenhower staff, Theodore Sorenson [q.v.], Walter Heller [q.v.], C. Douglas Dillon [q.v.] and Bell found that it would be impossible to avoid a deficit of some $2.8 billion. Bell was not pleased with the deficit, but, as he explained to the Congressional Joint Economic Committee in March 1961, he regarded the budget as an instrument of national policy rather than as a bookkeeping device to discourage expenditures. In a period of recession government spending was "an important part of a national effort to close the gap between our actual and potential output and to achieve adequate economic growth," he declared.

Along with Heller, Sorenson, Myer Feldman [q.v.] and Lawrence O'Brien [q.v.], Bell helped draft Kennedy's complete legislative program for 1962. One of the most important parts of the program was the request for a large tax cut. Although Bell thought it would leave a large budget deficit and stimulate inflation, he held that a tax cut of about $10 billion would finally end the recession of 1960-61. Balancing the budget, he said, "may itself contribute to bringing the recovery to a halt below full employment levels." Because of congressional opposition, the tax reduction was not enacted until February 1964.

Bell succeeded Fowler Hamilton [q.v.] as administrator of the Agency for International Development (AID) in November 1962. AID was a newly-created semiautonomous agency within the State Department, designed to coordinate and rationalize foreign aid programs.

AID's guiding principles owed much to the economic development theories of Walt W. Rostow [q.v.] and to the Ford Foundation's experience in the underdeveloped world. Whereas Eisenhower's foreign aid policy concentrated on grants intended for military and short-range purposes, the Kennedy Administration planned to offer long-term loans and credits to governments and native entrepreneurs. Strengthening the economic infrastructure by techniques such as improving the transportation system and providing universal access to quality education and health care would provide the base for an underdeveloped country's self-sustaining growth and ensure its more equal participation in the world economy. In addition, AID sought to train a cadre of experts in foreign aid. Attempts were made to enlist the skills of individuals in American private enterprise and thereby make foreign aid more representative of a national consensus.

As head of AID Bell had to work under constant public and congressional criticism. Congress cut Kennedy's $4.9 billion foreign aid request for fiscal 1963 to a final appropriation of $3.9 billion. Because military aid was reduced only slightly, economic aid suffered almost all of the $1-billion cut. To generate support for foreign economic assistance Kennedy appointed in December 1962 a bipartisan Citizens Committee to Strengthen the Security of the Free World headed by Gen. Lucius Clay [q.v.]. Although Kennedy hoped that the Committee's findings would support the need for an ambitious foreign aid program, the Clay Report, issued in March 1963, was an unexpectedly conservative document which concluded that the U.S. had attempted to do "too much for too many too soon."

Bell projected a foreign aid request of close to $5 billion for fiscal 1964, but by that time attacks on the program had grown even more vociferous. Congressional liberals, such as Sen. Wayne Morse (D, Ore.) [q.v.] turned against "waste" in foreign aid, while conservatives, such as Sen. Barry Goldwater (R, Ariz.) [q.v.], wanted to eliminate all economic foreign aid, saving only the military programs. Conscious of the mood of Congress, the Administration requested $4.5 billion. Bell then agreed that another $200 million could be taken from the AID budget proposal. The final appropriation was only $3 billion despite the protests of Bell and other members of the Administration. In addition, Congress added a series of provisions to the foreign aid bill which effectively limited presidential prerogatives.

During the Johnson Administration AID concentrated its programs in nations where American foreign policy interests were most directly at stake. With the widening of the Vietnam conflict in 1965, AID took responsibility for handling the economic assistance side of the large U.S. effort there. Bell resigned as AID head in June 1966 to become a Ford Foundation vice president. [See JOHNSON Volume]

[JCH]

BENNETT, WALLACE F(OSTER)
b. Nov. 13, 1898; Salt Lake City, Utah.
Republican Senator, Utah, 1951-75.

The son of Mormon pioneers, Wallace Bennett entered his family's plate and glass manufacturing business after graduating from the University of Utah. Beginning as a clerk he advanced through all phases of the business, taking over general management in 1932. Bennett's business interests also came to include a Ford dealership, a jewelry company, an investment concern and a bank. After serving as president of the National Association of Manufacturers (NAM) for 1949, Bennett was elected to the Senate as a Republican from Utah in 1950.

In the Senate Bennett advocated the same free enterprise views he had promoted for the NAM, opposing government restrictions on business and firmly defending "right-to-work" laws that allowed states to ban compulsory union shops. He became an influential proponent of pro-business views on the Finance Committee and the Banking and Currency Committee. Republican senators often looked to Bennett for conservative guidance on economic questions. [See TRUMAN, EISENHOWER Volumes]

Bennett was an active opponent of the area redevelopment bill promoted by Sen. Paul Douglas (D, Ill.) [q.v.] and the Kennedy Administration to invigorate economically depressed areas with federal loans and grants. Bennett disputed the wisdom of the program, arguing that many depressed areas were not suffering from a capital shortage but from inherent economic debilities which the federal government could not cure. Along with the Republican minority on the Banking and Currency Committee Bennett claimed that federal financing would be channeled into unsound projects. "Uncle Sam," he said in March 1961, "may well end up owning a host of second-hand empty buildings in so-called distressed areas." In May Congress voted to authorize $394 million for aid to depressed areas. In 1964 Bennett called the program "a political slush fund for the Democrats."

Bennett was more successful in his opposition to Douglas's "truth-in-lending" proposal to require merchants to furnish borrowers with full knowledge of finance charges and interest rates. Bennett said that he favored full disclosure but was against applying a single legislative formula to a wide variety of credit arrangements. He helped to defeat the measure in the Banking and Currency Committee in September

1962. Truth-in-lending legislation did not move out of the Committee until 1967 when a compromise version was passed.

Bennett consistently opposed the social welfare programs of the Kennedy Administration. He voted against the Administration's $2.5 billion aid-to-education bill in May 1961. He backed an amendment put forth by Sen. Strom Thurmond (R, S.C.) [q.v.] to prohibit withholding school aid from a district that practiced racial discrimination in its schools. Bennett opposed medicare in July 1962 and voted against mass transit aid in 1962 and 1963. He also opposed the nuclear test ban treaty in September 1963.

In 1963 the U.S. Chamber of Commerce praised Bennett as "our most outstanding spokesman, not just this year, but also in 1961 and 1962." Despite his impressive conservative credentials, Bennett faced a stiff primary challenge from Utah's right wing in 1962. He defeated Salt Lake City's militantly conservative mayor, J. Bracken Lee, in the Republican primary in September and won reelection in November over Rep. David King (D, Utah), a strong supporter of President Kennedy. Bennett remained one of the Senate's most influential Republican conservatives throughout the Johnson Administration. [See JOHNSON, NIXON Volumes]

[TO]

BERLE, ADOLF A(UGUSTUS), JR.

b. Jan. 29, 1895; Boston, Mass.
d. March 17, 1971; New York, N.Y.
Chairman, Interdepartmental Task Force on Latin America, January-July 1961.

The descendant of German liberals who fled to America in the 1850s, Berle received a rigorous education at home and entered Harvard College at the age of 14. After taking a law degree in 1916, he served in Army intelligence during the war and attended the Paris Peace Conference. Moving to New York City, Berle began a long teaching career, mainly at Columbia University, and became involved in a number of liberal causes, particularly in defense of American Indians. In 1932 he and Gardiner C. Means published *The Modern Corporation and Private Property,* an influential work which argued that ownership and control of capitalist enterprise had become divorced, hence concentrating excessive power in the hands of top management. He was one of Franklin D. Roosevelt's original "brain trusters," advising FDR in the 1932 campaign and preparing much of the early New Deal legislation. Until 1938 Berle also was involved in New York City government, where he helped Mayor Fiorello H. La Guardia reorganize the city's finances. He was assistant secretary of state for Latin American affairs through 1944 and then served as ambassador to Brazil, where he supported military insurgents who overthrew the dictatorship of Getulio Vargas in 1945. Since he was both an architect and an instrument of Roosevelt's Good Neighbor Policy, Berle earned a popularity in Latin America unusual for a North American. [See TRUMAN Volume]

During the 1950s Berle confined himself to his law practice, to his activity with the New York State Liberal Party and to participation in some of the studies sponsored by the Rockefeller Brothers Fund. Following the November 1960 elections, John F. Kennedy asked Berle to head a six-man task force designed to make recommendations on both immediate Latin American problems and long-range policy.

The recommendations, made in January 1961, found their most significant expression in the new Administration's Alliance for Progress, which marked a change from the Latin American policy pursued in the Eisenhower-Dulles years. The task force report, reflecting Berle's fear of Castro's Cuba, stated that the Communists intended to "convert the Latin American social revolution into a Marxist attack on the United States itself." Believing that the social revolution was inevitable, Berle advised the U.S. to decrease its support of right-wing dictatorships and openly support democratic-progressive political movements. To Berle, Latin America in 1960 resembled Europe in 1947. The situation called for a new Marshall Plan to defeat the Communist effort to bring the Cold War to this hemi-sphere. Although Berle wanted a massive economic and military aid program for Latin America, he emphasized the need for a dynamic ideology and philosophy to guide U.S. policy and counter the Communists. The Alliance was intended to be a more vigorous version of the Good Neighbor Policy.

In his autobiography Berle wrote that Richard N. Goodwin [q.v.], Kennedy's special assistant, had talked to him about becoming assistant secretary of state for Latin American affairs in December 1960, but Berle felt that he was too old for a "third-string office." His task force, in fact, advised that a State Department under-secretaryship for the Western Hemisphere be set up, "thus ending stepchild status of this area in U.S. policy." Berle, however, decided to serve as head of an inter-departmental task force on Latin America with authority at least equal to that of an assistant secretary of state. The task force was to be directly responsible to the President and the Secretary of State.

Berle served in his new post from January through July of 1961. He played no role in planning the Bay of Pigs invasion, although his advice was occasionally sol-icited. He wrote that he "did not dissent," although he disliked the covert nature of the Central Intelligence Agency's (CIA) plan and the Agency's indifference to the politics of the Cuban exiles whom they trained. Berle preferred that the U.S. gov-ernment and the CIA aid only those Cuban exiles who had been part of the 26th of July Movement, which he thought Castro had betrayed. He devoted much of the first three months explaining U.S. policy on Cuba to Latin American heads of state and to the Cuban exile groups.

When Berle left his post in July, he was on good terms with Kennedy but was dis-turbed that the State Department was so slow in implementing new policies. He had also warned the U.S. to take more forceful action against Castro with the cooperation of the other American nations, but he found that the Inter-American machinery, particu-larly the Organization of American States, was ineffective. Berle remained active until

his death, writing on Latin America and economics, offering his advice to the gov-ernment and participating in New York City politics.

[JCH]

For further information:
Adolf A. Berle, Jr., *Latin America: Diplomacy and Reality* (New York, 1962).
Beatrice Bishop Berle and Travis Beal Jacobs, eds., *Navigating the Rapids, 1919-1971: From the Papers of Adolf A. Berle* (New York, 1973).

BIBLE, ALAN D.
b. Nov. 20, 1909; Lovelock, Nev.
Democratic Senator, Nevada, 1954- .
Chairman, District of Columbia Commit-tee, 1957-68.

Attorney general of Nevada from 1942 to 1950, Alan Bible was elected to the Senate in 1954 to fill the seat vacated by the death of Sen. Patrick McCarran, a former law part-ner. During the campaign Bible promised to continue McCarran's efforts for higher wool, lead and zinc tariffs. Throughout the Eisenhower and Kennedy Administrations he voted as a moderate Democrat and estab-lished himself as a very effective but "low pro-file" senator.

Bible's committee assignments attested to his broad range of influence in the early 1960s: he sat on the committees on Appropriations, Interior and Insular Affairs and Select Small Business Committee. He sat on the Special Committee on Aging and the Democratic Steering Committee. He was chairman of the District of Columbia Committee, which reported a bill in September 1961 to enable residents of the District of Columbia over 18 years of age to vote in presidential elec-tions. The bill, proposed to implement the 23rd amendment giving capital residents the right to vote, was passed by the Senate after it was amended by a 38-36 vote to raise the minimum voting age to 21.

As a senator from the "Silver State," Bible was one of only 10 senators to vote against an Administration-backed repeal of the Silver Purchase Act of 1934 and subsequent amendments which had required the Secre-tary of the Treasury to buy domestically mined silver at $.91 cents per ounce. The new law also provided for the gradual removal of silver backing from U.S. paper currency. While not as liberal as most of his Democratic colleagues, Bible voted in favor of legislation desired by the Kennedy and Johnson Administrations more often than not. *Congressional Quarterly* reported that his votes supported the President's position 69% of the time in the 88th Congress. [See JOHNSON Volume]

[TO]

BIEMILLER, ANDREW J(OSEPH)
b. July 23, 1906; Sandusky, Ohio.
Director, Department of Legislation, AFL-CIO, 1956- .

A 1926 graduate of Cornell University, Biemiller taught history for a brief period at the University of Pennsylvania and at Syracuse. During the 1930s he was an organizer for the Wisconsin State Federation of Labor. From 1937 to 1942 he served in the Wisconsin state legislature. During World War II he was a labor specialist for the War Production Board. Biemiller won election to Congress as a Democrat in 1944. He was defeated in 1946, staged a successful comeback in 1948 but was defeated again in 1950 and 1952.

During the early 1950s, American Federation of Labor President George Meany [*q.v.*] recruited Biemiller to work on the merger of the AFL with the Congress of Industrial Organizations. The merger was completed in 1955 and Biemiller was subsequently named to head the AFL-CIO department of legislation. [See EISENHOWER Volume]

The basic political goals of the AFL-CIO were determined by the National Legislative Council under the chairmanship of Meany. Biemiller's office, consisting of five or six full-time lobbyists, and several representatives from the major international unions, was engaged in the daily effort to persuade senators and congressmen to vote in the interest of organized labor.

The Democratic Party was traditionally sensitive to AFL-CIO interests and Biemiller's department maintained close relations with the Kennedy Administration. During the 1960s Biemiller became a familiar figure on Capitol Hill, testifying on behalf of Administration manpower retraining, education and foreign aid bills.

The AFL-CIO was not entirely in agreement with the Administration on all issues. In an appearance before a Senate Labor and Public Welfare Committee subcommittee, in March 1961, Biemiller called himself a "reluctant critic" of the Administration's minimum wage bill. The Administration proposed that the minimum wage be increased to $1.25 over a three-year period; Biemiller argued that the increase should be effective immediately. However, the minimum wage law enacted in 1961 reflected the Administration's point of view.

During 1963 President Kennedy objected to labor's insistence that a Fair Employment Practices Commission (FEPC) be incorporated into the Administration's civil rights bill. In a June 1963 meeting with Biemiller, Kennedy argued that the FEPC provision would jeopardize the chances for enactment of the entire civil rights measure. Kennedy also suggested that economic growth was a far more important factor in creating jobs for minorities. However, labor and civil rights groups were reluctant to abandon their long-standing commitment to the FEPC; when finally enacted, Title VII of the 1964 Civil Rights Act banned discrimination in hiring on the basis of race, religion, sex or national origin and established an Equal Employment Opportunity Commission to enforce the provision.

During the Johnson years Biemiller maintained a close relationship with the White House staff. The AFL-CIO lobbied actively for Johnson Administration social welfare legislation, while also supporting the Administration's Vietnam war policy. Biemiller worked actively in Vice President Hubert H. Humphrey's [*q.v.*] 1968 campaign for the presidency. During 1969 and 1970 Biemiller played a crucial role in blocking the appointment of conservative Southern judges Clement F. Haynsworth and G. Harrold Carswell to the U.S. Supreme Court. [See JOHNSON, NIXON Volumes]

[JLW]

BISSELL, RICHARD M(ERVIN)
b. Sept. 18, 1909; Hartford, Conn.
Deputy Director of Plans, Central Intelligence Agency, 1959-62.

Educated at Groton, Yale and the London School of Economics, Bissell taught economics at Yale and the Massachusetts Institute of Technology. During World War II he worked for several government agencies supervising allied shipping. Bissell was appointed assistant administrator of the Marshall Plan in 1948 and served until 1951, including a brief tenure as acting administrator.

Bissell joined the Central Intelligence Agency (CIA) in 1954 as special assistant to Director Allen W. Dulles [q.v.]. He was one of the few top CIA officials without a long intelligence background. Bissell conceived and supervised the program of U-2 flights over the Soviet Union and other countries, helped develop the SR-71 high altitude surveillance plane and was an early advocate of surveillance satellites. He became CIA deputy director for plans in 1959, placing him in charge of covert activities. Among the projects he supervised was an unsuccessful effort, started in August 1960, to assassinate Congolese leader Patrice Lumumba.

On March 17, 1960 President Eisenhower ordered the CIA to help unify opposition to the Castro regime and to recruit and train a force of Cuban exiles capable of guerrilla action against the Cuban government. According to a Senate Select Committee report released in 1975, Bissell authorized two attempts on the lives of Cuban leaders in the summer of 1960. The first was aimed at Raul Castro, but authorization was rescinded before any action was taken. The second attempt was aimed at Fidel Castro and involved CIA cooperation with organized crime leaders Sam Giancana and John Roselli. Bissell claimed that Dulles was fully informed of these activities. It was unclear whether President Eisenhower had authorized or was aware of the plans.

Training of the exile force at a CIA camp in Guatemala and planning for landing them in Cuba were well under way when Bissell and Dulles briefed President-elect Kennedy on the project on Nov. 18, 1960. On Nov. 29, after a more detailed briefing, Kennedy ordered the planning to proceed. The 1975 Senate Committee report could not determine if Kennedy was ever informed of the plans to assassinate Castro. After a series of top-level meetings, at which Dulles and Bissell presented and defended the CIA invasion plan, Kennedy gave his approval for the action in early April 1961.

The CIA plan called for two air strikes against the Cuban air force, one before and one simultaneous with a landing at the Bay of Pigs. On April 15 exile pilots, flying U.S.-supplied B-26s based in Nicaragua, bombed Cuban air bases. One B-26 flew directly to Miami to establish a cover story that the raids had been made by defectors from the Cuban air force. American newspapers, however, soon questioned this account, which had already been presented to the U.N. Security Council by U.S. Ambassador Adlai E. Stevenson [q.v.]. At the urging of Secretary of State Dean Rusk [q.v.], Kennedy canceled the plans for a second wave of bombing attacks against the Cuban air force, although plans for air support of the actual invasion by the exile-flown B-26s remained in effect. On the night of April 16, hours before the scheduled landing, Bissell asked Rusk to recommend that the plans for additional attacks on the Cuban planes be reinstated. Rusk passed the CIA request on to Kennedy, but the President refused to reverse his decision. At that time Bissell and CIA Deputy Director General Charles P. Cabell declined to personally argue their case with Kennedy. However, at 4 a.m. Cabell called Kennedy in a final, unsuccessful attempt to win approval for a second bombing attack.

The April 17 invasion did not go well, and it was soon apparent that CIA planning had been seriously deficient. By April 18 the exile force was near defeat. At a midnight meeting with Kennedy and top Administration leaders, Bissell, supported by Chief of Naval Operations Adm. Arleigh A. Burke [q.v.], argued that the operation could still be saved by air attacks against the small Cuban air force, which had survived the first bombing attack and had been extremely effective against the invaders. Bissell proposed using carrier-based U.S. Navy planes for these raids. Other officials opposed the attacks. In a compromise, Kennedy refused to allow any bombing of Cuban air bases, but permitted six unmarked U.S. jets to provide an hour of protection for exile-flown B-26s flying air support missions over the invasion beachhead. (Due to an error in timing, the B-26s arrived after the jets had returned to their carriers and four B-26 flyers, all U.S. citizens employed by the CIA, were killed by Cuban fire.) By April 19 the invasion force was completely defeated.

According to the account offered by David Wise and Thomas B. Ross in *The Invisible Government*, Kennedy had been planning major changes in the CIA before the Cuban invasion and was considering Bissell for the directorship. After the Bay of Pigs the reorganization was delayed and the top CIA leadership quietly replaced. Dulles's resignation was accepted on Sept. 27, 1961, Cabell retired on Jan. 31, 1962 and Bissell resigned on Feb. 17, 1962. Bissell received a secret intelligence medal for his years of service and shortly thereafter became head of the Institute of Defense Analysis. He remained there until 1964 when he became an executive of the United Aircraft Corp.

[JBF]

For further information:
Arthur Schlesinger, Jr., *A Thousand Days* (Boston, 1965).
U.S. Senate, Select Committee to Study Intelligence Activities, *Alleged Assassination Plots Involving Foreign Leaders* (Washington, 1975).
David Wise and Thomas B. Ross, *The Invisible Government* (New York, 1964).

BLACK, EUGENE R(OBERT)

b. May 1, 1898; Atlanta, Ga.
President, International Bank for Reconstruction and Development, 1949-63.

A graduate of the University of Georgia in 1918, Black served as an ensign in the U.S. Navy during World War I. Following the war he became an investment banker and by 1933 was a vice president of Chase National Bank. Black was appointed undersecretary of the treasury in 1936 but returned to Chase a few months later because of the financial sacrifice that government service involved. During the postwar era he became increasingly active in the Chase Bank's international operations.

In 1947 President Harry Truman appointed Black an executive director of the World Bank at the insistence of John J. McCloy [q.v.], the Bank's president. McCloy was anxious to reverse the liberal lending policies of his predecessor and place the Bank in the hands of persons who could be depended on to pursue sound lending policies acceptable to the financial community.

In May 1949 Black was named president of the World Bank. During the 1950s he guided the institution in making loans for industrial, agricultural and power development, particularly in Europe and Asia. Black conceived of the bank in terms of a traditional lending institution rather than an instrument of foreign aid through which governments of capital-exporting states could assist underdeveloped areas. He remained with the bank until January 1963. [See EISENHOWER Volume]

In December 1962 President Kennedy, reacting to criticism of the newly created Agency for International Development and fearing that his 1963 foreign aid bill would have difficulty passing Congress, appointed Black to a committee of generally conservative businessmen asked to study the U.S. foreign aid program. Kennedy hoped that the panel would recommend the continuation of the program and generate support for it among businessmen and conservatives in Congress. The committee, however, reacted negatively to the proposals. Black, in particular, disapproved of bilateral foreign aid, fearing that it would clearly introduce international politics into the bank's development program. The final report of the committee, issued in March 1963, maintained that aid was indispensable to national security, but it disappointed Kennedy by suggesting that the total value of aid be reduced.

During the 1962 Pakistan-India fighting

over Kashmir, the U.S. proposed that Black act as mediator between the two countries. The Pakistanis accepted the proposal, but the Indians rejected it.

In August 1963 Black was named to a panel formed to study the development of a commercial supersonic airplane. The report, issued in March 1964, backed development but suggested a reorganization of the program under an independent agency directly responsible to the President and urged increasing the government's share in the cost of development.

During the Johnson Administration Black continued to serve on panels reviewing U.S. aid policy, particularly in Southeast Asia. [See JOHNSON Volume]

[EWS]

BLACK, HUGO L(AFAYETTE)
b. Feb. 27, 1886; Harlan, Ala.
d. Sept. 25, 1971; Bethesda, Md.
Associate Justice, U.S. Supreme Court, 1937-71.

A graduate of the University of Alabama Law School, Black practiced law in Birmingham and held several local offices before seeking election to the U.S. Senate in 1926. Campaigning for immigration restrictions, enforcement of prohibition and retention of federal control of the Muscle Shoals Dam, he defeated four candidates in the Democratic primary and was elected to the upper house in November. Reelected in 1932, he was a strong supporter of the New Deal and was President Franklin Roosevelt's first Supreme Court appointee in August 1937. Black's early years on the Court were dominated by issues arising from the New Deal, and he voted repeatedly to sustain federal and state economic and social welfare legislation.

Although he continued to influence economic, antitrust and labor law, Black became known primarily for his civil libertarian views and his judicial philosophy. In a dissent in the 1947 Adamson case, Black argued that the first eight amendments to the Constitution, which originally applied only to the federal government, had been extended to the states by the 14th Amend-

ment. Under this "total incorporation" doctrine, Black pressed especially for state recognition of such criminal rights guarantees in the Fifth and Sixth Amendments as the right to counsel. A constitutional literalist, Black held that the guarantees in the Bill of Rights were absolutes, which could not be abridged by the government. Black advocated his absolutist position most strongly with regard to the First Amendment, which he considered "the heart of the Bill of Rights." Throughout his years on the Court, he argued consistently against any government interference with freedom of speech and of the press. [See TRUMAN, EISENHOWER Volumes]

Although Black never persuaded a majority of the Court to accept fully his judicial doctrines, during the 1960s the Court often reached conclusions he supported. In the Gideon v. Wainwright decision of March 1963, for example, Justice Black, writing for a unanimous Court, overturned a 1942 ruling from which he had dissented and held that the states must supply free counsel to any indigent charged with a felony. Black had also dissented in a 1946 case where the majority of the Court ruled that apportionment of legislative districts was a political question in which federal courts should not intervene. In March 1962 a six-man majority in Baker v. Carr held that federal courts could try state legislative apportionment cases.

Black repeatedly insisted that "without deviation, without any ifs, buts, or whereases," freedom of speech meant the government could not for any reason regulate the views people expressed or wrote. Throughout the 1950s he dissented in cases where the majority, balancing freedom of speech against national security interests, upheld federal action against the Communist Party and its members. Black again dissented in two June 1961 cases where the Court sustained federal laws that required the Communist Party to register with the government and made it illegal to be an active member of a party advocating violent overthrow of the government. He dissented in two February 1961 cases in which the majority upheld the contempt-of-Congress convictions of two men who had refused to answer questions before a House Un-American Activities subcommittee. In the early 1960s, however, the Court began moving toward Black's position, and he concurred when the majority reversed similar contempt-of-Congress convictions in decisions in June 1961 and May 1962.

With his absolutist approach Justice Black argued that the First Amendment prohibited any government regulation of obscenity and of political expression. He voted against all censorship laws such as Chicago's movie censorship system, which the Court majority upheld in January 1961. In a controversial June 1962 decision, Black, speaking for the majority, held that the use of an official prayer in New York State's public schools violated the First Amendment. Black joined with the Court's majority in a January 1963 decision that nullified a Virginia law barring solicitation of legal business. The NAACP had been convicted under the law in a state court for advising Negroes to sue for their rights and suggesting the names of lawyers, many of whom were affiliated with the NAACP. The Court nullified the law on the grounds that litigation was a "form of political expression" and attempts to restrict it infringed on the NAACP's rights of free speech and association.

Black's literal interpretations of the Bill of Rights led him in most cases to take an expansive, liberal view of its provisions. With regard to the Fourth Amendment's prohibition against unreasonable searches and seizures, however, the Justice took a narrow approach. In 1949 he agreed with the majority that the Amendment did not require the states to exclude illegally seized evidence from their courts. Black was part of the five-man majority that overturned this ruling in June 1961, but in a concurring opinion he explained that he had changed his position only because he now considered the use of such evidence in court a violation of the Fifth Amendment's privilege against self-incrimination.

During the Johnson years the Court continued to move closer to Black's positions especially in the fields of criminal procedure and free speech. The fact that so many of Black's early dissents later became settled law, along with his ability to go directly to the heart of a problem, contributed to the assessment of Black as one of the foremost justices in the Court's history. Along with other legal scholars Paul Freund described Black as "without doubt the most influential of the many strong figures" who have sat on the Court since 1937. Many commentators also agreed with Chief Justice Earl Warren [q.v.] that Black's "attachment to the Constitution has been a passionate one" and that his "greatest contribution" has been in his "application of the Bill of Rights to a myriad of human relationships." [See JOHNSON, NIXON Volumes]

[CAB]

For further information:
Hugo Black, *A Constitutional Faith* (New York, 1968).
———, *One Man's Stand for Freedom: Mr. Justice Black and the Bill of Rights*, ed. Irving Dilliard (New York, 1963).
John P. Frank, "Hugo L. Black," in Leon Friedman and Fred L. Israel, eds., *The Justices of the United States Supreme Court, 1789-1969* (New York, 1969), Vol. 3
"Mr. Justice Black: Thirty Years in Retrospect," *UCLA Law Review*, 14 (1967), pp. 397-552.
Stephen P. Strickland, ed., *Hugo Black and the Supreme Court* (New York, 1967).

BLAKE, EUGENE CARSON
b. Nov. 7, 1906; St. Louis, Mo.
Clergyman.

Educated at Princeton and Edinburgh University, the Rev. Dr. Eugene Carson Blake took his first pastorate in 1932 in New York City. In 1951 he was elected to the first of a series of terms as the stated clerk of the General Assembly of the Presbyterian Church in the U.S.A., which became the United Presbyterian Church after a 1958 merger with another Presbyterian group. He served as a U.S. delegate to the World Council of Churches and between 1954 and 1957 was the elected president of the National Council of Churches of Christ in the U.S.A., an organization of Protestant and

Eastern Orthodox churches that took positions on social issues and furthered interdenominational cooperation.

Blake's official posts made him the most influential spokesman of liberal American Protestantism. During the 1950s he publicly attacked Sen. Joseph McCarthy (R, Wisc.) and consistently demanded strict maintenance of civil and human rights. Speaking for the World and National Councils of Churches, he advocated a world peace program which specifically backed the United Nations, disarmament and economic and technical assistance to the underdeveloped world. [See EISENHOWER Volume]

Characterized by the *New York Times* as the "personal symbol of modern ecumenical Christianity," Blake stressed social issues rather than theology. In his view, theological differences were less critical in the modern world than the threat to all religion from "atheistic Communism" and "humanistic secularism [and] moral collapse" in American society. In 1960 he proposed a merger of various Protestant denominations, which was received enthusiastically not only by the Presbyterians but also by the Episcopalians and Methodists. The merger scheme began to be discussed seriously in 1961 with the organization of the Consultation on Church Union and gained the interest of more denominations.

Blake also worked for interdenominational cooperation outside the framework of the National Council of Churches, particularly in the area of civil rights. In July 1963 he was arrested along with other prominent clergymen in an attempt to integrate a Maryland amusement park. The following month he spoke at the March on Washington.

During the 1960 campaign Blake's commitment to the separation of church and state had led him to publicly criticize those Protestants who opposed Kennedy because they feared that a Catholic president would undermine the church-state principle. Blake's position was vindicated when in the President's first month in office he offered a federal aid-to-education bill that excluded private and parochial schools. Blake supported the measure and criticized New York's Catholic archbishop, Francis Cardinal Spellman [*q.v.*], for demanding parity for parochial schools, thereby diminishing the program's chance of congressional approval. Blake also supported the June 1962 Supreme Court ruling banning prayer in the public schools.

Blake's outspoken liberalism earned him the hostility of conservative Protestants and extreme anti-Communist groups. In 1961 the John Birch Society charged that the Presbyterian Church and the National Council of Churches were sympathetic to Communism. Blake, who was personally implicated in the charge, assailed the Society for its "campaign of falsehoods". The following year, speaking as the chief executive officer of the Presbyterian Church, Blake urged church members not to join the Society and to fight Communism with Christian principles.

Blake continued as an activist in the civil rights movement and later became a persistent critic of U.S. policy in Vietnam. Replaced as the stated clerk of the Presbyterian General Assembly in 1966, he was elected secretary-general of the World Council of Churches in the same year, assuming, therefore, a larger role in international affairs. He served in that post until 1972. The liberalization of the Presbyterian Church, for which Blake was largely responsible, evoked considerable discontent among church members, leading to a secession movement and the formation of a new Southern-based denomination in 1973. [See JOHNSON Volume]

[JCH]

BLOUGH, ROGER M(ILES)
b. Jan. 19, 1904; Riverside, Pa.
Chairman, United States Steel Corp., 1955-69.

Roger Blough was the son of a truck farmer. He grew up in Pennsylvania, and graduated from Susquehanna University in 1925 and Yale Law School in 1931. After serving as a corporate lawyer with the Wall Street law firm of White and Case, Blough was made an executive vice president of U.S. Steel in 1951. In 1955 Blough was elected chairman of the board of U.S. Steel. The corporation was the world's largest maker of steel and provided one-third of total steel capacity in the U.S. Historically, U.S. Steel had been the pacesetter throughout the steel industry in setting prices.

In part because of his cordial relations with the Kennedy Administration, Blough in 1961 replaced Ralph J. Cordiner [q.v.], chairman of the board of General Electric Co. as head of the prestigious Business Advisory Council.

In March 1962, after intensive negotiations between Blough and United Steelworkers President David J. McDonald [q.v.], an anti-inflationary wage package was ratified by the union that provided for a modest 10-cent-an-hour increase in fringe benefits and did not include a wage increase. Secretary of Labor Arthur Goldberg [q.v.], who helped to negotiate the settlement, felt that the steel industry could absorb the small rise in wage costs without the necessity of a price increase. Most importantly, Goldberg believed that he had the tacit agreement of Blough and other major steel executives not to raise prices. After the pact was ratified on March 31, President Kennedy praised both management and labor for their "high industrial statesmanship." The settlement was generally regarded as a collective bargaining triumph for the Administration and one that would be a major factor in preventing an inflationary spiral as the recession of 1960-61 ended.

On the afternoon of April 10 Blough met briefly with President Kennedy and unexpectedly announced that U.S. Steel was raising its prices by $6 a ton. The reaction within the Administration after Blough's announcement was one of outrage. President Kennedy called it "a wholly unjustifiable and irresponsible defiance of the public interest." Secretary Goldberg called the action a "double cross" and offered to submit his resignation. After seven other major steel companies announced April 11 that they would follow U.S. Steel's traditional lead by also raising prices, the Administration took drastic and unparalleled measures to pressure the steel companies into a price

rollback. These actions included investigations by the FBI, Internal Revenue Service (IRS) and Federal Trade Commission (FTC), shifting defense contracts to smaller companies and launching an antitrust investigation by the Senate Judiciary Subcommittee on Antitrust and Monopoly, chaired by Sen. Estes Kefauver (D, Tenn.) [q.v.].

After his April 10 announcement to the President, Blough stated that while inflation was a matter of serious concern to the steel industry, its causes stemmed from poor government fiscal policies. Blough offered several reasons for the price increase, including serious inadequacies in depreciation allowances, the need to repay borrowings and pay dividends, as well as the need for extensive modernization of steel plant facilities. Blough also noted that U.S. Steel's profits as a percentage of sales had declined from 9.5% in 1957 to 5.7% in 1961. He conceded that the March 1962 agreement with labor was a modest one but felt that it exceeded productivity gains and thus would further squeeze U.S. Steel's profits. Blough declared that there had been no tacit agreement with the Administration not to raise prices and cited a September 1961 letter to President Kennedy, written in response to Kennedy's request that steel companies hold the price line, indicating in general terms the financial pressures which U.S. Steel felt obligated to meet in the pricing area.

The key to the Administration's strategy for rolling back the price increase lay in the fact that several small but profitable steel companies had not immediately followed U.S. Steel's lead. After Inland Steel, whose chairman was friendly with Secretary Goldberg, agreed not to raise prices, Kaiser Steel Co. and Armco Steel Corp. followed suit. Then on April 12, with the outcome of the steel crisis still in doubt, Blough made his first public concession to both Administration pressure and generally unfavorable public reaction. Blough defended the price increase and denied making "any commitment of any kind" to the Administration not to raise prices. However, Blough conceded that it would be a "very difficult" situation for U.S. Steel if some other major steel producer did not also raise its prices.

Early on April 13 Bethlehem Steel Co., the nation's second-largest steel maker, announced it was rescinding its price increase "in order to remain competitive" with Inland, Armco and Kaiser Steel. Bethlehem had lost a $5 million Pentagon defense contract to Lukens Steel Co. and its president had been criticized for earlier statements made to stockholders that a price rise would not be necessary.

After a tense meeting on April 13 between Goldberg and Blough, in which Goldberg presented a list of measures the Administration planned to take against the steel industry, Blough agreed to rescind U.S. Steel's price increase, which he did in a terse public announcement the same day.

The steel crisis sent shock waves through the business community and revived the "anti-business" label that the Administration hoped to avoid. A remark by President Kennedy April 10 that "my father always told me that steel men were sons-of-bitches. . . ." was taken as a slur against businessmen in general. Many businessmen were shocked by the raw display of presidential power during the steel crisis and were particularly worried about the implications of the Kennedy Administration's successful intervention in what they regarded as the private area of price-setting. Some felt Kennedy's action during the crisis was responsible in part for the stock market slump a month later.

It was Blough's belief that Kennedy's "vehement" reaction to the steel price increase was not prompted by fear of inflation but by a desire to maintain good relations with the labor movement. However, Blough made every effort after the crisis to renew cordial relations with the Administration, despite ongoing antitrust litigation and inquiries into secret price-fixing. In April 1963 the steel industry announced a "selective" price increase of $5 a ton, which the Administration decided not to challenge.

Blough continued as chairman of the board of U.S. Steel until 1969. In 1966 the NAACP sued the giant corporation for alleged job discrimination at its plant near Birmingham, Ala. The next year U.S. Steel agreed to a $21 million settlement of a 1964 antitrust suit involving the marketing of steel and concrete pipe. [See JOHNSON Volume]

[FHM]

For further information:
Roger M. Blough, *The Washington Embrace of Business* (New York, 1976).
Jim F. Heath, *John F. Kennedy and the Business Community* (Chicago, 1969).
Hobart Rowen, *The Free Enterprisers* (New York, 1964).

BOGGS, (THOMAS) HALE
b. Feb. 15, 1914; Long Beach, Miss.
d. Oct. 16, 1972; Alaska.
Democratic Representative, La., 1941-43, 1947-72; Chairman, Joint Economic Subcommittee on Foreign Economic Policy, 1957-72; Democratic Majority Whip, 1962-71.

After receiving his law degree from Tulane in 1937, Boggs began his political career in New Orleans as a member of the People's League, a business and professional organization formed to combat corruption among Huey Long's political heirs. First elected to Congress in 1940 as a reform candidate, Boggs was defeated in 1942 but returned to the House in 1946. Boggs was a protege of Speaker Sam Rayburn (D, Tex.) [q.v.] and in 1949 received a seat on the powerful House Ways and Means Committee. Boggs became chairman of the Ways and Means Subcommittee on Foreign Trade Policy in 1955 and the Joint Economic Subcommittee on Economic Foreign Policy in 1957. On both committees he championed lower tariffs and reduced trade restrictions.

Tariff reform was a major congressional issue in 1961. Boggs's Foreign Economic Policy Subcommittee released a series of study papers in November 1961, including one by former Secretary of State Christian A. Herter and Marshall plan architect Will Clayton advocating a "trade partnership with the European Common Market." Boggs's subcommittee also held two weeks of panel discussions in December and in January 1962 issued a report supporting liberal policies in line with the Administration's trade proposals. Boggs called the Administration's Trade Expansion Act of 1962, passed in September, "one of the most significant events of the century."

During the 1960s, Boggs achieved national prominence through his rise in the Democratic party hierarchy. In 1962 he was promoted from deputy Democratic whip, a post which the *New York Times* reported Speaker Rayburn had created especially for him, to House Democratic whip. President Johnson appointed Boggs to the Warren Commission investigation of the assassination of President Kennedy and to the President's Commission on the Causes and Prevention of Violence. Boggs also chaired the Platform Committee at the 1968 Democratic National Convention. He was elected House majority leader in January 1971. [See JOHNSON, NIXON Volumes]

[DKR]

BOHLEN, CHARLES E(USTIS)
b. Aug. 30, 1904; Clayton, N.Y.
d. Jan. 1, 1974; Washington, D.C.
Special Assistant for Soviet Affairs in the State Department, June 1960-August 1962; Ambassador to France, August 1962-December 1967.

The son of a wealthy sportsman, Charles Bohlen joined the foreign service in 1929, specializing in Soviet affairs. Bohlen was a staff member of the first U.S. embassy in the Soviet Union and served as a Russian translator at the Teheran, Yalta and Potsdam Conferences. Despite objections from Sen. Joseph McCarthy (R, Wisc.), who linked him with the "Truman-Acheson policies of appeasement," Bohlen was appointed ambassador to Moscow in 1953. In 1957 Secretary of State John Foster Dulles sent Bohlen to the Philippines amid rumors that the Ambassador was being "exiled" because he disagreed with Dulles's Russian policies. In 1960 he was made special assistant for Soviet affairs in the State Department. [See TRUMAN, EISENHOWER Volumes]

During the Kennedy Administration the new President, attracted by Bohlen's charm, shrewdness and breadth of experience, asked his advice on a wide range of foreign policy issues, especially those involving Soviet-American relations. Bohlen first served on the State Department task force studying Laos. There a civil war between American-supported Gen. Phoumi Nosavan and the neutralist Prince Souvanna Phouma threatened to permit a Communist takeover of the country. Bohlen advised the President to back the neutralists since the corrupt Phoumi regime had little popular support. On March 23, 1961, when continued military advances brought much of Laos under Communist control, Bohlen helped Kennedy draft a statement, aimed at the Soviet Union, asking for a ceasefire and warning that the U.S. would intervene if the military campaign continued.

Although Bohlen was only peripherally involved in the Kennedy Administration's decision to sponsor the April 1961 Bay of Pigs invasion of Cuba, the President consulted Bohlen on possible Soviet responses to the attack. Bohlen assured Kennedy that the Soviet Union would not act militarily but would merely use the invasion as political propaganda—provided the effort either succeeded or failed quickly. The invasion took place on April 17, and the next day Kennedy received a letter from Soviet Premier Nikita Khrushchev denouncing the attack. Bohlen helped Kennedy draft a reply, which stated that the Soviet Union should "recognize that free peoples in all parts of the world do not accept the claim of historical inevitability of Communist revolution."

In the summer of 1961 Kennedy asked Bohlen to accompany Lyndon Johnson [q.v.] to West Berlin, where the Vice President had been sent to boost the morale of the Berliners and assure them of American support in the face of Soviet and East German attempts to cut off access to the city. Upon returning from the Aug. 18-21 trip, Bohlen wrote a report to the President recommending that the U.S. be prepared to react vigorously, using any measures necessary short of war, to clear signs of harassment or attempts to erode Western rights in the city. He warned that any American hesitancy would depress morale in West Berlin.

Kennedy appointed Bohlen ambassador to France in August 1962. Before he could assume his post at the end of October, the Cuban missile crisis absorbed the attention of Washington policy-makers. As a member of the Executive Committee formed to advise Kennedy, Bohlen recommended reliance on diplomatic means to gain removal of the missiles from the island. Bohlen favored sending a carefully worded letter to Khrushchev requesting removal of the missiles. If the reply was not favorable, Bohlen advised informing our allies of our intentions and then asking Congress for a declaration of war. His advice was rejected and, on Oct. 23, the Administration ordered a "quarantine" of Cuba to prevent shipments of additional missiles and demand removal of those already in place.

Bohlen's tenure as ambassador to France was complicated by President Charles de Gaulle's desire to pursue an independent French foreign policy. The Ambassador, however, helped maintain good relations between the two countries by convincing Kennedy to avoid an open conflict with de Gaulle, no matter what the provocation.

Bohlen remained at his post during the first four years of the Johnson Administration. In December 1967 he returned to the U.S. as deputy undersecretary of state for political affairs. Because he was never close to Johnson, Bohlen was not consulted on a regular basis. He was, however, asked to advise the President during the Russian invasion of Czechoslovakia in August 1968. Bohlen retired from the foreign service in January 1969 and died five years later on Jan. 1, 1974. [See JOHNSON Volume]

[EWS]

For further information:
Charles Bohlen, *Witness to History, 1929-1969* (New York, 1973).

BOLLING, RICHARD W(ALKER)
b. May 17, 1916; New York, N.Y.
Democratic Representative, Mo. 1949- .

Born in New York City, Richard Bolling spent much of his boyhood in Huntsville, Ala. He studied at the University of the South and received an M.A. in English literature in 1939. After four years of military service overseas, he became director of student activities and veterans affairs at the University of Kansas City in Missouri, but left the academic community to become Midwestern director of Americans for Democratic Action in 1947. He ran for the House of Representatives in 1948 from Missouri's fifth (Kansas City) district, on a platform advocating repeal of the Taft-Hartley Act, and was elected over Republican incumbent Albert L. Reeves, Jr. Originally Bolling sat on the Joint Economic and the Banking and Currency Committees, but he left the latter for the powerful House Rules Committee in 1955. Although a liberal with an urban constituency, Bolling became a protege of Speaker of the House Sam Rayburn (D, Tex.) [*q.v.*] during the later years of the Eisenhower Administration.

Bolling was a leader of the Kennedy Administration's major congressional reform effort in early 1961: the expansion of the House Rules Committee from 12 to 15 members. Because of the requirement that most prospective legislation be reported through the Rules Committee, which issues "rules" determining the length of debate on a bill, the Committee and its conservative chairman, Howard W. Smith (D, Va.) [*q.v.*], possessed enormous power to obstruct liberal proposals indefinitely. With the support of the Kennedy Administration and Speaker Rayburn, Bolling helped to engineer an expansion of the Committee's membership in order to dilute the power of its conservative element. The reform passed on Jan. 31 by a vote of 217-212.

After Rayburn's death in November 1961, Bolling declared himself a candidate for the position of majority leader, but he withdrew on Jan. 3, 1962, and the House Democratic caucus elected Carl Albert (D, Okla.) [*q.v.*] to the post on Jan. 9. A reliable supporter of the Kennedy Administration, Bolling distinguished himself as a persistent proponent of internal House reform, which he advocated in his 1965 book *House Out of Order*. He claimed that "the House is not a training ground and a field of action for legislators, but a lobby for arrogant brokers of special privileges." Bolling recommended several reforms, including modification of the seniority system along with a strengthening of the Speaker and the party caucus. [See JOHNSON Volume]

[TO]

For further information:
Richard Bolling, *House Out of Order* (New York, 1965).

BONNER, HUBERT C(OVINGTON)
b. May 16, 1891; Washington, N.C.
d. Nov. 7, 1965; Washington, D.C.
Democratic Representative, N.C., 1940-65; Chairman, Merchant Marine and Fisheries Committee, 1955-65.

Bonner, a former congressional aide, was first elected to the House of Representatives in 1940. In Congress he represented a conservative eastern North Carolina district of small towns and textile mills until his death in 1965. While on Capitol Hill he compiled a record as an opponent of labor and civil rights legislation. A conservative on foreign policy, Bonner voted against lower tariffs and most foreign aid bills except those specifically designed to curb Communist aggression. [See EISENHOWER Volume] In 1962 Bonner successfully sponsored an amendment to the Foreign Aid Appropriations Act denying aid funds to nations whose vessels called at Cuban ports. During the Kennedy Administration he voted in favor of area redevelopment measures to provide funds for urban renewal and development. In 1964 Bonner supported mass transit legislation and the Johnson Administration's antipoverty program.

Bonner's major interest in Congress was the U.S. maritime industry. As chairman of the Merchant Marine and Fisheries Committee, he was a constant critic of what he believed were excessive wage demands of labor, the failure of management to automate and the unwillingness of government to broaden federal aid to the industry.

In October 1962 Bonner successfully sponsored a bill raising the federal subsidy given for reconditioning ships from 55% to 60%. The bill also continued the 55% ceiling on government cost-differential sub-sidies for domestic construction of new ships. However, he was forced to accept a two-year program rather than the three-year plan he had requested.

The 1962 strike of the specially trained crew of the nuclear ship *Savannah* just before launching convinced Bonner that compulsory arbitration was necessary in the industry. Bonner introduced a bill calling for this measure in 1964, but it was killed in committee because of opposition from the Administration and organized labor.

Shortly before his death in November 1965, Bonner announced plans to hold hearings on a measure to sever the Maritime Administration from the Department of Commerce. Believing that the Maritime Administration had failed to carry out the policies and laws laid down by Congress because it had been "deeply buried" in the bureaucracy of the Commerce Department, Bonner hoped it would become more efficient as an independent agency. His measure was never adopted.

[EWS]

BONTEMPO, SALVATORE A(NTHONY)
b. Aug. 14, 1909; Newark, N.J.
Administrator, Bureau of Security and Consular Affairs, June 1961-December 1961.

Bontempo was elected to the post of Newark city commissioner in 1953. He came to statewide attention in 1958 when Gov. Robert Meyner appointed him commissioner of New Jersey's Department of Conservation and Economic Development.

In 1960 Sen. John Kennedy asked Bontempo to join his presidential campaign as an adviser on natural resources matters. After Kennedy's inauguration, the President appointed him senior U.S. delegate to the United Nations disarmament conference in Geneva, and in June 1961 Bontempo became head of the State Department's Bureau of Security and Consular Affairs. In this post he was responsible for passports, visas and immigration and refugee policy as well as State Department security.

Because of the exodus from Castro's Cuba, U.S. refugee policy had become a politically sensitive issue. Although Bontempo's post was equivalent in rank to an assistant secretary's, his appointment did not require Senate confirmation. Some members of Congress felt they should have greater control over the post, and a bill was introduced in the Senate in July requiring that in the future the Bureau administrator be confirmed by the upper house. At the same time Rep. Francis E. Walter (D, Pa.) [q.v.], chairman of the House Un-American Activities Committee, introduced a bill to abolish the Bureau altogether. He attacked Bontempo and his deputy, Michel Cieplinski, as "totally unqualified political appointees." Walter implied that Bontempo was appointed in deference to the New Jersey Democratic organization and to Italian-Americans.

The Kennedy Administration decided that Bontempo ought to resign to avoid further criticism. Plans to appoint him as federal representative on the Delaware River Basin Commission, a $591-million development program, were also dropped. Bontempo resigned in December 1961 and was named chairman of the Braidburn Corporation in New Jersey. He remained active in state politics, however, and in 1969 became chairman of the New Jersey Democratic Committee.

[JCH]

BOUTWELL, ALBERT B(URTON)
b. Nov. 13, 1904; Montgomery, Ala.
Lieutenant Governor, Ala. 1959-63;
Mayor, Birmingham, Ala., 1963-67.

Boutwell was admitted to the Alabama bar in 1928 and opened a legal practice in Birmingham. He served as a member of the state Senate from 1946 to 1958. Chosen as the state's lieutenant governor in 1958, he filled that office for four years and gained a reputation as a moderate on racial issues.

In the Birmingham municipal elections held on April 2, 1963, Boutwell was elected mayor, leading a ticket that defeated the incumbent city administration of Mayor Arthur Hane and Police Commissioner Eugene "Bull" Connor [q.v.], both of whom were unyielding opponents of the civil rights movement. On the following day Martin Luther King [q.v.] and Fred L. Shuttlesworth [q.v.], both of the Southern Christian Leadership Conference, initiated a series of civil rights demonstrations in the city. During the month-and-a-half between the election and the new city administration's assumption of power, Mayor-elect Boutwell and local white leaders began quiet negotiations with King and other civil rights leaders. They also attempted to restrain Connor's use of force, but early in May the police began to employ dogs, nightsticks and pressure hoses against the civil rights marchers.

After these public attacks and the national and worldwide protest which ensued, the Kennedy Administration began to exert strong pressure on the local business elite to reach agreement with the civil rights leaders. On May 10 Shuttlesworth announced that a compromise plan to desegregate some public facilities and ease job discrimination had been devised. Mayor Hane denounced the white negotiators as a "bunch of quisling, gutless traitors," but Boutwell, although a segregationist, accepted the results. Contrasting the Mayor-elect with Hane and Connor, Martin Luther King said that Boutwell was at least "responsible enough to see the futility of massive resistance to desegregation."

On May 23, the day he took office, Boutwell announced his desire to meet with local blacks, and in mid-July the Mayor led a conference of black and white civic leaders. The meeting, which was picketed by the Ku Klux Klan and the White Citizens Council, created a biracial commission to recommend solutions for the city's racial problems. During the same month a U.S. district judge ordered the desegregation of Birmingham's schools in the fall. Boutwell, who opposed Gov. George Wallace's [q.v.] threats to block school desegregation in Alabama, was primarily concerned with maintaining order. He warned all outsiders, whether for or against integration, not to interfere in Birmingham's affairs. When protests directed against school integration culminated in the bombing of a Negro church in September 1963, killing four black girls, Boutwell described the incident as "just sickening."

During the remainder of Boutwell's administration, blacks gained access to the city's major public accommodations and to a modest number of jobs previously reserved for whites. About 600 black children attended formerly all-white schools. After protests flared over allegations of police brutality in early 1966, the Mayor urged black leaders to recruit qualified persons for employment on the all-white police force, and within a year a few blacks had been hired. In April 1965 an undetonated bomb, reputedly planted by white extremists, was discovered outside the Mayor's home on the same day that another exploded in the city. While some whites rejected any steps towards integration, Birmingham's growing black electorate rejected the slow pace of change. As a result, Boutwell was eliminated in the first round of the mayoral election of October 1967.

[MLL]

BOWLES, CHESTER
b. April 5, 1901; Springfield, Mass.
Undersecretary of State, January 1961-December 1961; President's Special Representative and Adviser on Asian, African and Latin American Affairs, December 1961-April 1963; Ambassador to India, May 1963-April 1969.

Born into a well-to-do family of Yankee manufacturers, Bowles was raised in a staunchly conservative household. After graduating from Choate School and then Yale University, Bowles tried journalism and considered a career in the Foreign Service before going to work as a copywriter in a New York advertising agency in 1925. In 1929 Bowles and William Benton opened a small agency of their own. They prospered despite, or perhaps because of, the business turmoil of the depression. After the war broke out, Bowles held a succession of administrative positions in Connecticut's rationing program. The public cooperation he achieved eventually led to his appointment as director of the federal Office of Price Administration. After

the war Bowles threw himself into state politics, winning the Democratic nomination and the gubernatorial election in 1948. When he lost his reelection campaign in 1950, President Truman named him ambassador to India, where he served until March 1953 [See TRUMAN Volume]. Bowles remained on the periphery of Connecticut and national politics, devoting himself to writing and traveling, until 1958 when he won election to the House of Representatives after failing to secure the nomination for the Senate. [See EISENHOWER Volume]

Despite Bowles's unimpressive record as a campaigner, in the fall of 1959 liberals began to boost him as a potential dark-horse contender for the Democratic presidential nomination. His outspoken advocacy of disarmament, aid for underdeveloped nations and accomodation with the Soviet Union and Communist China made him a liberal hero during the 1950s. Sen. John F. Kennedy recognized Bowles's symbolic importance, particularly to Adlai Stevenson's [q.v.] supporters, and began to court him in late 1959. In November Bowles announced his endorsement of Kennedy, the first by a nationally-prominent liberal. Kennedy announced in February 1960 that Bowles had agreed to serve as his chief adviser on foreign policy, leading some to believe Bowles might be the next Secretary of State.

The Democratic National Committee selected Bowles in February 1960 for another important position, chairmanship of the Convention's platform committee. Although Bowles performed the sensitive job credibly, it was by nature a thankless task, requiring the alienation of more petitioners than ever could be satisfied. Privately, Kennedy thought Bowles had included too many divisive specifics in the platform.

After the Convention, Bowles's influence in the Kennedy campaign steadily waned. Kennedy and his entourage placed a premium on a crisp, pragmatic and decisive approach to problems. Bowles tended to be wordy and idealistic. By refusing to campaign for Kennedy against his old friend Hubert Humphrey [q.v.] in the Wisconsin primary, Bowles had raised questions about his loyalty. His insistence on working fulltime in the presidential campaign, instead of running for reelection to Congress as Kennedy wished, was interpreted as an attempt to box the new President into offering him the State Department.

On Dec. 12 the President-elect announced his appointment of Dean Rusk [q.v.] as Secretary of State and Bowles as undersecretary. (Kennedy reportedly never seriously considered Bowles for the top position, regarding him as much too controversial, especially after such a close electoral victory.) For the transition, Kennedy gave Bowles special responsibility for finding talented New Frontier supporters to staff the State Department. Bowles has been credited for initiating many of the Administration's most notable foreign policy appointments, including those of Edward R. Murrow [q.v.] as head of the U.S. Information Agency, Abram Chayes [q.v.] as the Department's legal adviser, Roger Hilsman [q.v.] as Director of the Bureau of Intelligence and Research. Edwin Reischauer [q.v.] as ambassador to Japan and a long list of New Frontiersmen as envoys to the newly independent African states. The African appointments upset a plan by the outgoing Administration to use the posts to reward career foreign service officers on the verge of retirement. These deprived veterans formed a powerful anti-Bowles lobby inside Washington social circles.

To the surprise of many commentators, Bowles's confirmation roused little opposition in the Senate. He was closely questioned by members of the Senate Foreign Relations Committee on his position toward recognition of Communist China, but managed to evade the issue so effectively that one Washington newspaper reported he had leaned toward recognition while another reported he had opposed it. Only four conservative Republicans voted against his confirmation on the Senate floor on Jan. 23, 1961.

But Bowles was making enemies rapidly. His arguments in favor of establishing diplomatic relations with Mongolia stirred up the China lobby which successfully forced the abandonment of the plan in the summer of 1961. His circular letters to U.S. ambassadors urging them to coordinate all U.S. activities in

their countries won him the enmity of the Central Intelligence Agency, although the President himself was strongly in favor of ambassadorial supervision.

When reports of Bowles's opposition to the Bay of Pigs invasion leaked to the press, many White House insiders believed Bowles had breached Administration solidarity to gloat over the wisdom of his advice. The crisis in the Dominican Republic following the May 30, 1961, assassination of Rafael Trujillo brought Bowles into direct conflict with Robert Kennedy [q.v.] who, with both Rusk and the President out of the country, was demanding U.S. intervention. Although the President, reached in Paris, supported Bowles, his brother remained antagonistic.

The limits of Bowles's authority within the State Department caused constant friction with Rusk. Kennedy had directed Bowles to shake the Department out of its Eisenhower era lethargy. Rusk, however, favored a more cautious approach and hesitated to give Bowles wide authority to reform the Department. By May the President had concluded, as he told Arthur Schlesinger [q.v.], that Bowles was "not precise or decisive enough to get things done." Rusk began to hint in early July that Bowles might like to switch to a key embassy such as Chile or Brazil. When the *New York Times* reported July 17 that Kennedy was about to demand his resignation, Bowles's indignant friends rallied to his support, raising a storm of protest. Questioned about the report at a press conference July 19, Kennedy denied he had asked for Bowles's resignation, but also pointedly sidestepped any permanent commitment. Bowles left a few days later on an 18-day tour of Africa, the Middle East and Southeast Asia for regional meetings with U.S. ambassadors. Kennedy let the controversy die down, but the premature publicity had only postponed Bowles's ouster. The President had already settled on George Ball [q.v.] as a replacement.

The blow finally came in a general State Department reorganization announced over the Thanksgiving weekend. Worried that Bowles might publicly protest, Kennedy assigned Theodore Sorenson [q.v.] to "hold his hand a little, as one 'liberal' to another." Rusk broke the news on Sunday, Nov. 26, urging

Bowles to accept a position as roving ambassador. Bowles was tempted to quit and take his case to the public, but he negotiated a compromise with Kennedy through Sorenson by which he became the President's special representative and adviser on Asian, African and Latin American affairs, with the rank of ambassador.

Bowles spent the next few months on extensive fact-finding missions to the Middle East, Africa and Asia. In mid-1962 he drafted an elaborate but somewhat vague plan to head off American military involvement in Vietnam by neutralizing all of Southeast Asia. Although there was some discussion of the idea, it was rejected since the principle of regional neutralization had already been suggested to the other concerned governments without result. Bowles also sought to reshape the U.S. foreign aid program, ultimately recommending a set of specific criteria for the allocation of aid to insure that it was concentrated where it would have the most effect. Although the plan was widely praised in Congress and the press when it became public in October 1962, it was never fully implemented.

As a target for conservative attacks, Bowles was still a political liability in the White House. Sen. Barry Goldwater [q.v.] among others, urged his dismissal for urging "a soft policy toward communism." Bowles himself was dissatisfied with his new position. While it gave him access to Kennedy, it was a frustrating post far removed from the chain of command. Citing the Administration's alleged neglect of the underdeveloped world, Bowles submitted his resignation in December 1962. Kennedy suggested that instead of leaving the Administration, he return as ambassador to India. Accepting the offer after some initial reluctance, Bowles was designated ambassador on April 6, 1963. He arrived in New Delhi on July 17, where he served until April 1969. [See JOHNSON Volume]

[EWK]

For further information:
Chester Bowles, *Promises to Keep: My Years In Public Life 1941-1969* (New York, 1971).

BOYD, ALAN S(TEPHENSON)
b. July 10, 1922; Jacksonville, Fla.
Member, Civil Aeronautics Board, November 1959-May 1965; Chairman, Civil Aeronautics Board, February 1961-May 1965.

After service in the Army Troop Transport Command in World War II, Boyd earned a law degree from the University of Virginia in 1948. He returned to Florida where he practiced law and served on state commissions dealing with transportation development and regulation. In May 1959 President Eisenhower appointed Boyd, a Democrat, to fill a vacancy on the Civil Aeronautics Board (CAB).

President Kennedy designated Boyd as chairman of the CAB in February 1961. Kennedy reappointed him to a full six-year term one year later and redesignated him chairman in 1962 and 1963. Boyd's tenure on the CAB marked an important shift in the panel's functions. With the Federal Aviation Act of 1958, Congress had increased the power of the CAB to regulate the commercial airline industry and reasserted the board's authority to issue emergency subsidies to airlines in need of immediate financial assistance. Another reorganization of the CAB went into effect on July 3, 1961, which, like reforms in the administrative procedure of other regulatory agencies, permitted the chairman to delegate more authority to CAB staff members. This reform enabled Boyd to clear up a substantial backload of cases and redirect the activities of the five CAB members towards an evaluation of general policy issues.

The CAB turned its attention to declining airline industry profits in 1961. Inspired by impressive earnings in the early 1950s, the commercial lines had overestimated their potential markets and overexpanded services. As one response to the industry's dilemma, Boyd urged a reduction in the number of flights on main routes serviced by several lines. In July 1963 Boyd supported a panel majority which voted a controversial subsidy for Northeast Airlines. The CAB authorized the funds for the airline's unprofitable New England-Washington runs. The board ordered Northeast to discontinue its Florida flights in competition with Eastern. Massachusetts congressional and labor leaders unsuccessfully protested the CAB's action and demanded the restoration of Northeast's Florida trade.

With some reservations, Boyd endorsed airline mergers. In a November 1961 address at Hartford, Conn., he urged airline leaders to consider combination as the best available solution to the industry's financial difficulties. Despite his advocacy of greater consolidation, Boyd cast the deciding vote in a CAB decision against Eastern Airlines's request to merge with American in June 1963. A combination of such scale, the board ruled, might jeopardize effective competition in the industry.

From the beginning of his tenure as CAB chief, Boyd sought to increase the demand for airline services through lower fares. In May 1961 he opposed the Administration's proposed extension of the 10% excise tax on bus, train and airline tickets. He urged companies to lower charges voluntarily while experimenting with special rates for families and students.

Boyd's three-year effort as CAB chairman contributed to the recovery of the airline industry's profits. The total revenues for all lines for fiscal year 1964 nearly doubled the 1963 figures. The net income of United Air Lines rose from $8 million to $45.5 million in 1963. Only two companies—Eastern and Northeast —lost money in the fiscal 1964 period. Boyd left the CAB to become undersecretary of commerce in June 1965. Two years later President Johnson appointed Boyd to serve as the nation's first Secretary of Transportation. [See JOHNSON Volume]

[JLB]

BOYKIN, FRANK W(ILLIAM)

b. Feb. 21, 1885; Bladon Springs, Ala.
d. March 12, 1969; Washington, D.C.
Democratic Representative, Ala., 1935-63.

Boykin was initially elected to the U.S. House of Representatives in 1935 to fill a vacancy. At the beginning of the Kennedy Administration, he was the second-ranking member of the Merchant Marine and Fisheries Committee and the fourth-ranking member of the Veterans' Affairs Committee. He lost a May 1962 primary in which—as a result of redistricting—the nine incumbent Alabama representatives ran statewide for eight seats.

The following October a federal grand jury in Baltimore indicted Boykin and Rep. Thomas F. Johnson (D, Md.) [q.v.] on eight counts of conspiracy and conflict-of-interest charges. Boykin was accused of having received $250,000 as part of a real estate deal from J. Kenneth Edlin, a former officer of two Maryland savings and loan associations, in exchange for efforts in 1961 to influence the Justice Department to dismiss a 1959 mail fraud charge against Edlin. The indictment stated that an additional $3 million had gone to a company owned by Boykin as part of the land transaction. Edlin, who had pleaded no contest to the mail fraud charge in December 1961, was included in the indictment along with one of his business associates.

Maryland, the last state to establish effective supervision of savings and loan associations, had not adopted a strong regulatory statute until 1961. By the time of Boykin's indictment, 27 persons had been arrested in connection with Maryland savings and loan association scandals, several of the companies had gone into receivership and over $40 million in deposits had been jeopardized.

Boykin's trial was held in the United States District Court in Baltimore during the spring of 1963. Attorney General Robert F. Kennedy [q.v.] testified that Boykin had come to his office in 1961 to urge him to drop the Edlin indictment. On June 13, 1963 Boykin was found guilty on all eight counts. Johnson, Edlin and his associate were also convicted. Boykin received a $40,000 fine and six months probation in October. The court excused him from a jail sentence because of his ill health.

In December 1965 President Johnson granted Boykin a full pardon. Three senators and 34 House members, including most in the Alabama, Florida, Mississippi and South Carolina delegations, had written the President earlier in support of a pardon. Boykin died on March 12, 1969.

[MLL]

BRENNAN, WILLIAM J(OSEPH), JR.
b. April 25, 1906; Newark, N.J.
Associate Justice, U.S. Supreme Court,
1956-   .

The son of Irish immigrants, Brennan graduated from the Wharton School of Finance in 1928 and Harvard Law School, where he studied under Felix Frankfurter [*q.v.*], in 1931. He then joined the Newark, N.J., law firm of Pitney, Hardin and Skinner, becoming a partner in 1937 and an expert in labor law. Brennan was appointed to the New Jersey Superior Court in 1949, to the Court's Appellate Division in 1950 and in 1952 to the state Supreme Court, where he developed a reputation as a moderately liberal judge. Although a Democrat, Brennan was named to the U.S. Supreme Court by President Eisenhower and began serving on the Court under a recess appointment in October 1956. His appointment was confirmed by the Senate in March 1957.

In his early years on the Supreme Court Justice Brennan often played the role of a mediator between the Court's liberal and conservative wings, writing narrowly based opinions to assemble a majority. In the process, however, he generally aligned himself with the Court's liberal justices and demonstrated a strong commitment to the protection of individual liberties, especially to First Amendment freedoms, and to procedural fairness. Brennan also began his role as author of the Warren Court's opinions in major cases on obscenity in *Roth v. U.S.* in 1957. [See EISENHOWER Volume]

Justice Brennan joined with the majority in key Warren Court decisions expanding the procedural rights of criminal defendants, such as the June 1961 ruling in *Mapp v. Ohio* requiring state courts to exclude illegally seized evidence. In March 1963 Brennan wrote the majority opinion in *Fay v. Noia*, holding that a procedural default that precluded state court review of a criminal conviction did not bar federal court review of the conviction in habeas corpus proceedings. He dissented in a May 1963 case in which a government agent, wearing a secret recording device, had recorded a defendant's bribery offer. The majority held

this evidence was admissible in court, but Brennan saw a danger to individual liberty in electronic surveillance and insisted that the Fourth and Fifth Amendments afforded a "comprehensive right of personal liberty in the face of governmental intrusion."

With First Amendment rights in particular, Brennan demanded strict procedural standards from government to prevent intrusion into protected rights. In a June 1961 decision he argued that Missouri's censorship system was unconstitutional because it operated in a manner making it likely that non-obscene literature would be seized and taken out of circulation along with obscene literature. Similarly, Brennan's majority opinion in a February 1963 case overturned Rhode Island's quasi-governmental book censorship system because it set up an unconstitutional system of prior restraint. Brennan also wrote the majority opinion in a January 1963 case nullifying a Virginia law which barred solicitation of legal business because it had resulted in an unconstitutional restriction of the rights of free speech and association of the NAACP.

Brennan's most notable opinion in the Kennedy years was handed down in March 1962 in *Baker v. Carr*, a 6-2 decision holding that federal courts had the right and duty to try cases involving state legislative apportionment. Overturning a 1946 decision, Brennan's lengthy majority opinion ruled that malapportionment was a proper subject of judicial consideration and presented a justifiable cause of action. The decision launched an extensive process of reapportionment of state legislative and congressional districts, increasing the representation of cities at the expense of rural areas.

As a solid liberal majority emerged on the Warren Court in the early 1960s, Brennan abandoned the narrow ground of many of his early decisions and became more activist and creative in his opinions. During the Johnson Administration he wrote some of the Court's most significant opinions interpreting the First Amendment, especially in libel and obscenity law. In a 1966 decision, he put forward a new and expansive concept of congressional power under the Fourteenth Amendment. [See JOHNSON, NIXON Volumes]

[CAB]

For further information:
Archibald Cox, *The Warren Court* (Cambridge, Mass., 1968).
Stephen J. Friedman, ed., *An Affair with Freedom: William J. Brennan, Jr.* (New York, 1967).
———, "William J. Brennan, Jr.," in Leon Friedman and Fred L. Israel, eds., *The Justices of the United States Supreme Court, 1789-1969* (New York, 1969), Vol. IV

BRIDGES, HARRY (ALFRED RENTON)

b. Melbourne, Australia; July 28, 1901.
President, International Longshoremen's and Warehousemen's Union, 1937- .

Son of a prosperous Melbourne realtor, Bridges spent five years as a seaman before he began working on the San Francisco docks in 1922. Bridges was a member of the International Workers of the World and later was close to the Communist Party. He emerged in 1934 as the most important leader of the dock strike that triggered the famous San Francisco General Strike of the same year. By 1937 Bridges had led a group of rebellious Pacific Coast longshore locals out of the American Federation of Labor and into an independent International Longshoremen's and Warehousemen's Union (ILWU) affiliated with the new Congress of Industrial Organizations (CIO). During the 1930s and 1940s Bridges was one of the most important labor leaders on the West Coast. His 60,000-member ILWU was an important base of Communist strength within the CIO.

Beginning in 1939 Bridges fought a successful 16-year legal battle against deportation by the federal government. Although the Justice Department never proved that Bridges was a Communist, and therefore subject to denaturalization and deportation, the CIO expelled the ILWU in 1949 on charges that it was Communist-dominated.

Because of what he considered persecution by the Democrats during the 1940s and 1950s Bridges said he voted for the Republican presidential ticket in 1956 and 1960. [See TRUMAN, EISENHOWER Volumes]

In October 1960 Bridges signed a five-and-one-half-year collective bargaining contract with the Pacific Maritime Association (PMA), which had a far reaching impact on the nature of longshore work and the character of the industry. Known as the Mechanization and Modernization Agreement (M & M), the new contract suspended longstanding ILWU work rules, allowed for a reduction of the 14,000-man workforce on the docks and permitted virtually unlimited automation of the longshore work process. In return the PMA agreed to guarantee a 35-hour workweek for registered longshoremen and established a $29 million trust fund to be used for retirement pensions. Although an unusually large minority of the ILWU voted against the M & M Agreement because it would reduce the number of longshore jobs and speed the pace of work, the new contract was widely hailed in business and academic circles as an important step toward an increase in labor productivity and job security.

According to Bridges's biographer Charles Larrowe, the M & M Agreement was perhaps the last important step in the transformation of the ILWU president—or at least his public image—from that of "labor radical" to "labor statesman". Under Bridges's leadership the ILWU continued to give verbal and financial support to the civil rights and peace movements in the early 1960s, but the union was no longer in the forefront of social change on the West Coast. Bridges cooperated closely with the PMA in administration of the new M & M Agreement and fought a long legal and political challenge to his leadership from a group of predominantly black dissident longshoremen who were expelled from the union in June 1963.

Although Bridges renewed the M & M Agreement in 1966 and was appointed to the powerful San Francisco Port Commission in 1970, ILWU jurisdiction over containerized cargo came under increasing pressure from both the Teamsters Union and the PMA in the late 1960s. ILWU demands for a substantial wage increase and continued jurisdiction over packing and handling the new truck-length containers led to a half-year-long strike in 1971 and 1972. [See JOHNSON, NIXON Volumes]

[NNL]

For further information:
Charles P. Larrowe, *Harry Bridges, The Rise and Fall of Radical Labor in the United States* (New York, 1972).
Stanley Weir, "The ILWU: A Case Study in Bureaucracy", in Burton Hall, ed., *Autocracy and Insurgency in Organized Labor* (New Brunswick, 1972).

BRIDGES, (HENRY) STYLES
b. Sept. 9, 1898; West Pembroke, Me.
d. Nov. 26, 1961; Concord, N.H.
Republican Senator, N. H., 1937-61;
Chairman, Republican Policy
Committee, 1955-61.

Raised in rural Maine, Styles Bridges completed his education with a degree in agriculture from the state university in 1918. Shortly thereafter, Bridges moved to New Hampshire and eventually entered Republican politics. Elected governor in 1934 at the age of 36, he left office after two years to become a U. S. Senator. In the upper chamber, Bridges soon became recognized as one of his party's most vocal conservatives and a foe of organized labor. An outspoken anti-Communist even before the advent of the Cold War, Bridges in 1950 joined Sen. Joseph R. McCarthy (R, Wisc.) in accusing the Truman Administration of having condoned Communist gains in Europe and Asia. In the Republican 80th and 83rd Congresses, Bridges chaired the Senate Appropriations Committee. Beginning in 1955 he led the Senate Republican Policy Committee, the fourth-ranked Party leadership position and a post he held until his death. He repeatedly urged President Eisenhower to follow the guidance of the Party's Old Guard and actively supported conservative Everett M. Dirksen (R, Ill.) [q.v.] in his successful campaign for the Senate minority leadership in 1959. [See TRUMAN, EISENHOWER Volumes]

Until 1959 many observers had considered Bridges the real leader of the Senate Republicans. However, illness and personal loyalty to Dirksen limited Bridge's power after January 1959. Dirksen's biographer, Neil MacNeil, described Bridges as a loyal supporter of the minority leader; he declined to use his position as Policy Committee chairman to rival Dirksen's authority.

During 1961 Bridges continued as a spokesman for a strong anti-Communist policy. He criticized Kennedy's decision in March to end the Post Office Department's interception of non-first class mail sent from Communist nations. As the ranking Republican on the Senate Aeronautics and Space Committee, Bridges approved of the National Aeronautics and Space Administration request for $1.8 billion for fiscal 1962. He told the Senate in June 1961, "I do not believe we can afford to gamble" in America's space race with the Russians. He supported the President's strongly worded Berlin crisis message in July and twice in August attempted to prohibit all assistance to nations trading "strategic materials" with Communist countries. He co-sponsored a Senate resolution in late August urging the President to resume nuclear testing.

On Sept. 21 Bridges suffered a coronary attack while in Concord and died two months later. His third wife lost an opportunity to succeed him in the September 1962 Republican primary. In November Democrat Thomas J. McIntyre [q.v.] became the first member of his party to win election to the Senate from New Hampshire and served out the remaining four years of Bridges's term.

[JLB]

BRINKLEY, DAVID
b. July 10, 1920; Wilmington, N.C.
NBC News correspondent.

David Brinkley was the son of a North Carolina railroad worker. After graduating from high school in 1938, Brinkley worked as a reporter for the Wilmington, (N.C.) *Star-News* until 1940, when he joined the Army. Discharged in 1942, Brinkley was hired by the United Press news agency and for the next year served as a reporter with various Southern bureaus. While working in Nashville, Tenn., Brinkley studied English at Vanderbilt University.

Brinkley joined the National Broadcasting Company in 1943 in Washington, D.C. and the same year began doing television newscasts, although there were only a few hundred television sets in the city. Establishing a reputation for his pungent and economical style of reporting, Brinkley attained national celebrity when he teamed with newscaster Chet Huntley [q.v.] during the 1956 political conventions. In October 1956 the team took over the early-evening *NBC News* slot and after one month captured a 36% share of the national audience. The program was later renamed the Huntley-Brinkley Report with a carefully orchestrated format designed to portray Huntley, reporting from New York, as a conservative, and Brinkley, reporting from Washington, as an anti-establishment maverick, though both men shared the same liberal philosophy. Brinkley soon became known for his dry wit and terse broadcasting style.

In September 1963 the three major networks expanded their evening news formats from 15 to 30 minutes to reflect the growing audience for news, estimated at nearly 50 million viewers. To inaugurate the programs, President Kennedy granted interviews to the three major networks. Kennedy believed that the edited version of his first interview, with CBS correspondent Walter Cronkite [q.v.], had distorted his opinion of South Vietnamese President Ngo Dinh Diem and had left the impression that he had no confidence in that leader. Consequently, the President insisted that he exercise final approval of the televised version of his Huntley-Brinkley appearance. In the interview he told the reporters that he had no intention of reducing U.S. aid to Vietnam. Kennedy also supported the domino theory because the fall of South Vietnam "would give the impression that the wave of the future in Southeast Asia was China and the Communists."

During the late 1950s and throughout the 1960s, the team consistently led the competition from ABC and CBS in the Nielsen ratings and earned 10 Emmy and two Peabody awards. *David Brinkley's Journal* drew special praise for its concise commentaries on news events. It was Brinkley's opinion of television news that "some of the most successful 'news' on the air is not news at all. . . . Instead, it is often no more than a report on a mood, a feeling, a texture, a shape or a movement."

During the late 1960s and early 1970s, Brinkley co-anchored NBC News's coverage of such stories as the Watergate affair, the funeral of Lyndon B. Johnson [q.v.], the flights of Apollo 10 and 11 and the 1968 and 1972 national political conventions. When Chet Huntley retired from NBC in August 1970, Brinkley continued to anchor the new *NBC Nightly News* until August 1971, when he was replaced by veteran newsman John Chancellor. Five times a week Brinkley continued to present *David Brinkley's Journal* from Washington. [See NIXON Volume]

[FHM]

For further information:
Erik Barnouw, *The Image Empire* (New York, 1970).

BROWER, DAVID (ROSS)
b. July 1, 1912; Berkeley, Calif.
Executive Director, Sierra Club, 1952-69.

Brower developed a love of nature during family camping trips in the Sierra Nevada and walks with his blind mother in the still-wild Berkeley hills behind his home. Painfully shy, especially among older classmates, Brower dropped out of the University of California after one year. He made his first extended trip through the Sierra wilderness in 1933 and in the same year joined the Sierra Club, the West Coast conservation organization founded by John Muir. In the late 1930s Brower pioneered in the development of the modern sport of rock climbing and made numerous first ascents while employed on the staff of Yosemite National Park. He became an editor at the University of California Press in 1941. Two years later he joined the Army's 10th Mountain Division as an instructor in climbing techniques. After resuming his job as an editor after the war, Brower moved to the full-time position of executive director of the Sierra Club in 1952.

Since Muir's death in 1914 the Sierra Club had worked to interest people in the nation's wilderness but had largely ignored the cause of conservation. Brower transformed the Club into an activist political organization, one which attacked land developers, lumber and mining companies and government agencies, which, in Brower's opinion, were despoiling the wilderness. During Brower's tenure the Club's membership increased from 7,000 to 70,000 and its budget rose from $75,000 to $3 million a year. The organization became national in scope and Brower turned much of the Club's energy toward a vigorous lobbying and publicity effort on behalf of wilderness preservation legislation. Under Brower's direct supervision the Sierra Club also produced a series of lavish, expensive and highly praised photo-essay books in the 1960s. Brower chose the landscape photographs and selected or wrote much of the text. Although the books produced only marginal financial returns for the Club, they proved a forceful statement on behalf of wilderness values to an American public increasingly interested in the outdoor life.

The Sierra Club was an effective force in the enactment of conservation legislation in the early 1960s. Club lobbying efforts helped bring about the government's creation of the Cape Cod National Seashore in 1961 and the Point Reyes National Seashore in 1962. The former was the first park-type unit in the National Park System to be acquired predominantly through purchase and condemnation of private land. In 1961 Congress enacted another bill, strongly supported by the Sierra Club, that placed large virgin areas into a National Wilderness System free of roads and commercial activity. Although the Club failed in its 1963 effort to stop construction of the controversial Colorado River Glen Canyon Dam, its battle generated great interest in the Club's legislative activity. Stewart Udall [q.v.], Secretary of the Interior under Presidents Kennedy and Johnson, later called Brower "the most effective single person on the cutting edge of conservation in this country."

In the late 1960s Brower came under criticism from other members of the Sierra Club who opposed what they considered his extremist and financially irresponsible environmental campaigns. After the Sierra Club lost its tax-exempt status in 1968, more traditionally oriented members of the organization's board of directors took control of the Club and forced Brower's resignation. Brower then founded the John Muir Institute for Environmental Studies and Friends of the Earth. The former was a research and educational organization, while the latter was devoted to lobbying on conservation issues and campaigning for political candidates. [See JOHNSON, NIXON Volumes]

[JCH]

For further information:
John McPhee, *Encounters with the Archdruid: Narratives about a Conservationist and Three of His Natural Enemies* (New York, 1971).

BROWN, CLARENCE
b. July 14, 1893; Blanchester, Ohio.
d. Aug. 23, 1965; Washington, D.C.
Republican Representative, Ohio, 1939-65.

First elected to the House from central Ohio's seventh district, Brown was a loyal follower of Sen. Robert Taft (R, Ohio) until his death in 1953. By the late 1950s Brown was the ranking Republican on the powerful House Rules Committee. There he often worked with Chairman Howard W. Smith (D, Va.) [q.v.] to kill or delay liberal legislation. [See TRUMAN, EISENHOWER Volumes]

Kennedy Administration forces weakened conservative control of the Rules Committee in January 1961 by adding three new members to the body, thereby tipping the political balance toward the liberal-moderate faction. Despite this setback, Brown remained a leader of the Southern Democratic-Republican coalition in the House. In the early 1960s he was a leader of the coalition's often successful fight to block passage of Kennedy Administration legislation in the labor, education, tax reform and civil rights fields.

According to *Congressional Quarterly*, Brown voted against the Administration on more than 60% of the key House roll calls in the early 1960s. At the same time he voted with the conservative coalition an average of 80% of the time.

Brown was elected to another term in the House in 1964. He died on Aug. 23, 1965 and his House seat was subsequently filled by his son, Clarence Brown, Jr.

[FHM]

BROWN, EDMUND G(ERALD), SR.
b. April 21, 1905; San Francisco, Calif.
Governor, Calif., 1959-67.

"Pat" Brown was a product of San Francisco's public and parochial schools. He and began his political career as a Republican but switched to the Democrats in 1939. Working his way up through one of California's few solid party organizations, Brown won the post of San Francisco district attorney in 1943 and was elected California's attorney general in 1950 and 1954. The only Democrat holding statewide office during the period, Brown earned a reputation for honesty and strict enforcement of the law.

Brown was elected governor in 1958, defeating conservative Sen. William F. Knowland (R, Calif.). Calling himself a "responsible" liberal, Brown was strongly backed by organized labor, which mobilized its ranks to simultaneously help Brown and defeat a right-to-work initiative backed by his opponent. Brown's victory broke the pattern of Republican control of the state, which had prevailed for several decades. He was only the second Democratic governor of the century, and he carried with him the first Democratic majorities in both houses of the legislature since 1889. [See EISENHOWER Volume]

Brown claimed credit for a substantial amount of progressive legislation during his first term in office. In a period of great economic and population growth, his Administration expanded California's freeway system and public schools, passed a fair employment practices bill, increased jobless benefits and pensions for the blind and aged and enacted consumer protection legislation. Brown also succeeded in abolishing the state's cross-filing primary election system, which had allowed Californians to vote in either party's primary regardless of their own party registration. The net effect of the change was to increase the weight of the ideologically committed voters in both of California's political parties.

Two of Brown's most important achievements were the enactment of the California Water Project and the establishment of a "master plan" for higher education in the state. The $1.7 billion water program was designed to provide water from the northern part of the state for the burgeoning population of Southern California and the irrigated farmlands of the Central Valley. The education plan expanded the state's system of public higher education, which was the largest in the nation, to provide some type of college training for all of California's high school graduates.

Although Brown was chief executive of the nation's second largest state and titular head of its Democratic Party, his actual power was severely limited by the Democratic Party's weak structure in the state. Brown led the California delegation to the Democratic National Convention in Los Angeles in July 1960 as a favorite son, but agreed to turn over his votes to Sen. John F. Kennedy before the convention's first roll-call vote. However, he was unable to prevent about half of the California delegates from voting for Adlai E. Stevenson [*q.v.*] on the first ballot. Kennedy's loss of California in the November election increased doubts about Brown's effective political power, and the Kennedy Administration soon turned to the powerful Speaker of the State Assembly, Jesse Unruh [*q.v.*], as its chief political liaison in the state. As political journalist Lou Cannon noted some years later, the Kennedys did not understand that California politics lacked the tightly controlled machines of the East, and they unjustly blamed Brown for his inability to control the Party "organization."

Brown faced former Vice President Richard M. Nixon [*q.v.*] in the 1962 gubernatorial contest. Political observers considered the campaign one of the most bitter in the state's history. Nixon, who in his early California career had charged his opponents with being "soft on Communism," revived the issue against Brown. The Governor campaigned on his liberal record and charged that Nixon sought the governorship merely as a stepping stone to another presidential campaign. Brown defeated Nixon by winning almost 54% of the vote in November. At the time most commentators thought the defeat in his home state effectively ended Nixon's political career.

Brown's second term was more difficult than his first. Both liberals and conservatives found the Governor's brand of centrist politics inadequate after a series of dramatic political phenomena—the student revolt at Berkeley in 1964, the Watts riots in 1965 and the growing farmworker movement—brought new issues to the fore in California politics. Conservative Republicans benefited most from these new developments and in November 1966 Brown lost the gubernatorial election to Ronald Reagan, a former movie star and conservative political spokesman. Following his defeat Brown served as head of the National Commission for the Reform of Federal Criminal Laws. [See JOHNSON Volume]

[JCH]

BROWN, HAROLD
b. Sept. 19, 1927; New York, N.Y.
Director of Research and Engineering for the Department of Defense, May 1961-September 1965.
Air Force Secretary 1965-1969

Harold Brown was one of the experts dubbed "whiz kids" whom Secretary of Defense Robert S. McNamara [*q.v.*] asked to join the Pentagon staff when he took office. Prior to his appointment as director of defense research and engineering in May 1961, Brown, a nuclear physicist, had served as the director of the Livermore Laboratory, a University of California re-

search center for the development of atomic weapons. Earlier Brown had also acted as scientific consultant to the Pentagon and as technical adviser to the U.S. delegations to the Conferences for the Cessation of Nuclear Tests in 1958 and 1959.

As director of research, Brown was responsible for investigating all proposed technological projects. This position, always a high-ranking one, was given further status and influence under McNamara because of the Secretary's desire to modernize and coordinate the weapons systems of the various military services.

Although Brown had spent his life in weapons research, he believed that such weapons should not be constructed simply because the technology existed. Instead, he strongly insisted that technological developments should be generated in response to policy considerations. He was especially interested in weapons and means of warfare that could be used as alternatives to nuclear force.

Because of these ideas Brown was closely allied with McNamara in the Secretary's desire to build a multiservice fighter/bomber, the TFX. In his position as research director, Brown forced the Navy and Air Force to compromise their technical requirements so that one plane could be built for both services.

In a May 1963 hearing of the House Appropriations Subcommittee, Brown advocated the limited use of chemical and biological warfare as an intermediate step between conventional and nuclear weapons. Although sections of his testimony were closed, the public portions indicated that he was particularly interested in the use of psychologically disorienting non-lethal chemicals.

Brown supported McNamara's advocacy of the 1963 nuclear test ban treaty. He told a congressional committee in August 1963 that the treaty would not reduce American weapons superiority because the U.S. was ahead of Russia in the technological development of nuclear warheads that could be tested underground.

President Johnson appointed Brown as Air Force Secretary in September 1965. In that post Brown advocated limited bombing raids against North Vietnam, but after the military requested another 200,000 additional ground troops in February 1968 he supported de-escalation of the war. [See JOHNSON Volume]

In 1969 Brown resigned his position to become president of the California Institute of Technology.

[EWS]

BROWN, WINTHROP G(ILMAN)

b. July 12, 1907; Seal Harbor, Me.
Ambassador to Laos, July 1960-June 1962; Deputy Commandant for Foreign Affairs, National War College, June 1962-July 1964.

After receiving his law degree from Yale in 1929, Brown entered the New York firm of Platt, Taylor and Walker. During World War II he joined the staff of the Lend Lease Administration and represented that agency in missions in London and New Delhi. After the war he continued as a specialist in international economic policy for the State Department. In 1960 President Dwight D. Eisenhower appointed Brown ambassador to Laos.

Brown arrived in Laos at the end of July, one week before an Aug. 9 coup led by Laotian Air Force Capt. Kong Le toppled the government of the American-supported Gen. Phoumi Nosavan. Kong Le immediately turned over administrative power to the neutralist Prince Souvanna Phouma who formed a government opposed to Gen. Phoumi Nosavan's pro-Western orientation and militant anti-Communism. Phoumi refused to accept Souvanna's offer of a position in this new government. Instead, he decided to use his control of the Royal Laotian Army to retain domination of the country through a military campaign. The chaos created by this situation threatened to permit a Communist takeover of Laos by the Pathet Lao, which held much of the countryside.

In assessing the situation Brown questioned the possibility of building a pro-Western government in Laos. He believed that the corruption of the Phoumi regime had made it unpopular and that growing nationalist feelings in Laos demanded an independent foreign policy. Therefore, he recommended that the U.S. withdraw its support of Phoumi and back a coalition government proposed by Souvanna.

Despite a lack of firm direction from Washington, Brown worked to form a rightist-neutralist coalition in September and October 1960. He warned Phoumi that the U.S. would not support his campaign and attempted to persuade Souvanna to form a government that excluded Communists. In November 1960 the Ambassador was finally able to persuade Washington to cut off aid to Gen. Phoumi, but by that time the General had driven Souvanna into exile and Kong Le into an alliance with the Communists. [See EISENHOWER Volume]

During the Kennedy Administration Brown's attempts to form a neutralist-rightist coalition had the complete support of the President, who endorsed the proposal for a neutralist Laotian government in March 1961. In June 1961 the Geneva Conference convened to negotiate the formation of the neutralist-led coalition government. After that date Brown played only a minor role in creating the eventual coalition. Most of the actual policy-making decisions and negotiations were carried on by W. Averell Harriman [q.v.].

A coalition government, including representatives of all three political factions, was formed in June 1962. In this government, headed by neutralist Souvanna as prime minister, both the rightist Phoumi and the Communist leader Souphanouvong held posts as deputy premiers.

In 1964 Brown was appointed deputy commander of the National War College and from 1964 to 1967 served as ambassador to South Korea before becoming special assistant to the Secretary of State for liaison with state governments. In 1968 he was appointed deputy assistant secretary of state for East Asian and Pacific affairs. He retired from the foreign service in 1972.

[EWS]

For Further Information:
Charles A. Stevenson, *The End of Nowhere: American Policy Toward Laos Since 1954* (Boston, 1972).

BRUCE, DAVID K(IRKPATRICK) E(STE)

b. Feb. 12, 1898; Baltimore, Md.
Ambassador to Great Britain, February 1961-March 1969.

David Bruce, the senior ambassador during the Kennedy Administration, was born into a politically prominent Maryland family. Following his graduation from the University of Maryland Law School in 1926, Bruce practiced law in Baltimore and then entered public life as a member of the Maryland House of Delegates. From 1925 to 1927 he served as vice consul in Rome but quit to become an investment banker. At one time he was a director of 25 corporations. Bruce represented the American Red Cross in London in 1940 and for most of the war worked in the Office of Strategic Services in the European theater.

In 1947 Bruce became assistant secretary of commerce under his friend and business associate, W. Averell Harriman [q.v.]. He went to Paris to administer the Marshall Plan in 1948 and became ambassador to France one year later. In 1952 he served as undersecretary of state to Dean Acheson [q.v.]. Bruce participated in talks aimed at European military and economic integration during 1953 but despite his efforts to persuade the French of the benefits of multilateral defense, the French National Assembly refused to merge their forces into the European Defense Community. After a few years in private life, he returned to public service as ambassador to West Germany in 1957. Resigning in 1959, Bruce actively campaigned for Kennedy in 1960. [See TRUMAN, EISENHOWER Volumes]

Bruce was one of the leading contenders for the post of Secretary of State in the new administration, but according to historian Arthur Schlesinger, Jr. [q.v.], he was ruled out because of his age and his traditional European orientation in foreign affairs. However, Bruce was appointed ambassador to Great Britain in February 1961, becoming the first member of the Foreign Service to serve in the three top diplomatic posts in Europe. The Ambassador possessed sufficient personal wealth to underwrite the great expenses entailed in maintaining the London embassy. More importantly, the President had complete confidence that Bruce could improve the "special relationship" between the two Anglo-Saxon nations.

In 1956 this "special relationship" had been severely strained by the Suez crisis, but the friendship between President Dwight D. Eisenhower and British Prime Minister Harold Macmillan revived the image of an equal partnership based on common language and democratic traditions. Kennedy and Macmillan also developed a personal friendship; they met with each other seven times during Kennedy's abbreviated term and spoke frequently with each other over the telephone. The British ambassador to Washington, David Ormsby-Gore, had been Kennedy's personal friend since the 1930s. Not surprisingly, he had an access to Kennedy denied other ambassadors. Bruce occupied a similar position in London. As political scientist David Nunnerley noted, "Macmillan was in no doubt that whatever he said to Bruce . . . would receive the attention of the President."

Events of the early 1960s showed that the "special relationship" had grown weaker despite the good will of the two countries' top political leaders and their ambassadors. Britain, economically and militarily dependent on the U.S., had no power role within the European community. Although the British were America's best informed allies, the U.S. did not always quickly notify Britain of American actions.

In the Cuban missile crisis of October 1962, when the Kennedy Administration decided to blockade Cuba Bruce was informed of the decision only 24 hours before Kennedy announced it, but the British had learned of it earlier through their own intelligence channels. Bruce then had to explain the American position to Macmillan, who suffered a loss of prestige in Britain because he played no role in making the decision. The Prime Minister was also criticized by leaders of the British peace movement for accepting the U.S. analysis of the situation without any reservations. To protect the

United States' reputation and Macmillan's prestige Bruce released the first public photographs of the Cuban missile sites.

Apparent American indifference to British interests surfaced again in November and December 1962. In 1960 Eisenhower had offered to make the Skybolt missile available to the British as soon as it was perfected. The British, who had stopped work on their own missile system, accepted the offer because the Skybolt would have ensured them an independent nuclear deterrent through most of the 1960s. In 1962, however, Secretary of Defense Robert McNamara [q.v.] judged the Skybolt project inefficient and decided to cancel it. Bruce, inadequately informed of developments in Washington, was unable to alert Kennedy to the serious political consequences that a unilateral decision to end Skybolt would have for Macmillan's government. Kennedy attempted to correct the situation at a meeting with Macmillan in Nassau in December. He offered Britain the submarine-launched Polaris missile in place of the air-launched Skybolt. However, the offer was made under terms which could not conceal Britain's dependent role in the "special relationship."

The agreement angered French President Charles de Gaulle, who resented U.S. favoritism toward Great Britain. The "Europeanists" in the U.S. State and Defense Departments saw an independent British nuclear deterrent as an obstacle to a European multilateral nuclear force (MLF), then under construction. Bruce's position was ambivalent. On the one hand he saw the MLF as a step toward achieving a united Europe and interdependence in nuclear defense. Yet, at the same time, he understood the desire of many Britons to retain "great power" status. In view of the French determination to chart her own nuclear policy, there was no alternative to an independent British nuclear deterrent. The proposed multilateral force never materialized.

Bruce stayed on in London until 1969. In 1970 he represented the U.S. at the Vietnam peace talks in Paris and in 1972 he went to Peking as liaison officer to the People's Republic of China. [See JOHNSON, NIXON Volumes]

[JCH]

For further information:
David Nunnerley, *President Kennedy and Britain* (New York, 1972).

BUCKLEY, CHARLES A(NTHONY)
b. June 23, 1890; New York, N.Y.
d. Jan. 22, 1967; New York, N.Y.
Democratic Representative, N.Y., 1935-65; Chairman, Public Works Committee, 1955-65.

A bricklayer with his own construction business, Charles Buckley started in politics as a Democratic captain in a Bronx Assembly District in 1911. He held a variety of offices until his election to the House in 1934, serving a long political apprenticeship under Bronx Democratic leader Edward J. Flynn, Democratic National Chairman under Roosevelt and widely acknowledged to be one of the most skillful machine politicians in the nation. As Flynn's successor to the leadership of the Bronx Democratic organization, Buckley made full use of his congressional seat and his appointive powers as chairman of the Public Works Committee to reward his local supporters with federal patronage.

Buckley was an old friend of Joseph P. Kennedy [q.v.] and played a crucial role in lining up delegates to back John Kennedy at the Democratic National Convention in 1960. Kennedy's victory marked the apex of Buckley's influence, for the next year brought a series of sharp reverses in the Bronx. As head of the regular Democratic organization in the borough, Buckley was a major target of Mayor Robert F. Wagner's [q.v.] attacks on "bossism" in his campaign for reelection as mayor in 1961. Wagner's primary victory was a serious setback for Buckley, as was the election of a Republican, Joseph Periconi, to the Bronx borough presidency in November. Wagner's 1962 attempt to oust the organization's leaders was successful in every borough but the Bronx, where Buckley held on with public support from President Kennedy.

In Washington Buckley rarely opposed a

Kennedy Administration measure. His congressional performance, however, was most prominent for his persistent absenteeism. *Congressional Quarterly* reported that Buckley had the lowest voting participation score of any House member in 1961 and the third lowest in 1963. Buckley was also accused of padding the payroll of the Public Works Committee with his political supporters. Rep. James C. Cleveland (R, N.H.) [*q.v.*] charged in May 1964 that Buckley had nine aides on the Committee payroll who were paid $62,400 in 1963 despite the fact that "they were never known to serve or even to be seen by a member of the Committee." Another Committee member, Rep. James Harvey (R, Mich.) backed Cleveland's charges and added, "I have been on the Committee for three years. Frankly, I have never met Mr. Buckley." Buckley denied the payroll padding charges, saying: "I stand for good government . . . . They're not accountable to him [Cleveland]. They're accountable to me. I give them the work to do."

Buckley's chief local antagonists during the Kennedy years were the Bronx Reform Democrats. The culmination of their bitter struggle to win control over the borough's Democratic organization came in 1964 when Buckley was opposed for reelection by reformer Jonathan Bingham, who labeled Buckley "the Trujillo of the Bronx." In the June primary Bingham defeated Buckley by a 4,000-vote plurality. According to the *Almanac of American Politics*, "Buckley apparently refused to take Bingham's candidacy seriously. He could not believe that the scion of an aristocratic WASP family could beat him in a predominantly Jewish and Irish district." Buckley remained influential in Bronx politics until his death on Jan. 22, 1967.

[TO]

BUCKLEY, WILLIAM F(RANK), JR.
b. Nov. 24, 1925; New York, N.Y.
Editor-in-chief, *National Review*,
1955- .

William Buckley's father passed on to his ten children a rigidly conservative ideology, a strong Roman Catholic faith and a fortune from Latin American oil holdings estimated at $100 million. Buckley grew up on the family estate in Sharon, Conn., studied for a year at the University of Mexico and served in the Army during World War II. He entered Yale in 1946, studied history and economics and became chairman of the *Yale Daily News*. Under his editorship the paper increased its emphasis on religious news and conservative politics.

After his graduation in 1950 Buckley published *God and Man at Yale*, in which he attacked liberalism, the anti-religious faculty and what he regarded as Yale's lack of emphasis on conservative ideas. An immediate bestseller in 1951, Buckley's book was widely interpreted as an attack upon liberal education in general.

In the early 1950s Buckley established himself as a major figure in the conservative movement. He held several jobs with conservative organizations, including a position as regular panelist on ultra-conservative H. L. Hunt's [*q.v.*] radio show *Facts Forum*. In 1954 Buckley collaborated with his brother-in-law Brent Bozell on the controversial *McCarthy and his Enemies*, a book which acknowledged that Wisconsin Sen. Joseph McCarthy (R, Wisc.) had slandered reputations and indulged in "gratuitous sensationalism" but maintained that McCarthyism was a movement "around which men of good will and stern morality can close ranks."

With the aid of some 120 investors, Buckley founded the conservative magazine *National Review* in 1955. The aim of the magazine was to provide a conservative forum to compete with liberal magazines like the *Nation* and the *New Republic*. Editors and contributors to *National Review* included such writers and critics as Max Eastman, James Burnham and Whittaker Chambers—men who had once espoused left-wing causes. [See EISENHOWER Volume]

In September 1960, 100 young conservatives from 44 colleges gathered at the Buckley family home in Sharon to form the Young Americans for Freedom (YAF). The group drafted a statement of political philosophy that came to be known as "The Sharon Statement." Claiming 25,000 members, YAF advocated reduced federal spending, continued nuclear testing, withdrawal of U.S. aid to the Communist satellite states and a laissez-faire economic policy.

In the July 20, 1961 issue of *National Review*, Buckley described Pope John XXIII's encyclical *Mater et Magistra*—which advocated state welfare reforms—as a "venture in triviality." In a February 1962 *Review* editorial, Buckley attacked John Birch Society founder Robert Welch [*q.v.*]. While agreeing with the Society's stands against excessive union power, welfare and increased government authority, Buckley argued that Welch was entirely mistaken in asserting that former President Dwight D. Eisenhower was "an agent of the Communist conspiracy."

Buckley began the syndicated newspaper column "A Conservative Voice" in the spring of 1962 and later produced the column "On the Right" for syndicated distribution to more than 200 newspapers. Shortly after the Cuban missile crisis of October 1962, Buckley founded the Committee for the Monroe Doctrine, a group which opposed President Kennedy's assurance to the Soviets that the U.S. would not invade Cuba.

A strong opponent of federal civil rights laws, Buckley called the 1963 civil rights March on Washington a "mob deployment." He frequently criticized the United Nations, the Kennedy Administration, federal aid to public schools and court-ordered school integration. Describing himself as occupying the "dead center" of the conservative movement in the U.S., Buckley had become by the end of the Kennedy Administration one of the most prominent and intellectually resourceful conservative spokesmen in the nation.

A strong backer of Sen. Barry Goldwater's (R, Ariz.) [*q.v.*] presidential campaign in 1964, Buckley himself ran unsuccessfully for mayor of New York in 1965. He supported Richard Nixon's [*q.v.*] candidacy in 1968 and served as his brother James Buckley's campaign manager during his Senate race in New York in 1970. In 1972 Buckley tried unsuccessfully to rally conservative

support for the presidential candidacy of Rep. John Ashbrook (R, Ohio). [See JOHNSON, NIXON Volumes]

[FHM]

For further information:
William F. Buckley, *Up from Liberalism* (New York, 1959).
———, *The Jeweler's Eye* (New York, 1968).
John P. Diggins, *Up from Communism, Conservative Odysseys in American Intellectual History* (New York, 1975).
Charles Lam Markmann, *The Buckleys* (New York, 1973).

BUNCHE, RALPH J(OHNSON)
b. Aug. 7, 1904; Detroit, Mich.
d. Dec. 9, 1971; New York, N.Y.
United Nations Undersecretary for Special Political Affairs, 1957-71.

The son of a barber, Bunche was orphaned at the age of 13 and raised by his maternal grandmother in Los Angeles. Bunche graduated Phi Beta Kappa from the University of California at Los Angeles and in 1934 received a Ph.D. in government and international relations from Harvard, where his dissertation won the Tappan Prize as the best essay in the social sciences. From 1938 to 1940 Bunche served as Gunnar Myrdal's chief aide, gathering materials for *An American Dilemma,* Myrdal's celebrated study of race relations. During World War II Bunche moved from Howard University's political science department to the State Department's division of dependent area affairs, where he dealt with colonial problems. His State Department duties brought him into the planning of the United Nations, and in 1947 Bunche left the government to direct the new world body's trusteeship division.

During 1948 and 1949 Bunche helped mediate the Arab-Israeli war after Count Folke Bernadotte of Sweden was assassinated in Jerusalem. For this effort he became the first black to be awarded the Nobel Peace Prize. In 1956 Bunche organized and directed the deployment of 6,000 U.N. troops in the Suez area. He was promoted in 1957 to U.N. Undersecretary for Special Political Affairs serving as U.N. Secretary General Dag

Hammarskjold's principal troubleshooter. In 1960 Bunche directed the U.N.'s peacekeeping force in the Congo and sought to end the secession of the mineral-rich Katanga province. [See TRUMAN, EISENHOWER Volumes]

Hammarskjold's death in September 1961 en route to a meeting with Katanga's Premier Moise Tshombe aggravated a year-long organizational crisis at the U.N. In 1960 Soviet Premier Nikita Khrushchev had introduced a plan to abolish the office of secretary general and replace it with a "troika," a three-member executive board with representatives of the Communist, Western and neutralist blocs. Despite the unresolved crisis in the Congo, the Soviet Union was in no hurry to choose a new secretary general. In the absence of any formal charter provisions for temporary exercise of the secretary general's power, Bunche, U.N. Undersecretary for General Assembly Affairs Andrew Cordier [q.v.] and Hammarskjold's Chef de Cabinet Chakravarthi Narasimhan assumed responsibility for the day-to-day functioning of the U.N. Secretariat. On Oct. 24, 1961 this three-man group made an agreement between Katanga and the U.N. designed to restore peace in that province.

The big power deadlock over the abolition of the secretary generalship ended with the election of U Thant as acting U.N. secretary general on Nov. 3, 1961. After taking the oath of office, Thant announced that Bunche would be among his "principal advisers." Bunche returned to the Congo in December and brought Tshombe and Congolese Premier Cyrille Adoula together at Kitona, a U.N. operated air base southwest of Leopoldville where on Dec. 21 they signed an agreement placing Katanga under the rule of the Congolese central government. Upon his return to Katanga Tshombe repudiated the agreement and in January 1963 Bunche returned to the Congo to oversee the U.N. Army's capture of Elisabethville, Katanga and the reunification of the Congo.

Bunche continued to serve as a U.N. troubleshooter throughout the 1960s. He flew to Yemen in February 1963 to head off a possible civil war and in 1964 directed the U.N.

peacekeeping force on Cyprus. Bunche also lent his international prestige to the American civil rights movement. He served on the Board of Directors of the NAACP throughout this period and spoke at the 1963 March on Washington. [See JOHNSON Volume]

[DKR]

BUNDY, McGEORGE
b. March 30, 1919; Boston, Mass.
Special Assistant to the President for National Security Affairs, January 1961-February 1966.

Born into a distinguished New England family, Bundy grew up in a household where discussion of domestic policy and foreign affairs was a daily routine. His father, Harvey Bundy, had worked closely with Henry L. Stimson during several tours of high government service. Stimson proved a great influence on the younger Bundy, instilling in him a consciousness of the power of his class and the importance of disinterested public service.

A brilliant scholar, Bundy graduated first in his class from the Groton School and first from Yale in 1940. In 1941 he became a junior fellow at Harvard University. Bundy served in the Army during World War II and participated in the planning of the invasions of Sicily and France. Following his discharge in 1946, he helped Stimson research and write his autobiography. In April 1948 Bundy went to Washington to work for the agency responsible for implementing the Marshall Plan. He left government in September to join Thomas Dewey's presidential campaign as a foreign policy adviser. Following Dewey's defeat Bundy became a political analyst for the prestigious Council on Foreign Relations.

In 1949 Bundy was appointed a lecturer in government at Harvard, teaching a course in modern foreign policy that reflected many of Stimson's ideas. A teacher whose force of mind impressed those he met, Bundy rose rapidly within the department, becoming a full professor in 1954 without the usual academic credentials necessary for the position. The year before, Bundy had been appointed dean of arts and sciences, the second-ranking position at Harvard. There, as in other fields, he proved his ability through the adroit handling of the University's complicated bureaucracy and a faculty noted for its independent spirit.

A nominal Republican, Bundy backed Eisenhower in 1952 and 1956. However, he withdrew his support of the Republican Party after its 1960 nomination of Richard M. Nixon [q.v.]. Instead, Bundy helped organize a scientific and professional committee in support of Sen. John F. Kennedy. Following his election, Kennedy, impressed with Bundy's intellectual brilliance, organizational ability and philosophical pragmatism, offered him several positions in the State and Defense Departments and on the U.S. disarmament team. Bundy was not interested in these appointments but accepted one as the President's special assistant for national security affairs.

Bundy's position suited his philosophical background and prior experience. He was, in the words of Joseph Kraft, an "organizer of process," more interested in the process of informed decision-making than in advocating particular policies. It was Bundy's job to gather information from the Defense and State Departments and the intelligence agencies and present them to the President in a concise fashion. More importantly, he also controlled access to the President. These functions gave him great power in determining what issues received priority and the policy options from which Kennedy could choose. Bundy was also responsible for organizing the meetings of the National Security Council and helped assemble the task forces that Kennedy often used in place of State Department officials to deal with special diplomatic problems. Because of Bundy's background he generally drew men from the ranks of the academic and business establishments for these assignments and thus indirectly determined how many situations would be approached.

Bundy's influence became even greater following the April 1961 Bay of Pigs invasion. Angered by what he considered the State Department's poor advice during the months prior to the attack, Kennedy began relying more and more upon Bundy for foreign policy information and counsel. At Kennedy's urging Bundy reorganized and streamlined his staff and gathered at the White House a group of scholars and intellectuals such as Carl Kaysen [q.v.] and Ralph Dungan [q.v.] who became important forces in formulating Administration foreign policy. Bundy also set up a communications system that equaled those of the State and Defense Departments and permitted him to have the information available to these bureaucracies. By the end of 1961 he had come close to achieving what Arthur Schlesinger, Jr. [q.v.], described as Kennedy's desire to have a small semi-secret office to run foreign affairs "while maintaining the State Department as a facade . . . ." Bundy became, in Kennedy's words, one of his "inner circle," the very small group of advisers who the President consulted daily and whose counsel he trusted in times of crisis.

The role Bundy played in the Kennedy Administration was most evident during the Cuban missile crisis of 1962. Late in the afternoon of Oct. 15 Bundy was informed of the presence of Soviet missiles in Cuba. He delayed telling the President about this until the next morning, ostensibly to give the intelligence agencies time to compile all necessary data and to permit Kennedy to rest before dealing with a potential nuclear confrontation. Bundy was then instructed to set up the meetings of the Excom, a special panel to advise the President and gain bipartisan support for Administration action. This group included many men with long experience in foreign affairs, among them Dean Acheson [q.v.], Robert Lovett [q.v.] and John J. McCloy [q.v.].

At the meetings Bundy was anxious to keep the process of decision-making open until all policy ramifications had been explored. At the Oct. 17 meeting when majority sentiment seemed to favor an air strike to remove the missiles, Bundy advocated using a diplomatic approach. Two days later when sentiment favored a blockade, Bundy advocated an armed strike. Because a blockade was technically an act of war, Kennedy instituted a "quarantine" of Cuba on Oct. 23.

In the early 1960s Bundy began an involvement in Vietnam affairs that would grow during the remainder of his government service. Following the August 1963 attack on Buddhist dissidents by the regime of Ngo Dinh Diem, the Kennedy Administration began a reevaluation of American policy toward the South Vietnamese government. During the two-month debate on the subject, some advisers, such as Roger Hilsman [q.v.], advocated U.S. withdrawal of support in hope of precipitating a coup. Others, such as Secretary of Defense Robert McNamara [q.v.], insisted that the U.S. continue to support Diem but demand governmental reform. Bundy believed that the U.S. should not thwart any coup that seemed potentially successful but should have the "option of judging and warning on any plan with poor prospects of success." On Nov. 1 South Vietnamese generals staged a successful coup. The U.S. had given no direct aid to the rebels but made no move to stop the change in government.

Following Kennedy's assassination Bundy remained a special assistant to President Johnson and played a major role in the decision to send U.S. troops to the Dominican Republic in 1965. He was a major force in the formation of the Administration's Vietnam policy and advocated the bombing of North Vietnam in 1965. Unable to accommodate himself to Johnson's personality, Bundy left government in February 1966 to become president of the Ford Foundation. In 1968 Bundy came out in opposition to further troop increases in Vietnam and supported de-escalation. [See JOHNSON Volume]

[EWS]

For further information:

Graham Allison, *Essence of Decision* (Boston, 1971).
Patrick Anderson, *The Presidents' Men* (New York, 1968), pp. 260-275.
David Halberstam, *The Best and the Brightest* (New York, 1972).
Roger Hilsman, *To Move a Nation* (New York, 1967).
Joseph Kraft, *Profiles in Power* (New York, 1966), pp. 163-175.

BUNDY, WILLIAM P(UTNAM)

b. Sept. 24, 1917; Washington, D.C.
Deputy Assistant Secretary of Defense for International Security Affairs, January 1961-October 1963; Assistant Secretary of Defense for International Security Affairs, October 1963-February 1964.

As coordinator of military assistance programs during the Kennedy Administration, William Bundy often remained in the shadow of his younger brother, McGeorge Bundy [q.v.]. Yet, by the end of the decade, William Bundy emerged as one of the prime architects of and spokesmen for the Johnson Administration's policy in Southeast Asia. Born into a socially and politically prominent New England family, Bundy was raised in a milieu that stressed family position and personal achievement. An outstanding student, he attended Groton School and Yale University, from which he graduated in 1939.

After service in the Army, Bundy received a law degree from Harvard in 1947 and joined Covington and Burling, a Washington, D.C., law firm that traditionally supplied young lawyers for high government positions. In 1950 Bundy joined the Central Intelligence Agency (CIA), where he became a protege of CIA Director Allen Dulles [q.v.]. There he was assigned to the office of national estimates and was put in charge of overall evaluation of international intelligence. In 1960 Bundy took a leave of absence from the CIA to become staff director of President Dwight D. Eisenhower's Commission on National Goals, which had been established to formulate broad, long-term objectives and programs for the U.S. [See EISENHOWER Volume]

President Kennedy appointed Bundy deputy assistant secretary of defense in charge of international security affairs in January 1961. In this post he was responsible for coordinating military aid programs throughout the world. In the fall of 1962, when Communist China invaded disputed areas on its border with India, Bundy organized the shipment of American arms to India and attempted to get other U.S. allies to supply that country.

Shortly after assuming office Bundy began an involvement in Vietnam policy-making that would continue and increase during the Johnson Administration. Following the erosion of the South Vietnamese military position and the deterioration of morale in Saigon during 1961, President Ngo Dinh Diem asked the U.S. to sign a defense treaty and increase military aid to his country. Bundy was one of the officials chosen to make recommendations on the proposal. In an October 1961 memorandum to Secretary of Defense Robert S. McNamara [q.v.], Bundy told his superior, "It is now or never if we are to arrest the gains being made by the Viet Cong." He suggested that "an early hardhitting operation" would limit Communist expansion and give Diem a chance to reform and strengthen his government. In Bundy's opinion, any delay would lessen U.S. chances of success. Kennedy, reluctant to make a major U.S. commitment, decided not to send ground forces to Vietnam but to concentrate on prompt deployment of support troops and equipment in November 1961.

During the Johnson Administration Bundy became one of the President's principal policy advisers on Vietnam. Although he only reluctantly supported the Administration's large-scale troop commitments in 1964, Bundy backed increased American intervention during the last half of the decade. [See JOHNSON Volume]

In 1969 Bundy resigned his position as assistant secretary of state for Far Eastern and Pacific affairs to become a visiting professor at the Massachusetts Institute of Technology's Center for International Studies. In 1972 he became editor of *Foreign Affairs* quarterly.

[EWS]

BURDICK, QUENTIN N(ORTHRUP)
b. June 19, 1908; Munich, N.D.
Democratic Senator, N.D., 1960- .

A descendant of pioneer stock on both sides of his family, Burdick graduated from the University of Minnesota in 1931 and took his law degree from that university the next year. After several unsuccessful attempts to gain public office, he was elected to the U.S. House of Representatives in 1958 as the first Democratic congressman in North Dakota's history. Following the death of Sen. William Langer (R, N.D.) in 1959, Burdick won a special election to the Senate and was sworn in on Aug. 8, 1960.

Regarded as a liberal Democrat and a champion of the interests of the small farmer, Burdick supported Kennedy Administration legislation on more than 65% of key roll call votes. In 1961 he voted for the School Assistance Act, the extended Mexican farm labor program, the Peace Corps bill and the Area Redevelopment Act. As a member of the Labor and Public Welfare Committee, he opposed the amended National Defense Education Act because it included a provision for construction loans to private schools. In 1962 Burdick supported the Administration's civil rights and public works bills. He opposed the confirmation of John A. McCone [q.v.] as director of the Central Intelligence Agency because McCone had publicly urged U.S. resumption of nuclear testing in the atmosphere. On Sept. 24, 1963 Burdick voted to ratify unconditionally the limited nuclear test ban treaty, which ended all tests except those underground.

Burdick was reelected to the Senate in 1964 and 1970. [See JOHNSON, NIXON Volumes]

[FHM]

BURKE, ARLEIGH A(LBERT)
b. Oct. 19, 1901; Boulder, Colo.
Chief of Naval Operations, June 1955-August 1961.

Burke, a noted war hero and chief of naval organizational research and policy in the postwar years, was appointed chief of naval operations by President Dwight D. Eisenhower in 1955.

During the opening days of the Kennedy Administration, Burke was one of the military advisers who counseled the President to proceed with the proposed Bay of Pigs operation. When the April 17 assault floundered, the Admiral advised Kennedy to use

U.S. air strikes to help the Cuban brigade. The President rejected the proposal.

In May 1961 Burke became a member of a presidential commission ordered to study the failure of American intelligence to anticipate the Bay of Pigs disaster. The report emerged as a critique of the tactics but not the goals of the operation. The group's principal recommendation was that the Central Intelligence Agency should not undertake future operations where weapons larger than hand guns would be used.

Burke's vigorous anti-Communist point of view made him a central figure in the "muzzling" controversy of 1961. During the first week of the Kennedy Administration, the White House toned down a strong anti-Soviet speech that the Admiral intended to make. This curb, attacked by such conservatives as Sen. Barry Goldwater (R, Ariz.) [q.v.] and Sen. Strom Thurmond (D, Ga.) [q.v.], eventually led to a congressional probe of State Department censorship of high military officials and the content of military educational programs. On Jan. 23, 1962 Burke testified before the Senate Preparedness Subcommittee that he did not oppose censorship because unauthorized statements by high-ranking military men could be harmful to U.S. interests. In October, as a member of a Defense Department committee appointed to review muzzling charges, Burke reported that the educational programs, although weak, did not leave American troops ignorant of Communism as Senate conservatives had claimed.

Throughout his career Burke had stressed the importance of vigilance against what he thought was continued Communist aggression. After his retirement from the Navy in August 1961 to become a director of Texaco, he continued to play a prominent role in espousing the conservative position on U.S. relations with Communist nations. Burke spoke at a number of anti-Communist rallies including one sponsored by Dr. Fred Schwarz [q.v.] and his Christian Anti-Communism Crusade in June 1962. In May 1963 he became a member of the nonpartisan Citizens Committee for a Free Cuba, which warned against "growing Castro-Communist infiltration of Latin America." Before a Senate Foreign Relations Committee meeting held on Aug. 27, 1963, Burke testified against the limited nuclear test ban treaty, declaring that without an extensive system of inspection, which was not included in the agreement, the U.S. could never be certain whether the USSR was complying with the ban.

[EWS]

BURNS, JAMES MacGREGOR
b. Aug. 3, 1918; Melrose, Mass.
Political scientist.

James MacGregor Burns, a prominent proponent of strong presidential leadership in the 1950s and 1960s, was born and raised in rural Massachusetts. Following his graduation from Williams College in 1939, he studied for a year at the National Institute of Public Affairs and then returned to Williams as an instructor in political science. After the U.S. entered World War II, Burns worked for the National War Labor Board and then joined the Army in 1943, serving as a combat historian.

Following his discharge Burns studied at Harvard University where he was awarded his Ph.D. in 1947. That year he returned to Williams, eventually becoming a full professor of political science in 1953. While teaching Burns became active in politics, serving on Massachusetts's Little Hoover Commission in 1949 and acting as a delegate to the Democratic National Convention in 1952, 1956, and 1960. During 1958 he ran unsuccessfully for the U.S. House of Representatives. Burns associated himself politically with Sen. John F. Kennedy and in 1955 proposed that Kennedy seek nomination as the Democratic vice presidential candidate. In 1960 he wrote Kennedy's authorized biography, *John Kennedy: a Political Profile*, and during the Senator's presidential race campaigned for him through the Northeast and Midwest.

In a series of articles and several important books published in the 1950s and 1960s, Burns emerged as a proponent of strong presidential leadership as a key to the enactment of liberal and progressive legislation. Burns argued that the Constitution's series of checks and balances had contributed to the development of powerful independent party factions in Congress. These parochial and conservative congressional factions constituted virtually separate parties, distinct from the more liberal and national party factions that coalesced around the presidential Republicans and Democrats. Burns ascribed the failure of President Kennedy's liberal legislative program to the power of the conservatives in both "congressional parties." In his *Deadlock of Democracy; Four-Party Politics in America* (1963), Burns wrote, "We face a four-party system that compels government by consensus and coalition rather than a two-party system that allows the winning party to govern and the losers to oppose."

To resolve this "deadlock" Burns stressed the need for disciplined, centralized parties, somewhat in the manner of the British parliamentary system. He recommended that congressional power be curbed through reapportionment, the reform of the seniority system and abolition of the filibuster. He also favored national party membership, broad-based financing and strong grassroots party organizations. He urged repeal of the 22nd Amendment, which he believed crippled a second term president. Because off-year elections often resulted in a decline of presidential support in Congress, he suggested that representatives' terms be lengthened to four years. Finally Burns argued that "the cure for democracy is leadership . . . effective and exuberant leadership."

In 1965 Burns published *Presidential Government: The Crucible of Leadership* in which he answered critics who maintained that a strong presidency was a threat to individual liberty. He suggested that this problem could be overcome through the development of a united, responsible opposition that challenged the incumbent's values and developed its own definition of national purpose.

In 1956 Burns published *Roosevelt: the Lion and the Fox*, an award-winning biography that described how the development of a conservative coalition in Congress after 1938 crippled FDR's progressive New Deal program. In 1970 he completed the second volume of his history of the Administration, *Roosevelt: Soldier of Freedom.*

[NNL]

For further information:
James MacGregor Burns, *The Deadlock of Democracy: Four-Party Politics in America* (Englewood Cliffs, 1963).
———, *Presidential Government: The Crucible of Leadership* (Boston, 1965).

BURNS, JOHN A(NTHONY)
b. March 30, 1909; Fort Assiniboine, Mont.
d. April 5, 1975; Kaiwi, Oahu, Hawaii.
Democratic Governor, Hawaii, 1963-75.

The son of an Army infantry sergeant, Burns was raised in Hawaii and Kansas. As a captain in the Honolulu police department during World War II, he helped alleviate the discrimination suffered by Japanese-Americans under wartime martial law. Relying on his popularity among the Nisei population and on an alliance with the powerful International Longshoremen's and Warehousemen's Union (ILWU), which fostered multiracial unionism and opposed Hawaii's sharply stratified economic system, Burns reorganized the Hawaiian Democratic Party after the war. By 1954 his party was able to oust the predominantly Caucasian, plantation-backed Republican Party from its half-century control of the Hawaiian legislature.

Burns won election in his third bid for the office of territorial delegate to the U.S. Congress in November 1956. In Congress he smoothly handled the obstacles to Hawaii's application for statehood, including congressional fears of the state's nonwhite majority and the alleged Communist tendencies of the ILWU. Burns did not oppose Alaska's admission to the Union first, thus easing Hawaii's entry in 1959. In July 1959 only four months after President Eisenhower had signed the Hawaiian statehood bill, Burns lost a close election for state governor to the incumbent territorial governor, Republican William F. Quinn. [See EISENHOWER Volume]

In early 1960 Burns worked among Democratic state delegations in support of Sen. Lyndon Johnson's (D, Tex.) [q.v.] bid for the presidential nomination. In 1962 he again challenged Quinn for the governorship. With the Republican Party divided and Burns enjoying total ILWU support, he won an easy victory at the polls.

In his first years as governor, the Hawaiian economy underwent a spectacular burst of prosperity. Burns strengthened the Democratic hold on state politics and carried his protégés, many of them Japanese-Americans, into elective office. His actions helped make the Hawaiian Republican Party one of the weakest state organizations in the country. A master of what he called "consensus politics," Burns was reelected in 1966 and 1970. However, after learning that he was suffering from cancer, he decided not to run again in 1974. He was succeeded by his lieutenant-governor, George Ariyoshi, the nation's first nonwhite governor. Burns died on April 5, 1975. [See JOHNSON, NIXON Volumes]

[JCH]

For further information:
Tom Coffman, *Catch a Wave: A Case Study of Hawaii's New Politics* (Honolulu, 1973).

BUSH, PRESCOTT (SHELDON)
b. May 15, 1895; Columbus, Ohio.
d. Oct. 8, 1972; New York, N.Y.
Republican Senator, Conn., 1953-63.

A Yale graduate and World War I veteran, Prescott Bush entered banking after the war and in 1930 became a partner in Brown Brothers, Harriman in New York City. Maintaining a residence in Connecticut, he assumed the chairmanship of the state's Republican Finance Committee in 1947 and defeated Rep. Abraham A. Ribicoff (D, Conn.) [q.v.] for election to the Senate in 1952. He proved one of the Eisenhower Administration's most loyal Senate supporters, voting with the White House on over 90% of all votes in the 1953 session. [See EISENHOWER Volume]

Bush generally voted with his party in opposition to the Kennedy Administration, crossing the aisle only on foreign policy issues. He sought unsuccessfully to defeat the White House's 1961 aid-to-education bill in the Senate by introducing a compulsory desegregation amendment which he knew was unacceptable to Southern senators. Bush voted against the President's medicare bill in July 1962. He supported Kennedy, however, on the Treasury Department's proposed purchase of $100 million worth of United Nations bonds in April 1962. Bush approved of the creation of the Peace Corps as "a sounder approach than our foreign aid program" and "certainly . . . less expensive."

Bush attacked the Administration's Trade Expansion Bill in September 1962 and sought to maintain the "peril point" provision in the 1951 Trade Agreements Act. Under existing legislation, the President submitted to the Tariff Commission a list of items upon which he planned to negotiate reciprocal reductions, and the Commission informed him of the duty level or "peril point" below which a tariff cut might hurt an affected industry. The new White House bill, however, did not hold the President accountable to Congress for cuts below these "peril points." "Why do we have a Tariff Commission," Bush asked in September 1962, "if we are unwilling to trust its judgment on the safe limits for tariff change?" By only two votes the Senate defeated a Bush amendment that would have retained the "peril point" guidelines and compelled the President to explain a duty reduction to Congress. Lobbying efforts by the White House had effectively frustrated efforts to weaken the Trade Expansion Act. Only seven senators joined Bush in voting against the final bill.

In May 1962 the 67-year-old Bush, citing reasons of health, announced his decision not to run for reelection. Abraham Ribicoff [q.v.], Secretary of Health, Education and Welfare under Kennedy, captured his seat for the Democrats in the November election. One of the Connecticut Republican's sons, George Bush, later won election to the House from Texas and served in the Nixon and Ford Administrations.

[JLB]

BYRD, HARRY F(LOOD), SR.
b. June 10, 1887; Martinsburg, W. Va.
d. Oct. 20, 1966; Winchester, Va.
Democratic Senator, Va., 1933-65;
Chairman, Finance Committee, 1955-
65.

At the age of 15 Byrd left high school to
take over the management of his father's
bankrupt newspaper in Winchester, Va.,
which he saved by his insistence upon
meticulous frugality. Byrd grew up in a des-
titute Virginia which was struggling,
through draconian budget-cutting, to pay
the huge debts accumulated during the
Civil War. As a result of his personal experience and the influence of his political environment, Byrd would always be an unrelenting opponent of public debt and high
government expenditures.

After establishing himself as a successful
apple grower, he won a state Senate seat in
1919. In 1925 he was elected governor.
During his four-year term, Byrd skillfully
employed patronage to establish himself as
the leader of a powerful Democratic political machine. For almost 40 years Byrd's
rural-oriented organization, based on
county courthouses, maintained nearly unquestioned control of Virginia's politics. The
Party routinely nominated and elected
Byrd's choices for public office, and it uniformly endorsed his conservative policies of
"pay-as-you-go" financing, opposition to extensive government services and support of
racial separation. The organization gained a
reputation for producing consistently competent, honest and genteel conservatives in
Byrd's image, men who shunned the demagoguery of politicians from some of the
other Southern states.

Byrd was constitutionally barred from
succeeding himself as governor, but in 1933
he was appointed to the U.S. Senate,
where he would remain for over 30 years.
Applying his principles at the national
level, he opposed New Deal welfare spending programs. By the late 1940s Byrd was a
leader of the Southern Democratic-
Republican conservative coalition in Congress. His seniority enabled him to obtain
the chairmanship of the Senate Finance
Committee in 1955. Other consistently

reelected candidates of his machine, such as
Sen. A. Willis Robertson [q.v.] and Rep.
Howard W. Smith [q.v.], were also major
figures on Capitol Hill by this time. As a
group the Virginia delegation in Congress
was able to play an extremely effective role
in obstructing liberal legislation. [See TRU-
MAN Volume]

The Byrd machine suffered its first major
setback in Virginia when, early in 1959,
state and federal courts struck down the
state's school closing laws, which had been
passed the previous year to circumvent
court-ordered integration. After this defeat
Gov. J. Lindsay Almond, over the intransigent Byrd's objections, abandoned as hopeless the struggle to maintain all-white
schools. This division led to the coalescence
of a moderate group within the state's
Democratic machine. [See EISENHOWER
Volume]

Beginning in 1952 Byrd tacitly endorsed
Republican presidential candidates by declining to back the Democratic nominees,
whom he regarded as dangerously liberal.
As a result Adlai Stevenson [q.v.] lost the
state in 1952 and 1956, and John Kennedy
failed to carry it in 1960. A symbol of resistance to racial integration, Byrd in 1960 received the votes of 14 unpledged presidential electors in Mississippi and Alabama and
of one Republican presidential elector in
Oklahoma. Byrd continued his opposition to
Kennedy by consistently criticizing New
Frontier measures in the Senate. During
each of the three years of the Administration, Byrd was among the 10 Democratic
senators who most often voted against
Kennedy-backed bills. Described by Arthur
M. Schlesinger, Jr. [q.v.], in A Thousand
Days, as "the greatest balanced-budget
fundamentalist in the country," Byrd con-
stantly sought to reduce federal spending.
When Kennedy, in a special message to
Congress less than a month after his inauguration, proposed steps to remedy the nation's balance-of-payments deficit, Byrd approved of the thrust of the program but
added that "a much more positive and constructive effort must be made to reduce our
foreign economic aid." The following June
he described the Administration's moderate-income housing proposal as the

worst housing bill ever offered to Congress, denouncing what he called its "backdoor" and "sidedoor" spending provisions.

In 1962 he joined Sens. Albert Gore (D, Tenn.) [q.v.], Paul Douglas (D, Ill.) [q.v.] and other liberal Finance Committee members to form an unusual minority coalition against an Administration-sponsored 7% investment tax credit. The liberals opposed it as a "windfall" for business interests. Byrd did not oppose the measure primarily for this reason—although his rural-oriented political machine was not known in Virginia as a champion of business welfare—but, rather, because the loss of federal revenue it entailed would increase the federal deficit. The tax credit, considered the centerpiece of the Administration's 1962 tax bill, was approved by the Senate on Aug. 28 by a vote of 52-30.

In the early 1960s the Kennedy Administration's economic policy also called for sharp tax reductions in order to increase consumer demand and thereby stimulate the economy. Although the "New Economics," as its Keynesian-minded proponents termed it, forecast temporary budget deficits, Kennedy economic advisers thought that the resulting increase in taxable economic activity would eventually produce a budget surplus and a balanced federal budget over time. This program was anathema to Byrd. In January 1963 Budget Director Kermit Gordon [q.v.] presented a plan that called for a massive tax cut while rejecting compensatory spending reductions as "self-defeating." Byrd rejected the proposal and called for Gordon's ouster. Two months later Byrd asserted that federal spending could be reduced by more than $7 billion below the President's estimate for fiscal 1964. As a result of Byrd's opposition to the passage of the Kennedy tax-cut bill, which called for cuts of about $11.2 billion, the measure was delayed until February 1964.

As chairman of the Senate Finance Committee, Byrd was in a favorable position to block much of the social welfare legislation proposed by President Kennedy. In 1962 the Administration urged Congress to extend the duration of a law of the previous year that had expanded unemployment insurance coverage. Byrd's Committee, by declining to report the measure to the floor, helped to kill the proposal.

The fate of President Kennedy's medicare bill also illustrated the power that accrued to Byrd from his chairmanship. The health insurance plan was sent to Congress in 1961 and referred in the upper chamber to the Finance Committee. To stall its progress, Byrd gave hearings on the bill a low priority. As the 87th Congress approached its close, the Administration gained a floor vote on medicare by arranging for its attachment to a minor bill that was not under the Finance Committee's jurisdiction. But since the bypassing of a senior member such as Byrd violated the sensibilities of the protocol-minded Senate, some potential supporters were alienated and the bill was defeated by 52 to 48 on July 17, 1962.

Byrd won reelection to the Senate in 1964, but in the same year it appeared that his control over Virginia politics was slipping. By 1964 a growing urban and black vote was prodding the organization towards the political center, and the Virginia state Democratic convention endorsed Lyndon B. Johnson for reelection to the presidency against Byrd's wishes. Ill-health forced Byrd to resign from the Senate in November 1965. He died of a brain tumor on Oct. 20, 1966. [See JOHNSON Volume]

[MLL]

For further information:
J. Harvie Wilkinson III, *Harry Byrd and the Changing Face of Virginia Politics, 1945-1966* (Charlottesville, 1968).

BYRD, ROBERT C(ARLYLE)
b. Jan. 15, 1918; North Wilkesboro, N.C.
Democratic Senator, W. Va., 1959- .

Orphaned in infancy, Robert C. Byrd grew up on a West Virginia dirt farm. During World War II he worked as a shipyard welder and briefly belonged to the Ku Klux Klan. He won election to the West Virginia House of Delegates in 1946 and after serving in both houses of the state legislature, became a member of the U.S. House of Representatives from Charleston in 1953. In 1958 Byrd defeated an incumbent Republican for the U.S.

Senate with 59.2% of the vote and soon emerged as the most powerful Democrat in the state. [See EISENHOWER Volume]

Byrd supported Senate Majority Leader Lyndon B. Johnson (D, Tex.) [q.v.] for the 1960 Democratic presidential nomination. When Johnson declined to enter the West Virginia primary, Byrd actively worked for Sen. Hubert H. Humphrey (D, Minn.) [q.v.] against Sen. John F. Kennedy, the front-runner for the Party's nomination. Many observers expected Kennedy's Catholicism to hurt his chances in the overwhelmingly Protestant state but Byrd discounted any religious bias in his support of Johnson and Humphrey. "I wouldn't have supported Kennedy," Byrd remarked in 1972, "if he had been a Missionary Baptist." Despite the state's Protestantism, Kennedy swept the primary with 61% of the vote, carrying Byrd's home town of Sophia.

According to *Congressional Quarterly*, Byrd supported the Kennedy Administration in 1961-62 on 85% of the roll call votes for which the President announced a position. He voted against the nuclear test ban treaty in September 1963 and opposed the Administration's 1963 civil rights bill. After eight years of night classes, Byrd earned a law degree from American University in June 1963. Reelected in 1964 and 1970, Byrd became Secretary to the Senate Democratic Conference in 1967 and Majority Whip in 1971. [See JOHNSON, NIXON Volumes].

[JLB]

BYRNES, JOHN W(ILLIAM)
b. June 12, 1913; Green Bay, Wisc.
Republican Representative, Wisc.,
1945-73.

A graduate of the University of Wisconsin Law School, John Byrnes was appointed Wisconsin's special deputy commissioner for banking in 1938. Elected to the state Senate in 1940, he was named majority floor leader in 1943. He won election to the U.S. House of Representatives as a Republican in 1944 and in 1947 gained a position on the Ways and Means Committee, where he built a reputation as a fiscal conserva-tive. In 1959 Byrnes became chairman of the House Republican Policy Committee after helping Rep. Charles A. Halleck (R, Ind.) [q.v.] depose Rep. Joseph W. Martin (R, Mass.) as House minority leader. [See EISENHOWER Volume]

During the Kennedy Administration Byrnes was the leading House Republican spokesman on economic policy and, according to the *New York Times*, "second only to Mr. Halleck as a power among House Republicans." Byrnes frequently led Republican efforts to reduce or eliminate Kennedy Administration social welfare expenditures.

In April 1961 Byrnes tried to modify a Social Security bill that provided $780 million in new benefits by permitting men to retire at age 62 and raising benefits for the widowed. Byrnes introduced an amendment to eliminate those provisions. His substitute would have extended retirement benefits to currently ineligible workers age 72 or over and raised the earnings ceiling for Social Security recipients. The House rejected Byrnes's amendment by a voice vote and adopted the more liberal measure by a 400-14 vote. As he often did, Byrnes voted for the final bill after his substitute had been defeated.

In January 1962 Byrnes opposed the creation of a cabinet-level department of housing and urban affairs. He termed the new department a "fraud" that would solve "not one single urban problem." Byrnes accused the President of a "callous attempt" to exploit the racial issue by announcing his intention to appoint Housing Administrator Robert C. Weaver [q.v.], a Negro, as secretary of the proposed department.

Byrnes tried to halt a bill expanding the public assistance and child welfare programs reported by the Ways and Means Committee in March 1962. The bill embodied Administration proposals to expand the federal government's contribution to the federal-state matching fund, but the Committee added $140 million over the amount the President had requested. Byrnes proposed that the bill be sent back to committee, but Rep. Wilbur D. Mills (D, Ark.) [q.v.], chairman of the Committee, maintained that the Administration was not strongly opposed to the increase. The House rejected Byrnes's motion, 232-155 on March 15.

Byrnes lost another budget battle in June when he opposed the Administration's request to raise the national debt ceiling from $300 billion to $308 billion. Joining with other Republicans who criticized the measure as "fiscal irresponsibility," Byrnes claimed that the Administration had used "blackmail" to gain support for the bill. He said "any number" of congressmen had told him that the Defense Department had "advised" defense contractors in their districts that their contracts "may be in jeopardy" if the debt ceiling were not raised. Democrats answered that the warning was not "blackmail" but "a plain statement of fact." Byrnes's motion to cut the $8 billion increase to $6 billion was defeated, 201-118. In the same month Byrnes was unsuccessful in his attempt to modify the grant of tariff-cutting authority to the President contained in the Trade Expansion Act.

With his senior position on the Ways and Means Committee (he was second-ranking Republican in 1961-1962 and became ranking Republican in 1963), Byrnes exerted greater influence on tax policy than any other House Republican. Rep. Noah Mason (R, Ill.) was senior to Byrnes on the Committee before 1963, but Mason had a reputation as a "loner," and House Republicans often followed the more pragmatic Byrnes. While opposed to many of the Kennedy Administration's tax reform proposals, Byrnes usually worked with Mills to round up a consensus on the Committee behind compromise measures.

Byrnes joined the Treasury Department in opposition to Rep. Eugene Keogh's (D, N.Y.) [q.v.] plan to permit self-employed persons to set up tax-sheltered retirement funds. The Treasury estimated the measure would cost the government $358 million in lost revenue. The Committee passed the Keogh plan, 18-5 in May 1961, with Mills, Byrnes and three other Republicans in the minority. Byrnes assailed the Administration's proposal to close U.S. corporations' foreign "tax havens" by taxing the income

from such subsidiaries as normal income. He charged that the proposal indicated the U.S. was withdrawing from its position as a world economic leader. Byrnes and the House Republicans also opposed an extension of the 10% tax on passenger travel in June but were defeated, 196-189. In 1962, however, Congress eliminated all travel taxes except for a 5% levy on airline fares.

In 1963 Byrnes led the House Republican attack on President Kennedy's $10-billion tax cut and tax reform package. In September he accused the members of the Business Committee for Tax Reduction in 1963 of leading a "run on the Treasury." After Kennedy gave a televised address urging Americans to support the tax cut on Sept. 18, Byrnes gave the Republican response two days later over three national networks. He proposed to attach to the President's bill a provision that the tax cut would not take effect unless the federal budget was held to $97 billion for fiscal 1964. On Sept. 25 the House rejected Byrnes's motion to return the bill to committee, 226-199.

Byrnes suffered a personal embarrassment in November 1963 when he acknowledged that he had bought stock in the Mortgage Guarantee Insurance Corporation (MGIC) of Milwaukee at a preferential price after helping the company with a tax problem. Byrnes had bought the shares for $2,300 in September 1960; their value was $26,000 at the time of his admission. In an emotional speech to the House on Nov. 21 Byrnes denied "any unethical conduct." He said it was his duty as a congressman to help MGIC and maintained that he was initially unaware that his purchase of shares was restricted to company executives. Byrnes stated that, "to make amends and remove the slight possibility of doubt that I would knowingly profit from any transaction which . . . was not regular and above-board," he would sell the stock and devote the profits to a scholarship fund for college students.

Byrnes remained a key House Republican leader until his retirement in 1973. [See Johnson, Nixon Volumes]

[TO]

CABOT, JOHN M(OORS)
b. Dec. 11, 1901; Cambridge, Mass.
Ambassador to Brazil, May 1959-August 1961; Ambassador to Poland, December 1961-August 1965.

Born into the noted Cabot family of Boston, John Moors Cabot, following studies at Harvard and Oxford, entered the foreign service in 1927 as vice consul in Callao, Peru. Subsequently he served as third secretary in the Dominican Republic and then Mexico. From 1932 to 1941 Cabot was second secretary in Brazil, the Hague and Guatemala. In 1942 he was promoted to assistant chief of the Division of American Republics. Cabot occupied that post until 1944, when he was appointed chief of the Division of Caribbean and Central American Affairs. From 1945 to 1953 Cabot successively was charge d'affaires to Argentina and Yugoslavia and consul general in Shanghai. During brief service in 1953 as assistant secretary of state for inter-American affairs, Cabot warned against permitting Communists to monopolize the issue of social reform and warned that proposed import curbs on Latin American goods would only cause "resentment and despair" in the Hemisphere. He was appointed by President Dwight D. Eisenhower to successive ambassadorships in Sweden, Colombia and Brazil. [See EISENHOWER Volume]

Cabot shared with the new Kennedy Administration the belief that the U.S. ought to challenge the Communists in Latin America for leadership of social reform movements rather than simply defend reactionary regimes in the area. He was one of only 13 ambassadors whom Kennedy asked to remain at their posts. However, the newly elected regime of Brazilian President Janio Quadros, a vocal nationalist, strained U.S.-Brazilian relations and undermined Cabot's position. Seeking an independent international role for Brazil, Quadros rejected the suggestion made in March 1961 by Cabot and Adolf Berle, Jr. [q.v.], President Kennedy's chief Latin American adviser, that Brazil join the United States in taking action against Fidel Castro's Cuba. When Cabot asserted in July that, because of previous agreements, Brazil could not be considered an "uncommitted nation," Quadros attacked Cabot for "meddling" in Brazil's internal affairs. Kennedy removed Cabot in August 1961 in order to placate Quadros, but a few days later Quadros resigned the presidency, claiming that not only domestic elements but also foreigners, including Cabot, had interfered in his attempts to govern.

Cabot was named ambassador to Poland in December 1961 and was confirmed by the Senate in January 1962. The post had special significance because the U.S. used the Warsaw embassy to maintain contact with representatives of the People's Republic of China, a government with which the U.S. did not have formal diplomatic relations. In March 1962 Cabot resumed a series of secret talks with the Chinese, which had begun following the 1955 Geneva Conference on Indochina. The only official diplomatic contact between the two nations, these meetings were convened periodically during Cabot's tenure in Poland. The discussions covered disarmament, U.S. support of Nationalist China and Vietnam.

Cabot left his Warsaw post in August 1965 to become deputy commandant of the National War College. During the 1967-68 academic year he was a lecturer at the Fletcher School of Law and Diplomacy. Cabot subsequently retired, but he remained politically active, publicly defending U.S. involvement in Vietnam as late as 1972.   [JCH]

CANNON, CLARENCE
b. April 11, 1879; Elsberry, Mo.
d. May 12, 1964; Washington, D.C.
Democratic Representative, Mo. 1923-64; Chairman, Appropriations Committee, 1941-47, 1949-53, 1955-64.

A former confidential secretary to the speaker of the House, Cannon was first elected to Congress in 1922 as a representative of the "Little Dixie" district of northern Missouri. During his 40 years in the House, Cannon supported most civil rights and labor legislation. A strong believer in government economy and a defender of

Congress's right to control trade policy and regulate government spending, Cannon's position on trade and appropriations bills was determined by whether he believed the measure fiscally sound or whether it would decrease congressional power.

Except for those sessions of Congress when the Republicans were in the majority, Cannon served as chairman of the House Appropriations Committee from 1941 until his death. Known as "one of" the most stubborn men in Congress," he used his formidible parliamentary skills and almost total control of his Committee to cut appropriations and block what he considered excessive government spending. [See TRUMAN, EISENHOWER Volumes]

In 1961 Cannon emerged as a leading opponent of "backdoor spending," a term he used to define expenditures not specifically authorized by Congress. In the last legislative action of the session, he successfully rushed through Congress provisions in the Supplemental Appropriations Act for 1962 that prevented the use of the "backdoor spending" that had been enacted in the Area Redevelopment and Housing Acts. He also succeeded in deleting President Kennedy's request for long-term borrowing authority for development loans abroad under the Foreign Assistance Act.

In 1962 Cannon and Senate Appropriations Committee Chairman Carl Hayden (D, Ariz.) [q.v.] delayed final consideration of appropriations bills for over three months, from April to July, in a dispute over who should chair Senate-House conference committees and where the committees should meet. During the impasse several government agencies almost ran out of money and both houses were forced to pass stop-gap resolutions to provide funds to continue government operations. Under a truce finally arranged in July, conference meetings, alternately chaired by senators and representatives, took place on "neutral ground" half way between the House and Senate chambers.

Later in 1962 Cannon, objecting to spending increases for "pork barrel" projects, again delayed appropriations measures in a quarrel with the Senate that centered on the question of whether the upper house had a constitutional right to initiate appropriations in bills of its own or whether it could add to House-passed appropriations measures funds for items either not previously considered by the House or considered and turned down. The dispute was never settled, and the provisions for funding the projects were transferred to other bills. Cannon defended his delays by noting that it was a way of reducing expenditures, because government agencies, not knowing when they would receive new funds, had to spend cautiously.

In 1963 Cannon continued to press for government economy by cutting funds for new programs authorized under the Public Works Acceleration Act of 1962 and by unsuccessfully attempting to lower spending for Project Apollo. Cannon died in May 1964 at the age of 85.

[EWS]

CANNON, HOWARD W(ALTER)
b. Jan. 26, 1912; St. George, Utah.
Democratic Senator, Nev., 1959-   .

The son of a banker and farmer, Howard W. Cannon received a law degree from the University of Arizona in 1937 and opened a legal practice in Utah the following year. After service in the Air Force as a fighter pilot during World War II, Cannon moved to Nevada and became a partner in a Las Vegas law firm. Elected city attorney of Las Vegas in June 1949, he occupied that post for eight years.

In 1958 Cannon won the Democratic Party's nomination to oppose incumbent conservative Republican Sen. George W. Malone. Malone's connections were with the old mining interests in the northern and western areas of the state, interests that had long dominated Nevada's economy. Cannon's ties were to the new, growing and politically more liberal industrial interests of the state's southern region. Cannon denounced his rival as an isolationist and opponent of domestic social programs. Aided by his war record, support from organized labor and a national Democratic trend, Cannon defeated Malone with over 56% of the vote.

During the early 1960s Cannon voted as a moderately liberal Democrat. According to *Congressional Quarterly*, he backed the Kennedy Administration on 71% of key domestic roll call votes in the 87th Congress.

Cannon's most consuming interests, growing out of his experience in the Air Force, were aviation and the space program. In the early 1960s he served, by preference, as a member of both the Armed Services and the Aeronautical and Space Committees of the Senate. During the same years he was a brigadier general in the Air Force Reserve, a Senate adviser to the United Nations Committee on Peaceful Uses of Outer Space and a member of the Board of Governors of the National Rocket Club. During the summer of 1962 he supported an Administration bill to establish a private corporation to operate a satellite communications network. However, as a small-state senator Cannon voted against a motion to end a liberal filibuster against the measure.

Reelected to the Senate in 1964, Cannon supported the major Great Society programs of President Johnson. He also backed the Administration's Vietnam war policies and defended U.S. air strikes near the North Vietnam-China border in 1967. Elected to another term in 1970, Cannon spoke out strongly for both the SST and the space-shuttle program in 1971. He first received major national attention in the fall of 1973 when, as chairman of the Senate Rules Committee, he led its consideration of President Richard M. Nixon's [*q.v.*] nomination of Gerald R. Ford (R, Mich.) [*q.v.*] for vice president. The following fall, in the same capacity, he directed the hearings that preceded the confirmation of Nelson Rockefeller [*q.v.*] as President Ford's vice president. [See JOHNSON, NIXON Volumes]

[MLL]

CAPEHART, HOMER E(ARL)
b. June 6, 1897; Algiers, Ind.
Republican Senator, Ind., 1945-63.

Homer E. Capehart grew up on his father's tenant farm in Indiana. Following non-combat duty in World War I, Capehart successfully sold farm machinery, coin-operated popcorn vending machines and juke boxes throughout the Midwest. He reorganized a piano company and after financial difficulties in the early depression, turned it into a profitable record manufacturing concern. In 1944 Capehart won election to the U. S. Senate from Indiana and quickly emerged as one of the more conservative, anti-Communist Republican members, winning reelection in 1950 and 1956. [See TRUMAN, EISENHOWER Volumes]

During the 87th Congress Capehart was opposed to most Kennedy Administration legislation. He voted against medicare, housing subsidies and the 1961 school aid bill. According to *Congressional Quarterly*, Capehart supported Kennedy on only 18% of the key roll call votes for which the President's position had been announced. In the fall of 1962 Kennedy actively attempted to deny Capehart reelection and in October charged the Indiana Republican with a "19th century voting record" on domestic and foreign policy issues.

Capehart achieved national attention during the 1962 elections because of his sharp attack on the Administration's Cuban policy. Along with Senator Kenneth B. Keating (R, N.Y.), [*q.v.*] Capehart charged the White House with inaction against a Soviet military presence in Cuba. Capehart told an Indiana Republican gathering in late August that the Soviet Union had sent between "3,000 to 5,000" combat soliders to Cuba and he recommended an invasion of the island before "the hundreds of Russian troops [in Cuba] grow into hundreds of thousands." The White House immediately denied Capehart's allegations, and on Oct. 13, the President assailed the Senator in an Indianapolis speech and alluded to "these self-appointed generals and admirals who want to send somebody else's son to war."

The Administration had consistently dismissed the claims of Keating and Capehart as campaign rhetoric, but on Oct. 16 Kennedy learned from reconnaissance flights that the Russians had begun to build missile launching facilities on Cuba. A week later the President issued an ultimatum to Soviet leader Nikita Khruschchev demanding the removal of the missiles and announcing a naval "quarantine" of Cuba.

Although he had declined to follow Capehart's original suggestion and invade the island, Kennedy felt the actual existence of Soviet weapons on Cuba assured the Indiana Senator of reelection. "Would you believe it?" presidential advisor Theodore Sorenson [q.v.] reported the President as saying, "Homer Capehart is the Winston Churchill of our time." Long favored to win reelection over his 34-year-old opponent, state legislator Birch E. Bayh [q.v.], a confident Capehart all but withdrew from the campaign in the final week. With the active endorsement of the state AFL-CIO and a heavy, last minute television schedule, Bayh upset Capehart by a narrow 50.3% to 49.7% margin, surprising and delighting Kennedy Administration officials.

[JLB]

CAPLIN, MORTIMER M(AXWELL)
b. July 11, 1916; New York, N.Y.
Commissioner of Internal Revenue, February 1961-July 1964.

Mortimer Caplin graduated first in his class from the University of Virginia Law School in 1940. Except for combat service during World War II, he was associated with the New York law firm of Paul, Weiss, Rifkind, Wharton and Garrison until 1950. In that year he returned to the University of Virginia as a professor of law, specializing in tax and corporate law. Among his students were Robert F. Kennedy [q.v.] and Edward M. Kennedy [q.v.]. Caplin served on President-elect Kennedy's task force on taxation and was named Commissioner of Internal Revenue in February 1961.

In that month Caplin testified before the Senate Finance Committee in favor of sweeping tax reductions. He suggested cutting the rate for the highest income taxpayers from 90% to 60% and the rate for lowest income taxpayers from 20% to 10%. To make up the revenue loss, he advocated the revision of capital gains tax relief and the closing of such loopholes as the oil depletion allowance. Caplin also stated that he favored voluntary reporting by individuals of interest and dividend income rather than government withholding of taxes at the

source of such payments. The Kennedy Administration fought unsuccessfully for the withholding innovation in 1962.

As head of the Internal Revenue Service, Caplin played an important role in carrying out another 1962 tax reform: the tightening of expense-account deductions. The business community reacted to the new law with hostility and apprehension, particularly because of its requirements that strict records be kept of expenses such as luncheons, entertainment, lodging and other business deductions. Caplin assuaged much hostility by promulgating liberal regulations that spelled out what records must be kept and distinguished allowable deductions from "lavish and extravagant" expenditures.

Caplin was the first I.R.S. commissioner to prohibit the setting of quotas for tax collectors. He ruled out the awarding of promotions and pay raises on the basis of how many returns an employe audited or the amount of money he collected. Caplin retired as commissioner in July 1964 to return to private law practice.

[TO]

CAREY, JAMES B(ARRON)
b. Aug. 12, 1911; Philadelphia, Pa.
d. Sept. 1, 1973; Silver Spring, Md.
President, International Union of Electrical, Radio and Machine Workers, 1949-65.

While studying electrical engineering at night, Carey worked in a Philco Radio laboratory and led a successful strike there in 1933. Later that year the 22-year-old Carey was elected head of the Radio and Allied Trades National Labor Council, newly formed by the AFL and independent unions. Unwilling to follow the AFL's policy of assigning workers in the mass production industries to the federations' craft unions, Carey and others organized the United Electrical, Radio and Machine Workers of America (UE) in 1936 as an independent industrial union. Carey was elected first president of the UE, which soon thereafter affiliated with the CIO. In 1938 he was elected CIO national secretary and in 1942 Carey became general secretary-treasurer of the organization.

Within the UE, Carey, a liberal anti-Communist, faced growing opposition from a coalition of moderate and Communist local union leaders. In a dispute over American foreign policy and the role of Communists in the internal life of the union, Carey was ousted as UE president in 1941. Although Carey formed an opposition caucus, he was unable to regain control of the UE either during or after the war. In 1949 the UE was expelled from the CIO on charges of Communist domination and its charter turned over to Carey who then formed the rival International Union of Electrical Radio and Machine Workers (IUE). In the jurisdictional warfare that followed, electrical workers were divided among the UE, the IUE and several other unions. As a result no single industry-wide union existed, and the wages and working conditions of electrical workers declined relative to those in the steel and auto industries where powerful united unions existed. During the 1950s and early 1960s, Carey refused to coordinate bargaining strategy with the UE in disputes with electrical manufacturers despite repeated overtures from UE President James Matles. [See TRUMAN, EISENHOWER Volumes]

In the early 1960s Carey's leadership of the IUE was increasingly erratic and ineffective. IUE membership, which had stood as high as 425,000 in the mid-1950s, slipped 100,000 by 1962. On short notice Carey called a strike against General Electric in the fall of 1960. It proved a failure; many IUE members did not respond to his strike call, and the union almost lost its huge Schenectady local during the walkout. *New York Times* labor editor A. H. Raskin called the strike, resolved on GE's original terms, the "worst setback any union has received in a nationwide strike since World War II."

At the request of the IUE, the National Labor Relations Board brought charges against GE in early 1961 for unfair labor practices during the 1960 strike. The union charged GE with "Boulwarism," a term derived from the name of the GE vice president who established the company's rigid bargaining policy, which union members re-

ferred to as "bargaining by ultimatum" since the company's first offer was always its last. GE was also accused of attempting to bypass union negotiators by dealing directly with its unionized employes, a violation of the National Labor Relations Act.

GE agreed to allow its stockholders to vote on a union proposal that company executives who had recently been found guilty of violating federal antitrust laws be barred from serving the company. The proposal, backed by the IUE, was overwhelmingly voted down. In April 1961 Carey sent monopoly sets to GE officials jailed for price-fixing.

Carey had been a member of the AFL-CIO Unity Committee that negotiated the merger of the two labor federations in 1955. He was elected a vice president of the new organization and general secretary of the Industrial Union Department. Carey often joined Walter P. Reuther [*q.v.*] in the latter's frequent criticism of AFL-CIO President George Meany's [*q.v.*] leadership. In the early 1960s Carey supported Reuther's criticism of the building trades unions for their attempts to "raid" industrial union jurisdictions. In April 1961 Carey and Reuther called a meeting of industrial union leaders who agreed to work independently of the AFL-CIO in organizational and legislative matters. They proposed outside arbitration to resolve AFL-CIO jurisdictional disputes but later agreed to a compromise offered by Meany that involved a more limited form of arbitration.

Carey faced growing internal opposition from some of the highest officers of the IUE in the early 1960s. In 1962 and 1963 both the secretary-treasurer and the vice president of the union publicly broke with Carey and called for his ouster as union president. In the Midwest important IUE locals sought affiliation with the Teamsters. In 1965 Carey was defeated in an IUE presidential election by Paul Jennings. Carey supporters who counted the ballots first claimed he was the victor, but Carey resigned when Jennings's supporters challenged the election. Under Jennings the IUE initiated a united effort by 11 unions in the 1966 negotiations with GE and, in a subsequent strike, won a 5% wage increase. Carey left the IUE in 1965 and became a labor liaison representative of the United Nations Association of the U.S. He died in 1973.

[MDB]

CARROLL, JOHN A(LBERT)
b. July 30, 1901; Denver, Colo.
Democratic Senator, Colo. 1957-63.

A former Denver district attorney and congressman, Carroll served as one of Colorado's senators from 1957 to 1963. During his one term in the Senate he established a liberal record on civil rights, education, medical and social legislation. In both 1961 and 1962 the liberal Americans for Democratic Action gave him a rating of 100%.

As a member of the Judiciary Committee's Antitrust and Monopoly Subcommittee, Carroll was one of the senators who conducted investigations of price fixing in the electrical and drug industries in 1961. Following the drug probe Carroll signed the subcommittee's report that described drug prices as "unreasonable" and criticized state laws that required pharmacists to fill prescriptions according to expensive brand names ordered by physicians rather than with cheaper generically identified compounds. In 1962 Carroll supported the Drug Safety Act and unsuccessfully attempted to strengthen it by requiring doctors to tell their patients when they were using test drugs. During that session of Congress he also backed President Kennedy's program of medical care for the aged.

In 1962 Carroll supported the unsuccessful liberal Democratic filibuster against the Administration's communications satellite bill. Filibuster forces called the measure a "giveaway" to American Telephone and Telegraph and protested that the bill would involve private interests in foreign policy.

Carroll was defeated in his bid for reelection in 1962 by a group of young conservative Republicans, led by John Love [q.v.] and Peter Dominick [q.v.], who gained control of Colorado politics that year.

[EWS]

CARY, WILLIAM L(UCIUS)
b. Nov. 27, 1910; Columbus, Ohio
Chairman, Securities and Exchange Commission, March 1961-July 1964.

As chief regulator of the nation's securities markets, William L. Cary promoted the first major overhaul of securities regulation since the 1930s. A 1934 graduate of Yale Law School, Cary practiced law for a private firm and then for the Securities and Exchange Commission (SEC) and the Department of Justice. In 1944 and 1945 he served with the Office of Strategic Services in Rumania and Yugoslavia. After the war he taught tax and corporation law at Northwestern and Columbia Universities. In February 1961 President Kennedy, whose father, Joseph P. Kennedy [q.v.], had been the first chairman of the SEC, nominated Cary to be SEC chairman.

Congress established the SEC in 1934 to enforce the provisions of the Securities Exchange Act designed to protect the public from abuses in the nation's financial markets. Over the next 30 years the Commission devoted itself to enforcing disclosure of pertinent information about securities offered to the public and listed on the stock exchanges. After disclosure, the principle of "self-regulation" was paramount; the actual policing of the markets was mainly left to private associations such as the New York Stock Exchange (NYSE) and the National Association of Securities Dealers (NASD).

Cary took office at a time of growing criticism of the effectiveness of "self-regulation." The regulating associations had grown dangerously lax, it was charged, and the investing public was being victimized. Meanwhile, the SEC in its concentration on full disclosure was ignoring major changes in the securities business, such as the mushrooming growth in over-the-counter sales from $5 billion in 1949 to $39 billion in 1961. Stocks traded over the counter were not listed with the organized exchanges nor subject to the same SEC disclosure requirements, and the potential for fraud and misrepresentation was greater.

Cary acknowledged that there were serious flaws in stock market regulation. He appeared before the House Interstate and Foreign Commerce Committee in June 1961 to endorse a special investigation to determine whether the rules of securities associations adequately protected investors. He said the inquiry should focus on the over-the-counter market, the mutual fund business, and the rapid growth in the number of securities dealers who had "no particular qualifications" and were "not subject to the kind of supervision which insures high ethical standards." In August Congress authorized $750,000 to enable the SEC to set up an independent study group to conduct the first extensive investigation of the securities business since the landmark Pecora inquiry of the early 1930s. In October Cary named Chicago lawyer Milton Cohen [q.v.] to head a 65-man two-year probe of the industry.

Cary and the SEC moved to correct some abuses before the Cohen group had completed its work. In October 1961 the SEC ordered securities houses to investigate their employes' backgrounds more scrupulously to weed out those with records of unethical conduct. The next month Cary wrote an important decision widening the definition of "insider." Previously defined as directors, officers and major stockholders of a company issuing stock, "insiders" were prohibited from exploiting their privileged information for private gain. The new ruling widened the definition to include persons receiving special information through "insider" contacts.

The release of the Cohen study group's 5,400-page report in 1963 was a major event in the securities field. The report concluded that there were "grave abuses" in the markets but not "pervasive and fraudulent activity." Among the offenses noted by the study group were the lack of controls on over-the-counter trading, low standards permitting securities salesman of poor character and competence to enter the business, "high-pressure selling" by mutual fund operators and trading for personal profit by exchange "specialists," whose function was supposedly to stabilize the market by buying and selling against the prevailing trends. The Cohen report criticized the performance of "self-regulation," declaring the NASD had "fallen short of its potential as a self-regulatory agency," while the NYSE operated as a "private club" and leaned toward "tenderness rather than severity" in disciplining its members for ethical violations.

Cary and the SEC agreed with the Cohen group's criticisms and endorsed the great majority of its more than 100 reform recommendations. While affirming his commitment to self-regulation, Cary told Congress in the summer of 1963 that the Cohen report "demonstrates that irresponsible selling tactics, reckless investment advice, extravagant public relations and erratic markets for new issues thrive best when the lack of information is most marked."

For a year Cary and the SEC labored to persuade Congress to enact the study group's proposals into law. The final result was the Securities Acts Amendments of 1964, passed in August. The new law fell short of what the Cohen report had advocated but expanded the Commission's authority in two important areas: it enabled the SEC to enforce its full disclosure rules in the over-the-counter market and to set standards and qualifications for persons dealing in securities. The law did not attempt to reform mutual fund abuses or curb the activities of specialists and floor traders, exchange members who traded for personal gain on the floor. (The Cohen report had recommended the abolition of floor trading, a proposal Cary endorsed). Faced with congressional inaction on floor trading, Cary's SEC in August 1964 issued stringent new regulations under its existing authority that had the effect of cutting the number of floor traders from 300 to 30.

Business Week characterized Cary's Commission as "an exceptionally strong and dynamic one . . . that led to many breakthroughs in securities regulation and paved the way for others." Cary left the SEC on Aug. 20, 1964, the day the Securities Acts Amendments became law, and returned to his law professorship at Columbia University.

[TO]

For further information:
William L. Cary, *Politics and the Regulatory Agencies* (New York, 1967).

CASE, CLIFFORD P(HILIP)
b. April 16, 1904; Franklin Park, N.J.
Republican Senator, N.J., 1955- .

Case grew up in Poughkeepsie, N.Y., where his father was pastor of a Dutch Reformed Church. After completing his studies at Rutgers University and Columbia University Law School, he joined a Wall Street law firm. Entering local New Jersey politics in 1937, Case was elected to the U.S. House of Representatives in 1944 from Union County. Case's liberal Republicanism made him popular in highly industrialized, urban New Jersey and his reelection campaigns frequently won the endorsement of the Americans for Democratic Action (ADA) and organized labor.

In August 1953 Case resigned from the House to become the president of the Fund for the Republic, an organization designed to defend civil liberties and democratic procedures in the face of tensions generated by the Cold War. He left his new post in March 1954 to run for the U.S. Senate. Stressing his opposition to the investigative methods of Sen. Joseph R. McCarthy (R, Wisc.), Case narrowly defeated his liberal Democratic opponent in November. [See EISENHOWER Volume]

In 1960 Case faced a vocal conservative opposition and the indifference of local party organizations in his campaign for renomination. Conducting a casual campaign, Case identified himself with President Eisenhower and won an easy primary victory in May. In the general election organized labor did not endorse a Democrat but remained neutral, thereby greatly aiding Case's reelection effort. Case also enjoyed the financial backing of many wealthy Republicans from the Eastern establishment and won convincingly in November.

In the Senate Case was one of a small group of liberal Republicans, most of whom represented the highly urbanized states of the Northeast. Of this group, only Sen. Jacob Javits (R, N.Y.) [q.v.] rivaled Case in his support of liberal legislation. On the basis of positions taken on key legislation, Case earned ratings of 80%, 67% and 88% from the ADA for the three years of the Kennedy Administration. He sponsored or co-sponsored a voting rights bill in 1962 and a medicare bill and a GOP civil rights package in 1963. Case was one of only six Republicans to vote for the 1963 mass transit bill. In the area of foreign affairs he sought a relaxation of international tensions and supported the Kennedy Administration's program for long-term loans and development projects in the less developed nations.

Case was a consistent supporter of financial disclosure by officials in all three branches of government. He proposed that both elected and appointed office holders be required to publicly disclose their holdings and financial transactions. He also wanted the principle of disclosure applied to all oral or written communications from both the legislative and executive branches to regulatory agencies. Case was a major ally of Sen. Joseph Clark's (D, Pa.) [q.v.] largely unsuccessful 1963 efforts to overhaul the operation of Congress. Case believed that limiting the power of committee chairmen could be an important first step in democratizing the legislature and making it as effective as the executive branch in determining national policy.

An early supporter of New York Gov. Nelson Rockefeller [q.v.] for the 1964 Republican presidential nomination, Case refused to support the Party's nominee, conservative Sen. Barry Goldwater (R, Ariz.) [q.v.], in the general election. He later became an ardent critic of President Lyndon Johnson's [q.v.] Vietnam war policies. Despite the enmity of conservative Republicans and charges that he was "aloof" from local New Jersey politics, Case's popularity appeared to increase over the years. Political analysts credited his reputation for honesty and an unaffected style as well as his liberal credentials for his electoral success. Considered the greatest vote getter in the state's history, Case easily won reelection in 1966 and 1972. [See JOHNSON, NIXON Volumes]

[JCH]

For further information:
Neal R. Pierce, *The Megastates of America* (New York, 1972).

CASE, FRANCIS H(IGBEE)
b. Dec. 9, 1896; Everly, Iowa.
d. June 22, 1962; Bethesda, Md.
Republican Senator, S.D., 1951-62.

A graduate of Dakota Wesleyan University, Francis Case worked as a publicist for the Methodist Church in the early 1920s. He was editor and publisher of a South Dakota newspaper, *The Custer Chronicle*, and also a part-time rancher before his election to Congress in 1936. Representing a rural constituency, Case followed the Republican Party line in the House. After World War II he sponsored the Case Labor Disputes Act, a conservative enactment condemned by union leaders and vetoed by President Truman in June 1946.

Elected to the Senate in 1950, Case was described by the *New York Times* as "one of the most quiet and unobtrusive men in Washington politics." He emerged from the background only in 1956 when he created a furor with his revelation that oil industry lobbyists had offered him a $25,000 bribe for his vote on pending natural gas legislation. [See TRUMAN, EISENHOWER Volumes]

During the early 1960s Case served on the Armed Services Committee and was the ranking Republican on the Public Works Committee. He was a consistent supporter of positions favored by the conservative coalition of Republicans and Southern Democrats. Case was one of only four senators to vote against an emergency unemployment compensation bill in March 1961. An opponent of the Kennedy Administration's program of federal aid to education, Case offered an unsuccessful amendment in May that would have rebated 1% of federal taxes to states on the basis of their school-age population. In January 1962 Case joined 11 other senators in opposition to the appointment of John A. McCone [*q.v.*] as director of the Central Intelligence Agency. McCone had been termed unqualified and had been criticized for retaining extensive oil stock and shipping holdings. Case died of a heart attack on June 22, 1962.

[TO]

CAVANAGH, JEROME P(ATRICK)
b. June 16, 1928; Detroit, Mich.
Mayor, Detroit, Mich., 1962-70.

Jerome P. Cavanagh earned his B. A. and law degrees from the University of Detroit. Active in Democratic politics even before finishing college, he opposed the 1948 takeover of the state Democratic Party by a coalition of union leaders and liberals led by G. Mennen Williams [*q.v.*]. Cavanagh opened his own law office in 1954 and worked part-time as a sales representative for International Business Machines.

At the age of 33 Cavanagh upset incumbent Mayor Louis C. Miriani in the 1961 Detroit mayoral race. Although Miriani had the support of the city's two daily newspapers, the city's business establishment and the leadership of the United Auto Workers, his police department had alienated the black community in a recent "crime-wave" crackdown. Moreover, he had served as mayor during the recessions of 1957 and 1961, periods of double-digit unemployment for the auto-based Detroit economy. Cavanagh's campaign capitalized on the widespread discontent; he won the endorsement of the dissident all-black Trade Union Leadership Council and also appealed successfully to many second-generation immigrant workers. Cavanagh's ethnic support coupled with 85% of the black vote enabled him to overcome Miriani's organizational advantage in the November balloting.

Mayor Cavanagh championed the cause of Detroit blacks. He appointed a prominent black political science professor as city comptroller and in his first executive order forbade discrimination in municipal employment. In June 1963 he strongly endorsed an interracial civil rights march of some 125,000 area residents. Cavanagh's civil rights activities gained him the backing of the Democratic Party labor-liberals who had opposed him in 1961.

Cavanagh's first term held the promise that he represented a new generation of liberal, Kennedy-style mayors capable of reversing the decline of America's large industrial cities. He appointed a respected state supreme court justice to serve as police commissioner and persuaded the Republican-dominated state legislature to allow the city to enact a 1% income tax. By trimming the city's public works and sanitation department budgets and by winning additional federal aid, the young Mayor succeeded in reducing Detroit's financial difficulties to manageable proportions.

The Mayor's political future looked bright in the mid-1960s. He worked closely with both the Kennedy and Johnson Administrations for the enactment of new programs to aid the cities and then won for Detroit at least its share of the new federal money. "Cavanagh became America's most glamorous mayor" wrote the once hostile *Detroit Free Press*, "He was smart, shrewd, committed to social change, surrounded by a brilliant brain trust, a man who seemed to draw vitality from the very city air." Easily reelected in November 1965 Cavanagh won national recognition when he became the first man to serve simultaneously as head of both the National League of Cities and the U.S. Conference of Mayors.

Cavanagh's second term as Detroit mayor was far less successful than his first. Williams defeated him for the 1966 Democratic senatorial nomination, and he was embarrassed by his well-publicized divorce the next year. Cavanagh's political future virtually ended in July 1967 when Detroit erupted in the worst racial violence of the 1960s. He retired from politics at the end of his second term to return to his Detroit law practice. [See JOHNSON Volume]

[JLB]

CELEBREZZE, ANTHONY J(OSEPH)
b. Sept. 4, 1910; Anzi, Italy.
Mayor, Cleveland, Ohio, 1954-62; Secretary of Health, Education and Welfare, July 1962-August 1965.

Anthony J. Celebrezze grew up in the slums of Cleveland and worked his way through Ohio Northern Law School as a manual laborer for the New York Central Railroad. He entered politics in 1950 and won election to the Ohio Senate where he became a close ally of Gov. Frank J. Lausche (D, Ohio) [q.v.].

Three years later, Celebrezze won the endorsement of the influential *Cleveland Press* and defeated the local Democratic organization's candidate in the 1953 mayoralty primary, winning in the general election in November. In his only major political defeat, Celebrezze lost the 1958 Democratic gubernatorial primary to former Toledo Mayor Michael V. DiSalle [q.v.].

Like most large cities in the late 1950s and early 1960s, Cleveland suffered a loss in population and a decline in its economic growth rate. Celebrezze remained a popular mayor, however, and easily won reelection five times. He received an unprecedented 73.8% of the total vote in the 1961 election.

President Kennedy designated Celebrezze to succeed Abraham A. Ribicoff [q.v.] as Secretary of Health, Education and Welfare (HEW) in July 1962. The President wanted an Italian-American for a cabinet-level position and Celebrezze, who had requested appointment to the federal circuit court, well suited Kennedy's purposes. At cabinet meetings the President found Celebrezze more amusing than helpful, presidential advisor Theodore Sorenson [q.v.] wrote, with a tendency for analyzing "every world and national problem in terms of his experiences in Cleveland."

Yet Kennedy, who had known Celebrezze for many years, respected the Cleveland politician's skills as an urban administrator. With the aid of Undersecretary Wilbur J. Cohen [q.v.] and Education Commissioner Francis Keppel [q.v.], Celebrezze reorganized his 112-program department, once called "unmanageable" by Abraham Ribicoff. In January 1963 Celebrezze separated the public assistance and child health and welfare functions from the Social Security Administration and transferred these programs to a new Welfare Administration.

The HEW chief worked for the passage of the Administration's medicare and aid-to-education measures in 1962 and 1963. He told the House Education and Labor Committee in February 1963 that "dependence on traditional sources of financial support to education will no longer suffice in every community." Private and public universities, he added, required the "substantial and immediate aid" included in the White House education package to accommodate the needs of a rapidly increasing college age population. Failure to pass the Administration's medical care for the elderly bill, he warned in November 1963, represented a "major threat to the financial security and peace of mind of our older citizens."

The Administration included broad discretionary authority for HEW in its June 1963 civil rights bill. The White House measure enforced desegregation guidelines by granting HEW the power to deny funds for any federal program to states or institutions which practiced racial segregation. Celebrezze told the House Education and Labor Committee in July 1963 that he favored the prerogative for his department and called it "a tool that, handled with wisdom and justice, can contribute much toward our goal of equal opportunity for all."

Congress moved slowly on civil rights legislation and rejected medicare and the Administration's 1962 and 1963 aid-to-education bills. After the Democrats increased their congressional ranks following the 1964 elections, President Johnson reintroduced these measures with far greater success. Celebrezze continued as HEW Secretary until August 1965. [See JOHNSON Volume]

[JLB]

CELLER, EMANUEL
b. May 6, 1888; Brooklyn, N.Y.
Democratic Representative, N.Y., 1923-73; Chairman, Judiciary Committee, 1949-53, 1955-73.

A 1912 graduate of Columbia Law School, Celler practiced law in New York until 1922 when he ran for Congress in Brooklyn's 10th congressional district. His victory began a half-century career in the House where Celler established himself as a liberal Democrat and a staunch civil libertarian. He rose to the chairmanship of the House Judiciary Committee in 1949 and immediately took advantage of his position to establish a new subcommittee which focused on antitrust violations and other abuses by big business. As head of the subcommittee Celler conducted highly publicized investigations into insurance companies in 1949, the steel industry in 1950 and

monopoly practices in baseball in 1951. He coauthored the Celler-Kefauver Anti-Merger Act of 1950, a major piece of antitrust legislation. In the late 1950s Celler held hearings on government antitrust enforcement procedures and on the anti-competitive practices of regulatory agencies, particularly the Civil Aeronautics Board. Long an advocate of civil rights legislation, Celler was the principal architect of the 1957 Civil Rights Act, the first federal civil rights legislation in 82 years, and of the supplementary Civil Rights Act passed in 1960. [See TRUMAN, EISENHOWER Volumes]

Celler cooperated closely with the Kennedy Administration. He delayed passage of a federal judgeship bill from 1960 to 1961, thus giving Kennedy rather than Eisenhower the opportunity to make 70 new court appointments. In April 1962, when Kennedy clashed with the steel industry over a projected price increase, Celler added to government pressure on the steel companies by announcing that his antitrust subcommittee would hold hearings on the steel price situation. When the President's battle with steel ended, Celler quietly dropped his investigation. As early as August 1961 Celler had made clear his opposition to monopolization of the satellite communications industry; thus he supported the Administration's proposals for a satellite bill which would give the public, as well as the communications companies, the chance to invest in a new satellite corporation. When the final satellite communications bill came to a vote in the House in May 1962, Celler also backed an unsuccessful Administration effort to delete a portion of the bill which favored the private companies over the satellite corporation in the licensing of ground stations.

Celler played a key role in the development of civil rights legislation during the Kennedy Administration. He had prepared civil rights recommendations for Kennedy during his campaign for the presidency, and with Kennedy's backing, Celler sponsored the 24th Amendment, approved by Congress in August 1962 and ratified in 1964, which abolished the poll tax in federal elections. In February 1963 Kennedy sent Congress a modest civil rights bill limited largely to the protection of voting rights. Celler, who had proposed much stronger legislation in May 1961, urged Kennedy to broaden his bill to include public accommodations and employment. The rising tempo of the civil rights movement, in particular the April 1963 demonstrations in Birmingham, Ala. finally brought Kennedy to support legislation of the type Celler advocated. After Kennedy presented an expanded bill to Congress in June, Celler and the Administration worked closely to secure its passage. His judiciary subcommittee held hearings on Kennedy's measure during the fall of 1963, reporting out a bill much stronger than the Administration's on Oct. 21. Fearful that the subcommittee's proposal would fail in Congress, Kennedy worked out a compromise measure with Celler, who then shepherded it through the Judiciary Committee in late October. Celler also guided the bill, which became the landmark Civil Rights Act of 1964, through the full House in February 1964.

Celler played an important role in the passage of the 1965 Voting Rights Act, the Immigration and Naturalization Act of 1965, and the 1968 Civil Rights Act. Early in 1967 he headed a special committee that investigated Rep. Adam Clayton Powell's (D, N.Y.) [q.v.] fitness to serve in the House, and in 1967 and 1968, he sponsored the Johnson Administration's anti-crime and gun control bills. [See JOHNSON, NIXON Volumes]

[CAB]

CHARYK, JOSEPH V(INCENT)

b. Sept. 9, 1920; Canmore, Canada.
Undersecretary of the Air Force, January 1960-February 1963; President, Communications Satellite Corporation February 1963- .

A space scientist with a Ph.D. from the California Institute of Technology, Charyk taught aeronautics at Princeton University from 1946 to 1955. He then joined the missile research facilities of Lockheed Aircraft and Aeronautics Systems, Inc. and in 1959 accepted a one-year appointment as chief scientist of the U.S. Air Force. In January 1960 he was appointed undersecretary of the Air Force.

While undersecretary Charyk supported the Defense Department's grant of the TFX fighter/bomber contract to General Dynamics despite the lower cost of the Boeing Company's design. Charyk contended that the Boeing design was scientifically inferior to that of General Dynamics.

President Kennedy named Charyk president and chief operating officer of the Communications Satellite Corporation (Comsat) following its incorporation in February 1963. The corporation was a privately owned, profit-making company, established by Congress; it had been formed to create and maintain a global network of commercial communications satellites. In 1964 Comsat became the manager of the International Telecommunications Consortium. This system leased satellite service to any member of the International Telecommunications Union, an association that included virtually all nations except Communist China.

As president of Comsat Charyk was the technological expert responsible for the design of the actual satellite system adopted. This system relied on the placement of satellites in synchronous orbits circling the earth at a rate of speed and altitude that would keep each over a fixed point. The system was begun with the launching of the Early Bird satellite in April 1964. By 1970 Comsat had orbited satellites over every continent except Antarctica.

During the late 1960s Charyk was unable to maintain Comsat's domestic monopoly on the ownership of ground stations and satellites. In 1966 Comsat was required to share ownership of its transmission stations with communications carriers such as the American Telephone and Telegraph Company. Broadcasting networks and communications corporations were allowed to enter the satellite field in 1972.

[EWS]

For further information:
"Joseph V. Charyk," *Current Biography Yearbook*, 1970 (New York, 1971), pp. 77-80.

CHAYES, ABRAM
b. July 18, 1922; Chicago, Ill.
Legal Adviser, State Department, January 1961-August 1964.

After obtaining his law degree from Harvard in 1949, Chayes served as legal adviser to the governor of Connecticut and then as law clerk to Supreme Court Justice Felix Frankfurter [q.v.]. He joined the Washington law firm of Covington and Burling in 1952 and remained there until becoming professor of law at Harvard in 1955. In 1960 Chayes served as staff director of the Democratic Platform Committee.

Chayes was appointed legal adviser to the State Department in January 1961. Under President Kennedy this post encompassed far broader duties than its title implied. Because Kennedy used groups of trusted associates rather than the traditional State Department bureaucracy to advise him on foreign policy, Chayes often served as counselor and fact-finder for the President.

During the Berlin crisis of 1961, when the Russians threatened to sign a separate peace treaty with East Germany and create a "free city" in Berlin theoretically independent of Eastern or Western control, Chayes became a member of the informal body assigned to develop American policy alternatives. Opposing Dean Acheson's [q.v.] recommendation that the U.S. forego negotiations and concentrate on building up conventional and nuclear forces in preparation for a confrontation, Chayes advocated opening talks while increasing military strength. In his view this policy could prevent the crisis from precipitating a nuclear war and would also make the U.S. appear to be the peacemaker in the eyes of world opinion. Kennedy accepted Chayes's advice and in July 1961 publicly announced a policy based on both negotiation and a troop build-up.

Within the Administration Chayes was a leading advocate of giving American aid to Ghana for the construction of the Volta Dam. The project, originally conceived by British colonial administrators, had been undertaken by a consortium of American aluminium companies with the prospect of U.S. government participation. During the opening days of the Administration, Kennedy, sympathetic to the undertaking, assigned Chayes to negotiate the aid treaty. Just before the initialing of the agreement, opposition to the treaty arose in the press and from Congress because of President Kwame Nkrumah's presumed flirtation with the Soviet bloc. Despite this development Chayes and Kennedy remained in favor of granting the necessary aid. In October 1961 Chayes was sent to Ghana to investigate the situation and to provide "political cover" for a decision to proceed with the project. The agreement was signed in January 1962.

In May 1963 Chayes concluded a treaty with Indonesia, which had demanded eventual acquisition of American oil refining and distribution facilities in that country. Under the provisions of the agreement the American companies would retain control of foreign distribution, but Indonesia would have the right to nationalize refining facilities in 10 to 15 years. Later that year Chayes coordinated State Department efforts for congressional ratification of the partial nuclear test ban treaty that had been signed in August. The Senate approved the agreement in September 1963.

During the Johnson Administration Chayes helped open the June 1964 negotiations for Soviet participation in an international satellite system.

Chayes resigned as legal adviser for the State Department in June 1964. He returned to the Harvard faculty in 1965.

[EWS]

CHERRY, FRANCIS A(DAMS)
b. Sept. 5, 1908; Ft. Worth, Tex.
d. July 15, 1965; Washington, D.C.
Member, Subversive Activities Control Board, October 1955-July 1965.

Francis A. Cherry, former governor of Arkansas, served almost a decade as a member of the Subversive Activities Control Board (SACB). Son of a Texas railway conductor, Cherry attended Oklahoma Agricultural and Mechanical College and earned a law degree from the University of Arkansas in 1936. He subsequently practiced law in Jonesboro, Ark. and served as a judge in Arkansas's 12th chancery circuit.

When he ran for governor in the 1952 Democratic primary, Cherry relied on marathon radio broadcasts to publicize his candidacy. He won national attention by upsetting the incumbent, who had the endorsement of President Harry S. Truman.

As governor Cherry suggested that whatever the U.S. Supreme Court's decision in a pending school desegregation case, Arkansas would not become an "outlaw." In 1954, after a single two-year term, Cherry was defeated in the Democratic gubernatorial primary by Orval E. Faubus who subsequently attempted to thwart court-ordered school desegregation in Arkansas.

In September 1955 President Dwight D. Eisenhower appointed Cherry to the SACB and in 1960 reappointed him to another five-year term. Under the 1950 Internal Security Act, also known as the McCarran Act, "Communist-action organizations" and "Communist-front organizations" were required to register with the SACB. The SACB, in turn, was authorized to conduct investigations to determine an organization's relationship to the Communist Party. [See EISENHOWER Volume]

Cherry's best known investigation concerned the Union of Mine, Mill and Smelter Workers. In December 1961 he reported that many important members of this union's leadership were or had been members of the Communist Party. In May 1962 his findings were upheld by the entire SACB, and as a result the union became ineligible to represent employes under the National Labor Relations Act.

In January 1963 President Kennedy appointed Cherry to the chairmanship of the SACB, and he held that post until his death in July 1965. By that time, however, federal court rulings had made it increasingly difficult for the SACB to register Communist-front organizations. Congress was reluctant to appropriate funds for the agency and it was clearly on the decline.

[JLW]

CHURCH, FRANK (FORRESTER)
b. July 25, 1924; Boise, Ida.
Democratic Senator, Ida., 1957- .

Frank Church, son of a Boise sporting goods dealer, received a law degree from Stanford University in 1950 and then returned to his native city to practice with a prominent local firm. Church was active in Democratic Party politics and in 1956 defeated former U.S. Senator and 1948 Progressive Party vice presidential nominee Glen Taylor for the Democratic senatorial nomination. In November he won the general election, upsetting Republican Sen. Herman Welker, a supporter of Sen. Joseph McCarthy (R, Wisc.). Church was only 32 and the fourth youngest man in the history of the Senate. [See EISENHOWER Volume]

During the 1960s Church served on the Senate Foreign Relations and Interior and Insular Affairs Committees and the Special Committee on Aging. He established a liberal record, voting for the Kennedy Administration's school aid, minimum wage and medicare legislation.

In 1962 Church served as the floor manager of a bill to protect several million acres of wilderness from commercial and highway development. The wilderness bill passed the Senate but was defeated in the House. Although Church's advocacy of the measure sparked opposition from Idaho's mining, cattle and lumber interests, he easily won reelection in 1962. Church argued that his victory demonstrated a new voter awareness of the need for conservation. Although the wilderness bill finally became law in 1964, Church himself was not a consistent supporter of all conservation measures. He vacillated, for example, on the question of whether the Hells River Canyon should be dammed for hydroelectric power, a development conservationists firmly opposed.

As a member of the Foreign Relations Committee, Church advocated reduced expenditures for foreign aid. He called for a phasing out of aid to prosperous Western European nations and Japan and an end to military assistance to India, Pakistan, Turkey and Greece, nations that were likely to engage each other in hostilities.

Church favored much of the Johnson Administration's domestic social legislation but was among the most outspoken critics of its Vietnam war policy. In 1970 Church and Sen. John Sherman Cooper (R, Ky.) [q.v.] coauthored an amendment prohibiting the return of U.S. ground combat forces to Cambodia without the consent of the Senate. In 1975 Church headed a Senate select subcommittee to investigate alleged abuse of power by the Central Intelligence Agency and the Federal Bureau of Investigation.

In the spring of 1976 Church was an unsuccessful candidate for the Democratic presidential nomination. [See JOHNSON, NIXON Volumes]

[JLW]

CLARK, JOSEPH S(ILL), JR.
b. Oct. 21, 1901; Philadelphia, Pa.
Democratic Senator, Pa., 1957-69.

The son of a Philadelphia lawyer, Clark graduated from Harvard College in 1923 and from the University of Pennsylvania Law School in 1926. Opening a general law practice in Philadelphia, Clark broke with the Republican tradition of his family by supporting the New Deal. He served as deputy state attorney general during 1934 and 1935. After a distinguished service record in World War II, Clark entered local politics as a reform Democrat and became a leader of the liberal Americans for Democratic Action (ADA). In 1949 he broke the Republican stranglehold on Philadelphia by winning election as city controller. Two years later he was elected mayor. During Clark's mayoral term city and county governments were merged, efforts were made to replace patronage posts with civil service jobs and urban renewal projects were undertaken. Clark was succeeded as mayor in 1956 by his reform ally, Richardson Dilworth [q.v.], when he made a successful bid for the Senate. [See EISENHOWER Volume]

Often accorded a 100% rating from the ADA for his Senate voting record, Clark was an extremely energetic sponsor of liberal legislation, much of which failed to win congressional approval. Clark believed

Congress lagged behind the nation and the other branches of government and had come to constitute an obstacle to political and social progress.

While still a presidential candidate in 1960, John F. Kennedy asked Clark and Rep. Emanuel Celler (D, N.Y.) [q.v.] to draw up a civil rights bill to be introduced if Kennedy took office. Clark and Celler offered the bill in 1961, but the Administration, which needed the support of Southern Democrats to enact the rest of its legislative program, decided not to back the bill. However, Clark, who served on the Banking and Currency and the Labor and Public Welfare Committees in 1961, did act as floor manager for many of the most liberal Administration proposals. He was instrumental in getting Robert C. Weaver [q.v.] confirmed as administrator of the Housing and Home Finance Agency, and he introduced measures to create a cabinet-level Urban Affairs and Housing Department, to make the Civil Rights Commission a permanent body and to make $500,000 available annually for three years for city-planning and urban-studies fellowships. Most important was a Clark-sponsored Administration bill to retrain workers whose skills had been made obsolete by technological change. The Manpower Development and Training Act, enacted in March 1962, was one of the Administration's important legislative successes, the first peacetime effort by the federal government to assess the economy's labor requirements and train workers to fill those needs.

Following an easy reelection victory in November 1962, Clark took seats on the Senate Democratic Steering Committee and the Rules and Administration Committee and began an assault on the congressional "Establishment." Arguing that this establishment was the "antithesis of democracy," he challenged the seniority system, the power of committee chairmen, the filibuster and the generally slow pace at which Congress conducted its business. Clark claimed that, partly because of the power of Southerners on important committees, Congress had blocked the progressive policies of "modern" presidents such as Kennedy. Beginning in February 1963 Clark advanced a number of proposals, including creation of a joint committee to study congressional operations and recommend improvements, limitation of the age of Senate committee chairmen to 70, election of Senate committee chairmen by secret ballot of committee members at the beginning of each congressional session, a requirement that Senate debate be germane and limitation of a senator to three consecutive hours of debate on the request of another senator. With a few minor exceptions, all of Clark's reform proposals were rejected.

A severe critic of Johnson's Vietnam policy, Clark was defeated in his 1968 reelection bid by a young liberal Republican, Rep. Richard Schweiker (R, Pa.). Between 1969 and 1971 Clark was president of the World Federalists, U.S.A., and after 1969 chairman of the Coalition on National Priorities and Military Policy.

[JCH]

For further information:
Joseph S. Clark, *Congress: The Sapless Branch* (New York, 1964).

CLARK, TOM C(AMPBELL)
b. Sept. 23, 1899; Dallas, Tex.
Associate Justice, U.S. Supreme Court, 1949-67.

Clark received his law degree from the University of Texas in 1922 and after several years in private practice became the civil district attorney in Dallas County, Tex. A protégé of Sen. Tom Connally (D, Tex.) and Rep. Sam Rayburn (D, Tex.) [q.v.], Clark joined the Justice Department in 1937, becoming an assistant attorney general in 1943. During these years Clark helped coordinate the wartime evacuation of Japanese-Americans from the West Coast to inland relocation centers and oversaw much government antitrust and war frauds litigation. He cooperated closely with the Senate committee headed by Harry S Truman (D, Mo.) investigating the defense effort and promoted Truman's nomination as the Democratic vice presidential candidate in 1944. In May 1945 President Truman appointed Clark Attorney General.

As one of Truman's closest advisers on domestic issues, Clark was a vigorous, assertive Attorney General who instituted 160 antitrust cases and filed government amicus curiae briefs supporting expanded civil rights in the Supreme Court. He played a major role in the development of Truman's domestic anti-Communist program, drafted the first Attorney General's list of subversive political organizations and in 1948 initiated proceedings against American Communist Party leaders for violation of the Smith Act. Truman nominated Clark as a Supreme Court justice in 1949. Although the appointment met opposition from liberals who faulted Clark's record on civil rights and civil liberties, the Senate confirmed the nomination by a vote of 73-8.

Initially, Clark demonstrated little judicial independence on the Court. He usually voted in a conservative vein with Chief Justice Fred Vinson, another Truman appointee. Clark did vote against the President's position in the 1952 Steel Seizure Case and wrote the opinion of the Court in a 1952 case holding unconstitutional an Oklahoma loyalty statute. In general, however, Clark voted to uphold government regulatory authority and to sustain local, state and federal loyalty-security programs. Under Chief Justice Earl Warren [q.v.], Clark retained his conservative stance in loyalty-security matters, but he voted for the Warren Court's anti-segregation rulings and was often considered a "swing" vote between the Court's liberal and conservative blocs on other issues. With his strong background in antitrust law, Clark became the Court's specialist in this area. In addition, Clark exhibited greater confidence in his judicial ability and became increasingly independent and more innovative in his opinions. [See TRUMAN, EISENHOWER Volumes]

Loyalty-security issues remained important to Clark in the 1960s. He voted with a five man majority in two 1961 cases upholding the investigative powers of the House Un-American Activities Committee and the contempt-of-Congress convictions of witnesses who had refused to answer Committee questions. He was one of two dissenters the next year when the Court overturned the contempt convictions of six men who had refused to answer questions about Communism before congressional committees. In two five-to-four decisions in June 1961, Clark voted with the majority to sustain key provisions in the 1940 Smith Act and the 1950 Internal Security Act. He dissented in 1963 when the Court invalidated two federal laws that removed the citizenship of Americans who left the country to avoid military service.

Although he dissented in several cases that expanded the rights of criminal defendants in the early 1960s, Clark wrote the majority opinion in one of the Court's most significant criminal rights cases in 1961. Along with four other justices, Clark overturned previous Court rulings and, in *Mapp v. Ohio*, held that illegally obtained evidence was not admissible in state courts. He concurred in *Baker v. Carr* (1962), in which the Court overturned another long-standing precedent and ruled that apportionment of legislative districts was subject to federal court scrutiny.

Clark wrote the opinion of the Court in a five-to-four decision in January 1961 upholding a Chicago ordinance that barred the public showing of movies without prior approval of city censors. However, he agreed with a majority of the Court in June 1962 that prayer in the public schools violated the First Amendment. In June 1963 Clark wrote the majority opinion in two controversial cases holding unconstitutional state and local rules requiring recitation of the Lord's Prayer and Bible-reading in public schools. In that decision Clark ruled that the First Amendment committed the state to "a position of neutrality" in the "relationship between man and religion."

In the realm of civil rights, Clark regularly voted against segregation laws and state attempts to evade school desegregation. However, he dissented in 1963 when the Court nullified a Virginia law barring solicitation of legal business, a law which had been the basis for state prosecution of the National Association for the Advancement of Colored People. Clark was also unwilling to give constitutional protection to all civil rights demonstrators. He was the sole dissenter in a 1963 case, for example,

when the Court overturned the breach-of-the-peace convictions of nearly 200 blacks who had demonstrated against discriminatory state laws on the state capitol grounds in Columbia, S.C. While the majority held that the demonstrations were peaceful and had been protected by the 1st and 14th Amendments, Clark argued that the arrests had been justified because there was evidence that a "dangerous situation" had been developing and that the peace had been threatened.

In his remaining years on the Court, Clark wrote the majority opinion in the key cases sustaining the public accommodations section of the 1964 Civil Rights Act. He maintained his established position on loyalty-security questions, opposed the "one-man, one-vote" standard for reapportionment set up by the Court and often dissented from further expansion of criminal rights, most notably in *Miranda v. Arizona* (1966). Clark resigned from the Supreme Court in June 1967 shortly after his son, Ramsey Clark, was appointed Attorney General, to avoid any suspicion of conflict of interest. [See JOHNSON Volume]

[CAB]

For further information:
Richard Kirkendall, "Tom C. Clark," in Leon Friedman and Fred L. Israel, eds., *The Justices of the United States Supreme Court, 1789-1969* (New York, 1969), Vol. IV.

CLAY, LUCIUS D(UBIGNON)
b. April 23, 1897; Marietta, Ga.
Presidential Envoy to Berlin, August 1961-May 1962.

As the American general who had been deeply involved in the reconstruction of postwar Germany and had become the symbol of U.S. determination to break the Russian blockade of Berlin in 1948, Clay again represented the U.S. desire to protect that city during the crisis of 1961.

The son of a U.S. senator and descendent of the noted American statesman Henry Clay, Lucius graduated from West Point in 1918 and began his Army career as a military instructor and engineer. During World

War II he was appointed director of material and coordinated the production and movement of supplies to the battlefront. At the recommendation of Gen. Dwight D. Eisenhower, Clay was designated deputy military governor of American-occupied Germany in 1945. Two years later he became governor of the American zone and commanding general of U.S. forces in Europe. Clay retired from military service in 1949 and accepted a position as chairman of the board and chief executive officer of the Continental Can Company. During the 1950s he frequently advised the Eisenhower Administration on German affairs. [See TRUMAN, EISENHOWER Volumes]

In August 1961, when the Kremlin and East Germany threatened to cut off Western access to East Berlin and make Berlin a "free city," theoretically independent of both Eastern and Western control, Clay was sent as President Kennedy's personal representative to West Berlin. To assure Berlin of U.S. support and assert Western access rights into the Soviet sector, Clay, on a number of occasions, ordered American diplomats to drive into the Eastern zone. When East German authorities stopped American officials on Oct. 27, Clay ordered armed convoys to accompany the diplomats to ensure entry. In the ensuing crisis American and Soviet tanks faced each other across the border for the first time in the postwar era. American armored forces were withdrawn after the Soviet Union pulled back its tanks.

During the winter of 1962 U.S. newspapers reported that Clay was dissatisfied with the President's order that all major U.S. responses to Soviet measures be cleared in advance with Washington because the requirement prevented quick reaction to border incidents. According to these reports Clay believed the Communists would have torn down the Berlin wall in August 1961 if American officials had threatened its destruction. Clay subsequently denied the report. In May 1962, after the crisis subsided, he returned to the U.S. and resumed his business activities.

President Kennedy, hoping to gain support for his foreign aid proposals, appointed Clay head of a committee of generally con-

servative businessmen asked to study the program in December 1962. In a March 1963 report the committee stated that aid was indispensable to national security but recommended that aid operations be improved and assistance levels reduced. The report urged that aid not be given "inconsistent with our beliefs, democratic traditions and knowledge of economic organization and consequences" and advocated the curtailment of all projects undertaken as gifts to heads of state, gambles to maintain existing governments or grants to increase political leverage. The committee's recommendations were used by such conservative congressmen as Otto Passman (D, La.) [q.v.] as an excuse to reduce the 1963 foreign aid bill by over a third, the largest cut since the beginning of the foreign aid program in 1945.

In November 1965 Clay, along with 104 other well-known Americans, signed a statement supporting the Johnson Administration's policy on Vietnam. The statement declared that U.S. domestic critics "have a right to be heard but they impose on the rest of us the obligation to make unmistakably clear the nation's firm commitment in Vietnam."

In 1970 Clay retired as chairman of the board of the Continental Can Company.

[EWS]

CLEVELAND, (JAMES) HARLAN
b. Jan. 19, 1918; New York, N.Y.
Assistant Secretary of State for International Organization Affairs, January 1961-September 1965.

Prior to his appointment as assistant secretary of state for international organization affairs in January 1961, Cleveland had a varied career in government, the press and education. Two years after his graduation from Princeton in 1938, he became a writer for the Farm Security Administration and from 1944 to 1953 served in various relief agencies, including the United Nations Relief and Rehabilitation Administration, the United States Economic Cooperation Agency and the Mutual Security Agency. From 1955 to 1957 he was executive editor and then publisher of *The Reporter*. In 1957 Harlan Cleveland became the dean of the Maxwell Graduate School of Citizenship and Public Affairs at Syracuse University.

Cleveland was brought to Washington at the request of U.N. Ambassador Adlai Stevenson [q.v.] to be his high-level representative in the State Department bureaucracy. His most important task was to coordinate policy between the White House, the State Department and the U.N. mission. Occasionally he also acted as "ameliorator" in the often strained relations between Kennedy and Stevenson. During the early 1960s Cleveland aided Stevenson in writing many of his major U.N. policy statements, including those delivered during the Cuban missile crisis of October 1962. He also helped President Kennedy draft his September 1961 U.N. address, which included a proposal for "General and Complete Disarmament in a Peaceful World."

Cleveland and Assistant Secretary of State for African Affairs G. Mennen Williams [q.v.] were the leaders of the so-called New Africa Group, young members of the State Department anxious to have America back the growing nationalist movements in Africa. In the opening months of the Administration, these men were particularly concerned with the reunification of the Congo, where the secession of mineral-rich Katanga province shortly after Belgium had granted independence in June 1960 threatened the viability of the central government.

Cleveland successfully worked behind the scenes to gain allied support for the passage of the U.N. resolution of Feb. 21, 1961 that called for negotiation and reconciliation in the Congo. The resolution requested that military personnel—particularly Belgian troops and mercenaries—be withdrawn, that the Congolese parliament meet and that the U.N. take all appropriate measures to prevent civil war. However, all attempts at reconciliation failed.

Believing that this failure was the result of Katanga's military strength, Cleveland

and the New Africa Group pushed for the use of U.N. troops to end secession and attempted to influence the Administration and Congress to back their stand. The policy gained little support because of opposition from America's European allies, many of whom still had colonies in Africa, and because of a successful public relations campaign waged in Congress by the Katangan government.

By the summer of 1962, however, congressional criticism declined as it became increasingly evident that Katanga's leader, Moise Tshombe, did not want to negotiate. Cleveland and his group, therefore, began another diplomatic offensive. Learning from their earlier defeat, they now proposed a moderate plan for reunification backed by economic sanctions while they worked to gain support for the use of force if the measure failed. Their proposal, known as the U.N. Plan for National Reconciliation, called for the adoption of a federal constitution and the sharing of revenues between Katanga and the central government. An economic boycott of Katangan ore and the seizure of its foreign assets were to be used to force the province to accept this solution. In August 1962 the U.S. government gave public support to the plan with the implication that it also backed the economic sanctions. The measure, however, failed to achieve unification.

Having gained backing for military intervention in the summer and fall of 1962, Cleveland and the New Africa Group were able to get Administration approval for the use of force to end secession in December. In January 1963 U.N. troops, backed by the implied threat of American military support, succeeded in reunifying the Congo.

Cleveland was appointed ambassador to the North Atlantic Treaty Organization in July 1965. He left that post in April 1969 to become president of the University of Hawaii.

[EWS]

For further information:
Roger Hilsman, *To Move a Nation: The Politics of Foreign Policy in the Administration of John F. Kennedy* (New York, 1967).

CLIFFORD, CLARK (McADAMS)
b. Dec. 25, 1906; Fort Scott, Kan.
Lawyer.

Clark Clifford, influential adviser to three presidents, was born in Fort Scott, Kan. and grew up in St. Louis, Mo. Following his graduation from Washington University Law School in 1928, Clifford entered private law practice in St. Louis, specializing in corporation and labor law. He eventually became one of the most successful attorneys in that city. In 1944 Clifford was commissioned a lieutenant in the U.S. Naval Reserve and a year later became assistant to President Truman's naval aide, James K. Vardaman. He succeeded Vardaman in 1946.

Following the completion of his naval service in June 1946, Clifford was appointed special counsel to the President. While at the White House he played an important part in the formulation of postwar foreign and domestic policy. In 1946 he prepared a memorandum that was the basis for much of the Administration's increasingly hardline policy toward Russia. One year later he helped draft the Truman Doctrine and the National Security Act of 1947. Clifford also helped plan the political strategy that led to Truman's election in 1948 and that laid the basis for much Fair Deal legislation. In 1950 he resigned his post and returned to private law practice in Washington. [See TRUMAN Volume]

During the 1950s Clifford became one of the most influential lawyers in Washington, representing some of America's largest corporations in their dealings with the government. He also served as Sen. John F. Kennedy's personal attorney.

In 1960 Clifford joined Kennedy's presidential campaign as an adviser on strategy. He also counseled the candidate on the policy problems he would face if elected and on the organization of a White House staff. Following Kennedy's victory Clifford became his liaison to the Eisenhower Administration.

In May 1961 Kennedy appointed Clifford to the newly formed Foreign Intelligence Advisory Board. Disillusioned with the conduct of U.S. intelligence agencies during the planning of the disastrous Bay of Pigs invasion of Cuba in early 1961, the President had created this panel to oversee the activities of these bodies and look into possible ways of reorganizing them. Clifford became chairman of the panel in April 1963.

In the spring of 1962 the Kennedy Administration clashed with the steel industry over price increases instituted on April 10. Knowing that Clifford was respected by the corporations, many of which he had represented as an attorney, the President sent him to outline the government's demand for a price rollback. Clifford secretly met with U.S. Steel Chairman Roger Blough [q.v.] and was instrumental in forcing the corporation to rescind its price increase. In the early 1960s Clifford played a major role in the development of Comsat, the public-private corporation set up to manage communications satellites. Congress authorized this corporation in August 1962.

Clifford served as a trusted adviser to President Lyndon B. Johnson both in domestic and foreign affairs. In early 1968 he succeeded Robert S. McNamara [q.v.] as Secretary of Defense and was a decisive force in persuading Johnson to de-escalate the Vietnam war in March 1968. In January 1969 Clifford returned to his private law practice. [See JOHNSON Volume]

[EWS]

COHEN, MILTON H(OWARD)
b. Aug. 9, 1911; Milwaukee, Wisc.
Director of the Special Study of Securities Markets, October 1961-August 1963.

Milton Cohen guided the most extensive investigation of the stock market since the famed Pecora probe of the early 1930s, which led to the creation of the Securities and Exchange Commission (SEC). Cohen joined the SEC after graduating from Harvard Law School in 1935. Eight years later he was named head of the Commission's public utilities division and charged with the enormously complex task of dismantling the giant utility combines whose abuses had led to the Public Utility Holding Company

Act of 1935. Winning a reputation as a tough administrator, Cohen left the SEC in 1947 and joined a prestigious Chicago law firm.

In August 1961 Congress authorized $750,000 for the SEC to conduct a massive inquiry into the securities business. The Commission chairman, William Cary [q.v.], strongly favored the study and outlined as its main areas of focus, those developments that had come about in the market since the last full-scale study a generation earlier. These included the growth in the over-the-counter market, where securities not listed on the organized exchanges were issued, bought and sold for the most part beyond the SEC's purview; the mushrooming mutual fund business; the much-criticized activities of floor traders and exchange "specialists;" the deterioration of standards governing persons dealing in securities; and the laxity of the governmental and private associations regulating the stock market. In October Cary appointed Cohen to head a 65-man staff to analyze abuses and propose remedies.

After two years of study, the Cohen group produced in mid-1963 a 5,400-page report entitled the Special Study of the Securities Markets. The publication of the long-awaited study was attended by great interest and apprehension on Wall Street. In his letter of transmittal Cohen said that "the total picture emerging from our studies is one of basically strong institutions subject to many specific weaknesses and abuses." The report contained over 100 recommendations for reform.

Among the chief offenses detailed in the report were "high pressure selling" by mutual fund salesmen and purchase plans that victimized buyers, such as the "front-end load" plan that "loaded" commission payments into the early stages of installment contracts. The Cohen study also criticized the unregulated character of over-the-counter trading, the lax standards that permitted incompetent and unscrupulous salesmen to enter the securities business, and the practice of exchange "specialists" and "floor traders" buying and selling for their own profit in violation of their primary obligations.

The Special Study found fault with those institutions charged with regulating the stock market. It called the regulatory performance of the New York Stock Exchange (NYSE) "seriously unsatisfactory" in some areas, although in others it "provided constructive leadership." The NYSE, the study charged, operated like a "private club" and leaned "towards tenderness rather than severity" in disciplining members for violations that involved "ethical standards in dealing with customers." The National Association of Securities Dealers, in addition, had "fallen short of its potential as a self-regulating agency," while the SEC in its preoccupation with enforcing full disclosure gave insufficient attention to "changing market circumstances and regulatory needs."

Cohen returned to his Chicago law practice in August 1963. Cary and the SEC endorsed most of the Cohen group's findings and lobbied before Congress for passage of those reforms that could not be put into practice on the SEC's own authority. The Securities Acts Amendments of 1964, passed in August, were the fruits of the Cohen report. The two main sections of the 1964 law extended the SEC's jurisdiction to include over-the-counter trading and empowered the SEC to set standards and qualifications for persons dealing in securities. The new law failed to place curbs on mutual funds or exchange specialists or to abolish floor trading as the Special Study had urged. The SEC, however, issued stringent regulations that had the effect of drastically reducing the number of floor traders.

[TO]

COHEN, WILBUR J(OSEPH)
b. June 10, 1913; Milwaukee, Wisc.
Assistant Secretary of the Department of Health, Education and Welfare, April 1961-April 1965.

Cohen, son of a Milwaukee storekeeper, attended the University of Wisconsin and studied economics there under a group of distinguished professors that included Alexander Meiklejohn, Selig Perlman, Edward

A. Ross, Edwin Witte, and John R. Commons. After graduating in 1934, Cohen went to Washington to work as a research assistant to Witte, then the executive director of President Franklin D. Roosevelt's cabinet committee on economic security. Cohen also worked with Arthur Altmeyer and Labor Secretary Frances Perkins in drafting the 1935 Social Security Act. He served for many years thereafter as a technical adviser to the Social Security Board and from 1953 to 1956 as director of the Bureau of Research and Statistics of the Social Security Administration. Cohen was widely acknowledged as one of the leading authorities on social welfare policies and in 1956 became professor of public welfare at the University of Michigan.

In January 1961 President Kennedy named Cohen an assistant secretary in the Department of Health, Education and Welfare (HEW). His primary task was to win congressional approval of the basic legislation formulated within the Department. Cohen was known to favor broad expansion of the Social Security system, and his appointment met with bitter opposition from certain conservative congressmen and the powerful American Medical Association (AMA). As head of a Kennedy task force on health and Social Security, Cohen had recommended that hospital costs for the elderly be financed through the Social Security system. AMA President E. Vincent Askey denounced the proposal as a form of socialized medicine that would ultimately diminish the quality of health care in this country. Carl T. Curtis (R, Neb.) [q.v.] Cohen's leading critic in the Senate, argued that the Social Security system was already "too extensive and costly." Although Curtis opposed the appointment, Cohen was confirmed by the Senate in April 1961.

As assistant HEW secretary, Cohen won approval of bills authorizing increased federal appropriations for health care of veterans and Indians and for improved hospitals in the District of Columbia. Throughout 1963 Cohen and Commissioner of Education Francis Keppel [q.v.] worked for a number of Administration education bills that were passed shortly before or just after the President's death. These included the 1963 Higher Education Facilities Act, which established a five-year college building construction program funded by the federal government, the 1963 Vocational Education Act, which authorized the appropriation of $731 million for a broad five-year manpower training program and the 1964 Library Services Act, which made federal funds available for the maintenance and construction of libraries in cities as well as rural areas.

Cohen also helped win approval for measures relating to consumer protection, civil rights, mental health and water resources planning. However, during the Kennedy years he failed to win passage of the two measures most prized by the Administration: a medicare bill linking medical care for the aged to the Social Security system and an education bill authorizing federal aid to elementary and secondary schools. Progress on the education bill was thwarted by a controversy over the question of federal aid to parochial schools. The American Medical Association was a primary obstacle to passage of the medicare legislation.

The passage of both bills became possible following President Johnson's landslide election victory of November 1964, which brought the Democrats overwhelming majorities in the House and Senate. Cohen played a key role in the enactment of medicare and school aid legislation during 1965. He was promoted that year to the rank of HEW undersecretary and three years later succeeded John Gardner as Secretary. Cohen was named dean of the University of Michigan School of Education in January 1969. [See JOHNSON Volume]

[JLW]

COLLINS, JOHN F(REDERICK)
b. July 20, 1919; Boston, Mass.
Mayor, Boston, Mass., 1960-68.

Born in the Roxbury section of Boston, John F. Collins received his law degree from Suffolk University in 1941. After duty in counter-intelligence during World War II, he practiced law and served in the Massachusetts lower house, the General Court. Ten days before a November 1955 contest for the Boston City Council in which he had entered, Collins contracted bulbar poliomyelitis. The disease confined him to a wheel chair for the next 15 years of an active political life. Despite his illness, he won election to the city council and in November 1959, at age 40, upset a heavily favored opponent in a race for mayor of Boston.

Upon assuming office Collins concentrated on lowering the city's high property taxes. He cut the city budget through a freeze on the hiring of city employes and the reorganization of executive departments. His economy drives resulted in four separate property tax reductions in his first four-year term.

Collins's fiscal maneuvers had one central aim: the restoration of the city's deteriorating economic base. Like most large Eastern cities Boston had lost businesses, jobs and home-owners to the suburbs and other geographic regions in the 15 years after World War II. To reverse this trend, Collins closely cooperated with financial and corporation officials in the ambitious planning of new commercial centers in Boston. In January 1962 Collins persuaded the General Court to grant tax relief to the Prudential Life Insurance Co. for the construction of a $175-million Prudential Center. The "Prudential Law" allowed for the construction of the multi-purpose facility in the economically stagnant Back Bay area. Modeled after Rockefeller Center in New York, the Prudential Center included a 52-story office building, a 1,000-room hotel (the city's first new hotel since 1927), 75 retail shops and two 26-story apartment buildings. The legislation also served as a model for other, more modest commercial building projects through the 1960s.

In his designs for a "New Boston," Collins did not wholly rely on the private sector. At the Mayor's urging, the General Court reorganized and extended the scope of the Boston Development Authority. The Mayor also appointed the noted urban planner Edward J. Logue to head the agency. In a grand scheme, Logue and Collins arranged for the demolition of the 60-acre Scollay Square district, site of the old Howard burlesque theater. In its place they created Government Center; architect I. M. Pei drew up the overall plan that encompassed new state and federal office structures and a new city hall. Finished in 1969, Government Center spearheaded the area's reconstruction as a "walkway to the sea" that began at the Center, continued to the restored Faneuil Hall Market district and ended at a rebuilt waterfront.

Collins also worked to alleviate the city's serious shortage of adequate housing. Non-profit agencies cleared slums in Roxbury and Charlestown and built, Collins would later claim, more low-income and moderate-income housing in the 1960s than any other city in America. At the decade's end, however, large slum districts remained and the city's economy and population continued to decline.

Reducing property taxes and avoiding any serious scandals, Collins easily won reelection in November 1963. His further ambitions suffered a setback in the 1966 Democratic primary when former Gov. Endicott Peabody [q.v.] defeated the Boston Mayor for the Democratic senatorial nomination. Collins declined to run for reelection in 1967. He chaired the Massachusetts Committee for the Reelection of President Richard M. Nixon [q.v.] in 1972. [See JOHNSON Volume]

[JLB]

COLLINS, (THOMAS) LEROY
b. March 10, 1909; Tallahassee, Fla.
President, National Association of Broadcasters, January 1961-July 1964.

The son of a grocer, Leroy Collins built his political career in urban south Florida. After 16 years in the Florida legislature he won election as governor of Florida in 1954. Reelected to a four-year term in 1956, Collins challenged Supreme Court desegregation rulings in Florida courts but urged his fellow Southern governors to obey federal authority. Hailed by many political observers as "the voice of the New South," Collins chaired the June 1960 Democratic Convention. [See EISENHOWER Volume]

Between January 1961 and July 1964, Collins served as president of the National

Association of Broadcasters (NAB), which represented over 3,000 radio and television stations and the national networks. An occasionally independent spokesman, Collins criticized the television industry in May 1961 for being "too dependent" upon the rating services. He recommended that each station "take sides" by editorializing and called for more "blue ribbon programming" of drama, music and news specials. In November 1962 the former governor attacked cigarette commercials "designed primarily to influence young people" and urged the NAB to prohibit such advertisements in its code. Newton N. Minow [q.v.], the outspoken chairman of the Federal Communications Commission (FCC), frequently praised Collins's calls for the industry's self-improvement.

Despite Minow's friendly remarks and his own Democratic affiliation, Collins criticized the Kennedy Administration's communications policies. The NAB president testified against the Administration s plan to reorganize the Commission in June 1961. Collins told a House committee that he objected to a key provision of the plan that would have increased Minow's power to delegate authority. The House deleted the section and approved the rest of the Administration's plan in June. During the October 1962 Cuban missile crisis, the NAB president accused the White House of "news suppression."

Collins resigned as NAB president in July 1964 to become director of the Commerce Department's Community Relations Service, created under the 1964 Civil Rights Act and charged with coordinating the desegregation policies of communities affected by the statute. [See JOHNSON Volume]

[JLB]

COLMER, WILLIAM M(EYERS)
b. Feb. 11, 1890; Moss Point, Miss.
Democratic Representative, Miss., 1933-73.

During the 1930s Colmer supported Franklin D. Roosevelt's New Deal programs, but when the political climate of his Gulf Coast district later changed, he became an opponent of social welfare measures. Like almost all Mississippi politicians in the early 1960s, he was a bitter foe of bills directed against racial discrimination. At the Democratic National Convention in July 1960, Colmer and Rep. John Bell Williams (D, Miss.) [q.v.] announced they would support an independent slate of presidential electors because of their opposition to the civil rights plank in the national Democratic Party's platform.

At the beginning of the Kennedy Administration, Colmer was the second-ranking member of Rep. Howard Smith's (D, Va.) [q.v.] powerful Rules Committee, through which most bills had to pass before they reached the House floor. Dominated by a conservative Southern Democrat-Republican alliance, the Committee had frequently blocked liberal legislation during the 1950s.

One of President Kennedy's first goals was to weaken this coalition. In January 1961 House Speaker Sam Rayburn (D, Tex.) [q.v.], who was cooperating with the White House to attain this end, considered purging Colmer from the Committee on the ground that he had not supported the Democratic national ticket the previous year. However, this action would have raised the sensitive issue of how to deal with other Democratic representatives who had not backed the Kennedy candidacy in 1960. Instead, Rayburn promoted a plan, adopted by the House at the end of the month, to expand the membership of the Rules Committee from 12 to 15 and thereby create an eight-to-seven liberal majority.

However, when a liberal Committee member defected or was absent, the conservatives could succeed in blocking Administration proposals. In March 1963 the absence of a liberal Democrat enabled Smith and Colmer to combine with the panel's five Republicans to temporarily pigeonhole the Administration's medical training bill by producing a seven-to-seven vote on the question of sending the measure to the House floor. This provoked Kennedy. In a press conference the following day, he attacked the two Southerners by asserting that "the seven Democrats voted yes."

According to *Congressional Quarterly*, Colmer voted with the Southern Democrat-Republican conservative coalition 78%, 94% and 80% of the time on key House votes in 1961, 1962 and 1963, respectively. He generally opposed social welfare and civil rights proposals, contending that they would dangerously increase the power of the federal government. In May 1963 he opposed an Administration-endorsed equal-pay-for-women bill as a measure that would "set up another army of federal agents to go about snooping into every little, as well as every big business in the country. . . ."

In 1967 Colmer became chairman of the Rules Committee. He announced his retirement from political life in 1972. [See JOHNSON, NIXON Volumes]

[MLL]

CONNALLY, JOHN B(OWDEN), JR.
b. Feb. 27, 1917; Floresville, Tex.
Secretary of the Navy, January 1961-December 1961; Governor, Tex., 1963-69.

Connally grew up in a small farm town near San Antonio, one of seven children of a poor butcher and farmer. He attended the University of Texas at Austin where, according to a fellow-student, he was the type of person who made others "want him to be chairman of the board." Impressing people with his self-assured demeanor, suave manners and attractive appearance, he was elected student body president.

Connally was admitted to the Texas bar in 1938, and during the same year he became an aide to freshman Democratic Texas Rep. Lyndon B. Johnson [q.v.]. Entering the Navy in 1941 he served, among other assignments, as a legal assistant to Undersecretary of the Navy James V. Forrestal. In 1948 Connally managed Johnson's bitterly fought, controversial and narrowly successful campaign for the U.S. Senate. He served as Johnson's administrative assistant from January to October 1949.

In 1951 Connally moved to Fort Worth to become an attorney for billionaire Sid Richardson. The 1930s had witnessed the beginning of a great Texas oil boom, and the investment capital produced by oil profits made the state a leading manufacturer of petrochemicals, electronic equipment and defense-related hardware. Richardson was one of the major beneficiaries of the boom and of the industrialization which came in its wake. Connally's association with Richardson had a decisive impact upon the lawyer's career, helping him to accumulate a wide range of Texas business connections and a network of corporate directorships in Richardson-owned firms. Meanwhile, he served Richardson's economic empire in numerous capacities. One of his better known functions was that of a Washington lobbyist for a 1956 "fair-market-price" natural gas bill which, if it had not been vetoed by President Dwight D. Eisenhower, would have substantially increased the profits of the gas industry.

At the same time, Connally remained closely linked with the political career of Sen. Johnson, who in the 1950s became one of the most powerful figures on Capitol Hill. In 1956 he played a key role in helping Johnson supporters win elections to the state Democratic Party convention, thereby enabling the Senator to wrest control of the Texas organization from Gov. Allan Shivers. Four years later Connally managed Johnson's effort to become the Democratic presidential candidate.

In December 1961 President-elect Kennedy decided to nominate Connally as Secretary of the Navy. According to Arthur M. Schlesinger, Jr. [q.v.], the appointment represented the choice not of Vice President Johnson but of Kennedy's designee for Secretary of Defense, Robert S. McNamara [q.v.]. Nevertheless, Johnson's enthusiastic approval of McNamara's preference was also a significant factor in the choice of Connally.

The nomination produced substantial comment in the press because of Connally's close relationship to oil interests and the fact that the Navy was the industry's largest single customer. Sen. William Proxmire (D, Wisc.) [q.v.] contended that Connally's appointment would create a "conflict of interest," and he cast the only negative vote when the Senate approved the nomination on Jan. 23, 1961.

During his year in the sub-cabinet post, Connally felt that McNamara was usurping much of the authority traditionally belonging to the service secretaries themselves. He also came into conflict with McNamara over the controversial swing-wing fighter-bomber known as the TFX. In May Connally warned that the Air Force's specifications called for a plane that was too large and expensive for the Navy. But in the fall McNamara decided that only minimal changes would be made in the Air Force's specifications.

Connally resigned as Secretary of the Navy in December 1961. His major reason for departing was not his differences with McNamara but his desire to enter the Texas gubernatorial race in 1962. Connally had never run for elective office before and was not well-known to the electorate in his home state. Nevertheless, his extensive business and political connections in Texas brought him considerable financial backing and organizational support. He was the leader in the first round of the primary in May and faced liberal runner-up Don Yarborough in the June runoff.

The insurgent liberal faction of the state's Democratic Party, led by U.S. Sen. Ralph Yarborough [q.v.] (no relation to Don Yarborough), reviled Connally as a conservative pillar of Texas's business establishment. They feared that if Connally won the primary he would, because of his national connections with Lyndon Johnson, solidify conservative control of the Party machinery. Connally outspent Don Yarborough in the primary by $699,000 to $231,000. Furthermore, Connally's campaign was widely regarded as the best organized political effort in the history of Texas. During the first round of the primary he appeared on television every day to introduce himself to the voters, and during the runoff campaign he rode a special campaign train across the state to make personal contact with them.

Connally also skillfully designed his campaign rhetoric to appeal to a broad range of voters. He avoided identification as a doctrinaire conservative, emphasizing instead the pragmatic issues of business growth and the expansion of education. As a result, he cut into Yarborough's vote among blacks, Latins and liberals in rural and small town north and central Texas. His association with the Kennedy Administration also helped him to gain some liberal and moderate support. But Connally avoided endorsing major liberal objectives such as minimum wage legislation and a more progressive system of taxation and thereby was able to maintain his conservative core of support. With his fragile conservative, liberal and moderate coalition he defeated Yarborough with 51.2% of the vote. In the general election he faced conservative Republican Jack Cox. Concluding his campaign with a flamboyant non-stop, 48-hour airplane tour of the state, Connally won with 54.2% of the ballots.

During Connally's first year as governor he stressed the need for greater expenditures for higher education. In June 1963 he item-vetoed an appropriations bill and said that he would set aside the vetoed sums for the state's educational needs, guarding them "like an old mother hen." He accused the legislature of "short-changing" the colleges and universities of the state.

Connally was in the presidential limousine in Dallas the following Nov. 22 when President Kennedy was assassinated. The Governor suffered a serious chest wound, but he recovered. The assassination made public criticism of his administration more difficult and helped him easily win reelection in 1964 and 1966. Connally, however, continued to antagonize the state's liberals by his opposition to civil rights measures and social welfare legislation and his vehement support of the Vietnam war. [See JOHNSON Volume]

In 1969 he returned to the private practice of law. Two years later he became Secretary of the Treasury during the Republican administration of Richard Nixon. In May 1972 Connally resigned his post, and two months later he announced his support of Nixon's reelection bid. He switched his allegiance to the Republican Party during May 1973. Later in the month Connally became a special adviser to the President, but he resigned two months later. In July 1974 the Watergate grand jury indicted Connally for bribery and perjury in connection with an increase in federal milk price supports during his tenure as Treasury Secretary. He was acquitted the following April. [See NIXON Volume]

[MLL]

For further information:
Fred Gantt, Jr., *The Chief Executive in Texas: A Study in Gubernatorial Leadership* (Austin, 1964).
James R. Soukup, et al., *Party and Factional Division in Texas* (Austin, 1964).

CONNOR, (THEOPHILUS) EUGENE "BULL"

b. July 11, 1897; Selma, Ala.
d. March 10, 1973; Birmingham, Ala.
Commissioner of Public Safety, Birmingham, Ala., 1937-53, 1957-63.

Between 1926 and 1936 Connor acquired a large following as a radio sports broadcaster in Birmingham and received his nickname from the deep tone of his voice. Banking on his personal popularity, Connor was elected to the state legislature for one term in the mid-1930s and then won four consecutive terms as Birmingham's commissioner of public safety, serving from 1937 to 1953. He filled that post again from 1957 to 1963. As one of only three elected city officials, Connor, with his lengthy tenure in office, established himself as Birmingham's major public figure. According to the *New York Times*, he enhanced his influence by using his power to appoint temporary judges as a device for controlling the city's court system.

In the late 1950s and early 1960s Birmingham was known as one of the South's most rigidly segregated cities. And Connor earned a reputation as the unenlightened leader of its resistance to the civil rights movement. When an integrated Freedom Ride bus entered Birmingham on Mother's Day, May 14, 1961, it was received by a hostile white mob. Asked why the police were not present to prevent violence, Connor stated that most of the policemen were off duty to visit their mothers. Later in the year, when the manager of the city's bus terminal attempted to comply with an anti-discrimination directive of the Interstate Commerce Commission, Connor had him arrested.

In the fall of 1962 Birmingham's voters chose to replace the existing commissioner form of government with the mayor-city council system. Connor ran for mayor the following year but was defeated 29,000 to 21,000 by Albert Boutwell [*q.v.*] on April 2. However, Boutwell and the city councilmen did not assume their offices until May 23, 1963. During the interim Martin Luther King, Jr. [*q.v.*] and Fred Shuttlesworth [*q.v.*] led a series of civil rights demonstrations in Birmingham. Connor initially employed restraint in dealing with the protesters, but in early May his men began to use dogs, nightsticks and pressure hoses in an effort to crush the integration drive. After Shuttlesworth was injured and removed from the scene by ambulance, Connor remarked, "I waited a week to see Shuttlesworth get hit with a hose: I'm sorry I missed it. I wish they'd carried him away in a hearse."

Connor's strategy backfired. Many local white leaders were frightened by his methods and wanted a truce. The Kennedy Administration, responding to national and worldwide indignation against his methods, exerted strong pressure upon Birmingham's business community to negotiate with black leaders. On May 10 Shuttlesworth announced an agreement which provided for gradual desegregation of the city's major public accommodations and the hiring of blacks in jobs previously reserved for whites. President Kennedy, in a conversation with civil rights leaders shortly afterwards said, "I don't think you should be totally harsh on 'Bull' Connor. He has done more for civil rights than almost anybody else."

Connor remained an unyielding foe of integration after his defeat in Birmingham's municipal election. When Martin Luther King won the Nobel Peace Prize in 1964, Connor asserted, "They're scraping the bottom of the barrel. . . ." Three years later he defended his use of dogs against demonstrators in 1963 and urged they be employed against black rioters in the North. In

1964 Connor won a libel suit begun four years earlier against the *New York Times* over two April 1960 articles which depicted him as a repressive force in Birmingham's racial politics. The judgment was ultimately overturned by the U.S. Supreme Court on freedom-of-the-press grounds. Elected president of Alabama's Public Service Commission in 1964 and 1968, he was defeated in 1972 after the state's attorney general accused him of being a "tool" of the utility companies whose rates were regulated by the Commission. Connor died on March 10, 1973, shortly after suffering a stroke.

[MLL]

CONNOR, JOHN T(HOMAS)
b. Nov. 3, 1914; Syracuse, N.Y.
President, Merck & Company, 1955-65.

A graduate of Harvard Law School, John Connor joined the New York law firm of Cravath, de Gersdorff, Swaine & Wood in 1939. He went to Washington, D.C., in 1942 to serve as general counsel for the Office of Scientific Research and Development, where he set up a program for the development and production of penicillin, which involved a large number of government, university and commercial laboratories. As special assistant to Secretary of the Navy James V. Forrestal from 1945 to 1947 Connor dismantled the military penicillin program to integrate it with the private economy. Connor joined one of the largest drug manufacturers, Merck & Co., in 1947 as general attorney and became its president in 1955.

In December 1959 Connor represented Merck before Sen. Estes Kefauver's (D, Tenn.) [*q.v.*] investigation of the drug industry. "Unlike the drug industry generally," *Fortune* said, "Merck came out of the hearings virtually unnicked, thanks largely to Connor's fleet mind and air of candor." However, in February 1962 Connor accused Kefauver of "distortion, evasion and bias" in conducting the probe. Connor supported the compromise version of Kefauver's bill increasing government supervision of the drug industry. In October Connor stated that the new law would be effective "only to the extent that the Food and Drug Administration is strengthened in staff, facilities and organization."

A supporter of John F. Kennedy's presidential candidacy in 1960, Connor was also a fund raiser for New Jersey's liberal Republican senator, Clifford Case [*q.v.*], in that year. He was one of 13 prominent citizens named by Kennedy in October 1962 to set up and incorporate the Communications Satellite Corporation.

Connor played an important role during 1962 in the Justice Department's project to free the Cuban-held prisoners from the Bay of Pigs invasion partly in exchange for drugs contributed by private pharmaceutical firms, including Merck. As part of the ostensibly private deal the Internal Revenue Service gave a favorable tax ruling on the contribution, allowing each manufacturer to compute the amount of the charitable deduction based on the wholesale price of the drugs rather than on the cost of production. The difference between the two was often great in the drug business, and Merck made $300,000 on its wholesale-value donation of $2.5 million. Connor said in January 1963: "Without the tax rulings, absolutely nothing would have happened. The men would still be in prison."

In 1964 Connor was co-chairman of the National Independent Committee for Johnson and Humphrey. He left Merck to become Secretary of Commerce in January 1965. [See JOHNSON Volume]

[TO]

COOLEY, HAROLD D(UNBAR)
b. July 26, 1897, Nashville, N.C.
d. Jan. 15, 1974; Wilson, N.C.
Democratic Representative, N.C., 1934-67; Chairman, Agriculture Committee, 1949-53, 1955-67.

After attending North Carolina public schools and Yale Law, Cooley practiced at the bar until his election to Congress in a special 1934 election. During his long service in the House, Cooley associated himself with the "farm bloc" and helped write much of the Roosevelt, Truman and Eisenhower Administrations' agricultural legislation. [See TRUMAN, EISENHOWER Volumes]

As chairman of the powerful House Agriculture Committee in 1961 and 1962, Cooley backed Kennedy Administration proposals to impose sharp production and marketing controls in order to sustain the price of wheat, dairy products and feed grains. Despite Cooley's willingness to compromise with opponents of the Administration bill, the House narrowly defeated the measure in June 1962, primarily because 31 Southern Democrats defected from Administration ranks. When congressional liberals sought to strengthen the federal laws against child labor in farm work, Cooley supported efforts to weaken their bill, declaring, "There are no sweatshops on the farms of America. On the farms of our nation, children labor with their parents out under the blue skies." The bill's sponsors gave up their attempt Oct. 4, 1962 after a number of crippling amendments were added to the proposed legislation.

Following the deterioration in relations between the United States and Cuba in 1960, Cooley played a major role in reallocation of Cuba's lucrative sugar quota. Against the wishes of both the Eisenhower and Kennedy Administrations, Cooley kept much of the power to assign Cuba's quota in the hands of his committee. After intensive lobbying by representatives of foreign sugar interests, the House passed an extension of the Sugar Act in June 1962 that tripled the Dominican Republic's permanent quota and set allocations for 15 new nations. During debate on passage of the bill, the *New York Times* published secret documents of the recently deposed Trujillo regime indicating a pattern of cooperation between Cooley and the Dominican government on American sugar legislation. [See JOHNSON Volume]

[NNL]

COOPER, JOHN S(HERMAN)
b. Aug. 23, 1901; Somerset, Ky.
Republican Senator, Ky., 1946-49,
1952-55, 1956-73.

After earning a B.A. from Yale and a law degree from Harvard, Cooper returned to his native Kentucky and was elected to the state legislature in 1928. He served one term there before becoming a judge, first at the county and then at the circuit court level. Known as the "Poor Man's Judge," Cooper held this position for intervals in the 1940s and 1950s, returning to the post between terms as a U.N. delegate, ambassador to India and Nepal and U.S. senator. Cooper won special elections to fill Senate vacancies in 1946, 1952 and 1956, although he lost two regular Senate elections held during the period. He won his first full term by a wide margin in 1960 with the help of five professional campaign consultants sent to Kentucky by President Dwight D. Eisenhower. [See TRUMAN, EISENHOWER Volumes]

In the Senate Cooper won a reputation as a serious legislator and was praised by President Kennedy as an "outstanding Republican." *Congressional Quarterly* showed that during the years of the Kennedy Administration Cooper went against his party on more than one-third of the roll call votes. When questioned about his bipartisan voting record, he replied, "I reckon I'll vote as I see fit."

Cooper supported most civil rights legislation. Although he considered the 1962 voting literacy bill a violation of the states' right to determine voting qualifications, Cooper introduced an alternate bill in February 1963; it would have required equal enforcement of existing literacy examinations. He also opposed the public accommodation section of the Administration's 1963 civil rights bill because it did not differentiate between large and small businesses.

In May 1961 Cooper and Sen. Jacob Javits (R, N.Y.) [*q.v.*] cosponsored two unsuccessful amendments to an education appropriations bill, one to reduce overall aid and the other to distribute more aid to poorer states. During the same period, Cooper's proposal for U.S. grants for educational television passed the Senate but died in the House. After the failure of an attempt to bar federal aid to church-supervised schools from a higher education appropriation bill, Cooper and Sen. Sam Ervin (D, N.C.) [*q.v.*] managed to gain passage for an amendment allowing any taxpayer the right to bring a civil suit to test the constitutionality of any proposed grant to colleges.

Cooper favored long-term foreign development loans and was a major supporter of a $100-million loan to the U.N. in 1961. The Senate passed his bill to establish presidentially-appointed committees to review the effectiveness of foreign aid in June 1962.

Cooper was appointed to the Warren Commission investigating the assassination of President Kennedy in November 1963. He achieved national prominence as a leading opponent of the anti-ballistic missile system in 1968 and as a sponsor of an amendment with Sen. Frank Church (D, Ida.) [q.v.] in 1970 to prohibit the use of U.S. forces in Cambodia. He retired from the Senate in 1972. [See JOHNSON, NIXON Volumes]

[MDB]

CORDIER, ANDREW W(ELLINGTON)

b. March 3, 1901; Canton, Ohio.
d. July 13, 1975; New York, N.Y.
Executive Assistant to the Secretary General of the United Nations, 1946-61; Undersecretary for U.N. General Assembly Affairs, June 1961-March 1962; Dean of Columbia University School of International Affairs, March 1962-February 1972.

After serving as professor and chairman of the history department of Manchester College from 1923 to 1944, Cordier accepted the position of adviser on international security to the State Department. While at this post he became technical expert to the U.S. delegation to the United Nations Conference on International Organization in 1945 and the next year was appointed executive assistant to Secretary General Trygve Lie. During Lie's administration Cordier, as an American assistant to the Secretary General, was extremely influential both in Secretariat and General Assembly affairs. In his position Cordier was responsible for the coordination of all politi-

cal missions in Korea, Indonesia, India and Palestine.

Cordier retained his post after Dag Hammarskjold's election as Secretary General in 1953, but because of the Secretary's reluctance to delegate power, became an executor rather than initiator of policy. In that capacity Cordier was one of a group of Hammarskjold's close advisers, known as the Congo Club, who coordinated U.N. activities during the Congo crisis of 1960-64.

Four days after the declaration of Congolese independence in June 1960, President Joseph Kasavubu and Premier Patrice Lumumba, facing civil war with breakaway Katanga province, petitioned for U.N. troops to preserve order and prevent unilateral intervention by Belgium. On July 14, the U.N. voted to send a force and Cordier, in conjunction with Ralph Bunche [q.v.], was assigned to organize the effort. Over 16,000 troops under U.N. command were deployed in the area by September.

On Aug. 27 Hammarskjold sent Cordier to the Congo to survey the operation. While he was there the situation reached crisis proportions. On Sept. 5 Kasavubu dismissed Lumumba on the grounds that he was closely tied to the Soviet Union. Lumumba, in turn, denounced Kasavubu as a traitor. To prevent civil war Cordier, without Hammarskjold's prior consent, closed all airports, took over the radio station and granted funds to Congolese troops to assure their neutrality. These actions, justified in terms of preventing war, had the net effect of frustrating the radical aims of Lumumba and furthering those of the more moderate Kasavubu. As a result, the Soviet Union objected to the influence of American specialists in the Congo, and Hammarskjold agreed to replace both Cordier and Bunche with Africans.

In June 1961 Cordier resigned his position to facilitate the reorganization of the Secretariat staff and give it the wider geographical and ideological representation demanded by the Soviet Union. He was given the temporary post of undersecretary for General Assembly affairs. In that capacity Cordier controlled the day-to-day workings of the U.N. from Hammarskjold's death in September 1961 to the election of

U Thant in November 1961. With the other members of the Congo Club he also made important policy decisions to send fighter planes to protect U.N. forces in Katanga during September and to accept an October ceasefire between the U.N. and the secessionist province.

In March 1962 Cordier resigned from the U.N. to become dean of Columbia University's School of International Affairs and professor of international relations. In August 1968, following the student occupation of several campus buildings during the spring, Cordier became acting president of the University, eventually resigning the position in September 1970, when he was given the title president emeritus.

[EWS]

CORDINER, RALPH J(ARRON)
b. March 20, 1900; Walla Walla, Wash.
d. Dec. 4, 1973; Clearwater, Fla.
Chairman, General Electric Company, 1958-63.

Ralph Cordiner first came to General Electric (GE) in 1922. He became an expert in merchandising electrical appliances and a protege of executive Charles E. Wilson, who became GE president in 1940. Cordiner followed Wilson into a high position at the War Production Board during World War II. Elected a GE vice president in 1945, Cordiner worked out the details of a sweeping decentralization plan, which gave individual executives greater authority over their divisions. Cordiner succeeded Wilson as GE president in 1950.

During the 1950s GE played a central role in a criminal price-fixing and bid-rigging conspiracy involving electrical equipment manufacturers. On Feb. 7, 1961 seven high officers of the offending companies, including three GE executives, were given short jail terms for their roles in the conspiracy. Eight other GE officials were given suspended sentences and the company itself paid $437,500 of the $1,924,500 assessed in fines against the 29 companies.

Cordiner was not indicted, but his role was a subject of controversy during hearings held before Sen. Estes Kefauver's (D, Tenn.) [q.v.] Antitrust and Monopoly Subcommittee in the spring of 1961. One ex-GE vice president testified that Cordiner had known about the conspiracy, and another testified that Cordiner had no part in the affair. In June Cordiner testified that he "did not know of these secret violations of the law or condone such acts."

At the outset of the Kennedy Administration Cordiner was also chairman of the Business Advisory Council (BAC), a group of corporation executives serving as an advisory adjunct to the Department of Commerce. After the GE convictions Secretary of Commerce Luther Hodges [q.v.] called upon the BAC to replace Cordiner as chairman because of his firm's involvement in the conspiracy. Two weeks later Cordiner resigned as chairman and was succeeded by Roger Blough [q.v.] of U.S. Steel.

Cordiner retired as GE chairman in December 1963. The following August he was named head of the fund-raising drive for the presidential campaign of Sen. Barry Goldwater (R, Ariz.) [q.v.]. The *Chicago Tribune* reported in October that if elected Goldwater planned to appoint Cordiner as Secretary of the Treasury.

Cordiner died on Dec. 4, 1973.

[TO]

COTTON, NORRIS
b. May 11, 1900; Warren, N.H.
Republican Senator, N.H. 1954-74.

Cotton, a graduate of Phillips Exeter Academy and Wesleyan University, worked as an aide to Sen. George H. Moses (R, N.H.) while attending George Washington Law School. After graduating in 1928 Cotton returned to New Hampshire to practice law, first in Concord and later in Lebanon. He was elected to Congress in 1946 and served until 1954 when he entered the Senate. Over the next two decades, Cotton had little difficulty winning reelection.

Cotton once wryly described himself as a "stand-pat, conservative, hidebound, mossback Republican." In all his senatorial campaigns he won the support of the arch-conservative William Loeb [q.v.], publisher of the Manchester *Union Leader*, the most influential newspaper in the state.

Cotton, a consistent opponent of Kennedy Administration domestic policies, voted against federal aid to higher education, the minimum wage and manpower training bills. In foreign affairs he prided himself on his militant anti-Communism. In January 1961 he voted against the nomination of Chester Bowles [q.v.] as undersecretary of state because Bowles favored U.S. recognition of Communist China. In September 1963, however, he broke ranks with such conservatives as Sen. Barry Goldwater (R, Ariz.) [q.v.] and Sen. John Tower (R, Tex.) [q.v.] to vote for ratification of the nuclear test ban treaty.

Cotton became the ranking minority member of the Senate Commerce Committee in 1963. Over the next decade he generally opposed consumer protection measures favored by the Commerce Committee's Democratic majority.

In September 1963 Cotton called his first formal news conference in 17 years to announce his support for Sen. Goldwater for president. Cotton later helped manage Goldwater's 1964 New Hampshire primary campaign. The Arizona Senator outpolled his chief rival, New York Gov. Nelson Rockefeller [q.v.], but was defeated by a write-in vote for U.S. Ambassador to South Vietnam Henry Cabot Lodge [q.v.].

During the Johnson years Cotton generally opposed the Administration's domestic legislation while supporting its Vietnam war policy. He later became disillusioned with the war and opposed the Nixon Administration's military intervention in Cambodia and its support of the Nguyen Van Thieu regime. Cotton retired in 1974. [See JOHNSON, NIXON Volumes]

[JLW]

COUSINS, NORMAN
b. June 24, 1915; Union Hill, N.J.
Editor, *Saturday Review*, 1942-71.

Cousins graduated from Teachers College at Columbia University in 1933. The following year he began work in an editorial position on the *New York Post*. In 1935 he became the book critic for *Current History*. In 1940 Cousins was made executive editor of the *Saturday Review of Literature*, later known as *Saturday Review*, and in 1942 he became its editor. Cousins expanded the magazine to include feature articles on current events and literature and editorials on contemporary problems in addition to book reviews. By the 1960s the magazine had a circulation in excess of 500,000. Cousins's major concern after 1945 was the threat of nuclear war, and the magazine reflected his apprehension over the possibility of world destruction. Actively involved in the movement for international disarmament, he was one of the founders of the Committee for a Sane Nuclear Policy in 1957. [See EISENHOWER Volume]

Cousins believed that the arms race could be ended only with the establishment of a new world order. In July 1962 the editor wrote that the major problem facing man was not the nuclear bomb but the fact that "the human imagination has not yet expanded to the point where it comprehends its own essential unity. People are not yet aware of themselves as a single interdependent entity. . . ." Preoccupation with national interest, he asserted, had to give way to a "world consciousness" founded upon a "collective identity." In April 1962 Cousins, a member of the United World Federalists, wrote that for the purpose of creating a world rule of law the United Nations should be given sufficient authority "to underwrite national independence, to define and carry out a program of orderly and enforceable disarmament under proper safeguards [and] to create and coordinate a program for development of resources, especially in those areas most in need of such development."

Cousins regarded a cessation of nuclear testing as the first, important step towards the creation of international harmony. In September 1961, after the resumption of above-ground tests by the Soviet Union, he wrote, "Any nation that engages in atmospheric testing has in effect declared war on the human race." When the United States decided early in 1962 to resume tests in the atmosphere, Cousins stated that while the short run result might be an improvement in American military capacity, in the long run the rapid pace of improvements in the technology of armaments would make military security impossible. In July 1963 he was one of the founders of the Citizens Committee for a Nuclear Test Ban Treaty, which was formed to promote Senate ratification of the U.S.-Soviet test ban agreement.

In the late 1960s and early 1970s the causes which interested Cousins included the cessation of the bombing of North Vietnam and a negotiated settlement of the Indochina conflict, the pursuit of world peace, an end to racial discrimination and the control of environmental pollution. In November 1971 he resigned his post at *Saturday Review* because of an editorial dispute with its new owners. The following year he founded *World* magazine. In 1973 Cousins bought the then bankrupt *Saturday Review* and combined it with his new publication to form *Saturday Review/World*.

[MLL]

COX, ARCHIBALD

b. May 17, 1912; Plainfield, N.J.
U.S. Solicitor General, January 1961-July 1965.

Cox was a graduate of Harvard and the Harvard Law School. After several years in private practice, he joined the staff of the National Defense Mediation Board in 1941 and then served in the office of the Solicitor General from 1941 to 1943 and as an associate solicitor in the Department of Labor from 1943 to 1945. Following World War II Cox returned to Harvard Law School to teach and was made a professor in 1946.

A noted expert on labor law, Cox combined public service with teaching over the next 15 years. During the Korean war he served as co-chairman of the Construction Industry Stabilization Commission and then as head of the Wage Stabilization Board. He helped arbitrate several labor disputes during the 1950s and was an adviser to Sen. John F. Kennedy on labor legislation. During the 1960 presidential campaign Cox directed an academic team that did research and drafted speeches on major issues for Kennedy.

In December 1960 Kennedy named Cox as Solicitor General, the third highest position in the Justice Department. Cox oversaw all U.S. government litigation in the Supreme Court and determined which cases the government should appeal. Considered a brilliant and tireless worker, Cox developed a reputation for efficient administration of the Solicitor General's office. His department was known for the detailed and precise briefs it submitted to the Supreme Court. In oral argument before the Court, Cox displayed thorough preparation, a polished style and an occasional tendency to "lecture" the justices as though he were still a law professor.

Under Cox's direction, the U.S. government appeared as a friend of the court in several significant civil rights cases. Cox, for example, urged the Supreme Court to overturn the state convictions of sit-in demonstrators in a series of cases in the early 1960s, although the narrowly based grounds he offered for reversal were criticized by some civil rights advocates. He also intervened in *Baker v. Carr* to argue that the Court should abandon a 1946 precedent and hold that federal courts could try legislative apportionment cases. By a six to two vote the Supreme Court ruled in March 1962 that federal courts did have jurisdiction in apportionment suits. Some observers considered the government's support crucial in assembling a court majority for this position.

Cox also argued cases that led to the Supreme Court's "one-man, one-vote" standard of apportionment and cases involving the constitutionality of the 1964 Civil Rights Act. He resigned as Solicitor General in July 1965 and returned to teaching at Harvard Law School. In 1968 he headed the five-man commission that investigated the causes of disturbances at Columbia University in the spring of that year. He was appointed special prosecutor in the Watergate case in May 1973 but was fired in October, under President Nixon's [*q.v.*] orders, in a dispute over access to tapes of

White House conversations concerning the Watergate break in and coverup. [See JOHNSON, NIXON Volumes]

[CAB]

COX, W(ILLIAM) HAROLD
b. June 23, 1901; Indianola, Miss.
U.S. District Judge, Southern District of Mississippi, June 1961- .

Cox received his B.S. and LL.B. from the University of Mississippi and was admitted to the Mississippi bar in 1924. He practiced in Jackson until 1961 and served as chairman of the Hinds County Democratic Executive Committee from 1950 to 1961.

A long-time personal friend of Senator James O. Eastland (D, Miss.) [q.v.]—the two had been college roommates—Cox was named a district court judge in Mississippi in June of 1961. Both the President and Attorney General Robert Kennedy [q.v.] reportedly hoped Cox's appointment would placate Eastland, the powerful chairman of the Senate Judiciary Committee, and prepare the Senator to accept their selection of Thurgood Marshall [q.v.] the director of the NAACP Legal Defense and Educational Fund, for a Circuit Court judgeship. (Marshall was appointed to the Second Circuit Court in October 1961, but lengthy hearings by Eastland's Judiciary Committee postponed Senate confirmation of the nomination for nearly a year.) Although Eastland was an ardent segregationist, Cox himself had no public record on civil rights at the time of his nomination, and he assured Robert Kennedy in a private interview that he would uphold the Constitution in the realm of civil rights.

The meeting apparently convinced the Attorney General that Cox would rise above segregationist sentiments in dealing with civil rights cases. Once on the bench, however, Judge Cox handed down a string of anti-civil rights decisions and became the most famous of the segregationist Southern judges in the 1960s. Cox refused to overturn the conviction of five freedom riders in August, 1961, arguing that "their destination was Jackson but their objective was trouble." He issued an injunction barring the Congress of Racial Equality from encouraging blacks to use the McComb, Miss. interstate bus terminal, even after a 1961 Interstate Commerce Commission order required that all such facilities be integrated. Cox did hand down a temporary restraining order against race discrimination in an April 1962 voting rights case, but he generally ruled against blacks in voting rights suits brought by the Justice Department. In one instance, he attributed the fact that no blacks in a certain Mississippi county were registered though nearly 2,500 blacks of voting age lived there, to "the fact that Negros have not been interested to vote," and privately, he complained of having to spend most of his time "fooling with lousy cases" brought by the Justice Department's Civil Rights Division. As of March 1964, all but one of Cox's civil rights decisions had been reversed on appeal.

While Cox's appointment aroused little comment at the time it was made, his rulings created great resentment among civil rights workers in the 1960s, and Robert Kennedy, in his later years as senator from New York, was sharply criticized for having approved Cox's selection. [See JOHNSON Volume]

[CAB]

CRONKITE, WALTER L(ELAND),
b. Nov. 4, 1916; St. Joseph, Mo.
CBS News Correspondent.

Descended from Dutch-German ancestors, Walter Cronkite grew up in Kansas City, Mo., and Houston, Tex. He attended the University of Texas in Austin for two years while simultaneously working as the state capitol reporter for the Scripps-Howard bureau in 1935 and 1936. During World War II Cronkite had a distinguished career as a correspondent for United Press International. He was one of the first newsmen on the scene at the Normandy invasion. After a stint as a radio broadcaster in Washington, D.C., Cronkite joined the Columbia Broadcasting System in July 1950 as a member of the network's Washington staff and soon became one of its most important correspondents, acting as anchorman for the 1952 and 1956 political conventions. He also served as moderator for such popular CBS programs of the 1950s as *You Are There* and the *Morning Show*.

Renowned for a relaxed manner and a lucid style that was especially evident during "live" broadcast events, Cronkite remained CBS's chief anchorman during the early 1960s. When CBS became the first network to expand its evening news program from 15 to 30 minutes, President Kennedy took note of the event by granting Cronkite an exclusive interview on Sept. 2, 1963. The President hoped the interview would clarify his views to the public on Vietnam and the Buddhist crisis there. Kennedy told Cronkite that, "In the final analysis, it is their war. They are the ones who have to win it or lose it. We can help them . . . but they have to win it. . . ." The President said that if South Vietnamese President Ngo Dinh Diem made certain policy and "personnel" changes—meaning the removal of his brother and sister-in-law, Ngo Dinh Nhu and Madame Nhu, from power—he could regain the support of the Vietnamese people. According to White House Press Secretary Pierre Salinger [q.v.], Kennedy was later displeased with the Cronkite interview because he felt it cast South Vietnam's president in an unsympathetic light.

During the mid-1960s Cronkite's ratings dropped as a result of the popularity of NBC's Chet Huntley-David Brinkley news team, and he was removed from his customary position as anchorman for the 1964 political conventions. His eclipse was temporary, however, and by the late 1960s and early 1970s Cronkite was back covering such major news stories as the Vietnam war and the U.S. space program. By 1973 his evening news program was broadcast by 205 affiliated stations and led the competition with an estimated audience of 26 million. [See JOHNSON, NIXON Volumes]

[FHM]

For further information:
Erik Barnouw, *The Image Empire* (New York, 1970).
Edward J. Epstein, *News from Nowhere* (New York, 1973).

CRUIKSHANK, NELSON H(ALE)
b. June 21, 1902; Bradner, Ohio.
Director, Department of Social Security, AFL-CIO, 1955-65.

Nelson H. Cruikshank, a key aide to AFL-CIO President George Meany [q.v.], played an important role in organized labor's efforts to win enactment of medicare legislation in the 1960s.

A native of Ohio, Cruikshank attended Oberlin College and Ohio Wesleyan University. He won a master of divinity degree from the Union Theological Seminary in 1929. After serving as director of the social service department of the Brooklyn Federation of Churches in the early 1930s, Cruikshank joined the staff of the American Federation of Labor. As a political strategist for the AFL, Cruikshank developed a close working relationship with Meany, then the Federation's secretary-treasurer.

Following merger of the AFL with the Congress of Industrial Organizations in 1955, Cruikshank was named director of the new organization's department of social security. Meany gave Cruikshank broad authority to draw up a legislative program for the expansion of the Social Security system. Meany hoped thereby to demonstrate to the rank and file the solid political benefits that could be derived from the merger. During the Eisenhower Administration, Cruikshank lobbied successfully for legislation authorizing Social Security payments for permanently and totally disabled persons regardless of whether they had reached retirement age. Following this success Cruikshank proposed that the Social Security system be expanded to help defer the costs of hospitalization to the elderly. Known as medicare, this idea had the strong backing of organized labor but encountered stiff opposition from the American Medical Association (AMA). In the late 1950s Cruikshank organized a special labor committee on medicare to counter the AMA opposition.

In 1961 Rep. Cecil R. King (D, Calif.) [q.v.] and Sen. Clinton Anderson (D, N.M.) [q.v.] introduced medicare legislation supported by organized labor. Despite the enthusiastic support of the Kennedy Administration, it made no headway. The AMA was one obstacle; another was Rep. Wilbur D. Mills (D, Ark.) [q.v.], the powerful chairman of the House Ways and Means Committee, who seemed determined to prevent the King-Anderson bill from reaching the floor of the House.

In the summer of 1961 two AFL-CIO staff members began organizing the National Council of Senior Citizens (NCSC) to rally older persons in political support of medicare. Cruikshank was at first reluctant to channel labor funds into such an organization. He recalled the Townsend movement of the 1930s and feared that "we might create a sort of gerontocracy that would plague the government for one handout after another." Within a few months however, the NCSC had recruited half a million members, and Cruikshank's associates convinced him that in order to control the NCSC the AFL-CIO would be obliged to help support it. Cruikshank agreed and over the next five years, the AFL-CIO contributed over a half a million dollars to the senior citizens group.

Although NCSC proved to be a useful instrument in lobbying for medicare, it was at first unable to overcome the opposition of Mills and the AMA. However, following the massive Democratic congressional sweep in the 1964 elections, the Johnson Administration won passage of a medicare bill in the summer of 1965. Cruikshank served as a watchdog for labor's interests in the shaping of the bill, which in final form placed medicare under the Social Security system. Cruikshank retired from the AFL-CIO in October 1965 but later became head of the NCSC. He remained in Washington and continued to lobby actively on behalf of social welfare legislation.

[JLW]

CURRAN, JOSEPH E(DWIN)

b. March 1, 1906; New York, N.Y.
President, National Maritime Union, 1937-73.

Curran went to sea at 16. In 1935 he led a wildcat strike of crewmen on the S.S. *California*. The crew was eventually fired,

but the East Coast seamen's strike that followed led to the establishment of the National Maritime Union (NMU).

In 1937 Curran was elected as the first NMU president. Between 1938 and 1946 Curran worked closely with Communist Party members in leading the union; although he was never a member of the party, almost all of the other top NMU officers were. Curran ran for Congress on the American Labor Party ticket in 1940 but lost the election.

In 1946 Curran joined with a group of NMU leaders recently expelled from the Communist Party in a successful effort to oust those still in the Party from union office. Curran then turned against the maritime union's non-Communist radicals, including those with whom he had been recently allied, and by 1949 they too were forced out. After another split in the leadership in the early 1950s, Curran and NMU Treasurer Hedley Stone were the only leaders from the early days of the NMU still holding their top offices. [See TRUMAN, EISENHOWER Volumes]

Curran was reelected union president in 1960, but there were charges of election irregularities. Secretary of Labor James P. Mitchell began an investigation under the recently passed Landrum-Griffin Act and on Oct. 3, 1960 filed a suit to force a new election. The following year, however, the new Secretary of Labor, Arthur J. Goldberg [q.v.], dropped the suit in return for a stipulation in which Curran admitted some charges and agreed that future NMU elections would be conducted in accordance with the provisions of the Landrum-Griffin Act. In spite of frequent absences from the union's New York headquarters, Curran was in firm control of the union throughout the early 1960s. Although the NMU was relatively small, with 37,000 members in 1961, Curran was one of the highest paid union officials in the country.

On June 15, 1961, the NMU, the Seafarer's International Union (SIU), the National Marine Engineers' Beneficial Association (MEBA) and two other maritime unions struck U.S. ships. In addition to higher salaries and increased benefits, the unions were demanding that they be allowed to act as bargaining agents for about 25,000 seagoing personnel aboard some 700 American-owned foreign flag ships. On June 26 President Kennedy, citing the disruption of shipping to Hawaii and the delay of military shipments, invoked the Taft-Hartley Act to end the strike. He established a three-man inquiry panel, and at the request of the government, an injunction to halt the strike was issued on July 3. By July 5 most shipping had resumed.

By the time the injunction was issued, all of the unions except the MEBA had come to terms with a majority of the shipowners. The NMU and two smaller unions agreed to submit the issue of jurisdiction on foreign-flag ships to a panel, selected by Secretary of Labor Goldberg and empowered to present nonbinding recommendations. The NMU also agreed to a four-year wage settlement that provided an immediate 4% raise and annual 2¼% increases as well as a doubling of annual vacation time to 60 days and other improved benefits.

The NMU and the SIU had a long and bitter history of jurisdictional disputes, and throughout the strike there was considerable tension between the two unions. When on July 2 the MEBA, which was closely allied with the SIU, failed to reach a settlement with the shipowners, thus preventing the members of the other unions from returning to work, fights broke out among members of the rival unions.

Curran was a vice president of the AFL-CIO and in October 1961 was one of only three AFL-CIO executive council members to support a proposal by Transport Workers Union President Michael J. Quill [q.v.] to readmit the International Brotherhood of Teamsters to the federation. At the December 1961 AFL-CIO convention in Bal Harbour, Fla., Curran again was in a small minority supporting readmission of the Teamsters.

In an effort to further consolidate his control of the NMU, Curran had initiated a 1963 amendment to the union constitution limiting candidates for national office to those who had served at least one full term as a salaried union official. Although Curran remained in office until his retirement in

1973, in the late 1960s a growing opposition movement within the union challenged his authority, and charges of irregularities forced a 1969 rerun of the 1966 union election. [See JOHNSON, NIXON Volumes]

[JBF]

CURTIS, CARL T(HOMAS)
b. March 15, 1905; Kearney County, Neb.
Republican Senator, Neb., 1955- .

Curtis was elected in 1938 to the U.S. House of Representatives from Nebraska, a largely rural and consistently conservative state. In 1954 he won a seat in the Senate. There Curtis promoted legislation to extend Social Security coverage to a larger number of persons but was otherwise an opponent of domestic social welfare programs. [See EISENHOWER Volume]

During the early 1960s Curtis compiled one of the most conservative records in Congress. According to *Congressional Quarterly*, he was the most frequent Republican senatorial opponent of Kennedy-backed bills in 1962 and voted with the Southern Democratic-Republican conservative coalition 82%, 91% and 90% of the time in 1961, 1962 and 1963 respectively.

In 1961 Curtis unsuccessfully offered an amendment to reduce the number of persons covered by federal minimum-wage legislation. During the same year he assailed a bill expanding veterans' eligibility for National Service Life Insurance policies as weakening the private enterprise system. In 1962, as a member of the Senate Finance Committee, he resisted an Administration effort to tighten controls on the expense-account tax deductions of businesses. While opposing government spending directed at social ills, Curtis supported increased appropriations in the areas of agriculture and defense. In 1963 he voted against the nuclear test ban treaty with the Soviet Union.

Curtis almost uniformly rejected President Lyndon B. Johnson's social welfare programs but backed his Southeast Asia policies. He was a staunch supporter of the

Nixon Administration. Even after President Nixon, in August 1974, revealed his participation in the Watergate coverup, Curtis refused to call for his removal from office. [See JOHNSON, NIXON Volumes]

[MLL]

CURTIS, THOMAS B(RADFORD)
b. May 14, 1911; St. Louis, Mo.
Republican Representative, Mo., 1951-69.

Thomas Curtis grew up in Webster Groves, a suburb of St. Louis. After graduating from Dartmouth College and Washington University Law School, he joined his father's law firm in 1935. He made a number of unsuccessful bids for public office before his election to Congress in 1950 as a Republican from Missouri's twelfth district, which encompassed most of suburban St. Louis County. Joining the House Ways and Means Committee in 1953, Curtis gradually established himself as a leading Republican congressional spokesman on economic policy. [See EISENHOWER Volume]

When the 87th Congress convened in January 1961, Curtis was one of seven Republicans who issued a manifesto deploring any coalition with Southern Democrats opposing civil rights or other "constructive" legislation. In the January 1961 battle over the expansion of the Rules Committee, Curtis joined 21 other Republicans to supply House Speaker Sam Rayburn (D, Tex.) [q.v.] with the margin of victory needed to dilute the power of the conservative majority on the Rules Committee. "They blame the Rules Committee," Curtis told fellow Republicans, "Let's call their bluff by letting them rearrange the Committee."

Curtis consistently opposed social welfare and revenue measures that he believed contributed to unbalanced budgets. He was one of only 14 members to vote against a Social Security increase in May 1961. The bill permitted men to retire at age 62 and provided an estimated $780 million in new benefits. Curtis's motion to delete the early retirement provision was rejected by the full House in a voice vote.

The senior Republican representative on the Joint Economic Committee in 1962, Curtis issued a minority report with Sen. Prescott Bush (R, Conn.) [q.v.], opposing the delegation of additional tariff-cutting authority to President Kennedy. On the Ways and Means Committee Curtis led the fight against financing medical care for the aged through the Social Security system.

Unlike many conservatives, Curtis favored cuts in defense spending as well. In March 1963 he proposed a 5% reduction in all defense authorizations except those for submarines and the controversial RS-70 manned bomber. The House rejected the proposal, 258-149. When the House passed the $47 billion defense appropriation in June, 410-1, Curtis was the lone dissenter. He was one of only five congressmen to vote against a 17% military pay raise in October.

In 1963 Curtis was a leading House Republican opponent of President Kennedy's tax program. In response to Kennedy's call for a $11-billion tax cut and tax reform package, Curtis and the Republican minority on the Joint Economic Committee issued a report in March 1963 advocating a $7 to 8-billion cut of a different character. The Republicans envisioned a 40% corporate tax rate, as opposed to the 47% rate preferred by the Administration, and a $95-billion budget ceiling.

Curtis voted against the June 1963 extension of "temporary" corporate and excise rates, contending that Congress had a "moral obligation" to reduce temporary taxes before permanent ones. He vigorously opposed the Administration's "interest equalization tax" in August. The proposed levy, which Americans would pay when they purchased a foreign security, was intended to reduce the balance-of-payments deficit by making it more expensive for foreigners to obtain long-term capital inside the United States. Congress passed the tax in the summer of 1964.

Along with Rep. John Byrnes (R, Wisc.) [q.v.], Curtis led the Republican attack against the modified version of Kennedy's tax cut, passed 17-8 by the Ways and Means Committee on Sept. 10. Over national television on Sept. 21, 1963 Curtis criticized Kennedy for "advancing a new and untried fiscal theory for the United States, the theory of deficit financing," Byrnes's motion to return the $11.1-billion tax cut bill to committee was defeated, 226-199, on Sept. 25.

Curtis maintained his stance as a fiscal conservative through the Johnson Administration, frequently voting against spending proposals while backing civil rights legislation. He left the House after an unsuccessful run for the Senate in 1968. [See JOHNSON, NIXON Volumes]

[TO]

DALEY, RICHARD J(OSEPH)
b. May 15, 1902; Chicago, Ill.
Mayor, Chicago, Ill., 1955- .

Richard J. Daley was born in an Irish working-class neighborhood near the Union Stockyards not far from the house where he later resided as mayor. As a young man he joined the Hamburgs, a neighborhood gang—later an early source of his political strength. Daley served as president of the Hamburgs for 15 years.

Trained as a clerk and bookkeeper at the Christian Brothers De La Salle Institute, Daley later attended De Pauw University from which he earned a law degree in 1934. Daley was elected to the Illinois House of Representatives in 1936 and for the next decade served there and in the state Senate. As a state legislator he earned a reputation for reliability and a sense of discretion. These qualities won him appointment as Cook County comptroller, a position which gave him access to politically sensitive material on patronage and public works contracts. In 1953 he became chairman of the Cook County Democratic Central Committee and thus head of the Democratic Party in Chicago. In 1955, aided by Congressman William L. Dawson (D, Ill.) [q.v.], the powerful representative from Chicago's black wards, Daley was able to secure the mayoral nomination over the protests of incumbent Martin Kennelly. Daley was elected mayor that year and had little difficulty winning reelection.

As party leader and chief executive, Daley controlled thousands of jobs at local, county and state levels. Those appointed under Daley's patronage provided the Democratic organization and the Mayor with an army of workers at election time. Daley also won the support of organized labor and the Chicago business and financial community with an ambitious building program, which included high-rise apartments and offices, schools, police stations, and O'Hare International Airport. Daley-built expressways provided thousands of construction jobs and when completed sped shoppers to downtown businesses. The Mayor was widely credited with revitalizing the Loop at a time when the downtowns of other American cities were in decay. [See EISENHOWER Volume]

In 1960 Daley came to prominence as a power broker in national politics. Controlling an estimated three-quarters of the 69 Illinois delegate votes at the Democratic National Convention, he rejected Adlai Stevenson's [q.v.] late bid for a third presidential nomination and helped secure the first ballot nomination for Sen. John F. Kennedy. In the tightly contested November general election, the Cook County Democratic organization worked hard to turn out the urban vote; it swung Illinois into the Democratic column by a bare 10,000 votes. Benjamin Adamowski, the losing Republican candidate for state's attorney, charged that "Daley has stolen the White House." A limited and incomplete recount reduced Kennedy's margin of victory but failed to give Richard M. Nixon [q.v.] the 27 Illinois electoral votes.

Critics of Daley such as Mike Royko of The Chicago Daily News acknowledged the Mayor's political influence but argued that throughout the 1960s Daley showed little interest in providing the new hospitals, housing and improved educational opportunities needed by the city's poor. The Mayor was also charged with thwarting efforts to integrate housing and directing his urban renewal programs against the poor, especially blacks. Daley nonetheless managed to win the black vote by cultivating and promoting loyal followers.

Increased federal aid to cities during the Kennedy and Johnson Administrations had the effect of strengthening Daley's citywide base of support. City Hall dominated the new antipoverty programs, controlled new jobs opportunities in the poor black wards for organization loyalists and distributed urban renewal projects.

In the late 1960s Daley found himself on the defensive as the social turmoil of the era made itself felt in Chicago. The city's black west side ghetto was the scene of extensive rioting, looting and arson in mid-July 1966. A month later when black demonstrators under Martin Luther King [q.v.] marched into white ethnic neighborhoods to protest the city's patterns of residential segregation they were assaulted and pelted with rocks and debris.

Two years later Daley became the center of national attention when critics charged that he condoned the police department's heavy-handed suppression of anti-war demonstrators at the 1968 Democratic National Convention. In July 1972 Daley was humiliated when the Democratic National Convention, dominated by supporters of Sen. George McGovern (D, S.D.) [q.v.], refused to seat him and his slate of delegates and voted instead to seat an insurgent group headed by a liberal Chicago alderman. Following McGovern's overwhelming defeat in the 1972 election, the Democratic Party began to adopt a more centrist position, and Daley regained considerable influence within the party. [See JOHNSON, NIXON Volumes]

[JLW]

For further information:
Mike Royko, *Boss: Richard J. Daley of Chicago* (New York, 1971).

DAWSON, WILLIAM L(EVI)

b. April 26, 1886; Albany, Ga.
d. Nov. 9, 1970; Chicago, Ill.
Democratic Representative, Ill., 1943-70; Chairman, Government Operations Committee, 1949-53; 1955-70.

A veteran of World War I and a graduate of Fiske (magna cum laude) and the Kent School of Law, Dawson was admitted to the Illinois bar in 1920. He practiced law in Chicago. Dawson began his political career as a Republican, serving six years (1933-39) as alderman from Chicago's South Side. In 1939 he became a Democrat, in part because his black constituents, traditionally Republican, were deserting the party of Lincoln for that of Franklin D. Roosevelt. In 1942 he was elected to Congress as a Democrat representing the largest black ghetto in America. Dawson was then the only black on Capitol Hill. In 1949 he became the first black to head a regular standing congressional committee. [See TRUMAN Volume]

During the 1940s Dawson developed a powerful organization throughout Chicago's black neighborhoods. He was the man to see for low-paying patronage jobs or for help with housing, welfare or legal problems. Voters in Chicago's black wards responded with overwhelming support for Dawson and his handpicked aldermen. According to Chuck Stone, a former editor of *The Chicago Defender,* the Dawson machine also received payoffs from the numbers racket, bookmaking operations and organized prostitution, which he permitted to flourish on the South Side. As an executive of the Cook County (Chicago) Democratic party who commanded thousands of votes, Dawson could determine the fate of white as well as black office-seekers. In 1955, angered by alleged police brutality and interference with the policy-wheel operators in black wards, Dawson spurned incumbent Mayor Martin Kennelly and threw his support to challenger Richard J. Daley [q.v.]. Daley became mayor, and the single most important factor in his subsequent reelection victories was overwhelming support from Dawson's wards. In 1963 Daley was reelected with a margin of 139,000 votes of which 115,000 came from the Dawson machine.

In Congress Dawson initially worked to outlaw the poll tax and segregation in the armed forces, but during the 1950s he became increasingly alienated from the emerging civil rights movement. In 1956, when black Congressman Adam Clayton Powell (D, N.Y.) [q.v.] proposed to deny federal funds to segregated schools, Dawson opposed the so-called "Powell Amendment" on the grounds that it would destroy the chances of any federal aid to education. [See EISENHOWER Volume].

During the Kennedy years Dawson voted with other northern urban Democrats for the Administration's basic social welfare legislation. As chairman of the House Government Operations Committee, Dawson held hearings in May and June of 1961 on an Administration bill creating a cabinet-level urban affairs and housing department. Dawson supported the bill, and in August his committee reported out a version favored by the Administration. In effect, the bill would have elevated black Housing and Home Finance Administrator Robert C. Weaver [q.v.] to the cabinet. It met with broad Southern and conservative opposition. The bill was held up in Rep. Howard W. Smith's (D, Va.) [q.v.] House Rules Committee in 1961 and a year later was defeated on the floor. A federal Department of Housing and Urban Development, headed by Weaver, was created only in 1965 as part of the Johnson Administration's Great Society program.

During 1963 Dawson, a member of the House District of Columbia Committee, opposed legislation favored by the majority to provide the District police with broad latitude in making arrests; the legislation also set minimum mandatory penalties for certain crimes. Dawson and other opponents of the measure suggested that it would deprive suspects of their constitutional rights. The legislation passed the House but did not come to a vote in the Senate.

Throughout the 1960s a number of young blacks attempted to unseat the aging Dawson, but despite his silence on civil rights, he defeated all primary challenges by margins of at least two-to-one. At his death at 84, he was unbeaten. Judgments of Dawson's career differed drastically. To black activist Stokely Carmichael and political scientist Charles V. Hamilton he was the classic Uncle Tom, "a tool of the white Democratic power structure." To Henry Moon of the New York chapter of the NAACP, Dawson "was able to get things done without ballyhoo, without outblacking

others" and was a man who found jobs and opened up political opportunities within the Democratic Party. [See JOHNSON Volume]

[JLW]

For further information:
Chuck Stone, *Black Political Power in America* (New York, 1968).

DAY, J(AMES) EDWARD
b. Oct. 11, 1914; Jacksonville, Ill.
Postmaster General, January 1961-August 1963.

After graduating with honors from Harvard Law School in 1938, J. Edward Day worked in Chicago for Sidley, Austin, Burgess, and Harper and then for Adlai Stevenson's [q.v.] law firm. When Stevenson was elected governor of Illinois in 1948, Day served first as his legislative assistant and later as state insurance commissioner. Day joined the Prudential Insurance Company in 1953 and four years later took charge of Prudential's Western operations in Los Angeles.

In December 1960 President Kennedy announced Day's appointment as Postmaster General, a post traditionally reserved for professional politicians. Day had been a strong Kennedy supporter in 1960 but had not played a crucial role in the election. According to Theodore Sorenson [q.v.], Kennedy's special counsel, Day was appointed because Kennedy realized that the Post Office Department needed a skilled administrator. Historian Arthur Schlesinger, Jr. [q.v.], explained that Day was appointed because Kennedy felt that he ought to have at least one cabinet member from the West Coast.

As Postmaster General, Day attempted to cut costs, raise revenues and speed service. He reduced expenses by eliminating a number of consultants hired by the Post Office, by cutting back on expensive commemorative issues and by dropping costly experimentation with facsimile mail. Day introduced non-stop, night-time jet air mail service between California and the East Coast, but the efficiency of mail delivery still left much to be desired. At a testimonial dinner for Day, Kennedy wired a message "to be certain that [it] reaches you in the right place and the right time."

To reduce the size of the Post Office deficit, Day raised the rates for foreign mail, money orders and special delivery. He could not, however, raise the rates for domestic mail service without congressional approval. Over the strong objections of mail order houses, newspaper and magazine publishers, Congress authorized increases in both postal rates and the salaries of postal workers in October 1962.

One provision of the new legislation directed the Post Office to intercept Communist "propaganda" mail originating from foreign countries. The Post Office was obliged to deliver such mail only if the addressee served notice that he wished to receive it. (The provision was limited in scope since sealed first class letters and mail sent to libraries and other institutions was exempted from all interference.) Day and Kennedy opposed this provision, but the President signed the bill to secure the postal and salary increases.

Kennedy and Day were publicly opposed to all interference with mail delivery. On March 17, 1961 the President had ordered the Post Office to abandon its program, in existence since the early 1950s, which entailed the interception and confiscation of Communist propaganda. What was not well-known was that the Central Intelligence Agency (CIA) continued a program begun several years earlier, not merely to intercept, but to open first-class letters sent to American citizens from the Soviet Union. Whether Postmaster Day knew of the CIA activity remained unclear as late as 1976. According to *The Report of the Presidential Commission on CIA Activities Within the United States* (1975), Day met with Richard Helms [q.v.], then CIA deputy director for plans, CIA Director Allen Dulles [q.v.] and one other CIA official on Feb. 15, 1961. According to Helms's memorandum of the meeting, the CIA representative told Day of "the background development, and current status [of the mail project], withholding no relevant details." Day, testifying before the House Committee on the Post Office and Civil Service in May 1975,

stated that he and Dulles had met and that Dulles told him he had something "very secret" to talk about. Day recalled telling Dulles that he would rather not know about the secret, and so Dulles did not tell him. A note, apparently written by the chief of the mail project in August 1971, suggested that Dulles may indeed have withheld information from Day.

Day's relations with the Kennedy Administration were not entirely cordial. According to Sorensen, Day had a tendency to make uncleared and uncalled-for public statements embarrassing to the Administration. In addition Sorensen alleged that Day was incapable of dealing with partisan political problems. In August 1963 Day resigned to return to practice law.

[JLW]

For further information:
Theodore Sorensen, *Kennedy* (New York, 1965).

DEAN, ARTHUR H(OBSON)
b. Oct. 16, 1898; Ithaca, N.Y.
Chairman, U.S. Delegation to the Conference on Discontinuance of Nuclear Weapons Tests, February 1961-January 1962; Chairman, U.S. Delegation to the 18 Nation Disarmament Conference, January 1962-February 1963.

After graduating from Cornell Law School in 1923 Dean joined the law firm of Sullivan and Cromwell in which John Foster Dulles was a senior partner. In 1953 Dean accompanied Secretary of State Dulles to Korea. Later that year he returned as Dulles's special deputy in an unsuccessful attempt to arrange negotiations with the North Koreans. In 1958 and 1960 Dean represented the U.S. at the Geneva conference on the law of the sea.

In February 1961 President Kennedy appointed Dean representative to the Geneva talks on ending nuclear weapon tests. Because Kennedy was anxious to involve the U.N. in disarmament he also made Dean a representative to the U.N. General Assembly.

During the Kennedy Administration Dean was U.S. spokesman at the many unproductive test ban meetings held between the Soviet Union, Great Britain and the United States at Geneva and the United Nations. More importantly, he served as presidential adviser on disarmament and wrote several important weapons limitation proposals offered at the international conferences. One of Dean's first tasks was to help draft the statute creating the Arms Control and Disarmament Agency formed in September 1961. This autonomous agency was founded to coordinate government policy on nuclear testing and disarmament.

Dean had been appointed representative to the Conference on Discontinuance of Nuclear Weapons Tests at a low point in that body's history. The negotiations had been recessed since December 1960 because of a Soviet walkout over the U-2 spy plane incident. Although progress had been made on many substantive issues involving testing in the atmosphere, at sea and at high altitudes, negotiations were deadlocked over the conditions for an underground test ban. The Eisenhower Administration had called for frequent on-site inspections of possible testing areas by teams composed of representatives of all three participating nuclear powers. In addition, it had insisted that inspections be reciprocal. Each investigation in the U.S. would require one in the USSR. The Soviet Union, on the other hand, maintained the right to veto proposed inspections and demanded that inspection teams be composed of nationals of the country to be investigated.

At Kennedy's insistence Dean made a broad survey and reassessment of the government's entire arms control policy. After carefully studying the record of negotiations, Dean drafted the first complete American test ban treaty proposal. This document made major concessions to the Soviet position. It reduced the number of required annual inspections and granted parity between the Communist and Western blocs on inspection teams. Equally important, the U.S. conceded that inspections would not have to be reciprocal. The treaty proposal, presented in Geneva in April 1961, was rejected by the Soviet Union, which was about to start a series of large-scale nuclear tests.

In September 1961 Dean helped President Kennedy draft his "Proposal for General and Complete Disarmament in a Peaceful World." This plan called not only for nuclear disarmament but also for the eventual reduction of conventional weapons, leaving nations only those forces necessary to maintain internal order. Primary stress was put on the elimination of delivery vehicles for atomic weapons and for reciprocal measures to lessen the risk of war by accident. The measure was first presented by the President to the United Nations in September. In revised form Dean presented it at Geneva in April 1962. The Soviet Union rejected the proposed treaty as "utterly unacceptable" and declared it was drawn up to "give the West a military advantage over the Communist bloc."

During the analysis of U.S. disarmament policy made in the summer of 1962, Dean, although initially favoring a total test ban treaty, backed Llewellyn Thompson's [q.v.] suggestion that the U.S. should consider offering the Soviet Union a limited treaty. This proposal, backed by the U.S. Arms Control and Disarmament Agency, was adopted by the President. On Aug. 27, 1962, Dean tabled two plans in Geneva. One a partial, unsupervised ban covered high altitude, sea and atmospheric tests. The other was a comprehensive treaty which included provisions for on-site inspections. At the insistence of Dean the number of inspections was dropped from approximately 20 to 7 or 8. Both treaties were denounced by the Soviet Union, which wished to continue its testing series. Private talks on the issue continued between Dean and the Russian representative, Vasily Kuznetzov, during the winter but they remained stalemated on the number of inspections; the Russians wanted to drop the number to three per year.

Dean was not involved in the final negotiations that led to the signing of a partial nuclear test ban treaty in August 1963. In June 1963 Premier Nikita Khrushchev accepted Kennedy's suggestion that future disarmament talks be carried on through the leaders' personal emissaries in Moscow. Kennedy appointed Undersecretary of State for Political Affairs W. Averell Harriman

[*q.v.*] to head the U.S. delegation. By the end of July Harriman had arranged a partial test ban treaty initialed by both nations.

Dean returned to private law practice in February 1963. In July 1964 he was appointed chairman of the National Citizens Committee for Community Relations, an advisory committee formed to aid the director of the Community Relations Service in overseeing compliance with the Civil Rights Act of 1964. In the same year he became a member of a nonpartisan citizens panel formed to advise the President on foreign affairs and another panel created to study ways of halting the spread of nuclear weapons.

In March 1968 Johnson asked Dean to become a member of the Senior Advisory Group on Vietnam, convened to consider the military's request for over 200,000 more troops for Vietnam. The panel recommended rejection of the request and the de-escalation of the war. Johnson announced this change in policy on March 31, 1968.

[EWS]

For further information:
E(edson) L(ouis) M(illard) Burns, *A Seat at the Table* (Toronto, 1972).
Arthur Dean, *Test Ban and Disarmament; The Path of Negotiation* (New York, 1966).
Harold K. Jacobson, *Diplomats, Scientists and Politicians* (Ann Arbor, 1966).
Mary Milling Lepper, *Foreign Policy Formulation* (Columbus, 1971).

DELANEY, JAMES J.
b. March 19, 1901; New York, N.Y.
Democratic Representative, N.Y., 1945-   .

In 1932 Delaney received his law degree from St. John's University in New York City. From 1936 to 1944 he served as assistant district attorney of that borough. He was elected to Congress in 1945 from a district that included industrial areas such as Long Island City as well as tightly knit, overwhelmingly white residential neighborhoods with a large proportion of immigrant Catholics. In Congress Delaney built up a moderately liberal voting record. A con-sistent party regular, he acquired seniority on the powerful House Rules Committee.

Although he supported most of the Kennedy Administration's legislative program, Delaney played a crucial role in helping block Kennedy's 1961 aid-to-education bill. The measure called for grants of $2.3 billion for classroom construction and loans of $2.8 billion for colleges, but it excluded aid to private or parochial schools. The bill faced strong opposition from the Roman Catholic hierarchy, and Delaney generally represented their point of view on the issue in the Congress. Hoping to conciliate Catholics and others who favored aid to private schools, the Administration also sent Congress proposals for extending the National Defense Education Act (NDEA) of 1958, which provided for loans to private schools. However, Delaney feared that the NDEA extension would be defeated if it reached the House floor after the public-school aid bill had passed. In June, therefore, he joined the Rules Committee's five Republicans and two Southern Democrats in voting to withhold floor action on the public school bill until after the NDEA bill was reported. On July 18 he again joined conservatives on the Rules Committee, this time voting to table both education bills as well as a college aid bill. Proponents of the school aid bill invoked the rarely-used "Calendar Wednesday" procedure, which allowed committee chairman to call bills that had not been approved by the Rules Committee, but the compromise measure they put forth was soundly defeated by a coalition of Republicans, Southern Democrats and Catholic Democrats. In September Congress voted to extend NDEA.

In the late 1960s Delaney grew increasingly conservative. He supported Johnson and Nixon Administration Vietnam war policies, and by 1971 his ADA rating, which had averaged 82% in the 1960s, fell to 24%. In the 1970 congressional race Delaney won the endorsement of New York's growing Conservative Party. In 1972 he survived a primary challenge from a more liberal Democrat, and in 1974 he was reelected with 93% of the vote.

[MDB]

DEMPSEY, JOHN (NOEL)
b. Jan. 3, 1915; Cahir, Ireland
Governor, Conn., 1961-71.

John Dempsey, the first foreign-born governor of Connecticut in modern history, immigrated to that state from Ireland at the age of 10. Dempsey attended local public schools and spent one year at Providence College. At the age of 22 he entered politics, winning election as an alderman in his home town of Putnam, Conn. During the mid-1940s he served on the Connecticut Development Commission and acted as executive secretary for Rep. Chase Going Woodhouse (D). In 1947 Dempsey made an unsuccessful bid for lieutenant governor but won the office four years later. When Gov. Abraham Ribicoff [q.v.] joined John F. Kennedy's cabinet as Secretary of Health Education and Welfare in 1961, Dempsey became governor. He was elected in his own right in 1962.

During his tenure the previously little-known machine politician emerged as a progressive figure urging urban renewal, increased aid to education, expanded programs for juvenile delinquents and the mentally ill and assistance for the state's major commuter railroads. However, many of his proposals met with defeat because of opposition from a generally hostile legislature afraid of rising state expenditures.

Among state governors Dempsey was a leading proponent of civil rights legislation. During the massive Birmingham demonstrations in May 1963, Dempsey wired Alabama Gov. George Wallace [q.v.] to express his "deep dismay" over police attacks on black marchers there. (Wallace replied by wire the next day, "Mind your own affairs.") Two months later the National Governors Conference adopted, by a 38-3 vote, a compromise resolution introduced by Dempsey to give "top priority" to the civil rights issue. During the same month Dempsey signed into law a state bill banning discrimination in the sale of all housing and in all rentals except in owner-occupied, two-family dwellings, However, the statute was weaker than one originally proposed by the Governor that would have barred discrimination in all sales and rentals

and authorized the use of injunctions for enforcement.

In 1971 Dempsey retired from office. That year he became a consultant on environmental programs for the Southern New England Telephone Company. [See Johnson Volume]

[EWS]

DeSAPIO, CARMINE G(ERARD)
b. Dec. 10, 1908; New York, N.Y.
New York County Democratic Committee Chairman, 1949-61; New York National Democratic Committeeman, 1954-64.

After a political apprenticeship in New York's Greenwich Village under Sheriff Daniel E. Finn, Jr., DeSapio broke with his mentor and in 1943 won a seat on the executive committee of Tammany Hall, New York County's Democratic organization. In 1946 DeSapio was elected by the New York City Council to the city-wide Board of Elections and the next year was part of a group of four that took over effective leadership of Tammany Hall. Three years later he became sole head of Tammany in name and fact. According to a biography by Warren Moscow, DeSapio rose to power with the acquiescence of organized crime figures then powerful in the Manhattan Democratic Party, but as Tammany leader he advocated internal party reform, gave increased power to black and Puerto Rican political leaders and supported liberal social legislation. In 1953 DeSapio joined Bronx County leader Edward J. Flynn in backing Robert F. Wagner's [q.v.] primary challenge to incumbent Mayor Vincent R. Impelliteri. Wagner's victory and Flynn's death made DeSapio the leader of the party in both New York City and State. After DeSapio's candidate for governor, W. Averell Harriman [q.v.], was elected in 1954, DeSapio was appointed secretary of state, and became, according to Moscow, "possibly the most powerful political boss of recent times."

Harriman and DeSapio disagreed over the choice of a candidate for U.S. Senate at the

1958 state convention in Buffalo. DeSapio's candidate, Manhattan District Attorney Frank S. Hogan, was nominated after a floor fight, but along with Harriman he was defeated in the November balloting. Following the election, Thomas K. Finletter [q.v.], who had also sought the Senate nomination, Herbert H. Lehman [q.v.] and Eleanor Roosevelt [q.v.] formed the Committee for Democratic Voters, which united various reform groups and worked for DeSapio's ouster as party leader. [See EISENHOWER Volume]

DeSapio hoped to play a major role in the 1960 presidential nomination by keeping the New York state delegation neutral and then using its votes at the convention to provide the winning margin for some candidate. However, without DeSapio's knowledge Kennedy campaign aide John M. Bailey [q.v.] recruited a large number of upstate New York delegates, while Kennedy's father, Joseph P. Kennedy, did the same in the Bronx and Queens. DeSapio was thus forced to come out for Kennedy before the convention. His inability to control the New York delegation diminished his prestige and power. The new Kennedy Administration was willing to work with DeSapio, but Bailey demanded the ouster of New York State Democratic Chairman Michael H. Prendergast, who had reneged on an agreement with Kennedy during the campaign to allow Lehman to speak at a Kennedy rally. DeSapio refused to remove Prendergast, and thereafter DeSapio was denied control over federal patronage in New York State.

In 1961 Wagner broke with DeSapio and accepted the support of the increasingly powerful New York Democratic reform movement in his mayoral reelection bid. DeSapio and the other county leaders ran a slate headed by New York State Controller Arthur Levitt against Wagner in the September primary. Wagner made "bossism" the main campaign issue. In his own district, DeSapio was challenged for the district leadership by James E. Lanigan, a former Stevenson campaign aide backed by Stevenson, Lehman and Eleanor Roosevelt. In a record primary turnout, Wagner defeated Levitt by a three to two margin and DeSapio was defeated 6,165 to 4,245. Since only district leaders were eligible to serve as county leader,

under rules DeSapio himself wrote, DeSapio lost all his party posts except national committeeman, which he retained until 1964. In 1963 Lanigan chose not to run for reelection, and DeSapio ran against reform leader Edward R. Koch. DeSapio lost the September primary by 41 votes, but successfully challenged the election in court. However, he lost a new election against Koch in June 1964, 5,904 to 5,470. DeSapio failed in a final attempt to win back his district leadership in 1965.

On Dec. 13, 1969 DeSapio was convicted by a federal jury of having conspired to induce a public official to misuse his office in return for a cash bribe. The case involved New York Department of Water Supply Commissioner James L. Marcus, federal informer Herbert Itkin, a New York contractor and officials of Con Edison. After serving a 17-month sentence in the federal prison in Lewisburg, Pa., DeSapio was released in December 1972.

[JBF]

For further information:
Warren Moscow, *The Last of the Big-Time Bosses: The Life and Times of Carmine DeSapio and the Decline and Fall of Tammany Hall* (New York, 1971).

DILLON, C(LARENCE) DOUGLAS
b. Aug. 21, 1909; Geneva, Switzerland. Secretary of the Treasury, January 1961-March 1965.

C. Douglas Dillon was the most influential member of President Kennedy's economic policy-making team. His success in persuading the President that the nation's most pressing economic problem was the balance of payments deficit steered Administration policy along a moderate course and ruled out more adventurous liberal solutions to domestic problems.

Dillon came from a wealthy social background similar to that of Kennedy. His father made a fortune on Wall Street, building the firm of Dillon, Read & Company into one of the country's largest investment banks. Dillon attended Groton and Harvard before his father bought him a seat on the New York Stock Exchange for

$185,000 in 1931. After serving an apprenticeship with some smaller investment houses, he joined Dillon, Read as a vice president in 1938. He followed the company's president, James Forrestal, into the Navy Department in 1940 and saw action in the Pacific toward the end of the war.

As chairman of the board of Dillon, Read after the war, Dillon supervised the firm's far-flung domestic and foreign holdings and doubled its investment portfolio in six years. He was an active Republican, working with John Foster Dulles in the 1948 presidential campaign of Gov. Thomas E. Dewey and initiating a "draft Eisenhower" movement in New Jersey in 1951. In 1953 Eisenhower appointed Dillon ambassador to France, where he served until 1957, when Dulles recalled him to Washington to become undersecretary of state for economic affairs. He contributed heavily to the Republican presidential candidate, Vice President Richard M. Nixon [q.v.], in 1960 and was considered a natural appointment to a Nixon cabinet. [See EISENHOWER Volume]

President Kennedy's selection of Dillon as Secretary of the Treasury in January 1961 was an expression of his own deep concern with the balance of payments deficit and the resulting "gold drain." By placing a "sound money" man with Dillon's Wall Street, solidly Republican credentials in the top financial post of his Administration, Kennedy intended to reassure the financial community, which was apprehensive about the "easy money" proclivities of the incoming Democratic Administration. "The need for world confidence in the dollar, and the danger of a 'run on the bank' by dollar holders," said Theodore Sorenson [q.v.] in Kennedy, "were the decisive influence in his [the President's] choice of a Secretary of the Treasury."

Kennedy, moreover, shared Dillon's moderately conservative outlook on economic matters at the time of his appointment. Throughout the Kennedy Administration Dillon enjoyed easy access to the President and was one of Kennedy's few political associates who socialized with him as well.

The preoccupation of Kennedy and Dillon with the balance of payments question exerted a strong conservative pull on the Administration's overall economic policy. Swelling annual payments deficits since the late 1950s had left large deposits of dollars in the hands of foreigners, whose recurrent loss of "confidence" in the dollar's value led them to trade in dollars for American gold, the value of which was then fixed in relation to the dollar. The resulting "gold drain" alarmed the financial community and both the Kennedy and Johnson Administrations.

Anxious to solidify the standing of the dollar and stem the gold outflow, the Kennedy Administration tended to rule out economic initiatives that might increase inflation and thus undermine foreigners' confidence in the dollar. In the first two years of the Kennedy Administration, Dillon's success in maintaining the priority status of the payments deficit blocked the path of more aggressive fiscal and monetary stimulation of the economy or heavier spending on social programs.

The chief advocate of the latter approach within the Kennedy Administration was Walter W. Heller [q.v.], chairman of the President's Council of Economic Advisers (CEA). Heller and Dillon represented the two major opposing poles of economic thought in the Administration's policy-making councils. Heller advocated the active promotion of economic growth by the federal government employing the Keynesian techniques of fiscal stimulation via spending and tax cuts. Dillon voiced the Treasury's traditional opposition to deficit spending and generally resisted unorthodox proposals emanating from the CEA.

For the most part President Kennedy chose Dillon's cautious strategy over Heller's activist approach. Kennedy's decision in May 1961 not to recommend the substantial public works program urged by Heller and Secretary of Labor Arthur Goldberg [q.v.] was an important early victory for Dillon. In the jockeying over the size of the fiscal 1963 budget, Dillon's argument that another large deficit on top of the $7-billion deficit for fiscal 1962 might spark another crisis of confidence in the dollar won from Kennedy a pledge to keep the 1963 budget "strictly in balance." This resolve signified defeat for the CEA's expansionary fiscal strategy and left no room for increasing social welfare expenditures, since the Administration sought larger appropriations only in the areas of defense and space exploration. (As it turned out, the 1963 budget contained a $6.2 billion deficit.) For almost two years Dillon also succeeded in blocking Heller's proposal for a sizable tax cut. Later he joined President Kennedy in favoring the $10 billion fiscal stimulus.

A proponent of tax reform, Dillon oversaw the Treasury's formulation of a reform package in 1961 and 1962 and defended the program before Congress in 1962. He argued for Treasury proposals to withhold taxes on interest and dividend income, a device to curb widespread tax evasion, and advocated closing loopholes for foreign "tax haven" corporations and for businessmen deducting entertainment expenses. Much of the Administration's reform program was rejected or eliminated by Congress in the summer of 1962, but Dillon and the Administration endorsed the final package because it contained the feature they considered most important, the 7% investment tax credit.

Dillon said the tax credit was essential in order to enable American industry to modernize its plant and equipment and to bring it "abreast of its foreign competitors." Dillon also sponsored the Treasury's liberalization of depreciation guidelines, designed to permit businesses to claim greater tax deductions for depreciation of equipment and machinery. These guidelines, long sought by business, were promulgated by the Treasury in the summer of 1962. The investment credit and the changes in the depreciation timetables restored roughly $2.2 billion to corporate treasuries.

Together with the resourceful Undersecretary of the Treasury for Monetary Affairs Robert V. Roosa [q.v.], Dillon devised a complex series of measures to counteract the balance of payments deficit and the outflow of gold. Among the monetary solutions they tried were the prepayment of debts owed by European nations and the accumulation of foreign currencies by the Treasury to facilitate currency "swaps" during times of speculative pressure on the dollar. Controlling inflation and encouraging exports were broader elements in the balance of payments strategy. Dillon backed the Trade Expansion Act of 1962, which was designed to invigorate U.S. foreign trade by giving the President discretionary tariff-cutting authority.

Despite confident predictions by Dillon and Roosa in the fall of 1962 that the U.S. payments deficit would be eliminated by the end of 1963, the annual deficits continued unabated. In the summer of 1963 they advocated further steps: a rise in the Federal Reserve Board's discount rate and an "interest equalization tax." The increase in the discount rate from 3% to 3½% occurred in July 1963. Dillon, Roosa, and William McChesney Martin [q.v.], chairman of the Federal Reserve Board, hoped that the increase would forestall a flight of capital from the U.S. towards higher interest rates abroad. The "interest equalization tax" was a levy on foreign securities sold in the U.S., making it more expensive for foreigners to borrow in the U.S.

The Dillon-Roosa balance of payments strategy encountered opposition within the Administration. Their agile monetary maneuvers within a framework of traditional economics were substitutes for the sweeping reform of the international monetary system advocated by Heller and James Tobin on the CEA and also by individuals within the State Department. The monetary reformers advocated establishing a new international mechanism with the resources to expand international liquidity. Dillon and Roosa spearheaded the Treasury's opposition to such a scheme, denying that there was a serious liquidity shortage and arguing against any arrangement that involved a loss of sovereignty by the U.S. Dillon's adeptness at setting up roadblocks to ideas opposed by the Treasury became known as "dillontory" tactics around Washington. Sorenson recalled that Kennedy once remarked to Dillon, "The Treasury is very skillful at shooting down every balloon floated elsewhere in the Administration."

The Dillon-Roosa-Martin group likewise overcame efforts by Heller and Tobin to win Kennedy's support for lower short-term interest rates. The CEA believed that lower interest rates would stimulate the economy by making capital more available. In its view a strong economy would do more to arrest the balance of payments deficit than anti-inflationary measures.

Kennedy also used Dillon for foreign policy assignments. He made Dillon head of the American delegation sent to Punta del Este, Uruguay, to inaugurate the Alliance for Progress in August 1961. There Dillon pledged $20 billion in low-interest loans over the next 10 years to improve Latin America's living standards. "We welcome the revolution of rising expectations," Dillon said, "and we intend to transform it into a revolution of rising satisfactions." Dillon also sat on the National Security Council and took part in the tense deliberations during the Cuban missile crisis of October 1963.

Dillon's most significant shift in office was his conversion to Heller's view that sweeping tax cuts were needed to promote economic growth. By late 1962 Dillon had accepted the argument that high taxes were placing "shackles" on the economy. His evolution on the subject roughly paralleled President Kennedy's own developing views in favor of tax reductions. Nevertheless, Dillon still exerted a powerful restraining influence on the impact of the cut. Fearful that the budget deficit might become unmanageable if taxes were reduced by $10 billion at once, Dillon convinced Kennedy to spread the tax cut over three years. "To do it all at once and have a tremendous deficit," Dillon told the Advertising Council in March 1963, "would not inspire confidence in the rest of the world and could be very dangerous for our balance of payments."

Dillon further acted to brake the tax cut's fiscal momentum by insisting on revenue-raising reforms and a rigorous spending-control policy to accompany the reductions. He worked strenuously throughout 1963 to win passage of the Kennedy tax cut, defending the cut and the reforms before congressional committees. In the reform package Dillon placed special emphasis on a proposed 5% floor to be placed under all personal itemized deductions, a revision designed to recoup $2.3 billion for the Treasury. He also defended the Kennedy tax program before business audiences, and along with Treasury Undersecretary Henry Fowler [q.v.], prodded influential businessmen to form the Business Committee for Tax Reduction in 1963.

The Administration sacrificed the reforms, including the 5% floor, in the summer of 1963 in order to win passage in the House of a tax cut totaling $11.2 billion. The bill did not pass the Senate until after President Kennedy's death. In February 1964 President Johnson signed an $11.5 billion tax reduction, which cut personal income tax rates from the existing range of 20%-91% to 14%-70% and cut the corporate income tax from 52% to 48%.

Dillon retired as Treasury Secretary in March 1965. [See JOHNSON Volume]

[TO]

For further information:
E. Ray Canterbery, *Economics on a New Frontier* (Belmont, 1968).
Seymour Harris, *Economics of the Kennedy Years* (New York, 1964).
Hobart Rowen, *The Free Enterprisers: Kennedy, Johnson and the Business Establishment* (New York, 1964).

DILWORTH, RICHARDSON
b. Aug. 29, 1898; Pittsburgh, Pa.
Mayor, Philadelphia, Pa., January 1956-January 1962.

Born into an old Pittsburgh family, Dilworth earned A.B. and LL.B. degrees from Yale. His career as a Philadelphia trial lawyer, begun in 1927, was interrupted by war service in the Pacific theater. After the war Dilworth decided to enter reform politics in his adopted city as a Democrat, since the entrenched machine that dominated Philadelphia was Republican. Although Dilworth lost his bid for the mayoralty in 1947, he won election as city treasurer in 1949.

After an unsuccessful race for the governorship in 1950, Dilworth was elected district attorney in 1951 at the same time that his political ally and friend, Joseph Clark

[q.v.], became mayor. Together they initiated the longest reform period in Philadelphia's history. Dilworth succeeded Clark in 1955 and won reelection in 1959. Under the Clark-Dilworth administration Philadelphia reorganized its government, began to coordinate metropolitan public transportation, encouraged new industry and undertook large-scale programs in urban renewal and public housing. [See EISENHOWER Volume]

As a well-known liberal and as president of the U.S. Conference of Mayors, Dilworth spoke out nationally for the needs of cities. Testifying before the Senate Banking and Currency Subcommittee on Housing in April 1961, Dilworth endorsed a Kennedy-backed, four-year slum clearance program, but emphasized that he preferred a 10-year program and an increase in the federal share of urban renewal expenses from two-thirds to 80%. Dilworth was one of the first public officials to assert that, with a shrinking tax base, the cities required more federal aid. He was also a vocal supporter of Kennedy's plan to create a new cabinet-level department for housing and urban affairs.

As a result of a Philadelphia law which he had strongly supported, Dilworth was forced to resign as mayor when he announced his gubernatorial candidacy in January 1962. His candidacy was opposed by Rep. William Green, Jr. (D, Pa.) [q.v.], leader of the Philadelphia organization, but was backed by the statewide organization and by President Kennedy, who felt that he needed continued Democratic control of the state to ensure his reelection in 1964. Dilworth faced freshman Rep. William Scranton (R, Pa.) [q.v.] in the general election. The Scranton campaign capitalized on Dilworth's short temper and his penchant for making unequivocal statements on sensitive political issues. In addition, revelations of corruption in some Philadelphia agencies reflected badly on Dilworth, whose previous municipal campaigns had stressed honesty in government. Scranton defeated Dilworth with 55% of the vote in the November balloting, despite a Democratic edge in statewide voter registration.

After the 1962 elections Dilworth remained active in Philadelphia's business and civic circles. In 1965 his successor, Mayor James Tate, named him president of the Philadelphia School Board. Intent on instituting progressive educational reforms and answering the needs and demands of the city's black population, Dilworth came into conflict with the once reform-minded Tate and conservative police commissioner Frank Rizzo. Disturbed by the deterioration of Philadelphia's reform movement, Dilworth resigned from the school board in July 1971 in order to take a more active role in the city's political life and campaign against Rizzo, who was making his first, successful bid for mayor on the Democratic ticket.

[JCH]

For further information:
Kirk R. Petshak, *The Challenge of Urban Reform: Policies and Programs in Philadelphia* (Philadelphia, 1973).

DIRKSEN, EVERETT McKINLEY
b. Jan. 4, 1895; Pekin, Ill.
d. Sept. 7, 1969; Washington, D. C.
Republican Senator, Ill., 1951-69;
Senate Minority Leader, 1959-69.

Everett McKinley Dirksen grew up on his family's farm and attended the University of Minnesota. During World War I he served in the balloon corps, conducting air reconnaissance for the Army artillery. He returned to Pekin following the armistice and in 1932 won election to the House of Representatives as a Republican where he served until 1948. Dirksen generally supported his party's Eastern, internationalist wing. He endorsed Roosevelt's foreign policy on the eve of Pearl Harbor and played a key role in the passage of the first Marshall Plan appropriations in 1947.

Dirksen won an upset victory for the U. S. Senate in 1950. He allied himself with Sen. Joseph R. McCarthy, Jr. (R, Wisc.) and endorsed his frequent charges that Communists remained in the State Department. At the 1952 Republican National Convention, Dirksen bitterly denounced Gov. Thomas E. Dewey (R, N.Y.), leader of the presidential campaign of Gen. Dwight D. Eisenhower. In 1954 he supported the Bricker Amendment (to restrict the treaty-making powers of the President), which the Eisenhower Administration opposed, and voted against the censure of McCarthy.

Sponsored by the powerful conservative leader Sen. Styles Bridges (R, N.H.) [q.v.], Dirksen became Senate minority whip in January 1957, the party's second ranking position in the upper chamber. Two years later he won election as minority leader by defeating the liberal-moderate candidate John Sherman Cooper (R, Ky.) [q.v.]. Although the Democrats had won overwhelming majorities in both houses as a result of the 1958 elections, Dirksen frustrated the ambitious legislative program of Senate Majority Leader Lyndon B. Johnson (D, Tex.) [q.v.]. Despite his early opposition to Eisenhower, he proved an effective and loyal legislative leader. Dirksen established an unusual degree of party unity among his Republican colleagues, giving up his own choice committee assignments to younger or more liberal members, and employing flattery rather than threats to those reluctant to vote with the leadership. [See TRUMAN, EISENHOWER Volumes]

The Republicans' loss of the White House left Dirksen as the single most powerful GOP leader in Washington. The Senate leader played both a partisan and cooperative role with the new Administration. He frequently condemned the President's domestic policies in characteristically flowery prose and in an easily recognized, husky voice. "It may be called the New Frontier," he remarked in May 1961, "but the Kennedy program is the old New Deal taken out of an old warming oven." At the suggestion of former President Eisenhower, Dirksen and House Minority Leader Charles A. Halleck (R, Ind.) [q.v.] began a weekly review of Kennedy Administration policies, dubbed the "Ev and Charlie Show" by Washington journalists.

Dirksen led the Republican minority in defeating the Administration's proposals for an Urban Affairs Department, a new farm bill and school construction authorization. A fervent opponent of governmental regulation of business, Dirksen played an adversary role in the investigation chaired by Sen. Estes Kefauver (D, Tenn.) [q.v.] into the pricing policies of the drug industry. Dirksen fought Kefauver's efforts to increase regulation of drug companies and denounced his subcommittee's final report as a "monstrosity" in March 1962.

Dirksen consistently displayed a bipartisan attitude towards the Administration's foreign policy initiatives. In April 1961 he opposed Republican attacks on the White House for its role in the disastrous Bay of Pigs invasion and he strongly endorsed the President's policies in Laos and Berlin. The Illinois Republican continued to support foreign aid requests by the White House and worked for the Treasury Department purchase of $100 million worth of United Nations bonds in April 1962. More partisan Republican leaders, however, did not always approve of Dirksen's cooperative attitude. National Committee Chairman Rep. William E. Miller (R, N.Y. [q.v.] reportedly remarked that after Dirksen attended a White House foreign policy briefing, "He comes out with stars in his eyes, and there's nothing you can do with him." Sen. Barry M. Goldwater (R, Ariz.) [q.v.] termed Dirksen's stand on the U.N. bond issue "a surrender" while colleague Homer Capehart (R, Ind.) [q.v.] accused Dirksen of granting Kennedy "a blank check" over the same issue.

Dirksen's unqualified endorsement of Kennedy's foreign policy, however, did not go unrewarded. Amidst a close contest for re-election in October 1962, Dirksen received a presidential summons to Washington for a congressional briefing on the Cuban missile crisis. When senators advised the President to invade the Caribbean island and destroy missile sites, Dirksen helped end the debate when he inquired of Defense Secretary Robert S. McNamara [q.v.] about the casualty rate in such an attack. McNamara's estimates, heavy both in men and material, helped bolster the President's plan merely to blockade the island. Immediately following the meeting, Dirksen and other Republican congressional leaders drafted a statement endorsing Kennedy's action. A few days later, the President told Dirksen that he fully expected him to win reelection, a prediction which the Republican leader subsequently leaked to the press and which hampered the final stage of his Democratic opponent's campaign. Dirksen won reelection in 1962 with 52.9% of the vote.

The Kennedy Administration's negotiation of a nuclear test ban treaty with the Soviet Union in July 1963 presented Dirksen with the greatest single challenge to his bipartisan foreign policy commitment. Although public opinion surveys indicated strong support for the Treaty of Moscow, Dirksen initially opposed the agreement. When it became apparent that the opposition of powerful Democratic Sens. Richard Russell (D, Ga.) [q.v.] and John Stennis (D, Miss.) [q.v.] jeopardized Senate ratification of the treaty, the White House actively sought Dirksen's assistance. The Republican leader endorsed the treaty upon receiving the President's "unqualified and unequivocal assurances" that Kennedy would continue to support weapons development. Dirksen's position prevented Republican defections and countered the opposition of Russell and Stennis, assuring passage. By a vote of 80 to 19, the Senate ratified the Treaty of Moscow in September 1963 with only eight Republican votes against the pact compared to 11 nays by Democratic members.

Dirksen and Senate Majority Leader Mike Mansfield (D, Mont.) [q.v.] introduced an omnibus civil rights bill in June 1963. Their proposal included the right of a government agency to cut off federal funds to any state or institution which refused to comply with desegregation guidelines. Dirksen declined to support the President's request for a federal guarantee to blacks of the right to use all public accommodations, a provision he opposed on constitutional grounds and excluded from his bill.

However, during the legislative maneuvering over what became the Civil Rights Act of 1964, Dirksen changed his position on public accommodations. Seven months after Kennedy's death, Congress passed the first comprehensive civil rights measure since Reconstruction. During the Johnson years, Dirksen aided the Administration in the enactment of additional civil rights legislation while opposing most of the "Great Society" program. He endorsed Johnson's Vietnam policy and remained minority leader until his death in September 1969. [See JOHNSON, NIXON Volumes]

[JLB]

For further information:
Neil MacNeil, *Dirksen: Portrait of a Public Man* (New York, 1970).

DiSALLE, MICHAEL V(INCENT)
b. Jan. 6, 1908; New York, N.Y. Governor, Ohio, 1959-63.

At the age of three, Michael V. DiSalle moved to Toledo, Ohio from New York with his Italian immigrant parents. After studying law at Georgetown University, DiSalle began his career in local Democratic politics. The Toledo City Council appointed him mayor in 1947. He resigned in 1951 to serve under President Truman as Director of Price Stabilization, leaving Washington in 1952 to wage an unsuccessful campaign for the U. S. Senate against incumbent John W. Bricker (R, Ohio). Four years later, DiSalle lost the gubernatorial election to state Attorney General C. William O'Neill. In 1958, however, conservative business leaders placed a controversial referendum on the ballot to outlaw "closed" union-shop contracts under Section 14(b) of the Taft-Hartley Act. Aided by a large Democratic turnout generated by the state AFL-CIO, DiSalle defeated O'Neill in November 1958. [See EISENHOWER Volume]

As the Democratic governor of a large state, DiSalle played a key role in the nomination of Sen. John F. Kennedy at the 1960 Democratic convention. Kennedy wanted Ohio's 64 delegate votes and threatened to oppose the Governor in the state primary if DiSalle failed to endorse his candidacy. The Ohio Democratic leader had opposed Kennedy for the Democratic vice presidential nomination in 1956 and had held informal talks in 1959 with Sen. Stuart Symington (D, Mo.) [q.v.], another contender for the party's top prize. Withdrawing from a tentative commitment to the Kennedy forces in late 1959, DiSalle claimed that his endorsement of the Massachusetts senator early in the campaign would disrupt state party unity, possibly provoke a primary challenge from popular Sen. Frank J. Lausche (D, Ohio) [q.v.] or appear insignificant due to the governor's own Catholicism. In addition, DiSalle feared the wrath of his former boss, Harry S Truman [q.v.], who vehemently opposed Kennedy. Kennedy, however, was adamant about Ohio. His brother and campaign manager, Robert F. Kennedy [q.v.], reiterated their threat to precipitate a Kennedy-DiSalle primary battle and added that the Ohio Kennedy forces would oppose the Governor in an upcoming fight over control of the state party leadership. DiSalle finally relented in January 1960 and announced that he would run as a favorite son in favor of Kennedy.

Kennedy received the unanimous vote of the Ohio delegation at the Democratic National Convention thus helping to assure his first ballot nomination. Along with other important supporters, DiSalle encouraged Kennedy in his selection of Sen. Lyndon B. Johnson (D, Tex.) [q.v.] for the vice-presidential nomination. Although Kennedy campaigned extensively in Ohio, the state proved a disappointment in November when the efficient Ohio Republican organization reasserted its electoral supremacy by defeating the Kennedy-Johnson ticket with 53.3% of the vote.

DiSalle's performance as governor had in part contributed to Kennedy's failure to carry the state. In 1959 DiSalle inherited a huge budget deficit from his predecessors and raised the state sales tax, always an unpopular practice with Ohio voters. Republicans recaptured control of the state legislature in 1960 and the Democratic governor spent the remaining two years of his term locked in a prolonged argument over the state budget. A liberal Democrat in a normally Republican state, DiSalle proved a highly vulnerable candidate for reelection in 1962. In one of the state's most bitter gubernatorial contests, DiSalle accused his Republican opponent, State Auditor James A. Rhodes of misusing state and GOP funds. Rhodes, who promised not to raise taxes, defeated DiSalle by a record 555,669 vote margin.

In the aftermath of defeat, DiSalle resumed his law practice and published two books in 1966. In *The Power of Life or Death*, DiSalle

called for the abolition of capital punishment. (As governor, DiSalle had hired convicted murderers to work as household employes at the governor's mansion.) *Second Choice* combined a history of the vice presidency with some of DiSalle's own experiences in national Democratic politics. In July 1968 the former governor suddenly emerged as the official spokesman of the campaign to draft Sen. Edward M. Kennedy (D, Mass.) [q.v.] for President. On July 14 DiSalle announced that he planned to nominate Kennedy without his approval. The former governor established a Kennedy headquarters in his cramped hotel suite at the Democratic National convention in Chicago a month later. Kennedy, however, persuaded DiSalle not to make a nominating address and the move to draft the Massachusetts senator collapsed.

[JLB]

For further information:
Michael V. DiSalle, *Second Choice* (New York, 1966).

DIXON, PAUL RAND(ALL)
b. Sept. 29, 1913; Nashville, Tenn.
Chairman, Federal Trade Commission, February 1961-December 1969.

Paul Rand Dixon attended Vanderbilt University and received his law degree from the University of Florida in 1938. He immediately joined the staff of the Federal Trade Commission (FTC) as a trial attorney. Except for naval service during World War II, Dixon stayed with the Commission until 1957, when he was named chief counsel and staff director of Sen. Estes Kefauver's (D, Tenn.) [q.v.] Antitrust and Antimonopoly Subcommittee. Under Kefauver and Dixon the subcommittee carried out a number of highly publicized investigations of big business abuses, most notably price-fixing by drug companies and identical bidding by manufacturers of heavy electrical equipment. The Justice Department followed up the latter study, obtaining convictions against 45 of the colluding executives, seven of whom received jail terms in the most spectacular business scandal of the decade. Sponsored by

Kefauver, Dixon was appointed chairman of the FTC by President Kennedy in February 1961.

In the Clayton Act of 1914, Congress had given the FTC general responsibility for policing the market economy. The Commission was empowered to put a stop to "unfair trade practices" by means of "cease-and-desist" orders. The Celler-Kefauver Act of 1950 authorized it to prevent mergers whose effects might "substantially" lessen competition. A series of studies over the years had accused the FTC of investigative passivity, lax enforcement and preoccupation with trivial cases. Dixon, taking office with the image of a trustbuster, resolved to overcome the FTC's "inertia" and inaugurate a vigorous campaign against unfair trade practices.

Faced with a backlog of over 500 cases, Dixon sought and obtained from Congress in June 1961 a reorganization plan intended to streamline FTC procedures and expedite handling of future cases. The plan allowed the FTC's five commissioners to delegate more functions and gave the chairman, who administered the FTC in addition to deliberating with other commissioners, greater discretionary powers. Dixon was largely unsuccessful in his efforts to persuade Congress to grant the Commission itself greater powers. He failed to gain for the Commission the authority to issue temporary injunctions against proposed mergers and acquisitions. (Such authority would have circumvented the delay and litigation involved in seeking court orders.) He was also unsuccessful in his effort to empower the FTC to issue temporary cease-and-desist orders while cases were pending before the Commission. On his own authority Dixon opened FTC hearings to the public for the first time in the Commission's history.

With his offensive against misleading advertising, Dixon expanded the FTC's purview from the preservation of competition and the defense of small business to include the protection of the consuming public. Addressing the Advertising Federation of America in May 1961, he criticized advertisers guilty of "exaggerating claims for a product or falsely disparaging competing products," and promised "the victimized public . . . the hardest-hitting program of law enforcement that the Federal Trade Commission can develop."

Dixon also took the FTC into the area of deceptive packaging and labeling practices such as short-weighing and unsatisfactory contents designation. Arguing that current law restricted the FTC to prosecution of violators on a slow case-by-case basis, Dixon urged Congress during 1962 and 1963 to enact broad legislation to clarify business responsibility for fair packaging and accurate labeling. Sen. Philip A. Hart (D, Mich.) [q.v.] held hearings on the subject before the Antitrust and Monopoly Subcommittee, but no legislation was forthcoming.

The FTC initiated very few anti-merger cases during the Kennedy Administration. In the first two years of Dixon's tenure only one such complaint was issued. After President Johnson took office and asked regulatory agencies to concentrate on "helping, not harassing" businessmen, Dixon began to mellow in his approach to consumer protection. He remained as chairman through the Johnson Administration and the first year of the Nixon Administration. At that time a number of studies appeared finding severe fault with the operations of the Commission and with Dixon's performance as chairman. [See JOHNSON Volume]

[TO]

DOAR, JOHN M(ICHAEL)
b. Dec. 3, 1921; Minneapolis, Minn.
U.S. Assistant Attorney General, 1960-65.

A graduate of Princeton and the University of California, Berkeley Law School, Doar practiced law in New Richmond, Wisc., the town where he grew up, from 1950 to 1960. In the spring of 1960 he was appointed first assistant in the Civil Rights Division of the Justice Department, and although a Republican, he was retained in that post by the Kennedy Administration.

During the Freedom Rides in the summer of 1961, Doar won an injunction from the federal courts barring the Ku Klux Klan from interfering with the riders as they attempted to integrate interstate bus terminals. Throughout the Kennedy years Doar supervised many of the Justice Department's suits in the South to secure voting rights for blacks and to desegregate public schools and juries. Doar personally conducted the investigations which gathered evidence for court hearings in a number of these cases, developing a reputation for careful research and close attention to details.

Aside from litigation Doar became directly involved in several civil rights crises in the South. He was with James Meredith [q.v.] during three of Meredith's unsuccessful attempts to register at the University of Mississippi at Oxford in September 1962. On Sept. 30 he accompanied Meredith onto the University campus and stayed with him in his dormitory room that night while federal marshals and the National Guard quelled a riot outside. The next morning Doar escorted Meredith to the registrar's office where he was finally enrolled at the University.

Doar was also on hand on June 11, 1963, when two black students integrated the University of Alabama at Tuscaloosa. He accompanied one of the students onto campus and to his dormitory while Gov. George C. Wallace [q.v.] stood in the doorway of the University's registration hall in a final and futile attempt to block the entry of the students.

Four days later Doar was in Jackson, Miss., for the funeral of Medgar Evers [q.v.], the Mississippi NAACP field secretary who had been shot by a sniper outside his home on June 12. After the funeral several thousand blacks participated in a march of mourning in Jackson. Near its end a group of young blacks broke from the ranks and went down another street where they met a line of police who ordered them to disperse. As the crowd grew, some rocks and bottles were thrown, and the police moved forward and began making arrests. At this point Doar strode down the middle of the street between the line of police and the gathering of blacks, urging the crowd to remain calm, to stop the rock throwing and to leave the area. Several black leaders joined in Doar's appeal, and the crowd moved out without further violence.

In December 1964 Doar was named head of the Civil Rights Division in the Justice Department, a position he held until December 1967, when he resigned to become executive director of the Bedford Stuyvesant Development and Services Corporation. During 1974 Doar served as counsel to the House Judiciary Committee investigating possible impeachment of President Richard Nixon. [See JOHNSON, NIXON Volumes]

[CAB]

DODD, THOMAS J(OSEPH)
b. May 15, 1907; Norwich, Conn.
d. May 24, 1971; Old Lyme, Conn.
Democratic Senator, Conn., 1959-71.

After his graduation from Providence College in 1930 and then Yale Law School in 1933, Dodd worked for two years as a special agent for the FBI. He later served in the Justice Department as a special assistant to the Attorney General. After World War II he was named executive trial counsel to Robert H. Jackson, chief U.S. prosecutor for the Nuremberg war crimes tribunal.

Long interested in Connecticut state Democratic politics, Dodd held several posts within the state party organization and twice sought its gubernatorial nomination. Elected to the U.S. House of Representatives in 1952, Dodd was chosen the Democratic senatorial nominee in 1956, but he lost the general election to incumbent Sen. Prescott Bush (R, Conn.) [q.v.]. Less than a year later Dodd announced that he would seek the senate seat held by Sen. William A. Purtell (R, Conn.). Declaring that the major election issues were unemployment, inflation and the threat of Communism, Dodd defeated Purtell in the November 1958 election. In his first term in the Senate, Dodd was named to the Judiciary and Foreign Relations Committees. [See EISENHOWER Volume]

According to Congressional Quarterly, Dodd supported Kennedy Administration legislation on over 60% of all major issues. Regarded as a domestic liberal and a militant anti-Communist both at home and abroad, Dodd offered two Senate amendments in July 1961 that, he said, were designed to justify to the world U.S. "determination to keep Red China out of the United Nations." In August he was one of 13 senators to urge resumption of U.S. nuclear weapons testing, but he later voted for the 1963 limited test ban treaty. Dodd also proposed a bill in 1961 that would authorize the Attorney General, without a court order, to permit federal agents to make wiretaps in cases involving espionage, treason, sabotage, sedition and kidnapping. During early 1962 it was also reported that Dodd was a faculty member of a so-called "anti-Communism school" conducted in Oakland, Calif. from Jan. 29 to Feb. 2 by the right wing Christian Anti-Communism Crusade.

Early in 1962 Dodd's Senate Juvenile Delinquency Subcommittee conducted hearings concerning crime and violence on television and its possible impact on juvenile delinquency. Later Dodd charged that the television industry lacked imagination and responsibility to its viewers and accused the networks of thinking alike and of "jamming this stuff down the people's throat." Through his chairmanship of the Juvenile Delinquency Subcommittee, Dodd was active in pushing for stricter gun control laws. Interest in such laws stemmed from a March 1961 study by the subcommittee and was later strengthened by the assassinations of President John Kennedy [q.v.], Sen. Robert Kennedy (D, N.Y.) [q.v.] and Martin Luther King, [q.v.]. After much debate a watered-down gun control provision was written into the 1968 Omnibus Crime Control and Safe Streets Act.

In a widely publicized speech, Dodd denounced the November 1963 State Department dismissal of Otto F. Otepka [q.v.], chief of the Evaluation Division of the State Department's Office of Security. Otepka had allegedly passed classified documents concerning relaxed State Department security procedures to the Senate Judiciary Committee's Internal Security Subcommittee, of which Dodd was a member. Dodd stated that Otepka's only crime was that he had testified "honestly." The Senator warned that if the dismissal were allowed to stand it would become increasingly difficult to elicit any information from the executive branch.

On June 23, 1967 the Senate formally censured Dodd for "misuse of political funds." The censure, only the seventh in the Senate's history, stemmed from charges in more than 100 newspaper columns written by Drew Pearson [q.v.] and Jack Anderson between 1965 and 1967, alleging that Dodd had misused political campaign funds and employed his Senate position to help the overseas business dealings of Chicago public relations man Julius Klein. On Feb. 25, 1966 Dodd asked the Senate Select Committee on Standards and Practices to investigate the charges. After lengthy hearings the Committee found Dodd guilty, and he was formally censured by the full Senate by a vote of 92 to 5.

Campaigning as an Independent for reelection in 1970, Dodd was unseated by Republican Lowell Weicker. Dodd died on May 24, 1971. [See JOHNSON, NIXON Volumes]

[FHM]

DOMINICK, PETER H(OYT)

b. July 7, 1915; Stamford, Conn.
Republican Representative, Colo., 1961-63; Republican Senator, Colo., 1963-75.

Peter Dominick's grandfather, William, was a founder of the brokerage firm that later became Dominick and Dominick, Inc. His father, Gayer, was a partner in the firm and a director of several corporations. Dominick received undergraduate and law degrees from Yale and was an Army pilot during World War II. After the war he moved to Denver, where he practiced law and became active in the Republican Party. He was defeated in 1954 in an attempt to win a seat in the Colorado House of Representatives. Two years later he was successful in a second try, and he was reelected in 1958. In 1960 Dominick defeated Democratic Rep. Byron L. Johnson to win a U.S. House seat from a district that included part of suburban Denver. His winning margin of nearly 40,000 votes was somewhat less than the plurality in the district for the Republican presidential candidate, Richard M. Nixon [q.v.].

During his two years in the House, Dominick generally took conservative stands, supporting the conservative coalition on two-thirds of the votes. He generally opposed any expanded role for the federal government in domestic affairs. In 1961, however, he supported the Administration position that power transmission lines connecting government hydroelectric plants in the upper Colorado River basin should be built by the government rather than by private utilities. An amendment to a public works bill deleting funds for several of the lines was defeated when Dominick and 22 other Republicans backed the Administration. After much debate both houses approved the bill.

In 1962 Dominick won, without opposition, the Republican nomination to run against Sen. John A. Carroll (D, Colo.) [q.v.]. Dominick traveled widely during the campaign and organized an extensive door-to-door canvas and a major direct mail effort. He defeated Carroll, receiving 53.6% of the vote. In the Senate he continued his earlier voting pattern. As a member of the Banking and Currency Committee, he voted against reporting the Administration's 1963 request for a $500-million program of matching grants to aid urban mass transit. (The bill passed the full Senate on April 4, 1963 but never reached the House floor.) Dominick was also one of seven senators from the Western states to oppose a bill to establish a national wilderness preservation system. The bill passed the Senate in April, 1963 but later died in the House.

A lieutenant colonel in the Air Force Reserve, Dominick generally supported a strong military but voted to ratify the 1963 nuclear test ban treaty. That year he also introduced a successful amendment to the foreign aid bill that required annual appropriations of funds used in the development loan program and the Alliance for Progress, ending the use of revolving funds. Dominick was reelected to the Senate by a comfortable margin in 1968, but he was defeated in 1974 by Gary W. Hart. [See JOHNSON, NIXON Volumes]

[JBF]

DONOVAN, JAMES B(RITT)
b. Feb. 29, 1916; New York, N.Y.
d. Jan. 19, 1970; New York, N.Y.
Lawyer.

Donovan was a graduate of Fordham University and Harvard Law School. As a Navy officer during World War II he served as general counsel of the Office of Strategic Services and associate prosecutor at the principal Nuremberg war crimes trial. In 1951 Donovan, who specialized in insurance law, became a founding partner of the law firm of Watters, Cowen & Donovan. New York City Mayor Robert F. Wagner [q.v.] appointed Donovan to the city's Board of Education in September 1961, and Donovan was elected by the board as its vice president.

Upon the recommendation of the Brooklyn Bar Association, Donovan was assigned, in August 1957, as defense counsel for Rudolf Ivanovich Abel. Abel had been arrested in June of that year in New York City and charged with conspiracy to obtain and transmit United States defense secrets and failure to register as a Soviet agent. He was found guilty on Oct. 25, 1957, and sentenced to 30 years imprisonment and a $3,000 fine. Donovan appealed the conviction on the grounds that the government had used illegal search and seizure procedures, but on March 28, 1960, the Supreme Court rejected the appeal by a five-to-four vote.

At the time of the trial, Abel and Donovan had discussed the possibility of Abel's being exchanged for a Soviet-held United States spy, but no American of sufficient rank was then in a Soviet prison. However, when Central Intelligence Agency (CIA) U-2 pilot Francis Gary Powers [q.v.] was shot down over the Soviet Union on May 1, 1960, the situation changed. Powers's father, Oliver Powers, wrote to Abel suggesting an exchange of the two men. Donovan, acting in coordination with Administration officials, explored this possibility in a series of letters with a woman in East Germany who purported to be Abel's wife, but who Donovan believed was in fact a Soviet official. By May 1961 there were indications that the Soviet Union would consider a prisoner exchange.

Since the Soviets refused to acknowledge that Abel was an agent, negotiations could not take place through normal diplomatic channels. At the Kennedy Administration's request, Donovan met secretly with Soviet and East German representatives in East Berlin from Feb. 3 to Feb. 9, 1962. An agreement was reached to exchange Abel for Powers and an American student, Frederick L. Pryor, who was being held on espionage charges by East Germany. The Soviet representative also indicated that clemency for an American student, Marvin Makinen, held in the USSR, might be considered in the future. The actual prisoner exchange took place on the morning of Feb. 10 on the Glienicker Bridge connecting Potsdam and West Berlin. (Makinen was released on Oct. 11, 1963 as part of another prisoner exchange.)

Donovan also played a central role in the release of the men captured at the Bay of Pigs during the April 1961 CIA-sponsored invasion of Cuba. In March and April 1962 1,179 of the men were tried by Cuban military tribunals; each was sentenced to 30 years imprisonment or a fine ranging from $25,000 to $500,000. Soon after the trials, representatives of the U.S.-based Cuban Families Committee for the Liberty of Prisoners of War met with Castro, who indicated that commodities might be substituted for the cash fines, which totalled $62 million. Castro released 60 of the more seriously injured men in return for a pledge of $2.9 million for their fines. In June the Cuban Families Committee approached Attorney General Robert F. Kennedy [q.v.] for assistance in freeing more prisoners, and Kennedy referred them to Donovan.

Donovan met with Castro in Havana in late August and proposed that payment in drugs and baby food be substituted for the cash fines. Castro agreed to consider this possibility if the outstanding debt of $2.9 million for the earlier prisoner release was paid. Upon his return to the U.S. Donovan solicited agreements from Charles Pfizer and Merck, Sharpe & Dohme, two large pharmaceutical firms, to make major donations of drugs, while the CIA began to explore similar contributions with other drug manufacturers. Donovan returned to Cuba on Oct. 2 for further meetings with Castro, who agreed in principle to a drugs and baby food for prisoners exchange. But on Oct. 24 the U.S. began a blockade of Cuba, demanding the removal of Soviet missiles recently installed there. The negotiations to release the prisoners became stalled.

In late November the Cubans were still willing to participate in the proposed prisoner release, but the drug companies were no longer eager to be involved. At a Nov. 30 meeting of high officials from the Justice and State Departments, the Internal Revenue Service (IRS) and the CIA, the Administration decided to assume a major role in the proposed exchange. Central to the arrangements were highly favorable tax rulings given to corporate contributors to the exchange and assurances that no antitrust action would result from participation in the program. The Attorney General personally met with the heads of major drug companies on Dec. 7 and with the baby food manufacturers on Dec. 9.

In December Donovan resumed negotiations with the Cuban government by telephone. He returned to Havana on Dec. 18 and signed a memorandum of agreement with Castro on Dec. 21. It called for the release of all of the Bay of Pigs prisoners in exchange for $53 million (in retail value) of drugs and baby food. On Dec. 23 the first prisoners arrived in Miami. However, the next day Castro indicated that the exchange would be suspended until Cuba received the still unpaid $2.9 million in fines for the 60 men released in April. Robert Kennedy took personal charge of raising the money, and that same day $1 million was donated by Richard Cardinal Cushing, Roman Catholic Archbishop of Boston. The remainder was raised through a loan secured by Gen. Lucius D. Clay [q.v.], a sponsor of the Cuban Families Committee. At 9:35 p.m. Dec. 24 Donovan and the last of the 1,113 released men arrived in Miami.

Although both Donovan and the Administration claimed that the exchange had been privately arranged, Donovan had in fact worked closely with government officials. In addition to the tax arrangements, which according to an IRS estimate cost the government $20 million, the Department of Agriculture contributed 35 million pounds of surplus food for the exchange. Along with the prisoners themselves, Castro permitted thousands of their relatives to leave Cuba as well. As a result of further negotiations by Donovan in March and April 1963, Cuba also released 37 jailed U.S. citizens. (Three Cubans and a Cuban-American were released from New York jails as part of this arrangement.) On July 3, 1963, when the last shipment of medical supplies reached Cuba, the American Red Cross announced that 9,703 persons had left Cuba under arrangements negotiated by Donovan.

On Sept. 18, 1962, in the middle of his negotiations with Cuba, the New York State Democratic Party convention, meeting in Syracuse, nominated Donovan as its senatorial candidate. The following day Donovan received the Liberal Party nomination as well. He lost the Nov. 6 election to the incumbent, Sen. Jacob K. Javits (R, N.Y.) [q.v.], by nearly a million votes.

In December 1963 Donovan was elected president of the New York City Board of Education, where he served until June 1965. During his tenure Donovan was criticized by civil rights leaders for not developing an effective plan to desegregate the schools. Donovan served as president of Pratt Institute from October 1968 until his death in January 1970.

[JBF]

For further information:
James B. Donovan, *Strangers on a Bridge: The Case of Colonel Abel* (New York, 1964).
David Wise and Thomas B. Ross, *The Invisible Government* (New York, 1964).

DOUGLAS, PAUL H(OWARD)
b. March 26, 1892; Salem, Mass.
Democratic Senator, Ill. 1949-67.
Chairman, Joint Economic Committee, 1959-67.

Douglas was raised in rural Maine by his stepmother after she separated from his natural father, a traveling salesman, in 1898. After working his way through Bowdoin College, Douglas taught economics at several universities and earned a Ph.D. from Columbia in 1921. During the 1920s and 30s Douglas was a leading figure in the University of Chicago's stellar department of economics. As a labor economist he published several influential books, of which the most important were *Real Wages in the United States (1890-1926)* and *The Theory of Wages*, published in 1930 and 1934 respectively. During the depression Douglas served on state and federal advisory panels and helped draft the legislation that became the Social Security Act. In 1938 Douglas was elected Chicago alderman with the backing of both Hyde Park reformers and the Kelly-Nash machine. Defeated in the Democratic Senate primary in 1942, Douglas enlisted in the Marine Corps at the age of 50 and saw action in the Pacific.

With the backing of veterans' organizations and the Illinois branch of the Americans for Democratic Action (ADA), Douglas won election to the Senate in 1948. There he became a leader of liberal Democratic forces. He was an author of the landmark 1949 Housing Act and a prime opponent of "pork barrel" federal works spending. During the 1950s Douglas worked closely with the ADA, the NAACP and organized labor in a generally unsuccessful series of congressional battles designed to advance civil rights legislation, close tax loopholes, increase social security and minimum wage coverage and modify Senate Rule XXII to end Southern filibusters by imposition of cloture. During this period Douglas incurred the enmity of Senate Majority Leader Lyndon Johnson (D, Tex.) [q.v.] who denied him a seat on the Finance Committee until 1955. Douglas was elected chairman of the Joint Economic Committee in 1959. [See TRUMAN, EISENHOWER Volumes]

Since 1954 Douglas had sponsored legislation to aid "depressed areas" in Appalachia and other sections of the country where unemployment was at chronically high levels. In late 1960 President-elect Kennedy appointed Douglas chairman of a task force to study the problem. After hearings in West Virginia and Washington, D.C., Douglas recommended a doubling of surplus food distribution, reestablishment of a food stamp program, passage of an area redevelopment bill and extension of unemployment benefits to jobless workers whose standard benefits had been exhausted. With Administration backing most of Douglas's proposals quickly moved through Congress. At Kennedy's request Douglas agreed to accept Commerce Department control of the new Area Redevelopment Program, although he would have preferred administration by an independent government agency directly responsible to the President. The Senate passed the $389-million program March 15. After House action Kennedy signed the measure May 1.

Douglas was a strong opponent of what he called "tax truckholes" in the revenue code. With Sen. Albert Gore (D, Tenn.) [q.v.] Douglas fought to block tax relief for the shareholders of Christiana Securities Co., a DuPont family holding company about to receive by court order a large block of General Motors (GM) stock from the Du-Pont Co. Douglas and Gore argued that special tax treatment for Christiana and its DuPont family shareholders, who owned 8% of GM common stock, would only continue the monopoly situation. In order to discourage Christiana from a "pass-through" of GM stock to its shareholders, Douglas proposed an amendment to tax Christiana's GM stock at the full 25% capital gains rate rather than at the lower intercorporate dividend rate (which Douglas estimated as 8%). The intent of Douglas's proposal was to influence Christiana to sell the stock, but the amendment was defeated by a 72-18 vote on Jan. 23, 1962.

With other Senate liberals Douglas waged a generally unsuccessful effort to make Kennedy's 1962 tax revision bill a more progressive piece of legislation. He opposed the 7% investment tax credit on the ground that it merely opened a new tax loophole for large business enterprises. In addition Douglas and Gore thought it provided no "social control" over the purposes to which the deduction would be applied. Senate liberals were joined in their opposition to the tax credit by fiscal conservatives such as Sen. Harry Byrd (D, Va.) [q.v.] who opposed the provision because it would reduce federal revenues and increase the budget deficit. The 7% investment tax credit, considered the centerpiece of the Administration's 1962 tax bill, was approved by the Senate Aug. 28 by a vote of 52-30.

Douglas fought for the Administration's proposal to close another tax loophole and increase federal revenues by an estimated $800 million. He strongly supported a section of the 1962 Administration tax bill which proposed automatic withholding of taxes on dividends and interest payments. This withholding provision easily passed the House in April but was rejected by the Senate after building and loan associations generated one of the largest letter writing campaigns in legislative history. In a few weeks' time, Douglas received over 40,000 letters opposing interest and dividend withholding. In May the Senate Finance Committee voted against the withholding provision after the Administration leaked word that it was willing to abandon automatic taxation of such income in return for assured passage of the investment tax credit. The full Senate approved the Finance Committee amendment, removing withholding from the Administration tax bill on Aug. 29. At the same time Douglas also failed to eliminate what he considered tax loopholes expanding expense account deductions when the Senate voted to allow entertainment deductions "associated with" the active conduct of a trade or business. Douglas was among 11 Senate liberals who voted against the entire tax bill Oct. 2.

Douglas was also critical of the Kennedy Administration's new $10 billion tax reduction and reform proposal in 1963. As chairman of the Joint Economic Committee, Douglas announced in March that he thought the bill should offer more tax relief to low income groups. In October Douglas criticized the Administration for what he considered insufficient enthusiasm for tax reform. He told Secretary of the Treasury C. Douglas Dillon [q.v.] that if the Administration did not step up efforts to prevent congressional conservatives from gutting tax reform proposals, Senate liberals would have a difficult time voting for the Kennedy tax program. Despite these misgivings Douglas voted for the Kennedy-Johnson tax reduction bill in February 1964.

As a leading Senate liberal during the Kennedy years, Douglas was also actively involved in the fight for federal aid to education, a higher level of foreign aid, and truth in lending, wilderness preservation and civil rights legislation. His ADA rating in this period averaged 95%. Douglas continued in office until 1966 when Republican Charles Percy defeated him in a hard-fought senatorial contest in which Douglas's advanced age and his support of the Vietnam war and open housing were prominent issues. [See JOHNSON Volume]

[NNL]

For further information:
Paul H. Douglas, *In the Fullness of Time* (New York, 1971).

DOUGLAS, WILLIAM O(RVILLE)
b. Oct. 16, 1898; Maine, Minn.
Associate Justice, U.S. Supreme Court, 1939-75.

Raised by impoverished parents in Yakima, Wash., Douglas later worked his way through Columbia Law School and graduated second in his class in 1925. As a professor at Columbia and then at Yale Law School he became one of the nation's experts on corporate and financial law. Named a member of the Securities and Exchange Commission in 1936 and its chairman the next year, Douglas put into effect a thorough reorganization and reform of the stock exchange.

After President Roosevelt appointed Douglas to the Supreme Court in March 1939, he wrote some of the Court's most significant opinions in cases dealing with bankruptcy, antitrust and patent law. But Douglas became best known as an ardent protector of individual rights and liberties against the power of government. Douglas came to view First Amendment freedoms as particularly central to the preservation of democracy. He dissented repeatedly during the 1950s in cases where the majority sustained loyalty-security laws on the grounds that individual rights to free speech and thought had been violated. He was a leading advocate of the view that the guarantees of the Bill of Rights should be extended to the states, and he favored a broad reading of the rights in those amendments. Over the years any changes in Douglas's opinions were all in the direction of greater protection for constitutional liberties. He moved, for example, from the position that First Amendment rights should be balanced against governmental interests to the belief that the freedoms of speech and expression were absolutes upon which the government could not infringe. [See TRUMAN, EISENHOWER Volumes]

Douglas continued his defense of First Amendment freedoms in the Kennedy years. He dissented in two February 1961 cases where the majority upheld the contempt-of-Congress convictions of witnesses who had refused to answer questions before a House Un-American Activities Subcommittee. He also objected to two decisions in June 1961 sustaining provisions in federal anti-subversive laws. Douglas took an absolutist approach to freedom of religion in the 1960s and insisted that the First Amendment required the government to maintain a position of complete neutrality in regard to religion. He thus dissented in four May 1961 cases upholding state laws for Sunday closings of businesses, contending that the statutes enforced the Christian view of Sunday as a day of rest. Douglas concurred in Court decisions of June 1962 and June 1963 holding prayer and Bible-reading in public schools unconstitutional.

During these years Justice Douglas saw the Court adopt certain positions he had long espoused. He had objected to a 1949 decision holding that state courts did not have to exclude illegally seized evidence, and he concurred when the majority overturned that ruling in June 1961. In March 1962 the Court overruled a 1946 precedent from which Douglas had also dissented and held federal courts could try legislative apportionment cases. Douglas then wrote the majority opinion in a March 1963 decision that invalidated Georgia's county-unit system of voting and mandated in its place a "one man, one vote" standard of apportionment. As one of the strongest voices on the Court for guaranteeing all defendants the right to counsel, Douglas had repeatedly urged the Court to reject a 1942 ruling that the Sixth Amendment's right to counsel was not applicable to the states. In March 1963 the rest of the Court finally agreed with Douglas when they rendered a unanimous decision on the issue. Douglas himself wrote the majority opinion in another March 1963 case requiring the states to supply counsel to an indigent defendant for appeal of a criminal conviction. He was also the author of a February 1961 majority opinion holding that under an 1871 federal law policemen who violated a citizen's Fourth Amendment rights against unreasonable searches and seizures could be sued for damages in federal courts.

Douglas joined in later Warren Court rulings expanding the rights of criminal defendants and wrote the majority opinion in April 1965 and January 1967 cases broadening the application of the privilege against self-incrimination. His opinion for the Court in a June 1965 decision held that the Constitution guaranteed a right of privacy against government intrusion, and in later years Douglas continued to speak out for an absolute right to freedom of speech.

One of the most colorful and controversial justices in the Court's history, Douglas was as well-known for his activities off the bench as for those on it. An avid outdoorsman, he frequently went camping and mountain climbing well into his later years and was known as a strong environmentalist. Douglas was also a prolific author. He wrote popular books on topics ranging from international relations to accounts of his many travels at home and abroad.

Many liberals and radicals of the 1960s viewed Douglas as the justice most sympathetic to their point of view; conservatives were critical of the justice both for his outspoken liberalism and for his four marriages—three to women considerably younger than he. Although Douglas was the subject of three different impeachment attempts, the last in 1970, he easily survived them all. By the time of his retirement in November 1975 after suffering a stroke, he had served longer on the Supreme Court than any other justice in the nation's history. [See JOHNSON, NIXON Volumes]

Although sometimes criticized for his terse opinions, Douglas won praise from most legal commentators for the great range of his legal work and interests and for his growth while on the Court. He broadened, as one observer noted, "from the corporate financial specialist of the New Deal era to a sophisticated expert on important matters ranging from ecology and civil liberties to international relations." The "single most important phase" of Douglas's work on the Court, John P. Frank has written, was "in the field of individual liberty," and here he was "an extraordinarily dedicated and effective exponent of constitutional liberty for all."

[CAB]

For further information:
Vern Countryman, *The Judicial Record of Justice William O. Douglas* (Cambridge, Mass., 1974).
John P. Frank, "William O. Douglas," in Leon Friedman and Fred L. Israel, eds., *The Justices of the United States Supreme Court, 1789-1969* (New York, 1969). Vol. IV.
"Mr. Justice William O. Douglas," *Washington Law Review*, XXXIV (Spring, 1964), pp. 1-114.
"William O. Douglas," *Yale Law Journal*, LXXIII (May 1964), pp. 915-998.

DRYDEN, HUGH L(ATIMER)
b. July 2, 1898; Pocomoke City, Md.
d. Dec. 2, 1965; Washington, D.C.
Deputy Administrator, National Aeronautics and Space Administration, July 1958-December 1965.

Dryden, the highest ranking scientist in the National Aeronautics and Space Administration (NASA) during the Kennedy Administration, received his doctorate from Johns Hopkins in 1919. One year later he became director of the aerodynamics section of the National Bureau of Standards and was named the bureau's chief physicist in 1938. During World War II he served as a military adviser on aeronautical matters. Dryden became director of the National Advisory Committee on Aeronautics in 1949. When the National Aeronautics and Space Administration was formed in 1958, he became its deputy administrator.

Like many others in NASA, Dryden hoped that the Kennedy Administration would support an accelerated space program. When the Soviet Union put the first man in space in April 1961, he suggested to Kennedy that the U.S. launch a crash program similar to the wartime Manhattan Project in order to surpass the Russians in space.

John Glenn's [*q.v.*] orbital space flight

in February 1962 finally brought U.S. space achievements to the Soviet level. In March Dryden led the U.S. delegation in talks on space cooperation with the Soviets. The two delegations worked out a program of cooperation in meteorology, a world geomagnetic survey and communications satellites during May and June. One year later Kennedy, who feared that Congress would attempt to weaken any nuclear test ban treaty negotiated by the two governments, stated that he would "welcome" a joint moon venture with the Russians. In August 1963 it was reported that the Soviets had proposed such an effort to Dryden during the 1962 talks. NASA officials supported Kennedy's proposal, but congressional objections proved too strong, and the joint space venture was dropped by the Administration. Dryden died in December 1965.

Following the 1967 Apollo fire that killed three astronauts a congressional investigation revealed that Dryden, in conjunction with James Webb [q.v.], Robert Seamans and Robert Gilruth, had decided to award the prime Apollo contract to North American Aviation, although a NASA evaluation board had found Martin-Marietta technically superior. Webb said that they had awarded the contract to North American because their bid was lower and because the NASA evaluation board had not done "a complete job."

[MDB]

For further information:
Hugo Young, Bryan Silcock and Peter Dunn, *Journey to Tranquility: The Long Competitive Struggle to Reach the Moon* (Garden City, 1970).

DUBINSKY, DAVID
b. Feb. 22, 1892; Brest-Litovsk, Russian Poland (now USSR).
President, International Ladies Garment Workers Union, 1932-66.

Dubinsky led his first strike while working as a baker in Lodz, Poland. Arrested later as a labor agitator, he was exiled to Siberia but escaped and emigrated to the U.S. in 1911.

In New York Dubinsky learned the cloak-cutting trade, joined the International Ladies Garment Workers Union (ILGWU) and was active in the Socialist Party. He became involved in union affairs during a 1916 cloakmaker's strike and became a member of the union's executive board in 1922. Dubinsky tightly controlled the cutters' local and waged a successful 10-year internal union battle with the Communists. Assuming the duties of acting president in 1927, he was elected ILGWU president in 1932 and became a vice president of the American Federation of Labor in 1935.

In the two years following the enactment of the National Industrial Recovery Act of 1933, ILGWU membership grew from 40,000 to 200,000. In 1935 Dubinsky joined John L. Lewis and other industrial union advocates to form the Committee for Industrial Organization (CIO). Although Dubinsky strongly supported CIO organizing drives, he opposed the establishment of the CIO on a permanent basis as a separate federation. The ILGWU rejoined the AFL in 1940.

An ardent supporter of President Roosevelt, Dubinsky joined Sidney Hillman, Alex Rose [q.v.] and others in forming the American Labor Party (ALP) to support the New Deal nationally (while repudiating Tammany Hall Democrats in New York). Because of growing Communist strength in the ALP Dubinsky, Hillman and Rose left in 1944 to found the Liberal Party. Dubinsky helped form Americans for Democratic Action in 1947.

Dubinsky also played a major role in AFL international activities and helped organize the International Federation of Democratic Trade Unions. During the postwar years the ILGWU spent $3 million abroad, much of it going to Israel and to Italy, where Dubinsky helped facilitate the merger of Catholic and Socialist trade unions into one federation.

By 1949 the ILGWU's welfare programs were among the most extensive of any union in the country. It had established its own health centers, radio stations, a major housing project in New York and extensive recreational facilities. Under Dubinsky, who was never challenged for reelection, the union became a stronghold of labor liberalism. The ILGWU made large contributions to the national Democratic Party and the New York Liberal Party as well as to various civil rights organizations, the League for Industrial Democracy, the Jewish Labor Committee and other liberal groups throughout the 1950s and 1960s. [See TRUMAN, EISENHOWER Volumes]

During the 1960s the union's membership—mostly black, Puerto Rican and Italian—remained stable at about 440,000. Jews maintained their hold on leadership positions in the New York-based organization, and the union came under attack from civil rights groups charging racial discrimination. In 1962 Herbert Hill [q.v.], labor secretary of the NAACP, opened a drive to seek National Labor Relations Board decertification of unions practicing discrimination. In August Hill acted as a consultant to a special House subcommittee investigating the ILGWU. Hill maintained that the union condoned a low wage level in the New York garment trades in order to keep the industry in the city. This was at the expense of poorly-paid black and Puerto Rican workers who, he said, were discriminated against by an undemocratic union constitution. ILGWU officials denied these charges.

In May 1965, when Dubinsky was elected to his 12th term as union president, the ILGWU convention endorsed his call to support President Johnson's policy in both Vietnam and the Dominican Republic. Dubinsky retired in 1966 at age 74.

[MDB]

For further information:
Labor History Special Supplement (Spring 1968). Burton Hall, ed., Autocracy and Insurgency in Organized Labor (New Brunswick, 1972).

DUKE, ANGIER BIDDLE
b. Nov. 30, 1915; New York, N.Y.
Chief of Protocol for the State Department and the White House, January 1961-December 1964.

An heir to the American Tobacco Company fortune, Duke spent his early years traveling around the world before joining the Army during World War II. After the war he entered the foreign service and from 1952 to 1953 served as ambassador to El Salvador. During the 1950s he headed various private relief agencies, including the International Rescue Committee.

Duke was sworn in as chief of protocol in January 1961. During his term of office he was primarily interested in aiding African diplomats facing racial discrimination in the Washington area. Duke's concern was evident in his handling of a March 1961 incident in which a restaurant in Hagerstown, Md., refused to serve a diplomat from Sierra Leone. Instead of merely tendering an official apology, Duke and the town's mayor arranged a banquet for the visiting diplomat. The restaurant was subsequently desegregated. In August 1961 Duke quietly resigned from the exclusive Metropolitan Club in Washington in protest against its refusal to allow blacks as guests.

Duke was confirmed as ambassador to Spain in March 1965. One year later, in January 1966, the Navy lost a nuclear device in a crash off the Spanish coast. To assure the Spanish that the waters were safe, Duke and his family took a well publicized swim near the site of the accident. From January to September 1968 Duke again served as chief of protocol until being appointed ambassador to Denmark. He resigned this post at the beginning of the Nixon Administration in January 1969.

[EWS]

DULLES, ALLEN W(ELSH)
b. April 7, 1893; Watertown, N.Y.
d. Jan. 30, 1969; Washington, D.C.
Director of Central Intelligence, 1953-61.

Dulles's lifelong interest in foreign affairs was part of a strong family tradition. His maternal grandfather, John W. Foster, had been Secretary of State under President Benjamin Harrison, a post that both Dulles's uncle, Robert Lansing, and his older brother, John Foster Dulles, were also to hold. Another uncle, John Walsh, had been a minister to England, and Dulles's sister, Elinor Lansing Dulles, was later a State

Department official as well. Dulles's father was a Presbyterian minister.

After attending private schools in upstate New York and Paris and receiving B.A. and M.A. degrees from Princeton University, Dulles entered the diplomatic service in 1916. He served in a variety of posts abroad and was a member of the U.S. delegation to the Versailles Peace Conference. Following four years as chief of the State Department Division of Near Eastern Affairs, Dulles resigned from government service in 1926 to join his brother at the Wall Street law firm of Sullivan and Cromwell, where he remained for the next 15 years.

During World War II Dulles headed the ultra-secret Office of Strategic Services mission in Switzerland. He was subsequently a key figure in the establishment of the Central Intelligence Agency (CIA) after the war. Dulles later said that the act which set up the CIA "has given intelligence a more influential position in our government than intelligence enjoys in any other government of the world."

The CIA was initially an information-gathering agency, but partially as a result of a suggestion by Dulles, who in 1948 was appointed by President Truman as head of a three-man CIA review committee, the Agency was soon given authority and capacity to conduct covert operations abroad. In 1951 Dulles himself was placed in charge of these operations when he joined the CIA as deputy director for plans. [See TRUMAN Volume]

In February 1953 President Eisenhower appointed Dulles as Director of Central Intelligence, making him both head of the CIA and coordinator of all U.S. intelligence activity. During the Eisenhower Administration the CIA greatly expanded its operations and became centrally involved in establishing and executing U.S. foreign policy. This was in part the result of the close working relationship between Dulles and his brother John Foster Dulles, who was Secretary of State from 1953 to 1959. During these years the CIA often intervened in the domestic affairs of other countries. Intelligence-gathering operations were also expanded and new technological means of surveillance, such as the U-2 and SR-71 spy planes, were developed. Some CIA operations, such as the inspection and opening of mail sent from the Soviet Union to U.S. citizens, violated U.S. law.

On March 17, 1960 President Eisenhower ordered the CIA to help unify opposition to the Cuban government and to recruit and train a force of Cuban exiles capable of guerrilla action against it. Richard M. Bissell [q.v.], CIA deputy director for plans, was placed in charge of the project. According to a 1975 Senate Select Committee report, that summer Bissell also initiated attempts to kill Cuban leaders Raul and Fidel Castro. Bissell claiméd that Dulles was fully informed of these activities. The Senate Select Committee also reported that in August 1960 Dulles authorized a CIA effort to assassinate Congolese Premier Patrice Lumumba. (Lumumba was killed by Congolese rivals before the CIA plans were carried out.) It was unclear whether or not Eisenhower directly authorized these activities, or was fully aware of them. [See EISENHOWER Volume]

President-elect Kennedy announced that he would retain Dulles as Director of Central Intelligence on Nov. 10, 1960. Eight days later Dulles and Bissell briefed Kennedy on the training of the Cuban exile force, which was already well underway at a CIA camp in Guatemala, and on initial plans for landing them in Cuba. On Nov. 29, after a second more detailed briefing, Kennedy ordered the planning to proceed. It was unclear after the 1975 investigation whether Kennedy had been informed in this or in any other briefing of the parallel plans to assassinate Castro. After a series of top-level meetings, at which Dulles and Bissell presented and defended the CIA invasion plan, Kennedy gave his approval in early April 1961.

On the day of the invasion at the Bay of Pigs, Dulles was in Puerto Rico delivering a long-planned speech, which he apparently declined to cancel to avoid any suspicion that a major CIA operation was underway. Dulles was therefore not in Washington when Kennedy decided to cancel one of the two planned CIA air strikes. In Dulles's absence, Bissell was in charge of the Cuban operation, which ended in complete defeat for the invasion forces.

On April 22 Kennedy established a panel headed by retired Gen. Maxwell D. Taylor [q.v.] to investigate the CIA role in the Cuban invasion. Also serving on the panel were Dulles, Attorney General Robert F. Kennedy [q.v.] and Chief of Naval Operations Adm. Arleigh A. Burke [q.v.]. Members of the Taylor panel disagreed as to whether or not the invasion plans had had any chance of success. Dulles took a middle position, arguing that in spite of certain important problems, if the original plans had been followed, including both air strikes, the invasion might have succeeded. The panel recommended that the CIA be permitted to continue to conduct clandestine operations but not to undertake major paramilitary operations unless they could be plausibly denied.

During the early months of the Kennedy Administration, Dulles was also involved in efforts to bolster the deteriorating position of U.S.-supported forces in Laos, where the CIA had long been involved. During this period Dulles opposed the proposed establishment of the Defense Intelligence Agency (DIA), a plan supported by Secretary of Defense Robert S. McNamara [q.v.]. Dulles urged the continuation of individual military service intelligence agencies, each separately represented on the U.S. Intelligence Board, which he headed. Over Dulles's objections, McNamara proceeded in October 1961 with the creation of the DIA.

According to David Wise and Thomas B. Ross in *The Invisible Government*, Kennedy had been planning major changes in the CIA even before the Cuban invasion. After the failure of that project, the CIA leadership was quietly replaced. On July 31, 1961, Administration spokesman Pierre Salinger [q.v.] confirmed that Dulles would soon retire, and on Sept. 27 Kennedy accepted his resignation. (Bissell and CIA Deputy Director Gen. Charles P. Cabell also left the CIA in the following months.) On Nov. 28 Kennedy presented a National Security Medal to Dulles at the recently opened $46-million CIA headquarters in Langley, Va., which had been planned and con-structed during Dulles's tenure.

Following his resignation Dulles returned to his former law firm, Sullivan and Cromwell. In November 1963 President Johnson [q.v.] appointed Dulles to the Warren Commission charged with investigating the assassination of President Kennedy. In June 1964, following the disappearance of three civil rights workers in Philadelphia, Miss., Dulles went to Mississippi as Johnson's special emissary to evaluate "law observance problems." Dulles died in Washington, D.C. on Jan. 30, 1969.

[JBF]

For further information:
Allen W. Dulles, *The Craft of Intelligence* (New York, 1963).
David Wise and Thomas B. Ross, *The Invisible Government* (New York, 1964).
U.S. Senate, Select Committee to Study Intelligence Activities, *Alleged Assassination Plots Involving Foreign Leaders* (Washington, 1975).

DUNGAN, RALPH A(NTHONY)
b. April 22, 1923, Philadelphia, Pa.
Special Assistant to the President, January 1961-October 1964.

Ralph Dungan, aide to John F. Kennedy during both his Senate career and presidency, was born and raised in Philadelphia, Pa. Following his graduation from St. Joseph's College in 1950, Dungan studied at Princeton where he received a masters degree in public affairs in 1952. Dungan then served with the international division of the Bureau of the Budget's legislative reference service. From 1956 to 1957 he was a legislative assistant to Sen. Kennedy. Dungan later served on the staff of the Senate Labor and Public Welfare Committee and advised Kennedy on labor legislation and politics. During Kennedy's 1960 presidential campaign, Dungan served as a speech writer and liaison between Kennedy and labor leaders. After the election he aided Sargent Shriver [q.v.] in the Administration's talent hunt and advised him on political appointments.

In January 1961 Dungan joined the White House staff where he had a wide range of duties. He continued as chief talent scout for the Administration and as liaison with labor. Because Dungan was held in high regard by the Roman Catholic hierarchy, he was also used to explain Kennedy's positions to the church.

During 1961 Dungan followed developments in the Congo, where the secession of mineral-rich Katanga province shortly after independence in June 1960 threatened the viability of the central government. Dungan was one of the President's advisers who cautioned against American involvement in that civil war. Kennedy pursued this policy during most of 1961. However, by late fall Harlan Cleveland [q.v.] and the liberal New Africa Group in the State Department had convinced the President that force might be necessary to end the secession. In December U.N. troops, backed by the implied threat of American military support, succeeded in reunifying the Congo.

Throughout the Administration Dungan followed Latin American developments and foreign aid projects for the President. He helped choose the directors of the Agency for International Development, Hamilton Fowler [q.v.] and David Bell [q.v.], and helped Kennedy form the committee created to review U.S. foreign aid policy in December 1962.

In December 1964 President Lyndon B. Johnson [q.v.] made Dungan U.S. ambassador to Chile, a post in which he became known as a champion of political reform in Latin America. In June 1967 he resigned to become chancellor of higher education for the state of New Jersey.

[EWS]

DUTTON, FREDERICK G(ARY)
b. June 16, 1923; Julesburg, Colo.
Special Assistant to the President, January 1961-November 1961; Assistant Secretary of State for Congressional Relations, November 1961-December 1964.

Frederick Dutton graduated from the University of California, Berkeley, in 1946. Following the receipt of a law degree from Stanford in 1949, he entered private law

practice. Dutton served as chief assistant attorney general of California during 1957 and 1958 and from 1959 to 1960 was executive secretary to Democratic Gov. Edmund G. Brown [q.v.]. During the 1960 election he served as deputy national chairman of Citizens for Kennedy-Johnson.

In 1961 Dutton was brought to the White House as a special assistant to the President. There he served as secretary to the Cabinet and was responsible for coordinating the Administration's legislative programs on Capitol Hill. In addition, he was also expected to act as a buffer in the frequent clashes between those aides who had worked on Kennedy's Senate staff and those who had worked principally in organizing his campaigns.

In November 1961 Dutton was transferred to the State Department in the major reorganization that saw the ouster of Chester Bowles [q.v.] as undersecretary of state and his replacement by George Ball [q.v.]. There he handled relations with Capitol Hill and was responsible for guiding Administration foreign policy legislation through Congress. In 1962 Dutton helped negotiate the compromise bill that granted a $100-million loan to the United Nations. The next year he aided in efforts to win Senate ratification of the limited test ban treaty.

During 1964 Dutton served as executive director of the Platform Committee of the Democratic National Convention and director of research and planning for the Democratic presidential campaign. He resigned his government post in December 1964 to return to private law practice.

[EWS]

EASTLAND, JAMES O(LIVER)
b. Nov. 28, 1904; Doddsville, Miss.
Democratic Senator, Miss., 1941, 1943-   ;
Chairman, Judiciary Committee, 1956-   .

Eastland grew up in Mississippi, studied law at Vanderbilt University and at the University of Alabama, and was admitted to the Mississippi bar in 1927. He served in the state house of representatives from 1928 to 1932 and then spent the next nine years practicing law and running his family's 5,400-acre cotton plantation in Ruleville, Miss. Eastland was appointed U.S. Senator from Mississippi for 90 days in 1941 to fill a vacancy. In 1942 he ran for a full Senate term and won on a largely pro-agriculture platform. Reelected continuously after that, Eastland maintained a special interest in agriculture, working to advance the interests of cotton farmers in particular, and generally voted against labor and social welfare measures. An outspoken opponent of civil rights legislation, Eastland supported the States' Rights ticket in the 1948 presidential election and strongly denounced the Supreme Court's 1954 school desegregation decision. He became chairman of the Senate Judiciary Committee in 1956 and used that post to bottle up civil rights bills. The 1957 and 1960 Civil Rights Acts, both of which Eastland voted against, were passed only after the Senate leadership found ways to circumvent Eastland's Judiciary Committee. [See TRUMAN, EISENHOWER Volumes]

Although Mississippi for years had been ranked as one of the poorest states in the country, with educational levels and health standards below the national average, Eastland's conservative philosophy led him to oppose social welfare programs in the Kennedy years. He voted against the Administration bill to increase the minimum wage and extend minimum wage coverage in April 1961 and against an Administration school aid bill the next month. He voted to table and thus kill Kennedy's medical care for the aged bill in July 1962.

Eastland voted for a drug safety measure in August 1962, but only after he had played an important role in weakening the original version of the bill introduced by Sen. Estes Kefauver (D, Tenn.) [q.v.]. Most of the strong safety and antimonopoly provisions of the Kefauver bill were left out of a compromise measure written by representatives of the Administration, the drug industry, and Sens. Everett Dirksen (R, Ill.) [q.v.] and Eastland at a meeting from which Kefauver was excluded. When Kefauver later denounced both the meeting and the compromise bill, Eastland took full responsibility for calling the

meeting and said he had not asked Kefauver to attend because "I did not think he would make any agreement with respect to anything." Many of Kefauver's original safety provisions were restored to the drug bill, however, before Senate passage in October 1962.

Eastland's continuing interest in cotton was displayed when he successfully cosponsored an amendment to the 1961 minimum wage bill that exempted workers in cotton ginning from coverage. A member of the Agriculture and Forestry Committee, Eastland opposed the Administration's 1962 farm bill that sought mandatory production controls on wheat and feed grains. Many Southern Democrats feared that the feed grain controls would restrict the growth of the Southern dairy, poultry and livestock industries, and Eastland introduced an unsuccessful amendment to the bill on the Senate floor to exempt from controls farms using all the feed grains they produced.

Eastland maintained a vociferous opposition to civil rights in the early 1960s. He voted against the confirmation of Robert C. Weaver [q.v.] as administrator of the Housing and Home Finance Agency in 1961 alleging that Weaver, a black, had "a pro-Communist background." Eastland's Judiciary Committee handled all federal judicial appointments, and he was thus able to delay Senate confirmation of Thurgood Marshall's [q.v.] nomination to a circuit court judgeship for nearly a year. Eastland voted against a constitutional amendment to abolish the poll tax for federal elections in March 1962. He supported Mississippi Gov. Ross Barnett's [q.v.] efforts to prevent James Meredith's [q.v.] entry into the University of Mississippi in September 1962 and threatened a Judiciary Committee investigation of the federal government's intervention during the "Ole Miss" crisis. In January 1963 the Justice Department brought suit to end voting discrimination in Sunflower County, Miss., the site of Eastland's plantation, alleging that only 114 of more than 13,000 eligible blacks were registered to vote. Eastland decried the move, asserting that there was "no foundation in fact" for the charges of discrimination. He also denounced the Administration civil rights bill, introduced in Congress in June 1963, as a "grasp for power." One version of the bill was referred to the Judiciary Committee, which had never voluntarily reported out a civil rights measure during Eastland's chairmanship. After several days of hearings between July and September 1963, the Committee took no further action on the proposal. Eastland voted against an October 1963 bill to extend the life of the Civil Rights Commission for one year, claiming that the Commission "spews forth an unending series of fantastic and unconstitutional recommendations which would destroy our republican form of government."

A particularly ardent foe of both foreign and domestic Communism, Eastland was one of 19 Senators to vote against the nuclear test ban treaty with the Soviet Union in September 1963. Chairman of the Senate's Internal Security Subcommittee, Eastland was also a major critic of the Warren Court's decisions on internal security, civil rights and criminal law. From the mid-1950s on he repeatedly charged that the Supreme Court was "indoctrinated and brainwashed" by the left-wing and pro-Communist agitators. In a Senate address of May 1962, Eastland gave the results of a study intended to document the pro-Communist bias of the Court. According to Eastland's analysis, which presented "boxscores" showing how often each Supreme Court justice had voted "in favor of the position advocated by the Communist Party" from 1943 on, Justice Hugo Black [q.v.] was a consistent supporter of the "Communist position" and four other justices, including Earl Warren [q.v.], ruled for the "Communist stance" in a majority of cases. Eastland's charges were quickly denounced by other senators, including Hubert H. Humphrey (D, Minn.) [q.v.] and Thomas H. Kuchel (R, Calif.) [q.v.]. When the Supreme Court ruled in 1962 that prayer in public schools was a violation of the first amendment, Eastland immediately sponsored a constitutional amendment to nullify the decision.

During Johnson's Administration Eastland voted against the 1964 and 1968 Civil Rights Acts and the 1965 Voting Rights Act. He op-posed almost all of Johnson's school aid and anti-poverty programs and his medicare proposal, but was a strong supporter of the Administration's policy in Vietnam. [See JOHNSON, NIXON Volumes]

[CAB]

EATON, CYRUS S(TEPHEN)
b. Dec. 27, 1883; Pugwash,
Nova Scotia.
Industrialist.

Cyrus Eaton was a liberal, independent-minded and highly controversial industrialist who for more than 25 years advocated stronger ties between the U.S. and the Soviet Union, especially in the area of trade.

Eaton was of English descent and grew up in Pugwash, Nova Scotia. After briefly attending college, Eaton took a clerical job on the Ohio estate of multimillionaire, industrialist-philanthropist John D. Rockefeller. Eaton graduated from McMaster University, Toronto, in 1905, and under Rockefeller's asupices, started a long and immensely successful business career, first in utilities and then as chairman of the board of the Chesapeake & Ohio Railroad.

In the late 1940s Eaton, fearing the threat of nuclear warfare, worked to promote better East-West relations. He was denounced during this period as "the Kremlin's favorite capitalist," and his patriotism was frequently called into question. During the 1950s Eaton developed close friendships with several members of the Soviet leadership, including Soviet Premier Nikita Khrushchev. Shortly after the collapse of the Paris peace talks in May 1960, Eaton met briefly in Paris with Khrushchev, which prompted Sen. Thomas Dodd (D, Conn.) [q.v.] to ask for Eaton's prosecution under provisions of the Logan Act that barred private citizens from dealing with foreign governments on U.S. policy matters. In July of that year Eaton received the Lenin Peace Prize from the Soviet Union for "courageous service to the lofty idea of peaceful coexistence between the peoples." On the same day he received the prize, Eaton declared that U.S. policy toward Communist China was "wrong and dangerous" and "might lead to a world explosion."

Motivated by a strong belief that the use of nuclear weapons could be deterred only by better relations between the scientific communities in the U.S. and the Soviet Union, Eaton had financed a 1954 meeting of Soviet and U.S. atomic scientists at his boyhood home in Pugwash, Nova Scotia. The "Pugwash Conferences" were held annually during the 1950s and 1960s and provided informal exchanges among top scientists of the two countries. [See EISENHOWER Volume]

At the Pugwash Conference on disarmament in Moscow in December 1960, Soviet delegates indicated to U.S. economist Walt W. Rostow [q.v.] and scientist Jerome Wiesner [q.v.] that the Soviet Union might be willing to negotiate with the U.S. on arms control. According to historian Arthur Schlesinger, Jr. [q.v.], Premier Khrushchev had "given up" on President Eisenhower after the U-2 incident and the collapse of the Paris summit in May 1960, and was looking for ways to "semaphore his hopes for [President-elect] Kennedy." It was evident to many observers that Khrushchev had selected the Pugwash Conference, sponsored by his friend Eaton, as the ideal forum for such an overture.

During the 1960s and 1970s, Eaton was a vigorous opponent of the Vietnam war and a consistent critic of U.S. business methods. It was Eaton's belief that U.S. business invited economic collapse by refusing to acknowledge the legitimate demands of organized labor. While he described the business-labor situation as "incomprehensible," Eaton remained generally optimistic about the health and future of the American economy.

Eaton, then age 90, was named chairman emeritus of the Chesapeake & Ohio in 1973. His fortune was estimated at $200 millions.

[FHM]

EISENHOWER, DWIGHT D(AVID)
b. Oct. 14, 1890; Denison, Tex.
d. March 28, 1969; Washington, D.C.
President of the United States, 1953-61.

The third of seven sons born to a farming family of Swiss descent, Dwight D. Eisenhower grew up in Abilene, Kan., where he earned the nickname "Ike" and worked at a variety of jobs to help his brothers through college. In 1915 Eisenhower graduated from West Point. He served as a tank instructor during World War I and remained in the Army after the armistice. From 1929 to 1940 he worked under Army Chief of Staff Gen. Douglas A. MacArthur in Washington and in the Philippines when his chief went there to reorganize that country's defenses.

On the eve of America's participation in World War II, Eisenhower returned from the Philippines. He soon won a series of promotions that eventually led to his command of Allied forces on the Western Front. He oversaw the Allied invasions of North Africa in 1942, Sicily and Italy in 1943 and Normandy in 1944. In November 1945 President Harry S Truman named Eisenhower as Army Chief of Staff.

In the seven years following the end of World War II, Eisenhower moved from leadership positions in the Army to the worlds of education and politics. He resigned as Chief of Staff in February 1948 to become president of Columbia University. In 1951 he assumed command of forces newly organized under the North Atlantic Treaty Organization (NATO). In 1952 Eisenhower ran for the Republican presidential nomination and, in a closely fought contest, defeated conservative Sen. Robert A. Taft (R, Ohio). The most popular war leader since Grant, with a wide grin and a pleasing personality, Eisenhower easily defeated his Democratic opponent, Adlai E. Stevenson, both in 1952 and again in 1956. [See TRUMAN Volume]

Eisenhower's eight years in office proved less notable for accomplishment than for the deliberate avoidance of foreign and domestic conflict. Successful leaders of business, men characterized more for their administrative capacity than enthusiasm for innovation, dominated high appointive offices in his Administration. Despite his popularity Eisenhower possessed little sway over the conservative Old Guard of his own party, which often helped to defeat his modest legislative proposals in the Congress. By comparison with the social legislation passed under Democratic Administrations before and after him, Eisenhower took few initiatives and accomplished little in domestic policy areas.

On the international scene Eisenhower "waged" an uneasy peace. He forced the South Korean government to accept an armistice in 1953, thus ending a costly American-United Nations intervention in Asia. He proposed an "Atoms for Peace" program at the U.N. in 1953 and an "Open Skies" policy at the 1954 Geneva Peace Conference in the hope that the Soviet Union would agree to limit the production of atomic weapons and share nuclear secrets for peaceful purposes. His "new look" military budget reduced defense expenditures by laying far greater emphasis on more powerful nuclear weaponry at the expense of conventional Army and Navy systems.

Although Eisenhower spoke frequently of an end to the arms race, his Secretary of State, John Foster Dulles, stridently condemned Communism. Dulles negotiated regional mutual security alliances modeled after NATO and offered "massive nuclear retaliation" as the answer to Communist territorial expansion. Dulles's outward inflexibility restricted American policy towards recently independent, neutral nations that displayed less interest in the East-West political debate than in economic development.

Following Dulles's death in May 1959, Eisenhower engaged in a larger policymaking role both through personal trips abroad to neutral states and in summit meetings with Soviet leaders. Meaningful discussions with the Soviets ended in May 1960, however, when the USSR shot down an American U-2 spy plane over Russian territory. Eisenhower's admission that he knew of the spy flights prompted Soviet Party Chairman Nikita Khrushchev to withdraw from an important Paris summit conference. The incident damaged American prestige abroad and the Administration's standing at home. It dashed Eisenhower's hopes for a diplomatic triumph in his last year in office. [See EISENHOWER Volume]

Eisenhower limited his activity in the 1960 presidential race. He accepted the nomination of Richard M. Nixon [*q.v.*], his vice president, as more or less inevitable. But because Nixon preferred to campaign on his own merits and not as the popular President's former running mate, Eisenhower did not speak out in the Vice President's behalf. Only in the campaign's last week did the incumbent Republican President actively campaign for Nixon. An election night television appeal to West Coast voters helped Nixon carry California, but the intervention came too late. Sen. John F. Kennedy, who had feared Eisenhower's immense popularity and therefore only indirectly criticized his presidential leadership, narrowly defeated Nixon.

In his January 1961 farewell address, the most famous speech of his presidency, Eisenhower expressed anxiety over the creation of a Cold War "military-industrial complex" in America. The retiring leader regretted the "conjunction of an immense military establishment and a large arms industry" and warned that America "must guard against [its] unwarranted influence." He consistently opposed increases in defense spending by the Kennedy Administration in the early 1960s. In June 1962 Eisenhower criticized leaders of both parties in a public proposal that the defense budget "be substantially reduced". He also called upon NATO allies in November 1963 to share in the financial burden of Western Europe's defense and suggested that the U.S. withdraw five of its six divisions stationed in Europe.

Less than six months after leaving office, Eisenhower became embroiled in a controversy over who bore responsibility for the unsuccessful April 1961 invasion at the Bay of Pigs by anti-Castro Cubans. Although Kennedy accepted full responsibility for the Central Intelligence Agency operation, some Democratic partisans attributed the planning of the invasion to Eisenhower. In June 1961 the former President admitted that he had ordered the training and equipping of Cuban refugees in March 1960, but he added in September 1961 that "there was absolutely no planning for an invasion" of Cuba during his tenure in office. Kennedy Administration sources immediately challenged his assertion. Evidence revealed later largely discredited Eisenhower's claims of non-involvement.

Sensitive to the Kennedy Administration's criticisms of his presidency, Eisenhower responded with charges of his own. In May 1962 Eisenhower attacked Kennedy's call for a cabinet-level Urban Affairs Department as proof of his successor's efforts to augment his personal authority. Campaigning vigorously for Republicans in the month prior to the 1962 elections, Eisenhower accused Kennedy of favoring "one-party government" and termed his Administration a "clique" of "callow youths."

Despite his partisan flourishes Eisenhower endorsed the Administration's trade bill and U.N. loan proposal in 1962 and nuclear test ban treaty in 1963. The first volume of his presidential memoirs, *Mandate for Change*, was published in March 1963. Although he remained liked and respected in his last years, Eisenhower demonstrated little control over national events, including those within his own party. His health deteriorated steadily after 1964 and he died on March 28, 1969. [See JOHNSON Volume]

[JLB]

For further information:
Murray Kempton, "The Underestimation of Dwight D. Eisenhower," *Esquire* (September 1967), p. 108 +.
Arthur L. Larson, *Eisenhower, the President Nobody Knew* (New York, 1968).
Herbert S. Parmet, *Eisenhower and the American Crusades* (New York, 1972).

EISENHOWER, MILTON S(TOVER)
b. Sept. 15, 1899; Abilene, Kan.
President, Johns Hopkins University, 1956-67.

Milton Eisenhower, the younger brother of Dwight D. Eisenhower [*q.v.*], received a B.S. in industrial journalism from Kansas State University in 1924. During the same year he entered government service as U.S. vice consul in Edinbirgh, Scotland. From 1926 to 1941 he held important positions in the Department of Agriculture. In the early years of the war he directed the War Relocation Authority, which forcibly resettled Japanese-Americans. He also served in the Office of War Information. In 1943 Eisenhower became president of Kansas State College of Agriculture and Applied Science. He moved on to the presidency of Pennsylvania State University in 1950 and in 1956 to the Johns Hopkins University. Meanwhile, he assisted in the reorganization of the Department of Agriculture in 1945 and from 1946 to 1948 was chairman of the U.S. National Commission for the United Nations Economic and Social Council.

Considered more liberal and more intellectual than Dwight Eisenhower, Milton was his brother's admired and trusted adviser. He was active in the 1952 presidential campaign and during Dwight's two terms in office served on the President's Committee on Government Organization and, most prominently, acted as the President's personal representative and special ambassador to the nations of Latin America. Dean Rusk [*q.v.*], Arthur Schlesinger, Jr. [*q.v.*], and others later credited Eisenhower with initiating much of the new policy in Latin American relations that the Kennedy Administration later developed as the Alliance for Progress. [See EISENHOWER Volume]

In May 1961, shortly after the disastrous Bay of Pigs invasion of Cuba, President Kennedy approached Eisenhower to head the Tractors for Freedom Committee, together with Eleanor Roosevelt [*q.v.*] and Walter Reuther [*q.v.*]. The committee planned to negotiate with Fidel Castro the exchange of prisoners captured in the invasion for agricultural tractors. Many in the U.S. criticized the proposed exchange as a concession to blackmail, and public opinion was further incensed by Castro's insistence on terming the exchange an "indemnification." Within five weeks the controversial committee's efforts collapsed. The experience left Eisenhower bitter towards Kennedy. He claimed that the President failed to keep a promise that he would make it clear to the public that the committee was backed by the government.

Identified with the Eastern liberal wing of the Republican Party, Eisenhower served as chairman of the newly created Critical Issues Council of the Republican Citizens Committee in 1963. The council, which developed policy reports on major national issues, was the object of conservative attacks, and Sen. Barry Goldwater (R, Ariz.) [q.v.] tried to bring about the council's dissolution through the Republican National Committee. Eisenhower opposed the Goldwater faction in the Republican Party and at the 1964 National Convention nominated Pennsylvania Gov. William Scranton [q.v.] in an effort to prevent a Goldwater victory.

Eisenhower continued to speak out on public issues and served in a variety of offices. The Johnson Administration sent him on missions to Latin America, and in 1968 he headed the President's Commission on the Causes and Prevention of Violence. In 1967 Eisenhower became president emeritus of Johns Hopkins University, taking over active leadership of the school again in 1971-72. [See JOHNSON Volume]

[JCH]

For further information:
Milton S. Eisenhower, *The President Is Calling* (Garden City, N.Y., 1974).

ELLENDER, ALLEN J(OSEPH)
b. Sept. 24, 1890; Montegut, La.
d. July 27, 1972; Bethesda, Md.
Democratic Senator, La., 1937-72; Chairman, Agriculture and Forestry Committee, 1951-53, 1955-71.

After a career as a farmer-lawyer and district attorney, Ellender was elected to the Louisiana House of Representatives where he served for twelve years, the last four as speaker. Although he entered the legislature as an opponent of Huey Long, their alliance was cemented in 1929 when Ellender joined the defense at Long's impeachment trial. After Sen. Long's assassination in 1935, the Long organization slated Ellender for the Sen-

ate vacancy. Upon taking office Ellender was appointed to the Agriculture Committee and co-authored the Agricultural Adjustment Act of 1937. In 1951 Ellender became chairman of the Agriculture and Forestry Committee and in 1955 used his position as chairman to secure new sugar import quotas favorably to Louisiana's sugar industry. [See EISENHOWER Volume]

The Kennedy Administration sought to maintain farm income through mandatory "supply management controls" which would eliminate crop surpluses and reduce the cost of price supports without increasing consumer food prices. The Administration's 1961 feed grain proposal removed price support protection from farmers who refused to participate in the government's acreage retirement plan. The bill also gave the Secretary of Agriculture discretionary authority to sell federal grain stocks on the open market at less than support price. Unlike Midwestern Republican opponents of the measure such as Senator Roman Hruska (R, Neb.) [q.v.] who denounced the plan as a threat to the free marketplace, Ellender agreed with the Administration that corn farmers should be willing to accept acreage controls in return for price supports. Ellender first favored voluntary acreage reductions, but in 1962 supported mandatory feed grain controls in the Administration's Omnibus Farm Bill. However, Republican opponents of the bill forced Ellender to settle for an amendment empowering the Secretary of Agriculture to set price supports at up to 90% of parity in the final law.

A staunch Southern segregationist who led one of the three six-man teams which successfully filibustered against the 1962 voter literacy-test bill, Ellender's outspoken views on the race issue also engendered controversy abroad. At a Dec. 1, 1962 press conference in Salisbury, Southern Rhodesia, Ellender precipitated an international incident by stating that "the average African is incapable of leadership except through the assistance of Europeans." Four African governments barred Ellender from their countries and the State Department issued a statement disavowing his remarks as a reflection of American policy. The strained relationship between Ellender and the newly independent African states continued in 1963 when the ambassadors of 27 African nations responded to alleged racial slurs made by Ellender on a television program with a letter of protest to President Kennedy. During this period Ellender consistently proposed reducing foreign aid to Africa and suggested that Africa be maintained as a European sphere of influence. During the Johnson and Nixon years, Ellender's long tenure in office increased his Senate power. At the time of his death in 1972 Ellender was chairman of the powerful Appropriations Committee and President Pro Tempore of the Senate. [See JOHNSON, NIXON Volumes]

[DKR]

ELLIS, FRANK B(URTON)
b. Feb. 10, 1907; Covington, La.
Director, Office of Civil Defense and Mobilization, March 1961-February 1962; U.S. District Judge, Eastern Louisiana, April 1962- .

Ellis, a 1929 graduate of Louisiana State University Law School, practiced law in New Orleans for many years. He was a senior partner in the firm of Ellis, Lancaster and King. During the 1960 presidential race he campaigned effectively in Louisiana for Sen. John F. Kennedy.

The new President appointed Ellis Director of the Office of Civil Defense and Mobilization (OCDM) in March 1961. Ellis had hoped for a more prestigious position in the Administration but nonetheless took his new duties seriously and began an energetic campaign to educate the public about civil defense. At one point Ellis even considered seeking a testimonial from the Pope on behalf of a plan to install fallout shelters in church basements. The President, however, advised against making such a request, and Ellis canceled his trip to the Vatican.

According to Theodore Sorenson [q.v.], chief counsel to the President, Kennedy showed little interest in civil defense programs until after the Bay of Pigs fiasco of April 1961. In a May 25 address to Congress, the President called for a stepped-up shelter program to protect Americans from radioactive fallout in the event of a nuclear attack. Over Ellis's strong objections, Ken-

nedy transferred the shelter effort and much of the civil defense program from the OCDM to the Defense Department in July. The OCDM was renamed the Office of Emergency Planning and Ellis became its director. In this capacity he remained responsible for the stockpiling of strategic materials to be used during wartime or national emergency. In January 1962 Kennedy announced that the office had stockpiled materials $3.4 billion in excess of national requirements. Such stockpiling, the President suggested, could become the source of excessive and unconscionable profits, and Kennedy called for a congressional investigation of the matter.

Ellis was not linked to any wrong-doing in the probe. However, in February 1962 he resigned his post, and Kennedy nominated him to be U.S. District Judge for Eastern Louisiana. In May 1962, shortly after assuming his judgeshipl Ellis eased two important rulings in school integration cases. His predecessor, Judge J. Skelly Wright [q.v.], had ordered the first six grades of New Orleans schools to accept blacks by September 1962. Ellis, in modifying the order, required only integration of the first grade by the same date. The case was appealed to the U.S. Fifth Circuit Court, which compromised by issuing an integration order for the first three grades. In reversing another Wright decision, Ellis argued that Tulane University was a private, not a public institution, and therefore could not be forced by federal courts to admit Negroes nor could it be prevented from doing so by the state of Louisiana.

[JLW]

ENGLE, CLAIR
b. Sept. 21, 1911; Bakersfield, Calif.
d. July 30, 1964; Washington, D.C.
Democratic Senator, Calif., 1959-64.

Raised in Red Bluff in the upper Sacramento valley, Engle received his LL.B. in 1933 and in the same year began his political career as an assistant district attorney in his home county. He later won elections for district attorney and state senator. In a special election in the summer of 1943,

Engle became the first Democrat to represent the enormous second California congressional district.

In Congress Engle was known as an expert on water resources and electric power. He helped the mining industry and sponsored every piece of legislation during his congressional years that expanded the giant California Central Valley Reclamation Project. In 1955 Engle became the chairman of the House Committee on Interior and Insular Affairs. In 1958, a big Democratic year, he defeated Republican Gov. Goodwin Knight in the contest for the U.S. Senate. [See EISENHOWER Volume]

Accorded a 100% rating by the liberal Americans for Democratic Action in 1961, Engle was generally a loyal supporter of the Kennedy legislative program and almost always voted with the majority of his party. He supported federal aid to education, medical care for the aged and civil rights legislation.

Engle sat on the Senate Armed Services Committee, the Commerce Committee, the Select Small Business Committee and the Special Committee on Aging. Representing a state with a large defense industry, Engle defended California's economic interests from his seat on the Armed Services Committee. In 1961, for example, he unsuccessfully urged approval of a bill that would have granted federal research subsidies for the development of a supersonic civil aircraft, arguing that "private industry is not able to undertake development . . . within their own resources." In the following year he strenuously objected to the Defense Department's cancellation of the air-to-ground Skybolt missile program, most of which was contracted to the California-based Douglas Aircraft Corporation.

As a member of the Armed Services Subcommittee on National Stockpile and Naval Petroleum Reserves, Engle played an important role in the 1962 stockpile hearings. The most spectacular part of the investigation concerned the contract arrangements between the Hanna Coal and Ore Corporation and the U.S. government during the 1950s. Reflecting the Administration's position, Engle delivered a Senate speech in August in which he accused the Hanna Mining Co. of "deliberate misrepresentations" during the contract negotiations with the government in estimating the cost of producing nickel ore.

In 1963 it was discovered that Engle was seriously ill and required brain surgery. Although political observers had assumed that the popular Senator would face no serious opposition to his reelection, Engle announced in April 1964 that he would not run again. He attended Senate sessions in a wheelchair in June 1964 in order to vote for the civil rights bill. Engle died in Washington on July 30, 1964 and Pierre Salinger [q.v.], who had been President Kennedy's press secretary, filled out the remainder of the term.

[JCH]

ERVIN, SAM(UEL) J(AMES), JR.
b. Sept. 27, 1896; Morgantown, N.C.
Democratic Senator, N.C., 1954-75.

Sam Ervin, the senior senator from North Carolina and noted constitutional expert, was born and raised in Morgantown, N.C. Ervin attended the University of North Carolina and, following service in World War I, studied law at Harvard University where he graduated in 1922. For the next three decades he practiced law and served three terms as a state representative. Ervin was a judge in the Burke County Criminal Court from 1935 to 1937 and from 1948 to 1954 sat on the North Carolina Supreme Court. In 1954 he was appointed to the Senate and served there until his retirement from government service 21 years later. While in the upper house Ervin established a conservative record that reflected his strict constructionist view of the Constitution. [See EISENHOWER Volume]

During the Kennedy years this judicial viewpoint was the basis for his opposition to many important Administration proposals. In 1961 he voted against attempts to reorganize federal regulatory boards by making them more responsible to the President because he believed the measure was an unjustifiable increase in the power of the executive branch. That same year he unsuccessfully backed a motion to delete a provision from the Administration's unemployment compensation bill that would have enabled states to pool funds to increase benefits.

Ervin opposed the Kennedy Administration's college aid bills because he insisted that their provision for construction grants to parochial schools and loans to students attending religious institutions violated the constitutional provision for separation of church and state. In 1962 he unsuccessfully sponsored an amendment to the aid bill that would have permitted loans only to public colleges. The following year he offered a controversial amendment to the 1963 college aid bill that would have given an individual taxpayer the right to obtain a judicial review of the constitutionality of a specific loan or grant. Although approved by the Senate, the provision was dropped by the Senate-House conference committee.

The Senator also opposed Kennedy's civil rights measures on constitutional grounds. In a 1962 Senate Constitutional Rights Subcommittee meeting, Ervin denounced the Administration's proposal to curb voting discrimination through the regulation of literacy requirements as an unconstitutional attempt to deprive the states of their right to determine voter qualifications. A year later he opposed the public accommodations provision of the 1963 civil rights bill as an attempt to assume powers not granted the federal government either by the commerce clause or by the 14th Amendment to the Constitution.

The same philosophy that made him unpopular with liberals during the Kennedy Administration won Ervin liberal support at the end of the decade. As chairman of the Senate Constitutional Rights Subcommittee, Ervin held hearings on the rights of the mentally ill, criminals, military personnel and the American Indian. During the Johnson Administration the Senator supported measures designed to protect freedom of conscience and ensure the privacy of individuals against government and commercial surveillance. Ervin became na-

tionally prominent in 1973 when he headed the seven-man Senate committee formed to investigate the Watergate affair. He retired from Congress in January 1975. [See JOHNSON, NIXON Volumes]

[EWS]

ESTES, BILLIE SOL
b. Jan. 10, 1925; near Clyde, Tex.
Businessman; Member, National Cotton Advisory Committee, Department of Agriculture, July 1961-April 1962.

Billie Sol Estes, the son of an impoverished farmer and lay preacher, grew up in a spartan and fundamentalist household in West Texas. In 1951 Estes moved to Pecos, Tex., where a cotton boom was underway. Aided by federal price guarantees, within two years he became a prosperous cotton farmer with interests in a number of other enterprises. The National Junior Chamber of Commerce chose Estes, who quoted the Bible frequently and impressed many as a deeply religious man, as one of the ten outstanding young men in the country for 1953.

In his efforts to expand his commercial activities in the late 1950s, Estes was a ruthless competitor. He began to sell chemical fertilizer in 1957 and the following year commenced an effort to drive his competitors out of business by selling at below his wholesale cost. Estes hoped to monopolize the West Texas market in the long run, but in the meantime he accumulated huge debts to the fertilizer manufacturers from whom he was purchasing. He incurred additional debts by employing the same price-cutting strategy to induce farmers to store their grain in his elevators.

Late in 1959 Estes began to implement a fraudulent scheme for acquiring desperately needed funds by selling, and then leasing back, non-existent fertilizer tanks to West Texas farmers. He used his mortgages on the tanks to borrow from $22 to $30 million from commercial finance companies.

In 1960 Estes initiated a plan to expand his cotton lands by circumventing the federal government's allotment program, which was designed to limit the number of acres a farmer could devote to that crop. He sold land to farmers who possessed unused cotton allotments. Estes leased back the land and then, by an illegal prearrangement, the new owner defaulted on his first mortgage payment. The land, with the allotment that was now attached to it, reverted to Estes.

While building his fortune Estes was also becoming involved in Democratic Party affairs. In the late 1950s he began to contribute to the campaigns of Sen. Ralph Yarborough [q.v.] and Rep. J. T. Rutherford, both of Texas. From December 1960 to January 1962 he donated $12,300 to the national party, traveled to Washington frequently and made the acquaintance of many leading government officials. In July 1961 he was appointed to the Agriculture Department's National Cotton Advisory Committee.

In February 1962 the *Pecos Independent and Enterprise* published a series of articles describing Estes's fertilizer tank loans, which led to his arrest by the FBI on March 29. Soon the entire range of Estes's business affairs was exposed, including his dealings with the Agriculture Department. Early in 1961 it was revealed that the Department had permitted Estes to post a low bond for his participation in the government-subsidized grain storage program, basing its action upon a false and unverified financial statement submitted by Estes himself. The following December, despite a pending Department investigation of his accumulation of cotton allotments, Estes had been reappointed to the National Cotton Advisory Council. In January 1962 the Department had postponed an adverse ruling on the legality of his acquisitions.

These revelations, combined with Estes's links to the Democratic Party at the national level, produced the first important scandal of the Kennedy Administration. Republicans charged that the Agriculture Department had shown favoritism to Estes and noted that during the Department's investigation of his cotton dealings he had boasted of his influence with Vice President Lyndon Johnson [q.v.] and Secretary of Agriculture Orville A. Freeman [q.v.].

In 1962 Assistant Secretary of Labor Jerry R. Holleman and several minor Agriculture Department officials resigned or were dismissed because of favors they had received from Estes. Two Congressmen, J. R. Rutherford and H. Carl Anderson (R, Minn.) [q.v.], whose connections with Estes were widely publicized, lost their bids for reelection in the fall of 1962. But at a press conference in May, President Kennedy strongly defended Freeman, and neither the Secretary nor any other top-ranking Administration or Democratic Party figures was seriously tainted by the scandal.

The most significant congressional investigation of the affair was conducted in 1962 by Sen. John L. McClellan's (D, Ark.) [q.v.] Permanent Investigations Subcommittee of the Government Operations Committee. The Subcommittee concluded that the procedures and organizational structure of the Agriculture Department had to be revised to facilitate tighter control of farm programs, but it exonerated the Department of collusion with Estes.

In May 1962 the Agriculture Department fined Estes over a half million dollars for his cotton allotment dealings. He was convicted of fraud, theft and conspiracy by a Texas court in November 1962 and the following January was sentenced to eight years in prison. In March 1963 a federal jury found him guilty of mail fraud and conspiracy, for which he received a 15-year sentence. All charges in both trials stemmed from Estes's fertilizer tank operations. Estes remained free on bail pending appeals. The U.S. Supreme Court, in January 1965, refused to overturn the federal conviction. Five months later, however, it struck down the state verdict because the Texas trial had been televised over the defendant's objection.

In July 1971 Estes was released from prison after having served almost six and one-half years of his federal term. By the spring of 1975 he was employed by the Permian Petroleum Co. in Abilene, Tex. The following summer, according to a Dallas newspaper, the Internal Revenue Service, which had a $21-million tax lien on

Estes, was investigating him to determine if he had concealed assets in bank trusts and real estate.

[MLL]

For further information:
Julius Duscha, *Taxpayers' Hayride: The Farm Problem from the New Deal to the Billie Sol Estes Case* (Boston, 1964).
———, "Estes: Three-Sided Country Slicker," *Fortune* (July, 1962), pp. 166-70.

EVERS, MEDGAR W(ILEY)
b. July 2, 1925; Decatur, Miss.
d. June 12, 1963; Jackson, Miss.
Mississippi Field Secretary, NAACP, December 1954-June 1963.

After graduating from Alcorn A & M College in 1952, Evers took a job with a black-owned insurance company in Mound Bayou, Miss. At the same time he joined the NAACP and began organizing chapters of the Association in the Mississippi Delta. At an NAACP meeting late in 1953, Evers volunteered to try to desegregate the University of Mississippi. He applied to the University's Law School in January 1954, but when his application was rejected in September, Evers and the NAACP decided not to take his case to court.

Evers became the Association's first state field secretary in Mississippi in December 1954, and he opened an office in Jackson, the state capital, in January 1955. Over the next nine years Evers worked to increase NAACP membership and to encourage voter registration among Mississippi's blacks. He traveled throughout the state explaining the Supreme Court's 1954 school desegregation decision, showing black parents how to file petitions for desegregation with local school boards, the first step in implementing the Supreme Court ruling. While he organized the school board petition campaign, Evers also coordinated aid for black parents who signed petitions and were then subjected to economic reprisal for their action. He investigated the August 1955 lynching of 14-year-old Emmett Till, the murders of civil rights workers such as Lamar Smith in 1955 and Herbert Lee in 1961, and the charges of personal harassment and threats his office received from blacks throughout the state.

Once described as "the heartbeat of any integration activity in the state of Mississippi," Evers kept in touch with the increased tempo of civil rights work in the state during the Kennedy years. After 1960 the Student Nonviolent Coordinating Committee and the Congress of Racial Equality began voter registration drives in Mississippi. The Justice Department filed several voting discrimination suits and black students from colleges and high schools staged occasional sit-ins and protests. James Meredith [*q.v.*] called on Evers in the fall of 1960 and said he wanted to enter the University of Mississippi at Oxford, still an all-white institution. Evers encouraged him, put him in touch with NAACP attorneys and counseled and supported him until his graduation in 1963. Evers and his wife also signed a petition to the Jackson school board asking for desegregation of the city's schools in August 1962. When the board took no action, they joined in a federal court suit to integrate the schools, the first such case to be filed by individuals in Mississippi.

The next year Evers led a major antisegregation drive in Jackson. On May 12, 1963 a mass meeting called by the NAACP adopted a resolution demanding fair employment opportunities for blacks in city jobs, the desegregation of all public facilities and accommodations in Jackson, an end to discriminatory business practices and the appointment of a biracial committee to achieve these goals. Jackson Mayor Allen Thompson rejected all the demands the next day, and on May 17 Evers called for a consumer boycott which quickly spread from a few local products and one department store to all the stores in Jackson's main shopping area. The Mayor finally met with an NAACP committee on May 28, but when black leaders reported afterwards that he had agreed to several of their key demands, the Mayor denied their statements. Black college students in Jackson began sitting in at local lunch counters that day, and on May 30 a student march was attacked by the police and 600 were arrested.

According to his wife Evers was initially wary of the student protests and wanted the time and place of demonstrations carefully chosen and their purpose made clear. Evers and other adults in the black community were won over by the students' courage, however, and Evers was soon organizing protests and arranging bail for the jailed students. On June 1 he was arrested for picketing. Released from jail soon after, Evers led a daily campaign of mass meetings, marches, picketing and prayer vigils. On the evening of June 11, with the Jackson protests still in high gear, Evers listened to President Kennedy's nationwide address on civil rights, spoke at a mass rally in Jackson and then drove home. Around 12:20 a.m., as he walked from his car to the door of his house, Evers was shot in the back by a sniper. He died within an hour.

Evers had received little publicity for his work while alive, but his death made him a celebrated martyr of the civil rights movement. Funeral services were held in Jackson on June 15, and some 3,000 blacks marched that day behind a hearse bearing Evers's body. On June 19 Evers was buried in Arlington National Cemetery. The Jackson demonstrations he had led were suspended on June 17 while another local black leader met with President Kennedy in Washington. After a call from the President and Attorney General Robert Kennedy [q.v.], Mayor Thompson met with a committee of black leaders on June 18. Later he announced that the city would hire six blacks as policemen and eight as school crossing guards and would promote another eight blacks in the sanitation department. On June 23 the Federal Bureau of Investigation arrested Byron de la Beckwith, a fertilizer salesman from Greenwood, Miss., and a member of the segregationist White Citizens Council. He was indicted by a country grand jury in July in connection with Evers's murder and was tried twice early in 1964. After both trials ended in hung juries, he was free.

[CAB]

For further information:
Mrs. Medgar Evers with William Peters, *For Us, the Living* (Garden City, 1967).

FARMER, JAMES L(EONARD)
b. Jan. 12, 1920; Marshall, Tex.
National Director, Congress of Racial Equality, February 1961-March 1966.

After graduating from Wiley College in Texas in 1938, Farmer enrolled at the School of Religion at Howard University where he became well versed in pacifist thought. He received a Bachelor of Divinity degree in 1941 and then served as race relations secretary for the Fellowship of Reconciliation, a Christian pacifist organization, until 1945. While in this post he helped found the Congress of Racial Equality (CORE), first as a local Chicago group in the spring of 1942 and then as a national organization in June 1943. An interracial association, CORE applied Gandhian techniques of nonviolent direct action to racial segregation and discrimination in the U.S., pioneering the use of sit-ins and other forms of nonviolent protest. Farmer later worked as an organizer for several unions and as program director for the NAACP, but he remained in touch with CORE and its activities.

Farmer became national director of CORE on Feb. 1, 1961, and on March 13 he issued a call for a Freedom Ride through the South to challenge segregation at interstate bus terminals. Thirteen riders, including Farmer, left Washington by bus on May 4 with New Orleans as their destination. The first ride ended on May 14, however, after one bus was burned in Anniston, Ala., and several riders were severely beaten there and in Birmingham, Ala. On May 23, in Montgomery, Ala., Farmer and other rights leaders announced that the rides would continue despite threats of violence. Farmer and 26 other riders left for Jackson, Miss. the next day in two heavily guarded buses. There they were arrested when they tried to use the white waiting room at the bus terminal and, when found guilty of breach of the peace, elected to go to jail rather than pay their fines. Farmer spent 39 days in jail and then continued organizing more rides through the summer. As Farmer later noted, the Freedom Rides "catapulted CORE into fame," making it a major civil rights organization and Farmer a black leader of national stature. The rides ended after the Interstate Commerce Commission issued an order on Sept. 22 prohibiting segregation in all interstate bus terminals.

As CORE national director, Farmer traveled extensively to raise money, organize new CORE chapters and assist local action projects. In May 1963 he went to North Carolina to lead demonstrations and help coordinate protest movements in Greensboro, Durham and High Point. In each city Farmer led mass marches and boycotts until a biracial committee was appointed to work for the desegregation of public accommodations. Farmer went to Plaquemines, La., in August 1963 where local blacks aided by CORE workers had begun demonstrations to achieve desegregation in the town. The protests intensified on Aug. 19 when Farmer led a mass march of 500 blacks that was broken up by police. Farmer was arrested along with key local leaders and remained in jail until Aug. 29. He led another march of 600 blacks to the county courthouse on Sept. 1. This was also broken up by police using tear gas, fire hoses and electric cattle prods. State troopers then began a house-to-house search for the demonstration leaders, especially Farmer. Fearing that he would be killed if found, several local blacks hid Farmer in a hearse and took him over back roads to New Orleans. Farmer later described his escape during that "night of wild terror" as "a story book escape that was no story while I was living it."

Under Farmer CORE became known as one of the most militant and creative groups in the civil rights movement and he developed a reputation as a tough and audacious rights leader of great physical courage. Farmer was a co-chairman of the 1963 March on Washington, but he missed the Aug. 28 march since he was then in the Plaquemine jail.

Farmer led sit-ins at the New York World's Fair on its opening day in April 1964 and participated in highly publicized demonstrations in Bogalusa, La. in April and July of 1965. He resigned from CORE on March 1, 1966 intending to launch a program for improving literacy and job skills among the chronically unemployed. However, he eventually abandoned this project when an expected grant from the Office of Economic Opportunity did not materialize. [See JOHNSON, NIXON Volumes]

[CAB]

For further information:
August Meier and Elliott Rudwick, *CORE: A Study in the Civil Rights Movement, 1942-1968* (New York, 1973).

FEINSINGER, NATHAN P(AUL)
b. Sept. 20, 1902; New York, N.Y.
Labor arbitrator.

Born in Brooklyn, Feinsinger graduated from the University of Michigan in 1926 and received his law degree there in 1928. After a year of post-graduate work at Columbia University, he joined the law faculty at the University of Wisconsin and from 1937 to 1939 served as general counsel of the Wisconsin Labor Relations Board. Feinsinger's role in national labor disputes began with his appointment as associate general counsel of the National War Labor Board in 1942. In 1943 he helped resolve a United Mine Workers strike, and in 1946 President Truman appointed him to the fact-finding board that set the wage pattern in the decisive dispute between union and management in the steel industry. During the Korean War Truman appointed Feinsinger chairman of the newly reconstituted Wage Stabilization Board, a post he held until 1952, when he resumed his teaching duties. [See TRUMAN Volume]

Feinsinger was involved in several labor disputes in the early 1960s arising from increased automation in the transportation industry. In February 1961 President Kennedy chose him to head a commission to investigate a costly airline strike. The Flight Engineers International Association (FEIA) struck several major airline companies after a national mediation board ordered that flight crew members, represented by the FEIA and the Air Line Pilots Association, hold an election to choose one union as their bargaining representative instead of the existing two. The ruling came at a time when airlines were seeking to reduce cockpit crews from four—three pilots and one engineer—to three members. Engineers feared that representation by a single union would deprive them of seniority and that pilots would eventually replace them in the third cockpit seat.

On Feb. 17 the FEIA called a strike against Pan American, which immediately spread to six other major lines. The walkout ended at six of the seven lines on Feb. 23, when both sides agreed to submit the dispute to the commission headed by Feinsinger. In April the panel recommended that the unions merge and called for a "phasedown" of crew size from four to three. A second commission, appointed by Kennedy in November to avert a threatened strike by engineers at TWA, endorsed the Feinsinger recommendations, adding that engineers with some training as pilots should fill the third crew position. In 1962 the FEIA and the airlines reached agreements that reserved for engineers the first claim to the third seat.

Following a Supreme Court decision upholding the right of railroads to make sweeping work rule changes to eliminate unnecessary jobs, Kennedy appointed Feinsinger to the board formed to probe the matter. The panel suggested arbitration of some key issues and urged the elimination of most diesel locomotive firemen in freight and yard service. When negotiations failed Congress approved a bill requiring each side to submit key work rule issues to compulsory arbitration, delaying a strike by 180 days. A federal arbitration panel ruled in November that a total of 40,000 jobs were unnecessary and eventually could be eliminated.

Feinsinger later was appointed to a panel that mediated the 1966 New York City transit strike. He continued to teach at the University of Wisconsin Law School until 1973.

[MDB]

FELDMAN, MYER
b. June 22, 1917; Philadelphia, Pa.
Deputy Special Counsel to the President, January 1961-April 1964.

Following his graduation from the University of Pennsylvania's Wharton School of Business in 1935 and the receipt of his law degree from the University of Pennsylvania in 1938, Feldman entered private law practice in Philadelphia. In 1946 he was appointed special counsel and executive assistant to the chairman of the Securities and Exchange Commission. He remained in that post until 1954, when he became counsel to the Senate Banking and Currency Committee. In 1958 Feldman joined the legislative staff of Sen. John F. Kennedy and served in that capacity until Kennedy's election in 1960. During the presidential race he played an important role in researching and writing speeches and position papers and in furnishing Kennedy with information about Richard Nixon's [q.v.] record.

In January 1961 Feldman was appointed deputy special counsel to the President. As was the case with many of Kennedy's advisers, Feldman's area of responsibility was ill-defined, but he served primarily as liaison between regulatory agencies and the White House. It was his job to speak for the White House on matters before the agencies and counsel the President on tariff and trade issues. In addition he channeled business requests dealing with such problems as licenses and import quotas to appropriate agencies. He also advised the President on what action to take on many bills passed by Congress.

Feldman was responsible for drafting presidential proclamations and executive orders, and he assisted in the writing of the Administration's civil rights and consumer legislation. In 1962 he helped draft Kennedy's important transportation message, which proposed a fundamental reshaping of federal transportation policies by reducing Washington's role in intercity transportation and enlarging federal responsibility for urban transport. During the closing months of 1962 Feldman headed a presidential task force formed to analyze transportation problems in the Northeast. The panel's report, issued in December, recommended a comprehensive survey of transportation problems of the Northeastern urban corridor and urged the modernization of rail service to permit the use of high-speed automated trains.

That year Feldman also served as the

President's representative in the Administration's clash with Sen. Estes Kefauver (D, Tenn.) [q.v.], who was seeking legislation to increase federal control of drug safety standards and prices. Fearing that Kefauver's bills were too strong, Feldman arranged a secret meeting between legislative leaders, representatives of the Department of Health, Education and Welfare and drug manufacturers to write a bill acceptable to the industry. In violation of political courtesy, Kefauver was not asked to attend. The Senator later denounced the meeting in a speech before the upper house. Strong drug legislation was passed only after knowledge of the thalidomide tragedies generated strong public support for rigorous measures.

From time to time Feldman also dealt with Middle East problems. During the summer of 1961 he prodded the President into approving an American initiative, under U.N. auspices, to convince Israel and the Arab countries to accept a certain number of Palestinian refugees as a means of defusing tensions in the area. The plan failed when the Arabs rejected the proposal and Israel withdrew its initial support. Feldman also worked with Kennedy throughout his Administration in his unsuccessful attempts to open Arab-Israeli negotiations.

From April 1964 to January 1965 Feldman served as special counsel to President Johnson. Following his resignation he returned to private law practice.

[EWS]

For further information:
Lewis J. Paper, *The Promise and the Performance* (New York, 1975).

FELT, HARRY D(ONALD)
b. June 21, 1902; Topeka, Kan.
Commander-in-Chief, U.S. Armed Forces in the Pacific, May 1958-June 1964.

Adm. Harry D. Felt, a career naval officer, came to prominence as commander-in-chief of the U.S. armed forces in the Pacific during the early U.S. military in-

volvement in South Vietnam. In late September 1961 Felt and U.S. Ambassador to South Vietnam Frederick E. Nolting Jr. [q.v.] met in Saigon with South Vietnamese President Ngo Dinh Diem to discuss ways to cope with the stepped-up Communist guerrilla warfare throughout the countryside. Diem proposed the signing of a bilateral defense treaty by which the government of South Vietnam would receive increased military aid from the U.S. This request was forwarded to Washington, and in October 1961 President Kennedy responded by sending Gen. Maxwell D. Taylor [q.v.] to South Vietnam to investigate the political and military situation there.

Before his arrival Taylor stopped off in Honolulu to question Felt about the possibility of sending U.S. combat forces to South Vietnam. Felt did not give Taylor a definitive answer, but on Oct. 20 he cabled Washington to suggest that while the presence of American combat troops would greatly strengthen the Diem regime's ability to resist the Communist assault, it might also "stir [up a] fuss throughout Asia about the reintroduction of [a] force of white colonialism . . . and could trigger intensification of aggression." He advised that no combat troops be sent until all other means for helping the South Vietnamese government had been exhausted. (The *New York Times* reported on Dec. 20, 1961 that there were already 2,000 U.S. troops in South Vietnam serving as "military advisers.")

Felt and Secretary of Defense Robert S. McNamara [q.v.] met several times in Hawaii in 1962 to discuss the military situation in Vietnam. These conferences generally ended with public statements suggesting that South Vietnam, with American arms and military advisers, would defeat the Communists. Speaking in Saigon on Jan. 11, 1963, Felt maintained that while there were difficulties between the South Vietnamese and their American advisers, the defeat of the Communists was "inevitable." However, he was critical of reporters in Saigon who wrote pessimistic accounts of the war. "Get on the team," he told Malcolm Browne of the Associated Press, "Stop looking for the hole in the doughnut."

As early as January 1962 Felt also became critical of President Diem, who he thought did not have the support of the military and lacked the capacity or will to carry out much needed political and military reforms. He was particularly disturbed by the influence of Diem's brother and sister-in-law, Ngo Dinh Nhu and Madame Nhu, who during the spring and summer of 1963 had played a leading role in the suppression of the Buddhist opposition to his regime. Adm. Felt supported Ambassador Henry Cabot Lodge's [q.v.] position that the Nhus had to be removed from power in order to advance to the South Vietnamese war effort.

Late in August State Department officials instructed Lodge to inform a group of dissident South Vietnamese generals that the U.S. would not oppose the overthrow of the Diem regime. Felt dispatched a task force of American ships to the coast of South Vietnam to be ready to evacuate American dependents and civilians who might be endangered during a coup. The generals called off the coup in August, but by late October Felt once again put his evacuation team on the alert. Felt and Lodge paid Diem a courtesy call on Nov. 1, 1963 while coup units encircled Saigon. That afternoon the government was overthrown, and Diem and his brother were killed. (Madame Nhu was touring the U.S. at the time.)

As early as July 1962 Felt, under orders from Defense Secretary McNamara, had prepared a three-year plan under which the American role in Vietnam would be gradually eliminated as the South Vietnamese Army was strengthened. In accord with this plan 1,000 American troops were withdrawn in December 1963, but a worsening military situation prevented further reductions. When Felt retired in July 1964, there were more than 15,000 Americans in Vietnam.

[JLW]

For further information:
U.S. Department of Defense, *The Pentagon Papers*, Senator Gravel Edition (Boston, 1971), Vol. II.

FINDLEY, PAUL
b. June 23, 1921; Jacksonville, Ill.
Republican Representative, Ill., 1961-   .

Paul Findley, the publisher of the *Pike Press*, a small county weekly, was elected to Congress in 1960. His district in west central Illinois, a prosperous farming area, also included the state capital, Springfield, and the small cities of Alton and Quincy. This region sent Lincoln to Congress in 1846.

A fiscal conservative and staunch advocate of balanced budgets, Findley consistently opposed Kennedy Administration programs, including the federal aid to education, minimum wage and manpower training bills. In the spring of 1963 he spoke against the bill guaranteeing women equal pay for equal work. He argued that it cost more to employ women than men because of their high turnover and that the new legislation would only force employers to cut back their number of female workers.

As a member of the House Agriculture Committee, Findley denounced farm subsidy programs, attacked the Administration for meddling in farm business and deplored the fact that "the bureaucracy of government has replaced the discipline of the marketplace." Findley received national attention in the early 1960s for his opposition to granting Communist-bloc nations credits to purchase American agricultural products. He also opposed price supports for imported sugar, arguing that such measures as the 1962 Sugar Act helped finance and keep dictators like Raphael Trujillo in power.

The liberal Americans for Democratic Action gave Findley a zero rating for his voting record in 1961 and 1963. He consistently opposed the Johnson Administration's domestic policies. Unlike most Middle Western Republicans, however, Findley called for a review in 1967 of the President's power to wage war in Vietnam. He thought U.S. involvement in Southeast Asia a "fundamental mistake" but nonetheless voted consistently for war appropriations and opposed efforts to set a rigid timetable for withdrawal of American troops from the conflict. [See JOHNSON, NIXON Volumes]

[JLW]

FISHER, ADRIAN S(ANFORD)
b. Jan. 21, 1914; Memphis, Tenn.
Deputy Director, Arms Control and Disarmament Agency, October 1961-January 1969.

A Princeton and Harvard Law School graduate, Fisher served as law clerk to Supreme Court Justice Louis Brandeis in 1938 and Justice Felix Frankfurther [q.v.] in 1939. During the war he was assistant executive officer to the assistant secretary of war and served as technical adviser to the American judges at the Nuremberg war crimes trials. After the trials he joined the Washington law firm of Covington and Burling and later became vice president and counsel of the Washington Post Company.

President Kennedy appointed Fisher deputy to his disarmament adviser, John McCloy [q.v.] in February 1961. His chief duty at this post was to work with Congress in the Administration's efforts to pass the bill for the formation of the Arms Control and Disarmament Agency. The Agency, designed to coordinate and develop policy on disarmament and nuclear testing, was approved in September 1961. One month later Fisher was appointed deputy director.

Within the Agency Fisher served several functions. He continued his liaison with Congress, particularly the Senate Foreign Relations Committee; in addition he directed the gathering of basic information on the formation of disarmament policy. When Kennedy called for a reevaluation of American arms control policy in the summer of 1962, Fisher became chairman of the committee formed to analyze the advantages and risks of a partial, unsupervised test ban treaty. This group was also asked to prepare drafts of both a partial and a comprehensive treaty, which the President considered tabling simultaneously at Geneva.

Fisher's major concerns were with the problems of dectection, the possible detrimental effects a treaty could have on the development of nuclear technology and the influence such a treaty would have on U.S. military superiority. The group concluded that an agreement presented no real danger to the U.S. given the state of existing technology. A partial treaty would involve some risks, primarily because it would not stop the arms race and might contribute to the problems the U.S. faced in getting the Soviet Union to accept on-site inspection of underground testing areas. However a partial agreement also could prove to be an important first step toward more comprehensive treaties.

While developing this analysis Fisher continued his contacts with Congress. Interviews with senators, particularly Albert Gore (D, Tenn.) [q.v.] and Thomas Dodd (D, Conn.) [q.v.], convinced him that many on Capitol Hill opposed a comprehensive test ban treaty because, in their opinion, it failed to give the U.S. adequate safeguards against possible Soviet cheating. Consequently, Fisher became a proponent of a limited ban as the only one politically possible at the time. In August 1962 the U.S. delegation to the Geneva disarmament talks tabled both partial and comprehensive treaties; both were rejected by the Soviet Union.

In July 1963, after Premier Nikita Khrushchev indicated that he was willing to continue disarmament talks through private emissaries, Fisher accompanied Kennedy's representative, W. Averell Harriman [q.v.], to Moscow as his adviser. There, as chairman of the treaty drafting committee, he helped work out a system of multiple depositories designed to permit countries not having diplomatic relations with one of the three signatories to ratify the agreement. Clearly aimed at East Germany and the People's Republic of China, this document provided that each nation was free to sign in association with only those countries with which it had cordial relations. The treaty was initialed on July 25.

Fisher was one of the leaders of the Administration's fight for treaty ratification in August and September. In conjunction with his superior, William Foster [q.v.], he contacted individual senators to gain their backing and remained in the Senate gallery during floor debates to give support to Administration forces whenever needed.

Fisher retained his post as deputy director of the Arms Control and Disarmament

Agency throughout the Johnson Administration. He alternated with Foster as chief delegate to the 18 Nation Disarmament Conference in Geneva and helped negotiate the nuclear nonproliferation treaty of 1968. [See JOHNSON Volume]. Fisher left government service in January 1969 to return to private law practice and to accept the position of dean and professor of international law and international trade at Georgetown University Law Center.

[EWS]

For further information:

E(edson) L(ouis) M(illard) Burns, *A Seat at the Table* (Toronto, 1972).

Arthur Dean, *Test Ban and Disarmament: The Path of Negotiation* (New York, 1966).

Harold D. Jacobson, *Diplomats, Scientists and Politicians* (Ann Arbor, 1966).

Mary Milling Lepper, *Foreign Policy Formulation: A Case Study of the Nuclear Test Ban Treaty of 1963* (Columbus, 1971).

FONG, HIRAM L(EONG)

b. Oct. 1, 1907; Honolulu, Hawaii.
Republican Senator, Hawaii, 1959- .

The son of indentured plantation workers, Fong worked his way through the University of Hawaii and Harvard Law School. Returning to Honolulu in 1935, he formed the city's first multiracial law office, invested in diversified business interests, which eventually made him a millionaire, and began a political career by winning election to the Hawaiian Territorial Legislature. Fong's success story was an outstanding example of the upward mobility of many Chinese-Americans, the first nonwhite group to challenge the plantation elite's economic leadership on the islands.

Fong joined the Republican Party, the party of the white elite, but in the postwar era also maintained a working relationship with the powerful International Longshoremen's and Warehousemen's Union (ILWU). Speaker of the legislature from 1948 to 1954, Fong was easily elected to the U.S. Senate in Hawaii's first general election as a state in July 1959. Through the flip of a coin with Sen. Oren Long (D,

Hawaii) [*q.v.*], Fong won the title of senior senator and the full six year term.

In the Senate Fong was soon identified with the moderate Republican faction. During the 87th Congress he voted with the Kennedy Administration on about 50% of key roll-call votes, siding with the President more often on domestic issues than on foreign policy matters. Fong was one of only eight Republicans to support Kennedy's school-aid bill in May 1961. As a member of the Senate Post Office and Civil Service Committee, he was generally favorable to increased pay and benefits for civil service workers. A proponent of civil rights legislation, Fong voted to change the Senate's filibuster rule in February 1963 and in the following month joined six Senate colleagues in introducing a Republican civil rights "package."

Besides serving on the Senate Post Office and Civil Service Committee, Fong served on the Judiciary Commitee, the Public Works Committee, the Special Committee on Aging and the Republican Committee on Committees. In 1964 he was easily reelected to the Senate, but his conservative foreign policy stance, particularly his support of the Vietnam war, hurt his popularity in his home state. In the 1970 elections he relied on his personal organization—the Republican Party in Hawaii was almost totally ineffective—and the lukewarm backing of the ILWU to give him a narrow victory. [See JOHNSON, NIXON Volumes]

[JCH]

FORD, GERALD R(UDOLPH)

b. July 14, 1913; Omaha, Neb.
Republican Representative, Mich., 1949-73.

Gerald R. Ford, grew up in Grand Rapids, Mich., and in 1935 received his B.A. from the University of Michigan where he had starred as a football center. Declining offers from professional football teams, he earned a LL.B. from Yale in 1941 and served in the U.S. Navy during World War II. In 1948 Sen. Arthur H. Vandenberg (R, Mich.), leader of the Senate Republicans' internationalist wing, persuaded Ford to mount a successful challenge to an isolationist, incumbent representative in the GOP House primary. Ford easily won election twelve times and during the 1950s allied himself politically with Dwight D. Eisenhower and ideologically with Richard M. Nixon [q.v.]. "I don't know of anyone whose views on domestic and foreign policy," Nixon reportedly said in July 1960, "are more consonant with mine than Jerry [Ford]." Nixon listed Ford as among those men he seriously considered as a running mate in his unsuccessful 1960 presidential campaign. [See EISENHOWER Volume]

During the 87th Congress, Ford upheld the Vandenberg bipartisan tradition in foreign affairs. According to *Congressional Quarterly*, he supported Kennedy on 73% of the foreign policy votes for which the President announced a position, well above the Republican average. As a member of the House Appropriations Committee's Subcommittee on Foreign Operations Committee, which reviewed the Administration's foreign aid requests, Ford often opposed chairman Otto Passman (D, La.) [q.v.], a virulent foe of large foreign assistance authorizations. In September 1961 Passman's Committee voted to reduce the White House request for foreign military aid for fiscal 1962 by 17.5%. Against the Committee's recommendation, Ford offered an amendment approved by the House that restored the military aid funds sought by the White House. As the senior Republican on the Appropriations Committee's Department of Defense Subcommittee, he defended Defense Secretary Robert S. McNamara [q.v.] during the March 1963 debate over his department's refusal to acquiese to the Air Force's call for a RS-70 reconnaissance-strike plane.

Beginning in 1959 Ford served on the select congressional committee that authorized the secret budget of the Central Intelligence Agency. Informed of the CIA's role prior to the Bay of Pigs invasion in April 1961, Ford later declined to join some of his party colleagues in condemning Kennedy for the anti-Castro fiasco. In confidential talks with CIA Director John A. McCone [q.v.] in early October 1962, Ford offered support for an increase in the CIA's air reconnaissance missions over Cuba which later confirmed early reports of Soviet offensive missile sites on the island.

Despite his occasional aid to the Kennedy Administration on its foreign policy and intelligence operations, Ford maintained a conservative stance in domestic matters. He voted with the Republican-Southern Democratic conservative coalition on 64% of the votes during the 87th Congress. He opposed most of the Kennedy New Frontier legislation, voting against the area redevelopment and school aid appropriations in April 1961 and the omnibus housing bill in June 1961.

In January 1963 a coalition of young Republican House members challenged the authority of House Minority Leader Charles A. Halleck (R, Ind.) [q.v.] by opposing the re-election of Rep. Charles B. Hoeven (R, Iowa) as chairman of the Republican Conference Committee, the party's third-ranking leadership post. Led by Reps. Charles E. Goodell (R, N.Y.) [q.v.] and Robert P. Griffin (R, Mich), the "Young Turks" selected the handsome, athletic 49-year-old Ford as their candidate. He defeated the 67-year-old Hoeven by a vote of 87 to 78. Ford's candidacy represented an effort by younger conservative and liberal members to expand their role in Party decision making and to improve the public image of the GOP House leadership. The Young Turks denied that they intended to challenge Halleck directly, but Hoeven described himself as "the scapegoat and fall-guy" of a campaign to seize the House Republican leadership away from the incumbent leader. Ford worked hard to revitalize the Conference Committee and sought the views of both wings of the Party in the formulation of official Republican Party statements.

Ford agreed in December 1964 to run against Halleck for the minority leadership, and a month later the Young Turks again proved successful. Ford served as minority leader until December 1973 when President Nixon chose him to become vice president following the resignation of Spiro Agnew. He succeeded Nixon in August 1974. [See JOHNSON, NIXON Volumes]

[JLB]

For further information:
Richard H. Rovere, *A Ford, Not a Lincoln* (New York, 1975).

FORD, HENRY II
b. Sept. 4, 1917; Detroit, Mich.
Chairman and Chief Executive Officer,
Ford Motor Company, 1960-   .

Henry Ford II was the grandson of the legendary industrialist Henry Ford and the son of Ford Motor Co. President Edsel Ford. At the time of his father's death in May 1943, Ford, who majored in sociology at Yale, was serving in the U.S. Navy. He was released in August and began a management apprenticeship at Ford under the tutelage of his 80-year-old grandfather, who had resumed active management of the company. He was named president of Ford in 1945 at the age of 28. Unlike his grandfather, who was an autocratic manager and a bitter foe of unionism, the younger Ford developed a more flexible policy toward the demands of the United Automobile Workers (UAW). Ford also began a sweeping reform of the administrative structure of the company, hiring a specially-recruited "whiz kid" management team, which included Robert S. McNamara [q.v.], to modernize the firm's inefficient managerial system and production techniques. To a large extent Ford adopted the more decentralized structure of its giant rival, General Motors. [See TRUMAN, EISENHOWER Volumes]

Along with the rest of the auto industry, Ford's sales rose annually during the early 1960s. In January 1962 it announced an increase in the dividend rate per share from $.75 to $.90. According to *Fortune*, Ford had sales of $8.5 billion in 1963, ranking second in the auto industry behind General Motors and third among all U.S. corporations. In October 1961 the UAW engaged in its first company-wide strike against Ford in its 20-year relationship. The dispute revolved largely around such non-economic issues as job classifications for skilled-trades workers, local working conditions and the use of outside contractors.

During the early 1960s Ford sought to expand beyond the automobile industry and garner a share of U.S. defense contracts. In 1961 the company purchased Philco Corp. for what was then considered a bargain price of $94.6 million. Philco held several large military and National Aeronautics and Space Administration (NASA) contracts, but at the time Ford bought the company Philco was having severe internal problems with several product divisions, particularly its "glamor" electronic computer line. The company's financial situation stabilized somewhat in 1963 after it began to manufacture automobile radios for Ford.

Unlike other businessmen Ford defended the Kennedy Administration's call for an improvement in business ethics and urged executives in April 1961 to realize that morality was "not just avoiding price-fixing or conflict-of-interest." He served on President Kennedy's Advisory Committee on Labor-Management Policy, which submitted a report in January 1962 urging compensation, education and retraining for workers displaced by automation. Ford dissented from the report, however, and declared that the need for economic growth rather than unemployment assistance was the major problem. In the same month Ford spoke in favor of the Administration's proposals to grant the President broad tariff-negotiating powers.

In May 1962 Ford dissented from another Advisory Committee report, which recommended greater governmental power in labor-management disputes. Criticizing the alleged "monopoly" power of unions, Ford claimed that the government's collective bargaining policy already "grants excessive power to unions." With the steel crisis of April in mind, he also criticized the Administration for its tendency to "intervene directly in matters of collective bargaining and the economic decisions of business in an effort to hold the lid on costs and prices."

As co-chairman of the Business Committee for Tax Reduction in 1963, Ford was one of the most prominent corporate defenders of the President's controversial tax cut. He argued before the House Ways and Means Committee in February 1963 that cutting taxes was necessary "to stimulate the economy," but he advocated restricting federal spending in view of the increase in the national debt. He also opposed the Administration's proposed plan to increase the taxation of financial gains resulting from stock option plans, which he said "would effectively destroy the value of restricted stock options." He defended options on the grounds that they offered an incentive to top management to join and remain with a company. Ford was one of 26 business leaders to form a National Independent Committee for Johnson and Humphrey in September 1964. [See JOHNSON, NIXON Volumes]

[TO]

FORMAN, JAMES
b. Oct. 4, 1928; Chicago, Ill.
Executive Secretary, Student Nonviolent Coordinating Committee, October 1961-May 1966.

A 1957 graduate of Roosevelt University in Chicago, Forman did graduate work in African studies at Boston University and then taught for several years in Chicago public schools. In 1960 and 1961 he helped organize aid for black sharecroppers who had been evicted from their farms in Fayette County, Tenn., after registering to vote. In Tennessee Forman got to know members of the influential Nashville chapter of the Student Nonviolent Coordinating Committee (SNCC) and joined SNCC in October 1961. Shortly afterwards Forman was named executive secretary of the organization, and he spent much of the next six years at SNCC's Atlanta headquarters developing an effective communications system among SNCC workers, handling publicity, devising fund-raising mechanisms and helping establish policy.

Forman also spent time in the field, directly participating in SNCC demonstrations and voter registration drives. With other SNCC workers he launched a desegregation drive in Albany, Ga., in November 1961. The city's bus and railroad terminals were their first target. Three attempts to integrate the bus station were made in November, and on Dec. 10 Forman led a group of four blacks and five whites in a test of railroad facilities. Ignoring a conductor's order to segregate themselves, the group sat together on a Central of Georgia train from Atlanta to Albany. On arrival all entered the white waiting room at the Albany terminal where eight, including Forman,

were arrested. The test efforts and arrests galvanized the local black community to greater protest. In mid-December, the local leadership called in Martin Luther King [q.v.] to help lead and publicize the demonstrations, which continued through the summer of 1962.

Forman also joined in February 1962 demonstrations to desegregate the visitor's galleries at the state capitol building in Atlanta, Ga. He participated in a voter registration drive in Greenwood, Miss., begun by SNCC in February 1963, which resulted in several shootings and the harassment of registration workers. On March 27 Forman led 10 rights workers in a march on the county courthouse to protest the violence in Greenwood and to dramatize the right of blacks to register. The group was arrested; Forman and seven others were found guilty of disorderly conduct and given maximum sentences of four months in prison and a $200 fine. They were released from jail on April 4 after federal and city officials agreed that the federal government would postpone its voter discrimination suit against local officials in exchange for the release of the eight protesters.

Forman helped organize a May 1963 "Freedom Walk" originally undertaken in April by William Moore, a white Baltimore postal employe. Moore had planned a solitary pilgrimage from Chattanooga, Tenn., to Jackson, Miss., to deliver an appeal for integration to Mississippi Gov. Ross Barnett [q.v.]. When Moore was found murdered on April 24 near Attalla, Ala., SNCC and the Congress of Racial Equality decided to continue the march to protest Moore's murder. Ten people began the march on May 1 with Forman accompanying them to do logistical work. On May 3 they crossed into Alabama where they were arrested by state troopers on breach of peace charges.

Forman also participated in the May 1963 Birmingham demonstrations led by Martin Luther King and his Southern Christian Leadership Conference (SCLC), although by that time Forman and SNCC had become very critical of King. Forman wrote in his autobiography that King's participation in protests usually inhibited the development of local leadership and of a mass movement among Southern blacks. He charged that King and SCLC often dampened the militance of demonstrations to protect their own image and prestige. Forman joined in June 1963 protests in Danville, Va., aimed at desegregating municipal facilities and increasing municipal employment of blacks. He was present at the March on Washington in August 1963 where SNCC chairman John Lewis [q.v.] spoke as the organization's representative. When other march sponsors objected to Lewis's prepared address on the night before the march, Forman joined in the negotiations over the changes to be made in Lewis's speech and helped write the final, more moderate draft.

SNCC initiated another major voter registration drive in Selma, Ala., in September 1963. There Forman helped organize an Oct. 7 "Freedom Day" to protest voting discrimination against local blacks. Some 300 blacks came to the county courthouse in Selma and stood in line the entire day waiting to register. Local sheriff's deputies did not break up the queue, but they barred Forman and other SNCC workers from bringing any food or water to those on the registration line.

Forman helped plan the 1964 Mississippi Freedom Summer project and led March 1965 demonstrations in Montgomery, Ala., to protest the violence against civil rights marchers in Selma earlier in the month. He was replaced as executive secretary of SNCC in May 1966, but he remained an active member of the organization as it shifted to a more militant and nationalist position. [See JOHNSON Volume]

[CAB]

For further information:
James Forman, *The Making of Black Revolutionaries* (New York, 1972).

FORRESTAL, MICHAEL V(INCENT)
b. Nov. 26, 1927; New York, N.Y.
Presidential Assistant for Far Eastern Affairs, January 1962-July 1964.

Michael V. Forrestal served as a presidential adviser and was a close associate of W. Averell Harriman [q.v.] during the Kennedy Administration. Forrestal, the son of James V. Forrestal, the first U.S. Secretary of Defense, had been Harriman's assis-
tant when the Ambassador was director of the Marshall Plan from 1948 to 1950. At Harriman's suggestion Forrestal was brought to Washington from his New York law firm in January 1962 to serve as a senior staff member of the National Security Council under McGeorge Bundy [q.v.]. Harriman was in charge of the negotiations to neutralize Laos and wanted a personal liaison officer to the President.

In the first half of 1962, Harriman's efforts secured a neutralist government for Laos, established by the Geneva Agreements of 1962. Forrestal coordinated policy between the Ambassador, the President and other government agencies during their negotiations. In May 1963 he accompanied Abram Chayes [q.v.] to Indonesia to negotiate a treaty on the eventual nationalization of American oil interests in that country.

Forrestal's major concern during his tenure at the White House was America's growing commitment in Vietnam. After returning from a December 1962 fact-finding mission to that country with Roger Hilsman [q.v.], he reported doubts about the conduct of the war and the viability of President Ngo Dinh Diem's regime. In a joint report the two men concluded that the only people who supported Diem and his brother, Ngo Dinh Nhu, were Americans and Vietnamese leaders with close ties to the Diem family. Forrestal and Hilsman were skeptical about the optimistic assessment of the war offered by many high American officials and questioned the value of the strategic hamlet program as it was being carried out by Nhu. They foresaw a long and costly struggle and reported that Communist recruitment within the South was so successful that the war could be carried on without infiltration from the North.

Following the August 1963 attack by Nhu's secret police on Buddhist dissidents, Forrestal, in conjunction with George Ball [q.v.], Harriman and Hilsman, drafted the "August 24 Cable" sent to Henry Cabot Lodge [q.v.], the new ambassador to Vietnam. The message stated that "Diem must be given [a] chance to rid himself of Nhu" but cautioned that "if Diem remains obdurate and refuses, then we must face the possibility that Diem himself cannot be preserved." Lodge was also instructed to privately inform senior Vietnamese generals contemplating a coup that if Nhu remained in power the U.S. would "give them direct support in any interim period of breakdown [of the] central government mechanism." The coup failed to take place immediately because of the generals' inability to achieve a favorable balance of forces in the Saigon area. However, a coup was eventually carried out in November 1963.

Forrestal's influence declined during the Johnson Administration because the President entrusted Vietnam affairs to his closest senior advisers. In July 1964 Forrestal was moved to the State Department, where he worked on the Vietnam pacification program. In the fall of 1964 he and William Sullivan designed a plan, subsequently rejected by the Pentagon, to limit escalation of the air war through careful choice of bombing targets. Forrestal wrote a paper outlining the measures needed to achieve a negotiated settlement of the war during the winter of 1964, but the Administration never seriously considered it. In January 1965 he quietly left government to return to his law practice.

[EWS]

For further information:
U.S. Department of Defense, *The Pentagon Papers*, Senator Gravel Edition. (Boston, 1971), Vol. II.

FOSTER, WILLIAM C(HAPMAN)
b. April 27, 1897; Westfield, N.J.
Director, Arms Control and Disarmament Agency, September 1961-January 1969.

Prior to his appointment as director of the U.S. Arms Control and Disarmament Agency in September 1961, Foster had a varied career in government, serving as undersecretary of commerce, administrator of the Economic Cooperation Administration and deputy secretary of defense during the Truman Administration. He left government for private industry after

Eisenhower's 1952 election, and from 1953 to 1961 served as an executive for a number of large chemical corporations. In 1958 Foster headed the U.S. delegation to the abortive disarmament conference with the Soviet Union.

As head of the U.S. Arms Control and Disarmament Agency, Foster was responsible for running an autonomous department formed to coordinate government policy on disarmament and nuclear testing free from the influence of other federal agencies. Foster counseled the President on all major decisions involving nuclear policy. When the Soviet Union resumed atmospheric nuclear testing in September 1961, he advised the President to resume American atmospheric tests for two reasons: first, if America performed no new tests the Soviets might gain an important nuclear advantage from its testing series; second, if the USSR gained superiority it might be difficult to sustain U.S. support for a test ban treaty, particularly in the Senate, which would have to ratify the document. Although Kennedy resumed underground testing in September 1961, he held off the final decision to resume atmospheric tests until March 1962. In September 1961, Foster, along with Arthur Dean [*q.v.*], helped Kennedy prepare his U.N. address that included a proposal for "General and Complete Disarmament in a Peaceful World."

During the re-evaluation of American test ban policy made in the summer of 1962, Foster served as a member of the ad hoc committee formed to study U.S. options. At the group's meetings Foster backed two of the suggestions advanced: to present a simplified treaty involving an unsupervised ban on atmospheric, outer space and sea bed tests, and to propose a modified comprehensive treaty that provided for on-site inspection inside the Soviet Union but relied on internally coordinated and standardized national control posts.

Despite the fact that a partial test ban would not stop nuclear proliferation, Foster felt that the treaty would prevent tests that produced radioactive fallout and, therefore, caused the greatest concern. In addition, it would permit the U.S. to continue testing and thus maintain U.S. nuclear superiority. He also supported the second plan, which he believed would maintain pressure on the Soviets to accept inspection. Foster assured the committee that this measure was scientifically feasible and that the needed detection system could be put into operation immediately. These two proposals were tabled simultaneously in Geneva in August 1962 and were rejected by the Soviet Union.

Throughout the winter of 1962-63 Foster attempted unsuccessfully to break the deadlock, both in meetings with Russian officials in New York and in Geneva, where he replaced Arthur Dean as head of the U.S. delegation to the 18 Nation Disarmament Conference in February. However, the issue remained stalemated until June 1963 when Premier Nikita Khrushchev accepted Kennedy's personal suggestion that negotiations be carried on by private emissaries in Moscow. Because Kennedy had given repeated assurances to Congress that the Disarmament Agency would not appropriate the treaty-making functions of the State Department, Foster was not one of the men sent to Moscow. The delegation, led by W. Averell Harriman [q.v.], was able to conclude a limited test ban treaty by July 25.

Foster played an important role in the Administration's fight for treaty ratification. Under the direction of the President, an ad hoc committee composed of Foster, his deputy Adrian Fisher [q.v.] and several other top Administration officials was responsible for contacting individual senators and soliciting their support. At the treaty hearings held in August 1963, Foster was the only non-scientific expert to testify. He stressed that while there were real dangers in the test ban the risk of not signing the document were greater. He argued that it would constitute a significant step in achieving control over the spread of nuclear weapons, would eliminate radioactive fallout and would be the first step in bringing the arms race under control. To ensure continued support for the proposal, Foster or his deputy stayed in the gallery during the ratification debates to direct Administration forces when necessary. The test ban treaty was ratified in September 1963.

Foster retained his post as director of the Arms Control and Disarmament Agency throughout the Johnson Administration. In conjunction with Fisher, he served as chief delegate to the 18 Nation Disarmament Conference in Geneva and helped negotiate the nuclear nonproliferation treaty of 1968. Foster left government service in January 1969. He became president of Porter International Company in 1970.

[EWS]

For further information:
Edson L(ouis) M(illard) Burns, *A Seat at the Table* (Toronto, 1972).
Arthur Dean, *Test Ban and Disarmament: The Path of Negotiation* (New York, 1966).
Harold D. Jacobson, *Diplomats, Scientists and Politicians* (Ann Arbor, 1966).
Mary Milling Lepper, *Foreign Policy Formulation: A Case Study of the Nuclear Test Ban Treaty of 1963* (Columbus, 1971).

FOWLER, HENRY H(AMILL)
b. Sept. 5, 1908; Roanoke, Va.
Undersecretary of the Treasury,
January 1961-March 1964.

Following his graduation from Yale Law School in 1934, Henry Fowler became a counsel to the Tennessee Valley Authority, the first of many government positions he held under Democratic administrations. He served on several federal agencies and wartime boards until 1946, when he entered private law practice in Washington, D.C. He rejoined the government during the Korean War, becoming director of the Office of Defense Mobilization and a member of President Truman's National Security Council. During the Eisenhower Administration Fowler resumed his prosperous law practice and also served on the Democratic Advisory Council, a group formed by the Democratic National Committee to outline Party positions on National issues. [See TRUMAN Volume]

In January 1961 President Kennedy appointed Fowler undersecretary of the treasury. As second in command to Secretary of the Treasury C. Douglas Dillon [q.v.],

Fowler brought to the Administration's economic policymaking team long experience in administration and sophistication in Washington politics. He played a key role in selling Kennedy's economic policy to Congress and to the business community.

Fowler was among a group of high Administration officials commissioned by President Kennedy in September 1961 to improve the Administration's rapport with the corporation executives on the Business Council, an independent business advisory group. During the steel price-rise controversy of April 1962, Fowler joined Administration officials in pressuring steel officials to rescind the increase. Fowler also played an indirect role in government banking policy by recommending for the post of comptroller James J. Saxon [q.v.], who upset the status quo by liberalizing federal banking regulations.

Fowler devoted much of his attention to the Administration's tax program, especially to shepherding it through Congress. He was instrumental in instituting, in the summer of 1962, the accelerated depreciation allowances long urged by businessmen. He lobbied in Congress for reforms to check foreign "tax haven" corporations and for the "interest equalization tax," two measures intended to aid the balance-of-payments problem. Fowler devoted almost all his time in 1963 to winning approval for Kennedy's $11-billion tax cut. He was behind the formation of the influential Business Committee for a Tax Cut in 1963.

Fowler left the Treasury Department for his law practice in March 1964. He returned as President Johnson's Secretary of the Treasury in March 1965. [See JOHNSON Volume]

[TO]

FRANKFURTER, FELIX
b. Nov. 15, 1882; Vienna, Austria
d. Feb. 22, 1965; Washington, D.C.
Associate Justice, U.S. Supreme Court, 1939-62.

A Jewish immigrant who came to the United States at the age of 12, Frankfurter graduated from the College of the City of New York in 1902 and received a degree from Harvard Law School in 1906. He was then appointed an assistant U.S. attorney in New York under Henry. L. Stimson. When Stimson was named Secretary of War in 1911, Frankfurter accompanied him to Washington as his assistant. He subsequently served as chairman of the War Labor Policies Board in World War I and then as a presidential consultant at the 1919 Paris Peace Conference.

A member of the Harvard University law faculty from 1914 to 1939, Frankfurter developed a reputation as a brilliant legal scholar and an authority on the Supreme Court and administrative law. By the early 1930s he had also become known as an outspoken liberal; Frankfurter supported labor unions, assisted in fights for civil liberties and civil rights and publicly condemned as miscarriages of justice the trials of labor radical Tom Mooney and of Italian anarchists Nicola Sacco and Bartolomeo Vanzetti. Later Frankfurter was a confidant of President Franklin Roosevelt, advising him on legislation and executive appointments. Roosevelt named Frankfurter an associate justice of the Supreme Court in January 1939.

On the bench Frankfurter emerged as an articulate and persuasive advocate of a philosophy of judicial self-restraint. Drawing on his analysis of the Court during the 1920s and 1930s, Frankfurter repeatedly argued that the Court, as the "nondemocratic organ" of government, should uphold rationally supportable statutes designed to achieve "legitimate legislative" ends, no matter how strong the justices' personal dislike of the laws. As a result of this view, Frankfurter did not always vote on the side of the interests he had championed while a private citizen. He voted to uphold social and economic legislation of the New Deal, for example, but also to sustain state right-to-work and compulsory flag-salute laws. In Dennis v. U.S. (1951) Frankfurter also voted to uphold the criminal prosecution of Communist Party leaders under the Smith Act. He could find no constitutional basis for overturning what he considered a reasonable legislative judgment on the dangers of the Communist Party to internal security.

Frankfurter also insisted that the Court should be non-political and that certain issues were therefore not appropriate for judicial determination. Thus, in *Colegrove v. Green* (1946), Frankfurter held that the apportionment of legislative districts was an issue of "a peculiar political nature" and represented a "political thicket" which the Court should not enter. The justice did advocate a more activist court role in the realm of federal criminal procedure, where he believed the constitutional bases for Court rulings were clearer. He was the author in 1943 of the doctrine that confessions obtained from federal prisoners during unnecessary delays in their arraignments were inadmissible at trial, and he attached special importance to the Fourth Amendment's guarantee against unreasonable searches and seizures. Frankfurter used broader and less rigid standards in evaluating state criminal procedures, however. In *Wolf v. Colorado* (1949) Frankfurter held that state courts could admit illegally seized evidence that would not be admissible in federal courts. Throughout his career Frankfurter opposed the arguments, most prominently associated with Justice Hugo Black [*q.v.*], that the 14th Amendment made the first eight amendments to the Constitution fully applicable to the states and that there were absolutes in the Constitution, particularly in the First Amendment's guarantees of freedom of speech and religion. [See TRUMAN, EISENHOWER Volumes]

Frankfurter continued to emphasize the virtues of detachment, deliberation and reasoned restraint in his final years on the court. He voted with the majority in two 1961 cases, decided five to four, which upheld the investigative powers of the House Un-American Activities Committee and affirmed the contempt-of-Congress convictions of witnesses who had refused to answer Committee questions. In June 1961 Frankfurter wrote the majority opinion in another five-to-four decision upholding the requirement of the 1950 Internal Security Act for Communist organizations to register with the government. Although he recognized that registration and disclosure of

membership could infringe on the First Amendment's guarantee of free association in some circumstances, Frankfurter emphasized that this law applied only to U.S. branches of foreign-controlled organizations, and he sustained it as a reasonable legislative action. In the same month Frankfurter was part of another five man majority which upheld the provision of the 1940 Smith Act making it a crime to be an active member of a party advocating violent overthrow of the government.

In the same Court term Frankfurter voted to sustain a Chicago ordinance barring the public showing of movies without prior approval of city censors, which had been attacked as a violation of the First Amendment. In four cases challenging the constitutionality of state "blue laws," which prohibited certain types of business on Sundays, Frankfurter joined the majority in two cases to sustain the laws as secular rather than religious in character. He dissented, however, in two other cases brought by Orthodox Jews who observed their religious law by closing on Saturdays and objected to the state-enforced Sunday closings as an infringement on their freedom of worship.

In *Mapp v. Ohio*, decided in June 1961, a majority on the Court overturned Frankfurter's decision in the *Wolf* case and held that illegally seized evidence was inadmissible in state courts. Frankfurter dissented in *Mapp*, and he objected even more vehemently the next year when the Court overruled *Colegrove* and decided in *Baker v. Carr* that state legislative apportionment was subject to the constitutional scrutiny of the federal courts. In a 68-page dissent, Frankfurter assailed the majority for reversing a "uniform course of decision over the years" and for violating the precept of self-restraint in political matters. "There is not under our Constitution," he wrote, "a judicial remedy for every political mischief." The proper remedy for malapportionment was an aroused electorate which would act through the legislature, Frankfurter added, warning the Court that its decision would lead it into a "mathematical quagmire."

Frankfurter suffered a stroke while working in his chambers on April 5, 1962 and never recovered his health sufficiently to return to the bench. He resigned from the court on Aug. 28, 1962 and spent the next few years visiting with friends and carrying on his voluminous correspondence. He died of a heart attack in Washington on Feb. 22, 1965.

Reviewing Frankfurter's judicial career, all commentators agreed that the Justice's scholarly opinions had had a profound impact on the law. Many observers, such as the New York Times's Anthony Lewis, also noted the irony in Frankfurter's espousal of judicial self-restraint. He had been a vivacious, ebullient man who retained, beneath the robe, the strong convictions of his pre-court years. Frankfurter's critics argued that he had taken too narrow a view of the judicial function and had carried deference to the legislature too far. His supporters contended that Frankfurter had been a source for stability and moderation on the Court and that his efforts to prevent any abuse of judicial power had saved the Court from attacks which might have undermined its role.

[CAB]

For further information:
Albert M. Sacks, "Felix Frankfurter," in Leon Friedman and Fred L. Israel, eds., The Justices of the United States Supreme Court, 1789-1969 (New York, 1969), Vol. III.

FREEMAN, ORVILLE L(OTHROP)

b. March 9, 1918; Minneapolis, Minn.
Secretary of Agriculture, January 1961-January 1969.

Orville Freeman served in the Marine Corps in World War II and received A.B. and LL.B. degrees from the University of Minnesota. Following the war he practiced law in Minneapolis. He became a close political associate of Hubert H. Humphrey [q.v.], then mayor of Minneapolis and a leader in the Democratic-Farmer-Labor Party (DFL). With Humphrey Freeman helped make the DFL a powerful political organization that ended Republican dominance in the state. Unsuccessful in at-

tempts to win the governorship in 1950 and 1952, Freeman defeated the Republican incumbent in 1954, a year of big Democratic gains nationally. Reelected in 1956 and 1958, he compiled a progressive record as governor. [See EISENHOWER Volume]

When Humphrey dropped out of the race for the 1960 presidential nomination, Freeman threw his support to Sen. John F. Kennedy. To help win the crucial Minnesota delegate vote the Kennedy forces asked Freeman to deliver Kennedy's nomination speech at the Democratic National Convention in July. According to historian Arthur Schlesinger, Jr.[q.v.], Kennedy admired Freeman and would probably have asked him to be his running mate had Sen. Lyndon B. Johnson (D, Tex.) [q.v.] not accepted the vice presidential offer. Freeman's failure to win a fourth term as governor coupled with John Kennedy's November victory assured him a place in the new Administration. In January 1961 he became Secretary of Agriculture with responsibility for solving what Kennedy called "the major domestic problem. . .at the present time."

American agriculture suffered from chronic overproduction. Technological innovations exacerbated the problem in the 1950s, producing tremendous surpluses that were stored at government expense. Democratic farm policy traditionally advocated limitations on production and high price supports for farmers in order to keep their income at parity with non-farm income. This position generally appealed to small farmers, many of whom were represented by the National Farmers Union (NFU) and the National Grange. The Republicans, who were usually aligned with the large farmers and the American Farm Bureau Federation, charged that Democratic policy fostered inefficient farm units and interfered with the operation of a free market economy. The Democrats pointed out that the farm policy of President Dwight D. Eisenhower [q.v.] and his Secretary of Agriculture, Ezra Taft Benson, had kept price supports too low to ensure farmers an adequate income, but high enough—and with too few production controls—to saddle the Agriculture Department with budget expenses second only to the Defense Department.

Secretary Freeman's proposed farm program was the most comprehensive in history. It promised farmers "full parity of income" with non-farmers and contemplated more stringent production and sales limitations. Since technological efficiency had increased yield per acre, the Administration believed it imperative to have the power to set not only acreage limitations, but also to control the amount of a crop that would actually be marketed. In short, the Kennedy program aimed to cut production, increase farm incomes and distribute surpluses to the hungry on a large scale. With lower production, Freeman argued, farmers would get high prices and price supports would eventually become unnecessary. The Department's enormous budget could be cut and much of it put to other purposes, such as rural development, land conversion and research. The success of the program, observers noted, depended on the willingness of Congress—and especially Southern Democrats—and the farm community to considerably augment the authority of the Secretary of Agriculture.

In 1961 supply of farm products continued to outrun demand. In an effort to raise farm incomes immediately, Freeman, making use of special discretionary powers, raised the price support level for several commodities. One of the most important pieces of Administration legislation in 1961 was the Emergency Feed Grain Program, which proposed to cut corn and grain sorghum acreage by 25%. The Administration claimed the reduction would save the government $500 million in storage and price support costs. The bill was passed by Congress in March. Section Three of the law, though not as stringent as the Administration desired, allowed the Secretary to sell limited, but still substantial, amounts of surplus grain at as little as $1 a bushel. By keeping the market price low, Freeman was "warning" farmers to join the Department of Agriculture's acreage reduction program. Although Republicans objected to this expansion of the Secretary's power, the program was relatively successful, reducing acreage by 20 million acres and lowering pro-

duction by about 420 million bushels. Freeman hoped to make this temporary program control permanent instead of relying on price support purchases to maintain high market prices.

Later in 1961 Congress extended the feed grains retirement program into 1962 and passed a similar measure for wheat. The wheat provisions allowed the government to fine and withhold price supports from farmers who did not participate in the land retirement program. This made it unnecessary for the Secretary of Agriculture to sell surplus wheat at a low price in order to force farmers to cooperate.

At the beginning of 1962 Freeman was able to announce that net U.S. farm income had increased 9% in 1961 and that the government had cut its feed grains stocks for the first time since 1952. He offered a legislative program for the year that the Republican National Committee termed "the harshest in history . . . typical of the . . . Kennedy socialist philosophy . . . outright political blackmail." The Republicans and the American Farm Bureau lobby were able to defeat two parts of the plan. One recommended permanent mandatory acreage limitations for feed grains with severe penalties for overplanting. This was especially controversial because it had implications for the cattle, poultry and dairy industries, all of which were major consumers of feed grains. The second would have imposed sales quotas for dairy products with penalties for overselling.

The Administration won a significant victory, however, with passage of a permanent wheat program that would allow the Secretary, beginning in 1964, to set acreage allotments as low as he thought necessary to meet domestic and export needs. The Secretary was also authorized to conduct periodic referendums to give wheat farmers a choice between two systems of price supports.

The 1962 congressional investigation and court proceedings concerning the Texas financial empire of Billie Sol Estes [q.v.], who allegedly benefited from a close relationship with the Department of Agriculture, encouraged Republicans to press for

Freeman's resignation. Sen. Everett Dirksen (R, Ill.) [q.v.] charged that the Estes "manipulations" were "only a glaring symptom of a basic sickness. . .that has attached itself to the billions of handouts from the Agriculture Department." Yet, the Estes affair neither especially hurt the Administration nor curtailed Freeman's authority. Freeman attacked the Republican maneuvers as part of an attempt to defeat the Administration farm bill. He claimed that the government "lost no money through its business with Estes" and added that the Department had dismissed those officials who accepted favors from Estes. President Kennedy publicly affirmed his confidence in Freeman and Sen. John McClellan (D, Ark.) [q.v.], chairman of the Senate Government Operations Committee and of the Permanent Subcommittee on Investigations, commended Freeman for his "prompt action" on the Estes case and his "many administrative and procedural reforms" in the Department.

The May 1963 wheat farmers' national referendum proved the most important test of Administration farm policy. Since 1962 Freeman had campaigned for the Administration position in the referendum, the imposition of strict marketing controls for wheat. He warned that defeat of the controls would result in "low prices [that] would seriously impair" access to world markets, particularly the Common Market, for U.S. farm products. The NFU and the National Grange formed a "National Wheat Committee" to support the Freeman position, but the American Farm Bureau Federation, the largest farm group, and much of the Midwestern Republican press waged an intensive campaign against marketing controls. The opposition urged farmers to vote against a "licensed and regimented agriculture."

The new plan won only 47.8% of the vote, far short of the two-thirds necessary to put it into effect. It was the first time in the postwar period that marketing quotas had been rejected for a major crop. Because of the plan's defeat, wheat farmers lost an estimated $700 million on the next year's crop. The adverse vote also led to press speculation that Freeman would be transferred to another post. The $6 billion Agriculture Department budget was now more frequently criticized by urban Democrats, who indicated that they might no longer support the Kennedy farm program. Freeman denied rumors that he was expected to resign and declared that Kennedy wanted him to remain at his post.

Despite the referendum defeat some parts of the 1963 Administration farm program were successful. One bill, passed only a few days before the national wheat referendum, gave the Secretary the authority to order large acreage reductions for feed grains and deprived non-cooperating farmers of price supports. Most important politically was the October 1963 announcement of a wheat deal with the Soviet Union. It greatly improved Freeman's image, won the enthusiastic support of the vast majority of wheat farmers and promised to recoup some of the economic losses caused by the rejection of marketing controls.

Under Freeman the Department of Agriculture expanded its sphere of activity. His "rural renewal" proposals were designed to keep the rural unemployed and underemployed from flooding the crowded urban labor market by creating non-farm employment opportunities in the countryside. The Area Redevelopment Act of 1961 authorized federal money for the creation of new businesses and new uses of land and for vocational retraining in rural areas of chronic unemployment. Parts of the 1962 farm bill expanded government food donation programs at home and abroad and provided federal aid to farmers who converted crop land to non-farm income producing uses. The Food for Peace program disposed of large amounts of the U.S. farm surplus abroad and, as supporters pointed out, substituted food for the U.S. dollar as a form of foreign aid.

Freeman remained Secretary of Agriculture until the end of the Johnson Administration. He continued to expand the scope of the Department, particularly in increasing the numbers of citizens reached by the Food Stamp program, direct distribution programs and school breakfast programs. In recognition of the Department's new roles,

Freeman made several unsuccessful attempts to change its name to the Department of Food and Agriculture or the Department of Food, Agriculture, and Rural Affairs. In 1970 Freeman became president of the Business International Corporation. [See JOHNSON Volume]

[JCH]

FRELINGHUYSEN, PETER H. B.
b. Jan. 17, 1916; New York, N.Y.
Republican Representative, N.J., 1953-75.

A member of a patrician family of Dutch descent which produced three United States senators and a Secretary of State, Frelinghuysen graduated from Princeton and Yale Law School. In 1952 he won election to Congress from an affluent north central New Jersey district, the most Republican in the state.

A moderate Republican, Frelinghuysen frequently supported Kennedy Administration policies, particularly in foreign affairs. *Congressional Quarterly* reported that in the 87th Congress Frelinghuysen voted with the Administration on 82% of key foreign policy roll-call votes. He also consistently voted for civil rights legislation, although in 1963 he opposed the creation of the Equal Employment Opportunities Commission.

Frelinghuysen, who became the ranking Republican on the House Education and Labor Committee in 1963, devoted considerable attention to education legislation. In 1961 he unsuccessfully proposed an amendment to Kennedy's federal aid-to-education bill that would have barred granting federal funds to states where the public schools practiced racial or religious discrimination. He also failed to win approval for his recommendations that the states match federal funds on an equal basis and that public school teachers take a loyalty oath.

Also a member of the House Foreign Affairs Committee, Frelinghuysen in July 1962 proposed a ban on all foreign aid to Communist countries, but his measure was circumvented by an amendment offered by the committee chairman, Rep. Thomas Morgan (D, Pa.) [*q.v.*], which granted the President "discretionary" power to grant aid when he deemed it "vital" to U.S. security.

In 1965 Frelinghuysen made unsuccessful attempts to win the post of minority whip and the chairmanship of the House Republican Conference. In the late 1960s he increasingly turned his attention to foreign affairs, becoming the Party foreign policy spokesman in the House. Frelinghuysen's popularity declined in his district because of his unswerving support of Nixon's Vietnam policy. He decided not to seek reelection in 1974. [See JOHNSON, NIXON Volumes]

[JCH]

FULBRIGHT, J(AMES) WILLIAM
b. April 9, 1905; Sumner, Mo.
Democratic Senator, Ark., 1945-75.
Chairman, Foreign Relations
Committee, 1959-75.

J. William Fulbright, chairman of the Senate Foreign Relations Committee during the period of American involvement in Vietnam, was born in Sumner, Mo., and grew up in Fayetteville, Ark., where his family was socially and economically prominent. Following his graduation from the University of Arkansas in 1925, he studied at Oxford on a Rhodes scholarship and then returned to the U.S. in 1928 to take a law degree at George Washington University. Fulbright served as a lawyer for the Justice Department in 1934 and the next year was appointed instructor of law at George Washington. He returned to the University of Arkansas in 1936 as a member of its law faculty. From 1939 to 1941 Fulbright served as the president of that university. During his tenure he fought to upgrade academic standards in the face of state government indifference.

In 1942 Fulbright was elected to Congress where, as a member of the House Foreign Affairs Committee, he introduced the "Fulbright Resolution" calling for U.S. participation in an international organization to maintain peace. First elected to the Senate two years later, he was repeatedly returned to the upper house during the next two decades. As a representative from the deep South, Fulbright reflected the sentiments of his constituents on most domestic issues, compiling a conservative record on many legislative measures, especially those involving civil rights. However, the Senator's main preoccupation throughout his career was foreign affairs. Believing that world peace could be furthered through education, Fulbright sponsored the 1946 law that set up the international educational exchange program that bears his name. In 1954 he defended the program against Sen. Joseph McCarthy's (R, Wisc.) charges of Communist infiltration and was the only senator to oppose additional funds for McCarthy's hearings. In 1959 Fulbright became chairman of the Senate Foreign Relations Committee. [See TRUMAN, EISENHOWER Volumes]

Fulbright was widely mentioned as a possible choice for Secretary of State following John F. Kennedy's 1960 election. The President-elect admired his scholar's mind and supported Fulbright's demand for a reassessment of American foreign policy goals. Just as importantly, Fulbright could enhance the Administration's influence on Capitol Hill. However, the Senator was rejected for the post because his civil rights record would have made it difficult for him to deal with African nations and because his refusal to support an anti-Nasser foreign policy had alienated many in the Jewish community. In addition, Kennedy felt that Fulbright did not have the administrative experience necessary to lead a large bureaucracy.

During the Kennedy Administration Fulbright used his position as chairman of the Senate Foreign Relations Committee to advocate a reappraisal of the basic tenets upon which Soviet-American diplomacy had been conducted. In a series of speeches and articles and in two books, *Prospects for the West* (1963) and *Old Myths and New Realities* (1964), Fulbright urged the U.S. to abandon the postwar assumption that Russia and the U.S. were locked in uncompromising ideological combat. He thought this premise had produced continual confrontations between the two nuclear powers. Instead, the Senator recommended that the U.S. view relations with the Soviet Union in terms of traditional great power rivalry and use quiet diplomacy to settle differences.

Fulbright said America's goal should not be to change the Soviet Union's internal social, economic and political structure or destroy Communism but to block Russian imperialism. He maintained that although contemporary Soviet leaders were opportunists anxious to expand Soviet power, they were also rational individuals who would seek to fulfill this goal through the extension of their influence rather than through territorial conquest. Asserting that the West was the "ultimate determinant of the fortunes of Communism," Fulbright believed that America and her allies could prevent this expansion through a unified foreign policy that clearly defined Western interests and potential reactions to Soviet challenges. More importantly, the West could forestall Communist growth by strengthening its "internal free societies" through international cooperation "to make them impregnable to external ideological assault and at the same time magnetic examples of social justice and material well-being for the entire world."

The Senator played down the influence of Communism in the emerging nations, terming it "a scavenger" rather than an initiator of revolutions. He believed that upheavals in the Third World were the result of virulent nationalism and consequently that the Communists would find little future in the developing areas. The West could ensure Soviet failure through the use of foreign aid, not to bolster specific regimes, but to provide the basis for economic growth vital for the development of a "free society," according to Fulbright.

Fulbright's philosophy shaped his response to many of the foreign policy issues of the Kennedy Administration, particularly those involving Cuba. During the opening months of 1961 when the Administration debated whether to carry out a planned invasion of that island by U.S.-trained Cuban exiles, Fulbright opposed the action. In a

March 30 meeting with the President, the Senator questioned the exiles' political leadership and popular support and reminded Kennedy that, regardless of the outcome, the U.S. would be condemned as imperialist. He also cautioned that if the invasion succeeded the nation would find itself responsible for a bankrupt country in a grave state of disorder.

Fulbright maintained that the U.S. did not have to fear "competition from an unshaven megalomaniac" because Cuba would be unable to compete within the inter-American system. Instead of an invasion he recommended that the U.S. isolate the island from the rest of the hemisphere. The Senator again presented his objections to an attack in an April 4 meeting with the President and his highest military and civilian advisers. His recommendations went unheeded, and the invasion was launched on April 17. Two days later Castro crushed it.

Fulbright took a dramatically different stand during the Cuban missile crisis of 1962. At the Oct. 22 meeting with congressional leaders in which the President advised them of his decision to blockade the island to force removal of the missiles, Fulbright argued against the move. He agreed with Kennedy that decisive action was imperative to show the Soviet Union that the U.S. would not tolerate missiles so close to its territory. Yet, because of his belief that the U.S. should avoid direct military confrontation with Russia, he counseled an actual invasion as the most prudent step. The Senator maintained that since a blockade could lead to a clash with Russian ships, the President's measure would be more likely to provoke a nuclear war than an invasion in which Americans would presumably be fighting only Cubans. Kennedy did not accept this advice and on Oct. 24 instituted the naval "quarantine."

During the Kennedy Administration Fulbright began an involvement in Vietnam affairs which would become his major preoccupation for the remainder of his Senate career. In June 1961 he delivered a major address to the Senate which outlined his thoughts on the U.S. role in the nationalistic struggles of the developing nations. Citing the example of Vietnam, Fulbright argued that American aid to that country was only a "qualified success" because stress had been put on military rather than long-term economic assistance. As long as this emphasis continued, he thought, the effort was doomed to failure.

As the decade continued Fulbright became an increasingly vocal critic of the war. Although he supported the 1964 Gulf of Tonkin Resolution that gave President Johnson almost unlimited authority to send American troops to Vietnam, he gradually came to question the moral right of a world power to destroy a small country for what, in his view, were slight political gains. The Senator, therefore, used the Senate Foreign Relations Committee as a forum for the discussion of Johnson and Nixon Administration policies in Indochina. By the end of the decade Fulbright had become the preeminent symbol of growing congressional discontent with the war. In 1974 Fulbright failed in his bid for a sixth Senate term when he was defeated in the Arkansas Democratic primary. His defeat was attributed to his preoccupation with foreign affairs at the expense of his constituents' interests. [JOHNSON, NIXON Volumes]

[EWS]

For further information:
J. William Fulbright, *Prospects for the West,* (Cambridge, Mass., 1963).
———, *Old Myths and New Realities* (New York, 1964).
Haynes Johnson and Bernard M. Gwertzman, *Fulbright: the Dissenter* (New York, 1968).

FUNSTON, G(EORGE) KEITH
b. Oct. 12, 1910; Waterloo, Iowa.
President, New York Stock Exchange, 1951-67.

To the nation's 17 million shareholders, G. Keith Funston was the symbol of Wall Street. Yet Funston had no background in the securities business when he assumed the presidency of the New York Stock Exchange (NYSE) in 1951 at the age of 40. Reared in Sioux Falls, S. D., he attended Trinity College in Connecticut, where he graduated as class valedictorian in 1932. After earning an M.B.A. from the Harvard Graduate School of Business Administration, he worked from 1935 to 1940 for the American Radiator Company. During World War II Funston was a dollar-a-year man with the War Production Board, where he served as special assistant first to former investment banker Sydney Weinberg and then to chairman Donald Nelson. Chosen president of Trinity College at the war's end, Funston headed the small institution and served on the board of directors of seven corporations until 1951, when he was selected as NYSE president upon Weinberg's recommendation. [See EISENHOWER Volume]

Funston's tenure coincided with the greatest bull market in history. As head of the NYSE his role was to represent the stock exchange before Washington and the public. Besides providing the physical environment for buying and selling stocks, the NYSE was charged with responsibility for enforcing "self-regulation," policing its members' ethical behavior in areas outside the purview of the Securities and Exchange Commission (SEC). By the early 1960s the NYSE's self-regulation was coming under increasing criticism as lax and ineffective. Funston unsuccessfully opposed including the NYSE in the massive Special Study of the Securities Markets undertaken in the fall of 1961 under Chicago lawyer Milton Cohen [q.v.]. Funston was frequently at odds with Kennedy-appointed SEC Chairman William Cary [q.v.], who criticized the NYSE for its exclusiveness and self-protective attitudes.

The Cohen group's Special Study, released in 1963, found much to criticize in the NYSE. It characterized the NYSE's performance as a self-regulator as "seriously unsatisfactory" in some areas, although in others it "provided constructive leadership." The NYSE, it said, acted as a "private club" and leaned toward "tenderness rather than severity" in disciplining its members for violations that involved "ethical standards in dealing with customers." The report called for the reform of several abuses in stock trading, including excessive commissions paid by small investors buying and selling stocks in "odd lots" (less than 100 shares), floor "specialists" who did not fulfill their mandate to stabilize the market and "floor trading," in which an exchange member traded on the floor for his own account.

Funston supported the SEC-backed bill reforming securities regulation in 1963 and 1964 on the grounds that it would "reinforce. . .disclosure and self-regulation." He especially favored provisions extending the SEC's full disclosure authority to the "over-the-counter" market, an informal exchange network for stocks not listed on the organized exchanges. The bill did not mandate any sweeping revision of NYSE's procedures or responsibilities.

Funston left the NYSE in April 1967 to become chairman of the Olin Mathieson Chemical Corporation. [See JOHNSON Volume]

[TO]

GALBRAITH, JOHN KENNETH
b. Oct. 15, 1908; Iona Station, Canada. Economist; Ambassador to India, March 1961-June 1963.

John Kenneth Galbraith, an influential economist and ambassador to India during the Kennedy Administration, was born and raised in rural Ontario. Following his graduation from the University of Toronto in 1931, he studied economics at the University of California, Berkeley, where he earned a Ph.D. in 1934. During the next five years Galbraith taught at Harvard and then joined the economics department at Princeton.

After a year at Princeton Galbraith took the first of several government posts as a high-ranking policymaker in the wartime mobilization effort. In 1942 Galbraith was appointed deputy administrator of the Office of Price Administration. His vigorous and outspoken defense of price controls brought him under attack by congressional and business leaders, who objected to the comprehensive nature of the controls. In 1943 the criticism prompted his resignation. Two years later Galbraith headed the

Strategic Bombing Survey, which assessed the effects of wartime bombing on the warmaking capacity of the Axis powers. In the postwar period Galbraith also served as director of the State Department's Office of Economic Security Policy, which helped plan the economic recovery of Germany and Japan. [See TRUMAN Volume]

In 1949 Galbraith returned to Harvard. A Keynesian economist, Galbraith wrote a series of well received books during the 1950s and won a wide audience for his liberal critique of the American economy. In 1952 he published *American Capitalism: the Concept of Countervailing Power*. Three years later he wrote a popular history entitled *The Great Crash: 1929*. Both books argued for greater government regulation and stimulation of the economy as a method of sustaining stable economic growth. Galbraith wrote *The Affluent Society* in 1958. His most influential work, the book attacked what he believed was the economy's overemphasis on the production of private consumer goods and its neglect of public social expenditures. He proposed a transfer of resources from the private to the public sector to eliminate poverty, equalize social and economic opportunity and generate faster economic growth. [See EISENHOWER Volume]

A liberal Democrat, Galbraith worked on Adlai Stevenson's [*q.v.*] campaign staff in 1952 and 1956. From 1956 to 1960 he was chairman of the Democratic Advisory Council's economic panel. In 1960 Galbraith was an early supporter of Sen. John F. Kennedy's presidential nomination and worked to overcome distrust of the candidate within the Democratic Party's liberal wing. Following Kennedy's victory Galbraith served on the President's foreign economic policy task force and advised the Administration on important appointments.

In keeping with his desire to appoint capable men from outside the foreign service to high diplomatic posts, President Kennedy named Galbraith ambassador to India in March 1961. Kennedy chose the economist because of Galbraith's familiarity with India's staggering economic problems, his personal acquaintance with Indian Prime Minister Jawaharlal Nehru and his

prestige as an economic and social analyst. In addition, the President personally admired Galbraith for his intelligence, trenchant wit and independence and believed that as ambassador he could overcome the State Department's inertia to explore new policies toward India.

Galbraith came to India during a period when U.S.-Indian relations had been strained by the American policy of supplying military aid to Pakistan and by U.S. actions in Berlin and Laos. During the first years of his tenure, relations remained cool as a result of Nehru's personal antipathy to U.S. policies in Europe and Southern Asia and the State Department's refusal to abandon old policies and act on the Ambassador's recommendations. In the winter of 1961 Galbraith attempted to prevent India's military takeover of Goa by assuring Nehru that the U.S. considered the Portuguese colony an anachronism and would work to get Portugal out of the area. His attempt failed because the State Department was willing to offer only vague assurances that it would apply diplomatic pressure on Portugal. Relations were strained still further when the U.S. denounced the Indian annexation during U.N. debates but failed to condemn colonialism as Galbraith had recommended.

Following the outbreak of a China-India border conflict in October 1962, relations between the U.S. and India improved. In this period effective communications with Washington were briefly cut off during the Cuban missile crisis, and so Galbraith directed policy. Throughout the crucial months of October and November, he helped the aged, ill Nehru plan India's defenses and organized American military aid to that country. The Ambassador also directed diplomatic efforts designed to prevent a possible Pakistani attack on India.

Although Galbraith was not directly concerned with Southeast Asia, President Kennedy asked him to visit South Vietnam in November 1961 and make an independent assessment of the situation. In his report to the President, Galbraith described the decaying quality of the Diem regime, its lack of support and its ineffective administrative, military and political policies. He stressed that despite overwhelming military superiority South Vietnam's war effort was failing.

Galbraith believed that the war could be won with more effective leadership and urged the U.S. not to oppose any coup attempt. Until a coup took place, he said, the U.S. should "measurably reduce" its commitment to the regime and disassociate itself from the more controversial policies of the government such as the relocation of large numbers of rural families. Galbraith stressed that the U.S. must find a political rather than a military solution to the problem.

Because the military outlook improved during the summer of 1962, Kennedy did not have to consider sending U.S. combat troops and saw no urgent reason to consider Galbraith's advice on getting rid of Diem until the late summer of 1963.

Galbraith also remained in frequent contact with Kennedy on economic policy matters. He opposed the Administration's effort to stimulate the economy through a massive tax cut and instead favored the politically less popular effort to increase non-military public spending. Arguing from the point of view advanced in *The Affluent Society*, Galbraith described the 1962 tax cut proposed by the Council of Economic Advisers as "reactionary" Keynesianism.

On a trip to Washington in June 1962, Galbraith met briefly with the President. His diary recorded his objections to the proposed tax cut: "It is premature; money from tax reductions goes into the pockets of those who need it least; lower tax revenues will become a ceiling on spending. . . . I also stressed to the President the importance of realizing that in economics the majority is always wrong." Although Kennedy postponed advocacy of a tax cut in 1962 for reasons other than those advanced by Galbraith, he proposed an $11-billion cut the following year. It was enacted in early 1964.

In June 1963 Galbraith returned to Harvard. He published *The New Industrial State* (1965), a major work of economic history and analysis that argued for the nationalization of some industries, especially defense contractors, and favored a thorough system of wage and price controls. Galbraith was a sharp opponent of the war in Vietnam and in 1972 a warm supporter of Democratic presidential candidate George McGovern (D, S.D.) [*q.v.*]. [See JOHNSON, NIXON Volume]

[EWS]

For further information:
John Kenneth Galbraith, *Ambassador's Journal* (New York, 1969).

GATES, THOMAS S(OVEREIGN), JR.
b. April 10, 1906; Philadelphia, Pa.
President, Morgan Guaranty Trust Company, 1961-65.

The son of an investment banker, Thomas S. Gates, Jr., received his B.A. from the University of Pennsylvania in 1928 and then joined his father's firm, Drexel & Co., becoming a partner in 1940. During World War II Gates served as a naval officer in both the Pacific and European theaters. At war's end he returned to Drexel.

In October 1953 President Dwight D. Eisenhower [*q.v.*] named Gates to the first of four Defense Department posts he would hold under that Republican President. Between 1954 and 1959 he was undersecretary and then Secretary of the Navy. Gates served briefly as deputy secretary of defense in 1959 and as Secretary of Defense from December 1959 to the end of Eisenhower's second term. Although Gates was in office for a relatively short period, many Pentagon observers credited him with improving Defense Department efficiency and initiating many of the management innovations realized during the Kennedy Administration. Prior to and during the 1960 presidential campaign, however, Democratic spokesmen criticized Eisenhower and Gates for allegedly allowing the development of a "missile gap" in arms competition with the Soviet Union. Gates denied the charge but without telling effect. [See EISENHOWER Volume]

Despite his own attack on Eisenhower's defense policies and use of the missile gap allegation, John F. Kennedy was impressed with Gates's personal record and seriously contemplated retaining him at Defense. However, the President eventually nominated Ford Motor Company President Robert S. McNamara [q.v.] as Gates's successor. The outgoing Secretary fully cooperated with his replacement. Not wishing to commit McNamara to a last-minute Eisenhower Administration decision, Gates suspended Navy and Air Force projects for new supersonic aircraft and eliminated the proposed Skybolt missile system from the January 1961 defense budget.

Upon retiring as Secretary of Defense, Gates assumed the presidency of New York's Morgan Guaranty Trust Co., then the nation's sixth largest bank. The result of an April 1959 merger of Guaranty Trust and J.P. Morgan & Co., Morgan Guaranty functioned exclusively as a "wholesale" banker, offering services to other financial institutions and to corporations, including over half of the nation's largest 500. As a "bankers's bank," Morgan could not benefit from the growth of consumer (retail) banking, which accounted for a rising share of bank profits in the early 1960s. With Gates as president, however, the bank moved in several other directions to improve its profitability. Continuing a trend that began in the late 1950s, it shifted its assets from U.S. government securities to higher-yield loans, such as construction financing. Morgan also expanded its overseas investments, notably in Latin America.

In May 1962 the Federal Reserve Board denied Morgan Guaranty permission to merge with six upstate New York banks into what would have been the world's largest bank holding company. The Board's ruling, along with its similar judgment against First National City Bank of New York, frustrated the plans of New York City banks to expand their operations throughout the Empire State.

Gates generally remained out of the public eye during the Kennedy years. In November 1961 Eisenhower urged his last Secretary of Defense to seek the 1962 Republican nomination for governor of Pennsylvania, but Gates quickly denied any interest in the prospect. Yet, he did join a group of wealthy Pennsylvania Republicans in November 1963 sessions to plan a potential 1964 presidential race for Gov. William W. Scranton (R, Pa.) [q.v.].

Gates became board chairman of Morgan Guaranty in May 1965, retiring in January 1969 to become chairman of the board's executive committee. In the first months of the Nixon Administration, he headed the President's Commission on an All-Volunteer Armed Force. In March 1976 President Gerald R. Ford [q.v.] chose Gates to lead the United States liaison mission to China. [See JOHNSON, NIXON Volume]

[JLB]

GAVIN, JAMES M(AURICE)
b. March 22, 1907; New York, N.Y.
Ambassador to France, February 1961-August 1962.

James M. Gavin graduated from West Point in 1929. An early proponent of airborne operations, Gavin took personal command of the parachute combat team that spearheaded the Allied invasion of Sicily in July 1943. Promoted to brigadier general at age 36, he led the 82nd Airborne Division during the Normandy landing and in the Battle of the Bulge. Gavin remained in the Army following the war's end and in 1954 became the Army General Staff's chief of research and development and deputy chief of staff. He won promotion to lieutenant general in 1955. He soon found himself in conflict with the defense policies of the Eisenhower Administration, which emphasized massive nuclear retaliation at the expense of a more limited "conventional" warfare. In January 1958 Gavin resigned his commission in protest over Administration defense policy. [See EISENHOWER Volume]

Following his resignation Gavin became executive vice president and then president of Arthur D. Little, Inc., a Boston research and management firm. In December 1958 he joined a group of academic leaders advising presidential aspirant John F. Kennedy. With others, Gavin was an early proponent of a civilian Peace Corps for work in underdeveloped nations. He agreed with 1959 estimates that suggested that a "missile gap" existed between the U.S. and the Soviet Union. Kennedy later employed the allegation in his 1960 campaign.

In December 1960 Kennedy considered appointing Gavin as the administrator of the National Aeronautics and Space Administration, but Vice President-elect Lyndon B. Johnson [q.v.] opposed the designation of a former Army officer as head of the civilian agency. Kennedy then nominated Gavin as ambassador to France in February 1961. Many considered Gavin's appointment unusual because the former general possessed neither fluency in French nor the independent wealth necessary to entertain at the Paris embassy.

Gavin attempted to improve American relations with French President Charles deGaulle, who sought an independent French role in European defense and economic affairs. The Kennedy Administration complicated Gavin's task by seeking deGaulle's agreement to a Western European defense strategy which relied upon an exclusively Anglo-American nuclear deterrent. DeGaulle wanted France to have its own nuclear strike force, and he reaffirmed his policy of making France a nuclear power in a May 1962 press conference. Kennedy immediately rejected deGaulle's program and called for a continuance of the NATO nuclear force under American command.

In June 1962 Gavin reportedly recommended that the U.S. sell France nuclear equipment and information in exchange for French concessions to improve America's trade position with the European Common Market. Presidential adviser Maxwell D. Taylor [q.v.] and other military leaders agreed with Gavin's suggestion in the hope that deGaulle would cooperate with NATO defense plans. However the Administration failed to act on Gavin's proposal, and the General resigned his ambassadorship on Aug. 1, 1962. He offered as his reason for leaving the high cost of maintaining the American embassy.

Early in the Kennedy Administration, Gavin became involved in negotiations over the status of Laos. The General urged Kennedy in May 1961 not to commit American troops in the Laotian civil war. During the spring of 1961, Gavin held informal discussions with neutralist Laotian leader Prince Souvanna

Phouma in Paris. Gavin assured the Prince that the U.S. would shift its support from the rightwing General Phoumi Nosavan's government and agree to an independent and neutral Laos.

Gavin returned to Arthur D. Little following his diplomatic assignment and became chairman of the board in June 1964. Beginning in 1966 Gavin spoke out against the Johnson Administration's Vietnam war policies. He gained prominence as the advocate of the "enclave" theory which would have limited American ground forces to defensive operations and brought a halt to the bombing of North Vietnam. [See JOHNSON Volume]

[JLB]

For further information:
James M. Gavin, *War and Peace in the Space Age* (New York, 1958).
———. *Crisis Now* (New York, 1968).

GENEEN, HAROLD S(YDNEY)
b. Jan. 22, 1910; Bournemouth, England.
Chief Executive Officer, International Telephone and Telegraph Corporation, 1959- .

Harold Geneen's family moved from England to the U.S. when he was a year old. Geneen attended preparatory school in Connecticut and received a B.S. degree in accounting from New York University in 1934. Endowed with a keen business sense and a near photographic memory, Geneen spent eight years with an accounting firm, worked for various companies through the 1940s and early 1950s and then accepted the executive vice presidency of the Raytheon Manufacturing Company in 1956. At Raytheon Geneen more than quadrupled the Company's profits and instituted management and cost-effectiveness procedures that were later to make him renowned throughout the business community.

Assuming control of the sprawling International Telephone and Telegraph Corporation (ITT) in 1959, Geneen immediately instituted a sweeping internal reorganization designed to boost the conglomerate's stagnating yearly sales of $765 million, which had been accrued mainly from communications businesses held in a precarious confederation stretching around the world. Geneen created a system of strict accountability; all unit heads were required to draw up carefully monitored five-year plans and participate in grueling meetings held monthly in either New York or at the corporation's European headquarters in Brussels. Stating that "management must manage" and employing the personal slogan, "I want no surprises," Geneen proceeded to create a global business empire that took ITT from 47th place among industrial corporations in 1961 to 11th place in 1974 with sales of $8.5 billion.

During the early 1960s 82% of ITT's business was located outside the U.S. Disturbed over government expropriation of ITT communications systems in Cuba and Brazil, Geneen nevertheless stated confidently in a 1962 report that ITT "has in its time met and surmounted every device employed by governments to encourage their own industries and hamper those of foreigners."

The year 1963 marked an abrupt shift in direction for ITT. In March Geneen distributed an internal document entitled "Acquisition Philosophy;" it declared that instability in Europe and Latin America might prove potentially harmful to ITT's growth. Stating that ITT's earnings would "be subject to increasing pressures pricewise, sourcewise and ownershipwise," Geneen recommended an immediate policy of acquiring U.S. companies for ITT. (Geneen's fears of European instability were exaggerated; ITT's communications holdings in Europe proved extremely profitable during the 1960s). Geneen enlisted the services of the prominent investment banking firm of Lazard Freres to search for domestic investment opportunities. In 1962 Lazard purchased the ailing Avis Rent-a-Car Company, installed Robert Townsend as president and within five years transformed the Company into a profitable business. At that point ITT bought Avis for $52 million. ITT also expanded during the 1960s into such diversified areas as insurance, mutual funds, publishing and hotels. By 1974 ITT managed approximately 250 companies in 60 countries.

Geneen and ITT came under intense public scrutiny in 1972 after syndicated columnist Jack Anderson published a memo written by ITT Washington lobbyist Dita Beard. The memo connected the 1970 ITT acquisition of the Hartford Fire Insurance Co. with an ITT pledge of $400,000 for the 1972 Republican National Convention. ITT was further embarrassed when newspapers reported that the company had offered the Central Intelligence Agency funds to sabotage the election of Chilean President Salvador Allende because it was believed that Allende's new Marxist government would nationalize ITT telephone properties in Chile. [See JOHNSON, NIXON Volumes]

[FHM]

For further information:
Anthony Sampson, *The Sovereign State of ITT* (New York, 1973).

GILPATRIC, ROSWELL L(EAVITT)
b. Nov. 4, 1906; New York, N.Y.
Deputy Secretary of Defense, January 1961-January 1964.

After graduating from Yale College in 1928 and Yale Law School in 1931, Gilpatric joined the New York law firm Cravath, de Gersdorff, Swaine & Wood (later Cravath, Swaine & Moore). During World War II Gilpatric specialized in advising corporations involved in defense production. Gilpatric was appointed assistant secretary of the Air Force in May 1951 and that October was promoted to undersecretary. He was primarily responsible for production and procurement. [See TRUMAN Volume]

With the change of administration in 1953, Gilpatric returned to his law firm and represented many defense contractors in their dealings with the government. Gilpatric took part in the 1956-57 Rockefeller Brothers Fund study of the defense establishment that recommended increased weapons research and spending. In June 1960 he became chairman of the board of trustees of the newly created Aerospace Corporation, an Air Force-sponsored nonprofit organization active in ballistic missile development.

Gilpatric was an active Democrat, and after John F. Kennedy was nominated for president, he appointed Gilpatric to two study groups. One, headed by Paul H. Nitze [q.v.], concentrated on national defense and security, while the other, led by Sen. Stuart Symington (D, Mo.) [q.v.], prepared a report urging the unification of the top command structures of the separate Armed Services, eliminating the Joint Chiefs of Staff and increasing the power of the Secretary of Defense. Gilpatric, who had long advocated unification, played an important role in producing the report.

Kennedy considered appointing Gilpatric Secretary of Defense and after choosing Robert S. McNamara [q.v.] for the top defense post suggested that Gilpatric be made deputy secretary. Following a brief meeting with Gilpatric, McNamara agreed. The two men subsequently developed a close working relationship. Gilpatric's extensive contacts with the defense establishment and his smooth manner helped counteract McNamara's somewhat abrasive style.

Following the setback at the Bay of Pigs and the rapid deterioration of the U.S. position in Laos, on April 20, 1961 President Kennedy set up a task force headed by Gilpatric to come up with a plan to prevent a Communist triumph in Vietnam. A week later, on April 27, a first draft of the task force report was completed. It recommended a moderate increase in U.S. aid to the South Vietnamese armed forces but suggested that those forces should not be increased in size beyond a 20,000-man addition approved in January 1961. Further, the report suggested that the task force operations officer, Air Force Gen. Edward G. Lansdale [q.v.], be sent immediately to Vietnam to prepare further recommendations. Finally, it was suggested that the presidential task force take over the direction of U.S. policy in Vietnam, with Gilpatric in overall charge and Lansdale chief of operations in Saigon. An April 28 annex to the report, written in light of further setbacks in Laos, considerably changed its main points, suggesting an increase in the strength of the South Vietnamese army and the sending of U.S. ground troops to Vietnam to establish training centers. A May 1 draft added the idea that the U.S. publicly commit itself to intervention in Vietnam if necessary to prevent a Communist victory. Kennedy endorsed the original draft but took no action on the annex. The Lansdale trip, however, never took place, and the task force itself came increasingly under the control of the State Department. In the final May 6 task force report, largely prepared by State Department officials, Lansdale's future role was eliminated and the recommendations on U.S. troops and a public commitment were blurred although not eliminated.

In the fall of 1961 there was another major Administration re-examination of its Vietnam policy. Presidential advisers Gen. Maxwell Taylor [q.v.] and Walt W. Rostow [q.v.] were sent to Vietnam in mid-October as heads of a fact-finding mission. On their return, Taylor recommended the deployment of 8,000 U.S. combat troops in Vietnam to indicate America's readiness to support the Diem regime. In a memo to the President on Nov. 8, McNamara indicated that he, Gilpatric and the Joint Chiefs of Staff supported Taylor's position but felt troops should be sent only if coupled with a decisive commitment to prevent a Communist victory that included a willingness to send more troops and attack North Vietnam if necessary.

As the importance of the war grew, McNamara took over from Gilpatric the supervision of the Defense Department role in Vietnam policymaking. However, it was Gilpatric who approved for the Defense Department a controversial Aug. 24, 1963 State Department cable to Ambassador to South Vietnam Henry Cabot Lodge, Jr. [q.v.] that in effect gave American approval for a coup against South Vietnamese President Ngo Dinh Diem if Diem refused, as was expected, to eliminate from his government his brother, Ngo Dinh Nhu, and his sister-in-law, Madame Nhu. McNamara had been on vacation when the cable was sent. Along with several other top Administration figures also away from Washington at the time, McNamara expressed serious reservations about the cable upon returning. A new round of discussions on U.S. policy towards Diem was begun, and Lodge was asked to send more detailed information. Kennedy, who had approved the original cable, was angry at both the breakdown of the decision-making process and the collapse of an apparent policy consensus.

Gilpatric served on occasion as an Administration spokesman on defense policy. During the 1961 Berlin crisis, Gilpatric told a Washington press conference on June 6 that U.S. forces serving with NATO would use their nuclear weapons if Western Europe were in danger of being conquered by conventional Soviet forces. On Oct. 21 of that year Gilpatric laid to rest any lingering belief in a missile gap between the Soviet Union and the United States when he said the U.S. second-strike capability was "at least as extensive as what the Soviets can deliver by striking first."

Gilpatric supervised Defense Department procurement policies and the sale of weapons abroad. In October 1961 Gilpatric held a series of meetings with European defense ministers, successfully urging them to follow the U.S. lead in building up their armed forces and convincing them to do so by purchasing large quantities of U.S. military supplies. Gilpatric announced in September 1962 the agreement of the French, West German and Italian governments to make major U.S. arms purchases which, in addition to strengthening their forces, would help offset the drain on U.S. gold reserves resulting from the expense of stationing U.S. troops abroad.

During the Cuban missile crisis of October-November 1962, Gilpatric was a member of the Executive Committee of the National Security Council, a group Kennedy established to advise him on the management of the crisis. McNamara and Gilpatric, along with Undersecretary of State George Ball [q.v.], consistently opposed immediate direct armed action against the Cuban missile sites, an option Kennedy initially viewed with favor. At the key Oct. 20 Executive Committee meeting, at which the two main options were presented, a blockade of Cuba or air strikes against the sites, McNamara and Gilpatric supported the blockade. After arguments for both alternatives had been presented, Gilpatric summed up the situation, saying: "Essentially, Mr. President, this is a choice between limited action and unlimited action; and most of us think that it's better to start with limited action." Kennedy agreed with the majority and chose to "quarantine" the island with a naval blockade.

Kennedy retained the Executive Committee after the missile crisis was resolved to advise him on other defense matters. In February 1963 it met several times on the future of NATO and the U.S. plan for a multi-national nuclear force. During that month Gilpatric met with top European leaders to ascertain their views on the proposed force, but numerous complex problems and the opposition of France led to the eventual abandonment of the plan. In a major policy address delivered to a meeting of United Press International publishers and editors on Oct. 19, 1963, Gilpatric indicated that an upcoming U.S. military airlift exercise would show that the U.S. "should be able to make useful reductions in its heavy overseas military expenditures without diminishing its effective military strength or its capacity to apply that strength swiftly. . . ." Many felt that Gilpatric's speech indicated that the U.S. was considering reducing the size of its 230,000-man garrison in West Germany.

Gilpatric announced in March 1963 that he would soon resign his Defense post to return to private law practice, but his resignation was delayed by the prolonged TFX controversy. In November 1962 the Department of Defense awarded a contract for a new fighter plane, to be used by both the Air Force and the Navy, to General Dynamics Corp. General Dynamics had been in competition with the Boeing Co., and many military men had preferred the Boeing plane. The Boeing bid was also somewhat lower. Charges were made that political considerations had been involved in the decision. In February 1963 the Senate Permanent Investigations Subcommittee chaired by Sen. John L. McClellan (D, Ark.) [q.v.] began an investigation into the TFX contract that rapidly developed into a conflict between the subcommittee and top civilian Defense officials. Interviewed on the March 10 NBC-TV show Meet the Press, Gilpatric said he would "take an oath no political considerations" were involved in the TFX decision. Later that month, subcommittee investigators discovered that Cravath, Swaine &

Moore had done considerable legal work for General Dynamics since 1958, which included the period when Gilpatric was associated with the firm. On March 20 McNamara issued a statement indicating his "full confidence" in Gilpatric.

However when subcommittee hearings resumed in November, the Gilpatric issue was still unresolved. Subcommittee investigators discovered that Gilpatric had attended about half of the General Dynamics board meetings between 1958 and his appointment to the Defense Department and that although Gilpatric said that he had resigned from his law firm, insurance records indicated that he was only on a leave of absence. After considerable testimony subcommittee members on Nov. 20, in a 5-4 vote, expressed confidence in Gilpatric's role in the TFX contract award. A Justice Department investigation also cleared him of conflict-of-interest charges.

Gilpatric resigned his post as deputy secretary of Defense on Jan. 9, 1964 and returned to Cravath, Swaine & Moore as a senior partner. During the Johnson Administration Gilpatric served on an advisory panel on foreign policy and headed a panel studying ways to limit the proliferation of nuclear weapons. [See JOHNSON Volume]

[JBF]

GLEASON, THOMAS W(ILLIAM)
b. Nov. 8, 1900; New York, N.Y.
Executive Vice President, International Longshoremen's Association, 1961-63; President, International Longshoremen's Association, 1963- .

Gleason went to work on the New York docks at 15 and in 1919 joined the International Longshoremen's Association (ILA). He was appointed business agent of ILA Checkers' Local 1 in 1934 and later was elected president of the local. In 1953 the ILA was expelled from the AFL on charges of corruption. Shortly thereafter the union's president, Joseph P. Ryan, resigned, and with Gleason's support, William V. Bradley was elected to succeed him. Bradley appointed Gleason to the specially created post of general organizer. (The ILA was readmitted to the AFL-CIO in November 1959.) In 1961 Gleason was elected president of the ILA's Atlantic Coast Division and executive vice president of the 46,000-member union.

Gleason was the chief union negotiator in contract talks between the ILA and the New York Shipping Association that began in June 1962. The shippers wanted to reduce the size of work gangs, while the union, fearful of the effects of further automation, refused to comply. ILA members struck Atlantic and Gulf Coast ports on Oct. 1, but the strike was suspended on Oct. 4 when an injunction was issued under provisions of the Taft-Hartley Act, which President Kennedy had invoked. Following an 80-day "cooling off" period, the strike resumed on Dec. 24 and was not settled until Jan. 26, 1963. A compromise was reached on wages and benefits, and at the suggestion of a federal mediation panel, the issue of gang size was submitted for a two-year study.

In 1963 Gleason challenged Bradley for the ILA presidency. After a bitter campaign Bradley withdrew on the eve of the July 17 election to accept a salaried position as president emeritus.

The ILA leadership strongly supported the Cold War and had a tradition of refusing to handle trade with Communist countries. In October 1962 Gleason criticized President Kennedy's recently announced program to curb the use of U.S. or foreign ships in trade with Cuba as being too weak. Gleason declared that "more stringent action" was needed. He recommended that the ILA membership refuse to handle shipment to or from either Cuba or the USSR, which he called "the real culprit."

In September 1963, when the government was considering whether to permit the sale of wheat to the Soviet Union, Gleason told Administration officials that ILA members would "vigorously object to loading" the wheat. However, Gleason and the ILA executive council later agreed to permit the wheat to be loaded if at least one-half of it were carried in U.S. ships and if no Soviet ships were used. In February 1964, following a government waiver permitting more than one-half of a Soviet wheat purchase to be carried in non-U.S. vessels, the ILA refused to load any Soviet-bound wheat. However, a new agreement was reached after a nine-day boycott. Gleason continued to head the ILA throughout the Johnson and Nixon Administrations. [See JOHNSON, NIXON Volumes]

[JBF]

GLENN, JOHN H(ERSCHEL)
b. July 18, 1921; Cambridge, Ohio.
Astronaut.

Glenn became a naval pilot in the Marine Corps Reserve in 1943 and saw action in the Pacific. He remained on active duty through the Korean War. In 1954 Glenn became a naval test pilot and three years later set a speed record in the first non-stop trans-continental supersonic flight. In 1959 he was made a Marine lieutenant colonel.

In April 1959 Glenn and six others were chosen from 110 military test pilots to become America's first astronauts. Alan Shepard became the first American in space when his Mercury capsule made a suborbital flight in May 1961; Virgil Grissom's flight, also suborbital, followed in July. On Feb. 20, 1962 Glenn became the first American to orbit the earth, circling the globe three times in just under five hours.

Glenn's flight allayed fears that the U.S. lagged hopelessly behind the Russians in space technology. He was immediately hailed as a national hero. Parades welcomed him in Washington, D.C., New York City and his hometown, New Concord, Ohio, the U.S. Post Office issued a stamp commemorating his flight and New York City awarded him its medal of honor. On Feb. 26 Glenn addressed a joint session of Congress in support of the space program's long-range goals, saying that "exploration and the pursuit of knowledge have always paid dividends in the long run." A *New York Times* writer called Glenn "the Administration's star witness on Capitol Hill." His space capsule was placed in the Smithsonian Institute.

Glenn became a close friend of the Kennedy family. The President praised his religious beliefs as an illustration of a basic strength of the non-Communist world and members of the Senate Aeronautical and Space Sciences Committee said that his flight had helped revive religious values. Glenn, a former Sunday school teacher and an active member of the Presbyterian church, denied that he had prayed during the flight. "My peace has been made with my Maker for a number of years, so I had no particular worries along that line."

Glenn resigned as an astronaut to enter the Ohio Democratic senatorial primary in 1964. However, he withdrew from the race following a bathroom fall which caused a minor concussion that disturbed his sense of balance. He lost the 1970 primary but was elected to the Senate in 1974. [See NIXON Volume]

[MDB]

GOLDBERG, ARTHUR J(OSEPH)
b. Aug. 8, 1908; Chicago, Ill.
Secretary of Labor, January 1961-October 1962; Associate Justice, U.S. Supreme Court, October 1962-July 1965.

Goldberg was born into a large family of Russian-Jewish immigrants on Chicago's West Side. After working his way through college, he took a law degree in 1930 and served as an occasional counsel for a number of Chicago-area trade unions. Following service with the Office of Strategic Services during World War II, Goldberg was picked by Philip Murray in 1948 as general counsel for both the Congress of Industrial Organizations (CIO) and for the United Steelworkers of America (USW). Goldberg devised the legal procedures for expelling the Communist-dominated unions from the CIO in 1949 and in the early 1950s helped expedite the merger of the American Federation of Labor and the CIO. Goldberg was the principal author of the AFL-CIO ethical practices code and cooperated closely with Sen. John F. Kennedy during the 1958-59 McClellan Committee investigation of corrupt union practices. Goldberg achieved national recognition when he guided USW negotiations during the 116-day national steel strike in 1959 and 1960. [See TRUMAN, EISENHOWER Volumes]

Goldberg was among the earliest labor backers of John F. Kennedy's presidential primary campaign, and in December 1960 the new President chose Goldberg as his Secretary of Labor over five elected union officials nominated by AFL-CIO President George Meany [q.v.]. According to labor historian Thomas R. Brooks, Kennedy chose Goldberg because he needed a Secretary of Labor who could administer the reform provisions of the Landrum-Griffin Act, recently enacted over strong trade union opposition. Goldberg, who was "from the unions but not of them" was the "perfect appointee."

Goldberg was an activist Secretary ot Labor. During 1961 he personally intervened to settle a New York tugboat strike in January, a wildcat strike of flight engineers in February, a California agricultural work stoppage in March and a musicians' dispute at New York's Metropolitan Opera in August. In May 1961 Goldberg helped negotiate a no-strike, no-lockout pledge covering construction work at U.S. missile and space bases. President Kennedy then appointed Goldberg to chair an 11-man Missile Sites Labor Commission to handle subsequent labor disputes at the bases.

The principal economic problem facing Goldberg and Kennedy in 1961 was the lingering recession with its continuing 6.8% unemployment rate. At Kennedy's request Goldberg toured areas of high unemployment in five Midwestern states in February and reported that "we are in a full-fledged recession." The Department of Labor announced that "substantial and persistent" labor surpluses existed in 76 of 150 major industrial centers. Adopting the heretofore unsuccessful legislative proposals of Sen. Paul Douglas (D, Ill.) [q.v.] to aid these "depressed areas," the Administration backed a $389-million area redevelopment program in January 1961. Goldberg agreed that the new Redevelopment Agency be administered by the Secretary of Commerce, and he helped win the votes of conservative Southern congressmen by pointing out that federal money would be channeled into depressed areas of the rural South, as well as the high unemployment centers of the industrial North. The bill passed both houses of Congress in April and was signed by the President May 1.

During the spring of 1961 Goldberg also helped secure a 13-week extension of state unemployment benefits and a "pooling" of state tax revenues to spread the burden of increased expenditures among all 50 states. The Administration also won a substantial increase in the minimum wage (from $1 to $1.25 an hour over two years) in early May and extended minimum-wage coverage to an additional 3.6 million workers, the first such extension since 1938. In order to pump more purchasing power into the economy, the Administration won an $800 million increase in Social Security benefits in June. In August 1961 the Senate passed an Administration-sponsored manpower training bill, but the House delayed final passage of the compromise $435-million Manpower Development and Training Act until March 1962. The Act, administered by the Department of Labor, was designed to retrain workers displaced from their jobs by technological change or automation. A notable failure of the Kennedy-Goldberg legislative program came in May 1961 when the House rejected amendments aimed at protecting the wages and jobs of American farm workers. Instead, the lower chamber simply extended the "bracero" program which enabled California and Texas growers to import large numbers of poorly paid Mexican laborers.

Goldberg's term as Secretary of Labor coincided with an important increase in government supervision of peacetime labor-management relations. In the clearest statement of the Administration's labor policy, offered by Goldberg to a Feb. 23, 1962 luncheon of Chicago's Executive Club, the Secretary of Labor announced that the government "must increasingly provide guidelines" to ensure that future wage settlements were in the "public interest." Goldberg linked domestic labor-management peace and noninflationary settlements directly to the Kennedy Administration's ability to end the nation's balance of payments deficit and conduct a vigorous foreign policy. Despite opposition from the AFL-CIO, Goldberg defended the Administration's determination to hold future wage boosts to 3.2% per year, a figure which the Council of Economic Advisers (CEA) estimated equaled the average annual increase in worker productivity. Goldberg also opposed AFL-CIO efforts to secure the 35-hour week as a means of spreading employment and indirectly raising wages.

The most important application of the Kennedy-Goldberg labor policy came in the negotiations leading up to the 1962 collective bargaining agreement in steel. Goldberg hoped that by persuading the USW to accept a wage package within the 3.2% guideposts the Administration would then be in a position to prevent the industry from raising steel prices after the new contract went into effect on July 1, 1962. To this end Goldberg held several meetings with USW President David J. McDonald [q.v.] and U.S. Steel Chairman Roger Blough [q.v.] in the fall of 1961 and the winter of 1962. Goldberg helped get formal union-management negotiations started in February, several months before the USW contract expired. Urging a wage package based on a CEA analysis, Goldberg met with Blough on March 6 and proposed that the new contract provide for about 10 cents an hour in fringe benefits but no wage increase. Goldberg indicated to Blough that the Administration considered this figure, about 2.5%, well within the capacity of the industry to absorb without a price increase. (According to Kennedy Administration sources, neither Blough nor other steel industry leaders challenged this contention at the time.) Goldberg then urged the same wage package upon McDonald in a private conversation of March 12. McDonald, who had relied heavily upon Goldberg during industry negotiations all during the 1950s, accepted the package, the most modest contract improvement since 1942. Union and company formally ratified the agreement on March 31, and Kennedy praised both parties for their "high industrial statesmanship."

On the afternoon of April 10, Roger Blough met briefly with Kennedy and Goldberg at the White House and unexpectedly announced that U.S. Steel was raising its prices an average of $6 a ton. Kennedy was outraged and Goldberg called the U.S. Steel decision a "doublecross." When five other major steel firms followed suit the next day, Goldberg offered to resign as Secretary of Labor on the grounds that he could no longer preach wage restraint to any union. The President deferred Goldberg's offer and instead stepped up pressure to rescind the industry-wide price increase. Along with CEA Chairman Walter Heller [q.v.] and presidential assistant Theodore Sorenson [q.v.], Goldberg prepared the sharp verbal attack upon the price increases which Kennedy delivered at a dramatic press conference on April 11. With former Truman adviser Clark Clifford [q.v.], Goldberg met secretly with U.S. Steel executives during the next two days. Goldberg emphasized that the President could not "restrain the more fiery members of Congress" intent on harsh legislation unless the steel price raises were withdrawn. By the afternoon of April 14, after it became clear that some smaller steel makers had decided not to follow big steel's price lead, Bethlehem Steel announced it would rescind its price increase. A few hours later U.S. Steel followed suit.

In August 1962 Kennedy nominated Goldberg to fill the Supreme Court seat held for 23 years by Felix Frankfurter, who had recently suffered a stroke. The appointment, widely hailed in the press, came at a time when Goldberg's warm relationship with organized labor had begun to cool as a result of his vigorous wage restraint policies. The Senate confirmed the nomination in September with but one dissenting vote.

Goldberg spent 34 months on the bench. According to legal scholar Henry J. Abraham, the former Secretary of Labor showed a "zest for innovation in the law that left an imprint far out of proportion to the brief period he served." Goldberg first raised the specter of the unconstitutionality of the death penalty in October 1963 on the basis of the cruel and unusual punishment and due process of law clauses of the Constitution. He spoke for the Court's six-to-three majority in June 1964 that ruled denial of passports to members of the Communist Party "unconstitutional on its face." In the same month it was Goldberg who authored the Court's landmark five-to-four decision in *Escobedo v. Illinois*, holding that confessions cannot be used in court if police question a suspect without letting him consult a lawyer or without warning him that his answers may be used against him.

Most observers thought Goldberg's temperament activist rather than judicial, and the former Labor Secretary may have found his role on the Supreme Court somewhat confining. Goldberg continued to advise Presidents Kennedy and Johnson on national labor problems while he was on the bench and in July 1965 readily accepted Johnson's offer of appointment as ambassador to the United Nations. He resigned in April 1968 to aid Sen. Hubert Humphrey's (D, Minn.) [q.v.] campaign for the presidency and later spoke in opposition to American policy in Vietnam. Goldberg challenged Nelson Rockefeller [q.v.] in the 1970 New York gubernatorial election but failed to unseat the three-term Republican incumbent. [SEE JOHNSON, NIXON VOLUMES]

[NNL]

For further information:
Grant McConnell, *Steel and the Presidency—1962* (New York, 1963).
Theodore Sorenson, *Kennedy* (New York, 1965).

GOLDMANN, NAHUM
b. July 10, 1894; Wisznewo, Poland
President, World Zionist Organization, 1956-68.

Goldmann received a doctor of laws degree in 1920 and a Ph.D. in 1921 from the University of Heidelberg. From 1922 to 1934 he was publisher and coeditor of Eshkol, the first Hebrew language encyclopedia in Germany. He became a member of the Executive German Zionist Action Committee in 1929; his activities forced him to flee the Nazis five years later. In 1934 the Jewish Agency for Palestine, recognized by Britain as responsible for Jewish immigration and settlement in the Holy Land, appointed him its liaison officer with the League of Nations.

In 1940 Goldmann moved to the United States and became the director of the Washington, D.C., office of the Jewish Agency. During the early 1950s Goldmann was instrumental in obtaining for Israel, West German and Austrian reparations for property destruction suffered by Jews during the Hitler era. In May 1956 the World Zionist Congress elected him president of the New York-based World Zionist Organization.

Goldmann disagreed with Israeli leaders over some of the policies of the Jewish state. These differences took the form of political conflicts between Goldmann and Israeli Premier David Ben-Gurion in the early 1960s. In 1961 Goldmann criticized Israel's dependence on the West and contended that improved Israeli relations with the Soviet Union would force the Arabs to soften their position towards Israel. In March 1961 he visited Israel to help organize the Liberal Party as an opposition group to Ben-Gurion's dominant Mapai Party. In May 1962 a dispute arose between Ben-Gurion and Goldmann over the latter's more lenient position on the issue of readmitting Arab refugees to Israel.

These conflicts had their roots in a disagreement over the fundamental question of the relationship of the Zionist movement to the state of Israel. Ben-Gurion believed that the Zionist movement had completed its mission with the creation of the Jewish state and that all Zionists should settle in that country. Goldmann acknowledged the legitimacy of what he described in May 1962 as "the central position of Israel in Jewish life of today. . . ." But he rejected Ben-Gurion's call, in effect, for the dismantling of non-Israeli Jewish communities, stating in May 1961 that Zionists "have the full right to regard themselves as full citizens of their countries while at the same time helping build the State of Israel. . . ." He believed the Zionist movement should seek to strengthen the cohesion and distinctive identity of the world's Jewish communities and cement their interrelationships.

In November 1961 Goldmann described the American Jewish community as being in a state of "organized chaos," and he said it was "the only Jewish community in the world lacking a representative body." He contended that all American Zionist groups should be merged into one. In May 1962 he warned American Jews that their communities could not remain distinctive entities unless they regarded themselves not simply as one of many religious groups but as a people "which has many other elements and which is a unique people in this respect."

In November 1962 Goldmann urged that American Jews give top priority to education and cultural activities as a means of preserving all of the characteristics of Jewish social identity. In August 1961 Goldmann had criticized the majority of American Jews for opposing state aid to religious schools during the debate over President Kennedy's federal aid-to-education measures.

In 1965 Goldmann attracted attention by asserting that some fo the charges of anti-Semitism directed at the Soviet Union were exaggerated and that Soviet Jews would be best served if false assertions were avoided. Three years later his tenure as president of the World Zionist Organization ended. Shortly afterwards he became president of the World Jewish Congress. In 1970 the Israeli government rejected a reported offer by United Arab Republic President Gamal Nasser to hold peace talks with Goldmann. Premier Golda Meir cited Goldmann's opposition to Israeli policies in explaining the refusal. By that time Goldmann had concluded that Israel, whose policies towards the Arabs he regarded as inflexible, could best avoid the prospect of perpetual conflict by accepting neutralization under international guarantees.

[MLL]

GOLDWATER, BARRY M(ORRIS)
b. Jan. 1, 1909; Phoenix, Ariz.
Republican Senator, Ariz., 1953-65; 1969-   .

Heir to a Phoenix department store, Barry M. Goldwater left the University of Arizona after one year to run his family's business. After a tour of duty with the Army Transport Command during World War II, he won election to the Phoenix City Council in 1949. Three years later he upset Senate Majority Leader Ernest W. McFarland (D, Ariz.) despite the state's previously strong Democratic traditions. As one of the most conservative and anti-Communist Republicans, Goldwater defended Sen. Joseph R. McCarthy (R, Wisc.) and voted against his censure in December 1954. A member of the Senate Labor and Public Welfare Committee,

Goldwater frequently criticized leaders of organized labor. In 1958 he handily beat McFarland again despite a determined effort on his opponent's behalf by the state AFL-CIO. [See EISENHOWER Volume]

His 1958 triumph marked the beginning of his career as a national conservative spokesman. As chairman of the Senate Republican Campaign Committee, Goldwater's heavy speech-making schedule brought him before thousands of Republican Party members. During his eight years as chairman (1955-63), he proved one of the party's most effective fundraisers.

Goldwater's performance at the 1960 Republican National Convention confirmed his position as the leader of the Republican Party's conservative wing. The Arizona Senator led the conservative attack upon the pre-convention platform compromise reached by Vice President Richard M. Nixon [q.v.] and Gov. Nelson A. Rockefeller (R, N.Y.) [q.v.]. Goldwater accused Nixon of having participated in the "Munich of the Republican Party" by giving in to Rockefeller's demand for a more liberal party document. Enraged conservative delegates nominated Goldwater for president as a protest against Nixon's accommodation with the New York Governor. Aware of Nixon's overwhelming delegate strength, however, Goldwater asked that his name be withdrawn in an address calling for Party unity. He received ten votes from Louisiana on the first ballot.

Many conservative Republicans, long frustrated in GOP presidential politics, looked to Goldwater as the natural heir to the late Sen. Robert A. Taft (R, Ohio), who had three times sought and been denied the Party's highest honor. But Goldwater proved more militant in his anti-Communism and conservative on social welfare legislation than Taft. The Senator was also less pragmatic and more ideological than Taft. Unlike Taft, he promoted his views with evangelical fervor; his *Conscience of a Conservative*, published in 1960, sold over 700,000 copies in its first year, and ranked 23rd in sales of non-fiction works published between 1895 and 1965.

As a political leader Goldwater drew support from, and in turn applauded, the expansion in the early 1960s of diffuse ring-wing, anti-Communist groups separate from the regular Party. Goldwater, for example, often defended the John Birch Society (although he criticized its founder, Robert H. W. Welch, Jr. [q.v.]). In March 1962 Goldwater hailed as "the wave of the future" the Young Americans for Freedom, founded by journalist William F. Buckley, Jr. [q.v.], and others. Despite his identification with these and other rightist groups, Goldwater emphasized that the Republican Party should continue as the main vehicle of conservatism. He warned in May 1962 that President Kennedy's conduct during the steel price controversy the month before proved that Republicans had to win large gains in November "if this country is to be saved from Socialist regimentation."

In the Senate Goldwater often stood with only a small number of colleagues in his opposition to Kennedy Administration domestic policy proposals. As measured by Congressional Quarterly, Goldwater favored a smaller federal role in every roll-call vote in the 1961, 1962 and 1963 sessions of Congress. In April 1961 he voted against an increase in the federal minimum wage law, which the Senate approved 65-28. He cast negative votes on the Administration's 1961 and 1963 wilderness preservation bills, although the Senate twice voted for the proposal by overwhelming margins. With fellow conservative Sen. John Tower (R, Tex.) [q.v.], Goldwater frequently dissented on the Labor and Public Welfare Committee's recommendations.

Goldwater repeatedly demonstrated his strident anti-Communism on foreign policy issues. He joined three Republican colleagues in January 1961 in voting against the confirmation of Chester Bowles [q.v.] as undersecretary of state because of Bowles's positions on disarmament and the recognition of mainland China. During the 1962 congressional elections Goldwater attempted to make the Administration's Cuban policy an issue, and on Nov. 5 he claimed in a joint statement with Rep. Robert C. Wilson (R, Calif.) [q.v.] that Kennedy had pledged not to invade Cuba and had thus "locked Castro and Communism into Latin America and thrown away the key to their removal." After the naval blockade of Cuba, Goldwater frequently challenged Administration claims that its action had forced the Soviet Union to remove its offensive missiles and troops from the island.

During the debate on the nuclear test ban treaty in September 1963, Goldwater offered an amendment that would have made ratification contingent upon the removal of all Soviet troops and weapons from Cuba. The Senate rejected the Goldwater provision 75 to 17. Announcing that the test ban agreement would "erode our military strength," Goldwater took the side of those generals who publicly or privately opposed the Treaty of Moscow. He joined 18 other senators in voting against ratification of the agreement on Sept. 24, 1963. In October he also opposed a White House proposal to sell wheat to the Soviet Union.

Goldwater's attacks on Kennedy Administration measures solidified his command of the Republican right. In November 1961 political organizer F. Clifton White and others began a Draft Goldwater for President Committee, which effectively laid the groundwork for his presidential nomination in 1964. Gov. Rockefeller, however, enjoyed an early lead in the public opinion surveys. Goldwater, who loathed the prospect of a rigorous presidential race, came close in 1962 and early 1963 to renouncing a bid for the nomination. After repeated attempts to interest Goldwater in their campaign, White and his group sought an alternative to the Arizona Senator. To add to their frustration, Goldwater enjoyed a fleeting personal rapport with Rockefeller. Most Party rightists considered the New York Governor much too representative of the GOP's liberal Eastern Establishment. His remarriage to a woman 18 years his junior in May 1963 outraged enough Party members to cause a sharp decline in his national following. Before his remarriage Gallup polls of Republican voters found Rockefeller favored over Goldwater 59% to 41%. Polls taken in the early summer showed Goldwater topping his New York rival with 56% of the Republican vote.

At the same time that Goldwater's presidential stock rose, the rising tempo of civil rights activities in the South alienated many Southerners from the Kennedy Administration. Political observers and "Draft Goldwater" strategists claimed that Goldwater would sweep the South in 1964. In September 1963 *Time* speculated that "against Barry Goldwater, [Kennedy] can only be rated even."

Two factors, however, threatened to thwart the Goldwater strategy. First, the Senator's identification with the "radical right" and his votes against measures favored by a majority of his Party colleagues (such as the test ban treaty) appeared to place him outside the "political mainstream" of the GOP. Blaming Goldwater for his slide in the pre-primary opinion surveys, Rockefeller urged Republicans in a formal statement on July 14, 1963 to repudiate "well-drilled extremist elements boring within the [Republican] party." Clearly aimed at the Arizona Republican, Rockefeller's statement infuriated Goldwater and ended their briefly cordial association. Second, the Senator relied heavily upon ghost writers and hence frequently contradicted himself on major policy issues. L. Brent Bozell, brother-in-law of William F. Buckley, Jr., wrote the entire manuscript for *Conscience of a Conservative*, which Goldwater at first did not read, choosing instead to have another ghost writer approve it for him. "Oh hell, I have ghosts all over the place," he admitted in an August 1963 interview. Inconsistency or outright political gaffes—such as his advocacy in October 1963 of the sale of the Tennessee Valley Authority—later proved costly in the 1964 campaign.

In the fall of 1963 many analysts rated Goldwater the front-runner for the nomination, and some gave him a chance of an upset in November 1964. The Senator showed new interest in a presidential campaign, and both he and Kennedy looked forward to an issue-oriented contest. In 1964 he won the nomination after a bitter pre-convention struggle but lost the election to President Lyndon B. Johnson [q.v.] in an historic landslide. After semi-retirement from politics between 1964 and 1968, Goldwater again won election to the Senate in November 1968. [See JOHNSON, NIXON, Volumes]

[JLB]

For further information:
Robert Novak, *The Agony of the GOP 1964* (New York, 1965).
F. Clifton White, *Suite 3505; the Story of the Draft Goldwater Movement* (New Rochelle, 1967).

GONZALEZ, HENRY B(ARBOSA)
b. May 3, 1916; San Antonio, Tex.
Democratic Representative, Tex., 1961- .

Gonzalez won a seat on the San Antonio City Council in 1953. In 1956 he was elected to the state Senate, becoming the first citizen of Mexican descent to sit in that body in 110 years. The following year he conducted two filibusters against new laws designed to support and enforce racial segregation, a policy which had always been imposed against Mexican-Americans as well as blacks in Texas.

The Mexican-American vote in Texas had traditionally been controlled by the conservative Democratic machine which dominated state politics. Beginning in the late 1950s, however, the Latin vote began to swing towards more liberal candidates. Gonzalez both tapped this new mood and accelerated its progress. In 1958 he entered the Democratic gubernatorial primary and won nine of the 36 counties with more than a 40% Latin population. Two years later he played a major role in the creation of the "Viva Kennedy" organization, which helped the national Democratic ticket capture the great majority of Texas's Mexican-American counties.

Gonzalez's relationship with the minority liberal faction within the state Democratic Party was not uniformly friendly. Early in 1961 he ran in a special, non-partisan election for Vice President Lyndon Johnson's [q.v.] U.S. Senate seat, but the liberal Democrats of Texas organization endorsed Maury Maverick, Jr., and Gonzalez received only about 9% of the vote. This reinforced the feeling of many Latins that minorities were not being offered an equal partnership in the liberal coalition.

Later in the year he won the Democratic nomination for a vacant seat in the U.S. House of Representatives from San Antonio, whose population was more than 40% Mexican-American. Shortly before the general election, Gonzalez received an endorsement from President Kennedy and the active campaign assistance of Vice President Johnson, which helped him defeat his Republican opponent by 52,885 to 42,553 votes. He thereby became the nation's first Mexican-American congressman. In succeeding years he won reelection with little or no opposition.

Gonzalez entered Congress in January 1962 and was a strong supporter of Kennedy Administration programs. According to *Congressional Quarterly*, he supported the President on 87% and 93% of the key votes in 1962 and 1963, respectively. In the latter year he voted against the Southern Democrat-Republican conservative coalition on 100% of the major roll-call votes in the House.

During the Johnson Administration Gonzalez lost the favor of some liberals by refusing to oppose the Vietnam war. As a result he opened another breach with the Texas liberals in 1968 when he endorsed Hubert Humphrey [q.v.] for the presidency at the same time that Sen. Ralph Yarborough [q.v.], the leader of the Texas liberals, endorsed peace candidate Sen. Eugene McCarthy (D, Minn.) [q.v.]. In the late 1960s and early 1970s younger, more militant Mexican-Americans denounced Gonzalez as a member of the establishment, but they were unable to prevent his consistent electoral success. [See JOHNSON Volume]

[MLL]

GOODELL, CHARLES E(LLSWORTH)
b. March 16, 1926; Jamestown, N.Y.
Republican Representative, N.Y., 1959-68.

Goodell received his law degree from Yale in 1951 and in 1952 took a masters degree there in government. A congressional liaison assistant with the Department of Justice in 1954-55, he subsequently practiced law in Jamestown, N.Y., In 1959 he won a special election to fill a vacant congressional seat.

Goodell soon established a reputation as an energetic congressman. According to *Congressional Quarterly*, he voted with the conservative coalition 72% of the time in 1961 and 1962 and 53% of the time in 1963. On the Education and Labor Committee he helped cut the Kennedy Administration's $900-million scholarship program by two-thirds. Later Goodell was a leading Republican critic of the Administration's 1963 Youth Conservation Corps plan. His 1961 proposal for a preschool education program for lower-income areas, however, laid the legislative basis for what later became Project Head Start, enacted four years later.

Goodell cosponsored the Administration's manpower retraining development program and was instrumental in gaining House clearance for the measure in February 1961. In July 1962, however, he succeeded in deleting a provision from an equal-pay-for-women bill that would have barred employers from lowering wages in order to equalize them. He voted against the Administration's successful foreign aid bill in July 1962 because it granted assistance to nations which he regarded as pro-Communist.

In January 1963 Goodell and Reps. Gerald Ford (R, Mich.) [q.v.] and Robert Griffin (R, Mich.) led a "Young Turks" challenge which ousted Rep. Charles Hoeven (R, Iowa) as chairman of the House Republican Conference. The secret vote demonstrated the growing strength of the younger, somewhat less conservative faction.

A congressman until 1968, Goodell became chairman of the newly-formed Republican Planning and Research Committee in 1965. After Gov. Nelson Rockefeller [q.v.] appointed him to fill the seat of the assassinated Sen. Robert F. Kennedy (D., N.Y.) [q.v.], he shifted somewhat to the left and took an increasingly outspoken stand against American involvement in the Vietnam war. Goodell ran for reelection in 1970 but was defeated in a three-way race by the Conservative Party's candidate, James L. Buckley. [See JOHNSON, NIXON Volumes]

[MDB]

GOODMAN, PAUL
b. Sept. 9, 1911; New York, N.Y.
d. Aug. 2, 1972; North Stratford, N.H.
Social critic.

Goodman grew up in the New York City slums and attended the City College of New York, where he was first attracted to the communitarian anarchist principles of Peter Kropotkin. It was characteristic of his anti-institutional perspective that Goodman eschewed a conventional career. After his dismissal from the University of Chicago graduate program in English because of his undisguised homosexual activity, Goodman taught at progressive schools, practiced Gestalt therapy and wrote novels, short stories, poetry, literary criticism and essays in sociology, linguistics and constitutional law. He collaborated with his brother, Percival, in writing *Communitas* (1947), which suggested that rational urban planning could be a workable alternative to what they saw as the chaotic and destructive growth of the capitalist city.

In the late 1950s Goodman completed *Growing Up Absurd: Problems of Youth in the Organized System*. His manuscript was rejected by 19 publishers before Norman Podhoretz [*q.v.*] decided to serialize it in *Commentary* in 1960. A critical success, the book was published later in the year by Random House.

In *Growing Up Absurd* Goodman confidently analyzed a problem that baffled many of his contemporaries: why so many young people were uninterested in careers and why so many were unhappy in the midst of an affluent America. Describing the subculture of juvenile delinquents, beatniks and other disaffected young people, Goodman implied that their alienation was neither essentially perverse nor aberrant. Their disaffection was a genuinely human response, he argued, since work, education and even leisure-time activities had become dehumanized in American society.

Most jobs, according to Goodman, were boring and wasteful of human and material resources because they were built on an artificial system of values characterized by the profit motive, status-consciousness and a debased popular culture. Goodman believed that the traditional solution to the youth "problem"—mainly expensive programs aimed at socialization—would prove a failure because these programs could not compensate for what the U.S. lacked in values, sensitivity to human needs and a vision of the future. The system, Goodman thought, had to be radically changed.

In 1962 Goodman extended his discussion of alienated youth by publishing *The Community of Scholars*, his first book on education. He asserted that the size of the American educational bureaucracy stifled student curiosity for learning. He argued that only in smaller units could students and faculty find a sense of community and enhance the creativity of the learning process.

No longer generally considered an eccentric or crank in the mid-1960s, Goodman was taken seriously by the American intellectual and academic communities. Goodman's emergence as a widely read social critic marked an important stage in the development of the New Left. By the end of the decade his influence was seen in the period's experiments in communal living, establishment of decentralized and "free schools" and in the efforts of many young people to become more active in neighborhood life. Goodman died on Aug. 2, 1972. [See JOHNSON Volume]

[JCH]

For further information:
Paul Goodman, *Growing Up Absurd: Problems of Youth in the Organized System* (New York, 1960).
———, *The Community of Scholars* (New York, 1962).

GOODWIN, RICHARD N(ARADHOF)

b. Dec. 7, 1931; Boston, Mass.

Assistant Special Counsel to the President, January 1961-November 1961; Deputy Assistant Secretary of State for Inter-American Affairs, November 1961-July 1962; Director, the International Peace Corps Secretariat, December 1962-January 1964.

The son of a Lithuanian Jewish immigrant, Goodwin graduated first in his class from both Tufts University and Harvard Law School, where he was president of the Law Review. In 1958 he clerked for Supreme Court Justice Felix Frankfurter [q.v.]. The next year he worked as counsel to the House Interstate and Foreign Commerce Subcommittee on Legislative Oversight, which investigated rigged television quiz shows and radio payola. In November 1959 he joined the speechwriting staff of Sen. John F. Kennedy, who began his formal presidential campaign three months later.

During the 1960 campaign Goodwin and Theodore Sorenson [q.v.] wrote most of Kennedy's speeches. Goodwin impressed Kennedy with his quick intelligence, capacity for work and a knack for phrasemaking. He invented the term Alliance of Progress, which Kennedy used in his speeches to refer to his projected aid program for Latin America. Following the November 1960 elections Goodwin organized a task force, under the chairmanship of Adolf A. Berle, [q.v.], to draw up the Alliance for Progress program. With Kennedy's inauguration in January 1961, Goodwin was named White House assistant special counsel specializing in Latin American affairs. Although Goodwin spoke no Spanish and had never visited the region, Kennedy assumed that Goodwin's intelligence and sympathy for New Frontier ideals would compensate for any lack of expertise.

Goodwin served on a White House Latin American task force under Berle. He supported Berle's belief that the U.S. ought to clearly align itself with democratic governments and movements, opposing right-wing dictatorships as well as Castroite revolutions. However, he differed with Berle in recommending that long-term economic development projects were a greater help to democracy in Latin America than direct U.S. support of democratic revolutionary movements.

The White House group found it difficult to induce the State Department to adopt the new goals and ideals. Berle quit his post in disgust in July 1961 because of what he considered State's slowness to reorient its approach. State Department officials had resented his interference and especially disliked Goodwin for his youth, his unfamiliarity with Latin America and for what they saw as his preoccupation with self-promotion. According to the historian and White House aide Arthur Schlesinger, Jr. [q.v.], with whom Goodwin worked closely on Latin American policy, many officials found him "abrasive. . .and often impatient; those whom he overrode called him arrogant. . . . He had friends in high places and could therefore cut through the. . .red tape that bogged down others, and they, of course, resented him for that."

Goodwin's standing in the new Administration was advanced following the Bay of Pigs fiasco in April 1961. Henceforth, Kennedy decided to rely less on the Pentagon, the CIA and other experts and more on his own staff, many of whom, including Goodwin, had expressed reservations about the invasion operation.

In May 1961 Goodwin and Schlesinger began preparations for the conference of the Inter-American Economic and Social Council scheduled to meet in August at Punta del Este, Uruguay. At the conference all the Latin American nations except Cuba agreed to join the Alliance for Progress. The beginning of intensive efforts to achieve economic development under U.S. leadership and the apparent isolation of Cuba made the conference a great diplomatic success for the United States, but on his return to Washington Goodwin came under congressional fire for an allegedly lengthy and unauthorized meeting with the Cuban delegate, Ernesto "Che" Guevara. Questioned by the Senate Foreign Relations Subcommittee on Latin America, Goodwin explained that he had spoken with Guevara for less than a half-hour at a diplomatic cocktail party and not, as some had thought, at a three-hour conference aimed at U.S.-Cuban reconciliation. Foreign representatives corroborated Goodwin's explanation, adding that Goodwin had rejected Guevara's attempts to cultivate him. Goodwin also satisfied the subcommittee by taking a "hard-line" against Cuba, recommending economic and political isolation of the island.

Goodwin continued to write speeches on civil rights and domestic affairs for Kennedy, but Latin America constituted his major area of interest. In November 1961 he left the White House to become deputy assistant secretary of state for inter-American affairs. Sen. Barry Goldwater (R, Ariz.) [q.v.] criticized the appointment because he believed Goodwin to be "soft on Communism," while others noted his youth and inexperience. At the time, the appointment was interpreted as part of a "shake-up" of the State Department intended to make it a more pliable tool of the Administration and to overcome the divisions and conflicts of authority between State and the White House.

Goodwin's new post greatly reduced his influence in the government. Disliked by many Department officials, he was isolated in the bureaucracy. Edwin Martin [q.v.], the assistant secretary of state for inter-American affairs, found it necessary to diminish Goodwin's sphere of activity in order to advance State Department reorganization. Restless at State, Goodwin began to work with Sargent Shriver's [q.v.] Peace Corps on a temporary basis in July 1962. In December he was able to set up his own agency under the auspices of the Corps. The small International Peace Corps Secretariat advised other nations on how to establish their own peace corps. Shortly before Kennedy's assassination in November 1963, Goodwin was slated to become presidential adviser on the arts.

After a trial period Goodwin found a secure position on the Johnson staff. He wrote many of President Lyndon Johnson's [q.v.] speeches and coined the "Great Society" and "War on Poverty" slogans. In December 1964 he was named a special assistant to the President. Disenchanted with Johnson's Vietnam policy, he resigned in September 1965 to become a fellow at Wesleyan University. Increasingly vocal in his opposion to the war, Goodwin worked for the presidential campaigns of both Sen. Eugene McCarthy (D, Minn.) [q.v.] and Sen. Robert F. Kennedy (D, N.Y.) [q.v.] in 1968. Later earning a living as a journalist and author, he became increasingly pessimistic about the future of American politics. [See JOHNSON Volume]

[JCH]

GORDON, KERMIT
b. July 3, 1916; Philadelphia, Pa.
Member, Council of Economic Advisers, January 1961-November 1962; Director of the Budget, November 1962-April 1965.

A Rhodes scholar, Kermit Gordon worked in the Office of Price Administration and then the Office of Strategic Services during World War II. He began teaching economics at Williams College in 1946 and also served as a State Department consultant until 1953. President Kennedy appointed Gordon to his Council of Economic Advisers (CEA) early in 1961 at the behest of the Council's chairman, Walter W. Heller [q.v.]. Gordon, like his fellow CEA members Heller and James Tobin [q.v.], was a Keynesian economist who favored using the fiscal resources of the federal government to stimulate full employment and rapid economic growth. The CEA sought to win over both the public and President Kennedy himself to the aggressive fiscal policies of the "new economics." In their view stimulative spending and tax cuts should take precedence over the traditional imperative to balance the federal budget.

Within the CEA Gordon's main areas of responsibility were problems of wage-price relations, foreign aid and trade, and natural resources. As chairman of an ad hoc committee on housing credit, he helped shape the Housing Act of 1961. He was also involved in the drafting of the Trade Expansion Act of 1962. Gordon left the CEA in November 1962 to become Director of the Budget following the resignation of David Bell [q.v.].

Gordon played a prominent role in defending Kennedy's deficit budget for 1964, which contained a controversial $13.6 billion in tax reductions for individuals and corporations. He opposed conservative plans to cut expenditures to compensate for the revenue lost in the tax cut. At a Jan. 29, 1963 hearing of the Joint Economic Committee of Congress, Gordon argued that such action would be "self-defeating." He warned that an attempt to balance the budget under current conditions could push the unemployment rate toward 10% (compared to 5.6% in 1962) and reduce the gross national product by $50-60 billion annually. Upon reading newspaper accounts of Gordon's testimony, Sen. Harry F. Byrd (D, Va.) [q.v.], conservative chairman of the Senate Finance Committee, called for Gordon's ouster. Kennedy kept him on as Budget Director, and the House passed the tax bill before the President's assassination in November. Gordon and Heller then helped persuade President Johnson to support the measure, which he signed after Senate passage in February 1964. Gordon remained Budget Director until April 1965. He was named president of the Brookings Institution in March 1967. [See JOHNSON Volume]

[TO]

GORDON, LINCOLN
b. Sept. 10, 1913; New York, N.Y.
Ambassador to Brazil, August 1961-January 1966.

Educated at New York's Ethical Culture School, the Fieldston School and Harvard College, Gordon received his Ph.D. in economics from Balliol College, Oxford, in 1936. His dissertation was published in 1938 as *The Public Corporation in Great Britain*. Taking a leave from his teaching duties at Harvard University in 1941, Gordon served as an economist with the War Production Board from 1942 to 1945. Subsequently, he was a delegate to the United Nations Atomic Energy Commission, worked on the Marshall Plan and served as a State Department consultant. In 1950 he left Harvard to work full-time with the

North Atlantic Treaty Organization. Between 1952 and 1955 he handled economic affairs in the London embassy. In 1959 the Ford Foundation sent Gordon to Argentina, Brazil and Chile on a short exploratory mission.

Soon after his November 1960 election victory, President-elect Kennedy invited Gordon to join a Latin American task force. Although not a Latin American specialist, Gordon had considerable diplomatic experience and possessed the type of flexible expertise that the Kennedys admired. The task force set the guidelines for Kennedy's Alliance for Progress, a program which promised U.S. support for economic development and political and social reform in Latin America. Gordon, however, differed with the political emphasis of task force chairman Adolf A. Berle, Jr. [q.v.]. Berle wanted the U.S. to form a "democratic international" to help organize and aid Latin American political parties committed to revolutionizing their own societies on democratic, anti-Communist lines. Gordon emphasized economic development as a prerequisite to social change and believed that the promise of U.S. economic aid would induce incumbent governments to initiate agrarian reform, income redistribution, education projects, etc. To a considerable degree the Gordon emphasis, considered more practical, became characteristic of the Alliance and Kennedy's Latin American policy. Gordon's concern that economic aid be used for development marked a break with the Eisenhower policy, which had favored military and short-term emergency aid.

In May and June 1961 Gordon, as chief U.S. economic adviser, worked with Latin American representatives in planning the August meeting of the Inter-American Economic and Social Council. Gordon then attended the conference at Punta del Este, Uruguay, where all the Latin American nations, with the exception of Cuba, agreed to join the U.S.-sponsored Alliance for Progress. Upon his return to Washington Gordon was appointed ambassador to Brazil to replace Ambassador John M. Cabot [q.v.], who had been severely criticized by Brazil's new president, Janio Quadros.

As Latin America's largest country and a potential international power, Brazil was one of the most sensitive embassy posts in the hemisphere. Quadros, a brilliant politician but an erratic statesman, wanted to chart an independent foreign policy and alienated many Kennedy advisers by his aggressive rhetoric. He hesitated to join the U.S. in taking action against Fidel Castro's Cuba, and his nationalist instincts rejected the Alliance's implication that Brazil was an underdeveloped nation. When Gordon arrived in Brazil in October, Quadros had already been out of office more than a month, having served only eight months of a five-year term. In his resignation note he attacked the meddling of foreign powers in Brazil's internal affairs.

Quadros was succeeded by Vice President Joao Goulart, whom some U.S. policymakers suspected of Communist sympathies. Conservative elements in the Brazilian congress and military, failing in their efforts to prevent him from taking power, temporarily succeeded in limiting Goulart's authority. The nationalist left meanwhile pressured him to maintain Brazil's high rate of inflation and initiate radical social programs. Gordon urged, with little success, that Goulart control inflation on the grounds that price stability was essential to orderly economic development under the guidelines set up by the Alliance for Progress.

Nationalization of U.S.-owned industries became a diplomatic issue in 1962. The unwillingness of Leonel Brizola, the leftist governor of the state of Rio Grande do Sul and Goulart's brother-in-law, to satisfactorily compensate an expropriated International Telephone & Telegraph Co. (IT&T) subsidiary exacerbated U.S.-Brazilian relations early in the year. At the urging of IT&T President Harold Geneen [q.v.] and Sen. Bourke Hickenlooper (R, Iowa) [q.v.], the U.S. Congress passed an amendment to the Foreign Assistance Act of 1962 that required the President to suspend all economic assistance to nations which expropriated the property of a U.S. company. Gordon, who was not opposed to nationalization if reasonable compensation were offered, convinced Goulart to reach an agreement with IT&T. The accord salvaged economic aid for Goulart's government but hurt him politically, drawing sharp attacks from both the nationalist left and right.

In 1963 Gordon and Kennedy made a last effort to save Goulart from his economic and political difficulties. David Bell [q.v.], the administrator of the Agency for International Development, and Santiago Dantas, the Brazilian finance minister, agreed to an aid package dependent upon Goulart's taking austerity measures to control inflation. The measures were unpopular with all sectors of the Brazilian political spectrum, and Goulart, in search of support, threw in his lot with the left and the labor unions. U.S. economic aid subsequently came to a complete halt.

Gordon, fearing that Communists had infiltrated the Goulart government, gave his support to military and middle class groups planning the overthrow of Goulart. A military coup forced Goulart out of office on March 31, 1964. The Ambassador, who had criticized Goulart's disregard for constitutional procedures, was shocked by the repressive excesses of the new military regime and considered resigning his post. However, he reached an understanding with Humberto Castelo Branco, the new president, and helped arrange a massive increase in Brazil's foreign aid allotment.

Gordon stayed on as ambassador until 1966, when he returned to Washington to direct Latin American policy as assistant secretary of state for inter-American affairs. He became president of Johns Hopkins University in 1967 and four years later returned to teaching and research, first at Johns Hopkins and subsequently at the Woodrow Wilson International Center at Princeton University.

[JCH]

For further information:
Jerome Levinson and Juan de Onis, *The Alliance That Lost Its Way: A Critical Report on the Alliance for Progress* (Chicago, 1970).

GORE, ALBERT A(RNOLD)
b. Dec. 26, 1907; Granville, Tenn.
Democratic Senator, Tenn., 1953-71.

A country school teacher who studied law at the Nashville YMCA's night law school, Albert Gore was elected to Congress as a New Deal supporter from Secretary of State Cordell Hull's old district in 1938. The liberal Gore combined populist oratory with diligent study of economic issues. Elected to the Senate in 1952 against the aged Sen. Kenneth McKellar (D, Tenn.), representative of the state's once powerful Crump machine, Gore matched the outspoken liberalism of his fellow Tennessean, Democratic Sen. Estes Kefauver [q.v.]. Gore and Kefauver were two of the three senators from the states of the old Confederacy who refused in 1956 to sign the Southern manifesto protesting the Supreme Court's decision banning school segregation. [See TRUMAN, EISENHOWER Volumes]

Although in general sympathy with the economic and social goals of the Kennedy Administration, Gore was frequently in opposition to its moderate reform approach. In a November 1960 letter to President Kennedy, he warned against the appointment of Wall Street Republican C. Douglas Dillon [q.v.] as Secretary of the Treasury. The appointment of an "affable easy-goer" like Dillon, Gore said, would mean that "glaring tax loopholes would not be closed; that fiscal policies, monetary policies, and economic policies would not be very different" from the Eisenhower Administration. Gore later said of Dillon: "I draw my views from Hull and Jackson and Roosevelt and Truman. His views are from Mellon and Hoover and Wall Street." Gore later wrote that Kennedy had "an awesome regard or a kind of mystical respect for the financier and the big businessman."

Gore stood outside the Senate "Establishment" as well. He opposed a proposal in January 1961 that Vice President Lyndon Johnson [q.v.] continue to preside over the Senate Democratic Caucus. Gore insisted on a roll-call vote, which he lost, but Johnson did not attempt to retain the caucus post after the bitter dispute. Gore's proposal that the Senate Democratic Conference elect members of the Democratic Steering and Policy Committee rather than have them appointed by the leadership led Majority Leader Mike Mansfield (D, Mont.) [q.v.] to threaten his resignation if the proposal were adopted. Mansfield accepted a compromise that allowed the Democratic Conference to confirm or challenge his appointments.

Gore's overall voting record was not the most liberal in the Senate (the liberal Americans for Democratic Action gave him a 79% score for the Kennedy years), but his crusading zeal placed him in the liberal forefront on many issues. In March 1961 Gore helped lead the Administration forces against an amendment by Sen. Harry Byrd (D, Va.) [q.v.], chairman of the Finance Committee, to limit emergency unemployment compensation. Byrd's amendment passed the Finance Committee, 11-2, but was defeated in the Senate, 44-42.

Along with Sen. Paul Douglas (D, Ill.) [q.v.], Gore was the most determined tax reformer in the Senate. Together they waged a constant battle against a wide variety of tax deductions, most notably the oil depletion allowance, arguing that such provisions eroded the tax base and benefited only the well-to-do. They usually lost in the conservative Finance Committee and often attracted only a handful of supporters on the Senate floor.

Gore played a crucial role in the struggle over the Administration's 1962 tax reform package. He defended the proposal to withhold taxes on interest and dividend income at the source of such payments in order to curb a common form of tax evasion. The reform, not a new tax but a change in the method of collection, aroused savings and loan associations to conduct one of the most intensive lobbying campaigns in history to defeat the proposal. The Finance Committee, whose members received thousands of letters against the plan, voted 10 to 5 in July to eliminate the withholding provision from the bill.

The Finance Committee also modified a House-passed limitation of business deductions for entertainment expenses. Such deductions were disallowed by the House unless they were "directly related" to active conduct of the business; the Senate added "or associated with." Gore said the three extra words "would wreck the bill so far as correcting expense account abuses is concerned."

Gore opposed the Administration's central tax innovation, the 7% investment tax credit intended to encourage modernization of plants and equipment. He said it was merely another loophole and another example of the "trickle-down" economic theory aimed at providing advantages to corporations and the wealthy to stimulate investment and to indirectly create jobs. An unusual alliance of tax reform liberals and fiscal conservatives tried to defeat the provision in August but lost, 52-30. Gore opposed the 1962 tax bill as a whole, arguing that Kennedy's major recommendations had been "ignored or watered down." Yet, Gore complained, the Administration "lifted not a finger" on the Senate floor to restore interest and dividend withholding or tighten business deductions. The Administration sacrificed these reforms to win approval of the investment tax credit.

Gore and Douglas led losing battles against two other major tax preferences enacted in 1962. They opposed a provision to allow self-employed persons to set up tax-sheltered retirement plans, arguing that the tax benefits would accrue mostly to affluent doctors and lawyers. The bill passed the Senate in September, 75-4, with Douglas and Gore in the minority. They also fought to block tax relief for the Christiana Securities Corp., a Du Pont family holding company about to receive a large block of General Motors (GM) stock by court order. Gore and Douglas argued that special tax treatment for Christiana was inequitable and would perpetuate the Du Pont family's inordinate influence in GM, which the court was trying to diminish. Douglas's proposal to tax Christiana's GM stock at the full 25% capital gains rate rather than at the lower intercorporate dividend rate (which he estimated as 8%) lost, 72-18, in January 1962.

Gore was one of a small group of liberal senators who attempted to conduct a filibuster against an Administration-backed bill to charter a private corporation to own and operate a satellite communications system. The bill's opponents maintained that a private corporation would be dominated by the American Telephone & Telegraph Co. (AT&T) and would represent a "giveaway" of the millions of tax dollars already spent on research and development. They urged government ownership of the satellite system. In the first such action since 1927, the Senate envoked cloture and the private version passed by a vote of 66-11 in August 1962.

A member of the Foreign Relations Committee, Gore generally backed the Administration's foreign policy. However, he caused a controversy after the April 1961 Bay of Pigs fiasco when he called upon President Kennedy to replace the Joint Chiefs of Staff for their part in leading Kennedy to believe that the operation was feasible. Gore enthusiastically supported the Administration's 1963 nuclear test ban treaty; he had been the first senator to propose such a treaty in 1958.

Gore was a vocal opponent of Kennedy's 1963 $11-billion tax cut. Arguing that tax reforms should take preference over tax reductions, Gore held that a tax cut would stir a conservative movement to cut spending as well. He believed that the tax plan was conceived by Secretary Dillon to benefit corporations and wealthy individuals.

During the Johnson Administration Gore continued his fervent advocacy of tax reform, backed the Great Society's social welfare programs and became a critic of the Vietnam war. He lost his Senate seat to conservative Rep. William E. Brock III (R, Tenn.) in 1970. [See JOHNSON, NIXON Volumes]

[TO]

For further information:
Albert Gore, *Let the Glory Out: My South and its Politics* (New York, 1972).
Neal R. Peirce, *The Border South States: People, Politics, and Power in the Five States of the Border South* (New York, 1975).

GRAHAM, BILLY (WILLIAM FRANKLIN)

b. Nov. 7, 1918; Charlotte, N.C.
Evangelist.

Billy Graham was raised on a farm outside Charlotte, N.C. During a revival held in Charlotte, the 16-year-old Graham experienced what he later described as a spiritual awakening and made "his decision for Christ." After graduating from Florida Bible College and the fundamentalist Wheaton College in Illinois, Graham found his calling as an evangelist.

Graham attained national prominence in the fall of 1949 when the Hearst papers publicized his successful revival in Los Angeles. He distinguished himself from other American evangelists through his early and effective use of radio and television and by his appeal to urban audiences. At mass rallies at home and abroad he pleaded with sinners and skeptics to stand up and come forward to demonstrate their new found peace and abiding sense of salvation through Christ. By the late 1950s polls indicated that he was one of America's "most admired" men. President Harry Truman [q.v.] first invited Graham to the White House, and the pastor later played an occasional round of golf with President Dwight D. Eisenhower [q.v.].

During the 1960 presidential primaries when it became evident that anti-Catholic feeling might dash John F. Kennedy's hopes for the nomination, Theodore Sorenson [q.v.] and Pierre Salinger [q.v.], two Kennedy aides, approached Graham with a request that, as a leading Protestant, he sign a petition calling for religious toleration. According to Sorensen Graham refused, arguing that his signature would only inflame the issue. Sorensen bitterly noted that later during the campaign Graham made negative comments on the Catholic Church. Five days before the 1960 election, Graham appeared at a rally for Vice President Richard M. Nixon [q.v.].

Despite his support for Nixon Graham's relations with the Kennedy Administration were generally cordial. The President invited him to preside at prayer breakfasts at the White House. An outspoken foe of Communism, Graham supported the Kennedy Administration's blockade of Cuba during the October 1962 missile crisis.

As a Southern Baptist with millions of followers around the country, Graham's views on the race question were closely watched. In the early 1950s Graham ordered that his rallies be desegregated and blacks be hired for his staff. In May 1961 he denounced the beatings of freedom riders in the South but advised civil rights leader Martin Luther King [q.v.] "to put the brakes on a little bit." Graham argued that integration would ultimately be achieved not through sit-ins and civil disobedience but through Christian fellowship. Graham was a regular visitor to the White House during the Administrations of both Lyndon Johnson [q.v.] and Richard Nixon. [See JOHNSON, NIXON Volumes]

[JLW]

GRAHAM, PHILIP L(ESLIE)

b. July 18, 1915; Terry, S.D.
d. Aug. 3, 1963; Washington, D.C.
Publisher, Washington Post, 1946-63; Chairman of the Board, Newsweek, 1961-63.

Philip Graham was the son of a South Dakota mining engineer. During the 1920s his family moved to Florida. Graham graduated from the University of Florida in 1936. After taking a degree at Harvard Law School, he served as a clerk to Supreme Court Justices Stanley Reed and Felix Frankfurter [q.v.].

In 1940 Graham married Katharine Meyer, the daughter of Eugene Meyer, owner of the struggling Washington Post. After serving in the U.S. Army during World War II, Graham became associate publisher of the Post and then publisher in 1946 at the age of 31. The Post merged with its principal competition, the Times-Herald, in 1954, and during the 1950s and 1960s the paper's circulation grew to over 400,000. Graham controlled the business end of the Post operation as well as its editorial policy. Although liberal in its editorial policy, the *Post* did not endorse a presidential candidate in 1960.

Graham was an influential figure in Washington political and social circles. Through his close personal friendships with Sen. Lyndon Johnson (D, Texas) [*q.v.*] —with whom he had worked on the 1957 Civil Rights Act—Sen. John Kennedy and Adlai Stevenson [*q.v.*], Graham had access to each of the major presidential contenders during the 1960 Democratic National Convention and acted as chief liaison in the formation of the Kennedy-Johnson Democratic ticket at the convention.

In the interregnum between Kennedy's election and inauguration, Graham successfully urged the President-elect to appoint Republican C. Douglas Dillion [*q.v.*] as Secretary of the Treasury despite the fear of many Kennedy advisers that Dillon would resign in a few months and then express public dissatisfaction with the new Administration. Graham unsuccessfully boosted diplomat David Bruce [*q.v.*] for Secretary of State after the choice narrowed down to Sen. J. William Fulbright (D, Ark.) [*q.v.*], Dean Rusk [*q.v.*] and Bruce. In 1962 Graham attempted to persuade Kennedy to shift Rusk to the U.N., name Adlai Stevenson as ambassador to Great Britain and appoint Bruce as Rusk's replacement at State.

In March 1961 the Washington Post Company acquired a 59% interest in *Newsweek* magazine for $9 million. The following year the Post Company purchased *Art News*, a widely-read monthly art magazine, and *Portfolio*, an art quarterly. In addition, the Washington Post Company controlled television stations WTOP in Washington and WJXT in Jacksonville, Fla., as well as a news service owned jointly with the *Los Angeles Times*.

In October 1962 President Kennedy appointed Graham and 13 other prominent citizens to organize the private corporation that was to own and operate the U.S. part of a global satellite communications system (Comsat). Graham also attempted to mediate the 114-day New York newspaper strike in early 1963, but the New York City newspaper publishers objected to his participation.

Described by Arthur Schlesinger, Jr. [*q.v.*], as a man of extraordinary vitality, audacity and charm, Graham was subject to frequent debilitating fits of depression, which finally resulted in his hospitalization. On Aug. 3, 1963 Graham, on leave from the hospital, committed suicide.

[FHM]

GREEN, EDITH S(TARRETT)
b. Jan. 17, 1910; Trent, S.D.
Democratic Representative, Ore., 1954-74.

Edith Green, a liberal representative from the Oregon district that included most of Portland and some of its suburbs, had been an English teacher and radio commentator before her election to Congress in 1954. As ranking member of the House Education and Labor Committee, Green chaired the Subcommittee on Special Education, earning the title of "Mrs. Education" in the 1950s. [See EISENHOWER Volume]

Green supported nearly all of the Kennedy Administration's proposed legislation and sponsored important college aid bills. In 1962 she sponsored a proposal to authorize $900 million in federal grants and $600 million in loans for college construction. Although both chambers passed versions of the measure, a House-Senate conference committee was unable to arrange a compromise on the bill. The following year she successfully sponsored a similar proposal, authorizing the first extensive federal expenditures for higher education since the National Defense Education Act of 1958. In 1961 Green was one of six representatives to vote against appropriations for the House Un-American Activities Committee.

Green remained a powerful influence on the shaping of education legislation, but she grew increasingly conservative on domestic issues; her Americans for Democratic Action rating fell to 38% in 1971. In the late 1960s she became an opponent of the

Johnson Administration's Vietnam policies. [See JOHNSON, NIXON Volumes]

[MDB]

For further information:
Hope Chamberlin, *A Minority of Members: Women in the U.S. Congress* (New York, 1973).

GREEN, WILLIAM J., JR.
b. March 5, 1910; Philadelphia, Pa.
d. Dec. 21, 1963, Philadelphia, Pa.
Democratic Representative, Pa., 1945-47; 1949-63.

The son of a saloon-keeper, William J. Green, Jr. was first elected to Congress from Philadelphia's fifth district in 1944. Defeated in 1946, he was reelected in 1948 and in each succeeding election. He exerted his greatest influence, however, not in Washington but in Philadelphia where he was one of the most powerful bosses ever to head Philadelphia's Democrats. He joined with Richardson Dilworth [q.v.] and Joseph S. Clark [q.v.] in 1951 to overthrow 68 years of Republican rule in the city. Elected Democratic city chairman in 1956, Green was described by the *New York Times* as "a gruff, iron-fisted party disciplinarian" who "shaped a coalition of ward politicians and social blue-bloods into one of the nation's most powerful Democratic machines."

Green was an important supporter of John F. Kennedy for the Democratic nomination in 1960. The high point of his tenure as party leader came when Philadelphia gave Kennedy a 331,000-vote edge over Richard M. Nixon [q.v.] in November, a margin that enabled Kennedy to carry Pennsylvania by 116,000 votes and capture its 29 electoral votes. In 1963 Green induced President Kennedy to campaign in Philadelphia for Mayor James Tate. Their efforts were credited with producing Tate's victorious margin of 68,000 votes in the face of a strong Republican challenge. In Congress Green sat on the House Ways and Means Committee and was a reliable supporter of Kennedy's legislative program. He died of a pancreas and gall bladder ailment on Dec. 21, 1963.

[TO]

GREENBERG, JACK
b. Dec. 22, 1924; New York, N.Y.
Director-Counsel, NAACP Legal Defense and Educational Fund, October 1961- .

A graduate of Columbia College and Columbia Law School, Greenberg joined the Legal Defense and Educational Fund of the NAACP in 1949. Greenberg worked on Fund cases that integrated Southern law schools and graduate schools in the early 1950s. He handled a case challenging racial segregation in Delaware public schools that was decided by the Supreme Court in 1954 as part of its landmark ruling in *Brown v. Board of Education*. Greenberg later argued more school desegregation cases and worked on *Cooper v. Aaron*, the 1958 Supreme Court case ordering school desegregation in Little Rock, Ark. In 1960 he assisted in writing the brief for *Boynton v. Virginia* in which the Supreme Court held segregation at interstate bus terminals illegal. The decision spurred the organization of the 1961 Freedom Rides. During the 1950s Greenberg served as chief assistant to Thurgood Marshall [q.v.], then director-counsel of the Fund. When Marshall was appointed to a federal circuit court judgeship in October 1961, Greenberg was named the Fund's new director.

From 1961 through 1963 Greenberg oversaw court suits leading to James Meredith's [q.v.] admission to the University of Mississippi in September 1962 and to the desegregation of the Universities of Georgia and Alabama and Clemson College in South Carolina. The Fund also represented thousands of nonviolent civil rights demonstrators arrested in the South in the early 1960s. Greenberg argued *Garner v. Louisiana*, the first case involving sit-in demonstrators to reach the Supreme Court, and in December 1961 the Court unanimously overturned the conviction of 16 blacks arrested in Louisiana sit-ins. Over the next five years the Fund took 45 similar cases to the Supreme Court, winning virtually all of them. In 1963 the Fund also successfully challenged segregation in hospitals receiving federal funds and Southern city ordinances requiring segregation in public accommodations.

A strong proponent of the view that litigation can achieve social change, Greenberg inaugurated in 1965 a Fund campaign to win greater rights for prisoners and to outlaw the death penalty. In 1967 he founded the National Office for the Rights of the Indigent to assert the rights of the poor in court. [See JOHNSON, NIXON Volumes]

[CAB]

GROSS, H(AROLD) R(OYCE)
b. June 30, 1899; Arispe, Iowa
Republican Representative, Iowa,
1949- .

H.R. Gross was raised on a farm in southern Iowa. After service overseas in World War I, he worked on various newspapers from 1921 to 1935. He was a radio news commentator for the next 13 years, billed as "the man with the fastest tongue on radio." Elected to Congress in 1948 from Iowa's agricultural third district, Gross established himself as an isolationist, a backer of high agricultural price supports, and a determined opponent of what he considered administration extravagance. Gross waged his campaign for government frugality through Democratic and Republican administrations alike and often excoriated his congressional colleagues for overspending, unnecessary travel "junkets," and unwarranted recesses.

Gross greeted the Kennedy Administration by criticizing the Defense Department for having provided a military driver for the actors Frank Sinatra [q.v.] and Peter Lawford at the inauguration. In March 1961 he opposed restoring former President Eisenhower [q.v.] to the rank of a five-star general unless Congress stipulated that Eisenhower would receive only his $25,000 presidential pension and not also receive his $20,543 Army salary. Gross was a consistent opponent of the New Frontier program. *Congressional Quarterly* reported that Gross's anti-Administration votes placed him among the top five House opponents of Administration programs. In July 1962 he called upon Kennedy to fire Navy Secretary Fred Korth [q.v.] on the grounds that North had shown favoritism in

awarding the TFX fighter plane contract to General Dynamics, which would build the plane in Korth's native Fort Worth. A member of the Post Office and Civil Service Committee, Gross voted against salary increases for postal workers and postage rate raises in October 1962.

Gross was also a foe of the Administration's foreign policy. From January to September 1962, he waged an unsuccessful campaign to reduce the U.S. subscription to the United Nations bond issue from $100 million to $64 million and to bar any U.S. loans until all U.N. members had paid their share of the world organization's expenses. In April the House rejected his amendment to limit U.S. contributions to the U.N.'s Congo operations. He also opposed the creation of the Peace Corps, which he characterized as "a haven for draft dodgers." In November 1963 he opposed a $20 million authorization for the Arms Control and Disarmament Agency declaring, "I am not ready to disarm the United States . . . so that we become the prey and slaves of any other power in the world." From his seat on the House Foreign Affairs Committee, which he assumed in 1963, Gross continued during the Johnson Administration his persistent battle against foreign aid as part of his general war for economy in government. [See JOHNSON Volume]

[TO]

GRUENING, ERNEST H(ENRY)
b. Feb. 6, 1887; New York, N.Y.
d. June 26, 1974; Washington, D.C.
Democratic Senator, Alaska, 1959-69.

Although he graduated from Harvard Medical School in 1912, Gruening became a journalist. During the 1920s and 1930s he edited several liberal journals, including *The Nation* and the *New York Herald Tribune*. He was a strong advocate of racial equality and birth control and an opponent of American military intervention in Latin America. In 1928 he published a sympathetic and widely read account of the Mexican Revolution, *Mexico and its Heritage*.

Gruening was in charge of public relations for Robert LaFollette's 1924 presidential campaign and supported Herbert Hoover in 1928, but the New Deal years cemented his loyalty to the Democratic Party. Roosevelt sent Gruening to the 1933 Inter-American Conference and then appointed him director of territories and island possessions. He helped administer New Deal recovery programs in Puerto Rico during the mid-1930s.

As governor of Alaska from 1939 to 1952, Gruening pressed for construction of the Alcan Highway, anti-discrimination legislation aimed at protecting Alaska's Indians and a tax system intended to weaken the influence of absentee businessmen. In 1950 he testified before the Senate Interior and Insular Affairs Committee on behalf of statehood and campaigned actively for that cause. [See TRUMAN, EISENHOWER Volumes]

As Alaska's first U.S. senator, elected following the granting of statehood in 1959, he represented the state's interests as a developing area with high transportation costs. He increased his state's share of federal funds to construct housing and junior college facilities and won appropriations for the replacement of a ship funded by the Bureau of Indian Affairs that served Alaskan ports not served by commercial lines. With less success he sought federal incentives for gold mining.

Gruening and other Senate liberals, including Sens. Estes Kefauver (D, Tenn.) [q.v.], Wayne Morse (D, Ore.) [q.v.] and Maurine Neuberger (D, Ore.) [q.v.], opposed the Administration-backed communications satellite bill in July 1962 because the proposed satellite system would be largely privately owned and controlled. The group staged a liberal filibuster and provoked the Senate's first successful vote of cloture in 35 years. The Senate also rejected a Gruening amendment to the National Aeronautics and Space Administration bill that would have required the American Telephone and Telegraph Company to reimburse the government for research and development costs of the satellite system.

Gruening worked for greater congressional supervision of foreign aid and increased restrictions on executive policy-making during the early 1960s. In August 1961 the Senate accepted his amendment to limit Development Loan Fund interest rates on refinancing loans to 5% above the rate charged for the original U.S. loan to the recipient country. Declaring that restrictions on expenditures abroad should be subject to the same stipulations in effect domestically, he offered a proposal in June 1962 that would have banned federal appropriations to repair or maintain foreign highways built with federal funds. The Senate rejected his proposal by a vote of 39-42.

Gruening and Morse led the attack on Kennedy's foreign aid bill in 1963. Stating that "Congress. . .has a definite responsibility to decide how the foreign aid funds are to be spent," he advocated congressional review of an individual country's needs and of appropriations for specific projects above $1 million. With support from Sens. Kenneth Keating (R, N.Y.) [q.v.] and Jacob Javits (R, N.Y.) [q.v.], he successfully sponsored an amendment in November 1963 barring aid in any form to countries engaging in or preparing for military aggression. (This amendment was aimed at the United Arab Republic.) Gruening also worked with Sen. Joseph Clark (D, Pa.) [q.v.] for government support of birth control programs, and he co-sponsored a bill in August 1963 increasing federal research programs on contraception.

Gruening achieved national recognition in August 1964 when he and Morse cast the only dissenting votes against the Gulf of Tonkin Resolution. In subsequent years he was an opponent of American military involvement in Vietnam. Gruening remained in the Senate until 1968 when, at 81, he lost the Alaska Democratic primary to Mike Gravel. [See JOHNSON Volume]

[MDB]

For further information:
Ernest Gruening, *Many Battles* (New York, 1973).

HAGGERTY, CORNELIUS J(OSEPH)
b. Jan. 10, 1894, Boston, Mass.
d. Oct. 10, 1971, Palm Springs, Calif.
President, AFL-CIO Building and Construction Trades Department, 1960-70.

Cornelius Haggerty, the son of Irish immigrants, grew up in Boston. After a brief attempt at a singing career, he became a lather's apprentice in 1913 and, two years later, a journeyman. He was soon elected president of his local of the International Union of Wood, Wire and Metal Lathers. Haggerty served in the Navy during World War I and then moved to California. In 1933 he was elected secretary of the Los Angeles Building and Construction Trades Council and from 1937 to 1943 served as president of the California State Federation of Labor. During World War II he was a member of several state and regional labor boards. Usually a supporter of the Democratic Party, Haggerty was named a regent of the University of California by Republican Gov. Earl Warren [q.v.]. In 1960 he became president of the AFL-CIO Building and Construction Trades Department.

Within the AFL-CIO leadership Haggerty was a close ally of President George Meany [q.v.] and served as a spokesman for the more conservative craft unions in the federation. He clashed frequently with United Auto Workers (UAW) President Walter Reuther [q.v.], who headed the AFL-CIO Industrial Union Department. At the November 1961 Building and Construction Trades Department convention, Haggerty charged that Reuther was trying to "kidnap" the craft unions' jurisdiction. He called for a settlement of jurisdictional disputes based on a voluntary agreement between the conflicting unions. A plan was approved at the AFL-CIO convention the following month to settle disputes through internal mediation and arbitration, with final power resting with the AFL-CIO executive council. However, the issue was not fully resolved and later contributed to Reuther's decision to withdraw the UAW from the federation.

After local strikes at missile construction sites had alarmed the Kennedy Administration, Haggerty succeeded in bringing the authority to strike these sites under his close supervision. In May 1961 an agreement was reached with the missile industry and contractors for a no-strike, no-lockout plan. A Missile Sites Labor Commission, chaired by Secretary of Labor Arthur Goldberg [q.v.], was appointed by President Kennedy to handle future labor disputes in the field.

During the early 1960s civil rights groups charged the construction trades with racial discrimination. Responding to this pressure the Labor Department's Bureau of Apprenticeship and Training issued new rules to bar racial discrimination in federally sponsored apprenticeship programs. Both labor and management groups objected to the Labor Department's plan, which included intensified efforts to encourage minority group applicants for apprenticeship programs. In August 1963 an agreement on a compromise plan was reached under which labor and management pledged that an applicant's qualifications would be the "sole standard" in choosing apprenticeship candidates and that openings would be publicly listed. Haggerty was appointed to a panel established to supervise the plan's implementation. However, he warned several months later that false hopes for increased apprenticeship openings had been raised because government projections of the industry's manpower needs had been set "unrealistically high."

Haggerty retired from union affairs in 1970 and died of cancer the following year.

[MDB]

HALABY, NAJEEB E(LIAS)
b. Nov. 19, 1915; Dallas, Tex.
Administrator, Federal Aviation Agency, March 1961-June 1965.

Najeeb Halaby, the son of a Syrian immigrant, grew up in Dallas, Tex. He graduated from Stanford University in 1937 and Yale Law School in 1940. After service as a test pilot during World War II, Halaby served in advisory capacities with the Departments of State and Defense until 1953, when he joined the Rockefeller Brothers, Inc., a philanthropic organization. While pursuing a business career Halaby maintained his interest in aviation and in 1955 and 1956 was vice chairman of a White House study group that prepared a plan for modernizing U.S. airway facilities. The study group also recommended creation of a federal agency to oversee air safety. As a result, the Federal Aviation Agency (FAA) was formed in 1958.

With a budget of $700 million in 1961, the FAA had responsibility for administering regulations affecting air safety, navigation and traffic, and for conducting research in airport and traffic control. The FAA administrator also had the power to invoke fines of up to $1,000 a day for continuing violations of safety regulations and to temporarily suspend an airline's license pending hearings. Under the 1958 act creating the FAA, the Civil Aeronautics Board (CAB) retained control over regulations governing airline routes and fares.

Sworn in as FAA administrator in March 1961, Halaby immediately decentralized the Agency, transferring more authority to its regional offices. He continued the policy of requiring mandatory retirement of pilots at age 60.

After an Eastern Airlines plane was hijacked and flown to Cuba on July 24, 1961, Halaby recommended amendments to the Federal Aviation Act that would make it a crime equivalent to piracy to commandeer an airplane and a federal crime to attack, intimidate or interfere with aircraft crew members. The rash of airplane hijackings in the late 1960s and early 1970s prompted the Nixon Administration to begin placing U.S. marshals on selected international and domestic commercial flights and resulted in a law making criminal penalties mandatory for persons committing air piracy.

In November 1961 President Kennedy ordered Halaby to implement a $500 million air safety program, which required that an airplane weighing over 6.5 tons be equipped with a special radio "beacon" to transmit its altitude to traffic control centers in response to impulses sent from ground radar. The program also included various other safety measures for aircraft.

The FAA recommended to Congress in September 1964 a $1.5 billion expenditure to build 727 new landing facilities with major emphasis on heliports and local airports. Halaby stated that the movement of industries to suburban areas had increased the need for "neighborhood-type" airports.

Halaby resigned as administrator of the FAA in June 1965 and was replaced by William F. McKee. In 1968 he was named president of Pan American World Airways. [See JOHNSON Volume]

[FHM]

HALBERSTAM, DAVID
b. April 10, 1934; New York, N.Y.
Foreign Correspondent, *New York Times,* 1961-66.

The son of an Army surgeon, David Halberstam spent his childhood on various military posts but went to high school in Yonkers, N.Y. He attended Harvard, served as managing editor of the *Crimson* and graduated in 1955. Believing that civil rights would be the major issue of the late 1950s, Halberstam joined the staff of the West Point, Miss., *Daily Times Leader.* Shortly thereafter he began four years as a reporter with the Nashville *Tennessean.*

In the fall of 1960 he joined the *New York Times.* After six months in Washington and a year in the Congo, the 28-year-old Halberstam succeeded veteran *Times* foreign correspondent Homer Bigart in Vietnam. Halberstam arrived in Saigon in September 1962 at a particularly difficult time for journalists covering the war. Although American troop strength had increased to 16,000 and economic aid had risen to over $500 million, the war was not going well for the South Vietnamese government. American correspondents who accurately reported this state of affairs were coming under increasing suspicion by the regime of Ngo Dinh Diem. *Newsweek* reporter Francois Sully, for example, had just been expelled from the country for writing an unflattering article about the powerful Madame Ngo Dinh Nhu, Diem's sister-in-law.

With colleagues Malcolm Browne of the Associated Press and Neil Sheehan of United Press International, Halberstam began to investigate and report the deteriorating military situation in strategic areas such as the Mekong Delta. This small corps of American reporters also reported that Diem's regime was aloof, autocratic and indifferent to the needs of most of the population. They gave opposition groups in the large Buddhist community better press coverage than either Diem or American mission officials would have liked.

The incident which finally drew national attention to what columnist Joseph Alsop [q.v.] derisively called a group of "young crusaders" was the first major battle of the Vietnam war at Ap Bac in January 1963, during which a South Vietnamese division was routed by a small force of insurgents. Halberstam reported the battle in detail, including the deaths of three American military advisers killed while trying to induce reluctant Vietnamese soldiers to fight. Halberstam, Browne and Sheehan wrote stories quoting one of the U.S. advisers, Lt. Col. John Vann, on the enemy's combat skill and the cowardice of the South Vietnamese troops.

After writing the Ap Bac story Halberstam was subject to personal attacks. During the summer of 1963 the Pentagon began to monitor Halberstam's sources and record his whereabouts, contacts and telephone conversations. Meanwhile, White House Press Secretary Pierre Salinger [q.v.] declared that press reports from Vietnam were "emotional and inaccurate." When in late October 1963 New York Times publisher Arthur Ochs Sulzberger [q.v.] paid a courtesy call on John F. Kennedy, the President asked Sulzberger to reassign Halberstam because he was, in the Chief Executive's words, "too close to the story, too involved." Sulzberger refused to shift Halberstam, although the reporter left Vietnam in early 1964 to spend a year at the Times's New York bureau.

For his reporting in Vietnam Halberstam shared a 1964 Pultizer Prize with Browne. In 1965 he published The Making of a Quagmire, a personal account of his fifteen months in Vietnam. The book was an im-

mediate success. As Bert Cochran later wrote in The Nation, ". . .it had an electrifying effect on a new generation of dissenters. It opened the eyes of a wider public to the sordid activities concealed by official [bombast]." Although critical of U.S. failures in Vietnam, Halberstam defended the essential thrust of American policy: "A strategic country in a key area, it [Vietnam] is perhaps one of only five or six nations in the world that is truly vital to U.S. interests."

Halberstam was assigned in January 1965 to the Warsaw bureau of the Times. Expelled in December because of reports distressing to the Polish government, he returned to the New York bureau of his newspaper but soon resigned to become a contributing editor of Harper's magazine. After writing profiles of McGeorge Bundy [q.v.] and Robert McNamara [q.v.] for Harper's, Halberstam wrote The Best and the Brightest, a best-selling indictment of American Vietnam policy published in 1972.

[FHM]

For further information:
David Halberstam, The Making of a Quagmire (New York, 1965).
———, The Best and the Brightest (New York, 1972).

HALL, GUS
b. Oct. 8, 1910; Iron, Minn.
General Secretary, Communist Party, U.S.A., 1959- .

Hall was born Avro Kusta Halberg in a small town in Minnesota's Mesabi iron range. His parents were Finnish immigrants and charter members of the American Communist Party. Hall himself joined the party at 17. 1936 he became an organizer for the Steel Workers Organizing Committee and the following year was a leader of the Little Steel strike in Warren, Ohio. Soon afterward he resigned his union post to become a full-time Communist organizer. After serving in the Navy during World War II, Hall became general secretary of the Ohio Communist Party in 1947. The next year he was indicted with 11 other Communist leaders under the 1940 Smith Act for conspiring to teach and advocate the violent overthrow of the government. He was convicted in October 1949. While out on bail, Hall became acting national secretary of the Party when National Secretary Eugene Dennis was jailed. Hall's own conviction was upheld by the Supreme Court in July 1951, and Hall fled the country. Captured in Mexico, he was imprisoned from October 1951 to March 1957 in a federal penitentiary. While Hall was in prison, the Communist Party suffered a sharp decline, both from intense government harassment and from internal factionalism and disillusionment following Khrushchev's 1956 denunciation of Stalin and that year's Soviet invasion of Hungary. At a December 1959 Communist Party convention in New York, Hall, whose imprisonment had kept him out of the factional dispute, was elected to replace Dennis as general secretary, the leading party post.

Throughout the Kennedy Administration, the Communist Party remained under legal attack. In June 1961 the Supreme Court ruled in a 5-4 decision that under the 1950 Internal Security Act (McCarran Act), the Communist Party had to file registration documents, including a complete list of its members. In a re-interpretation of the 1940 Smith Act, the Court also ruled that simply being an active member of the Communist Party could be a federal crime. Following the Court decisions, Hall announced that the Party would not register as required nor would it submit membership lists. That December the Communist Party was indicted for failing to register, and in March 1962 Hall and Party National Secretary Benjamin J. Davis were individually indicted on similar charges. (In December 1963 a federal appeals court overturned the conviction of the Communist Party for failing to register, and in November 1965 the Supreme Court unanimously ruled that the provisions of the McCarran Act requiring individual members of the Communist Party to register with the federal government violated the Fifth Amendment protection against self-incrimination.)

Although Hall traveled widely in the early 1960s, speaking at meetings and on several college campuses, the Communist Party took largely cautious and defensive public stands.

Some party members, led by Milton Rosen and Mort Scheer, argued that the party should be more aggressive, openly advocating Communism and recruiting members on that basis. These individuals were sympathetic to China in the developing Sino-Soviet dispute, while Hall and the majority of the party were pro-Soviet. Beginning in late 1961 the dissident members were expelled, and in July 1962 they formed the Progressive Labor Movement.

In the late 1960s, with legal obstacles largely removed and many Americans caught up in protest movements, the Communist Party began to increase its size and reduce its political isolation. Hall continued as Party head and in 1972 was the Communist Party candidate for President. [See JOHNSON, NIXON Volumes]

[JBF]

HALL, PAUL
b. Aug. 21, 1914; Ingelnook, Ala.
President, Seafarers International Union, 1957- .

Hall went to sea as an engine wiper in the early 1930s. In November 1938 he was among the founding members of the Seafarers International Union (SIU), established as an AFL rival to the left-wing, CIO-affiliated National Maritime Union (NMU). During World War II Hall served as an oiler in the merchant marine and following the war became a SIU official. He became chief officer of the union's Atlantic, Gulf, Great Lakes and Inland Waters District, one of two component units of the SIU, in 1948. Following the federation's 1953 expulsion of the International Longshoremen's Association (ILA) on corruption charges, Hall was chief organizer of the AFL's unsuccessful effort to establish a new longshoremen's union. After the death of SIU President Harry Lundeberg in January 1957, Hall became president of both the SIU and the AFL-CIO Maritime Trades Department.

In January 1961 Hall led a two-week strike of members of the SIU and two other unions against New York City tugboats and ferries. The strike was ended when Secretary of Labor Arthur Goldberg [*q.v.*] negotiated a truce between the unions and the companies involved.

In the late 1950s and early 1960s, the various U.S. maritime unions, including the SIU, were faced with the problem of "runaway shipping," the registration of U.S. ships under foreign flags to avoid higher U.S. taxes and labor costs. To meet this problem Hall and NMU President Joseph E. Curran [*q.v.*], his longtime rival in a series of jurisdictional disputes, agreed to a truce in January 1959. Later that year they jointly founded the International Maritime Workers Union in a drive to organize sailors on U.S.-owned, foreign-flag ships. However, the truce soon collapsed, and the new union was formally dissolved in May 1961.

On June 15, 1961 the SIU, the NMU, the National Marine Engineers' Beneficial Association (MEBA) and two other maritime unions began a major strike, idling about one-quarter of the U.S. merchant fleet. The unions sought higher wages, increased benefits and the right to organize and bargain for seagoing personnel on foreign-flag ships owned by U.S. companies. Citing the disruption of shipping to Hawaii and delays in military shipping, President Kennedy invoked the Taft-Hartley Act on June 26 and appointed a three-man inquiry board.

The inquiry board attempted to mediate the dispute, and by July 2 all of the unions except the MEBA, which was closely allied with the SIU, had reached agreements with a majority of the shipowners. However, with the MEBA still on strike, no resumption of shipping was possible. On July 3, at the request of the government, an injunction was issued ordering a halt to the strike, and by July 5 most shipping had resumed.

The continuing rivalry between the SIU and the NMU and the fragmentation of the maritime labor force along craft, geographic and dual union lines resulted in a complex pattern of shifting alliances among U.S. maritime unions and between those unions and a variety of international labor organizations. Hall also was involved in jurisdictional conflicts with the Teamsters and the Canadian Maritime Union. In 1960 the Canadian Labor Congress expelled the SIU of Canada for raiding and for establishing a rival maritime union in Canada. The conflict between the unions was intense and at times violent. In November 1963 the Canadian government established a trusteeship over all five Canadian maritime unions and removed SIU of Canada President Harold C. Banks. Hall opposed the trusteeship and Banks's ouster but later came to an agreement with the trustees leading to the eventual restoration of SIU control over its Canadian affiliate. In January 1962 Hall issued an SIU charter to a Chicago taxi drivers local formerly affiliated with the International Brotherhood of Teamsters, and a raiding war between those two unions followed.

A longtime anti-Communist, Hall cooperated in 1962 with an ILA boycott of foreign ships that traded with Cuba. The next year he became a member of the anti-Castro Citizens Committee for a Free Cuba. Hall continued to head the SIU during the Johnson and Nixon Administrations and was a strong supporter of President Nixon. [See NIXON Volume]

[JBF]

HALLECK, CHARLES A(BRAHAM)
b. Aug. 22, 1900; Demotte, Ind.
Republican Representative, Ind., 1935-69; House Minority Leader, 1959-65.

After graduating first in his class from Indiana University Law School, Charles A. Halleck entered Republican state politics in 1924. He won a special election to fill a House vacancy in 1935 and served successively until his retirement in 1969. Although generally conservative and a wholehearted isolationist, Halleck first gained national attention by nominating fellow Hoosier Wendell L. Willkie, candidate of the GOP's Eastern internationalist wing, for president at the 1940 Republican National Convention.

Halleck loyally campaigned for his Party colleagues, rose steadily on House seniority lists and became House majority leader following the election of Joseph W. Martin, Jr. (R, Mass.) as Speaker in January 1947. In the wake of the GOP's disastrous showing in the 1958 congressional elections, Halleck narrowly defeated Martin for the minority leadership in a January 1959 secret ballot. [See TRUMAN, EISENHOWER Volumes]

Halleck's deposition of Martin marked the end of a cooperative relationship between the GOP leadership and House Speaker Sam Rayburn (D, Tex.) [q.v.]. To gain his victory, Halleck pledged to younger members a share in Party policymaking decisions, while he promised to all Republicans a more partisan opposition to the Democrats. A liberal Democratic colleague remarked that Halleck "fights with whatever he has, and he makes maximum use of his troops." As a counterpart to Rayburn's famous "Board of Education" meetings with his favorite Democrats, Halleck started "the Clinic" of Republican leaders.

With the start of the Kennedy Administration, Halleck joined Senate Minority Leader Everett M. Dirksen (R, Ill.) [q.v.] in a weekly press conference review of the new President's proposals. Reporters quickly dubbed the Republican leadership's program "the Ev and Charlie Show" much to Halleck's annoyance. Within a year the weekly series had attracted national news coverage for the Republican party.

The Kennedy Administration won an early victory over Halleck and conservative Democrats in January 1961 when the House voted 217 to 212 to enlarge the powerful Rules Committee. The Rules Committee effectively determined the terms of debate on important legislation reaching the floor, and Committee Chairman Howard W. Smith (D, Va.) [q.v.] frequently allied himself with Halleck in preventing liberal legislation from receiving favorable action. The White House persuaded Speaker Rayburn to lead its fight to enlarge the Committee from 12 to 15 members, a move designed to weaken the conservatives' control. Although the House Republican Policy Committee voted overwhelmingly against Rayburn's plan, Halleck failed to prevent 22 GOP members from supporting the Speaker's proposal.

The Rules Committee vote, however, proved a deceptive triumph for the new President. Halleck skillfully aligned Republicans and Southern Democrats in opposition to most of the Kennedy Administration's legislative program. He successfully led the conservative coalition in defeating the President's school aid bill (April 1961), omnibus housing bill (June 1961), a proposal to create a housing and urban development department (January 1962) and farm bill (June 1962).

Halleck surprised the White House in the summer of 1963 by becoming a strong advocate of the Administration's civil rights bill. The Republican leader worked hard to provide the conservative GOP votes that were needed to overcome Southern opposition. Both the President and Attorney General Robert F. Kennedy [q.v.] praised Halleck for his labors in October 1963. The efforts of Halleck and Rep. William McCulloch (R, Ohio) [q.v.], senior Republican on the Judiciary Committee, bore fruit in February 1964 when the House overwhelmingly passed a civil rights measure with provisions opposed Dirksen and many conservative Republican senators.

Halleck lost what proved an important challenge to his authority in January 1963. Although the House leader had expanded both the size and scope of the House Republican Conference (Policy) Committee, he had failed to satisfy some of his younger or more liberal colleagues. In January Rep. Gerald R. Ford, Jr. (R, Mich.) [q.v.] ran against Rep. Charles B. Hoeven (R, Iowa), Halleck's choice for Conference Committee chairman. Ford won the support of younger conservative and liberal members and defeated Hoeven by eight votes. Two years later, Ford unseated Halleck as Republican minority leader. [See JOHNSON Volume]

[JLB]

For further information:
Henry Z. Scheele, *Charlie Halleck* (New York, 1966).
Neil MacNeil, *Dirksen: Portrait of a Public Man* (New York, 1970).

HAMILTON, (MILO) FOWLER
b. May 7, 1911; Kansas City, Mo.
Administrator, Agency for International
Development, September 1961-
November 1962.

A Rhodes scholar and international
lawyer, Hamilton entered government service in 1938 as special assistant to the Attorney General. During World War II he
directed the "enemy" section of the
economic warfare division from the London
embassy. He returned to legal practice in
New York City in 1946. Except for a brief
period in 1956, when Hamilton served as
general counsel to the Senate Armed Services Subcommittee on the Air Force, he
did not participate in government again
until 1961.

During the 1960 elections Hamilton
worked as a fund raiser for the Democratic
Party in New York. Because of this and the
fact that he was director of the Foreign Policy World Affairs Center, a member of the
Council on Foreign Relations and a colleague of George Ball [q.v.], it was expected that he would be offered some
foreign policy post in the new Administration. In July 1961 the press suggested that
Hamilton would succeed Allen Dulles [q.v.]
as head of the Central Intelligence Agency.
Instead, Hamilton became the first head of
the Agency for International Development
(AID) in September after George D.
Woods, Kennedy's initial candidate for the
post, met with Senate opposition. He was
considered sufficiently conservative to make
a revamped foreign aid program palatable
to critical congressmen.

The creation of AID gave new stature to
the foreign aid program. Coordinating the
International Cooperation Administration
(ICA), the Development Loan Fund (DLF),
Food for Peace and various other agencies
that dispensed assistance abroad, AID
aimed at both greater efficiency and a more
systematic foreign aid policy.

The men of the New Frontier had
criticized the "shotgun" method of foreign
aid practiced by their predecessors because
it provided military and economic assistance
out of a mixture of fear of Communism and
humanitarian instincts. Although its arguments for providing foreign aid were not
markedly new, the Kennedy Administration sought to rationalize the program's
aims and methods of implementation.
Long-term development projects and loans
were preferred to grants intended to alleviate emergency situations. Long-term assistance, it was thought, would allow a
foreign nation to undertake self-sustaining
economic growth and enable it to leave the
ranks of the underdeveloped countries.
Along with economic growth democratic
political institutions would develop, making
the recipient nation an ally of the United
States capable of resisting the appeals of
both Communist and rightwing dictatorships. The State Department, of which AID
was a part, would encourage democracy in
the recipient nation while AID would promote economic growth.

Hamilton successfully changed the structure of existing foreign aid programs. He
reversed the 65-35 grant-to-loan ratio of the
Eisenhower Administration and concentrated funds in countries that showed the
greatest willingness to cooperate and the
greatest likelihood of achieving self-
sustaining economic growth. In fiscal 1962,
for example, 80% of over $1 billion in de-
velopment loans went to six countries (India, Pakistan, Brazil, Chile, Ghana and Israel). Eleven countries facing Communist
subversion got $703 million or 75% of sup-
porting assistance.

Although Hamilton changed the aid program's operations, he failed to reorganize
the agencies involved. Morale was low.
Some foreign aid veterans resented taking
orders from an outsider. Hamilton quar-
reled with other colleagues, including his
friend and chief deputy, Walter L. Lingle,
Jr., a former Procter and Gamble executive, who left AID to join the National
Aeronautics and Space Administration. His
desire to dismiss Teodoro Moscoso [q.v.] as
head of AID's Latin American division in
favor of a stronger administrator irritated
many liberals. In addition, Hamilton's conservative image failed to mollify right-of-
center congressmen. Rep. Otto Passman
(D, La.) [q.v.], chairman of the House Appropriations Subcommittee on Foreign Aid,

attacked economic assistance in general and AID's sluggishness in particular. Although bureaucratic delay was partly due to legislative restrictions, even Kennedy was unhappy with the slowness of AID's operation.

Since Hamilton and the Administration agreed that a new AID head might be better able to win congressional approval of the fiscal 1964 foreign aid request, he resigned in November 1962 to allow his successor time to prepare the new budget. Government service also entailed an economic loss for Hamilton, which he did not want to sustain beyond one year. Citing the difficulties he had encountered, Hamilton recommended that the administrative and organizational functions of the AID administrator be divided. He specifically suggested that a permanent advisory group on foreign aid be appointed by the President to handle the problems of reorganization. Although he returned to his law practice, Hamilton maintained an influential role in foreign policy formulation through his membership in a number of foreign affairs organizations.

[JCH]

HARKINS, PAUL D(ONAL)
b. May 15, 1904; Boston, Mass.
Commander, United States Military Assistance Command, Vietnam, January 1962-June 1964.

A West Point graduate, Harkins served first with the cavalry and then during World War II as an assistant to Gen. George S. Patton, whose writings he later edited. After the war he spent five years at West Point, rising to commandant of cadets under Gen. Maxwell D. Taylor [q.v.]. He served in Korea for three years, again under Taylor, and after several years at the Pentagon assumed command of NATO land forces in southeastern Europe in 1957. He became deputy commander and chief of staff of U.S. Army forces in the Pacific in September 1960.

In November 1961 the Kennedy Administration, following a fact-finding mission to Vietnam led by presidential advisers Maxwell

Taylor and Walt W. Rostow [q.v.], decided to send a major military advisory and support team to Vietnam. Harkins was chosen in January 1962 to head a new Military Advisory Command in Vietnam which would supervise the already existing Military Assistance Advisory Group as well as all other U.S. military activity. Harkins was promoted from lieutenant general to full general and arrived in Saigon on Feb. 13, 1962. In May of that year, as the U.S. position in Laos deteriorated, Harkins flew to Thailand to meet with U.S. officials and Thai Premier Sarit Thanarat. An agreement was reached for stationing American troops in Thailand, and on May 15 Harkins was given the additional job of commander of a new U.S. Military Advisory Command in Thailand.

Harkins's main area of responsibility, however, remained defeating the Communist forces in Vietnam. Although the Kennedy Administration was in theory committed to counter-insurgency warfare, the new commander in Vietnam had neither training nor experience in anti-guerrilla fighting. In fact, according to David Halberstam's The Best and the Brightest, "No one . . . could have been more conventional than Harkins." Harkins's formula for winning the war was to kill as many insurgents as possible.

Harkins was, in the words of journalist Frances Fitzgerald, "eternally optimistic," and accepted without question inflated enemy casualty figures submitted by South Vietnamese commanders. As a result, Washington officials received a seriously distorted picture of the war effort. However, Taylor, appointed chairman of the Joint Chiefs of Staff in July 1962 and an old friend of Harkins, apparently encouraged the practice of optimistic assessments. By late 1962 and early 1963 several United States Army officers in field positions in Vietnam were protesting Harkins's continually positive and inaccurate reports, and they began to submit more pessimistic appraisals. Harkins was infuriated and refused to circulate their reports. Harkins was also a strong advocate of the use of napalm, defoliants and free-fire zones. Although President Kennedy had reservations about these measures, he approved their limited use.

Harkins had a close working relationship with United States Ambassador to South Vietnam Frederick S. Nolting [q.v.], but his relationship with Henry Cabot Lodge [q.v.], who replaced Nolting in August 1963, was not good. Lodge did not share the enthusiasm of Harkins and Nolting for the Diem regime. When a number of Vietnamese generals led by Duong Van Minh planned a coup against Diem in late August, Harkins argued that Diem should be given a final chance to disassociate himself from his unpopular brother and sister-in-law, Ngo Dinh Nhu and Madame Nhu. Lodge disagreed, but the Vietnamese generals themselves cancelled the plot.

In late September Secretary of Defense Robert S. McNamara [q.v.] and Taylor made an inspection trip to Vietnam, and the sharp differences between Harkins and Lodge were immediately evident. The military command was confident about the direction of the war, while Lodge stressed the uncertainties of the political situation and raised questions about some of the military data.

When coup plans were revived by the Minh group in October, Harkins again expressed serious reservations. Lodge, however, still felt that a new government was needed, and he stopped consulting with Harkins or keeping him fully informed about the planned coup. Harkins was irate when he realized what Lodge was doing. He continued to argue that, in spite of Diem's loss of support, the war was going well. In a cable to Taylor on Oct. 30 he questioned whether it would be wise to risk a known quantity, Diem, for an unknown one. "I have seen no batting order proposed by any of the coup groups," he reported. Harkins doubted that any of the generals themselves had sufficient stature to lead the fight against Communism. (Diem was overthrown two days later and was killed along with his brother Nhu.)

During a December 1963 inspection trip, McNamara was disturbed by the inaccurate reporting of the field situation, and on his return to Washington he requested that the Central Intelligence Agency send a special team to Vietnam to study the reporting problem. By early 1964 a decision had apparently been made to replace Harkins, but he was allowed to remain at his post until June. At his final Saigon press conference Harkins conceded that despite two and one half years of massive U.S. aid, Communist military strength had continued to increase. He nevertheless expressed confidence in the progress of the war. On June 22 President Johnson gave Harkins an oak-leaf cluster for his distinguished service medal, and at Johnson's request Harkins delayed his retirement until August to serve as a Pentagon adviser.

[JBF]

For further information:
David Halberstam, *The Best and the Brightest* (New York, 1972)
U. S. Department of Defense, *The Pentagon Papers*, Senator Gravel Edition (Boston 1971), Vol. II.

HARLAN, JOHN MARSHALL
b. May 20, 1899; Chicago, Ill.
d. Dec. 29, 1971; Washington, D.C.
Associate Justice, U.S. Supreme Court, 1955-71.

The grandson of a Supreme Court justice, for whom he was named, John Marshall Harlan graduated from Princeton University in 1920. He then studied jurisprudence as a Rhodes scholar at Oxford, and he took his law degree from New York University Law School in 1924. For over 25 years Harlan was a member of a prestigious Wall Street law firm where most of his practice dealt with corporate and antitrust matters. He also served as an assistant U.S. attorney in the southern district of New York and as the special prosecutor in a New York State investigation of municipal graft during the 1920s. Head of the Operational Analysis Section of the Eighth Air Force in World War II, Harlan was chief counsel for the New York Crime Commission from 1951 to 1953.

Harlan, a life long Republican, was named judge of the U.S. Second Circuit Court of Appeals in January 1954. President Dwight D. Eisenhower [q.v.] then appointed him to the U.S. Supreme Court in November 1954, and his nomination was confirmed in March 1955. On the bench Harlan espoused constitutional doctrines similar to those of Justice Felix Frankfurter [q.v.], with whom he had a close personal and intellectual relationship. Harlan wrote several important opinions for the Court in the 1950s, such as the majority opinion in the 1957 *Yates* case, which overturned the convictions of Communist Party leaders under the Smith Act on the grounds that the trial judge had erred in his charge to the jury. [See EISENHOWER Volume]

During the 1960s Harlan served less often as spokesman for the Court because his judicial philosophy was at odds with that of the liberal, activist majority that emerged on the Warren Court. Harlan placed a high value on stability in the law and on adherence to precedent, and he rarely voted to overturn past decisions even if he personally disagreed with them. He also insisted that the Court had only a limited role in the federal system.

In criminal rights cases, for example, Harlan opposed the nationalization of state criminal procedures by extending the guarantees in the Bill of Rights to the states. He argued that the due process clause of the 14th Amendment only required that such state procedures meet a test of "fundamental fairness." Thus, Harlan dissented in June 1961 when the majority overturned a 1949 decision and applied to the states the rule that illegally seized evidence was inadmissible in court. He objected in June 1963 when the Court held that state and local law officers were subject to the same constitutional standards as federal agents in conducting searches and seizures. Harlan's view of due process, however, also led him to join with the majority in June 1963 to reverse a 21-year-old ruling and require the states to supply free counsel to indigent criminal defendants.

Justice Harlan's majority opinion in two June 1961 cases upheld a provision in the 1940 Smith Act making it a crime to belong to an organization advocating violent overthrow of the government. Harlan rejected claims that the law violated the First and Fifth Amendments. He ruled that the statute made illegal only active, not passive, membership in the Communist Party, a de-

cision that made future prosecutions under the act extremely difficult. Harlan consistently voted to sustain the authority of congressional committees to investigate possible subversive activities and associations. In March 1963 he voted to uphold similar powers for a state legislative committee.

In line with his views on the Court's limited role in a federal system, Harlan opposed extending the Court's jurisdiction into areas that he believed the Constitution left to the other branches of government. He therefore dissented in March 1962 when the majority overturned a 1946 ruling and held that federal courts could try legislative apportionment cases. Harlan insisted that the federal courts had no jurisdiction in such suits and labeled the majority decision "an adventure in judicial experimentation."

Although generally wary of broadening the Court's jurisdiction and of invalidating federal or state legislation on constitutional grounds, Harlan occasionally ruled against laws limiting personal freedom. He dissented in June 1961 when the Court refused to review a case challenging a state anti-contraceptive law on the grounds that the issue was not justiciable. Harlan joined with the majority in June 1962 and June 1963 decisions holding prayer and Bible-reading in public schools a violation of the First Amendment. In December 1961, when the Court overturned the breach of the peace convictions of 16 blacks involved in lunch counter sit-ins, Harlan entered a concurring opinion asserting that the sit-ins were comparable to verbal expression protected by the First Amendment. He voted to overturn similar convictions from civil rights demonstrations in February 1963 but changed course in later years.

In the remaining years of the Warren Court, Harlan was a frequent dissenter, objecting to the majority's "one-man, one-vote" standard for legislative apportionment and to numerous criminal rights rulings. He voted to uphold state laws on obscenity but to overturn a Connecticut statute prohibiting the use of contraceptives by married couples. [See JOHNSON Volume]

Even those who disagreed with Harlan's views generally praised his legal craftsmanship. The clarity, competence and learning in Harlan's opinions won him recognition as the leading scholar on the Court in the 1960s. Harlan's judicial philosophy caused him to object to most of the Warren Court's major innovations and made him a dissenter rather than a leader on the bench. That same philosophy, legal scholar Norman Dorsen has written, also made Harlan "a conservative conscience to a highly active Court" who rendered "conspicuous service" by acting as a critical and "restraining force during a period of rapid change."

[CAB]

For further information:
Norman Dorsen, "John Marshall Harlan," in Leon Friedman and Fred L. Israel, eds., *The Justices of the United States Supreme Court, 1789-1969* (New York, 1969), Vol. IV.
David L. Shapiro, ed., *The Evolution of a Judicial Philosophy: Selected Opinions and Papers of Justice John Marshall Harlan* (Cambridge, Mass., 1969).
"Mr. Justice Harlan," *Harvard Law Review*, LXXXV (December, 1971), pp. 369-391.

HARRIMAN, W(ILLIAM) AVERELL
b. Nov. 15, 1891; New York, N.Y.
Ambassador at Large, January 1961-November 1961; Assistant Secretary of State for Far Eastern Affairs, November 1961-March 1963; Undersecretary of State for Political Affairs, March 1963-February 1965.

As the heir to a vast railroad fortune built by his father, Edward H. Harriman, William Averell attended Groton and Yale and routinely advanced to the board of the family-controlled Union Pacific. Turning to international finance in the early 1920s, Harriman was among the first American capitalists to seek business concessions with the new Soviet government. At home he entered Democratic Party politics and held a series of business advisory posts under the early New Deal. President Roosevelt picked Harriman in March 1941 as his special representative in Great Britain to expedite Lend-Lease shipments. In August of the same year, FDR sent Harriman to the USSR where he remained until 1946,

first as minister and then as ambassador. Harriman attended all of the Big Three wartime conferences, remained in frequent contact with both Churchill and Stalin and won a permanent place in America's foreign policy establishment. After a brief period as ambassador to Great Britain in 1946, Harriman helped administer the Marshall Plan in Europe and served as President Truman's national security adviser during the Korean War. In 1954 Harriman won the governorship of New York, but most commentators considered him a poor politician; his crushing defeat by Nelson Rockefeller [*q.v.*] in 1958 set the stage for almost a generation of Republican rule in the state. Harriman also failed in his attempts to win the Democratic nomination for president in 1952 and 1956. [See TRUMAN, EISENHOWER Volumes]

In large part because of Harriman's age, 69, John F. Kennedy passed him over for a high diplomatic post in the new Administration. Instead Kennedy offered him a roving ambassadorship. Still vital, hard-working and ambitious, Harriman accepted, ready, in his own words, "to start at the bottom and work your way up." The President first assigned Harriman to help resolve the lingering political-military crisis in Laos. By 1960 American support of a rightwing strongman, Gen. Phoumi Nosavan, had pushed neutralist Premier Souvanna Phouma into a working relationship with the Soviets and had inadvertently driven neutralist army elements into an accommodation with the Communist-led Pathet Lao insurgency. Gen. Phoumi's troops were in retreat, and the Pathet Lao had overrun the strategic Plain of Jars by February 1961, threatening the Laotian administrative and royal capitals at Vientiane and Luang Prabang. In early 1961 Harriman was among those in the new Administration who urged the neutralization of Laos as a solution to the crisis there. He met with Soviet Premier Nikita Khrushchev in February and reported to Washington that the Russian leader had made it plain that he did not want a war over Laos. After Harriman met with Souvanna Phouma in New Delhi in March, he recommended that the Administration support Souvanna's efforts to form a new neutralist government. At the same time Harriman urged a limited commitment of troops to Thailand to underline American opposition to a total Communist takeover in Laos. His proposal was offered in opposition to suggestions from the Joint Chiefs of Staff that up to 60,000 troops be deployed in Laos. Kennedy publicly adopted Harriman's perspective on March 23, 1961 when he called for "a truly neutral government, not a Cold War pawn" in Laos.

In May 1961 Kennedy appointed Harriman as the American representative to the reconvened Geneva conference on Laos, where he spent the rest of the year attempting to negotiate a coalition neutralist government among the three Laotian factions. Despite Soviet support for the idea of a neutral Laos, the Geneva negotiations proceeded slowly. Gen. Phoumi, backed by American military aid and encouraged by some American representatives in Laos, created obstacles, demanding control of key defense and interior posts in the new government. Kennedy's promotion of Harriman from ambassador at large to assistant secretary of state for Far Eastern affairs in November 1961 helped Harriman apply increasing pressure on Phoumi. He first persuaded Kennedy to cut off the money used to pay the Laotian general's troops in February 1962 and then insisted that all United States agencies in Laos replace every American who was a personal friend of Phoumi's. During this period Harriman earned the nickname "the Crocodile" from his colleagues who had their "heads snapped off" when he regarded their ideas as stupid or irrevelant.

The Pathet Lao captured the town of Nam Tha in May 1962, decisively defeating 3,000 of Phoumi's best troops. During this offensive Harriman again supported an American show of force in Indochina, which this time included transfer of the Seventh Fleet into the Gulf of Siam and an airlift of another 1,800 troops to Thailand. The new Pathet Lao offensive, combined with Harriman's year-long pressure, finally forced Phoumi to yield in June 1962 to a neutralist-dominated government headed by Souvanna Phouma. The next month the United States and thirteen other nations signed the Geneva accords neutralizing Laos. Although these agreements were violated by North Vietnam and China (and eventually, as later revealed, by the United States), Harriman defended the accords with the Kennedy Administration because the settlement won the Laotian neutralists away from an alliance with the Pathet Lao and prevented a great power confrontation in the small Asian nation.

Following the conclusion of the Laotian negotiations, Harriman handled several important diplomatic assignments for the Kennedy Administration. When China invaded the mountainous regions along India's northern frontier in October 1962, Prime Minister Jawaharlal Nehru asked for Western support. Harriman led an American delegation to the subcontinent to survey Indian military requirements. Along with United States Ambassador John Kenneth Galbraith [q.v.], Harriman pressed for a resolution of India's dispute with Pakistan over Kashmir to ensure that military aid to the subcontinent would not pit one American-supplied army against another. Before American pressure could win results, the Chinese declared a unilateral ceasefire, and the incentive for resolving the India-Pakistan dispute evaporated.

Kennedy promoted Harriman to undersecretary of state for political affairs in March 1963 and two months later put him in charge of negotiating the nuclear test ban treaty with the Soviets in Moscow. Reportedly, Khrushchev recognized that Kennedy's appointment of the former ambassador to the Soviet Union to head the American delegation signaled the President's serious intention to reach an agreement. Harriman carried out his assignment in Moscow with characteristic restraint and toughness; a member of the British delegation called him "the great man of the meeting." By July 23 Harriman had persuaded the Soviets to drop their demand that a NATO-Warsaw Pact nonaggression treaty be signed simultaneously with the test ban agreement. (The United States and Britain objected to the nonaggression pact idea because it would have implied Western recognition of East Germany and a permanent division of Europe.) Harriman also assured the Russians that the signatures of China and France were not vital to a successful test ban treaty. On July 25 Harriman initialed the treaty for the United States in Moscow, and it was ratified by the Senate and signed by President Kennedy on Oct. 7, 1963.

As the American role in Vietnam expanded, Harriman maintained a skeptical attitude toward a purely military solution to the civil war there. Along with Roger Hilsman [q.v.], the new assistant secretary of state for Far Eastern affairs, and Michael Forrestal [q.v.], a White House aide assigned to work on Vietnam, Harriman repeatedly questioned the military's optimistic reports on the progress of the counterinsurgency program in Southeast Asia. During the spring and summer of 1963, this "Harriman group" urged that the Administration separate the American effort in Vietnam from the fortunes of the increasingly repressive Ngo Dinh Diem regime. The turning point in American policy came in August 1963 after Diem's secret police, led by his brother, Ngo Dinh Nhu, began a crackdown on opposition Buddhists in Saigon and Hue. With Undersecretary of State George Ball [q.v.], Harriman, Hilsman and Forrestal drafted a cable to Saigon Aug. 24 instructing Ambassador Henry Cabot Lodge [q.v.] on U.S. policy. The message stated that Diem must be "given [a] chance to rid himself of Nhu," but if he refused the U.S. had to "face the possibility that Diem himself cannot be preserved." Lodge was also instructed to inform leading South Vietnamese generals that the U.S. would not support the government unless reforms were made. In addition, he was given permission to tell the generals that U.S. would give them "direct support" in case of a "breakdown" in the central government. Because of dissention among the President's advisers, these instructions were canceled on Aug. 20 and Lodge was ordered to work for reform of the regime. A coup toppled the Diem government on Nov. 1.

With Kennedy's assassination and the continuing escalation of the war in Vietnam, Harriman's influence in government declined until President Johnson called on the former governor to serve as chairman of the American delegation to the Paris peace talks on Vietnam in May 1968. [See JOHNSON, NIXON Volumes]

[NNL]

HARRINGTON, (EDWARD) MICHAEL

b. Feb. 24, 1928; St. Louis, Mo.
Member, National Executive Committee, Socialist Party, 1960-72.

Raised in a middle-class, Democratic, Irish-Catholic home, Harrington attended parochial schools and Holy Cross College. During a year at Yale Law School and later as a graduate student at the University of Chicago, Harrington developed an interest in socialism. In 1951 he came to New York City and worked for a year with the Catholic Worker movement. Soon afterward Harrington joined the Young Peoples' Socialist League, and later became a leading member of the Socialist Party. During this period Harrington considered himself a revolutionary socialist, equally opposed to both Western capitalism and the Communist regimes of Asia and Europe. He was active in various civil rights, civil liberties and peace groups throughout the 1950s.

In 1959, at the suggestion of Commentary editor Anatole Shub, Harrington began research on poverty in the United States and published a report in the July 1959 issue of the magazine entitled "Our Fifty Million Poor." Later Harrington expanded his study of the problem into a book, The Other America: Poverty in the United States, published in March 1962. Harrington argued that within America's "affluent society" a quarter of the population remained in poverty. These "invisible poor" were "maimed in body and spirit, existing at levels beneath those necessary for human decency. . .without adequate housing and education and medical care." Living in a demoralizing subculture, the poor themselves were unable to break out of their cycle of deprivation and despair or call attention to their plight. Only an aroused larger society, he wrote, could initiate action to alleviate the suffering of America's poor.

The initial reception accorded The Other America was modest if favorable, but a review by Dwight MacDonald in The New Yorker in January 1963 introduced the book to a much wider audience. Later that year the work was given a special George Polk Award for achievement in journalism. President Kennedy, interested in the poverty problem since his 1960 West Virginia primary campaign, asked Walter Heller [q.v.], chairman of the Council of Economic Advisers, about recent writing on the problem. Heller gave him Harrington's book, which Kennedy read and remembered. Shortly afterward, Kennedy decided to make poverty in the United States a major concern of his Administration, leading eventually to the establishment of the Office of Economic Opportunity in 1964.

A friend of Bayard Rustin [q.v.]. Martin Luther King, Jr. [q.v.] and other civil rights leaders, Harrington helped organize the 1960 "March on the Conventions." By demonstrating at the national nominating conventions, these leaders hoped to dramatize their demands and increase the pressure for strong civil rights planks in the national platforms. Working in Los Angeles, Harrington helped organize a march of 5,000 people and a 24-hour vigil at the Democratic Convention, which received widespread publicity.

By the early 1960s Harrington had become convinced that socialists should work to "realign" the forces inside the Democratic Party in a more progressive direction by building a coalition of labor, liberal and civil rights groups, rather than follow the traditional socialist policy of running independent candidates. Although he did not support Kennedy in the 1960 election, Harrington later endorsed other Democratic candidates, and supported Johnson in 1964.

Throughout 1961 and 1962 Harrington also worked with the young leaders of the Student Nonviolent Coordinating Committee and tried to spread the democratic, anti-Communist, socialist viewpoint to which he had long adhered. In the spring of 1962 Harrington became a member of the Student Activities Board of the League for Industrial Democracy (LID) and chief liaison to LID's youth affiliate, the recently renamed Students for a Democratic Society (SDS). Harrington attened the June 1962 SDS convention at Port Huron, Mich. as a LID representative and vigorously opposed the inclusion in the Port Huron Statement of an attack on American liberalism juxtaposed with only mild criticism of the Soviet Union. At a special LID hearing following the SDS convention, Harrington chastized SDS for seating an observer from a Communist Party youth group. Harrington

and the majority of the LID Board decided to cut off funds to SDS and change the locks at the SDS office. Although an immediate break was avoided, relations between LID and its youth affiliate remained tense and were eventually severed in 1966. [See JOHNSON Volume]

[JBF]

For further information:
Michael Harrington: *Fragments of the Century: A Social Autobiography* (New York, 1973).

HARRIS, LOUIS
b. Jan. 6, 1921; New Haven, Conn.
Pollster.

Harris, the son of a real estate developer, majored in economics at the University of North Carolina and wrote for the college paper. After service in the Navy during World War II, Harris joined the liberal American Veterans Committee and worked as the organization's program director for several months in 1946 and 1947. There he came in contact with pollster Elmo Roper and joined his organization, first as writer and researcher and later as a partner.

In 1956 he left to form Louis Harris and Associates, a public opinion and market research company. Harris took his first political polls for columnists Joseph and Stewart Alsop [q.v.] and in 1958 worked for Sen. John F. Kennedy in his Massachusetts reelection campaign.

Harris came to national prominence in 1960 after Kennedy engaged his organization to sample public response during the Senator's bid for the Democratic presidential nomination. Harris soon became a Kennedy partisan and a member of the inner circle that mapped campaign strategy. An early Harris poll in West Virginia was instrumental in convincing Kennedy to enter the primary there. After extensive polling in the state, Harris advised Kennedy that he could counter the potential religious bias of the state's predominantly Protestant voters by projecting himself as an all-out liberal Democrat.

Harris also took a special poll in the early fall shortly before Kennedy's series of televised debates with Republican presidential candidate Richard Nixon [q.v.]. The pollster advised Kennedy to show a friendlier and warmer manner and to emphasize his maturity by offering well structured and slowly spoken answers to questions posed during the debates.

Harris polls were characterized by a sophistication that distinguished them from those of competitors George Gallup and Elmo Roper. His polls sought to probe basic attitudes, biases and political reasons behind the initial responses of those interviewed. Harris also pioneered in the close analysis of voting returns at the precinct level, a technique that often accurately revealed shifts in political sentiment by various ethnic and religious groups from one election to another.

By the mid-1960s Harris had firmly established himself as a political pollster and manager, usually for Democratic or liberal Republican candidates. He replaced Roper as public opinion analyst for the Columbia Broadcasting System in 1962, and the next year he began writing weekly columns for *Newsweek*. Another column which he wrote for the *Washington Post* was syndicated in 100 newspapers.

[NNL]

HARRIS, OREN
b. Dec. 20, 1903; Belton, Ark.
Democratic Representative, Ark.,
1941-66; Chairman, Interstate and
Foreign Commerce Committee, 1956-
66.

Harris received a law degree in 1930 and three years later became deputy prosecuting attorney of Union County, Ark. In 1936 he was elected prosecuting attorney of the state's 13th judicial district. Four years later Harris defeated the incumbent Democratic U.S. representative in Arkansas's seventh congressional district and easily won the general election. As a member of the Interstate and Foreign Commerce Committee, to which he was appointed in 1943,

Harris sponsored a bill in 1949 exempting independent natural gas producers from the rate and service regulations of the Federal Power Commission (FPC). A measure similar to Harris's was passed by Congress but vetoed by President Harry S Truman. In 1956 Harris became chairman of the Commerce Committee. [See EISENHOWER Volume]

The Commerce panel had jurisdiction over legislation pertaining to federal regulatory agencies. The agencies were under congressional control to a considerable degree, and Harris generally opposed bills increasing presidential power over them. Early in 1961 Harris objected to a Kennedy Administration bill to increase the authority of the chairman of the Federal Communications Commission (FCC), who was appointed by the President, over the agency's commissioners. In June 1961 the House defeated the Kennedy plan by a vote of 323 to 77, in part as a result of Harris's opposition.

Harris also fought what he regarded as too much control of private enterprise by the regulatory agencies. In June 1961 he introduced a bill to relax federal restraints on natural gas producers. The measure would have required the FPC to base gas rates on a "reasonable market price" rather than on the cost of discovery and production. The bill, however, died in the House.

In September 1963 Harris denounced an FCC directive requiring broadcasters to present the views of both sides in disputes involving racial segregation. He asserted that such a directive would inexorably lead the Commission to "interject itself into programming on a day-to-day basis." During the fall of 1963 Harris also expressed his opposition to an Administration-supported bill to expand the Securities and Exchange Commission's (SEC) policing power over securities trading. The proposed bill placed securities firms doing strictly intrastate business under the jurisdiction of the SEC and gave the Commission authority to set both financial and personnel standards for securities firms.

In July 1963 the Senate had passed the SEC bill in essentially the form favored by the Administration. But Harris held the bill in the Commerce Committee until May

1964. As reported out by the panel, the measure exempted insurance companies, which had lobbied strongly against the bill, from SEC jurisdiction. The amended bill also gave securities dealers the option of joining the National Association of Securities Dealers or submitting themselves to SEC supervision. The final bill, which was signed by the President in August 1964, incorporated the Commerce Committee's amendments.

In July 1965 President Lyndon B. Johnson [q.v.] nominated Harris to be a federal district judge in Arkansas; the Senate confirmed the nomination in August. Harris resigned from the House to assume the judgeship in February 1966. [See JOHNSON Volume]

[MLL]

HART, PHILIP A(LOYSIUS)
b. Dec. 10, 1912; Bryn Mawr, Pa.
Democratic Senator, Mich., 1959-76.

Philip Hart, the son of a Pennsylvania banker, attended Georgetown University. After receiving his law degree from the University of Michigan in 1937, he began private practice in Detroit. He was seriously wounded at the invasion of Normandy during World War II and returned to law practice after the war. Hart entered government in 1949 as Michigan's corporation and securities commissioner. In 1953 he became legal adviser to Gov. G. Mennen Williams [q.v.], a former law school classmate, and was elected lieutenant governor in 1954 and 1956. With strong labor support Hart ran successfully for the Senate in 1958. In that and subsequent campaigns Hart was aided by the inherited wealth of his wife, the former Jane Briggs, daughter of Walter Briggs, the auto parts millionaire and owner of the Detroit Tigers baseball team.

In the Senate Hart earned a reputation as one of that chamber's most liberal members, with a special interest in civil rights and consumer protection. *Congressional Quarterly* reported that in 1963 he was one of the Senate's two most frequent opponents of measures favored by the conservative coalition. He supported the Kennedy Administration's major legislative requests, including the area redevelopment bill in January 1961 and medicare in July 1962. Hart introduced the Administration's package of voter rights proposals in April 1963.

As a member of the Judiciary Committee's Subcommittee on Antitrust and Monopoly, Hart supported subcommittee chairman Estes Kefauver's (D, Tenn.) [q.v.] attack on prescription drug prices in June 1961. When the Judiciary Committee voted nine to two in March 1962 to refer Kefauver's bill to amend the drug antitrust laws to conservative Sen. John McClellan's (D, Ark.) [q.v.] patents subcommittee, Hart and Kefauver were in the minority.

Hart moderated subcommittee hearings in 1961, 1962 and 1963, investigating misleading packaging and labeling practices such as short-weighting and unsatisfactory contents designation. In March 1963 the Senator proposed a bill to prohibit such deceptive practices. After repeated rebuffs Congress finally passed "truth-in-packaging" legislation in October 1966.

Following Kefauver's death in August 1963, Hart assumed the chairmanship of the Judiciary Committee's antitrust subcommittee. He shared Kefauver's opposition to corporate power but had less devotion to the interests of small business than some antitrust enthusiasts. Hart stated: "I have never held the notion that bigness per se is bad and that smallness is necessarily good. My interest is basically in a consumer-oriented committee."

The performance of the antitrust subcommittee under Hart reflected his temperamental differences from his predecessor. The flamboyant Kefauver had conducted headline-making investigations into concentrations of industrial power, notably in the electrical, drug and steel fields. Under Hart, who was conspicuous in the Senate for his reserved, judicious style, the subcommittee receded from public attention, although he held numerous hearings on the problems of industrial concentration and the growth of conglomerates. The volume of testimony resulted in little legislation, however, because the Committee's conservative Chairman Sen. James Eastland (D, Miss.) [*q.v.*], was disinclined to strengthen the antitrust laws. [See JOHNSON Volume]

[TO]

HARTKE, R(UPERT) VANCE
b. May 31, 1919; Stendal, Ind.
Democratic Senator, Ind., 1959- .

Vance Hartke was raised in a small mining town in southwestern Indiana. After service in the Coast Guard during World War II, he returned to his studies at the Indiana University Law School, from which he graduated in 1948. Hartke then practiced law in Evansville, Ind., while earning a reputation as a skilled organizer for the local Democratic Party. He was elected mayor of Evansville in 1955 and three years later, after a strenuous campaign, won election to the U.S. Senate. He was the first Democrat to represent Indiana in the upper house in 20 years.

Hartke proved to be a strong supporter of the Kennedy Administration, voting for its school aid, minimum wage, housing and medicare bills. From 1961 to 1963 the liberal Americans for Democratic Action gave him high ratings. Hartke served on the powerful Senate Commerce and Finance Committees; but lacking seniority, he did not play an influential role in the Senate during the Kennedy years.

In 1961 Hartke successfully amended Social Security legislation, raising to $1,800 the limit on earnings of retired persons exempted from benefit deductions. As a member of the Senate District of Columbia Committee, he served as floor manager for the 1962 law that abolished the mandatory death penalty for first degree murder convictions in Washington, D.C. As a member of the Finance Committee, he supported a key provision of the Administration's 1962 tax revision bill requiring automatic withholding of taxes on interest and dividend payments. This provision was defeated on the floor of the Senate following intensive lobbying against it by savings and loan as-

sociations. Hartke also supported an Administration measure permitting businesses a 7% tax deduction to defer the cost of newly purchased equipment.

Hartke represented a state where the manufacture of steel was an important industry. In April 1963 he introduced legislation requiring manufacturers to label containers made with foreign steel with the metal's country of origin. Hartke hoped thereby to encourage greater purchases of the domestic product. Congress took no action on the bill.

In 1964 Hartke won reelection with 55% of the vote, a substantial margin for a liberal running in an essentially conservative state. During the campaign Hartke received large cash contributions from a Chicago-based mail order firm. A year later he requested and won appointment to the Senate Post Office Committee where he worked to forestall planned postal rate increases for third class mail. Hartke's opponents charged that he was guilty of conflict of interest; this coupled with his outspoken opposition to American involvement in Vietnam made his reelection in 1970 problematical. Hartke defeated his opponent by only 4,235 votes; his claim to his seat was not finally settled until 18 months after the election. [See JOHNSON, NIXON Volumes]

[JLW]

HATFIELD, MARK O(DUM)
b. July 22, 1922; Dallas, Ore.
Governor, Ore., 1959-67.

Mark O. Hatfield, the son of a Southern Pacific Railway blacksmith, was raised in Salem, Ore. He attended Willamette University in Salem, served in the Navy during World War II and did graduate work at Stanford University. In 1949 he began a seven-year career as a political science teacher at Willamette. At the same time he proved adept in practical politics. In 1950 he won election to the state House of Representatives and in 1954 to the state Senate. He was elected secretary of state in 1956 and three years later became the youngest governor in Oregon history.

Hatfield had been a youthful admirer of Wendell Willkie, the 1940 Republican presidential nominee. Like Willkie, Hatfield considered himself an internationalist. On domestic issues Hatfield usually was associated with such moderate Republicans as New York Gov. Nelson Rockefeller [q.v.] and Michigan Gov. George Romney [q.v.].

As governor, Hatfield played an active role in Oregon's economic development, helping particularly to expand the state's trade with the Far East. He also backed legislation for construction of state community colleges and favored public rather than private development of the Columbia River basin hydroelectric project. He opposed state right-to-work laws and blocked a proposed effort by the legislature to impose a state sales tax because he believed it placed an unfair burden on the poor.

Early in his political career Hatfield earned a reputation as a strong civil rights advocate. As a young state legislator he had cosponsored a public accommodations bill in the Oregon House of Representatives. Speaking before the National Governors Conference in July 1963, he pleaded for a "meaningful civil rights resolution."

During the early 1960s Hatfield emerged as a promising future candidate for the Republican presidential or vice presidential nomination. In 1960 he nominated Vice President Richard Nixon [q.v.] for president at the Republican National Convention, and four years later he delivered the keynote address at the Republican Convention in San Francisco. He supported Sen. Barry Goldwater's (R, Ariz.) [q.v.] presidential bid that year even though Goldwater's conservatism was alien to his own political outlook.

During the mid-1960s Hatfield became a vigorous opponent of American involvement in the Vietnam war. As a result his standing with Republican Party leaders declined sharply. When he ran for the Senate in 1966, the popular Hatfield was barely able to defeat Rep. Robert Duncan (D, Ore.), a supporter of the war. As a senator during the Johnson and Nixon Administrations, Hatfield remained a strong opponent of the Vietnam war and sponsored legislation that proposed a fixed date for a cutoff of war funding. [See JOHNSON, NIXON Volumes]

[JLW]

HAYDEN, CARL T(RUMBULL)
b. Oct. 2, 1877; Tempe, Ariz.
d. Jan. 25, 1972; Mesa, Ariz.
Democratic Senator, Ariz., 1926-69;
Chairman, Appropriations Committee, 1955-69.

Carl Hayden served in Congress longer than any other member in U.S. history. Born 35 years before Arizona achieved statehood, Hayden graduated from Stanford University with Herbert Hoover in 1900. He served as a councilman and county sheriff until 1912, when he was elected Arizona's first representative. Elected to the Senate in 1926, Hayden did not make a single speech on the floor during his first 21 years in office. Nevertheless, he became known as a dogged champion of legislation to improve roads and irrigation in his home state. He was the father of the bill to establish the Grand Canyon National Park and was coauthor in the 1950s of the legislation that led to the interstate highway system. [See TRUMAN, EISENHOWER Volumes]

According to Congressional Quarterly, Hayden supported Kennedy Administration legislation on nearly 70% of all major issues. As chairman of the Senate Appropriations Committee, Hayden became involved in a bitter dispute in 1962 with fellow octogenarian Rep. Clarence Cannon (D, Mo.) [q.v.], chairman of the House Appropriations Committee. The major issues concerned the Senate's right under the U.S. Constitution to initiate appropriations bills of its own and to make additions to House-passed appropriations. These important questions were overshadowed during the feud by the minor issue of where Senate-House conference committees on appropriations bills should meet and which branch should provide chairmen for conferences.

The Senate-House conflict held up appropriations for three months in 1962 from

April to July. During the procedural crisis several government agencies, including the Small Business Administration and the U.S. Secret Service, nearly exhausted their funds. On June 28 both branches passed supplemental appropriations to continue government operations, but late in the session a Senate-House disagreement over agricultural research funds resulted in a three-week deadlock on the agriculture approprations bill. In October the Senate adopted a resolution asserting its "coequal power" with the House to originate appropriations bills. The Senate-House dispute waned during the next year, but it was a contributing factor in the nearly 12 months Congress took to clear appropriations for 1963.

During the period between President Kennedy's assassination in November 1963 and Lyndon Johnson's [q.v.] inauguration in January 1965, Hayden was President Pro Tempore of the Senate and third in line for presidential succession after House Speaker John McCormack (D, Mass.) [q.v.]. During the Johnson years Hayden supported the President on civil rights, medicare and social security, as well as on foreign aid appropriations.

The crowning achievement of Hayden's career came with the 1968 passage of the $892 million Central Arizona Project, a 400-mile system of dams and aqueducts designed to divert water from Lake Hasavu, behind the Parker Dam on the Colorado River, to the populous areas in and around Phoenix and Tucson.

Declining to seek reelection in 1968, Hayden returned to Arizona where he died in January 1972 at the age of 94. [See JOHNSON VOLUME]

[FHM]

HEBERT, F(ELIX) EDWARD
b. Oct. 12, 1901; New Orleans, La.
Democratic Representative, La., 1941- .

Between 1917 and 1940 Hebert worked as a sportswriter, a columnist and an editor of New Orleans newspapers. In June 1939 as city editor of the *New Orleans States*, Hebert wrote a series of articles exposing state house corruption which resulted in conviction of a number of officials including Gov. Richard W. Leche. The next year Hebert won New Orleans's first district congressional seat and in subsequent elections faced little if any opposition. In Congress Hebert associated with other Southern Democrats supporting Roosevelt and Truman in foreign affairs, but he opposed their liberal domestic programs. A firm segregationist, Hebert supported Strom Thurmond [q.v.] in the 1948 presidential election. In the 1950s Hebert gained prominence as chairman of the House Armed Services Special Investigations Subcommittee. In 1951 he headed an investigation of Defense Department procurement procedures, and in 1959 he led a well-publicized probe of the "munitions lobby" which exposed defense industry use of retired officers as lobbyists and salesmen. [See TRUMAN, EISENHOWER Volumes]

As a ranking member of the Armed Services Committee, Hebert consistently backed large military budgets and represented the armed forces viewpoint in Congress, often opposing the Kennedy Administration's attempt to assert greater civilian control over military affairs. As chairman of the House Armed Services Reserve Forces Subcommittee, Hebert was centrally involved in the 1962 controversy over the reduction and reorganization of the National Guard and Army Reserve. Although the Department of Defense had been seeking a reorganization of reserve forces for several years, the call-up of reserve units during the 1961 Berlin crisis brought a new urgency to the issue. On April 4, 1962 the Defense Department announced a plan to reduce the total Army Reserve and National Guard strength to 642,000, eliminating or downgrading some units and closing 150 armories, in an effort to build a smaller, but better equipped and prepared reserve force.

Severely criticized by the National Guard, the American Legion, and many state governors, the Defense Department proposal was rejected by Hebert's subcommittee after hearings in the spring of 1962. Instead, a subcommittee report called for larger reserve force appropriations and no force reduction.

In late November the Defense Department capitulated, agreeing to an increased target strength of 700,000.

The next year Hebert again clashed with the Kennedy Administration over the development of the RS-70 manned bomber. The Administration, and particularly Secretary of Defense Robert S. McNamara [q.v.], opposed the development of new bombers, hoping to put greater emphasis on guided missile systems. During the House debate in March 1963 Hebert said: "I-got-all-the-answers-McNamara is not the last word in military strategy." The final version of the bill, signed into law on May 23, 1963, included the $364 million appropriation for the RS-70 that its proponents had sought. After initial opposition, Hebert supported the Administration's 1963 proposal for a $191 million fallout shelter construction program, which eventually passed the House but died in the Senate.

Hebert opposed the growing civil rights movement, and in April 1962 he defended the plan of the segregationist Citizens Council of Greater New Orleans to give free, one-way tickets to blacks seeking to leave New Orleans for Northern cities. In response to a protest from the NAACP, Hebert said that the plan represented a true "Freedom Ride" and accused the NAACP of not wanting "these free people in the North."

As a segregationist, Hebert was caught in a dilemma when in December 1963, Rep. Otis R. Pike (D, N.Y.) tried to amend a ROTC bill to bar participation by segregated schools. The bill, which Hebert initially supported, would have "vitalized" ROTC at the college level and continued and expanded the high school ROTC program that the Defense Department had been planning to drop. When Hebert learned of Pike's proposed amendment, he attempted to suspend House rules, preventing any amendments to the bill. His motion failed to achieve the two-thirds vote needed, and Hebert let the entire ROTC bill die rather than risk passing a measure fostering integration. In the next session of Congress, Hebert succeeded in passing the bill without the anti-segregation clause. [See JOHNSON Volume]

[JBF]

HELLER, WALTER W(OLFGANG)
b. Aug. 27, 1915; Buffalo, N.Y.
Chairman, Council of Economic Advisers, January 1961-November 1964.

After earning his Ph.D in economics from the University of Wisconsin, Heller served in the Treasury Department's division of tax research during World War II, where he helped install the new withholding tax system. He left the Treasury in 1946 to teach economics at the University of Minnesota, although he remained a Treasury consultant afterwards and was involved in drafting tax legislation during the Korean War. From 1955 to 1960 he was an economic adviser to Gov. Orville Freeman [q.v.] of Minnesota and consultant to the Minnesota Department of Taxation.

It was on the strength of recommendations by Gov. Freeman and the economist Paul A. Samuelson [q.v.] that President Kennedy chose Heller to be chairman of his Council of Economic Advisers (CEA). (Heller selected economists James Tobin [q.v.] and Kermit Gordon [q.v.] to serve with him on the CEA.) At a press conference on Dec. 23, 1960 announcing his appointment, Heller said the Kennedy Administration's task was to "put the economy back on the track of full employment and satisfactory growth." Heller stressed that the current recession and 7% unemployment level represented an incomplete recovery from the more serious recession of 1957-58.

Heller argued within the Administration that the major problem was not, as some cabinet and Federal Reserve officials argued, chronic unemployment due to technological displacement, but insufficient aggregate demand. High taxes were stalling recovery by draining purchasing power and investment capital. His solution to this problem of "fiscal drag" was an application of Keynesian economics: stimulate expansion via a tax cut and aggressive federal spending. Heller's fiscal approach to economic recovery distinguished him from those who favored monetary measures, those who advocated intensive job training to attack "structural" unemployment and those who believed in the necessity of a balanced budget. In a report submitted to the Joint Economic Committee of Congress in March 1961, Heller defended the concept of deficit spending: "The success of fiscal or budget policies cannot be measured only by whether the budget is in the black or in the red. . . . If at the end of this year the unemployment ratio is still near 7%, our fiscal policies would have to be viewed with great concern, even if there is little or no deficit in the budget." The "real challenge" of U.S. economic policy, he said, lay in closing an estimated $50 billion gap in 1961 between production and potential output, not merely in reversing the current decline.

Heller did much to propagate the "new economics," but the President was not immediately won over to his program. Kennedy, for example, favored a $3 billion tax increase in July 1961 during the Berlin crisis to finance the military mobilization; a conference with Keynesian Paul Samuelson on July 27 helped to change the President's mind. Heller was instrumental in conceiving and pushing many of the Administration's short-run, anti-recession measures through Congress. He convinced the President that an increase in social security payments should be made in April 1961 but that the increase in contributions to pay for the program should be postponed until January 1962 in order not to deflate the slow economic advance of 1961.

Heller unsuccessfully argued for lower interest rates on the grounds that the "tight money" policy of the Eisenhower Administration had inhibited recovery. He was unable to convince the Federal Reserve Board and its chairman, William McChesney Martin [q.v.], to institute an "easy" monetary policy, however, for they feared that lower short-term interest rates would cause foreign investors to withdraw their capital and thus aggravate the balance of payments deficit. Martin and C. Douglas Dillon [q.v.], Secretary of the Treasury, were the main opponents within the Administration of the deficit spending advocated by Heller, arguing that unbalanced budgets would be inflationary and also exacerbate the balance of payments problem. Foreign bankers, they maintained, would lose confidence in the value of the dollar and withdraw their funds from U.S. institutions.

The CEA Annual Report for 1962 was a broad rationale for the economic policies subsequently pursued by the Kennedy and Johnson Administrations. (Kennedy often used Heller to stake out a position before he himself was prepared to embrace it publicly.) The report appealed for a comparatively easy money policy, an 8% tax credit for new plant and equipment, liberalized depreciation allowances and presidential authority for temporary income tax reductions and public works expenditures as anti-recession weapons. To restrain inflation the CEA offered wage-price guideposts for industry and labor which were intended to tie any pay increases to advances in productivity.

Heller and the CEA were leading participants in the Administration's 72-hour campaign in April 1962 to force U.S. Steel to rescind its announced price increase. In conjunction with Labor Department economists, they developed the argument that a price rise was not necessary and would aggravate inflation, worsen the steel industry's position vis-a-vis foreign competition and thus add to the country's balance of payments deficit. The CEA proposed that the Administration urge smaller producers such as Inland, Armco, and Kaiser to hold the price line. Heller maintained an active two-way flow of information with Joseph Hall, a member of Armco's board, during the crisis. When the large steel companies announced price increases in April and September 1963, Heller counseled the President to respond mildly because the increases were "selective" and not across-the-board.

A member of a special five-man "core" group that included Theodore Sorenson [q.v.], Myer Feldman [q.v.], Lawrence O'Brien [q.v.] and David Bell [q.v.], Heller helped draft Kennedy's complete legislative program for 1962. The CEA played an important role in drafting the Trade Expansion Act, which gave the president authority to reduce tariff barriers.

Heller's most significant contribution to the Kennedy program was in the area of tax reduction, for which he had lobbied within the Administration since his appointment, finally winning the President's commitment to a tax cut in August 1962. In January 1963 Kennedy called for extensive tax cuts totalling $13.6 billion—$11 billion for individuals, the rest for corporations—plus the closing of various loopholes to reduce the net loss to the Treasury to $10.2 billion. Heller argued within the Administration and then before Congress that such a large reduction was vital for economic growth and that the immediate deficit it caused would be more than offset by the increase in taxable income which would follow greater prosperity. Heller awkwardly provoked conservative Administration critics on Jan. 28, 1963 when he told the Joint Economic Committee that there was a need for "public education in economics" to counter the American "basic puritanical" aversion to tax reduction and deficit spending. An $11.2 billion tax cut passed the House in September 1963 but was held up in the Senate Finance Committee, chaired by Sen. Harry Flood Byrd (D, Va.) [q.v.], one of the leading fiscal conservatives in the Senate. The Kennedy tax program did not pass the Senate until after the President's death; President Johnson signed an $11.5-billion tax reduction act on Feb. 26, 1964. Heller resigned as Chairman of the CEA in November 1964. [See JOHNSON Volume].

[TO]

For further information:
E. Ray Canterbery, *Economics on a New Frontier* (Belmont, Calif., 1968).
Edward S. Flash, Jr., *Economic Advice and Presidential Leadership* (New York, 1965).
Walter W. Heller, *New Dimensions of Political Economy* (New York, 1966).

HELMS, RICHARD M(cGARRAH)
b. March 30, 1913; St. David's, Pa.
Deputy to the Director for Plans, Central Intelligence Agency, 1952-62; Deputy Director for Plans, 1962-65.

Richard Helms grew up in an upper middle class family, which lived first in New Jersey and then Europe, where Helms received his secondary education. On his return to the U.S., Helms entered Williams College and graduated in 1935. He then worked as a correspondent for the United Press and later as advertising director of the Indianapolis *Times*.

Commissioned a lieutenant in the Navy in 1942, Helms was transferred to the Office of Strategic Services one year later. After his discharge in 1946 he remained in intelligence work, joining the Strategic Services Unit of the Department of War. The following year he helped organize the Central Intelligence Agency and during the 1950s became one of its key staff officers. During those early years he reportedly worked on covert operations or "plans" and helped recruit and train top agents.

In 1952 Helms was appointed deputy to the chief of the plans division. Although his exact functions were never made public, he was said to have supervised U.S. espionage in the Soviet Union, including the U-2 reconnaissance flights. Sometime during the 1950s, Helms also became involved in the CIA's program of domestic surveillance, which included the opening of mail and the compiling of files on 10,000 private American citizens in violation of the CIA's 1947 charter. Helms reportedly opposed the establishment of a CIA Domestic Operations Division in 1962.

According to a 1975 Senate report, between 1960 and 1965 Helms helped to plan the assassinations of Congolese Premier Patrice Lumumba and Cuban Premier Fidel Castro. The first of the plots against Castro employed underworld crime figure John Roselli to carry out the assignment. Other plots involved the use of explosives, high-powered rifles and poisoned ball-point pens and cigars to assassinate the Cuban leader. In January 1963 a skin-diving suit contaminated with a poisonous fungus was prepared as a gift to be given to Castro by James Donovan [q.v.], who was then negotiating for the release of Cuban prisoners taken during the Bay of Pigs invasion. The plan failed because Donovan decided to give Castro an uncontaminated suit.

Although Helms, Richard Bissell [q.v.] and CIA Director Allen Dulles [q.v.] were implicated in these plots, the 1975 Senate Select Intelligence Committee investigating the assassination plans could not determine whether Presidents Dwight D. Eisenhower [q.v.], John Kennedy or Lyndon B. Johnson [q.v.] were aware of them. Helms testified that the presidents under whom he served had never asked him to consider assassination. The investigation revealed that Helms had withheld information from Johnson and Attorney General Robert Kennedy [q.v.] and did not tell John McCone

[*q.v.*] of the CIA's use of underworld figures to kill Castro when McCone became CIA director in 1961.

According to ex-CIA employee Victor Marchetti, Helms was involved in the planning of the April 1961 Bay of Pigs invasion, but his participation was not documented. Helms was promoted to deputy director for plans in February 1962 upon the resignation of Richard Bissell [*q.v.*], who had planned the ill-fated invasion.

In 1966 Helms was appointed director of Central Intelligence. During his tenure the Agency continued its domestic surveillance, assassination planning and involvement in the internal politics of such countries as Chile, Italy and Laos. Because the Agency's system of executive command and control was ambiguous. Helm's connection with these activities remained unclear. In 1973 he was confirmed as ambassador to Iran. As CIA operations were revealed during the 1970s, Helms came under increased criticism from Congress. Several members of Congress urged the Ambassador's recall in light of the revelations and his misleading testimony before congressional committees. [See JOHNSON, NIXON Volume]

[EWS]

For further information:
Victor Marchetti and John D. Marks, *The CIA and the Cult of Intelligence* (New York, 1974).
Commission on CIA Activities within the United States (Rockefeller Commission), *Report to the President* (Washington, 1975).
U.S. Senate Select Committee on Intelligence Activities, *Alleged Assassination Plots Involving Foreign Leaders* (Washington, 1975).

HENRY, AARON E(DD)

b. July 2, 1922; Coahoma County, Miss.
President, Mississippi Conference of Branches of the NAACP, 1960- ; President, Council of Federated Organizations, Miss., 1962-65.

Henry grew up in Clarksdale in the Mississippi delta and graduated from Xavier University in 1950. A pharmacist, he re-turned to Clarksdale and opened a drugstore, which became one of the leading black businesses in the city. In 1952 Henry helped organize the Clarksdale branch of the NAACP, and in 1960 he became president of the Mississippi Conference of NAACP Branches. Henry worked closely with Medgar Evers [*q.v.*], the NAACP's state field secretary, in efforts to register black voters, organize new NAACP branches and investigate charges of harassment and intimidation from blacks throughout the state.

As a leader of civil rights activity in Mississippi, Henry was repeatedly harassed and arrested. The windows of his drug store were broken innumerable times, and in 1963 his home and his store were both badly damaged by bomb explosions. Henry was convicted of conspiring to harm public trade in January 1962 after he led Clarksdale blacks in a citywide boycott of white merchants. Two months later he was convicted of disturbing the peace for allegedly having made indecent advances on an 18-year-old white youth who had hitched a ride in his car. When the civil rights leader accused the Clarksdale police chief and the county attorney of having concocted the charge, they sued him for libel and won $40,000 from local courts. The U.S. Supreme Court later overturned both the disturbance of the peace conviction and the libel judgment.

Henry was an early supporter of James Meredith [*q.v.*] in his legal battle to enter the University of Mississippi. After Meredith had finally enrolled at the University in October 1962, Henry denied charges that the NAACP had handpicked Meredith to desegregate the school.

In the spring of 1962 Henry was elected president of the Council of Federated Organizations (COFO), a coalition of the NAACP and other civil rights groups in the state established to conduct a unified voter registration campaign. Henry worked closely with Robert P. Moses [*q.v.*], project director of COFO and Mississippi field secretary for the Student Nonviolent Coordinating Committee, in planning and organizing voter registration projects throughout the state. COFO first concentrated its efforts in Greenwood, but late in the summer of 1963 it branched out from that delta town and began organizing a statewide "Freedom Ballot," a mock election to be held in November to coincide with the regular state elections. Open to all blacks of voting age, the COFO election was designed to call national attention to the disfranchisement of blacks in Mississippi and to educate blacks about the potential power of the vote. Henry ran as the Freedom candidate for governor on a platform declaring that poor whites as well as blacks suffered under the state's existing political and economic leadership. Some 80,000 votes were cast for Henry on the Freedom Ballot, a figure four times larger than the number of blacks then officially registered to vote in the state.

Henry participated in the 1964 Mississippi Freedom Summer Project and was a leader in organizing the state Freedom Democratic Party (MFDP). He headed the MFDP delegation that unsuccessfully challenged the seating of the regular Mississippi delegation at the Democratic National Convention in August 1964. Although the NAACP and Henry severed relations with COFO early in 1965, Henry remained active in voter registration work. In 1968 he headed the insurgent delegation from Mississippi that successfully unseated the regular state delegation at the August Democratic National Convention. [See JOHNSON Volume]

[CAB]

HESBURGH, THEODORE M(AR-TIN)

b. May 25, 1917; Syracuse, N.Y.
President, University of Notre Dame, June 1952- ; Member, United States Civil Rights Commission, November 1957-November 1972.

Ordained a Roman Catholic priest in 1943, Hesburgh taught theology at Notre Dame before becoming the school's president in 1952. He upgraded the academic reputation of the school, long famous for its football teams, and secularized its faculty and administration. An outspoken liberal, Hesburgh typified a new generation of Roman Catholic intellectuals who rejected the traditional conservatism once dominant in the Church hierarchy. Already active in national education circles, Hesburgh was appointed by President Dwight D. Eisenhower [q.v.] to the newly formed United States Commission on Civil Rights (CRC) in November 1957.

Father Hesburgh came into greater prominence in the 1960s as the movements to extend civil rights to blacks and other minorities and to further ecumenical cooperation between Catholics and other religious groups both gathered momentum. The CRC often recommended legislation more comprehensive than anything Congress or the President was willing to enact, and Hesburgh distinguished himself by making especially strong statements on civil rights issues. When the Commission issued a January 1961 report charging the "federal government [with] a heavy responsibility for. . .discrimination against. . .Negroes" and advising that federal aid be withheld from public colleges and universities that practice discrimination, Hesburgh and two other Commission members urged that the ban also be applied to private colleges.

Hesburgh also added his own statement to a November 1961 CRC report on the shortcomings of the criminal justice system's treatment of minority groups. Noting that the Commission had, perhaps, overemphasized discrimination in the South, he attacked Northern builders and real estate brokers who profited from blighted housing while ignoring the "moral dimension" of their work. Hesburgh scored the "hypocrisy" of the government's propaganda war with the Communists in the largely non-white underdeveloped world, while "democracy and civil liberties were not fully practiced in the U.S." He stated that America's failure to realize national ideals subverted its institutions and the nation's moral character more effectively than the efforts of the Communists themselves.

During the 1960s Hesburgh served on a great number of boards and committees, including those of the Rockefeller Foundation, the Carnegie Foundation for the Advancement of Teaching and the Association of American Colleges. In February 1969 Hesburgh announced a "get-tough" policy for dealing with possible campus disorders at Notre Dame, which earned the praise of President Richard Nixon [q.v.]. Named chairman of the CRC in March 1969, Hesburgh later came into conflict with the President over Nixon's policy of "benign neglect" in the civil rights field. Angered by Nixon's use of busing as a campaign issue, Hesburgh resigned his post in November 1972 following the President's reelection. [See JOHNSON, NIXON Volumes]

[JCH]

HICKENLOOPER, BOURKE B(LAKEMORE)

b. July 21, 1896; Blockton, Iowa.
d. Sept. 4, 1971; Shelter Island, N.Y.
Republican Senator, Iowa, 1945-69.
Chairman, Republican Policy Committee, 1962-69.

A former state legislator and governor of Iowa, Hickenlooper served in the Senate from 1945 until his retirement in 1969. While in the Senate Hickenlooper compiled what the *New York Times* described as a "moderately conservative" voting record. As representative of an agricultural state dependent on corn and hay prices, Hickenlooper favored high price supports on these commodities while opposing acreage restrictions on planting. The greatest legislative achievement of the first half of his Senate career came in 1954 when he cosponsored the Atomic Energy Act, which initiated the private development of nuclear power for peaceful use. [See TRUMAN, EISENHOWER Volumes]

Hickenlooper supported most of the civil rights legislation passed in the late 1950s and early 1960s. He reflected the conservative Protestant ethic of many of his constituents in his opposition to domestic welfare programs. He therefore voted against such Kennedy Administration measures as medicare and aid to education. Hickenlooper voted in agreement with the conservative Americans for Constitutional Action more than three-quarters of the time in the three years during which Kennedy was president.

In 1962 Hickenlooper successfully added a controversial amendment to the foreign aid bill of that year. His amendment provided that the U.S. automatically deny aid to a foreign country that expropriated the property of a U.S. citizen holding valid contracts unless the country took appropriate steps toward adequate compensation within six months. The application of the "Hickenlooper amendment" was generally opposed by Presidents Kennedy and Johnson, and it was invoked only once during the 1960s—against Ceylon in 1963.

During the mid and late 1960s Hickenlooper worked with Sen. J. William Fulbright (D, Ark.) [q.v.] to pass the heatedly debated consular treaty with the Soviet Union in 1967. Hickenlooper supported the Johnson Administration's policy in Vietnam and, as chairman of the Republican Policy Committee, was careful to stress that most Republicans backed the President. Hickenlooper retired in 1969 and died two years later. [See JOHNSON Volume]

[EWS]

HILL, HERBERT

b. Jan. 24, 1924; New York, N.Y.
Labor Secretary, NAACP, 1951- .

While preparing for a career in music, his father's profession, Hill was captivated by the dramatic labor organizing struggles in the late 1930s. He soon plunged into radical politics and dropped out of New York University to help organize a local of the steel workers union. In 1948 Hill—who is white—joined the staff of the NAACP and in 1951 was named the Association's labor secretary, in charge of coordinating work against discrimination by private employers and labor unions.

With the rise of the civil rights movement in the 1950s, minority group workers pressed for access to high-paying jobs in industries where a pattern of employer or union discrimination had prevailed. During the Kennedy years,

Hill used legal, political and economic tactics to open up employment opportunities for black and Puerto Rican workers. In 1961 President Kennedy issued an executive order barring discrimination by government contractors. Hill filed repeated claims with the newly created Equal Employment Opportunities Committee (EEOC) charging that large defense contractors were willfully violating the order. Assistant Labor Secretary Jerry R. Holleman met with Hill in April 1961 and pledged cancellation of contracts with any employer who refused to comply with the presidential order. Eight leading defense contractors, including Boeing, Douglas and General Electric, signed agreements with the EEOC in July 1961 guaranteeing racial equality in hiring and promotions. Eventually, 52 leading defense contractors pledged non-discrimination. The next year Hill attacked the corporate promises as producing "more publicity than progress."

Hill also increased NAACP pressure on organized labor. In 1959 Hill had sent a public memorandum to AFL-CIO President George Meany [q.v.] charging that the newly merged labor federation had failed to eliminate racial discrimination and segregation in several affiliated unions. Hill renewed his charges in the early 1960s, declaring that the "decade-long attempt to resolve these problems within the labor movement itself" had resulted in "negligible" progress. He cited the machinists, railway clerks, carpenters, electrical workers, operating engineers, plumbers and boilermakers among those unions that practiced "a broad pattern of racial discrimination and segregation" by excluding blacks, maintaining segregated locals, separate racial seniority lines and limiting opportunities in apprentice training for members of racial minorities. In August 1962 Hill charged before a congressional investigating committee that the traditionally liberal International Ladies Garment Workers Union discriminated against black and Puerto Rican workers in New York City. Hill began a campaign in October 1962 to convince the National Labor Relations Board to decertify those unions that rejected NAACP appeals to end discriminatory practices. He filed decertification petitions against the Seafarers International Union, the Brotherhood of Railway Trainmen and an Atlanta local of the United Steelworkers of America.

Hill's criticism and the decertification drive evoked an angry response from established labor leaders. In November 1962 George Meany, United Auto Workers President Walter Reuther [q.v.], and A. Philip Randolph [q.v.], the AFL-CIO's only Negro vice president, all attacked Hill and the NAACP's union decertification project as destructive of trade unionism. Meany announced Nov. 13 that the AFL-CIO wanted to work with the NAACP but "could not under the circumstances we are faced with by their labor secretary." Charles S. Zimmerman, an ILGWU vice president, resigned as a member of the NAACP's Legal Defense and Education Fund because of Hill's criticism of the garment workers leadership.

NAACP Executive Secretary Roy Wilkins [q.v.] backed Hill in his conflict with union leaders, refusing to allow deteriorating relations between the Negro protest group and the AFL-CIO to inhibit demands for more minority hiring, especially in the nearly all-white building and construction trades. Keeping step with a rising wave of black protest, Hill announced in May 1963 that the NAACP would launch mass actions against construction trade unions that excluded blacks from membership. Picket lines were set up at construction sites in New York, Cleveland and other northern cities during the spring and summer of 1963, halting work in many instances. The protests won a rapid government response. On June 4 President Kennedy ordered a review of all federal construction programs aimed at ending discriminatory hiring practices. Labor Secretary Willard Wirtz [q.v.] announced the same day that "contracts will be cancelled or they will not be let" wherever he encountered opposition to the President's program. In return, Hill announced the NAACP would suspend its picketing of federal construction projects. His most important local victory in the summer of 1963 came in Cleveland where a coalition of civil rights groups reached agreement with a city-wide plumbers union substantially increasing the number of minority members admitted to the union's apprentice program and hiring hall.

In the mid and late 1960s Hill continued to

lead a campaign of picketing and protest directed at the building trades, which he said had made "only token adjustments" to civil rights demands. [See JOHNSON Volume]

[NNL]

HILL, LISTER
b. Dec. 29, 1894; Montgomery, Ala.
Democratic Senator, Ala., 1938-69;
Chairman, Labor and Welfare Committee, 1955-69.

Hill, the son of a prominent surgeon, came from a wealthy family that dominated the politics of Montgomery, Ala. In 1923, after serving as president of the Montgomery Board of Education, he won a special election to fill a vacant seat in the House of Representatives. In the House Hill supported New Deal programs, and particularly the Tennessee Valley Authority, which played a crucial role in promoting the economic development of northern Alabama.

Hill ran for a vacant Senate seat in 1937 as an ally of President Roosevelt. At the time the New Deal was losing favor with many political leaders of the rural South, who opposed the Administration's federal wages-and-hours program. But with urban and labor support Hill defeated his right-wing opponent, who reflected the views of the Ku Klux Klan.

After World War II Hill's primary legislative interests were in the area of medical and mental health. His major legislative accomplishment was the Hill-Burton Act of 1946, which provided federal grants for hospital construction and which was extended and expanded in subsequent decades. Hill became chairman of the Senate Labor and Welfare Committee in 1955. In that post and as chairman of the Appropriations Committee's Subcommittee for Health and Welfare Agencies, he was able to substantially increase federal health expenditures. [See TRUMAN, EISENHOWER Volumes]

By the early 1960s Hill and fellow Alabama Sen. John J. Sparkman [q.v.] were among the few remaining Deep South politicians who backed domestic social welfare legislation. According to *Congressional Quarterly*, he backed bills supported by the Kennedy Administration on 78% of key Senate roll-call votes in 1961. During that year he voted for such Kennedy-endorsed measures as the area redevelopment, minimum wage, housing and school aid bills.

Hill faced strong opposition in his 1962 reelection bid from conservative Republican James D. Martin; he won by only 6,803 votes out of a total of 397,071 cast. From that year onward, apparently in response to this impressive challenge in an overwhelmingly Democratic state, Hill brought his voting record into closer conformity with the views of his rural and more conservative constituents. He continued to vote for social welfare programs that aided rural areas while opposing urban-oriented measures such as the mass transit and youth employment bills of 1963.

However, Hill did not abate his efforts on behalf of health legislation in the 1960s. In 1963 he was the floor manager of the medical training aid bill. Contending that the number of graduating physicians would have to increase 50% by 1975 to maintain the existing physician-population ratio, he asserted a "compelling need" for the bill and opposed efforts by the American Medical Association lobby to weaken it. During the same year he was the floor manager of a bill to provide grants to private and public mental health institutions. In floor debate Hill said that conditions for the mentally ill had "changed very little since the first public mental health hospital was opened. . .in 1773."

Hill consistently opposed measures aimed against racial discrimination. In March 1962 he criticized a bill to bar the arbitrary use of literacy tests in voter registration for federal elections, declaring that Congress had no authority to determine the qualifications of voters. During the same month he opposed a proposed constitutional amendment to eliminate the poll tax as a qualification for voting in federal elections and primaries and denied that the Alabama poll tax disqualified anyone from voting.

During the Johnson Administration Hill continued to promote health legislation and social welfare measures of benefit to rural regions while voting against civil rights measures and bills directed at urban problems. In January 1968, at the age of 73, Hill announced that he would not run for reelection. [See JOHNSON Volume]

[MLL]

HILSMAN, ROGER
b. Nov. 23, 1919; Waco, Tex.
Director, State Department Bureau of Intelligence and Research, February 1961-May 1963; Undersecretary of State for Political Affairs, May 1963-February 1964.

One of the architects of early Kennedy Administration policy on Vietnam, Roger Hilsman eventually left government service because of his opposition to the conduct of the war. Following service with the famed Merrill's Marauders and the Office of Strategic Services during the war, Hilsman entered Yale University where he earned a Ph.D. in international relations in 1951. During the Korean War he took part in planning for the North Atlantic Treaty Organization.

After teaching international politics at Princeton University from 1953 to 1956, Hilsman accepted an appointment as chief of the foreign affairs division of the Library of Congress's legislative reference service. President Kennedy appointed him director of the State Department's Bureau of Intelligence and Research in February 1961. This agency was responsible for making an immediate analysis of current foreign developments for the guidance of top policymakers and for conducting research for long-term planning. In the early 1960s Hilsman and his staff were primarily concerned with the development of American policy toward Laos, Indonesia, the Congo and Cuba.

During the Kennedy Administration Hilsman became increasingly involved in the growing war in Vietnam. In January 1962 when the Administration was attempting to formulate basic strategy in Vietnam, Hilsman presented a plan for conducting the war entitled "A Strategic Concept for South Vietnam." This proposal defined the struggle against the Communists as essentially a political rather than a military one and recommended that policies designed to win the allegiance of the rural population be the prime focus of any joint American-South Vietnamese effort. One important aspect of his plan was the use of strategic hamlets to provide villagers with security and to give the South Vietnamese government toeholds from which they could eventually extend their control throughout the countryside. He recommended that the South Vietnamese military adopt guerrilla tactics rather than employ conventional ground troops and bombing raids. The strategic hamlet program was begun in the spring of 1962, but it proved ineffective.

After returning from a December 1962 fact-finding mission to Vietnam with Michael Forrestal [q.v.], Hilsman reported doubts about the conduct of the war and the viability of President Ngo Dinh Diem's regime. In a joint report the two men concluded that the only people who supported Diem and his brother, Ngo Dinh Nhu, were Americans and Vietnamese leaders with close ties to the Diem family. They were skeptical about the optimistic assessment of the war offered by many high American officials and questioned the value of the strategic hamlet program as it was being carried out by Nhu. Hilsman and Forrestal foresaw a long and costly struggle and reported that Communist recruitment within the South was so successful that the war could be carried on without infiltration from the North. In July meetings with the President's chief advisers, Hilsman began discussing the ramifications of a possible coup.

Following the August 1963 attack by Nhu's secret police on Buddhist dissidents, Hilsman, in conjunction with George Ball [q.v.], Averell Harriman [q.v.] and Forrestal, drafted the "August 24 Cable" sent to Henry Cabot Lodge [q.v.], the new ambassador to Vietnam. The message stated that Diem must be "given [a] chance to rid himself of Nhu" but cautioned that "if Diem remains obdurate and refuses, then we must face the possibility that Diem himself cannot be preserved." Lodge was also instructed to privately inform senior Vietnamese generals contemplating a coup that if Nhu remained the U.S. would "give them direct support in any interim period of breakdown [of the] central government mechanism." The coup failed to take place immediately because of the generals' inability to achieve a favorable balance of forces in the Saigon area. However, a coup was carried out in November 1963.

In February 1964 Hilsman, out of favor with President Lyndon Johnson, [q.v.], Secretary of State Dean Rusk [q.v.] and the military because of his views and the aggressive way he presented them, resigned his State Department post. That fall he joined the department of public law and government at Columbia University. Three years later he published To Move a Nation, which described the process of foreign policy formulation under Kennedy and criticized the Johnson Administration's escalation of the Vietnam war into a general ground and air conflict.

[EWS]

For further information:
Roger Hilsman, To Move a Nation: The Politics of Foreign Policy in the Administration of John F. Kennedy (New York, 1967).

HITCH, CHARLES J(OHNSTON)
b. Jan. 9, 1910; Boonville, Mo.
Assistant Secretary of Defense, February 1961-August 1965.

During the 1960s Charles J. Hitch, an economist, revolutionized cost accounting procedures in the Pentagon. Hitch was raised in Boonville, a small town in central Missouri where his father was a teacher and administrator at Kemper Military School and College. Hitch studied at Kemper through the junior college level. In 1931 he graduated from the University of Arizona; he then did graduate work in economics at Harvard University and in 1933 went to Oxford as a Rhodes scholar. Hitch subsequently served as a tutor and fellow at Queen's College, Oxford.

During World War II Hitch was a staff economist for the Lend-Lease Administration, served on the War Production Board and in 1943 joined the Office of Strategic Services. In 1948 he became head of the economics division of the Rand Corporation, a non-profit organization that specialized in research for the Atomic Energy Commission, the Defense Department and later for the National Aeronautics and Space Administration.

In 1960 Hitch and Ronald N. McKean published The Economics of Defense in the Nuclear Age, a study of how budgetary reforms could reduce Defense Department costs. The book impressed Secretary of Defense Robert S. McNamara [q.v.], who invited Hitch to become assistant secretary of defense for budgetary affairs. Hitch joined the Department in February 1961 and within six months outlined a plan for the drastic restructuring of Pentagon budgets. Hitch argued that various budget requests, which traditionally had been submitted separately by the Army, Navy, Air Force and other services, should be grouped together into categories: missile systems, civil defense, research and development and so forth. This innovation would permit planners to eliminate waste and duplication between the various services. Hitch also proposed that all budget requests include five-year rather than the conventional one-year cost estimates to eliminate long-term cost overruns.

The Hitch scheme, known as the Planning-Programming-Budgeting System (PPBS), required centralized planning in the office of the Secretary of Defense and a reduction in the independence of the service secretaries. This was precisely the goal of Secretary McNamara, and he accepted PPBS enthusiastically. The system was first applied to the 1963 budget and then to subsequent Defense Department budgets. PPBS was credited with helping the Department to reduce costs substantially.

Hitch left the Pentagon in August 1965 to become vice president in charge of finance for the University of California. After the University's Board of Regents dismissed Clark Kerr [q.v.] in early 1967, Hitch was picked as his successor. He assumed his new post during a tumultuous period when conservative California Gov. Ronald Reagan and many state legislators were attacking the University for its high costs and its faculty and students for their participation in anti-war and other radical activity. Hitch was unable to prevent Reagan from making substantial cuts in the University budget and imposing student tuition. He was somewhat more successful in resisting the efforts of the Governor and some Regents to limit academic freedom and student civil liberties at the nine-campus university. [See JOHNSON Volume]

[JLW]

For further information:
"Charles J. Hitch," *Current Biography Yearbook*, 1970 (New York, 1971), pp. 184-187.

HODGES, LUTHER H(ARTWELL)
b. March 9, 1898; Pittsylvania County, Va.
d. Oct. 6, 1974; Chapel Hill, N.C.
Secretary of Commerce, January 1961-December 1964.

Born on a tenant farm in Virginia, Luther Hodges grew up in Leaksville, N. C. He worked his way through the University of North Carolina and was voted "best all-around man" for his wide participation in athletic and extracurricular activities. In 1919 Hodges became secretary to the general manager of Marshall Field & Company's eight textile mills in the Leaksville area. Hodges advanced steadily in the company, becoming general manager of all its textile mills in 1939. He retired in 1950 as a vice president.

Hodges's government career began in 1944 with his appointment to the Office of Price Administration, where he headed the textile division. Elected lieutenant governor of North Carolina in 1952, Hodges became governor in 1954 when Gov. William B. Umstead died. During his six-year tenure as governor Hodges won a national reputation for attracting industry to North Carolina. He worked energetically, publicizing such industrial advantages as tax incentives, lower wage scales and loans made available by his privately financed creation, the Business Development Corp. An oppo-

nent of integration, Hodges became known as a racial moderate because he produced an accommodation with the Supreme Court's 1954 desegregation decision that avoided violence. [See EISENHOWER Volume]

During the 1960 presidential campaign Hodges actively supported Sen. John F. Kennedy's candidacy. He played a key role in swinging the Carolinas to Kennedy, particularly by winning over Spencer Lover, head of the powerful Burlington Industries, to the Kennedy camp. With much of the business community apprehensive about his incoming Administration, Kennedy appointed the 63-year-old Hodges Secretary of Commerce in the hope that his business background and famed salesmanship would help to assuage business fears.

There was soon tension, however, between Hodges and leaders of big business who sat on the Business Advisory Council (BAC). Created as part of the Commerce Department in 1933, the BAC was composed of prominent businessmen and was intended to serve as a bridge between business and the federal government. Hodges induced the BAC in the spring of 1961 to find a new chairman because its current chairman, Ralph J. Cordiner [q.v.] of the General Electric Co., headed a firm at the center of a criminal price-fixing conspiracy. The BAC replaced Cordiner with Roger Blough [q.v.] of U.S. Steel but balked at Hodges's other suggestions that it be made more representative by including small businessmen in its membership and that its secret meetings be opened more often to the press. The BAC originally complied with Hodges's proposals but in July 1961 voted to break with the Commerce Department and change its name to the Business Council. President Kennedy accepted the change, however, and did not follow up Hodges's threat to form a new BAC.

Congress's decision in the spring of 1961 to place the newly created Area Redevelopment Administration (ARA) in the Commerce Department was a victory for Hodges. The ARA was authorized to spend $400 million in loans and grants in regions beset by chronic unemployment. The bill's chief sponsor, Sen. Paul Douglas (D, Ill.) [q.v.], fearing that the Commerce Department was business-dominated and hostile to his program, had long fought to have area redevelopment funds administered by an independent agency. He consented to Commerce Department jurisdiction at the urging of President Kennedy, who had been persuaded by Hodges. Hodges also convinced Congress in May to create the U.S. Travel Service in an effort to attract more foreign tourists.

Hodges was one of the less influential members of the Kennedy cabinet, serving more as an enthusiastic defender of Administration programs than as an architect of its policies. He joined the Administration's offensive against the steel price rise in April 1962, calling it "a disservice to the country and to the business community as a whole." The Secretary also testified before Congress in support of Kennedy's proposed $11 billion tax reduction in February 1963.

Hodges played a leading part in the passage of the Trade Expansion Act of 1962. The act authorized the President to cut tariffs on certain goods in order to stimulate foreign trade. Throughout his tenure at the Commerce Department, Hodges was an active promoter of increased exports. He created a new unit within the Department in October 1962 to help U.S. business compete in foreign markets and began a series of commercial trade fairs at which American businessmen could display their wares abroad and seek orders. During his term U.S. exports rose from under $20 billion a year to $25 billion. Hodges advocated more trade with the Soviet Union in non-strategic goods, "Sell them anything they can eat, drink, or smoke," was his slogan.

Hodges retired as Commerce Secretary in December 1964 and became chairman of Financial Consultants International, a mutual fund. He died of a heart attack in October 1974.

[TO]

For further information:
Carl Rieser, "Luther Hodges Wants to Be Friends," *Fortune* (August, 1961), pp. 106-109+.

HOFFA, JAMES R(IDDLE)

b. Feb. 14, 1913; Brazil, Ind.
d. presumed July, 1975.
President, International Brotherhood of Teamsters, Chauffeurs, Warehousemen and Helpers of America, 1957-67.

Hoffa's father, an itinerant coal driller, died when the boy was seven. In the seventh grade Hoffa quit school to help pay the family bills. He soon became a union organizer and at age 17 gained control of Teamster Local 299, the largest local in Detroit. In the mid-1950s Hoffa became president of the newly formed Central Conference of Teamsters, with 650,000 dues-paying members, and a vice president of the national union, then led by his ally David Beck. From early 1957 on, the union was the target of investigations by the Justice Department and the Senate Permanent Investigations Subcommittee chaired by Sen. John L. McClellan (D, Ark.) [q.v.]. The Subcommittee's hearings aired charges that underworld figures were deeply involved in union affairs at both the local and national level and that the leadership had misappropriated large amounts of union funds. Indicted for tax fraud and for other crimes, Beck quit his post, and Hoffa was elected president of the 1.3-million-member union in October 1957. [See EISENHOWER Volume]

The appointment of Robert F. Kennedy [q.v.], as the new Attorney General ensured that any legal infractions by Hoffa would be vigorously prosecuted under the new Administration because, as former counsel to the McClellan Committee, Kennedy developed a strong commitment to eliminating corruption in the Teamsters Union. Within a few days of Kennedy's confirmation, a special team of young attorneys was established in the Justice Department to probe the activities of alleged labor racketeers. Before President John F. Kennedy took office, Hoffa's activities were again spotlighted by the Senate subcommittee. The latest allegations, stated by Chairman McClellan as the hearings reopened on Jan. 10, 1961, charged that New York Teamsters Local 239 was secretly dominated—"with knowledge and consent" of Hoffa—by an alleged mobster and ex-Teamster official named Antonio (Tony Ducks) Corallo. Witnesses also testified that Hoffa had refused to investigate charges that some $200,000 had been misappropriated from the treasury of Philadelphia Teamsters Local 107. Officials from both locals refused to testify on the charges, asserting their Fifth Amendment privilege. But Hoffa, testifying for the 15th and 16th times before the McClellan panel, defended both locals and his own refusal to bar convicted felons from holding office in the union. A report based on the hearings, issued July 25, 1962, accused Hoffa of "defiant indifference to the interests of the rank-and-file members of Local 239, whose treasury was being exploited and misused by corrupt and dishonest officials." Hoffa denounced the report as "a lie."

Despite temporary victories Hoffa's legal plight increased during the early 1960s. An indictment for mail fraud accusing Hoffa of misusing union funds to finance a Florida land development scheme (Sun Valley, Inc.) was dismissed July 13, 1961 on the ground that the grand jury that issued the indictment had not been properly impaneled. However, a federal grand jury reindicted Hoffa and an associate on Oct. 11, adding new charges of telephone and telegraph fraud. The charges were eventually dismissed by U.S. Judge Joseph P. Lieb on Jan. 4, 1963.

On Oct. 22, 1962 Hoffa went on trial in Nashville, Tenn., on charges of accepting over $1 million from a trucking firm in violation of the Taft-Hartley Act. Judge William E. Miller declared a mistrial Dec. 23 and ordered a special grand jury investigation of what he described as three "illegal and improper attempts" by "close labor union associates of the defendant" to tamper with the jury. The investigation resulted in an indictment May 9, 1963, accusing Hoffa and six associates of conspiring and attempting to bribe jurors to vote for an acquittal. (The indictment was the 60th indictment on information filed against Teamster officials and employees since the Kennedy Administration took office.)

On Nov. 12, 1963 the Supreme Court refused to consider Hoffa's requests for a dismissal of the indictment because of the alleged exclusion of minorities and unionists from the grand jury or for removal of the trial to another venue because of adverse publicity about him in the Nashville area. Another federal grand jury indicted Hoffa and seven associates in Chicago June 4, 1963 on charges of fraudulently obtaining $20 million in loans from a Teamsters pension fund and diverting $1 million of it for their own benefit. Hoffa was accused of using at least $100,000 from the fund to rid himself of financial involvement in the Sun Valley project.

Hoffa was convicted on the jury-tampering and the fraud charges in March 1964. After the Supreme Court rejected his appeal, Hoffa began serving an eight-year sentence on the jury-tampering charge in 1967. He was convicted in July 1964 on the pension fraud charges by a Chicago jury and sentenced to five years in prison.

The legal difficulties of Hoffa and David Beck were primarily responsible for the Teamsters' expulsion, on unethical practices charges, from the AFL-CIO in 1957. Hoffa's attempt to win readmission to the Federation was rejected by a decisive 24-3 vote by the organization's executive council Oct. 10, 1961. A resolution barring reentry was passed unanimously by the AFL-CIO convention in December 1961.

Despite Hoffa's problems with the government and the rest of organized labor, his leadership of the Teamsters Union was marked by a successful drive toward centralization and membership growth. During his presidency the union remained the largest in the nation, growing by over half-a-million members to a total of almost two million in the late 1960s. Hoffa also limited the power of the regional vice presidents, curbed wildcat strikes and standardized contracts. He was reelected by an overwhelming margin to his second five-year term as president at the union's July 1961 convention. The same convention passed a new constitution that strengthened Hoffa's control over local unions, increased his salary by 50% and provided for the payment of his mounting legal expenses. Hoffa defeated several local union insurgencies in the early 1960s and secured his greatest personal triumph when he negotiated in January 1964 the trucking industry's first national contract.

After Hoffa entered Lewisburg Federal Penitentiary in March 1967, Teamsters General Vice President Frank E. Fitzsimmons completed Hoffa's presidential term and in 1971 was elected Teamsters Union president in his own right. President Richard M. Nixon [q.v.] commuted Hoffa's sentence on December 1971 under conditions that barred Hoffa from union activity until 1980. Hoffa disappeared in July 1975, at a time when he was regrouping his forces for an attempt to regain control of the union. It was widely believed that he had been murdered. [See JOHNSON, NIXON Volumes]

[EWK]

For further information:
Ralph and Estelle James, *Hoffa and the Teamsters* (New York, 1965).
Walter Sheridan, *The Fall and Rise of Jimmy Hoffa*, (New York, 1972).

HOLIFIELD, CHET (CHESTER) (EARL)
b. Dec. 3, 1903; Mayfield, Ky.
Democratic Representative, Calif., 1943-75; Chairman, Joint Committee on Atomic Energy, 1961-63, 1965-67, 1969-71.

Holifield was first elected to the House of Representatives in 1942. For his entire tenure in Congress he represented California's 19th district, a predominantly blue-collar area in Los Angeles County with a large Mexican-American community. Holifield was a member of the House liberal faction that organized the Democratic Study Group in the late 1950s. He served as its chairman in 1960. [See EISENHOWER Volume]

Holifield generally backed the proposals of President John F. Kennedy on the House floor. According to *Congressional Quarterly*, he voted against Administration positions on only 5%, 2% and 4% of key House roll-call votes in 1961, 1962 and 1963, respectively.

During the 1960s Holifield rotated the chairmanship of the Joint Committee on Atomic Energy with Sen. John O. Pastore (D, R.I.) [q.v.], the senior senator on the panel. As a ranking member of the Joint Committee, Holifield was, in the early 1960s, one of the leading congressional supporters of the Administration's multi-billion-dollar fallout shelter program. Congress's failure to adopt the plan led him to declare in July 1962, "If we do nothing and stand unprepared, the very life of the nation is at stake."

In his Committee Holifield was a strong supporter of public power. In 1961 and 1962 he backed an Administration plan to permit the Atomic Energy Commission to add electric generating facilities to its new plutonium production reactor in Hanford, Wash. Conservatives blocked the proposal in the House in 1961, but the measure was passed the following year.

After 1965 Holifield came under increasing attack from former liberal allies for, among other things, his strong support of the Vietnam war and of Pentagon appropriation requests. In 1971 he became chairman of the House Government Operations Committee. In 1974 Holifield announced that he would not seek reelection. [See JOHNSON, NIXON Volumes]

[MLL]

HOLLAND, SPESSARD L(INDSEY)
b. July 10, 1892; Bartow, Fla.
d. Nov. 6, 1971; Bartow, Fla.
Democratic Senator, Fla. 1946-70.

Spessard L. Holland, a veteran of World War I, earned a law degree at the University of Florida in 1916 and that year began practicing law in his hometown of Bartow, Fla. He subsequently served as Polk County prosecutor, county judge and, from 1932 to 1940, as state senator. As governor of Florida from 1941 to 1945, he earned a reputation for his financial acumen, turning a state fiscal deficit into a surplus by the end of his term.

Holland was appointed to the U.S. Senate in September 1946 to fill an unexpired term; two months later Holland won election on his own. Over the next 24 years he had little difficulty winning reelection despite a reputation as "the most monotonous orator in the Senate." According to the *New York Times,* "he never changed the inflection of his voice. . .[and] droned on in a manner that would send some of his fellow senators from the floor during filibusters against civil rights legislation during the 1950s." During the 1960s Holland served on the Aeronautical and Space Sciences, Agriculture and Appropriations Committees. But despite his seniority he never attained the chairmanship of a major committee.

Holland considered himself a "moderate liberal" although his voting record was distinctly conservative. He opposed the Kennedy Administration's major social welfare policies, voting against school aid, minimum wage and medicare legislation. He did support the 1963 nuclear test ban treaty and the Administration's communications satellite corporation bill. The Americans for Democratic Action, a liberal group, gave Holland a zero rating in 1961.

Holland was solicitous of the interests of Florida's citrus and vegetable farmers and opposed efforts by Sen. Eugene J. McCarthy (D, Minn.) [*q.v.*] and other Senate liberals to compel those farmers to pay their Mexican and West Indian laborers 90% of the state or national average farm wage.

Although Holland opposed most civil rights legislation, he differed from many of his Southern colleagues on the question of the poll tax. Beginning in 1949 and in every subsequent congressional session, Holland introduced a constitutional amendment to outlaw the poll tax—a device used by many Southern states to prevent poor blacks from voting. Because of the solid opposition of Southern senators, Holland's bill was not reported out of the Senate Judiciary Committee until 1962. That year the anti-poll tax amendment won the support of the Kennedy Administration and passed both houses of Congress despite the opposition of both Southern conservatives and certain

pro-civil rights liberals. The NAACP and other groups argued that the Holland amendment "would provide an immutable precedent for shunting all further civil rights legislation to the amendment procedure." By February 1964 three-quarters of the states had ratified the anti-poll tax measure and it became the 24th Amendment to the Constitution. The fear of civil rights groups that Congress had committed itself to the cumbersome amendment process to rectify other abuses in the area of civil and voting rights proved unfounded. Congress passed the Civil Rights Act in 1964 and the Voting Rights Act a year later. Holland opposed both measures.

During the Johnson years Holland opposed much of the Administration's domestic legilsation while supporting its Vietnam war policy. Holland retired from the Senate in 1970 and died a year later in his hometown. [See JOHNSON Volume]

[JLW]

HOLLINGS, ERNEST F(REDERICK)
b. Jan. 1, 1922; Charleston, S.C.
Governor, S. C., 1959-63.

Ernest Hollings grew up in the port city of Charleston, S.C. After his graduation from the Citadel in 1942, he served in the U.S. Army during World War II and then received a degree from the University of South Carolina Law School in 1947. Hollings was elected Democratic state assembly man in 1948, lieutenant governor in 1954 and governor four years later. Under South Carolina law a governor was not allowed to succeed himself.

In what was then regarded as a politically dangerous move, Hollings supported the presidential candidacy of Sen. John F. Kennedy in 1960. Kennedy carried South Carolina by only 10,000 votes in the general election.

During his four-year term Hollings earned a reputation as a consistent but moderate opponent of civil rights. Many observers credited Hollings with reducing racial strife in South Carolina during a period of increased tensions in most other

Southern states. Although Hollings filibustered against a liberal civil rights resolution at the July 1962 Governors Conference, the next year he declared in his farewell address before the South Carolina General Assembly that the state was "running out of courts" in its fight against desegregation of schools and that when all the legal battles were over there had to be "progress with dignity" in South Carolina. Hollings's statement stood in marked contrast to that of Alabama Gov. George Wallace [q.v.], who in an inaugural speech nine days later pledged "segregation now, segregation tomorrow and segregation forever."

During his governorship Hollings undertook a massive industrialization program for South Carolina to raise the standard of living in an economically depressed state where workers earned only about three-quarters of the national average income. Hollings believed that with his program for investment in new industries "the money would trickle right down to the humblest man in the state."

In 1962 Hollings lost the Democratic senatorial primary election to incumbent Sen. Olin D. Johnston (D, S.C.) [q.v.]. After leaving office in 1963 Hollings became a state legislator and subsequently practiced law for several years before winning a 1966 special election to the U.S. Senate in which he captured 98% of the black vote. During the two years preceding his reelection in 1968, Hollings compiled one of the most conservative voting records of any Southern senator. [See JOHNSON, NIXON Volumes]

[FHM]

HOOVER, J(OHN) EDGAR

b. Jan. 1, 1895; Washington, D.C.
d. May 2, 1972; Washington, D.C.
Director, Federal Bureau of Investigation, 1924-72.

J. Edgar Hoover served as director of the FBI under every president from Coolidge to Nixon. During the Kennedy years Hoover clashed frequently with his superior, Attorney General Robert F. Kennedy [q.v.], who attempted to bring the Bureau under his control. Hoover, nonetheless, maintained his autonomy and continued to dominate the FBI as he had for more than a generation.

Hoover was raised in Washington, D.C., where his father worked for the Coast and Geodetic Survey. In 1913 he graduated from Central High School as class valedictorian. He then went to work as an indexer for the Library of Congress while studying law at night at George Washington University. After receiving his law degree in 1916, he joined the Justice Department as a clerk. Hoover distinguished himself by his enthusiasm, thoroughness and willingness to work overtime. In 1919 he was named special assistant to Attorney General A. Mitchell Palmer, who was then engaged in rounding up thousands of alleged Communists and revolutionaries for possible deportation under the provisions of the Wartime Sedition Act. As head of the newly created General Intelligence Division of the Justice Department's Bureau of Investigation, Hoover was successful in his efforts to deport well-known anarchists Emma Goldman and Alexander Berkman, as well as Ludwig Martens, the unofficial representative of the new Soviet government.

In 1921 Hoover was appointed assistant director of the Bureau of Investigation (the name was changed to the Federal Bureau of Investigation in 1935), and three years later he was named director. He assumed the directorship at a time when the Bureau had been demoralized by revelations linking it to the scandals of the Harding Administration. Hoover improved morale and recruited an honest and well-disciplined staff. During the 1920s the Bureau's authority was limited to investigating crimes against the federal government; its agents lacked even the authority to make arrests and carry arms. In May 1932 Congress passed legislation empowering the Bureau to investigate bank robberies, kidnapings that were unsolved after seven days and extortion cases which involved use of the telephone. Bureau agents were also authorized to carry guns and make arrests.

During the 1930s J. Edgar Hoover became a national hero as the press recorded the exploits of the Bureau agents, or "G-men," who arrested "Baby Face" Nelson, John Dillinger, "Pretty Boy" Floyd and other "public enemies." Hoover meanwhile was building the FBI into a major resource and educational center for local police agencies. He established a massive fingerprint file (1925), a major crime laboratory (1932) and a police academy (1935) for the training of local law enforcement officials. In 1939 President Roosevelt further increased the authority of the FBI, giving it the power to investigate espionage and sabotage.

After World War II the FBI became increasingly involved in investigating alleged Communist subversion within the U.S. Information gathered by FBI agents played an important part in the prosecution of Julius and Ethel Rosenberg and Alger Hiss. In the popular mind the suppression of Communism had become the FBI's preeminent responsibility by the end of the 1950s. [See TRUMAN, EISENHOWER Volumes]

In the Kennedy years Hoover, as head of a 13,000-man agency, was a formidable political figure. He was virtually immune from criticism on Capitol Hill and maintained close relations with House Speaker John McCormack (D, Mass.) [q.v.] and Rep. John J. Rooney (D, N.Y.) [q.v.], chairman of the House appropriations subcommittee responsible for approving Justice Department budgets. Throughout the entire postwar period Hoover's budget requests were never cut by Congress.

Hoover's position within the FBI was so secure that President-elect John F. Kennedy approved his reappointment even before naming his brother Robert, Attorney General. Relations between Robert Kennedy and Hoover were at first cordial. Hoover for many years had been a friend of Kennedy's father, Joseph P. Kennedy [q.v.]. However, as Robert Kennedy attempted to exert his authority over the FBI—an agency which absorbed more than 40% of the Justice Department's budget—his differences with Hoover became evident. Hoover, who had been accustomed to speaking directly with presidents, was now forced to communicate through the Attorney General's office. He also resented the rule stipulating that FBI press releases be cleared through the Justice Department Information Office.

One of the major areas of contention between Kennedy and Hoover concerned organized crime. The Attorney General wished to make a concerted effort to suppress crime syndicates, but Hoover remained skeptical of their very existence. "No single individual or coalition of racketeers," he said, "dominates organized crime across the nation." Hoover opposed Kennedy's suggestion that the Internal Revenue Service be used to investigate taxpayers who possibly might be associated with organized crime. He also thwarted Kennedy's bid to establish a group within the Justice Department, but outside the jurisdiction of the Bureau, to investigate organized crime. Hoover eventually agreed to establish a special division within the Bureau to work exclusively on organized crime investigations.

Hoover was unsympathetic to the civil rights movement. At a cabinet meeting in 1956, he suggested that the U.S. Supreme Court's 1954 school desegregation decision had been unfair to the South, and he frequently asserted that Communists were attempting to infiltrate the NAACP. When Robert Kennedy announced in 1961 that all branches of the Justice Department should hire more blacks and other minorities, Hoover was reluctant to comply, arguing that the hiring of minorities would force the Bureau to lower its standards. The FBI did begin to hire more blacks and Puerto Ricans in the 1960s, but few held the prestigious rank of "agent."

As the tempo of the civil rights movement rose in the South, the FBI made little effort to protect civil rights workers even when they were in great danger. In 1961, during an attempt to integrate a bus depot in Montgomery, Ala., FBI agents took notes as they watched a mob knock unconscious a special assistant to Robert Kennedy. The agents made no effort to interfere with Alabama state police, who barred three blacks from registering to vote in 1963. Hoover explained that the FBI was an investigative unit, not a national police force, and that peace-keeping was a matter for the local police. In general, members of the Justice Department, including Burke Marshall [q.v.], head of the civil rights division, accepted this argument. Only after the slaying of three civil rights workers in Meridian, Miss., in the summer of 1964 did the FBI begin to make its presence felt in civil rights cases.

One of the most controversial aspects of FBI investigative work concerned its wiretapping of telephones and use of secret electronic listening devices to record private conversations. In 1961 and 1962 Attorney General Kennedy asked Congress to grant him the power to authorize wiretapping without a court order in cases involving national security. The proposed legislation, which had Hoover's support, failed to win approval on Capitol Hill. Nevertheless, according to a 1976 report of the Senate Select Committee on Intelligence Activities, the Kennedy Administration—without explicit legislative or judicial approval—ordered the FBI to wiretap a congressional staff member, three Agriculture Department officials, a lobbyist and a Washington law firm. In October 1963 the FBI began tapping Martin Luther King's [q.v.] phone lines; the taps remained in effect until April 1965. Robert Kennedy authorized these actions.

According to Sanford J. Ungar, a student of the Bureau, Hoover personally detested Dr. King, whom he considered a dangerous demagogue and associate of known Communists. He used information acquired from the tap to attempt to discredit King as a civil rights leader. In November 1964, shortly before King was to receive the Nobel Peace Prize, the FBI sent the black leader a note implying that he ought to commit suicide. In an effort to break up King's marriage, the Bureau also sent to King's wife tape-recorded evidence of her husband's alleged infidelity.

In 1956 the FBI began a program that entailed deliberate efforts to disrupt alleged subversive organizations by creating dissension within them. This Counter Intelligence Program, known as COINTELPRO, was first directed against the Communist Party.

In October 1961 Hoover also ordered agents to begin a "disruptive program" against the Socialist Workers Party (SWP), a small Trotskyist organization. The FBI frequently attempted to embarrass SWP members, publicizing the prison record of an SWP candidate for the New York City Council and fabricating evidence that certain SWP leaders had stolen money earmarked for a civil rights defense fund.

At 1:45 P.M. Nov. 22, 1963, Hoover called Robert Kennedy at his home in Virginia. According to William Manchester's *Death of a President,* Hoover declared, "I have news for you, the President has been shot." Following the President's death the FBI conducted an investigation of the assassination and in December 1963 issued a five-volume report that concluded that a single gunman, Lee Harvey Oswald [q.v.], acting without accomplices, had murdered the President. The Warren Commission subsequently upheld this finding but criticized the Bureau for having failed to inform the Secret Service that the FBI file on Oswald suggested that he might be a potential assassin. It was later revealed that Oswald had sent a note to the FBI threatening to blow up the Dallas police station if FBI agents did not cease questioning his wife about his Cuban and Soviet contacts. The FBI had withheld the note from the Warren Commission and destroyed it. There was some speculation concerning the possibility that Hoover had personally ordered the note destroyed to protect the Bureau's reputation.

Following the assassination Robert Kennedy's relations with Hoover deteriorated rapidly. Indeed, the two men never spoke again. Hoover, thereafter, maintained direct contact with President Johnson.

During the late 1960s the FBI under Hoover directed its disruptive COINTELPRO campaign against the Ku Klux Klan, black power groups and anti-war organizations. It continued a campaign of harassment against Dr. King, and at the request of President Johnson it conducted "name checks" on his critics. In May 1964 Johnson waived mandatory retirement for Hoover. President Nixon did likewise in 1971. [See JOHNSON Volume]

In the Nixon years Administration officials argued that the FBI was not sufficiently aggressive in its campaign against anti-war student organizations, and it consequently encouraged the Central Intelligence Agency to infilitrate and disrupt these groups. Hoover's reputation declined in the years immediately before and after his death as a consequence of revelations of widespread illegal activities carried out by the Bureau. He died May 2, 1972. [See NIXON Volume]

[JLW]

For further information:
Jerry J. Berman and Morton H. Halperin, eds., *The Abuses of The Intelligence Agencies* (Washington, 1975).
Victor S. Navasky, *Kennedy Justice* (New York, 1971).
Sanford Ungar, *FBI* (Boston, 1975)
U.S. Senate, Select Committee on Intelligence Activities, *Report* (Washington, 1976).

HRUSKA, ROMAN L(EE)
b. Aug. 16, 1904; David City, Neb.
Republican Senator, Neb., 1954- .

A former county official and U.S. representative, Hruska resigned his House seat in 1954 to fill a Senate vacancy created by the death of Hugh Butler. In Congress Hruska opposed such domestic social welfare programs as medicare and school aid and earned a national reputation as an opponent of most new social programs. Coming from an agricultural state with an economy dependent on cattle raising and feed grain production, Hruska voted consistently for price supports and measures to limit meat imports. The Senator voted against foreign economic aid proposals but favored military aid to nations fighting alleged Communist aggression. Hruska was one of the Senate's most consistent supporters of the conservative coalition of Republicans and Southern Democrats and voted with them over 84% of the time on key roll call votes during the Kennedy Administration.

In 1961 Hruska was a member of the Judiciary Antitrust and Monopoly Subcommittee that investigated pricing in the drug industry. A strong supporter of business, Hruska criticized the subcommittee's final report, which termed prescription drug prices "unreasonable" in relation to production costs and attributed high prices to control of the market by a few giants. The Senator claimed that competition did exist and that brand name prescriptions gave corporations the profits needed for research.

During the last half of the decade, Hruska emerged as one of the chief opponents of gun control in the Senate. He was a consistent supporter of the Johnson Administration's policy in Vietnam but opposed extending the Indochina war into Laos. In 1970 the Senator gained national attention during hearings on the nomination of Federal District Judge G. Harrold Carswell to the Supreme Court when he remarked that mediocre people deserved representation on the high court. [See JOHNSON, NIXON Volumes]

[EWS]

HUGHES, H(ENRY) STUART
b. May 7, 1916 New York, N.Y.
Historian, peace activist.

The grandson of Chief Justice Charles Evans Hughes, H. Stuart Hughes graduated from Amherst in 1936 and took his Ph.D. in European history from Harvard in 1940. During World War II Hughes directed the Research and Analysis Branch of the Office of Strategic Services for the Mediterranean and Germany. After the war he headed the State Department's Division of Research for Europe. Hughes left governmental service in 1948 to return to university teaching, serving as assistant professor at Harvard until 1952, associate professor and department chairman at Stanford between 1952 and 1957, and full professor at Harvard beginning in 1957. An authority on Italy and European intellectual history, Hughes's writings included *Oswald Spengler* (1952), *The United States and Italy*

(1953), and *Consciousness and Society* (1958).

Freely labeling himself a socialist, Hughes was a national sponsor of the Committee for a Sane Nuclear Policy (SANE) and frequently criticized the Kennedy Administration's foreign policy. Following the April 1961 Bay of Pigs invasion, Hughes wrote a letter to Kennedy, signed by 70 prominent academicians, calling for the normalization of relations with Cuba and the reversal of "the present shift towards American military intervention." In a collection of essays published a year later, Hughes decried tensions between the U.S. and the Soviet Union. "We have more in common with the Russians than either side realizes," Hughes wrote, "[an] interest in stopping the drift towards the thermonuclear warfare before its too late."

Hughes ran for the U.S. Senate in Massachusetts in 1962 as the candidate of the state's Political Action for Peace Committee. His regular party opposition proved formidable: the Democrats nominated Edward M. Kennedy [*q.v.*], brother of the President, and the Republicans chose George C. Lodge, son of former Senator and United Nations Ambassador Henry Cabot Lodge [*q.v.*]. Despite the odds, Hughes conducted a vigorous campaign, assailing the Administration's resumption of nuclear tests and its October naval quarantine of Cuba. Hughes also supported a 32-hour workweek to reduce unemployment. Many political observers watched the contest as a test of the size of the "peace vote." The Harvard faculty divided between Lodge and Hughes, with scant support for the President's youngest brother. In the November election Kennedy overwhelmed Lodge. Hughes came in a distant third, pulling only 2.3% of the vote.

Hughes persisted in his call for an easing of East-West tensions and later opposed large-scale military intervention in Vietnam. Chosen Gurney Professor of History and Political Science at Harvard in 1969, Hughes resigned from the faculty in 1975 in a dispute concerning the denial of tenure to his wife. He became professor of history at the University at San Diego later that year.

[JLB]

For further information:
H. Stuart Hughes, *An Approach to Peace* (New York, 1962).

HUGHES, HOWARD R(OBARD)
b. Dec. 24, 1905; Houston, Tex.
d. April 5, 1976; Aboard an Acapulco-Houston flight.
Industrialist.

The son of a multi-millionaire developer of oil-well drilling equipment, Howard Hughes briefly attended Rice Institute in Houston and the California Institute of Technology before assuming control of the Hughes Tool Co. upon his father's death. With an income estimated at $2 million per year, Hughes turned to filmmaking in the late 1920s and early 1930s and produced a series of Hollywood movies including *Scarface* and *The Front Page*.

In 1935 Hughes founded the Hughes Aircraft Co. and subsequently established a reputation as an aviator. Two years later his interest in the infant aircraft industry led him to purchase Trans World Airlines (TWA), which he developed into the first intercontinental air carrier. In 1948 Hughes purchased RKO Pictures, winning public attention in the late 1940s with his assertions of Communist influence in the postwar movie industry. In 1952 he assumed an hermitic, mysterious and rumor-filled existence, traveling in several U.S. states and foreign countries. [See TRUMAN, EISENHOWER Volumes]

During the late 1950s TWA, by then increasingly uncompetitive in the new field of commercial jet aircraft, began to lose large amounts of money—$4 million in the first quarter of 1959 alone—and Hughes was forced to turn to several prominent lending institutions for financial aid. While he still owned 78% of TWA stock and theoretically should have been in direct control of the airline, rigid contractual arrangements had in fact passed operation of the company from Hughes to the lending institutions and an independent-minded board of directors by 1961.

Seeking to further neutralize what they considered Hughes's authoritarian and incompetent management, the board of directors of TWA filed a civil antitrust suit in U.S. District Court in New York against Hughes himself and the Hughes Tool Co. on June 30, 1961. TWA alleged that Hughes and Raymond M. Holliday, director of Hughes Tool Co., had conspired since 1939 to seize control of the airline "for their own purposes" and had restrained trade by forcing TWA to buy aircraft equipment only from Hughes Tool. The suit also charged that the Atlas Corp., a company in which Hughes owned 11% of the stock and which in turn controlled 56% of Northeast Airlines, had conspired to force a merger between that struggling trunk line and TWA on terms advantageous to the defendants. The proposed merger, according to TWA, would have increased TWA's requirement for aircraft, which could only have been met by increased purchases of aircraft equipment owned by or contracted for by Hughes Tool Co.

On Feb. 13, 1962 Hughes and Hughes Tool Co. filed a $366-million countersuit against TWA, two TWA executives and four financial institutions, charging that the lending institutions had illegally gained control of TWA. The suit also sought a return of TWA control to Hughes. The twin suits touched off an intricate 11-year legal battle. On Sept. 21, 1968 Hughes was ordered to pay TWA $137.6 million in damages, but that ruling was overturned by the U.S. Supreme Court on Jan. 10, 1973. The Court's ruling hinged on the narrow, ancillary judgment that Hughes's financial dealings had at all times been approved by the Civil Aeronautics Board (CAB); therefore, the Court ruled, TWA could not collect on previous antitrust judgments in its favor.

The clandestine nature of so many of Hughes's business dealings became public in the late 1960s and 1970s. In 1956 Hughes had loaned Richard Nixon's [q.v.] brother Donald $250.000. The Nixon connection with Hughes had been a minor issue in the 1960 presidential campaign, but the importance of the Hughes loan was not made fully clear until 1973 when the *Washington Post* revealed that from the early days of the Nixon Administration, the Secret Service had wiretapped Donald Nixon's telephone and kept him under physical surveillance to guard the Administration against embarrassment over Donald Nixon's continuing financial involvement with Hughes.

After a group of stockholders won a lawsuit charging that Hughes had illegally used TWA to finance other investments, Hughes abruptly and without public explanation sold his TWA stock in May 1966 for $546.5 million in the second-largest stock transaction in U.S. history. During the late 1960s Hughes turned his business attention toward purchasing $250 million worth of property in Nevada.

Following years of poor health Hughes died on board a chartered jet in transit from Acapulco, Mexico to Houston in April 1976. At his death he was estimated to be worth $1.5 billion. [See NIXON Volume]

[FHM]

For further information:
Albert B. Gerber, *Bashful Billionaire* (New York, 1967).

HUGHES, RICHARD J(OSEPH)
b. Aug. 10, 1909; Florence, N.J.
Governor, N.J., 1962-70.

The son of a New Jersey Democratic politician, Hughes received his law degree in 1931 and began working for the Democratic Party in strongly Republican Mercer County. Defeated in a 1938 congressional election, he was appointed assistant U.S. attorney for New Jersey in 1939. Hughes became Mercer County Court judge in 1948 and a member of the appellate division of New Jersey's Superior Court in 1957. Financial and family responsibilities forced him to resign and resume his law practice in the same year. His clients included some of the nation's largest drug corporations and the Association of New Jersey Railroads.

Although relatively unknown to New Jersey's voters, Hughes's years of Party service enabled him to secure the gubernatorial endorsement of state Democratic leaders in February 1961. In the general election Hughes campaigned against former Secretary of Labor James P. Mitchell on a platform of increased civil defense facilities, aid to education and urban and suburban development. Hughes's campaign was aided by appearances by such national figures as former President Harry S Truman [q.v.], Secretary of Labor Arthur Goldberg [q.v.] and President Kennedy. Large turnouts in Democratic strongholds helped make Hughes the state's first Roman Catholic governor.

The most controversial issue during Hughes's governorship was New Jersey's attempt to integrate its public schools. This effort focused largely on the suburban community of Englewood. On Feb. 1, 1962 the local board of education refused to admit nine black children to a predominantly white elementary school. An all night sit-in was held at city hall, and on Feb. 5 Paul Zuber filed suit in a U.S. district court seeking to bar Englewood from maintaining a "racially segregated" elementary school. On Feb. 6 Hughes charged that the Englewood protest could lead to "violence" and at a Democratic fund raising dinner urged legislators to join him in enacting state civil rights laws to end bias in education and housing. Zuber's suit was dismissed on July 9 on the ground that all available state remedies had not been sought. When school reopened in September black students boycotted the segregated Lincoln elementary school. On Sept. 6 Hughes urged the board to present a plan for "reasonable desegregation" and said he was certain the courts would eventually require the city to desegregate. The NAACP filed a petition with the state commissioner of education on Sept. 8 accusing the Englewood board of education of maintaining a separate school without equal educational opportunities for black children. In February Zuber began a five-month boycott, and in June Hughes convened a statewide conference on racial problems. On July 2 the state commissioner of education ordered the Englewood Board of Education to adopt an integration plan. The same day

Hughes threatened to cut off aid to Englewood and other school districts that failed to comply with the commissioner's instructions.

Hughes suffered a temporary political setback in the November 1963 election when voters turned down his proposal for a $750 million bond issue to finance the construction of highways and educational facilities. But in November 1965 he was reelected with a plurality unprecedented in the state's history. [See JOHNSON Volume]

[DKR]

HUMPHREY, GEORGE M(AGOFFIN)
b. March 8, 1890; Cheboygan, Mich.
d. Jan. 20, 1970; Cleveland, Ohio.
Industrialist.

George Humphrey, Secretary of the Treasury during the Eisenhower Administration, grew up in central Michigan. He graduated from high school in 1908 and earned a law degree from the University of Michigan four years later. Humphrey was admitted to the Michigan bar in 1912 and practiced law in his father's Saginaw law firm before joining M.A. Hanna and Company, coal and iron shippers, as general counsel in 1918. Humphrey was named president of the Company in 1929. He subsequently became a major leader in the coal, iron and steel industry and a prominent spokesman for business interests.

In 1953 President Dwight D. Eisenhower named Humphrey to the post of Secretary of the Treasury, where the industrialist earned a reputation as a fiscal conservative who advocated the restoration of "sound money" policies and a balanced budget. He left the Treasury post in 1957 to return to honorary chairmanship of the Hanna Company and its subsidiaries. [See EISENHOWER Volume]

In 1962 the Kennedy Administration began an investigation of the national stockpile, which was composed of essential goods accumulated to meet estimated needs in the event of war. In January 1962 the President stated that the total stockpile amounted to $7.7 billion worth of materials—more than twice what was estimated for emergency requirements.

In March 1962, at Kennedy's request, the Senate Armed Services National Stockpile and Naval Petroleum Resources Subcommittee, chaired by Sen. Stuart Symington (D, Mo.) [q.v.], began hearings into the intricate financial transactions related to the stockpile. The Subcommittee focused on contracts between the government and M.A. Hanna Co. signed in 1953, at the height of the Korean War. The transaction resulted in enormous profits for the Hanna Company and its nickel ore mining and smelting subsidiaries. The contracts were signed four days before President Eisenhower's inauguration at a time when George Humphrey was Eisenhower's designated Secretary of the Treasury and still serving as a top Hanna executive.

During the hearings Eisenhower came to the defense of his beleaguered former Treasury Secretary, declaring, "If Secretary Humphrey ever did a dishonest thing in his life, I'm ready to mount the cross and you can put the nails and spear in me." However, a supervising accountant from the General Accounting Office (GAO) testified that the Hanna contracts between 1954 and 1961 had earned, before taxes, profits of 457% and that Hanna had sold nickel ore to the U.S. government at a profit rate of 57.4% of sales, or $15 million. It was later revealed that between January 1953 and April 1961, Humphrey's Hanna stock had increased by nearly $6 million in market value.

In 1963 the Symington subcommittee published a draft report charging that there was costly waste and mismanagement in the stockpile program and hinted that high officials in the Eisenhower Administration had acted improperly in aiding stockpile suppliers. The report also stated that some suppliers had earned "excessive and unconscionable profits," especially during the Korean War. The report cited the nickel industry in general and the M.A. Hanna Company and its subsidiaries in particular.

Humphrey stated in 1962 that the Symington hearings were politically motivated by the Kennedy Administration and a year later denounced the subcommittee report as "a warmed-over version of the unfounded and biased insinuations and charges . . . for the purpose of creating political propaganda."

On Oct. 31, 1963 Symington introduced a bill to revise existing stockpiling legislation and to provide for reduction of excess stockpile materials. In 1966 Congress enacted 23 separate Johnson Administration bills authorizing disposal of materials from the national stockpile. The bills allowed the orderly transfer to industries of materials not needed for long-range national emergencies, but which might be necessary to meet shortages brought on by the expanding war in Vietnam.

Humphrey continued as M.A. Hanna's honorary chairman of the board until his death in January 1970.

[FHM]

For further information:
Herbert S. Parmet, *Eisenhower and the American Crusades* (New York, 1972).

HUMPHREY, HUBERT H(ORATIO)
b. May 27, 1911; Wallace, S. D.
Democratic Senator, Minn., 1949-65;
Senate Majority Whip, 1961-65.

Hubert Humphrey was Congress's most outspoken champion of the welfare state. For many he was the premier symbol of postwar American liberalism, a senator who combined persistent advocacy of domestic social reform with unwavering anti-Communism. As Senate majority whip during the Kennedy Administration, Humphrey placed his crusading zeal behind passage of the Administration's program.

The son of a South Dakota druggist, Humphrey was profoundly influenced by his father's reverence for William Jennings Bryan and Woodrow Wilson. He was a star debater and class valedictorian in high school, but he had to leave the University of Minnesota early in the Depression to work in his father's drugstore. He became a registered pharmacist and managed the store while his father participated actively in South Dakota Democratic Party politics.

Humphrey returned to the University of Minnesota in 1937, earning his B.A. in 1939 and an M.A. in political science from Louisiana State University a year later. His master's thesis, entitled, "The Political Philosophy of the New Deal," was a glowing tribute to Franklin D. Roosevelt's response to the Depression.

Humphrey abandoned his teaching career to plunge into Minnesota politics. He played a key role in the 1944 merger of the Farmer-Labor and Democratic Parties and won election as mayor of Minneapolis the next year. As mayor he waged an anti-vice war, created the first municipal fair employment practices commission in the United States, expanded the city's housing program and took an active part in settling strikes. Reelected in 1947 Humphrey helped to organize the liberal, anti-Communist Americans for Democratic Action (ADA) and fought a successful battle to purge the Communist faction from the Democratic-Farmer-Labor party. He gained national attention at the 1948 Democratic National Convention with a stirring oration in favor of a strong civil rights plank, one of the most memorable convention speeches of modern times. In November Minnesota voters elected Humphrey to the Senate over a conservative Republican incumbent.

Humphrey quickly moved into the vanguard of the Senate's liberal minority, promoting a wide variety of social welfare, civil rights, tax reform and pro-labor legislation. The first bill he introduced was a proposal to establish medical care for the aged financed through the Social Security system, finally enacted as medicare in 1965. In his early career powerful Senate conservatives were alienated by Humphrey's aggressive debating style and effusive liberalism, and their hostility reduced his effectiveness.

In the 1950s he eased his way into the Senate "establishment," toning down his fervid ideological approach and working closely with Democratic leader Sen. Lyndon Johnson (D, Tex.) [q.v.], who used Humphrey as his liaison with liberals and intellectuals. Humphrey, moreover, outdid some conservatives on anti-Communist issues. For example, he introduced the Communist Control Act of 1954 which virtually outlawed the Communist Party. In foreign affairs he softened his anti-Communism with Wilsonian idealism. He became a leading advocate of disarmament and distribution of surplus food to needy nations. [See TRUMAN, EISENHOWER Volumes]

Humphrey began his first run for the presidency on Dec. 30, 1959. He was the first candidate to declare in the 1960 campaign. Only he and Sen. John F. Kennedy campaigned actively in the 18 months prior to the nominating convention in July. The West Virginia primary in May was the crucial test. The state's depressed economic condition and Kennedy's Catholicism were important issues, but the campaign soon slipped into bitter personal attacks. Humphrey highlighted Kennedy's wealth and contrasted it with his own campaign's impoverished condition, while Kennedy partisans, particularly Franklin D. Roosevelt, Jr. [q.v.], accused Humphrey of being a draft-dodger during World War II. (Humphrey had been deferred because of a double hernia and color blindness.) Kennedy won a smashing victory with 60.8% of the vote compared to Humphrey's 39.2%. Humphrey supported Kennedy after the latter's nomination in June and was himself reelected to his third Senate term in November.

Humphrey reached the peak of his influence in the Senate during the Kennedy Administration. With his selection as assistant majority leader, or majority whip, he channeled his kinetic legislative energy in support of the Administration's program. It was the majority whip's task to round up votes for the Administration's measures, and Humphrey plunged into the job with characteristic exuberance, becoming a more effective advocate for the Kennedy program, in the eyes of many senators, than Majority Leader Sen. Mike Mansfield (D, Mont.) [q.v.], who was as reserved as Humphrey was extroverted. Humphrey also served on the Foreign Relations, Appropriations, Government Operations and Small Business Committees.

Humphrey's new position in the Senate

hierarchy enabled him to win passage of proposals he had been advocating for years. He had proposed the Peace Corps and the Food for Peace programs during the Eisenhower years and saw them enacted in 1961. He was also a moving force behind the creation of the Arms Control and Disarmament Agency in that year. Humphrey's crowning achievement was the passage of the nuclear test ban treaty, a measure that he struggled to keep alive during the late 1950s, sold to President Kennedy and pushed through the Senate in September 1963.

In the domestic area Humphrey was a pivotal figure in the enactment of much of the Administration's anti-recession and social welfare measures. He was floor manager for the 1961 minimum wage and aid-to-education bills and arranged a compromise to ensure passage of Sen. Paul Douglas's (D, Ill.) [q.v.] area redevelopment bill. In 1962 he strongly backed the investment tax credit, the centerpiece of the Administration's tax bill, but lost the fight for medicare in July. In the spring and summer of 1962 Humphrey was one of the leading voices urging Kennedy to propose a substantial tax cut.

The compromises that came with Humphrey's leadership position earned him the criticism of some liberal allies and praise from unaccustomed sources. *Business Week*, in June 1963, approved of Humphrey's new pragmatic style in an article entitled, "Firebrand Senator Cools Down." The article praised his August 1962 efforts to win passage of the Communications Satellite Act, which set up a private corporation to own and operate a satellite communications system. A group of liberal senators had conducted a filibuster against the measure, calling it a "giveaway" to the American Telephone and Telegraph Co. and urging public ownership of the system. Humphrey told *Business Week*, "I now think it's better for me to sit inside, at the seat of power, instead of waving banners outside."

In the aftermath of President Kennedy's assassination, Humphrey helped smooth the transition to the Johnson Administration by advising the new President and serving again as his link to suspicious liberals and intellectuals within the Democratic Party. In his last year as majority whip, he worked tirelessly to win passage of the Kennedy-Johnson $11-billion tax cut and was floor manager of the historic Civil Rights Act of 1964, the climax of Humphrey's long advocacy of the cause of equal rights. He diligently cultivated Senate Minority Leader Everett Dirksen (R, Ill.) [q.v.] and worked out a compromise with the Republican leader that broke the 57-day Southern filibuster on June 10.

Chosen by Johnson as his vice presidential running mate in August 1964 and elected in November, Humphrey was an enthusiastic defender of Johnson's domestic and foreign policies throughout the next four years. His unwavering support for Johnson's Vietnam policy cost him the support of many anti-war Democrats in his 1968 presidential campaign. Humphrey lost the election to Republican Richard M. Nixon [q.v.] by a narrow margin. He returned to the Senate in 1971. [See JOHNSON, NIXON Volumes]

[TO]

For further information:
Albert Eisele, *Almost to the Presidency: A Biography of Two American Politicians* (Blue Earth, Minn., 1972).
Winthrop Griffith, *Humphrey: A Candid Biography* (New York, 1965).
Robert Sherrill and Harry Ernst, *The Drugstore Liberal* (New York, 1968).

HUNT, H(AROLDSON) L(AFAYETTE)
b. Feb. 17, 1889; Vandalia, Ill.
d. Nov. 29, 1974; Dallas, Tex.
Industrialist.

At the time of his death H.L. Hunt had an estimated fortune of $3 billion and was the nation's wealthiest man. Hunt grew up on a small farm in Illinois and received only a fifth grade education. He struck it rich in 1930 by acquiring East Texas land holdings that proved to contain what were then the world's largest known oil deposits. Hunt founded the Dallas-based Hunt Oil Company in 1936 and saw it develop into the nation's largest independent producer of oil and natural gas, giving him an estimated income in the late 1960s of $1 million a week.

A charming, somewhat reclusive eccentric who lived frugally and carried his lunch to work in a brown paper bag, Hunt became well-known in the 1950s and 1960s as one of the nation's most powerful supporters of ultraconservative causes. In 1951 he founded "Facts Forum," a nonprofit educational foundation originally intended to teach conservation and practical farming. It later turned into a platform for Hunt's zealous crusade against Communism and liberalism. Hunt's message was disseminated by radio and television as well as through the mass distribution of books that vigorously supported the politics of Sen. Joseph McCarthy (R, Wisc.) while violently attacking such organizations as the United Nations. Facts Forum ended in 1956 but was revived again in 1958 under a new name, "Life Line." The organization subsequently lost its tax-exempt status when the Internal Revenue Service decided it was "devoted to political commentary."

Despite his own conservative views Hunt made an effort to maintain cordial relations with many prominent liberal politicians. He supported Lyndon Johnson's [q.v.] 1960 presidential candidacy because Johnson advocated the continuation of the tax-saving oil depletion allowance. Following John F. Kennedy's nomination in July, Hunt reluctantly supported the Democratic ticket, but after the 1961 Bay of Pigs fiasco Hunt declared that it was just as well the invasion failed because it was "just one Communist government trying to overthrow another." According to an October 1963 article by Washington Post columnist Marquis Childs, President Kennedy was extremely upset that some of the country's richest men, including Hunt, used their wealth to spread right-wing propaganda while paying little or no income tax.

Hunt supported Sen. Barry Goldwater's (R, Ariz.) [q.v.] presidential candidacy in 1964. He continued to subsidize Life Line throughout the 1960s and early 1970s, and also directed a group called The Youth Freedom Speakers, which enrolled up to 20,000 young people, mainly in the Southwest, to take Hunt's message of "God, Country, Christianity, and Freedom" to civic groups and schools.

By 1967 Hunt's newspaper column, Hunt for Truth, was carried by an estimated 80 newspapers and his radio program by over 500 stations with an audience of some five million. Hunt died in November 1974, and his immense wealth in oil and real estate was distributed among his six children.

[FHM]

For further information:
"H. L. Hunt," Current Biography Yearbook, 1970 (New York, 1971), pp. 191-194.

HUNTLEY, CHESTER R(OBERT)
b. Dec. 10, 1911; Cardwell, Mont.
d. March 20, 1974; Bozeman, Mont.
NBC News correspondent, 1956-70.

The son of a railroad telegrapher, Chet Huntley grew up on a Montana ranch near the Canadian border. After a brief stint as a premedical student at the University of Montana, Huntley transferred to the University of Washington and graduated from there in 1934. While still a student Huntley became program director of Seattle radio station KPCB and subsequently took a succession of jobs with radio stations in the Northwest before joining the Columbia Broadcasting System's (CBS) Los Angeles affiliate in 1939.

Huntley joined the National Broadcasting Company in 1955 and first teamed with fellow broadcast journalist David Brinkley [q.v.] during the 1956 political conventions. The team proved so successful that they replaced John Cameron Swayze in October 1956 with their own early-evening news program, later called the Huntley-Brinkley Report, with Huntley in New York and Brinkley in Washington. According to the program's creator Reuven Frank, the format of the show was carefully designed during the late 1950s and throughout the 1960s to create a "balance of tension" between Huntley and Brinkley, casting Brinkley as the "anti-establishment maverick" and Huntley as the conservative "defender of the status quo," even though both men shared the same liberal philosophy. Edward Jay Epstein later noted that both newscasters developed such a tight organizational image that instead of their personal views bearing upon the presentation of the news exactly the reverse happened.

In September 1963 the three major television networks expanded their evening news format from 15 minutes to half an hour to reflect the growing audience for news, estimated at nearly 50 million people. To inaugurate the programs President Kennedy granted interviews to the three networks. Kennedy believed that his edited interview with CBS reporter Walter Cronkite [q.v.] had distorted his opinion of South Vietnamese President Ngo Dinh Diem and had given the impression that he did not trust that leader. Consequently, the President insisted that he give final approval to the edited version to be televized on the Huntley-Brinkley program. Kennedy told the reporters that he had no intention of reducing U.S. aid to Vietnam and that he supported the "domino theory." The President maintained that if South Vietnam succumbed it "would give the impression that the wave of the future in Southeast Asia was China and the Communists."

The great popularity of the Huntley-Brinkley news team was emphasized during the 1964 political conventions when rival CBS replaced its veteran correspondent Walter Cronkite with an anchor team of Roger Mudd and Robert Trout. General hostility toward newsmen was evident during the Republican National Convention where press movement was heavily restricted and many Goldwater supporters wore buttons that read "Stamp Out Huntley-Brinkley."

In March 1967 Huntley was the only network newsman who refused to honor picket lines set up by the American Federation of Television and Radio Artists (AFTRA), who were then striking over higher wages and announcer staffing at FM radio stations. Huntley stated that AFTRA was not qualified as a bargaining agent or representative of network news broadcasters. His colleague, David Brinkley, honored the striking announcers' picket lines.

Although Huntley had been frequently mentioned as a candidate for the U.S. Senate from Montana, he announced in February 1970 that he would retire from NBC to become chairman of a firm planning to develop a large recreation area in Montana. The project, called Big Sky, subsequently caused controversy with environmentalists who felt that the facility would destroy the natural beauty of the area.

Shortly before his retirement from NBC, Huntley said in a widely publicized interview for the July 17, 1970 issue of *Life* magazine that he had observed President Richard M. Nixon "under many circumstances" and "the shallowness of the man overwhelms me; the fact that he is President frightens me." Later Huntley apologized to Nixon in a letter and denied the remarks attributed to him.

Huntley died of cancer on March 20, 1974, while preparing to dedicate the Big Sky recreational complex.

[FHM]

For further information:
Erik Barnouw, *Tube of Plenty* (New York, 1975).
Edward Jay Epstein, *News from Nowhere* (New York, 1973).

HUTCHESON, MAURICE A(LBERT)
b. May 7, 1897; Saginaw County, Mich.
President, United Brotherhood of Carpenters and Joiners of America, 1952-72.

Hutcheson's father, William L. Hutcheson, was president of the United Brotherhood of Carpenters and Joiners of America (UBC) from 1913 to 1952. Maurice Hutcheson became a carpenter's apprentice in 1914 and worked as a journeyman carpenter from 1918 until 1928 when he was appointed a UBC auditor. In 1938 he was elected first vice president of the UBC, a position he held until 1952 when he became president of the union upon his father's death.

In 1953 Hutcheson, a lifelong Republican, became an AFL vice president and a member of the executive council, a position he retained after the AFL-CIO merger in 1955. Hutcheson was convicted of contempt of Congress in 1958 when he refused to answer questions before the Select Senate Committee on Improper Activities in the Field of Labor-Management Relations. Already under indictment for allegedly bribing an Indiana state official to obtain information on proposed highway routes, he pleaded the Fifth Amendment when the Committee asked if he had used union funds to attempt to fix the bribery case. No disciplinary action was taken by the union, and AFL-CIO President George Meany [q.v.] and other labor leaders urged a reduced sentence, which the court granted in February 1964. Hutcheson was convicted in the higway case in 1960 and sentenced to 2-to-14 years imprisonment. This verdict was overturned in October 1963 when the Indiana Supreme Court ruled that the conviction had been based on insufficient evidence. [See EISENHOWER Volume]

Hutcheson and other union leaders resisted efforts by civil rights groups and the U.S. Labor Department to eliminate racial discrimination in the construction trades. In July 1963 the Labor Department's Bureau of Apprenticeship and Training issued new rules for federally sponsored apprenticeship programs that denied aid to programs found to discriminate. The Labor Department also issued an appeal to program directors to intensify efforts to obtain minority group applicants. When labor and management groups in the construction industry objected to the new rules, Labor Secretary W. Willard Wirtz [q.v.] agreed to a compromise plan. The plan required that craft unions review their apprenticeship programs to ensure that an applicant's qualifications were the "sole standard" used in selection of candidates and that notice of apprentice openings be listed publicly. Hutcheson was appointed to a panel established by the labor and management Construction Industry Joint Conference to administer the compromise plan.

Hutcheson was pardoned by President Lyndon B. Johnson [q.v.] in 1964 for his contempt of Congress conviction. He retired as UBC president in 1972.

[MDB]

HUTCHINS, ROBERT M(AYNARD)
b. Jan. 17, 1899; New York, N.Y.
President, Center for the Study of Democratic Institutions, 1959-74, 1975- .

Hutchins was the son of a Presbyterian minister. He entered Oberlin College at 16, served in World War I and received his A.B. and LL.B. degrees from Yale. At the age of 29 Hutchins was appointed dean of Yale Law School, and at 30 he was named president of the University of Chicago. At Chicago in the 1930s Hutchins undertook drastic reforms that angered many faculty and alumni. He abolished intercollegiate football, pioneered the "Great Books" program, introduced college-level study for high school sophomores and revamped the graduate school. All his efforts were directed to moving the University away from overspecialization and activities that Hutchins considered irrelevant to the University's true purpose. Hutchins believed that a liberal arts program with a core of required courses was a student's best preparation for an active and intelligent role in society.

A member of the America First Committee before Pearl Harbor, Hutchins later supported the Allied war effort and the creation of the United Nations. While chancellor at Chicago from 1945 to 1951, he became an outspoken defender of academic freedom and an opponent of loyalty oaths for university professors. In 1951 Hutchins joined the Ford Foundation as associate director and in 1954 became president of the Foundation's Fund for the Republic. After the Fund became independent Hutchins helped establish the Center for the Study of Democratic Institutions in 1959 at Santa Barbara, Calif., and was named its first president. [See TRUMAN, EISENHOWER Volumes]

Hutchins's establishment of the Center grew out of his disappointment with the university as a critical institution in American life. In opposition to Clark Kerr's [q.v.] "service station" concept of the "multiversity," the Center brought together distinguished scholars to examine "the major institutions of the 20th century in the light of their impact on the possibilities for the continued existence of democracy." In the early 1960s the Center discussed six areas of concern in its Basic Issues Program: corporations, labor unions, religious institutions, defense, mass media and the political process. The Center was not concerned with conventional research, which it left to the universities, but with "objective and disinterested thought" on issues it considered of fundamental concern for the survival of democracy. It frequently involved practicing politicians in its activities, distributed thousands of topical pamphlets reporting Center discussions and published a journal, *The Center.*

Under the Center's auspices in the early 1960s, Michael Harrington [*q.v.*], author of *The Other America*, led discussions on the future of organized labor. Adolf Berle, Jr. [*q.v.*], and Andrew Hacker took up the question of the shift in corporate power from owners to managers, and Adlai Stevenson [*q.v.*] and Justice William O. Douglas [*q.v.*] considered the "American character." Hutchins himself was particularly concerned with the "two faces of federalism," the problem of whether social progress could best be advanced through decentralization or through expanded social welfare programs at the federal level. Others who participated in Center discussions at the time included Eric Goldman, Clark Kerr, Henry R. Luce [*q.v.*], Paul Jacobs and Reinhold Niebuhr [*q.v.*].

Hutchins found it difficult to raise money after the termination of the initial $15 million grant from the Ford Foundation in 1962. In addition, the Center faced constant criticism for its liberalism and elitism. Extreme right-wingers called the Center "the little Moscow on the hill," while some critics on the left characterized it as an "intellectual Disneyland."

In 1962 Hutchins became the Center's board chairman, while he continued to serve as president. He became a life senior fellow in 1974 but returned as president in 1975.

[JCH]

For further information:
Robert M. Hutchins, *Higher Learning in America* (New Haven, 1961).

JACKSON, HENRY M(ARTIN)
b. May 31, 1912; Everett, Wash.
Democratic Senator, Wash., 1953- ;
Chairman, Interior and Insular Affairs Committee, 1963- .

The son of Norwegian immigrants, Jackson received a law degree from the University of Washington in 1935 and three years later was elected prosecuting attorney of Snohomish County, Wash. In 1940 he was elected to the U.S. House of Representatives where he compiled a liberal record, voting for social welfare measures, against the creation of the House Un-American Activities Committee and in support of President Harry S. Truman's veto of the Internal Security Act in 1950.

Working against the Republican landslide of 1952, Jackson won a seat in the U.S. Senate. As a member of the upper house, he continued to support liberal domestic legislation, but his major interest turned to foreign policy and military matters. While Jackson rejected Sen. Joseph R. McCarthy's (R, Wisc.) contention that domestic Communist subversion represented a major threat, he became best known for his vociferous insistence, as a member of the Armed Services Committee, upon the maintenance of American military superiority over the Soviet Union. In 1959 he was appointed, at his own request, to chair the newly created Government Operations Committee's National Policy Machinery Subcommittee, which conducted a two-year investigation of the government's Cold War policy. As a result of this investigation, Jackson became intimately acquainted with the inner workings of the Defense and State Departments. Some political observers attributed the intensity of Jackson's interest in military affairs and support of large defense expenditures to the presence of major defense industries in his state, the Boeing aircraft company being the most prominent. [See EISENHOWER Volume]

At the 1960 Democratic national convention Sen. John. F. Kennedy gave consideration to Jackson as a possible vice presidential running mate. However, Jackson was passed over partly because he had only been able to deliver 14½ of his state's 27 convention votes to Kennedy. Instead, he was asked to run the presidential campaign as chairman of the Democratic National Committee. He accepted the post but found that Robert F. Kennedy [q.v.] was the real director of the Kennedy election effort and so resigned the chairmanship before John Kennedy's inauguration. During the Kennedy Administration relations between the Senator and President remained cool and, despite his familiarity with military and foreign policy, Jackson was rarely consulted on these matters.

During the early 1960s Jackson expressed reservations about some of the Kennedy Administration's efforts to improve relations with the Soviet Union and control the arms race. In 1961 he joined conservatives in a nearly successful effort to prevent the creation of the Arms Control and Disarmament Agency. In March 1962 Jackson won widespread publicity as the result of a speech at the National Press Club in which he criticized what he considered to be "the undue influence of U.N. considerations in our national decision making." He argued that American military power, not the United Nations, was the foundation of world peace. The following year Jackson expressed reservations about the nuclear test ban treaty with the Soviet Union. He ultimately backed the agreement but interpreted it as a loose commitment that could be unilaterally abrogated.

Jackson also clashed with the Administration over the Pentagon's November 1962 decision to award General Dynamics rather than Boeing the contract to build the swing-wing TFX fighter/bomber plane. When Jackson, a member of the Government Operations Subcommittee on Investigations, called for an examination of the matter, Secretary of Defense Robert S. McNamara [q.v.] suggested to Government Operations Committee chairman John J. McClellan (D, Ark.) [q.v.] that Jackson was acting merely to assuage his constituents, especially those connected with Boeing. During the subcommittee investigation from February to November 1963, most members, including Jackson, were critical of the Pentagon decision.

During the Johnson years Jackson was a firm supporter of the Vietnam war. In 1968 he declined President-elect Richard M. Nixon's offer to appoint him Secretary of Defense. Jackson backed the Nixon Administration's Southeast Asia policies and voted for construction of the Safeguard antiballistic missile system (ABM) in 1969 and the supersonic jet transport (SST), a Boeing project, in 1970. He also identified himself with support of Israel and of the rights of Soviet Jews. In 1972 Jackson entered the race for the Democratic presidential nomination but was eliminated after the first few primaries. Four years later he again unsuccessfully sought the nomination. [See JOHNSON, NIXON Volumes]

[MLL]

For further information:
Peter J. Ognibene, *Scoop: The Life and Politics of Henry M. Jackson* (New York, 1975).

JACOBS, JANE (BUTZNER)
b. May 4, 1916; Scranton, Pa.
Author.

With the publication in 1961 of *The Death and Life of Great American Cities*, Jane Jacobs established herself as a leading critic of city planning, public housing and urban renewal programs. The former Jane Butzner was the daughter of a Scranton physician. After graduating from high school she worked as a reporter for *The Scranton Tribune*. "I was so damn glad to get out of school," she said later, "I couldn't even think of going to college." At 18 she left Scranton for New York City, where she worked as a secretary, helped manufacture candy and began writing freelance magazine articles about working class neighborhoods. In 1944 she married Robert H. Jacobs, Jr., an architect. Jacobs later credited her husband with giving her the education necessary to become a successful writer on architecture. From 1952 to 1962 she served as an associate editor of *The Architectural Forum*.

In 1947 the Jacobs family moved to Hudson Street in the western part of New York's Greenwich Village. The style of life in this diverse and lively neighborhood of factory lofts, small shops, brownstones and walk-up apartments had a profound influence on Jacobs's ideas. Indeed, *The Death and Life of Great American Cities* was a defense of old neighborhoods like the West Village and the North End in Boston and an attack on urban renewal projects, which had been planned to replace them.

Jacobs argued that traditional city planners, in their desire to impose order, cleanliness and quiet, were destroying the city. One of the central aims of planners was to separate residential from industrial and commercial land use. Jacobs argued that a mixture of homes, shops and businesses was necessary to generate the kind of activity that made for a safe and interesting neighborhood. Streets aswarm with children, tradesmen and peddlers might appear chaotic to planners, but they were far safer than the clean, empty superblocks that could be found in urban renewal areas. High-rise housing projects might have light and airy apartments, but they were so immense that they destroyed the social relationships that made a neighborhood a good place to live. "Low-income projects," she noted, "become worse centers of delinquency, vandalism and general hopelessness than the slums they were supposed to replace."

Jacobs applied her ideas in a practical political fashion. As chairman of the Committee to Save the West Village, she forced New York City to abandon its plan to redevelop a 14-block area in her neighborhood. She also helped block construction of the planned Lower Manhattan Expressway, which she believed would destroy many decent neighborhoods.

Jacobs's ideas were controversial. Civic leaders and planners argued that she had romanticized life in older neighborhoods plagued by run-down housing from which tenants were desperate to escape. High-rise projects, her critics argued, were the only practical means of housing the thousands who needed new and better living quarters.

Despite such criticism Jacobs's ideas began to have extensive influence by the late 1960s. Planners conceded that massive high-rise housing projects often contributed to social disorders; new urban renewal projects were planned to include smaller buildings more compatible with the social needs of the tenants. Further, there was an increased interest in the need for "mixed uses" in the making of viable neighborhoods.

In 1969 Jacobs published *The Economy of Cities*, which attempted to construct a theoretical foundation for her ideas. Citing many examples from ancient Anatolia to modern New York City, she argued that economic development had always originated in urban areas. Continued progress was dependent on the development of new kinds of work usually generated by small enterprises. To remain vital, she wrote, cities must maintain this type of business and the seeming inefficiency it produced. Jacobs contended, however, that American city officials were destroying diversity in their desire for efficiency and were producing a stagnation that would ultimately affect the country as a whole.

By the end of the decade Jacobs had left her home in Greenwich Village and moved to Toronto, a city that she believed "hasn't destroyed itself."

[JLW]

For further information:
Jane Jacobs, *The Death and Life of Great American Cities* (New York, 1961).
——, *The Economy of Cities* (New York, 1969).

JAVITS, JACOB K(OPPEL)
b. May 18, 1904; New York, N.Y.
Republican Senator, N.Y., 1957- .

The son of a tenement janitor and Tammany Hall ward heeler on New York City's Lower East Side, Javits held part-time jobs while studying law at New York University. After he was admitted to the bar in 1927, his older brother and he established a law firm specializing in bankruptcy and corporate reorganization. During World War II he served in the Chemical Warfare Service in Washington, D.C.

A supporter of Fiorello La Guardia, Javits joined the Republican Party during the 1930s. In 1945 he was the chief of research for a Republican mayoral candidate in New York City. The following year he received his party's nomination in an Upper West Side congressional district. Running on a liberal platform, he was the first Republican to carry the district since 1920. In the House of Representatives Javits generally voted against the Republican majority on major bills. He opposed the successful effort to override President Truman's veto of the Taft-Hartley Act in 1947, favored anti-poll tax bills in 1947 and 1949 and voted against appropriations for the House Un-American Activities Committee in 1948.

Javits defeated Democrat Franklin D. Roosevelt, Jr. [q.v.], in a race for New York State attorney general in 1954. Two years later, with the backing of such liberally inclined New York business executives as David Rockefeller [q.v.], Thomas Watson [q.v.] and John Hay Whitney, he won the Republican senatorial nomination and defeated New York City Mayor Robert F. Wagner, Jr. [q.v.], by almost a half-million votes. In the Senate Javits continued to function as a Republican maverick, supporting progressive social legislation. [See EISENHOWER Volume]

Javits consistently won a large share of New York City's vote because of his liberal positions and Jewish religious affiliation, while his party label enabled him to carry easily the traditionally Republican regions upstate. One of the most successful vote-getters in New York State's history, he won his 1962 reelection bid by almost a million votes over James B. Donovan [q.v.] and accomplished the rare Republican feat of carrying New York City.

But in the Senate Javits's liberalism and his combative style barred him from entering the ranks of the chamber's Republican leadership. Finding himself isolated within the small liberal faction of the minority party, the energetic Javits attempted to compensate for his lack of power by serving on as many committees as possible and by informing himself about and speaking on a broad range of issues.

In his 1960 book *Discrimination-U.S.A.*, Javits wrote that "racial segregation or discrimination is inconsistent with freedom," and during the early 1960s he uniformly supported civil rights measures. He backed an effort to ease the Senate rule for ending filibusters in 1961, supported a bill barring the discriminatory use of literacy tests in federal elections the following year and praised the civil rights bill proposed by President Kennedy in June 1963. During each of those years he also offered civil rights riders aimed at prohibiting the use of federal funds by segregated institutions and facilities.

Javits offered an amendment in 1961 to expand the number of workers covered by minimum wage legislation. In 1962 he co-sponsored with Sen. Clinton P. Anderson (D, N.M.) [q.v.] an Administration-backed Social Security medicare bill. The next year Javits was the only Republican on the Banking and Currency Committee who supported a mass transit aid bill and was one of six Republicans who voted for the measure on the Senate floor.

A strong supporter of Israel, Javits in 1963 introduced with Sen. Kenneth B. Keating (R, N.Y.) [q.v.] a foreign aid amendment prohibiting assistance to any country engaging in or preparing for military aggression against the United States or any U.S. aid recipient. The amendment was aimed primarily at the United Arab Republic.

Although Javits was best known as a supporter of liberal legislation, he regarded himself as one who steered a middle course between a Republican right that favored laissez-faire policies and a Democratic left that supported ever-increasing government control of the economy. He contended that the Republican Party should support a mixed economy in which business and government would cooperate to further the national welfare.

Javits's position on the Administration's 1962 communications satellite bill illustrated his views. The bill provided for private ownership of the satellite system and public controls over the corporation. A small group of Senate liberals favored public ownership and filibustered against the measure, while conservatives were against the controls. Javits supported the bill and voted to end the filibuster. In his 1964 *Order of Battle* he cited the bill as promoting the kind of partnership between government and private enterprise that he favored.

Javits also attempted to advance cooperation between government and business by linking foreign aid with private investment. In 1961 he proposed an amendment requiring the President, whenever feasible, to administer foreign aid through private channels. The following year he introduced a foreign aid amendment to raise from $10 million to $25 million the maximum private loan to other countries that could be guaranteed by the U.S. government. In 1963 he offered an amendment to establish an advisory committee on private enterprise in foreign aid.

A supporter of Gov. Nelson A. Rockefeller's [q.v.] 1964 presidential bid, Javits declined to endorse the candidacy of conservative Republican Sen. Barry M. Goldwater (R, Ariz.) [q.v.]. In the mid-1960s he was, despite his religion, considered a possible vice presidential running mate of Gov. George Romney [q.v.] for 1968, but as Romney's hopes for the Republican nomination faded so did the possibility of a place on the national ticket for the Senator. In 1968 he was again reelected by a margin of over a million votes.

Initially a supporter of the Vietnam war, Javits expressed doubts about its conduct in 1967 and backed the 1970 Cooper-Church amendment to bar funds for U.S. forces in Cambodia. Some opponents of the war, however, believed that he was insufficiently outspoken in his criticism of the conflict. In the late 1960s and early 1970s Javits became a leading advocate of consumer protection legislation. In 1974 he was reelected to a fourth term in the Senate.

[MLL]

JENNINGS, W(ILLIAM) PAT
b. Aug. 20, 1919; Smyth County, Va.
Democratic Representative, Va., 1955-67.

Chosen sheriff of Smyth County in 1947 and again in 1951, Jennings served in that post until 1954, when he won election to the U.S. House of Representatives in the state's ninth congressional district as a Democrat. During the course of his 12 years in the House, Jennings was one of the few elected officials from Virginia who did not support the conservative fiscal, social welfare and racial policies of U.S. Sen. Harry Byrd's [q.v.] dominant Democratic machine.

Jennings's electoral success resulted from the atypical history, geography and demography of his distrct. It was located in the mountainous southwestern region of the state, an area that had long been politically at odds with the lowlands, where the Byrd organization's strength was greatest. There had been much Unionist sentiment in the area during the Civil War, and ever since that time the Republicans had possessed a considerable following in the region. Because blacks composed only 2.7% of the population, the district's whites did not consider racial integration a major threat or issue. Coal mining was a major industry in the region, and it was one of the few areas of the state where organized labor had made significant inroads.

Jennings was the most liberal member of Virginia's congressional delegation. According to *Congressional Quarterly* he supported the Kennedy Administration on key House votes 77%, 80% and 76% of the time in 1961, 1962 and 1963, respectively. Jennings first indicated his strong support of the Administration during its initial month in office. With the backing of House Speaker Sam Rayburn (D, Tex.) [q.v.], President Kennedy sought to enlarge the House Rules Committee. The purpose of the plan was to create a liberal majority on the powerful Committee and thereby prevent its Southern Democrat and Republican members, led by Jennings's fellow-Virginian Chairman Howard W. Smith [q.v.], from blocking social welfare legislation. On Jan. 31, 1961 the House voted 217 to 212 to expand the Committee; Jennings was the only Virginia representative to support the proposal.

During January 1963 the House Democratic caucus chose Jennings and Rep. Ross Bass (D, Tenn.), another Southern liberal, to fill vacancies on the important

Ways and Means Committee. This represented an effort by pro-Administration forces supporting the Administration to reduce the power of conservatives on that Committee. Jennings reaffirmed his liberal credentials in October 1963 when he was the only Virginia representative to support the one-year extension of the life of the U.S. Commission on Civil Rights.

The growth of Virginia's urban and black vote had seriously weakened the Byrd machine by the mid-1960s, and in the 1966 Democratic primaries moderates defeated Rep. Smith and Sen. A. Willis Robertson [q.v.], both conservative stalwarts of the Byrd Organization. But in the ninth district this trend worked to Jennings's disadvantage. As the Byrd machine declined, many of its supporters in his district transferred their allegiance to the already strong Republican Party. As a result, Jennings lost his 1966 reelection bid to William C. Wampler, a conservative Republican. Jennings was chosen House Clerk in each Congress after defeat, and his election to that post was taken as a sign of the growing strength of the liberal Democratic Study Group within the House Democratic Caucus.

[MLL]

JOHNSON, LYNDON B(AINES)
b. Aug. 27, 1908; Stonewall, Tex.
d. Jan. 22, 1973; Stonewall, Tex.
Vice President of the United States, January 1961-November 1963; President of the United States, November 1963-January 1969.

Lyndon Johnson was born on a farm in the hill country of south-central Texas. He attended local public schools, graduated from Southwest Texas State Teachers College in 1930 and the next year became secretary to a Texas congressman. While in Washington Johnson was urged to pursue a political career by Rep. Sam Rayburn (D, Tex.) [q.v.], later Speaker of the House of Representatives. In 1934 he married Claudia Alta Taylor, known as Lady Bird, an accomplished woman who was credited

with being a steadying influence on the sometimes mercurial Johnson.

In 1935 President Franklin Roosevelt appointed Johnson Texas state administrator of the National Youth Administration, a New Deal relief agency for young people. The job also provided Johnson with a wide political base for his successful congressional campaign in 1937. He ran on a strong New Deal platform rooted in a personal relationship with Roosevelt, who Johnson later declared "was like a daddy to me." Johnson's political career was interrupted by service with the Navy in World War II. In 1948 he won a bitterly fought Democratic primary runoff election for the U.S. Senate by 87 votes out of one million cast and then went on to defeat his Republican opponent in the general election. [See TRUMAN Volume]

Befriended by powerful Sen. Richard Russell (D, Ga.) [q.v.], a member of the Senate "Establishment," Johnson rose quickly through the Senate hierarchy, attaining the post of Senate minority leader in 1953 and majority leader two years later. In 1955 he made a rapid recovery from a massive heart attack.

As majority leader Johnson established a near-legendary reputation for his command of the legislative process and his assessment of the needs, ambitions and weaknesses of individual senators. As his own national ambitions increased, Johnson's political stance moved from conservative to moderate. He guided a number of programs through Congress in opposition to the Eisenhower Administration during the 1950s and helped gain passage for the Civil Rights Acts of 1957 and 1960, despite considerable Southern opposition.

Johnson's 1960 presidential strategy was to remain aloof from the primaries in the hope that the announced candidates, Sen. John F. Kennedy (D, Mass.) and Sen Hubert H. Humphrey (D, Minn.) [q.v.], would either drop out of the race or become deadlocked before reaching the convention. However, it was evident from the start that the kind of direct personal power Johnson exerted in the U.S. Senate was not suitable to a national political campaign. The big-city political machines, labor unions and black voters were already solidly behind the Kennedy candidacy, and Johnson's attempts to portray himself as a responsible legislative leader and Kennedy as a youthful dilettante were unsuccessful. On July 5 Johnson announced his candidacy for the Democratic presidential nomination. On July 13 Kennedy won the Democratic presidential nomination at the Los Angeles convention with 806 delegates to Johnson's 409.

With the presidential nomination secured Kennedy surprised his northern liberal and labor backers by selecting Johnson as his running mate, although Johnson had declared repeatedly that he would not accept the second spot on the ticket. It was Kennedy's belief that Johnson would help win Southern and Western votes in the general election. Johnson's nomination was generally considered to be a critical factor in the Kennedy-Johnson ticket's narrow margin of victory over Vice President Richard M. Nixon [q.v.] and Henry Cabot Lodge [q.v.] in the November election. [See EISENHOWER Volume]

Immediately after the election Johnson sought to broaden the powers of the vice presidency by exerting the same control over Senate Democrats that he had exercised as majority leader. Acting on Johnson's suggestion the new Senate majority leader, Mike Mansfield (D, Mont.) [q.v.], proposed at a Jan. 3, 1961 Senate Democratic caucus that the Vice President be made the presiding officer of all formal Senate Democratic conferences. However, liberal Democrats balked and quickly tabled the motion.

Shortly after the Jan. 20 inauguration, Johnson attempted to strengthen his powers within the executive branch by drafting an executive order stipulating that the Vice President was to have "general supervision" over certain governmental areas, particularly the National Aeronautics and Space Administration (NASA). The President declined to sign the order. According to columnists Rowland Evans and Robert Novak [q.v.], from then on Johnson "did absolutely nothing to advance the Kennedy legislative program." Johnson later told biographer Doris Kearns that the vice presidency "is filled with trips around the world, chauffeurs, men saluting, people clapping, chairmanships of councils, but in the end, it is nothing. I detested every minute of it."

On March 6, 1961 Johnson was designated chairman of the newly created President's Committee on Equal Opportunity, established to prevent racial discrimination in employment by businesses having contracts with the federal government. In late 1962 Attorney General Robert F. Kennedy [q.v.] and Secretary of Labor Willard Wirtz [q.v.] urged Johnson to move faster in the equal employment field, despite notable gains already achieved in the area, including a February 1962 agreement by 31 leading defense contractors to eliminate job discrimination. Later that year Wirtz, angered at Johnson's reluctance to act, began to systematically reduce the Committee's influence by transferring many of its functions to government agencies that had large defense contracts with private business.

Johnson's main influence as Vice President was as chairman of the National Aeronautics and Space Council, which was organized to formulate space policy and mediate disputes between military and civilian leaders. He was instrumental in securing the February 1961 appointment of Texas businessman James E. Webb [q.v.] as director of NASA, and he participated in all major decisions involving the space program during the Kennedy Administration.

Replying to critics angered over the cost of the moon program, Johnson warned in October 1963 that abandonment of the effort would be tantamount to a "conspicuous withdrawal and retreat." He denied that quitting the program "would cost less" than an expensive moon landing and asserted that the U.S. had paid heavily "in loss of confidence in the dollar and in international prestige" for permitting an initial series of Communist successes in space to create the false impression that technological leadership had passed from the West to the East."

In association with his Space Council duties, Johnson was also chairman of a committee to study the supersonic transport (SST). The question of financing the prototype brought him into direct conflict with Secretary of Defense Robert McNamara [q.v.] and others within the Administration who believed that private industry should pay for at least one-third of the project. Johnson wanted a large, if not total, federal underwriting of the costs.

During his vice presidency Johnson visited more than 34 countries on trips likened to domestic campaign swings. Their main function was to spread goodwill rather than to initiate policy. The widely publicized 1961 U.S. visit of a camel driver, whom Johnson had met on an earlier trip to Pakistan, vividly illustrated to many observers Johnson's decline in power and prestige since his days as majority leader.

The Vice President's most important trip was his May 1961 mission to Southeast Asia to help formulate U.S. aid policy for South Vietnam. On May 12, 1961 Johnson addressed the South Vietnamese General Assembly and declared that the U.S. was ready "immediately" to help expand South Vietnam's armed forces and to "meet the needs of your people on education, rural development, new industry and long-range economic development."

In both 1962 and 1963 there were persistent rumors, denied by President Kennedy, that Johnson would be "dropped" from the 1964 national Democratic ticket. Fuel was added to the rumors in the fall of 1963 when Robert G. Baker [q.v.], former secretary to the Majority and Johnson protege, was charged with having used his job and political influence for his own personal gain.

On Nov. 21, 1963 President Kennedy flew to Texas with Johnson on a precampaign swing designed to reconcile rival factions of the Texas Democratic Party. The next day, Nov. 22, Kennedy was assassinated while riding in a Dallas motorcade. At 2:39 p.m. the same day, Lyndon Johnson was sworn in aboard Air Force One as the 36th President of the United States. In a brief address to the nation that evening at Andrews Air Force Base in Washington, Johnson said, "This is a sad time for all people. We have suffered a loss that cannot be weighed. . . . I will do my best, that is all I can do. I ask for your help and God's."

During the early weeks of his Administration, Johnson earned unanimous praise for his success in maintaining national stability. He initiated a series of conferences with congressional leaders, cabinet members and advisers, reaffirmed U.S. commitments in foreign affairs, asked the cabinet and important Kennedy staffers to remain in service and pledged on Nov. 28 "to work for a new American greatness." The next month Johnson established the Warren Commission to investigate the Kennedy assassination. During the following year Johnson secured congressional passage for several dormant Kennedy legislative proposals, including the tax-cut bill and the 1964 Civil Rights Act.

Johnson was elected to a full presidential term in 1964, defeating Republican presidential candidate Sen. Barry Goldwater (R, Ariz.) [q.v.] by an electoral margin of 486 to 52. With that mandate and a large Democratic congressional majority, Johnson pushed through a number of "Great Society" measures over the next two years, including the medicare bill, the 1965 Voting Rights Act and the $1.3 billion aid-to-education bill.

Johnson's major problem as President was the war in Vietnam. After congressional approval of the 1964 Gulf of Tonkin Resolution giving the President the authority to take "all necessary measures" to prevent North Vietnamese attacks against U.S. troops in South Vietnam, Johnson and his advisers increasingly turned their attention from domestic affairs to the conduct of the Vietnam war.

During the mid and late 1960s a strong anti-war movement gathered momentum in the U.S. In March 1968 Sen. Eugene McCarthy (D, Minn.) [q.v.] barely lost the New Hampshire Democratic presidential primary to President Johnson, in what amounted to a stinging defeat for the President. On March 31, 1968 Johnson announced to the nation that he would not seek a second term but would utilize the remainder of his incumbency to search for peace in Vietnam.

In January 1969, after the election of Richard M. Nixon as President, Johnson retired to his Texas ranch to work on his memoirs and to oversee the construction of the Johnson Library at the University of Texas. During the next four years Johnson's health declined. He died of a heart attack in January 1973. [See JOHNSON, NIXON Volumes]

[FHM]

For further information:

Rowland Evans and Robert Novak, *Lyndon B. Johnson: The Exercise of Power* (New York, 1966).
Eric Goldman, *The Tragedy of Lyndon Johnson* (New York, 1969).
Doris Kearns, *Lyndon Johnson and the American Dream* (New York, 1976).

JOHNSON, PAUL B(URNEY), JR.
b. Jan. 23, 1916; Hattiesburg, Miss.
Lieutenant Governor, Miss., 1960-64.

The son of a Mississippi congressman and governor, Johnson received his law degree from the University of Mississippi in 1940 and practiced in Jackson and Hattiesburg until 1948. In that year he supported the regular Democratic rather than the States' Rights ticket in the presidential election and was appointed an assistant U.S. attorney in Mississippi, serving until 1951. He ran for lieutenant governor in 1959 and won both the Democratic primary and the November election.

Johnson received little attention outside his state until September 1962 when he joined Mississippi Gov. Ross Barnett [q.v.] in defying federal court orders for the enrollment of James Meredith [q.v.] at the University of Mississippi. Barnett twice denied Meredith admission to the University in late September, and on Sept. 26 Johnson blocked Meredith's third attempt to register. Backed by some 35 state troopers and county sheriffs, Johnson stopped Meredith and accompanying federal officials two blocks from the entrance to the Oxford campus. Declaring he was acting in Barnett's "stead, by his direction, and under his instructions," Johnson read a proclamation denying Meredith entry to the University. Later the same day the U.S. Fifth Circuit Court of Appeals cited Johnson for contempt. The Court found him guilty of civil contempt on Sept. 29 and ordered him to comply with its desegregation orders or face a $5,000-per-day fine. Meanwhile Johnson participated in the behind-the-scenes negotiations between Barnett and Attorney General Robert F. Kennedy [q.v.]. On Sept. 30 Meredith entered the campus under an arrangement worked out by Barnett and Justice Department officials. Around 8 p.m., however, a riot broke out at the University, and Barnett sent Johnson to Oxford to aid in ending the disturbance. The riot, in which two men were killed, lasted into the early morning hours and was quelled only after President Kennedy called in the National Guard, 3,000 federal troops and 400 U.S. marshals.

Meredith finally enrolled on Oct. 1 at 8 a.m., but the Fifth Circuit Court refused to drop the contempt charges against Johnson. In December 1962, at the explicit request of the Court, the Justice Department filed additional criminal contempt-of-court charges against Johnson and Barnett. The Kennedys reportedly did not want to press the case against either official for fear of sparking another federal-state confrontation. In the end the Fifth Circuit Court dismissed the charges against both Johnson and Barnett in a 4-3 ruling in May 1965.

Johnson ran for governor in 1963 as a militant segregationist, emphasizing his obstructionist role in the "Ole Miss" crisis throughout the campaign. With backing from Barnett and Sen. James O. Eastland (D, Miss.) [q.v.], Johnson defeated a more moderate candidate in the Aug. 27 Democratic primary runoff and was easily elected in November. In contrast to his strong campaign statements on race, Johnson delivered a moderate inaugural address in January 1964. Concerned with improving Mississippi's national image, Johnson used legal means only to fight desegregation and civil rights measures throughout his term, abandoning the tactic of defiance used in the Meredith crisis and taking a strong stand against lawlessness and disorder. [See JOHNSON Volume]

[CAB]

For further information:
Walter Lord, *The Past That Would Not Die* (New York, 1965).

JOHNSON, THOMAS F(RANCIS)
b. June 26, 1909; Worcester County, Md.
Democratic Representative, Md.,
1959-63.

First elected to the U.S. House of Representatives in 1958, Johnson, a moderate liberal, supported the Kennedy Administration on 83% and 77% of key House votes in 1961 and 1962, according to *Congressional Quarterly.*

On Oct. 16, 1962 a federal grand jury in Baltimore indicted Johnson and Rep. Frank W. Boykin (D, Ala.) [*q.v.*] on eight counts of conspiracy and conflict of interest charges. Johnson was accused of having received nearly $25,000 between June 1960 and October 1961 from J. Kenneth Edlin, a former officer of two Maryland savings and loan associations, in exchange for efforts to influence the Justice Department to dismiss a 1959 mail fraud charge against Edlin. One count of the indictment asserted that Johnson's attempts to assist Edlin included a June 30, 1960 speech on the House floor defending the integrity of Maryland savings and loan associations, which had been involved in a number of scandals.

Johnson had been favored to win reelection in November 1962. But as a result of the indictment he lost to Republican Rogers C.B. Morton by 33,664 votes to 29,653.

Johnson's trial was held in the U.S. District Court in Baltimore during the spring of 1963. Attorney General Robert F. Kennedy [*q.v.*] testified that Johnson had come to his office in 1961 to urge that the indictment of Edlin be dropped. Johnson was found guilty on all counts in June and the following October received a six-month jail term and a $5,000 fine. Boykin, Edlin and an associate of the latter were also convicted.

Johnson appealed the verdict and in February 1965 the U.S. Supreme Court overturned his conviction on the grounds that speeches on the floor of Congress were privileged and not subject to criminal sanctions. It ruled that Johnson could be tried again if the charges did not question his proper legislative functions.

In January 1968 Johnson was convicted again on the seven remaining counts of the original indictment. In April 1970, after losing another appeal to the Supreme Court, Johnson began serving his six-month term. He was paroled four months later. In April 1972 a former member of the United States Parole Board, testifying before the House Judiciary Committee, stated that Attorney General John N. Mitchell and Deputy Attorney General Richard G. Kleindienst had pressured G.J. Reed, the Parole Board chairman, to parole Johnson. Reed denied the allegation.

[MLL]

JOHNSON, U(RAL) ALEXIS
b. Oct. 17, 1908; Falun, Kan.
Deputy Undersecretary of State for Political Affairs, April 1961-July 1964, September 1965-July 1966.

U. Alexis Johnson, a career diplomat, was an expert on Far Eastern affairs. After joining the State Department in 1935, he served in Japan, Korea, China and Manchuria before the war. With the exception of a wartime assignment in Brazil and a tour of duty as ambassador to Czechoslovakia from 1953 to 1958, he continued to concentrate on Far Eastern affairs throughout the postwar period. When President Kennedy appointed him deputy undersecretary of state for political affairs in April 1961, Johnson became the highest-ranking career foreign service officer in the State Department.

In October 1961 Johnson began an involvement in Vietnam affairs that would become the major focus of his attention throughout the decade. Following the erosion of the South Vietnamese military position and the deterioration of morale in Saigon during 1961, President Ngo Dinh Diem asked the U.S. to sign a defense treaty and increase military aid to his country. Johnson was one of the officials chosen to make recommendations on the proposal. In a document entitled the "Concept of Intervention in Vietnam," he advised an increased troop commitment to achieve what he believed to be the ultimate objective of "defeating the Vietcong and rendering Vietnam secure under a non-Communist government." Johnson "guessed" three divisions would be the ultimate force needed for the mission. However, he cautioned that the plan's viability was dependent on the degree to which the South Vietnamese government accelerated its own defense program.

Despite his recommendation and others made by Gen. Maxwell Taylor [q.v.] and presidential adviser Walt W. Rostow [q.v.], Kennedy decided in November 1961 to defer a major commitment of ground forces and concentrate on prompt deployment of support troops and equipment. During April 1962 this policy was paralleled by the strategic hamlet program, a plan that sought to relocate much of the rural population into fortified villages, which could be used as defense, political and educational units by the Saigon government. By the spring of 1963 Johnson announced that the war was being handled successfully and that the strategic hamlet program "was the most important reason for guarded optimism."

In January 1962 Johnson became a member of the Special Group Counterinsurgency created at the suggestion of Gen. Taylor to integrate the government's effort to support counterinsurgency measures in Laos, South Vietnam and Thailand. This group was concerned mainly with keeping the importance of counterinsurgency before the Defense and State Departments and with training personnel for guerrilla warfare.

Following the discovery of Soviet missiles in Cuba in October 1962, Johnson served as a member of Excom, the special bipartisan committee formed to advise Kennedy on the crisis. When the President decided to use a blockade to force the missile withdrawal, Johnson, along with Undersecretary of State George Ball [q.v.] and Assistant Secretary of State Edwin Martin [q.v.], was designated to inform American allies, prepare for the meeting of the Organization of American States called to discuss the issue and write a legal justification for the action.

During the Johnson Administration the undersecretary continued his involvement in Vietnam both in Washington and as dep-

uty ambassador in Saigon. In July 1966 he succeeded Edwin Reischauer [q.v.] as ambassador to Japan. President Richard M. Nixon appointed Johnson chief of the U.S. delegation to the strategic Arms Limitation Talks (SALT) in 1973. [See JOHNSON, NIXON Volumes]

[EWS]

JOHNSTON, OLIN D(EWITT)
b. Nov. 18, 1896; Honea Path, S.C.
d. April 18, 1965; Columbia, S.C.
Democratic Senator, S.C., 1945-65.

Olin Johnston grew up in rural South Carolina. He served with the U.S. Army in World War I and then graduated from Wofford College in 1921. Johnston received an M.A. degree in rural economics from the University of South Carolina in 1923 and a Law degree from that University the next year.

After a career in local politics, including an unsuccessful bid for the governorship in 1930, Johnston was elected governor in 1934. Although a vigorous supporter of most New Deal programs, Johnston also earned a reputation as a militant segregationist. In 1945 Johnston was elected to the U.S. Senate. Four years later he became chairman of the Post Office and Civil Service Committee.

During the Kennedy Administration Johnston voted with the conservative coalition on over 60% of all major issues, according to Congressional Quarterly. In 1962 he defeated Gov. Ernest Hollings [q.v.] in the Democratic senatorial primary and went on to defeat his Republican opponent in the general election. The same year Johnston cosponsored a constitutional amendment to nullify the Supreme Court's decision banning prayer in public schools.

In 1963 Johnston supported ratification of the nuclear test ban treaty. He declared that rejection of the treaty would be "telling the world it must look forward only to an endless dark age of cold war and ever-threatening nuclear attack." Johnston maintained a militant stand against civil rights legislation and joined with other Southern Democrats in 1963 to prevent the Kennedy

Administration's civil rights bill from reaching the Senate floor. He voted against the 1964 Civil Rights Act. Later the same year he supported. the Social Security and medicare bills.

After Johnston's death in April 1965, South Carolina Gov. Donald S. Russell assumed the vacated Senate seat. The next year Russell lost the Democratic primary to Ernest Hollings.

[FHM]

JORDAN, B(ENJAMIN) EVERETT

b. Sept. 8, 1896; Ramseur, N.C.
d. March 15, 1974; Saxapahaw, N.C.
Democratic Senator, N.C., 1958-73;
Chairman, Rules and Administration
Committee, 1963-73.

A wealthy North Carolina textile manufacturer, Jordan began to participate in Democratic state politics as a fund raiser in the mid-1930s. From 1949 to 1954 he served as chairman of the Democratic State Executive Committee. Originally associated with the Party's liberal wing, he moved into its conservative faction during the early 1950s. In April 1958 Gov. Luther Hodges appointed Jordan to fill a U.S. Senate vacancy created by the death of W. Kerr Scott. The following November Jordan was elected to complete the final two years of Kerr's term.

During the early 1960s Jordan compiled a conservative voting record on Capitol Hill, although he supported the Administration's federal school aid bill in 1961 and the following year voted for a constitutional amendment banning the use of the poll tax in federal elections. According to *Congressional Quarterly*, Jordan supported the Senate's conservative coalition on 95%, 91% and 86% of roll-call votes in 1961, 1962 and 1963, respectively.

In 1963 Jordan succeeded Majority Leader Mike Mansfield (D, Mont.) [*q.v.*] as chairman of the Senate Rules and Administration Committee. During the last days of the Kennedy presidency, the Committee began an investigation of the activities of Bobby Baker [*q.v.*], secretary to the senate majority, who had been accused

in a civil suit of using his influence to obtain government contracts.

The Committee completed its investigation in 1965. The majority report, signed by Jordan, asserted that Baker had been guilty of "gross improprieties." But it cleared Baker of some of the charges against him and did not implicate President Johnson, who as Senate majority leader until his assumption of the vice presidency in 1961 had worked closely with Baker. The Committee's three Republicans charged that the majority report was a whitewash. [See JOHNSON Volume]

In 1972 Rep. Nick Galifianakis (D, N.C.), who had a more liberal voting record than Jordan, defeated the incumbent in the Democratic senatorial primary. Jordan died in Saxapahaw, N.C., on March 15, 1974. [See NIXON Volume]

[MLL]

JUDD, WALTER H(ENRY)

b. Sept. 25, 1898; Rising City, Neb.
Republican Representative, Minn.,
1943-63.

Walter H. Judd earned B.A. and M.D. degrees at the University of Nebraska. After an internship in Omaha, he left for China to become a medical missionary. With the exception of a four-year leave of absence, during part of which he taught surgery for the Mayo Foundation at Minneapolis, Judd worked in Fukien Province as a doctor and hospital superintendent from 1925 until 1938. Six months after the Japanese Army invaded Fukien, Judd returned to the United States and toured the nation warning of Japanese aggression and calling for support of the Nationalist government of Chiang Kai-shek.

Judd won election to the House from Minneapolis in 1942, and his China experience established his reputation as an expert on the Far East. He vigorously advocated American aid to the Nationalists, first against the Japanese and ultimately against the Communist Chinese, whom he declared in June 1945 were "Communists first and Chinese second." After Chiang's defeat and exile from the mainland in 1949, Judd became identified with the domestic "China Lobby" composed of business, editorial and congressional leaders who strongly endorsed the Nationalist regime on Taiwan. In 1953 Judd helped form the Committee of One Million against the admission of Communist China to the United Nations. The group organized a massive letter-writing campaign to Congress and the State Department opposing any normalization of relations with mainland China. [See EISENHOWER Volume]

Judd's prominence as an orator won him the keynote speakership at the 1960 Republican National Convention. He delivered a strong, anti-Communist attack on the Democrats and was supported by some delegates for the vice presidential nomination (Eisenhower had considered Judd for the vice presidency in 1952). Nixon strategists utilized Judd as a spokesman during the 1960 campaign, and just 48 hours before the voting the former physician charged that Democratic presidential nominee John F. Kennedy suffered from Addison's disease and insisted that this affliction disqualified him for the presidency.

Judd opposed features of the Kennedy Administration's program without being among its most resolute foes, speaking out forcefully, however, against the President's plan to expand the size of the House Rules Committee in January 1961. As the senior Republican on the House Foreign Affairs Committee, Judd frequently met with Kennedy. He supported the White House on its proposal to have the Treasury Department purchase $100 million worth of United Nations bonds in September 1962, although most House Republicans voted against the authorization. Despite his reputation as a rigid anti-Communist and conservative, *Congressional Quarterly* ranked Judd fourth among GOP House members in support of the Administration on 1962 roll-call votes.

Judd attended the June 1962 meeting of the "All-Republican Conference" of Party leaders at the farm of Dwight D. Eisenhower [*q.v.*]. He also participated in the Christian Anti-Communist Crusade led by an Australian physician, Fred C. Schwarz [*q.v.*]. Judd and Sen. Thomas J. Dodd (D, Conn.) [*q.v.*] belonged to the "Faculty" of Schwarz anti-Communism school. Along with Senator Barry M. Goldwater (R, Ariz.)

[*q.v.*], Judd criticized the right-wing John Birch Society's founder Robert H. Welch [*q.v.*] as unfit to lead an effective anti-Communist movement.

Following the 1960 census, redistricting reduced the number of Republican voters in Judd's congressional district. After serving in the House for two decades, the Minneapolis physician lost reelection to a Democratic state legislator with just under 45% of the total vote. Political commentators judged Judd's defeat as a major upset and an unanticipated triumph for the Kennedy Administration. Despite the loss of his seat, Judd remained active in national Republican politics and a strong opponent of Communist China. [See JOHNSON Volume]

[JLB]

KAHN, HERMAN
b. Feb. 15, 1922; Bayonne, N.J.
Director, Hudson Institute, September, 1961-   .

Herman Kahn's rise to prominence as a nuclear strategist coincided with the Kennedy Administration's increased emphasis on civil defense and the fallout shelter program. After publication of *On Thermonuclear War* in 1960, Kahn emerged as the nation's foremost authority in the arcane and highly complex fields of systems analysis and games theory, especially as such methods could be applied to an actual nuclear attack and its aftermath.

The son of Jewish immigrants, Herman Kahn spent his childhood in New York City before attending high school in Los Angeles. He served in the Army during World War II and graduated from the University of California, Los Angeles in 1945. He took his master's degree from the California Institute of Technology three years later. In 1948 Kahn was named a senior physicist with the Rand Corporation, a nonprofit research organization working on U.S. Air Force contracts. At Rand during the 1950s Kahn became experienced in the fields of operations research and systems analysis as well as in the use of applied mathematics to solve various game theories of strategic warfare.

Kahn's controversial 1960 book, *On Thermonuclear War*, was drawn from a lecture series given at Princeton in 1959. The central thesis of the book and also that of his later work, *Thinking About the Unthinkable* (1962), was that nuclear war could be conducted as rationally as conventional warfare, and he dismissed those who thought the use of nuclear weapons in another war tantamount to the end of civilization. It was his belief that there were "degrees of awfulness" in a nuclear exchange with the Soviet Union. He urged American policymakers to recognize that they held a series of options in the conduct of such a war that fell short of a total nuclear holocaust.

As part of this strategy Kahn advocated the building of a massive civil defense program to add flexibility to the conduct of U.S. foreign policy. Kahn thought such a civil defense program necessary to prepare people for the possibility of limited nuclear war so that "normal and hopeful lives would not be precluded for the survivors" of such a conflict. Illustrative of the deep divisions within the nuclear establishment, *On Thermonuclear War* was described by one prominent critic as "instructive and absorbing" and by another as "a moral tract on mass murder."

In September 1961 Kahn left Rand to found his own "think tank," the Hudson Institute. The new research firm received grants from a number of business and research organizations and furnished information on military strategy, civil defense and national security matters.

A vigorous supporter of Kennedy Administration civil defense measures, Kahn was particularly interested in the Administration's program to provide fallout shelters for an estimated 50 million people in the U.S. Kahn himself conceived a $200-billion shelter plan with caverns a thousand feet underground capable of withstanding direct hits by nuclear bombs of up to five megatons and near-misses by larger bombs. Such a shelter would contain an economic and industrial complex "to provide a base for rebuilding the country" after an attack.

Frequently criticized for his seemingly blithe approach to nuclear devastation,

Kahn continued through the 1960s to expound his theories of defense strategy and was a strong supporter of the Nixon Administration's Safeguard antiballistic missile system.

[FHM]

KAPPEL, FREDERICK R(USSELL)

b. Jan. 14, 1902; Albert Lea, Minn.
Chairman and Chief Executive, American Telephone and Telegraph Corporation August 1961-January 1967.

Frederick Kappel joined the Northwestern Bell Telephone Company, a subsidiary of American Telephone & Telegraph (AT&T), immediately after graduating from the University of Minnesota in 1924 with a degree in electrical engineering. An "operations" man, Kappel rose steadily through Northwestern's ranks, moving to New York as an AT&T vice president in 1949. He was chosen president of AT&T's manufacturing and supply unit, the Western Electric Company, in 1953 and president of AT&T itself in 1956. In that year Kappel handled the final stages of negotiations with the government permitting AT&T to keep Western Electric. The Justice Department had been trying to divest the corporation of its manufacturing subsidiary since 1949. Kappel was elevated to chairman of AT&T in August 1961.

With assets of $28 billion in 1962, AT&T was the largest private enterprise in the world. It had the greatest number of shareholders (2,200,000) and employes (730,000). In the 10 years preceding 1963, AT&T's 13% annual rate of growth in net income was the second highest of any U.S. corporation. With his elevation to the company presidency, Kappel initiated the greatest expansion program in the history of American business. In 1962, for example, AT&T's $3 billion outlay for capital construction dwarfed that of any other company. Kappel continued AT&T's historic policies, financing expansion more through stock issues than debt and paying high dividends on its shares.

The political question of greatest interest

to AT&T during the Kennedy Administration was the ownership and operation of the new communications satellite system. In 1960 AT&T outlined a proposal for a worldwide telephone and television system using 50 low-orbit satellites. The company recommended that it own and operate the system. The antitrust division of the Department of Justice, however, objected to an AT&T-owned system, fearing both the company's monopoly power and the possibility that AT&T might charge the costs of a satellite system to its domestic telephone customers. Senate liberals favoring government ownership unsuccessfully tried to filibuster an Administration compromise to allow private ownership of the system but with public membership on its board of directors. The measure passed in August 1962. AT&T was allocated a 30% participation in the ownership, the remainder going to other international communications carriers.

Saturday Review selected Kappel as its Businessman of the Year in 1963. That same month he became chairman of the Business Council, a group of 175 prominent business executives advising the President on economic policy. In that position Kappel urged greater corporate employment of blacks in October 1963. He was also a member of the Business Committee for Tax Reduction in 1963. Kappel resigned as AT&T Chairman in January 1967. [See JOHNSON Volume]

[TO]

KATZENBACH, NICHOLAS deB(EL-LEVILLE)

b. Jan. 17, 1922; Philadelphia, Pa.
U.S. Assistant Attorney General, January 1961-April 1962; U.S. Deputy Attorney General, April 1962-September 1964.

After graduating from Princeton University in 1945 and Yale Law School in 1947, Katzenbach spent two years at Oxford University as a Rhodes scholar. He served as an attorney-adviser in the office of general counsel of the Air Force from 1950 to 1952

and as a part-time consultant to the same office during the next four years. During the latter period Katzenbach also taught at Yale Law School and then, from 1956 to 1960, at the University of Chicago Law School.

Katzenbach was appointed assistant attorney general in charge of the Justice Department's Office of Legal Counsel on Jan. 26, 1961. He helped draft new wiretapping legislation and the Kennedy Administration's foreign trade program. Skillful at negotiation and compromise, Katzenbach played a key role in the development of the Communications Satellite Act of August 1962. Controversy over the legislation had centered on whether the new satellite system should be privately or governmentally owned. Katzenbach was credited with devising a compromise proposal to establish a private satellite corporation whose stock would be equally divided between communications companies and the general public.

Following Byron White's [*q.v.*] appointment to the Supreme Court, Katzenbach was named deputy attorney general, the second highest post in the Justice Department, on April 2, 1962. In September of that year, when state officials attempted to block the court-ordered enrollment of James Meredith [*q.v.*] at the University of Mississippi, Katzenbach went to the state to direct personally the Justice Department's operations. He oversaw the force of federal marshals who accompanied Meredith onto the campus in Oxford, Miss., on Sept. 30. He also joined in the decision to call in federal troops when a riot erupted there that night, and he remained in constant contact with Attorney General Robert F. Kennedy [*q.v.*] in Washington throughout the crisis.

Katzenbach was present during another civil rights crisis in Tuscaloosa, Ala., in June 1963. Fulfilling a campaign pledge, Alabama Gov. George C. Wallace [*q.v.*] tried to thwart court-ordered desegregation of the University of Alabama. In a historic confrontation on June 11, Wallace stood in the doorway of the University's registration center, blocking the entry of Katzenbach and two black students. Katzenbach read a presidential proclamation ordering Wallace to comply with the federal court orders for desegregation and asked him to step aside. When Wallace refused Katzenbach withdrew and accompanied one of the two students to her dormitory. President Kennedy then federalized the Alabama National Guard and later that day Wallace stepped aside and let the students register on orders of the National Guard commander.

During the October 1962 Cuban missile crisis, Katzenbach drafted a legal brief in support of President Kennedy's decision to "quarantine" Cuba. On Dec. 21, 1962 private negotiators, who had behind-the-scenes support from the Kennedy Administration, reached an agreement with the Castro regime for the release of prisoners captured during the April 1961 Bay of Pigs invasion. Katzenbach was part of a four-man team appointed by the Attorney General that coordinated a major government effort to gather and transport quickly the medical and food supplies promised to Cuba in exchange for the prisoners.

In 1964 Katzenbach achieved a compromise settlement in a long-standing dispute between the U.S. government and Interhandel, a Swiss holding company, over ownership of the General Aniline and Film Corporation. He played a major role in the lengthy negotiations with Congress over the provisions of the 1964 Civil Rights Act. Katzenbach also worked closely with the Warren Commission in its 10 month investigation of President Kennedy's assassination.

Upon the resignation of Robert Kennedy in September 1964, Katzenbach was named acting Attorney General. He was appointed Attorney General on Jan. 28, 1965. He had a significant part in drafting the 1965 Voting Rights Act and the Johnson Administration's anti-crime proposals of 1965. Named undersecretary of state in September 1966, Katzenbach traveled as a presidential envoy on several important diplomatic missions, primarily in Europe. He resigned that post in November 1968 and in 1969 became a vice president and general counsel of International Business Machines Corporation. [See JOHNSON Volume]

[CAB]

KAYSEN, CARL
b. March 5, 1920; Philadelphia, Pa.
Deputy Special Assistant to the President for National Security Affairs, November 1961-December 1963.

An economist by training, Kaysen served as a foreign policy adviser to the President during the Kennedy Administration. Following his graduation from the University of Pennsylvania in 1940, he worked for the National Bureau of Economic Research before becoming an economist in the Office of Strategic Services in 1942. After the war Kaysen joined the faculty of Harvard University. A specialist in U.S. antitrust policy, he rose to the rank of professor of economics in 1957. President Kennedy appointed Kaysen a White House assistant in November 1961.

Although virtually unknown by the public, Kaysen was called "one of the really influential figures inside the Administration" by journalist Joseph Kraft. Kraft attributed his effectiveness to the fact that he was not a "celebrity" and could therefore maintain good relations with both the White House and the State Department bureaucracy.

During the Berlin crisis of the summer of 1961, when the USSR threatened to cut off access to the city and make Berlin a "free city" ostensibly independent of Eastern or Western control, Kaysen was one of Kennedy's advisers who rejected Dean Acheson's [q.v.] analysis of the situation. Believing that negotiations would be a sign of weakness, Acheson maintained that the U.S. had to build up both its conventional and nuclear forces in preparation for an armed confrontation with the Soviet Union. Instead, Kaysen recommended a plan supplementing a military buildup with negotiations. President Kennedy publicly outlined a U.S. policy based on Kaysen's proposals in July 1961.

During 1961 and 1962 Kaysen helped organize the movement in the State Department, the Council of Economic Advisers and the Bureau of the Budget for a reorganization of American foreign trade policy to stem the growing U.S. deficit in its international balance of payments. This movement culminated in the Trade Expansion Act of 1962, which cut tariffs from 50% to 100% on many foreign goods and gave the President wide discretionary powers to retaliate against foreign import restrictions.

Kaysen was one of the major officials pressing for a nuclear test ban treaty during the Kennedy Administration. Working from the White House he helped coordinate the efforts of various government agencies and lobbying groups in support of a total test ban agreement. When the Russians rejected this in the spring of 1962, Kaysen was one of the advisers who recommended that the U.S. offer the USSR a partial ban outlawing tests in the atmosphere, the sea and in outer space. Kaysen accompanied Ambassador Averell Harriman [q.v.] on the Moscow mission that resulted in the signing of a partial test ban agreement in August 1963. During the ratification hearings on the treaty, he coordinated the Administration's effort at the behest of Secretary of Defense Robert S. McNamara [q.v.]. The treaty was approved by the Senate in September 1963.

Kaysen returned to Harvard in 1964. In 1966 he became director of the Institute for Advanced Studies at Princeton.

[EWS]

KEATING, KENNETH B(ARNARD)
b. May 18, 1900; Lima, N.Y.
d. May 5, 1975; New York, N.Y.
Republican Senator, N.Y., 1959-65.

Kenneth Keating, the junior senator from New York during the Kennedy Administration, began his political career as a member of the House of Representatives in 1946. There, as a congressman from New York's conservative upstate region, he compiled a record as a strong anti-Communist and proponent of law enforcement measures but also as a supporter of many domestic welfare bills and civil rights proposals.

In 1958 Keating was elected to the Senate on the coattails of Nelson Rockefeller [q.v.], who won the governorship that year by a wide margin. While in the upper house the Senator attempted to broaden his support and extend his political base to New York City by voting more liberally, particularly on domestic legislation. During the Kennedy Administration he was one of the President's most consistent Republican supporters in the Senate.

Keating gained prominence in the summer of 1962 as a vocal critic of the Kennedy Administration's "do-nothing" Cuban policy. Keating received refugee reports in August that the Soviet Union was increasing its weapons buildup in Cuba, and the Senator soon began a campaign to force the government into some form of "action." On Oct. 10 he issued a public statement charging that Russia was installing offensive missiles on the island. Despite attempts to check Keating's claims, the Central Intelligence Agency (CIA) could not verify them, and Keating refused to disclose his sources. Without substantiation President Kennedy refused to act on the reports. On Oct. 14 the CIA received photographic evidence of the existence of missiles on the island. One week later Kennedy announced a U.S. blockade of the island until the weapons were removed.

Keating's action in the pre-crisis period was widely criticized as an attempt to "make political hay" in the fall election campaign. In November the Senator, fearing that he would also be charged with either peddling unfounded rumors or failing to give the government information vital to national security, attempted to justify his action. Keating maintained that he had verified the rumors with a government official who had "access to reliable information." When asked why high-level intelligence officers were ignorant of the reports, Keating implied that the official had concealed the information from his superiors. Despite continued pressure the Senator refused to divulge the identity of his informant.

Keating lost his race for reelection to Robert F. Kennedy [q.v.] in 1964. One year later he was elected to the New York State Court of Appeals and served there until 1969 when President Richard M. Nixon appointed him ambassador to India. Keating resigned the post in 1972 to work for the reelection of the President. From 1973 until his death in May 1975, he was ambassador to Israel. [See NIXON Volume]

[EWS]

KEFAUVER, C(AREY) ESTES
b. July 26, 1903; Madisonville, Tenn.
d. Aug. 10, 1963; Bethesda, Md.
Democratic Senator, Tenn., 1949-63;
Chairman, Judiciary Subcommittee on
Antitrust and Monopoly, 1957-63.

Born into a socially prominent Tennessee family, Estes Kefauver took his law degree at Yale and returned to Chattanooga where over the next 12 years he established one of the city's most successful corporate legal practices. After brief tenure as state Commissioner of Finance and Taxation, Kefauver won a special election to Congress in 1939 as a New Deal Democrat. Kefauver gained national recognition as chairman of a postwar House subcommittee on small business which investigated economic concentration in American industry. He was also a consistent advocate of the Tennessee Valley Authority and other public power projects.

In 1947 Kefauver assembled a coalition of union, women's, Negro and professional groups and waged a successful nine-month senatorial primary campaign against the Memphis-based political machine of Tennessee Democratic "boss" Ed Crump. (It was during this campaign that Kefauver adopted the coonskin cap as his political trademark after Crump attacked him as a "pet coon".)

Kefauver's national reputation grew during his early years in the Senate. He coauthored the 1950 Kefauver-Celler Act to regulate corporate purchases of competitors' assets. In 1950 and 1951 he chaired a special Senate committee appointed to investigate organized crime. The "Kefauver Committee" generated little new information on the problem, but the televised hearings increased Kefauver's national exposure and helped him win several Northern state primaries in his unsuccessful quest for the 1952 Democratic presidential nomination. Defeated by Adlai Stevenson [q.v.], Kefauver again ran for the Party's presidential nomination in 1956. The Democratic Convention again chose Stevenson, but the Tennessee Senator won a dramatic second ballot victory over John F. Kennedy for the vice presidential nomination. In 1956 Sen. Kefauver campaigned primarily in the Midwest and the West, vigorously attacking

President Eisenhower's farm program.

The defeat of the Stevenson-Kefauver ticket and the prospect of a difficult Senate primary fight in August 1960 attracted national attentions back to Tennessee. The Senate primary fight in August 1960 attacked national interest because Kefauver's independence from the Senate's Southern bloc and his support of the 1960 voting rights bill were viewed as issues that would test the Democratic national ticket's November chances in the South. A massive turnout gave Kefauver an overwhelming primary victory, which the anti-Kefauver *Nashville Banner* called "one of the most surprising votes in Tennessee's political history." Kefauver called his primary success "an indication that the South wants to go ahead with the New Frontiers advocated by our Democratic candidate." In the fall of 1960 Kefauver campaigned for the national ticket for 38 days in 16 states and was singled out by Drew Pearson [q.v.] as one of the five men who worked hardest to elect John F. Kennedy President.

In 1958 Kefauver became chairman of the Judiciary Subcommittee on antitrust and monopoly and in December 1959 began hearings on the prescription drug industry as part of the subcommittee's ongoing investigation of economic concentration in American industry. By this time Kefauver was considered, in the words of biographer Joseph B. Gorman, "a walking legend by at least a score of his Democratic colleagues" who "could personally deliver at least 10 votes on any issue by the sheer force of his reputation as champion of the public interest."

As a result of the subcommittee's examination of the drug industry, Kefauver introduced an omnibus bill in April 1961 to tighten federal antitrust, patent and health laws affecting the prescription drug industry. The bill's history was a stormy one. The committee's hearings and its 1961 report had been denounced by subcommittee member Everett Dirksen (R, Ill.) [q.v.] as a "monstrosity." After the subcommittee reported Kefauver's bill to the full Judiciary Committee in March 1962, the Kennedy Administration sought to bypass Kefauver by sending its own measure to the House. The Administration again compromised when officials from the Department of Health, Education and Welfare met secretly with representatives of Everett Dirksen, James Eastland (D, Miss) [q.v.] and the drug industry to hammer out a bill acceptable to all parties present. Kefauver first learned of the meeting three days later when the Judiciary Committee met to consider his bill and he discovered that the coalition he had assembled now supported the weaker compromise measure. Declaring that "I've never been so disturbed by double dealing in all my life," Kefauver demanded and received that afternoon a delay in a vote on the Interior Department's annual appropriation so that he could address the Senate. Despite the last minute pleas of presidential adviser Myer Feldman [q.v.] and Bobby Baker [q.v.], secretary to the Senate majority, Kefauver charged that the Administration's cooperation with opponents of the measure had "just about knocked this bill right out of the ring." Sen. Eastland replied by accepting responsibility for calling the secret meeting, explaining that Kefauver had not been invited "because I thought it would be a futile act. I did not think he would make any agreement with respect to anything."

Kefauver carried his fight for a strong bill to the Senate floor, where in July 1962 his efforts were aided by the publicity given to the many birth deformities caused by thalidomide, a sedative taken by women during pregnancy. The thalidomide revelations contributed to a stronger bill's unanimous passage in both chambers in early October. President Kennedy signed it Oct. 9, 1962. The Kefauver-Harris Act contained many of the Tennessee Senator's original proposals. Kefauver told the *New York Times* that "as far as getting safer, better tested, more accurately advertised drugs, it's an excellent bill." But the law did not include Kefauver's proposals to reduce exclusive patent ownership of a drug from 17 to 3 years, lower drug prices or provide for government licensing of drug manufactures. Despite these drawbacks the *Times* singled out Kefauver as "the hero of this victory."

Kefauver also clashed with the Kennedy Administration over its communications satellite program. He maintained that the plan to turn at least a major part of the satellite communications industry over to the American Telephone and Telegraph Company encouraged monopoly and subsidized the corporation at taxpayers' expense. He was one of three Senators to sign a letter to the President urging that space communications experimentation and research be undertaken by the federal government. From July 26 to July 31, 1962 Kefauver led a "liberal filibuster" in an attempt to keep the bill from becoming the pending business of the Senate. Kefauver lost the 1962 battle over private versus public development of space communications but pursued the issue during the August 1963 debate over the National Aeronautics and Space Administration's appropriation. On Aug. 8 Kefauver introduced an amendment designed to prevent government space research from becoming a "free gift" to the new Communications Satellite Corporation. During the debate Kefauver suffered a mild heart attack. He was hospitalized, but before surgery was performed his aorta burst and he died on Aug. 10.

[DKR]

For further information:
Joseph B. Gorman, *Estes Kefauver* (New York, 1971).

KELSEY, FRANCES O(LDHAM)
b. July 24, 1914; Vancouver Island, Canada.
Medical Officer, Food and Drug Administration, 1960-   .

During the early 1960s Dr. Frances O. Kelsey, a medical officer with the Food and Drug Administration, won fame for her efforts to prevent distribution in the United States of thalidomide, a drug subsequently discovered to produce grave birth defects.

She did her undergraduate work at McGill University in Montreal, coming to the U.S. in the mid-1930s to study pharmacology under the distinguished Dr. E.M.K. Geiling at the University of Chicago. After taking her doctorate from Chicago in 1938, she remained to teach in the school's department of pharmacology. In 1944 she married a departmental colleague, Dr. F. Ellis Kelsey. Frances Kelsey subsequently won an M.D. from the University of Chicago Medical School. When her husband took a teaching job at the University of South Dakota Medical School in 1952, she engaged in an extensive private practice, traveling widely throughout South Dakota. At the same time she held the post of associate professor of pharmacology at the University of South Dakota Medical School. In 1960, when her husband won appointment to the National Institutes of Health in Washington, D.C., Frances Kelsey took a position with the Food and Drug Administration (FDA).

Working in an uncarpeted office in a temporary barracks building constructed during World War II, Kelsey was responsible for evaluating the applications of pharmaceutical firms for licenses to market new drugs. In September 1960 she received a request from the William S. Merrell Company to market thalidomide, a drug first developed in West Germany and sold widely throughout Europe. Physicians commonly prescribed thalidomide as a "safe" sleeping pill because an overdose would not result in death.

Kelsey noted that the physiological effects of thalidomide on laboratory animals was somewhat different from drugs that it chemically resembled. She withheld permission to market the drug pending further tests of its safety. The Merrell company charged that Kelsey was over-cautious and undertook a major lobbying effort to win approval of its drug. Nevertheless, Kelsey's superiors in the FDA supported her stand, and by the end of 1961 she was vindicated. In November of that year a West German scientist issued a report suggesting that pregnant women who took thalidomide risked giving birth to infants with severely deformed limbs. Subsequently, this report was widely confirmed.

Kelsey was hailed as a great public servant who had saved the American public from disaster. In August 1962 President Kennedy granted her the Award for Distinguished Federal Civilian Service.

As a result of the thalidomide episode, Congress was moved to pass long-delayed legislation placing the drug industry under greater governmental control. Testifying before a Senate subcommittee in August 1962,

Kelsey suggested that the FDA needed authority, not simply to control the marketing, but also the testing of drugs. This authority was granted in legislation passed in October 1962. In December of that year Dr. Kelsey was named head of a new division of the FDA formed to test new drugs.

[JLW]

KENNAN, GEORGE F(ROST)
b. Feb. 16, 1904; Milwaukee, Wisc.
Ambassador to Yugoslavia, May 1961-July 1963.

Kennan entered the foreign service in 1926, serving over the next two decades in nearly a dozen Eastern and Central European posts. Two tours of duty in Moscow (1933-35; 1944-46) secured his recognition as an expert on Soviet-American relations. The reports he filed during his second stay in Moscow outlined his recommendations for a policy to resist Soviet expansionism that came to be known as "containment." These reports, published in modified form under the name "X" in the journal Foreign Affairs in July 1947, led to appointments as director of the State Department's policy planning staff and subsequently as counselor to the Department. Kennan returned to Moscow as ambassador in 1952, but the Soviets demanded his recall a few months later after he publicly chided them for their treatment of Western diplomats. Shortly after arriving back in the U.S., Kennan publicly dissented from views expressed by John Foster Dulles, President-elect Eisenhower's designated Secretary of State. The incident resulted in his premature retirement from the Foreign Service. [See TRUMAN Volume]

During the Eisenhower Administration Kennan taught and wrote at the Institute for Advanced Studies at Princeton University. In 1957 his call for the unification of a disarmed and neutralized Germany provoked a bitter debate both in the U.S. and Europe. Sen. John F. Kennedy wrote Kennan in February 1958 to express admiration for the general tenor of his remarks and reservations on many of the specific recommendations. [See EISENHOWER Volume]

Three days after his inauguration Kennedy

offered Kennan the ambassadorship to either Yugoslavia or Poland. Kennan accepted the Belgrade post and was officially designated ambassador on Feb. 8, 1961. A few days later Kennan and other former ambassadors to the Soviet Union met with the President for a reevaluation of U.S. policy toward the USSR in the light of Soviet Premier Nikita Khrushchev's conciliatory statements since Kennedy's election. Although Kennan—and perhaps the other ambassadors—were professionally skeptical about summit diplomacy, the immediate outcome of the meeting was an invitation to Khrushchev for a face-to-face meeting with the President. (The meeting, held in Vienna June 3-4, 1961, increased tensions between the two countries.)

When Kennan arrived in Belgrade in early May 1961, U.S.-Yugoslav relations were deteriorating as rapidly as Soviet-Yugoslav relations were improving. President Tito's vehement denunciation of the Bay of Pigs invasion in April and his indulgent comments on the Soviet Union's resumption of atmospheric nuclear testing in September fueled congressional antagonism toward Yugoslavia's Communist regime. Bending to the prevailing mood, the Administration delayed the sale of surplus wheat requested by Yugoslavia under the Food for Peace program. The delay infuriated Tito, who saw it as an attempt to force his country to change its foreign policy. An agreement on the sale was finally signed in April 1962.

Kennan's first months in Belgrade were further complicated by congressional opposition to the delivery of the final components for 130 obsolescent U.S. F-86D jet fighters purchased during the Eisenhower Administration. When the sale was revealed in October 1961, Sen. John Tower (R, Tex.) [q.v.], asserting that it was "foolish to sell arms to the enemy," urged a total aid embargo on Yugoslavia. Backed by Sen. Henry Jackson (D, Wash.) [q.v.] and other legislators, Tower demanded that four pilots and five technicians being trained in Texas be sent home to Yugoslavia. After Kennedy publicly hinted that he too doubted the wisdom of the sale, Kennan flew back to Washington and extracted an oral commitment from the President that the delivery would be carried out. (He reported in his memoirs, however, that the components still had not arrived when he resigned in 1963.)

Congressional attempts to manage U.S.-Yugoslav relations continued to frustrate Kennan during 1962. Sen. William Proxmire (D, Wisc.) [q.v.] introduced an amendment to the foreign aid bill in June 1962 to bar all aid to Yugoslavia. A week later the House Ways and Means Committee added a restriction to the trade expansion bill canceling Yugoslavia's most-favored-nation status. Kennan, convinced these actions could severely damage Yugoslavia's economy and jeopardize repayment of its debts to the U.S., returned to Washington July 1 for urgent consultations with the President. With Kennedy's approval he lobbied for a week on Capitol Hill and took the Administration's case to the press.

Kennedy had released Kennan's confidential assessment describing the congressional proposals as "little short of tragic" to the New York Times in mid-June. Proxmire replied, castigating Tito in a letter-to-the-editor. In a letter to the Times and a long article in the Washington Post, Kennan warned that "vindictive" measures would only force Yugoslavia closer to the Soviet Union. The Administration effectively mobilized Senate allies to add a loophole to the Proxmire amendment giving the President wide discretion in its implementation. Assured that his efforts had been successful, Kennan left for Belgrade at the end of July. On Sept. 27 he received a telephone call over an open circuit from a State Department official informing him that the Senate-House conference committee had retained the most-favored-nation restriction and that only Kennan's personal appeal to Kennedy for presidential intervention could reverse the decision. Aware that the Yugoslavs had monitored the conversation, Kennan immediately called Kennedy. The President sympathized but merely transferred the call to Wilbur Mills [q.v.], chairman of the House Ways and Means Committee. Mills proved unreceptive, and on Oct. 4 the bill with the restriction still intact was signed into law.

Kennan concluded that this rejection of his advice had destroyed his credibility in full view of the Yugoslav government. Two weeks later he decided to resign as soon as possible. He later wrote that Congress had made a major contribution to the Soviet-Yugoslav reconciliation signaled by Tito's December 1962 visit to Moscow, where he received a warm ovation from the Supreme Soviet. Kennan's resignation was announced May 17, 1963. He returned to the U.S. in July to resume his academic career at Princeton. During the Johnson Administration Kennan was a forceful critic of U.S. policy in Indochina, notably in his testimony before the Senate Foreign Relations Committee in 1966. [See JOHNSON Volume]

[EWK]

For further information:
George F. Kennan, *Memoirs: 1960-1963* (Boston, 1972).

KENNEDY, EDWARD M(OORE)
b. Feb. 22, 1932; Brookline, Mass.
Democratic Senator, Mass., 1962- .

Edward Kennedy, the youngest of the nine children of multimillionaire financier Joseph Kennedy [q.v.], was the brother of President John F. Kennedy and Attorney General Robert F. Kennedy [q.v.].

Like the rest of the Kennedy children, Edward was encouraged from an early age to take a strong interest in public affairs. Kennedy attended schools in England and America before entering Harvard in 1951. During his freshman year he was suspended for cheating on a Spanish exam and subsequently served two years in the U.S. Army before returning to Harvard. After his graduation in 1956 Kennedy went on to take his law degree from the University of Virginia Law School in 1959.

Kennedy's first important participation in politics came when he served as his brother's campaign manager in Sen. John Kennedy's 1958 reelection race. Already actively seeking the 1960 Democratic presidential nomination, John Kennedy spent less than 17 days in Massachusetts but won an impressive victory. During the 1960 presidential campaign Edward Kennedy was put in charge of the Kennedy campaign in the Mountain and Pacific states. Richard Nixon [q.v.] took all but three of those states in the November election.

After his victory John Kennedy negotiated the appointment of staunch Kennedy-supporter Benjamin A. Smith to fill his own vacant Senate seat until the next statewide election, by which time his youngest brother would be 30, the age required for election to the Senate. Meanwhile, Edward Kennedy began to groom himself for political office. In December 1960 he traveled to Africa on a "fact-finding" mission with three members of the Senate Foreign Relations Committee; then he took his first job as a dollar-a-year assistant prosecutor in the Suffolk County (Mass.) district attorney's office.

Amid Republican and liberal accusations of "nepotism" and charges that the Kennedy family was attempting to start a political dynasty, Edward Kennedy announced his candidacy for the Senate in 1962. His opponent in the Democratic primary was Edward J. McCormack, Massachusetts attorney general and nephew of House Speaker John McCormack (D, Mass.) [q.v.]. According to President Kennedy's aide Theodore Sorensen [q.v.], the President's biggest worry during his brother's campaign was that it would place a strain on his own cordial relations with the Speaker, but both men remained generally aloof from the contest. The voters' negative reaction to Edward McCormack's ferocious personal attacks on Kennedy's youth and inexperience contributed to an easy Kennedy victory in the Democratic primary. Kennedy went on to win the general election with 57% of the vote over the equally inexperienced George Cabot Lodge, son of Henry Cabot Lodge [q.v.].

According to one of Edward Kennedy's biographers, Theo Lippman, Jr., Kennedy's "performance in the two years [of his brother's unexpired term] is barely visible in any records of government activity." Sworn in on Jan. 9, 1963, Kennedy was determined to fit smoothly into the Senate "establishment" by courting such senior senators as James Eastland (D, Miss.) [q.v.] and Richard Russell (D, Ga.) [q.v.]. Appointed to the Judiciary and the Labor and Public Welfare Committees, Kennedy supported the President on most major issues in 1963. He was particularly interested in securing defense contracts for Massachusetts. Kennedy pursued the matter with such zeal that Sen. Kenneth Keating (R, N.Y.) [*q.v.*] accused him of trying to lure contracts away from New York State. In 1963 Kennedy supported mass transit and wilderness preservation bills and voted for ratification of the nuclear test ban treaty. He was presiding over the Senate on Nov. 22, 1963 when word came that his brother had been assassinated in Dallas.

Reelected in 1964 despite severe injuries suffered in a plane crash, Kennedy played a major role during the Johnson Administration in the revision of U.S. immigration laws and in the drive to give 18-year-olds the vote. In the late 1960s Kennedy was one of the main backers of national health insurance legislation. An opponent of the Vietnam war, he became particularly identified with alleviating the plight of the Vietnamese refugees.

Many observers believed that Kennedy was content to pursue a career in the Senate while helping his brother, Sen. Robert Kennedy (D, N.Y.), gain national office. But in June 1968 Robert Kennedy, then an active presidential candidate, was assassinated in Los Angeles. At the 1968 Democratic National Convention, Edward Kennedy refused to allow his name to be put in nomination, but he remained a major Democratic presidential contender until he was involved in a July 1969 automobile accident on Chappaquiddick Island, off Martha's Vineyard, Mass., in which a young woman was drowned.

In 1969 Kennedy defeated Sen. Russell Long (D, La.) [*q.v.*] for the post of majority whip. He was easily reelected to the Senate in 1970. Aided by a strong political organization in Massachusetts, a competent staff and the lingering attractions of the Kennedy mystique, Edward Kennedy emerged as one of the most powerful members of the U.S. Senate in the early 1970s. [See JOHNSON, NIXON Volumes]

[FHM]

For further information:
James McGregor Burns, *Edward Kennedy and the Camelot Legacy* (New York, 1976).
Theo Lippman, Jr., *Senator Ted Kennedy* (New York, 1976).

KENNEDY, JACQUELINE (LEE BOUVIER)

b. July 28, 1929; Southampton, N.Y.
First Lady, January 1961-November 1963.

Descended from a French family that came to the U.S. during the Revolutionary War, Jacqueline Bouvier grew up in New York City and spent her summers in fashionable East Hampton, Long Island. After her parents' divorce and her mother's subsequent marriage to wealthy Washington stockbroker Hugh D. Auchincloss in 1942, she lived at the Auchincloss estates in Newport, R.I., and Virginia. After a junior year of study at the Sorbonne pursuing an interest in art, she graduated from George Washington University in Washington in 1951. First introduced to Sen. John Kennedy in 1952, the couple married on Sept. 12, 1953 in one of the most publicized society weddings of that year.

During Kennedy's campaign for the 1960 Democratic presidential nomination, Mrs. Kennedy often accompanied her husband on campaign trips through primary states. However, due to a pregnancy, she did not attend the Democratic National Convention in Los Angeles in July 1960. During the presidential campaign itself she gave political tea parties, wrote a newspaper column called "Campaign Wife" and stressed her private role as wife of the candidate and mother of three-year-old Caroline Kennedy. John F. Kennedy, Jr., was born in November 1960, shortly after the election.

It was Mrs. Kennedy's stated belief that "whoever lives in the White House must preserve its traditions, enhance it, and leave something of herself there." During her husband's tenure she made an effort to restore the White House as a period mansion of the 18th and 19th centuries. She appointed a curator to catalog historical items and created a Fine Arts Committee for the White House composed of art and historical experts. Her interest and expertise in this area were highlighted on Feb. 14, 1962, when she conducted an hour-long televised tour of the White House, commenting on the furnishings and the history of the rooms. The show subsequently received special Emmy and Peabody awards.

During the Administration Mrs. Kennedy was instrumental in lessening the formality of state occasions by including an admixture of writers, artists and prominent musicians at White House functions. She was also a trend-setter in fashion and turned out to be a surprising political and diplomatic asset to the President once the public became accustomed to a young and elegant, if somewhat aloof, First Lady. Her trip to Paris with the President in June 1961 and a visit to India in March 1962 were accounted goodwill triumphs for the U.S.

In November 1963 Mrs. Kennedy accompanied the President to Texas in her first real public appearance since the death of her prematurely born son, Patrick, the previous August. She was sitting beside the President when he was shot to death in an open car on Nov. 22, 1963 in Dallas. Later the same day she witnessed the swearing-in of President Johnson [q.v.] aboard Air Force One. Mrs. Kennedy's conduct and bearing during the aftermath of the assassination earned her worldwide respect and contributed to the power of the Kennedy mystique in the 1960s.

In 1967 Mrs. Kennedy was involved in legal action concerning William Manchester's book *The Death of a President*, portions of which she regarded as a violation of her privacy and wished deleted. In October 1968 she married Greek shipping magnate Aristotle Onassis. [See JOHNSON Volume]

[FHM]

For further information:
Kenneth P. O'Donnell and David F. Powers, *Johnny, We Hardly Knew Ye* (New York, 1970).
Pierre Salinger, *With Kennedy* (New York, 1966).

KENNEDY, JOHN F(ITZGERALD)
b. May 29, 1917; Brookline, Mass.
d. Nov. 22, 1963; Dallas, Tex.
President of the United States, January 1961-November 1963.

By the end of the 19th century both of John F. Kennedy's grandfathers were important figures in the world of Boston Democratic politics. His father, who was the first member of the Irish Catholic family to attend and graduate from Harvard, turned his considerable talents to business. In the 1920s Joseph Kennedy [q.v.] amassed a fortune in banking, securities speculation and the new motion picture industry. His social and financial success enabled the Kennedy children to penetrate the bastions of New England and New York society.

John F. Kennedy attended Choate, spent a year at Princeton and then went to Harvard, where he graduated in 1940. While John was still in college his father was appointed ambassador to Great Britain, and John Kennedy spent several vacations and part of a school year in England and on the continent. Out of these experiences came a senior thesis, which recounted and condemned England's prewar policy of appeasement. Published as *Why England Slept*, it became a best-seller in 1940.

After a brief attendance at Stanford Business School in 1941, Kennedy enlisted in the Navy. He served as the commander of a torpedo boat, which was sunk in a 1943 South Pacific engagement heavily publicized in Kennedy's subsequent political career.

Upon his discharge from the service, Kennedy worked for a few months as a journalist before he plunged into a campaign for Boston's 11th district U.S. House seat. Backed by his father, who had long held political ambitions for his sons, Kennedy waged a well planned, vigorous effort, which proved a prototype of his future campaigns. Elected with little difficulty from the predominantly Irish-Italian district, Kennedy usually voted with other Northern liberals in Congress. His tenure in the lower chamber was a conventional one, although he created a small furor in 1949 when he attacked President Harry S Truman [q.v.] and the State Department for what he considered the unnecessary loss of mainland China to the Communists.

In 1952 Kennedy ran against the popular incumbent senator from Massachusetts, Republican Henry Cabot Lodge [q.v.]. Despite Dwight D. Eisenhower's [q.v.] easy win the state, Kennedy demonstrated remarkable popularity by defeating Lodge by approximately 70,000 votes.

As a senator, Kennedy's first few years in office were marked by pivotal personal and political events that shaped his future career. In September 1953 he married Jacqueline Lee Bouvier [q.v.], a beautiful, cultured woman of 24 who would later gain an immense following as the First Lady. The next year Kennedy underwent a long, difficult back operation in October. His hospitalization and lengthy recuperation forced his absence from Senate business when the upper house debated censure of Sen. Joseph McCarthy (R, Wisc.). Although Kennedy had earlier opposed some of McCarthy's methods, he considered the Wisconsin Senator popular in heavily Catholic Massachusetts, and he therefore took advantage of his absence to avoid taking a stand when the Senate voted censure in December 1954. Kennedy later endorsed the Senate's vote, but his equivocation on the issue made him suspect in some sections of the liberal and intellectual community when he ran for President five years later.

During the months when he was convalescing from his back operation, Kennedy wrote *Profiles in Courage*, a study of fidelity to political principle by seven American politicians over a 150-year period. The book, published in early 1956, was a bestseller and gave Kennedy important national exposure.

Kennedy nominated Adlai Stevenson [q.v.] for President at the Democratic National Convention in 1956. When Stevenson threw the vice presidential nomination open to the Convention, Kennedy and a few aides organized a spirited campaign for the second place on the ticket. They lost to Sen. Estes Kefauver (D, Tenn.) [q.v.] on the third ballot, but Kennedy again achieved widespread political recognition.

Kennedy immediately began to lay the groundwork for a 1960 presidential campaign. Over the next three years, he made some 1,000 speeches in all parts of the nation, demonstrated his formidable popularity by winning reelection to the Senate by almost a million votes in 1958 and carefully built a national legislative record that would

appeal to Democratic Party liberals and moderates. [See EISENHOWER Volume]

By the time he officially announced his candidacy in January 1960, Kennedy held a slight edge in the opinion polls over his chief rivals, Sens. Hubert Humphrey (D, Minn.) [q.v.], Lyndon Johnson (D, Tex.) [q.v.] and Stuart Symington (D, Mo.) [q.v.]. In addition to his substantial personal and family wealth, Kennedy's greatest asset was a tightly knit, brilliantly staffed campaign organization. His brother Robert Kennedy [q.v.] served as campaign manager; legislative aide Theodore Sorenson [q.v.] wrote many of his speeches; experienced political professionals Lawrence O'Brien [q.v.] and Kenneth O'Donnell [q.v.] took on the often delicate task of winning the candidate support among other powerful forces in the Democratic Party.

Kennedy and his staff decided that the candidate's youth and his Catholicism were the two greatest obstacles to the nomination. Their strategy, therefore, was to prove Kennedy's electability by entering and winning a series of Democratic state primaries. Two contests were crucial—Wisconsin in April and West Virginia in May. Against Sen. Humphrey Kennedy carried Wisconsin by a relatively close four-to-three margin, but an analysis of the vote indicated that Catholics and Protestants divided heavily along religious lines when marking their ballots. This made West Virginia, with a 95% Protestant population, even more decisive. Kennedy mounted a major organizational and financial effort in the state and surprised political observers by capturing 61% of the vote, thereby convincing Humphrey to withdraw as an active contender.

By the time the Los Angeles Democratic National Convention opened in July, Kennedy had won delegates in seven state primaries and had lined up the vital support of such important political leaders as Chicago Mayor Richard Daley [q.v.], Pennsylvania Gov. David Lawrence [q.v.] and Ohio Gov. Michael DiSalle [q.v.]. On the first ballot Kennedy captured the nomination with 806 votes to 409 for his chief rival, Lyndon Johnson, who received most of his support from the South and West. To balance the ticket Kennedy then selected Johnson as his vice presidential running mate, a choice that provoked immediate if transitory anger among many liberals in the party.

In the general election campaign neither Kennedy nor his Republican opponent, Vice President Richard M. Nixon [q.v.], could find an issue that sharply divided them. Both thought foreign policy the over-riding issue in the election. Both favored a strong defense and vigorous diplomacy to ensure continued American leadership of the West. Although Kennedy took a some-what less aggressive stand than did his rival on the need to defend Nationalist China's island outposts, the Democratic candidate criticized the Republicans for not taking stronger action against Cuba, and he warned of an ominous, but later disproven, "missile gap" between the U.S. and the USSR. At home Kennedy promised to "get the country moving again," although he avoided direct attacks on President Eisenhower because he recognized and feared the incumbent's immense popularity. "Rarely in American history," wrote jour-nalist Theodore White [q.v.] "has there been a political campaign that discussed is-sues less or clarified them less."

Despite a lack of political controversy, Kennedy's presidential campaign was one of the most effective and resourceful in recent history. He defused the religious issue by declaring his adherence to the "absolute" separation of church and state before a televised meeting of the Houston Ministe-rial Association in September. Late the next month Kennedy won new support in the black community when he made a sym-pathetic phone call to Mrs. Martin Luther King [q.v.] after her husband was jailed in a civil rights incident. (Meanwhile, Robert Kennedy called the local judge and secured King's release.)

Kennedy's charm, wit and sophistication won him the respect of much of the working press, while his boyish good looks and glamorous family and associates excited campaign crowds and brought the word "charisma" into vogue. Many political ob-servers thought the turning point in the campaign came on Sept. 26 during the first of four televised debates between the two candidates. Kennedy, who had sought the debate, proved confident and vigorous, while his opponent, still recovering from a two-week hospital stay, appeared hesitant and weary. Neither candidate "won" the debate, but Kennedy's cool, relaxed style proved attractive to many viewers.

In the election a record turnout gave Kennedy the victory by a mere 113,057 vote margin—the smallest of the 20th cen-tury. He carried fewer states than Nixon but defeated his opponent in the electorial college, 219 to 303, because the Democratic Party carried most of the big industrial states as well as the Deep South. Political analysts later reported that the religious issue had had a major impact on voting pat-terns. Kennedy lost much of Protestant Ap-palachia, but probably more than counter-balanced these defections by capturing a solid Catholic vote in the urban North.

Kennedy assumed the presidency deter-mined to give the office the activist orienta-tion he thought it lacked under Eisenhower. The President, Kennedy had declared in his campaign, "must be pre-pared to exercise the fullest powers of his office—all that are specified and some that are not." Decision making in the White House would be "tough-minded" and "pragmatic," unswayed by sentimentality, ideology or the pull of interest and faction. Kennedy later spelled out the rationale be-hind his self-confidence. "Most of the prob-lems. . .that we now face," he told a Yale audience in June 1962, "are technical prob-lems, are administrative problems. They are very sophisticated judgments which do not lend themselves to the great sort of 'passionate movements' which have stirred this country so often in the past."

The new President assembled a cabinet that reflected his own sense of political realism and pragmatic liberalism. Kennedy appointed many of his early liberal backers to top domestic policy posts. Connecticut Gov. Abraham Ribicoff [q.v.] took over the Department of Health, Education and Wel-fare, and AFL-CIO Counsel Arthur Goldberg [q.v.] was put in charge at Labor. Other liberals like Stewart Udall [q.v.] (Interior) and Orville Freeman

[*q.v.*] (Agriculture) also joined the cabinet.

But Kennedy ignored the liberal wing of his party when he chose men to fill the offices he considered sensitive. Amid some controversy he appointed his brother Robert as Attorney General. He unhesitatingly reappointed conservatives Allen Dulles [*q.v.*] and J. Edgar Hoover [*q.v.*] to lead the CIA and FBI. Finally, Kennedy gave individuals closely associated with the Eastern Establishment the posts he thought most vital. Moderate Republicans Robert S. McNamara [*q.v.*] and C. Douglas Dillon [*q.v.*] were appointed to head the Departments of Defense and the Treasury. Kennedy chose the rather colorless head of the Rockefeller Foundation, Dean Rusk [*q.v.*], as Secretary of State. The new President planned to conduct American diplomacy himself and saw in Rusk a man who would administer the State Department without threatening White House dominance in international affairs.

Kennedy considered the conduct of foreign affairs his most important responsibility and his most difficult challenge. In an inaugural address devoted almost exclusively to world affairs, he pledged the nation "to pay any price, bear any burden, meet any hardship, support any friend, oppose any foe, to assure the survival and success of liberty." Kennedy thought the Cold War was at its "hour of maximum danger," and he called for sacrifice and commitment by all citizens. In what became the most memorable line in a speech that many historians then considered the best since Lincoln's, Kennedy proclaimed, "Ask not what your country can do for you, ask what you can do for your country."

With his most influential foreign policy advisers, Gen. Maxwell Taylor [*q.v.*], McGeorge Bundy [*q.v.*] and Robert McNamara—"the best and the brightest" as David Halberstam [*q.v.*] would later call them—the President sought a new and more effective strategy for countering the Communist military and political threat. These New Frontiersmen held their fiscally conservative and ideologically rigid predecessors responsible for a dangerous overreliance upon the nuclear deterrent. Kennedy foreign policy strategists sought a more "flexible" response to the Communists, one that would counter the enemy regardless of the form its offensive took: local brushfire insurgencies, ideological warfare or diplomatic maneuver.

The Peace Corps, Food for Peace, the Alliance for Progress, economic aid for underdeveloped nations and for the dissident Communist regimes of Yugoslavia and Poland were programs inaugurated or increased by the Administration as part of its more flexible strategy in the Cold War. At the same time Kennedy favored an expanded military establishment possessing sufficient conventional, nuclear and counterinsurgency forces to effectively oppose any level of Communist aggression. During the first six months of his presidency, Kennedy asked for and received $6 billion in additional military appropriations from Congress. In all, the defense budget rose from $43 to $56 billion while Kennedy was in office.

During his first year Kennedy faced a difficult series of diplomatic and military pressures and reverses. He accepted the neutralization of Laos in early 1961 as the most advantageous solution to a troublesome local situation. In April the President suffered a personal humiliation when a CIA-planned exile invasion of Cuba was routed at the Bay of Pigs. Later in the spring the Soviets stepped up their pressure on West Berlin and demanded that the West recognize as permanent the postwar division of Germany. When Kennedy met with Nikita Khrushchev in Vienna in June, the new President appeared shaken by the Russian leader's intransigence and believed he had failed to make a strong impression on the Premier.

While Kennedy could do little to rectify the American situation in Laos or Cuba, he was determined to demonstrate U.S. firmness in Berlin. In July the President reaffirmed the American will to defend West Berlin by ordering 250,000 reservists to active duty and asking Congress for another increase in the military budget. At the same time he outlined a sweeping civil defense program designed to show the Russians America's willingness to risk nuclear war over the German city. (The USSR responded to the crisis by building the "Berlin Wall" in August and letting the issue of a German settlement die by the end of the year.)

By the fall the Communist insurgency in South Vietnam had begun to seriously weaken the American-backed regime there. Kennedy sent two of his most trusted advisers, Walt W. Rostow [q.v.] and Maxwell Taylor, to survey the situation. Upon their return Kennedy agreed to sharply increase the level of American military and economic assistance and to dispatch an additional 400 military counterinsurgency specialists there. Most historians have concluded that the stalemate in Laos, the defeat at the Bay of Pigs and the Soviet pressure on Berlin contributed to Kennedy's determination to avoid a defeat in Vietnam. Although he never authorized a full-scale commitment of U.S. ground troops to Vietnam, the number of American military "advisers" there increased from 700 to over 15,000 during his term in office.

Kennedy confronted his most serious Cold War crisis in October 1962 when American intelligence discovered that the Soviets had begun to install offensive missiles in Cuba. Working closely with his brother Robert, Kennedy rejected the views of his advisers who favored an immediate air strike, but he also opposed an extended period of negotiations or a public tradeoff of Soviet missiles in Cuba for American rockets in Italy or Turkey. Instead, Kennedy and a special committee of the National Security Council, which met each day to "manage" the crisis, decided to impose a "quarantine" of the island, which went into effect on Oct. 24. On Oct. 28 the Soviets turned back from the potential naval confrontation and agreed to remove their Cuban missiles. We were "eyeball to eyeball," said Dean Rusk, "They blinked first." Kennedy thought the successful resolution of the missile crisis a triumph for the mode of cool, rational decision making characteristic of the New Frontier. Nevertheless, he had been sobered by the imminence of nuclear war. "I want no crowing and not a word of gloating," Kennedy told his staff.

When Khruschev later suggested that negotiations be reopened toward a long-deferred nuclear test ban treaty, Kennedy quickly assented. Disagreement over on-site inspection of underground nuclear tests stalled the talks, but in a speech delivered at American University on June 10, 1963 Kennedy announced that he was sending Averell Harriman [q.v.] to Moscow to negotiate a more limited test ban agreement excluding the controversial underground tests.

The American University speech was one of Kennedy's most notable addresses. Avoiding the Cold War rhetoric he often had used in the past, Kennedy expressed his admiration for the Russian people and affirmed the common interest of both nations in avoiding nuclear holocaust. In July a limited nuclear test ban agreement was initialed in Moscow and, with surprisingly little domestic opposition, ratified by the Senate in September. Although the test ban treaty did nothing to stop the arms race, it ended the poisonous radioactive pollution of the atmosphere. It was Kennedy's most enduring achievement in foreign affairs.

Kennedy sought to act boldly in the diplomatic arena, but he was far more timid at home, especially in his relationship with Congress. The election had given him no popular mandate; in fact, the Democrats lost 20 seats in the House in 1960. In Congress a coalition of Southern Democrats and Republicans dominated much of the legislative process. Special Assistant Arthur Schlesinger, Jr. [q.v.], reported Kennedy "sensitive, perhaps overly sensitive, to the limitations imposed by Congress on the presidential power of maneuver." The New Frontier, therefore, shaped its legislative program in a cautious fashion. Truman-era programs—such as health insurance for the aged, medicare and federal aid to education—were reintroduced, but no new civil rights or labor legislation was sent to Capitol Hill from the White House.

The President began 1961 with a modest victory: backed by Speaker Sam Rayburn [q.v.], Administration forces in the House succeeded in expanding the Rules Committee by adding three new liberal members, thereby shifting control of that important Committee to a majority more favorable to the White House. Despite their success in the Rules Committee fight, Kennedy forces in the House were unable to move a medicare bill out of the Ways and Means Committee, and they were forced to accept a substantial reduction in coverage under a new minimum wage law passed in March. A modest aid-to-depressed-areas bill was passed in April, but Kennedy suffered a major legislative defeat in July when his aid-to-education bill was bottled up in the Rules Committee. (The Catholic church hierarchy was instrumental in this setback; it opposed any bill that did not provide aid for parochial schools.) With this defeat, wrote Tom Wicker, "Kennedy had lost Congress." By the time of his assassination, little additional social legislation had been passed.

Taking office in the midst of the fourth postwar recession, Kennedy gave economic recovery and sustained growth a personal priority second only to foreign affairs. His two most important economic advisers were Treasury Secretary Dillon and Walter Heller [q.v.], the Keynesian economist who headed the Council of Economic Advisers (CEA). During his first two years Kennedy deferred to Dillon's conservative fears that an overly stimulative fiscal policy would upset the balance of payments and ignite a round of inflation. The Administration's economic legislation was, therefore, of a limited and orthodox scope, including modest increases in the budget for social programs, a 7% investment tax-credit for business and the Trade Expansion Act in 1962. Though Congress passed most of these proposals, the economy remained sluggish into early 1963 when Kennedy finally agreed to Heller's long deferred suggestion for a $10 billion tax cut to stimulate economic growth. The business community quickly backed the innovation, but fiscal conservatives in Congress delayed its passage until 1964. Combined with the mounting military and space expenditures of the mid-1960s, the Kennedy tax cut provided much of the basis for the longest period of sustained economic growth in the postwar era.

Kennedy's stimulative economic policies made his Administration acutely sensitive to inflationary pressures. Since most trade unionists considered Kennedy a friendly chief executive, they agreed to keep wage increases within what the CEA considered non-inflationary wage guideposts. Ironically, it was the Administration's downward pressure on wages that led to a dramatic confrontation with the steel industry over prices. Kennedy had personally used his prestige with labor to keep the 1962 round of wage increases in the steel industry the lowest in 20 years. The President was, therefore, enraged when U.S. Steel and other major producers announced a $6-a-ton price increase on April 10.

"My father always told me that all steelmen were sons of bitches," Kennedy told his close advisers. By mobilizing the resources of the executive branch and by putting his personal influence on the line, Kennedy forced a rollback in prices during the next 72 hours. The President's standing rose among liberals but declined among businessmen. After the stock market plunged in late May, Kennedy worked hard to regain the confidence of the business community. When the steel industry "selectively" raised prices in September 1963, Kennedy and his advisers thought it wise to take no action and avoid another confrontation.

Because the President hoped to enlist Southern support for his domestic economic programs, he moved cautiously in the field of civil rights. He made frequent personal efforts to befriend powerful Southern congressmen and appointed several segregationist Southerners to federal judgeships in the deep South. He also delayed signing for almost two years an executive order, promised in his campaign, to ban segregation in federally subsidized housing. The President was sympathetic to the demands of black Americans, but he mistrusted the passions aroused by the civil rights issue and the unpredictable impact of the movement on his ability to command the political initiative. Kennedy and his brother consistently urged moderation on black leaders, especially with regard to public marches and demonstrations.

The rising tempo of the movement in the South soon forced the Administration to put its weight behind Negro demands. Federal marshals were used to ensure the integration of the Universities of Mississippi and Alabama. In April and May 1963 massive and tumultuous demonstrations in Birmingham forced Kennedy to commit himself to the legislative battle over civil rights he had long sought to avoid. Declaring that the issue was "moral" as well as "legal," in June Kennedy submitted a civil rights bill to Congress far stronger than any he had contemplated before. Although the bill, chiefly designed to desegregate public accommodations, was blocked by Southern resistance for almost a year, Kennedy enjoyed an unprecedented popularity among black Americans at the time of his death.

Looking forward to a sharp, issue-oriented campaign against the probable Republican presidential candidate, Sen. Barry Goldwater (R, Ariz.) [q.v.], Kennedy scheduled a series of political trips beginning in the fall of 1963. Among the most important was a four-day visit to Texas, where he hoped to unite the Democratic Party in the state by moderating the long-standing feud between factions identified with conservative Gov. John Connally [q.v.] and liberal Sen. Ralph Yarborough [q.v.]. While riding in a Dallas motorcade early on the afternoon of Nov. 22, Kennedy was shot and killed with a high-powered rifle fired by Lee Harvey Oswald [q.v.]. A series of public and private investigations over the next decade found no conclusive proof that the President's assassin, a man of erratic political views, did not act alone.

In the aftermath of the assassination, Kennedy's popular reputation reached heights unsurpassed in the last century, except by Lincoln and Franklin Roosevelt. "He left a myth," wrote Richard Neustadt in 1964, "[of] the vibrant, youthful leader cut down senselessly before his time." Award-winning biographies by presidential aides Arthur Schlesinger and Theodore Sorenson ably defended Kennedy as a pragmatic liberal who used a powerful intellect and growing political sensibility to break a new and progressive path in American politics.

Although the public's warm remembrance of Kennedy hardly wavered over the next decade, scholarly estimates of his policies fell in the late 1960s. Escalation of the Vietnam war cast Kennedy's early military commitment to Indochina and his Administration's aggressive Cold War posture into an unfavorable light. In the early 1970s President Nixon's abuses of executive authority prompted many historians to reconsider Kennedy's own favorable attitude toward the expansion and use of presidential power. Finally, a series of revelations concerning illegal CIA and FBI activity during the early 1960s further diminished the luster of Kennedy's years in office.

[NNL]

For further information:
James T. Crown, *The Kennedy Literature: a Bibliographical Essay on John F. Kennedy* (New York, 1968).

Henry Fairlie, *The Kennedy Promise* (New York, 1973).

Roger Hilsman, *To Move a Nation: the Politics of Foreign Policy in the Administration of John F. Kennedy* (Garden City, 1967).

Lewis J. Paper, *The Promise and the Performance* (New York, 1975).

Arthur M. Schlesinger, Jr., *A Thousand Days* (New York, 1965).

Theodore C. Sorensen, *Kennedy* (New York, 1965).

Richard J. Walton, *Cold War and Counterrevolution* (New York, 1972).

Theodore White, *The Making of the President 1960* (New York, 1961).

KENNEDY, JOSEPH P(ATRICK)
b. Sept. 6, 1888; Boston, Mass.
d. Nov. 18, 1969; Hyannis Port, Mass.
Businessman.

The multimillionaire father of one U.S. president and two U.S. senators, Joseph Kennedy grew up in Boston where his own father, Patrick Kennedy, operated several East Boston saloons and was a power in local politics. Determined that his son should not be hampered by prejudice against Irish Catholics, the elder Kennedy sent Joseph to the fashionable Boston Latin School and then to Harvard, where he majored in economics and graduated in 1912.

During the next 25 years Kennedy controlled a variety of immensely successful business enterprises and amassed a fortune estimated at $200 million. By World War I he had become the youngest bank president in U.S. history. In the 1920s he moved into the infant motion picture business—earning $5 million in three years—while at the same time speculating with great success on Wall Street.

Unlike most successful businessmen Joseph Kennedy backed much of the New Deal reform program of Franklin D. Roosevelt in the 1930s, and he contributed heavily to the President's campaigns in 1932 and 1936. In response to this political and financial support, Roosevelt appointed Kennedy the first chairman of the Securities Exchange Commission in 1934, chairman of the Maritime Commission in 1937 and ambassador to Great Britain in 1938. Representing U.S. interests in England during a crucial period in Anglo-American relations, Kennedy stirred a bitter controversy in the U.S. over his staunchly isolationist and, some thought, anti-Semitic views. In 1940 he resigned his post.

After World War II Kennedy expanded his fortune by successfully investing in New York real estate and Texas oil. He also employed his considerable political and financial influence on behalf of his son, John Kennedy, to win election first to the House of Representatives in 1946 and then to the Senate in 1952. Joseph Kennedy was instrumental in persuading powerful Sen. Joseph McCarthy (R, Wisc.), not to enter Massachusetts to campaign for John Kennedy's opponent.

In the 1960 campaign John Kennedy viewed his father as a political liability. Liberal suspicions of Kennedy's presidential candidacy focused on the extent to which the father exerted political and financial influence over his son. While Joseph Kennedy believed that the principal issue in the presidential campaign was whether a Catholic could be elected president, the main concern among Kennedy campaign staffers was that the elder Kennedy's alleged anti-Semitism would effect the Jewish vote in populous Northeastern States.

After his son's election, Joseph Kennedy emerged from a seclusion that he had maintained since 1952. President Kennedy often consulted his father on matters related to U.S. business, and the elder Kennedy recommended the appointemnt of Dean Rusk [q.v.] as Secretary of State. Mainly, however, Kennedy was content to bask in the glow of his son's success.

On Dec. 19, 1961 Kennedy suffered a severely debilitating stroke that left him a complete invalid until his death in November 1969.

[FHM]

Richard J. Whalen, *The Founding Father* (New York, 1964).

KENNEDY, ROBERT F(RANCIS)
b. Nov. 20, 1925; Brookline, Mass.
d. June 6, 1968; Los Angeles, Calif.
Attorney General, January 1961–September 1964.

The seventh of nine children, Robert Kennedy graduated from Harvard in 1948 and the University of Virginia Law School in 1951. He then served briefly as an attorney in the Criminal Division of the Justice Department, leaving in 1952 to manage his brother John F. Kennedy's successful campaign for U.S. senator from Massachusetts. In January 1952 he was named an assistant counsel for the Senate Permanent Subcommittee on Investigations, then chaired by Sen. Joseph McCarthy (R, Wisc.), but he resigned the post in July because of disagreement with the subcommittee's procedures. Kennedy rejoined the subcommittee in February 1954 as chief counsel for the Democratic minority and became chief counsel in January 1955 when Sen. John L. McClellan (D, Ark.) [q.v.] became chairman. From 1957 to 1959 he was chief counsel for McClellan's Senate Rackets Committee, which investigated crime and corruption in the union movement. Beginning in November 1959 Kennedy served as manager for his brother's presidential campaign. [See EISENHOWER Volume]

On Dec. 16, 1960 the President-elect

named his brother Attorney General. The appointment was widely criticized as nepotistic. Some also called Robert Kennedy, then 35, too inexperienced in the law and too ruthless a prosecutor and politician to be Attorney General. During his four years as head of the Justice Department, Kennedy would repeatedly encounter charges that he was arrogant, power-hungry and ruthless, although he impressed many legal observers as the best Attorney General in years.

By all accounts Kennedy assembled a distinguished and capable staff that produced legal work of high quality. A man of action who valued courage, achievement and excellence, Kennedy ran the Department in an informal manner. He delegated much authority, made himself visible and accessible throughout the Department and was open to ideas and suggestions from his subordinates. Ignoring jurisdictional boundaries, Kennedy put his aides to work wherever they could be of use, sending men from the Organized Crime Section, for example, into Mississippi to investigate the Ku Klux Klan.

In addition, Kennedy was frequently credited with having established Justice Department control over J. Edgar Hoover [q.v.] and the FBI, largely because of his special relationship with the President. For the first time in years, FBI communications with the White House went through the Attorney General's office, and Kennedy involved the Bureau in areas such as civil rights and organized crime that it had previously avoided. Although acknowledging that Kennedy had an impact on the FBI, Victor Navasky has challenged the view that the Attorney General effectively asserted his authority over the Bureau. Kennedy and his aides, Navasky has argued, learned how to manipulate the FBI, but Hoover retained control of the agency, and the Bureau's resistance to change kept its usefulness in civil rights, for example, well below its potential.

From the Rackets Committee investigations, Kennedy had developed a special interest in organized crime. When he became Attorney General, he made a drive against it his top priority. He increased the budget and manpower of the Organized Crime Section and sent out special prosecutors to investigate, indict and try cases against top rackets figures. Kennedy attempted to mobilize public opinion, won passage in Congress of a package of anti-crime bills in 1961 and 1962 and for the first time won cooperation from other government agencies in the anti-racketeering effort. In 1960 the Justice Department had secured convictions of 14 organized crime figures; in Kennedy's last year as Attorney General, some 325 racketeers were convicted.

The McClellan Committee's work had also convinced Kennedy that James R. Hoffa [q.v.] and the Teamsters Union he headed were involved in criminal activities. As Attorney General he recruited a special group of attorneys in the Labor and Racketeering Divisions who investigated and prosecuted Hoffa, ultimately winning two convictions in 1964 on charges of jury tampering and misuse of union pension funds. The Justice Department also successfully prosecuted 115 other Teamster officials or their close associates during Kennedy's years as Attorney General.

Although the Supreme Court upheld the Hoffa convictions, many commentators charged Kennedy with abusing his power by concentrating so many resources on one individual.

Kennedy was also criticized as being insensitive to civil liberties. In 1961 he endorsed a broad bill to legalize wiretapping that was opposed by civil liberties groups. Under an arrangement dating back to Franklin Roosevelt's Administration, Kennedy also authorized wiretaps by the FBI in cases involving national security. The most celebrated example of this, revealed in later years, was a tap on civil rights leader Martin Luther King [q.v.], which Kennedy authorized in October 1963, apparently because of the FBI's insistence that there was a Communist effort to influence King and his organization. When evidence of illegal electronic surveillance by the FBI first came to light in 1966, Kennedy denied ever having authorized it and claimed he never had been informed of the FBI's bugging practices. Even strong Kennedy supporters who fully believe his account of events admit that he failed in not examining more closely and supervising more vigilantly the FBI's surveillance methods.

In 1962, however, the Justice Department proposed wiretap legislation that contained safeguards lacking in its 1961 bill. These won support from some civil liberties organizations. Kennedy favored the removal of security restrictions on travel to Communist countries and on visas for entry into the U.S. He also had his Department draft legislation abolishing the national origins quota system for immigrants. The Attorney General built a strong record of impartiality in prosecuting political figures for wrongdoing. During his tenure the Justice Department brought numerous Democratic political figures to trial, including several, such as James Landis [q.v.], with close political or family ties to the Kennedys.

In April 1961 Kennedy appointed a committee of distinguished attorneys to study the quality of justice afforded the poor in federal courts. Based on the committee's findings he established an Office of Criminal Justice in the Justice Department. He also sponsored the Criminal Justice Act, passed in August 1964, which provided paid counsel for indigent defendants in federal courts. Beginning in May 1961 Kennedy headed a Cabinet-level committee on juvenile delinquency, which originated the concept of community action and control later incorporated into the war on poverty programs. The Attorney General also contributed to the intellectual aura of the New Frontier by holding monthly seminars at which an expert on some topic would address Administration officials at Hickory Hill, the home of Kennedy's large and ever-growing family.

The Justice Department was the center of most civil rights action in the Kennedy Administration, and the Attorney General and Assistant Attorney General Burke Marshall [q.v.], head of the Department's Civil Rights Division, gave special emphasis to securing voting rights for blacks. They significantly increased the number of voting rights suits brought by the Department and encouraged civil rights organizations to launch a major voter registration project in the Southern states.

Kennedy's personal involvement in and commitment to civil rights increased as he responded to various crises in the South, beginning with the Freedom Rides in the spring of 1961. After the riders were attacked in Montgomery, Ala. on May 20, Kennedy sent in federal marshals to prevent further violence. He petitioned the Interstate Commerce Commission to issue an order desegregating interstate bus and rail terminals and ultimately, through negotiation and court action, integrated transportation facilities in the South. In the fall of 1962, Kennedy negotiated with Mississippi Gov. Ross Barnett [q.v.] to secure the peaceful admission of James Meredith [q.v.] to the University of Mississippi. He dispatched several assistants to the state to aid the desegregation effort and advised the President to call in federal troops when rioting against Meredith's admission erupted on the university campus Sept. 30. The Attorney General sent Burke Marshall to Birmingham, Ala. in May 1963 to try to work out a desegregation agreement that would end the demonstrations led by Martin Luther King. Later that spring he oversaw the effort to enforce court-ordered desegregation of the University of Alabama, opposed by Alabama Gov. George C. Wallace [q.v.].

According to Arthur Schlesinger Jr. [q.v.], civil rights had become Robert Kennedy's top domestic priority by the summer of 1963. The Administration's civil rights bill of June 1963 was formulated by the Justice Department largely on Kennedy's initiative. In extensive congressional testimony, public speeches and meetings with various interest groups, the Attorney General worked for passage of the bill. Enacted in July 1964, shortly before Kennedy left the Justice Department, the Civil Rights Act has been ranked as one of his major achievements.

Kennedy's record of action in support of civil rights was partly offset, however, by the appointment of several segregationist judges, such as W. Harold Cox [q.v.], to federal courts in the South. Civil rights advocates also criticized Kennedy for not having the FBI and Justice Department do more to protect civil rights workers in the South from harassment and assault. Most were unpersuaded by his argument that the federal government did not have authority to act as they wanted. The Department's emphasis on negotiation during civil rights crises was also criticized as tending to maintain the status quo rather than advance black rights. However resourceful and effective, many of Kennedy's civil rights activities came in response to crises rather than on his own initiative. Still, Mississippi rights leader Charles Evers asserted that Kennedy did more to help blacks win their rights "than any other public official" and more than "all other U.S. attorney generals put together."

As the brother of the President, Robert Kennedy had influence and power not available to other high Administration officials. He had the full confidence of President Kennedy and the strong rapport, friendship and loyalty between the two made the Attorney General the President's alter ego and his closest adviser and aide. After the unsuccessful Bay of Pigs invasion of April 1961, President Kennedy included his brother in the decision-making process on all crucial foreign and domestic policy questions. Among other tasks, the Attorney General carried out diplomatic missions to Europe and the Far East, encouraged the development of a counterinsurgency force in the military, kept an eye on overseas intelligence operations, advised on civil rights policy and dealt with many state party chairmen and political bosses around the country.

The Cuban missile crisis of October 1962 supplied perhaps the best example of Robert Kennedy's influential advisory role. He was a member of Excom, the group that met to consider the U.S. response to the discovery of Soviet offensive missiles in Cuba. In the early deliberations the Attorney General strongly opposed proposals for a general air strike and invasion of Cuba and supported the idea of a "quarantine." Acting as unofficial chairman of the committee in the President's absence, Kennedy was a major force in securing a consensus within the group on the decision to blockade Cuba. On Oct. 26 a letter from Soviet Premier Nikita Khrushchev suggested a bargain in which Soviet missiles would be withdrawn from Cuba in return for an American pledge not to invade the island. It was followed the next day, however, by a second letter demanding the withdrawal of American missiles in Turkey in exchange for removal of the Cuban missiles. During a debate in ExCom over the American response to the second Khrushchev proposal, Robert Kennedy devised the idea of ignoring the second letter and responding favorably to the first. The Attorney General helped draft the President's reply and then personally delivered a copy of it, along with a strong warning, to the Soviet Ambassador to the U.S. The next day Khrushchev agreed to the American proposal for removal of the Cuban missiles in exchange for an end to the blockade and a promise that the U.S. would not attack Cuba.

His brother's assassination in Dallas on Nov. 22, 1963 was a shattering loss to Robert Kennedy, and he temporarily left most Justice Department duties and decisions to his subordinates. John Kennedy's death reportedly led the Attorney General to reconsider his goals and to redefine his role. He resigned as Attorney General on Sept. 3, 1964 to run successfully for U.S. senator from New York. He built a liberal record in the Senate, giving special attention to the problems of the urban poor, and gradually emerged as an outspoken critic of President Johnson's policies in Vietnam. In March 1968 Kennedy entered the race for the Democratic presidential nomination. He won primaries in Indiana and Nebraska but lost the Oregon primary election. Then on June 5, while celebrating the victory he had just won in California, Kennedy was shot by Sirhan B. Sirhan, a Jordanian-born Arab living in California. He died the next day. [See JOHNSON Volume]

As Attorney General, Kennedy's greatest strength, according to Victor Navasky, was "his personal quest for excellence and his ability to use the best ideas provided him. He had an inspirational quality that brought out the best" in those who worked with him and infused the Justice Department with virtually unprecedented elan, energy and purpose.

[CAB]

For further information:
Robert F. Kennedy, *The Pursuit of Justice*, ed. by Theodore J. Lowi (New York, 1964).
———, *Thirteen Days: A Memoir of the Cuban Missile Crisis* (New York, 1969).
Victor S. Navasky, *Kennedy Justice* (New York, 1971).
William V. Shannon, *The Heir Apparent: Robert Kennedy and the Struggle for Power* (New York, 1967).

KEOGH, EUGENE J(AMES)
b. Aug. 30, 1907; New York, N.Y.
Democratic Representative, N.Y., 1937-67.

A graduate of New York University and Fordham University Law School, Keogh won election to Congress in 1936 from a solidly Democratic district in Brooklyn. As a ranking member of the powerful House Ways and Means Committee, Keogh was particularly active in sponsoring tax legislation. His most important enactment, later called the Keogh Plan, set up a tax-sheltered pension plan for small businessmen and professionals. Keogh first sponsored the bill in 1957, but did not secure its passage until 1962 over the opposition of President Kennedy and Treasury Department officials who feared a loss of revenue. In general, however, Keogh loyally supported Kennedy's legislative program.

In May 1962 a Brooklyn federal court heard two government witnesses testify that Keogh tried to intercede with a federal judge on behalf of a jukebox operator convicted in a bankruptcy swindle. Although Keogh's brother, New York Supreme Court Justice James Vincent Keogh, and two others were convicted in June 1962 of conspiracy to "fix" a federal court sentence, Rep. Keogh denied the allegations and was never indicted. Nevertheless, the charges initiated a series of attacks on Keogh's integrity. In March 1964 columnists Drew

Pearson [*q.v.*] and Jack Anderson asserted that Keogh was unduly influenced by the receipt of money and special favors. The *New York Times* attacked Keogh for his unwillingness to either divest himself of his business interests, which included a law practice, title insurance company, real estate firm and two banks, or publicly divulge his net assets and sources of income. Keogh announced in April 1965 that he would not seek reelection in 1966, and at the same time he stated that there was too much public concern about the conflict of interest issue.

Keogh left Congress in 1967 to return to his law practice and many business concerns.

[JCH]

KEPPEL, FRANCIS
b. April 16, 1916, New York, N.Y.
Commissioner of Education, March 1963-September 1965.

Francis Keppel, son of a former dean of Columbia College, attended Groton and graduated from Harvard in 1938. After studying sculpture in Rome for a short while, he returned to Harvard where he served as dean of freshmen and, after the war, as assistant to the provost of the University. Harvard President James B. Conant named Keppel dean of the Harvard graduate school in 1948. Over the next 14 years Keppel increased the size, endowment and prestige of the school and developed an innovative master of arts in teaching degree (MAT). The widely emulated Harvard MAT program de-emphasized the pedagogical curriculum traditionally found in teachers colleges, requiring instead that graduate students in education acquire a deeper understanding of their teaching specialty.

In November 1962 President Kennedy chose Keppel to succeed Sterling M. McMurrin [*q.v.*] as commissioner of education. At the time Keppel assumed his post, the National Education Association (NEA), representing over a million elementary and secondary public school teachers, and the National Catholic Welfare

Conference (NCWC), representing paro-chial schools, were bitterly divided over the question of whether federal funds should be appropriated for sectarian education. This conflict had prevented the Administration not only from passing an elementary and secondary education aid bill, but also from aiding higher education. The President appealed to Keppel to mediate between the two groups, a task at which he proved remarkably adept.

In his *Education in National Politics,* Norman C. Thomas credits Keppel with facilitating enactment of the Higher Education Facilities Act (HEFA) and the Vocational Education Act, both passed during 1963. HEFA established a five-year college building program; money was made available to private as well as public institutions, although not for facilities used for religious purposes. The Vocational Education Act authorized the appropriation of $731 million for a broad, five-year program to help workers learn new job skills.

During the summer of 1963 Keppel testified on behalf of Administration manpower training legislation to enable those unemployed who lacked the reading skills to take advantage of job training programs to receive basic education courses. This legislation became law in December 1963. He also spoke on behalf of the Library Services Act, which made federal funds available for libraries in cities as well as rural areas.

Keppel's skill in winning congressional approval of Kennedy education bills and his growing influence within both the NEA and NCWC impressed President Lyndon B. Johnson [q.v.]. Shortly after the elections in November 1964 Johnson suggested to Keppel that he frame an elementary and secondary school aid bill acceptable to both public and parochial school groups. Keppel's proposal, the Elementary and Secondary Education Act, was passed by the Congress in April 1965. Keppel was named assistant secretary of health, education and welfare in September 1965. He served in that position until April 1966, when he resigned to become chairman and chief executive of the General Learning Corporation. [See JOHNSON Volume]

[JLW]

KERNER, OTTO
b. August 15, 1908; Chicago, Ill.
d. May 9, 1976; Chicago, Ill.
Governor, Ill., 1961-68.

Otto Kerner was the son of a U.S. Court of Appeals judge. He attended Chicago public schools, took a B.A. from Brown University and attended Trinity College Cambridge. In 1934 he received a law degree from Northwestern University and subsequently practiced corporate law in Chicago for many years. In 1947 Kerner was appointed U.S. attorney general for the Northern District of Illinois. In 1954 he was elected county judge for Cook County and reelected in 1958. In 1960, with the support of Chicago Mayor Richard J. Daley, [q.v.], Kerner won the Democratic gubernatorial nomination and overwhelmed incumbent Gov. William G. Stratton in the general election.

During his first term Kerner won enactment of a state fair employment practices act, a revision of the criminal code and consumer credit laws and a program establishing statewide mental health clinics. Under Kerner Illinois also established its first state board of higher education. Kerner's programs generally had the support of Mayor Daley who controlled many votes in the state legislature. The two men did not, however, agree on all issues. For example, in 1961 Kerner turned down a Daley request that Illinois cities share in revenues derived from an increased state sales tax.

In 1964 Kerner won reelection, defeating Republican candidate Charles Percy by some 200,000 votes. During his second term Kerner was forced to deal repeatedly with riots in Chicago and other Illinois cities. In 1965, 1966 and 1968 Kerner ordered Illinois National Guardsmen into Chicago to quell riots in the city's black neighborhoods. In 1967 the guardsmen were dispatched to Cairo, a racially troubled city in southern Illinois.

In July 1967 President Lyndon B. Johnson [q.v.] appointed Kerner chairman of the Special Commission on Civil Disorders to probe the causes of riots in American cities. The famed "Kerner Commission" report, issued in February 1968, attributed the riots to poverty and despair resulting from "white racism" and called for massive federal appropriations to improve the quality of life in the ghetto. [See JOHNSON Volume]

In May 1968 Kerner resigned from the governorship to become a judge on the Seventh Circuit U.S. Court of Appeals, the same post his father had held.

In December 1971 Kerner was indicted on charges of bribery, fraud, conspiracy, and income tax evasion arising from his purchase and sale of race track stock while governor of Illinois. A race track owner and a former Illinois State Racing Board chairman testified that in 1962 Kerner and his revenue director, Theodore J. Isaacs, were given the opportunity to purchase race track stock at a very low price, reaping windfall profits. In exchange for the favor, Kerner intervened with the State Racing Board to ensure that the race track owner would be assigned prime dates on which to hold races.

Kerner was sentenced to three years in prison in April 1973 and fined $50,000 for his part in the scandal. He appealed his sentence on the ground that a federal judge could not be tried until first impeached. This appeal was dismissed by the U.S. Supreme Court, and in July 1974 Kerner began serving his sentence. In March 1975 the U.S. Parole Board granted Kerner's release on medical grounds; that month he underwent surgery for removal of a cancerous lung. He died on May 9, 1976.

[JLW]

KERR, CLARK
b. May 17, 1911; Stony Creek, Pa.
President, University of California, 1958-67.

Kerr graduated from Swathmore College in 1932 and then took a Ph.D. in economics from the University of California, Berkeley. He taught at Stanford and the University of Washington in the early 1940s, acquiring a reputation as a leading labor economist and arbitrator. In 1945 Kerr returned to the University of California to become the first director of the Institute of Industrial Rela-

tions. With other influential social and political scientists of the late 1940s and 1950s, Dr. Kerr argued that given rational discourse and the willingness to compromise strikes and other forms of social conflict would decline in a fully industrialized society. In 1952 Kerr was appointed chancellor of the Berkeley campus and in 1958 president of the seven-campus University of California.

Kerr's tenure as president coincided with the accelerated growth of California's public higher educational system, the nation's largest. He presided over a near doubling of the University's 50,000-student enrollment, the dramatic expansion of several campuses and a growing consensus among many scholars that the University's faculty and the quality of its research made it the "most distinguished" in the country. Kerr devised a master plan to coordinate the programs of the state's junior colleges, four-year colleges and the University. The result was an hierarchical system in which the top 12% of California's high school graduates were admitted to the University, the top third to the colleges and the remainder to the two-year junior colleges.

With the California system of higher education considered by many as a model for the nation, Kerr reached his greatest influence in the early 1960s. In 1963 he gave a series of lectures at Harvard which were published the same year as *The Uses of the University*. In these lectures he justified the role of the "multiversity"—a term coined by Kerr—in contemporary American society. Kerr argued that a great university was of necessity elitist, but its existence was justified in a nation dedicated to an egalitarian philosophy by its role as a "prime instrument of national purpose," a "service station" to society. The multiversity's central place in a highly industrialized society was based upon its role as a trainer of skilled manpower, a source of applied research and a protector of free inquiry. Kerr recognized that the modern university had many constituencies: government, industry, faculty, students, the general public. He saw the university administrator's role as one which mediated among the demands of these groups.

In his Harvard lectures Kerr admitted that undergraduates might be unable to find a sense of security and identity in the new multiversity. Although he recognized that the students were the least influential component of the multiversity, he offered no immediate solutions to improving the undergraduate's situation. When student protests against University of California regulations curbing on-campus political activities broke out at Berkeley, Kerr was unable to conclusively settle the conflict. In December 1964 the bulk of the Berkeley faculty sided with the "free speech" demands of the students, and Kerr was forced to acquiesce in opening the campus to virtually unlimited student political advocacy. Student activism made Kerr's role as a mediator between university and state government impossible. In the 1966 gubernatorial election conservative Ronald Reagan successfully used Kerr's "softness" in dealing with student unrest as a campaign issue. In January 1967 Reagan persuaded the University's Board of Regents to dismiss Kerr from his post. Following his dismissal he served as chairman of the Carnegie Commission on Higher Education. [See JOHNSON Volume]

[JCH]

For further information:

Clark Kerr, *The Uses of the University* (Cambridge, Mass., 1963).

Seymour Martin Lipset and Sheldon S. Wolin, eds., *The Berkeley Student Revolt* (Garden City, 1965).

KERR, ROBERT S(AMUEL)
b. Sept. 11, 1896; Ada, Okla.
d. Jan. 1, 1963; Washington, D.C.
Democratic Senator, Okla., 1949-63.

Robert S. Kerr was born in the proverbial log cabin in Indian Territory, later the state of Oklahoma. After attending three Oklahoma colleges and serving overseas in World War I, Kerr passed the state bar examination in 1922. He entered the oil drilling business of his brother-in-law in 1925 and bought him out the next year. Kerr's successful campaign to persuade the voters of Oklahoma City to approve drilling within city limits and his lucrative contracts with the Continental Oil Co. and the Phillips Petroleum Co. made him a millionaire by the end of the Depression. He formed Kerr-McGee Industries, Inc. out of a partnership with oil geologist Dean McGee; the company expanded into all phases of the oil business, except distribution, and obtained interests in other natural resources as well, including gas, helium, potash, berylium and uranium.

Elected Democratic governor of Oklahoma in 1942, Kerr was the keynote speaker at the Democratic National Convention in 1944. Kerr was elected to the Senate in 1948, where he generally endorsed Truman Administration policies. He emerged as the chief senatorial spokesman for the oil and gas industry in an unsuccessful 1950 fight to exempt natural gas from federal regulation. [See TRUMAN Volume]

In the 1950s Kerr consolidated his power within the Senate and enlarged his personal fortune. He was an influential member of the Public Works Committee and the Finance Committee, and his close relationship with Majority Leader Lyndon Johnson (D, Tex.) [*q.v.*] placed him at the center of the directorate which dominated the Senate. He bluntly stated his purpose in politics: "I represent the financial institutions of Oklahoma, and I am interested in them, and they know that, and this is the reason they elect me."[See EISENHOWER Volume]

Kerr supported Johnson's campaign for the Democratic presidential nomination in 1960 and argued unsuccessfully against Johnson's decision to accept second place on the ticket. Nevertheless, Johnson's resignation from the Senate cleared the way for Kerr to replace him as chairman of the Aeronautical and Space Sciences Committee. Following President Kennedy's request for an acceleration in the space program, the Committee doubled appropriations for the National Aeronautics and Space Administration from $914 million in fiscal 1961 to $1.8 billion in 1962. According to *The Almanac of American Politics*, "Kerr made sure that valuable NASA contracts went to Oklahoma corporations." In 1961 Kerr supported the Administration's programs to increase school aid and federal housing subsidies, but voted against a 13-week extension of unemployment benefits to be financed by a national "pool" of employer contributions. Kerr voted instead for Sen. Harry Flood Byrd's (D, Va.) [q.v.] amendment to let each state pay for its own costs under the program, an alternative which opponents charged would arbitrarily penalize those states hit hardest by the recession. Kerr also opposed the effort of Senate liberals to modify the filibuster rule in September 1961.

According to Congressional Quarterly, Kerr "reached the pinnacle of his power in the Senate" during the second session of the 87th Congress. Kerr played a major role in the controversy over the establishment of the new Communications Satellite Corporation. In January 1962 he proposed a bill which would have consigned complete ownership and operation of the system to private industry. Proponents of public ownership called Kerr's bill a "giveaway" to the American Telephone and Telegraph Co., whose Telstar satellite had successfully transmitted television pictures between two continents. When Senate liberals tried to stymie his proposal via a filibuster, Kerr voted on Aug. 14 in favor of cloture, a procedure he had consistently opposed when civil rights bills were on the floor. The motion carried, 63-27, and for the first time since 1927 the Senate voted to invoke cloture. The final law provided for private ownership, with a board of 15 directors, of whom three were to be appointed by the President.

Kerr also guided through the Finance Committee and the Senate much Administration-backed legislation, including the Trade Expansion Act of 1962, which gave the President extensive authority to reduce tariffs, and a tax law which contained a 7% investment tax credit. He managed Administration measures raising the debt ceiling and augmenting public assistance to the needy. Kerr stressed in conference that the federal matching funds be passed on to the recipients and not be used by the states to reduce their own welfare costs. He also favored accelerating public works expenditures to stimulate the economy.

Kerr disagreed with the Administration over funding of a medical care for the aged plan. The Kerr-Mills enactment of 1960 had financed federal matching funds to the states for the medically needy aged out of general revenues. Kennedy's medicare proposal would have financed a larger program of such assistance out of increased Social Security contributions, but Kerr engineered its defeat in July 1962. Despite this conflict, Kerr's overall voting record became increasingly pro-Administration: Congressional Quarterly reported that Kerr voted with the Administration 59% of the time in 1961 and 74% in 1962. Kerr died of a heart attack on Jan. 1, 1963.

[TO]

KEYSERLING, LEON H.
b. Jan. 22, 1908; Charleston, S.C.
Economist.

A graduate of Harvard Law School, Leon Keyserling left the economics faculty at Columbia University in 1933 to become secretary to Sen. Robert F. Wagner (D, N.Y.), sponsor of much of the far-reaching social legislation of the New Deal era. Keyserling was an expert in federal housing programs when President Truman appointed him in 1946 to his Council of Economics Advisers (CEA), of which he served as chairman from 1950 to 1953. As a member and then chairman of the CEA, Keyserling gave the Council an active political orientation. He was an aggressive supporter of Fair Deal legislative programs, wage and price controls and federal fiscal policies designed to implement the goals of the Full Employment Act of 1946, which Keyserling had helped to shape. [See TRUMAN Volume]

During the Kennedy years Keyserling was a liberal critic of the Administration's economic policy. Representing the Americans for Democratic Action (ADA), he called for a massive housing program in April 1961 and in June criticized the Administration's economic proposals as insufficient to restore full-capacity production and employment. At an April 1962 ADA convention Keyserling characterized the Administration as too timid and conservative, placing undue emphasis on balanced budgets and the balance of payments. Testifying before the Senate Finance Committee in the same month, he opposed the 7% investment tax credit on the grounds that business needed not "capital help" but bigger markets. He argued that "useful expenditures and/or tax cuts to stimulate consumer demand would be infinitely more beneficial to the economy" than the tax credit. In August 1962 and February 1963, Keyserling called for a quick, "one-shot" tax cut of $7 billion concentrated in the lowest income brackets, a $3 billion increase in federal spending and a liberalization of monetary policy by lowering interest rates. Keyserling praised the goals of President Johnson's anti-poverty program but criticized its limited scope. With the support of civil rights leaders A. Philip Randolph [q.v.] and Bayard Rustin [q.v.], he prepared a $185-billion "freedom budget" in 1966 designed to eliminate poverty in 10 years. Given the mushrooming costs of the Vietnam war, however, the ambitious proposal stood little chance of adoption.

[TO]

KHEEL, THEODORE W(OODROW)
b. May 9, 1914, New York, N.Y.
Labor arbitrator.

The son of a Brooklyn, N.Y., businessman, Kheel took a law degree from Cornell in 1937 and the next year joined the legal staff of the National Labor Relations Board. During World War II he began a career as an arbitrator, rising to executive director of the National War Labor Board in 1944. After brief service in the administration of New York Mayor William O'Dwyer, Kheel was appointed impartial arbitrator of labor-management relations for New York City's private bus lines in 1949. In 1956 he assumed a similar role for the city's public transit system. Kheel was president of the National Urban League from 1956 to 1960.

As an arbitrator and mediator, Kheel played a key role in preventing or ending a series of New York City strikes in the early 1960s. In December 1961 Kheel ordered the New York City Transit Authority to delay the introduction of an automated shuttle subway train to prevent a subway strike threatened by Transport Workers Union President Michael J. Quill [q.v.]. Serving as New York Mayor Robert F. Wagner's [q.v.] special labor adviser, Kheel helped draft the recommenda-

tions that served as the basis for the March 1963 agreement ending New York City's 114-day newspaper strike and played a central role in securing ratification by the unions involved. In both the transit and the newspaper negotiations, Kheel handled the problem of new technology by permitting management to introduce automated equipment but not to lay off redundant workers. In September 1963 Kheel served on a mediation panel that helped prevent a New York City teachers' strike.

As arbitrator for the National Maritime Union, Kheel settled a 1962 strike aboard the nuclear-powered vessel *Savannah* and helped end an inter-union dispute that tied up the liner *America* for four months in 1963. Kheel also served on the presidential mediation board that brought an end to the 34-day East and Gulf Coast longshoremen's strike in January 1963.

A Democrat, Kheel was campaign coordinator for Mayor Wagner's 1961 reelection campaign. He was a member of the President's Committee on Equal Opportunity Employment in 1962 and 1963. In later years Kheel continued his activities as a labor mediator and arbitrator. [See JOHNSON Volume]

[JBF]

KING, CECIL R(HODES)
b. Jan. 13, 1898; Youngstown, N.Y.
d. March 17, 1974; Inglewood, Calif.
Democratic Representative, Calif., 1942-69.

King migrated to Southern California with his family at the age of ten. He served in the Canadian Army during World War I, went into business after the war and then entered politics as a Democratic state assemblyman in 1932. Ten years later he won a special election to the House of Representatives from an industrialized and predominantly working-class Los Angeles district. A loyal and generally liberal Democrat, King easily won reelection through the late 1940s and 1950s. In 1961 he became the second-ranking Democrat on the Ways and Means Committee, perhaps the single most powerful House panel. Congressional observers characterized King as a diligent worker and rather quiet legislator.

During the Kennedy years King consistently backed Administration policy. According to *Congressional Quarterly*, he supported Kennedy on 96% of the roll-call votes for which the Administration announced a position. Indeed, in 1962 only nine other representatives equaled or surpassed King's pro-Administration score.

With Sen. Eugene J. McCarthy (D, Minn.) [q.v.], King submitted an Administration plan for a reorganization of federal-state unemployment compensation. Presented in June 1961, the proposed law represented the most systematic revision of the unemployment insurance program since its creation in the 1930s. Essentially, the McCarthy-King bill would have boosted unemployment benefits, extended their duration and increased the taxes necessary to pay for them. However, neither house approved the plan.

Beginning in February 1961 King cosponsored a bill to provide medical insurance for the aged, medicare. Introduced by King and Sen. Clinton P. Anderson (D, N.M.) [q.v.], the King-Anderson medicare plan was to finance hospital and out-patient care for old age assistance beneficiaries through increased Social Security taxes. Kennedy had endorsed the medicare concept in December 1960, and normally the ranking Democrat on the Ways and Means Committee would have sponsored White House legislation dealing with taxation. However chairman Wilbur D. Mills (D, Ark.) [q.v.] opposed medicare; King, as the second-ranking Democratic member, initiated the White House version. Mills's intransigence, bolstered by the opposition of other conservative Democrats and most Republicans, delayed passage of the King-Anderson bill through the Kennedy presidency. King joined other medicare proponents in blaming the spirited lobbying campaign of the American Medical Association for delaying the bill's enactment into law until 1965. King retired from Congress in 1969.

[JLB]

KING, JOHN W(ILLIAM)
b. Oct. 10, 1918; Manchester, N.H.
Governor, N.H., 1963-69.

A graduate of Harvard and Columbia University Law School, John King practiced law in New York City from 1943 to 1948. He returned to his hometown of Manchester in 1948, taught a course in business law at St. Anselm's College, practiced law and became active in Democratic Party politics. He won election to the New Hampshire General Court (the state legislature) in 1956 and from 1959 to 1962 served as the lower chamber's minority leader.

King had little difficulty winning the Democratic gubernatorial primary in September 1962, but under normal circumstances he would have stood little chance against the Republican nominee in the general election two months later. No Democrat had been elected governor of New Hampshire in 40 years. In 1962, however, the Republican Party was badly divided as a result of a bitter primary contest between State Rep. John Pillsbury and the incumbent governor, Wesley Powell. Pillsbury won the primary with the support of the arch-conservative William Loeb [q.v.] publisher of the *Manchester Union-Leader*. Gov. Powell then urged his supporters to vote for King. With Powell's help, King won the election by 40,000 votes.

During the campaign King had pledged increased state aid for public schools without imposing a state sales or income tax. King proposed instead that New Hampshire institute a sweepstakes lottery on a local option basis with the profits to be used exclusively for educational purposes. The lottery bill passed the General Court, and King signed it into law April 30, 1963. A year later the state held a referendum on the bill, and voters approved it overwhelmingly. New Hampshire thus became the first state since Louisiana in 1894 to operate a lottery. Later, New York, New Jersey and Connecticut also turned to lotteries as a new source of revenue.

King became a popular figure in New Hampshire and twice won reelection in 1964 and 1966. In 1968 he was defeated in his bid for the Senate by Sen. Norris Cotton (R, N.H.) [*q.v.*]. With the expiration of his term as governor, King returned to his legal practice in Manchester. He was later named to the New Hampshire Supreme Court. [See JOHNSON Volume]

[JLW]

KING, MARTIN LUTHER, JR.
b. Jan. 15, 1929; Atlanta, Ga.
d. April 4, 1968; Memphis, Tenn.
President, Southern Christian Leadership Conference, 1957-68.

Born and raised in Atlanta, Ga., where his father was pastor of the prestigious Ebenezer Baptist Church, King enrolled at Morehouse College in 1944. He decided to enter the ministry during his junior year and was ordained in his father's church in 1947. After receiving his B.A. from Morehouse in 1948, King studied at Crozer Theological Seminary in Chester, Pa., and was class valedictorian when awarded his divinity degree in 1951. He then began doctoral studies in systematic theology at Boston University and received a Ph.D. in June 1955.

King's first involvement in the civil rights movement occurred following his September 1954 move to Montgomery, Ala., to become pastor of the Dexter Avenue Baptist Church. On Dec. 5, 1955 the black community in Montgomery began a boycott of the city's segregated buses and formed the Montgomery Improvement Association (MIA) to continue the protest. King was elected president of the MIA the same day. A dynamic and well-educated minister who would be an effective spokesman for the boycott, King was also new enough in Montgomery to be unidentified with any one faction in the black community and young enough to be able to relocate should there be strong retribution against the boycott leader from whites. He led the year-long protest, which ended in victory after the Supreme Court ordered desegregation of the city's buses in November 1956.

The historic Montgomery boycott made King a national figure and furthered the development of his philosophy of nonvio-lent resistance. King's studies in theology and philosophy had first introduced him to the principles of Gandhian civil disobedience. As King explained in *Stride Toward Freedom*, nonviolence emerged gradually as the ideological framework within which the Montgomery civil rights struggle was fought. A month-long trip to India in February 1959 deepened King's knowledge of and commitment to nonviolence, and by 1960 he was the most prominent exponent of nonviolent direct action within the civil rights movement. Nonviolent resistance to segregation and discrimination, King contended, brought those evils into the open and forced the community to confront them. It enabled blacks to challenge injustice but also called on them to have "compassion and understanding for those who hate us" and to "struggle without hating." If nonviolence allowed blacks to "transmute hatred," it also transformed their oppressors. By remaining nonviolent in the face of white resistance and brutality, by matching "your capacity to inflict suffering with our capacity to endure suffering," King asserted, civil rights demonstrators appealed to the heart and the "conscience of the great decent majority" and won them over. Early in 1957 King helped found and was elected president of the Southern Christian Leadership Conference (SCLC), an organization established to coordinate direct action protests in the South and committed to a philosophy of nonviolence. [See EISENHOWER Volume]

In January 1960 King left Montgomery for Atlanta, where the SCLC had its headquarters, to become co-pastor at his father's church. When the student sit-ins began the next month, King welcomed the nonviolent protests. He issued a call for a conference of student leaders to be held in Raleigh, N.C. in April 1960; the meeting, financed by the SCLC, ultimately led to the formation of the Student Nonviolent Coordinating Committee (SNCC). In October King was arrested by officials of DeKalb County, Ga., for allegedly violating a one-year probation he was serving because of a conviction arising from a protest demonstration and was sentenced to four months at hard labor in a rural penal camp. His imprisonment caused a nationwide protest and on Oct. 26 presidential candidate John Kennedy and his brother Robert [q.v.] intervened and helped arrange for King's release. Coming in the last days of the 1960 campaign, the incident has been credited with swinging black voters solidly behind Kennedy.

The Congress of Racial Equality (CORE) launched the Freedom Rides, a protest designed to challenge segregation at Southern bus terminals, in May 1961. When a mob attacked the riders as they arrived in Montgomery, Ala. on May 20, King rushed to the city and the next day addressed a mass meeting in support of the rides. With James Farmer [q.v.] of CORE and other civil rights leaders, he announced on May 23 that the protests would continue despite threats of more violence. King was named chairman of a Freedom Rides Coordinating Committee organized in May, and he rejected Attorney General Robert Kennedy's call for a "cooling off" period at the end of the month. King never went on one of the Freedom Rides, however, and CORE and SNCC were far more active in the protest than King and the SCLC.

In mid-December 1961 King was called into Albany, Ga. to help direct an anti-segregation campaign there. With the aid of some SNCC organizers, the city's blacks had formed the Albany Movement in November and had launched a series of demonstrations. King led a march to the county courthouse in Albany on Dec. 16. When he was arrested, he refused bond and announced he would stay in jail rather than pay a fine if convicted. Two days later, however, a truce was declared and King accepted bail. The truce, arranged by several local leaders who mistrusted King and his aides, won blacks only a promise that their grievances would be heard by the city commission. King later regretted having accepted bail for such an ineffectual agreement.

The truce collapsed in January, and King spent the next six months shuttling back and forth between Atlanta and Albany, where he oversaw a renewal of periodic demonstrations. Late in February he was tried and found guilty of the charges stemming from his December arrest. In July he was sentenced to a fine of $178 or 45 days in prison. King chose prison but was released three days later when someone anonymously paid his fine. At this juncture, with complaints about his leadership growing, King decided to concentrate on Albany. From mid-July through August, he and his top aides in the SCLC directed a series of daily marches and protests that attracted national publicity. The campaign tapered off in September, and by the end of the year the Albany movement had won no tangible gains. It was judged a clear defeat for King.

King used the lessons learned in Albany to prepare for the next major desegregation campaign in Birmingham, Ala., during the spring of 1963. Unlike Albany, the campaign in Birmingham was preceded by careful reconnaissance work and planning, by meetings with local black leaders to ensure unity and by intensive training of the black population in nonviolent techniques. King quietly raised funds and contacted other civil rights organizations, sympathetic religious leaders and reporters in the months before the campaign. The SCLC decided to focus its efforts on Birmingham's business community rather than attack all targets of segregation at once as it had in Albany. The starting date was twice delayed until city elections had been held.

The campaign began on April 3, 1963 when the SCLC issued a "Birmingham Manifesto" detailing blacks' grievances. Demonstrations began at segregated lunch counters and a boycott of downtown stores started the same day. A series of daily mass marches was begun on April 6. Four days later the city obtained an injunction against further demonstrations which specifically cited King. On April 12, Good Friday, King led a march toward city hall in defiance of the injunction, was arrested en route and was placed in solitary confinement. In prison King wrote his later famous "Letter from a Birmingham Jail." Addressed to some fellow clergymen who had publicly criticized King's tactics in Birmingham, the letter rebutted charges that the Birmingham campaign was untimely and unwise and detailed the injustices blacks suffered in that city and elsewhere. It explained the methods and goals of nonviolent direct action and criticized white moderates and the white church for their lack of moral leadership and courage on the race issue. Released on bond on April 20, King was tried six days later for defying the injunction and convicted of criminal contempt but was given time to file an appeal before having to serve his five-day sentence.

The Birmingham campaign reached a turning point on May 2 when King launched a new phase of the protests in which children, ranging in age from six to 16, began mass marches in the city. The same day the relative restraint exercised by Commissioner of Public Safety Eugene "Bull" Connor [q.v.] and his police officers ended. Over 900 children were arrested on May 2 and the next day, as nearly 1,000 demonstrators of all ages prepared to march. They were savagely attacked by police with nightsticks, by snarling police dogs and by high pressure fire hoses. Similar police actions, occurring over the next four days, were recorded by newspaper and television cameras. National public opinion shifted decisively toward King and the SCLC. President Kennedy sent Assistant Attorney General Burke Marshall [q.v.] to Birmingham on May 4 to try to negotiate a settlement but his efforts were unavailing until May 7. On that day two demonstrations involving several thousand blacks flared into an open riot in response to police assaults. Faced with the threat of continued civil disorders, white leaders in Birmingham asked for and were granted a truce that evening. On May 10 an agreement was announced which called for phased integration of the city's business facilities, the upgrading of black workers and the establishment of a permanent biracial committee. Late that evening, however, bombs exploded at the home of King's brother, the Rev. A.D. King, and at the Gaston Motel, headquarters for the SCLC campaign. As news of the bombings spread, a riot broke out in Birmingham, which lasted until the early morning hours.

The May 10 agreement survived the bombings and riot, but Birmingham's blacks achieved only limited gains from their victory. The city's white leaders tried to evade key points of the settlement and interpreted its terms as narrowly as possible. Outside Birmingham the campaign had enormous impact and significance. As historians August Meier and Elliott Rudwick have noted, Birmingham "compelled the United States to face the problem of Southern discrimination in a way it had never done before." Birmingham was a turning point for the Kennedy Administration, forcing it to take forthright action on civil rights. In a national television address on June 11, President Kennedy delivered his most positive statement to date on behalf of black Americans, publicly labeling racial discrimination a national and a moral issue. He announced that he would ask Congress for major civil rights legislation, and on June 19 he sent Congress a civil rights bill dealing with public accommodations, school desegregation, and employment. Birmingham also stirred blacks throughout the South, and over the summer of 1963 demonstrations similar to Birmingham's spread from one Southern city to the next.

Birmingham reestablished King's leadership in the civil rights movement after the failure of Albany. He went on a triumphal speaking tour from California to New York in June and aided a desegregation drive in Danville, Va. during the summer. King endorsed A. Philip Randolph's [q.v.] proposal for a mass March on Washington, helped plan the march and joined other rights leaders in a meeting with President Kennedy on June 22. At the Aug. 28 march, King addressed 250,000 people assembled at the Lincoln Memorial, delivering a speech which drew heavily on both Biblical and American democratic themes. His classic "I Have a Dream" speech eloquently set forth King's vision of full equality and freedom for black Americans and was the most remembered speech of the March.

On Sept. 15, 1963 a bomb exploded at a black church in Birmingham killing four young black girls. King immediately called for federal troops to be sent into the city to prevent a "racial holocaust." He threatened a resumption of demonstrations in Birmingham but was reportedly dissuaded from this by moderate black leaders in the city and by Kennedy's decision to send an advisory team to Birmingham to conduct negotiations between black and white leaders. Instead, King decided to focus on Atlanta, and in October he joined other local black leaders in a demand that the pace of desegregation in that city be increased. The rejection of the demands led to a series of demonstrations in Atlanta in December and January in which King joined.

By the end of 1963 King had achieved enormous stature. In January 1964 *Time* magazine selected King its Man of the Year, and in December 1964 he was awarded the Nobel Peace Prize. To the general public, King was clearly the symbolic leader of the civil rights movement, and within the movement he occupied a unique position. King was criticized by more conservative blacks for being too militant in forcing confrontations and by more radical blacks, particularly the students in SNCC, for being too cautious, too compromising, too willing to settle for only minimal black gains. But throughout the early 1960s King balanced the demands of each group and served as a powerful bridge between the activist and traditional wings of the black protest movement.

King also served as an extraordinary symbol to both blacks and whites and as a unique channel of communication between the races. He articulated the aspirations of Southern blacks for full equality better than any black leader of the day and he communicated those aspirations to whites more effectively than anyone else. To many whites King seemed a militant, but his willingness to negotiate and compromise also made him appear a "responsible" activist and gave him respectability among white moderates. His philosophy of nonviolence combined a challenge to white society with a promise of its salvation. King repeatedly argued that nonviolence would awaken the conscience of America and make the nation live up to its democratic and religious ideals. By presenting justice to blacks as a benefit for both races, by promising love rather than revenge from the oppressed for the oppressors, King was able to develop and exploit whites' feelings of guilt without alienating them.

It became increasingly difficult for King to continue this role during the latter half of the decade when the civil rights movement began to fragment, when black radicalism and violence increased and when white opposition to black gains outside the South intensified. As the focus of black protest shifted from the small town South to the urban North, King and the SCLC searched for a method to adapt nonviolent resistance to a new set of problems. King led major campaigns in St. Augustine, Fla., Selma, Ala. and Chicago during these years and was an early opponent of the war in Vietnam. During the 1960s he was the target of a six-year FBI campaign which attempted to discredit him. In November 1975 a Senate Select Committee on Intelligence revealed that the Bureau had repeatedly tapped King's telephone, bugged his hotel rooms and had anonymously sent him two tapes that had recorded his alleged infidelities and a letter implying that he should commit suicide. King was assassinated in Memphis, Tenn., on April 4, 1968. [See JOHNSON Volume]

[CAB]

For further information:
Lerone Bennett, Jr., *What Manner of Man: A Biography of Martin Luther King, Jr.* (Chicago, 1968).
Martin Luther King, Jr., *Stride Toward Freedom: The Montgomery Story* (New York, 1958).
———, *Why We Can't Wait* (New York, 1964).
David Lewis, *King: A Critical Biography* (New York, 1970).
August Meier, "On the Role of Martin Luther King," *New Politics*, IV (Winter, 1965), pp. 52-59.

KOHLER, FOY D.
b. Feb. 15, 1908; Oakwood, Ohio.
Assistant Secretary of State for European Affairs, January 1959-July 1962; Ambassador to the Soviet Union, July 1962-September 1966.

A foreign service officer since his graduation from Ohio State University in 1931, Kohler became a Soviet specialist following a tour of duty in Moscow from 1947 to

1949. During the 1950s he served on the policy planning staff of the State Department and was counselor at Ankara before becoming deputy assistant secretary of state in 1958. Kohler was appointed assistant secretary of state for European affairs in January 1959 and remained in that post until July 1962.

As one of the major State Department officials concerned with European affairs, Kohler played an important part in day-to-day attempts to coordinate allied policy during the Berlin crisis of 1961 and 1962. The four major Western allies were divided on how to handle Moscow's harassment of West Berlin and its threat to sign a peace treaty with East Germany. The United States and Britain wished to negotiate as quickly as possible to prevent the crisis from escalating into a nuclear war. On the other hand, the French and Germans believed that any seeming rush to negotiate would make the West appear weak in Moscow's eyes. Despite Kohler's own belief that the United States should use military measures if necessary to protect access to Berlin, he had the task of trying to convince the hardline Germans and French to accept the U.S. proposal.

During the late summer of 1961, Kohler helped prepare the agenda for the Big Four Conference of Western foreign ministers called to try to reduce policy differences. Kohler, however, did not play a significant part in the September talks, at which the American delegation was headed by Secretary of State Dean Rusk [q.v.]. Despite Kohler's continued attempts, allied policy on Berlin remained uncoordinated.

Kohler was appointed ambassador to the Soviet Union in July 1962. Despite the fact that several other candidates had a better knowledge of the Russian language and culture, Kennedy, at the urging of Soviet experts Charles Bohlen [q.v.] and Llwellyn Thompson [q.v.], chose Kohler because of his expertise on the Berlin situation. In announcing the appointment, Kennedy stressed that Kohler's mission would be to induce Moscow to negotiate on Berlin and sign a nuclear test ban treaty. Although Kohler was able to interest Premier Nikita Khrushchev in the possibility of Berlin dis-

cussions in the fall of 1962, the talks were never opened because of the Soviet refusal to compromise on the issue.

Kohler's experience in handling his disarmament assignment reflected many of the frustrations that State Department officers and ambassadors faced during the Kennedy Administration. Most major negotiations of the period were not carried on through the traditional embassy channels but pointed to deal with particular problems. Thus, Kohler laid the groundwork for the July 1963 Moscow talks that led to the signing of a partial nuclear test ban treaty in August 1963, but the actual negotiations were handled by W. Averell Harriman [q.v.], who had been chosen by the President to deal with that situation.

For the first two years of the Johnson Administration, Kohler continued at his Moscow post. During that period relations between the U.S. and the USSR became increasingly strained because of America's growing involvement in the Vietnam war. When President Johnson sought to involve the Soviet Union in bringing about North Vietnamese-U.S. negotiations in 1966, Kohler was replaced by Llwellyn Thompson, a diplomat highly respected by the Russians and a friend of many Kremlin leaders. Kohler returned to Washington as undersecretary of state for political affairs. He resigned this post in December 1967 to take a teaching position at the Center for Advanced International Studies at the University of Miami. In addition to his academic work, he remained a consultant to the Defense and State Departments.

[EWS]

KORTH, FRED
b. Sept. 9, 1909; Yorktown, Tex.
Secretary of the Navy, January 1962-October 1963.

Son of a Texas banker and rancher, Korth practiced law in Fort Worth during the 1930s and served in the Air Transport Corps in the war. After a brief tenure as an assistant secretary of the Army in the early 1950s, Korth returned to Texas to head the Continental National Bank of Fort Worth.

There he became influential in state Democratic Party affairs. With Kennedy's election in 1960, Korth returned to Washington to serve as an aide to Army Secretary Elvis J. Stahr, Jr. [q.v.]. In January 1962 he succeeded fellow Texan John Connally [q.v.] as Secretary of the Navy.

Korth came to national attention in the summer of 1963 for his role in the controversy over the development of the planned TFX jet fighter. In June he appeared before the Senate Permanent Investigations Subcommittee to support the decision of Secretary of Defense Robert S. McNamara [q.v.] to award the prime contract for the TFX to the General Dynamics Corporation. McNamara's decision was considered controversial because many officers in both the Navy and the Air Force thought the Boeing Corporation could build a better airplane at lower cost.

Senators John J. Williams (R, Del.) [q.v.] and John L. McClellan (D, Ark.) [q.v.] argued that Korth and Deputy Secretary of Defense Roswell Gilpatric [q.v.], two of McNamara's principal advisers, should not have been involved in the contract decision because of conflicting business interests. In Gilpatric's case General Dynamics was an important client of the law firm with which he had been associated.

Korth's situation was more complicated. The Navy Secretary was on close terms with top executives of General Dynamics, whose Convair Division was located in Forth Worth. Shortly before he became Navy Secretary, the Continental National Bank—in which Korth retained a $160,000 interest—loaned General Dynamics $400,000. Korth argued that his bank's loan to General Dynamics was only part of a much larger transaction involving a $20 million loan to the corporation by the Chase Manhattan Bank of New York. He also claimed that his stock interest in Continental National was insignificant when viewed in the context of the bank's total business. The Justice Department upheld Korth in the fall of 1963 when it ruled that a conflict of interest case should not be brought against him. The Department also cleared Gilpatric of wrong-doing.

Korth resigned as Navy Secretary in Oc-tober 1963. At first it was believed that the resignation stemmed from his differences with McNamara over Korth's advocacy of the use of nuclear propulsion for surface ships. (McNamara thought nuclear power was not worth the cost.) However, the *New York Times* reported on Oct. 19 that the White House had asked Korth to resign for violating the code of ethics established in 1961 for high Administration officials. While serving as Navy Secretary, Korth had solicited business for Continental National Bank and had offered to entertain some clients of the bank on the Navy's official yacht, *Sequoia*.

After his resignation Korth began a private legal practice in Washington, D.C.

[JLW]

KRULAK, VICTOR H(AROLD)

b. Jan. 7, 1913; Denver, Colo.
Special Assistant for Counter-insurgency and Special Activities, Office of the Joint Chiefs of Staff, February 1962-January 1964.

Victor Krulak, an adviser to the Pentagon during the Kennedy Administration, graduated from the U.S. Naval Academy at Annapolis in 1934 and saw service in World War II and Korea as a Marine. He was named a brigadier general in July 1956 and three years later was promoted to major general. In 1959 Krulak was given command of the Marine Corps Recruit Depot in San Diego.

In February 1962 Gen. Krulak was appointed special adviser on guerrilla warfare to the Joint Chiefs of Staff. At that post he represented the military at high-level meetings on Vietnam and served on fact-finding missions for the President. During policy meetings the General, reflecting the opinion of the military commanders in Vietnam, offered consistently optimistic reports on the conduct of the war. His political skills made him a powerful proponent of this position within the President's circle of advisers.

In the meetings held to formulate the U.S. response to the Diem regime's attack on Buddhists in August 1963, Krulak supported the Defense Department's position that the U.S. should continue to back Diem but insist upon reform of his government. He opposed suggestions that the U.S. might have to withdraw support from the regime.

In September 1963 Krulak and a State Department representative, Joseph Mendenhall, flew to Saigon to study the effect of Diem's conduct on the war. Upon returning Krulak reported that the war, although affected by the political crisis, was progressing well, and he recommended a continuation of existing policies. Mendenhall, on the other hand, reported a virtual breakdown in the civil government and a distrust of the Diem regime that threatened the war effort. The division reflected in these two opinions continued throughout the Kennedy Administration and hampered effective response to developments in Vietnam.

From March 1964 until his retirement in May 1968, Gen. Krulak served as commander of the Fleet Marine Force in the Pacific. In 1969 he became president of the Copley News Service in San Diego.

[EWS]

KUCHEL, THOMAS H(ENRY)
b. Aug. 15, 1910; Anaheim, Calif.
Republican Senator, Calif., 1953-69.

Kuchel was a member of the family that helped found the town of Anaheim in 1859 and owned and edited the Anaheim *Gazette*. He opened a law practice in his home town in 1935. The following year Orange County elected him to the first of a series of terms in the state Assembly and Senate. After wartime service in the Navy, Kuchel was appointed state controller by Republican Gov. Earl Warren [q.v.] in February 1946, and in November he won election to a full term. Warren again appointed him to an elective office when Richard Nixon [q.v.] vacated his U.S. Senate seat in 1952 in order to become vice president.

Kuchel was a conservative in his first years in the Senate. He was one of the minority of senators, for example, to vote against the censure of Sen. Joseph McCarthy (R, Wisc.) in 1954. In time, however, he moderated his positions, due in part to his desire to seize the political center in a state where, despite a large majority of registered Democrats, ticket-splitting was common. [See EISENHOWER Volume]

In the Senate Kuchel sat on the Appropriations Committee and the Interior and Insular Affairs Committee. Beginning in 1959 he held the influential post of Senate Republican whip. As whip he was responsible for getting out the Republican vote on issues on which the Party position had been determined by the Republican Policy Committee. However, Kuchel often voted against the majority of his party. He took liberal positions on such key legislative issues of the early 1960s as federal aid to education, mass transit, the United Nations loan and nuclear disarmament. In 1961 he cosponsored a bill to weaken Senate filibusters and in 1963 cosponsored both a medical-care-for-the-aged bill and a GOP civil rights package.

Following two electoral setbacks in 1958 and 1960, the solid California Republican organization fashioned by Earl Warren began to fall apart. Extreme conservatives, especially in Orange County, attacked Kuchel for his liberalism and lack of party loyalty, and they initiated efforts to unseat him in the 1962 primary. In 1961 Rep. John Rousselot (R, Calif.) [q.v.], a member of the John Birch Society, announced his intention to oppose Kuchel the following June. In response to right-wing criticism, Kuchel attacked the John Birch Society in a March 1961 Senate speech calling for a congressional investigation of the Society. He became an outspoken critic of what he called right-wing "fright peddlers." Richard Nixon, who assumed an important position in the California Republican Party after his 1960 presidential defeat, defended Kuchel from right-wing attacks in the interest of party unity. Nixon arranged a January 1962 conference with Rousselot and other conservative critics and persuaded them to drop a primary challenge to the Senator. Kuchel then went on to easily win the June 1962 primary.

Despite his efforts on Kuchel's behalf,

Nixon sought to dominate the state party, and for a time it was rumored that he wanted Kuchel to step aside so that he could claim his old Senate seat. Therefore, Kuchel and Nixon, who was running for governor, refused to support each other in the general elections. Kuchel, winning a substantial part of the registered Democratic electorate, defeated his liberal Democratic opponent by a margin larger than Gov. Edmund G. Brown's [q.v.] edge over Nixon.

Although Kuchel had defeated right-wing opponents in 1962, won reelection and remained the highest California Republican officeholder, his position in the state party became progressively more isolated as conservatives assumed greater control of the state organization. In 1964 Kuchel supported New York Gov. Nelson Rockefeller [q.v.] in a losing presidential primary contest against conservative Sen. Barry Goldwater (R, Ariz.) [q.v.]. He refused to support the Republican presidential and senatorial candidates, Goldwater and George Murphy, in the November elections, and in 1966 he did not back Ronald Reagan in the gubernatorial contest. In the 1968 Republican primary another conservative, State Superintendent of Public Instruction Dr. Max Rafferty, narrowly defeated Kuchel. Kuchel returned to legal practice with a Beverly Hills firm in 1969. [See JOHNSON Volume]

[JCH]

LAIRD, MELVIN R(OBERT)
b. Sept. 1, 1922; Omaha, Neb.
Republican Representative, Wisc., 1953-69.

Both of Laird's parents were influential members of the Wisconsin Republican Party, and his mother's family held considerable lumber and sawmill interests in the northern part of the state. Laird graduated from Carleton College, served in the Navy and, at the age of 23, won a seat in the Wisconsin Senate vacated by the death of his father. A hardworking state legislator and a supporter of Sen. Robert Taft (R, Ohio), Laird successfully ran for the U.S.

House of Representatives in 1952, winning election from the dairy farming and lumber producing seventh district of north central Wisconsin. In the House Laird was assigned first to the Appropriations Committee and later to the Agriculture Committee. On both powerful bodies he effectively represented the interests of the Wisconsin dairy industry. [See EISENHOWER Volume]

Tough-minded and articulate, Laird became a spokesman for a pragmatic Republican conservatism in the early 1960s. He worked closely with Gerald Ford (R, Mich.) [q.v.] in the House and strongly supported Richard Nixon [q.v.] in the national political arena. At the 1960 Republican National Convention, Laird represented Nixon's interests by guiding the candidate's moderate platform, outlined during a Manhattan meeting with New York Gov. Nelson Rockefeller [q.v.], through an often rebellious, conservative platform committee.

During the Kennedy years Laird emerged as a Republican Party authority on military affairs. Long a proponent of an expanded Polaris submarine fleet, Laird headed a 1961 Republican naval warfare task force whose recommendations were later adopted by the Defense Department. The next year Laird wrote A House Divided: America's Strategy Gap, a work that called for greater defense spending and a closer unity of foreign policy and military strategy. As chairman of a House-Senate Republican Committee, Laird was the author of the "Declaration of Republican Principles and Policy" of March 1962. The Declaration, designed to dispel the negative image of the Republican Party, called for a reduction of taxes on business, a cut in non-defense spending and an offensive in Cold War propaganda.

Although the conservative Americans for Constitutional Action rated Laird's House voting record at over 90% "correct" during the early 1960s, the Wisconsin Representative was not a partisan of Sen. Barry Goldwater (R, Ariz.) [q.v.]. He engineered the favorite son candidacy of Rep. John F. Byrnes (R, Wisc.) [q.v.] before the 1964 Republican convention and impartially chaired the platform committee at the convention.

A strong supporter of the Vietnam war and the Republican Party's foremost congressional expert on military affairs, Laird was reelected without opposition during the remainder of the decade. He resigned his House seat in early 1969 to become Secretary of Defense in the new Nixon Administration. During his four-year tenure at Defense, the number of American ground troops in Vietnam declined by several hundred thousand, but the air war expanded into Cambodia, Laos and North Vietnam. Laird resigned in late 1972, later becoming a presidential adviser in the midst of the Watergate affair. [See JOHNSON, NIXON Volumes]

[NNL]

LANDIS, JAMES M(cCAULEY)
b. Sept. 25, 1899; Tokyo, Japan
d. July 30, 1964; Harrison, N.Y.
Presidential Assistant on Regulatory Agencies, January 1961-September 1961.

The son of a Presbyterian minister, Landis was born and raised in Tokyo. In 1925, after graduating from Harvard Law School and serving a year as law clerk for Supreme Court Justice Louis Brandeis, he joined the Harvard Law School faculty. Appointed to the Federal Trade Commission in 1933, Landis became a Securities and Exchange Commission member in 1934 and served as its chairman from 1935 to 1937. In 1937 he left government to become dean of the Harvard Law School. He was appointed director of the Office of Civil Defense in 1942 and served as Civil Aeronautics Board chairman from 1946 to 1947. In the years that followed Landis entered private law practice and worked for Joseph Kennedy, Sr. [q.v.], helping to run the Kennedy business operations. [See TRUMAN Volume]

In 1960 President-elect Kennedy appointed Landis chairman of a panel to investigate charges that federal regulatory agencies had been protecting the businesses they were supposed to regulate. Landis's report, scoring the agencies' performance, provided the basis for the President's April 1961 message proposing legislative and administrative reform. The message, drafted by Landis, criticized each agency's tendency to concern itself solely with the industry over which it had control rather than deal with the interrelation of its industry and the total economy. Other agency weaknesses Landis cited included the vagueness of the chairman's area of responsibility and excessive delays and workloads. The document proposed that all agency chairmen serve at the President's pleasure and have the authority to staff and distribute agency funds. It also urged that workloads be reduced and the quality of inspectors be improved.

Charging that the Administration's plan would create a "czar in the White House" and establish a "direct chain of political command" over the independent agencies, many congressmen opposed the measure. However, by the end of the 1961 legislative session, Congress had passed statutes streamlining and speeding up agency procedures for the Civil Aeronautics Board, the Federal Trade Commission, the Federal Maritime Board and the Federal Home Loan Bank Board. Modified versions of the Kennedy proposals were also passed for the Securities and Exchange Commission and the Federal Communications Commission.

In September 1961 Landis resigned as the President's special assistant because he was under investigation for income tax evasion. Two years later, in August 1963, he pleaded guilty to charges of failing to file federal income tax returns for the years 1956 to 1960. Landis asserted that he had filled out the returns and put the necessary money in his checking account each year but had neglected to file the returns or pay the taxes he owed. He offered the explanation that he had been so engrossed in public affairs that he had forgotten to file the returns until the Internal Revenue Service summoned him. When called he made what he believed to be a full settlement of the principal owed. Landis was found guilty and sentenced to a term of 30 days in jail. Because he was under psychiatric care, he served his sentence in a federal public health service hospital. On July 30, 1964

Landis was found dead in the swimming pool of his home in Westchester County, N.Y. Following an autopsy, the coroner ruled that he had been the victim of accidental drowning.

[EWS]

LANDRUM, PHIL(LIP) M(ITCHELL)
b. Sept. 10, 1907; Martin, Ga.
Democratic Representative, Ga., 1953- .

A Georgia country lawyer, school superintendent and executive assistant to Gov. M.E. Thompson, Landrum first won election to Congress in 1952. He represented a slice of Appalachia with an economy based on low-wage poultry raising and the textile manufacturing industry. Landrum was first assigned to the Education and Labor Committee where he generally opposed desegregation proposals and higher minimum wage legislation in the 1950s. Landrum achieved national fame in 1959 when he coauthored with Rep. Robert Griffith (R, Mich.) the Landrum-Griffin Labor-Management and Disclosure Act. The new law, which extended the precedents set by the Taft-Hartley Act a decade earlier, was bitterly opposed by organized labor and congressional liberals. The statute required greater financial disclosure by trade union officials, curbed picketing rights and assured internal opponents of existing union leaders recourse to the courts. [See EISENHOWER Volume]

Landrum was a spokesman for the nonunion Southern textile industry in the 1960s. He strongly supported restrictions on textile imports and opposed increases in the minimum wage. To play a more effective role in the development of trade legislation that affected the industry, Landrum sought a seat on the Ways and Means Committee, but the animosity that existed between organized labor and the Georgia Congressman delayed his admission to that powerful body. In January 1963 Landrum and House Democratic leaders agreed that in return for a seat on the Committee the Congressman would help deliver the votes of Georgia's Democratic delegation in favor of a permanent expansion and liberalization of the House Rules Committee. The Georgia Representative kept his part of the legislative "deal," but a coalition of labor-backed liberals and intransigent Southern conservatives defeated Landrum for the Ways and Means seat in the House Democratic caucus. Landrum finally won election to the Committee in early 1965.

Although his district frequently voted for the Republican candidate in presidential elections, Landrum was never seriously challenged for reelection in the 1960s. He opposed the 1964 and 1965 Civil Rights Acts and generally voted with the Southern Democratic-Republican conservative coalition in Congress. [See JOHNSON Volume]

[NNL]

LANSDALE, EDWARD G.
b. Feb. 6, 1908; Detroit, Mich.
Air Force Officer, 1947-63.

Lansdale, a former advertising executive, served in the Office of Strategic Services during World War II and later in the United States Air Force. After the war he was sent on a special assignment to the Philippines where he worked with Filipino Defense Secretary Ramon Magsaysay in undermining the Huk rebellion with a program of social reform and military action. Lansdale went to Vietnam in 1954 as head of the United States Military Mission and later as chief of the Saigon station for domestic affairs of the Central Intelligence Agency. During the 1954 Geneva negotiations, Lansdale unsuccessfully attempted to thwart a Viet Minh takeover in northern Vietnam, using sabotage and psychological warfare. In southern Vietnam Lansdale strongly backed Premier Ngo Dinh Diem, and it was largely Lansdale's influence that won official American support for Diem. Lansdale lived in the presidential palace and was one of Diem's closest advisers until he left Vietnam in 1956. It was the Lansdale of this era who was the model for Colonel Hillindale in the best-selling novel by Eugene Burdick, *The Ugly American*. [See EISENHOWER Volume]

In January 1961 Lansdale, then assistant to the Secretary of Defense for special operations, returned to Vietnam on an inspection mission planned by the outgoing Eisenhower Administration. Lansdale's report, written on his return, was pessimistic about the situation. While critical of Diem, it was even more critical of the United States for failing to give him full support. Lansdale recommended the immediate adoption of social, economic, political and military programs in Vietnam that would indicate American support for Diem and help stabilize the countryside. He also recommended the replacement of United States Ambassador to Vietnam Elbridge Durbow and the transfer of supervision of American Vietnam policy to a special team operation outside of normal bureaucratic channels. Newly appointed presidential adviser Walt W. Rostow [q.v.] gave Lansdale's report to President Kennedy. According to State Department official Roger Hilsman [q.v.], Kennedy was so impressed with it that he considered appointing Lansdale as the next ambassador to Vietnam. High-level opposition within the Administration, however, blocked the appointment.

Possibly as a result of a suggestion by Lansdale, President Kennedy appointed on April 20, 1961 a task force headed by Deputy Secretary of Defense Roswell Gilpatric [q.v.] to consider ways of preventing a Communist victory in Vietnam. Lansdale was the group's operations officer, and the first draft of the task force report, issued April 27, closely followed Lansdale's earlier suggestions. It recommended a modest increase in U.S. aid to South Vietnam and proposed that the supervision of American policy be transferred to a permanent task force, with Gilpatric in overall charge and Lansdale as chief of operations in Saigon. The report also suggested that Lansdale be sent immediately to Saigon to develop further recommendations.

The final May 6 draft of the task force report was written by Undersecretary of State George Ball [q.v.]. It eliminated Lansdale's future role and sharply downgraded the importance of the task force. Furthermore, Secretary of Defense Robert S. McNamara [q.v.] revised the report to stipulate that Lansdale should go to Vietnam only on the receipt of an invitation from the American ambassador, an invitation he never received. However, in offering support to Diem without demanding any specific reforms or concessions, the report followed Lansdale's position that Washington should try to reinforce Diem's confidence in the U.S. through increased support. This was an important change of policy from the January 1961 counterinsurgency plan, which made aid to Diem contingent on certain military and civilian reforms.

In October 1961 Kennedy sent a mission headed by Gen. Maxwell Taylor [q.v.] and Rostow to Vietnam to determine whether or not the United States should commit ground troops to Vietnam. Kennedy had also asked Lansdale to make a similar trip, and he was included in the Taylor-Rostow mission. Taylor, who disliked Lansdale, assigned him to explore the possibility of building a fence along Vietnam's borders to prevent infiltration, an idea fundamentally at odds with Lansdale's approach to the war. However, in his appendix to the mission's final report, Lansdale concurred with the recommendation that the U.S. commit several thousand ground troops to Vietnam. Twice during the Taylor-Rostow mission Diem requested that Lansdale be assigned to Vietnam, and after its return he twice repeated the request. However the Administration declined to comply with Diem's wishes in spite of Lansdale's own eagerness to return to Vietnam.

Lansdale did return to Vietnam in August 1965 with Henry Cabot Lodge [q.v.], who was beginning his second assignment as U.S. ambassador. Lansdale advocated a greater emphasis on pacification programs, a position Lodge shared, but personally he had little say about top policy decisions.

In an interview with the *New York Times* on May 30, 1975, Lansdale reported that in November 1961, Attorney General Robert F. Kennedy [q.v.], acting on behalf of the President, requested that he prepare contingency plans to depose Cuban Premier Fidel Castro. According to Lansdale, the plans centered on recruiting a group of Cuban exiles to return to Cuba to organize popular uprisings against Castro. Lansdale said that to his knowledge, the anti-Castro plans were never put into operation.

[JBF]

LARSON, LEONARD W(INFIELD)
b. May 22, 1898; Clarksfield, Minn.
President, American Medical Association, June 1961-June 1962.

Dr. Leonard W. Larson, as head of the American Medical Association (AMA), was a key foe of the Kennedy Administration's proposed medicare legislation. The son of Norwegian immigrants, Larson was born and raised in a small town in southeastern Minnesota. He earned his M.D. from the University of Minnesota School of Medicine in 1922 and for many years was associated with the Quain and Ramstad Clinic in Bismarck, N.D.

During the mid-1950s Larson, as a member of the AMA board of trustees, headed a committee investigating various health insurance schemes. The Larson committee issued a report in 1959 that, for the first time in the history of the AMA, endorsed private prepaid group clinics. The report, however, opposed the use of the Social Security system to finance national health insurance.

Dr. Larson became president of the AMA in June 1962. As president he repeatedly attacked the Administration's King-Anderson bill, which proposed expanding the Social Security system to provide funds to help defer the medical expenses of the elderly. Larson suggested that such a measure might eventually lead to socialized medicine and undermine the personal relationship between doctor and patient.

In May 1962 President Kennedy, in a televised mass rally at Madison Square Garden in New York City, appealed for passage of the King-Anderson bill. Larson requested equal time from the networks, charging that the Administration was carrying out "the biggest lobbying campaign this nation has ever seen." The networks rejected his request. The AMA then rented Madison Square Garden and bought an hour of prime television time to present the case of organized medicine. On May 21, 1962 Larson stood before 18,000 empty seats as an announcer explained to television viewers that "these seats are yours. There will be no pageant. But there will be an appeal to you from the physicians of America." Larson then appealed for a system of private medicine in which patients were treated "individually and intimately" not "as numbers." Larson was followed by Dr. Edward R. Annis [q.v.], the head of the AMA speakers bureau, who systematically attacked the King-Anderson bill.

As an alternative to the Administration bill, Larson and the AMA supported the Kerr-Mills Act, which had become effective in October 1960. This law provided federal matching funds to states that desired to broaden the scope of programs providing medical care for the aged. By February 1962 some 23 states had established programs under provisions of the Kerr-Mills Act, but there were widespread complaints that the vast majority of older persons failed to benefit from the legislation.

Larson's term as AMA president expired in June 1962, and he was succeeded by Dr. Annis.

[JLW]

LAUSCHE, FRANK J(OHN)
b. Nov. 14, 1895; Cleveland, Ohio.
Democratic Senator, Ohio, 1957-69.

The son of Slovenian immigrants, Frank J. Lausche worked as a streetlamp lighter, court interpreter and semi-professional baseball player before receiving a LL.B. degree from a Cleveland Law School in 1920. After nine years on the Cleveland municipal bench, Lausche, a Democrat, won election as mayor in 1941. Three years later he won the first of five terms as governor of Ohio. Lausche's frugality with state money and his cheery, nonpartisan campaign style made him popular with Republican voters. In November 1956 Lausche unseated Sen. George H. Bender (R, Ohio) in the first of two successful campaigns for the U.S. Senate. [See TRUMAN, EISENHOWER Volumes]

Lausche continued his conservative record in Washington. According to *Congressional Quarterly*, during the 87th Congress he voted with the Administration on only 41% of the roll calls for which the President announced a position. (The average for all Democrats was 64%). In 1963 Lausche's pro-Administration margin fell to 32%. He voted with the conservative coalition of Southern Democrats and Republicans on 58% of the group's roll-call votes during the 87th Congress and on 81% in 1963, the highest mark of any Northern Democrat that year. Lausche was joined by only 11 Democrats in voting against the President's area redevelopment measure in March 1961 and by only 12 party colleagues in opposing the Administration's school-aid bill in April 1961. He voted against the creation of a Housing and Urban Development Department in February 1962 and the ratification of the nuclear test ban treaty in September 1963. In his memoirs Lausche's liberal colleague Sen. Paul H. Douglas (D, Ill.) [q.v.] referred to him as "the Northern Harry Byrd [q.v.]."

As a member of the Senate Foreign Relations Committee, Lausche opposed the Administration's request for aid to Communist Yugoslavia. Despite pleas from U.S. Ambassador George Kennan [q.v.] in June 1962, Lausche proposed a modification of an amendment offered by Sen. William Proxmire (D, Wisc.) [q.v.] that prohibited the President from furnishing economic or military aid to nations under "Communist domination." The Senate approved the Proxmire-Lausche amendment to the fiscal 1963 foreign aid appropriation, but House and Senate conferees weakened the prohibition in the final authorization bill.

Lausche had greater success in his opposition to the Administration's 1962 and 1963 mass transit proposals. In an April 1962 transportation message, Kennedy asked Congress for a $500 million, three-year, grant-in-aid program for urban transit assistance. In September Lausche, a member of the Senate Commerce Committee, denounced the President's plan as "a mere beginning" that would ultimately cost "billions of dollars." He described the transit measure as a "coercive force" that would destroy the private transportation industry. The only committee member present at the bill's Sept. 17 hearings, Lausche ordered the bill to the floor without recommendation, a move that effectively killed the measure.

Senate Administration allies reintroduced the White House's transit bill in 1963, and again Lausche emerged as its chief opponent. In April he termed the urban transit proposal "nothing more than a vote-buying device" for Northeastern politicians and accused the Eastern rail lines of having initiated the legislation. Lausche offered an amendment to the White House measure to eliminate all federal grants, but the Senate rejected his provision by a vote of 41-57 and passed the Administration's bill. The House, however, failed to vote on the Senate version.

Despite his independence from New Frontier policies, Lausche won Kennedy's endorsement in his 1962 senatorial campaign and, as in other statewide contests, overwhelmed his Republican foe. In his second term Lausche voted even more conservatively. His opposition to organized labor's legislative program angered both the Ohio AFL-CIO and the state Democratic leadership. Together they helped to deny him renomination in the May 1968 Democratic primary. [See JOHNSON Volume]

[JLB]

LAWRENCE, DAVID L(EO)
b. June 18, 1889; Pittsburgh, Pa.
d. Nov. 21, 1966; Pittsburgh, Pa.
Governor, Pa., 1959-63.

The son of a teamster, David L. Lawrence quit school at the age of 14 to work as an office boy for the leader of the Pittsburgh Democratic Party. He became chairman of the Allegheny County (Pittsburgh) Democratic Party in 1920 and 14 years later assumed the chairmanship of the state Democratic committee. In 1945 he won the first of four terms, a record, as mayor of Pittsburgh and started an ambitious campaign to revive local industries and neighborhoods, curtail air pollution and improve transportation. Judged by many to be one of the last of the big city bosses, Lawrence proved to be an able city administrator. A 1958 *Fortune* magazine survey ranked Pittsburgh among the eight best-run cities in America. In 1958 state Democrats divided over the selection of a gubernatorial nominee, and Lawrence agreed to run, at age 69, as the unity candidate. He defeated his Republican opponent, a pretzel manufacturer, by 80,000 votes. [See TRUMAN, EISENHOWER Volumes]

Long prominent in national Democratic politics, Lawrence had supported Adlai E. Stevenson [q.v.] for his party's 1952 and 1956 presidential nominations and privately favored him in 1960. Lawrence opposed the candidacy of John F. Kennedy because, although a Catholic officeholder himself, he did not believe that a member of the Roman Catholic faith could win national office. Kennedy, who needed Lawrence's endorsement to win support from Pennsylvania's 81-member delegation at the Democratic National Convention, decided not to challenge the Governor directly by entering his state's primary. Nevertheless, Kennedy won 71.5% of the vote in the non-binding Pennsylvania contest in April as a write-in candidate.

Although Kennedy's primary triumphs in Pennsylvania and elsewhere impressed him, Lawrence refused to commit his delegation to any candidate up to the Convention's first ballot. By July 11, however, Kennedy had won the endorsement of Rep. William J. Green, Jr. (D, Pa.) [q.v.], the influential Philadelphia Democratic leader, and the support of a large number of individual Pennsylvania delegates. When it appeared that he could no longer keep his delegation unpledged, Lawrence agreed to back Kennedy. The 68 votes Kennedy received from Pennsylvania, along with those from other large industrial states, assured him of a first ballot victory.

At the Democratic Convention Lawrence led a delegation of Party leaders that urged Kennedy to select Senate Majority Leader Lyndon B. Johnson (D, Tex.) [q.v.] as his running mate. Kennedy agreed to Lawrence's recommendation, and the Governor nominated Johnson before the Convention. During the general election campaign, Lawrence's control over state patronage provided the national ticket with funds and precinct workers, helping Kennedy to carry Pennsylvania with 51.1% of the vote.

As governor, Lawrence presided over a state hard hit by the effects of the 1957-58 recession and the 116-day 1959 nationwide steel strike. Throughout his term in office, unemployment remained a serious problem. State revenues fell, and the state, despite

reductions in expenditures in 1959, had to borrow over a half billion dollars to finance the fiscal 1961 budget. At congressional hearings in January and February 1961, Lawrence testified in favor of the Administration's area redevelopment bill designed to assist localities with high rates of unemployment.

With the governors of New York, New Jersey and Delaware, Lawrence joined in signing a 100-year "Delaware Water Compact" in February 1961. The four state executives agreed to plan collectively for the development of the entire 12,750-square-mile Delaware River Basin region through the construction of multiple-use reservoirs and dams. Congress agreed to provide partial funding of the project in September 1961. The same month, Lawrence appointed the first woman to the Pennsylvania Supreme Court.

State law prevented Lawrence from succeeding himself, and the Republican gubernatorial nominee, Rep. William W. Scranton (R, Pa.) [q.v.], ended eight years of Democratic rule in 1962 with a 486,000-vote margin of victory. Following his retirement Lawrence continued to play a role in national and state politics, chairing the credentials committee at the Democratic National Convention in August 1964. He failed, however, to prevent a wealthy, liberal anti-organization candidate, Milton J. Shapp, from upsetting the state Party leadership's choice in the 1966 gubernatorial primary. Shapp lost the election in November. Lawrence suffered a heart attack on Nov. 4, 1966 and died Nov. 21.

[JLB]

LEE, RICHARD C(HARLES)
b. March 12, 1916; New Haven, Conn.
Mayor, New Haven, Conn., 1954-70.

During the Kennedy years New Haven under Mayor Richard C. Lee became a model city, demonstrating how urban renewal programs could revive the commercial life of decaying downtown areas.

Lee was born and raised in a working-class section of New Haven. After graduating from high school in 1935, he won a job as a city hall reporter for the *New Haven*

Journal-Courier. Running as a Democrat in 1939, Lee was elected as a city alderman. During World War II he was inducted into the Army but served only a short time before receiving a medical discharge. In 1943 he went to work for the *Yale News Digest* and subsequently served as the director of the University's public relations service. After two unsuccessful campaigns for mayor—in 1951 he lost by only two votes—he was finally elected in 1953.

Lee's plan for the redevelopment of New Haven was based on the assumption that well-to-do suburbanites would shop downtown only if the stores were readily accessible by automobile. Lee quickly won authorization for a project crucial to his plans: the construction of a superhighway linking the Connecticut Turnpike to the heart of downtown. He then initiated massive slum clearance projects to permit the widening of local streets and construction of new offices, department stores, middle-income apartments and parking garages. He hired Edward J. Logue, a talented attorney, to supervise the redevelopment program. To finance these projects Lee and Logue applied for federal assistance under the 1954 Housing Act. The two soon won national reputations for their expertise in the field of urban renewal. During the 1960 presidential campaign Lee served as an urban affairs adviser to John F. Kennedy. [See EISENHOWER Volume]

During the early 1960s Lee became increasingly concerned with the plight of New Haven's poor, who failed to benefit from the commercial revival. (Indeed, the city's slum clearance programs had forced hundreds of poor families from their homes.) During 1962 Lee's administration helped establish Community Progress Inc. (CPI), a private antipoverty program which received a $2.5 million grant from the Ford Foundation. CPI sponsored prekindergarten classes, job placement and retraining programs. In June 1963 it received a $300,000 grant from the Labor Department, and it subsequently became the first local antipoverty program to receive a grant from the Johnson Administration's Office of Economic Opportunity.

Lee also attempted to call attention to the problems of the city's growing black population. In July 1960 he suggested that blacks should stall traffic on the expressways to force homeward-bound commuters onto local streets where they could observe the ghetto's wretched housing. Lee's proposal was widely condemned as irresponsible and it cost him thousands of votes in the 1961 mayoral election.

Lee also received national attention in September 1963 when he criticised Yale students for having invited Alabama Gov. George C. Wallace [*q.v.*], a segregationist, to address the Yale Political Union. He declared that if Wallace came to New Haven he would be "officially unwelcome." Wallace eventually declined the invitation, but Lee was widely attacked by students, civil libertarians and conservatives.

During the Johnson years Lee was widely recognized as a figure of national importance. Thanks to his efforts New Haven was receiving more federal urban renewal assistance than any city in the country on a per capita basis. In fact, it received a great deal more money than several cities many times its size. The Lee Administration's housing redevelopment and rent subsidy programs won the praise of Secretary of Housing and Urban Development Robert C. Weaver [*q.v.*], who, in January 1966, declared that New Haven came "closest to our dream of a slumless city." On Aug. 19, 1967 the dream was shattered when New Haven's black ghetto exploded with five days of rioting, looting and arson. [See JOHNSON Volume]

Lee won reelection in 1968 but the riot had seriously tarnished his reputation. In 1970, after eight terms as mayor, he retired.

[JLW]

LEHMAN, HERBERT H(ENRY)
b. March 28, 1878; New York, N.Y.
d. Dec. 5, 1963; New York, N.Y.
Former New York Governor; Adviser, New York Committee for Democratic Voters, January 1959-November 1961.

Lehman, the son of wealthy German Jewish immigrants, worked for a textile firm and volunteered at New York's Henry

Street Settlement before becoming a partner in Lehman Brothers, his family's vestment banking firm, in 1908. He directed the relief programs of the Jewish Joint Distribution Committee when World War I began and in 1917 joined the U.S. Army, serving as an adiministrative aide and attaining the rank of colonel. After the war he returned to Lehman Brothers and also acted as a labor mediator in the garment industry. He became known as a leading philanthropist during this era.

Lehman worked for Alfred E. Smith's election as governor in 1926, was elected lieutenant governor in 1928 and succeeded Franklin D. Roosevelt in the statehouse in 1932. He was a strong supporter of the New Deal during the 1930s and was named by FDR as director-general of the United Nations Relief and Rehabilitation Administration after he left Albany in 1943. Elected to the U.S. Senate in a 1949 special election, Lehman became a major advocate of liberal foreign and domestic policies in the early Cold War era. He was a leading opponent of the 1952 McCarran-Walter Immigration Act, and in 1954 he joined in the effort to censure Sen. Joseph R. McCarthy (R, Wisc.) and strip him of his committee chairmanships. Lehman favored trade with the Soviet bloc and opposed the mutual defense treaty between the U.S. and Nationalist China. He was also a strong supporter of civil rights legislation during the 1950s. [See TRUMAN Volume]

After retiring from the Senate Herbert Lehman became active in the ongoing struggle between New York's regular and reform Democrats. He attributed Nelson Rockefeller's [q.v.] 1958 gubernatorial victory to domination of the state Democrats by "old-style party professionals," such as Tammany Hall leader Carmine DeSapio [q.v.]. Early in 1959 he joined Eleanor Roosevelt [q.v.] and other liberals in forming the New York Committee for Democratic Voters (NYCDV) to reform the Democratic Party and, they hoped, to oust Party boss DeSapio. The substantial gains made by the reform group in the 1959 and 1960 primaries were described by the *New York Times* as a "major blow to Mr. DeSapio's

political prestige." [See EISENHOWER Volume]

Lehman, termed the "patriarch of the reform movement" by the *Times*, favored liberal support for Mayor Robert F. Wagner [q.v.]. Wagner, who had been DeSapio's ally called for his former patron's resignation in early 1961. In June Lehman told the general committee of the NYCDV, many of whom remained critical of the Mayor's performance despite his repudiation of DeSapio, that a primary battle against Wagner would destroy the reform movement. When Wagner declared his candidacy in June, Lehman endorsed him immediately and called his candidacy an opportunity "to free this city with one blow from the shackles of the boss system." In July the general committee of the NYCDV, apparently heeding Lehman's admonitions to be "realistic," voted to endorse Wagner. The Tammany candidate, State Controller Arthur Levitt, was defeated in September by a three-to-two margin in a record primary turnout. The reformers were also successful in the contests for the leadership of most of Manhattan's districts, including DeSapio's. DeSapio was also disqualified as county leader since only district leaders were eligible for this post. He failed in his attempts to regain his district leadership in 1963 and 1965.

Following the reelection of Wagner in November, Lehman resigned as adviser to the NYCDV. He remained an elder statesmen of New York reform politics until he died of a heart attack at 85 in late 1963.

[MDB]

For further information:
Warren Moscow, *The Last of the Big-Time Bosses: The Life and Times of Carmine DeSapio* (New York, 1971).
Allan Nevins, *Herbert H. Lehman and His Era* (New York, 1963).

LEMAY, CURTIS E(MERSON)
b. Nov. 15, 1906; Columbus, Ohio.
Air Force Chief of Staff, June 1961-January 1965.

Curtis LeMay, the eldest of seven children of a poor Ohio family, dreamed from childhood of becoming a flyer. At the age of four or five he caught sight of his first plane and recalled "its wonderful sound and force. . .a thing of wood and metal, piercing the air. . .something unique and in a way divine." LeMay had hoped to attend West Point, but failing to win an appointment, he studied engineering at Ohio State University. In 1928 he joined the Army and won the chance to study flying. LeMay rose through the ranks and at the age of 37 became a major general in the Army Air Corps.

An innovator in the use of strategic bombers, LeMay played an important role in planning the devastating B-29 raids on Tokyo in the last months of World War II. LeMay became the commander of the American Air Force in Europe in 1947, directed the Berlin airlift for several months in 1948 and later that year became commanding general of the Strategic Air Command (SAC). The SAC bombers, airborne around the globe 24 hours a day, were thought by defense specialists in the 1950s to represent the United States' prime deterrent against Soviet attack.

By the time LeMay succeeded Gen. Thomas D. White as Air Force chief of staff in June 1961, he had become embroiled with the Kennedy Administration over the question of manned bomber production. From the mid-1950s onward, as emphasis on missile production increased, LeMay became one of the most effective advocates on Capitol Hill for continued and expanded appropriations for new aircraft. In July 1961 LeMay's testimony before the Senate Armed Services Committee was instrumental in the congressional decision to appropriate funds, far in excess of Defense Department requests, for the construction of B-52s, B-58s and for the development of the new RS-70 bomber. Although Secretary of Defense Robert S. McNamara [q.v.] thought that "missiles will be able to do anything bombers can do cheaper," LeMay argued for the continuing usefulness of the manned bomber. They would serve to "mop up" after a missile assault and alone could "show the flag" and demonstrate American power to other nations.

LeMay had little difficulty winning con-

gressional appropriations for bomber research and development, but Secretary of Defense McNamara was reluctant to spend the money. Of the $1.7 billion appropriated for the B-70, $510 million had been diverted by McNamara to other purposes by 1963. LeMay also attacked the Administration for favoring the development of the Navy's Polaris submarine missile over the Air Force's Minuteman and for the Defense Department's selection of the General Dynamics Corporation as the prime contractor for the construction of the controversial TFX experimental fighter. In testimony before the Senate Preparedness Subcommittee in the summer of 1963, LeMay supported the nuclear test ban treaty but only because the pact with the Russians had already been signed. LeMay expressed the fear that the treaty might put the U.S. at a serious military disadvantage.

LeMay's attacks on the Defense Department were welcomed by conservative Republicans like Sen. Barry Goldwater (R, Ariz.) [q.v.], who stated in 1964 that he would "rather put my faith in a man like General LeMay than a man like McNamara who puts his primary reliance on computers." High officials in both the Kennedy and Johnson Administrations feared that LeMay might become a formidable political threat upon his retirement; therefore, his tour of duty at the Pentagon was repeatedly extended.

After his retirement in 1965 LeMay became an outspoken critic of the Johnson Administration's restrictions on bombing raids in both North and South Vietnam. In October 1968 George C. Wallace [q.v.] chose LeMay to be his vice presidential running mate on the American Independent Party ticket. LeMay's calls for a massive air assault on North Vietnam and his refusal to rule out the use of nuclear weapons were thought by many observers to have done the Wallace candidacy considerable harm. [See JOHNSON Volume]

[JLW]

For further information:
Curtis LeMay with McKinley Kantor, *Mission With LeMay: My Story* (New York, 1965).

LEMNITZER, LYMAN L.

b. Aug. 29, 1899; Honesdale, Pa.
Chairman, Joint Chiefs of Staff, October 1960-July 1962; Supreme Allied Commander, Europe, January 1963-June 1969.

After a distinguished career in which he served in a series of command positions in Europe and the Far East, Gen. Lemnitzer was appointed Army Chief of Staff in 1959 and chairman of the Joint Chiefs of Staff in 1960.

In January 1961 Lemnitzer was one of the men who first advised Kennedy of the existence of a secret plan to invade Cuba. Despite a lack of in-depth study by the Defense Department, the General, along with the other Joint Chiefs, personally endorsed the attack, insisting that it must go through immediately or be abandoned because of the continuing Cuban-Soviet military build-up. Initially giving the President assurances that U.S. troops would not have to be committed, Lemnitzer was one of the Chiefs who later asked Kennedy to introduce American air and naval power to back the Cuban brigade after the April 17 invasion faltered. Because of his failure to anticipate the defeat, several senators, led by Sen. Albert Gore [q.v.], urged Lemnitzer's replacement.

As a result of this experience with Congress, Lemnitzer refused to commit himself to a particular policy during the early days of the Laotian crisis in the spring of 1961. He did, however, urge the President to avoid a ground war in Asia unless he was willing to commit large numbers of troops and possibly use nuclear weapons. Despite his belief that only a large-scale war would be effective in Asia, he continually underestimated the commitment necessary in both Laos and South Vietnam. As late as November 1961 he advised Kennedy that 40,000 troops would be sufficient to win the war.

In July 1962 Lemnitzer was designated to succeed Lauris Norstad [q.v.] as Supreme Commander, Allied Forces, Europe. His nomination provoked anger among those allies who had not been consulted and who felt Norstad was being removed because his ideas for supplying the North Atlantic Treaty Organization (NATO) with nuclear weapons were not approved by the Administration. As commander, Lemnitzer advocated many of his predecessor's proposals, including the need for having nuclear missiles under NATO control. He retired from the Army and from his position as commander of NATO in June 1969. [See JOHNSON Volume]

[EWS]

LEWIS, JOHN

b. Feb. 21, 1940; Troy, Ala.
Chairman, Student Nonviolent Coordinating Committee, June 1963-May 1966.

Born on a small farm in Alabama, Lewis became a Baptist minister at age 16. He graduated from the American Baptist Seminary in Nashville and later studied philosophy at Fisk University. In 1959, while a seminary student in Nashville, Lewis met regularly with other students in a series of workshops on nonviolence sponsored by the Nashville Christian Leadership Conference and the Fellowship of Reconciliation. When the sit-in movement to desegregate Southern luncheon counters began in February 1960, Lewis immediately joined the Nashville sit-ins. He was a founder of the Student Nonviolent Coordinating Committee (SNCC), established in April 1960, which grew out of the sit-ins.

Lewis was one of 13 persons on the first Freedom Ride to challenge segregation at interstate bus terminals in May 1961. Organized by the Congress of Racial Equality, the ride began on May 4 in Washington, D.C., with New Orleans as its destination. When the riders reached Rock Hill, S.C., Lewis was beaten as he entered the white waiting room at the bus station. More violence, including the beating of several other riders and the burning of a bus, erupted at Anniston and Birmingham, Ala. As a result the ride was discontinued on May 15 in Birmingham. Lewis went back to Nashville where he and his SNCC colleagues decided that the ride should be resumed and continued until its original New Orleans destination was reached. Lewis and nine other students returned to Birmingham by bus on May 17 where they were arrested and driven back to the Tennessee border the next day by local police. On May 19 all 10 were back in Birmingham. This time they went on to Montgomery where Lewis was again beaten and arrested on May 20. Throughout the summer Lewis participated in more Freedom Rides, which helped produce a September 1961 order from the Interstate Commerce Commission desegregating all interstate bus terminals.

Lewis abandoned his studies at Fisk when elected chairman of SNCC in June 1963. He represented the organization at the Aug. 28, 1963 March on Washington. The address he prepared for that day labeled the Administration's civil rights bill "too little and too late" and warned that "we will march throughout the South, through the heart of Dixie, the way Sherman did. We shall pursue our own 'scorched earth' policy and burn Jim Crow to the ground—nonviolently." When this text was circulated on the evening of Aug. 27, the other march sponsors, upset by Lewis's criticism of the Kennedy Administration and his angry tone, insisted that its contents be changed. Lewis, who had been jailed over 20 times for his civil rights activities by the date of the march, complied but still delivered the most radical speech of the day. He asserted that American politics was "dominated by politicians who build their career on immoral compromising and ally themselves with open forms of political, economic and social exploitation." He also warned that if Congress failed to pass meaningful civil rights legislation, "we will march through the South, through the streets of Jackson . . . Danville . . . Cambridge . . . Birmingham" with "the spirit of love and with the spirit of dignity that we have shown here today." The same day Lewis joined nine other rights leaders in a meeting with President Kennedy where they discussed the Administration's civil rights bill, then pending in Congress.

Lewis participated in a series of civil rights demonstrations in 1964 and 1965, refusing to endorse a July 1964 call, agreed to by several other civil rights leaders, for a

"moratorium" on demonstrations during the presidential election campaign. In March 1965 he helped lead the Selma to Montgomery march. Lewis was voted out as chairman of SNCC a year later and replaced by the more militant Stokely Carmichael. [See JOHNSON Volume]

[CAB]

LINCOLN, MURRAY D(ANFORTH)
b. April 18, 1892; Raynham, Mass.
d. Nov. 7, 1966; Columbus, Ohio.
President, Nationwide Insurance Company, 1955-64.

A graduate of Massachusetts Agricultural College, Murray Lincoln devoted much of his life to promoting producer and consumer cooperatives. He left his position as agricultural agent for a Cleveland bank in 1920 to become executive secretary of the Ohio Farm Bureau Federation, where he served until 1948. In response to farmers' complaints about paying excessive automobile insurance rates, Lincoln organized the Farm Bureau Mutual Automobile Insurance Company in 1926 with $10,000 in capital provided by dues from the Farm Bureau Federation. In the 1930s he organized similar concerns for fire and life insurance. Named the Nationwide Insurance Companies in 1955, these entities had $600 million in assets by 1961.

During World War II Lincoln was a leader of the liberal bloc in the American Farm Bureau Federation. After the war he emerged as a prominent internationalist and a pioneer in the humanitarian distribution of U.S. agricultural surpluses to needy nations. Lincoln was a founder and the president from 1945 to 1957 of the Cooperative for American Remittance to Europe, popularly known as CARE. He served on numerous advisory committees for President Truman and was a director of Americans for Democratic Action (ADA). Described by the *New York Times* as "part evangelist and part Yankee trader," Lincoln was also president of the Cooperative League of America from 1941 to 1965. [See TRUMAN, EISENHOWER Volumes]

In late 1960 Lincoln headed a task force

on the proposed Food for Peace program for President-elect Kennedy. The task force report in January 1961 urged that the U.S. expand its global food program and give, or sell at cut-rate prices, at least $3 billion worth of surplus food annually to poorer nations. During 1961 Food for Peace distributed 60 billion pounds of surplus commodities and fed 64 million people. In 1961 Lincoln was also appointed to the Peace Corps Advisory Council and the Citizens Committee for International Development, a group formed to win public approval of Kennedy's foreign aid program.

In November 1962 Lincoln became involved in a controversy over a television show sponsored by Nationwide, Howard K. Smith's ABC-TV documentary, "The Political Obituary of Richard M. Nixon." Many conservatives criticized the show for including an interview with Alger Hiss, an ex-State Department official whom Nixon had branded a Communist in the 1940s. Lincoln defended his company's decision not to censor the program and criticized those who favored such censorship.

Lincoln retired as Nationwide president in 1964. He died on Nov. 7, 1966.

[TO]

LINDSAY, JOHN V(LIET)
b. Nov. 24, 1921, New York, N.Y.
Republican Representative, N.Y., 1959-65; Mayor, New York, N.Y., 1965-73.

The son of an investment banker, Lindsay graduated from Yale in 1943 and joined the Naval Reserve. After receiving his law degree from Yale in 1948, he served as executive assistant to U.S. Attorney General Herbert Brownell from 1953 to 1956. Campaigning on a platform calling for more "aggressive leadership . . . in Congress to carry forward the Eisenhower program," Lindsay defeated a Republican Party regular in a 1958 primary race to represent Manhattan's East Side "Silk Stocking" district. He won the general election and soon established himself as an independent, liberal Republican congressman.

A member of the Judiciary Committee,

Lindsay won a reputation as a progressive on civil liberties issues. In 1961 he blocked one bill that would have publicized the conveyance of Communist propaganda through the U.S. mails and another that would have barred from waterfront employment anyone refusing to answer the questions of a congressional committee or federal agency concerning subversive activities. In January 1962 Lindsay and Rep. William F. Ryan (D, N.Y.) [q.v.] cast the only votes against a provision forbidding the U.S. Postal System to handle Communist propaganda. He blocked a House Un-American Activities Committee (HUAC) bill in May 1962 that would have authorized the Secretary of Defense to establish a security program in defense industries. In August 1963 Lindsay proposed the creation of a joint congressional watchdog committee to improve what he called "cursory and sporadic surveillance" of the Central Intelligence Agency (CIA). The proposed committee was to study problems arising from conflicts between the CIA's information gathering and special operations functions. That year he also proposed that HUAC's functions be transferred to the Judiciary Committee.

Lindsay was a strong supporter of civil rights laws. He was one of seven House Republicans to issue a statement against any Party alliance with Southern Democrats opposing civil rights and other "constructive" legislation in early 1961. In March 1962 he called for a broad voting rights bill to allow states the right to deny the franchise only on the grounds of age, length of residence or imprisonment. In January 1963 he sponsored a Republican civil rights bill to make the Civil Rights Commission a permanent agency and to increase its powers.

Lindsay's liberalism (Americans for Democratic Action gave him an 88% rating in 1962) weakened his ties with the Republican Party. He refused to support Sen. Barry M. Goldwater (R, Ariz.) [q.v.] for president in 1964, and in his campaign for the New York mayoralty in 1965 he won the Liberal as well as Republican endorsement. Lindsay won the election as a fusion candidate. Lindsay's controversial performance as mayor alienated New York's white middle class, and he failed to capture the Republican designation for reelection in 1969. However, he won a plurality as the Liberal nominee. Lindsay later declared himself a Democrat, and in 1972 he made an unsuccessful bid for the Democratic presidential nomination. [See JOHNSON, NIXON Volumes]

[MDB]

For further information:
Daniel E. Button, Lindsay, A Man for Tomorrow (New York, 1965).

LIPPMANN, WALTER
b. Sept. 23, 1889; New York, N.Y.
d. Dec. 14, 1974; New York, N.Y.
Journalist.

Walter Lippmann, a seminal force in American liberalism for over 50 years, articulated many of the major movements in American political philosophy and politics during the 20th century. Lippmann was born into a well-to-do family of German-Jewish ancestry. From 1906 to 1910 he studied at Harvard, where he was deeply influenced by William James's pragmatism and George Santayana's belief in an "aesthetic aristocracy." While at Harvard Lippmann joined the Socialist Club and graduated from the University with a deep commitment toward many of the social reforms of the era.

After working with Lincoln Steffens at Everybody's Magazine, Lippmann flirted briefly with municipal socialism, but by 1914, when he wrote Drift and Mastery, he had become openly hostile to the doctrine. That same year Lippmann joined Herbert Croly in founding the New Republic, a progressive journal that supported the activist presidency advocated by Theodore Roosevelt and Woodrow Wilson. During World War I the young journalist served as assistant to Secretary of War Newton Baker and aided President Wilson in drawing up his famous Fourteen Points.

During the 1920s Lippmann edited the liberal New York World but also published more books which reflected a growing postwar pessimism with democracy. Lippmann's influence grew still further after 1931, when he began writing his column "Today and Tomorrow" for the Republican New York Herald Tribune. Lippmann opposed most of Franklin D. Roosevelt's New Deal programs because he feared them as statist and potentially totalitiarian in their content. After 1937 Lippmann turned his attention to foreign affairs and urged the U.S. to prepare for war.

Lippmann's prestige increased after the war and he emerged as one of America's most respected political critics. In foreign affairs he was a realist and took the view that Soviet expansion was molded more by traditional Russian expansionism than by Communist ideology. [See TRUMAN, EISENHOWER Volumes]

Because of his calm, impersonal and almost aloof journalistic style, as well as his access to government decision-makers, Walter Lippmann influenced Washington's critical taste more than any other journalist of his time. During the 1960 presidential campaign, Lippmann hailed John Kennedy as the first candidate since Franklin D. Roosevelt who could stir and unite the American people. Many observers felt Lippmann's endorsement lent the Kennedy campaign a special air of legitimacy.

In the early 1960s, however, Lippmann became increasingly critical of the President. Kennedy's cautious economic policies caused him to write in June 1961 that the President was carrying on "in all its essentials the Eisenhower economic philosophy. . . .It's like the Eisenhower Administration 30 years younger."

Lippmann also opposed the Administration's October 1962 decision to blockade Cuba to force the removal of Soviet missiles from that island. He suggested that the risk of nuclear confrontation was unnecessary and that the U.S. should quietly negotiate to exchange Soviet missiles in Cuba for American missiles in Turkey.

In 1963 Lippmann shifted his column from the Herald Tribune to Newsweek. During the next five years his fear that the U.S. would become involved in an Asian land war led him to criticize the Vietnam policies of both the Kennedy and Johnson

Administrations. Though often regarded as "the dean of American liberal journalists," many of his admirers chose to ignore his dislike of popular democracy and his shift from an early liberalism to an almost despairing conservatism in his later years.

Lippmann retired from *Newsweek* in 1968. He died in December 1974.

[FHM]

LODGE, HENRY CABOT
b. July 5, 1902; Nahant, Mass.
Ambassador to Vietnam, August 1963-April 1964, July 1965-April 1967.

Henry Cabot Lodge, the U.S. ambassador to South Vietnam during the closing days of the Kennedy Administration, was born into a distinguished New England family that traced its ancestry back to the Massachusetts Bay Colony. After the death of his father in 1909, Lodge was raised by his grandfather, Henry Cabot Lodge, Sr., the powerful Republican senator who opposed U.S. entry into the League of Nations after World War I.

Following his graduation from Harvard in 1924, Lodge worked as a reporter and then editorial writer for the *New York Herald Tribune*. From 1933 to 1937 he served in the Massachusetts House of Representatives. Lodge was first elected to the U.S. Senate in 1936 and, with the exception of periods of service in the Army from 1941 to 1942 and from 1944 to 1945, remained there for the next 15 years. In 1951 he helped persuade Dwight D. Eisenhower to run for the Republican presidential nomination and later managed Eisenhower's primary campaign. Because of his work for Eisenhower, Lodge neglected his own political career and was defeated for reelection in 1952 by John F. Kennedy. From 1953 to 1960 the former Senator served as ambassador to the U.N., representing the U.S. in important debates on Suez, Lebanon and Hungary and in clashes with the Soviet Union on disarmament and espionage. [See TRUMAN, EISENHOWER Volumes]

In 1960 Richard M. Nixon [*q.v.*] chose Lodge as his vice presidential running mate. Nixon assumed that Lodge's East Coast connections would balance his own strength in the West and Midwest and that Lodge's liberalism would offset his more conservative image. More importantly, Lodge's work at the U.N. had made him a popular figure, and Nixon hoped he would be a valuable asset in a campaign in which foreign policy would be an important issue.

Lodge's conduct during the campaign was the subject of controversy among Republicans. Supporters pointed to polls showing that he was more popular than the presidential candidates and claimed that he aided the Republican election effort. His detractors criticized his refusal to campaign aggressively and maintained that a Harlem speech promising to put a black in the cabinet undermined Nixon's Southern campaign.

A year after his defeat, in November 1961, Lodge became director general of the Atlantic Institute then being founded by European and American statesmen and industrialists to plan for a united European-American-Canadian economic community. During the next year he worked with high level policymakers to advance these objectives, but the project remained stillborn because of French President Charles de Gaulle's nationalistic policies.

In June 1963 President Kennedy, anxious to gain bipartisan support for American involvement in Vietnam, appointed Lodge ambassador to Saigon. While at that post Lodge served not only as an executor but also as an important formulator of policy. The Ambassador arrived in Saigon on Aug. 22 during the crisis precipitated by the Diem regime's attack on Buddhist dissidents. This attack, carried out by President Ngo Dinh Diem's brother, Ngo Dinh Nhu, generated fierce criticism not only from foreign governments but also from elements within Vietnam. Several American observers also thought the attack threatened the military effort in that country. After assessing the situation, Lodge came to the conclusion that the war could not be won with the unpopular regime. In the ensuing months he worked to convince Washington that it should be replaced.

Two days after his arrival the Ambassador

was instructed by State Department officials to tell Diem that he must "rid himself of Nhu" and to inform military leaders that if Diem did not, the U.S. would "give them direct support in any interim period [of the] breakdown [of the] central government." Lodge approved of the plan but proposed to forego what he believed to be a futile attempt to approach Diem and, instead, state the U.S. position only to the generals, thus throwing U.S. support behind a coup. However, the message, written by George Ball [q.v.], Michael Forrestal [q.v.], Roger Hilsman [q.v.] and Averell Harriman [q.v.], had not been adequately studied by the Secretaries of Defense and State or the Chairman of the Joint Chiefs of Staff who, upon reflection, questioned the efficacy of a coup. The State Department sent Lodge a message canceling the previous communications and ordering him to work for the reform of the Diem regime. The suggested coup did not take place because the Vietnamese generals were unable to achieve a favorable balance of forces in the Saigon area and because several believed that the U.S. had leaked information about their plot to Diem and Nhu.

Despite Washington's decision Lodge remained convinced that the war would not be won with Diem, and he tried to persuade Washington that a new, more popular government was necessary. During September he carried on a secret correspondence with Kennedy in which he presented his pessimistic view of the situation and suggested the need for change. In addition, he gave Secretary of Defense Robert S. McNamara [q.v.] extensive briefings during the Secretary's September visit to undercut the military's uniformly optimistic reports to Washington.

In Saigon Lodge worked on what he regarded as futile attempts to force Diem to reform. Through press leaks he informed the government that the U.S. would have to withdraw its support if Diem did not institute necessary changes. During the first week in October, Washington, on advice given earlier by Lodge, deferred approval of a portion of the foreign aid program as a threat of possible further cuts unless Nhu was removed. At Lodge's suggestion John

Richardson, the Central Intelligence Agency chief in Saigon who had been a supporter of Diem, was returned to Washington on Oct. 5, ostensibly because his cover identity had been compromised. In a more controversial move Lodge, with the permission of Washington, informed the South Vietnamese government on Oct. 17 that U.S. aid for Diem's private guard, which had been used in August to put down the Buddhists, would be suspended until it was transferred to field combat.

South Vietnamese generals interpreted these actions as a green light for a coup and in the beginning of October approached Lodge's aides to ask about the U.S. stand on a change of government. On Oct. 5 the Ambassador indirectly informed them that the U.S. would not thwart any proposed coup. Whether this was done before or after receiving an Oct. 5 message from the President ordering him not to give active "covert encouragement to a coup" but to "identify and contact possible alternative leadership" is unclear.

As the coup took shape during the last days of October, Lodge worked to forestall any attempt by Washington to oppose it. On Oct. 30, when several of the President's advisers decided to make one last attempt to deal with Diem and asked Lodge to delay or call off the coup, he informed them that the matter was in Vietnamese hands and he could do nothing to prevent it. A successful coup took place on Nov. 1.

During the months following the coup, Lodge remained an important force in Vietnamese politics, attempting to aid in the establishment of a stable government and pushing for needed reforms. In May 1964 he resigned his post to return home to try to prevent the nomination of Sen. Barry Goldwater (R, Ariz.) [q.v.] as the Republican presidential candidate.

In July 1965 Lodge was again appointed ambassador to Vietnam where he worked to develop the pacification program and to find a formula that would bring the North Vietnamese to the negotiating table. He served at that post until April 1967. From April 1968 until January 1969 Lodge was ambassador to West Germany. He served as the U.S. chief negotiator at the Paris

Peace Talks from January 1969 until June 1970. In June 1970 Lodge was named presidential envoy to the Vatican. [See JOHNSON, NIXON Volumes]

[EWS]

For further information:
Alden Hatch, *The Lodges of Massachusetts* (New York, 1973).
Henry Cabot Lodge, *The Storm Has Many Eyes* (New York, 1973).
William J. Miller, *Henry Cabot Lodge* (New York, 1967).

LOEB, JAMES (ISAAC), JR.

b. August 18, 1908; Chicago, Ill.
Ambassador to Peru, April 1961-November 1962; Consultant to the State Department, November 1962-June 1963; Ambassador to Guinea, June 1963-August 1965.

A graduate of Dartmouth and Northwestern, Loeb decided not to join his father's insurance business, but instead he became a teacher of Romance languages. In May 1941, while an instructor in a New York high school, Loeb helped found the Union for Democratic Action, an organization of liberals and intellectuals formed to mobilize other progressives against the threat posed by European fascism. Rejected by the military for health reasons, Loeb served as executive director of the organization, which in 1947 was transformed into Americans for Democratic Action (ADA) with Loeb as national director. He also helped organize the Inter-American Association for Democracy and Freedom, founded in Havana in 1950, and established friendships with many of Latin America's political reformers, including Romulo Betancourt of Venezuela.

In 1951 Loeb left his post in the ADA to serve for two years as a foreign policy adviser to the Truman Administration. During the Eisenhower years Loeb was the editor and co-publisher of an upstate New York newspaper. He remained involved in liberal politics and assisted New York Gov. W. Averell Harriman [q.v.] in his unsuccessful reelection campaign against Nelson Rocke-

feller [q.v.] in 1958. [See TRUMAN Volume]

Although he worked for Sen. Hubert Humphrey (D, Minn.) [q.v.] in the 1960 Democratic presidential primaries, Loeb was named by President Kennedy to be ambassador to Peru in April 1961, largely because of his liberal credentials and foreign policy experience. Loeb and Assistant Secretary of State for Inter-American Affairs Edwin Martin [q.v.] agreed that the Administration must follow a policy throughout Latin America consistent with the ideals and aims of the Alliance for Progress. These included support of democratic governments and social reform and opposition to military overthrow of elected governments.

As early as December 1961 Loeb saw that the tense Peruvian political situation might test the consistency of the new U.S. policy. With Peruvian presidential elections scheduled for June 1962, Loeb and Martin began to draw up plans for actions the U.S. might take should the army interfere in the Peruvian political process. Their task was complicated by the fact that two of the major parties committed to democracy and social change, the Popular Action Party of Fernando Belaunde Terry and the American Popular Revolutionary Alliance (APRA) of the old populist and fierce anti-Communist, Victor Raul Haya de la Torre, were at apparently irreconcilable odds. When APRA won the largest vote share of any single party in the June elections, the military, hostile to Haya de la Torre and supported by Popular Action, charged fraud and removed the incumbent civilian government. Loeb, who had close ties with APRA, was adamant in his opposition to military coups, and he and Martin persuaded Kennedy to suspend diplomatic relations and economic aid.

This policy appeared successful; the military junta restored civil liberties, reached a modus vivendi with APRA and scheduled new elections for the following year. The U.S. then agreed to resume diplomatic relations in August, although military aid remained suspended. Loeb, who was recalled to Washington in late July, could not return to Peru, since he had earned the enmity of the junta and of the U.S. business community in Peru. Some critics charged that, although the U.S. stand was principled and justified, the Kennedy Administration encouraged military rebellion when it had failed to act as firmly in a similar situation in Argentina in March 1962. Others, including Sen. Ernest Gruening (D, Alaska) [q.v.], attacked the U.S. military foreign aid program since it strengthened rebellious and undemocratic armies, such as Peru's.

Loeb formally resigned his post in November 1962 and in June 1963 was named ambassador to Guinea. Loeb left government service in 1965 to resume his career as a journalist.

[JCH]

LOEB, WILLIAM
b. Dec. 26, 1905; Washington, D.C.
Publisher, *Manchester Union Leader*, 1948- .

Loeb's father was a private secretary to President Theodore Roosevelt, and the younger Loeb grew up in fashionable Oyster Bay, N.Y., attended the Hotchkiss School and graduated from Williams College in 1927. After two years at Harvard Law, Loeb took a variety of newspaper jobs before purchasing a string of small New England newspapers in the 1940s and 1950s. Loeb bought a share in New Hampshire's *Manchester Union Leader* in 1946 and gained full control of the newspaper in 1948, using it as a forum for his arch-conservative and often erratic views on U.S. politics. As the only New Hampshire newspaper with a statewide circulation, the *Union Leader* exercised an important influence on the state's politics and, once every four years during the presidential primary, on national politics as well.

Using highly personal, front-page editorials, Loeb supported Robert Taft (R, Ohio) and Joseph McCarthy (R, Wisc.) in the 1950s. Late in the decade Loeb attacked the national political aspirations of Sen. John F. Kennedy and during the New Hampshire presidential primary in March 1960 supported a ballpoint-pen manufac-

turer from Chicago named Paul C. Fisher. It was an indication of hardcore New Hampshire support for Loeb's conservative ideas that the unknown Fisher received almost 13% of the Democratic vote in the March 8 primary.

On Nov. 2, 1960, six days before the presidential election, Loeb stated in an editorial that Kennedy "whose father has a half a billion dollars and whose family has $40,000 weddings," was incapable of understanding the problems of the average citizen. In a Nov. 7 speech in Manchester, Kennedy called Loeb "irresponsible" and stated that the publisher had no regard for the truth. Kennedy's strategy was to attack Loeb 24 hours before the presidential election, so that the publisher—who lived in Massachusetts—would not have a chance to write an editorial reply before his newspaper's deadline. In the New Hampshire presidential balloting, Kennedy received 135,000 votes, the highest total for any Democrat in history, but he failed to carry the state. After the new President's inauguration Loeb called him "the No. 1 liar in the United States."

During the Kennedy years Loeb was involved with antitrust suits between one of his newspapers, the Haverhill (Mass.) *Journal*, and a group of anti-Loeb New England publishers who had purchased the rival *Gazette*. Because of his effort to entice Haverhill merchants into signing long-term advertising contracts with the *Journal*, Loeb was fined $3 million, an amount which he borrowed in installments from the Teamsters Union. In the early 1960s Loeb gave vigorous editorial support to Teamster President James R. Hoffa [q.v.] in his running legal battle with Attorney General Robert F. Kennedy [q.v.].

Viewing himself as a last bastion of the traditional American way of life, Loeb proffered a somewhat eccentric ideology. A vigorous anti-Communist who saw a Soviet menace on a global scale, he nevertheless denounced the far-right John Birch Society and called its leader, Robert Welch [q.v.], a "bloody nut." In 1963 Loeb headed the Coordinating Committee for Fundamental Human Freedoms, a lobby against the civil rights bill. He was also a vigorous opponent of increased taxation in New Hampshire.

Loeb gave editorial support to the presidential candidacies of Sen. Barry Goldwater (R, Ariz.) [q.v.] in 1964, Richard Nixon [q.v.] in 1968 and Los Angeles Mayor Sam Yorty [q.v.] in 1972. [See JOHNSON Volume]

[FHM]

For further information:
Kevin Cash, *Who the hell is William Loeb?* (Manchester, 1975)

LOEVINGER, LEE
b. April 24, 1913; St. Paul, Minn.
Assistant Attorney General, Antitrust Division, February 1961-May 1963; Commissioner, Federal Communications Commission, May 1963-July 1968.

Lee Loevinger was the son of a St. Paul district court judge who had helped organize Minnesota's Farmer-Labor Party. He took his law degree in 1936 and entered the federal government as an attorney with the National Labor Relations Board. He moved to the Antitrust Division of the Justice Department during the tenure of Thurman Arnold, who initiated a sweeping antitrust campaign before the war.

Loevinger returned to private practice after the war. He established a reputation for representing private plaintiffs in tripledamage antitrust suits, usually against larger companies. In 1949 he published *The Law of Free Enterprise*, which argued for an energetic federal antitrust policy to curb the power of monopolies and stimulate competition. Gov. Orville Freeman [q.v.], a former law partner, appointed Loevinger to the Minnesota Supreme Court in 1960, where he served for a year until President Kennedy chose him to be assistant attorney general in charge of antitrust matters in February 1961.

"I believe in antitrust almost as a secular religion," Loevinger had told Attorney General Robert Kennedy [q.v.]. *Business Week* and the *Wall Street Journal* interpreted the appointments of such individuals as Loevinger and Paul Rand Dixon [q.v.],

chairman of the Federal Trade Commission, as indications that the Kennedy Administration intended to embark upon an aggressive antitrust offensive. In his *John F. Kennedy and the Business Community*, Jim F. Heath characterized Loevinger as "the Administration member who worried big business the most."

Loevinger worked to improve antitrust investigative techniques by reorganizing the Antitrust Division and testifying before Congress in favor of legislation to require businesses to turn their records over to the Justice Department for use in civil antitrust investigations. Such a bill finally passed in September 1962. Loevinger also favored legislation requiring companies intending to merge their operations to give a 60-day, pre-merger notification to federal antitrust agencies, but Congress took no action on the proposal. Through 1961 Loevinger spoke several times before Congress against the restriction of the proposed Communications Satellite Corp. to international communications carriers. Arguing that this restriction would give the American Telephone and Telegraph Company (AT&T) a monopoly over the new system, Loevinger argued that domestic as well as international carriers should be given an opportunity to participate in the ownership of a satellite system.

Loevinger filed 73 suits during his first fiscal year in office and 62 in his second, many of which were aimed at criminal price-fixing. Prominent among Loevinger's efforts were two criminal cases against General Motors, one charging monopoly in the manufacture of diesel locomotives and the other a conspiracy to impede the sale of Chevrolet cars at discounts in the Los Angeles area. He filed eight civil suits against General Electric (G.E.), a continuation of the Eisenhower Administration's successful prosecution of G.E. for criminal price-fixing. In his attacks on bank mergers, Loevinger departed from the policy of the preceding administration, which had argued that the Clayton Act did not apply to such combinations.

Despite such activity, the Antitrust Division under Loevinger fulfilled neither the fears of big business nor the hopes of antitrust advocates. The number of suits filed did not differ appreciably from the total in the last years of the Eisenhower Administration. Loevinger, arguing that sheer quantity of cases was a deceptive yardstick, had promised earlier that the Kennedy antitrust record would reveal a greater number of major prosecutions, but no spectacular suits were initiated. Loevinger had suggested that the Justice Department might attempt divestiture actions against G.E., "Big Steel," and AT&T, but no such action was taken against those companies. Attorney General Kennedy disavowed the possibility of an AT&T suit, soon after Loevinger's remark in August 1961 that his division was investigating the possibility of compelling AT&T to drop its international subsidiaries. (Loevinger's remark had sent the company's stock plummeting six points.)

Loevinger attributed his division's undramatic results to a shortage of manpower. He also maintained that spectacular cases had been avoided for fear of damaging business confidence and inhibiting economic recovery. The Administration became especially cautious in this regard after the steel price controversy of April 1962. Loevinger was replaced as antitrust chief in May 1963 by William Orrick [q.v.].

According to Heath, "businessmen regarded Loevinger as a 'crusader' and sensed that his transfer signaled a transition in antitrust policy." President Kennedy appointed Loevinger to the Federal Communications Commission, where he served for the next five years.

[TO]

LONG, EDWARD V(AUGHAN)

b. July 18, 1908; Whiteside, Mo.
d. Nov. 6, 1972; Clarksville, Mo.
Democratic Senator, Mo., 1961-69.

Descended from Missouri settlers, Edward Long briefly attended the University of Missouri and then studied law at Culver-Stockton College before his admission to the Missouri bar in 1932. Active in local politics, Long was elected to the Missouri General Assembly in 1946 where he

served for 10 years before winning election as lieutenant governor in 1956. After the death of Sen. Thomas C. Hennings, Jr. (D, Mo.) in September 1960, Long was appointed to fill his vacant seat. He defeated his Republican opponent in the November 1961 special election.

Assigned to both the Judiciary and Banking and Currency Committees, Long, a moderate liberal, supported Kennedy Administration legislation on over 60% of all major issues, according to Congressional Quarterly. In September 1961 he cosponsored an unsuccessful amendment to a clean elections bill that would have required political committees to make financial reports and also would have limited individual campaign contributions to $20,000.

As a majority member of the Judiciary Committee's Antitrust and Monopoly Subcommittee, Long supported legislation requiring owners of drug patents to grant manufacturing licenses to other qualified companies after three years of exclusive proprietorship. Long was also an active proponent of the drug reform bill that became the 1962 Federal Food, Drug and Cosmetic Act. In the wake of the controversy over the drug thalidomide, the Act required "substantial evidence" of a drug's effectiveness and permitted the Secretary of Health, Education and Welfare to immediately remove a drug from the market if it presented an imminent hazard to the public health. However, Long generally disapproved of what he regarded as excessive federal intervention in private enterprise and acted to prevent two important 1963 Senate investigations into the drug industry.

Elected to a full term in 1962, Long was one of the senators who unsuccessfully voted in January 1963 to modify Senate Rule 22 so that fewer than the required two-thirds majority could invoke the cloture rule in the event of a filibuster. In March 1964 he was named a floor captain of that section of the Johnson Administration's civil rights bill covering the Civil Rights Commission.

Long supported major Johnson Administration domestic and foreign policy legislation. On Oct. 25, 1967 he was cleared by the Senate Select Committee on Standards and Conduct of charges that he had used his position to help Teamsters President James R. Hoffa [*q.v.*]. Committee Chairman John Stennis (D, Miss.) [*q.v.*] stated that the Committee had "found no facts" to show that a *Life* magazine article charging Long with taking $48,000 in payments for legal services from Morris A. Shenker, one of Hoffa's attorneys, "had any connection" with Long's "activities as a member of the Senate." The *Life* article, however, was regarded as a decisive factor in Long's defeat by Thomas Eagleton in the 1968 Democratic senatorial primary. After his defeat Long returned to private business. He died on Nov. 6, 1972. [See JOHNSON Volume]

[FHM]

LONG, OREN E(THELBURT)
b. March 4, 1889; Altoona, Kans.
d. May 6, 1965; Honolulu, Hawaii.
Democratic Senator, Hawaii, 1959-63.

Long first went to Hawaii in 1917 as a settlement house worker. The holder of two M.A. degrees, he served in a number of the territory's administrative posts in education and public welfare during his career. In 1951 President Truman appointed him territorial governor. Long left office in 1953 when a Republican administration was inaugurated in Washington.

Always a strong proponent of statehood, Long was honored by fellow Democrats with a senatorial nomination when Hawaii became a state in 1959. He was elected in July 1959, but, by the flip of a coin, he lost the title of senior senator and the longer term of office to Republican Sen. Hiram Fong [*q.v.*].

In the Senate Long was a member of the Interior and Insular Affairs Committee and the Public Works Committee. A self-defined liberal, he earned ratings of 80% in 1961 and 83% in 1962 from the Americans for Democratic Action. He voted in favor of civil rights, federal school aid and minimum wage legislation and was a faithful supporter of the Kennedy Administration's legislative program.

Long announced his retirement in 1962,

indicating that he wished to be succeeded by Rep. Daniel Inouye (D, Hawaii), one of the major architects of Hawaii's resurgent Democratic Party. Inouye won the election that fall. Long died on May 6, 1965.

[JCH]

LONG, RUSSELL B(ILLIU)
b. Nov. 3, 1918; Shreveport, La.
Democratic Senator, La., 1949- .

As the eldest son of Huey Long, the Louisiana populist who dominated state politics in the 1920s and 1930s, Russell Long was marked for a political career. After law school and World War II naval service, Long aided his uncle Earl K. Long's gubernatorial campaign in 1947. The following year Long was elected U.S. Senator after a barnstorming effort reminiscent of his father's campaigns. In Congress Long sought the membership in the Senate's "inner club" which had been denied his father. His entree was eased by repeated reelection against token opposition and by appointment to the powerful Finance and Foreign Relations Committees.

In 1961 Long chaired the Senate's Small Business Subcommittee on Monopoly which conducted hearings on the possible antitrust violations involved in the American Telephone and Telegraph Co.'s participation in the satellite communications project. Long charged that the Federal Communications Commission was "getting ready to put this thing into the hands of the biggest and most powerful monopoly in America" and called for reconsideration of a government-owned satellite communications system. The following year Long took his attack to the Senate floor where he joined nine other Democratic senators in a short-lived filibuster against the communications satellite bill.

Long's close ties to the oil industry reflected the industry's importance in Louisiana politics. Long succeeded Rep. Sam Rayburn (D, Tex.) [*q.v.*] and Sen. Robert Kerr (D, Okla.) [*q.v.*] as the oil industry's principal spokesman in Congress during the debate over the passage of the Trade Expansion Act of 1962. In October of that year Long reported that private conversations with President Kennedy had resulted in an "understanding" that the Administration would continue, and in some cases strengthen, oil import quotas. As a result of this agreement with Kennedy, senators from oil producing states supported the trade bill which gave the President authority to lower tariff restrictions on a variety of imports.

During the Kennedy years Long adopted an aggressive outlook in foreign affairs. In response to the Brazilian seizure of an International Telephone and Telegraph subsidiary in February 1962, Long sponsored legislation halting aid to any country that seized U.S. property. In 1963 Long was the only member of the Senate Foreign Relations Committee to vote in committee against ratification of the limited nuclear test ban treaty. On the Senate floor Long and Sen. John Tower (R, Tex.) [q.v.] co-sponsored an "understanding" which declared that the treaty did not affect the right of the United States to resort to nuclear weapons in the event of war. The understanding was defeated, and Long voted against ratification of the treaty.

Despite their differences President Kennedy selected Long, the second-ranking member of the Finance Committee, to conduct the floor fight for the Administration's $11.5-billion tax reduction bill. Long skillfully guided the bill to adoption in 1964. This success and his ascension to the positions of assistant Senate majority leader and chairman of the Finance Committee marked Long as a rising figure in the Senate during the early years of the Johnson Administration. [See JOHNSON Volume]

[DKR]

LOVESTONE, JAY
b. 1898, Lithuania.
Director, Free Trade Union Committee, 1944-63.

In 1908 Jacob Leibstein emigrated to the U.S. and changed his name to Lovestone. A left-wing socialist and a graduate of City College of New York, Lovestone was among the founders of the American Communist Party in 1919. He first served as editor of the Party's theoretical journal and then became its general secretary. Out-

flanked in an intraparty dispute, Lovestone was removed from office by Stalin at the 1928 Communist International Congress. He then led a small anti-Stalin Communist group popularily known as the "Lovestonites." Lovestone's involvement in factional battles in the early CIO attracted the attention of International Ladies Garment Workers Union (ILGWU) President David Dubinsky [q.v.], who recognized that Lovestone's intimate knowledge of the Communist Party could help him combat Communists in the ILGWU. "I know the communists better than they know themselves," Lovestone once remarked.

Described by a reporter as "a real mystery man, whose personality is part cloak and dagger, part cloak and suit," Lovestone became director of the ILGWU's international affairs program, the most active in the labor movement. After helping numerous European labor leaders escape from Axis countries, the ILGWU recruited many of them into the Office of Strategic Services, the forerunner of the CIA, following the outbreak of war. With the ILGWU back in the AFL after 1940, Lovestone became a confidant of federation Secretary-Treasurer George Meany [q.v.] and in 1944 helped start the Free Trade Union Committee (FTUC), which was designed to counter Communist influence in foreign labor groups by supporting non-Communist unions and labor federations in postwar Europe. During the postwar years the CIA contributed nearly $2 million annually for the FTUC's anti-Communist activities in France and Italy alone. The opposition of Walter Reuther [q.v.] and other CIO leaders to Lovestone's methods, particularly his collaboration with the CIA, prevented Meany from naming him director of international affairs after the 1955 AFL-CIO merger. However, as head of the FTUC Lovestone maintained a firm grip on foreign labor operations. He shifted his focus of activity increasingly to Latin America in the late 1950s. [See TRUMAN, EISENHOWER Volumes]

Responding to Fidel Castro's successful revolution in Cuba, President Kennedy called for a program in 1961 "through which the talents and experience of the U.S. labor movement could be brought to bear on the danger that Castro. . .might undermine the Latin American labor movement." In August 1961 the AFL-CIO chartered the American Institute for Free Labor Development (AIFLD), whose declared purpose was to assist "in the development of free democratic trade union structures in Latin America." Of the AIFLD's 1962 income, 62% was supplied by the U.S. government, the remainder coming from corporations and the AFL-CIO International Affairs Division. Between 1961 and 1968 the government contributed $15.4 million through the Agency for International Development. As Meany's chief international adviser, Lovestone developed AIFLD's program, supporting anti-Communist unions and labor federations where they already existed and helping to create them where they did not. The Institute ran an extensive program to train Latin American leaders in American-style trade unionism and helped plan and finance union housing projects, credit unions, banks and other projects in Latin American countries.

Directed by Serafino Romuladi [q.v.], AIFLD helped promote a general strike in British Guiana in April 1963, which led to the overthrow of the radical regime of President Cheddi Jagan in 1964. The 80-day strike, which some observers described as a lockout of workers sympathetic to Jagan, was later revealed to have been financed by the CIA at a rate of $30,000 to $50,000 a week in the beginning and later at about $130,000 a week.

Appointed director of the AFL-CIO International Affairs Department in 1964, Lovestone continued to support U.S. intervention in Latin America throughout the 1960s. AIFLD worked to overthrow the Joao Goulart regime in Brazil and the Juan Bosch government in the Dominican Republic. In 1965 Lovestone and Meany helped launch the African-American Labor Center whose educational activities were modeled on those of AIFLD. A strong supporter of the Vietnam war policies of both Presidents Johnson and Nixon, Lovestone

remained director of international affairs through the early 1970s. [See JOHNSON Volume]

[MDB]

For further information:
Henry W. Berger, "American Labor Overseas," *The Nation*, Jan. 16, 1967.
Sidney Lens, "Lovestone Diplomacy," *The Nation* (July 5, 1965).
Ronald Radosh, *American Labor and U.S. Foreign Policy* (New York, 1969).

LOVETT, ROBERT A(BERCROMBIE)
b. Sept. 14, 1895; Huntsville, Tex.
Investment banker.

Termed "a leader of the American Establishment" by historian Arthur Schlesinger, Jr., Lovett played a major role in the formation of postwar military and foreign policy. The son of the president of the Union Pacific Railroad, he attended the exclusive Hill School before entering Yale in 1914. Following service in the Air Corps during World War I, Lovett joined his father-in-law's banking and investment firm, Brown Brothers; in 1931 he was instrumental in bringing about its merger with the Harriman firm to form Brown Brothers, Harriman and Company.

An early advocate of increasing American air power, Lovett worked to develop the Air Corps into a semi-autonomous branch of the Army when he served as assistant secretary of war from 1941 to 1945. While undersecretary of state two years later, he gained a reputation for being Secretary of State George C. Marshall's "ace troubleshooter" and served as acting Secretary of State during Marshall's numerous absences. Again working under Marshall, Lovett was named deputy secretary of defense in 1950 and one year later replaced the General as Secretary of Defense. In 1953 he resigned his post to return to his investment banking firm.

Although Lovett had not voted for Kennedy in the 1960 election, the President-elect, attracted by Lovett's urbane realism, lack of ideology and his vast experience, offered the banker his choice of the three top cabinet portfolios—State, Defense or

Treasury. Lovett refused the appointments because of ill-health and never held a government post during the Kennedy Administration. Instead, Kennedy used him as an adviser on important appointments and counselor on foreign and defense policy.

During the months prior to the inauguration, the former Secretary of Defense served as a link between Kennedy and many of the prominent officials of the Marshall era. Lovett also introduced the President to sources of talent unknown to him because of the business community's coolness toward Kennedy and his family. Lovett was one of the major supporters of Dean Rusk's [q.v.] appointment as Secretary of State. When the offer was made Lovett convinced the Rockefeller Foundation to make Rusk, who was then Foundation president, a financial settlement that enabled him to accept the appointment.

As a former high-ranking government official, Lovett often testified at congressional investigations on the Administration's behalf. He appeared at the August 1961 Senate Foreign Relations Committee hearings on the formation of a disarmament agency where he spoke in favor of the measure. During the January 1962 Senate Preparedness Subcommittee probe of State Department censorship of high military officials, he testified in favor of departmental review of officials' speeches necessary for continuity in foreign policy.

Lovett was among the former high-ranking diplomats serving on Excom, the committee formed to advise the President following the discovery of Soviet missiles on Cuba in October 1962. Within that group he was a sharp critic of U.N. Ambassador Adlai Stevenson's [q.v.] proposal to give up the Guantanamo naval base and withdraw Jupiter missiles from Turkey and Italy in return for removal of Soviet missiles from Cuba.

In December 1962, following attacks by conservative senators on Kennedy's foreign aid program, the President formed a committee of conservative businessmen, headed by Lucius Clay [q.v.], to investigate the system and presumably recommend its continuance. As a prominent Wall Street investment banker, Lovett became a member

of that body. According to Schlesinger, Lovett's chief contribution to its deliberations "lay in elegantly sarcastic phrases: 'There has been a feeling that we are trying to do too much for too many too soon, that we are overextended in resources and undercompensated in results, and that no end of foreign aid is either in sight or in mind.' " The committee stressed that the program was indispensable to American security, but it recommended that aid operations be improved and the level of assistance reduced.

Because Lyndon B. Johnson [q.v.] did not maintain close contacts with the Eastern business community, Lovett's influence declined during the last half of the decade. He did, however, serve on two committees created in 1964 to advise the President—a nonpartisan citizen's panel on foreign policy and a panel to study ways of halting the spread of nuclear weapons.

[EWS]

LUCE, HENRY R(OBINSON)
b. April 3, 1898; Tengchow, China.
d. Feb. 28, 1967; Phoenix, Ariz.
Editor-in-chief, *Time* and Time Inc., 1923-64.

Luce, the son of a Presbyterian missionary, lived in China until he was 14 and graduated Phi Beta Kappa from Yale in 1920. Luce and Briton Hadden edited the *Yale Daily News* while in college and in 1923 founded *Time*, the weekly news magazine. Despite Hadden's death in 1929 and the Depression, Luce's young publishing concern flourished with the addition of *Fortune* in 1930 and *Life* in 1936. Soon the largest magazine publishing company in America, Time-Life's total circulation ran to 12 million in 1960. *Time*, in particular, set a pattern for weekly news reporting. Containing no editorial page, *Time* nonetheless combined a summary of the week's events with the philosophy of Henry R. Luce, an internationalist Republican and firm anti-Communist. [See TRUMAN, EISENHOWER Volumes]

Despite his long association with the Kennedy family, Luce publications supported

Vice President Richard M. Nixon [*q.v.*] in the 1960 presidential campaign. Luce had written a highly flattering introduction to Kennedy's 1940 book, *Why England Slept*, and received assurances from the candidate's father, Joseph P. Kennedy [*q.v.*], in June 1960 that "no son of mine could ever be a goddamn liberal." But Luce considered Nixon the more resolute anti-Communist, and *Life* endorsed the Vice President in October.

For all its influence, Luce's publishing empire faced serious problems in the new decade. Production costs had risen, while subscriptions declined and advertising revenues fell because of competition from television networks. In May 1961 and April 1962, Time Inc. representatives testified against the President's recommendation for a 45% postal rate increase on magazines. In October 1962 Congress reduced the Administration's proposed magazine rate increase to 35.1% and passed the post office revenue bill.

Luce applauded any evidence of Kennedy's anti-Communism. In January 1962 *Time* praised the President for having demoted Undersecretary of State Chester Bowles [*q.v.*], who had a reputation for advocating a conciliatory policy toward the Soviet Union and China. *Time* characterized Bowles as "the wrong man" for such a high foreign policy post. The Luce magazines heralded Kennedy's conduct during the October 1962 Cuban missile crisis. "In sharp contrast to frustration in Vietnam, murkiness in Laos and stalemate in Berlin," *Life* editorialized, "this was action with honor."

Long identified with America's "China Lobby," Luce contributed $1,000 in 1961 to the "Committee of One Million Against the Admission of Communist China to the United Nations." In part because of the influential publisher's opposition to the mainland Chinese regime, Kennedy delayed a shift in America's policy of opposition to Communist Chinese membership in the U.N. At the same time Luce publications defended the regime of South Vietnamese President Ngo Dinh Diem and his controversial sister-in-law, Madame Nhu. According to W.A. Swanberg, *Time* editors fre-

quently "bowdlerized" dispatches from their own Saigon bureau that criticized Diem and the course of the war.

Although often rigidly anti-Communist the Luce press led the news media in its investigations of domestic right-wing extremism. *Time* had been the first national magazine, according to Luce biographer John Kobler, to devote attention to the extreme anti-Communist John Birch Society. In September 1961 *Life* criticized the Christian Anti-Communist Crusade of Dr. Fred Schwarz [*q.v.*] and provoked an angry response from the Doctor's sympathizers, including the board chairman of the Schick Safety Razor Company, Patrick J. Frawley, Jr., who demanded that *Life* retract its condemnation of Schwarz. According to Kobler, Luce feared an advertising boycott of his magazine by right-wing businessmen. He therefore reluctantly ordered *Life* publisher C.D. Jackson to appear at a Schwarz rally in Hollywood, Calif., in October. Before an audience of 15,000 Jackson expressed praise for Schwarz and regrets that his magazine had offered an "oversimplified misinterpretation" of his movement.

Time proclaimed Kennedy its "Man of the Year" in January 1962, but "during most of his time in the Presidency," Kennedy aide Kenneth P. O'Donnell [*q.v.*] later wrote, the President "was convinced that the editors of *Time* were picking on him." A *Time* evaluation of Kennedy's first hundred days in office found little for which to praise the new President. Even in mourning the *Time* issue that covered the President's assassination suggested that he might be known "less for the substance of his achievements than for [his] style."

In April 1964 Luce retired as editor-in-chief of Time, Inc. Serving as editorial chairman, he wielded control over his publication's editorial direction until his death in February 1967. [See JOHNSON Volume]

[JLB]

For further information:
John Kobler, *Luce* (Garden City, 1968).
W.A. Swanberg, *Luce and His Empire* (New York, 1972).

McCARTHY, EUGENE J(OSEPH)
b. March 29, 1916; Watkins, Minn.
Democratic Senator, Minn., 1959-71.

In the 13 years following his graduation from St. John's University in Minnesota in 1935, Eugene McCarthy taught economics and sociology at Catholic high schools and colleges. He also spent nine months in a monastery as a Benedictine novice in 1942-43. McCarthy was teaching sociology at St. Thomas College in St. Paul in 1947 when he entered politics in support of Hubert Humphrey [q.v.], who was leading a fight against the Communist-led wing of Minnesota's Democratic Farmer-Labor Party (DFL). After leading a successful drive to take control of the DFL in St. Paul and Ramsey County, McCarthy won election to the House of Representatives in 1948.

In the House McCarthy compiled a liberal, pro-labor voting record. His intelligence and pragmatism won him the approval of House Speaker Sam Rayburn [q.v.], who had him placed on the important Ways and Means Committee in 1953. Beginning in 1956 McCarthy organized an informal caucus of liberal House Democrats, later institutionalized as the Democratic Study Group, which agitated for liberal legislative alternatives to Republican policies. McCarthy entered the Senate after winning an upset victory over a Republican incumbent in 1958, a contest regarded as a portentous demonstration of the willingness of a Protestant electorate to elect a Catholic to high office. [See EISENHOWER Volume]

During the 1960 presidential campaign McCarthy worked for several candidates. Originally he backed his Minnesota colleague, Sen. Humphrey. Following Humphrey's withdrawal from the race in May subsequent to his defeat in the West Virginia primary, McCarthy refused to support Sen. John F. Kennedy. At the opening day of the Democratic National Convention in July, Sen. Robert Kerr (D, Okla.) [q.v.] announced that McCarthy was "all out for Lyndon Johnson." Nevertheless, at the Convention McCarthy gained national attention with his nominating speech for Adlai Stevenson [q.v.], appealing to the delegates, "Do not leave this prophet without honor in his own party." The speech was considered the most memorable oration of the Convention. McCarthy campaigned vigorously for Kennedy following the latter's nomination.

With his scholarly demeanor and air of detachment, McCarthy stood apart from his counterparts in the Senate's liberal bloc. He usually backed legislation favored by the liberal Americans for Democratic Action, voting for school aid, medical care for the aged and other social reforms of the Kennedy Administration. Many observers, however, considered McCarthy to be inattentive to the practical details of legislative procedure.

McCarthy's most sustained efforts were in the areas of unemployment and migrant farm worker legislation. He had been chairman of the Senate Special Committee on Unemployment Problems, whose 4,000-page report issued in March 1960 foreshadowed many of the legislative remedies proposed by the Kennedy and Johnson Administrations. In June 1961 McCarthy introduced an Administration-backed bill to reform the federal-state unemployment compensation system and impose minimum federal standards on state programs. McCarthy's measure did not pass in that year or in 1962 and 1963 when he reintroduced it.

McCarthy's efforts on behalf of Mexican-American agricultural laborers were continued in September 1961 when he sponsored an amendment to require that each imported Mexican worker be paid at least 90% of the prevailing wage in the area. The Senate accepted the amendment by a 42-40 vote, but it was abandoned in conference. His amendment suffered the same fate in August 1963 after being passed, 44-43. From his seat on the Agricultural Committee, McCarthy also supported Administration farm programs and attempted to increase price supports for dairy producers.

Although McCarthy's position on the powerful Finance Committee gave him potential influence in the struggle of some Senate liberals to close tax loopholes favoring corporations and wealthy individuals, he never became a crusader for tax reform in the manner of his colleagues Sens. Paul Douglas (D, Ill.) [q.v.] and Albert Gore (D, Tenn.) [q.v.]. Douglas considered McCarthy a "disappointment" because of his support of certain tax preferences, particularly his votes to retain the 27½% oil depletion allowance. "He never voted for our progressive tax policies," Douglas said in 1971. "That is, to me, the acid test of domestic liberalism."

McCarthy lined up against the tax reformers on some of the key tax votes of 1962. He voted to eliminate the Administration's provision to cut tax evasion by withholding taxes on interest and dividend payments; he voted for the 7% investment tax credit and for a special measure to reduce taxes on the DuPont family's huge capital gains realized in the court-ordered sale of its General Motors stock; and he added a special provision of his own to the 1962 act for the benefit of the Twin Cities Rapid Transit Company of Minneapolis-St. Paul. The amendment, vetoed in 1961 by President Kennedy but protected in 1962 by its inclusion in the omnibus tax bill, enabled the bus company to enjoy full tax deductions for losses suffered due to the fraudulent activities of the previous management.

McCarthy was an early advocate of closer congressional oversight of U.S. intelligence agencies. During the Johnson Administration McCarthy stood out for his vocal opposition to the Vietnam war. His strong showing as an anti-war candidate in the New Hampshire Democratic presidential primary in March 1968 was credited with convincing President Johnson not to run for reelection. McCarthy's ultimately unsuccessful campaign was distinctive for its reliance on legions of youthful and idealistic volunteers instead of on the professionals of the regular party organization. McCarthy retired from the Senate in January 1971. In 1976 he ran for president as an independent. [See JOHNSON, NIXON Volumes]

[TO]

For further information:
Albert Eisele, *Almost to the Presidency* (Blue Earth, Minn., 1972).

McCLELLAN, JOHN L(ITTLE)
b. Feb. 25, 1896; Sheridan, Ark.
Democratic Senator, Ark., 1943- ;
Chairman, Government Operations Committee, 1949-53, 1955-72.

McClellan studied in his father's law office for five years and then entered private practice at the age of 17. He served as city attorney of Malvern, Ark., from 1920 to 1926 and as prosecuting attorney of the state's seventh judicial district from 1927 to 1930. In 1934 McClellan was elected to the U.S. House of Representatives, where he supported most New Deal policies. In 1938 he was defeated in the Democratic senatorial primary and returned to private law practice. Four years later he won a seat in the Senate.

During the postwar period McClellan opposed civil rights legislation and compiled a generally conservative voting record, but he backed such liberal legislation as the national forestry program, Social Security and federal aid to hospitals. He first came to national attention as the ranking minority member, from 1953 to 1955, on the Government Operations Committee and its Permanent Investigations Subcommittee, both chaired by Sen. Joseph R. McCarthy (R, Wisc.). As the leader of the Committee's Democrats, McClellan led protests against what he charged were Sen. McCarthy's undemocratic methods. McClellan gained further publicity as chairman of the Select Committee on Improper Activities in the Labor and Management Fields. From 1957 to 1960 the ad hoc panel investigated corruption in labor unions and particularly in the International Brotherhood of Teamsters. [See TRUMAN, EISENHOWER Volumes]

By 1960 McClellan had established a reputation as a stern, effective and fair investigator, and for the next decade his senatorial career centered around his role as chairman of the Permanent Investigations Subcommittee.

In April and May 1961 the panel held hearings on work stoppages at missile bases and test sites. McClellan concluded that labor unions had been "gouging the government" and said that remedial legislation might be necessary. In response to the subcommittee's investigation, President Kennedy announced on May 26 the creation of an 11-member commission to develop procedures for preventing strikes at military and space installations.

During the summer of the following year, the subcommittee investigated the relationship between Texas businessman Billy Sol Estes [q.v.] and Agriculture Department officials to determine why Estes's illegally acquired cotton allotments had not been canceled by the Department until after his arrest on other charges in March 1962. The Estes case represented the first major scandal of the Kennedy Administration, and Republicans charged that the Department had shown favoritism towards Estes and demanded the resignation of Secretary of Agriculture Orville L. Freeman [q.v.]. But McClellan concluded that the Department's delay in acting on the Estes matter was attributable more to inefficiency and lack of discipline than to corruption, and he praised Freeman for canceling the allotments swiftly upon receiving the facts of the case. The subcommittee's 1964 report reflected the chairman's views, while the minority report of the panel's Republicans charged that Estes had accumulated substantial influence within the Department of Agriculture.

In September and October 1963 Joseph Valachi, convicted murderer and self-described former member of a crime syndicate, testified on the structure and operations of organized crime in one of the Investigations Subcommittee's most publicized probes. At the beginning of the hearings, McClellan had declared that Valachi might provide valuable information for fighting crime, but many law enforcement officials stated that his testimony contained nothing new.

From February through November of the same year the subcommittee held closed hearings concerning reports of pressure and favoritism in the Defense Department's award of the multi-billion dollar TFX swing-wing fighter plane contract to General Dynamics. McClellan considered himself a friend of the Administration, but the panel's probe uncovered damaging evidence against the Department of Defense. The investigation revealed, among other things, that Secretary of Defense Robert S. McNamara [q.v.] selected General Dynamics in November 1962 after four studies by the Air Force and Navy and a Pentagon study had concluded that Boeing's design was superior and less expensive; that McNamara, who claimed that the General Dynamics design would save one billion dollars, had not followed his usual procedure of ordering independent cost studies; and that two of McNamara's principal advisers, Deputy Secretary of Defense Roswell L. Gilpatric [q.v.] and Navy Secretary Fred Korth [q.v.], had had connections with General Dynamics.

The controversial nature of the hearings produced considerable acrimony. In March McClellan accused the Defense Department of attempting to try the case in the press. During the same month McNamara charged that the investigation had "needlessly undermined public confidence" in high-level Defense Department officials, and three months later columnists Rowland Evans, Jr. and Robert D. Novak [q.v.] wrote that McClellan was employing "injudicious tactics" and that his purpose was to force McNamara's resignation. The attack prompted both Democrats and Republicans to come to McClellan's defense, but the probe was terminated in November upon the assassination of President Kennedy.

In 1964 the Investigations Subcommittee examined missile procurement policies and criticized the payment of allegedly excessive profits to companies for work that they farmed out to subcontractors. In 1967 the panel began hearings on race-related riots and other civil disturbances. During the mid and late 1960s and early 1970s, McClellan was critical of Supreme Court decisions that, in his opinion, expanded the rights of criminal suspects at the expense of effective law enforcement. In August 1972 after the death of Sen. Allen J. Ellender (D, La.) [q.v.], chairman of the Appropriations Committee, McClellan gave up his Government Operations post to become head of the Appropriations panel. [See JOHNSON, NIXON Volumes]

[MLL]

McCLOSKEY, MATTHEW H(ENRY)

b. 1893; Wheeling, W. Va.
d. April 26, 1972; Philadelphia, Pa.
Treasurer, Democratic National Committee, January 1955-April 1962; Ambassador to Ireland, July 1962-January 1964.

Matthew McCloskey quit school at the age of 15 and entered the building trades. His firm, McCloskey & Company, headquartered in Philadelphia, became one of the nation's leading construction contractors, building hotels, office buildings and high-rise apartments, and in the process changing the skyline of Philadelphia. McCloskey involved himself in politics as a premier fund raiser for the Democratic Party, chiefly in Pennsylvania from 1935 to 1955 and nationally after 1955, when he was chosen treasurer of the Democratic National Committee. McCloskey's contribution to the art of fund raising was the invention in 1935 of the $100-a-plate fund-raising dinner. At a June 1962 testimonial dinner for McCloskey attended by the hierarchy of the Democratic Party, Presidents Kennedy and Truman lauded McCloskey for his fundraising contributions to their respective elections.

Kennedy's nomination of McCloskey as ambassador to Ireland in June 1962 encountered opposition in the Senate. Sen. John Williams (R, Del.) [q.v.] protested that the Foreign Relations Committee had not thoroughly considered McCloskey's alleged connection with a 1946 surplus shipyard sale, in which an associate of McCloskey's had made a $25,000 payoff to a Maritime Commission official. McCloskey denied any connection with the incident, and Williams's motion to recommit the nomination to committee was defeated, 62-30; McCloskey was then confirmed. He served as ambassador until January 1964, when he resigned to aid President Johnson's reelection campaign.

Upon his return McCloskey was drawn into the celebrated Bobby Baker [q.v.] case. In the first phase of the Rules Committee's investigation of the sundry improprieties of the former secretary to the Senate majority, McCloskey's name was mentioned, but the Committee voted not to call him as a witness. In September 1964, however, Sen. Williams charged that McCloskey had arranged with Baker to make an illegal $25,000 contribution to the 1960 Democratic campaign in order to secure the $20 million contract to build the District of Columbia stadium. The $25,000 was concealed, Williams said, as an overpayment on a performance bond for a project handled by insurance man Don Reynolds, a Baker associate. The Senate voted to reopen the Baker probe following Williams's accusation.

When the Rules Committee's hearings resumed in December, Reynolds testified that he had been the "bagman" for the transaction. He produced the bill for the performance bond together with McCloskey's payment check, which was $35,000 in excess of the bill. (Reynolds claimed a $10,000 commission on the deal.) McCloskey denied Reynolds's charges, saying that the insurance man "hasn't told the truth once." McCloskey maintained that the overpayment was an honest "goof" stemming from a bookkeeping error and the mistaken belief that Reynolds was to be paid for liability insurance as well as the performance bond. The Rules Committee, in effect, chose to believe McCloskey over Reynolds, whose credibility had been questioned by the FBI. In June 1965 its majority report—with the Republican minority dissenting—found McCloskey and his company not guilty of any wrongdoing.

McCloskey's firm, which was building the new U.S. mint in Philadelphia and was working on the renovation of the east front of the Capitol around the time of the Baker scandal, received sharp criticism for its work on other federal projects. In January 1964 the Department of Justice sued McCloskey & Co. for $4.9 million for its faulty construction of the Boston Veterans Hospital. The company paid the government $1.6 million in a March 1967 settlement. Another McCloskey project, the Rayburn House Office Building, completed in 1965, was marred by gigantic cost overruns.

McCloskey died of cancer in 1972.

[TO]

McCLOY, JOHN J(AY)
b. March 31, 1895; Philadelphia, Pa.
Presidential Disarmament Adviser,
January 1961-October 1961; Director,
U.S. Arms Control and Disarmament
Agency, September 1961-October 1961.

One of the architects of American foreign
policy in the Roosevelt and Truman Administrations, John J. McCloy served as
presidential consultant and adviser on disarmament during the Kennedy years. After
graduating from Harvard Law School in
1921, McCloy worked in several New York
law firms specializing in international corporate law. In 1940 he accepted the position of consultant to Secretary of War
Henry L. Stimson and a year later became
assistant secretary of war. McCloy resigned
his post in 1946 to resume private law practice but remained there for only one year
before becoming head of the World Bank.
In 1949 he was appointed military governor
and high commissioner for Germany.
McCloy left Germany in 1952 and for the
next nine years served as chairman of the
Chase Manhattan Bank. In 1962 he returned to private practice to handle international legal problems for many of
America's largest oil companies. From 1953
to 1965 he was also chairman of the Ford
Foundation. [See TRUMAN, EISENHOWER
Volumes]

In January 1961 President-elect Kennedy
appointed McCloy, a Republican, his principal disarmament adviser and negotiator.
While at that post McCloy drafted the bill
that led to the establishment of the U.S.
Arms Control and Disarmament Agency in
September 1961. The Agency was designed
to coordinate government policy on disarmament and nuclear testing free from the
influence of other federal bodies.

McCloy's primary responsibility during
1961 was to negotiate conditions under
which the stalemated East-West disarmament talks could resume. Working through
the summer of 1961, he finally got the
Soviet Union to agree to a declaration of
principles to govern formal negotiations.
This agreement was submitted to the U.N.
in September. However, the ensuing disarmament discussions proved futile. In Oc-

tober McCloy resigned his post, terming
his diplomatic activity "the most discouraging exercise in disarmament negotiations"
since World War II. Six months later he
was appointed to the General Advisory
Committee of the U.S. Arms Control and
Disarmament Agency.

Following President Kennedy's October
1962 announcement of a Cuban blockade to
force the removal of Soviet missiles from
that island, McCloy was asked to take part
in U.N. negotiations on the terms of inspection for the weapons' removal. Kennedy,
anxious to have bipartisan support for his
policy and fearing that U.N. Ambassador
Adlai Stevenson [q.v.] would be too conciliatory, wished the tough-minded Republican to be part of the three-man team
pressing American demands for the withdrawal of both Soviet missiles and bombers
under supervised conditions. The talks
proved unproductive and the question of
inspection was solved only in December,
when Nikita Khrushchev agreed to remove
the missiles and bombers and permit aerial
observation and counting of the weapons as
they left.

McCloy served on several presidential
commissions during the Johnson Administration. In late 1963 Johnson [q.v.] appointed him to the Warren Commission
probing the death of John F. Kennedy. A
year later he joined panels dealing with
ways of forestalling the spread of nuclear
weapons and ensuring world peace. During
1966 McCloy acted as a presidential consultant on NATO and was envoy to the multilateral talks held to renegotiate financial
arrangements for German compensation of
its allies, whose troops helped protect that
country. In 1968 Johnson asked McCloy to
become a member of the Senior Advisory
Group on Vietnam, which recommended
de-escalation of the war in March of that
year. [See JOHNSON Volume]

In 1974 a Senate investigation of the petroleum industry revealed that McCloy had
been in the forefront of attempts to unite
U.S. oil companies in their dealings with
the producing nations since 1961. He had
also used his influence to obtain Justice
Department approval for the plan in 1971.

McCloy's efforts proved fruitless because the U.S. ambassador to Iran had agreed to a suggestion by the Shah that the oil companies conclude separate price arrangements with the producing states.

[EWS]

McCONE, JOHN A(LEX)

b. Jan. 4, 1902; San Francisco, Calif.
Director of Central Intelligence, November 1961-April 1965.

John McCone, director of the Central Intelligence Agency (CIA) during the Kennedy Administration, was born into a prosperous San Francisco family. He graduated from the University of California in 1922 and that year joined Llewellyn Iron Works, working in blue collar positions before becoming an executive. McCone left the steel business in 1937 to form an engineering concern specializing in the design and construction of petroleum refineries and power plants. When the war broke out in Europe in 1939, McCone joined a corporation that built merchant ships and planes. His remarkable financial success in that business prompted contemporary criticism of McCone as a war profiteer.

McCone entered government service in 1947 as a member of President Harry Truman's Air Policy Commission. In 1948 he became deputy to Secretary of Defense James Forrestal and worked closely with the Secretary in the creation of the CIA. He was named undersecretary of the Air Force in 1950. While in Washington McCone gained a reputation as a militant anti-Communist and strong supporter of the doctrine of massive retaliation. He left government in 1951 but returned to serve as chairman of the Atomic Energy Commission from 1958 to 1961. [See EISENHOWER Volume]

In September 1961 President Kennedy appointed McCone director of the CIA to succeed Allen Dulles [q.v.], who had retired following the abortive Bay of Pigs invasion. Kennedy chose the conservative Republican not only because of his reputation as a good manager but also because the President felt vulnerable to an attack from the conservative wing of the Republican Party following the Bay of Pigs fiasco. McCone's appointment was intended to quiet these critics and ensure approval of future CIA actions on Capitol Hill. However, liberals within the Administration were appalled by the choice and were convinced that McCone's reporting would reflect a right-wing bias.

McCone proved himself an able administrator even in the eyes of such liberals as Roger Hilsman [q.v.]. Reversing his predecessor's stand, McCone did not try to make the Agency dominant in foreign policy formation and instead worked to repair relations with the State Department and Congress. He also succeeded in improving Agency morale, which was low following the Cuban invasion.

Although conservative on many issues, McCone did not let his personal attitudes bias intelligence estimates. He was not, however, above using his official position to further his views outside the Agency. According to David Halberstam, McCone secretly opposed the nuclear test ban treaty of 1963 and lent CIA atomic energy experts to conservative Sen. John Stennis (D, Miss.) [q.v.] to help him make a case against the agreement. In public, however, the Director testified in favor of the treaty, which was ratified by the Senate in September 1963.

McCone became one of Kennedy's advisers during the 1962 Cuban missile crisis. As early as August 1962 he had received reports that Soviet anti-aircraft missiles were being introduced into Cuba and had ordered intelligence flights over the island stepped up. On Aug. 22 McCone told the President that he believed the USSR was installing offensive missiles on the island. Kennedy, however, dismissed this warning as the fears of an overzealous anti-Communist.

Having voiced his suspicions McCone, who had just remarried, left on a wedding trip to Europe. During his absence several U-2 spy planes strayed or were shot down over Russia and China. Consequently, flights over western Cuba were stopped to reduce the probability of loss and a resulting public outcry. While in Europe and after his return, McCone lobbied for resumption of the overflights. They were finally resumed on Oct. 4. Ten days later flights over western Cuba revealed the presence of offensive missiles.

In the policy debate that followed this revelation, McCone was a member of Excom, the special group formed to advise the President and gain bipartisan support for Administration action. In conjunction with Paul Nitze [q.v.], Dean Acheson [q.v.] and the Joint Chiefs, McCone recommended the use of air strikes to remove the missiles, but Kennedy rejected the idea and instead instituted a "quarantine" of Cuba on Oct. 23.

As the U.S. became increasingly involved in Vietnam, a larger portion of McCone's time was devoted to activities in that country. In the policy meetings that followed the Diem regime's crackdown on Buddhists in August 1963, McCone was among the Kennedy advisers who cautioned against support of a coup. Instead he suggested that the U.S. maintain Diem but insist on reforms. This policy was carried out while conditions were established that would permit a successful coup without direct American intervention.

In 1974 and 1975 a Senate investigation revealed that while McCone was head of the CIA the Agency had carried on the illegal surveillance of over 10,000 American citizens and had made several unsuccessful attempts to assassinate foreign leaders, including Patrice Lumumba and Fidel Castro. Because the system of executive command and control was purposely ambiguous to permit "plausible denial," McCone's exact role in these plots remained undetermined. In 1975 hearings before the Senate Select Committee on Intelligence, McCone testified that he had not been aware of the efforts and had not authorized plots against the Cuban dictator. The Committee report attributed the assassination attempts to vague orders that were subject to differing interpretations by the subordinates responsible for carrying them out.

During the Johnson Administration McCone opposed the introduction of American combat troops into Vietnam. He felt that if the armed services were forced to continue fighting under the constraints imposed by the Administration the war would be unwinnable. In April 1965 McCone resigned from the CIA. During the remainder of the decade, he served on the government panel investigating the Watts riots and testified on urban violence before congressional committees. [See JOHNSON, Volume]

[EWS]

For further information:
Graham Allison, *Essence of Decision: Explaining the Cuban Missile Crisis* (Boston, 1971).
U.S. Senate Select Committee on Intelligence Activities, *Alleged Assassination Plots Involving Foreign Leaders* (Washington, 1975).
David Wise and Thomas B. Ross, *The Invisible Government* (New York, 1964).

McCORMACK, JOHN W(ILLIAM)
b. Dec. 21, 1891; Boston, Mass.
Democratic Representative, Mass., 1928-71; House Majority Leader, 1940-47, 1949-53, 1955-62; Speaker of the House, 1962-71.

McCormack, who grew up in the poor, tightly knit Irish community of South Boston, left school to go to work at age 13 after his father died. He read law and passed his bar exams when he was 21. In 1917 McCormack was elected a delegate to the Massachusetts Constitutional Convention. Three years later he was elected to the state legislature and served there for six years. In 1926 McCormack ran unsuccessfully for the U.S. House of Representatives, but two years later he won a special election to fill a House vacancy.

In Congress McCormack was a strong supporter of New Deal programs and worked closely with the House Democratic leadership as a member of the important Ways and Means Committee. When Majority Leader Sam Rayburn [q.v.] became Speaker of the House in 1940, McCormack moved into Rayburn's former post.

As majority leader, McCormack gained a reputation as a good soldier who was an unswervingly loyal deputy to Rayburn. He made many political friendships in the

House by helping to procure committee assignments for colleagues and influencing the scheduling of their bills. McCormack also became known for his sharply partisan debating style. [See TRUMAN, EISENHOWER Volumes]

McCormack and Sen. John F. Kennedy, leaders of opposing factions within the Massachusetts Democratic Party, were not close political allies. Nevertheless, McCormack was the chairman of his state's pro-Kennedy delegation at the Democratic National Convention of 1960, and as majority leader he backed almost all Administration programs in 1961. But he was a devout Catholic with close ties to many of the Church's high clerics, and in 1961 he favored adding parochial school assistance to the Administration's aid-to-education package, a course opposed by President Kennedy. As a result of controversy over aid to parochial schools, the program did not clear the House in 1961.

On Aug. 31, 1961, after Rayburn became ill, McCormack was elected Speaker Pro Tempore. Rayburn died on Oct. 2, and on Jan. 10, 1962 McCormack, drawing upon the political IOUs he had accumulated as majority leader, won the election to succeed him. McCormack was the first Catholic and, at age 70, the second oldest man to win election to the speakership.

The Speaker of the House was in a position to exert great influence upon the flow of legislation. He had the right to refuse recognition to representatives wishing to speak and could also refuse to entertain motions from the floor. The most important foundation of a Speaker's power, however, was the informal influence he exercised over his colleagues.

According to the *New York Times*, McCormack, despite the numerous ties he had established with his fellow representatives over many years, "never developed, either through disinclination or inability, the same sort of elaborate network of information and rewards that enabled Mr. Rayburn to keep the House a relatively tightly run political apparatus." Many of his associates, and particularly the younger liberals of the House, regarded him as an un-

dynamic and ineffectual leader. Some believed that McCormack was too old to exercise the functions of his position.

If McCormack was a weak leader, it was not due to a lack of partisan dedication to the passage of Administration bills. Early in 1963 some of the younger Republican House leaders asked for increased minority staffing. McCormack defended existing arrangements, asserting that the purpose of the Democratic Congress was to enact President Kennedy's programs. Enlarging the prerogatives of the minority, he said, could hamper the House in performing this function.

While McCormack consistently supported New Frontier domestic programs, his fervent anti-Communism set him at odds with President Kennedy over one major issue in 1963. The Administration opposed the production of the planned Nike-Zeus anti-missile system, believing it would be ineffective against advanced missile penetration aids. McCormack joined a group of conservative senators and representatives who favored prompt deployment of the system, and in February he exhorted the House, "Close the gap in our missile posture; muzzle the mad-dog missile threat of the Soviet Union; loose the Zeus through America's magnificent production lines, now."

After the assassination of President Kennedy, McCormack was first in line to succeed President Lyndon Johnson under the Presidential Succession Act of 1947. Some politicians and political observers, feeling that McCormack lacked the innovative and leadership ability needed by a chief executive, believed he should resign the speakership.

During the mid and late 1960s, McCormack came under increasing fire for his allegedly ineffective leadership and for his support of the Vietnam war. In 1969 his administrative assistant and one of his friends were linked with influence-peddling activities, and in January 1970 they were indicted. In May 1970 McCormack announced that he would not seek reelection. [See JOHNSON, NIXON Volumes]

[MLL]

McCULLOCH, WILLIAM M.
b. Nov. 24, 1901; Holmes County, Ohio.
Republican Representative, Ohio, 1947-73.

After earning a law degree from Ohio Northern University, William M. McCulloch practiced law in Piqua, Ohio. In 1932 he was elected to the first of six terms in the Ohio House of Representatives. A Republican, McCulloch led the house minority between 1936 and 1939 and served as speaker from 1939 to 1944. He won election to Congress in a 1947 special election. The ranking Republican on the Judiciary Committee by 1959, McCulloch worked closely with Committee Chairman Emanuel Celler (D, N.Y.) [q.v.] for the enactment of the 1960 civil rights law.

McCulloch, who represented a conservative rural constituency, voted against nearly every significant piece of New Frontier legislation. He opposed the Kennedy Administration's successful campaign to enlarge the Rules Committee in January 1961. He voted against raising the minimum wage in May 1961, aid to education in August 1961, the creation of an urban affairs department in February 1962 and the income tax cut in September 1963. He also joined in GOP efforts to reduce foreign aid appropriations in August 1961 and July 1962. The liberal Americans for Democratic Action gave McCulloch zero ratings on its list of key votes for 1961, 1962 and 1963.

Dissatisfied with the 1957 and 1960 civil rights statutes, the Administration and a group of liberal Democratic Judiciary Committee members clashed in 1963 over a new, comprehensive law guaranteeing minority rights. The President's modest proposal of June 1963, designed not to offend powerful Southern Democrats, required the desegregation of Southern schools under the threat of a federal aid cutoff. At the same time, Judiciary Committee liberals recommended a bill that went well beyond the White House legislation to strictly prohibit discrimination in public accommodations and employment practices. Southern and conservative Republican panel members supported the liberal version in the belief that it would never win approval in the full House.

To prevent the liberal bill from winning Committee endorsement, Kennedy and his brother, Attorney General Robert F. Kennedy [q.v.], won the full cooperation of McCulloch in writing a compromise measure. In October Attorney General Kennedy testified against the liberal proposal. Although the bill finally approved by the Committee in October eliminated some liberal demands, it included a ban against discrimination in employment and the threat to withhold federal aid to localities violating federal civil rights statutes. The Administration's strategy worked. By a wide margin, the most detailed civil rights bill in 90 years passed the House in February 1964 and became law following Senate approval in June.

Confessing that the final Judiciary Committee bill proved a "better bill than the Administration's," Robert Kennedy praised the work of McCulloch, without which the "possibility of civil rights legislation in Congress would have been remote." Later accounts of the 1963 negotiations between the White House and the Judiciary Committee by presidential aides Theodore Sorenson [q.v.] and Lawrence O'Brien [q.v.] confirmed the decisive role played by McCulloch in the passage of the legislation. Throughout the rest of the decade, McCulloch took part in the shaping of additional civil rights legislation, and he later criticized the Nixon Administration's opposition to a simple extension of the 1965 Voting Rights Act. McCulloch retired in 1973. [See JOHNSON, NIXON Volumes]

[JLB]

McDONALD, DAVID J(OHN)
b. Nov. 22, 1902; Pittsburgh, Pa.
President, United Steelworkers of America, 1952-65.

The son of a skilled Irish Catholic steelworker, McDonald was encouraged by his family to work his way out of the mills and into a white collar occupation. In 1922 he became the personal secretary to Philip Murray, then a United Mine Workers Union vice president. McDonald worked closely with Murray during the bitter coal strikes of the 1920s, the UMW's successful organizing drives of the early New Deal era and the formation of the Congress of Industrial Organizations. After CIO President John L. Lewis appointed Murray to head the organizing drive in steel, McDonald became secretary-treasurer of the new union. Murray died in 1952, and McDonald immediately succeeded his mentor as president of the million-member United Steelworkers of America (USW). Although McDonald favored a spirit of labor-management "mutual trusteeship" for the steel industry, increasing employer resistance to USW wage demands precipitated three major strikes in the 1950s. The 1959 shutdown lasted 116 days and required Eisenhower Administration intervention to settle. McDonald's power was also challenged in 1957 when Donald Rarick, a little known grievance committeeman, won 35% of the vote in the USW's biennial presidential election. [See EISENHOWER Volume]

Although John F. Kennedy refused to back USW proposals for a 32-hour work week, McDonald strongly endorsed the Massachusetts Senator for the Democratic presidential nomination in 1960. McDonald controlled an estimated 100 steelworker-union delegates to the Los Angeles convention, perhaps the largest single bloc, and he instructed them to favor Kennedy on the first ballot. Unlike others in the AFL-CIO leadership, McDonald supported Lyndon B. Johnson (D, Tex.) [q.v.] for the vice presidential nomination. He worked with Robert Kennedy [q.v.] to ensure Johnson's selection by convention delegates after John Kennedy had publicly announced his choice. The new President chose Arthur Goldberg [q.v.], the USW's counsel, as his Secretary of Labor.

During Kennedy's first year in office McDonald cooperated with the Administration to mesh USW bargaining strategy with the government's overall economic policy. As the economy recovered from the recession of 1960-61, President Kennedy and his economic advisers feared that renewed prosperity would bring a new round of inflation. They urged that all collective bargaining settlements be limited to the annual increase in

productivity, then estimated to average about 3.2%. The Administration thought that such limited wage increments would not require compensating price increases. In September 1961 and again in January 1962, Kennedy asked the USW and the steel industry to reach an accord on their next contract within these wage-price guidelines. With the help of Arthur Goldberg, USW negotiations with the steel industry began in February 1962. Ignoring opposition from his 170-member wage policy committee, McDonald reached agreement with the industry on March 31. The new two-year contract contained 10 cents an hour in fringe benefits, but no across-the-board wage increase, the first such settlement since 1942. Union economists estimated the contract to be well within the 3.2% wage guidelines. Kennedy lauded the USW's "high industrial statesmanship," and Iron Age, an industry publication, found the agreement "closer to the company position than any recent settlement."

On April 10, 1962 Roger M. Blough [q.v.], chairman of the board of United States Steel, announced a price increase of six dollars a ton. Five other major steel firms followed suit the next day. President Kennedy strongly denounced the price rise in a news conference April 11. He attacked the "tiny handful of steel executives whose pursuit of private power and profit exceeds their sense of public responsibility." Privately he told McDonald, "You have been screwed and I've been screwed." After intense pressure from the White House and the announcement of antitrust investigations by the Justice Department and two congressional committees, the major steel companies rescinded their price increases April 13.

In June 1963 McDonald again negotiated a steel contract that contained no across-the-board wage increase. The settlement sought to stem the decline in industry employment by liberalizing vacation benefits and prohibiting outside contracting of work. But the agreement proved unpopular with many in the union because it represented a cut in "real" steelworker take-home pay. Moreover a section of the union's top leadership objected to the new contract chiefly because McDonald had bypassed the USW executive board and negotiated the settlement in secret through a labor-management "Human Relations Committee," established in 1960 to study day-to-day problems in the plants. USW Secretary-Treasurer I.W. Abel challenged McDonald for the union presidency in late 1964. Campaigning on a program to "restore rank-and-file control over basic policy" Abel defeated McDonald in a close race in Frebruary 1965. [See JOHNSON Volume]

[NNL]

For further information:
John Herling, *Right to Challenge, People and Power in the Steelworkers Union* (New York, 1972).
David J. McDonald, *Union Man* (New York, 1969).

McGARR, LIONEL C(HARLES)
b. March 5, 1904; Yuma, Ariz.
Commander, Military Assistance Advisory Group, South Vietnam, September 1960-March 1962.

The former head of the Army Command and General Staff College, Lt. Gen. Lionel C. McGarr served as the chief American military adviser to the South Vietnamese Army during the period when the United States became more directly involved in the Vietnam war.

When McGarr took command of the 700-man U.S. Military Assistance Advisory Group in September 1960, Communist guerrillas were increasing their activity throughout the South Vietnamese countryside and threatening the stability of the government of South Vietnamese President Ngo Dinh Diem. The armed forces of South Vietnam, consisting of three distinct bodies—the Civil Guard, the Self Defense Corps and the regular army—were in disarray. The Civil Guard and Self Defense Corps, controlled variously by President Diem, the minister of the interior and the province chiefs, were paramilitary units designed to police local areas and protect them from attack by Communist guerrillas.

According to McGarr these units were so ineffective that the regular army was forced to spend three quarters of its time in "static guard and security roles." McGarr

favored strengthening the Civil Guard and Self-Defense Corps by placing them under direct army command to enable the regular forces to assume the offensive against the enemy. McGarr's ideas were embodied in a counterinsurgency plan for Vietnam, which President Kennedy approved in January 1961 shortly after he took office. Under this plan the U.S. offered South Vietnam $28.4 million to increase the size of its army and another $12.7 million to train, equip and supply the 32,000-man Civil Guard. Although these appropriations were welcomed by the Diem regime, the South Vietnamese government refused to unify its command structure as McGarr had suggested.

By the spring of 1961 the number of men serving under McGarr had been increased to 1,600, and he began to argue that American combat troops as well as advisers were needed to win the war. Gen. Maxwell D. Taylor [*q.v.*], who conferred with McGarr on a special fact-finding mission to South Vietnam in October 1961, agreed. McGarr suggested that serious flooding in the Mekong Delta would enable the U.S. to bring its combat forces to Vietnam posing as relief workers. This idea was rejected by both Washington and Saigon. Instead, the Diem regime requested increased subsidies for its own army and American helicopter pilots to aid in combat missions.

In September 1961 McGarr's staff prepared a report that outlined a method for securing the allegiance of rural areas dominated by the Communists. This report became the basis of "Operation Sunrise," or the strategic hamlet program. This effort entailed moving an intelligence team into a hamlet to define its military significance, its political outlook and its economic needs. The South Vietnamese Army would then attack and clear the area of Communist guerrillas. Finally, the hamlet would be placed under civilian control while social and economic reforms were instituted to secure the loyalty of the rural population.

McGarr, although committed to the strategic hamlet program, showed little concern with the economic and social reforms upon which the project's success depended. His first priority was to clear the Communists from their jungle retreats, especially in War Zone D, northwest of Saigon. At a January 1962 Honolulu meeting, McGarr told Secretary of Defense Robert S. McNamara [q.v.] that with two divisions of the South Vietnamese Army he would be able to "clean out" the guerrillas in War Zone D.

McNamara had grave doubts about such an action. According to his biographer, Henry Trewhitt, one of McNamara's aides passed him a note reading, "This man is insane," and the Defense Secretary nodded in approval.

The strategic hamlet program was put into effect in March 1962, but by the end of 1963 it had proved a failure. According to documents later reprinted in the *Pentagon Papers*, the South Vietnamese government overextended itself, particularly in areas that were consistently vulnerable to guerrilla attack. In February 1962 Gen. Paul D. Harkins [q.v.] was named head of a new unit, the U.S. Military Assistance Command, with McGarr as his subordinate. Two months later McGarr retired from the Army as scheduled.

[JLW]

For further information:
David G. Marr, "The Rise and Fall of 'Counterinsurgency'—1961-64," *The Pentagon Papers, Critical Essays* (Boston, 1972).
U.S. Department of Defense, *The Pentagon Papers*, Senator Gravel Edition (Boston, 1971), Vol. II.

McGEE, GALE W(ILLIAM)
b. March 17, 1915; Lincoln, Neb.
Democratic Senator, Wyo., 1959- .

Born and raised in Nebraska, Gale W. McGee graduated from Nebraska State Teachers College in 1936. Specializing in American diplomatic history, McGee earned a M.A. from the University of Colorado in 1939 and a Ph.D. from the University of Chicago in 1947. A year before completing graduate work, McGee accepted a professorship at the University of Wyoming. An accomplished speaker, he toured the state and nation giving lectures on foreign policy and Communism. During a leave of absence in 1952-53, McGee studied Soviet foreign policy

for the Council on Foreign Relations. With the endorsement of Eleanor Roosevelt [q.v.], McGee made his first try for public office in 1958 and unseated Sen. Frank A. Barrett (R, Wyo.) with 50.8% of the vote.

Though committed to Senate Majority Leader Lyndon B. Johnson (D, Tex.) [q.v.] in the race for the 1960 Democratic presidential nomination, McGee later declared himself neutral and his state's convention delegation gave John F. Kennedy the votes necessary for victory. McGee generally supported the new President's legislative program. He voted for the Administration's aid-to-education bill in May 1961 and introduced a resolution in favor of the President's call for a cabinet-level department of housing and urban development in January 1962. The Western Democrat voted with the White House on its medical care for the elderly proposal in July 1962 and the nuclear test ban treaty in September 1963.

McGee defended the Administration's United Nations policy during the Senate debate over the purchase of a $100-million U.N. bond issue in April 1962. A month earlier Sen. Henry M. Jackson (D, Wash.) [q.v.] had attacked the State Department's U.N. policy and had called for greater reliance on the North Atlantic Treaty Organization. McGee reiterated the President's own, mildly critical response to Jackson by warning that his colleague's arguments against the world organization "will be seized upon by the wrong people for the wrong reasons." McGee easily won reelection in his normally Republican state in 1964 and strongly supported Johnson's Vietnam war policies. [See JOHNSON, NIXON Volumes]

[JLB]

McGOVERN, GEORGE S(TANLEY)
b. July 19, 1922; Avon, S.D.
Director, Food for Peace Program, January 1961-July 1962; Democratic Senator, S.D., 1963- .

The son of a Methodist minister, George McGovern grew up in Mitchell, S.D., where he excelled at debating in high school and at Dakota Wesleyan University. After service as a bomber pilot during

World War II, McGovern trained for the ministry but abandoned it to undertake graduate work in history at Northwestern University. While there he supported the third-party presidential candidacy of Henry Wallace in 1948 and wrote a study of a Colorado coal strike sympathetic to the striking miners. (Northwestern awarded him his Ph.D. in 1953.)

McGovern taught history and political science at Dakota Wesleyan from 1949 to 1953, leaving to become executive secretary of the state Democratic Party. He was the only full-time organizer for the weak South Dakota Democrats, who then held only two out of 110 seats in the state legislature. Touring the thinly populated state alone by automobile, McGovern laboriously rebuilt the Party apparatus. In the 1954 elections Democrats increased their representation in the legislature to 25 seats. Alongside the party organization McGovern built a personal following as well. He ran for Congress in 1956 on a liberal platform, attacking the unpopular farm policies of Republican Secretary of Agriculture Ezra Taft Benson, and won an upset victory over the Republican incumbent. Reelected in 1958, McGovern ran for the Senate against Sen. Karl E. Mundt [q.v.] in 1960 but lost to the conservative Republican in a sharp ideological confrontation.

President Kennedy rewarded McGovern's support of the Kennedy-Johnson ticket by appointing him director of the Administration's Food for Peace program. The program, until then known as the Agricultural Trade Development & Assistance Act, or PL 480, involved the coordination of nine different agencies and departments dispensing American food around the globe. Besides its humanitarian value the government's food program helped to dispose of America's enormous farm surpluses, reduce the government's storage costs and indirectly subsidize the maritime industry. McGovern and other liberal Democrats had criticized the "surplus disposal" orientation of the government program during the Eisenhower Administration. Campaigning for "more effective use of our God-given abundance in a hungry world," McGovern often warned that

"hunger and Communism go hand in hand."

In February and March 1961 McGovern toured Brazil and Argentina to gauge their needs and to assure their officials that the U.S. was not using the program to "dump" surpluses and compete with their domestic agriculture. McGovern lobbied for the program's expansion, urging the President in April 1961 to endorse a five-year, $11 billion effort to feed the hungry and clothe the ragged of the world. Although he was more a coordinator of the program than a director, McGovern's access to the President enabled him to accentuate its humanitarian role and to keep Food for Peace from being absorbed by other departments. During 1961 Food for Peace distributed 60 billion pounds of surplus commodities and fed 64 million people, ten million more than it had reached the previous year. Arthur Schlesinger, Jr. [q.v.] judged it "the greatest unseen weapon of Kennedy's third world policy."

In April 1962 McGovern announced his candidacy for the seat of Sen. Francis Case (R, S.D.) [q.v.]. When Case died in June, Lt. Gov. Joseph H. Bottum became McGovern's Republican opponent. In the campaign Bottum attacked and McGovern defended the Kennedy Administration. With more than 250,000 ballots cast, McGovern was the victor by only 504 votes. He requested and was assigned to the Agriculture and Forestry Committee and the Interior and Insular Affairs Committee.

McGovern immediately emerged as a critic of American foreign policy. His maiden speech in March 1963 attacked U.S. Latin American policy for its "dangerous Castro fixation." Drawing from his experience on Food for Peace, he called for greater attention to "real problems"—like "depressed commodity prices, land reform and population pressures"—and denounced such military adventures as the "ill-conceived Bay of Pigs invasion." In August McGovern introduced an amendment to cut $5 billion from the $53.6 billion defense budget, but it was easily defeated.

McGovern was the first man to speak out against the Vietnam war on the floor of the Senate. In a September 1963 speech advocating nuclear disarmament, McGovern included a five-paragraph aside on the Vietnam conflict. Calling U.S. policy there one of "moral debacle and political defeat," he said that "we find American money and arms used to suppress the very liberties we went in to defend." Although McGovern voted for the Tonkin Gulf Resolution in August 1964, he became one of the Senate's most vocal critics of the Johnson Administration's escalation of the fighting.

McGovern belatedly sought the Democratic presidential nomination in August 1968 but finished a distant third in the convention balloting. After a long "dark horse" candidacy beginning in 1971, McGovern won a series of primaries and captured the nomination in 1972. [See JOHNSON, NIXON Volumes]

[TO]

For further information:
Robert Sam Anson, *McGovern: A Biography* (New York, 1972).

McINTYRE, THOMAS J(AMES)
b. Feb. 20, 1915; Laconia, N.H.
Democratic Senator, N.H., 1963- .

Thomas McIntyre, a graduate of Dartmouth and the Boston University Law School, practiced law for many years in his hometown of Laconia. He served as mayor of Laconia from 1949 to 1951 and was active in statewide Democratic politics. New Hampshire, however, was steadfastly Republican, and McIntyre seemed to have little chance of attaining high office. In November 1961 Sen. Styles Bridges (R, N.H.) [*q.v.*] died, and a special election was scheduled a year later to pick a successor to fill out Bridges's unexpired term. McIntyre won the Democratic senatorial nomination without opposition. Republicans, however, engaged in a bitter four-way primary fight that so weakened and divided the Party that McIntyre was able to defeat the Republican candidate, Rep. Perkins Bass (R, N.H.), by a slim majority.

During his freshman year McIntyre generally supported Kennedy Administration domestic legislation, voting for increased area redevelopment aid, the youth em-

ployment bill and the national service corps. He opposed the Administration's request for more mass transit aid. McIntyre established a reputation as a strong advocate of atomic submarines. In April 1963 he endorsed an amendment by Sen. Margaret Chase Smith (R, Me.) [*q.v.*] to add $134 million to a defense procurement bill for two additional atomic submarines. He voted in favor of the nuclear test ban treaty.

McIntyre generally supported the Johnson Administration's social welfare legislation as well as its Vietnam war policy. He also consistently defended New Hampshire's interests in the Senate, attempting to win support for higher tariffs on textiles and shoes to protect his state's industry from foreign competition. He also vigorously opposed the efforts of Secretary of Defense Robert S. McNamara [*q.v.*] to close the naval base at Portsmouth, N.H. [See JOHNSON Volume]

[JLW]

McMILLAN, JOHN L(ANNEAU)
b. April 12, 1898; Mullins, S.C.
Democratic Representative, S.C., 1939-72; Chairman, District of Columbia Committee, 1948-72.

John McMillan grew up on a farm in the heart of South Carolina's tobacco region. He served in the U.S. Navy during World War I, graduated from the University of North Carolina and then took a degree from the University of South Carolina Law School in 1923. That same year McMillan went to Washington as secretary to the Democratic congressman from South Carolina's sixth district. McMillan was elected to the House from the same district in 1938 and assumed the chairmanship of the District of Columbia Committee in 1948. He also served as vice chairman of the Agricultural Committee, where he guarded the interests of South Carolina's tobacco industry.

The District Committee was controlled by Southern Democrats who opposed home rule for the nation's capital on ostensibly constitutional grounds. The District of Columbia ranked ninth in population among U.S. cities, with a 63% black majority. Many observers felt that Southern opposition to home rule was based on the fear that black control of the municipal government would establish a precedent for black political power in the South.

Described by journalist Neal Peirce as a man who was "doing his best to run Washington like a South Carolina plantation," McMillan repeatedly stated that home rule was backed by "Communist sympathizers" who hoped to take over the city. The District of Columbia Committee successfully blocked passage of home-rule legislation from 1949 to 1967. Through enactment of the 23rd Amendment in 1961, which McMillan vigorously opposed, District of Columbia residents were given the right to vote in presidential elections.

No action was taken on the home-rule question during the Kennedy Administration. McMillan supported the conservative coalition in Congress on 75% and 78% of all major issues in 1961 and 1962, respectively, and on 100% of the key issues in 1963, according to *Congressional Quarterly*.

· In 1967 President Johnson [q.v.], frustrated in his attempts to get home-rule legislation through McMillan's Committee, used authority granted to the President under the Reorganization Act to alter the city government of Washington, which had previously been governed by Congress and a three-member board of commissioners. The three commissioners were replaced by a single commissioner, or "mayor," a deputy commissioner and a city council. In September 1967 Johnson named a black, Walter E. Washington, as District of Columbia commissioner and appointed a majority of five black members to the nine-member city council.

After winning a close primary race in 1970, McMillan lost the 1972 primary to a Democratic state legislator who had the support of organized labor and the black community. [See JOHNSON, NIXON Volumes]

[FHM]

For further information:
Drew Pearson and Jack Anderson, *The Case Against Congress* (New York, 1968).

McMURRIN, STERLING M(OSS)
b. Jan. 12, 1914; Woods Cross, Utah.
Commissioner of Education, April 1961-September 1962.

McMurrin, a Mormon, graduated from the University of Utah in 1937 and for the next eight years served in the department of education of the Church of Jesus Christ of the Latter-Day Saints. He received a Ph.D. from the University of Southern California in 1946. Two years later he was named a full professor of philosophy at the University of Utah and in 1960 became the school's academic vice president.

Secretary of Health, Education, and Welfare designate Abraham Ribicoff [q.v.] named McMurrin as Commissioner of Education in January 1961. McMurrin later confided that at the time he knew little about the position. Unlike most previous commissioners McMurrin had never been a public school administrator or a member of the National Education Association (NEA), the million-member organization that represented elementary and secondary public school teachers.

In his swearing-in ceremony in April 1961, McMurrin charged that American education was "soft," "flabby" and "easy." He called for a return to rigorous courses in the fundamentals, implicitly attacking "life adjustment" courses and the trappings of progressive education. He criticized the "dead leveling" of students in American schools and issued a call for excellence in education. American teaching was not up to standard, he said, because American teachers were underpaid.

McMurrin had a hand in drawing up Administration education bills, but the job of guiding them through Congress was left to Ribicoff and his assistant, Wilbur J. Cohen [q.v.]. "I was to look after education," said McMurrin, "and he [Ribicoff] was to look after the politics."

In the spring of 1961 McMurrin testified before Senate and House subcommittees on behalf of the Administration's bill for the extension and amendment of the 1958 National Defense Education Act (NDEA). Noting that the quality of English instruction was "alarmingly deficient in our schools," McMurrin pointed out that under the Administration bill college students majoring in English would—like foreign language students—be eligible for NDEA grants and loans. He also suggested that school "physical fitness" programs be eligible for NDEA grants.

The most controversial provision of the NDEA bill provided that federal funds be made available for private and parochial elementary and secondary school construction. According to *Congressional Quarterly* the Administration "tacitly" supported this provision, hoping thereby to remove the religious issue from the general public school aid bill. McMurrin himself offered no testimony on the proposal. The school construction provision provoked bitter opposition, which wrecked the Kennedy NDEA bill. Congress eventually passed a simple two-year extension of the NDEA without the amendments supported by the Administration.

During 1961 and 1962 education bills made little headway in Congress because of conflicts between Protestant and Catholic and public and private school groups over the issue of federal aid to parochial schools. McMurrin also blamed the failure of these bills on the NEA. In October 1962, shortly after he left office, McMurrin maintained that the NEA "is not interested in higher education, is cool to private schools and is pathologically opposed to parochial schools." He charged that it was dominated by a hierarchy unresponsive to the membership and bent on controlling American educational policy. He blamed the failure of an Administration aid-to-higher-education bill on lack of NEA support.

Some educational commentators suggested that the conflict between the NEA and McMurrin hastened his departure from office. He denied these charges, suggesting instead that he wished to return to teaching. He left Washington in October 1962 to become the provost and a professor at the University of Utah.

[JLW]

McNAMARA, PATRICK V(INCENT)
b. Oct. 4, 1894; North Weymouth, Mass.
d. April 30, 1966; Washington, D.C.
Democratic Senator, Mich., 1955-66.

A pipe-fitter by trade, McNamara served as president of Detroit Pipe Fitters Local 636 of the American Federation of Labor for 20 years prior to his election to the Senate in 1954. He was also employed by a Michigan mechanical contracting firm as head of labor relations and vice president in charge of sales. His career in public office began comparatively late in life with his election to the Detroit Common Council in 1946 and then to the Detroit Board of Education in 1949. McNamara was given little chance when he announced his candidacy in 1954 for the Democratic senatorial nomination against former Sen. Blair Moody. But Moody's sudden death on July 20 left McNamara the only Democrat in the field, and he went on to defeat the incumbent Republican, Homer Ferguson (R, Mich.), with a platform advocating repeal of the Taft-Hartley Act and federal aid for schools. He was assigned to the Senate Labor and Public Welfare Committee and Public Works Committee. In 1957 he was named to the special Senate committee investigating labor (Senate Rackets Committee). McNamara quit in April 1958, denouncing the committee for persecuting the labor movement. [See EISENHOWER Volume]

During the Kennedy Administration McNamara was a strong supporter of aid to education, wages and hours legislation and medical aid for the aged. In February 1961 he introduced the Administration's bill to raise the minimum wage from $1 to $1.25 an hour and expand coverage to include an additional 4.3 million workers. He successfully sponsored the Work Hours Act in July 1962 to replace with a single statute a series of federal "eight-hour laws" enacted between 1892 and 1940. The new statute required that overtime rates be paid on federal projects for any work in excess of 40 hours a week, thus ending what McNamara called "all too many instances in which contractors would observe an eight-hour day for their employes, but kept those workers on the job seven days a week." McNamara's advocacy of subsidies for elementary and secondary education was less effective: his amendment to a college aid bill to provide $650 million for construction of grade schools and high schools was rejected by the Senate in February 1962.

McNamara was a strong advocate of the Social Security approach to medicare. In January 1963, as chairman of the Special Senate Committee on Aging, he criticized the Kerr-Mills Act of 1960 (which provided aid to the states to help the "medically indigent") as "too little, too late and to too few." McNamara was one of only four senators to vote against a law which allowed self-employed persons to defer taxes on their contributions to retirement funds. He opposed it on the grounds that it gave an unjust financial break to doctors and lawyers. McNamara was an administration loyalist during the Kennedy and Johnson years. *Congressional Quarterly* reported that his voting record was conssistently among the 10 highest in support of White House bills from 1961 until his death in 1966. [See JOHNSON Volume]

[TO]

McNAMARA, ROBERT S(TRANGE)
b. June 9, 1916; San Francisco, Calif.
Secretary of Defense, January 1961-February 1968.

Robert S. McNamara, Secretary of Defense under Presidents Kennedy and Johnson, was one of the most controversial cabinet members of the postwar era. During the Kennedy years he won recognition for his efforts to bring the armed forces under strong civilian control. Under President Johnson he became a leading architect of American strategy in Vietnam.

McNamara, son of the sales manager of a wholesale shoe business, was raised in a middle-class section of Oakland. From grammar school to the University of California, Berkeley, to the Harvard Business School, McNamara was an outstanding student. After taking his M.B.A. in 1939, McNamara worked briefly for a San Francisco accounting firm. The next year he returned to Harvard to accept a teaching post in the business school.

McNamara was rejected for service in World War II because of poor vision. He remained at Harvard to instruct Army Air Corps officers in statistical techniques useful for the management of the war effort. After a year of teaching McNamara flew to England to aid the Air Corps in directing the planning and logistical effort that supported bomber operations. In March 1943 he was assigned the rank of captain in the Air Corps and subsequently was promoted to lieutenant colonel. While serving in the Far East at the end of the war, McNamara won praise for his pioneering efforts in the assessment of the effects of B-29 bombing raids on Japan.

In 1945 McNamara joined a group of young Army officers, later dubbed the "whiz kids," who offered their managerial services to the financially troubled Ford Motor Company. As general manager and vice president of the automotive division of Ford in the 1950s, McNamara supported the development of the Falcon, a compact economical automobile, and the four-door version of the Thunderbird, a luxury car, both of which were financial successes. In November 1960 McNamara was named company president, the first man outside of the Ford family to hold that position.

McNamara, a registered Republican, had held his new post for only a month when President-elect John F. Kennedy invited him to take a high cabinet post in the new Administration. McNamara had been suggested to Kennedy by Robert Lovett [*q.v.*], a leading New York banker upon whom Kennedy relied for advice on staffing many of his top policymaking positions. Offered the choice of either the Treasury or the Defense Department, McNamara chose the latter because he considered it the greater challenge.

Shortly after he assumed office in January 1961, McNamara made it plain that he would not, as had most of his predecessors, serve passively as a referee mediating between the conflicting interests of the Army, Navy and Air Force. McNamara argued that many operations of the Pentagon were grossly inefficient because the three armed services were working at cross purposes, duplicating efforts that cost the taxpayers billions of dollars. McNamara enlarged his personal staff and moved to centralize decision making authority, thereby under-cutting the power of the subordinate Army, Navy and Air Force Secretaries. He also created several new divisions controlled by civilians to deal with the common needs of the armed services. McNamara created a Defense Intelligence Agency to evaluate the intelligence operations of all three ser-vices and a Defense Supply Agency to pur-chase standardized items for use by the Army, Navy and Air Force.

A key element in McNamara's reorgani-zation of the Pentagon was the planning-programming-budgeting system (PPBS), which was developed in the latter half of 1961 by Defense Department Comptroller Charles Hitch [q.v.] and Alain Enthoven, a weapons systems analyst. Under the PPBS the budgets of the different branches of the military were coordinated to elimi-nate duplication or waste, particularly in the purchase or development of weaponry. For example, the cost-advantages of the Navy's Polaris missile, the Air Force's Min-uteman and the proposed RS-70 bomber, under the PPBS system, could be more easily compared. The system was applied to the 1963 and subsequent defense budgets.

As a result of these cost-effectiveness studies, McNamara refused to spend funds appropriated by Congress during 1961 and 1962 for development of the RS-70 bomber, a project favored by Air Force Chief of Staff Gen. Curtis LeMay [q.v.]. McNamara also vetoed construction of nuclear power plants for naval ships. Citing studies by his analysts, McNamara questioned whether the benefits of nuclear-powered vessels outweighed their additional costs. (It was not until 1966 that McNamara would tell a congressional committee that the cost-effectiveness of nuclear propulsion had been raised to the point where their use was justified for aircraft carriers.)

McNamara's budgetary and organizational reforms were highly controversial. Influen-tial congressmen and military officers were angered because the new Defense Depart-ment techniques threatened military bases or weapons systems with which they were identified. When, in the interests of effi-ciency, McNamara sought to merge the Na-tional Guard and the Army Reserves into one system, powerful conservative leaders in Congress like Rep. F. Edward Hebert (D, La.) [q.v.] delayed and eventually frustrated his proposals. McNamara's abrupt and unilateral decision to cancel develop-ment of the Skybolt missile, upon which Britain had been counting as a prime nu-clear weapons system, created momentary tensions between the two allies and con-tributed to the fall of the Conservative gov-ernment in 1964.

The most controversial weapons de-velopment project of the Kennedy years concerned the so-called TFX (Tactical Fighter Experimental). In 1961 McNamara and his civilian aides argued that a new jet fighter with "swing wings" could be de-veloped to meet the needs of both the Air Force and the Navy. Military men were skeptical, but in October 1961 the Defense Department invited a number of companies to submit plans for such an aircraft. By De-cember the choice had been narrowed down to Boeing and General Dynamics. In November 1962 the Defense Department awarded the contract to General Dynamics, despite the fact that military selection boards had found the Boeing design prefer-able. Early in 1963 the Senate Government Operations Subcommittee began an investi-gation of the award of the TFX contract. In testifying before the subcommittee McNamara suggested that the General Dynamics plane was more suitable than the Boeing aircraft for use by both services; he also argued that the technical innovations in the Boeing plane were impractical and that the cost of the Boeing design had been grossly underestimated.

The TFX hearings, which lasted nine months, embarrassed McNamara. Long-smoldering differences between the civilian and military men in the Pentagon were thoroughly publicized. In addition, officials who sided with McNamara—Deputy De-fense Secretary Roswell L. Gilpatric [q.v.], Navy Secretary Fred Korth [q.v.] and Air Force Secretary Eugene M. Zuckert [q.v.]—were forced to defend themselves against subcommittee charges that they were guilty of conflict of interest in supporting the General Dynamics bid. General Dynamics eventually built the TFX, but it proved to be far more costly than Defense Department estimates and, because of various structural problems, did not perform as expected.

McNamara once told an aide that "the military feels it has to have every bright shiny new gadget that comes along no matter how much it costs. I think we ought to buy what we need." He argued that the U.S. should not automatically deploy every new potential weapons system, since the Soviet Union would have to duplicate or counter it and our security would not be truly enhanced. For this reason he cautioned against the deployment of a costly and possibly ineffective anti-ballistic missile system until the Russians themselves had shown signs of doing so. He favored an end to the arms race and strongly supported the 1963 nuclear test ban treaty, which he thought might lead to arms limitations talks between the U.S. and the Soviet Union.

Despite McNamara's reluctance to build new weapons systems, the Defense Department budget rose from $45.9 billion in 1960 to $53.6 billion in 1964. This increase was dictated by two major Defense Department objectives. The first called for the U.S. to develop the capability to absorb a nuclear attack and still retain the ability to launch a devastating counterattack. This "second strike" capability, McNamara argued, would help prevent accidental nuclear war because it would reduce the pressure on the U.S. to retaliate on the basis of ambiguous radar information merely suggesting an enemy nuclear attack. McNamara urged that to ensure second-strike capability, the U.S. should replace its vulnerable, liquid-fuel Intercontinental Ballistic Missiles (ICBMs) with the solid-fuel Polaris and Minutemen ICBMs, which would be widely dispersed and could be fired quickly from underground or from submarines. McNamara also called for a stepped-up fallout shelter construction program to minimize loss of life following a nuclear attack.

McNamara's second goal was to develop a large and highly mobile striking force, which would permit the U.S. to deal with guerrilla or conventional wars without having to resort to nuclear weapons. The Eisenhower Administration's doctrine of "massive retaliation," he suggested, had limited American foreign policy options and increased the probability of a nuclear confrontation. In developing a "flexible response" capability, McNamara won approval for a 300,000-man increase in U.S. fighting strength and authorization for a vast buildup in U.S. capacity to airlift troops.

McNamara considered the Administration's handling of the Cuban missile crisis in October 1962 an example of the successful use of a "flexible response" strategy. When the Pentagon learned that the Soviet Union was erecting long-range missile sites in Cuba, the Administration did not immediately attack the launch pads as some military officers proposed. Instead, it demanded that the sites be dismantled and imposed "quarantine" around the island to turn back Soviet missile transport ships. McNamara carefully supervised the deployment and conduct of the blockade ships to ensure that unnecessary clashes with the Soviets would be avoided. After the U.S. Navy intercepted two ships on the high seas, the Russians agreed to withdraw their missiles from Cuba.

As a result of the buildup of conventional armed forces and development of contingency plans for brushfire wars, McNamara was reasonably confident of his Department's ability to deal with Communist guerrilla activity in Vietnam. The Defense Department rather than the State Department assumed primary responsibility for Vietnam affairs, because President Kennedy had greater confidence in the abilities of McNamara than in those of Secretary of State Dean Rusk [q.v.]. In addition, McNamara had already assumed important diplomatic responsibilities, particularly in his efforts to shore up the divided North Atlantic Treaty Organization. Finally, throughout the 1950s U.S. relations with Vietnam had been considered more of a military than a political problem, and the same attitude prevailed in the 1960s.

At the end of 1961 there were an estimated 2,000 American troops in South Vietnam training Vietnamese military personnel and operating aircraft, transport and communications facilities. In the spring of 1962 McNamara stated that the U.S. had no plans for introducing combat forces into South Vietnam, although Americans already there were authorized to fire if fired upon. In the fall of 1963 McNamara and Gen. Maxwell D. Taylor [q.v.] visited Saigon and then advised President Kennedy that the main U.S. military role in Vietnam could be completed by the end of 1965, although there might be a continuing need for U.S. advisers for some time thereafter. At the time of President Kennedy's death, there were some 15,000 American advisers in South Vietnam.

Within a year, however, it had become clear to McNamara that the war against the Communist guerrillas and their North Vietnamese allies could not be won quickly or easily. Vietnam soon became his overwhelming preoccupation. In the spring of 1964 Sen. Wayne Morse (D, Ore.) [q.v.] dubbed the conflict "McNamara's war."

"I think it is a very important war," replied McNamara in April 1964, "and I am pleased to be identified with it and do whatever I can to win it." McNamara was subsequently involved in the key decisions that led in 1965 to the commitment of U.S. combat troops to South Vietnam and to sustained U.S. bombing of North Vietnam. Over the next two years he was caught between the views of his Joint Chiefs of Staff, who urged him to authorize ceaseless and wide-ranging bombing of the North, and the views of civilian advisers, who argued that the bombing was useless and inhumane. By 1967 more than half a million American troops were involved in a conflict that was costing the U.S. $2.5 billion a month.

McNamara announced his resignation as Defense Secretary late in 1967. In March of the following year, he became president of the World Bank, a largely U.S.-supported organization devoted to lending money to underdeveloped countries. [See JOHNSON, NIXON Volumes]

[JWL]

For further information:
James M. Roherty, *Decisions of Robert S. McNamara: A Study of the Role of the Secretary of Defense* (Miami, 1970).
Henry L. Trewhitt, *McNamara: His Ordeal in the Pentagon* (New York, 1971).

McNAUGHTON, JOHN T(HEODORE)

b. Nov. 21, 1921; Bicknell, Ind.
d. July 19, 1967; Hendersonville, N.C.
Special Assistant for Disarmament Affairs, International Security Affairs, Department of Defense, July 1961-September 1961; Deputy Assistant Secretary of Defense for International Security Affairs, October 1961-June 1962; General Counsel, Department of Defense, July 1962-June 1964;

John T. McNaughton, a Rhodes scholar, was a professor of law at Harvard from 1956 to 1961. In July 1961 he joined the Defense Department, where he specialized in problems relating to arms control and disarmament. According to the journalist David Halberstam, McNaughton became "one of the two or three most important men in government in the fight to limit the arms race. . . ," a judgment with which Secretary of Defense Robert S. McNamara [q.v.] later concurred. Precisely because he worked in the Defense Department, McNaughton exercised considerable influence in urging restraint in the development of new weapons systems.

McNaughton outlined his ideas on disarmament in a December 1962 speech before the International Arms Control Symposium at the University of Michigan. He argued that the U.S. alone, without negotiations with the Soviet Union, could take steps to limit the arms race and enhance the security of both nations. For example, he noted, the U.S. had already taken elaborate precautions to prevent the firing by accident or mis-calculation of its nuclear weapons.

McNaughton also stressed that it was of crucial importance for the security of both nations that the U.S. be able to survive a surprise attack; otherwise it would be under great pressure to launch a nuclear strike on the basis of ambiguous radar information merely suggesting a Soviet attack. McNaughton supported an extensive civil defense program to protect "tens of millions of people from death caused by fall-out. . . ." He also justified the development and deployment of the Minuteman Inter-continental Ballistic Missile on the ground that it could be dispersed, thereby drawing Russian missiles away from cities.

The failure of the Soviet Union to sign a disarmament pact, said McNaughton, should not be taken by the U.S. as the pre-text for pursuing a policy of unbridled ex-pansion and development of new weapons systems. He pointed out that the develop-ment of such systems did not in the long run contribute to security and only served to escalate the arms race at great cost to both nations. McNamara's reluctance to start the development of the anti-ballistic missile system has been attributed to a similar belief in the desirability of such re-straint.

In July 1963 McNaughton joined a group under the direction of Undersecretary of State for Political Affairs W. Averell Harri-man [q.v.] that traveled to Moscow and successfully negotiated a treaty with the Soviet Union barring the above-ground testing of atomic weapons. In August McNaughton helped to lobby for passage of the treaty in the Senate. The agreement was ratified in September.

McNaughton was named an assistant sec-retary of defense in June 1964 and shortly thereafter became deeply involved in the strategic planning for the Vietnam war. In July 1967 McNaughton, his wife and younger son died in an airplane crash. [See JOHNSON Volume]

[JLW]

For further information:
William W. Kaufmann, *The McNamara Strategy* (New York, 1964).

MAGNUSON, WARREN G(RANT)
b. April 12, 1905; Moorhead, Minn.
Democratic Senator, Wash., 1944- .

Orphaned in infancy, Magnuson was raised by an immigrant Scandinavian fami-ly. At 19 he left home and settled in Seat-tle, where he received his law degree from the University of Washington in 1929. Elected to the state legislature in 1932, Magnuson sponsored the nation's first un-employment compensation law. He served as county prosecutor in Seattle from 1934 until his election to Congress in 1936.

In Washington Magnuson strove to apply the remedies of the New Deal to his state's economy. Water development projects for Washington soon became a dominant inter-est for Magnuson. He won election to the Senate in 1944 and continued to promote federally operated dams and power projects for his state, although his efforts to establish a single administration for the Columbia River modeled on the Tennessee River Val-ley Authority proved unsuccessful. During the 1950s he opposed the Republican policy of "partnership" between government and private enterprise for water and power projects, denouncing what he called "giveaways" to "favored corporations." Strongly supported by organized labor, Magnuson fought against the more restric-tive provisions of the Taft-Hartley Act in 1947 and introduced a bill in 1950 that re-stored the maritime union hiring hall.

Because his state's economy relied heavi-ly on federal defense contracts and re-source development, Magnuson's seniority on key committees and his ability to deliver federal programs made him an extremely valuable representative for his constituency. In 1955 he became chairman of the power-ful Interstate and Foreign Com-merce Committee (later renamed the Commerce Committee). Along with liberal social lesislation Magnuson favored large defense expenditures, and both he and Sen. Henry Jackson (D, Wash.) [q.v.] were sometimes called "the Senators from Boe-ing." [See TRUMAN, EISENHOWER Volumes]

During the early 1960s Magnuson con-tinued to focus on legislation designed to boost Washington's economy, particularly its aerospace, shipbuilding and extractive industries. In 1961 he led a contingent of Northwest congressmen who sought Kennedy's support for limitations on imported Canadian lumber. Kennedy agreed to support repeal of the Jones Act, which forbade the shipment of U.S. lumber on foreign vessels to Puerto Rico; the repeal was accomplished the following year. Magnuson was also successful in obtaining federal appropriations to aid Northwest lumbering. In 1962 he introduced an amendment that tripled federal funds for forest service acquisition of timber roads in national parks.

Magnuson was a leading Senate proponent of large aerospace expenditures. In the summer of 1963 he was one of several senators named in the testimony of Air Force Secretary Eugene Zuckert [q.v.] in a Senate investigation of the awarding of the TFX fighter-plane contract. Magnuson, like the others, had contacted Zuckert during the contract competition and stated that he wanted to know where the contract was going to be awarded.

Because he thought the U.S. was "losing more and more dollars to travel-conscious countries," Magnuson introduced the U.S. Travel Service Act, which became law in June 1961. The bill authorized nearly $8 million dollars for expansion of the Commerce Department's travel promotion activities and development of tourist facilities in the U.S. He had previously won a federal grant of $10 million for the 1962 Seattle World's Fair.

In June 1961 Magnuson acted as floor manager for an oceanographic research bill, which would have coordinated existing oceanography programs under a Division of Marine Sciences in the National Science Foundation. The Senate approved the bill, but no further action was taken, and a 1962 version that won passage in both houses was pocket vetoed. Magnuson argued that the programs would help the U.S. catch up with the Soviet Union in this area and that the results of increased research would provide valuable defense information.

Usually elected by a wide margin, Magnuson received only 52% of the vote in his 1962 campaign. An overhaul of his staff soon followed, and Magnuson's legislative emphasis began to shift from the specific needs of his state to issues of broader national significance. After the Senate Judiciary Committee, headed by Sen. James Eastland (D, Miss.) [q.v.], failed to report an Administration civil rights bill, Magnuson held hearings in the Commerce Committee, which in October ordered a version reported that included a controversial provision desegregating public accommodations. Fearing a Southern filibuster against the measure, however, the Committee did not release the report until 1964, when Magnuson managed the section's passage on the Senate floor.

During the late 1960s Magnuson played a leading role in consumer and environmental legislation, although he also favored federal aid for the Boeing supersonic transport plane. A close friend of President Lyndon Johnson [q.v.], Magnuson supported his Administration's Indochina policies but shifted to an anti-war position in the early 1970s. He was reelected in 1974 with a 65% majority. [See JOHNSON, NIXON Volumes]

[MDB]

MAHON, GEORGE H(ERMAN)
b. Sept. 22, 1900; Mahon, La.
Democratic Representative, Tex., 1935- .
Chairman, Department of Defense Appropriations Subcommittee, 1949-53, 1955- .

As a child George Mahon migrated with his parents to rural West Texas. Mahon received B.A. and LL.B. degrees from Texas universities and then entered politics, successively winning election as a district attorney, judge and representative from the newly formed 19th congressional district. Mahon supported most of Roosevelt's defense and agriculture programs. As the chairman or ranking Democrat on the House Defense Appropriations Subcommittee beginning in 1949, Mahon urged larger military expenditures and opposed efforts by the Eisenhower Administration to trim the military budget. [See EISENHOWER Volume]

During the Kennedy years Mahon backed the White House when it sought to raise defense appropriations. Soon after the inauguration, he declared that the "missile gap," an issue in the 1960 election, "is real." In June 1962 his subcommitee approved a fiscal 1963 defense budget of $48.1 billion, the largest such outlay since the Korean War. Agreeing to an Administration request to raise the national debt ceiling at the same time, Mahon warned Republican opponents that if Congress failed to increase the debt limit "probably one-half" of the accompanying budget reduction "would go in defense, and I think it would be unthinkable at this period in our history."

Mahon defended Defense Secretary Robert S. McNamara [q.v.] in the controversy surrounding his award of the TFX fighter bomber contract to General Dynamics in Ft. Worth, Tex. Republicans criticized the Defense Department's decision and accused the Administration of favoritism to Texas business and financial interests. In June 1963 Mahon declared that McNamara "undoubtedly selected [General Dynamics] because he felt it would be in the best interest of defense and the taxpayer." With the death of House Appropriations Committee Chairman Clarence Cannon (D, Mo.) [q.v.], Mahon assumed the leadership of the powerful committee in May 1964. [See JOHNSON NIXON Volumes]

[JLB]

MAILER, NORMAN
b. Jan. 31, 1923; Long Branch, N.J.
Novelist, journalist.

Mailer grew up in Brooklyn, graduated from Harvard with a degree in aeronautical engineering and served as an infantryman in the Army during World War II. Out of his military experiences in the Philippines came the 1948 bestseller *The Naked and the Dead*, a massive naturalistic novel about men in combat that catapulted the 25-year-old author to national literary fame. After a brief stint as a Hollywood scriptwriter, Mailer returned in the early 1950s to New York, where he helped to found the *Village Voice*, a weekly Greenwich Village newspaper for which Mailer wrote essays on the philosophy of "hip" and "American existentialism." He also published two more

novels in the 1950s, *Barbary Shore* (1951) and *The Deer Park* (1955), both of which received unfavorable reviews and sold poorly.

A cultural and political radical, Mailer gained a wide reputation in the 1950s and 1960s as a critic of American society, especially for what he saw as the "totalitarian" aspects of its mass culture. Mailer once wrote, "Everytime one sees a bad television show, one is watching the nation get ready for the day when a Hitler will come." Mailer had a volcanic and unpredictable personality. In November 1960 he won widespread notoriety when, after an all-night party, he was arrested for stabbing and seriously wounding his wife with a penknife.

In the early 1960s Mailer began a monthly political column for *Esquire* magazine, of which the best-known article was entitled "Superman Comes to the Supermarket," an evocation and glamorization of John F. Kennedy as well as a report on the 1960 Democratic National Convention. His essay was significant because it explained Kennedy's appeal not only to Mailer but also to a wide circle of radical and ex-radical intellectuals who shared the author's distaste for the culture of the 1950s. Mailer, who found little political difference between Kennedy and his Republican opponent Richard Nixon [q.v.], supported the Democratic candidate for non-political reasons. "I knew that if he [Kennedy] became President it would be an existential event," wrote Mailer, "he would touch the depths in American life which were uncharted. . . . Regardless of his overt politics, America's tortured psychotic search for security would finally be torn loose from the feverish ghosts of its old generals, its MacArthurs and Eisenhowers. . . ."

Many of Mailer's articles and columns in the early 1960s, collected in the *Presidential Papers*, criticized the young President for not living up to either his political or existential greatness. Mailer participated in demonstrations against the Administration following the abortive Bay of Pigs invasion of Cuba in April 1961. He later found in Fidel Castro the "existential" qualities he decided were lacking in Kennedy.

With the growth of political and cultural radicalism in the late 1960s, Mailer's presence in the American left was felt more strongly. His public personality increasingly pervaded his view of politics, both in his award-winning books *Armies of the Night* and *Miami and the Siege of Chicago* (both 1968) and in his unsuccessful seriocomic run for mayor of New York in 1969. [See JOHNSON, NIXON Volumes]

[NNL]

For further information:
Leo Brandy, ed., *Mailer: a Collection of Critical Essays* (New York, 1972).
Robert F. Lucid, ed., *Norman Mailer: The Man and His Work* (New York, 1972).
Norman Mailer, *Presidential Papers* (New York, 1963).

MALCOLM X
b. May 19, 1925; Omaha, Neb.
d. Feb. 21, 1965; New York, N.Y.
Black Muslim leader.

Malcom X was born Malcolm Little in Omaha, Neb., where his father was a Baptist minister and an organizer for Marcus Garvey's United Negro Improvement Association. Raised primarily in Michigan, Little moved to Boston to live with a half-sister after his father died. He developed a reputation in the black ghettos of Boston and New York City as a "hustler" and was sentenced to prison for burglary in February 1946. In jail he discovered the teachings of Black Muslim leader Elijah Muhammad [*q.v.*] and changed his name to Malcom X. Released from prison in August 1952, Malcolm settled in Detroit where he was appointed assistant minister of Muslim Temple No. 1. He was placed in charge of the Muslims' New York temple in 1954 and in 1963 became the Muslims' first "national minister."

During the early 1960s Malcom X's forceful indictment of white society and the civil rights movement created an unprecedented amount of public interest in the Black Muslims. Regarded by many as a proponent of "racism in reverse," Malcolm was a controversial figure among white and black people alike during this period. When civil

rights leader Paul Zuber invited Malcolm X to attend an Aug. 18, 1962 anti-segregation rally in Englewood, N.J., the invitation was denounced by white municipal officials and by some black ministers who urged their congregations not to attend the rally. Malcolm X first accepted but then declined the invitation because of what he considered "the narrow-mindedness of some of [Englewood's] . . . Negro ministers."

Malcolm X replaced the ailing Elijah Muhammad as the main speaker at the Muslims' national convention in 1963. In his speech he repeated the traditional Black Muslim demands for "everything we need to start our own independent civilization." For the first time he also appealed for unity in the fight for civil rights and for cooperation between the Muslims, the NAACP and the Congress of Racial Equality. Historian William O'Neil maintained that Malcolm's increasing desire for a "popular front" contributed to the split between Malcolm X and Elijah Muhammad.

The rift between the two leading Black Muslims became public knowledge in December 1963 when Muhammad publicly silenced Malcolm X for 90 days as punishment for his statement that President Kennedy's assassination was a case of "chickens coming home to roost." When rumors of indefinite suspension were heard within the Muslim organization, Malcolm requested that Muhammad clarify his status. Unsatisfied with a subsequent "clarification," Malcolm X announced on March 8, 1964 that he was leaving the Muslims to form an organization that would stress "black nationalism as a political concept and form of social action against the oppressors." He was assassinated by men thought to be linked with the Muslims on Feb. 21, 1965 before his Organization of Afro-American Unity was firmly established. [See JOHNSON Volume]

[DKR]

For further information:
George Breitman, *The Last Year of Malcolm X* (New York, 1967).
Malcolm X and Alex Haley, *Autobiography of Malcolm X* (New York, 1965).

MANN, THOMAS (CLIFTON)
b. Nov. 11, 1912; Laredo, Tex.
Assistant Secretary of State for Inter-American Affairs, July 1960-March 1961; Ambassador to Mexico, March 1961-December 1963.

Growing up in the border town of Laredo, Mann learned to speak Spanish almost as fluently as English. After working in the family law firm, he joined the State Department in 1942, specializing in Latin American and economic affairs. On the advice of Spruille Braden, he became a Foreign Service officer in 1947, attaining ambassadorial rank in El Salvador in 1955.

Mann was named assistant secretary of state for economic affairs in 1957. Describing himself as a "pragmatist," he maintained that he was sometimes willing to ignore the "free enterprise" ideal in working to control the prices of Latin American commodities. His most significant success came in 1958, when he got Latin American coffee-producing countries to attempt to stabilize quotas and prices. A year later he brought African nations into the agreement. In 1960 Mann helped negotiate the Act of Bogota, an inter-American declaration that foreshadowed the Alliance for Progress. Along with C. Douglas Dillon [q.v.] he set a pattern in President Dwight D. Eisenhower's Latin American policy that provided a basis for some of the policies of the Kennedy Administration. [See EISENHOWER Volume]

According to Arthur Schlesinger, Jr. [q.v.] Mann was skeptical of the idealism of the New Frontier and the Alliance for Progress but was a "good bureaucrat and ready enough to go along with" Kennedy policies. Mann was also skeptical of the CIA's Cuban invasion plan but, like many others, felt it was impossible to stop preparations that had proceeded so far. Like Kennedy, he was wary of the Latin American reaction and wanted to make the U.S. involvement appear minimal.

Appointed ambassador to Mexico in March 1961, Mann had to deal with two persistent problems plaguing U.S.-Mexican relations: Mexico's land claim to the Chamizal section of El Paso, Tex., and Mexico's annoyance over the excessive amounts of salts in the irrigation water that flowed from the Colorado River into Mexico. Mann resolved the first problem by negotiating the Chamizal Treaty of 1963, which ceded part of El Paso to Mexico. The second problem was not successfully settled despite talks between Kennedy and Mexican President Lopez, a $20 million U.S. agricultural loan and grants from the Ford and Rockefeller Foundations.

In December 1963 President Lyndon B. Johnson [q.v.] named Mann as assistant secretary of state for inter-American affairs. In addition, Mann was to head the Alliance for Progress and coordinate Latin American policy among the various departments. Observers credited Mann with the creation of a distinctive Johnson Latin American policy, which some believed to be a regression from the idealism of the Kennedy years. Mann emphasized private U.S. investment in Latin American and did not feel the U.S. should exclusively aid democratic governments or only those that sponsored social and economic reforms. Instead, he believed economic development must precede political and social progress in many countries. Mann left government service in 1966 to lecture and in 1967 became president of the Automobile Manufacturers Association. [See JOHNSON Volume]

[JCH]

MANNING, ROBERT J(OSEPH)
b. Dec. 25, 1919; Binghamton, N.Y.
Assistant Secretary of State for Public Affairs, March 1962-June 1964.

A former senior editor of *Time* magazine, Robert Manning was Sunday editor of the *New York Herald Tribune* in March 1962 when he was named assistant secretary of state for public affairs. In his new capacity Manning acted as press secretary for Secretary of State Dean Rusk [q.v.] and as liaison between the press and the State Department. Kennedy's press secretary, Pierre Salinger [q.v.], credited Manning with building the "most efficient press operation the State Department has ever known."

Manning came into some prominence during and after the Cuban missile crisis of October 1962. The Administration gave Manning responsibility for preventing leaks to the press of any diplomatic information that would be of value to the Soviets and the Cubans. On Oct. 31 the President instituted a policy requiring all State Department officials to report by memorandum to Manning all their contacts with the press. A similar policy had been put into effect in the Defense Department four days earlier, but both Manning and Salinger thought the policy unnecessary for the State Department and correctly predicted that the press would charge the Administration with censorship. Manning's counterpart in the Defense Department, Arthur Sylvester [q.v.], exacerbated the tension between the press and the Administration by arguing that the "generation of news . . . becomes one weapon in a strained situation."

After the Cuban crisis Kennedy helped restore better press relations by suspending the security policy for the State Department. Manning, however, pointed out that the media's criticism of the policy had ignored the fact that the temporary procedure had not required Department officials to receive advance permission for press contacts. On the other hand, he did not believe that it was in the public interest for State Department officials to disclose isolated bits of news during an emergency. While there was a need for "the democratic public to know the facts. . . . ," Manning said, officials sometimes served the public "by protecting a national policy from failure through premature disclosure."

In October 1963 Manning flew to Vietnam after nine Western newsmen, including four Americans, had been beaten by Vietnamese police while covering a Buddhist demonstration in Saigon. Although failing to solve the immediate problems, Manning sent Secretary Rusk a memorandum on his return that considered the problems of how a democratic society should govern its relations with the press in the context of the Cold War. Manning argued for a "relaxation of some—but not all—of the strictures still imposed on American coverage of the Vietnamese situation" and for a more "relaxed attitude on the part of U.S. officials to the reports and assessments of the U.S. press." He suggested that the arrival of the new ambassador to South Vietnam, Henry Cabot Lodge [q.v.], could serve as the beginning of a new and more productive relationship between the media and U.S. government officials in Saigon.

Manning resigned in June 1964 to become executive editor of the *Atlantic Monthly*.

[JCH]

MANSFIELD, MIKE (MICHAEL) (JOSEPH)
b. March 16, 1903; New York, N.Y.
Democratic Senator, Mont., 1953-   ;
Senate Majority Leader, 1961-   ;
Chairman, Rules and Administration Committee, 1961-63.

After his mother died three-year-old Mansfield was sent to live with relatives in Montana. From 1918 to 1922 he served successively in the Navy, Army and Marines. For the next eight years he worked as a miner and mining engineer in Montana. Mansfield received B.A. and M.A. degrees from Montana State University in 1933 and 1934. He remained there to teach Latin American and Far Eastern history.

Mansfield lost a Democratic congressional primary in 1940 but won a seat in the U.S. House of Representatives two years later. Interested in foreign affairs as a result of his academic background, the freshman Congressman was assigned to the Foreign Relations Committee. At President Roosevelt's request, he made a tour of inspection in China in 1944. A supporter of President Harry Truman's foreign policy, Mansfield served on the United States delegation to the 1951-52 session of the United Nations General Assembly.

In 1952 Mansfield defeated an incumbent Republican senator and entered the upper house of Congress the following year. He was immediately assigned a seat on that body's foreign relations panel. In 1957 Senate Majority Leader Lyndon B. Johnson [q.v.] chose Mansfield as his assistant, or whip. Johnson allegedly chose Mansfield because the latter was a political moderate and an unassertive man, unlikely to challenge the majority leader's authority. [See EISENHOWER Volume]

In January 1961 Johnson assumed the vice presidency and the Senate Democratic caucus chose Mansfield to succeed him. The Montana Senator inherited a position that, although unrecognized by either the Constitution or the Senate rules, gave its occupant great potential power. By tradition the majority leader had nearly total control over the scheduling of bills and considerable influence over committee appointments and policy through the chairmanship of his party's Steering and Policy Committees and of the full Party conference.

Johnson, a forceful and dominant leader, used all of the powers at his disposal to shape legislation and control the votes of his Democratic colleagues. He served as floor manager of almost every major bill and as the Democrats' chief strategist, parliamentarian and whip. Mansfield, however, assumed his position as a Democratic Administration took office and therefore shared with the White House the role of directing the Senate majority. Furthermore, he had a mild-mannered and scholarly disposition, preferring to win votes by persuasion rather than by cajolery and threats, which were often Johnson's most effective techniques.

Unlike Johnson, Mansfield dispersed the power of his office. He left the arrangement of deals and the use of pressure to his whip, Sen. Hubert H. Humphrey (D, Minn.) [q.v.]. He allowed committee chairmen to act as floor managers for their own bills. Mansfield also generally avoided intricate parliamentary maneuvering and long sessions as means of bending the upper house to his will.

A number of Democratic senators regarded Mansfield as an indecisive and ineffective leader. Criticism to that effect came to the surface in November 1963 during a long debate on the Kennedy Administration's foreign aid requests. Sen. Thomas J. Dodd (D, Conn.) [q.v.] asserted, "The Senate should be in session longer hours, and be working harder. Mike Mansfield is a gentleman. . . . But I worry about his leadership. . . . He must say 'No' at times. He must say 'Yes' at times." Liberal Democratic senators often criticized him for working too closely with Minority Leader Everett M. Dirksen (R, Ill.) [q.v.].

Mansfield's defenders contended that the respect he demonstrated for each senator and the universal affection in which he was held enabled him to exercise considerable influence. They also argued that, since many Senate Democrats were Southern conservatives, he often had to cooperate with Dirksen to win Republican votes for Administration measures. Mansfield's supporters noted that under his guidance the Senate passed the controversial aid-to-education bills of 1961 and mass transit and area redevelopment bills of 1963, all of which were blocked in the House.

Although Mansfield usually served as a spokesman for Kennedy Administration views, his interest in foreign affairs sometimes induced him to present his own ideas in that area. In June 1961 he suggested that Berlin be made a free, neutralized city under international guarantees and protection. American diplomats hastened to assure distraught West German officials that the Majority Leader was speaking only for himself.

During the Johnson Administration Mansfield became increasingly critical of the Vietnam war and had strained relations with the President. After the Republicans gained control of the White House in 1969, he employed his leadership role somewhat more assertively. Mansfield argued for a retrenchment of American commitments abroad, and in 1971 he pushed through the Democratic Policy Committee a resolution calling for an end to American involvement in Indochina. He urged the Senate to retrieve from the executive what he believed was its declining power in the conduct of foreign affairs. In March 1976 Mansfield announced that he would not seek reelection that year. [See JOHNSON, NIXON Volumes]

[MLL]

MARSHALL, BURKE
b. Oct. 1, 1922; Plainfield, N.J.
U.S. Assistant Attorney General in charge of the Civil Rights Division, February 1961-December 1964.

A 1943 graduate of Yale University, Marshall was a Japanese language expert for the Army in World War II. After receiving a degree from Yale Law School in 1951, he became a member of a Washington law firm where he specialized in antitrust work. An attorney with an excellent reputation, he was named assistant attorney general in charge of the Justice Department's Civil Rights Division on Feb. 2, 1961.

Marshall, a quiet and cool-headed man and a skillful negotiator, was a key figure in the development of the Kennedy Administration's civil rights policies and its handling of racial crises in the South. He viewed the right to vote as the key to securing other civil rights and significantly stepped up the voting rights work of the Justice Department. While only 10 voter discrimination suits were filed by the Eisenhower Administration, Marshall's division had filed 42 such cases by mid-1963. Marshall also urged the leaders of civil rights organizations to undertake a voter registration campaign in the South in 1961. His proposals helped lead to a foundation-financed Voter Education Project, which began in April 1962.

When the freedom riders—protesters challenging segregated transportation—were attacked by mobs in Anniston and Birmingham, Ala. on May 14, 1961, Marshall joined with other Administration officials in working out means to protect the riders from further violence and to end segregated travel facilities. He personally reached an agreement in October 1961 with three railroads for desegregation of their Southern terminals. Marshall also followed James Meredith's [q.v.] court suit seeking integration of the University of Mississippi from its start. When state officials attempted to block Meredith's court-ordered admission to the school in the fall of 1962, Marshall participated in negotiations with Gov. Ross Barnett [q.v.] to try to secure Meredith's peaceful enrollment and helped to coordinate the federal government's activities during the crisis from Washington.

In April 1963 Martin Luther King [q.v.] began leading civil rights demonstrations in Birmingham, Ala. The historic protest escalated in May and was met with increasing police repression. Marshall arrived in Birmingham on May 4 as President Kennedy's personal representative and began mediating behind the scenes, trying to get city officials, white businessmen and black leaders to confer. His negotiating efforts ultimately led to a May 10 desegregation agreement between white and black leaders. In the summer of 1963, Marshall also helped to arrange a desegregation agreement ending some four months of demonstrations in Cambridge, Md. In addition he worked to forestall crises by quietly touring Southern cities and conferring with local officials to help prepare for peaceful school desegregation. Marshall also aided in drafting the Kennedy civil rights bill introduced in Congress in June 1963 and worked to secure its passage.

According to journalist Benjamin Muse, Marshall was an "official of quiet tact and effectiveness, who enjoyed to a rare degree the respect of all parties to civil rights disputes." Both he and the Administration, however, were often criticized for their policies. The voting rights suits, for example, were labeled "ineffective in ending voting discrimination" by Howard Zinn, and Marshall himself admitted in 1964 that the federal government had not yet succeeded "in making the right to vote real" for blacks in Mississippi and in large parts of Alabama and Louisiana. Some rights workers also charged that the mediation efforts of Marshall and his colleagues in racial disputes were aimed more at restoring order and tranquility than at advancing black civil rights.

The greatest criticism centered on the federal government's failure to protect civil rights workers and local blacks in the South from both private and official harassment and assault. Many of those who participated in the voter registration campaign encouraged by Marshall were especially bitter about the Justice Department's inaction. Marshall countered with the argument that under a federal system of government, many of the assaults on rights workers were outside the reach of the national government. He insisted that the Constitution afforded no basis for sending special federal agents throughout the deep South as some urged. Legal experts were divided on the validity of this view, but Marshall adhered to it, even though he recognized that it caused great frustration and resentment against the government among civil rights workers.

Marshall resigned his post on Dec. 18, 1964 and then spent several months aiding Vice President Hubert H. Humphrey [q.v.] in coordinating overall federal civil rights policy. He worked with Justice Department officials in overseeing federal activities during the March 1965 Selma march. Marshall joined the International Business Machines Corp. (IBM) as vice president and general counsel in June 1965. President Johnson named him chairman of a National Advisory Commission on Selective Service in July 1966. [See JOHNSON Volume]

[CAB]

For further information:
Burke Marshall, *Federalism and Civil Rights* (New York, 1964).

MARSHALL, THURGOOD
b. July 2, 1908; Baltimore, Md.
Director-Counsel, NAACP Legal Defense and Educational Fund, 1940-61; U.S. Circuit Judge, Second Circuit Court of Appeals, 1961-65.

Valedictorian of the class of 1933 at Howard University Law School, Marshall was named assistant special counsel of the National Association for the Advancement of Colored People (NAACP) in 1936, special counsel in 1938 and director-counsel of the newly created NAACP Legal Defense and Educational Fund in 1940. In the latter two positions Marshall coordinated the entire NAACP legal program and led the organization to a series of U.S. Supreme Court victories in cases challenging racial segregation and discrimination. Marshall's most notable success was the 1954

school desegregation decision in *Brown v. Board of Education,* but his other significant victories included a 1944 Supreme Court decision invalidating white Democratic primaries and a 1948 decision ending state court enforcement of racially restrictive covenants in housing. Marshall argued 32 cases before the Supreme Court as NAACP counsel and won substantive victories in 27. [See TRUMAN, EISENHOWER Volumes]

President Kennedy nominated Marshall for a judgeship on the Second Circuit Court of Appeals on Sept. 23, 1961, and Marshall began serving in October under a recess appointment. Under the chairmanship of Sen. James O. Eastland (D, Miss.) [q.v.], who opposed Marshall's appointment, the Senate Judiciary Committee delayed hearings on the nomination for nearly eight months and then held six days of hearings stretched out over four months. The Committee finally approved his appointment on Sept. 7, 1962 by an 11-4 vote, and the full Senate confirmed the nomination on Sept. 11 by a vote of 54 to 16. All of the opposition came from Southern Democrats.

As a new judge, Marshall had little opportunity to write majority opinions in significant civil or individual rights cases, and most of his written decisions concerned such areas as federal tort claims, admiralty law or patent and trademark cases. However, his votes on the Court and the opinions he did write identified him as a liberal jurist who usually granted the government broad powers in economic matters but barred it from infringing on the constitutional rights of the individual.

Marshall was not actively involved in the civil rights movement after his appointment to the court. However, he remained a symbol of the NAACP's achievements through legal action. President Johnson appointed Marshall U.S. solicitor general in July 1965 and an associate justice of the U.S. Supreme Court in June 1967. Marshall was the first black to hold either post. [See JOHNSON, NIXON Volumes]

[CAB]

For further information:
Randall W. Bland, *Private Pressure on Public Law: The Legal Career of Justice Thurgood Marshall* (Port Washington, 1973).

MARTIN, EDWIN M(cCAMMON)
b. May 21, 1908; Dayton, Ohio.
Assistant Secretary of State for Economic Affairs, August 1960-May 1962; Assistant Secretary of State for Inter-American Affairs, May 1962-December 1963.

A graduate of Northwestern University, Martin worked as a government economist during the war until he joined the Office of Strategic Services in 1944. He began his State Department career in 1945, first working in the area of Japan and Korea and later gaining experience in Europe and international trade. Eisenhower appointed him to assistant secretary of state in 1960.

Authority for Latin American policy was diffuse in the Kennedy Administration's first year. The State Department bureaucracy was sensitive to any White House infringement on its authority and disliked the rapid pace at which Kennedy's Latin American advisers, particularly Richard Goodwin [q.v.], sought to redirect policy. It was hoped that Martin, noted for his toughness and organizational ability as well as for his commitment to the Alliance for Progress, would run a tighter ship than his predecessor, Robert F. Woodward. Soon after his appointment as assistant secretary of state for inter-American affairs, he was able to concentrate greater authority in his own office and to sharply curtail the activities of Goodwin, then serving as his deputy.

Many observers saw Martin's appointment as a move to reinforce the Alliance for Progress. Yet, in his first crisis as assistant secretary of state, Martin's efforts to follow a liberal policy were rejected. In March 1962 Martin advised Kennedy not to recognize the military regime that had just overthrown the constitutional government of Arturo Frondizi in Argentina. Such a position would have been consistent with the Alliance's—and Kennedy's—avowed support for democratic governments and its opposition to military dictatorships. However, believing that Frondizi's cause was not popular with the Argentine people, DeLesseps Morrison [q.v.], ambassador to the Organization of American States (OAS),

and Sens. Wayne Morse (D, Ore.) [q.v.] and Bourke Hickenlooper (R, Ia.) [q.v.] convinced Kennedy to recognize the military regime as the constitutional continuation of the Frondizi government.

But when a similar crisis occurred in Peru in July 1962, Martin and Ambassador to Peru James Loeb [q.v.] successfully put pressure on the military junta to restore civil liberties and set up free elections in return for diplomatic recognition and renewal of economic aid. Ironically, Martin, who was a consistent opponent of military regimes, was widely criticized in October 1963 when he praised the "restraint" of certain military governments in respect to civil liberties. Meanwhile, vocal anti-Communists Sen. Everett Dirksen (R, Ill.) [q.v.] and Rep. Charles Halleck (R, Ind.) [q.v.] claimed that the Kennedy-Martin policy of favoring democratic governments had "wreaked havoc" in the hemisphere.

During the Cuban missile crisis of October 1962, Martin was a member of the executive committee of the National Security Council. A staunch proponent of the need for cooperative action in the hemisphere, he was able to get the OAS to unanimously (19-0) endorse a resolution that described the presence of Soviet missile sites in Cuba as a threat to the security of the Americas. The resolution also called for multilateral action to eliminate their presence on the island.

Martin resigned his position in December 1963. President Johnson gave his successor, Thomas C. Mann [q.v.], even greater authority in the Latin American area. Martin was named ambassador to Argentina in January 1964. Despite Martin's opposition to the military coup which overthrew the constitutional president, Arturo Illia, in June 1966, the U.S. recognized the new military government after a short suspension of relations. The recognition was viewed as typical of Johnson's pragmatic approach to Latin American relations. Martin resigned in November 1967 to become chairman of the Development Assistance Committee, a multinational body coordinating aid to developing countries.

[JCH]

MARTIN, JOHN BARTLOW
b. Aug. 4, 1915; Hamilton, Ohio.
Ambassador to the Dominican Republic, March 1962-January 1964.

In the 1950s Martin won fame as a free-lance journalist writing factual crime stories. Active as a leader in the crusade for prison reform, Martin also worked intensively in Adlai Stevenson's [q.v.] presidential campaigns in 1952 and 1956 and wrote a 1952 campaign biography, *Adlai Stevenson*.

Associated with John F. Kennedy as a speechwriter during the 1960 presidential campaign, Martin was later confirmed as Kennedy's ambassador to the Dominican Republic on March 1, 1962. Martin's tenure as ambassador coincided with an era of Dominican political instability. In 1961 the 31-year rule of right wing dictator Rafael Trujillo ended with his assassination. Trujillo's successor, Dr. Joaquin Balaguer, failed to democratize the political system, and the influence of the Trujillo family and the old oligarchy remained strong. The Organization of American States (OAS), acting with U.S. approval, pressured the Trujillo family to flee the country by November 1961. In January 1962 rioting forced Balaguer to step aside. By February a seven-man council of state committed to holding free elections proved acceptable to the U.S., and the Kennedy Administration resumed military and economic aid.

In the December 1962 elections Juan Bosch of the social democratic *Partido Revoluncionario Dominicano* (PRD) emerged the winner. The Kennedy Administration was committed to Bosch and to making a democratic Dominican Republic a showcase for the Alliance for Progress. Yet Martin, who had told Bosch that the U.S. would use its "influence to see that [the] government is not dominated by the military or by police," later characterized the PRD as "too doctrinaire" and Bosch himself as "emotionally unstable." Martin did not feel that Bosch attacked Communist "subversion" with sufficient energy, while he feared tht Bosch was alienating the army, the church and the landowners too quickly with his liberalization measures.

The U.S. State Department, long suspicious of Bosch and influenced by Martin's reports, therefore took no action when a September 1963 military coup overthrew Bosch, although Martin had asked that a U.S. aircraft carrier be sent to Dominican waters to deter the conspirators. Despite the Department's previous apathy, the U.S. immediately broke diplomatic relations with the Dominican Republic, halted all economic aid and recalled Martin to Washington. Martin recommended that the U.S. recognize the new junta after a waiting period, and diplomatic relations were resumed in December 1963, three weeks after Lyndon B. Johnson [q.v.] became president. Martin resigned his post in January 1964. He joined the Johnson campaign staff later in the year.

In April 1965 a pro-Bosch constitutionalist army group revolted against the Dominican junta government. Johnson soon sent in U.S. Marines to "protect and evacuate" Americans. On May 2 he sent Martin to arrange a ceasefire and mediate between the warring factions. Martin, concerned over what he considered a Communist threat, tried to form a provisional government committed to holding elections. However, his choice of Antonio Imbert to head the new government was so unpalatable even to many conservative Dominicans that Martin was soon replaced by a team of presidential representatives, including Cyrus Vance [q.v.], McGeorge Bundy [q.v.] and Thomas C. Mann [q.v.]. The situation was not stabilized until the OAS Peace Committee arranged a provisional government acceptable to all factions. The interim regime took power in September 1965. Elections were held the following June. Martin, however, had left the Dominican Republic at the end of May 1965 to return to teaching and writing. He worked for Robert F. Kennedy [q.v.] and, after Kennedy's death, for Hubert H. Humphrey [q.v.] in their 1968 election bids.

[JCH]

For further information:
John Bartlow Martin, *Overtaken by Events: The Dominican Crisis from the Fall of Trujillo to the Civil War* (Garden City, 1966).

MARTIN, WILLIAM McCHESNEY
b. Dec. 17, 1906; St. Louis, Mo.
Chairman, Board of Governors of the
Federal Reserve System, 1951-70.

As chief custodian of the nation's money
supply, William McChesney Martin was a
figure of great controversy throughout the
1950s and 1960s. To conservatives, Martin
was the symbol of financial integrity, while
many liberal Democrats held his "tight
money" policies responsible for the recessions
of the Eisenhower Administration. Despite
some accommodation to demands for
monetary "ease" in the early 1960s, Martin
remained throughout the Kennedy Administration a powerful conservative influence on the course of economic policy.

Martin grew up within the Federal Reserve tradition. His father, a St. Louis
banker, aided in the drafting of the Federal
Reserve Act of 1913 and became president
of the Federal Reserve Bank of St. Louis.
The product of a strict Presbyterian up-
bringing, Martin attended Yale University
and received his B.A. in 1928. He spent a
year as a clerk at the St. Louis Federal Reserve Bank, moving on to become head of
the statistical department of a St. Louis
brokerage firm. In 1931 Martin acquired a
seat on the New York Stock Exchange
(NYSE) to become his firm's Wall Street
representative.

In a remarkable breakthrough for a man
of 31, Martin became president of the Exchange in 1938. The first salaried president
of the NYSE, he took office in an atmosphere of scandal and pledged full cooperation with the Securities and Exchange
Commission. Martin was inducted into the
Army as a private in 1941. During World
War II he served in an important administrative role with the Munitions Allocation
Board and supervised much of the Russian
Lend-Lease program. In November 1945
President Truman made him a director of
the Export-Import Bank, which granted
loans to foreign countries. Appointed assistant secretary of the Treasury in 1949, Martin engineered a famous "accord" between
the Treasury Department and the Federal
Reserve which freed the Federal Reserve
Board, fearful of becoming "an engine of inflation," from "pegging" the bond market to
enable the Truman Administration to borrow at low interest rates. In 1951 Truman
named Martin chairman of the Board of
Governors of the Federal Reserve System.
"Independent" of the national administrations, Martin and the Federal Reserve pursued a conservative course designed to halt
the threat of inflation by keeping interest
rates high. [See TRUMAN, EISENHOWER
Volumes]

Martin's policies were an issue in the
1960 presidential campaign. The Democratic platform stated in July, "As the first step
in speeding economic growth a Democratic
president will put an end to the present
high interest, tight money policy." Democratic candidate Sen. John F. Kennedy reiterated that tight money had been the main
cause of the Eisenhower recessions, while
his advisers spoke of pressuring or firing
Martin if he attempted to block Kennedy's
liberal economic programs. In contrast, Republican candidate Richard M. Nixon
[q.v.] pledged never to tamper with the
"independence" of the Federal Reserve.
The Fed's "independence" was a volatile
issue in the financial community; in the
words of economist James Tobin [q.v.],
"The Federal Reserve to some is the last
citadel protecting the dollar and the country from disaster."

In September 1960 Kennedy began to
temper his rhetoric concerning the Federal
Reserve. Acknowledging that the institution
had been granted a degree of independence
by the Federal Reserve Act, he said that its
Board of Governors and the President
"should work together to achieve national
economic goals." Kennedy's decision to assign priority status to correcting the balance
of payments deficit and strengthening the
dollar was a policy welcomed by Martin.

The President and Martin had a smooth
relationship after their first meeting in February 1961. Kennedy's economics were
more orthodox and Martin's less intransigent than the other had expected. Unlike
Eisenhower, Kennedy integrated Martin
into the top-level economic policy making
team that included Secretary of the Treasury C. Douglas Dillon [q.v.] and Chairman of the President's Council of Economic

Advisers (CEA) Walter W. Heller [q.v.]. Martin exerted a strong conservative pull on Administration policy, generally adding weight to Dillon's position and opposing the more liberal counsel of Heller and the CEA, who favored more aggressive deficit-spending and liberal monetary policies.

Early in the Kennedy Administration Martin made an important accommodation by abandoning the Federal Reserve's controversial "bills only" policy by which it bought only short-term government obligations. Participating in what became known as "Operation Twist," Martin agreed to buy issues with longer terms of maturity and thus help drive down long-term interest rates. The Administration hoped to stimulate investment in this way, while maintaining short-term rates at a relatively high level to prevent funds from fleeing abroad in search of higher interest rates. The latter aspect of the policy was more in accord with Martin's beliefs and his concern over the balance of payments deficit.

Proof of the Kennedy-Martin concord was Kennedy's reappointment of Martin as chairman of the Federal Reserve Board of Governors in February 1963. Kennedy needed Martin, the symbol of the sound dollar, to stay in office while the dollar's position was deteriorating. More importantly, the Federal Reserve under Martin was acting in concert with the Administration's expansionary fiscal and monetary policies. Martin approved of Kennedy's veto of a temporary tax cut to spur the economy in 1962 and eventually supported Kennedy's $11 billion tax cut in 1963. He agreed to allow some increase in bank reserves in order not to cancel out the tax cut's stimulative effect, but he also moved to tighten money through higher interest rates to control inflation and stem the payments deficit. Despite opposition by Democrats in Congress, Kennedy and Dillon supported the Federal Reserve Board's decision in July 1963 to force a substantial rise—from 3% to 3.5%—in the discount rate. The increase was dramatic, the first since August 1960. Kennedy defended it and said it "should have little, if any, adverse effect on our economy."

Hobart Rowen summarized Martin's per-formance in *The Free Enterprisers: Kennedy, Johnson and the Business Establishment*: "In the Kennedy Administration, Martin's Federal Reserve did not try to run a course independent of the White House, although it did not move along the always-easy money lines urged by Representative [Wright] Patman [q.v.], or even along the more modest expansionary path urged by Walter Heller."

Martin's "tight money" policy became a subject of greater controversy during the Johnson Administration. He resigned in early 1970 and was succeeded by the equally conservative Arthur Burns. [See JOHNSON, NIXON Volumes]

[TO]

MATHIAS, CHARLES McC(RUDY),
b. July 24, 1922; Frederick, Md.
Republican Representative, Md., 1961-69.

A former city attorney for Frederick and member of the Maryland House of Delegates, Charles Mathias was elected to Congress in 1960. His district was a traditionally Southern Democratic one of suburbs and farms. In national elections the district voted for conservative Republicans. This background was reflected in Mathias's early voting record. During the Kennedy Administration the Congressman voted against many of the President's domestic proposals, including housing subsidies, area redevelopment and aid to education, but he supported the chief executive on most foreign policy matters.

As a member of the District of Columbia Committee, Mathias was concerned with the affairs of the capital, which adjoined his district. In 1962 he introduced legislation to give the District a non-voting delegate in the House as a step toward home rule. The House approved the measure in 1970.

Mathias, who also served on the Judiciary Committee, was one of the legislators responsible for shaping civil rights legislation and introducing the 1963 bill that was a forerunner of the Civil Rights Act of 1964. The Congressman also introduced a bill in 1963 requiring that no congressional district within a state vary from any other by more than 20% in population. Less than a year later the Supreme Court ruled that districts had to be "substantially equal."

During the last half of the decade, Mathias earned a reputation as a Republican maverick because of his stand on civil rights and his opposition to the Vietnam war. In 1966 he became a center of controversy when he added a compromise amendment to exempt the sale of individual homes and small multiple dwellings from the open housing provisions of the civil rights bill in an attempt to save the total proposal. The amended bill was passed by the House but was killed by a Senate filibuster. In 1968 he was elected to the U.S. Senate where he continued to push for congressional reform and to oppose delays in ending the Vietnam war. [See JOHNSON, NIXON Volumes]

[EWS]

MEANY, GEORGE
b. Aug. 16, 1894; New York, N.Y.
Prsident, AFL-CIO, 1955-   .

Meany grew up in a large Irish-Catholic family in the Bronx. At 16 he entered his father's trade as a plumber's apprentice and joined the union when he became eligible as a journeyman. Meany won his first full-time union office in 1922 as business agent of Plumber's Union Local 463. Twelve years later he was elected local president; more importantly, he also won election as president of the New York Federation of Labor. His statewide post put him in close contact with the Democratic Party, the Roosevelt Administration and the national leadership of the American Federation of Labor (AFL). Meany proved an adept lobbyist and politician, and in 1940 AFL President William Green chose him as secretary-treasurer of the Federation.

Meany took over an increasing amount of the AFL's day-to-day activity in the postwar years and became especially involved in the Federation's foreign activities. He worked closely with the American government in helping set up anti-Communist trade unions in Western Europe and Japan and was instrumental in the formation of the pro-Western International Confederation of Free Trade Unions in 1949. [See TRUMAN Volume]

After Green's death in 1952 Meany was elected AFL president. Although a firm "business unionist" with great loyalty to the craft traditions of the AFL, Meany was less hostile to the rival Congress of Industrial Organizations than others in the Federation hierarchy. He opened merger negotiations with the CIO in 1953 and two years later reached a unity agreement. Since the AFL was nearly twice as large as the CIO, Meany assumed the presidency of the new AFL-CIO, while CIO President Walter Reuther [q.v.] took command of a newly created Industrial Union Department (IUD) within the merged labor federation. In 1957 Meany, with the support of the old CIO unions, took the lead in expelling the AFL-CIO's largest affiliate, the International Brotherhood of Teamsters, on corruption charges. [See EISENHOWER Volume]

Meany often projected an image of one who held capricious and autocratic power over the trade union movement. He was the chief public spokesman for the 12.4 million members of the AFL-CIO; he dominated the Federation's policymaking executive council; and in the early 1960s he spoke frequently and directly with President Kennedy on executive appointments of interest to labor. But Meany's authority was carefully delimited by the federated structure of the AFL-CIO itself. He had virtually no power to influence individual union bargaining and strike activities or the political strategy adopted by individual international unions affiliated with the AFL-CIO. He had only limited authority to umpire jurisdictional disputes between affiliated unions or to combat segregation within a local union. Meany's only real power over the internal affairs of an affiliate was to recommend expulsion, and this Meany was extremely reluctant to do after exclusion of the Teamsters from the Federation proved ineffective in reforming that union.

In the early 1960s Meany's leadership of the AFL-CIO executive board was unsuccessfully challenged on two issues. The first was civil rights. Historically, the AFL-CIO had adopted several anti-discrimination statutes, but A. Philip Randolph [q.v.], president of the Brotherhood of Sleeping Car Porters and the only black on the executive council, thought Meany insufficiently vigorous in the enforcement of this policy. Many craft locals excluded blacks from their membership, and in the South official AFL-CIO state bodies frequently held segregated conventions. In June 1961 Randolph submitted a report detailing AFL-CIO "tokenism in civil rights" and charging that there was "a crisis of confidence between the leaders of Negroes and labor." Randolph called for expulsion of those unions that continued to practice discrimination.

Meany responded to these charges by seeking to undercut Randolph's standing within the AFL-CIO. He appointed a committee that investigated Randolph's charges and produced a resolution in October "censuring" the black leader for "causing the gap that has developed between organized labor and the Negro community." Meany asserted, "We can only get moving on civil rights if he [Randolph] comes over to our side and stops throwing bricks at us." Later Meany and Randolph met privately and reached a compromise. The AFL-CIO dropped its censure resolution and at its convention in December 1961 adopted a resolution that called for "appropriate action" by the executive council against unions that persisted in discriminatory practices. Meany admitted that "pockets of discrimination" existed in the union movement and in 1963 threw the AFL-CIO's weight behind the inclusion of a fair employment practices commission in the Kennedy Administration's civil rights bill.

Despite his gradual shift toward a more determined civil rights stand, Meany mistrusted the social activism of the black movement. Although he invited Martin Luther King [q.v.] to speak at the 1961 AFL-CIO convention, Meany was cool to most civil rights demonstrations. In August 1963 he was instrumental in the AFL-CIO's decision not to endorse the March on Washington but rather to make participation a "matter of individual union determi-

nation." (Randolph called the resolution a "masterpiece of noncommital noncommitment.")

Meany also clashed with some other union leaders over the apparent stagnation of the AFL-CIO in the early 1960s. As a result of the expulsion of the Teamsters and the recession of 1957-58, the Federation had fewer members in 1960 than it had had at the time of merger. Jurisdictional disputes between craft and industrial unions consumed much of the time of the AFL-CIO executive council. Meanwhile, the labor federation lost another 100,000 members in the first two years of the new decade; the proportion of non-farm workers in its ranks dropped to 18% of the total workforce.

Walter Reuther, president of the United Auto Workers, was Meany's most formidable opponent within the AFL-CIO. Reuther held Meany responsible for failing to curb craft union jurisdictional raids, and he urged Meany to use his authority to throw Federation resources into large-scale organizing drives. He attacked Meany's $50,000 annual salary and his penchant for holding executive council meetings in Bal Harbor, Fla., rather than in cities of the industrial North.

Meany took only limited steps to meet Reuther's criticisms. In late 1961 he threw his personal prestige behind a compromise agreement that imposed new restrictions upon craft union jurisdictional claims against workers already organized in industrial unions. But Meany thought organizing new workers was the primary responsibility of each international affiliate, and he was unwilling to ask individual unions to abandon their jurisdictional claims in joint organizing drives. Moreover, Meany thought Reuther's criticisms chiefly designed to advance his chances of one day succeeding to the AFL-CIO presidency. Meany, therefore, carefully guarded his authority vis-a-vis the UAW leader. He blocked Reuther's appointment to the U.S. United Nations delegation in 1961 and for several months in 1962 delayed seating a Reuther nominee on the AFL-CIO executive council.

Meany's relationship with the Kennedy Administration was also frequently strained.

Although Meany backed Kennedy even before the Democratic National Convention, he was bitterly disappointed that the nominee chose Sen. Lyndon Johnson (D, Tex.) [q.v.] as his vice presidential running mate. He was also disappointed in Kennedy's choice of former CIO counsel Arthur Goldberg [q.v.] as Secretary of Labor. Meany had preferred that an elected union official be offered the post.

Despite Kennedy's failure to consult Meany on these two selections, the President regularly spoke with the AFL-CIO leader on issues of concern to labor, and he frequently deferred to Meany's wishes concerning lesser executive branch appointments of interest to the Federation. Meany strongly backed most Kennedy Administration social welfare and economic legislation. He put AFL-CIO lobbyists to work in support of Kennedy's bills to increase Social Security payments, to aid depressed areas and to provide federal aid to education. The AFL-CIO was particularly active in the unsuccessful fight for medicare during the Kennedy years.

In 1961 the AFL-CIO applauded Kennedy Administration efforts to stimulate the economy, but Meany soon concluded that economic policymakers were giving too much weight to the problem of inflation and too little to the continuing high rate of unemployment. AFL-CIO suggestions for a substantial increase in the minimum wage, a public works program and a $100 personal income tax cut were either ignored or rejected by the Administration. In February 1962 the AFL-CIO executive council officially described Administration efforts to combat unemployment as "overly timid."

The next month Meany announced that since Kennedy was not taking the steps necessary to lower sharply the unemployment rate, labor would open a drive for a shorter workweek as a means of spreading the available work. "If this means 35, 34, 33 or 30 hours a week or less so be it," Meany announced at a Building and Construction Trades Department convention in Washington. For the next two years Meany argued repeatedly for a national 35-hour week, but both the President and Secretary

Goldberg opposed the demand on the ground that it would lower productivity. Meany also differed with the Administration over Goldberg's frequent declarations that the government had the right to assert the "national interest" in collective bargaining negotiations. The Administration's 3.2% anti-inflation wage guideposts were similarly viewed by Meany as unfair to organized labor.

Differences with the Kennedy Administration over domestic economic policy did not disturb the AFL-CIO's close working relationship with the government on foreign policy matters. Meany was a staunch anti-Communist who closely followed political developments in the international labor movement. The State Department gave Meany a substantial say in the selection of labor liaison officers in U.S. embassies abroad, and the AFL-CIO itself devoted one-quarter of its entire budget to its International Affairs Department.

After Fidel Castro came to power in Cuba, Meany and International Affairs Director Jay Lovestone [q.v.] turned increasing attention to the labor movements of Latin America. The keystone of this effort was the American Institute for Free Labor Development (AIFLD), whose declared purpose was to assist in the "development of free democratic trade union structures in Latin America." Established in the summer of 1961, AIFLD had representatives of business as well as labor and government on its board of directors. "While unions and management may quarrel over the terms of a contract," Meany declared to a business group in early 1962, "they should stand together in the great struggle of our time, the struggle that will determine the future and perhaps the survival of mankind."

AIFLD had close ties to the Agency for International Development and received almost 90% of its funding from it in the mid-1960s. AIFLD supplied funds to anti-Communist labor unions and operated a system of schools for trade union leaders in Latin America. In 1963 and 1964 Institute-trained labor leaders played a crucial role in the overthrow of the Cheddi Jagan regime in British Guiana and the Joao Goulart government in Brazil.

During the next decade Meany's virtually unchallenged control of the AFL-CIO assured that the American labor movement would continue as a strong supporter of the Vietnam war policies of Presidents Johnson and Richard M. Nixon [q.v.]. In 1968 Meany mobilized AFL-CIO efforts on behalf of Sen. Hubert Humphrey's (D, Minn.) [q.v.] presidential candidacy. Four years later he played an equally aggressive role in withholding the AFL-CIO's endorsement and resources from liberal anti-war Sen. George McGovern (D, S.D.) [q.v.] in his 1972 presidential campaign. [See JOHNSON, NIXON Volumes]

[NNL]

For further information:
Joseph C. Goulden, *Meany* (New York, 1972).
Ronald Radosh, *American Labor and United States Foreign Policy* (New York, 1969).

MERCHANT, LIVINGSTON T(ALLMADGE)

b. Nov. 23, 1903; New York, N.Y.
d. May 15, 1976; Washington, D.C.
Ambassador to Canada, April 1956-October 1958; February 1961-April 1962; Undersecretary of State for Political Affairs, October 1958-February 1961; Special Representative for Multilateral Force Negotiations, January-March 1963.

The descendant of a prominent colonial family, Livingston Merchant served as an investment counselor before becoming a State Department official specializing in European security affairs. From April 1956 to October 1958 he served as ambassador to Canada, leaving that post when appointed undersecretary of state for political affairs. [See EISENHOWER Volume] In February 1961 President Kennedy sent Merchant on his second tour of duty as ambassador to Canada, where he served until his retirement from the foreign service in April 1962.

In January 1963 Kennedy called Merchant out of retirement to become special representative for multilateral force negotiations. The idea of a North Atlantic Treaty Organization (NATO) Multilateral Nuclear Force (MLF) had first been aired publicly by Secretary of State Christian Herter in 1960 and then by President Kennedy in an Ottawa speech in May 1961. Although it was only vaguely developed, Kennedy made the plan one of the chief articles of the December 1962 Nassau accord between the U.S. and Great Britain. In a hastily improvised measure designed to bolster Prime Minister Harold Macmillan's domestic political position and soothe British indignation at American refusal to continue supporting Skybolt (a joint missile project), Kennedy offered Britain Polaris missiles in a NATO context. Under the agreement British submarines armed with missiles would be assigned to NATO until a multinational and multilateral force was developed. The proposal was also designed to further Kennedy's attempt to stop a French atomic buildup and forestall German demands for an independent nuclear deterrent.

Merchant outlined the MLF proposal to the NATO Permanent Council on Feb. 27, 1963. The plan envisioned the joint construction and operation of a fleet of 25 warships equipped with Polaris missiles and manned by mixed crews representing at least three participating nations with each crew containing an American contingent. All major participants would have a veto over the use of the missiles. Although agreeing to the measure in principle, European NATO representatives received the proposal without enthusiasm, insisting on first developing a multinational force.

In March Merchant was sent to Europe on a series of what were intended to be small, quiet meetings to explore backing for the proposal. Instead, the mission grew to 32 people traveling throughout Europe on what appeared to be a major diplomatic campaign. Although Kennedy intended to assert no pressure on the allies, Merchant's mission gave the appearance of coercion and turned many Europeans against the project. Even before the February NATO meeting, France had rejected the measure. In March Italy, in the middle of an election campaign, refused to commit itself. Greece and Turkey told Merchant they could not afford it; and, despite assurances to Merchant, Britain began backing away, unwilling to commit itself for financial, political and strategic reasons. Only West Germany gave its approval, but the prospect of a Washington-Bonn operation was unacceptable to the allies. As Merchant's mission continued, reporters labeled the plan the "multilateral farce."

At the end of March Merchant reported back to Kennedy and then resigned to head the Glen Falls Insurance Company. Negotiations on the MLF continued throughout the rest of 1963, both at the May ministerial meeting of the Atlantic Council in Ottawa and at a U.S.-German summit conference in June. At that meeting German Chancellor Konrad Adenauer, withdrawing full support of MLF, urged Kennedy to postpone further discussion of the proposal, and the plan was informally dropped. President Lyndon B. Johnson [q.v.] formally renounced the measure in December 1966.

From 1965 to 1968 Merchant served as American executive director of the International Bank for Reconstruction and Development.

[EWS]

MEREDITH, JAMES H(OWARD)
b. June 25, 1933; Kosciusko, Miss.
Civil rights activist.

Meredith grew up on a Mississippi farm and, after graduating from high school in 1951, spent nine years in the Air Force. He returned to Mississippi in August 1960 and enrolled that fall at all-black Jackson State College to complete the college studies he had begun while in the military. Sometime during the semester Meredith decided to try to enter the all-white University of Mississippi at Oxford, the state's best public college. In his account of this effort, *Three Years in Mississippi*, published in 1966, Meredith wrote that he believed he had a "divine responsibility," a "mission," to help "break the system of 'White Supremacy' " in Mississippi and direct "civilization toward a destiny of humaneness." He sent his application for admission to Oxford in January 1961, intiating a 17-month fight to desegregate the University of Mississippi.

After months of correspondence the University denied admission to Meredith in May 1961. With the aid of Constance Baker Motley [q.v.] and Jack Greenberg [q.v.], attorneys for the NAACP Legal Defense Fund, Meredith brought suit against University officials in federal district court, charging the denial was because of his race. Judge Sidney C. Mize turned down Meredith's request for a preliminary injunction in December 1961. After a trial on the merits, Mize ruled on Feb. 3, 1962 that the University was "not a racially segregated institution" and that Meredith had not been refused admission because of his race. The Fifth Circuit Court in New Orleans reversed this decision on June 25, ordering Meredith admitted to the school. U.S. District Judge Ben Cameron, sitting in Mississippi, stayed this order four times during the summer. The Fifth Circuit Court vacated three of the stays, and on Sept. 10, 1962, Supreme Court Justice Hugo Black [q.v.] nullified the fourth and ordered the University to admit Meredith.

Meredith wired the University's registrar on Sept. 11 that he would enroll on Sept. 20. On the night of Sept. 13, in a statewide television and radio address, Mississippi Gov. Ross Barnett [q.v.] promised to oppose Meredith's entrance to the University and began a series of state efforts to block implementation of the federal court orders. On Sept. 19 a Mississippi state court issued an injunction barring Meredith from the University. The same day the state legislature passed a law that no one convicted of a crime could attend a state university. The next day a justice of the peace in Jackson convicted Meredith in absentia on a charge of false voter registration and ordered him arrested. The U.S. Justice Department, which had formally entered Meredith's case on Sept. 18, got federal court orders on the 20th voiding the state court injunction and the conviction. Late that afternoon Meredith made his first attempt to register in Oxford and was met by Gov. Barnett, who had been appointed special registrar for Meredith by the University's board of trustees. Barnett read Meredith and accompanying federal officials a state proclamation refusing him admission to the University. The Justice Department then moved for contempt citations against the University's trustees and top officials. At a hearing before the Fifth Circuit Court on Sept. 24, the trustees agreed to enroll Meredith the next day. On the 25th the Fifth Circuit enjoined Barnett from blocking Meredith's admission, but when Meredith tried to register that day, this time at the trustees' office in Jackson, Barnett refused to accept copies of the Circuit Court's injunction and again denied Meredith admission to the University. The Justice Department applied to the Circuit Court for a contempt citation against Barnett.

While this action was pending Meredith made two more unsuccessful attempts to register in Oxford. A Sept. 26 try was blocked by Lt. Gov. Paul B. Johnson [q.v.], and the Justice Department called off another effort on Sept. 27 because of possible violence at the University.

The Fifth Circuit Court found Barnett guilty of civil contempt on Sept. 28 and directed him to comply with earlier court orders by Oct. 2 or be fined $10,000 a day. Behind the scenes the Justice Department had been negotiating with Barnett in an effort to find a peaceful and safe way to enroll Meredith. President Kennedy entered these negotiations on Sept. 29 with three phone calls to the Governor. Kennedy also federalized Mississippi's National Guard, ordered Army units to Memphis in case more forces were needed to protect Meredith and issued a proclamation to the government and people of Mississippi calling on them to cease all obstruction to the federal court orders.

Meredith flew from Memphis to Oxford on Sept. 30 and was taken to his dormitory room around 6 p.m. Barnett made a statement at 9 p.m., indicating that his resistance to Meredith's admission was over. That night a 24-man guard protected Meredith in his room, and 300 federal marshals and a force of Mississippi state troopers were on the University campus. President Kennedy addressed the nation on television at 10 p.m. and appealed to the University's students to preserve both the law and the peace. However, a riot on the campus had already erupted around 8 p.m. Before it was over early the next morning, Kennedy had called in both the National Guard and the Army. Two men died in the rioting; over 350 were injured. At 8 a.m. on Oct. 1, Meredith was escorted to the registrar's office by federal officials and finally enrolled. The crisis at "Ole Miss" posed the most serious state challenge to federal authority since the events in Little Rock in 1957. Although Kennedy regretted having to use troops, his actions upheld the supremacy of the federal courts and the Constitution over state power. They also represented a victory for the civil rights movement because the Kennedy Administration had acted decisively to protect the constitutional rights of a black citizen.

Throughout the crisis Meredith, a quiet and introspective person, had remained controlled and composed. Justice Department attorney John Doar [q.v.], who accompanied Meredith on four of his five registration attempts, said later that Meredith took everything "calmly and coolly." Meredith displayed the same quiet courage throughout the semester as he underwent harassment, threats and ostracism. He announced on Jan. 7, 1963 that he would not return for the spring semester at the University unless "very definite and positive changes" were made to make his situation more conducive to learning. On Jan. 30 Meredith said he had decided to enroll for a second term, and he registered the next day without incident. Protected throughout his months at the University by federal marshals, Meredith completed his studies during the summer term and graduated on Aug. 18, 1963 with a B.A. in political science.

Although Meredith was widely acclaimed for his entry into "Ole Miss," he was publicly rebuked for the views he expressed at the convention of the NAACP in Chicago in July 1963. Speaking at the organization's Youth Freedom Fund banquet, Meredith critized "the low quality and ineffectiveness of our Negro youth leaders" and reportedly told his audience that "anyone of you burr-heads out there" could be successful in business or politics "if you only believe."

The head of the NAACP's college division immediately attacked Meredith for these statements and won a standing ovation from the assembly.

Meredith left Mississippi following his graduation but returned in June 1966 for a march from Memphis, Tenn., to Jackson, Miss., to encourage voter registration among Mississippi's blacks. Meredith was shot from ambush on the second day of the march. While he recuperated civil rights leaders, including Martin Luther King [q.v.] and Stokely Carmichael, continued Meredith's march. Meredith rejoined them and marched with them into Jackson on June 26. [See JOHNSON Volume]

[CAB]

For further information:
Walter Lord, *The Past That Would Not Die* (New York, 1965).

METCALF, LEE
b. Jan. 28, 1911; Stevensville, Mont.
Democratic Senator, Mont., 1961- .

As the junior senator from the predominantly rural state of Montana, Lee Metcalf was often overshadowed by the state's Democratic senior senator, Mike Mansfield [q.v.], the Senate majority leader. Yet he earned a reputation in the upper house as a vigorous supporter of many social welfare and conservation measures and as a persistent critic of private utility companies. Prior to his election to the U.S. House in 1952, Metcalf had served as a state legislator and associate justice of the Montana Supreme Court. In the House of Representatives he was known as one of Congress's "young Turk" liberals who promoted domestic social legislation and reform of congressional procedures. In 1960 he was elected to the Senate. [See EISENHOWER Volume]

During the Kennedy Administration Metcalf was one of the President's five or six most consistent supporters, backing Administration measures over 80% of the time. In his first years in the Senate, Metcalf focused his attention on conservation issues and private utility company regulation. In 1962 he introduced a "save our streams"

bill designed to protect natural recreation facilities, fish and wildlife from destruction by federal highway building programs. The measure was never passed, but its major provision, requiring the Secretary of the Interior to satisfy himself that recreation resources had been considered in highway planning, was later introduced into the National Environmental Policy Act of 1970. Metcalf also supported the early Senate attempts to preserve wilderness areas, which resulted in the eventual passage of the Wilderness Act of 1964.

An opponent of private utility companies because he believed they overcharged consumers, Metcalf in 1963 unsuccessfully fought for the construction of a federal dam with commercial power production facilities for the southern Montana region.

During the late 1960s and early 1970s, Metcalf continued to be a strong supporter of conservation and consumer legislation as well as a backer of educational reform. In addition, he campaigned for reassertion of congressional authority over the budget as a way of curbing excessive presidential power. [See JOHNSON, NIXON Volumes]

[EWS]

MILLER, GEORGE P(AUL)
b. Jan. 15, 1891; San Francisco, Calif.
Democratic Representative, Calif., 1945-73; Chairman, Science and Astronautics Committee, 1961-73.

Initially elected to Congress in 1944, Miller represented California's eighth district, which included southern Oakland, several of the city's suburbs and part of rural Alameda county. Most of the district's voters belonged to white blue-collar families. In the 1940s and 1950s Miller compiled a moderately liberal voting record. He was interested in scientific matters and in the late 1950s was the chairman of the Merchant Marine and Fisheries Committee's Subcommittee on Oceanography.

During the presidency of John F. Kennedy, Miller generally backed Administration positions. According to *Congressional Quarterly* he supported the Administration on 82%, 75% and 83% of key House roll-call votes in 1961, 1962 and 1963, respectively. With the death of Rep. Overton Brooks (D, La.) in September 1961, Miller assumed the chairmanship of the Science and Astronautics Committee. He was an enthusiastic supporter of the space program. In a speech to the American Astronautical Society in January 1962, Miller defended the $20-billion race to the moon on the ground that its by-products would "have economic, social and defense values far in excess of the original cost." In the fall of 1963, when some congressmen criticized costly and recurring technical defects in the National Aeronautics and Space Administration's programs, Miller chided his colleagues for attacking "those things you do not understand." He contended that certain mistakes in the U.S. space effort had led to increased experience and knowledge in space technology.

During the Johnson and Nixon Administrations, Miller supported the Vietnam war and large military expenditures while continuing to back the space program. Disenchantment with the war, the military establishment and the space program increased among Democratic liberals during the late 1960s and early 1970s, and Miller lost the 1972 Democratic primary in his district to a candidate who articulated this trend. [See JOHNSON, NIXON Volumes]

[MLL]

MILLER, WILLIAM E(DWARD)
b. March 22, 1914; Lockport, N. Y.
Republican Representative, N.Y., 1951-65; Chairman, Republican National Committee, June 1961-July 1964.

A janitor's son and a Roman Catholic, William E. Miller received his B.A. from Notre Dame in 1935 and his law degree, with honors, from Union University Law School in 1938. After serving with Army intelligence during World War II, he was an assistant prosecutor for the United States at the Nuremberg war crimes trials in 1946. In November 1950 Miller won election to the first of seven consecutive terms in the House of Representatives.

Miller supported Rep. Charles A. Halleck (R, Ind.) [q.v.] for the House minority leadership in January 1959. In return, Halleck supported him for the chairmanship of the Republican Congressional Campaign Committee one year later. Miller campaigned in 34 states on behalf of GOP congressional candidates in 1960, and the Party gained 22 seats in November despite its loss of the White House. Many Party leaders credited Miller with the Party's House victories, and in June 1961 he became chairman of the Republican National Committee.

Miller quickly established himself as a frequent and sharp critic of the Kennedy Administration. Unlike many GOP leaders who advocated "bipartisanship" in international affairs, Miller attacked the President's foreign policy. On June 11, 1961 the Party chairman termed Kennedy's failure to provide airpower for the anti-Castro Bay of Pigs invasion "a most tragic mistake." In October 1961 Miller listed eight "constructive" GOP proposals for the improvement of Kennedy's foreign policy, which included the removal of Undersecretary of State Chester Bowles [q.v.] and United Nations Ambassador Adlai E. Stevenson [q.v.], whom Miller called "completely inept." Both men had called for greater efforts to ease East-West tensions. The New York Congressman termed State Department official W. Averell Harriman [q.v.] as the man who "loused up Laos" and called White House press secretary Pierre Salinger [q.v.] "the thinking man's filter." The President himself, Miller declared, was "the foundering father of the New Frontier." Stung by Miller's barbs, Kennedy urged Democratic National Committee Chairman John M. Bailey [q.v.] to take on Miller in what the President described in October 1961 as a politicians' "battle of the mimeograph."

Miller hoped to strengthen GOP organization and win control of the House for the party in the 1962 elections. Under his leadership, the National Committee eliminated a $750,000 debt from the 1960 campaign, but in November 1962 the GOP gained only six seats in the House while losing four in the Senate. The GOP captured governorships in several large industrial states, although the total number of Republican governors remained the same. Miller's own re-election proved surprisingly close, with the Party chairman winning only 52% of the total vote, his closest margin of victory in any campaign. Moderate and liberal Republicans criticized Miller for spending national committee funds on "Operation Dixie," which sought to establish a Republican Party presence in the South. In 1962 the GOP increased its House vote in the South to a level 244% above its 1958 total, but support from Southern blacks slipped drastically.

In Congress as in national politics, Miller was a partisan Republican. He voted against the Administration's school aid bill in April 1961 and its omnibus housing measure in June 1961. He attacked the Kennedy medicare program and favored a voluntary health insurance plan as an alternative to the Administration's bill. As the second ranking Republican on the Judiciary Committee, Miller co-sponsored the party leadership's 1963 civil rights bill introduced by Rep. John V. Lindsey (R, N.Y.) [q.v.]. However, Miller voted on only 49% of the House roll calls in 1963 and no major piece of legislation bore his name in the 14 years he spent in the House.

By early 1963 Gov. Nelson A. Rockefeller (R, N.Y.) [q.v.] had emerged as the clear leader in the race for the 1964 GOP presidential nomination. Although not part of Rockefeller's state organization, Miller hoped Party conservatives would reconcile themselves to a Rockefeller nomination, and in 1963 he urged conservative Sen. Barry M. Goldwater (R, Ariz.) [q.v.] to run as the Governor's running mate. While acknowledging that Goldwater might himself run for first place on the ticket, Miller suggested that "there are many areas of agreement between Rockefeller and Goldwater" which would make a joint ticket possible in 1964. Fearing adverse voter reaction, the Party chairman helped persuade Rockefeller not to remarry prior to the 1962 elections. Miller's political instincts later proved correct when the Governor's marriage to a 36-year-old divorcee in May 1963

severely weakened his presidential prospects. Miller declined to run for reelection to the House in 1964 and ran instead as the Republican candidate for vice president with Goldwater. [See JOHNSON Volume]

[JLB]

MILLS, C(HARLES) WRIGHT
b. Aug. 28, 1916; Waco, Tex.
d. March 20, 1962; Nyack, N.Y.
Sociologist.

Raised in Texas and educated at the University of Wisconsin, Mills emerged in the 1950s as a principal radical critic of postwar American society. His work influenced much of the social analysis made by the New Left in the early 1960s. After taking his Ph.D. in 1941, Mills taught at the University of Maryland and, after 1945, at Columbia, where he soon earned a reputation as an iconoclastic and combative lecturer and writer who rebelled against the conservative mood in postwar academic circles.

Drawing upon the methodology of Karl Marx and Max Weber, Mills sought to identify the changing sources of political power in America in order to trace a strategy for its radical transformation. His *New Men of Power* (1948) emphasized the strategic position that leaders of the organized working class had achieved in the social structure, while his *White Collar* (1951) explored the powerlessness and "false consciousness" of the new middle class. In his most controversial book, *The Power Elite* (1956), Mills argued that America was ruled by a small group of men joined by family, education and class interest.

His analysis of this interconnected military-governmental-corporate elite challenged the dominant view of other contemporary social scientists who emphasized the pluralistic character of American politics. In the next few years Mills waged an increasingly bitter intellectual contest against those he described as "smug conservatives, tired liberals and disillusioned radicals" who, he charged, had reached a comfortable accommodation with the status quo in the West.

In the late 1950s and early 1960s, Mills wrote a series of popular and polemical books in which he argued his political point of view with new urgency and broke entirely with the methods of academic sociology. His *Sociological Imagination* (1959) ridiculed the assumptions of value-free social science, while his *Causes of World War III* (1958) bitterly indicted the ruling elite for taking the world to the brink of nuclear disaster. *Listen, Yankee!* (1960), published after a trip to Cuba, was a spirited defense of the revolution there and did much to generate enthusiasm for the new regime among the student left in the United States.

By the early 1960s Mills had abandoned his earlier view that the industrial working class had the potential to transform society. Agreeing with more conservative thinkers who held that postwar U.S. capitalism was a relatively stable system, Mills argued that the working class had become a basically conservative force, hostile to both revolution and radical reforms. He rejected the traditional Marxist conception of the working class as romanticism; in its place he sought another "possible, immediate, radical agency of change." Writing a 1960 "Letter to the New Left," Mills linked the recent student rebellions in Turkey and Korea with the Cuban revolution and the student sit-in movement in the American South. "Who is it that is thinking and acting in radical ways?" he asked. "All over the world . . . the answer's the same: it is the young intelligentsia."

Mills died of a heart attack in March 1962. Despite his premature death, historians of the American left have stressed his influence on the development of the New Left and the radicalism of the 1960s. In a sympathetic critique of the sociologist's work, historian Peter Clecak wrote that "Mills almost single-handedly reopened the debate over the sources and distribution of power in America." Tom Hayden relied heavily upon Mills's analysis of American society when he drafted the Students for a Democratic Society's (SDS) Port Huron Statement in the spring of 1962. Three years later Jack Newfield reported that, along with Albert Camus, Mills was the author whose works were most widely known by SDS members.

[NNL]

For further information:
Peter Clecak, *Radical Paradoxes, Dilemmas of the American Left: 1945-1970* (New York, 1973).
G. William Domhoff and Hoyt B. Ballard, eds., *C. Wright Mills and the Power Elite* (Boston, 1968).

MILLS, WILBUR D(AIGH)
b. May 24, 1909; Kensett, Ark.
Democratic Representative, Ark., 1939-   ; Chairman, Ways and Means Committee, 1957-74.

Wilbur Mills was one of the most powerful men in Congress. As the respected chairman of the most important committee in the House, handling legislation relating to taxes, social security and foreign trade, Mills stood in the path of the Kennedy Administration's economic program. Whether shaping or obstructing Administration measures, he left a major imprint on the economic legislation of the 1960s.

The son of a country banker, Mills attended Arkansas public schools and Methodist-affiliated Hendrix College before moving on to the Harvard Law School. He returned to Arkansas after receiving his degree in 1933, taking a job as a cashier in his father's bank because of the Depression. In 1934 he was elected county and probate judge for White County, where he served until his election to the House of Representatives in 1938. Mills was reelected in every subsequent election with little or no opposition.

Joining the tax-writing Ways and Means Committee in 1943, Mills industriously applied himself to his committee labors, becoming by the 1950s the House's foremost tax expert. He compiled a moderate voting record overall and joined his Southern colleagues in voting against all civil rights proposals. In late 1957 Mills became chairman of the Ways and Means Committee. [See TRUMAN, EISENHOWER Volumes]

The peculiar structure of the Ways and Means Committee and the Committee's prestige and unique prerogatives within the House enabled Mills to exert extraordinary influence on the writing of tax laws. The Ways and Means Committee also functioned as the Committee on Committees, doling out committee assignments to all the members of the House, with Mills at the center of this crucial process. The fact that Ways and Means, alone among House committees, had no subcommittees further centralized power in Mills's hands. Bills emerging from the Ways and Means Committee, moreover, operated on the House floor under a "closed rule," meaning that no amendments were permitted, only total approval or flat rejection.

The result was almost always approval, in part because of Mills's mystique. No congressman could match his vast knowledge of the tax laws. Most stood in awe of his mastery of the complex subject matter, and many owed their grasp of complicated bills to Mills's lucid explanations, which at times brought members of both parties to their feet in applause. Equally important to Mills's success on the floor of the House was his consensus-seeking approach in the Committee. He refused to report out controversial measures by narrow majorities, preferring to delay and excise or water down controversial features until he had attained unanimity or a large majority. By compromising in the Committee, he managed to forestall potential opposition in the House. Consistently smooth passage of measures introduced by Mills enhanced his aura of power. Conversely, his fear that a defeat on the floor would diminish that aura often led him to pursue a strategy of delay on important legislation until he felt assured of a safe majority in the House.

During the Kennedy Administration Mills held a pivotal position in the enactment of the Administration's economic program. Fearing Mills's great power, Kennedy strategists delayed submitting important proposals to the House until they conformed to Mills's standards of political moderation. (Mills backed major bills endorsed by the liberal Americans for Democratic Action 59% of the time during the Kennedy years.) Once a measure had won his support he was a powerful ally, but his opposition could be deadly. In a joking tribute to Mills's influence, President Kennedy in October 1963 referred to a story in the *New York Times* suggesting that the President, while dedicating an Arkansas dam, would sing "Down by the Old Mill Stream" or any other tune requested by Wilbur Mills. "I would be delighted," Kennedy said, but Mills had not asked him to.

In April 1961 Mills introduced the Administration's bill to increase Social Security benefits and lower the retirement age from 65 to 62, but the Ways and Means Committee raised both benefits and the payroll tax less than the Administration desired. The measure passed the House without amendment, 400-14. Mills was the floor manager in March 1962 for Administration welfare measures that made far-reaching changes in the federal-state public assistance and child welfare programs. The bill, which increased welfare benefits and enlarged the federal government's role, passed the House, 320-69.

Mills subjected Kennedy's tax proposals to lengthy deliberations. Presented to Congress in April 1961, Kennedy's initial tax revision bill was not reported out of the Ways and Means Committee until March 1962. The Committee's version contained the Administration's key provisions in modified form: a 7% investment tax credit designed to spur investment in plant and equipment (the credit was reduced and narrowed by the Committee), disallowance of various expense-account deductions by businessmen and the withholding of taxes on interest and dividend income.

As the floor manager of the omnibus tax bill, Mills defended the withholding reform to halt the "vast leakage" of some $850 million in tax revenue through failure to report such income. The tax measure passed the House, 219-196, after vigorous debate. In the summer the Senate eliminated the withholding provision and diluted the expense account reforms but approved the key provision, the investment tax credit. The Senate also passed the self-employed retirement income plan, or "Keogh Plan," which allowed self-employed persons to set up tax-sheltered retirement plans. This bill had previously passed the Ways and Means Committee over Mills's opposition, demonstrating that the chairman, however dominant, was not invincible.

Mills also guided through the House the centerpiece of the Administration's 1962 legislative program, the Trade Expansion Act. He managed to preserve all the major provisions requested by the President through a nine-month congressional struggle. The House finally passed the bill, 256-91, in October. The new law authorized the President to cut tariffs in order to stimulate the nation's foreign trade.

Mills succeeded in blocking the Kennedy Administration's medicare plan to provide medical care for the aged financed through the Social Security system. Medicare was intended to replace the existing system of federal matching grants to the states for such care, the so-called Kerr-Mills Plan of which Mills had been the co-author. Mills doubted the fiscal prudence of medicare, but his basic objection was less principled than practical: he felt that the measure would not pass the House. With characteristic caution he resisted reporting the proposal out of his Committee even if a slim majority could be obtained. He did not wish to be the swing vote on the Committee, thus drawing the wrath of the medical establishment upon himself. After the 1964 elections returned pro-medicare majorities to the Ways and Means Committee and the House, Mills shifted to support of the program in 1965 and became the prime House architect of the final legislation.

Mills followed a similar course on Kennedy's 1963 tax cut, opposing the measure until he felt Congress was ready and until his own conservative fiscal views were sufficiently appeased by Administration concessions, then shaping the legislation and steering it through the House. His opposition figured prominently in President Kennedy's decision not to push for a massive tax cut in 1962. Instead, Kennedy assiduously cultivated Mills's support for a sizeable cut to stimulate the economy in 1963. Mills agreed to back the proposal when it was combined with revenue-raising tax reforms and a pledge to limit federal spending. In December 1962 Kennedy said the Administration intended to follow Mills's suggestion to link tax reduction with "increased control of the rise in expenditures."

In public Mills declared that tax reform was his main goal in backing the tax cut. "The function of taxation," he told the House, "is to raise revenue. . . . I do not go along with economists who think of taxation as an instrument for manipulating the economy." The Administration's tax package presented to the Committee in early 1963 contained several significant reform provisions designed to narrow loopholes available to wealthy individuals. After the customary exhaustive study and prolonged deliberation by the Ways and Means Committee through much of 1963, the Committee reported out in August an $11 billion tax cut bill almost entirely sheared of its reform elements. The Administration and Mills agreed to sacrifice the reforms to win approval of the reduction. Declaring the cut "fiscally responsible," Mills presented the Administration's position in the House and used his influence to persuade Southern Democrats not to support a Republican motion to send the bill back to Committee. The Republican motion to recommit failed by a 226-199 vote on Sept. 24, and the measure was adopted.

Despite his public avowal of tax reform and his periodic endorsement of sweeping revision of the tax code and elimination of tax preferences, Mills never accomplished major tax reform during his tenure as chairman. With his overall political outlook growing more conservative during the Johnson Administration, his habit of extended study and his search for consensus served to smother tax reform possibilities within the Ways and Means Committee. Mills maintained his formidable influence throughout the Johnson years and played a key role in delaying, shaping and passing major Administration programs.

Mills resigned as chairman of the Ways and Means Committee in December 1974 after a highly publicized incident in which he was linked with an Argentine stripper and then hospitalized for alcoholism and exhaustion. [See JOHNSON, NIXON Volumes]

[TO]

For further information:
John F. Manley, *The Politics of Finance: The House Ways and Means Committee* (Boston, 1970).

MINOW, NEWTON N(ORMAN)
b. Jan. 17, 1926; Milwaukee, Wisc.
Chairman, Federal Communications Commission, March 1961-June 1963.

After serving in the Army Signal Corps in World War II, Newton N. Minow took a law degree from Northwestern University, where he graduated first in his class. He then clerked for Chief Justice Fred Vinson. In 1955 he joined the Chicago law firm of Adlai E. Stevenson [*q.v.*] and assisted his senior partner in his 1956 presidential campaign. Minow's work for the Kennedy-Johnson ticket in Illinois during the 1960 election won high praise from R. Sargent Shriver [*q.v.*], the President's brother-in-law. In January 1961 Kennedy designated Minow, then 34, to serve as chairman of the Federal Communications Commission (FCC).

Minow assumed the FCC chairmanship at a time when the agency responsible for the regulation of radio and television appeared to have scant impact on the industries subject to its supervision. In a strongly worded address to the National Association of Broadcasters in May 1961, Minow surprised his audience by condemning television as a "vast wasteland" of Western badmen, private eyes, cartoons, and "endless commercials." He accused broadcasters of an excessive dependence upon TV program ratings which "don't tell us what the public might watch if they were offered half a dozen additional choices." To achieve better television, Minow promised that the FCC would take its station-licensing power far more seriously.

The "vast wasteland" address provoked an angry response from both the television industry and many anti-Administration congressmen. In June 1961 the House re-jected the section of the President's proposed reorganization plan for the FCC, endorsed by Minow, which increased the chairman's powers in delegating authority. House speaker Sam Rayburn (D, Tex.) [*q.v.*] opposed strengthening the powers of the chairman, and Rep. William H. Avery (R, Kan.) claimed this provision would create "a one-man Commission in the chairman" and allow the President to "dominate" the FCC through a "czar."

Despite the House defeat, Minow persisted in his attempts to improve the quality of television. Kennedy repeatedly praised Minow's verbal blasts at television programming as "one of the really important things" being done on the New Frontier. Beginning in June 1961 the FCC tightened its television station license-renewal standards to take into account the station's community affairs programming. In the next two years Minow's agency revoked 14 licenses and renewed 26 others on a short-term basis.

The FCC chairman consistently voiced concern over the quality of children's TV, and in September 1961 he announced that the Antitrust Division of the Justice Department would permit the three national networks to work together to provide one daily educational children's program. Each network, however, eventually introduced its own "quality" children's program. Minow and the FCC encouraged the establishment of adult educational television stations, and in 1961 he took a personal hand in securing one for New York City. Congress voted the first funds for construction of educational TV facilities in April 1962.

Minow favored greater station competition in each community as a spur to program quality. In January 1962 he warned that TV faced either "more competition or more regulation," and he suggested that greater use of the ultra-high-frequency (UHF) channels represented the "least painful" means of upgrading industry quality. Minow told Congress in March 1962 that the additional UHF channels (14 through 83) would create "a television system which will serve all the people, encourage local outlets, foster competition—

particularly in the larger markets—and meet educational needs." The three national networks joined Minow and endorsed a bill that compelled TV manufacturers to place UHF receivers on all sets. Congress passed the UHF law in June 1962. Minow optimistically predicted in September that "UHF will change the face and voice of television in the present decade."

The FCC also attempted to stabilize the financially volatile condition of the AM radio industry. In 1960 over one-third of all AM stations reported a loss while another 30% each earned less than $5,000. Minow thought that the sale of failing stations had created "jungle markets over-populated by quick-buck operators." Beginning in April 1962 the FCC placed severe restrictions on the sale of new AM licenses. In September 1962 the FCC set new FM radio standards designed "to ease the crowding in AM" and make FM stereo "a fine new service."

Beyond his chiding industry management, Minow felt by the spring of 1963 that only increasing the FCC's power could realize his major goal of vitalizing the TV "wasteland." In April 1963 the FCC head proposed that Congress enact legislation to establish financial penalties for the "over-commercialization" of radio and TV by setting limits on advertisements. He also recommended that Congress reorganize the FCC's functions. In a letter to Kennedy in May 1963, Minow called for the formation of an administrative court within the FCC for daily operations and the appointment of a single administrator who "would not be hamstrung by such wide splits among agency members." Congress failed to act on either of his recommendations, and Minow resigned from the FCC on June 1, 1963 to become executive vice president and general counsel of *Encyclopedia Britannica.*

Minow's impact on the quality of television proved limited. TV failed to change substantially during the 1960s despite the advance of UHF stations and the expansion of educational TV. But his successor, E. William Henry, commented in June 1963 that when Minow had assumed office two years before "complacent and self-satisfied" industry leaders "needed a real shock." Minow, Henry observed, "did very well in

giving them that shock." Minow left *Encyclopedia Britannica* in 1965 to resume the practice of law in Chicago.

[JLB]

For further information:
Eric Barnouw, *The Image Empire* (New York, 1970), Vol. III.
Newton N. Minow, *Equal Time* (New York, 1965).

MITCHELL, CLARENCE M.
b. March 8, 1911; Baltimore, Md.
Director, Washington Bureau, NAACP, 1950-   .

Mitchell, a black lawyer, served on the Fair Employment Practices Committee and the War Manpower Commission during World War II. Immediately after the war he was appointed to head the newly created labor department of the NAACP and in 1950 became the director of the NAACP's Washington bureau. His major function in that post was to serve as the organization's lobbyist for civil rights measures in the legislative and executive branches of the federal government.

The NAACP and other civil rights groups were dissatisfied with the Kennedy Administration's failure to introduce significant civil rights legislation during the early 1960s. In July 1961 Mitchell denounced the President for ignoring the civil rights pledges of the 1960 Democratic national platform, and he repeated his criticism at the NAACP's annual membership meeting in January 1962. The only difference between the Democratic and Republican Parties in the area of civil rights, he charged at the meeting, was that "the Democrats have more Negroes who can explain why we don't need such rights."

In November 1962 the President issued an executive order barring discrimination in federally aided housing. But the following April Mitchell charged that the order was not being enforced, and he placed the blame on the President himself, asserting, "The tempo is always taken by the President. . . . I have been in Washington a long time, and I know this is true under any Administration, under any program. If the President wants it to move, it will move."

Meanwhile, in 1962 and early 1963 Mitchell, who met frequently with liberal congressmen and senators to map civil rights strategy, appeared before the House Education and Labor Committee and other congressional panels in support of measures to combat racial discrimination. His proposals included anti-bias riders added to federal school-aid bills and a national fair employment practices law. However, the Administration did not support these proposals, and they were not passed by Congress.

Southern civil rights protests in the early 1960s and the violent white reaction to them enlarged the national constituency for anti-discrimination laws, and in June 1963 President Kennedy sent a civil rights bill to Congress. The major sections of the bill provided for the desegregation of public accommodations, the withholding of federal aid from all programs and activities in which racial discrimination was practiced and federal initiation of public school desegregation suits.

A House Judiciary Committee subcommittee strengthened the bill, but the Administration felt that the added provisions would deprive the measure of the Republican votes needed for passage. In October 1963 Attorney General Robert F. Kennedy [q.v.] urged the subcommittee to delete sections that expanded the President's definition of public accommodations and that permitted the Justice Department to seek injunctions against local police authorities that employed violent tactics against civil rights demonstrators.

Mitchell asserted, as he had on earlier occasions, that the difficulty in securing passage of effective civil rights laws was not a lack of support for such measures but the unwillingness of President Kennedy to vigorously press for them. He denounced the Attorney General's suggestions and said, "There is no reason for this kind of sellout. . . . The Administration should be in there fighting for the subcommittee bill."

On the whole, Mitchell was pleased with President Johnson's successful efforts on behalf of civil rights legislation in the areas of public accommodations, voting rights and housing discrimination. He frequently defended the Administration's antipoverty program against Republican attacks. However, Mitchell denounced the Nixon Administration for what he regarded as its efforts to turn back the tide of civil rights progress in order to win Southern segregationist votes. [See JOHNSON, NIXON Volumes]

[MLL]

MONRONEY, A(LMER) S(TILLWELL) MIKE
b. March 2, 1902; Oklahoma City, Okla.
Democratic Senator, Okla., 1951-69.

Mike Monroney, an effective advocate of aviation interests on Capitol Hill, was born into a pioneer Oklahoma family. Following his graduation from the University of Oklahoma in 1924, he became a political reporter for the *Oklahoma News* before taking over the family furniture business. In 1938 Monroney was elected to the House of Representatives and served there until he became a senator in 1951.

During the 1940s Monroney gained a reputation as a congressional reformer, sponsoring legislation to eliminate the filibuster, modify the seniority rules and limit the power of the House Rules Committee. While in the House he was a supporter of most New Deal and Fair Deal legislation and as a senator continued to back most progressive legislation during the Eisenhower and Kennedy Administrations. In 1963 he was one of President Kennedy's most consistent supporters in the upper house. [See TRUMAN, EISENHOWER Volumes]

As chairman of the Senate Commerce Committee's Aviation Subcommittee, Monroney worked to aid the industry, which played an important part in the Oklahoma economy. In 1961 he supported the Kennedy Administration's reorganization of the Civil Aeronautics Board, which was designed to make it more efficient in dealing with vital industry problems.

The following year Monroney voted against a bill that eliminated transportation taxes on bus and train fares but only lowered those on airlines. The measure also contained a provision that would have financially hurt the airlines by stipulating that the elimination take place several months before the reduction. Although unable to prevent the bill's passage, Monroney was able to force the required rate changes to take place simultaneously. The same year he sponsored amendments to the Supplemental Airlines Act, which placed strict regulations on those carriers.

In 1963 Monroney's subcommittee held hearings on the need for congressional funding of a supersonic transport (SST) program. The probe led to the adoption of a bill providing $60 million for the plane. Throughout the Kennedy Administration he also worked for funds to improve airports and increase aviation safety.

Monroney remained in the Senate during the Johnson years and continued his fight for congressional reform. Although an effective politician who had obtained large amounts of federal funds for Oklahoma, Monroney lost touch with his constituents and was defeated for reelection in 1968. [See JOHNSON Volume]

[EWS]

MORALES CARRION, ARTURO
b. Nov. 16, 1913; Havana, Cuba.
Deputy Assistant Secretary of State for Inter-American Affairs, February 1961-January 1964.

Morales Carrion, an historian who received his Ph.D. from Columbia University in 1950, was a resident of Puerto Rico. He worked for the U.S. State Department during World War II and during the 1950s was part of Puerto Rican Gov. Luis Munoz Marin's [q.v.] inner circle as the Commonwealth's undersecretary of state.

John F. Kennedy solicited the advice of Munoz in his efforts to redirect U.S. Latin American policy. The Munoz government offered Washington a pool of talented officials who could effectively represent the U.S. to the Latin nations and better sympathize with Latin problems than citizens from the mainland. The Kennedy Adminis-

tration also wanted to use Puerto Rico, which had successfully combined liberal democracy and economic development, as a model alternative to Communism for the rest of Latin America.

Soon after his election Kennedy asked two members of the Munoz staff, Morales Carrion and Teodoro Moscoso [q.v.], to join a Latin American task force under Adolf A. Berle, Jr. [q.v.]. The result of their deliberations was the Alliance for Progress, the Kennedy program to achieve long-range economic development and political democracy in Latin America. Morales Carrion, along with Berle and Moscoso, emphasized the need to support the democratic left in Latin America and oppose all forms of dictatorship. He advocated close U.S. ties with the reformist democratic governments of Colombia and Venezuela, with whose leaders he maintained personal friendships.

In February 1961 Morales Carrion was named deputy assistant secretary of state for inter-American affairs. He was expected to concentrate on cultural affairs and take occasional political assignments. During Morales Carrion's tenure the Latin American view of the United States, particularly among the intellectuals, greatly improved, and Kennedy attained considerable personal popularity throughout the hemisphere. Morales Carrion strongly encouraged Kennedy to make a Latin American goodwill tour in December 1961. Despite some misgivings from the State Department, the trip proved a great success.

In August 1961 Morales Carrion was a member of the U.S. delegation at the Inter-American Economic and Social Council conference in Punta del Este, Uruguay. Historian Arthur Schlesinger, Jr. [q.v.], who was also a member of the delegation, credited Morales Carrion and Lincoln Gordon [q.v.] with rounding up the votes necessary to win hemisphere approval of the Alliance for Progress.

In November 1961 Morales Carrion was sent to the Dominican Republic to settle the chaotic political situation that followed the overthrow of longtime dictator Rafael Trujillo. Morales Carrion was personally opposed to the incumbent government of

Joaquin Balaguer and supported what Schlesinger termed "the democratic opposition," but he worked to convince Balaguer to form a coalition government acceptable to all factions to undertake political democratization. President Kennedy's personal intervention in December finally broke the deadlock, and Balaguer agreed to form a council of state which held democratic elections the following year.

Until 1964 Morales Carrion remained in the State Department, where some reporters, such as Tad Szulc of the *New York Times*, thought that his skills were underutilized. He later worked for both the Organization of American States and the Pan American Union in Washington.

[ICH]

MORGAN, HOWARD V.

b. 1914; Tillamook, Ore.
Commissioner, Federal Power Commission, June 1961-June 1963.

Prior to 1961 Howard Morgan had spent most of his adult life in the field of transportation and public utility regulation, building a reputation as an advocate of public power systems. He served as Oregon's public utility commissioner and state chairman of the Democratic Party before his nomination by President Kennedy to the Federal Power Commission (FPC) in January 1961. Morgan's failure to list two minor arrests in 1936 and 1937 on his federal employment forms sparked a controversy during Senate Commerce Committee hearings on his nomination in May. With an undercurrent of hostility to his public power views beneath the bitter partisan debate over this omission, the Senate confirmed Morgan in June by a 57-27 vote.

In his two years on the FPC, Morgan emerged as a maverick opposed to many of the Commission majority's decisions. His most prominent act as commissioner was his resignation, announced in January 1963 in a highly publicized letter to President Kennedy. Implying that his fellow commissioners were dominated by the private utilities, Morgan asked the President not to reappoint him when his term expired in

June. Utility regulation, Morgan said, "can easily become a fraud upon the public and a protective shield behind which monopoly may operate to the public detriment," especially since the agency was manned by "ordinary men" who "yield too quickly to the present-day urge toward conformity, timidity and personal security."

Morgan's charges were disputed by FPC Chairman Joseph Swidler [q.v.], who called himself "a consumer's man second to none." Before a special House investigative subcommittee in March, Morgan attempted to buttress his general accusations with specific instances. As an example of what he described as the Commission's attitude that "we mustn't investigate because we would disturb industry," Morgan cited the FPC's approval of the Idaho Power Company's request to construct a dam on the Snake River. Morgan had dissented from the majority's decision, arguing that the power produced would be surplus and that the FPC should investigate the company's solvency. Morgan added that the FPC commissioners had become "captives of the staff who are captives of the chairman who in turn is a captive of the White House." Subcommittee Republicans attacked Morgan's stand while Democrats John E. Moss (D, Calif.) [q.v.] and Oren Harris (D, Ark.) [q.v.] defended the commissioner.

Returning to Oregon after his FPC term ended, Morgan ran on an anti-war platform in Oregon's Democratic senatorial primary in May 1966 but was defeated by Rep. Robert Duncan (D, Ore.), a supporter of the war.

[TO]

MORGAN, THOMAS E(LLSWORTH)

b. Oct. 13, 1906; Ellsworth, Pa.
Democratic Representative, Pa., 1945- ; Chairman, Committee on Foreign Affairs, 1958- .

A practicing physician, "Doc" Morgan grew up in the depressed coal-mining districts of southwestern Pennsylvania. His father was an organizer for the United Mine Workers. Following medical studies and an internship in Detroit, young Morgan became involved in Democratic politics. By 1939 he had assumed the leadership of the local Democratic organization in the Fredericktown, Pa., area and in 1944 was selected to run for Congress. Since his district was overwhelmingly Democratic, Morgan never faced serious opposition in subsequent general elections. He consistently voted with his party and was an especially vigorous advocate of measures that were supported by organized labor. In 1958 Morgan became chairman of the House Foreign Affairs Committee. [See EISENHOWER Volume]

Described as an "organization man" by the *New York Times*, Morgan was chiefly concerned with winning congressional approval for the Administration's foreign policy program in the early 1960s. Morgan, who was said not to have an enemy in either party, was a successful champion of a bipartisan foreign policy. Despite substantial cuts in each of Kennedy's foreign aid packages, Morgan was able to win approval for some controversial proposals, including the Administration's 1961 long-term development loan fund request. The following year Morgan helped preserve President Kennedy's foreign policy flexibility by successfully proposing an amendment to a foreign aid measure that maintained the President's discretionary authority to make assistance available to any one of 18 Communist nations if he thought it "vital" to U.S. security.

Morgan voted for bills backed by the White House on more than 85% of key House rollcall votes during the years of the Kennedy Administration. He also earned one of the highest voting participation records in Congress.

Morgan supported without qualification the Vietnam war policies of President Lyndon Johnson [q.v.] during the late 1960s. As a consequence he was often compared unfavorably with his Senate counterpart, Sen. J. William Fulbright (D, Ark.) [q.v.], whose Senate Foreign Relations Committee undertook critical investigations of the war. [See JOHNSON, NIXON Volumes]

[JCH]

MORRISON, DeLESSEPS S(TORY)

b. Jan. 18, 1912; New Roads, La.
d. May 22, 1964; Ciudad Victoria, Mexico.
Ambassador to the Organization of American States, June 1961-September 1963.

A descendant of Ferdinand deLesseps, builder of the Suez Canal, and the son of Jacob Haight Morrison, a district attorney and political leader in Louisiana's Pointe Coupee Parish (County), DeLesseps Morrison earned an LL.B. from Lousiana State University in 1934. Beginning in 1936 he became involved in "good government" groups in New Orleans opposed to the Louisiana political machine of Huey Long. After distinguished service in the Army during World War II, Morrison returned to New Orleans politics. He became the city's "boy mayor" in 1946 when he swept an entrenched regime from City Hall in an upset victory. Heading a reform administration, Morrison improved both the image and the economy of New Orleans and was elected to four terms as mayor. [See TRUMAN, EISENHOWER Volumes]

During his tenure as mayor Morrison expanded the port facilities of New Orleans in an effort to attract trade with Latin America. Because his projects diverted a substantial portion of U.S.-Latin American trade away from other U.S. ports, Morrison campaigned for a total increase in overall trade. He met personally with Latin American political leaders and was one of the few American politicians publicly friendly with Argentina's Juan Peron and the Dominican Republic's Rafael Trujillo. Because of both his Latin American contacts and his reputation as a reformer, Kennedy appointed Morrison ambassador to the Organization of American States (OAS) in June 1961.

Morrison surprised many observers by taking a more conservative position on foreign policy issues than many of the Administration's other Latin American advisers. Before the OAS meeting in Punta del Este, Uruguay in January 1962, Morrison, along with Sen. Bourke Hickenlooper (R, Iowa) [q.v.] and Rep. Armistead Selden (D, Ala.), urged the U.S. to seek immediate diplomatic and economic sanctions against Cuba even if such important Latin American nations as Brazil, Mexico and Argentina refused to go along. A more cautious strategy, recommended by Dean Rusk [q.v.], Richard Goodwin [q.v.] and Arthur Schlesinger, Jr. [q.v.], succeeded in getting the votes of the big states on policy resolutions that excluded Cuba from the hemispheric community and initiated steps to combat Cuban subversion.

In March 1962 Morrison, Hickenlooper and Sen. Wayne Morse (D, Ore.)] q.v.] convinced Kennedy not to condemn the Argentine military's overthrow of President Arturo Frondizi's constitutional government. This action stymied the efforts of Assistant Secretary of State for Inter-American Affairs Edwin Martin [q.v.] to pursue a policy of consistent opposition to all military coups.

Morrison resigned his ambassadorship in September 1963 in order to make his third attempt to win the Louisiana Democratic gubernatorial nomination. In the December primary Morrison ran first, but he lost to Long family protege John J. McKeithen in the January runoff election. As in the past, Morrison, a Catholic and an urbanite with a reputation as a racial moderate, ran poorly among rural white Protestants in the northern part of the state.

Morrison died when his chartered plane crashed in dense fog 27 miles from Ciudad Victoria, Mexico on May 22, 1964.

[JCH]

For further information:
DeLesseps S. Morrison, *Latin American Mission: An Adventure in Hemisphere Diplomacy*, ed. by Gerald Frank (New York, 1965).

MORSE, WAYNE (LYMAN)
b. Oct. 20, 1900; Madison, Wisc.
d. July 22, 1974; Portland, Ore.
Republican Senator, Ore., 1945-52;
Independent Senator, Ore., 1952-55;
Democratic Senator, Ore., 1955-69.

Morse majored in labor economics at the University of Wisconsin, graduating in 1923. From 1924 to 1928 he was an assistant professor of argumentation at the University of Minnesota, and he received his law degree there in 1928. In 1929 Morse became an assistant professor of law at the University of Oregon. Two years later he was appointed dean of the University's law school.

During the 1930s Morse served as an arbitrator in West Coast labor disputes, and by 1940 he was one of the nation's most prominent labor relations experts. In January 1942 he was appointed a public member of the National War Labor Board. Although Morse was a liberal who sympathized with the interests of labor, he resigned from the panel two years later in protest against what he regarded as unwarranted concessions to John L. Lewis's United Mine Workers.

Later in the year Morse defeated the incumbent U.S. senator in Oregon's Republican primary and went on to defeat his Democratic opponent. In the Senate he was a contentious and fiercely independent liberal who often refused to modify strongly held views for the sake of legislative compromise. Morse's opponents, while acknowledging his intelligence and legal expertise, regarded him as a rigid, humorless egotist, and he alienated many senators by what they felt was his self-righteous and scornful attitude towards those who disagreed with him. His propensity for antagonizing his colleagues barred him from playing a major leadership role in the Senate. But Morse's admirers saw him as a fearless maverick who placed principle over expediency and who served as a watchdog against injustice.

Morse was an early backer of Dwight D. Eisenhower for the 1952 Republican presidential nomination. But he abandoned his support of Eisenhower when the Party's National Convention adopted what he considered a "reactionary" platform. In October 1952 he resigned from the Republican Party and became an independent. A persistent critic of the Eisenhower Administration, in April 1953 he led a liberal filibuster against a bill giving the states title to offshore oil. The following year he denounced President Eisenhower's peacetime atomic energy bill as a "give-away to big business" and again directed a filibuster. Early in 1955 Morse joined the Democratic

Party, giving it the decisive vote needed to organize the Senate.

Morse was a strong believer in the settlement of international disputes through multilateral cooperation and a system of world law. In 1946 he successfully pressed for American participation in the World Court. In the 1950s he criticized Secretary of State John Foster Dulles for bypassing the United Nations in his diplomatic efforts.

A supporter of civil rights measures, Morse, as a member of the District of Columbia Committee, was the chief Senate proponent of home rule for the nation's capital, whose population in the 1950s was approximately 50% black. He voted against the 1957 civil rights bill on the grounds that it was too weak. [See TRUMAN, EISENHOWER Volumes]

In December 1959 Morse announced he would seek the Democratic presidential nomination. He attacked Sens. John F. Kennedy, Hubert H. Humphrey (D, Minn.) [q.v.] and other presidential aspirants in his party as "phony liberals." Morse's criticism of Kennedy focused upon the latter's role in the formulation of the 1959 Landrum-Griffin labor bill, which was the legislative response to Sen. John J. McClellan's (D, Ark.) [q.v.] investigation of union corruption. Morse denounced the bill as imposing excessive restrictions upon the activity and power of the labor movement. His presidential effort collapsed after he suffered successive primary defeats in the District of Columbia, Maryland and his home state.

Under the Kennedy Administration the White House was occupied for the first time by a president who belonged to the same party as Morse, who was then chairman of the Labor and Public Welfare Committee's Education Subcommittee and of the Foreign Relations Committee's American Republics Affairs Subcommittee. Political observers wondered whether Morse would abandon his role as a loner in the Senate and promote Administration legislation or continue to act as a dissenter. In practice he did both, serving as a pragmatic conciliator on most matters within the jurisdiction of his subcommittees, while at the same time acting as an independent critic in many other legislative areas.

In 1961 Morse successfully guided controversial Administration school-aid bills through the Senate. Aid to private schools was supported by Catholic organizations but opposed by many individuals and groups as a breach of the constitutionally mandated separation of church and state. President Kennedy opposed such assistance, and while Morse personally favored private school loans, he cooperated with the Administration in rebuffing efforts to add such loans to its school-aid package. He also successfully opposed an attempt to attach a rider requiring the withholding of funds from states with segregated schools. Morse took the pragmatic view that the bills could not pass with such a proviso.

During the early days of the Kennedy Administration, however, Morse demonstrated that he was not abandoning his accustomed role as a gadfly. In March 1961 he opposed the nomination of Charles M. Meriwether of Alabama as a director of the Export-Import Bank because of the nominee's past connections with a Grand Dragon of the Ku Klux Klan and with retired Admiral John Crommelin, also a promoter of racist causes. Failing to win significant support for his fight against the Meriwether appointment, Morse, at a Foreign Relations Committee hearing, shouted, "Where are the other flaming liberals? . . . In seventeen years I've never backed away from a fight. . . ." He was widely criticized for giving exaggerated importance to the matter, and William V. Shannon of the liberal *New York Post* wrote that the Senator could not distinguish between "bad minnows" and "bad whales." Many observers believed that Morse's lack of discrimination in choosing causes reduced his effectiveness as a dissenter.

During the spring of 1961 President Kennedy accepted a House-Senate conference report excluding laundry workers from coverage under an Administration minimum wage bill in order to win the Southern votes necessary for passage of the measure. Morse, who was one of the conferees, refused to sign the report as a gesture of protest against the exclusion of the laundry workers.

In July and August of the following year, Morse led a liberal filibuster against an Administration bill creating a private corporation to establish, own and operate a communications satellite network. He and other liberals argued that the bill represented a gift to private enterprise of millions of the taxpayers' dollars spent on research and development, and they warned that the corporation would be dominated by the American Telephone & Telegraph Co. On Aug. 14 the Senate, for the first time since 1927, invoked cloture to limit debate, and the bill was passed later in the month.

In 1963 Morse unsuccessfully sought to prohibit Alliance for Progress aid to any country whose government had come to power through the forcible overthrow of a prior government chosen in a democratic election. He believed that aid to Israel, Taiwan and Turkey was no longer necessary, but Congress traditionally opposed attacking foreign aid programs on a country-by-country basis. Congress did, however, take the unusual step of cutting off aid to Indonesia, whose president was described by Morse as "one of the most corrupt men on the face of the earth." Although Administration requests were substantially reduced, Morse led the opposition to the final aid bill because he felt that levels of assistance were still too high and that essential reforms had not been made.

During the mid-1960s Morse was best known for his vehement opposition to the Vietnam war. In August 1964 he and Sen. Ernest Gruening (D, Alaska) [q.v.] were the only opponents of the Tonkin Gulf Resolution on Capitol Hill. Morse subsequently attacked the war as unconstitutional and immoral and in 1966 denounced President Johnson as "power-mad." On March 1, 1966 the Senate rejected a Morse amendment to repeal the Tonkin Resolution by a vote of 92 to 5. Critics of Morse contended that he had once again undercut his own cause by taking an extreme position. They noted that Senate moderates who opposed escalation of the war but who did not want to repudiate totally the President had been forced to vote with the Administration.

In 1968 Morse's defeat at the hands of Republican challenger Robert W. Packwood was attributed in large measure to the incumbent's views on the war. Four years later Morse won the Democratic senatorial primary but lost the election to incumbent Sen. Mark O. Hatfield (R, Ore.) [q.v.]. In 1974 Morse again won the senatorial primary. However, on July 22, in the midst of his election campaign, he died of kidney failure. [See JOHNSON Voooollume]

[MLL]

For further information:
A. Robert Smith, *The Tiger in the Senate: The Biography of Wayne Morse* (Garden City, 1962).

MORTON, THRUSTON B(ALLARD)
b. Aug. 19, 1907; Louisville, Ky.
Republican Senator, Ky., 1957-69;
Chairman, Republican National Committee, 1959-61.

Thruston B. Morton, a seventh generation Kentuckian, received a B.A. in 1929 from Yale University. After working for several years in his family's milling firm and serving in the Navy during World War II, Morton won election to the House three times beginning in 1946. He voted with the GOP's liberal internationalist wing and in 1952 supported Gen. Dwight D. Eisenhower for the Republican presidential nomination. The new Republican President appointed Morton assistant secretary of state for congressional relations in January 1953. Three years later Morton ran for the U.S. Senate as a "modern Republican," closely identifying himself with the Eisenhower Administration. He unseated Assistant Senate Majority Leader Earle C. Clements (D, Ky.). In the Senate Morton's support of Eisenhower Administration programs was the most consistent of any member in the chamber. [See EISENHOWER Volume]

In April 1959 Eisenhower selected him to serve as chairman of the Republican National Committee. A year later Republican presidential nominee Richard M. Nixon [q.v.] briefly considered Morton as his running mate but chose instead United Nations Ambassador Henry Cabot Lodge [q.v.]. As chairman of the National Committee during the 1960 campaign, Morton attacked Nixon's Democratic opponent, John F. Kennedy, for having given "aid and comfort to the Communists" by attacking America's "pace." Following the close Kennedy-Nixon vote, Morton accused the Democrats of massive vote frauds, particularly in Illinois, and sought an investigation of the results there and in several other key states. However, an Illinois election board composed of five Republicans and one Democrat certified the Kennedy vote in December 1960, thus ensuring the Democratic candidate's victory in the Electoral College.

According to *Congressional Quarterly*, Morton supported Kennedy on only 35% of the Senate roll calls on which the President had declared his position in the 87th Congress. He voted for the President's minimum wage bill in April 1961 but against the Administration's school aid appropriation in May 1961 and omnibus housing measure in June 1961. He fought passage of Kennedy's medical care for the aged plan in July 1962.

Morton resigned as National Committee chairman in April 1961 to devote full attention to his reelection campaign in 1962. Because Morton had won in a close contest in 1956, national Democratic strategists waged an aggressive effort for Morton's opponent, Lt. Gov. Wilson Wyatt, one of the two first co-chairmen of the liberal Americans for Democratic Action (ADA), Former President Harry S Truman [q.v.] and Kennedy both made appearances in Kentucky on Wyatt's behalf, while Eisenhower campaigned for Morton. In a hard-fought and bitter contest, the Morton forces attacked Wyatt for his ADA affiliation. A widely circulated Morton pamphlet alleged that the ADA held strongly pro-Communist sympathies. Morton himself said Wyatt's election "would give comfort and support to his old ADA friends who represent the policy of soft talk and concessions." Capturing 52.8% of the vote, Morton won what observers described as a surprisingly easy triumph.

Supporting the Administration's nuclear test ban treaty in September 1963, Morton continued to vote as a middle-of-the-road Republican. During the Johnson years, Morton voted against most Great Society legislation and came to criticize the President's escalation of the war in Vietnam. In poor health, Morton declined to seek reelection in 1968. [See JOHNSON Volume]

[JLB]

MOSCOSO (MORA RODRIGUEZ), (JOSE) TEODORO

b. Nov. 26, 1910; Barcelona, Spain.
Ambassador to Venezuela, March-November 1961; Coordinator, Alliance for Progress, November 1961-May 1964.

Although born in Spain, Moscoso grew up in Ponce, Puerto Rico, where his father owned a retail drug firm. After graduating from the University of Michigan, Moscoso worked for the family business and then in 1942 became the first president of the Puerto Rico Industrial Development Company, a government corporation designed to attract industry to the island. In the same year Gov. Rexford G. Tugwell also appointed Moscoso the housing administrator for Puerto Rico. The island's first elected governor, Luis Munoz Marin [q.v.], asked Moscoso to head Puerto Rico's Economic Development Administration in 1950, a post he held until 1961. Together with Munoz, Moscoso is credited with making "Operation Bootstrap" a success, decreasing unemployment, increasing the per capita income and expanding the government's social services.

Soon after John F. Kennedy was elected, the new President chose Moscoso and another Puerto Rican, Arturo Morales Carrion [q.v.], to work under Adolf A. Berle, Jr. [q.v.] on a task force formed to recommend a Latin American policy for the new Administration. In March 1961 Moscoso became the first Puerto Rican to be named a United States ambassador. His post, Venezuela, was a delicate one, for the democratic government of President Romulo Betancourt was threatened both from the extreme right wing and from Castro-inspired guerrillas. On June 14 Moscoso was forced to remain in Caracas's Central University for more than two hours while anti-American students set fire to his automobile outside the building. Moscoso, unruffled, indicated that he could understand the students' anger and frustration. In November he was named to more important positions: coordinator of the new Alliance for Progress and assistant administrator for Latin America in the Agency for International Development (AID). The Alliance was to operate through AID, which was part of the State Department.

Drawing on the advice of the Berle task force and his special assistant, Richard N. Goodwin [q.v.], Kennedy formally proposed the Alliance in March 1961. It was to be a 10-year, 10-point program "to build a hemisphere where all men can hope for the same high standard of living—and all men can live out their lives in dignity and in freedom." With an eye to Castro's brand of Communism and the brutal right-wing dictatorship of Trujillo, Kennedy said that the Alliance offers "our special friendship to the people of Cuba and the Dominican Republic . . . and the hope that they will soon rejoin the society of free men. . . ."

The Alliance for Progress became a hemispheric venture at the Inter-American Economic and Social Conference in Punta del Este, Uruguay in August 1961. Moscoso was an appropriate choice for coordinator of the program. Puerto Rican economic development, which he had helped to fashion, was thought to be a model for the rest of Latin America. Opposed to both Communism and the land-owning oligarchies, Moscoso frequently voiced his humanitarian commitment to achieving social justice for all people. Under the program a Latin American nation not only had to commit a certain portion of its own budget to development programs to get a matching grant of U.S. aid but also had to draw up programs that encouraged social change, such as agrarian land redistribution. Speaking in October 1962, Moscoso warned that Latin American countries that had not made a "substantial advance" in agrarian reforms would have "difficulty" in getting Alliance aid. He became the Alliance's leading publicist, writing articles, meeting with Latin American leaders and defending the Alliance before the American Congress. As coordinator he worked closely with other agencies, such as the Inter-American Bank, the Food for Peace program, the Peace Corps and the United States Information Agency.

Moscoso left the Alliance in May 1964, criticizing the Johnson Administration for neglecting the political meaning of the Alliance and stressing only "money, skills and bureaucrats." Although he continued to offer criticisms of U.S. foreign policy, he dedicated himself to business interests in Puerto Rico after 1964.

[JCH]

MOSES, ROBERT
b. Dec. 18, 1888; New Haven, Conn.
Chairman, New York State Council of Parks, 1924-62; Chairman, Triborough Bridge and Tunnel Authority, 1936-68; Chairman, New York State Power Authority, 1954-62; President, New York World's Fair Corporation, 1960-67.

Raised in a wealthy German-Jewish family and educated at Yale, Oxford and Columbia Universities, Moses first became politically active as an advocate of civil service reform and government reorganization. Joining New York Gov. Alfred E. Smith's second administration in 1924, Moses took over New York's poorly run and meager state park system and soon planned and built a series of widely praised Long Island beaches and parks and two major parkways connecting them to New York City. Moses became New York City's first city-wide commissioner of parks in 1934, while retaining his various state posts. With federal New Deal money, Moses undertook a program of park, highway and bridge construction on an unprecedented scale. A pioneer in the use of independent, bond-issuing public authorities to build and run public works projects, Moses, as head of several such authorities, was able to build an independent power base largely outside the control of elected officials. In the postwar years Moses effectively controlled public construction in New York City (and much of the state) and by 1959 simultaneously held 12 state and city posts. Between 1924 and 1968 Moses supervised a staggering total of $27 billion in public construction (in 1968 dollars). According to his biographer, Robert A. Caro, "Robert Moses was America's greatest builder . . . shaper of the greatest city in the New World." [See TRUMAN, EISENHOWER Volumes]

By 1959, however, Moses was under attack for a series of scandals involving New York City's slum clearance program, which he headed. When offered the presidency of the proposed New York World's Fair, Moses accepted, leaving the troubled urban renewal program. At the same time, in May 1960, he resigned from his other city appointments. Moses suffered setbacks in 1961 and 1962 when his plans for a Lower Manhattan Expressway and a road on Fire Island were blocked by opponents. In December 1962 New York Gov. Nelson A. Rockefeller [q.v.] sought to replace Moses, then 74, as chairman of the State Council of Parks with his own brother, Laurance S. Rockefeller. Resisting, Moses threatened to resign all his state posts, a tactic that had worked with previous governors. To Moses's surprise and dismay, Rockefeller accepted his resignation from four park posts and his chairmanship of the State Power Authority.

Initially, Moses's main interest in the World's Fair was his plan to use the anticipated profits to build a string of parks extending from the Fair's Queens site. He was thus less concerned with the details of the two-year exposition itself. Planning for the Fair did not go smoothly. When Moses denounced the Bureau of International Expositions, a European group coordinating international fairs, for failing to give the New York Fair official sanction, the bureau responded by requesting that its member nations not participate, and all but Spain followed this recommendation.

The New York press, once favorably disposed towards Moses, was by now more critical and charged him with favoritism in the assignment of Fair contracts. Moses's blunt replies led to further recriminations. Finally, the New York World's Fair ended with a large deficit and badly tarnished Moses's reputation and popularity. In 1968 he lost his last post when the Triborough Bridge and Tunnel Authority was dissolved. [See JOHNSON Volume]

[JBF]

For further information:
Robert A. Caro, *The Power Broker: Robert Moses and the Fall of New York* (New York, 1974).
Robert Moses, *Public Works: A Dangerous Trade* (New York, 1970).

MOSES, ROBERT P(ARRIS)
b. Jan. 23, 1935; New York, N.Y.
Field Secretary, Mississippi Student Nonviolent Coordinating Committee, 1961-65; Director, Mississippi Council of Federated Organizations, 1962-65.

Born and raised in Harlem, Moses graduated from New York's Stuyvesant High School in 1952 and from Hamilton College in 1956. He received a master's degree in philosophy from Harvard University the next year and then taught mathematics at Horace Mann, an elite private school in New York City. Intrigued by the Southern student sit-ins from the time they began in February 1960, Moses went to Atlanta that summer as a volunteer for the recently organized Student Nonviolent Coordinating Committee (SNCC). Late in the summer he traveled through Alabama and Mississippi recruiting for SNCC. In Cleveland, Miss., he met Amzie Moore, head of the local chapter of the NAACP. Moore convinced Moses that he should return to Mississippi the next summer to launch a voter registration campaign. In July 1961 Moses, by then a fulltime SNCC worker, moved into Amite and Pike Counties in southwestern Mississippi to start registration drives.

Alone at the outset, Moses was the first member of SNCC to undertake civil rights work in a deep South black community on a long-term basis. He opened voter registration schools in the two counties in August 1961 and began accompanying small groups of local blacks to voting registrars' offices. Along with other SNCC workers and local blacks who associated with them, Moses was repeatedly harassed, beaten and jailed. In late October 1961 Moses was found guilty of disturbing the peace after leading a protest march in McComb, Miss. In jail until Dec. 6, Moses found on his release that the violence and intimidation had deterred nearly all the blacks in Amite and Pike Counties from joining the registration drive. Early in 1962 Moses left the region and moved to Jackson, Miss., where SNCC set up its state headquarters.

In the spring of 1962 SNCC joined several other civil rights organizations in Mississippi in a Council of Federated Organizations (COFO). Established to conduct a unified voter registration project in the state, COFO was staffed mainly by SNCC workers. Moses was named project director. From the COFO office in Jackson, Moses drew up the plans for voter registration projects in various parts of the state and served as unofficial campaign manager for the Rev. R. L. Smith, a black Jackson minister who ran unsuccessfully for Congress in the June 1962 Democratic primary. Moses spent most of the summer doing registration work in Cleveland, Miss. but moved the center of COFO activity to Greenwood the following spring after a shooting incident outside that Mississippi delta town seriously wounded a black civil rights worker. (Moses was almost killed in the same nightrider assault.)

Moses was also a key organizer of the November 1963 Freedom Ballot, a mock election sponsored by COFO and open to all blacks over 21. The COFO election was designed to demonstrate the magnitude of the denial of black voting rights in Mississippi and to prove that large numbers of blacks in the state did want to vote. Moses served as campaign manager for Aaron Henry [q.v.] and Rev. Ed King, the Freedom candidates for governor and lieutenant governor, and directed the black and white student volunteers from Northern universities who canvassed throughout the state. Some 80,000 votes were cast in the Freedom Ballot, held simultaneously with the regular state elections.

The Freedom Ballot paved the way for both the 1964 Mississippi Freedom Summer Project and the state Freedom Democratic Party (MFDP). Moses, who had directed the summer project, also accompanied MFDP delegates to the August 1964 Democratic Convention where they challenged the seating of Mississippi's regular delegation. Well before 1964, however, Bob Moses had become a legendary figure within SNCC and the student movement. Because of his pioneer role in Mississippi, his hard work there and the courage and ability he displayed, Moses acquired what SNCC executive secretary James Forman [q.v.] described as an "almost Jesus-like aura" among many civil rights workers and Mississippi blacks. Partly because of the stature he had achieved, which he feared would damage rather than aid the movement, Moses changed his name to Robert Parris and left both Mississippi and SNCC early in 1965. [See JOHNSON Volume]

[CAB]

For further information:
Howard Zinn, *SNCC: The New Abolitionists* (Boston, 1964).

MOSS, FRANK E(DWARD)
b. Sept. 23, 1911; Holladay, Utah.
Democratic Senator, Utah, 1959- .

A devout Mormon, Moss received his law degree from George Washington University in 1937 and then worked with the Securities and Exchange Commission. In 1940 he won election as a Salt Lake City judge and served as a judge advocate in the Air Force during World War II. He was Salt Lake's county attorney until his election to the Senate in 1958.

A liberal with strong labor support, Moss won his Senate seat in 1958 with a plurality of 38% when a former Republican governor ran as an independent and split the state's traditionally conservative vote. Moss an energetic representative of his state's natural resource interests, served on the Interior and Insular Affairs Committee and as chairman of its Subcommittee on Irrigation and Reclamation. In the early 1960s Moss advocated a cabinet-level department of natural resources, and President Kennedy remarked that Moss "has preached the doctrine of the wise use of water with, I think, more vigor than almost any other member of the U.S. Senate." Moss played an important role in the development of several irrigation and reclamation projects as well as in the creation of Canyonlands National Park, which was established in 1964. However, he argued against those he called "stand-pat conservationists," who criticized the bill because it did not ban mineral, oil and gas exploration in the park.

Described by the *New York Times* as "a leading champion of the consumer in Congress," Moss cosponsored truth-in-lending legislation and favored controls on political campaign contributions. During his first term he began to work for the ban on television cigarette advertising. This brought him increased electoral support from Utah Mormons, for whom smoking was a sin.

Moss was a strong supporter of the Kennedy Administration's legislative program. During 1962 he ranked among the Democratic senators who voted most consistently with their party majority. Describing himself as a "cautious liberal," Moss opposed lowering the defense budget but argued for a federal ban on state right-to-work laws.

By concentrating on issues of resource development and water supply, Moss was able to defend his seat in 1964 and 1970 despite Utah's traditional conservatism. [See JOHNSON, NIXON Volumes]

[MDB]

MOSS, JOHN E(MERSON)
b. April 13, 1913; Hiawatha, Utah.
Democratic Representative, Calif.,
1953-   .

Moss ran a retail appliance business in Sacramento and was active in local Democratic politics before serving in the Navy during World War II. After the war he joined his brother's real estate firm and won election to the California State Assembly in 1948. Moss was first elected to Congress in 1952 where, as a self-described "really liberal Democrat," he represented Sacramento County.

A strong supporter of the Kennedy Administration's legislative program, Moss was

primarily concerned with public access to government information. In August 1961 he protested that the new code of ethics for federal workers seriously restricted the employes "duty" to make information available to the public. In response to his complaint the White House announced that the code would not forbid the release of unclassified information to either the public or the press. As chairman of the Special Subcommittee on Public Information, Moss held hearings in March 1963 to evaluate charges that the executive branch had tried to "manage" news coverage, especially during the 1962 Cuban missile crisis, by withholding information or giving false information. The hearings concentrated on controversial policies of the Departments of State and Defense, since both had required that their officials report all conversations with newsmen. In addition, the Defense Department required that a public information official be present during all interviews. Seven newsmen participated in a panel as part of the hearing, but no report was released.

During the late 1960s Moss continued to press for greater availability of public information. His efforts culminated in the Freedom of Information Act of 1966. Maintaining a liberal voting record, he became an increasingly active proponent of consumer interests and held his seat in Congress through the mid-1970s. [See JOHNSON, NIXON Volumes]

[MDB]

MUNDT, KARL E(RNST)
b. June 3, 1900; Humboldt, S.D.
d. Aug. 16, 1974; Washington, D.C.
Republican Senator, S.D., 1949-72.

Karl Mundt, a former speech teacher, was first elected to Congress in 1938. There he emerged as an ardent anti-Communist. In 1948 the Congressman became known nationally when he presided over the House Un-American Activities Committee hearings into the Alger Hiss case. That same year Mundt, in conjunction with Richard M. Nixon (R, Calif.) [*q.v.*], sponsored the measure requiring the registration of Communist-front organizations and their officers that became part of the Internal Security Act of 1950. Mundt was elected to the Senate in 1948 and carried on his anti-Communist policies in the upper house. In 1954 he served as chairman of the Senate Investigation Committee during the Army-McCarthy hearings. Three years later he voted against the Senate censure of Joseph McCarthy (R, Wisc.). [See TRUMAN, EISENHOWER Volumes]

After the mid-1950s Mundt's name disappeared from national prominence, but he remained a powerful spokesman for the prevailing conservative views of postwar South Dakota. Mundt voted consistently with the conservative coalition of Southern Democrats and Republicans, supporting that group over 90% of the time on key roll call votes during the Kennedy years. Although conservative on most domestic issues, he backed civil rights measures, farm subsidy bills and legislation for international cooperation.

As a member of the Permanent Investigation Subcommittee, Mundt was involved in two of the most prominent investigations of the Kennedy Adminstration, the probes into the affairs of Texas financier Billie Sol Estes [q.v.] and the awarding of TFX jet-fighter contracts. In 1962 the subcommittee held hearings into the relationship between the Agriculture Department and Estes, then under indictment for fraud in connection with his grain storage and cotton allotment dealings. At these meetings Mundt and Sen. Carl T. Curtis (R, Neb.) [q.v.], the other Republican on the subcommittee, were vigorous critics of the Agriculture Department. In what some Democrats saw as an attempt to embarass the Administration and force the resignation of Secretary of Agriculture Orville Freeman [q.v.], Mundt accused the Department of "complete capitulation to Estes," particularly in its reappointment of the Texan to a local cotton allotment board while he was under investigation.

The subcommittee report, issued in 1964, put the blame for Estes's manipulation on bureaucratic inertia and not on favoritism by the Agriculture Department. However, in a separate statement Mundt and Curtis maintained that Estes had received favored treatment on the county and state levels and in Washington.

The 1963 investigation of TFX contract awards was instituted when Congress learned that the Defense Department had given the contract for the multi-service fighter-bomber to General Dynamics despite a lower bid by Boeing. Mundt accused several high Pentagon officials, including Deputy Secretary of Defense Roswell Gilpatric [q.v.] and Secretary of the Navy Fred Korth [q.v.], of acting to benefit their own interests in the matter. Gilpatric had worked for the law firm that represented General Dynamics; Korth had an interest in a bank that lent General Dynamics money. However, the Justice Department cleared them of wrongdoing.

Although a supporter of the expanding war in Indochina, Mundt denounced the 1968 mission of the captured American spy ship *Pueblo*. His criticism was viewed as an indication that even the most hard-line anti-Communists in Congress feared that the U.S. was overcommitted in Southeast Asia.

In 1969 Mundt suffered a debilitating stroke that prevented him from appearing on the Senate floor or at committee meetings. However, the Senator refused to resign. Two years later, in a precedent-setting decision, the Senate relieved him of his posts as ranking Republican on the Government Operations Committee and second-ranking minority member of the Foreign Relations and Appropriations Committees. Mundt died in the capital in August 1974. [See JOHNSON, NIXON Volumes]

[EWS]

MUNOZ MARIN, LUIS
b. Feb. 18, 1898; San Juan, Puerto Rico.
Governor, Puerto Rico, 1948-64.

The son of Luis Munoz Rivera, "the George Washington of Puerto Rico," Munoz Marin spent much of his youth in the U.S., becoming a member of the Puerto Rican Socialist Party and earning a reputation as a New York-based freelance writer, editor and translator. By 1926 Munoz was active in island politics and won election to the Puerto Rican Senate in 1932 as a Liberal. His stateside contacts helped him to bring New Deal money to Puerto Rico, which in turn added to his growing political popularity. In 1948 he founded the Popular Democratic Party (PPD), which mobilized the support of the *jibaro* country people to become the dominant political force on the island.

Munoz became Puerto Rico's first elected governor in 1948. He presided over the unprecedented program of economic development, nicknamed "Operation Bootstrap," which coordinated public and private investment and fostered the 1952 transformation of Puerto Rico from a U.S. territory to an associated commonwealth. At the same time he had created a powerful political machine personally loyal to him. Political scientist Henry Wells described Munoz as "both a democrat and a *caudillo* . . . a gifted teacher of democratic values and a skilled practitioner of authoritarian values." [See TRUMAN, EISENHOWER Volumes]

In 1960 Puerto Rican politics played a small role in the U.S. presidential race. As the Governor sought his fourth term, President Dwight D. Eisenhower publicly endorsed Munoz's Republican Statehood Party (PER) opponent, Luis Ferre. Ferre's party was formally aligned with the mainland Republicans, who were to make Puerto Rican statehood part of their 1960 platform, but the Puerto Rican legislature and press protested Eisenhower's "improper intervention" in island politics. Puerto Rico's three Catholic bishops were also criticized for their "meddling." The bishops wanted to guarantee support for the new Catholic Action Party (PAC) and declared that a vote for the PPD—which supported Puerto Rico's birth control program and the exclusion of religious instruction from the public schools—could mean excommunication from the Church for the voter. Sensitive to mainland concern about possible Church interference in secular politics, Sen. John F. Kennedy and other prominent American Catholics, including Cardinals Francis Spellman [q.v.] and Richard Cushing

[q.v.], affirmed their fidelity to the principle of church-state separation. The churchmen denied that the bishops could excommunicate a PPD voter. Although the two episodes had a negligible impact on the Kennedy-Nixon contest, Munoz won a large sympathy vote. The PAC failed to win enough votes to qualify for future ballots, and PER gains came at the expense of the Independist Party (PIP), while the PPD held firm at about 58%. Munoz and the bishops were subsequently reconciled.

The Kennedy Administration, planning a more active U.S. role in Latin America, saw Puerto Rico as a bridge to the Latin nations and a source of talent for shaping the new policies. Two of the Governor's closest advisers, Arturo Morales Carrion [q.v.] and Teodoro Moscoso [q.v.], joined the Administration, the latter heading the Alliance for Progress. Munoz also cultivated his friendships with Romulo Betancourt and Juan Bosch, Latin American leaders of the democratic stamp Kennedy hoped to encourage.

Most importantly, Kennedy believed that the image of Puerto Rico's economic prosperity and political democracy achieved in conjunction with the U.S. would counter the potential appeal of Castro's Cuba. Kennedy and Munoz agreed in a series of letters in 1962 that a plebiscite was needed to refute charges by, as Munoz put it, "enemies and misguided friends" of the United States and Puerto Rico "that the commonwealth was not the free choice of the people of Puerto Rico acting in their sovereign capacity." Puerto Rican voters were to express their preference to independence, statehood or a continuation of the commonwealth association. Although Munoz had once been a strong advocate of independence, he now envisioned the commonwealth as a permanent status, since it offered the most favorable level of federal economic aid and local autonomy.

Despite Kennedy's plans, the plebiscite was not held until 1967. Meanwhile, Munoz had refused a fifth term as governor in 1964 and returned to the island's Senate. His vigorous campaign on behalf of the commonwealth position yielded a 60% vote for that alternative, but many groups favoring independence did not participate in the plebiscite. Also, PPD strength and commonwealth sentiment were concentrated in the rural areas, while the cities and the middle class leaned more heavily towards statehood. In 1968 Ferre and his pro-statehood New Progressive Party captured the governorship. Munoz went into retirement, returning in 1972 to help the PPD regain control of the government.

[JCH]

For further information see:
Gordon K. Lewis, *Puerto Rico: Freedom and Power in the Caribbean* (New York, 1963).
Henry Wells, *The Modernization of Puerto Rico: A Political Study of Changing Values and Institutions* (Cambridge, Mass., 1969).

MURROW, EDWARD R(OSCOE)
b. April 25, 1908; Greensboro, N.C.
d. April 27, 1965; Pawling, N.Y.
Director, U.S. Information Agency, March 1961-January 1964.

After working his way through college, Murrow served as president of the National Student Federation and as an assistant director of an international education philanthropy. In 1935 he began a long and famous career with the Columbia Broadcasting System (CBS). Stationed in London during the Battle of Britain in 1940, Murrow gained national recognition for his dramatic radio accounts of the London blitz. He returned to the United States following World War II and conducted regular newscasts over CBS radio beginning in 1947. Moving to television in November 1951, Murrow's *See It Now* program established innovative and professional standards for television news broadcasting. Although he considered himself a reporter rather than a commentator, Murrow's televised investigation of Sen. Joseph R. McCarthy (R, Wisc.) in March 1954 is usually credited with being one of the most important turning points in the Senator's downfall. [See EISENHOWER Volume]

As the size of the television audience expanded in the late 1950s, industry leaders devoted more and more air time to lucrative entertainment shows at the expense of news and public affairs programming. Murrow became increasingly disenchanted with the attitude of the CBS management and in January 1961 accepted President Kennedy's offer to serve as director of the U.S. Information Agency (USIA), charged with the promotion of America's image abroad.

At Murrow's request, Kennedy agreed to make USIA independent of the State Department and to appoint him to the National Security Council (NSC). Murrow expected the White House to inform him of any activity which might affect the nation's prestige overseas. He sought to be "in on the takeoffs and not just the crash landings." His assignment to the NSC and his fame as a newscaster greatly boosted the morale of USIA, which had been shattered by McCarthy in the early 1950s. Murrow promised to provide the world with an objective portrait of America, "We cannot be effective in telling the American story abroad," he said in February 1961, "if we tell it only in superlatives."

Almost immediately after taking office in March 1961, however, Murrow tried to prevent the British Broadcasting Corp. (BBC) from showing a CBS news documentary that he had helped to produce. *Harvest of Shame*, televised in the U.S. on Thanksgiving Day 1960, had exposed the sordid living and working conditions of America's migratory farm workers, much to the annoyance of many farm state congressmen. In March 1961 Murrow asked an old colleague at the BBC as "a personal favor" not to schedule the film over British television. The BBC denied Murrow's request and the American Civil Liberties Union attacked his intercession. He quickly admitted that his action had been "both foolish and futile."

Despite the *Harvest* controversy, Murrow devoted much of his time to battling with the Washington bureaucracy. Following the March 1962 manned orbital mission flown by Col. John H. Glenn, Jr. [*q.v.*], the USIA director suggested that his agency display *Friendship-7*, Glenn's spacecraft, around the world for U.S. propaganda purposes. However, officials of the National Aeronautics and Space Administration (NASA) had already promised to deliver *Friendship-7* to the Seattle World's Fair. In a step unusual for a USIA director, Murrow went directly to Kennedy who overruled NASA in favor of USIA. The *Friendship-7* display proved one of the agency's great successes. Murrow was also skilled in his relations with Congress, winning congressional approval to increase the number of USIA posts from 199 to 298 during his years with the agency.

In September 1961 Kennedy consulted with the full NSC over whether the U.S. should follow the Soviet Union's course and resume atmospheric testing of nuclear weapons. In opposition to the recommendation of Secretary of State Dean Rusk [*q.v.*], Murrow argued against an immediate renewal of American tests which he thought would "destroy the advantages of the greatest propaganda gift we have had in a long time." Rusk reversed himself following Murrow's comment, and Kennedy delayed ordering American atmospheric tests for eight months during which USIA exploited the Soviets' resumption against a background of worldwide concern over nuclear fallout. The American resumption of atmospheric tests in early 1962 brought the cancellation by the Soviet Union of a U.S.-USSR television exchange between Kennedy and Soviet Premier Nikita Khrushchev. Presidential Press Secretary Pierre Salinger [*q.v.*] and Murrow had negotiated the planned exchange with Soviet officials under which each of the two leaders were to have addressed the people of the other's nation in March 1962.

Illness limited Murrow's role in Administration policymaking after the summer of 1962. Recuperation from pneumonia kept the USIA chief away from Washington during the October 1962 Cuban missile crisis, and two lung cancer operations in 1963 further weakened Murrow's ability to lead his agency. Ten weeks after Kennedy's death, Murrow resigned. He never regained his health and died of brain cancer in April 1965.

[JLB]

For further information:
Alexander Kendrick, *Prime Time: The Life of Edward R. Murrow* (Boston, 1969).

MUSKIE, EDMUND S(IXTUS)

b. March 28, 1914; Rumsford, Me.
Democratic Senator, Me., 1959-   .

The son of a Polish immigrant tailor, Muskie excelled as a student and won a scholarship to Cornell Law School in 1936. Following naval service in the war, Muskie advanced rapidly in Maine's Democratic Party. By 1948 he was the Party's floor leader in the state House of Representatives. Running for the governorship in 1954, he scored a surprising victory over incumbent Republican Burton M. Cross. Muskie's two terms as governor revitalized the state Democratic Party. In 1958 he again upset a Republican opponent, Frederick G. Payne, to become Maine's first Democratic Senator since 1911. As a freshman Muskie rejected Majority Leader Lyndon Johnson's (D, Tex.) [*q.v.*] advice and voted with Senate liberals in an unsuccessful 1959 attempt to modify the filibuster rule. After the vote Johnson pointedly ignored Muskie's request for a seat on the prestigious Foreign Relations Committee and instead assigned him to the fourth, fifth and sixth committee choices he had listed: Banking and Currency, Public Works and Government Operations.

Muskie was one of the first in the Senate to endorse John F. Kennedy for president in 1960. At the Democratic Party's Los Angeles Convention he helped swing the Maine delegation to Kennedy, thereby ensuring a solid New England vote for the Massachusetts Senator. During Kennedy's Administration Muskie backed the President's aid-to-education, civil rights and medical care proposals and strongly supported the nuclear test ban treaty. He was also a vocal advocate of federal subsidization of the financially troubled New Haven Railroad. Muskie voted for Kennedy's liberal 1962 trade act but insisted that the President retain authority to impose quotas on certain foreign imports. Muskie was particularly concerned with maintaining the viability of New England's shoe manufacturing industry in the face of Italian imports. According to *Congressional Quarterly*, Muskie was among the six most consistent supporters of Kennedy's legislative program in

1962 and 1963, voting for the President's proposals on 83% and 88% of all roll-call votes.

During the Kennedy years Muskie's influence in the Senate gradually increased, and he achieved a reputation as a liberal who "does his homework." In 1962 the deaths of two senior Democrats on the Public Works Committee made a Muskie ally, Pat McNamara (D, Mich.) [q.v.], chairman. McNamara appointed Muskie head of a newly created subcommittee on air and water pollution, and he soon became the Senate's recognized expert in the field. Muskie was the chief sponsor and floor manager of the Water Quality Act of 1963. The new law provided matching grants to states and localities to build sewage treatment plants and appropriated $20 million a year for three years to finance research. The act also set up a Water Pollution Control Administration under an assistant secretary of health. During 1963 Muskie's subcommittee held public hearings in cities across the country, dramatizing the urgency of the air and water pollution problem and helping to create a growing nation constituency for stronger environmental legislation. In 1968 Muskie was the Democratic Party's vice presidential candidate. [See JOHNSON, NIXON Volumes]

[NNL]

For further information:
David Nevin, *Muskie of Maine* (New York, 1972).

MUSTE, A(BRAHAM) J(OHANNES)
b. Jan. 8, 1885; Zierikzee, Netherlands.
d. Feb. 11, 1967; New York, N.Y.
Clergyman, peace activist.

Muste grew up in Michigan and was ordained as a Dutch Reformed minister in 1909. His first position brought him to New York where, in 1916, he joined the Fellowship of Reconciliation, a nondenominational pacifist group. A socialist and an opponent of World War I, Muste allied himself with the cause of labor radicalism over the next two decades. He was a leader of the 1919 Lawrence, Mass. textile strike, director of the Brookwood Labor School in the 1920s

and an organizer of the victorious Toledo Auto-Lite strike of 1934.

Muste's influence declined in the late 1930s because he opposed U.S. entry into World War II and counseled pacifists to refuse to register for the draft. However, by the late 1950s his ideas again became widely known through the new peace movement. With David Dellinger and Bayard Rustin [q.v.], he founded the magazine *Liberation* in 1956. The next year he became chairman of the Committee for Nonviolent Action. Muste's pacifism influenced Martin Luther King, Jr. [q.v.], who joined the Fellowship of Reconciliation at this time. [See TRUMAN, EISENHOWER Volumes]

Muste was chairman of the committee that organized a San Francisco-to-Moscow Walk for Peace, begun in December 1960. Prior to their arrival he had negotiated with the Soviet Union to allow the marchers to present their position for a period of five days. The international group of marchers, who urged unilateral disarmament and an end to nuclear testing, arrived in Moscow in October 1961. During their stay members of the group debated with Moscow University students, distributed literature concerning disarmament and met with Premier Nikita Khrushchev's wife. However, they were denied permission to speak in Red Square.

In 1962 Muste and Norman Thomas [q.v.] co-chaired the Hiroshima Day Committee. On Aug. 6 marchers opposed to nuclear tests brought petitions to the American and Soviet U.N. missions. Participating groups included the Sane Nuclear Policy Committee, the War Resisters League and Women Strike for Peace. Muste was also co-chairman of the United Easter Peace Demonstrations Committee in April 1963 and helped to organize a Quebec-Washington-Guantanamo Walk for Peace, which began in September.

During the mid-1960s Muste continued to work for pacifist causes and actively opposed U.S. involvement in Vietnam. He traveled to Hanoi in early 1967 and met with Ho Chi Minh to discuss the possibility of negotiations between North Vietnam and the U.S. Before his death that year he described himself as "an unrepentant unilateralist, on political as well as moral grounds." [See JOHNSON Volume]

[MDB]

For further information:
Nat Hentoff, *Peace Agitator: The Story of A. J. Muste* (New York, 1963).

NELSON, GAYLORD A(NTON)
b. June 4, 1916; Clear Lake, Wisc.
Democratic Senator, Wisc., 1963- .

Gaylord Nelson grew up in a small Wisconsin village. His father was a country doctor and a devoted supporter of Sen. Robert M. LaFollette's Progressive Party. After earning a law degree and serving in the Pacific during World War II, Nelson ran as a Republican in 1946 for a seat in the Wisconsin state Assembly. He lost, along with many other followers of Sen. Robert M. LaFollette, Jr., but he was elected as a Democrat to the state Senate in 1948. After 10 years service Nelson ran for the governorship and was elected the first Democrat to fill that post in Wisconsin since 1932. Gov. Nelson attacked industrial polluters and launched an Outdoor Resources Acquisition Program, financed by a penny tax on cigarettes. The program committed the state to a $50 million land acquisition program to preserve wild and unspoiled areas against developers. He also carried out the first major reform of the state's tax system in 50 years, introducing a state sales tax. Nelson was elected to the U.S. Senate in 1962 over the incumbent Republican, Sen. Alexander Wiley (R, Wisc.) [q.v.].

As a Senator, Nelson aligned himself with the bloc of liberal Democrats. In 1963 he voted in favor of federal matching grants for mass transit, modification of the cloture rule and the nuclear test ban treaty. He also favored Sen. William Proxmire's (D, Wisc.) [q.v.] amendment to cut the funds of the National Aeronautics and Space Administration by $90 million, which passed 40-39 in November.

Nelson's major efforts as a freshman senator were in the areas of conservation and environmental protection. His maiden speech in October was in support of a ban on polluting detergents. In April 1963 he voted for an Administration-backed bill designed to block exploitation of the remaining wilderness areas in the U.S. Both measures passed the Senate but were stalled in the House throughout 1963. In an interview published in the *Washington Monthly* in July 1975, Nelson maintained that he had tried in 1963 to alert President Kennedy to the enormity of the environmental crisis, but Kennedy "just didn't understand the issue." During the Johnson years Nelson widened his environmental targets to include DDT, industrial pollution of the Great Lakes and strip mining. [See JOHNSON, NIXON Volumes]

[TO]

NEUBERGER, MAURINE B(ROWN)
b. Jan. 9, 1907; Cloverdale, Ore.
Democratic Senator, Ore., 1960-66.

After working as an English and physical education teacher in Oregon's public schools, Maurine Neuberger joined her husband Richard in the Oregon legislature in 1951. As a state representative she sponsored bills on education and consumer protection. The Neubergers supported themselves as a journalistic team until Richard's election to the U.S. Senate as a Democrat in 1954. In Washington she worked as his unpaid assistant, helping with research and public relations. When he died in March 1960, Maurine Neuberger was elected first to fulfill her husband's unexpired term and then, in November, for a full Senate term.

While supporting most of the Kennedy Administration's major legislation, Neuberger established a record as an independent liberal. She opposed the Administration's communications satellite bill because it gave effective control of the new system to American Telephone and Telegraph Corp. and other private companies. Neuberger joined nine other senators who attempted to block passage of the bill in July 1962 by staging a "liberal filibuster." Their use of the unlimited debate rule provoked the Senate's first successful cloture vote in 35 years.

Neuberger was also a frequently dissenting member of the Agriculture and Forestry Committee. In September 1961 and July 1963 she opposed the extension of laws that authorized the recruitment of Mexican workers for U.S. farms. Along with other Senate liberals and the Labor Department, Neuberger held that extension of the current law merely intensified the problems of American migrant workers and was therefore only acceptable if accompanied by new protective labor legislation.

Active on a variety of congressional reform issues, Neuberger sponsored an unsuccessful bill in March 1961 to provide federal funds for election campaigns and to require disclosure of candidates' other financial sources. Over strong opposition her proposal to extend anti-billboard provisions in federal highway programs in June 1961 won Senate approval. She was responsible for a provision in the 1963 Clean Air Act requiring that information resulting from federally funded research be available to the public. She also won increased appropriations for the Women's Bureau of the Labor Department. The 1963 tax reform bill included her amendment which, for the first time, allowed working mothers to deduct the cost of child care from their taxable income.

Neuberger won a victory for the depressed Pacific Northwest lumber industry with the repeal of the Jones Act, which had restricted the shipment of lumber between U.S. ports to American ships. Over the protest of West Coast shipping interests, Congress repealed the act in November 1962, thereby enabling the lumber industry to regain its market in Puerto Rico by paying cheaper rates on Canadian ships.

Neuberger wrote *Smoke Screen: Tobacco and the Public Welfare* in 1963 and worked for federal controls on cigarette advertising. Retiring from the Senate in 1966, she continued to campaign against smoking and was later appointed chairwoman of the Citizen's Advisory Council on the Status of Women. [See JOHNSON Volume]

[MDB]

For further information:
Hope Chamberlin, *A Minority of Members: Women in the U.S. Congress* (New York, 1973).

NEUSTADT, RICHARD E(LLIOT)
b. June 27, 1919; Philadelphia, Pa.
Presidential consultant.

Richard E. Neustadt, author of *Presidential Power: The Politics of Leadership* (1960), was an adviser to presidents Kennedy and Johnson. He was raised in San Francisco and Washington, D.C., where his father, a Social Security Board official, served as an adviser to President Franklin D. Roosevelt. The excitement of the New Deal kindled in Neustadt a lifelong interest in Democratic Party politics and the presidency.

Neustadt won a B.A. from the University of California, Berkeley in 1939 and an M.A. from Harvard University in 1941. Following service in the Navy in World War II, he worked for the Bureau of the Budget in Washington, D.C. In 1950 he joined the White House staff as a policy and administrative adviser. Harvard granted Neustadt a Ph.D. in government the next year, and at the close of the Truman Administration, he began his teaching career. Neustadt taught for a year at Cornell University and from 1954 to 1964 at Columbia University.

In April 1960 Neustadt's *Presidential Power* was published. The book attracted little attention until autumn when newspapers reported that the Democratic presidential nominee, Sen. John F. Kennedy, was reading it. *Presidential Power* then became a best-seller. Neustadt's study was a plea for decisive presidential leadership. He challenged the commonplace notion that the modern presidency had become too great a burden for any one man. Through an analysis of the key decisions of the Roosevelt, Truman and Eisenhower Administrations, he explained how a strong chief executive might shape policy according to his wishes. He concluded that the key to presidential power was "the power to persuade." The powerful president, skilled in the art of bargaining, could utilize public opinion and patronage to win senators, congressmen, labor officials and businessmen to his point of view. For Neustadt, Franklin D. Roosevelt was the very model of an active president; Dwight D. Eisenhower exemplified a passive one.

The book had particular appeal to liberals who believed that an active president would press for progressive social legislation.

In September 1960 Neustadt, at Kennedy's request, undertook a study of the problems the new Administration would face upon assuming office. Neustadt subsequently worked to organize the White House staff and advise the President on appointments. Kennedy asked him to join his Administration, but Neustadt preferred to serve as a part-time, $75-a-day consultant to the White House while continuing to teach at Columbia and, during 1961-62, at Oxford. Neustadt also served during both the Kennedy and Johnson Administrations as a consultant on organizational problems for the State Department, the Atomic Energy Commission and the Bureau of the Budget. During 1963 he completed a major study of the cancellation of the Skybolt missile project. Britain had been relying on the Skybolt to give it an independent nuclear strike force, and the U.S. cancellation of the project created a furor there, temporarily undermining Britain's relations with the U.S. In 1964 Neustadt also wrote a lengthy analysis of the problem of utilizing crews from different NATO countries to man nuclear submarines.

In March 1963 Neustadt testified before a Senate subcommittee established to review Administration procedures for national security matters. He told the subcommittee that in an age of nuclear missiles a president simply did not have the time to consult with Congress on the decision to wage war. "When it comes to risking war," he said, "technology modified the Constitution." Neustadt pointed out, however, that in crisis situations the President's own staff would, like Congress, serve to check and balance decision-making. As an example Neustadt cited the responsible behavior of the White House staff during the Cuban missile crisis.

Shortly after the President's death Neustadt offered what he called "a premature appraisal" of Kennedy's performance. Neustadt argued that despite having served only two years and 10 months, Kennedy had proved to be a far more active and vital president than his predecessor. Neustadt credited Kennedy with laying the foundations for the poverty and civil rights legislation passed during the Johnson Administration. Kennedy's great achievement, however, was that "he pioneered in handling nuclear confrontations." His skill, coolness and tact in the Cuban missile crisis was an example of "what presidents must do to minimize the risk of war through mutual miscalculation." This, Neustadt concluded, was Kennedy's major contribution to the presidency.

In 1965 Neustadt joined the Harvard faculty to serve as the first director of the Institute of Politics at the John F. Kennedy School of Government. Until 1966 he remained as a special consultant to President Lyndon B. Johnson and carried out a number of studies in foreign and domestic policy.

[JLW]

For further information:
Richard E. Neustadt, *Presidential Power: The Politics of Leadership* (New York, 1960).
———, "Kennedy in the Presidency: a Premature Appraisal," *Political Science Quarterly* LXXIX (September, 1964), pp. 321-334.

NIEBUHR, REINHOLD
b. June 21, 1892; Wright City, Mo.
d. June 1, 1971; Stockbridge, Mass.
Theologian.

Following ordination as a minister by the Evangelical Synod of North America in 1915, Niebuhr took up a pastorate in industrial Detroit where he became active in labor, socialist and pacifist movements. In 1928 he joined the faculty of Union Theological Seminary and sharpened his critique of liberal Protestantism and the secular society whose values it justified. In his *Moral Man and Immoral Society* (1932), written during his most radical period, he abandoned pacifism as historically irrelevant and politically unsuited to confront contemporary social problems. Niebuhr broke with the Socialist Party in 1940 when he advocated American aid to the allies. He then founded a biweekly, *Christianity and*

Crisis, in which he denounced the pacifism of a "sentimentalized Christianity" that refused to take action against Nazi tyranny. In 1941 he helped found the Union for Democratic Action as an organization designed to mobilize ex-pacifist liberals to support a war against Germany.

After World War II Niebuhr won recognition as the most influential American theologian. Political scientist Hans Morgenthau described Niebuhr as "perhaps the only creative political philosopher [in American thought] since Calhoun." Niebuhr developed a philosophical rationale for anti-Communist liberalism that conformed with his "realist" neo-orthodox theology. Just as his theology emphasized original sin, his politics attacked what he thought to be the utopianism and simple faith in human progress characteristic of socialist and some liberal thought. Niebuhr "toughened" American liberalism, supported a strong defense posture and took a "pragmatic" approach to social issues while avoiding political cynicism. He was a founder of the Americans for Democratic Action. [See TRUMAN, EISENHOWER Volumes]

Niebuhr's influence on a generation of liberals was evident in the Kennedy Administration's resolute conduct of the Cold War and its concern for civil rights. In his writings of the early 1960s, he continued his attacks on the utopianism of historical liberalism. In his *Reinhold Niebuhr on Politics* (1960), he wrote that "liberalism is in short a kind of blindness . . . which does not see the perennial difference between human actions and aspirations, the perennial source of conflict between life and life, the inevitable tragedy of human existence, the irreducible irrationality of human behavior and the tortuous character of human history."

As early as 1965 Niebuhr opposed U.S. policy in Vietnam. Speaking in 1967 he called the war a "fantastic adventure of United States imperialism" but added that he wanted an "American presence in Southeast Asia [based in] perhaps Thailand."

Unfriendly to the Nixon Administration, Niebuhr severely criticized President Nixon for holding interdenominational religious services in the White House. Not only was Nixon circumventing the Bill of Rights, wrote Niebuhr, but he was also attempting to prevent any criticism of his Administration on religious grounds.

Because of his age Niebuhr in 1966 decided to take a less active role on *Christianity and Crisis* by becoming a special contributing editor. He died on June 1, 1971.

[JCH]

For further information:
Nathan A. Scott, Jr., *Reinhold Niebuhr* (Minneapolis, 1963).
Ronald H. Stone, *Reinhold Niebuhr: Prophet to Politicians* (Nashville, 1972).

NITZE, PAUL H(ENRY)

b. Jan. 16, 1907; Amherst, Mass.
Assistant Secretary of Defense for International Security Affairs, January 1961-October 1963; Secretary of the Navy, November 1963-June 1967.

An investment banker before World War II, Paul Nitze went to Washington in 1940 as an expert on economics. After 1946 he advanced to top policymaking positions in the State Department. There he helped prepare the congressional legislation responsible for the Marshall Plan and, in 1950, drafted "NSC-68," the first comprehensive review of U.S. national security policy. Based on the belief that the Soviet Union would pursue an aggressive foreign policy, this document asked the U.S. to accept primary responsibility for the defense of the non-Communist world. To accomplish this mission the defense budget would have to be increased threefold so that a flexible response, permitting the use of either conventional forces or nuclear weapons, could be maintained. This idea fell from favor during the Eisenhower years when attempts to cut the defense budget resulted in a policy, termed "massive retaliation" by Secretary of State John Foster Dulles, that relied primarily on nuclear weapons. [See TRUMAN Volume]

Because of Sen. Joseph McCarthy's (R, Wisc.) opposition to his appointment as assistant secretary of defense, Nitze remained out of government during the Eisenhower years. He returned to public service in 1959 when the Senate Foreign Relations Committee asked him to study the impact of long-range missiles and future weapons systems on the United States. In 1961 Nitze headed John F. Kennedy's pre-election task force on national defense problems. In both the Committee and task force reports, Nitze reiterated his belief that the U.S. had to assume a more diversified defense posture to provide a real alternative to the massive nuclear deterrent strategy of the Dulles era.

On Dec. 24, 1960 Kennedy appointed Nitze assistant secretary of defense for international security affairs. In this position Nitze urged NATO to move away from reliance on American nuclear power and organize a multilateral conventional and nuclear force (MLF) of its own.

During the Berlin crisis of 1961, Nitze headed the Berlin task force created to handle strategy in a possible showdown with Russia. As chairman, Nitze warned the Russians that the West would use "all their strategic capabilities" to protect Berlin.

A member of the Executive Committee of the National Security Council charged with policy analysis during the Cuban missile crisis of October 1962, Nitze was one of the advisers who advocated immediate military action to rid Cuba of Soviet missiles. He opposed the Cuban blockade suggested by the more moderate Attorney General Robert F. Kennedy [q.v.] and Secretary of Defense Robert S. McNamara [q.v.]. Believing that military action was inevitable, Nitze and some of Kennedy's other advisers urged air strikes before the Soviet missiles were operational, when attempts to remove them would necessitate a massive attack that could lead to nuclear war.

In February 1963 Nitze, along with special presidential assistant Walt W. Rostow [q.v.], was assigned the task of analyzing the government's response to the crisis. Nitze concluded that his previous position had been in error because it overestimated the possibility that nuclear war would have resulted from a delay in air strikes.

In November 1963 Nitze became secretary of the Navy. During his tenure he was one of the major advocates of the ill-fated TFX, a multi-service fighter/bomber. A proponent of a negotiated peace in Vietnam and a de-escalation of the ground war, Nitze helped Robert McNamara write in April 1967 the so-called San Antonio Formula designed to bring the North Vietnamese to the negotiating table. In March 1968 he was a member of the President's Ad Hoc Task Force on Vietnam formed to study the military's proposal for massive troop increases following the Communist Tet offensive. Within this group he continued to oppose escalation. [See JOHNSON Volume]

Nitze served as deputy secretary of defense from June 1967 to January 1969. In November 1969 he went to Helsinki as a member of the U.S. delegation to the Strategic Arms Limitation Talks (SALT).

[EWS]

NIXON, RICHARD M(ILHOUS)
b. Jan. 9, 1913; Yorba Linda, Calif.
Vice President of the United States, 1953-61.

Nixon grew up in Whittier, Calif., where he worked in the family grocery store and attended public schools and Whittier College. A competitive student, he won a scholarship to Duke University Law School. After graduation in 1937 Nixon practiced law in Whittier until 1942, when he went to work for the Office of Price Administration in Washington for seven months and then joined the Navy.

Soon after he left the service, Nixon was nominated as the Republican Party's candidate for a seat in Congress from California's 12th district. He conducted an aggressive, personal campaign in which he capitalized on anti-Communist sentiment by questioning the patriotism of his opponent, Rep. Jerry Voorhis (D, Calif.). Nixon defeated Voorhis and in Congress became identified with a new postwar brand of Southern California conservatism. As a member of the House Un-American Activities Committee, Nixon gained national recognition in the sensational investigation of Alger Hiss, a former State Department official, which eventually led to Hiss's conviction on perjury charges. Nominated as the Republican candidate in the 1950 U.S. Senate race against Rep. Helen Gahagan Douglas (D, Calif.), Nixon won after a bitter campaign in which he accused his opponent of being "soft on Communism." [See TRUMAN Volume]

Nixon's questionable campaign tactics earned him the nickname of "Tricky Dick" in liberal circles, but his vehement anti-Communism made him a respected national figure in the Cold War climate of the early 1950s. At the 1952 Republican National Convention Nixon was nominated for vice president to give a conservative balance to a ticket headed by former Gen. Dwight D. Eisenhower [q.v.], the choice of the Republican Eastern Establishment.

Elected in 1952 and reelected in 1956, Nixon wielded very little real power, but he received more public exposure than most vice presidents. Partly because of Eisenhower's desire to appear "above" politics, Nixon acted as the chief Republican Party spokesman and campaigned extensively for state and local candidates in off-year elections. When Eisenhower was incapacitated by illness, Nixon assumed many of the ceremonial functions of the presidency. He also acted as liaison between the White House and Congress and traveled abroad as Eisenhower's representative. An attack on Nixon and his wife by a left-wing mob in Caracas, Venezuela, in 1958 and Nixon's "kitchen debate" with Soviet Premier Nikita Khrushchev in Moscow in 1959 reinforced the Vice President's stature as a spokesman for the West. By 1958, when he began to lay plans for a 1960 presidential race, polls showed that Nixon was already the overwhelming choice of a majority of registered Republicans. [See EISENHOWER Volume]

Only New York Gov. Nelson Rockefeller [q.v.] constituted an obstacle to an easy Nixon victory at the 1960 Republican National Convention. Although Rockefeller decided not to challenge Nixon's nomination, success in November still required the full support of the New York Governor and the liberal wing of the Party, which had long been hostile to Nixon. In July 1960, only a few days before the Convention,

Nixon visited Rockefeller at the Governor's New York City triplex to discuss their differences and offer him the vice presidential nomination. The Governor turned down the offer but insisted upon a rewriting of the Republican Party platform. Although the "Treaty of Fifth Avenue" was termed a "Munich" by conservative Sen. Barry Goldwater (R, Ariz.) [q.v.], Nixon in fact conceded only minor changes in the platform—mainly stronger commitments to military preparedness and a greater emphasis on economic growth—while winning the backing of Eastern liberals and moderates. He easily quieted dissension on the Platform Committee, won the nomination and chose Henry Cabot Lodge [q.v.], ambassador to the United Nations and an Easterner, as his running mate.

Public opinion polls taken in early August 1960 showed that a slim majority of voters preferred Nixon to Sen. John F. Kennedy in the presidential contest. Nixon had the advantage of greater national recognition, claimed to possess executive experience and had the personal blessing of the still-popular incumbent President.

Yet Nixon's campaign failed to develop as he had hoped. He could find no issue on which he sharply disagreed with Kennedy. On foreign policy questions Nixon was unable to outflank Kennedy on the right since both candidates accepted the basic tenets of U.S. Cold War strategy and employed similar rhetoric. Not only was Nixon unable to accuse Kennedy of "softness" toward the Communist threat, but he found himself on the defensive when Kennedy called for tougher policies against Fidel Castro's Cuba and a strengthening of U.S. nuclear defenses. Nixon took a more aggressive stance on defense of Nationalist China's island outposts, but the issue excited little voter interest.

According to most political observers, the turning point in the campaign came on Sept. 26 when the candidates met for the first of four nationally televised debates. At the time Nixon was still leading in the public opinion polls, but on television he projected a tired appearance, which contrasted sharply with Kennedy's crisp style and good looks. Neither candidate "won" the debate, but the verbal confrontation proved a distinct advantage to Kennedy because it enabled some 70 million viewers to see the Democratic candidate as the mature and forceful equal of the Vice President in face-to-face debate.

After the first television debate the momentum of the Nixon campaign slowed considerably. Increased unemployment in October and the absence of Eisenhower on the campaign trail damaged Nixon's chances. The President's response to a question from the press that, if given a week, he might be able to cite one contribution Nixon had made to his Administration, was used by Democrats to imply that the President lacked confidence in Nixon's ability. Nixon supporters claimed that poor health kept Eisenhower from active campaigning. When Eisenhower spoke publicly in Nixon's behalf during the last week of the campaign, it was already too late to reverse the trend.

In the election a record turnout gave Kennedy a plurality of 113,057—the smallest of the century—but a comfortable electoral vote margin of 303 to 219. Nixon won more states, but Kennedy took the industrial North and most of the South. Although there was post-election evidence that fraud in Illinois and Texas had given the votes of those key states to Kennedy by narrow margins, Nixon recognized that any investigation would be both time consuming and divisive. He therefore conceded defeat. He later declined Kennedy's offer of a temporary foreign assignment. In January 1961 he retired to private life.

From a multitude of attractive employment offers, Nixon chose to join the Los Angeles law firm of Adams, Dugue and Hazeltine. His annual income of $200,000 far exceeded the salaries he had received in government. In addition, his new position was politically advantageous because Earl Adams was one of his oldest political allies, and the firm's clients included some of California's largest corporations. Nixon retained part of his old power base in his home state and, as titular leader of the Republican Party, continued to receive national media coverage. Between June 1961 and April 1962, he wrote a series of news-paper columns for the *Los Angeles Times-Mirror* Syndicate, which afforded him a public forum from which to criticize the Kennedy Administration.

Nixon also worked on a book, published in March 1962 as *Six Crises*. The work focused on the major political events of his career and included a defense of his role in the Hiss case and an analysis of his 1960 defeat. Some reviewers found it a revealing exposure of the "real" Nixon hidden under a wholly political exterior. *New Republic* writer William Costello called it a stark revelation of the restless, frustrated, diffident psyche of the protagonist" who "wraps himself in a cloak of masochism." *Six Crises* was a financial success and helped keep Nixon's name in the national spotlight.

Encouraged by political friends and convinced that he needed an important elective office from which to launch another presidential campaign, Nixon announced his candidacy for the governorship of California in September 1961. Since he was leader of the national Republican Party and had cultivated a new image as a centrist and conciliator of party factions, Nixon expected unified support from the state Party. However, three other Republicans, including former Gov. Goodwin Knight, an old Nixon rival, declared their intention to enter the June 1962 primary. Extreme right-wing Republicans attacked Nixon for being "soft on Communism," partly because of his criticism of the John Birch Society. Knight and another candidate dropped out in the course of the race, but Nixon did not defeat his conservative opponent in June by as large a vote as he had hoped. Still, he expected to win in November against his colorless Democratic opponent, Gov. Edmund G. Brown [*q.v.*].

Nixon was unable to find a controversial issue upon which to peg his campaign. His promise to clean up "the mess in Sacramento" proved ineffective; Brown was generally considered both an honest politician and a successful practitioner of the legislative process. Nixon attempted to identify Brown with leftist elements late in the campaign, but this aggressive use of the anti-Communist issue probably worked to his opponent's advantage. The Democrats, in turn, asserted that Nixon only wanted to use the governorship to become president. They also embarrassed Nixon by publicizing a loan made by millionaire Howard Hughes [q.v.] to Nixon's brother, Donald, in 1956. Nixon lost badly in the November election—by about 300,000 votes—and many commentators asserted that his political career was finished.

In his concession speech the following morning, Nixon shocked assembled reporters with an emotional and confused outburst in which he attacked the press for biased reporting throughout his career. Nearing the end of his speech, he said, "I leave you gentlemen now, and you will now write it. You will interpret it. That's your right. But as I leave you I want you to know—just think how much you're going to be missing. You won't have Nixon to kick around any more, because, gentlemen, this is my last press conference. . . ." Many thought that this speech, as much as the electoral defeat, finished Nixon's political career and permanently ruined his relationship with press.

In June 1963 Nixon moved to New York City and joined the prestigious law firm of Mudge, Stern, Baldwin and Todd. He continued to speak out on national issues and to visit political leaders abroad. He assumed the role of an "elder statesman" in the Republican Party and attempted to conciliate its liberal and conservative factions.

Nixon campaigned loyally for the Party's national ticket in 1964 and, following the disastrous Republican defeat that year, became the Party's leading fund raiser. He worked hard for Republican candidates in 1966, captured the Party's nomination in 1968 and in a three-way race won the presidential election in November. Although Nixon was reelected by a landslide in 1972, revelations of criminal misconduct by him and his staff in the coverup of the Watergate affair forced Nixon to resign the presidency in August 1974. [See JOHNSON, NIXON Volumes]

[JCH]

For further information:
Earl Mazo and Stephen Hess, *Nixon: A Political Portrait* (New York, 1968).

NOLTING, FREDERICK E(RNEST), JR.

b. Aug. 24, 1911; Richmond, Va.
Ambassador to South Vietnam, March 1961-August 1963.

After serving in the Navy during World War II, Nolting joined the State Department in 1946, specializing in European affairs. He was assigned in 1955 to the U.S. delegation to the North Atlantic Treaty Organization in Paris. In 1957 he was promoted to deputy chief of mission, serving in that capacity until February 1961.

President Kennedy's decision to name Nolting to replace Elbridge Durbrow as ambassador to South Vietnam was opposed by some members of the new Administration. Chester Bowles [q.v.], the undersecretary of state, objected that Nolting had no experience in Asia and was too conservative to serve as a liberal administration's representative in a critical post. When Nolting was sounded out about the possibility of being switched to another post, he objected strenuously. Rather than risk a potentially embarrassing row over the issue, Kennedy decided to go ahead with Nolting's appointment, officially designating him for the post on Feb. 17, 1961.

Nolting arrived in Saigon March 15 in agreement with his instructions to avoid antagonizing President Ngo Dinh Diem, his brother, Ngo Dinh Nhu, and his sister-in-law, Madame Nhu. (Durbrow's blunt criticism of the regime and his suggestion that Nhu go into voluntary exile had made him virtually *persona non grata* by the end of his tour of duty.) Believing that overt pressure would only stiffen Diem's opposition to reforms, Nolting sought to win his cooperation with assurances of unconditional American support.

Nolting's reports during his first six months in Saigon that the war against the Communist guerrillas was being won failed to prepare the Administration for the government's major defeats and its request for U.S. combat troops in the autumn of 1961. A fact-finding mission sent to Vietnam returned with recommendations that the U.S. press Diem for more reforms, increase its military assistance program and commit 8,000 ground troops to Vietnam. Kennedy rejected the request for troops and ordered Nolting to insist on the reforms as a condition of increased aid. Eventually, after tense negotiations, Diem agreed to carry out the reforms in exchange for a letter from Kennedy, made public Dec. 15, promising that "we shall promptly increase our assistance to your defense effort." When the reforms did not materialize in the early months of 1962, the Administration was persuaded by Nolting that further pressure would be futile and unnecessary since the military situation had improved thanks to increased U.S. aid. Homer Bigart of the *New York Times* wrote at the time that Nolting's policy could be summarized in a phrase: "Sink or swim with Ngo Dinh Diem." Addressing a South Vietnamese group Feb. 15, the Ambassador declared, "My government fully supports your elected constitutional government" despite criticism by those he described as misguided "skeptics." The only hope for success against the guerrillas, he added, lay with "the dedicated and courageous leadership of your president."

The American press corps and Nolting were often at odds. The Ambassador considered reports that the war was going badly and that corruption was rife as unpatriotic, demoralizing and a threat to U.S.-Vietnamese relations. He withheld embassy cooperation from critical reporters, interceding only reluctantly when the Diem government expelled or harassed American newsmen. The government's attempt to herd peasants into "strategic hamlets" ringed by barbed wire was a major point of contention, with Nolting defending it as a striking success and many reporters attacking it as a repressive failure. (In 1963, when the program was clearly failing, its principal sponsor, Ngo Dinh Nhu, tried to tie the U.S. to the program by naming one of the hamlets after Nolting. The Ambassador sought to decline this honor but finally presided over a dedication ceremony. The Communists overran the hamlet soon after.)

While Nolting was away on an Aegean holiday in June 1963, the simmering protest against the regime led by Buddhist monks reached a crisis. Deputy Chief of Mission William Trueheart, an old friend of Nolting's, reported to Washington that the government was totally isolated. President Kennedy, who had already decided that Nolting should be replaced, directed Trueheart to warn Diem sternly against further religious oppression.

Nolting, anxious to retire because of pressing family responsibilities, learned when he passed through Washington on his way to Saigon that he was about to be replaced by Henry Cabot Lodge [*q.v.*]. (Lodge's appointment was announced June 27.) Arriving in Saigon for a final attempt to exert his influence before Lodge took over, Nolting found Diem sullen and unresponsive. Nolting accused Trueheart of disloyalty and blamed him for destroying his good relations with the South Vietnamese. After coaxing some minor concessions from Diem, he publicly defended the regime's record on the religious issue. Just before Nolting left for Washington Aug. 15, Diem promised the Ambassador that there would be no more attacks on the Buddhists. Six days later government troops attacked the Buddhist pagodas, beating monks, desecrating holy relics and presenting Lodge with a *fait accompli* when he arrived the next day. The attack on the pagodas led to a reversal of U.S. policy toward Diem and, ultimately, to a benevolent view of the military coup that ousted him in November.

Nolting was included for a few months in White House policy meetings on Vietnam after he returned to Washington. He fought hard for continued support for Diem, but the tide of opinion within the Administration was running against him. The coup and murder of Diem ended the opportunity for further debate. Nolting worked on a special intelligence survey under the aegis of the Central Intelligence Agency during early 1964, retiring from government service later in the year to become a vice president in the Paris office of the Morgan Guaranty Trust Co.

[EWK]

NORSTAD, LAURIS
b. March 24, 1907; Minneapolis, Minn.
Supreme Commander, Allied Forces, Europe, April 1956-January 1963.

Lauris Norstad, son of a Norwegian Lutheran minister, became the youngest man in U.S. history to attain the rank of four star general. He achieved the rank as a result of his work as planner of the air campaign against Japan in 1944 and 1945, as shaper of an independent air corps from 1945 to 1947 and as commander in chief of Allied forces in Central Europe in 1952. In 1956 he was named Supreme Commander of Allied Forces, Europe. Although termed a military post the job was essentially the diplomatic one of keeping the North Atlantic Treaty Organization (NATO) unified during a period of extreme stress generated by changing U.S. policy, growing demands for fuller European participation in the alliance and by Russian threats against Berlin. [See EISENHOWER Volume]

As Supreme Commander Norstad was able to develop close working ties with alliance governments because of his willingness to take positions independent of American policy. Reflecting the growing European belief that NATO was too dependent on U.S. military power, Norstad proposed in 1959 that the alliance build its own nuclear force. While still defending the "shield theory," which called for the maintenance of conventional troops in Europe as first deterrent against Russian attack, he also felt the possession of land-based ballistic missiles was an important symbol of power necessary for NATO in an atomic age.

During the Berlin crisis of 1961, Norstad continued to stress the importance Europeans placed on the potential use of nuclear weapons. In his communications with Kennedy he urged the President to assure our allies that we would be willing to take whatever measures were necessary to defend Berlin by indicating a readiness to use nuclear weapons in a confrontation. Kennedy's refusal to heed his advice led to an increased determination on the part of Britain and Germany to build up European atomic forces. As a result of this development and Norstad's continued campaign, strongly supported by the West Germans, Kennedy was forced to develop a plan for sharing nuclear weapons. Under the terms of this measure, outlined in the Nassau pact of December 1961, America would commit Polaris submarines to a multilateral NATO nuclear force. To prevent the use of weapons for national purposes, each country in the alliance would have a veto over

the use of the nuclear-armed missiles.

Kennedy's proposal, more limited than the one envisioned by Norstad, generated a break that prompted the Commander's early resignation. The General, feeling that the veto clause would prevent immediate action in case of attack, championed a plan in which a majority decision by NATO's three nuclear powers—Britain, France and the U.S.—would determine if an atomic strike should be launched. In addition, he believed that reliance on Polaris submarines would not be as strong a psychological deterrent to Russian aggression as European land-based missiles.

Initially intending to retire in November 1962, Norstad was asked by Kennedy to delay his action until January 1963 because of the Cuban missile crisis. Norstad became president of Owens-Corning Fiberglass Corp. in 1964, but he continued his campaign for an independent NATO nuclear force, pressing the issue in a Republican Party platform paper on NATO delivered in April 1964 and in hearings before Sen. Henry Jackson's (D, Wash.) [q.v.] Subcommittee on National Security and International Operations in May 1966.

[EWS]

O'BRIEN, LAWRENCE F(RANCIS)
b. July 7, 1917; Springfield, Mass.
Special Assistant to the President for Congressional Relations and Personnel, January 1961-August 1965.

O'Brien's father, a leader of the local Democratic organization, began training his 11-year-old son as a campaign worker in Gov. Alfred E. Smith's presidential campaign of 1928. After World War II O'Brien managed three congressional campaigns for his friend Foster Furcolo in 1946, 1948 and 1950. Furcolo won the seat in 1948, and O'Brien accompanied him to Washington to serve as his administrative assistant. Returning to Springfield after the 1950 election, O'Brien became director of organization for John F. Kennedy's 1952 Senate campaign. Kennedy's upset victory over the popular Republican incumbent, Henry Cabot Lodge [q.v.], was widely attributed to O'Brien's painstaking creation of an independent statewide organization and skillful mobilization of volunteers. He repeated his achievement in Kennedy's reelection campaign of 1958, running up an 874,608-vote margin of victory that thrust Kennedy into presidential contention. Between elections O'Brien looked after his family's real estate holdings and acted as a public relations consultant in Springfield.

In April 1959 O'Brien began touring the country to lay the foundations of Kennedy's bid for the Democratic presidential nomination, focusing on such key primary states as New Hampshire, Wisconsin, Indiana, West Virginia, Nebraska and Oregon. A 64-page book known as O'Brien's Manual—containing detailed instructions for registration drives, telephone campaigns and literature distribution systems—ensured that the Kennedy organization in each state followed the model that had proven its success in the Massachusetts campaigns. Under O'Brien's guidance, crucial victories were won against Sen. Hubert Humphrey (D, Minn.) [q.v.] in Wisconsin and West Virginia. While charges that Kennedy had bought a primary victory with his father's money and aspersions cast on Humphrey's war record by Kennedy campaigner Franklin Delano Roosevelt, Jr. [q.v.] were bitterly debated after the West Virginia election, the 61-39% margin of victory in a heavily Protestant state convinced many party leaders that Kennedy's Catholicism was not an insurmountable handicap. Theodore H. White wrote in *The Making of the President 1960* that O'Brien's organization of the West Virginia campaign was "a masterpiece in the art of primaries."

O'Brien's innovative tactics were vigorously applied at the Democratic National Convention. Files were compiled on each of the 4,509 delegates and alternates; liaison people were placed in each delegation; floor representatives were linked to the Kennedy headquarters by a complex telephone and walkie-talkie communications system. With Kennedy's first-ballot nomination, O'Brien's convention tactics were vindicated. They have since been adopted virtually intact by the major candidates at both parties' national conventions. In the general election campaign against Vice President Richard M. Nixon [q.v.], O'Brien successfully applied on a national level the organizational scheme and procedures that had been perfected in the state primaries.

Soon after his narrow victory, the President-elect assigned O'Brien to find talented campaign supporters to fill positions in the new Administration. O'Brien's appointment as special assistant to the President for congressional relations and personnel was officially announced Jan. 2, 1961. (He reportedly had rejected a position as deputy postmaster general in December 1960.)

O'Brien immediately devoted himself to systematizing relations between the White House and Capitol Hill. Opposed by a strong conservative coalition of Republicans and Southern Democrats, the Kennedy legislative program clearly would require deft but intensive lobbying to be enacted. With the support of the President, O'Brien coordinated the efforts of the congressional liaison offices located in more than forty federal departments and agencies, insisting that they work in concert for the President's legislative priorities instead of for the vested interests of their own agencies and departments. O'Brien initiated a system requiring each liaison office to submit weekly reports of its congressional activity for the previous week and plans for the week ahead. Detailed files were compiled on each member of Congress covering voting records, prejudices, favorite projects and political friends.

The Administration's first, and in many ways, most crucial test in Congress was over a procedural question, enlargement of the House Rules Committee. Led by the chairman, Howard Smith (D, Va.) [q.v.], the conservative majority on the Committee had the power to bottle up liberal legislation in committee, as it had done for many years, preventing a vote in the House. House Speaker Sam Rayburn (D, Tex.) [q.v.] had agreed in a December 1960 meeting to a plan to add three new members to the Committee, thereby giving liberals and moderates a majority. Four days after the inauguration Rayburn told O'Brien and Kennedy that he didn't have the votes to carry out the plan. O'Brien immediately mobilized members of the cabinet, Southern governors and the AFL-CIO to convince a small group of wavering Southern Democrats and liberal Republicans to support the President's position. The House voted 217-212 Jan. 31 to increase the Committee membership from 12 to 15.

The next critical test for Kennedy's legislative program came in April 1961 in the House over a proposal to raise the minimum wage from $1 to $1.25 an hour and extend coverage to an additional four million workers. With the bill facing certain defeat in the House, O'Brien devised a compromise breaking the increase into two steps—raising the minimum wage to $1.15 immediately and to $1.25 two years later—and dropping some 450,000 workers from the plan to extend coverage. The final version of the bill incorporating O'Brien's compromises passed the House and Senate May 3.

Other key legislative victories won under O'Brien's management during the first year of the Kennedy Administration included a $389 million area development program (passed by voice vote in the Senate April 20 and a 223-193 House vote April 26), an omnibus housing bill (passed June 28 by a 53-38 Senate vote and a 229-176 House vote), a two-year extension of the Civil Rights Commission and establishment of the Arms Control and Disarmament Agency, the Peace Corps and the Alliance for Progress.

O'Brien's tight supervision of the executive branch's relations with Congress was decisive in the passage (House, June 28; Senate, Sept. 19) of the Trade Expansion Act of 1962 by wide margins. A 10-man White House task force, put together by O'Brien, orchestrated support for the bill from business, labor and government departments, quelling the traditional rivalries on trade legislation between the Departments of State, Commerce, Agriculture and Labor that had frustrated earlier efforts at reform.

The other legislative achievements won in 1962 with O'Brien's assistance included passage of the communications satellite bill (House, May 3; Senate, Aug, 17) following a liberal filibuster in the Senate, a $100 million loan authorization for the U.N., a $435 million manpower retraining program (Senate, March 8; House, March 13), a constitutional amendment barring the poll tax (Senate, March 27; House, Aug. 27) and the reduction of funds for the RS-70 bomber. (This followed a widely reported walk in the White House rose garden by the President with Rep. Carl Vinson [D, Ga.] [q.v.], the bomber's principal advocate.) In 1963 the Administration's only major legislative victory was Senate approval of the nuclear test ban treaty by an 80-14 vote Sept. 24. However, according to O'Brien, even before Kennedy was assassinated, significant breakthroughs were evident in the drive to enact civil rights legislation, medicare and an aid plan for elementary and secondary education. But the failure to pass these priority measures and to secure congressional approval for a department of urban affairs left gaps in O'Brien's record of legislative achievement.

While canvassing for support on Capitol Hill, O'Brien also presided over patronage at the White House, a position that strengthened his legislative efforts. As he later wrote in his memoirs, O'Brien called legislators when patronage requests were granted while Democratic National Chairman John Bailey [q.v.] broke the news when they were denied.

During the 1962 midterm elections, O'Brien had the additional duty of planning and coordinating President Kennedy's activities on behalf of Democratic candidates. Democrats gained two seats in the Senate and lost only five in the House, an unusually strong showing for an incumbent president's party in a midterm election.

Political considerations accounted for O'Brien's presence in Dallas when the President was assassinated on Nov. 22, 1963. Kennedy's trip was intended to reconcile differences among Texas Democrats in preparation for the 1964 presidential campaign. O'Brien went along to help patch up the long-standing patronage feud between Vice President Lyndon Johnson [q.v.] and Sen. Ralph Yarborough [q.v.].

O'Brien remained in Washington after Kennedy's death, first serving President Johnson as his special assistant for congressional relations and later as Postmaster General. [See JOHNSON Volume] After Nixon became president, O'Brien was elected chairman of the Democratic National Committee.

As the holder of that office, he was the principal intended victim of the wiretapping plans of the Watergate burglars. [See NIXON Volume]

[EWK]

For further information:
Patrick Anderson, *The President's Men* (New York, 1968).
Lawrence F. O'Brien, *No Final Victories* (New York, 1968).
Theodore H. White, *The Making of the President 1960* (New York, 1962).

O'DONNELL, KENNETH (PATRICK)
b. March 4, 1924; Worcester, Mass.
White House Special Assistant, January 1961-January 1965.

The son of Irish-Catholic parents, Kenneth O'Donnell grew up in Boston, served in the U.S. Army Air Force during World War II and then graduated from Harvard with a degree in politics and government. His relationship with John F. Kennedy began with Kennedy's first race for Congress in 1946 and continued through Kennedy's successful Senate campaigns. Robert Kennedy [q.v.], who had been a friend of O'Donnell's at Harvard, rescued him from a career as a paper salesman by bringing him to Washington to serve as a special assistant to the Senate Rackets Committee in 1957. In the presidential campaign of 1960, O'Donnell played a major role as one of John Kennedy's chief political tacticians.

During the Kennedy Administration O'Donnell was an integral part of what the press referred to as "the Irish Mafia"—a group of Kennedy advisers, including Lawrence O'Brien [q.v.] and David Powers [q.v.], who served as Kennedy's political operatives. As appointments secretary, O'Donnell controlled access to the President—a job which, according to journalist Patrick Anderson, he performed in such a cold manner that top aides often preferred to circumvent him.

The job of appointments secretary gave O'Donnell wide and often concealed powers. In addition to controlling access to the President, O'Donnell directed use of White House limousines and helicopters, allocated White House office space, served as liaison with the FBI and Secret Service, handled the logistics of all presidential trips and helped dispense political patronage. White House Press Secretary Pierre Salinger [q.v.] and presidential adviser Arthur Schlesinger, Jr. [q.v.] considered O'Donnell a strong, liberal influence on Kennedy and believed that O'Donnell had helped to bridge the gap between Kennedy advisers from the Harvard academic community and those from the Irish-Catholic sector of Massachusetts politics.

In November 1963 O'Donnell handled the political arrangements for Kennedy's trip to Texas, designed to end the disruptive political feud between conservative and liberal factions of the Texas Democratic Party. Although some urged Kennedy not to visit Dallas because of that city's reputation for extremism, O'Donnell told the President that the whole purpose of the trip would be negated if Texas's second-largest city was bypassed. In the aftermath of Kennedy's assassination, O'Donnell was instrumental in seeing to it that, despite interference from local officials, Kennedy's body was returned immediately to Washington.

While among the most vigorous opponents of Johnson's 1960 vice presidential nomination, O'Donnell remained on the Johnson staff the longest of all the old Kennedy team. Although Johnson readily acknowledged that O'Donnell's first loyalty was to the political ambitions of Robert Kennedy, he needed O'Donnell as a link to big-city Democratic leaders, who were virtually unknown to the new President. O'Donnell resigned from Johnson's staff on Jan. 16, 1965 and the next year ran in the Democratic gubernatorial primary in Massachusetts, losing to Edward McCormack by nearly 100,000 votes. In 1970 O'Donnell collaborated with former White House special assistant David Powers on *Johnny, We Hardly Knew Ye*, a memoir that described the Irish-Catholic milieu from which the career of John Kennedy developed. [See JOHNSON Volume]

[FHM]

For further information:
Kenneth P. O'Donnell and David F. Powers, *Johnny, We Hardly Knew Ye* (New York, 1970).

ORRICK, WILLIAM H(ORSLEY), JR.

b. Oct. 10, 1915; San Francisco, Calif.
Assistant Attorney General, Civil Division, January 1961-June 1962; Deputy Secretary of State for Administration, June 1962-May 1963; Assistant Attorney General, Antitrust Division, May 1963-April 1965.

A graduate of Yale University and the University of California Law School, William Orrick was chairman of the Northern California Kennedy campaign committee. President Kennedy appointed Orrick assistant attorney general in charge of the Civil Division of the Justice Department which handled all the non-criminal lawsuits to which the United States was a party. This included a wide variety of legal actions, such as admiralty suits, patents and claims against the federal government. In June 1962 Orrick moved to the State Department as deputy secretary of state for administration.

Orrick replaced Lee Loevinger [q.v.] as chief of the Justice Department's Antitrust Division in May 1963. Loevinger had the image of an antitrust crusader and had been unpopular with big business. Orrick was a proven administrator but had no background in antitrust. He initiated a study of the dozen most-concentrated industries and suggested in April 1964 that his division was contemplating major divestiture suits against mergers that had resulted in anti-competitive, industrial concentrations. However, no major actions were taken during Orrick's two-year tenure. The overall number of cases filed dropped to 43 in 1965, from an annual average of 69 for the prior six years.

The Kennedy Administration had gradually softened its antitrust approach, partly out of a fear that highly publicized prosecutions would injure business confidence and inhibit economic recovery. In the next administration neither President Johnson nor Attorney General Nicholas Katzenbach [q.v.] had a special enthusiasm for antitrust prosecutions. Katzenbach vetoed the filing of several major anti-merger suits prepared by the Antitrust Division under Orrick. These included actions against the merger of the Pennsylvania and New York Central Railroads, the merger of two Louisiana rice-milling companies and the acquisition of the New York Yankees by the Columbia Broadcasting System. The Antitrust Division also unsuccessfully sought to file a suit to divest the American Telephone and Telegraph Corp. of the Western Electric Company. Orrick retired to private practice in April 1965.

[TO]

OSWALD, LEE HARVEY

b. Oct. 18, 1939; New Orleans, La.
d. Nov. 24, 1963; Dallas, Tex.
Presumed assassin of President John F. Kennedy.

Born two months after his father's death, Oswald experienced a difficult childhood in New Orleans and Fort Worth. Oswald's mother was forced to place three-year-old Lee Harvey, his brother and stepbrother in a New Orleans orphanage so that she could go to work. When Oswald was 12 the family moved to New York, but he refused to attend school and was placed in a home for truants. For three weeks he was under psychiatric observation and was found to be tense, withdrawn and evasive but above average in intelligence. There was no evidence to suggest that he was potentially dangerous. In January 1954 the Oswalds left New York City and returned to New Orleans where Lee Harvey finished the ninth grade.

Two years later he joined the Marines, according to his half brother, "to get from out and under . . . the yoke of oppression from [his] mother." Oswald served in Japan, attaining a sharpshooter's rating. He was twice convicted in summary courts martial for failure to register a weapon and for using profanity to a noncommissioned officer. In September 1959 he was honorably transferred at his own request to the Marine Corps Reserve, ostensibly to care for his mother who had been injured at work. A month later he appeared at the American embassy in Moscow to renounce his American citizenship and to affirm his allegiance to the Soviet Union. Oswald had been interested in Communism since the age of 15 or 16 and had begun studying and reading Russian newspapers while in the Marines. In a letter to his brother shortly after his defection, he explained, "America is a dieing [sic] country and I do not wish to be a part of it, nor do I ever again wish to be used as a tool in its military aggression."

Soviet officials were at first reluctant to accept Oswald, but after he attempted suicide he was permitted to remain and was given a factory job in Minsk and a stipend, which enabled him to live better than the average Soviet worker. Oswald married a young pharmacist Marina Nicholaevna Prusakova, but after two and a half years he grew disillusioned with the Soviet Union, partly because he resented the high standard of living enjoyed by party officials. In January 1962 Oswald wrote to Sen. John Tower (R, Tex.) [q.v.] suggesting that the Soviets were preventing him and his family from leaving Russia. This letter was turned over to the State Department, and six months later the American embassy advanced Oswald the money—later repaid—that he needed to return to the U.S. with his wife and infant daughter. Oswald worked for a few months as a sheet-metal worker in Fort Worth and later for a photographic firm in Dallas, from which he was discharged in April 1963.

A search of Oswald's papers later revealed that, while in Dallas on April 10, 1963, he shot at and barely missed Edwin A. Walker [q.v.], the retired U.S. Army major general known for his right-wing views. Oswald was not apprehended and late in April left for New Orleans, where he began distributing literature supporting the Cuban revolution and Fidel Castro. Oswald, representing himself as the secretary of the fictitious New Orleans chapter of the Fair Play for Cuba Committee, was twice arrested in New Orleans while fighting in the streets with anti-Castro Cuban exiles.

In October 1963 Oswald took a job as a $50-a-week employee of the Texas School Book Depository in Dallas and rented a room in the city under an assumed name. His wife, then expecting a second child, was living at the home of a friend in Irving, a suburb of Dallas. In October and early November 1963 James Hosty, an FBI agent, interviewed Marina Oswald and the friend with whom she was staying in regard to Oswald's pro-Cuban activities. Oswald, apparently angered by this interview, hand-delivered a letter around Nov. 12 to the Dallas office of the FBI threatening to blow up the city police headquarters if the FBI did not stop its interviews.

According to the Warren Commission, which investigated the assassination of John F. Kennedy, Oswald stood at the sixth floor window of the Texas School Book Depository at about 12:30 p.m. on Nov. 22 and fired three shots that killed President Kennedy and wounded Texas Gov. John Connally [q.v.], who was riding with him in the same car. An elevator operator who had taken Oswald to the top of the building gave police his description. Forty-five minutes after the assassination, Dallas police officer J. D. Tippit, attempting to arrest a man fitting Oswald's description, was shot four times and died instantly. Oswald was arrested in a Dallas movie theater at 2:15 p.m. He was armed with a revolver later identified as the one that killed Tippit. At 7:10 p.m. he was charged with the murder of Tippit and, at 1:30 a.m. the next morning with the murder of the President. Oswald denied that he had committed either crime.

On Sunday Nov. 24, 1963, as Oswald was being taken to a car to take him from the city jail to the Dallas County jail, Jack Ruby, a Dallas nightclub proprietor, brushed past Oswald's escort and fatally shot Oswald in the stomach. The incident was televised live around the country.

Appointed by President Lyndon B. Johnson [q.v.], a commission under the chairmanship of Chief Justice Earl Warren [q.v.] began an investigation of the assassination on Nov. 29, 1963. A year later it issued a report that declared that Oswald, acting entirely alone, had murdered the President and Tippit and wounded Gov. Connally.

Over the next decade critics of the Warren Commission argued that the gun found on the sixth floor of the school book depository might not have been Oswald's. They also claimed that—given the speed of the presidential limousine, its distance from the depository and the time needed to aim and fire—even a highly skilled marksman could not have singlehandedly wounded Gov. Connally and killed the President. Some believed that Oswald had been a CIA or FBI informer; some were convinced that he was part of a left or right-wing conspiracy to murder Kennedy. Whatever the truth of these allegations, the belief was widespread that the Warren Commission investigation had been inadequate. In the fall of 1975 a committee of Congress had begun to reexamine certain questions relating to the assassination and the enigmatic life of Lee Harvey Oswald.

[JLW]

For further information:
Report of the President's Commission on the Assassination of President John F. Kennedy (The Warren Commission Report), (Washington, 1964).
Mark Lane, *Rush to Judgment* (New York, 1966).
William Manchester, *The Death of a President* (New York, 1967).

OTEPKA, OTTO F(RED)

b. May 6, 1915; Chicago, Ill.
Chief Security Evaluator, Department of State, 1953-63.

Otto Otepka worked as a clerk for the Farm Credit Administration and the Internal Revenue Service while he earned his law degree from Catholic University. After graduation in 1942 he became a wartime investigator and security officer for the Civil Service Commission. In 1953 he was recruited for the post of chief security evaluator at the State Department by Scott McLeod, one of the Department's most zealous investigators in the Eisenhower Administration's campaign to rid the government of "security risks." Otepka held the position throughout the aggressive antisubversive campaign of Sen. Joseph R. McCarthy (R, Wisc.)

During the Kennedy Administration Otepka disagreed with other State Department officials over the use of emergency security procedures. In its first two years the Administration granted "emergency

security clearance" on 150 occasions, and Otepka was reported to have demanded more stringent procedures. (Only five such security clearances were given during the entire Eisenhower Administration.) Otepka became a conservative cause celebre when Secretary of State Dean Rusk [*q.v.*] dismissed him from his post in November 1963 on the grounds that he had violated departmental regulations in giving confidential security information to the Senate Internal Security Subcommittee.

Otepka replied that the charges were "without foundation and should be dismissed." He admitted giving classified documents to J.G. Sourwine, chief counsel for the subcommittee, but only at Sourwine's request and after Sourwine had informed him that his testimony conflicted with that of his immediate superior. Deputy Assistant Secretary of State John F. Reilly. Otepka said he was "shocked and amazed" at Reilly's statements and sent Sourwine a 39-page memorandum with the documents as exhibits. Otepka also accused the Department of tapping his telephone and surreptitiously searching his office.

Otepka's dismissal was denounced in a Senate speech Nov. 5 by Sen. Thomas J. Dodd (D, Conn.) [*q.v.*], a member of the subcommittee, Dodd said Otepka's only crime was that he had testified "honestly" and warned that if the ouster was allowed to stand "it will become impossible or exceedingly difficult to elicit any information from employes of the executive branch that bears on disloyalty, malfeasance. . .or other wrongdoing by their superiors." Dodd charged that Otepka's superiors had tapped his telephone although Department witnesses had "denied under oath" before the subcommittee that this had been done.

On the day following Dodd's speech, two Department officials accused by Dodd wrote letters to the subcommittee to "amplify" their testimony. Reilly and David I. Hill, who had denied in July and August any knowledge of tampering with Otepka's telephone, said on Nov. 6 that they had participated in March in a "survey for the feasibility of intercepting conversations in Otepka's office" by connecting wires from his telephone to a laboratory listening post within the Department. They said that the wires were disconnected due to technical difficulties and after other evidence was obtained from Otepka's trash basket. Reilly and Hill submitted their resignations Nov. 18.

The Otepka case became a campaign issue in 1964 when Republican presidential candidate Sen. Barry Goldwater (R, Ariz.) [q.v.] charged Oct. 29 that the State Department "has coddled the liars, the wire tappers, the brutal abusers of government power who tried to railroad Otto F. Otepka." President Richard M. Nixon appointed Otepka to a $36,000-a-year position on the Subversive Activities Control Board in March 1969.

[TO]

PASSMAN, OTTO E(RNEST)

b. June 27, 1900; Washington Parish, La.

Democratic Representative, La., 1947- ; Chairman, Foreign Operations Subcommittee of the House Appropriations Committee, 1955- .

After establishing himself as a successful Louisiana businessman, Passman was elected to the House of Representatives from that state's fifth district in 1946. He consistently opposed civil rights measures and usually voted with the Southern Democrat-Republican conservative coalition.

Passman became a member of the House Appropriations Committee in 1949 and soon was an outspoken foe of foreign aid programs and a master of their fiscal intricacies. In 1955 Rep. Clarence Cannon (D, Mo.) [q.v.], the conservative chairman of the Appropriations Committee, appointed Passman to head that panel's Foreign Operations Subcommittee, which initiated congressional consideration of foreign aid appropriations bills. In Passman's largely agricultural, cotton-growing district, there were few industries that benefited from foreign aid. In addition, there were no military bases or defense plants which a federal administration could threaten to remove or choke off as a means

of influencing his views. As a result, little effective pressure was exerted upon Passman to modify his opposition to foreign aid. By the end of the Eisenhower presidency, Passman, with the support of Cannon, had achieved considerable success in reducing that Administration's annual foreign assistance requests. [See EISENHOWER Volume]

Passman refused to support John F. Kennedy's presidential campaign in 1960. In January 1961 House Democratic leaders considered but decided against punishing those conservative Democrats who had not backed Kennedy by stripping them of their seniority. Passman went on to become the most formidable congressional opponent of the new President's foreign aid programs.

In a foreign aid message to Congress on March 22, 1961, President Kennedy stated that the East-West struggle for world influence necessitated substantial foreign assistance allotments. He particularly stressed the importance of a long-term, coordinated economic aid program for the underdeveloped nations to demonstrate that "economic growth and political democracy can develop hand in hand." As one means of accomplishing this purpose, Kennedy proposed to unify the administration of assistance programs through the creation of the Agency for International Development (AID).

Passman's views were diametrically opposed to those of the President. In August 1961 he asserted, "In principle I am very much against foreign aid." The following month he explained that, in his view, foreign assistance represented a threat to the American economy because "our national debt exceeds by $23 billion all public debts of all other nations. . . . We are bleeding the American people and dissipating our resources."

In an article he wrote for the *New York Times Magazine* of July 7, 1963, Passman declared that America could not win friends or earn respect through foreign aid, which he called "a weak policy, bordering on appeasement." He particularly opposed aid to those underdeveloped nations whose foreign policies were not consistently pro-American. But much of the Kennedy Administration's military and economic aid was directed towards nonaligned, economically backward countries. In the fall of 1962 Passman's subcommittee issued a report that condemned assistance to the "so-called neutral nations" that had criticized the U.S. at the Belgrade Conference of September 1961.

The fundamental structure and goals of foreign aid agencies and programs were largely determined by foreign aid authorization bills, which originated in the House and Senate Foreign Relations Committees. The 1961 authorization bill complied with Kennedy's request for the establishment of AID. But Passman's Foreign Operations Subcommittee had initial jurisdiction over foreign aid appropriations bills, which provided the funds for assistance programs. Most of the subcommittee's members sympathized with the Chairman's views. Furthermore, Passman, who was known for his long and sometimes derisive interrogation of foreign aid officials, monopolized most of the time allotted for the questioning of witnesses. As a result of his commanding role on the subcommittee and the support he received from Cannon, Passman succeeded in substantially reducing all of the Kennedy Administration's annual aid requests. Largely as a result of Passman's initiative, Congress cut Administration requests by about 18% in both 1961 and 1962.

In December 1962 President Kennedy appointed a bipartisan committee, headed by retired Gen. Lucius D. Clay [q.v.], to study the foreign aid program. The President expected that the panel would provide support for expanded foreign assistance. Instead, the Clay Committee's ambiguous report of March 1963 provided enemies of foreign aid with arguments for reductions. Passman commented that he was "surprised and pleased" by the report, and his subcommittee reduced the Administration's $4.5 billion aid proposal to $2.8 billion. The final bill provided for $3 billion in assistance. This represented a 33.8% cut, the largest since the beginning of the foreign aid program in 1945.

Rep. Cannon died in the spring of the following year and was replaced as Appropriations Committee chairman by George H.

Mahon (D, Tex.) [q.v.]. Mahon did not support Passman's effort to cut President Johnson's 1964 foreign aid request, and the President made intensive efforts to win congressional support for the Administration's assistance program. The House, as a result, rejected Passman's proposed reductions for the first time since his assumption of the subcommittee chairmanship. The following year Mahon revamped the subcommittee's membership to weaken Passman's influence on the panel. Congress sharply reduced the Administration's foreign aid requests during the last three years of Johnson's presidency, and Passman remained the most outspoken congressional foe of foreign aid. But he never regained the great power he had held before 1964. In January 1975 liberals in the House Democratic Caucus failed in a bid to remove Passman from the Foreign Operations Subcommittee chairmanship. [See JOHNSON, NIXON Volumes]

[MLL]

For further information:
Otto Passman, "Why I am Opposed to Foreign Aid," *New York Times Magazine* (July 7, 1963), pp. 16-17.
Rowland Evans, Jr., "Louisiana's Passman: The Scourge of Foreign Aid," *Harper's* (January 1962), pp. 78-83.

PASTORE, JOHN O(RLANDO)
b. March 17, 1907; Providence, R.I.
Democratic Senator, R.I., 1950- .

The first Italian-American ever elected to the U.S. Senate, John Pastore was the son of a Providence, R.I., tailor. After his graduation from Northeastern University Law School in 1931 and a career in local politics, Pastore was elected lieutenant governor and then in 1945 assumed the governorship upon the resignation of Gov. J. Howard McGrath. The biggest vote-getter in Rhode Island's history, Pastore was elected to the U.S. Senate in 1950. [See EISENHOWER Volume]

According to *Congressional Quarterly*, Pastore supported Kennedy Administration legislation on over 70% of all major issues. As chairman of the Communications Subcommittee of the Senate Commerce Committee, Pastore was a powerful voice in the regulation of television and other broadcast media. In July 1961 he sponsored a bill amending the Communications Act of 1934 to provide for reorganization of the Federal Communications Commission (FCC) and to expedite the Commission's handling of major cases. The bill did not, however, provide the increased authority for the FCC chairman that the Administration had requested. Subsequently, Pastore's Subcommittee conducted widely publicized hearings on the impact of televised sex and violence, especially on children.

As vice chairman of the Joint Atomic Energy Committee, Pastore was active in supporting the 1963 limited nuclear test ban treaty. During the Senate's debate on ratification, Pastore, long known for his volatile temperament, appealed to undecided senators to support the treaty and declared that, "If by their vote they . . . kill the treaty, God help us, God help us!"The treaty was ratified by the Senate on Sept. 24, 1963.

In 1963 Pastore was floor manager of the Administration bill to put the Communications Satellite Corp. (Comsat) under private ownership. During the Communications Subcommittee hearings on the measure, Pastore criticized Dr. Hugh L. Dryden, deputy National Aeronautics and Space Administration (NASA) administrator, who testified that the government expected to pay for a large part of the research required to inaugurate the satellite system. Pastore stated that the research expense should be paid by stockholders, since in the end they would receive the profits from the corporation. The Comsat bill was signed into law on Aug. 31 over objections of 10 liberal senators who believed that the space communications industry, in effect, would be turned over to the American Telephone and Telegraph Co., a major partner in Comsat. which had developed the Telstar satellite.

During the Johnson years Pastore supported the President on major domestic legislation and was a strong backer of the Vietnam war. He was reelected in both 1968 and 1974. [See JOHNSON, NIXON Volumes]   [FHM]

PATMAN, (JOHN WILLIAM) WRIGHT

b. Aug. 6, 1893; Patman's Switch, Tex.
d. March 7, 1976; Bethesda, Md.
Democratic Representative, Tex., 1929-76; Chairman, Banking and Currency Committe, 1963-75.

Wright Patman was the most persistent congressional opponent of the concentration of economic power in the hands of major commercial banks and Federal Reserve officials. Patman adhered for a lifetime to the anti-Wall Street populism prevalent at the turn of the century in the rural Texas of his youth. A cotton farmer before entering the Army in World War I, he served as a member of the state legislature and then as Texarkana district attorney before his election to the House of Representatives from his northeast Texas district in 1928.

In Congress Patman quickly emerged as the figure of controversy he was to remain for over four decades in Washington. In the early 1930s he called for the impeachment of President Hoover's Secretary of the Treasury, Andrew Mellon, after charging the wealthy financier with pervasive conflicts of interest. Patman next sponsored a controversial veterans bonus intended to boost purchasing power and end the Depression. Opposed by the Hoover and Roosevelt Administrations and pushed relentlessly by Patman, the bonus bill, providing $2.2 billion to World War I veterans, finally passed Congress over President Roosevelt's veto in 1935. Payment of the bonus, however, did not affect the Depression; Patman blamed the Federal Reserve for nullifying its effect by doubling bank reserve requirements and thus cutting consumer purchasing power at the same time.

Patman was a leading actor in other dramatic legislative achievements of the modern era. He was the coauthor of the 1936 Robinson-Patman Act designed to prevent chain stores from driving small retailers out of business by forbidding price discrimination in favor of large-volume dealers. Patman championed the small businessman in his successful efforts to establish the Small Business Administration and, during World

War II, backed the principle that small businesses had a right to share in defense contracts. Since the mid-1930s Patman had advocated legislation finally enacted as the Employment Act of 1946, a landmark measure that created the Council of Economic Advisers and the Joint Economic Committee of Congress and that asserted "maximum employment, production and purchasing power" as the permanent objectives of national policy. [See TRUMAN, EISENHOWER Volumes]

By the early 1960s Patman was conspicuous chiefly for his attacks on the power of large commercial banks and the policies of the Federal Reserve Board. At the outset of the Kennedy Administration, Patman was serving as chairman of the Select Committee on Small Business, alternate chairman of the Joint Economic Committee and was the ranking Democrat on the Banking and Currency Committee. His ascension to the chairmanship of the Banking and Currency Committee in January 1963 gave him a prominent forum to carry out a crusade for his unorthodox monetary views.

The major offense of the Federal Reserve, in Patman's view, was its policy of tight money and high interest rates. He blamed this effort to constrict the money supply for unemployment. In response to those bankers who argued that high interest rates were necessary because of the threat of inflation and the balance of payments deficit, Patman said in November 1962 that such spectres were "phony, fake issues . . . for the sole and only purpose of keeping interest rates high." Patman advocated lowering interest rates to stimulate the economy. To check inflation, he advised the Federal Reserve to raise bank reserve requirements rather than raise interest rates.

The Kennedy Administration shared Patman's desire for lower interest rates to a degree, but his structural criticism of the Federal Reserve System and his proposed solutions were considered too radical and were never endorsed by Kennedy or any other President. The major shortcoming of the Federal Reserve, Patman argued, was its domination by powerful private banking interests. In his view, the two con-

spired to keep interest rates artificially high, swelling bank profits but injuring small businessmen and farmers in need of cheap credit. Patman proposed a drastic restructuring of the Federal Reserve to end its "independence" from Congress and the Executive, curb the influence of the financial community and enable the Administration to coordinate fiscal and monetary policy. "I would have the monetary system in the charge of and directed by public servants, who owe no allegiance to any group," Patman said in November 1962. On the first day of every session Patman introduced a perennially unsuccessful Federal Reserve reform bill.

Patman's tenure as chairman of the Banking and Currency Committee was characterized by a steady stream of investigative studies. In January 1963 Patman issued a report critical of the concentration of control in banking. The study explored the "unadvertised connections" between banks through stockholdings of third-party "nominee accounts," dummy corporations that concealed the true ownership of bank stock. His energetic investigation of the banking system was a marked change from his predecessors' policies. Under Rep. Brent Spence (D, Ky.), the Committee's budget never had exceeded $200,000 per Congress. The Banking Committee's operating funds tripled to $608,000 in Patman's first two years as chairman. Sharp interrogation of banking and Federal Reserve officials was another hallmark of Patman's chairmanship. The main results of his tenure, nevertheless, were limited to study and exposure, for his major reform proposals were not adopted.

Patman was a defender of small local banks and savings and loan associations against the competition of the big national banks. He was vehemently opposed to the establishment of branch banks and vowed that Comptroller of the Currency James Saxon's [q.v.] proposal to permit branch banks where states had prohibited them would pass "over my dead body."

Patman's other major target was the tax-exempt foundation. In 1961, through his Small Business Committee, he began the most comprehensive investigation of private foundations ever undertaken. The Committee's findings appeared in a series of interim reports issued over the decade, detailing abuses and irregularities in the operations of the 534 foundations studied. In the first report, issued in August 1962, Patman charged that many foundations were too big, were virtually unregulated and were abusing their tax-exempt status.

Foundations often cited their philanthropic function, Patman said, while their founders and benefactors exploited their organizations' tax-exempt status for the benefit of themselves, family members and business associates. He accused foundations of accumulating excessive income, of making improper loans to wealthy investors, and of being vehicles for trading in securities and dodging capital gains taxes. Patman held that in many cases private foundations stagnated under the perpetual control and management of the founders' families.

A supporter of fiscal activism on the part of the government, Patman backed efforts of the Kennedy Administration to stimulate the economy. He was instrumental in the April 1961 passage of the Area Redevelopment Act intended to spur the revival of economically depressed areas with government loans and grants. Patman fought unsuccessfully for increased funding for the program in June 1963. In September of that year he voted for Kennedy's stimulative $11 billion tax cut. The liberal Americans for Democratic Action (ADA) calculated that Patman voted for measures favored by the ADA 80% of the time in 1961, 50% in 1962, and 73% in 1963.

Despite rumblings of hostility among the Banking Committee's Democratic majority over his maverick politics and his autocratic style as chairman, Patman persevered in his populist crusade against the moneyed interests throughout the Johnson and Nixon Administrations. He was unseated as chairman by the House Democratic caucus in January 1975. Patman died of pneumonia on March 7, 1976. [See JOHNSON, NIXON Volumes]

[TO]

PATTERSON, JOHN (MALCOLM)
b. Sept. 27, 1921; Goldville, Ala.
Governor, Ala., 1959-63.

After receiving his law degree from the University of Alabama in 1949, Patterson joined his father's law practice in Phenix City. In June 1954 his father was murdered while trying to drive racketeers out of the vice-ridden town. Patterson then ran for state attorney general and, once in office, launched a nationally publicized effort to clean up Phenix City. A committed segregationist, Attorney General Patterson also initiated a court suit in 1956 to ban the NAACP in Alabama and took legal action against the black community's boycott of stores in Tuskegee and buses in Montgomery. Patterson entered the race for governor in 1958 and campaigned on a segregationist platform, receiving the endorsement of the Ku Klux Klan. He defeated Circuit Judge George C. Wallace [q.v.] in the June 3 Democratic runoff primary and easily won the November election.

Inaugurated in January 1959, Patterson quickly became known for his firm defense of segregation. He led state officials in defying the U.S. Civil Rights Commission when it attempted to investigate complaints of voter discrimination in Alabama. He supported legislation designed to curb black voter registration in the state and denounced federal school desegregation suits. Patterson also condemned the student sit-ins of 1960; as chairman of the Alabama Board of Education, he ordered the expulsion of several students who had joined sit-ins from Albama State College for Negroes. Patterson opposed all talk of a Southern third-party movement in 1960, however, and was an early supporter of John F. Kennedy for the Democratic presidential nomination. [See EISENHOWER Volume]

In May 1961 the Congress of Racial Equality launched a series of Freedom Rides in an effort to integrate interstate bus facilities. The first group of riders reached Anniston, Ala., on May 14, where a mob attacked them and fire-bombed one of the two buses on which they were traveling.

Later the same day the freedom riders were again attacked and beaten by a crowd of whites in Birmingham. Following these incidents both the President and Attorney General Robert F. Kennedy [q.v.] tried to secure assurances from Patterson that the riders would be protected in Alabama, but he refused to speak with them and released a statement saying he would not guarantee the riders "safe passage" in the state. Justice Department aide John Seigenthaler, sent to Montgomery on May 19 as President Kennedy's personal representative, finally won from Patterson a promise of protection for the riders when they continued their journey. When the riders entered Montgomery on May 20, however, no police were present and a mob of 200, which eventually grew to about 1,000 people, assaulted the riders. Police arrived 10 minutes later, but it took over an hour to end the riot. The Kennedys then ordered 400 federal marshals into Montgomery under the direction of Deputy Attorney General Byron R. White [q.v.]. In a telegram to the Attorney General, which did not take note of any of the disturbances in Alabama, Patterson protested this action saying the state did "not need" and did "not want" the help of federal marshals.

The next evening Martin Luther King [q.v.] addressed a mass metting in support of the freedom riders at Montgomery's First Baptist Church while federal marshals stood outside. A crowd of about 1,000 whites assembled outside the church, apparently intending to attack the congregation, and at 10 p.m. White notified Attorney General Kennedy that more men were needed. Kennedy called the Governor and, with a second riot threatening, Patterson finally declared martial law and called out the National Guard. The 800 Guardsmen sent into Montgomery that night helped protect the church, but the congregation inside was not able to leave safely until 6 the next morning. When the Freedom Rides resumed on May 24, the Alabama National Guard commander rode on their bus, and other Guardsmen and state police supplied an escort until the riders reached the Mississippi line. As more riders entered the city, the Guardsmen remained on duty in Montgomery until Patterson ended martial law on May 29.

In September 1962 Patterson publicly supported Mississippi Gov. Ross Barnett's [q.v.] efforts to block the court-ordered enrollment of James Meredith [q.v.] at the University of Mississippi. Throughout his term Patterson had pending a million-dollar libel suit against the *New York Times* and four black ministers. Filed in May 1960, his suit charged that a March 1960 advertisement in the *Times*, which criticized Alabama officials and sought to raise funds for civil rights causes, contained "false and defamatory" information. The case was eventually dismissed after the Supreme Court in March 1964 reversed the libel judgment in a companion case brought by another Alabama official. Patterson's term ended in January 1963, and he was succeeded in office by George C. Wallace. Patterson ran again for governor in 1966 but polled only about 4% of the vote in the May Democratic primary.

[CAB]

PATTON, JAMES G(EORGE)
b. Nov. 8, 1902; Bazar, Kan.
President, National Farmers Union, 1940-66.

James Patton, head of the National Farmers Union, was the son of a populist farmer. Patton earned a business administration degree in 1929 and was working for a life insurance company in 1931 when he proposed a cooperative insurance program to the Colorado Farmers Union. He then worked for the farmers' organization, became its president in 1938 and in 1940 was elected president of the National Farmers Union (NFU). Patton revitalized the NFU, expanded its membership and brought it into a close alliance with the Roosevelt Administration and organized labor.

Patton was an active liberal whose political interests extended far beyond the area of farm policy. In the early postwar period he argued in favor of federal aid to education and universal health care. He believed that land reform ought to be part of U.S. foreign aid programs and was partly responsible for the creation of the United Nations Food and Agricultural Organization in 1945. Patton's proposals for maintaining full employment and full production in the postwar economy constituted the basis for the Employment Act of 1946. He served the Truman Administration on many assignments. He was, for example, on the public advisory board that helped administer the Marshall Plan. Patton remained active as a government consultant during the Eisenhower Administration, but his differences with Secretary of Agriculture Ezra Taft Benson lessened his influence. [See TRUMAN, EISENHOWER Volumes]

By 1961 the NFU represented approximately 250,000 families, mainly from the small farms of the Great Plains and Rocky Mountains. Though smaller and less wealthy than the conservative American Farm Bureau Federation, the NFU had an effective lobbyist in Patton whose influence increased with the return of the Democrats to power. Secretary of Agriculture Orville Freeman [q.v.] met with Patton in February 1961 and put many of Patton's proposals into the Administration's farm package. These included increased price-support levels, rural antipoverty programs and expansion of surplus food distribution programs abroad. Patton also won an explicit commitment from the Administration to maintain the small family farm. When the Committee for Economic Development issued a farm plan in July 1962 recommending the reduction of the number of U.S. farms from 3.9 to 1.2 million within a five-year period and the elimination of price supports, Patton's sharp rejection of the plan was seconded by Secretary Freeman. Patton in turn supported Freeman's 1963 efforts to win the wheat farmers' endorsement of strict marketing controls. The NFU and the National Grange combined to form a National Wheat Committee to campaign for the Administration position, which they felt would ensure high prices and access to world markets, but farmers rejected the new controls in a May referendum. Later in 1963 the NFU unequivocally supported the Administration's plans to sell wheat to the Soviet Union.

Patton remained active outside the area of domestic agricultural policy. He served as a consultant to the Department of Health, Education and Welfare's panel on vocational education in 1961 and committee on the aged in 1962. In a March 1963 speech demanding government revitalization of the economy, he recommended a "vast public works program," a tax cut and development of a world food policy to stabilize farm prices and provide food for underdeveloped countries. He also proposed a World Economic Union to lower trade barriers among the Western nations. Patton's proposal for a world food bank for the distribution of surpluses was approved by the U.N.'s Food and Agricultural Organization in December 1961.

Patton retired from the presidency of the NFU in 1966. Between 1967 and 1969 he was president of the United World Federalists and from 1971 to 1973 served as a special consultant to the Pennsylvania Department of Agriculture.

[JCH]

PAULING, LINUS C(ARL)
b. Feb. 28, 1901, Portland, Ore.
Chemist, peace activist.

Pauling completed his doctoral work at the California Institute of Technology in 1925 and later worked with Neils Bohr on quantum mechanics. His theory of "resonating" molecules led to the development of various plastics, drugs and synthetic fibers.

At Caltech in the 1930s Pauling began to study the chemical structure of proteins, and during World War II he worked on explosives and served as a medical research consultant. After the war he was a member of the Research Board for National Security and was also a trustee of the Emergency Committee of Atomic Scientists, which favored international atomic energy controls.

Pauling was a leading scientific opponent of nuclear testing in the 1950s. He was among the scientists who attended the international Pugwash conferences on disarmament, and in 1957 he drafted a petition calling for "an international agreement to stop all testing of nuclear weapons." Support for this position grew when Dr. Albert Schweitzer broadcast an appeal for a ban on testing, and Pauling presented the petition, signed by over 11,000 scientists, to the U.N. in 1958. His book *No More War!*, published in the same year, warned that the U.S. and the Soviet Union had more than enough nuclear weapons to destroy each other completely and that atomic tests produced radioactive strontium 90 and carbon 14, which could cause cancer, leukemia and birth defects.

Because of his work for disarmament, Pauling was labeled a Communist by Sen. Joseph McCarthy (R, Wisc.) and was investigated later by the Senate Internal Security Subcommittee. In 1952 and 1954 the State Department denied him a passport, but he was issued one after he won the 1954 Nobel Prize in chemistry. To accusations concerning his political beliefs, Pauling replied "I am not even a theoretical Marxist." [See EISENHOWER Volume]

Following resumption of atomic tests by the Soviet Union in September 1961, Pauling cabled Premier Nikita Khrushchev in September urging him to "cancel the new tests and announced expansion of the Soviet arsenal." Pauling denounced renewed atmospheric testing by the U.S. as a "monstrous immorality" and in April 1962 joined a protest march near the White House a day before he was to be a guest at a presidential dinner for Nobel Prize winners and other American notables.

In May 1963 Pauling objected to large-scale, space-program expenditures because he thought the scientific benefits "will be very small compared to putting that money into medical research or other basic scientific research . . . [or] in underdeveloped countries."

The day a partial nuclear test ban went into effect, Oct. 10, 1963, it was announced that Pauling had won the 1962 Nobel Peace Prize. "For many years it has not been respectable to work for peace," he said. "Perhaps the Norwegian Nobel Prize committee's action will help to make it respectable." When he received the award in December, Pauling called for admission of Communist China into the U.N. and an end to the research, development and use of biological and chemical weapons.

In 1963 Pauling took leave from Caltech to join the Center for the Study of Democratic Institutions, where he continued to work for general disarmament. As the war in Vietnam escalated, Pauling voiced his opposition to U.S. involvement there and participated in the movement for American withdrawal. In 1967 he joined Herbert Marcuse, Noam Chomsky, Dr. Benjamin Spock and others in a "call to resist illegitimate authority," which attacked the war as unconstitutional and urged resistance to the draft. Pauling returned to Caltech in 1967 to resume his scientific research.

[MDB]

For further information:
Robert Gilpin, *American Scientists and Nuclear Weapons Policy* (Princeton, 1962).

PEABODY, ENDICOTT
b. Feb. 15, 1920; Lawrence, Mass.
Governor, Mass., 1963-65.

A member of one of Massachusetts's most distinguished families and a direct descendant of John Endecott, one of the founders of Massachusetts Bay Colony, Peabody served as reform governor of the state during the mid-1960s. Following his graduation from Groton, which his grandfather had founded, Peabody attended Harvard University. Upon graduation in 1942 he was commissioned a lieutenant in the Navy's Submarine Corps. Peabody became interested in politics during the war, and after his graduation from Harvard Law School in 1948 became politically active as a Democrat. He ran successfully for a seat on the Governor's Council in 1954 but failed in successive attempts to win the Democratic nomination for attorney general in 1956 and 1958 and for governor in 1960.

Running on a reform program that scored Republican Gov. John A. Volpe's [q.v.] inability to deal with government corruption and institute needed reform, Peabody won the gubernatorial race in 1962. He was also aided by the indirect intervention of the Kennedy family who did not want an "All-Green" ticket of Irishmen, which could offend other ethnic groups in the year when Edward M. Kennedy [q.v.] was first running for the U.S. Senate. In a state strained by ethnic tensions, Peabody became a symbol of nonethnic integrity.

While in office Peabody undertook a program of reform designed to increase the power of the governor. He asked and got the legislature to grant him control over the appointment of state department heads. Peabody also gained approval for a constitutional amendment that deprived the Executive Council, which had become dominated by many old machine politicians, of all power except the approval of pardons and ratification of judicial appointments. Another amendment extended the gubernatorial term to four years with the governor and lieutenant governor elected as a team. In addition, the legislature approved tax reform measures and highway safety recommendations. However, Peabody could not gain support for a program aiding education through tax reform and for the abolition of capital punishment.

Despite his legislative record Peabody was denied the gubernatorial renomination in 1964. In analyzing his defeat, the *New York Times* attributed it to his failure to overcome the "image of trying too hard to be all things to all men" and to his steadfast advocacy of the abolition of the death penalty at a time when several policemen had been killed in holdups around Boston. After his defeat Peabody returned to private law practice and served on various presidential commissions.

[EWS]

PEARSON, DREW (ANDREW RUSSELL)
b. Dec. 13, 1896; Evanston, Ill.
d. Sept. 1, 1969; Washington, D.C.
Syndicated columnist.

For more than 30 years Drew Pearson was the most prominent "muckraking" journalist in the nation. He was the son of a Quaker professor and in 1919 graduated from Swarthmore College. A foreign correspondent until 1929 when he joined the staff of the Baltimore *Sun*, Pearson first gained re-

nown through his 1931 expose, *The Washington Merry-Go-Round*, written with journalist Robert Allen. In 1932 Allen and Pearson collaborated on a column of the same name, which by 1942 was syndicated in 350 papers. A self-described liberal, Pearson supported civil rights, domestic welfare programs, foreign aid and East-West detente, but his column mainly specialized in exposing the private lives of public figures and in searching out corruption in government, often with merciless zeal and occasional inadequate regard for accuracy. [See TRUMAN, EISENHOWER Volumes]

During the Kennedy Administration Pearson praised President Kennedy for his intelligence but delighted in reviving the Kennedy connection with the late Sen. Joseph McCarthy (R, Wisc.) and detailing the allegedly unscrupulous business dealings of Joseph Kennedy [q.v.]. Pearson also attributed the government's increased aid to the Diem regime in South Vietnam to Kennedy's Catholicism.

In August 1961 Soviet Premier Nikita Khrushchev held an exclusive interview with Pearson, in which the Premier told the columnist that he was "ready at any moment" to negotiate with Western leaders on a realistic settlement of the Berlin question. Khrushchev said the Soviet Union was willing to guarantee "free city" status for West Berlin and to station a token Soviet force there alongside U.S., British and French troops. Khrushchev warned Pearson that unless the Western powers signed a peace treaty with East Germany, their further access to West Berlin would be dependent on that country's permission.

The impact of a Pearson expose was vividly illustrated in November 1961 when deputy Federal Housing Administration Commissioner James B. Cash announced on Nov. 20 that he had been fired after it became known that Pearson's column the next day would report that Cash had lost $7,000 in a card game at a builders' convention.

During the late 1960s Pearson's column was instrumental in exposing the financial misconduct of Sen. Thomas Dodd (D, Conn.) [q.v.]; the expsoure eventually led to Senate hearings and Dodd's official censure. By 1969 Pearson's column was syndicated by more than 650 newspapers, making it the most widely read column in the U.S.

When Pearson died in September 1969, his column was taken over by longtime associate Jack Anderson. [See JOHNSON Volume]

[FHM]

For further information:
Oliver Pilat, *Drew Pearson* (New York, 1973).

PELL, CLAIBORNE (DEBORDA)
b. Nov. 22, 1918; New York, N.Y.
Democratic Senator, R.I., 1960- .

Born into a wealthy and prominent Newport family, Claiborne Pell attended the fashionable St. George's School, graduated from Princeton in 1940 and served in the Coast Guard during World War II. After being commissioned in the Foreign Service in 1946, Pell served at various foreign embassies during the late 1940s and early 1950s. He then became a limited partner with a prominent investment banking firm.

Pell first gained political recognition through his ability as a state Democratic fund-raiser and his job as consultant to the Democratic National Committee from 1953 to 1960. After popular but aged Sen. Theodore F. Green (D, R.I.) announced his retirement in 1960, Pell entered the Democratic senatorial primary against two former Rhode Island governors. A Protestant in a state that was 60% Catholic, Pell called attention to his foreign affairs experience, aligned himself with John F. Kennedy's presidential candidacy, and received an unexpected 61% of the vote in the primary election. Pell went on to win the general election with a record 69% of the vote.

Regarded as a liberal, Pell was named to the Senate's important Labor and Public Welfare Committee, where he generally supported Kennedy Administration domestic programs, particularly in the area of education. In foreign affairs Pell strongly supported a proposed Senate investigation of the Central Intelligence Agency after the 1961 Bay of Pigs fiasco. In 1963 he advocated that the Western nations accept the permanent division of Germany into East and West and recommended that in exchange for such recognition the Soviets create an international zone linking Berlin to West Germany.

An early critic of the Vietnam war, Pell was a member of the four-man panel that issued a February 1963 Senate report questioning the high level of U.S. military and economic aid to the South Vietnamese government. The report also stated, "There is no interest of the U.S. in Vietnam which would justify . . . the conversion of the war . . . into an American war to be fought primarily with American lives."

Pell was floor manager of the 1963 Senate bill that, in a modified version, became the National Arts and Cultural Development Act of 1964, establishing a National Council on the Arts and providing for federal matching grants and nonprofit professional groups to promote the arts. During the Johnson Administration Pell strongly supported passage of the 1965 High Speed Ground-Transportation Act, providing $90 million for the study of advanced ground-transportation systems.

Named to the Senate Foreign Relations Committee in 1965, Pell remained a quiet but firm critic of the Vietnam war during the Johnson years. He was reelected to the Senate in 1966 and 1972. [See JOHNSON, NIXON Volumes]

[FHM]

PEREZ, LEANDER H(ENRY)
b. 1891; Plaquemines Parish, La.
d. March 19, 1969; Plaquemines Parish, La.
President, Plaquemines Parish Commission Council, 1961-67.

Perez graduated from Tulane Law School in 1914 and five years later became a district judge in his native Plaquemines Parish, La., a swampy area along the Mississippi River between New Orleans and the Gulf of Mexico. In 1924 Perez was elected district attorney for Plaquemines and St. Bernard Parishes, a post he held for the next 36 years. He used this position as a power base to become the almost undisputed political boss of Plaquemines and a major influence in Louisiana politics, within both the state Democratic Party and the state legislature.

Perez's friend and political ally, U.S. Rep. Edward Hebert (D, La.) [q.v.], described him as a "benevolent dictator." His biographer, James Conaway, wrote, "Louisiana politics is traditionally ruthless and highly professional . . . but he brought to it a particularly aggressive style, unhampered by either subjective or purely moral considerations."

Perez resisted any outside encroachment upon his parish authority. When in 1943 the state's governor appointed a sheriff not to Perez's liking, he set up a flaming blockade to prevent the appointee from entering the parish. Thirteen years later, when Gov. Earl Long appointed a ward official of whom Perez disapproved, he abolished the ward. His local opponents were suppressed through harassment and intimidation and frequently driven out of the parish.

An unabashed racist, Perez helped to organize the States' Rights Party in 1948 and the White Citizens Councils in 1954. As national pressure for racial integration increased in the late 1950s, he became progressively more vitriolic in his public statements, charging that Communists and "Zionist Jews" were behind the desegregation movement.

In 1960 Perez resigned his post as district attorney but retained his preeminent position within the parish. He was succeeded by his son Leander, Jr., and in 1961 Perez himself became president of the Plaquemines Parish commission council, the newly created governing body of the district.

In 1961 he urged Louisiana citizens not to cooperate with FBI agents entering the parish to investigate voting discrimination against blacks, who composed about 25% of the region's population. Perez also began, during the same year, to sanction the use of force in resisting integration. In February 1961 he spoke before a segregationist rally in Atlanta, Ga. "The national government is the enemy of the people," Perez stated, asserting that Southerners had no choice "but to rise up in physical opposition."

In March 1962 Archbishop Joseph Rummel, whose New Orleans diocese included Plaquemines Parish, ordered the desegregation of diocesan schools. The following month he excommunicated Perez for his adamant opposition to integration. Perez commented to an associate, "I had trouble with my Archbishop. I said, 'If you think you can send me to hell, I'll ask you to go to hell.' " New Orleans's Catholic schools were desegregated, but an explosion damaged one of the parochial schools in Plaquemines after a series of inflammatory speeches by Perez, and the integration effort was abandoned in the parish. Meanwhile, in the early 1960s the state legislature, under pressure from Perez, was passing a series of bills to delay court-ordered integration of public schools. Many of the bills were written by Perez himself.

In the summer of 1963 Perez denounced Defense Secretary Robert S. McNamara's [q.v.] order authorizing military commanders to declare segregated facilities near bases off limits. In retaliation, the parish council, at Perez's behest, approved an ordinance prohibiting bars from admitting or serving military personnel from the nearby Belle Chase naval base.

As a result of his own steadfast resistance to integration and the difficulty encountered by civil rights workers in organizing the predominantly rural Plaquemines Parish, Leander Perez successfully prevented significant steps toward desegregation during the early 1960s. Federal government pressure against Perez and other parish segregationists increased in the mid 1960s. After 1964 school integration began, and black voter registration increased rapidly. Perez remained a radical segregationist, however, and strongly supported the presidential candidacy of Alabama Gov. George Wallace [q.v.] in 1968. [See JOHNSON Volume]

[MLL]

For further information:
James Conaway, *Judge: The Life and Times of Leander Perez* (New York, 1973).
Numan V. Bartley, *The Rise of Massive Resistance: Race and Politics in the South during the 1950's* (Baton Rouge, 1969).

PIKE, JAMES A(LBERT)
b. Feb. 14, 1913; Oklahoma City, Okla.
d. Sept., 1969; Israel.
Protestant Episcopal Bishop of
California, 1958-66.

Raised in Los Angeles as a Roman
Catholic, Pike studied for the priesthood
but soon turned to a legal career. While
serving in the U.S. Navy during World
War II, he renewed his interest in religion
and was ordained an Episcopalian priest
in 1946. Dean of the Cathedral of St. John
the Divine and a professor of religion at
Columbia University in the early 1950s,
Pike became well known for his iconoclastic
views through numerous books and articles
and his own television show. He was most
notable for his championship of planned
parenthood, the state of Israel and civil
rights. He spoke out against censorship of
books and films and, though in favor of
legal restrictions against members of the
Communist Party, attacked the methods of
the House Un-American Activities Committee.
Pike soon attracted the enmity of conservative
Protestants.

In February 1961 a group of Georgia
clergymen charged Pike, then the Episcopal
bishop of California, with heresy and
communism. The charges were a response
to the Bishop's characterization of the Garden
of Eden and the virgin birth of Christ
as "myths" that churchmen should be free
to accept or reject. Pike denied the charges
and suggested that he might file a counterclaim
in the Episcopal House of Bishops
accusing the Georgians of maintaining
segregated churches, "a heresy worth discussing."
Other Episcopal bishops came to
Pike's defense, but the heresy accusation
would plague him later in the 1960s.

Pike was active in U.S. groups opposed
to Fidel Castro's Communist regime in
Cuba. In June 1962 he joined a committee
designed to raise money to ransom prisoners
captured in the April 1961 Bay of
Pigs invasion, and in 1963 he helped establish
a nonpartisan Citizens Committee for a
Free Cuba.

Unlike many liberal American clergymen,
Bishop Pike attacked the Supreme Court's
June 1962 decision banning prayer in the
public schools. Testifying before the Senate
Judiciary Committee in August 1962, he argued
that the Court's decision "distorted
the meaning of the First Amendment" and
urged Congress to approve an amendment
allowing school prayer, thus preventing the
high court from "desecrating the nation."

In the mid and late 1960s Pike participated
in the civil rights and anti-war
movements. In May 1966 he became a resident
member of the Center for the Study
of Democratic Institutions in Santa Barbara,
Calif. In the same month, as pressure grew
for a heresy trial, he relinquished his bishopric.
Although there was no trial, his increasingly
unorthodox theological views prompted
a conference of Episcopalian bishops to
censure his "irresponsibility." He subsequently
moved further from mainstream
Protestantism when he attempted to contact
his dead son through mediums and
spiritualists. He decided to leave the
church in 1969. During a research expedition
to Israel, Pike's car stalled in the Judean
wilderness. His body was discovered
five days later, on Sept. 7, 1969. Death was
attributed to exposure. [See JOHNSON
Volume]

[JCH]

PITTMAN, STEUART L(ANSING)
b. June 6, 1919; Albany, N.Y.
Assistant Secretary of Defense for Civil
Defense, September 1961-March 1964.

Prior to his appointment to the Pentagon
in September 1961, Pittman, a Washington
lawyer, had been a consultant to a number
of government agencies and groups, including
the Second Hoover Commission on
Governmental Reorganization in 1958. In
its recommendations to Congress, this body
urged the establishment of the Office of
Defense and Civilian Mobilization to make
a master plan for national protection against
nuclear attack. During the late 1950s some
progress was made in the testing of an alert
system, but efforts on a fallout shelter program
were meager.

The development of a fallout shelter program
became the chief concern of Pittman
after he was appointed assistant secretary of

defense for civil defense. In December 1961 Pittman announced the start of a nationwide survey of space for community shelters for 20 million people and gave his own endorsement to a family shelter program. For $100 to $150, Pittman explained, the average family could build a shelter on a do-it-yourself basis. Pittman's remarks added fuel to the national controversy over the types of shelters, individual or community, to be built and about the need for shelters at all.

In the spring of 1962, Kennedy sent Congress a request for $689 million to implement a community shelter program. Only one-sixth of this amount was granted when the bill passed in September. During the Cuban missile crisis of October 1962, Pittman, with New York Gov. Nelson A. Rockefeller [q.v.] and members of the Governors Conference Civil Defense Committee, announced a three-month emergency program to help identify and set up shelters. Despite the crisis, congressional opposition to a large-scale shelter program remained strong. In the spring of 1963 members of the House Armed Services Committee, assigned to investigate requests for further appropriations, opposed the new funding request. Only after hearing testimony from Pittman and other Defense Department officials that the program would save millions of lives did the Committee unanimously support the measure. Rep. Edward Hebert (D, La.) [q.v.], revealing the change in opinions, said, "I cannot recall a similar experience in my 23 years in Congress."

Pittman resigned his office in March 1964 to return to private law practice. The plan for federal subsidization of shelter construction died in 1964, when the Senate shelved a bill for further appropriations.

[EWS]

PODHORETZ, NORMAN
b. Jan. 16, 1930; New York, N.Y.
Editor, *Commentary*, 1960-   .

Norman Podhoretz wrote in his autobiography, *Making It*, that the dream of his youth was to be a "great and famous poet."

After he entered Columbia College at the age of 16, his poetic ambitions were deflated, and he decided, instead, to become a literary critic. He received a B.A. from Columbia in 1950 and obtained another degree from Cambridge University in 1952, but he discontinued graduate studies in order to serve as a reviewer for *Commentary* magazine.

Commentary was founded in 1945 by the non-Zionist American Jewish Committee. Under the editorship of Eliot Cohen, it provided a forum for what Podhoretz called "the family," a group of mainly Jewish left-wing, but anti-Communist, intellectuals. The group included Lionel Trilling, Nathan Glazer, Leslie Fiedler, Irving Howe, Irving Kristol, Alfred Kazin, Dwight Macdonald and Mary McCarthy. By the late 1950s, however, members of the group wrote less frequently for the magazine and readership declined. Podhoretz himself resigned his associate editorship in 1958 to go into other publishing ventures, but he returned as editor in 1960 following Cohen's suicide.

Podhoretz announced a new orientation for *Commentary*, changing its format and serializing Paul Goodman's [q.v.] *Growing Up Absurd* in his first issues as editor. The Goodman serialization was especially indicative of Podhoretz's intentions to make the new *Commentary* less academic, less parochially Jewish, more leftist and more critical of the status quo than it had been under Cohen. Members of the "family" contributed more frequently, while such writers as Michael Harrington [q.v.] and Hannah Arendt [q.v.] began to appear. Podhoretz's belief that *Commentary* was keeping in step with a changing social and political climate was partly confirmed by a growth in circulation from 18,000 in 1958 to 42,000 in 1960 and to amost 60,000 in 1966. Its influence grew accordingly, with President Kennedy numbering himself among its readers and admirers.

Podhoretz departed from his usual role of literary critic for that of social essayist with the publication of "My Negro Problem—and Ours" in the February 1963 issue of *Commentary*. The controversial article described his irritation with liberal integrationist rhetoric and was written from the vantage point of his own youth spent "in an 'integrated' slum neighborhood where it was the Negroes who persecuted the whites and not the other way around."

In the mid and late 1960s Podhoretz was critical of the New Left for what he believed was its lack of understanding of Communist totalitarianism. The tone of *Commentary* became more conservative, and it served as a literary home for disenchanted leftists. In January 1968 Podhoretz's *Making It* was published. A confessional autobiography, it described what he considered the "dirty little secret" of the times: the ambition and desire for praise motivating literary intellectuals such as himself. [See JOHNSON Volume]

[JCH]

For further information:
Norman Podhoretz, *Doings and Undoings: The Fifties and After in American Writing* (New York, 1964).
———, *Making It* (New York, 1968).
———, ed., *The Commentary Reader* (New York, 1966).

POWELL, ADAM CLAYTON, JR.
b. Nov. 29, 1908, New Haven, Conn.
d. April 4, 1972, Miami, Fla.
Democratic Representative, N.Y., 1945-67, 1969; Chairman, Education and Labor Committee, 1961-67.

At the age of 29 Adam Clayton Powell, Jr., a graduate of Colgate with a master's degree from Columbia, succeeded his father as pastor of Harlem's Abyssinian Baptist Church. During the 1930s and 1940s Powell turned the Abyssinian, the largest Protestant congregation in the country, into a center of social activism. Powell set up soup kitchens for the needy, organized a bus boycott, which compelled the Transport Workers Union to accept Negro drivers, and used similar tactics to win concessions from the telephone company and Harlem merchants. In 1941 he became the first Negro elected to the New York City Council and four years later took his seat in Congress as the representative from central Harlem.

The pulpit afforded a skilled orator like Powell an exceptional political opportunity to appear weekly before a mass audience. The Abyssinian provided its congregation with a variety of social services, and the congregation served Powell's political machine, helping its pastor to overwhelm all challengers in his Harlem district.

When Powell took office in 1945 there was only one other Negro congressman, William L. Dawson (D, Ill) [*q.v.*] of Chicago. The discreet and tactful Dawson, attentive to his congressional business got on well with the House "Establishment," even the segregationists. Powell, in sharp contrast, considered himself the "first bad nigger in Congress" and forced his way into formerly segregated restaurants, baths, showers and barber shops. More troubling to his liberal supporters was Powell's attendance record, among the worst in Congress, and his penchant for congressionally financed vacations. "As a member of Congress," Powell once said, "I have done nothing more than any other member, and by the grace of God, I intend to do not one bit less."

During the 1950s Powell became known for his efforts to bar federal appropriations to state projects that continued a pattern of racial discrimination. The so-called "Powell Amendment" to a 1956 school construction bill seriously divided liberal Democrats because it forced them to choose between federal aid to education and de facto support of segregated school systems. Because Adlai Stevenson [*q.v.*] opposed the amendment and refused to discuss the matter, Powell thought Stevenson soft on civil rights and broke party ranks in 1956 to support the reelection of President Dwight D. Eisenhower.

Shortly before Powell became chairman of the House Committee on Education and Labor in 1961, the *New York Times* wrote that his "miserable record as a legislator and his extreme absenteeism all tend to disqualify him as a reasonable and effective chairman." During his six years as chairman, however, he headed a remarkably productive committee. Powell had supported Lyndon B. Johnson's [*q.v.*] presidential candidacy in 1960, but his relations with the Kennedy Administration were generally cordial. During a House-Senate conference in 1961, Powell rescued the minimum wage bill and helped secure its enactment for the Administration. In 1961 Powell also prodded the Administration into supporting legislation, passed a year later, granting the Secretary of Labor increased power to investigate the management of workers' pension and trust funds.

Powell generally supported the Administration's education bills and did not obstruct their passage with antisegregation amendments. To win Catholic backing for Administration education bills denying aid to private and parochial schools, Powell supported additional legislation offering parochial schools low-interest loans in lieu of direct federal aid. The effort failed in 1961. In 1963 Powell persuaded the Kennedy Administration to break its omnibus education bill into separate measures, which were then reported from his committee and passed. They dealt with aid for the construction of college buildings, for vocational education, for training of teachers of handicapped children and for aid to federally impacted areas.

At the very moment when as a committee chairman Powell held greater power than any other elected Negro official, he became entangled in the difficulties that ultimately wrecked his political career. During a March 6, 1960 television show, Powell off-handedly referred to Mrs. Esther James as a "bag-woman," or graft collector, for the New York City police. Mrs. James sued Powell for defamation and in April 1963 won a $211,500 judgment against him, which he refused to pay. He was held in contempt of court and escaped punishment only by absenting himself from New York.

While the James case was in the courts, newspapers revealed that in the summer of 1962 Powell, accompanied by two young women from his staff, had taken a six-week European vacation paid for with Committee funds.

In the early 1960s Powell became a center of controversy as a result of his praise for black militant Malcom X [q.v.]; he also appealed in March 1963 for blacks to boycott all civil rights organizations, including the NAACP, "not totally controlled by us."

In January 1967 a congressional committee began an investigation of Powell's contempt of court conviction and his alleged misuse of committee funds. He was formally expelled from the House in March. Black leaders from around the country denounced the action as racist. In April a special election was held in Powell's district to fill his seat, but Powell was reelected by a margin of 7 to 1. Nevertheless, Powell's seat remained vacant for two years. In January 1969 he was permitted to return to the House, and six months later the U.S. Supreme Court ruled that his expulsion had been unconstitutional. Powell felt vindicated but lost his seat in 1970 to Charles B. Rangel (D, N.Y.). Powell died three years later in Miami. [See JOHNSON Volume]

Adam Clayton Powell Jr., was among the most controversial politicians of his time. To journalist Theodore White [q.v.], he was "the most egregious and frightening" exception to the general excellence of black elected officials. To Chuck Stone, Powell's chief congressional assistant, he was "a mercurial personality who wavered erratically between tub-thumping militancy and cowardly silence," a man so driven by "hedonistic compulsions" that he undermined his role as a black leader. Julius Lester, a black author, also remembered Powell as a man who during the 1950s "gave blacks a national voice" when others were quietly submissive and deferential.

[JLW]

For further information:
Adam Clayton Powell, Jr., *Adam by Adam* New York, 1971).
Chuck Stone, *Black Political Power in America* (New York, 1970).

POWERS, BERTRAM A(NTHONY)
b. March 8, 1922; Cambridge, Mass.
President, Local 6, International Typographical Union, 1961-   .

Bertram A. Powers, head of Local 6 of the typographers union, called a strike that shut down New York City newspapers for 114 days in 1962 and 1963. Powers was born into a poor family in Cambridge, Mass. He learned printing at Fitchburg State Teachers College and later worked as an apprentice in Boston, Chicago, Detroit and New Haven. After completing his apprenticeship he came to New York City in 1946, took a job as a typesetter and joined Big Six, the powerful 11,000-member local of the International Typographical Union (ITU).

Powers became active in union politics and in 1953 won his first full-time office as vice president of the local. He earned a reputation for militancy by arguing that ITU wage settlements were unfairly and unnecessarily tied to the contracts negotiated first by the weaker and less aggressive white-collar Newspaper Guild.

Powers was elected Big Six president in May 1961. During 1962 he was unable to negotiate a settlement with the New York Publishers Association, and on Dec. 8, 1962 his local struck four major New York daily newspapers. Other New York dailies and two Long Island papers, all members of the Publishers Association, shut down voluntarily in support of the struck papers. The strike was the first called by the ITU against New York newspapers since 1883.

The union asked for a substantial wage increase, but the most difficult issue of the strike involved the introduction of automated and computerized typesetting equipment. The publishers saw the use of this new technology as an essential means of cutting their production costs and competing more effectively with magazines and television. The ITU membership viewed the new automated machinery as a threat to their jobs.

A total of 19,000 New York newspaper employees were directly affected by the strike. As the walkout wore on the city's retail trade, theatres and restaurants suffered a marked decline. On Feb. 21, 1963 President Kennedy said the strike had "long since passed the point of toleration." He warned that Powers and his union "were attempting to impose a settlement which could shut down several newspapers and throw thousands out of work." Powers replied that the President was "ill-advised."

Labor Secretary W. Willard Wirtz [q.v.] and William E. Simkin [q.v.], director of the Federal Mediation and Conciliation Service, suggested that compulsory arbitration might be the only way to settle the walkout. However, in March 1963 New York Mayor Robert F. Wagner [q.v.] helped arrange a settlement that brought the strike to an end on the 31st of the month.

Big Six won a wage and benefit package of $12.63 a week and common expiration dates for all newspaper union contracts. But the ITU local agreed for the first time to allow limited use of computerized typesetting equipment. The effects of the strike forced the New York Mirror to cease publication later in the year. It also contributed to the subsequent demise of the New York Herald-Tribune and the Journal-American.

Over the next decade Powers fought a rear-guard battle against the use of automated equipment by the three remaining New York City daily newspapers. In negotiations over a new contract in 1973 and 1974, however, the ITU made the decision to trade control over the pace of automation for a substantial wage increase, an early retirement bonus and guarantees of lifetime job security for currently employed printers. Ratified by the Big Six membership in June 1974, the new contract provided for a staged automation of the pressroom and a sharp reduction in the number of typographical jobs over the next 10 years.

[JLW]

"Bertram A. Powers," Current Biobraphy Yearbook, 1974 (New York, 1975), pp. 324-327.

POWERS, DAVID F(RANCIS)
b. April 25, 1911; Charlestown, Mass.
White House Special Assistant, January 1961-January 1965.

Powers grew up in the Charlestown waterfront district of Boston and attended public school in that city. He served in the Army Air Force during World War II. In 1946 Powers met young John F. Kennedy at the start of Kennedy's first political campaign for a seat from Massachusetts' 11th congressional district. During the early days of what proved to be a close 17-year personal and political relationship, Powers served as an effective liaison between Kennedy and the "three-decker tenement" Irish poor of Charlestown and Boston's North End. According to former White House Press Secretary Pierre Salinger [q.v.], Powers "was with John F. Kennedy more than any other man from that time until the assassination." He was a political operative in each of Kennedy's subsequent political campaigns.

During the Administration Powers served as assistant to Appointments Secretary Kenneth P. O'Donnell [q.v.]. His main functions were to escort prominent visitors to the President's office and to help keep the President's appointments schedule running smoothly. However, according to author Patrick Anderson, Powers was "on the payroll primarily because he amused the President" with Irish anecdotes, stories, songs and a phenomenal memory for things political. Described by Arthur Schlesinger, Jr. [q.v.] as "a man of exceptional sweetness and fidelity," Powers became something of a legend during the Kennedy Administration for his indifference toward the rank or station of those whom he met in his task as the White House's unofficial "greeter." To the visiting Shah of Iran, Powers once declared: "I want you to know you're my kind of Shah." On another occasion, Powers introduced Prime Minister Harold Macmillan to the President as "the greatest name in England."

During the Administration Powers was a member in good standing of what the Washington press corps called "the Irish Mafia," which included Kenneth O'Donnell, Lawrence O'Brien [q.v.] and others with a Boston Irish background who served as Kennedy's political strategists and companions.

On Nov. 22, 1963 Powers was riding in the motorcade in Dallas when Kennedy was killed. He was later instrumental in making arrangements for the state funeral of the President. After Kennedy's death Powers continued as a White House special assistant until January 1965, when he resigned to become curator of the Kennedy Library in Massachusetts.

[FHM]

For further information:
Kenneth P. O'Donnell and David F. Powers, *Johnny, We Hardly Knew Ye* (Boston, 1970).

POWERS, FRANCIS GARY
b. Aug. 17, 1929; Burdine, Ky.
Central Intelligence Agency Employe, 1956-62.

After six years in the U.S. Air Force, Powers was hired in January 1956 by the Central Intelligence Agency (CIA) as a test pilot for the new U-2 espionage plane. In November of that year he and other CIA pilots began making high-altitude flights over the Soviet Union and the Middle East, in what the *New York Times* later called "the most successful reconnaissance espionage project in history." On May 1, 1960 Powers was shot down near Sverdlovsk, deep inside the Soviet Union, by a surface-to-air missile. Although the United States initially denied that the U-2 was on a spy flight, Soviet Premier Nikita Khrushchev's disclosure that Powers had been captured and was alive forced the United States to acknowledge the purpose of the flight.

The long-planned East-West Summit meeting, which opened in Paris on May 16, collapsed when Khrushchev refused to attend further meetings unless President Eisenhower formally apologized for the U-2 flight, which Eisenhower refused to do. At a Soviet trial that August, Powers pleaded guilty to a charge of espionage and was sentenced to 10 years confinement. [See EISENHOWER Volume]

Powers was released by the Soviet Union on Feb. 10, 1962 in an exchange for the United States-held Soviet spy Rudolph Abel. The exchange had been negotiated by Abel's American lawyer, James B. Donovan [q.v.]. Upon his release, Powers was criticized by the press, American Legion officials and several members of Congress for not having destroyed his plane or used a CIA-supplied, curare-soaked pin to kill himself. His apparent cooperation with the

Soviets at his trial was criticized and many suggested that he not be given the back pay his CIA contract called for. However, a CIA inquiry headed by retired federal Judge E. Barrett Prettyman [q.v.] found "that Mr. Powers lived up to the terms of his employment. . .and in his obligations as an American under circumstances in which he found himself." Powers testified before the Senate Armed Services Committee on March 6, 1962, giving details of his flight and trial. Committee members seemed satisfied with his testimony, and several commended him for his conduct after capture.

Powers left the CIA in October 1962 to join Lockheed Aircraft, makers of the U-2, as a test pilot. He published an account of his experiences in 1970.

[JBF]

For further information:
Francis Gary Powers with Curt Gentry, *Operation Overflight: The U-2 Spy Pilot Tells His Story For the First Time* (New York, 1970).

PRETTYMAN, E(LIJAH) BARRETT
b. Aug. 23, 1891; Lexington, Va.
d. Aug. 4, 1971; Washington, D.C.
U.S. Court of Appeals Judge, 1945-71.

Judge E. Barrett Prettyman, who served on several presidential advisory panels during the Kennedy Administration, graduated from Randolph-Macon College in 1910, was admitted to the Virginia bar in 1915 and for the next two years practiced law in Hopewell, Va. Following service in the U.S. Army during World War I, Prettyman became a special attorney for the Internal Revenue Department. For the next 26 years he alternated between government service and private law practice. In 1945 he was appointed a judge of the U.S. Court of Appeals for Washington, D.C. During the 1950s Prettyman headed the President's Conference on Administrative Procedure and handed down important decisions upholding the constitutionality of the 1950 McCarran Act. [See EISENHOWER Volume]

In April 1961 President Kennedy appointed Prettyman head of the Administrative Conference, which was formed to rec-

ommend improvements in the administration of federal agencies. The panel report, issued in January 1963, did not call for sweeping reform, but did urge streamlining procedures to speed up decision making, strengthen enforcement powers and prevent the use of improper influence in the agencies.

Prettyman headed the 1962 board of inquiry formed to investigate U-2 spy-plane pilot Francis Gary Powers's [q.v.] conduct while a prisoner of the Russians. The board's report, made public in March 1962, exonerated Powers of charges that he had not complied with instructions when he revealed the nature of his mission and his connection with the Central Ingelligence Agency.

The following year the Judge headed the President's Advisory Commission on Narcotics and Drug Abuse. In an April 4 interim report the Commission recommended strict control of hard drugs and the creation of a special Justice Department-Treasury Department unit to launch a "massive attack" against importers and large-scale distributors of narcotics. It also urged increased research into drug use, lighter penalties for narcotics users and small pushers, dissemination of accurate data on drug abuse, and a joint U.S.-Mexican commission to fight drug smuggling.

In 1967 Prettyman was on the U.S. Appeals Court that reversed the 1965 conviction of a U.S. Communist Party member for failing to register with the government as an agent of the Soviet Union as required by the McCarran Act. Prettyman died in August of 1971.

[EWS]

PROXMIRE, (EDWARD) WILLIAM
b. Nov. 11, 1915; Lake Forest, Ill.
Democratic Senator, Wisc., 1957-   .

Voted the "most energetic" and "biggest grind" by his high school classmates, Proxmire earned degrees at Yale and Harvard before serving in the Army Counterintelligence Corps during World War II. He moved to Wisconsin in 1949 and ran successfully for the state Assembly as a Democrat the next year. He earned a reputation during the 1950s as an uncommonly productive legislator, a foe of Sen. Joseph McCarthy (R, Wisc.), and a perennial loser in gubernatorial elections. Proxmire won a surprising victory over his twice-victorious opponent for governor, Walter J. Kohler, in a special election held in 1957 to fill the seat left vacant by the death of Sen. McCarthy. Named to the Senate Banking Committee but passed over for the Finance Committee, the iconoclastic Proxmire alienated Senate Majority Leader Lyndon Johnson in February 1958 when he criticized his "unwholesome and arbitrary power" and demanded more frequent Democratic Party caucuses. [See EISENHOWER Volume]

The Kennedy Administration was three days old when Proxmire first distinguished himself as a liberal gadfly. Opposing the confirmation of John Connally [q.v.] as Secretary of the Navy, Proxmire argued that Connally's associations with the oil industry, especially his current position as co-executor of the estate of Texas oilman Sid Richardson, constituted a "conflict of interest." He was the only Senator to vote against Connally's confirmation. In August Proxmire held the Senate floor for 34½ hours in an unsuccessful attempt to halt the confirmation of Lawrence J. O'Connor, Jr., whom he called "an oil-and-gas man with a built-in bias," to the Federal Power Commission. The following month, for similar reasons, he opposed the appointment of Jerome J. O'Brien, a vice president of Humble Oil and Refining Company, to be director of the Office of Oil and Gas of the Interior Department.

Proxmire favored Administration school aid and medicare programs, and he was a consistent supporter of civil rights, but his dogged espousal of a balanced budget marked him as a maverick among liberals. In October 1961 he claimed that President Kennedy had "backed away" from his pledge that he would balance the budget even if it required higher taxes. A member of the Joint Economic Committee, Proxmire filed a separate report in March 1962 opposing the proposed investment tax credit and the grant of emergency authority to

the President to cut taxes and institute public works. Proxmire's amendments in August to eliminate the investment credit from the tax revision bill were rejected by the Senate.

Proxmire waged a relentless but often futile struggle to reduce federal expenditures. He was one of only two Northern senators to vote against a proposal in March 1961 to have the federal government finance a 13-week extension of unemployment benefits from a nationwide "pool" of employer contributions. He proposed unsuccessful amendments in April 1962 to eliminate federal funds for the New York World's Fair, in July to reduce appropriations for the Department of Health, Education and Welfare, and in October to cut the Maritime Commission's ship construction program. In March 1963 he voted against the mass transit grant-in-aid program and later in the year was one of a handful of senators to oppose defense budget appropriations for long-range manned bombers, mid-range ballistic missiles, and the supersonic transport (SST). However, his amendment to reduce funds for the National Aeronautics and Space Administration was accepted on Nov. 20 by a vote of 40 to 39. Throughout the 1960s Proxmire persisted in his assaults on the budget as a member of the Appropriations Committee and as chairman of the Joint Economic Committee's Subcommittee on Economy in Government. Focusing more sharply on waste and mismanagement in Pentagon weapons buying, he publicized a $2-billion cost overrun in the production of the C-5A cargo plane and was instrumental in the Senate vote to kill the SST in 1970. Proxmire also led Senate opposition to requests for government assistance from Lockheed Aircraft, manufacturer of the C-5A. The company's mismanagement, he charged amounted to "a deliberate and calculated policy of financial brinksmanship." [See JOHNSON, NIXON Volumes]

[TO]

For further information:
Jay G. Sykes, *Proxmire* (Washington, 1972).
Drew Pearson and Jack Anderson, *The Case Against Congress* (New York, 1968).

QUILL, MICHAEL J(OSEPH)
b. Sept. 18, 1905; Gourtloughera, Ireland.
d. Jan. 28, 1966; New York, N.Y.
President, Transport Workers Union, 1935-66.

Quill was active as a youth in the Irish Republican Army. He came to New York in 1926 and worked on the subway system. Influenced by the writings of Irish socialist James Connolly, Quill advocated militant unionism and, in April 1934, joined forces with a group of Communist Party organizers, led by John Santos, to form the Transport Workers Union (TWU). He was elected union president the next year. Quill also served three terms on the New York City Council between 1937 and 1949, twice representing the American Labor Party and once as an independent. Quill broke with the Communist Party in March 1948 and, after a bitter, year-long struggle, won control of the union. Although he often threatened transit strikes, Quill usually negotiated contracts without actually calling out his members. [See TRUMAN Volume]

At the October 1961 TWU convention, Quill called for the "socialization" of railroads, transit lines, airlines and utilities, the formation of a national labor party, and equal rights and opportunities for blacks. Re-elected to a four-year term, Quill also called for the readmission of the International Brotherhood of Teamsters to the AFL-CIO, and invited Teamster President James R. Hoffa [q.v.] to address the gathering. However, at a meeting of the AFL-CIO Executive Council on Oct. 10, Quill's resolution to readmit the Teamsters was defeated, 24-3, and that decision was confirmed at the next month's AFL-CIO convention in Bal Harbour, Fla.

Quill feared the effect of automation on the transit industry, and in negotiations with the New York City Transit Authority and New York's private bus lines in 1961 the union demanded a four-day, 32-hour week. Quill also threatened an immediate strike if the Transit Authority put its automatic shuttle subway into operation. The shuttle issue was settled on Dec. 13 when arbitrator Theodore W. Kheel [q.v.] or-dered the authority to postpone the introduction of the experimental train. Contracts between the union and the Transit Authority and the union and most of the private bus lines were agreed upon in late December, maintaining a 40 hour, five-day workweek but guaranteeing no layoffs. The Fifth Avenue Coach Line, however, did not approve the contract until after a four-day strike in January 1962 and a city agreement to permit the line to end transfer tickets. A month later, a new management group at the company announced that it would lay off 1,500 workers. As soon as the layoffs began, on March 1, the 6,500 TWU members struck. Three weeks later a settlement was reached when New York City permanently took over the struck lines.

In January 1963 Quill led a 20-day TWU strike against Philadelphia's transit system. During the strike, Philadelphia Mayor James H. Tate filed a $250,000 defamation-of-character suit against Quill, after Quill allegedly said in a television interview that Tate was a servant of Philadelphia bookmakers.

Although a strike on New York's transit system was avoided at the last minute in January 1964, two years later Quill led a 12-day shutdown of New York buses and subways, during which he was jailed. He died shortly afterward. [See JOHNSON Volume]

[JBF]

For further information:
L. H. Whittemore, *The Man Who Ran the Subways: The Story of Mike Quill* (New York, 1968).

RANDOLPH, A(SA) PHILIP
b. April 15, 1889; Crescent City, Fla.
President, Brotherhood of Sleeping Car Porters, 1929-68.

After an adolescence as a brilliant student and amateur dramatist, Randolph left his father's ministerial household in Florida to join the growing prewar migration of Southern Negroes to Harlem. Soon after his arrival in 1911 he joined the Socialist Party and plunged into radical politics. With

Chandler Owen, Randolph founded the anti-war journal *The Messenger,* which became a pillar of Harlem's Negro Renaissance in the early 1920s. Long a partisan of black trade unionism, Randolph joined forces with a group of Pullman porters in 1925 to begin an epic 12-year struggle to organize the Brotherhood of Sleeping Car Porters. With recognition of the union in 1937, the cool and dignified Randolph became the most widely respected black leader of his time. In June 1941 Randolph's threat of a march on Washington by 100,000 blacks wrestled from a reluctant Roosevelt Administration an executive order banning racial discrimination in federal employment and in defense industries. Randolph's postwar protest campaign against segregation in the armed forces helped pressure President Truman into issuing another executive order, in July 1948, ordering integration of the military services. [See TRUMAN Volume]

During the late 1950s Randolph also prodded the newly merged AFL-CIO to take more vigorous action to end discrimination among its affiliated unions. Tensions between Randolph and AFL-CIO President George Meany [q.v.] reached a climax at the labor federation's September 1959 convention when Randolph and other Brotherhood officials introduced a motion demanding that racially segregated local unions be "liquidated." In an angry and well publicized exchange on the convention floor, Meany asked Randolph, "Who in the hell appointed you as the guardian of all the Negroes in America?" [See EISENHOWER Volume]

As a consequence of the slow progress made by the AFL-CIO in ending racial discrimination, Randolph joined with other black trade unionists to organize the Negro American Labor Council (NALC) in November 1959. As president of the new organization, Randolph said discrimination had "reached the stage of institutionalization in the labor movement," but he nevertheless sought to work within the AFL-CIO to change these conditions. During his four-year tenure as NALC president, Randolph was challenged by younger militants in the black labor organization who wished to adopt a more combative posture toward the AFL-CIO

leadership. As the *New York Times* put it in October 1961, Randolph was involved in a "two-front battle," fighting to restrain elements within the NALC and obliged, on the other hand, to maintain his pressure against the organized labor movement itself. Meany identified Randolph with what he termed NALC "dual-union" militants. The AFL-CIO executive council censured Randolph in October 1961 after he had again urged the labor federation to take disciplinary action against racially segregated unions. Meany told the press Oct. 12, "We can only get moving on civil rights if he [Randolph] comes to our side and stops throwing bricks at us."

This rebuke to Randolph was strongly denounced by civil rights leaders Roy Wilkins [q.v.] and Martin Luther King [q.v.] and by Daniel Schulder, president of the New York chapter of the Association of Catholic Trade Unionists. Randolph deplored the tendency of AFL-CIO leaders "to equate opposition to trade union policies with opposition to the trade union movement." Meany met for the first time with an NALC delegation at the December 1961 AFL-CIO convention. At the same meeting the Federation effectively rescinded its motion censuring Randolph and passed a civil rights resolution, which Randolph praised as the best adopted in his 35-year association with organized labor. In November 1962 Randolph opposed a NAACP-sponsored campaign to decertify trade union locals that discriminated against minority workers. He reaffirmed his conviction that "we must carry out our fight within the house of labor."

As a socialist and trade unionist, Randolph emphasized an economic solution to America's racial problems. With Bayard Rustin [q.v.], a radical pacifist who had helped organize the 1941 march on Washington movement, Randolph began planning in December 1962 for a new Washington march. The mass protest was designed to link the demand for strong federal civil rights legislation with the labor movement's call for full employment, a higher minimum wage and a guaranteed income. In February 1963 Rustin and Randolph publicly announced plans for a summer march of

100,000 people, whose slogan would be "jobs and freedom now." During the spring of 1963 Randolph recruited an impressive array of liberal, labor, religious and civil rights organizations in support of the march. According to Murray Kempton, the 74-year-old Randolph was uniquely suited for this task because "alone among the leaders [of the civil rights movement] he neither feels hostility for nor excites it in any other of them." When NAACP Executive Secretary Roy Wilkins objected to Rustin's prominent role in organizing the march, Randolph agreed to assume the title national director, with Rustin as his deputy.

After civil rights demonstrations in Birmingham, Ala. sparked a series of often violent clashes across the South, President Kennedy asked black leaders to the White House on June 22. He requested them to call off their march on the grounds that any disorders at the demonstration could stiffen the resistance of congressional conservatives to pending civil rights legislation. "With great dignity," reported Arthur Schlesinger, Jr. [q.v.], Randolph replied to the President, "The Negroes are already in the streets. It is very likely impossible to get them off." He told Kennedy that the only alternative to the current march was a new black leadership which "cares neither about civil rights nor about nonviolence." The march, which Kennedy eventually endorsed, took place as scheduled on Aug. 28, 1963. An estimated 210,000 participated in the orderly and peaceful demonstration. Randolph chaired the march's Lincoln Memorial assemblage and, in the last major speech of his life, emphasized the link between the fulfillment of civil rights demands and the need for fundamental economic and social changes in American society.

During the remaining years of the 1960s Randolph's advanced age forced him to retire from day-to-day participation in the civil rights and labor movements. In September 1968 he formally resigned as president of the Brotherhood of Sleeping Car Porters. [See JOHNSON Volume]

[NNL]

For further information:
Jervis Anderson, A. Philip Randolph (New York, 1972).

RANDOLPH, JENNINGS
b. March 8, 1902; Salem, W. Va.
Democratic Senator, W. Va., 1958- .

Randolph worked as a journalist before joining the faculty of Davis and Elkins College at Elkins, W.Va., in 1926, where he became head of the department of public speaking and journalism. He lost an election for the U.S. House of Representatives in 1930 but made a successful bid for a House seat two years later. Randolph was a strong supporter of New Deal domestic legislation. He was interested in aviation and sponsored bills dealing with air mail delivery, civilian pilot training and federal aid to airports.

Randolph was defeated in the 1946 Republican electoral sweep. For the next decade he was an assistant to the president and director of public relations for Capital Airlines. In 1958 Randolph was elected to fill a vacant Senate seat, and two years later he won a full term.

During the early 1960s Randolph generally supported social welfare measures, but he identified himself particularly with legislation pertaining to West Virginia's economic problems. West Virginia was the second leading coal-producing state in the nation, and more of its residents were employed in coal mining than in any other occupation. But mechanization of the mines after World War II had produced considerable unemployment, encouraging a population decline of 13% between 1950 and 1970.

In 1961 Randolph supported an area redevelopment bill aimed at depressed regions like West Virginia. Testifying in favor of the measure before the Senate Banking and Currency Committee, he asserted, "I can attest to the fact that joblessness in West Virginia, long chronic, also remains as chronic today. . . ." During the same year Randolph defended a manpower retraining bill, arguing that "automation and technological changes have made obsolete the skills of literally hundreds of thousands of Americans. . . ." Two years later he backed a new area redevelopment bill. In 1963 Randolph and Sen. George McGovern (D, S.D.) [q.v.] were the only Senators who voted for the latter's amendment to cut over $2 billion from defense appropriations. McGovern argued that the funds were needed for social programs.

In 1965 Randolph played a key role in securing Senate passage of the Appalachian development bill. The following year he became chairman of the powerful Public Works Committee. Although Randolph continued to support most social welfare legislation during the late 1960s and early 1970s, he was accused by some of representing the views of coal operators regarding mine health and safety hazards and air and water pollution caused by coal mining. [See JOHNSON, NIXON Volumes]

[MLL]

RAUH, JOSEPH L(OUIS), JR.
b. Jan. 3, 1911; Cincinnati, Ohio.
Vice Chairman, Americans for Democratic Action, 1952-55, 1957- .

Rauh graduated from Harvard Law School in 1935 and served as an enforcement attorney for the Wage and Hour Administration and counsel for the Lend-Lease Administration before joining Gen. Douglas MacArthur's staff in 1942. In 1947 he entered private law practice. During the same year Rauh was one of the founders of Americans for Democratic Action (ADA), a liberal anti-Communist organization intended to prevent the Communist-influenced Progressive Party of former Vice President Henry A. Wallace from dominating left-of-center politics. Rauh was chairman of the ADA's executive committee from 1947 to 1952, when he was elected a national vice chairman. From 1955 to 1957 he was chairman of the organization, and in the latter year he resumed his vice chairmanship.

Rauh was an advocate of liberal causes in his private law practice as well as in his capacity as an ADA leader. Among his first clients were Walter Reuther's [q.v.] United Auto Workers and A. Philip Randolph's [q.v.] Brotherhood of Sleeping Car Porters. In the late 1940s and the 1950s, Rauh defended government employes charged under loyalty-security programs. In

1957 he carried the case of *Watkins v. United States* to the Supreme Court and won a decision denying the right of the House Un-American Activities Committee to employ its investigative powers simply for the purpose of exposure. [See TRUMAN, EISENHOWER Volumes]

In the race for the 1960 Democratic presidential nomination, Rauh and ADA preferred Sen. Hubert H. Humphrey (D, Minn.) [q.v.], a former vice chairman of the group, over Sen. John F. Kennedy, who was not associated with the organization and whose record was not as consistently liberal as the Minnesota Senator's. Relations between ADA and the Kennedy Administration were not close. Rauh was the chief public spokesman for the group during the early 1960s, and his statements in those years reflected ADA's attempt to push the New Frontier towards the left.

At a workshop of the General Assembly of the Union of American Hebrew Congregations in November 1961, Rauh criticized what he said was the continued flow of federal money to construct racially segregated housing. The following April he denounced the Administration for backing conservative John B. Connally [q.v.] in the Texas Democratic gubernatorial primary over liberal Don Yarborough. Rauh charged that the only reason for the President's support of Connally, whom he described as an opponent of federal aid to education and of a national medical care program for the aged, was the Texan's close relationship to Vice President Lyndon B. Johnson [q.v.].

At a national ADA convention in May 1962, Rauh denounced President Kennedy's bill to legalize wiretapping in certain instances as "the greatest threat to civil liberties in America today." Three months later he testified before the Senate Foreign Relations Committee against the Administration's plan for private operation of a communications satellite system, which he called "probably one of the biggest giveaways in the history of our nation." He claimed that the proposal conflicted with the 1960 Democratic national platform, which had pledged to protect the people against the growth of monopoly.

In private practice Rauh continued to act

on behalf of social reform during the early 1960s. In 1962 he handled the case of a developer of integrated housing whose land had been condemned by the town of Deerfield, Ill., a suburb of Chicago, for the ostensible purpose of building a park. When the Illinois Supreme Court decided in December 1962 that the condemnation was legal since a need for parks had been demonstrated, Rauh commented, "This ruling is a direct encouragement of the use of the power of eminent domain to keep Negroes out of all white areas."

At the August 1964 Democratic National Convention, Rauh represented the Mississippi Freedom Democratic Party in that organization's effort to seat its integrated delegation. During the same year he became general counsel to the Leadership Conference on Civil Rights, a group that formulated and lobbied for anti-discrimination legislation. In the late 1960s and early 1970s he was a legal representative of dissident elements in W. A. (Tony) Boyle's United Mine Workers. [See JOHNSON, NIXON Volume]

[MLL]

RAYBURN, SAM(UEL) T(ALIAFERRO)

b. Jan. 6, 1882; Kingston, Tenn.
d. Nov. 16, 1961; Bonham, Tex.
Democratic Representative, Tex., 1913-61; Speaker of the House, 1940-47, 1949-53, 1955-61.

The son of a Confederate veteran, Sam Rayburn grew up on a cotton farm in Texas. He served in the Texas House of Representatives from 1906 to 1912 and was chosen speaker in 1910, the youngest man in Texas history ever to hold that post. Elected to Congress in 1912, Rayburn served for 48 continuous years, the longest tenure in the history of the House. Rayburn, who became a lieutenant of Speaker John Nance Garner, served as chairman of the House Interstate and Foreign Commerce Committee from 1931 to 1937. An ardent New Dealer, he authored or co-sponsored such controversial legislation as the Securities Exchange Act of 1934, the Public Utility Holding Company Act of 1935 and the bill establishing the Rural Electrification Administration. He was elected speaker in 1940 and reelected every term afterwards, except for 1947-48 and 1953-54 when Republican majorities controlled the House. Rayburn's length of service as speaker was also a House record, more than doubling the tenure of Henry Clay, his nearest rival.

Through a political career that spanned several generations and some of the most dramatic legislative battles of the twentieth century, Rayburn solidifed his reputation as a partisan Democrat but also as an able compromiser. "To get along, go along," was his famous aphorism for freshmen congressmen. Although it was his responsibility to build majorities for Democratic legislation, Rayburn maintained that he never asked a representative to violate his convictions or destroy his political career. Although one of the most powerful speakers in history, Rayburn's influence rested on an informal and, as his successor John McCormack (D, Mass.) [q.v.] was to discover, ephemeral foundation. Richard Bolling (D, Mo.) [q.v.], a former protege of Rayburn, described the nature of Rayburn's power in *House Out of Order*: "There was hardly a member, however strong a political opponent, for whom he had not done a favor. . . .Rayburn knew that the speakership had been shorn of much of its substantive power. Therefore he built up in place of it, a vast backlog of political IOU's." [See TRUMAN, EISENHOWER Volumes]

Rayburn was a strong supporter in 1960 of the presidential candicacy of fellow Texan Lyndon B. Johnson (D, Tex.) [q.v.], another former protege. Rayburn disliked John F. Kennedy and feared that an Eastern Catholic at the head of the Democratic ticket would repeat the Alfred E. Smith debacle of 1928. At the Democratic National Convention in July he was firmly against Johnson's acceptance of second place on the ticket. However, Rayburn's fear of a Nixon victory later helped moderate his opposition, and he campaigned vigorously for the Kennedy-Johnson ticket.

The most important task facing Rayburn at the start of the Kennedy Administration in

January 1961 was the reform of the House Rules Committee. The Committee, under its conservative chairman Howard Smith (D, Va.) [q.v.], had long bottled up liberal legislation by refusing, often by a 6-6 tie vote, to issue the "rule" necessary to accompany each bill to the House floor. The fate of much of the New Frontier program hung on the outcome of this early battle. As the leader of the reform forces, Rayburn considered two strategic alternatives: purging a Committee conservative, William D. Colmer (D, Miss.) [q.v.], who had refused to support his party's national ticket in 1960, or enlarging the Committee to 15 members, thus creating an 8-7 liberal majority. Rayburn chose the latter course, which required the approval of the entire House. Rayburn then made one of his rare appearances as a debater before the House, arguing that "the House, on great measures, should be allowed to work its will." After an intensely bitter struggle, the Rayburn forces defeated a coalition of Republicans and Southern Democrats by a vote of 217-212 on Jan. 31. Rayburn added to the Committee two pro-Administration Democrats, Reps. Carl Elliott (D, Ala.) and B.F. Sisk (D, Calif.).

The closeness of the Rules Committee result foreshadowed the difficulty Rayburn would experience in steering much Kennedy legislation through the House. Maintaining in February 1961 that the economic situation was "the most urgent since the Great Depression," Rayburn fought with mixed success for much of the New Frontier program. According to Rayburn's biographer, Alfred Steinberg, the Administration's emergency farm price support program passed the House 209-202 in March "only after Rayburn appealed personally at the last minute to seven members who opposed it." The area redevelopment bill and the $4.9 billion Housing Act of 1961 passed in May and June by somewhat larger majorities. However, Rayburn could dislodge neither the Administration's medicare plan from the House Ways and Means Committee nor its aid-to-education bill from the Rules Committee, where Rep. James Delaney (D, N.Y.) [q.v.] championed aid to parochial schools.

One of Rayburn's most trying ordeals came in his struggle to pass the Administration's requested increase in the minimum wage from $1.00 to $1.25 an hour and expand its coverage to an additional 4.3 million workers. In the face of conservative Republican and Southern Democratic opposition, Rayburn and Democratic whip Carl Albert (D, Okla) [q.v.] wrote a compromise version that added only 3.6 million workers, but it lost by 185 to 186 in March. The House then approved, 216 to 203, a "coalition" substitute raising the minimum to $1.15 and limiting new coverage to 1.3 million workers at $1 per hour. The Senate passed a bill much closer to the Administration version, however, and the bill that emerged from the House-Senate conference committee (with Rayburn choosing the House members) was in effect the Rayburn-Albert measure. This version, raising the minimum to $1.25 and including 3.6 million new workers (and excluding 140,000 laundry workers and 305,000 employes of auto and farm equipment dealers), passed the House on May 3, 230 to 196. In the Senate debate Sen. Wayne Morse (D, Ore.) [q.v.], who had refused to sign the conference report, complained that the exclusion of "laundry workers because they're mostly black" was "exploitation" and charged that Rayburn and Rep. Carl Vinson (D, Ga.) [q.v.] had told the conferees that "there would be no bill in the House at all with laundry workers covered."

Rayburn opposed the Administration's plan to reorganize the Federal Communications Commission (FCC) in June. He charged that the White House was trying to usurp congressional authority over regulatory agencies and establish one-man "dictatorship" by agency chairmen. The FCC reorganization was rejected by the House, 323 to 77. This legislative dispute was one indication of Rayburn's growing estrangement from the leaders of the Kennedy Administration, which was widened by his more conservative political orientation, the enormous generation gap between the septuagenarian Rayburn and the Kennedy people and his belief that Vice President Johnson was being slighted in the new Administration.

Rayburn was suffering from cancer in 1961, and his growing weakness reduced his effectiveness after the middle of the year. He flew home to Bonham, Tex., on Aug. 31 and never returned to Washington. He died Nov. 16.

[TO]

For further information:
Alfred Steinberg, *Sam Rayburn* (New York, 1975).

REISCHAUER, EDWIN O(LDFATHER)
b. Oct. 15, 1910; Tokyo, Japan.
Ambassador to Japan, April 1961-July 1966.

Born in Tokyo to American missionary parents, Edwin Reischauer spent his formative years in Japan, coming to the United States for the first time at the age of 16 to attend Oberlin College. He received his Ph.D. in Far Eastern languages from Harvard in 1938. He was an instructor there until 1942 and then worked as a senior research analyst for the State and War Departments before joining the Army in 1943. After the war Reischauer became the chairman of the State Department's Japan-Korea secretariat and special assistant to the director of the office of Far Eastern affairs before resuming his Harvard career. Appointed associate professor of Far Eastern languages in 1946, he became professor of Japanese history in 1950 and director of the Harvard-Yenching Institute in 1956.

While at Harvard he was the author of four Asian studies: *Japan, Past and Present* (1946), *The United States and Japan* (1950), *Wanted: An Asian Policy* (1955) and *East Asia: The Great Tradition* (1960) as well as several basic Japanese language texts. Reischauer also created a comprehensive chart, showing the epochs and stages of Asian history by nation, which proved invaluable to scholars. He was one of the few Western scholars to suggest that democratic institutions were not foreign to Japan but had begun with the industrial revolution and had taken hold in 1868, when the power of the feudal shogunate was broken.

In his writings and public statements Reischauer was critical of U.S. Asian policy, particularly the lack of adequate economic aid to Okinawa, trade restrictions on Japanese goods and the failure of the United States to offer a comprehensive philosophical framework for Japanese democracy. In addition, he criticized the U.S. government's tacit approval of Prime Minister Nobusuke Kishi's decision to push the unpopular Japanese-American Mutual Security Treaty (granting the U.S. use of Japanese bases as staging areas for Asian military operations with the consent of Japan) through the Diet. Kishi's action eventually led to riots and the cancellation of President Dwight D. Eisenhower's proposed visit to Japan in 1960.

In April 1961 President Kennedy, acting on the recommendation of Chester Bowles [*q.v.*], appointed Reischauer ambassador to Japan. The move was opposed by the State Department's career officers who felt they had been overlooked in the appointment. However, Kennedy thought the move useful to improve Japanese-American relations, which had been strained by a long period of American indifference and by the Mutual Security Treaty crisis.

As ambassador, Reischauer was not the source but the instrument of policy. Nevertheless, his expertise permitted him to mold policy on two issues: the Japanese need for foreign trade and more liberal American economic aid to Okinawa. During his tenure in Tokyo the two countries arranged annual meetings of cabinet members to discuss vital trade and economic questions and special committees to look into scientific and cultural matters of mutual concern. Despite tension generated by the resumption of atomic testing, congressional threats to tax Japanese textiles and U.S. insistence that Japan play a larger role in Asian affairs, Reischauer was generally credited with strengthening ties between the two countries.

Reischauer's major impact on Japan was not the result of his direct diplomatic activity but of his political philosophy and prestige as a scholar. He believed Japan was of particular importance to the United States as a test case designed to prove that "democracy is an article for export." Reischauer saw that country as a "great ideological battleground" involved in a conflict between modern patterns of democracy and "glittering totalitarianism." Although democratic forms had been established in Japan since the 19th century, postwar tensions seriously threatened continued democratic growth. Reischauer did not see his mission as speaking solely in terms of U.S. desires and interests. Instead, he sought to convince the Japanese that it was in their own interest to support democracy and strengthen the alliance between the two countries.

He thought the central problem of Japanese-American relations was to break down Japanese stereotypes of Americans as "capitalists" and "imperialists" and change the rigid attitudes of the country's intellectuals, who, according to Reischauer, were passive, pure theoreticians aloof from society. In his view, the majority were Marxists, tied to a mid-19th century dialectic that provided a comprehensive philosophy in the face of a dramatic postwar change in value systems. Reischauer, therefore, believed that the major purpose of his mission was to establish a continuing dialogue designed to convince intellectuals of American interest in their opinions and problems. Because of Reischauer's knowledge of the language, his understanding of Japanese problems and, most importantly, his scholarly position, the Japanese permitted him to express controversial opinions. In July 1966 he resigned his post to return to Harvard.

During the Johnson era Reischauer became a leading academic critic of the Administration's handling of the Vietnam war, advocating de-escalation without "resorting to either of the dangerous alternatives of withdrawal or major escalation." He also proposed a revised American Far Eastern policy based on a renunciation of its role as "the leader" in Asia. During the 1960s and 1970s, Reischauer continued his scholarly work, producing several monographs on foreign policy as well as a work on education. [See JOHNSON Volume]

[EWS]

RESTON, JAMES B(ARRETT)

b. Nov. 3, 1909; Clydebank, Scotland.
New York Times columnist, 1961- .

James Reston, for many years the most powerful and influential reporter at the *New York Times*, graduated from the University of Illinois in 1932, joined the Associated Press as a sportswriter and theater critic in 1934 and then became a reporter with the London bureau of the *Times* during the war. Reston helped organize the London branch of the Office of War Information during World War II, returning to the U.S. in 1942 as assistant to *Times* publisher Arthur Hays Sulzberger. In 1944 Reston joined the Washington bureau under columnist Arthur Krock. As a top reporter on the Washington news team, Reston earned a Pulitzer Prize in 1945. He established a warm relationship with the Ochs family, which had owned the *Times* since 1896, and with Krock, who in 1953 named Reston to head the Washington bureau. Under his leadership the bureau gained considerable power within the *Times* organization.

In April 1961 veteran Latin American correspondent Tad Szulc filed a story with the *Times* describing the Central Intelligence Agency's recruitment of Cuban nationals to take part in an invasion of the island. Szulc indicated that an invasion was imminent. After heated debate within the New York office, publisher Orville Dryfoos consulted with Reston, and the two men decided to tone down the story. They agreed not to mention the CIA's part in the invasion preparations, not to include the probable date of the invasion and not to reveal detailed plans for an initial air strike on Cuba to be carried out from Guatemala. Szulc's article, which originally was to have been a multi-column story on page one of the *Times*, was considerably shortened, given a smaller headline and published on April 7, 1961. According to historian Arthur Schlesinger, Jr. [*q.v.*], Reston felt that publishing Szulc's story "would alert Castro, in which case the *Times* would be responsible for casualties on the beach, or else the expedition would be canceled, in which case the *Times* would be responsible for grave interference with national policy."

Shortly before the Cuban missile crisis of October 1962, Reston wrote a story that took note of increased U.S. troop movements and speculated that a crisis was brewing in Cuba over nuclear missiles. President Kennedy telephoned Orville Dryfoos to say that publication of Reston's story would produce an ultimatum from Moscow before the plan to "quarantine" Cuba could be implemented. Dryfoos and Reston agreed not to print the story.

Arthur Ochs Sulzberger [q.v.] took over as publisher of the *Times* in June 1963 and initiated a complete reorganization of the newspaper. In 1964 Reston became an associate editor and was succeeded in the Washington bureau by Tom Wicker. In 1968 Reston was named executive editor and subsequently a vice president of the New York Times Company.

After his appointment as executive editor, Reston sought to create a more reflective attitude toward daily news events in the *Times*. He requested more stories on youth and on the "silent majority" and insisted that the paper carry front-page interviews with prominent men of ideas such as Andre Malraux and C. P. Snow. In his columns Reston displayed a cautiously optimistic, if somewhat detached and dispassionate, attitude toward world events.

[FHM]

For further information:
Gay Talese, *The Kingdom and the Power* (New York, 1969).

REUSS, HENRY S(CHOELLKOPF)
b. Feb. 22, 1912, Milwaukee, Wisc.
Democratic Representative, Wisc., 1955- .

The grandson of a Wisconsin bank president who had emigrated from Germany in 1848, Henry Reuss grew up in Milwaukee, where he practiced law after earning an LL.B. from Harvard in 1936. After wartime service with the Office of Price Administration and the Army, Reuss resumed his law practice and served on the board of directors of several companies, including a Milwaukee bank. A Republican until 1950,

Reuss switched to the Democratic Party in that year because he considered Sen. Joseph McCarthy (R, Wisc.) "a disgrace to Wisconsin." He helped to organize an anti-McCarthy movement in the state and ran unsuccessfully for the offices of state attorney general in 1950 and U.S. senator in 1952. Reuss won election to the House of Representatives from Milwaukee's fifth district in 1954 against a pro-McCarthy Republican incumbent, Rep. Charles J. Kersten.

Reuss was a consistent congressional liberal and in the Kennedy years a reliable supporter of the President's legislative program. An early advocate of the Peace Corps idea, Reuss was cited by President Kennedy in his March 1, 1961 message to Congress proposing creation of the Corps. In March and April of 1961 he called for investigations of the John Birch Society and Maj. Gen. Edwin A. Walker [q.v.], the right-wing commander of the 24th Army Division in Germany.

Reuss was an early environmentalist, sponsoring a bill in 1955 to prevent the Secretary of the Interior from disposing of the national wildlife refuges without the approval of Congress. His 1961 amendment to a farm bill to prohibit subsidized drainage of farm wetlands where such drainage would harm wildlife was passed by the House in July but dropped in conference the next month. Reuss proposed the measure again in 1962 and saw it signed into law on Oct. 2 of that year. He also proposed a bill in March 1963 to ban synthetic detergents that did not decompose sufficiently to prevent pollution of the nation's rivers and lakes.

A member of the House Banking and Currency Committee and the Joint Economic Committee, Reuss became a House expert in the subjects of trade and finance. In December 1962 Reuss blamed the "gold drain" on European countries, which were accumulating gold and dollars instead of spending their rising export income on imports, on contributions to mutual defense costs and on long-term aid to developing countries. Reuss supported legislation in 1964 to stem this gold outflow and as chairman of the International Finance Subcommittee of the Banking and Currency Committee continued his efforts in this area throughout the Johnson years. [See JOHNSON, NIXON Volumes]

[TO]

REUTHER, WALTER P.
b. Sept. 1, 1907; Wheeling, W. Va.
d. May 10, 1970; Pellston, Mich.
President, United Automobile Workers, 1946-70.

Reuther's father, Valentine, was an emigre German socialist who became an important trade union leader in the upper Ohio Valley. After completing high school in Wheeling, Walter Reuther moved to Detroit in 1926 and became a skilled tool and die worker at the Ford Motor Company. Discharged for union activity in 1931, Reuther joined the Socialist Party, attended Wayne University and campaigned actively for Norman Thomas's presidential candidacy in 1932. With his brother Victor, Reuther then embarked on a three-year world tour during which he worked for 18 months in a Russian auto factory. Returning to Detroit in late 1935, Walter, Victor and another brother, Roy, plunged into organizational work for the fledgling UAW. Walter Reuther was first elected to the UAW executive board in 1936 but only achieved real power in the union after he helped organize 30,000 auto workers on Detroit's West Side early the next year.

With the approach of the war in 1940, Reuther and his brothers resigned from the Socialist Party, broke their temporary alliance with the Communists and, along with other like-minded unionists, formed their own caucus in the UAW. Reuther backed the no-strike pledge during the war but, as head of the union's General Motors Department, led the UAW in an aggressive 113-day postwar work stoppage against the giant auto maker. His articulate leadership of the GM strike won for Reuther the support of the union's restive postwar membership, a national reputation as a leader of the non-Communist left and the presidency of the million-member UAW in March 1946. During the next year and a half the Reuther caucus consolidated its control of the union in a bitter factional fight against a coalition of union leaders who were strongly supported by the Communists.

Over the next decade Reuther helped found the liberal anti-Communist Americans for Democratic Action (ADA), became a power in the national Democratic Party and served as president of the Congress of Industrial Organizations from 1952 until its merger with the American Federation of Labor in 1955. He also negotiated for the UAW a series of collective bargaining agreements which won for the union such pace-setting contract innovations as a cost-of-living escalator clause (1948), company-funded pensions keyed to Social Security (1949) and supplemental unemployment benefits (1955). The recession of 1958 cut UAW membership from 1.5 to 1.1 million members, ended union efforts to win a shorter workweek and enabled auto company management to regain much of its control over production standards in the shops. [See TRUMAN, EISENHOWER Volumes]

When the UAW faced the auto corporations in the 1961 round of contract talks, it had not fully recovered from the recession of 1958. Reuther therefore opposed rank-and-file demands for an immediate reduction in the workweek to 30 hours (with no loss in pay). Instead, he proposed at the UAW's April collective bargaining convention that organized labor back a drive for a wage law that would authorize gradual reduction of the 40-hour week during periods of serious unemployment. (The Kennedy Administration opposed such a law.) Reuther also announced that a major contract demand would be replacement of hourly wages with an annual salary.

On Sept. 6, 1961 the UAW and General Motors reached tentative agreement on an annual six-cent-an-hour pay rise (2½%) over the next three years, cost-of-living allowances adjusted on a quarterly basis, improvements in supplemental unemployment benefits and increases in company-funded pensions. The contract settlement did not include a reduction in the workweek or a substitution of salaries for the traditional hourly pay. In addition, the national contract did not resolve local grievances over working conditions in GM plants. A series of wildcat strikes began immediately after announcement of the national accord. By Sept. 11, 92 of 129 GM plants were on strike. Reuther maintained control of the strike movement by formally authorizing these work stoppages, but on Sept. 20 he ratified the UAW-GM pact and announced that the international union would not authorize a company-wide work stoppage in support of the 59 local strikes still in progress. To end them, Reuther called UAW officials from 26 locals to Detroit on Sept. 22. After working with top GM officials to resolve the remaining disputes, Reuther gave the 10 locals blocking final accord one day to negotiate local agreements. On Sept. 25 Reuther ordered the last five striking unions to return to work.

After negotiators for Ford and the UAW reached accord in early October on an economic package similar to GM's, a company-wide agreement was again held up as a result of local plant disputes over production standards and job classifications. To settle these conflicts, Reuther authorized on Oct. 3 the first company-wide strike at Ford in two decades. National agreement on economic issues was announced a week later by Reuther and Ford officials. Although about 25 local bargaining pacts were still unsigned, the UAW's national Ford council approved a full three-year contract Oct. 12. In November widespread local strikes at Chrylser were averted when Reuther emphasized local bargaining issues before reaching agreement with the financially weak automaker on an economic package similar to the ones signed by Ford and GM earlier in the fall.

The significance of the 1961 round of contract negotiations with the auto Big Three was in the emphasis local union leaders gave to the resolution of non-economic grievances involving production standards and working conditions. Reuther was often criticized by rank-and-file unionists for his handling of these issues and encountered for the first time since the late 1940s important and widespread internal union opposition to his policies. "Reuther no longer has the magic touch with the ranks that characterized his rise to the top," wrote labor journalist and former Chrysler union official B. J. Widick, "and most of his associates admit it, at least privately."

During the early 1960s Reuther was also involved in an intermittent dispute with AFL-CIO President George Meany [q.v.]. After the merger of the two labor federations in 1955, Reuther was elected head of the new organization's Industrial Union Department, but the auto union leader soon found his power in the AFL-CIO inferior to that of Meany and the craft unionists who supported him. In the spring of 1961 Reuther repeatedly criticized the building trades for trying to "raid" long-standing industrial union jurisdictions. At one point Reuther threatened to lead an industrial union walkout from the August 1961 AFL-CIO Executive Council meeting unless the craft unions agreed to outside arbitration of jurisdictional disputes. At Meany's urging the Council worked out a compromise resolution involving a limited form of arbitration, but the outcome of the entire incident was, in the words of Reuther's biographers Frank Cormier and William J. Eaton, a "sharp reversal for Reuther in the internal power struggle."

Although Reuther was a prominent Kennedy supporter in the early 1960s, Meany insisted that all presidential appointments involving labor move through his office. Hence, Meany was able to veto Adlai Stevenson's [q.v.] appointment of Reuther to the American U.N. delegation in early 1961 and to block Reuther's own choice for undersecretary of labor in 1962. Meany also vetoed Reuther's selection of Ralph Helstein, president of the Packinghouse Workers, for a seat on the AFL-CIO Executive Council in August 1962. Reuther contended that the old CIO unions had the right to name anyone to fill a vacancy caused by the death or resignation of a former CIO man. Meany, however, thought Helstein's union still employed some Communists in staff positions and mustered a majority of the Executive Council to block Reuther's nominee.

Reuther sought to identify the UAW with the civil rights movement in the early 1960s and generally backed integrationist efforts within the AFL-CIO. He supported A. Philip Randolph's [*q.v.*] fight to pass a strong anti-segregation resolution in 1961 and in August 1963 called the AFL-CIO's failure to forthrightly endorse the March on Washington "anemic." The UAW provided major financial and organizational support for the March, and Reuther delivered the only speech by a representative of organized labor at the Aug. 28 demonstration.

In Detroit area politics, however, the UAW was often at odds with the predominantly black Trade Union Leadership Caucus (TULC). The caucus, which numbered some seven to nine thousand, successfully backed the candidacy of Jerome Cavanagh [*q.v.*] in the 1961 Detroit Mayorality contest against a more conservative UAW-endorsed opponent. Partly in response to TULC agitation, Reuther chose Nelson Jack Edwards, a veteran black UAW staff man, as his candidate for the union's executive board in May 1962.

During the Kennedy years Reuther stood somewhat closer to the President than other labor leaders. He agreed with the Administration's efforts to reduce unemployment primarily through stimulation of the economy (rather than through reduction of the workweek to 35 hours, which was the official AFL-CIO position) and enthusiastically supported Kennedy Administration efforts to reduce tensions with the Communist world. After Fidel Castro proposed in May 1961 that the prisoners taken following the abortive Bay of Pigs invasion might be exchanged for earth-moving equipment, Kennedy asked Reuther to set up a private committee to raise funds and seek release of the men held captive. Reuther named a bipartisan Tractors for Freedom Committee, which included Eleanor Roosevelt [*q.v.*] and Milton Eisenhower [*q.v.*]. The rescue effort failed, however, when Castro told a Reuther emissary, Pat Greathouse of the UAW, that he wanted heavy earth-moving machinery, not simply the farm tractors the committee was prepared to purchase. (In 1962 and 1963 all of the prisoners and many members of their families were freed after a separate exchange was arranged.)

In 1964 Reuther was a strong supporter of Lyndon Johnson's [*q.v.*] presidential campaign and helped organize liberal and labor support for his civil rights and Great Society legislative programs. Reuther supported the war in Vietnam in 1965 but gradually took a more "dovish" position in 1966 and 1967. His disagreements with Meany grew more intense during the second half of the 1960s, and in 1968 Reuther formally withdrew the UAW from the AFL-CIO itself. Reuther, his wife and four others were killed near Pellston, Mich. on May 9, 1970 when their chartered jet crashed on landing. [See JOHNSON, NIXON Volumes]

[NNL]

For further information:
Frank Cormier and William J. Eaton, *Reuther* (Englewood Cliffs, 1970).
Victor Reuther, *The Brothers Reuther and the UAW* (New York, 1976).
Jack Stieber, *Governing the UAW* (New York, 1962).
B. J. Widick, *Labor Today* (New York, 1964).

RHODES, JOHN J(ACOB)
b. Sept. 18, 1916; Council Grove, Kan.
Republican Representative, Ariz., 1953-   .

Rhodes received a law degree from Harvard in 1941 and after World War II helped establish an insurance company in Arizona. In 1952 he was elected to the U.S. House of Representatives from Arizona's first district, which included Phoenix and the surrounding area. The population of Phoenix grew from just over 100,000 in 1950 to almost 600,000 in 1970, largely as a result of an influx of Midwesterners and Southerners with conservative political leanings. Rhodes's voting record in Congress paralleled the views of these constituents.

According to *Congressional Quarterly*, Rhodes supported the House's conservative coalition on 87%, 94% and 80% of roll-call votes in 1961, 1962 and 1963, respectively, and generally opposed bills supported by the Kennedy Administration during those years.

Rhodes favored a limited role for the national government. In October 1961 he voted against federal construction of high-power transmission lines from the Upper Colorado River Basin Project to the areas receiving electricity from the project. Rhodes was the only representative from the five states directly affected who favored private over public construction of the lines. In June of the following year, he opposed a national vaccination program, claiming that the matter was "a problem for the states to deal with. . . ."

Rhodes generally opposed social welfare and other programs directed at the problems of the poor. During House debate in March 1961 over a Kennedy-backed minimum wage increase from $1.00 to $1.25, Rhodes asserted that the increment would probably produce inflation, business failures and layoffs.

As a member of the Appropriations Committee's Foreign Operations Subcommittee, Rhodes usually aligned himself with the views of subcommittee chairman Otto E. Passman (D, La.) [q.v.], who invariably favored large cuts in annual Administration foreign aid requests.

In 1965 Rhodes participated in a successful revolt of the younger House Republicans against Minority Leader Charles A. Halleck (R, Ind.) [q.v.]. The House Republican Conference elected Rep. Gerald R. Ford (R, Mich.) [q.v.] to the minority leadership post in January, and later in the month Rhodes succeeded Rep. John W. Byrnes (R, Wisc.) [q.v.] as chairman of the House Republican Policy Committee, which recommended and tried to enforce party positions on issues before the House. When Ford became vice president in 1973, Rhodes was chosen House minority leader. [See JOHNSON, NIXON Volumes]

[MLL]

RIBICOFF, ABRAHAM A(LEXANDER)

b. April 9, 1910; New Britain, Conn.
Secretary of Health, Education
and Welfare, January 1961-July 1962;
Democratic Senator, Conn., 1963-   .

The son of poor Polish-Jewish immigrants, Ribicoff was born in a tenement in New Britain, Conn. After graduating from high school, he worked in a buckle and zipper factory to earn money to attend New York University. Within a year he was named Midwestern representative of the zipper company and settled in Chicago, where he attended the University of Chicago at night.

After graduating from the University of Chicago Law School in 1933, he returned to Connecticut to practice law, first in Kensington, later in Hartford. In 1938 he won election to the lower house of the Connecticut General Assembly. He served two terms. From 1941 to 1943 and from 1945 to 1947, Ribicoff was a police court judge in Hartford. He was elected to Congress in 1948 and won reelection two years later. While serving in the House Ribicoff established an enduring friendship with Rep. John F. Kennedy (D, Mass.). In 1952 Ribicoff abandoned his House seat to run for the Senate. He was narrowly defeated by incumbent Sen. Prescott Bush (R, Conn.) [q.v.].

Two years later Ribicoff was elected governor of Connecticut. While governor he gained national prominence for a much publicized traffic safety campaign which resulted in the suspension of thousands of licenses for drunken or reckless driving. He also devoted considerable attention to increasing the efficiency of state and local government. In 1956 Ribicoff was reelected to another four-year term as governor.

During the 1956 Democratic National Convention, Ribicoff supported Kennedy's vice presidential bid. Kennedy lost the nomination, but Ribicoff and Connecticut Democratic Party Chairman John Bailey began planning strategy for Kennedy's 1960 presidential campaign. [See EISENHOWER Volume]

Ribicoff was among the first public officials to endorse Kennedy for President. In June 1960 he worked to rally support for Kennedy at the National Governors Conference. A month later Ribicoff and Robert Kennedy [q.v.] served as floor managers for their candidate at the Democratic National Convention in Los Angeles.

After the 1960 elections Kennedy offered Ribicoff his pick of cabinet posts, including the attorney generalship. According to Kennedy biographers Arthur Schlesinger, Jr. [q.v.], and Theodore Sorensen [q.v.], Ribicoff felt it would be unwise for a Jewish attorney general to undertake the controversial task of prosecuting civil rights and school desegregation cases in the South. Ribicoff chose instead to head the Department of Health, Education and Welfare.

One of Ribicoff's major tasks as secretary of HEW was to win congressional approval of the Administration's medicare and school aid bills. During 1961 and 1962 Ribicoff and his talented Assistant Secretary Wilbur H. Cohen [q.v.] worked for the enactment of the medicare bill sponsored by Sen. Clinton Anderson (D, N.M.) [q.v.] and Rep. Cecil R. King (D, Calif.) [q.v.]. The King-Anderson bill made provision for the use of Social Security funds to help defray the hospitalization costs of the elderly. Ribicoff and Cohen were unable to win passage of the legislation because of the powerful opposition of the American Medical Association. Furthermore, Rep. Wilbur Mills (D, Ark.) [q.v.], the influential chairman of the House Ways and Means Committee, seemed determined to prevent the medicare bill from reaching the floor of the house. (A version of the medicare bill was not enacted until the summer of 1965.)

Ribicoff and Cohen were unable to win enactment of a bill authorizing federal aid to elementary and secondary schools because of conflict over the question of whether private and parochial schools should receive federal assistance. Groups like the National Catholic Welfare Conference demanded assistance for parochial schools, while the National Educational Association, representing a million public school teachers, was bitterly opposed to such aid.

Ribicoff believed that his major legislative achievement as chief of HEW was the revision of the 1935 Social Security Act. Under that law the federal government could release aid-to-dependent-children (ADC) funds only in cases where there was only one caretaker—usually the mother—in the home. If a husband and wife were living under the same roof, no funds were allowed even in cases of destitution. Ribicoff thought the law thereby encouraged fathers to leave home to establish ADC eligibility for their families. Ribicoff and Cohen supported the 1962 Public Welfare Amendments to the Social Security Act that authorized federal assistance for needy two-parent families. The new amendments, however, did not compel states to broaden their ADC programs, and many continued to exclude two-parent families.

One of the most difficult problems with which Ribicoff had to deal was the question of whether federal aid to segregated school systems should be continued. When Rep. Adam Clayton Powell Jr., (D, N.Y.), [q.v.] became chairman of the House Committee on Education and Labor in 1961, he established an ad hoc Subcommittee on Integration in Federally Assisted Education specifically to force Ribicoff to cut off aid to segregated school systems. However, Ribicoff, the HEW legal staff and the Justice Department all argued that, despite the 1954 Supreme Court decision ordering school desegregation with "all deliberate speed," HEW could not legally withhold funds from segregated schools without specific congressional authorization. Ribicoff was also aware that if he cut off aid, he would lose support of Southern congressmen and senators for the Administration's general school aid bill.

Ribicoff did believe, however, that HEW could exercise its authority over "impacted" schools, those especially subsidized by the federal government because of the enrollment of large numbers of children from military bases. In March 1962 he announced that segregated schools were "unsuitable" for these children. He stated that the U.S. Commissioner of Education was being authorized to build and operate public schools on bases currently served by segregated schools. Ribicoff 's order did not formally bar parents from sending their children to segregated schools but directed that if the children were withdrawn from such schools, federal aid to the school district would also be withdrawn.

Among his other accomplishments as HEW secretary, Ribicoff won congressional approval of legislation establishing a program of federal aid for educational television stations and supported the 1961 Juvenile Delinquency and Youth Offenses Control Act, which authorized $10 million for a three-year HEW program for the development of techniques to control or prevent juvenile delinquency. Ribicoff also lobbied successfully for increased appropriations for dental research, for the licensing and use of the Sabin oral polio vaccine, and for increased screening of milk, water, food and the air for the presence of radioactive contamination.

Ribicoff found the task of administering his sprawling agency a frustrating experience. In resigning his post to undertake what proved to be a successful campaign for the Senate, he suggested that HEW was so big and diverse that it was unmanageable. He felt so strongly on the matter that as a senator he introduced legislation to dismantle HEW into three separate departments. Congress, however, did not act on the Ribicoff proposals.

In the Senate Ribicoff was counted on by both the Kennedy and Johnson Administrations for support of major social welfare legislation. He consistently won high ratings from the liberal Americans for Democratic Action. Until 1968 Ribicoff generally supported the Johnson Administration's Vietnam war policies. During the 1968 Democratic National Convention in Chicago, however, Ribicoff won national attention by condemning the city's police for their "Gestapo tactics" toward anti-war demonstrators. While presiding over the convention, he denounced Chicago's Mayor Richard J. Daley [q.v.] who he said was responsible for the "bloodbath taking place in the streets." Ribicoff was subsequently identified with the anti-war bloc in the Senate. [See JOHNSON, NIXON Volumes]

[JLW]

RICHARDSON, GLORIA (HAYS)
b. May 6, 1922; Baltimore, Md.
Civil rights leader.

The daughter of a prosperous druggist and a graduate of all-black Howard University, Richardson grew up in Cambridge, Md. The town of 14,000 was on Maryland's Eastern Shore, a region that was historically more Southern in outlook than the rest of the state.

Cambridge's blacks, who constituted one-fourth of the population, had the vote by the early 1960s. But the town's public facilities were still segregated. In 1962 Richardson joined the Cambridge Nonviolent Action Committee (CNAC), a civil rights group. Several months later she became president of the organization, becoming the only woman in the country to head a local black protest movement.

During the spring of 1963 Richardson began leading demonstrations to integrate public accommodations. The protests led to violence in early July, culminating on July 12 when, after whites had thrown eggs at the demonstrators, blacks and whites exchanged gunshots. Six whites were injured. The violence in Cambridge represented one of the first instances in which Southern blacks employed force against whites in connection with civil rights activities.

After the shootings Richardson and white officials met with Attorney General Robert F. Kennedy [q.v.]. They agreed to a halt in demonstrations, desegregation of public facilities and a referendum on a local ordinance to outlaw segregation. Shortly before the Oct. 1 vote, however, Richardson reversed her position on the referendum and urged blacks to boycott it. She said it was "wrong to put our constitutional rights to the vote of a white majority." The desegregation ordinance was defeated, 1,720 to 1,994, with only 40% of the registered blacks voting.

Richardson seemed uncertain of her strategy on a number of occasions during the integration struggle. Some observers attributed her indecisiveness to behind-the-scenes influence by male black leaders in Cambridge. Richardson herself, speaking of the rallies in which she participated, said, "When I get on the platform . . . and the men are all there, I just feel there is nothing more to say."

In August 1964 Richardson married and resigned from CNAC. During subsequent years she was not politically active.

[MLL]

RICKOVER, HYMAN G(EORGE)
b. Jan. 27, 1900; Makow, Russia.
Director of Naval Research, Atomic
Energy Commission; Director of Nuclear Propulsion, Navy Bureau of Ships,
1953- .

A Russian immigrant raised in Chicago,
Hyman Rickover was credited with the development of the world's first atomic submarine. Upon graduation from Annapolis in
1922, Rickover served in routine assignments before being sent to work on an
atomic submarine project for the Atomic
Energy Commission. As a result of this experience he pressed for the development of a
nuclear submarine in the late 1940s. In the
face of naval opposition, Rickover managed
to get congressional approval for the building
of the *Nautilus* in 1952. When it appeared to
many government officials that the Navy had
refused to promote Rickover from captain
to vice admiral in 1951 and 1952 because
of his abrasive advocacy of nuclear submarines, Congress organized an investigation
which resulted in his promotion in 1953.

During the 1950s Rickover campaigned
for the development of a nuclear Navy
while directing the construction of several
nuclear ships and supervising the building
of the first large-scale atomic power plant.
As a result of his experience in recruiting
men for his staff and coping with poor
workmanship by civilian contractors, Rickover became a leading critic of American
education. The Admiral maintained that the
schools failed to teach Americans to use
their minds fully or to instill in them the
desire for excellence required by an advanced technological society. His views
were published in a book entitled *Education and Freedom* (1959). [See EISENHOWER Volume]

During the Kennedy Administration Rickover strongly advocated the construction of
a second nuclear carrier, a project opposed
by Secretary of Defense Robert S. McNamara [*q.v.*]. In testimony given before the
Joint Congressional Committee on Atomic
Energy in April 1962, Rickover challenged
the Secretary's major contention that the
project was too costly, pointing out that
in the case of nuclear submarine development multiple production had brought costs
down. Despite widespread support from
naval officers commanding nuclear ships,
the carrier was not built because of
McNamara's opposition.

In May 1962 the House Appropriations
Committee asked Rickover to testify on his
investigations of the American and English
educational systems. He praised the quality
of the English schools and recommended
several steps to improve American education, including the placement of school direction in the hands of highly qualified
teachers rather than administrators. He also
suggested the government use grants to
raise national educational quality by making
acceptance of government standards and inspection a condition for awarding funds. Finally, Rickover recommended a series of
nationwide examinations leading to a national diploma so that officials could
monitor local performance.

In February 1963 Kennedy asked Rickover to advise him on the type of ships
that should be used for the President's proposed NATO multilateral nuclear force.
Kennedy had originally suggested that
NATO rely on nuclear submarines to carry
the missiles, but Rickover convinced him
that the proposal would cause security
problems and that surface vessels equipped
with missiles should be substituted.

Although scheduled to retire in 1964 at
the mandatory age of 64, Rickover was retained on active duty by presidential order.
During the Johnson years Rickover campaigned against the close connection between the military and business, which he
said resulted in the Navy's acceptance of
inferior materials. [See JOHNSON Volume]

[EWS]

ROBERTSON, A. WILLIS
b. May 27, 1887; Martinsburg, W. Va.
d. Nov. 1, 1971; Lexington, Va.
Democratic Senator, Va., 1946-66;
Chairman, Banking and Currency
Committee, 1959-66.

Robertson served in the Virginia Senate
from 1916 to 1922 and for the next six years
was the commonwealth's attorney for

Rockbridge County. In 1932 he won election to the U.S. House of Representatives, where he sat until chosen to fill the unexpired U.S. Senate seat of Carter Glass in 1946. Robertson was reelected for full terms in 1948, 1954 and 1960 with the support of Virginia's conservative Byrd machine.

According to Virginia historian J. Harvie Wilkinson, Robertson "personified Spartan discipline, pioneer individualism [and] Puritan and Calvinist morality." He was as conservative as his colleague Sen. Harry F. Byrd [q.v.], whose Democratic machine dominated Virginia's politics from the late 1920s to the mid-1960s. Like Byrd, Robertson opposed extension of federal power, social welfare programs and racial integration. However, he was not on close terms with Byrd or the other organization leaders, and it was the strength of his own extensive, informal network of supporters and friends that forced the machine to back him in 1946. [See TRUMAN, EISENHOWER Volumes]

In 1959 Robertson became one of the leading spokesmen for Capitol Hill's Southern Democrat-Republican coalition when he obtained the chairmanship of the Senate Banking and Currency Committee. At the beginning of the Kennedy Administration, he was also a high ranking member of the Senate Appropriations Committee. Unlike Sen. Byrd, he gave nominal endorsement to Sen. John F. Kennedy's presidential candidacy in 1960 as an act of party loyalty. However, he persistently opposed Administration programs in the Congress. According to *Congressional Quarterly,* Robertson was among the three Senate Democrats who most often voted against Kennedy-supported bills in 1962 and 1963.

As chairman of the Banking and Currency Committee, the fiscally conservative Robertson sought to block Kennedy welfare-spending programs, but the liberals on the Committee generally prevailed. During the spring of 1961 he denounced the Administration's housing bill as "extravagant and inflationary," but his Committee overrode him, and the measure ultimately became law. In June 1963

Robertson opposed Kennedy's Area Redevelopment Act (ARA) for aiding regions with high unemployment rates, asserting that rejection of ARA and other unsound spending schemes would produce more jobs than their adoption. Again he was in a minority on his Committee, and the bill was passed by both houses of Congress. Rep. Howard W. Smith (D, Va.) [q.v.], Robertson's fellow-Virginian and chairman of the House Rules Committee, played a more effective role in blocking Kennedy's programs. In 1962 Robertson failed to prevent his Committee from reporting favorably on an Administration-sponsored mass transportation bill, but Smith succeeded in bottling it up in his Rules Committee. In September 1962 he and the majority of a subcommittee of the Banking and Currency Committee voted to kill a truth-in-lending bill, which was opposed by many banks. In contrast to his views on social welfare spending, Robertson favored large expenditures for defense. During August 1961 he defended Congress's additions to President Kennedy's military budget.

During the Johnson Administration Robertson continued to oppose poverty legislation, which he claimed would "breed and foster reliance on the government." By 1966, however, Virginia's electorate was moving towards the political center because of the increasing numbers of urban and black voters. Furthermore, William B. Spong, Jr., Robertson's moderate opponent in the Democratic primary of that year, effectively employed the charge that the incumbent, in return for his support of their interests in the Senate, was receiving large campaign contributions from banks. Robertson lost the primary by 611 votes out of over 433,000 cast. After his defeat he became a consultant to the International Bank for Reconstruction and Development. He died on Nov. 1, 1971. [See JOHNSON Volume]

[MLL]

For further information:
J. Harvie Wilkinson III, *Harry Byrd and the Changing Face of Virginia Politics, 1945-1966* (Charlottesville, 1968).

ROCKEFELLER, DAVID
b. June 12, 1915; New York, N.Y.
President, Chase Manhattan Bank, 1960-69.

David Rockefeller was born into one of the wealthiest families in the U.S. His grandfather, John D. Rockefeller, had amassed a fortune from petroleum estimated at $800 million. His father, John D. Rockefeller, Jr., built Rockefeller Center, reconstructed colonial Williamsburg, Va., and consolidated and increased the family's wealth, leaving the bulk of it to his six children.

Rockefeller graduated from Harvard in 1936, briefly attended the London School of Economics and took his doctorate in economics from the University of Chicago in 1940. After several public service jobs and duty with the U.S. Army during World War II, he joined the Chase National (after 1955 the Chase Manhattan) Bank in 1946, as an assistant manager in the foreign department. The Rockefeller family held a controlling interest in the Chase National, and David worked his way quickly up through the ranks. By 1960 he was president and chairman of the executive committee of the bank and one of the chief spokesmen for business in the U.S. With assets of $13 billion, 28 foreign branches of its own and a global network of 50,000 correspondent banking offices, the Chase Manhattan was the second-largest bank in the U.S., only smaller than the California-based Bank of America. It exerted direct (minority) control over more than 50 U.S. companies, and, through a system of interlocking directorates, influenced the decision-making policies of many more. During the early 1960s Rockefeller increased the overseas operations of Chase, establishing close banking ties particularly with Latin America.

Rockefeller was a strong opponent of minimum wage legislation, less stringent bank credit policies toward lower income borrowers and the 35-hour workweek. A supporter of Richard Nixon [q.v.] during the 1960 presidential campaign because he felt that the Democratic platform would be distrusted abroad, Rockefeller, neverthe-less, supported many Kennedy Administration tax programs. In July 1962 President Kennedy, in a widely publicized exchange of letters with Rockefeller, stated that the key to increased business profits was increased use of capacity. Kennedy called attention to his own proposal for a 7% plant-investment tax program Rockefeller supported the measure and in turn urged higher interest rates, corporate tax cuts, more efficient control of government expenditures and an effort to balance the budget. On April 25, 1963 Rockefeller was one of a group of prominent business leaders, calling themselves the Business Committee for Tax Reduction, who met with President Kennedy to support the President's call for a $10 billion tax cut. The Committee urged that the tax cut take effect "as early as possible," but refrained from supporting the Administration's entire tax bill, which included provisions for tax reform.

Under Rockefeller's leadership the assets of the Chase Manhattan Bank grew from $13 billion to $23 billion between 1960 and 1969, as Rockefeller's influence within the business community increased. He served as a director and trustee of many companies and philantropic organizations. With his brother, New York Gov. Nelson A. Rockefeller [q.v.], he championed urban renewal projects for New York City. He also served as chairman of the Downtown Lower Manhattan Association. This group was instrumental in planning the 110-story World Trade Center and the Chase Manhattan Plaza. In 1969 Rockefeller succeeded George Champion as Chase's chairman of the board. During the early 1970s Chase Manhattan's earnings growth was inferior to that of most of its major competitors because of reverses suffered in its domestic real estate operations. Nevertheless, profits remained stable. Behind Bank of America and Citibank, Chase Manhattan ranked as the third-largest bank in the U.S. [See JOHNSON, NIXON Volumes]

[FHM]

For further information:
Meyer Kutz, *Rockefeller Power* (New York, 1974).

ROCKEFELLER, NELSON A(LDRICH)

b. July 8, 1908; Bar Harbor, Me.
Governor, N.Y., 1959-73.

Nelson Rockefeller was a grandson of John D. Rockefeller, the founder of the Standard Oil Company of New Jersey and one of the wealthiest men in the world. The second of the five sons of John D. Rockefeller, Jr., a strict Baptist who devoted most of his public activity to the family's philanthropies, Nelson was taught thrift, self-reliance and a sense of social responsibility in his youth.

After graduating from Dartmouth College in 1930, Nelson worked in the Rockefellers Chase National Bank and leased space in the new Rockefeller Center complex in Manhattan. From 1935 to 1940 he was a director of the Creole Petroleum Corporation, a Standard Oil affiliate with extensive holdings in Venezuela. His experience in that post convinced him of the need for comprehensive economic assistance to Latin America to alleviate poverty and improve the climate for investment by North American corporations.

Because of Rockefeller's interest in Latin America, President Roosevelt appointed him to head the Office of the Coordinator of Inter-American Affairs in 1940. Rockefeller held that post for four years and then served as assistant secretary of state in charge of Latin American relations. After World War II he founded private organizations that sought to promote Latin American economic development by granting technological aid and encouraging private investment.

From 1950 to 1951 Rockefeller advised President Truman on the implementation of the Point Four program. During the Eisenhower presidency he served as undersecretary of health, education and welfare from 1953 to 1954 and as a special assistant to the President from 1954 to 1955. Regarded as too liberal by many members of the Administration and critical of what he felt were the President's short-range, stopgap policies, Rockefeller left Washington at the end of 1955.

In 1956 Rockefeller decided to run for the governorship of New York, and for the next two years he cultivated contacts with Republican state and local leaders in his capacity as chairman of the Committee on the Preparation of the State Constitutional Convention. Some influential Republicans believed that the Rockefeller name would be an insuperable bar to his election. The negative impact of Rockefeller's wealth upon his 1958 campaign, however, was blunted by the fact that incumbent Gov. W. Averell Harriman [q.v.] was also a multimillionaire. Rockefeller, outspending his rival by nearly a million dollars, won the election by over half-a-million votes. Planning to introduce an ambitious array of social welfare spending programs, Rockefeller successfully pressed the legislature for tax increases early in 1959 in order to establish pay-as-you-go financing under a state constitution that mandated a balanced budget. [See EISENHOWER Volume]

Because of his tax proposals Rockefeller gained a reputation across the country for fiscal responsibility. In 1959 Rockefeller sent out political feelers to ascertain his chances for heading a 1960 national Republican ticket. Discovering that Vice President Richard M. Nixon [q.v.] had overwhelming support, Rockefeller announced on Dec. 26, 1959 that he was withdrawing his name from consideration for the Republican presidential nomination.

However, Rockefeller had established himself as a leader of the Eastern, liberal wing of the Republican Party, and he attempted to influence the formulation of the Party's national platform for 1960. On July 19, shortly before the Republican Convention, he presented a program of his own to the GOP Platform Committee. He asserted that the Soviet Union had surpassed the United States in a number of key areas of weaponry and called for increased defense spending. He also proposed tax revision to promote investment, a compulsory arbitration system for strikes threatening the national welfare, an acceleration of desegregation in all areas, federal aid to education and a health insurance program within the Social Security system. Rockefeller warned that if his proposals were not adopted by the Platform Committee, he would fight for them on the convention floor. On July 25 Nixon conferred with the Governor at the latter's Fifth Avenue apartment in New York City and accepted almost all of the proposals. Outraged conservatives, regarding the agreement as symbolic of the Eastern establishment's power within the Republican Party, denounced what became known as the "Treaty of Fifth Avenue." Sen. Barry M. Goldwater (R, Ariz.) [q.v.] described it as "the Munich of the Republican Party."

During his first five years as governor, Rockefeller, with the concurrence of a Republican-controlled legislature, accelerated or created a large number of social welfare programs. He increased the state's middle-income housing program from 2,360 units in 1958 to over 31,000 units in 1963. Rockefeller established the state's first uniform minimum wage of $1 an hour in 1960 and increased it to $1.15 in 1962. State financial aid to education was expanded from about $600 million in fiscal 1958-59 to about $1 billion in fiscal 1963-64. He established a program to expand the state university system from a capacity of 42,000 students in 1959 to a projected 160,000 by the early 1970s. A school-to-employment program (STEP) to deter juvenile delinquency and a youth employment service (YES) to find part-time jobs for young people were initiated. He successfully pressed for civil rights legislation to bar discrimination in the areas of housing, lending and public accommodations.

Alarmed by Soviet military progress Rockefeller was a zealous advocate of the construction of fallout shelters to protect citizens in the event of a nuclear attack. In April 1961 he signed a bill granting up to $100 in real estate tax exemptions to homeowners building shelters. In November of the same year, the legislature, without public hearings or debate, passed a hastily drawn-up bill providing $100 million in state matching funds for schools and colleges that decided to construct shelters. Some liberals criticized fallout shelters as ineffective and as creating a fatalistic acceptance of the inevitability of nuclear war. Few individuals or institutions took advantage of the state's shelter programs.

In 1962 Rockefeller ran for reelection against Robert S. Morgenthau, U.S. Attorney for the southern district of New York. A self-assured, quick-witted campaigner with the common touch, the incumbent easily defeated his bland challenger by 529,000 votes. During the campaign Rockefeller pledged that there would be no tax hikes, but to preserve pay-as-you-go financing he called for increases in automobile and liquor licensing fees in 1963, asserting that they were not taxes. In the face of the opposition that ensued, Rockefeller had to scale-down his request for fee increases and reduce the budget by $40 million.

From 1960 onward Rockefeller had his sights on the 1964 Republican presidential nomination. In October 1961 polls showed him ahead of conservative Republican leader Barry Goldwater as a choice of the Party's voters, but they also showed Nixon leading both men. In November 1961 he and his wife, Mary Todhunter Clark Rockefeller, announced their separation and planned divorce. The Governor's popularity dipped sharply but soon recovered. His reelection as governor in 1962, combined with Nixon's defeat in his bid for the California governorship, made Rockefeller the front-runner in the polls. But in May 1963 Rockefeller married Margaretta "Happy" Fitler Murphy, who was almost 20 years younger than the Governor and who had received a divorce one month earlier without gaining custody of her children. His remarriage provoked an extremely unfavorable popular reaction that dogged Rockefeller for the remainder of his presidential race.

Meanwhile, right-wing supporters of Sen. Goldwater gained strength within the Party, dominating the Young Republicans convention in San Francisco in June 1963. The following month Rockefeller issued a manifesto warning that "the Republican Party is in real danger of subversion by a radical, well-financed and highly disciplined minority." He charged that this minority was led by "the Birchers and others of the radical right lunatic fringe—every bit as dangerous . . . as the radical left. . . ." On Nov. 7, he formally announced his candidacy for Republican presidential nomination.

Rockefeller's drive for the nomination, culminating in a narrow loss to Goldwater in the June 1964 California primary, was unsuccessful. The Governor refused to endorse Goldwater in the 1964 general election. Another Rockefeller bid for the presidency in 1968 also failed.

During the late 1960s and early 1970s, Rockefeller moved toward the right. He "recanted" his views on social welfare spending, asserting that the state had gone beyond its financial means. Rockefeller called for crackdowns on welfare cheating and successfully advocated mandatory life sentences for certain categories of narcotics offenders. In 1971 he refused to negotiate with rebellious Attica state prison inmates and sent in heavily armed state troopers to crush the uprising. Liberals criticized his political shift and also frowned upon his promotion of large construction projects, such as the Albany mall and the aborted Rye-Oyster Bay Bridge over Long Island Sound. Many observers regarded Rockefeller's change of views as an effort to win conservative Republican support for a future presidential bid.

In 1973 Rockefeller resigned the governorship of New York and set up a study group called the Commission for Critical Choices for Americans. In August 1974 President Ford nominated him for the vice presidency. At Rockefeller's congressional confirmation hearings he stated that his personal wealth and that of his wife and his children totaled about $230 million. A family spokesman placed the wealth of all of the Rockefellers at well over $1 billion. Some observers placed the figure at $5 billion. The Congress confirmed Rockefeller's nomination in December 1974. In November 1975 he announced that he did not wish to be renominated for the vice presidency in 1976. [See JOHNSON, NIXON Volumes]

[MLL]

For further information:
Robert H. Connery and Gerald Benjamin, eds., *Governing New York State: The Rockefeller Years* (New York, 1974).
James Desmond, *Nelson Rockefeller: A Political Biography* (New York, 1964).

ROCKWELL, GEORGE LINCOLN
b. March 9, 1918; Bloomington, Ill.
d. Aug. 25, 1967; Arlington, Va.
Commander, American Nazi Party.

Rockwell was the son of George "Doc" Rockwell, a well-known vaudeville comedian of the 1920s and 1930s. His parents were generally on tour, and Rockwell spent much of his youth traveling with them until their divorce. In the late 1930s he attended Brown University, where he did art work for the college's humor magazine. A psychiatrist later described his drawings of that period as reflecting a preoccupation with "the recurrent themes of death, cannibalism, blood and bombing." Rockwell contended that he had merely been imitating cartoonist Charles Addams.

In 1940 Rockwell left Brown to join the Navy. Following the war he established a successful advertising agency but left after a quarrel with his partners. When the Korean conflict began he was recalled to naval service and attained the rank of commander. Until this time Rockwell had remained generally apolitical, but in the early 1950s he became interested in racist and anti-Semitic literature. After reading *Mein Kampf* he regarded himself as a disciple of Adolf Hitler. In 1958, while still in the Navy, he organized a fascist group, which by 1960 called itself the American Nazi Party.

Believing that Communism was a Jewish-inspired movement, Rockwell at different times advocated either the sterilization or extermination of American Jews. He also asserted the superiority of the "white race" and favored the deportation of blacks to Africa.

Rockwell frequently staged grotesque and provocative demonstrations. In one case he provided his supporters with gorilla suits and pro-civil rights placards. Often donning stormtrooper uniforms with swastika armbands, the Nazis received a hostile reception from even racist and extreme right-wing groups. Throughout the period of Rockwell's leadership, the Party's membership was generally estimated at below 100.

In May 1960 New York City's Parks Commissioner Newbold Morris denied

Rockwell a speaking permit on the grounds that the preaching of hatred might produce rioting. But the following February the Appellate Division of the New York State Supreme Court supported Rockwell's right to speak, ruling that the prior restraint of speech could not be imposed "unless it is demonstrated on a record that such expression will immediately and irreparably create injury to the public weal." In November 1961 the U.S. Supreme Court refused to reverse this decision.

Whatever his constitutional rights Rockwell's efforts to present his views were generally unsuccessful. In February 1960 the Navy discharged him because of his efforts to propagate Nazism. During the following January he was stoned in Boston while trying to picket the film "Exodus," which dealt with the establishment of the state of Israel. Later in the year, while on what he described as a "hate tour" of the South, Rockwell was arrested for disorderly conduct while attempting to demonstrate against the same movie. In 1962 the state of Virginia, in which the Nazis had established their headquarters, passed a law revoking the Party's charter. During the August 1963 civil rights March on Washington, however, Rockwell and a small group of followers were permitted to hold a counter-demonstration.

On Aug. 25, 1967 Rockwell was shot and killed in Arlington, Va., by a former Party member who had been expelled from the organization the previous spring. [See JOHNSON Volume]

[MLL]

For further information:
Fred. C. Shapiro, "The Last Word (We Hope) on George Lincoln Rockwell," *Esquire* (February, 1967), pp. 101-105.

ROMNEY, GEORGE W(ILCKEN)
b. July 8, 1907; Chihuahua, Mex.
Chairman of the Board and President, American Motors Corporation, 1954-62; Governor, Mich., 1963-69.

Born to a poor, American Mormon family in Mexico, George W. Romney grew up in Texas and Idaho and attended the University of Utah and George Washington University. Romney served as an aide to Sen. David I. Walsh (D, Mass.) in 1929-30 and remained in Washington to lobby for the aluminum industry until 1939 when he accepted a job with the Automobile Manufacturers Association. In 1948 Romney was appointed special assistant to the board chairman of Nash-Kelvinator and six years later became the president and board chairman of its successor firm, American Motors (AMC). During his years at AMC, Romney's advocacy of the compact car over what he termed "the Dinosaur in your driveway" helped the company overcome serious financial problems and emerge in the late 1950s as a profitable operation. [See EISENHOWER Volume]

Beginning in 1959, Romney became actively involved in statewide reform and GOP politics. He led the formation of a non-partisan "Citizens for Michigan" committee in June 1959 which sought to reorganize state government by writing a new state constitution. In November 1960 voters endorsed the group's proposal for a constitutional convention, and Romney served as a delegate and vice president of the convention when it met in 1961 and 1962. Even before the convention completed its work, Romney announced his candidacy for governor as a Republican. Under Gov. G. Mennen Williams (1949-61) [*q.v.*] and John B. Swainson (1961-63), state Democrats in alliance with the United Auto Workers (UAW) had held the governor's mansion for 14 years. High unemployment and Romney's non-partisan appeal, however, proved decisive in the November 1962 election, and he defeated Swainson with 51.4% of the total vote.

Despite the UAW's opposition in April 1963, Michigan voters approved the constitution drafted by the convention. The new charter extended the term of elected state officials from two to four years and made the appointment of non-elective department heads subject to Senate confirmation. It increased urban representation in the legislature, created a permanent civil rights commission and prohibited state budget deficits and a graduated income tax.

Voter approval of the new constitution in

April enhanced Romney's national prestige, and many Party leaders envisioned the moderate Republican governor as an alternative to liberal Gov. Nelson A. Rockefeller (R, N.Y.) [q.v.] or conservative Sen. Barry M. Goldwater (R, Ariz.) [q.v.]. Even before Romney's successful gubernatorial campaign, former President Dwight D. Eisenhower [q.v.] and former Vice President Richard M. Nixon [q.v.] had promoted Romney as a presidential prospect. Although he disavowed any interest in national office, Romney did make political appearances outside Michigan in April and May 1963. By the summer his support among Republican voters for the 1964 presidential nomination rose to 25%, an impressive mark for a newly elected politician.

After May 1963, however, Romney abandoned any effort to win a national constituency and declined to set up a national campaign organization. The *Detroit News,* which had strongly endorsed him for governor in 1962, opposed a presidential drive by the state's new chief executive, and a tax fight with the Michigan legislature forced Romney's attention away from national politics. Romney had promised state tax reform during his gubernatorial campaign, and in the fall of 1963 he proposed that the state adopt a flat-rate individual and corporate income tax. But he failed to persuade conservative Republican legislators to support his tax package and by November the state legislature had rejected it. The defeat seriously damaged his standing among those Republican leaders who had previously advocated his candidacy for president.

Like many moderate and liberal Republicans, Romney criticized the right-wing John Birch Society and called for the GOP to maintain a positive attitude toward civil rights legislation. During his 1962 campaign for governor, Romney forced the resignation of a district Party leader who belonged to the Birch Society. In June 1963 Romney joined in a civil rights march favoring open housing in the wealthy and racially exclusive Detroit suburb of Grosse Point.

Romney won reelection as governor in 1964 and election to a four-year term two years later. He actively campaigned for the 1968 Republican presidential nomination but withdrew from the race two weeks before the first primary. Romney served as Secretary of Housing and Urban Development through the first Nixon Administration. [See JOHNSON, NIXON Volumes]

[JLB]

For further information:
Clark R. Mollenhoff, *George Romney* (New York, 1968).
Robert D. Novak, *The Agony of the GOP 1964* (New York, 1965).

ROMUALDI, SERAFINO
b. Nov. 18, 1900; Bastia Umbra, Italy.
d. Nov. 11, 1967, Mexico City, Mexico.
Director, Amerian Institute for Free Labor Development, 1961- .

An active socialist, Romualdi fled his native Italy after Mussolini came to power. He arrived in New York in 1923 and joined the Anti-Fascist League, which drew much of its support from the Italian locals of the International Ladies Garment Workers Union (ILGWU) and the Amalgamated Clothing Workers of America (ACWA). In 1933 he joined the ILGWU's editorial staff. Striving to counter pro-Fascist sentiment in the Italian communities of South America, Italian groups based in the U.S. sent Romualdi on a Latin American tour in early 1941. Following the declaration of war by the U.S., Romualdi returned to South America as an agent of the U.S. Bureau of Latin American Research. While still affiliated with the ILGWU, he was sent to Italy after the fall of the Fascist government as an agent of the Office of Strategic Services, the forerunner of the Central Intelligence Agency (CIA). Romualdi was responsible for directing financial contributions from American labor groups to non-Communist labor and political groups in Italy. These contributions flowed, in large part, from the CIA, and over $2 million a year was spent on anti-Communist activities in Italy and France alone.

In 1945 Romualdi became the Latin American director for the AFL's international activities division, the newly established Free Trade Union Committee. In Latin America he continued the AFL policy of support for non-Communist labor groups abroad. Denouncing Guatemala's elected president, Jacobo Arbenz, as a Communist in 1954, Romualdi brought local labor leaders opposed to the Arbenz regime into cooperation with army officers who led a CIA-financed coup against Arbenz in June. Romualdi, however, was dismayed by the anti-labor repression that followed, reducing Guatemalan workers to what he called "conditions of servitude if not actual slavery."

Fearing the impact of the Cuban revolution in other parts of Latin America, President Kennedy called in 1961 for a program "through which the talents and experience of the U.S. labor movement could be brought to bear on the danger that Castro . . . might undermine the Latin American labor movement." The structure formed was the American Institute for Free Labor Development (AIFLD), chartered by the AFL-CIO with Romualdi as its director. Although AFL-CIO President George Meany [q.v.] claimed that the Institute was supported "in almost equal shares, by industry, labor and government," 62% of its original funding came from the government, mostly through the Agency for International Development (AID). The remainder was supplied by corporations and the AFL-CIO International Affairs division. Through AID the government contributed $15.4 million to the AIFLD between 1961 and 1968. As part of its educational program, AIFLD began to operate a system of training schools for Latin American labor leaders "with particular emphasis on the theme of democracy versus totalitarianism." The Institute also provided loans to Latin American unions for housing projects, credit unions, banks and other social programs.

Under Romualdi's leadership AIFLD played a major role in the overthrow of the elected regime of Cheddi Jagan, the radical president of British Guiana. During the course of an 80-day general strike declared by Jagan's opponents in the spring of 1963, Romualdi put at the disposal of the strike committee the services of six graduates of the American Institute. He also helped channel CIA money to the strike leadership. As a result of the political turmoil in

Guiana, the more moderate opposition party leader, Forbes Birnham, came to power in 1964.

Romualdi retired from AIFLD in 1965, but remained a consultant to the Institute until his death in 1967.

[MDB]

For further information:
Ronald Radosh, *American Labor and United States Foreign Policy* (New York, 1969).
Serafino Romualdi, *Presidents and Peons* (New York, 1967).

ROONEY, JOHN J(AMES)
b. Nov. 29, 1903; New York, N.Y.
Democratic Representative, N.Y., 1944-75.

John Rooney, the son of Irish immigrants, was born in the declining central district of Brooklyn and educated in local Catholic schools. He received his law degree from Fordham University in 1925 and over the next 14 years pursued a successful career specializing in civil law. In 1940 he was appointed as assistant district attorney of New York City.

In 1944 Rooney was chosen by the regular Democratic machine to run in a special election to fill a U.S. House seat vacated by the death of Thomas H. Cullen. Elected in June 1944, he represented a polyglot district of mixed ethnic and economic groups from poor Irish and Hasidic Jews to wealthy third-generation Americans.

Rooney was appointed to the House Committee on Appropriations in 1946 and served on the subcommittee that oversaw the budgets of the State and Justice Departments, the judiciary and other federal agencies. From 1949 until his retirement in 1975, with the exception of two years when Congress was controlled by the Republicans, Rooney served as chairman of the subcommittee. As the dominant force on that panel, he championed economy, particularly in the State Department. However, he remained a friend of the Federal Maritime Administration, the Antitrust Division of the Justice Department and, especially, the FBI. During his years as chairman, Rooney approved virtually without question all budget requests from the Bureau. [See TRUMAN, EISENHOWER Volumes]

Rooney was a close friend of FBI Director J. Edgar Hoover [q.v.], who often consulted the Congressman when some official sanction was necessary for special projects. Rooney's approval was viewed in the FBI as tantamount to congressional authorization. According to historian Sanford Ungar, Rooney was told about some of the Bureau's controversial counterintelligence programs during the 1950s and 1960s. Because of the similarity in their political beliefs they rarely disagreed on policy.

On most domestic legislation Rooney's voting reflected the needs of his constituents. He consistently supported labor and civil rights legislation and backed medicare, urban renewal and child care measures that could help the depressed sections of his district. In analyzing Rooney's voting pattern one political reporter pointed out that it reflected special loyalties to Brooklyn, Ireland, the Roman Catholic Church, the FBI and Israel.

Although an opponent of most State Department spending, Rooney, at the request of President Kennedy, worked to increase representation allowances given diplomats. This measure, supplementing embassy entertainment funds, passed in March 1961, permitting qualified men who were not independently wealthy to accept important diplomatic posts.

During the remainder of his tenure in the House, Rooney continued to back liberal domestic legislation while supporting the Johnson Administration's policy in Vietnam. His 1972 primary battle proved the focus for an unsuccessful attempt by reform elements in New York's Democratic party to oust the entrenched machine politician. [See NIXON Volume]

Rooney retired in January 1975 after 31 years in the House.

[EWS]

For further information:
Sanford J. Ungar, *FBI* (Boston, 1975).

ROOSA, ROBERT V(INCENT)

b. June 21, 1918; Marquette, Mich.
Undersecretary of the Treasury for Monetary Affairs, January 1961-November 1964.

Robert Roosa joined the research department of the Federal Reserve Bank of New York in 1941. He remained with the bank, except for wartime service, for the next 20 years, rising to the position of vice president for research in 1956. Regarded as a brilliant theorist on Wall Street and well-respected in international financial circles, Roosa was appointed undersecretary of the treasury for monetary affairs in January 1961. Roosa's appointment was interpreted in the financial community as a sign that the Kennedy Administration was serious about combating the balance of payments deficit and as an indication that there would be closer cooperation between the Treasury Department and the Federal Reserve.

Roosa's predecessors in the post had been occupied chiefly with the management of the national debt. Roosa, however, devoted himself to halting the gold outflow and strengthening the international standing of the dollar, problems that deeply vexed President Kennedy. In August 1963 *Business Week* characterized Roosa as the "de facto head of a coalition of conservative central bankers and economists" and as the "chief financial strategist in the New Frontier."

The central problem confronting Roosa was the gold outflow, the root cause of which was the growth in dollar holdings abroad since World War II. Large balance of payments deficits persisted during the Kennedy Administration despite efforts to arrest the problem by curbing domestic inflation and tying some 80% of foreign aid to purchases of goods in the United States. Since dollars were convertible into gold, Roosa had to devise a host of strategies to reduce the incentive for gold conversion.

Roosa led the U.S. into active involvement in the foreign exchange market. Under Roosa the Treasury began to purchase and hoard foreign currencies. In times of stress—during a movement to "dump" dollars for gold or for foreign currencies with premiums—such reserves would be used to neutralize the speculative pressure on the dollar. Roosa also worked to reduce the gold outflow by selling Treasury bonds denominated in foreign currencies (called "Roosa bonds"), another technique of adding to the Treasury's accumulation of foreign currencies. To help arrest the balance of payments deficit, he negotiated with European governments in 1962 for the prepayment of $662 million of debts owed the U.S. government.

In October 1962 Roosa testified in favor of a bill passed by Congress permitting American commercial banks to pay a higher interest rate on short-term deposits of foreign governments. The measure was designed to help maintain foreign dollar accounts in the U.S. and discourage conversion of the accounts into gold.

Frustration at the persistence of the gold drain and fear that the elaborate Roosa Plan might unravel led the Administration to advocate additional remedies in the summer of 1963. Roosa backed the Federal Reserve Board's increase in the discount rate from 3% to 3½% in July 1963 in the hope of discouraging the flight of short-term capital towards higher interest rates abroad. The next month he argued in favor of the Administration's "interest equalization tax," a levy on foreign securities sold in the U.S. The tax, passed by Congress in August 1964, was intended to help stem the balance of payments deficit by making it more expensive for foreigners to borrow funds in the U.S.

Roosa's innovative schemes operated within a framework of traditional monetary thought. He resolutely opposed devaluation of the dollar as a solution to balance of payments and gold outflow problems. Within the Administration he spearheaded the Treasury Department's resistance to proposals for sweeping international monetary reform emanating from the Council of Economic Advisers. Monetary reformers envisioned a great increase in international liquidity through unorthodox measures such as the creation of new supra-national credit machinery. Countries with balance of payments difficulties would then have greater freedom to pursue expansionary economic

policies. Dismissing the notion of a dire international liquidity shortage, Roosa advocated working within the existing system by adding to the reserves of the International Monetary Fund. In May 1962 he argued against any "synthetic currency device created by an extra-national authority bearing neither the responsibilities nor the disciplines of sovereignty." Supported by Secretary of the Treasury C. Douglas Dillon [q.v.], Roosa was successful in persuading President Kennedy to follow his more conservative approach to monetary problems.

Roosa left the Treasury Department in November 1964 to become a partner in the New York investment banking firm of Brown Brothers, Harriman & Company.

[TO]

ROOSEVELT, (ANNA) ELEANOR
b. Oct. 11, 1884; New York, N.Y.
d. Nov. 7, 1962; New York, N.Y.
Delegate to the United Nations General Assembly, March 1961-November 1962.

Eleanor Roosevelt, the niece of one president and the wife of another, achieved a national reputation as a liberal spokeswoman during Franklin D. Roosevelt's years as president. Closely identified with Negro, labor and women's groups, she often served as the Roosevelt Administration's liaison with these New Deal constituencies.

After FDR's death President Truman appointed Eleanor Roosevelt a delegate to the U.N. General Assembly. There she was instrumental in drafting the Human Rights Commission's Declaration of Human Rights in 1948. A member of the Democratic Party's liberal wing, Roosevelt was also a founding member of the Americans for Democratic Action in 1947 and later an enthusiastic supporter of Adlai Stevenson [q.v.] in his 1952 and 1956 campaigns for the presidency. In the late 1950s she helped to found the Democratic Party reform movement in New York. A strong supporter of Mayor Robert F. Wagner's [q.v.] primary campaign in September 1961, she was influential in the defeat of Tammany Hall leader Carmine De Sapio [q.v.] in that election. [See TRUMAN, EISENHOWER Volumes]

In early 1960 Roosevelt unsuccessfully attempted to persuade Sen. John F. Kennedy to accept the vice presidential spot on a ticket again headed by Adlai Stevenson. She believed that Kennedy lacked the commitment and maturity to be president. Her coolness toward Kennedy also stemmed from her intense personal dislike of his father, Joseph P. Kennedy [q.v.], and in her view, the younger Kennedy's "soft" stand on McCarthyism during the early 1950s. Despite her disappointment over Kennedy's failure to appoint Stevenson Secretary of State, Mrs. Roosevelt's enthusiasm for the young President increased after his inaugural address; at his urging, she kept in close correspondence with him until her death.

On Stevenson's recommendation, Roosevelt was appointed a delegate to the U.N. General Assembly in March 1961. Seventy-seven years old and in failing health, Eleanor Roosevelt still maintained a vigorous work schedule. After Fidel Castro proposed in May 1961 that the Bay of Pigs prisoners be exchanged for 500 tractors, President Kennedy initiated the private Tractors for Freedom Committee, chaired by Roosevelt, Walter Reuther [q.v.] and Milton Eisenhower [q.v.]. The project soon collapsed, however, due both to Republican opposition and to Castro's insistence upon receiving heavy earth-moving machinery rather than the light farm tractors the Committee was prepared to purchase.

Although President Kennedy appointed Roosevelt to a series of highly visible posts, such as the Commission on the Status of Women and the Advisory Council of the Peace Corps, she had little influence on Administration policy. Her recommendation that the U.S. continue a moratorium on nuclear tests after the Soviet Union resumed testing was rejected. Her 1962 suggestion that the issue of the war in Vietnam be taken before the United Nations was never seriously considered. Kennedy referred Roosevelt to the State Department, where a spokesman told individuals representing her that the U.N. was incapable of taking "any action" on Vietnam.

Efforts were made before and after Eleanor Roosevelt's death to secure for her the Nobel Peace Prize. After her death on Nov. 7, 1962 Presidents John Kennedy, Dwight D. Eisenhower and Harry Truman attended her funeral at Hyde Park.

[FHM]

For further information:
Joseph Lash, *Eleanor: The Years Alone* (New York, 1972).

ROOSEVELT, FRANKLIN D(ELANO), JR.
b. Aug. 17, 1914; Campobello Island, Canada.
Undersecretary of Commerce, March 1963 -May 1965.

The son of Franklin Delano and Eleanor Roosevelt [q.v.], Franklin D. Roosevelt, Jr., attended Groton, Harvard and the University of Virginia Law School and earned a Silver Star while in the Navy during World War II. Roosevelt helped in the formation of the liberal Americans for Democratic Action in 1947 and won an impressive, hard fought race for Congress in New York City's Upper West Side in May 1949. A promising career in New York politics ended unexpectedly in November 1954 when Rep. Jacob K. Javits (R, N.Y.) [q.v.] defeated Roosevelt in a race for the post of state attorney general. Resuming his law practice, Roosevelt alienated many of his old liberal backers by accepting a legal retainer of $150,000 from Rafael Trujillo, the Dominican Republic dictator. [See TRUMAN, EISENHOWER Volumes]

Roosevelt actively campaigned for Sen. John F. Kennedy early in the battle for the 1960 Democratic presidential nomination. Making his greatest contribution to the Senator's effort in the May West Virginia primary, Roosevelt took full advantage of his famous name and occasionally overshadowed the candidate in joint appearances. He criticized Kennedy's opponent, Sen. Hubert H. Humphrey (D, Minn.) [q.v.] for not having served in the armed forces during World War II, in contrast to the Massachusetts Democrat's heroism as a torpedo boat commander. His implied charge of "draft-dodging" deeply hurt Humphrey, who lost the West Virginia contest and his hopes for the Party's first prize. Following the state balloting, Roosevelt apologized for the remark.

Victory in West Virginia greatly aided Kennedy's quest for the nomination. After his election the new President hoped to find a place for Roosevelt in his Administration. Defense Secretary-designate Robert S. McNamara [q.v.] rejected Kennedy's suggestion that Roosevelt be named secretary of the Navy, and Roosevelt himself declined the President's offer of an ambassadorship or directorship of the Civil Defense Office. Instead, Roosevelt remained in New York, while making diplomatic appearances on the President's behalf in Tanganyika and West Berlin.

In January 1963 Kennedy finally placed Roosevelt in the administration as undersecretary of commerce. Assuming office in March Roosevelt took on a variety of roles with the full expectation of succeeding his aging superior, Luther D. Hodges [q.v.]. Appointed chairman of the new Appalachian Regional Commission in April, Roosevelt led in planning for the poverty-stricken region's economic development. His work anticipated President Johnson's aid-to-Appalachia programs. In October and November 1963 Roosevelt participated in negotiations with the Soviet Union for the sale of $250 million worth of U.S. wheat. He testified on Nov. 22 against a bill sponsored by Sen. Karl E. Mundt (R, S.D.) [q.v.] that would have denied credit to Communist grain buyers.

With his Commerce Department appointment, Roosevelt became an intimate of the Kennedy family, sailing with the President at Newport and accompanying Jacqueline Kennedy [q.v.] to Greece in October following the death of her second son Patrick. On the trip Greek shipping magnate Aristotle Onassis entertained Roosevelt and Mrs. Kennedy, an action criticized by Rep. Oliver P. Bolton (R, Ohio) as improper in view of Onassis's shipping interests and the Commerce Department's jurisdiction over the U. S. Maritime Administration.

Roosevelt never became Secretary of Commerce and failed in a move to reenter New York politics. Declining to promote Roosevelt upon Hodges's resignation in December 1964, President Johnson instead named him chairman of the Equal Employment Opportunity Commission (EEOC) six months later. Roosevelt left the EEOC in May 1966 to seek the New York Democratic gubernatorial nomination. Failing in that goal he ran as the Liberal Party nominee and finished fourth. He retired from politics following his 1966 defeat. [See JOHNSON Volume]

[JLB]

For further information:
Mitchell Levitas, "Rise, Fall and_____of FDR, Jr.," The New York Times Magazine (Oct. 23, 1966, p. 27.

ROSE, ALEX
b. Oct. 15, 1898; Warsaw, Poland.
President, United Hatters, Cap and Millinery Workers International Union, 1950- ; Vice-chairman, Liberal Party, 1944- .

The son of a well-to-do tanner, Rose left Poland hoping to study medicine in the U.S. Cut off from his parents' support by World War I, he became a millinery worker. Rose, who had been active in the Labor Zionist Organization, joined the Jewish Legion of the British Army in 1918 and served in the Middle East for two years. Returning to the U.S. in 1924, he defeated a Communist-backed opponent in a race for secretary-treasurer of his local in the Cloth Hat, Cap and Millinery Workers Union. By 1927 he was a union vice president, a position he retained when the union merged with the United Hatters of North American to form the United Hatters, Cap and Millinery Workers International Union in 1934.

In 1950 Rose was appointed president by the union's executive board and was subsequently elected to the post. Rose eschewed confrontations with employers stating, "The class struggle is a thing of the past in my union and in many others . . . . Our union has demonstrated its willingness and capacity to render constructive service in stabilizing our industry." During the 1950s the union loaned large sums to faltering hat manufacturers, purchased real estate in New York's millinery district, and became the largest stockholder in the Merrimac Hat Corporation, preventing its liquidation.

With International Ladies Garment Workers Union President David Dubinsky [q.v.] and others, Rose helped form the American Labor Party (ALP) in 1936, offering New Yorkers the opportunity to support the New Deal without voting the Democratic, and therefore Tammany, line. Serving as ALP state secretary until 1944, he and Dubinsky then withdrew because the Party had come under Communist influence. They formed the Liberal Party and continued to support Democrats in most major elections. Although the Party ran an occasional congressional candidate, its major influence was in its impact on the Democrats. The Party actively sponsored urban renewal, reapportionment, civil rights and rent control legislation. [See TRUMAN, EISENHOWER Volumes]

Factional conflicts among the Democrats enlarged the power of New York Liberals in the early 1960s. In 1959 former Gov. Herbert H. Lehman [q.v.] and Eleanor Roosevelt [q.v.] formed the New York Committee for Democratic Voters to break the power of the Tammany bosses, especially Carmine DeSapio [q.v.] and Charles Buckley [q.v.]. New York Mayor Robert F. Wagner [q.v.], formerly allied with DeSapio, also sought to disassociate himself from the Tammany leader early in 1961. Wagner, seeking reelection, turned to Rose for advice, hoping to win the support of reform Democrats. The Liberal Party endorsed Wagner at its June convention where Rose and Dubinsky rejected charges that the union leaders' presence on the dais intimidated other delegates. Wagner won the election easily. Rose claimed that Liberal Party endorsement also had given the edge to the Republican candidate for the Bronx borough presidency, enabling him to defeat the Buckley-supported Democratic candidate there. In 1962 the Liberals endorsed the Democratic candidates for gov-

ernor and senator, Robert Morgenthau and James R. Donovan [q.v.], who lost to Republicans Nelson A. Rockefeller [q.v.] and Jacob Javits [q.v.].

During the late 1960s Rose and Dubinsky continued to dominate the Liberal Party, which broke away from its usual practice of supporting Democratic candidates and successfully ran John V. Lindsay [q.v.] for two terms as mayor.

[MDB]

For further information:
Warren Moscow, *The Last of the Big-Time Bosses: The Life and Times of Carmine DeSapio* (New York, 1971).
Stephen D. Isaacs, *Jews and American Politics* (Garden City, 1974).

ROSTOW, WALT W(HITMAN)
b. Oct. 7, 1916; New York, N.Y.
Deputy Special Assistant to the President for National Security Affairs, January-December 1961; Chairman, State Department Policy Planning Council, December 1961-April 1966.

The son of Russian-Jewish immigrants, Rostow attended Yale University as an undergraduate and graduate student. He received his Ph.D. there in 1940, after having spent two years at Oxford as a Rhodes scholar. During World War II he was an officer in the Office of Strategic Services and helped select bombing targets in Germany. Following the war he served briefly in the State Department and from 1947 to 1949 was assistant to the executive secretary of the Economic Commission for Europe. From 1950 to 1960 Rostow taught economics at the Massachusetts Institute of Technology (MIT) and after 1951 was associated with its Central Intelligence Agency-supported Center for International Studies.

Rostow's chief academic interests were the process of economic growth and the direction of United States foreign policy. His best-known book, *The Stages of Economic Growth: A Non-Communist Manifesto* (1960), was an effort to present an economic interpretation of history that challenged Marxist theories of development. Rostow argued that economic growth was a multi-staged process stimulated by a widespread desire for the improvement of life as well as the search for profit by the middle class. The past industrialization of Europe and the U.S. and the contemporary development of Asia, Africa and Latin America followed the same pattern. After the creation of pre-conditions for growth in a formerly traditional society, rapid growth in a few sectors such as railroads or textiles caused an economic "take-off" towards industrialization and modernization, while later maturation led to "the age of high mass consumption."

Rostow did occasional work as a consultant for the Eisenhower Administration and in 1958 regularly began to provide Sen. John F. Kennedy with ideas and research on foreign affairs. During the 1960 presidential campaign, he was on Kennedy's informal academic advisory council and was credited with writing two widely used Kennedy campaign slogans: "The New Frontier" and "Let's Get This Country Moving Again."

Shortly after the election Rostow and Jerome B. Wiesner [q.v.], a fellow MIT professor active in the Kennedy campaign, attended a scholarly conference in the Soviet Union. In a meeting with First Deputy Soviet Foreign Minister Vasily V. Kuznetsov, they urged the release of two U.S. pilots, who had been shot down over the Soviet Union in July 1960, as "an essential first step towards better United States-Soviet relations." The pilots were released on Jan. 25, 1961.

In planning his new Administration Kennedy originally intended to appoint Rostow head of the State Department Policy Planning Council, but Secretary of State-designate Dean Rusk [q.v.] preferred to have an old friend, George McGhee, in the post. Kennedy finally appointed Rostow deputy to McGeorge Bundy [q.v.], the special assistant to the President for national security affairs. In this post Rostow had a major role in advising the President on foreign policy options and planning.

Shortly after the inauguration Rostow was given a report on conditions in Vietnam, prepared in the final days of the Eisenhower Administration by Brig. Gen. Edward G. Lansdale [q.v.]. Lansdale, who was pessimistic about the situation, anticipated the possibility of a major crisis in the near future and urged a major expansion of U.S. programs in that country. Rostow believed Lansdale's report to be of crucial importance; on Feb. 2 he gave it to the President, who was greatly impressed by it. The report was the first step in a major Administration examination of Vietnam policy.

Rostow believed that Communist insurgents were "scavangers of the modernization process," preying on dislocations and discontent inherent in the transitional stages of economic growth. He believed that the situation was particularly difficult for pro-Western forces in South Vietnam and Laos because he thought the guerrilla wars were being waged from foreign bases. Rostow argued that the U.S. had to speed the modernization process in these countries and, in the interim before full modernization was achieved, stop guerrilla infiltration by either diplomatic or military means or take direct action against its sources. Rostow was thus one of the earliest Administration figures to urge the consideration of bombing North Vietnam or invading and occupying its southern regions. According to David Halberstam [q.v.] in *The Best and the Brightest*, Rostow was "genuinely enthusiastic about a guerrilla confrontation" in South Vietnam.

In a memorandum to the President on April 12, 1961, Rostow urged "gearing up the whole Vietnam operation" by appointing a full-time coordinator in Washington, increasing aid and sending a group of Special Forces advisers to South Vietnam, making personnel changes in the U.S. aid program and scheduling a vice-presidential trip to Vietnam. Many of these recommendations, including the trip, were eventually accepted. Shortly after reading this memorandum Kennedy appointed a task force headed by Deputy Secretary of Defense Roswell Gilpatric [q.v.] to reevaluate U.S. Vietnam policy. The task force recommended a moderate increase in U.S. aid but did not clearly call for U.S. ground troops to be sent to Vietnam.

Rostow was the White House representative on an inter-departmental task force on Laos established in January 1961. During the crisis that spring, which resulted from military setbacks experienced by the U.S.-backed rightist troops, Rostow generally advocated firm military and political action against the Communist forces. Reacting to a subsequent crisis in May 1962, Rostow advocated bombing North Vietnam, which he believed to be largely in control of the Laotian Communists. In both cases, however, diplomatic solutions were reached before any major military steps were taken by the United States.

In September 1961 there was an increase in insurgent action in Vietnam, and on Oct. 1 South Vietnamese President Ngo Dinh Diem requested a bilateral treaty with the U.S. A number of different proposals were considered by the Administration during this period, including one prepared by Rostow to send a Southeast Asian Treaty Organization force of 25,000 men to guard the Lao-Vietnamese border. Rostow's proposal was rejected in early October by the Joint Chiefs of Staff, who introduced their own plan to send U.S. troops to either Laos or the central highlands of Vietnam. On Oct. 11 Kennedy decided to send presidential adviser Gen. Maxwell Taylor [q.v.] and Rostow to Vietnam to investigate various possible plans for increasing U.S. involvement, including for the introduction of U.S. combat troops.

Although Rostow did not prepare a personal draft, he was one of the principal authors of the mission's main report, issued on Nov. 3. The tone of this document was characterized in *The Pentagon Papers* as combining "urgency with optimism." The report recommended a series of reforms in the Saigon government and military, an increase in U.S. military aid and the deployment of additional U.S. advisers at all levels of the South Vietnamese government, changing the U.S. role from an advisory one to one of "limited partnership." In a separate, top secret report, Taylor recommended the introduction of 8,000 U.S. combat troops. With the exception of Taylor's call for the introduction of ground troops, most of the mission's recommendations were put into effect.

As part of a high-level shuffle of White House and State Department officials on Nov. 26, 1961, Rostow was appointed a State Department counselor and chairman of the Department's Policy Planning Council. In this position he was in charge of long-range analysis and planning for a broad spectrum of foreign policy aras but was no longer directly involved in the White House decision-making process and no longer centrally involved in Vietnam policy.

One of Rostow's new projects was a program to increase the viability and attractiveness of West Berlin in the face of the construction of the Berlin Wall. He also attended various international planning conferences and in February 1962 attended a meeting of the NATO Permanent Council to seek support for the U.S. policy toward Latin America, particulary for a ban on trade with Cuba.

At the request of Kennedy and Rusk, Rostow made a week-long trip to India and Pakistan in April 1963 to explore the possibilities for a settlement of their dispute over Kashmir and encourage both sides to sincerely seek a negotiated solution. However, in his report to Kennedy, Rostow was deeply pessimistic about the possibility for a peaceful resolution of the dispute in the near future.

In May 1964 Rostow was given the additional post of U.S. representative to the Inter-American Committee on the Alliance for Progress. In April 1966 he succeeded Bundy as special assistant to the President for national security affairs, and he served in that post for the remainder of the Johnson Administration. In 1969 he returned to the academic life as a professor of economics and history at the University of Texas. [See JOHNSON Volume]

[JBF]

For further information:
David Halberstam, *The Best and the Brightest* (New York, 1972).
W. W. Rostow, *The Diffusion of Power, 1957-1972* (New York, 1972).
U.S. Department of Defense, *The Pentagon Papers*, Senator Gravel Edition (Boston, 1971), Vol. II.

ROUSSELOT, JOHN H(ARBIN)
b. Nov. 1, 1927; Los Angeles, Calif.
Republican Representative, Calif.,
1961-63; Western District Governor,
John Birch Society, 1963-64.

Rousselot operated a public relations consulting firm in Los Angeles from 1954 to 1958. In 1958 he became the director of public information for the Federal Housing Administration in Washington. He resigned from that post early in 1960. Later in the year he successfully ran for Congress from a conservative suburban district in Los Angeles county.

In March 1961 the existence of the ultra-conservative, anti-Communist John Birch Society, established in 1958, became widely known to the general public. On March 8 Sen. Milton R. Young (R, N.D.) [q.v.] revealed that its founder, Robert H. W. Welch [q.v.] had written in 1955 that President Dwight D. Eisenhower and other high government officials were agents of a world Communist conspiracy which had deeply infiltrated all levels of the federal government. A month later Rousselot and Rep. Edgar Hiestand (R, Calif.) acknowledged that they were members of the Society.

Rousselot said he had joined the organization in the fall of the previous year. Denying that the Society was an extremist group, he asserted that its purpose was to educate Americans about the danger of Communism and teach them how to combat that threat by legal means. In a 1967 interview for *Encounter* magazine, he said that his experience as a federal official had led to his decision to join the Society. While working in Washington, Rousselot explained, he had become convinced that many national officeholders were Communist agents or their dupes. He further justified his mistrust of federal officials by claiming that "government is inevitably an enemy of freedom.

Rousselot compiled an extremely conservative record in Congress. According to *Congressional Quarterly*, he never voted against the House conservative coalition of Republicans and Southern Democrats during those two years. He favored a militantly anti-Communist foreign policy, urging President Kennedy in August 1961 to "eliminate the Communist threat in Cuba." When in the spring of 1962 it was reported that Walt W. Rostow [q.v.], chairman of the State Department's Policy Planning Board, had asserted that Soviet foreign policy was mellowing, Rousselot urged that his background be investigated.

In 1962 Rousselot and Hiestand, the only two acknowledged Birch Society members in Congress, were unsuccessful in their reelection bids. Their defeats resulted from the gerrymandering of their districts by the Democratic-controlled California legislature and from the Society's reputation as an irresponsible, semi-secret organization that recklessly accused innocent persons of being Communist sympathizers.

Shortly after his electoral defeat Rousselot became the Western district governor of the Birch Society. In March 1963 he stated that the major goals of the organization included the removal of the United Nations from the United States as a check on Soviet espionage, an investigation of the State Department "to find out why it doesn't take a strong stand against the Communist conspiracy" and the impeachment of Chief Justice Earl Warren [q.v.] "for a long series of decisions favorable to Communist objectives." Rousselot also favored restricting university education and opposed the Peace Corps as "an extension of socialism because it is controlled by the colleges." At the same time he tried to modify the organization's unfavorable image by asserting that the group did not seek to infiltrate and capture the Republican Party and that, while the group established "ad hoc committees" for particular causes, it disapproved of the use of "front" organizations in the "deceptive" Communist sense.

In 1964 Rousselot became the national public relations director of the Birch Society. He resigned that position in 1967 to return to private business. In 1970 he was again elected to the House of Representatives from Los Angeles county and was reelected in 1972 and 1974. [See JOHNSON Volume]

[MLL]

ROWAN, CARL T(HOMAS)

b. Aug. 11, 1925; Ravenscroft, Tenn.
Deputy Assistant Secretary of State for
Public Affairs, February, 1961-January
1963; Ambassador to Finland, January
1963-January 1964.

Born into a poor Southern black family,
Rowan held menial jobs before entering
Tennessee Agricultural and Industrial State
College in 1942. While at college he passed
the Navy examinations for the officer-
training program and in 1944 became one
of the first blacks to earn a naval commission. After the war Rowan went on to win
his B.A. from Oberlin College and his M.A.
in journalism from the University of Minnesota.

In 1948 Rowan joined the staff of the
Minneapolis Tribune, where he achieved
acclaim for his reporting on Southern blacks
and on social conditions in Asian countries.
His articles became the basis for three
books: South of Freedom (1952), The Pitiful
and the Proud (1956) and Go South to Sor-
row (1957).

Rowan became senior press officer for the
State Department in February 1961 when
he assumed the position of deputy assistant
secretary of state for public affairs. In
January 1962 he became a center of controversy when Washington's exclusive Cos-
mos Club rejected his nomination for
membership because of his race. In reaction 12 club members, many holding high
government positions, resigned. Several
days later the club passed a resolution opposing racial or religious discrimination in
the admission of new members, but the rejection of Rowan was not withdrawn.

During his tenure at the State Department, Rowan became a leading advocate of
improving relations between the press and
American officials in Saigon. At his urging
the Administration appointed Charles
Davis, a man sympathetic to press problems, as head of the U.S. Information Service in South Vietnam in February 1962.
On Feb. 21, 1962 Rowan, in conjunction
with Pierre Salinger [q.v.] and Arthur Sylvester [q.v.], drafted a memorandum designed to liberalize the Administration's
press policy. The document, known as

Cable 1006, urged the ambassador and
commanding general to see the press as
frequently as possible. It also noted that although criticism of the Diem regime could
not be cut off, it should be pointed out to
the press that this type of reporting made
the American task in Vietnam difficult. The
memo concluded by warning that press de-
scriptions of certain battles as "decisive"
were inaccurate and likely to give a false
impression of the growing war.

During hearings on the Administration's
press policies held before a House subcommittee on information in late 1963, the
cable—attributed solely to Rowan—was
termed a failure. Reporters severely
criticized it as merely recognizing reporters'
right to cover the war but not aiding them
in doing so.

In January 1963 Rowan was appointed
ambassador to Finland. There he won the
admiration of the Finnish people by can-
didly talking about racial problems in the
United States.

A year later President Lyndon B.
Johnson appointed Rowan director of the
U.S. Information Agency (USIA) after the
death of Edward R. Murrow [q.v.]. By accepting the job Rowan became the first
black to hold a seat on the National Security Council. In June 1964 he participated
in the top-level Honolulu Conference on
Vietnam. As USIA director he left the actual administration of the Agency to subordinates and concentrated on directing the
reporting of the Vietnam war. To cover the
conflict Rowan switched more than a
hundred men to posts in Vietnam, deplet-
ing the Agency's ranks elsewhere.

In 1964 intra-agency tensions emerged as
Henry Loomis, the former director of the
Voice of America, accused Rowam of permitting President Johnson to dictate news
coverage on Vietnam. Rowan resigned his
post in July 1965 citing financial need.
However, rumors circulated around the
capital that President Johnson had asked
him to step down to quiet growing criticism. After leaving government service
Rowan became Washington columnist for
the Chicago Daily News and wrote a widely
circulated political column for the Publishers Newspaper Syndicate.

[EWS]

RUSK, (DAVID) DEAN
b. Feb. 9, 1909; Cherokee County, Ga.
Secretary of State, January 1961-
January 1969.

Dean Rusk, Secretary of State during
most of the 1960s, spent his early years in
poverty. He was the son of an ordained
Presbyterian minister who had left the
ministry because of ill-health and was
forced to eke out a living as a farmer and
mail carrier. Rusk worked his way through
Davidson College and, following his graduation in 1931, studied at Oxford on a Rhodes
Scholarship. Returning to the U.S. in 1934,
he joined the political science department
of California's Mills College. Rusk became
dean of the faculty in 1938.

In 1943 Rusk served with the infantry in
the China-Burma-India theater and eventually became deputy chief of staff to Gen.
Joseph Stilwell. While in the Army he became a protege of Gen. George Marshall
who admired the young man's diplomatic
ability. After his discharge in 1946 Rusk, at
the behest of Marshall, joined the State
Department as assistant chief of the division
of international security affairs. Several
months later he became special assistant to
Secretary of War Robert P. Patterson. In
1947 he returned to the State Department
as director of the office of special political
affairs. During the next five years Rusk
served as a close aide to Robert Lovett
[q.v.] and Dean Acheson [q.v.]. In 1950
he was appointed assistant secretary of state
for Far Eastern affairs. In this position Rusk
helped formulate policy during the Korean
conflict, supporting military action in Korea
but opposing the expansion of the war into
Communist China.

Rusk left the State Department to become president of the Rockefeller Foundation in 1952. During his tenure he helped
expand the Foundation's projects to aid underdeveloped nations in Asia, Africa and
Latin America in solving agricultural and
public health problems.

Following his election in 1960 President
Kennedy appointed Rusk his Secretary of
State. Kennedy, who considered foreign affairs his personal responsibility, was determined to dominate foreign policy formulation during his Administration. He did not
want a Secretary who might overshadow
him and so rejected such prominent individuals as Adlai Stevenson [q.v.] and
Chester Bowles [q.v.] for the position. Instead, he selected the relatively obscure
Dean Rusk, a man, moreover, who agreed
with the President's conception of policymaking. In addition, Rusk's appointment
had the support of members of the powerful New York-based Eastern establishment
with whom Kennedy wanted to develop close
connections.

Rusk inherited an organization beset by
problems. The postwar growth of the State
Department had resulted in the development of an unwieldy bureaucracy that by
1961 threatened the effectiveness of U.S.
policy. In addition, rivalry between the
State and Defense Departments for dominant influence in foreign affairs had often
crippled policymaking. More importantly,
the McCarthyite anti-Communist crusades
of the 1940s and 1950s had driven many
capable men, particularly those knowledgeable about the Soviet Union and China,
from the Department. These attacks had
also inbred timidity and political orthodoxy
in those who remained. Consequently there
was little creativity within the Department.
(Kennedy considered State a "bowl full of
jelly.")

During the Kennedy Administration Rusk
attempted to make the Department more
responsive to new policy trends and to the
wishes of the President. Although he had
only limited success in reforming the
bureaucracy, Rusk, at the urging of the
President, did permit such subordinates as
Roger Hilsman [q.v.], G. Mennen Williams [q.v.] and Theodore Moscoso [q.v.]
to tentatively explore new policies toward
Asia, Africa and Latin America. In addition,
Rusk quietly improved relations between
State, Congress and the Central Intelligence Agency and moderated the rivalry
between the State and Defense Departments. Critics claimed, however, that
Rusk's cooperation with Defense was not so
much the result of a conscious effort as it
was of his inability to assert himself.

Despite his position and long tenure—he
served the second longest term of any Sec-

retary of State in the 20th Century—Rusk had little impact on foreign policy formulation. Because Kennedy sought to be his own Secretary of State, he personally directed day-to-day policymaking on many major issues, such as the East-West conflict over Berlin in the summer of 1961. Kennedy was also reluctant to rely on the traditional Department bureaucracy and instead appointed task forces made up of men both from in and out of government to deal with particular problems. Often these groups were composed of close personal friends and aides. Rusk, neither close to Kennedy nor constitutionally equipped to bypass the bureaucracy, was rarely given a role in these task forces.

Rusk's lack of impact can also be attributed to his personality and his conception of the role of Secretary of State. Rusk was by nature a reserved, unassertive man whose chief virtues were patience, the ability to handle detail and express himself clearly. These qualities served him well during private negotiations and earned him praise, even from his critics, as a supreme "technical diplomat." However, those who worked with Rusk also complained of his lack of imagination, creativity and qualities of leadership.

To a great degree, these qualities were not vital for the role that Rusk envisioned for himself as Secretary of State. Rusk believed that the Secretary should be the personal adviser of the President. It was the President who defined the nation's overall goals and objectives. The assistant secretaries of state with their expert knowledge of particular regions were the formulators and advocates of specific policies and the managers of the Department. The Secretary's job was to stay above the daily business of the Department and remain at the President's side as a judge of policy alternatives.

Consequently Rusk refused to advocate specific policies during most of the important crises of the Kennedy Administration. During the March 1961 debates over the proposed invasion of Cuba by U.S.-trained Cuban exiles, Rusk, in the words of Arthur Schlesinger, Jr. [q.v.], merely listened "inscrutably through the discussions, confin-

ing himself to gentle warnings about possible excesses." The Secretary, however, did caution that the invasion might result in a national and international loss of faith in the new President. To avoid this he suggested that someone make the decision to launch the invasion in the President's absence—someone who could be sacrificed if the plan failed. Although several aides urged Rusk to clearly voice his doubts about the invasion, the Secretary took no action. The invasion was launched on April 17 and was crushed two days later.

Rusk again played little part in the policy discussions that followed the discovery of Soviet offensive missiles in Cuba in October 1962. The Secretary did not join the early meetings of the Excom, the group formed specifically to advise the President in the crisis. At the meetings he did attend, Rusk advocated no particular response but opposed informing the Russians of U.S. knowledge of the missiles. He believed that such a step would permit the Soviets to act before the U.S. had formulated policy. Only at the Oct. 18 meeting did Rusk suggest a course of action, but his stand was extremely inconsistent. At the morning meeting he argued against an air strike to destroy the weapons. However, at the evening session he urged a limited air attack after informing U.S. allies. By the end of the meeting he had backed away from that position as well. On Oct. 23 Kennedy, at the suggestion of Attorney General Robert Kennedy [q.v.] and Secretary of Defense Robert McNamara [q.v.], instituted a "quarantine" of the island to force the removal of the missiles.

During the Kennedy Administration Rusk attempted to keep the State Department out of Vietnam affairs, believing that American involvement in that country was primarily a military problem. However, by 1963 he had become entangled in the conflict that would occupy his attention for the remainder of the decade.

Following the Diem regime's attack on dissident Buddhists in August 1963, American foreign policy advisers began a reevaluation of U.S. support of the regime. The President's highest advisers were divided on possible courses of action. Some, such as

McNamara, wished to press Diem for reform. Others, such as Rusk, believed that a change of government might be necessary. The initial instructions sent to Ambassador Henry Cabot Lodge [*q.v.*] on Aug. 24, 1963 reflected the State Department's position. Lodge was told that Diem should be given every chance to "rid himself" of elements hostile to reform but that if he remained obdurate the U.S. "must face the possibility that Diem himself cannot be preserved." The Ambassador was also instructed to privately inform military leaders that the U.S. would not continue to support the government of South Vietnam unless reforms were made. At the insistence of Rusk, he was also given permission to tell the generals that the U.S. "would give them direct support in any interim period of breakdown [of the] central government."

Because of dissension among the President's advisers, these instructions were canceled on Aug. 30, and Lodge was ordered to work for reform of the regime. The policy debate continued throughout the fall of 1963. However, Rusk remained a shadowy figure in these discussions, leaving subordinates such as Lodge and Hilsman to expound the need for change. South Vietnamese generals overthrew the Diem regime on Nov. 1.

During the Johnson Administration Rusk helped implement the President's Vietnam policy and became one of its most eloquent defenders. Rusk left office in January 1969 and later became a professor of international law at the University of Georgia. [See JOHNSON Volume]

[EWS]

RUSSELL, RICHARD B(REVARD)
b. Nov. 2, 1897; Winder, Ga.
d. Jan. 21, 1971; Washington, D.C.
Democratic Senator, Ga., 1933-71;
Chairman, Armed Services
Committee, 1951-53, 1955-69.

Russell received a law degree from the University of Georgia at Athens in 1918. Three years later he was elected to the state Assembly and in 1927 became its speaker. In 1930 Russell was elected governor of Georgia on an economy platform. While in office he drastically reduced the number of executive departments and commissions in an effort to reduce the state budget.

In 1932 Russell won an election to fill a vacant U.S. Senate seat. He was a supporter of most New Deal programs, helping to pass bills creating the Rural Electrification Administration and the Farmers Home Administration. Russell also drew up the legislation establishing the first nationwide school lunch program. As a Senate authority on national security affairs, he helped bring many military installations to Georgia. After World War II, however, he became an opponent of social welfare programs, explaining later, "I'm a reactionary when times are good. . . .In a depression, I'm a liberal.

Throughout his Senate career Russell was an unrelenting foe of civil rights measures. In 1935 and 1937 he led filibusters against anti-lynching bills, and in 1942 he was one of four Southern senators who filibustered to save the poll tax. By the late 1940s Russell was solidly established as the leader of the Southern bloc in the upper house of Congress, and at the 1948 Democratic National Convention he was put forward as his region's candidate for the Party's presidential nomination. However, he refused to join the Dixiecrat bolt from the national Party after the nomination of President Harry S Truman.

Despite Russell's strong identification with the dissident Southern wing of the Democratic Party, he was highly respected by almost all senators. A member of a patrician family, he was known for his dignified bearing and courteousness as well as for his formidable intelligence, and he was widely regarded as the embodiment of the best traditions of the upper house. Aided by this reputation and a single-minded dedication to his work (he never married), an intimate knowledge of parliamentary procedure and his leadership of the powerful Southern senatorial caucus, Russell became one of the most influential members of Congress in the 1940s and 1950s.

Russell reached the peak of his prestige in 1951, when he chaired an investigation of President Truman's removal of Gen. Douglas MacArthur from his Korean command. He was credited with defusing a potentially explosive situation by tactfully handling the matter. The following year Russell made a serious bid for the Democratic presidential nomination but was hampered by his identification with Southern interests and received only 294 out of 1,200 votes at the Democratic National Convention. He was somewhat embittered by the loss and in 1953 declined an opportunity to become Senate majority leader, preferring to serve as a spokesman for the South rather than as a national party figure. Instead he successfully promoted Sen. Lyndon B. Johnson (D, Tex.) [*q.v.*] for the post of majority leader.

Russell became chairman of the Senate Armed Services Committee in 1951 and in that position played a major national role in the area of military affairs in the 1950s and 1960s. This role was bolstered by his membership on the Appropriations Committee. An advocate of large military expenditures, Russell felt that the Eisenhower Administration was excessively cost-conscious and was placing too much emphasis on nuclear deterrence as its prime military strategy. [See TRUMAN, EISENHOWER Volumes]

In 1960 Russell, who vehemently opposed the civil rights plank in the Democratic national platform, initially declined to campaign for the Kennedy-Johnson ticket. However, he ultimately relented at the request of Johnson, who over the years had established an intimate friendship with Russell.

Russell was an opponent of many Kennedy Administration programs, including most social welfare measures, all civil rights proposals and some military policies. Russell's power was declining in the 1960s as the Southern delegation in Congress became less ideologically conservative with the election of younger and more moderate men. However, he remained a formidable figure during those years. In addition to his Armed Services Committee chairmanship and second-ranking position on the Appropriations and Aeronautical and Space Sciences Committees, he was a member of the Democratic Policy Committee and led the conservative majority on the Democratic Steering Committee, which distributed committee assignments. Furthermore, as Meg Greenfield observed in *The Reporter*, "He is the unofficial chairman of what amounts to an interlocking directorate of Southern committee and subcommittee chairmen without whose cooperation it is not possible to run the Senate."

In 1961 the Kennedy Administration decided to halt development of manned bombers. But Russell, who still believed that excessive reliance upon missiles was foolhardy, held lengthy hearings on the matter in the Armed Services Committee, and the panel added $525 million to Administration defense appropriations requests for the continued procurement of bombers. In 1963 Russell played a key role in adding over $350 million in extra funds for development of the RS-70, a missile-carrying reconnaissance plane. The additional appropriation had been sought by the Air Force but opposed by the Administration.

Believing that a large military establishment was essential to American security, Russell feared that steps towards disarmament and reliance upon the U.N. to maintain peace would result in a weakening of the nation's defenses. In 1961 he unsuccessfully opposed creation of the Arms Control and Disarmament Agency, arguing that its establishment was inappropriate at a time of mounting international tension and a U.S. arms buildup. In April 1962, during a Senate debate over American appropriations for the United Nations, he described that organization as "a frail reed on which to rest in the hope of deterring Communist aggression. . . ." Favoring a strong unilateral response to what he regarded as Communist provocations, Russell strongly urged President Kennedy to invade Cuba during the October missile crisis. In 1963 he opposed the nuclear test ban treaty, arguing that the agreement would preserve the Soviet lead in high-yield weaponry while permitting the Russians to catch up to America in low-yield research through underground testing.

Russell continued to lead the Southern

opposition to civil rights measures during the early 1960s. In 1962 he directed a successful filibuster against a bill to bar the arbitrary use of literacy tests against persons seeking to register to vote in federal elections. Defending the filibuster during a debate over cloture, he asserted, "The Founding Fathers intended . . . that the Senate should remain the one bulwark of our government against precipitate actions of the mob. . . ."

When President Kennedy introduced a public accommodations civil rights bill in June 1963, Russell declared that he believed in equality before the law for all Americans but that the Administration measure would use federal power "to compel the mingling of the races in social activities to achieve the nebulous aim of social equality." Such compulsion, he asserted, "would amount to a complete denial of the inalienable rights of the individual to choose or select his associates."

During the Johnson Administration Russell continued to lead anti-civil rights forces; despite repeated defeats and the growing size of the black electorate in Georgia, he refused to modify his views. But regardless of Russell's opposition to the large majority of President Johnson's Great Society programs as well as to his anti-discrimination measures, the two men remained close friends.

Although supporting a strong national defense and swift, decisive military actions such as the invasion of Santo Domingo in 1965, Russell was wary of American involvement in protracted foreign wars and had strong misgivings concerning the escalation of the conflict in Vietnam. However, he believed that the American commitment in Indochina, once made, had to be honored, and he backed President Johnson's Vietnam positions. In 1966 he warned that Americans would not indefinitely support a policy that did not promise foreseeable victory. After the Communists' Tet offensive early in 1968, Russell declared that he would not back the sending of additional ground troops to Vietnam unless there was a dramatic escalation of the air war. [See JOHNSON Volume]

In 1969 Russell stepped down as chair-man of the Armed Services Committee to head the Appropriations Committee. During the same year he became President Pro Tempore of the Senate. On Jan. 21, 1971, while still a senator, he died of respiratory insufficiency after a month-and-a-half of hospitalization. [See NIXON Volume]

[MLL]

For further information:
Frederic W. Collins, "Senator Russell 'in the Last Ditch'," *The New York Times Magazine* (Oct. 20, 1963), pp. 16+.
Meg Greenfield, "The Man Who Leads the Southern Senators," *The Reporter* (May 21, 1964), pp. 17-21.

RUSTIN, BAYARD
b. March 17, 1910; West Chester, Pa.
Civil rights leader.

An illegitimate child, Rustin was raised by his grandparents in West Chester, Pa. His grandmother belonged to the Society of Friends, and he was influenced by the Quakers' pacifist principles. Rustin later recalled that when traveling with his high school football team he was physically ejected from a restaurant because of his race; Rustin decided at that point never to accept segregation.

Rustin joined the Young Communist League (YCL) in 1936 because he believed that it was committed to peace and to equal rights for blacks. He came to New York City as an organizer for the League in 1938 and attended the City College of New York at night. Rustin left the YCL in 1941 when, after the Nazi invasion of the Soviet Union, the Communists abandoned their opposition to World War II and called for the subordination of all social protest to the cause of defeating Germany.

Upon leaving the YCL Rustin became a socialist and joined the Fellowship of Reconciliation, a pacifist nondenominational religious group that opposed the war and racial injustice. In 1941 Rustin worked with A. Philip Randolph [*q.v.*], president of the Brotherhood of Sleeping Car Porters, in planning a march on Washington to demand fair employment practices in the nation's rapidly growing defense industries.

The march itself was canceled when President Roosevelt issued an executive order banning racial discrimination by defense contractors. During the early 1940s Rustin also participated in the founding of the Congress of Racial Equality (CORE), an offshoot of the Fellowship of Reconciliation. In 1947 he helped organize and participated in CORE's first Freedom Ride into the South. At about the same time Rustin became director of Randolph's Committee Against Discrimination in the Armed Forces, which played a major role in securing President Harry S Truman's 1948 executive order prohibiting discrimination in the armed forces.

During World War II Rustin was a conscientious objector and served more than two years in jail. He became executive secretary of the War Resisters League in 1953 and in 1958 went to England to assist the Campaign for Nuclear Disarmament in organizing the first of its annual Aldermaston to London "ban the bomb" peace marches.

During the 1950s Rustin became one of the leading strategists of the civil rights movement. In 1955 he played a key role in organizing the Montgomery, Ala., bus boycott led by Rev. Martin Luther King, Jr. [q.v.], and he subsequently drafted the plan for what became the Southern Christian Leadership Conference. In the late 1950s he served as an adviser to King. [See EISENHOWER Volume]

In 1960 Rustin, acting on behalf of King and Randolph, organized civil rights demonstrations at the Democratic and Republican national conventions. Because Rep. Adam Clayton Powell, Jr., (D, N.Y.) [q.v.] informed King that he would publicly denounce Rustin for his radical background and alleged homosexuality unless King fired him, Rustin agreed to leave the project in the interest of harmony. For the next two years rumors circulated that Rustin was a "draft-dodging Communist." Randolph, with whom he had established a close working relationship over the previous two decades, was the only leader who kept up his ties with Rustin.

During the winter of 1962-63 Randolph asked Rustin to draw up plans for a mass march on Washington. Believing that blacks could overcome their second-class citizenship only through basic economic and social reforms, Rustin contended that the demonstration should concentrate on demands for federal action in the areas of jobs, housing and education. The Birmingham demonstrations of April and May 1963 further convinced him that such demands were the order of the day. In June Rustin contended that those protests represented a watershed for the civil rights movement because they were the first to involve masses of black workers who, not satisfied with token integration of public accommodations, insisted upon equal opportunity and full employment.

The original plans for the march reflected Rustin's views. But during the two months preceding the demonstration, march leaders shifted its emphasis from economic and social reforms to traditional civil rights objectives in order to secure the support of moderate blacks such as Roy Wilkins [q.v.], executive director of the NAACP.

Randolph had planned to make Rustin the director of the march, but Wilkins felt that Rustin's radical background might expose the project to unnecessary attack. In the spring of 1963 Randolph agreed to be the official director of the march, but he appointed Rustin to serve as his deputy, and the latter was the actual organizer of the demonstration.

Rustin was successful in gaining the support of approximately 100 civil rights, religious and labor organizations for the march, although the AFL-CIO, fearing possible disorders, declined to endorse the demonstration. On Aug. 28 an unprecedented 200,000 to 250,000 persons participated in a well-ordered and peaceful March on Washington for Jobs and Freedom.

In the mid-1960s Rustin contended that coalition politics within the framework of the Democratic Party was the only feasible means by which blacks could gain economic and social justice. As a minority, he said, blacks acting on their own could not exert sufficient power to influence the federal government to provide decent jobs, housing and education. Viewing political struggle as essentially a conflict between the interests of workers and of business rather than between races, he urged an alliance of blacks with the established AFL-CIO leadership for the purpose of radically reforming American society. He believed black separatism would merely strengthen the position of a few black businessmen within the Negro community.

In 1964 Rustin became executive director of the newly created A. Philip Randolph Institute. In that post he attempted to bring black youths into union apprenticeship training programs and to solidify the political links between blacks and unions. [See JOHNSON, NIXON Volumes]

[MLL]

For further information:
Thomas R. Brooks, *Walls Come Tumbling Down: A History of the Civil Rights Movement, 1940-1970* (Englewood Cliffs, 1974).
Bayard Rustin, *Down the Line: The Collected Writings of Bayard Rustin* (Chicago, 1971).

RYAN, WILLIAM FITTS
b. June 28, 1922; Albion, N.Y.
d. Sept. 17, 1972; New York, N.Y.
Democratic Representative, N.Y., 1961-72.

After receiving his law degree from Columbia University, Ryan served as an assistant district attorney under Manhattan D.A. Frank S. Hogan from 1950 to 1957. In the latter year Ryan helped found an anti-Tammany Democratic club, and was elected as a district leader, the only one opposed to the Party leadership in Manhattan. Reelected two years later, he joined forces with the newly organized Democratic reform movement, headed by former New York Gov. Herbert H. Lehman [q.v.], Eleanor Roosevelt [q.v.] and Thomas K. Finletter, in opposing Manhattan County Democratic leader Carmine G. DeSapio [q.v.], de facto head of the New York State party. In September 1960 Ryan won a major victory for the reformers when he defeated the organization candidate, Rep. Ludwig Teller (D, N.Y.), in a primary fight in Manhattan's Upper West Side 20th congressional district. Ryan's continual identification of Teller as "DeSapio's candidate"

was the main campaign issue, and his victory was influential in Mayor Robert F. Wagner's [q.v.] decision to break with De-Sapio the next year. In the general election Ryan defeated Teller, who ran on the Liberal Party line, and Republican Morris Aarons by a plurality of 25,000 votes.

Ryan's outspoken liberalism reflected the political orientation of his district but often put him at odds with the vast majority of Congress. In March 1961 Ryan was one of only six congressmen to vote against the $331,000 appropriation for the House Un-American Activities Committee (HUAC). The same month Ryan and fellow New York Rep. John V. Lindsay (R, N.Y.) [q.v.] were alone in opposing a measure to forbid anyone refusing to testify before Congress or a federal agency about subversive activities from working on waterfront facilities or merchant ships. (The bill was not acted on in the Senate.) In September 1961 Ryan and Lindsay were again the only House opponents of a bill that, in effect, required propaganda from foreign countries to be intercepted if it was labeled as such. The bill, which failed to clear the Senate, would have reversed the effect of a March 17, 1961 directive from President Kennedy ending the interception of non-first class mail from Communist countries. The next year Lindsay and Ryan once again were the only House opponents of a provision in a postal bill, signed into law Oct. 11, 1962, that banned from all but first class mail any material deemed by the Attorney General to be Communist propaganda. Along with Rep. Thomas L. Ashley (D, Ohio), Ryan was the only House member to speak against a 1961 congressional resolution calling for the continued exclusion of the People's Republic of China from the United Nations.

Ryan backed most of the Kennedy Administration's legislative program and was a strong supporter of civil rights. In his first year in Congress he helped secure the nomination and confirmation of Robert C. Weaver [q.v.] as administrator of the Housing and Home Finance Agency, making him the highest-ranking black in the executive branch. He also joined civil rights leaders and the Administration in successfully seeking an Interstate Commerce Commission ruling ending segregation on interstate buses and at bus terminals following the 1961 Freedom Rides in the South. Ryan introduced a number of unsuccessful amendments to ban the use of federal funds for segregated hospitals, school programs or Civil War centennials, as well as two unsuccessful bills to ban discrimination in housing in Washington, D.C. Ryan proposed in May 1961 and again two years later the creation of a permanent civil rights commission to investigate and seek court orders against discrimination.

Ryan opposed the 1962 Kennedy Administration bill creating the profit-making Communications Satellite Corporation, a private company with substantial public investment. Ryan called the bill the "greatest giveaway of the space age" and argued that full public ownership of communication satellites was the only way to "protect the national interest and to allow the public to enjoy the full benefits of this new technology which has been developed with public funds."

When the New York legislature redrew Manhattan district lines following the 1960 census, Ryan's district was eliminated in a move that he charged was designed to weaken the reform Democratic movement. Ryan ran in a newly expanded, adjacent district against the organization-backed incumbent, Rep. Herbert Zelenko, defeating him in the 1962 primary by 8,000 votes and going on to win the general election by nearly 60,000 votes.

In the new Congress Ryan continued to oppose appropriations for HUAC, this time joined by 19 other representatives, and to advocate a "legislative war on discrimination." In April 1963 he and Sen. Harrison Williams, Jr. (D, N.J.) [q.v.] introduced identical bills to protect migrant farm workers. During the Johnson and Nixon Administrations, Ryan was a strong critic of United States intervention in Vietnam. Although he failed in his 1965 primary campaign for the New York City Democratic mayoral nomination, he was returned to Congress by large margins until his death in September 1972. [See JOHNSON, NIXON Volumes]   [JBF]

SALINGER, PIERRE E(MIL GEORGE)

b. June 14, 1925; San Francisco, Calif.
White House Press Secretary, January 1961-March 1964.

After service in the Navy during World War II, Salinger graduated from the University of San Francisco in 1947. He became night city editor of the *San Francisco Chronicle* in 1950 and then was appointed West Coast editor and contributing editor to *Collier's* magazine in 1955. During the 1950s Salinger established a reputation as an investigative reporter and also became active in state and national politics. He served as press officer for Adlai Stevenson's [q.v.] California campaign in 1952 and supported Robert Graves for California governor in 1954.

Salinger first became acquainted with the Kennedys when Robert Kennedy [q.v.] hired him as an investigator for the Senate Rackets Committee in 1957. Sen. John F. Kennedy served on this Committee and during his 1960 presidential campaign made Salinger his press secretary. On Nov. 10, 1960 Salinger, at 35, became the youngest White House press secretary in history. Columnist William White noted in a 1961 article for *Harper's* that Salinger's predecessor, James Hagerty, ran the White House press room during the Eisenhower Administration "like an Army orderly room." Salinger, on the other hand, conveyed "an essentially lighthearted atmosphere." Early in the Kennedy Administration Salinger recommended the use of "live" television and radio broadcasts of presidential press conferences, a completely fresh idea at the time.

Kennedy policy dictated greater centralization of top-level information. In the wake of the Cuban missile crisis, this led to charges of "news management." Salinger vigorously denied these charges, but in early 1963 the House Government Information Subcommittee conducted hearings on the Kennedy Administration's handling of news information, especially during the recent crisis. An invited witness, James Reston [q.v.] of the *New York Times*, testified that the problem of news management was not as bad as some newsmen had indicated during the crisis, but Charles S. Rowe of the AP Managing Editors Association said, "The public has never been told the full story of the Cuba blockade." Many of the newsmen who attended the hearings had been particularly upset by Assistant Secretary of Defense Arthur Sylvester's [q.v.] December 1962 statement that the government has "a right, if necessary, to lie to save itself when it's going up into nuclear war." In a speech before the National Press Club on March 22, 1963, Salinger denied that the Administration had lied to the public during the Cuban missile crisis and proposed a "fundamental study" to determine whether the media was managing news.

Unlike James Hagerty, Salinger had virtually no influence on either domestic or foreign policy. After President Kennedy's death he stayed on as White House press secretary until March 1964, when he resigned to assume the Senate seat in California vacated by Democrat Clair Engle [q.v.]. In the 1964 senatorial race Salinger lost decisively to Republican George Murphy. [See JOHNSON Volume]

[FHM]

For further information:
Pierre Salinger, *With Kennedy* (New York, 1966).

SALTONSTALL, LEVERETT

b. Sept. 1, 1892; Chestnut Hill, Mass.
Republican Senator, Mass., 1944-67.

Descended from English and Irish colonial settlers, Leverett Saltonstall was born into one of the wealthiest and most politically prominent families in Massachusetts. A graduate of Harvard in 1914 and Harvard Law School three years later, Saltonstall served in World War I and then practiced law in Boston. He first entered local politics as a successful candidate for the Newton, Mass., board of aldermen. Saltonstall rose quickly in the Yankee-dominated Republican Party, attaining the governorship in 1938. In 1944 he ran successfully for the Senate, where he earned a reputation as a liberal and an internationalist. During the Eisenhower Administration Saltonstall held

several important Senate posts, including chairmanship of the Armed Services Committee in 1953 and 1954, Republican whip and assistant Republican Senate leader. [See TRUMAN, EISENHOWER Volumes]

Saltonstall and Sen. John Kennedy maintained a personal cordiality throughout their Senate careers. During Saltonstall's 1960 reelection campaign Kennedy declined to endorse Saltonstall's Democratic opponent, and Kennedy reportedly considered naming Saltonstall ambassador to Canada if the Republican lost his bid for reelection. Saltonstall won by 300,000 votes. During the Kennedy years Saltonstall maintained a moderately liberal voting record. He was a member of the Senate Appropriations Committee, the ranking Republican on the Armed Services Committee and chairman of the GOP conference. By 1963 Saltonstall was one of the three senior Republicans in the Senate, but despite his rank he exerted little influence.

In 1961 Saltonstall was a reluctant supporter of the provision in the foreign aid bill that permitted the Administration to borrow from the Treasury to finance long-term development loans. Saltonstall had favored a plan that would enable Congress to veto individual loans. However, Foreign Relations Committee Chairman J. William Fulbright (D, Ark.) [q.v.] assured Saltonstall and other recalcitrant supporters that the controversial provision would not mean that Congress had given up control of its foreign aid program.

In July 1962 Saltonstall voted to table Kennedy's medicare bill after Senate rejection of his proposal that $500 million a year in federal matching funds be granted to the states for health insurance for the aged. The next month Saltonstall voted for cloture on the pending communications satellite bill, which had been filibustered by 10 liberal senators who felt that a major part of the space communications industry would be turned over to the American Telephone and Telegraph Corporation, a major partner in Comsat. Declared Saltonstall, "I think the Senate has debated this matter almost to the point of absurdity."

Saltonstall remained uncommitted on the nuclear test ban treaty throughout much of

1963, but after the Senate Preparedness Subcommittee, chaired by Sen. John Stennis (D, Miss.) [q.v.], issued a report on Sept. 9 charging that the pact "would affect adversely the future quality of this nation's arms," Saltonstall called the report "overly adverse." He voted for ratification of the treaty on Sept. 24.

During the Johnson Administration Saltonstall supported the President's Vietnam policies. He voted against medicare and for the 1964 civil rights bill. In 1965 he was reelected GOP conference chairman. Pressure from the Massachusetts Republican Party, which supported the quickening political aspirations of Massachusetts Attorney General Edward Brooke, led Saltonstall to announce his retirement from the Senate in December 1965. Brooke was elected to the seat in 1966 and became the first black to serve in the Senate since Reconstruction. [See JOHNSON Volume]

[FHM]

SAMUELSON, PAUL A(NTHONY)
b. May 15, 1915; Gary, Ind.
Economist.

Paul Samuelson was the author of an immensely popular economics textbook and a prolific disseminator of Keynesian economic thought in both popular and professional journals. President Kennedy often consulted him for advice on economic policy and key appointments.

Samuelson earned his Ph.D in economics at Harvard during the 1930s under the tutelage of Alvin Hansen, the most prominent exponent of Keynesian economics in America. The British economist John Maynard Keynes had argued that the cycles of boom and depression characteristic of capitalism were not inevitable but could be moderated by government fiscal action. He urged deficit spending to combat economic slack and heavy unemployment and a government budget surplus when inflation was the primary threat. The adjustment of interest rates was also part of the Keynesian prescription for economic stability.

Samuelson promoted these concepts in his textbook, *Economics: An Intro-*

ductory Analysis, first published in 1948 and destined to become the most widely read economics textbook in America. He also served as a frequent consultant to government agencies, wrote often on current issues and taught economics at the Massachusetts Institute of Technology.

In December 1960 Samuelson, described as "Kennedy's favorite economist" by economic journalist Hobart Rowen, turned down the President-elect's offer to become chairman of the President's Council of Economic Advisers (CEA). Samuelson recommended Walter W. Heller [q.v.] for the post instead and also proposed economist Robert V. Roosa [q.v.] for the critical position of under secretary of the treasury for economic affairs.

Samuelson did agree to Kennedy's request that he head a special task force on economic policy to draw up proposals for combating the current recession. The task force included a blue-ribbon array of economists: Walter Heller, James Tobin [q.v.], Otto Eckstein and Joseph Pechman [q.v.], along with Kennedy's under secretary of the treasury, Henry Fowler [q.v.]. Its January 1961 report, written mainly by Samuelson, outlined a moderate Keynesian approach to ending the recession and stimulating economic growth. It served to guide Administration action in 1961.

Samuelson advocated two "lines of defense" against recession and the economy's "basic sluggishness." The first line of defense was increased spending on social programs: expanded unemployment compensation, school and housing construction, aid to depressed areas and acceleration of public works projects already authorized. The task force's report also suggested a monetary remedy, which became known as "Operation Twist" when the Administration put it into operation. This plan was an attempt to keep short-term interest rates high—in the hope of attracting foreign deposits and stemming the balance of payments deficit—while keeping long-term rates low in the belief that investment in plant and equipment, and thus economic growth, would be stimulated by easier borrowing over the long term.

Samuelson's second line of defense was a

temporary tax cut of 3% or 4%, to be enacted if the economic stagnation persisted. Kennedy rejected this alternative during the first half of his Administration, along with Samuelson's corollary suggestion that the President ask Congress for discretionary authority to raise or lower taxes. Samuelson's report did not include a plea for the massive public works program favored by some Keynesians and liberal reformers. Economist Robert Lekachman, in *The Age of Keynes*, characterized the task force report as "a notably mild policy brew for liberal economists to offer to a liberal President."

In the summer of 1961 Samuelson played a key role in the effort of Kennedy's economic advisers to persuade the President not to raise taxes by $3 billion to pay for the increased defense spending motivated by the Berlin crisis of July 1961. Heller and the CEA economists argued strenuously against the move, which many of Kennedy's political advisers favored to counter Republican criticism of deficit spending. Heller arranged for Samuelson to accompany Kennedy on a flight from Hyannisport to Washington, D.C. in order to buttress their case. Arguing that a tax increase would abort the nascent economic recovery, Samuelson helped to dissuade the President from raising taxes.

During 1962 Samuelson added his voice to those calling for sizeable tax cuts to prevent another recession and to promote economic growth by stimulating aggregate demand. Kennedy conferred with Samuelson on several occasions before announcing in August 1962 his intention to propose a substantial tax reduction in January 1963.

Not as close to the center of power during the Johnson Administration, Samuelson continued to reach a wide audience for his mainstream liberal economics through a *Newsweek* column and revised editions of his famous textbook. [See JOHNSON, NIXON Volumes]

[TO]

For further information:
Paul Samuelson, *The Samuelson Sampler* (Glen Ridge, New Jersey, 1973).

SANDERS, CARL E(DWARD)
b. May 15, 1925; Augusta, Ga.
Governor, Ga., 1963-67.

Sanders received his law degree from the University of Georgia in 1947 and joined an Augusta law firm. Elected to the state Assembly in 1954 and to the state Senate in 1956, he became president pro tempore of the latter body in 1960. During the administration of Gov. S. Ernest Vandiver (1959-63) [*q.v.*], Sanders became known as a racial moderate for his support of "open school" bills, which barred the closing of the state's public schools in order to avoid integration.

In 1962 Sanders entered the Democratic gubernatorial primary against former Gov. Marvin Griffin, a white supremacist who vowed undying opposition to integration. Sanders's greatest strength was in the urban centers of the state, which were more inclined to accept federal pressure for integration. His campaign also focused on alleged corruption in the Griffin Administration. Furthermore, Sanders was aided by a federal court decision in the spring of 1962 that voided the state's rural-biased county unit voting system. He defeated Griffin by over 100,000 votes and ran unopposed in the general election.

As governor, Sanders did not support integration, and in July 1963 he declared his opposition to the Kennedy Administration's civil rights bill. Nevertheless, he reiterated his determination to keep the schools open. Primarily interested in preserving social harmony and promoting Georgia's economic growth, Sanders declared shortly after his election, "I am determined that during my administration this state will move ahead—fast." He asserted that one of his major goals was to give all of Georgia's children the opportunity to attend college, and in 1963 he successfully pressed the legislature for greater appropriations for both secondary schools and higher education.

Barred by the state's constitution from running for reelection in 1966, Sanders considered challenging U.S. Sen. Richard Russell [*q.v.*] in the Democratic primary of that year. But political trends were running against racial moderates in Georgia, and Sanders abandoned the effort. In 1970 he entered the Democratic gubernatorial primary but was defeated by Jimmy Carter. [See JOHNSON Volume]

[MLL]

SANFORD, (JAMES) TERRY
b. Aug. 20, 1917; Laurinburg, N.C.
Governor, N.C., 1961-65.

Terry Sanford, a champion of state educational reform, was born in the rich cotton-land of southeastern North Carolina. He attended the University of North Carolina and two years after his graduation in 1939 joined the FBI. During the war Sanford enlisted in the Army and participated in five campaigns in Italy, France, Belgium and Germany. Following his discharge he studied law at the University of North Carolina, receiving his degree in 1946. For the next two years he served as assistant director of the Institute of Government at Chapel Hill.

From 1948 until his election in 1960, Sanford practiced law while becoming active in state politics. During the 1950s he served as a member of the North Carolina State Ports Authority and as a state senator. In 1954 he managed the successful U.S. Senate campaign of W. Kerr Scott and succeeded in building his own effective political organization.

In 1960 Sanford played an important role in bringing about Sen. John F. Kennedy's nomination at the Democratic National Convention. He was the first Southern leader at the meeting to abandon Sen. Lyndon B. Johnson [q.v.] and join the Kennedy camp. Sanford also seconded Kennedy's nomination on the floor of the convention.

During his 1960 gubernatorial campaign Sanford ran on a progressive platform that emphasized the need for attracting new industry to the state and for increasing spending on education. He played down the race issue, urging token integration in North Carolina public schools to avoid both court fights and racial violence. Sanford declared, "We need massive intelligence, not massive resistance." Drawing the votes of city dwell-

ers, organized labor, businessmen and blacks, he won the November general election by more than 77,000 votes.

While in office Sanford worked to build new community colleges and technical institutes and to expand the university system. He also raised salaries for teachers and increased funds for libraries and other educational facilities. To finance these improvements Sanford persuaded the legislature to pass a sales tax on food. Sanford also won grants from the Ford and Reynolds Foundations and the Carnegie Corporation for experimental programs for disadvantaged and specially gifted children.

While championing education Sanford also worked for federal aid to Appalachia and sponsored measures to end job discrimination against blacks. Following racial distrubances in the state during 1963, he pledged to end bias in hiring for state jobs and pleaded for open hiring in industry.

Under North Carolina law Sanford was not permitted to succeed himself and so retired from state government in 1965. During the late 1960s he served on several federal education panels and in 1969 was named president of Duke University. In 1972 and 1976 Sanford made unsuccessful bids for the Democratic presidential nomination. [See JOHNSON, NIXON Volumes]

[EWS]

SAXON, JAMES J(OSEPH)
b. April 13, 1914; Toledo, Ohio.
Comptroller of the Currency, November 1961-January 1967.

James J. Saxon disrupted the banking status quo more than any federal regulatory official in a generation. He first came to Washington in 1937 to work in the office of the comptroller. For the next 15 years Saxon held a wide variety of posts in the Treasury Department, including service as chief aide to Secretary of the Treasury John W. Snyder during the Truman Administration. He left the government in 1952 to become assistant to the chairman of the Democratic National Committee. After the 1952 elections Saxon, who had obtained his law degree from the Georgetown University

Law School in 1950, joined the Washington office of the American Bankers Association as assistant general counsel. In 1956 he became an attorney for the First National Bank of Chicago. Upon the recommendation of Undersecretary of the Treasury Henry H. Fowler [q.v.], Saxon was appointed comptroller of the currency by President Kennedy in November 1961.

Outspoken and combative, Saxon jeopardized his nomination, which had yet to be confirmed by the Senate, when he publicly attacked the Justice Department in January 1962 for starting antitrust actions against certain banks without forewarning him. He denounced the Department's "hard-core antitrust zealots" and threatened to retaliate by withholding information from its Antitrust Division, for whom "the antitrust laws come first and the Ten Commandments come second." Attorney General Robert Kennedy [q.v.] questioned Saxon's "stability" for airing an interagency dispute in public and suggested that the President withdraw Saxon's nomination. Secretary of the Treasury C. Douglas Dillon [q.v.] intervened, however, arranging for Saxon and the Attorney General to repair the rift. The Senate confirmed Saxon in February 1962.

The comptroller of the currency was the chief supervisor of the nation's 4,500 nationally-chartered banks. Saxon came to the post determined to liberalize the elaborate network of regulations that governed banking operations. Believing that regulation should be restricted to preserving bank solvency and liquidity, he wanted to give national banks more freedom to expand and compete. Saxon quickly appointed a 24-man commission to survey banking problems and recommend reforms.

In September 1962 the commission issued a 189-page report, soon known as the Saxon Report, proposing a series of sweeping reforms. It was the first major blueprint for the reorganization of the banking system since 1933. Among the suggested revisions were proposals to transfer certain regulatory functions from the Federal Reserve to the comptroller and to place state banks under the purview of the Federal Deposit Insurance Corporation (FDIC). Saxon also backed a host of

changes to broaden banks' freedom to loan, borrow and invest.

Most controversial by far was Saxon's proposal to allow national banks to establish branches even where they were prohibited by state law. State bankers excoriated Saxon for threatening the "dual-banking" system of state and nationally-chartered banks. The small banks' champion in Congress, House Banking and Currency Committee Chairman Rep. Wright Patman (D, Tex.) [q.v.], vowed that Saxon's reform would pass only "over my dead body." In the spring of 1963 Patman conducted lively hearings on Saxon's proposals and his rulings as comptroller. In defense of his regulatory innovations, Saxon said, "Enclaves of monopoly and stagnant, unprogressive banks should not . . . be safeguarded."

Patman succeeded in blocking almost all of Saxon's legislative suggestions. But with the support of the national banking community, Saxon partly circumvented the congressional impasse, mostly by administrative rulings. He issued a flurry of new regulations that expanded banks' lending powers. Saxon permitted banks to engage in a wide variety of business activities "incidental" to banking. Among these were the functions of credit card, insurance and equipment leasing companies.

Saxon embarked upon a determined policy of freely chartering new banks and bank branches. He cut the time required to approve a new bank charter from nine months to 75 days. In his first three years he chartered 434 new banks, compared to the 227 by his predecessors in the Treasury Department had chartered in the previous 10 years. Saxon's liberalization of national bank regulations sparked a movement by state banks to gain national charters.

Saxon's bold innovations and his brusque style brought him into conflict with the rest of Washington's banking regulatory apparatus. He engaged in policy and jurisdictional battles with the Federal Reserve, the FDIC and the Justice Department. Nevertheless, reported *Fortune*, although "Saxon's squabbles were an occasional annoyance to the White House, . . . the President approved the main thrust of the

Saxon policies and his tenure was never endangered." Saxon resigned as comptroller in January 1967. [See JOHNSON Volume]

[TO]

For further information:
Irwin Ross, "Scrappy, Happy James J. Saxon," *Fortune* (April 1966), p. 162 +.

SCALI, JOHN A(LFRED)
b. April 27, 1918; Canton, Ohio.
ABC News correspondent, 1961-71.

After his graduation from Boston University in 1942, John Scali became a reporter for the Boston *Herald*. In 1944 he joined the Associated Press and was assigned to the AP's Washington bureau where he remained for 17 years, earning a reputation as an indefatigable, aggressive and ambitious reporter. In February 1961 Scali was named State Department correspondent for ABC News.

On Oct. 22, 1962 President Kennedy announced the presence of Soviet offensive missiles in Cuba and imposed an arms "quarantine" on that country. Four days later, at the height of the missile crisis, Scali was contacted by Alexander S. Fomin, a top official at the Soviet embassy in Washington. Fomin was not only a friend of Premier Nikita Khrushchev's but a full colonel in the Soviet intelligence organization, the KGB. Aware that Scali was highly regarded in the Kennedy Administration and in frequent contact with Secretary of State Dean Rusk [*q.v.*], Fomin believed that the veteran newsman could act as an unofficial liaison between the White House and the Kremlin during the crisis. Fomin informed Scali that the Soviets would be willing to dismantle their missile bases under U.N. supervision provided the U.S. agreed not to invade Cuba.

Scali promptly relayed Fomin's message to Assistant Secretary of State Roger Hilsman [*q.v.*], who in turn informed Rusk. The Secretary of State discussed the proposal with members of Excom, the high-level Administration committee assembled for the crisis, and then instructed Scali to tell Fomin that there were "real possibilities" in the Soviet proposal. At 6

p.m. on Oct. 26, President Kennedy received a conciliatory letter from Krushchev that echoed Fomin's proposal, but on Oct. 27, in a second letter broadcast via Radio Moscow, Khrushchev further stipulated that the U.S. must dismantle its missile bases in Turkey.

Scali met again with Fomin the morning of Oct. 28. Acting on his own initiative Scali called Khrushchev's second letter "a dirty, rotten, lousy, stinking double-cross." The members of Excom, meanwhile, at the suggestion of Attorney General Robert Kennedy [*q.v.*], had decided to ignore Khrushchev's second letter and accept his more conciliatory proposal of Oct. 26. That decision proved to be the turning point of the Cuban missile crisis; on Oct. 28 Khrushchev announced the missiles were being withdrawn.

After the crisis Scali was denied permission to publish details of his part in the negotiations because President Kennedy regarded the contact with Fomin as too valuable to be jeopardized. Shortly after Kennedy's assassination the story of Scali's role in the Cuban missile crisis was "scooped" by Robert Donovan of the Los Angeles *Times* and Marguerite Higgins of *Newsday*. Describing his long enforced silence to a *New York Post* reporter nearly two years later, Scali said, "At times like that a reporter has no choice. Because whatever he can do to save humanity from destruction, even just an ounce worth, he must do—and that's not just patriotic flag-waving."

Scali continued at ABC until 1971, narrating various news programs for the network and pioneering the "subjective analysis" approach to television news "specials." In April 1971 he accepted a post in the Nixon Administration as senior White House consultant on foreign affairs information policy. In December 1972 Scali succeeded George Bush as the U.S. permanent representative at the U.N., a post he held until 1974.

[FHM]

For further information:
Graham T. Allison, *Essence of Decision* (Boston, 1971).

SCHLESINGER, ARTHUR M(EIER), JR.

b. Oct. 15, 1917; Columbus, Ohio.
Special Assistant to the President, January 1961-January 1964.

Schlesinger spent most of his youth in Cambridge, Mass., where his father was a professor of history at Harvard. After graduating from that college in 1938, Schlesinger studied at Oxford and again at Harvard as a junior fellow. During the war he worked for the Office of War Information and the Office of Strategic Services. In his spare time Schlesinger wrote *The Age of Jackson*, for which he won the Pulitzer Prize for history in 1946. As a member of the Harvard faculty, Schlesinger spent much of the next 14 years on an ambitious multi-volume project entitled *The Age of Roosevelt*.

Influenced by the theology of Reinhold Niebuhr [*q.v.*], Schlesinger emerged in the early postwar era as a leading spokesman for American liberalism. As a founder of the anti-Communist Americans for Democratic Action in 1947 and as the author of the influential *The Vital Center* in 1949, Schlesinger argued that liberals should adopt an "unsentimental" approach to politics, rejecting the utopian solutions of both the totalitarian left and the romantic right. In his works on Jackson and Roosevelt, Schlesinger sought to demonstrate that American liberalism was most successful when allied with a strong president who used his power in a pragmatic fashion. [See TRUMAN, EISENHOWER Volumes]

Although Schlesinger had served as a speech writer for Adlai Stevenson [*q.v.*] in 1952 and 1956, he switched his allegiance to John F. Kennedy in the late 1950s and helped recruit a group of New York-Boston intellectuals and scholars for the Kennedy "brain trust" in 1959. During the 1960 campaign Schlesinger wrote speeches for the Democratic Party nominee and published a short campaign biography favorably contrasting Kennedy with his Republican opponent, Richard M. Nixon [*q.v.*]. After the election Kennedy asked Schlesinger to join his staff as a special assistant to the president, and he was sworn in on Jan. 30, 1961.

Schlesinger's first assignment for Kennedy was to travel to South America with Food for Peace Program Director George McGovern [*q.v.*] in February. The two men discussed food and development problems with leaders of Brazil and Argentina, and then Schlesinger continued on alone to Bolivia, Peru and Venezuela as the President's personal representative. Schlesinger's report to Kennedy helped advance planning for the Alliance for Progress, designed to promote economic development and progressive democracy and counter the influence of Cuban-backed Communist movements.

Upon his return from South America in early March, Schlesinger first became aware of plans for an invasion of Cuba by exiles trained in Guatemala by the Central Intelligence Agency. At Kennedy's request Schlesinger quickly prepared a White Paper on Cuba that endorsed the Cuban revolution against Fulgencio Batista but condemned the direction in which Fidel Castro had led it. The White Paper admitted past errors in American relations with the island and called upon Castro to break his connection with Communism and return to the democratic goals of the revolution.

Schlesinger also sat in on the series of top-level discussions in late March and early April at which the final decision to go ahead with the invasion was reached. Although Schlesinger would have favored an American-sponsored overthrow of Castro by a "surgical stroke" if it could have been easily done, he argued that the planned military operation would either fail or lead to a prolonged civil war. In either case, he said, such intervention would destroy the good will the new Administration was trying to develop in Latin America.

During the weeks immediately before the April 17 invasion, Schlesinger was in frequent contact with the Cuban Revolutionary Council, the exile group in titular command of the Cuban brigade training in Guatemala. Schlesinger and Adolph Berle [*q.v.*] met with members of the Council in Miami and New York, urging them to adopt a policy of social reform for Cuba that would offer "not a restoration but a liberation" of their homeland. After the failure of the Bay of Pigs invasion, Schlesinger and Berle flew to Opa-Locka, Fla. to break the news to the Council members waiting there and then fly them back to Washington for a personal meeting with President Kennedy.

During the rest of the Administration, Schlesinger remained one of the few White House staff members assigned to follow Latin American developments. He helped formulate American policy calling for the economic and political isolation of Cuba in 1961 and 1962 and helped write Secretary of State Dean Rusk's [q.v.] speech at the January 1962 meeting of the Organization of American States (OAS) that called for a hemispheric trade boycott of the island. During the Cuban missile crisis in October 1962, Kennedy assigned Schlesinger to work with Adlai Stevenson on the preparation of a speech to the U.N. reflecting the Administration's demand that the Soviet Union immediately remove its long-range rockets from the island.

Two months after Kennedy's assassination Schlesinger resigned his post as a White House special assistant and began work on a history of the Administration. His best-selling *A Thousand Days: John F. Kennedy in the White House* was published in 1965 and won the Pulitzer Prize for biography the next year. Although critical of Kennedy for an occasional misjudgement or mistake, the work viewed the Administration as one embodying "the life-affirming, life-enhancing, zest, the brilliance, the wit, the cool commitment [and] the steady purpose" of the young President.

Returning to academic life in 1966, Schlesinger voiced measured criticism of the Vietnam war policy of Presidents Johnson and Nixon. He served as a presidential campaign adviser to both Sen. Robert Kennedy (D, N.Y.) [q.v.] in 1968 and Sen. George McGovern (D, S.D.) in 1972. [See JOHNSON, NIXON Volumes]

[NNL]

For further information:
Arthur M. Schlesinger, Jr., *A Thousand Days* (Boston, 1965).

SCHWARZ, FRED(ERICK) C(HARLES)

b. Jan. 15, 1913; Brisbane, Australia.
President, Christian Anti-Communist Crusade.

Dr. Fred Schwarz's father was a Viennese Jew who emigrated to Australia in 1905 and became a convert to the Plymouth Brethren, a Baptist sect. Schwarz won degrees in science, art, and medicine at the University of Queensland and also became a lay Baptist preacher. He practiced medicine and gained a local reputation as an anti-Communist evangelist, making his first American lecture tour in 1950 at the request of the Rev. Dr. Carl McIntire of Collingswood, N.J. Along with W.E. Pietsch, a radio preacher in Waterloo, Iowa, Schwarz organized the Christian Anti-Communist Crusade in 1953, with Pietsch as president (until his death in 1960) and Schwarz as director. Schwarz gained prominence when he was called to testify before the House Committee on Un-American Activities on May 29, 1957 as an "expert" witness on Communism.

Schwarz's testimony was expanded in 1960 into a book, *You Can Trust the Communists (to be Communists)*. He claimed 750,000 copies in print by 1962. His thesis was that Communists were single-minded ideologues who had set 1973 as their date for the conquest of America. Schwarz frequently employed medical analogies in his campaign to educate the public about Communists: "They are extremely trustworthy. You can trust a cancer cell to obey the law of its lawless growth."

Besides his book, Schwarz disseminated his message by staging rallies and conducting anti-Communist "schools." His most successful rally was a televised one held in the Hollywood Bowl on October 1961 before 15,000 cheering participants. It featured a host of celebrities, including George Murphy, Ronald Reagan, Roy Rogers, and Ozzie and Harriet Nelson. He sponsored a less successful rally in June 1962 in New York's Madison Square Garden, filling only 8,000 of the Garden's 18,000 seats; featured speakers included Herbert A. Philbrick, an ex-FBI undercover agent in the Communist Party, Eugene Lyons, a senior editor of the Reader's Digest, and singer Pat Boone.

About 13,600 persons were reported to have attended an anti-Communist school conducted in Oakland, Calif., Jan. 29-Feb. 2, 1962. Faculty members included Sen. Thomas Dodd (D, Conn.) [q.v.], Rep. Walter H. Judd (R, Minn.) [q.v.] and Maj. Gen. William F. Dean. In New York, however, only 830 persons paid to attend a school at the 2,760-seat Carnegie Hall in August. Unlike such political action groups as the John Birch Society, Schwarz's organization espoused no specific political goals and took no part in electoral politics, concentrating instead on alerting the public to what it considered the general dangers of Communism.

[TO]

SCOTT, HUGH D(OGGETT)
b. Nov. 11, 1900; Fredericksburg, Va.
Republican Senator, Pa., 1959-   .

Hugh Scott graduated from Randolph-Macon College in 1919 and in 1922 received his LL.B. from the University of Virginia. He began law practice in Philadelphia and between 1926 and 1941 was assistant district attorney of that city. Elected to the House of Representatives in 1940 and 1942 and continuously after 1946, Scott chaired the Republican National Committee in the late 1940s. In 1952 he joined Dwight D. Eisenhower's personal staff, serving as chairman of the headquarters committee during the presidential campaign. Scott was first elected to the Senate in November 1958, outmaneuvering the state Party's Old Guard to get the nomination. [See TRUMAN, EISENHOWER Volumes]

As a first-term senator during the Kennedy Administration, Scott was assigned to the Commerce and Judiciary Committees but played his most significant role in the Senate through his work with a small group of Republican "liberals" or "moderates," most of whom came from the Northeast. Scott was consistent in his support of civil rights, frequently breaking with his own

party to support the Kennedy Administration. In March 1963 he was joined by six other Republican moderates in sponsoring 12 bills aimed at implementing the 1961 recommendations of the Civil Rights Commission. The Republicans stated that they were taking the initiative since the President's February civil rights message had fallen "far short" of the Commission's recommendations.

Scott's efforts to broaden the Republican Party's base of support in Pennsylvania, which had long been dominated by the railroads and heavy industry, often led him to back bills favorable to labor and lower-income groups. In March 1961 Scott was one of only five Republicans to vote for an Administration-sponsored unemployment insurance measure. In April of the same year, Scott voted to raise the minimum wage and extend its coverage. He voted again with a small Republican minority in April 1963 in favor of an Administration mass transit aid package. On the other hand, in May 1962 Scott successfully opposed a Kennedy proposal to institute a withholding tax on interest and dividends, and in September of the same year he voted to block a Judiciary Committee inquiry into steel industry price increases.

Scott consistently approved high defense appropriations but was one of the few Republicans who also supported Kennedy's innovations in the foreign aid program, including long-term development loans and the Peace Corps. In September 1963 he backed the treaty banning nuclear tests in the atmosphere, but at the same time he played the role of a persistent partisan critic of the Administration's Cuban policy.

In Pennsylvania Scott tried to move the Republican Party to a more liberal stance and a more youthful, modern image. When, in 1962, the Old Guard planned to run the colorless party "regular" Judge Robert Woodside for governor, Scott feared a Republican defeat that would hurt his own reelection chances in 1964. He therefore obtained the support of Dwight Eisenhower, who then lived in Gettysburg, Pa., in opposing Woodside's nomination and even offered to run for governor himself to keep the office from a "few hungry men." By the end of February all GOP factions agreed to run the young, relatively liberal Rep. William Scranton (R, Pa.) [q.v.] for governor and the conservative Rep. James Van Zandt (R, Pa.) for the Senate. Scranton's smashing November victory over Democrat Richardson Dilworth [q.v.] combined with Van Zandt's loss to Sen. Joseph Clark (D, Pa.) [q.v.] increased Scott's power in the Party and changed the complexion of the state organization.

Scott was narrowly reelected in 1964. Under a Republican president in January 1969, he was elected Senate minority whip and in September was chosen minority leader. His voting and policy positions subsequently became increasingly conservative. In November 1970 he was again reelected by a small margin. Compromised by his unquestioning defense of Nixon during the 1973-74 Watergate investigations and by the 1975 disclosure that he had been receiving an annual fee from the Gulf Oil Corporation, Scott announced in December 1975 that he would not seek another term. [See JOHNSON, NIXON Volumes]

[JCH]

SCRANTON, WILLIAM W(ARREN)
b. July 19, 1917; Madison, Conn.
Republican Representative, Pa., 1961-63; Governor, Pa., 1963-67.

Scion of a family of Pennsylvania steelmakers, William W. Scranton attended the Hotchkiss School and received degrees from Yale and Yale Law School. Returning from Army service to Scranton, Pa., at the end of World War II, he worked to revitalize local industry while investing successfully in the new cable television business. Between 1959 and 1960, Scranton served on the personal staff of the Secretary of State, first of John Foster Dulles and then of Christian A. Herter. In 1960 Republican leaders persuaded Scranton to oppose incumbent Rep. Stanley A. Prokop (D, Pa.). Although at first reluctant to make the race, Scranton went on to wage a vigorous campaign and upset Prokop by 17,000 votes despite John F. Kennedy's substantial victory in the same northeastern Pennsyl-

vania district.

Scranton proved a liberal Republican during the 87th Congress. In the 1961 session, he voted with the White House to enlarge the House Rules Committee, to increase the minimum wage and to establish the Peace Corps. Scranton supported Kennedy during the April 1962 steel price crisis by condemning U.S. Steel's price increases as "wrong for Pennsylvania, wrong for America, wrong for the free world."

Despite his occasional endorsements of Kennedy policies, Scranton's style appealed to Pennsylvania Republican strategists. "Perhaps the superficial similarities to John F. Kennedy—the diffidence, the aristocratic manner, the boyishness—intrigued the party leaders," wrote columnist Robert D. Novak. Pennyslvania resident Dwight D. Eisenhower [q.v.] and other prominent GOP figures encouraged Scranton to seek the 1962 Republican gubernatorial nomination. When all 67 GOP county chairmen endorsed his nomination, Scranton agreed to run and led a united Pennsylvania Party to victory over Philadelphia Mayor Richardson Dilworth [q.v.] by a landslide margin of 486,000 votes in November 1962.

Victory made Scranton the first Republican governor of the state in eight years and a possible contender for the 1964 Republican presidential nomination. As governor, Scranton increased by 17,000 the number of state employes under Pennsylvania's civil service merit system. He persuaded the state legislature to raise the sales tax and to double state appropriations for education. Although he consistently denied any interest in running for the presidency, by the fall of 1963 a group of Eastern Republicans led by Tom McCabe, Sr., chairman of the board of the Scott Paper Company, had begun the informal organization of a Scranton presidential committee. At the same time, Scranton blocked efforts by supporters of conservative Sen. Barry M. Goldwater (R, Ariz.) [q.v.] to win places on Pennsylvania's delegation to the 1964 Republican National Convention.

Beginning one month prior to the Party's July 1964 convention, Scranton fought a bitter and futile campaign to deny Goldwater the presidential nomination. Scranton retired from public life at the end of his term as governor but served as an occasional adviser to Presidents Richard M. Nixon and Gerald R. Ford, Jr. In March 1976 he became U.S. ambassador to the United Nations. [See JOHNSON, NIXON Volumes]

[JLB]

SEABORG, GLENN T(HEODORE)
b. April 19, 1912; Ishpeming, Mich.
Chemist; Chairman, Atomic Energy Commission, January 1961-August 1971.

After earning his doctorate in nuclear chemistry at the University of California, Berkeley, in 1937, Seaborg joined the faculty there. His discovery of the element plutonium in 1940 provided a new source of fissionable material for nuclear energy. In 1941 he joined the Manhattan Project's work on the atomic bomb and, from 1946 to 1950, served on the general advisory board of the Atomic Energy Commission (AEC). After the war Seaborg returned to Berkeley where he discovered several more transuranium elements. Seaborg won the 1951 Nobel Prize for chemistry and the AECs Enrico Fermi Award in 1959.

Seaborg was appointed chairman of the AEC by President Kennedy in January 1961. The Commission, whose 1961 budget was $2.5 billion, was responsible for contracting with private corporations to develop nuclear projects for military and civilian use. In 1960 both the AEC and Congress's Joint Committee on Atomic Energy began to study the possibility of a conflict of interest between the AEC's operational and regulatory functions. A University of Michigan study calling for the establishment of a separate regulatory agency was reviewed by the Joint Committee in March 1961, and formal hearings were set for June. In late March, however, Seaborg announced that "the Commission had acted to separate its regulatory function from the operational and developmental functions at general management level." When the hearings took place the Joint Committee agreed to allow the AEC to maintain its regulatory function.

In September 1961, after a three-year moratorium, the Soviet Union resumed atmospheric nuclear tests. Seaborg asserted in October that "we are still ahead of the Russians with respect to our [nuclear] stockpile and know-how," but he added that they would move ahead if they continued to test in the atmosphere. Seaborg, who favored the resumption of U.S. atmospheric tests, was a member of the Federal Radiation Council, which released a report in June 1962 on possible effects of radiation from atmospheric explosions. While critics such as Linus Pauling [q.v.] argued that above-ground explosions should be banned because they caused gross birth defects, leukemia and bone cancer, the Council concluded that only a small percentage of the total number of such cases was directly attributable to nuclear fallout. Its findings, which had been available to Kennedy since February, had reportedly weighed heavily in his decision to resume atmospheric testing in the Pacific in April 1962.

Seaborg also served on the Committee of Principals, a body created to advise the President on the conduct of nuclear test ban negotiations with the Soviet Union. The group, which included military and intelligence officials, recommended in July 1962 that the President change his position on the monitoring of the proposed American-British-Soviet treaty. One month later Kennedy, who had earlier pressed for an internationally manned detection system, adopted the Committee's proposal to accept national policing. In August 1963 Senate hearings Seaborg spoke for ratification of the partial nuclear test ban treaty, which was approved in September.

In the late 1960s the AEC came under fire from critics who thought its safeguards inadequate. Seaborg resigned as its chairman in 1971 and returned to the University of California. He was succeeded by James Schlesinger. [See JOHNSON, NIXON Volumes]

[MDB]

For further information:
H. Peter Metzger, *The Atomic Establishment* (New York, 1972).

SHOUP, DAVID M(ONROE)
b. December 30, 1904; Battle Ground, Ind.
Commandant, Marine Corps, January 1960-December 1963.

Unlike many of the men who became members of the Joint Chiefs of Staff, Shoup was not closely associated with the military in his early years. He went to a small Methodist college, DePauw University, where he enrolled in the Reserve Officers Training Corps only because it paid his room rent. After graduation in 1926 Shoup joined the Marines, serving in various sea and shore assignments before being sent to the Pacific in 1943. There he won the Medal of Honor and developed a reputation for bravery and leadership that eventually made him one of the most respected Marine Corps commanders.

After the war Shoup served in command positions in the Pacific and at the Pentagon. Following the drowning of six Marines on a disciplinary night march at the Parris Island, S.C., boot camp, he was named to the newly created post of inspector-general of recruit training in May 1956. In 1959 President Eisenhower, passing over 10 more senior generals, nominated him as commandant of the Marine Corps for the four-year term mandated by law.

During the opening days of the Kennedy Administration, Shoup was the one member of the Joint Chiefs of Staff to counsel against the proposed Cuban invasion because he thought it militarily unfeasible with the limited number of troops in the Cuban brigade.

As commandant, Shoup achieved national recognition in the "muzzling" probe conducted by Sen. Strom Thurmond (D, S.C.) [q.v.] and the Senate Preparedness Subcommittee in December 1961. The investigation focused on the questions of State Department censorship of high military leaders, the content of military education programs and the role of the military in educating the civilian population on the "menace of the Cold War." Although all the Joint Chiefs testified at the hearings, Shoup became a central figure because subcommittee investigators, without his permission, had given a group of Marines a difficult questionnaire intended to determine whether they understood the "Communist menace" and if Shoup was taking a "soft" stand on Communism.

In testimony given before the subcommittee on Jan. 30, 1962, Shoup told the members that he approved of censorship because of "the changing and sometimes extremely delicate international situation." He expressed his strong disapproval of the subcommittee questionnaire, saying it was a "needless waste of time." Asked if the Marines were given special indoctrination in Communism, Shoup said, "Our training system has only one objective—to produce combat-ready Marines to carry out any mission assigned to the Corps. We still continue to teach fighting, but not hate." The force of Shoup's testimony ended any further subcommittee attempts to investigate the Marine Corps.

In August 1963 Shoup testified before the Senate Foreign Relations Committee in favor of the limited nuclear test ban treaty signed on Aug. 5 by the U.S., Britain and the Soviet Union. With other members of the Joint Chiefs, he cautioned that the agreement be accepted only with the adoption of three safeguards: continuance of comprehensive underground testing, maintenance of laboratory facilities and resources necessary for the prompt resumption of atmospheric tests and improvement of equipment to detect violations.

At the end of 1963 Shoup retired as commandant and became director of the United Services Life Insurance Co. During the latter years of the decade, he became increasingly critical of what he believed to be growing military interference in civilian policymaking decisions. He opposed the Johnson Administration's conduct of the Vietnam war, saying it was "pure unadulterated poppycock" to believe that a military presence in South Vietnam was necessary for American defense. Shoup said a victory over North Vietnam could be achieved but only by committing "genocide on that poor country." [See JOHNSON Volume]

[EWS]

SHRIVER, R(OBERT) SARGENT
b. Nov. 9, 1915; Westminster, Md.
Director, Peace Corps, March 1961-
February 1964.

Shriver was born into an old Maryland family which traced its origins to the 17th century Catholic founders of the colony. From 1934 to 1938 he attended Yale as an undergraduate and received his law degree there in 1941. Shriver was employed briefly with a New York law firm before joining the Navy. After his discharge in 1945 he became an assistant editor of *Newsweek* magazine.

In 1946 Shriver joined Joseph P. Kennedy's [q.v.] business organization and two years later was appointed assistant general manager of Kennedy's Chicago Merchandise Mart, then the largest commercial building in the world. In 1953 Shriver married Kennedy's daughter, Eunice Mary Kennedy. From 1955 to 1960 he served on the Chicago Board of Education. During his years in the Midwest, Shriver became prominent in Democratic politics and was mentioned as a possible Democratic candidate for the governorship of Illinois in 1960.

In April 1960 Shriver joined John F. Kennedy's presidential campaign staff. Although not one of Kennedy's top advisers, he was important as a liaison between the field forces and the Democratic National Committee and between the Kennedy and Johnson staffs. Shriver also functioned as a fund raiser and was active in promoting the candidate in urban areas. Following Kennedy's election Shriver headed the Administration's talent hunt, a systematic attempt to recruit personnel for high government posts.

During the new Administration Shriver served as organizer and first director of the Peace Corps. The establishment of such a volunteer group, first suggested by Sen. Hubert H. Humphrey (D, Minn.) [q.v.], was promised during the last days of Kennedy's campaign. After the inauguration Shriver immediately began developing plans for the agency. According to proposals outlined during the first two months of 1961, the Peace Corps would serve two purposes. It would present the inhabitants of under-developed countries with a more balanced picture of Americans and counteract the prevalent stereotypes of complacent Americans afraid to do manual work. It would also give young Americans a first hand view of conditions in other parts of the world and provide a future core of knowledgeable individuals for foreign affairs positions. The Corps, staffed primarily by college and post-college-age volunteers, would serve in a country only at the invitation of its government. Peace Corps members would work as teachers, nurses and construction workers and would adopt the living standard of their counterparts in the host country.

From its inception Shriver was determined to make the Corps an organization independent of other government agencies. This was formally achieved when Kennedy made it a semi-autonomous branch of the State Department in August 1961. Equally important, Shriver received the assurances of the President and of Central Intelligence Agency (CIA) Director Allen Dulles [q.v.] that the Agency would not attempt to use the Peace Corps as a front for its overseas work. Shriver established strict criteria for enlistment that excluded anyone who had had even the remotest connection with the CIA. During orientation periods new recruits were also impressed with the need to report attempts to use the Corps by the Agency.

Following the establishment of the organization on a pilot basis by executive order in March, Shriver lobbied for approval of the Corps on Capitol Hill. There it met strong opposition from many congressmen who believed that the organization would be a haven for "fuzzy-minded idealists and malcontents." Still others feared that the Soviet bloc would view it as part of an American crusade to increase U.S. influence in the developing world. With little aid from the White House, Shriver quieted these fears. Congress established a permanent Peace Corps in September 1961 and funded it with a $40 million appropriation.

The Peace Corps became one of the most popular programs of the Kennedy Administration. By 1964 over 100,000 men and women had applied to join the organization, and the program had been expanded from 500-1,000 members in 1961 to 10,000 in 1964. Many of the men and women who served in the Corps believed that it provided a way of putting their idealism to work by doing something worthwhile for others. To many, both in the U.S. and abroad, it served as a symbol of the Administration's idealism and desire to aid developing countries without ulterior motives. However, by the end of the decade the appeal of the Corps had declined. Anti-Vietnam war activists and radicals became suspicious of its goals and several foreign governments expelled groups of Peace Corps workers from their countries.

In February 1964 Shriver was appointed to head President Johnson's war on poverty. From 1968 to 1970 he served as ambassador to France. Shriver was Sen. George McGovern's (D, S.D.) [q.v.] running mate during the 1972 presidential race. In 1976 he made a brief, unsuccessful attempt to win the Democratic nomination for president. [See JOHNSON, NIXON Volumes]

[EWS]

For further information:
Robert A. Liston, *Sargent Shriver: a Candid Portrait* (New York, 1964).
Sargent Shriver, *Point of the Lance* (New York, 1964).

SHUMAN, CHARLES B(AKER)
b. April 27, 1907; Sullivan, Ill.
President, American Farm Bureau Federation, 1954-70.

Shuman grew up on a farm that had been in his family since 1853. He earned B.S. and M.S. degrees in agriculture at the University of Illinois and became active in farm organizations in the 1930s. Shuman said that in those years he "learned about bureaucracy." Although a registered Democrat, he was an enemy of government controls in agriculture. A director of the American Farm Bureau Federation since 1945 and its elected president since 1954, Shuman helped move that organization away from support of New Deal farm policies. During the Eisenhower Administration Shuman and the Farm Bureau backed Secretary of Agriculture Ezra Taft Benson's flexible price support policy and rejected Democratic demands for a return to a fixed rate of 90% of parity. [See EISENHOWER Volume]

With a membership of 1.6 million farm families, the Farm Bureau was far larger than its two major rival organizations, the National Farmers' Union (NFU) and the National Grange. Observers characterized it as the representative of the large commercial farmers, and some critics charged that Shuman had made the Farm Bureau an agent of big business. Shuman claimed that the Farm Bureau represented a cross section of the American farming community. However, members of the Farm Bureau tended to own larger, more prosperous farms and advocated more conservative policies than the members of the NFU and the National Grange.

Shuman was a persistent and often effective critic of the farm policies of the Kennedy Administration and of Secretary of Agriculture Orville L. Freeman [q.v.]. He objected to the Administration's efforts to force farmers to cut production of basic crops (wheat and feed grains) in order to keep market prices high. Secretary Freeman asserted that the Farm Bureau did not represent the views of farmers, since, if its opposition to Kennedy farm legislation were successful, there would be "a return to the lower incomes and higher costs of the discredited Benson program." Shuman argued that, on the contrary, the elimination of controls would ultimately increase U.S. farm incomes. The extraordinary productivity of American agriculture would assure it a large share of the world market, he said, if only farmers were allowed to produce as much as they wanted in accordance with the laws of supply and demand. Shuman criticized the Administration's not always successful efforts to expand the market for U.S. farm products abroad.

Shuman's biggest victory over the Administration came in the national wheat referendum held in May 1963. Freeman, the NFU and the National Grange asked wheat farmers to accept strict marketing controls to ensure both a high price and access to world markets. However, the Farm Bureau and the Midwestern Republican press waged an intensive campaign against the Administration. The new plan won only 48% of the vote, far short of the two-thirds necessary to put it into effect. The defeat represented the first rejection of marketing quotas for a major crop in the postwar period.

In October 1963 Shuman hesitated to criticize the proposed sale of U.S. wheat to the Soviet Union because of the sale's popularity in the wheat belt, but he argued that the decision to approve the sale should have been made by Congress rather than President Kennedy.

Shuman retired from the presidency of the American Farm Bureau Federation in 1970, but he remained active on the boards of a number of agencies and companies, including the Export-Import Bank, the Economic Development Administration, the Illinois Power Company and the Chicago Mercantile Exchange. [See JOHNSON Volume]

[JCH]

SHUTTLESWORTH, FRED L(EE)
b. March 18, 1922; Mugler, Ala.
Secretary, Southern Christian Leadership Conference, 1957-70; President, Alabama Christian Movement for Human Rights, 1956-70.

Pastor of the First Baptist and then the Bethel Baptist Church in Birmingham, Ala., during the 1950s, Shuttlesworth was an active member of the Alabama NAACP until 1956 when the state legislature outlawed the organization. Shuttlesworth then organized the Alabama Christian Movement for Human Rights (ACMHR) and, as its president, led efforts to desegregate Birmingham's buses, schools and parks in the late 1950s. Along with Martin Luther King [q.v.], Shuttlesworth organized the Southern Christian Leadership Conference (SCLC) in 1957 and was elected its first secretary.

In 1960 Shuttlesworth became pastor of the Revelation Baptist Church in Cincinnati, Ohio, but he remained active in Birmingham and was a key aide to King. When the first of the Freedom Rides ended in violence at Anniston and Birmingham, Ala. on May 14, 1961, Shuttlesworth helped arrange for the riders' safe passage out of Alabama. When the rides, which were aimed at desegregating interstate transportation facilities, were continued, Shuttlesworth joined them and was arrested on May 17 in Birmingham and on May 25 in Montgomery, Ala. He headed an SCLC nonviolent training center in Birmingham during the early 1960s and backed student-led sit-ins and boycotts there in 1960 and 1962.

At a May 1962 board meeting of the SCLC, Shuttlesworth proposed that the SCLC join with his ACMHR in an anti-segregation campaign in Birmingham. The suggestion led to the dramatic Birmingham demonstrations, which began on April 3, 1963 and were led by King and Shuttlesworth. Once described as "one of the most articulate and fastest-talking leaders of the Negro drive for equality in the South," Shuttlesworth addressed daily mass meetings in Birmingham, led demonstrations and marches, and was arrested on April 6 and again on April 12. He was also injured in a May 7 demonstration when police turned fire hoses on the crowd and a stream of water hit Shuttlesworth, lifting him up and throwing him against the side of a building. Despite his injuries Shuttlesworth participated in the negotiations between Birmingham's black and white leadership, and on May 10 he announced the terms of the agreement they had reached.

Following the Sept. 15 bombing of a black church in Birmingham which killed four young girls, Shuttlesworth organized protests in the city, met in Washington with President Kennedy on Sept. 19 and, after two more bombings in Birmingham, called for federal troops to be sent into the city. The historic events in Birmingham contributed to President Kennedy's decision to seek strong civil rights legislation and created support for the passage of a new federal law. The spring demonstrations also increased the momentum of the civil rights movement. During the summer of 1963, desegregation drives emerged in numerous Southern cities, including Danville, Va., where Shuttlesworth helped lead the campaign.

Shuttlesworth led more demonstrations in Birmingham over the next three years and participated in an SCLC campaign in St. Augustine, Fla., in the summer of 1964. During the 1960s Shuttlesworth's six convictions resulting from his civil rights work were overturned by the Supreme Court. [See JOHNSON Volume]

[CAB]

SIKES, ROBERT L. F.
b. June 3, 1906; Isabella, Ga.
Democratic Representative, Fla., 1941-   .

Robert Sikes was a newspaper publisher and a state legislator before his election to the House from Florida's first district in 1940. His district covered the western panhandle in northern Florida and closely resembled—socially and politically—its northern neighbors, Alabama and Georgia. Sikes's moderate voting record in Congress gradually grew more conservative during the Truman and Eisenhower Administrations. Strategically positioned on the Appropriations Committee's Subcommittees on Defense and Military Construction, Sikes managed to gain for the first district one of the heaviest concentrations of military installations in the nation.

Sikes's seniority on the Appropriations Committee made him one of the more powerful House conservatives during the Kennedy Administration. The liberal Americans for Democratic Action (ADA) gave him ratings of only 20% in 1961, 13% in 1962 and 33% in 1963 for his votes on legislation the ADA favored. Sikes was an active foe of civil rights legislation and, as a brigadier general in the Army Reserve, was a strong defender of military spending. He was the leading congressional proponent of appropriations for chemical, biological and radiological warfare.

Sikes became chairman of the Military Construction Subcommittee in 1965. In 1976 he was the target of an investigation by the House Committee on Standards of Official Conduct into conflict of interest charges relating to his undisclosed ownership of stock in a defense contractor and his sponsorship of legislation in 1961-62 to aid his Florida land development company. [See JOHNSON, NIXON Volumes]

[TO]

SIMKIN, WILLIAM E(DWARD)
b. Jan. 13, 1907; Merrifield, N.Y.
Director, Federal Mediation and Conciliation Service, 1961-69.

While teaching at the Wharton School of Finance and Commerce at the University of Pennsylvania in the late 1930s, Simkin became an associate of Professor George W. Taylor, the well-known labor arbitrator. He shortly thereafter began a long career in labor mediation, including service on the National War Labor Board and other government panels.

On Feb. 2, 1961 President Kennedy appointed Simkin director of the Federal Mediation and Conciliation Service (FMCS). An independent agency within the executive branch, the FMCS was notified of pending labor contract changes in collective bargaining agreements that affected interstate commerce. The FMCS entered any case that developed negotiating problems whether or not it was invited by the concerned parties. However, it could not enforce settlements—its only instruments were persuasion and the prestige of the federal government.

Simkin was mainly an administrator, but during the Kennedy Administration he personally intervened in some of the more crucial negotiations. He was able to delay strike action in a number of cases, including one in the automobile industry in 1961 and another in the aerospace industry in July 1962. His intervention helped settle the Boeing Company-International Association of Machinists dispute in April 1963 and the strike of the Oil, Chemical and Atomic Workers International Union against the Shell Oil Company in August 1963. Simkin, however, was ineffective in his efforts to negotiate an end to the long New York City newspaper strike of 1962-63. The length of the newspaper strike—and other strikes during the period—caused Simkin to fear that the public would become "discouraged and demand drastic changes" in bargaining methods.

Simkin stayed on at the FMC until 1969, when he became a lecturer at the Harvard School of Business Administration. Beginning in 1970 he was chairman of the Federal Reserve System's labor relations panel and in the following year became chairman of the State Department's Foreign Service Grievance Board. [See JOHNSON Volume]

[JCH]

SINATRA, FRANK (FRANCIS ALBERT)
b. Dec. 12, 1917; Hoboken, N.J.
Entertainer.

Frank Sinatra was the son of a Hoboken fireman. In the early 1940s he gained an idolatrous nationwide audience of "bobby-soxers" for his uniquely intimate vocal style. His career went into eclipse late in the decade but revived after he won a 1953 Academy Award for best supporting actor in the film *From Here to Eternity*. For the next 20 years Sinatra continued at the top of his profession with nightclub acts, television shows, recordings and films. His yearly income was estimated at $4 million. In the early 1960s Sinatra and several other show business stars, including singers Dean Martin and Sammy Davis, Jr., became known as the "Rat Pack" and frequently performed together.

A longtime Democrat, Sinatra was an early and active supporter of the presidential candidacy of Sen. John F. Kennedy, to whom he had been introduced by Kennedy in-law, actor and sometime "Rat Pack" member Peter Lawford. Sinatra urged liberals in Hollywood to support Kennedy, organized benefits on Kennedy's behalf and accompanied the Senator on several campaign trips. After the election he escorted Jacqueline Kennedy [q.v.] to the Inaugural Gala, where ticket prices ranged from $100 to $10,000. The gala raised $1.4 million to help pay off the Democratic Party's campaign debts.

During the next two years Kennedy became a close friend of Sinatra's and often stayed at the entertainer's house in Palm Springs, Calif. However, late in the Administration Sinatra's reputed connections with organized crime led to a cooling-off between the two men. According to many observers the friendship was terminated in September 1963 after the Nevada State Gaming Commission charged that Sinatra had violated state law by permitting Mafia leader Sam Giancana to use the gambling facilities of Cal-Neva Lodge, of which Sinatra was the principal stockholder. After the commission ordered Sinatra to sever his financial interests in the state's gambling industry, the entertainer announced that he was divesting himself of his gambling holdings and would confine his investments to the entertainment industry.

In April 1976 the *New York Times* reported in a series of investigative articles that during the Kennedy Administration Attorney General Robert F. Kennedy [q.v.] had blocked Justice Department inquiries into the nature and extent of Sinatra's Mafia connections and into his relationship with Judith Campbell Exner, who was an intimate friend of Mafia leaders Sam Giancana and John Roselli. According to the Senate Committee on Intelligence Activities, in the early 1960s both Roselli and Giancana had been involved in Central Intelligence Agency plots to assassinate Cuban Prime Minister Fidel Castro.

Early in 1976 Exner publicly acknowledged that she had had a two-year affair with President Kennedy from 1960 until 1962. She said she had been introduced to Kennedy in Las Vegas by Sinatra and that several weeks later Sinatra had introduced her to Giancana and Roselli. Exner speculated that Sinatra had wanted to "set up a [Mafia] Connection" with the White House.

According to the *Times*, Attorney General Kennedy's motives for discouraging the Sinatra investigation were a matter of considerable controversy among Justice Department attorneys during the early 1960s. Many believed that Robert Kennedy's reluctance to pursue the investigation stemmed from President Kennedy's close personal friendship with the entertainer and his gratitude for Sinatra's extensive efforts on behalf of the Kennedy campaign. However, Herbert J. Miller, then assistant attorney general in charge of the Criminal Division, stated: "You have to remember this was in 1962 when we [the Justice Department] were just getting into the organized-crime fight. The FBI was just coming around to the idea that there was a Mafia."

In October 1969 the New Jersey State Commission of Investigation, which was conducting an inquiry into organized crime in New Jersey, issued a warrant for Sinatra's arrest after he refused to appear before the Commission to answer questions about crime in the state. Sinatra declared that he was "not willing to be part of any three-ring circus." Three months later Sinatra agreed to testify before the Commission after the U.S. Supreme Court refused to set aside the subpoena directing him to appear.

During the Nixon Administration Sinatra developed a close personal friendship with Vice President Spiro Agnew. In 1972 he contributed $14,000 to President Richard M. Nixon's reelection campaign. [See NIXON Volume]

[FHM]

SMATHERS, GEORGE A(RMISTEAD)

b. Nov. 14, 1913; Atlantic City, N.J.
Democratic Senator, Fla., 1951-69.

George Smathers, an influential senator from Florida and close friend of Presidents Kennedy and Johnson, was raised in Miami. Following his graduation from the University of Florida Law School in 1938, he entered private law practice. Through the influence of Sen. Claude Pepper (D, Fla.), Smathers was appointed assistant U.S. district attorney for Dade County in 1940. After service in World War II, he was made a special assistant to the U.S. Attorney General. In 1946 Smathers was elected to the House of Representatives where he earned a reputation as a liberal.

In 1950 Smathers, backed by business interests opposed to Pepper's liberal stand on taxes and labor legislation, won the Democratic senatorial nomination from Pepper. During what was called one of the dirtiest campaigns of the postwar period, Smathers dropped his liberal stance on social issues and accused Pepper of being a Communist sympathizer. In November Smathers won the general election. [See TRUMAN Volume]

Through his friendship with Senate Majority Leader Lyndon B. Johnson (D, Tex.) [q.v.], Smathers became a powerful member of what was known as the Senate "Establishment," the small group of senators who made committee assignments and could often decide the fate of important legislations. [See EISENHOWER Volume]

Smathers voted against most of the civil rights bills and domestic social legislation of the Kennedy years. Although a personal friend of Kennedy, he often failed to exert his influence on behalf of the President or even appear for some close votes on Administration-backed measures. In 1963, for example, his absence was a factor in the Senate's reduction of funds for the space program by a 40-to-39 vote.

During the 1960s Robert Sherrill, a political commentator, maintained that a major force behind Smather's voring pattern was his desire to aid his law firm's clients and help the large companies that had contributed to his election campaigns. He pointed to Smathers's 1961 amendment to the Foreign Assistance Act that granted funds for housing projects in Latin America, which his friends would underwrite. In 1962 Smathers added an amendment to the Internal Revenue Code that resulted in the saving of millions of dollars in taxes for the DuPont family, which had backed his first Senate campaign.

During the Johnson Administration Smathers remained a powerful force in the Senate and frequently served as an adviser to the President. In 1964 he was cited as a business partner of Bobby Baker [q.v.], the former senate majority secretary then under investigation for fraud. Although exonerated of impropriety in the matter, Smathers was politically hurt by the incident. In the late 1960s many of his business dealings became widely known, and charges of influence peddling were frequently aimed at him. Claiming poor health, Smathers announced that he would not seek reelection in 1968. [See JOHNSON Volume]

[EWS]

For further information:
Robert Sherrill, *Gothic Politics in the Deep South* (New York, 1968).

SMITH, HOWARD W(ORTH)
b. Feb. 2, 1883; Broad Run, Va.
Democratic Representative, Va., 1931-67; Chairman, Rules Committee, 1955-67.

Smith first entered public life as the commonwealth's attorney for Alexandria, Va., in 1918. Four years later he became judge of the corporation court of that city and in 1928 was appointed judge of the state's 16th Circuit Court. In 1930 he won election to Congress and served there for 36 consecutive years. Smith had an unprepossessing personality but was gifted with extraordinary political skills. By mid-century he had become one of the chief lieutenant's of Sen. Harry Byrd's [q.v.] powerful, conservative Democratic political machine in Virginia.

As a congressman Smith voiced his own and the Byrd organization's opposition to the extension of federal power, social welfare spending and racial integration. In 1955 he became chairman of the powerful House Rules Committee, which, since the late 1930s, had been dominated by a conservative coalition of Southern Democrats and Republicans. Most bills passing from their original committee to the House floor stopped at the Rules Committee, which determined the length and manner of the floor debate. As its chairman Smith played a major role in blocking liberal legislation, for the panel could determine whether a bill would be subject to amendment before the full House or whether it would reach the floor at all. [See EISENHOWER Volume]

President Kennedy made liberalization of the House Rules Committee one of the first tasks of his new Administration. Following a strategy devised by Speaker Sam Rayburn (D, Tex.) [q.v.], the Democratic leadership in the House proposed to "pack" the Committee by adding three new members, two of whom were deemed moderate to liberal. In what was considered a test of the new Administration's strength, and Kennedy's first legislative victory, the House voted 217 to 212 on Jan. 31, 1961 to increase the Committee's membership from 12 to 15. This gave liberals an 8-to-7 majority. In January 1963 the House voted 235 to 196 to make this arrangement permanent. Smith, arguing unsuccessfully against expansion, said that conservative control of the panel would enable the country to consider measures carefully and would help to prevent deficit spending.

The enlargement of the Rules Committee reduced the power of Smith and his Southern Democratic-Republican coalition, but it by no means eliminated that power. The 8-7 liberal majority was tenuous, particularly when a special issue influenced normally liberal members. On July 18, 1961 the Committee voted 8-7 to table an Administration public school aid bill. The decisive vote was provided by Rep. James Delaney (D, N.Y.) [q.v.], a Catholic and normally a liberal, who voted with the conservatives after the Catholic hierarchy denounced the measure because it did not include aid to parochial schools. On the other hand, the Administration was able to win a number of straight liberal-conservative votes. In August 1962 the Committee decided by an 8-6 margin, with Smith in opposition, to report out a Kennedy-backed public works bill. By 8-7 the body again overrode Smith in April 1963 when it voted out a bill to subsidize medical training.

However, Smith's effectiveness did not depend entirely upon majority support in the Committee. As chairman he had considerable independent power to determine the pace at which the panel acted. He could often bury bills that he disliked or, by allowing them to accumulate, give their supporters enough time to promote only a few of them on the floor. An Administration-sponsored urban mass transportation bill failed to reach the floor in either 1962 or 1963 because the Rules Committee did not act upon it. The committee also took no action on two youth training bills proposed by President Kennedy in June 1962.

Smith was an adamant foe of any civil rights-related legislation. His successful opposition to Kennedy's public school aid bill stemmed largely from his belief that it would be used to compel school integration. In June 1961 Smith asserted, "This is not a bill to aid education. It is a bill to aid the NAACP. . . ." In 1962 he denounced Congress's approval of a constitutional amendment barring payment of a poll tax as a condition for voting in federal elections.

In January 1965 the House adopted a rule that enabled the committee with original jurisdiction over a bill to circumvent the Rules Committee. The new proviso significantly weakened Smith's impact upon legislation. As a result of redistricting, which added moderate suburban areas to his constituency, and a growing black electorate, Smith was narrowly defeated in the 1966 Democratic primary. [See JOHNSON Volume]

[MLL]

SMITH, MARGARET CHASE
b. Dec. 14, 1897; Skowhegan, Me.
Republican Senator, Me., 1949-73.

After a varied career in business and local Republican politics, Smith won election to the U. S. House of Representatives in 1940, filling a vacancy created by her husband's death. She served four full terms in the House and advanced to the Senate in 1948. Smith built a record as an independent in domestic affairs, often supporting liberal Democratic legislation. As a representative, she voted for extension of the Social Security Act and against establishment of a permanent House Un-American Activities Committee. In the Senate she voted for such Democratic proposals as aid to depressed areas and federally subsidized housing. Although an advocate of a strong military defense and a staunch anti-Communist, Smith was repelled by the tactics of Sen. Joseph

McCarthy (R, Wisc.). In her first major address to the Senate on June 1, 1950, Smith assailed the Wisconsin Senator with a "declaration of conscience" formulated by herself and six other Republican senators. In her widely publicized attack Smith accused McCarthy of reducing the Senate to a "forum of hate and character assassination." In 1954 she voted for his censure by the Senate. [See TRUMAN, EISENHOWER Volumes]

Elected to a third Senate term in 1960, Smith soon clashed with the Kennedy Administration over defense strategy. When the Administration announced plans in 1961 to modernize and increase conventional military forces, Smith interpreted the new policy as an indication of an apparent lack of will to use nuclear weapons if circumstances required it. During a Senate speech on Sept. 21, 1961, she charged Kennedy with virtually telling the Soviet Union that he would never resort to nuclear warfare, arguing that this approach would diminish America's "nuclear credibility" and weaken the nation's capacity to deal with the Russians. Administration spokesmen, including Defense Secretary Robert McNamara [q.v.] and Attorney General Robert Kennedy [q.v.], promptly denied Smith's allegations and asserted that the President was prepared to use nuclear weapons if necessary. Soviet Premier Nikita S. Khrushchev responded more vehemently to Smith's speech; he labeled the Main Republican "the devil in a disguise of a woman" and accused her of "savage hatred" of the Soviet bloc.

Smith also remained at odds with other sections of Kennedy's foreign policy program. She voted against the President's nominee for head of the Export-Import Bank in March 1961 and in January 1962 was one of the two Republicans to vote against confirmation of John A. McCone [q.v.] as director of the Central Intelligence Agency. Smith was one of a small minority of senators to oppose the nuclear test ban treaty in October 1963. She feared it would place the United States at a military and technical disadvantage in future arms development. Despite these differences with the Administration, Smith favored measures to extend foreign aid and supported the Defense Department's efforts in 1962 to review the public statements of military officers before delivery or publication. As a member of the Preparedness Investigating Subcommittee, she defended the Administration against charges that the review policy "muzzled" military leaders who spoke out against Communism.

During the 87th Congress Smith was one of the five Republican senators who voted most consistently for Kennedy Administration programs. In 1963 *Congressional Quarterly* reported that her support of the President's domestic proposals was exceeded among Senate Republicans only by New York's Jacob Javits [*q.v.*] and Kenneth Keating [*q.v.*]. Smith opposed Kennedy's medicare program but voted in favor of the Administration's area redevelopment, school aid, minimum wage and communication satellite proposals. She also favored efforts to change Senate Rule 22 which required a two-thirds vote of the members present to invoke cloture and end debate. [See JOHNSON, NIXON Volumes]

[CAB]

For further information:
Margaret Chase Smith, *Declaration of Conscience* (New York, 1972).

SMYLIE, ROBERT E.
b. Oct. 31, 1914; Marcus, Ida.
Governor, Ida., 1955-67.

Robert E. Smylie, a graduate of the College of Idaho, took a law degree at George Washington University in 1942. After service in the Coast Guard during World War II, he returned to Idaho where he became active in the Republican Party while practicing law. In 1947 the governor of Idaho appointed him attorney general to complete the term of the deceased incumbent. A year later Smylie won election as attorney general, a post he held for the next six years. In his successful bid for the Idaho governorship in 1954, Smylie urged private rather than federal development of the hydroelectric power facilities in the Hell's Canyon area of the Snake River. [See EISENHOWER Volume]

As governor Smylie was generally regarded as a capable administrator. He worked to revamp the Idaho tax system, supported state aid for local schools and favored an extensive park and recreation program. Although Smylie was a vigorous opponent of local efforts to promote gambling in Idaho, in 1963 the state Supreme Court upheld the constitutionality of a para-mutual betting law, which the state legislature had passed over a Smylie veto.

In September 1963 Smylie served as acting chairman of the newly formed Republican Governors Association. The group issued a statement asserting that the "single most important domestic challenge" facing the nation was the need to provide a job for every able-bodied American. It called for an immediate tax cut coupled with action to hold federal spending at current levels. A year later Smylie was named chairman of the Republican Governors Association.

Smylie was generally associated with the moderate wing of the Republican Party, and when Sen. Barry M. Goldwater (R, Ariz.) [*q.v.*] won the 1964 Republican presidential nomination, the Governor supported him with reluctance. Following Goldwater's devastating defeat Smylie initiated a successful movement to remove Dean Burch, a Goldwater supporter, as head of the Republican National Committee. Smylie also denounced the right-wing John Birch Society and called for the Republican Party to adopt a more centrist political stance. As a result of this activity, Smylie thoroughly alienated conservative Idaho Republicans. They subsequently supported his opponent in the 1966 Republican gubernatorial primary, and Smylie was routed. At the expiration of his term, he retired to private life and his legal practice in Boise. [See JOHNSON Volume]

[JLW]

SORENSEN, THEODORE (CHAIKIN)
b. May 8, 1928; Lincoln, Neb.
Special Counsel to the President,
January 1961-January 1964.

Theodore Sorensen, John F. Kennedy's closest aide throughout his senate and presidential career, was born into a politically liberal family in Lincoln, Neb. The son of a crusading lawyer and reformer, Sorensen was raised in the progressive tradition of Sen. George W. Norris (D, Neb.), a close friend of his father's. A liberal maverick in his own right, Sorensen registered with the draft as a noncombatant in 1945 and later campaigned for the integration of universities and municipal facilities in Nebraska.

Following his graduation from the University of Nebraska Law School in 1951, Sorensen went to Washington as an attorney for the Federal Security Agency. One year later he became a staff researcher for the joint congressional subcommittee studying railroad pensions. In 1953 Sorensen joined the staff of newly elected Sen. John F. Kennedy, where he helped research and draft legislation. He also prepared the background material for Kennedy's best-selling *Profiles in Courage*.

Sorensen's relationship with Kennedy was one of total loyalty and dedication. Although not a close social friend of the Senator's, he became Kennedy's political alter ego, willingly submitting his personal interests to Kennedy's political ambition. Sorensen later stated that "for those 11 years he was the only human being who mattered to me."

According to journalist Patrick Anderson, Sorensen was a liberalizing influence on the Senator, particularly in the areas of civil rights, international relations and social welfare. The aide drew Kennedy from the conservative positions he had taken while influenced by his father to more moderate stands on many issues. At the same time Kennedy steered the idealistic Sorensen toward a more pragmatic political philosophy. Gradually the two men's philosophies merged until "no one—not even Sorensen—was sure just where his thoughts left and Kennedy's began."

Not personally aggressive in presenting his ideas, Sorensen primarily influenced Kennedy through his facility as a speech writer. He believed that he could use his writing to educate Kennedy, present him with policy choices not previously considered and force him to take a stand on the issues.

Sorensen remained Kennedy's closest adviser during the presidency, a position emphasized by his title, Special Counsel to the President. At the White House Sorensen's duties became more varied. He remained the chief White House speech writer, helping Kennedy to forge a style of public speaking that often captured the nation's imagination and contributed to the flavor of pragmatic optimism that characterized his presidency. Sorensen was credited with writing some of Kennedy's most notable speeches, including the inaugural address and the American University speech of June 1963.

Because of Kennedy's distrust of the federal bureaucracy, Sorensen and his staff were responsible for shaping much of the Administration's legislative program, particularly its aid-to-education proposals. He was also the spokesman for Kennedy on all but the most important day-to-day issues and served as Kennedy's chief aide in domestic crises. During the summer of 1961, when Kennedy contemplated a tax increase to pay for the military buildup in Berlin, Sorensen advised him against the idea as bad politics and conservative economics. In April 1962 he helped coordinate the Administration's drive for a price rollback following steel industry rate increases.

After the abortive Bay of Pigs invasion of Cuba in April 1961, Sorensen's influence increased further. Angered by what he considered poor advice from the State and Defense Departments during the months prior to the attack, Kennedy increasingly relied on such trusted aides as Sorensen. The aide, therefore, began advising the President on such foreign policy matters as the American response to the Soviet challenge in Berlin and Communist expansion in Laos during 1961 and 1962. In each of these situations Sorensen urged Kennedy to avoid confrontation and the use of military force and to work for a peaceful solution to the problem.

Sorensen played a leading role in policy formation following the discovery of Soviet missiles in Cuba on Oct. 14, 1962. In the policy meetings of Excom, the special group of advisers gathered to counsel the President in the crisis and gain bipartisan support for Administration policy, participants had divided over two courses of action: an air strike against the missile bases or a blockade of Cuba to force removal of the weapons. Following the tentative decision made on Oct. 18 to recommend the blockade, Sorensen, anxious to gain a stronger consensus for the policy, offered to draft speeches on both proposals. These statements and his discussions with the Excom members convinced many of those recommending stronger action that a blockade was only the beginning of the U.S. response, and that if it did not force removal of the weapons an air strike would be the next step. This became the core of the plan that Kennedy approved on Oct. 20.

Following Kennedy's death Sorensen left the White House and spent the next two years writing *Kennedy*, a glowing description of the White House years that was published in 1965. In the prologue Sorensen said that the book was "my substitute for the book he [Kennedy] was going to write." Sorensen, initially indecisive about a prospective career, traveled and lectured before joining a leading New York law firm in 1966. In 1970 he made an unsuccessful bid for the Democratic Senate nomination from New York.

[EWS]

For further information:
Patrick Andersen, *The Presidents' Men* (New York, 1968), pp. 276-298.
Theodore Sorensen, *Kennedy* (New York, 1965).

SPARKMAN, JOHN J(ACKSON)

b. Dec. 20, 1899; Morgan County, Ala.
Democratic Senator, Ala., 1946-   ;
Chairman, Select Small Business Committee, 1950-53, 1955-67; Chairman, Housing Subcommittee of the Senate Banking and Currency Committee, 1955-   .

Sparkman received a legal degree from the University of Alabama in 1923 and began a law practice in Huntsville, Ala., two years later. In 1936 he was elected to the U.S. House of Representatives. Sparkman was a supporter of New Deal programs and was particularly interested in the creation of the Tennessee Valley Authority, which played a major role in the development of the northern Alabama region that he represented.

In 1946 Sparkman won a special election to fill a Senate vacancy created by the death of John H. Bankhead. During the postwar period most Southerners on Capitol Hill opposed liberal domestic measures, but Sparkman continued to favor many public works and other spending programs. As a member of the Joint Committee on Housing and the chairman of the Banking and Currency Committee's Housing Subcommittee, he played a key role in the passage of almost all housing legislation in the late 1940s and the 1950s. Because of his relatively liberal voting record, Sparkman was chosen as Adlai E. Stevenson's [*q.v.*] vice-presidential running mate in 1952.

Although Sparkman did not employ demagoguery in discussing the race issue, he opposed civil rights legislation as consistently as his more conservative Southern colleagues. In 1956 he assisted in the drafting of the "Southern Manifesto," which vowed resistance to the Supreme Court's 1954 school desegregation decision. [See TRUMAN, EISENHOWER Volumes]

Sparkman remained uniformly opposed to civil rights measures during the early 1960s, but he supported most major Kennedy-backed legislation. He also favored many of President Kennedy's efforts to reduce East-West tensions. In 1961 a number of Southern Democrats and conservative Republicans criticized an Administration bill to create an Arms Control and Disarmament Agency, but Sparkman warned in September that "if we do not begin to limit armaments, we shall surely continue the present path to mutual destruction." The following year he was the floor manager of a bill authorizing President Kennedy to loan the United Nations up to $100 million. In September 1963 Sparkman voted for the nuclear test ban treaty.

Sparkman voted against medicare in July 1962 but supported most of the Administration's other domestic programs. In the spring of 1963 he was the floor manager of

President Kennedy's bill to provide aid to states and localities for mass transit. Speaking of the urban transportation problem, Sparkman asserted, "The longer we delay in recognizing that this is a real crisis the costlier it will be."

In 1961 Sparkman, as chairman of the Housing Subcommittee, was the Senate sponsor of the Administration's omnibus housing bill. The measure, which became law in June, was designed to reduce urban blight and congestion, improve housing for low and moderate-income families and stimulate the construction industry to counter the 1960-61 recession. Many senators objected to the bill's provisions for loans to promote the building of moderate-income sales and rental housing. Sparkman beat back an attempt to delete that section of the measure, stating that 65% of American families had incomes too low to buy most Federal Housing Administration units and too high to qualify for low-cost public housing.

As chairman of the Select Small Business Committee, Sparkman backed increased funding for the Small Business Administration (SBA). During the spring of 1962 Sen. William Proxmire (D, Wisc.) [q.v.], chairman of the Banking and Currency Committee's Small Business Subcommittee, attempted to reduce the amount of money available to the SBA for small business loans on the ground that most small businesses did not need or use the agency's funds. Sparkman replied that the SBA needed a cushion to meet emergency demands. In November 1963 he was the floor manager of a bill to increase SBA aid to small businesses. In both cases the Senate approved the level of funding favored by Sparkman.

In 1967 Sparkman became chairman of the Banking and Currency Committee. During the late 1960s his voting record became increasingly conservative. In 1972 he narrowly avoided a primary runoff against an opponent who accused him of being too close to big banking interests. In 1975 he gave up his Banking and Currency chairmanship to become head of the Foreign Relations Committee. [See JOHNSON, NIXON Volumes]   [MLL]

SPELLMAN, FRANCIS J(OSEPH)
b. May 4, 1889; Whitman, Mass.
d. Dec. 2, 1967; New York, N.Y.
Roman Catholic Archbishop of New York, 1939-67.

Trained in Rome and ordained a Roman Catholic priest in 1916, Spellman was named archbishop of New York in 1939. In 1946 he became a cardinal. With the movement of Catholics into the middle-class and into national political life in the postwar era, Spellman became one of the most powerful American clergymen. A successful fund raiser, he built churches and schools in New York and helped finance Catholic missionary work abroad. As military vicar-general of the U.S. armed forces, he visited American troops around the world and was often identified with the interests of the American military. Cardinal Spellman strongly supported American policy in the Cold War, and in 1953 he defended Sen. Joseph McCarthy's (R, Wisc.) anti-Communist congressional investigations. With the assistance of Joseph Kennedy [q.v.], Spellman helped influence the Eisenhower Administration in 1955 to give full support to the South Vietnam regime of Ngo Dinh Diem, marking the growth of serious interest in stopping the growth of Communism in Southeast Asia. [See TRUMAN, EISENHOWER Volumes]

Although President Kennedy was a Catholic, the Cardinal disagreed sharply with him on two issues that Spellman considered vital to the welfare of American Catholics. In March 1961 he attacked Kennedy's proposed federal school-aid program because it would have excluded Catholic schools from benefit eligibility. Wishing to avoid any charge that he was meddling in politics, Spellman refused to take a position on the constitutionality of federal aid, but he did state that "should [there] be any federal aid, then certainly any legislation should conform to principles of social justice, equal treatment and non-discrimination." He added that it was "unthinkable that any American child be denied the federal funds alloted to other children . . . .because his parents choose for him a God-centered education."

In February 1962 Spellman predicted that the Kennedy school-aid program would result in the end of the parochial school system, but a majority of Protestant and Jewish clergymen backed the President and warned that Spellman's stubborn opposition could hurt the chances of a secular federal aid program. The Cardinal also came into conflict with Kennedy and other religious leaders when he attacked the Supreme Court's June 1962 decision banning prayer in the public schools.

Spellman had long been a supporter of civil rights and interdenominational cooperation, but he found it difficult to keep pace with many of the other changes introduced in the 1960s. His anti-Communism prevented him from adapting to the more liberal Vatican foreign policy advocated by Pope John XXIII. He opposed some of the innovations of the Vatican Council, including the introduction of English into the church liturgy. The election of a Catholic president also did much to end the minority-consciousness of American Catholics, bringing into focus divisions within American Catholicism. Liberal Catholics, including both clergy and laymen, began to challenge Spellman's role as an official spokesman for Catholicism.

Spellman's influence continued to decline under the Johnson Administration. His strong support for the Vietnam war brought him into conflict with Pope Paul VI and aggravated his battle with Catholic anti-war activists in the U.S. In October 1966 Spellman offered to resign as archbishop because of his age, but Pope Paul urged him to stay on. The Cardinal died of a stroke on Dec. 2, 1967. [See JOHNSON Volume]

[JCH]

STAHR, ELVIS J(ACOB), JR.
b. March 9, 1916; Hickman, Ky.
Secretary of the Army, January 1961-June 1962.

A distinguished lawyer and educator, Elvis Stahr took a leave of absence from his post as president of West Virginia University to become Army Secretary in January 1961. Previously he had been a practicing lawyer, professor of law, provost and dean of the college of law at the University of Kentucky and vice chancellor of the University of Pittsburgh. He had also served in 1951 and 1952 as special Assistant for reserve forces in the Department of the Army.

In an interview given after his resignation, Stahr admitted that as Secretary of the Army he had had little to do with policy formation on the major issues confronting his department: the Berlin crisis of 1961, the decision to form specialized military units to help underdeveloped countries strengthen their national security and the planning of nuclear strategy. His political role was confined to defending Administration action in calling up reserve troops during the Berlin crisis and admonishing Gen. Edwin A. Walker [q.v.] for making derogatory statements about prominent Americans. In 1961 Stahr appealed for rapid production of the Army's Nike-Zeus antimissile system, warning of increased Russian missile development.

While in office Stahr became critical of Secretary Robert S. McNamara's [q.v.] personal control of the Defense Department, calling it "overreaching." He opposed McNamara's tendency to make even the smallest decisions himself, feeling it established a dangerous precedent. Although praising the Defense Secretary's performance, Stahr believed that decision making should have been left decentralized so that the Department could operate effectively when men of lesser abilities held McNamara's post. Along with the Secretaries of the Air Force and Navy, he protested a tendency on the part of some of McNamara's aides to deal directly with the service secretaries' subordinates, leaving the secretaries themselves without knowledge of policy.

Although rumors suggested that Stahr's resignation in June 1962 was the result of disagreements with McNamara, the former Secretary insisted it was to take "the once in a lifetime opportunity of becoming the president of Indiana University."

[EWS]

STANTON, FRANK
b. March 20, 1908; Muskegon, Mich.
President, Columbia Broadcasting System, 1946-73.

From audience surveys to ashtrays Frank Stanton exerted direct operational control over the Columbia Broadcasting System (CBS) for three decades. He presided over the growth of CBS into the largest advertising and communications operation in the nation and saw the company's earnings climb from $22 million in 1961 to over $100 million in 1974.

Stanton grew up in Ohio and graduated from Ohio Wesleyan in 1930. He took a master's degree from Ohio State in 1932 and then received a doctorate in psychology from that university three years later. Stanton's doctoral thesis, outlining a new method of gauging audience reaction to radio programs, caught the eye of a CBS executive, who gave Stanton a job with the company. Working his way quickly up through the ranks, Stanton became director of research, vice president and general manager and, finally, president of CBS in 1946.

The most visible and articulate of the three network presidents, Stanton expressed his views on censorship, network policy and the rules and regulations of the Federal Communications Commission (FCC) before a number of Senate investigating committees during the 1950s and 1960s. He was instrumental in persuading Congress to lift the FCC's "equal time" rule, requiring networks to provide equal time to presidential candidates from both major and minor parties, so that the two leading presidential candidates in 1960, Sen. John F. Kennedy and Vice President Richard M. Nixon [q.v.], could hold televised debates. Later he advocated that the "equal time" rule be permanently abandoned.

Stanton was angered by FCC chairman Newton Minow's [q.v.] May 1961 description of television as a "vast wasteland" full of commercials and prime-time blandness. The Commission chairman's view was contrary to Stanton's stated belief that "what the media do is to hold a mirror up to society and try to report it as faithfully as possible."

During the 1960s CBS consistently led the other networks in both ratings and profits. CBS expanded its nightly news coverage to 30 minutes in 1963 but was frequently criticized for what Erik Barnouw called its "unrelentingly though cheerfully familiar" program fare, such as The Beverly Hillbillies, a popular comedy series of the early and mid-1960s.

As the executive at CBS directly in charge of the company's organizational development during the 1960s, Stanton was responsible for CBS's diversification program, which included the $11 million purchase of the New York Yankees baseball club in 1964—subsequently sold in 1973—and the publishing firm of Holt, Rinehart & Winston, Inc. in 1967. Within CBS Stanton introduced a decentralization plan that divided the company into seven units, each responsible for the use of its own profits. He also supervised the planning (including such details as elevator lights and ashtrays) of the CBS building completed in 1965.

Stanton was acutely sensitive to the criticism and possible encroachments of the FCC and worried that the Commission might become too politicized. In the wake of Vice President Spiro T. Agnew's attacks on media "bias" in the networks' news coverage of the Nixon Administration, Stanton stated in November 1969 that economic, legal and psychological methods were available to the government that were even more damaging to the media than outright censorship. "Nor is their actual employment necessary to achieve their ends," declared Stanton." To have them dangling like swords over the media can do harm even more irreparable than overt action."

Stanton retired from CBS in 1973. The same year he was named chief officer of the American Red Cross. [See JOHNSON, NIXON Volumes]

[FHM]

For further information:
Robert Metz, CBS: Reflections in a Bloodshot Eye (New York, 1975).
Erik Barnouw, The Image Empire (New York, 1970).

STENNIS, JOHN C(ORNELIUS)
b. Aug. 3, 1901; Kemper County, Miss.
Democratic Senator, Miss., 1947- .

The son of a farmer and merchant in Kemper County, Miss., Stennis received a degree from the University of Virginia law school in 1928. During the same year he won a seat in the Mississippi House of Representatives. Three years later Stennis was elected prosecutor for the state's 16th judicial district. In 1937 he became a circuit court judge.

U.S. Sen. Theodore Bilbo of Mississippi, one of the most notorious racial demagogues in the history of the South, died in 1947, and Stennis won the contest for the vacant seat. He campaigned on an agricultural platform and did not mention the race issue, thereby receiving the support of the state's liberals and black community leaders. But in the Senate he was a staunch segregationist. Stennis's maiden speech was a strong anti-civil rights statement, and in 1956 he helped to draft the "Southern Manifesto," which pledged resistance to the Supreme Court's 1954 school desegregation decision.

Stennis's views in the late 1940s and the 1950s were consistently conservative. He favored a strongly anti-Communist foreign policy and opposed most social welfare legislation. But during those years Stennis, a courtly and dignified man who was regarded as a personification of Southern gentility, acquired a reputation for fairness and personal integrity that transcended his political outlook. He won public esteem in 1954 when he served on the committee inquiring into the conduct of Sen. Joseph R. McCarthy (R, Wisc.). Believing that the maintenance of high standards of behavior in the Senate should supercede political partisanship, Stennis denounced what he regarded to be McCarthy's vituperative and reckless method of charging government officials and private citizens with Communist sympathies. In November 1954 he became the first Democrat to call for McCarthy's censure on the Senate floor. [See TRUMAN, EISENHOWER Volumes]

Stennis became a member of the Armed

Services Committee in 1955, and in 1961 he succeeded Lyndon B. Johnson [q.v.] as chairman of that panel's Preparedness Investigating Subcommittee when Johnson became vice president. During the first five months of 1962, he enhanced his reputation for rising above partisan politics when the subcommittee investigated State Department and Pentagon control of the public utterances and troop-indoctrination activities of military officers. The probe was sparked by the June 1961 reprimand of Maj. Gen. Edwin A. Walker [q.v.], a member of the John Birch Society, for allegedly indoctrinating his troops in an anti-Communist, right-wing viewpoint that condemned America's postwar foreign policy. Walker subsequently resigned from the Army, and in August 1961 Sen. Strom Thurmond (D, S.C.) [q.v.] charged that the Administration was seeking to "muzzle" anti-Communist military officers. He introduced a Senate resolution asking for an inquiry. Many observers feared that the subcommittee's investigation might create explosively emotional issues reminiscent of the McCarthy era. But, according to James K. Batten's account in The New York Times Magazine, Stennis "earned the gratitude of many apprehensive colleagues—and Thurmond's lasting disdain—for keeping a tight rein on what could have turned into a sensational witch-hunt." The panel's final report defended civilian review of the speeches and indoctrination programs of military personnel but urged that the standards of review be made more uniform.

During the early 1960s Stennis continued to compile a conservative voting record. In 1961 and 1962, according to Congressional Quarterly, he was among the three Senate Democrats who voted most frequently against Administration-sponsored bills. He opposed most New Frontier domestic programs and all civil rights measures. In 1962 Stennis led one of the three Southern teams organized in the Senate to filibuster against a bill barring the discriminatory use of literacy tests in voter registration for federal elections. During the same year he argued against a proposed constitutional amendment barring the payment of a poll tax as a requirement for voting in a federal election, asserting that "voting is a privilege; it is not a right."

Stennis's major interest was in the area of national defense, and he favored a strong military establishment. In 1961 he supported, against Administration wishes, the addition of over a half-billion dollars for the building of long-range bombers to President Kennedy's military authorization request. Stennis stated that testimony before his Preparedness Investigating Subcommittee had convinced him that manned bombers would be the country's major deterrent weapon for the foreseeable future. Two years later he opposed an effort by Sen. J. William Fulbright (D, Ark.) [q.v.] to prevent an increase in the budget of the National Aeronautics and Space Administration. Stennis contended that the military value of the space program made it indispensable to the nation's security.

In the aftermath of the investigation of Bobby Baker's [q.v.] influence-peddling activities, Stennis was chosen to head the newly created Senate Select Committee on Standards and Conduct. Two years later the Committee investigated charges that Sen. Thomas J. Dodd (D, Conn.) [q.v.] had diverted campaign funds for personal use. The panel, with Stennis's concurrence, recommended the censure of Dodd by the Senate.

Stennis had initial misgivings over the escalation of American involvement in Vietnam. However, he believed that the American commitment in Southeast Asia had to be honored and favored an intensified use of air power. In 1969 he succeeded Sen. Richard B. Russell (D, Ga.) [q.v.] as chairman of the Armed Services Committee and became the leading Senate defender of high military expenditures.

In January 1973 Stennis was shot and seriously wounded during a robbery attempt in front of his home in Washington, D.C., but he recovered rapidly. [See JOHNSON, NIXON Volumes]

[MLL]

For further information:
James K. Batten, "Why the Pentagon Pays Homage to John Cornelius Stennis," *The New York Times Magazine* (Nov. 23, 1969), pp. 44-5+.

STEVENSON, ADLAI E(WING)

b. Feb. 5, 1900; Los Angeles, Calif.
d. July 14, 1965; London, England.
Ambassador to the United Nations, January 1961-July 1965.

Born into a family whose ancestors included a vice president, an intimate of Abraham Lincoln and an associate justice of the U.S. Supreme Court, Stevenson entered politics in 1948. He had served as personal assistant to the Secretary of the Navy in World War II and as a planner of the U.N. organizational conference in 1945.

Although almost unknown when he ran for governor of Illinois in 1948, Stevenson received an unprecedented plurality in the election. As governor he successfully worked to rid the state administration of its long established corruption, improve state social services and fight for progressive laws against the opposition of a Republican-controlled legislature.

By 1952 Stevenson had emerged as a prominent figure in the Democratic Party and in July received his Party's presidential nomination in one of the few genuine drafts in American political history. Hampered by the necessity of defending Truman's unpopular domestic and foreign programs and by Eisenhower's tremendous personal popularity, Stevenson lost the election by a wide margin.

Stevenson again won the Democratic presidential nomination in 1956. Campaigning on a liberal platform that criticized the failure of Eisenhower's domestic social programs, scored the control of government by big business and denounced nuclear brinksmanship, he called for the desegregation of public schools, a moratorium on hydrogen bomb tests and an end to the draft. His unpopular stands on these issues, together with Eisenhower's continued popularity and a poorly planned campaign, again cost him the election.

Although Stevenson had announced he would not be a candidate in 1960, many in the liberal wing of the Democratic Party still hoped to nominate him once again as their Party's presidential candidate. A draft-Stevenson movement led by George Ball [q.v.], Thomas Finletter and Sen.

Mike Monroney (D, Okla.) [q.v.] assembled thousands of enthusiastic supporters at the July Democratic National Convention in Los Angeles. Massive demonstrations for Stevenson took place outside the convention and on indoor balconies on the evening of July 11. The next day Sen. Eugene McCarthy (D, Minn.) [q.v.] gave a ringing nomination speech for Stevenson, imploring the delegates, "Do not reject this man who has made us all proud to be Democrats. Do not reject this prophet without honor in his own party." Despite this support Stevenson never formally declared his candidacy and his backers failed to win sufficient delegates to prevent Sen. John F. Kennedy's nomination on the first ballot.

In the 1960 campaign Stevenson helped to bridge the gap between Kennedy and the liberal Democrats whose support was vital for victory in the anticipated close race. Many liberals, including Eleanor Roosevelt [q.v.], thought that Kennedy was devoid of commitment and too willing to compromise on moral issues, but Stevenson's support convinced the influential liberals to support the Party's candidate, if with a show of reluctance.

Throughout the campaign Stevenson anticipated that for services rendered, as well as past experience, he would be Kennedy's choice for Secretary of State. However, that office was denied him when the President-elect made it clear that, in effect, he wished to be his own Secretary of State and did not want a Secretary with a constituency of his own. Kennedy also believed that Stevenson's stands on controversial issues would increase his problems in dealing with a deeply conservative Congress. Equally important in Kennedy's refusal to offer Stevenson the office was the lack of personal rapport between the two men. According to Arthur Schlesinger, Jr. [q.v.], Kennedy found Stevenson "prissy" and "indecisive." He viewed Stevenson's refusal to announce his candidacy for the Democratic nomination as an indication of a lack of "toughness," which Kennedy sought in his appointees.

Instead of State, Kennedy appointed Stevenson as ambassador to the United Nations. The ambassadorship was a post of cabinet rank, but it was not a policymaking

office. The White House did not consult the Ambassador during the planning stages of the Cuban Bay of Pigs operation in April 1961 and misinformed him about the invasion's American character. As a consequence, Stevenson told the Security Council on April 17 that the U.S. had committed no aggression against Cuba. When it became apparent that the U.S. had been heavily involved in training and equipping the Cuban exile group, Stevenson was enraged. President Kennedy later described his failure to inform Stevenson as a "communications failure."

The Bay of Pigs episode had far-reaching repercussions on Stevenson's position. Although his personal integrity at the U.N. was not questioned, his power within the Administration's policymaking councils was limited still further. As a result of the bad advice given Kennedy on the invasion by many of his counselors, the President centralized policy-making functions in the hands of a few trusted White House advisers. Stevenson, therefore, found himself in the humiliating position of having his speeches censored by men with less foreign affairs experience than himself and being forced to support policies he had had no voice in making.

To placate the unhappy Ambassador, Kennedy included Stevenson in policy-making discussions during the Cuban missile crisis of 1962. Stevenson strongly opposed a "surgical" air strike to eliminate the missiles and recommended that Cuba be demilitarized and its integrity guaranteed by the United Nations.

A report of Stevenson's views during the crisis, written by newspaper columnist Charles Bartlett in collaboration with Stewart Alsop [q.v.] damaged relations between Kennedy and the Ambassador still further. Quoting an unnamed official, Bartlett reported that "Adlai wanted a Munich," a complete American capitulation to the Soviets on the issue of offensive missiles. Bartlett's close personal friendship with Kennedy gave the article a special significance, and the report caused a major furor. Both Kennedy and Stevenson vigorously denied the story. Kennedy, however, was slow in coming to Stevenson's defense.

On Oct. 24, 1963, while attending a United Nations Day rally in Dallas, Stevenson was heckled, hit by a sign and spat upon. He wrote to historian Arthur Schlesinger, Jr. [q.v.], "There is something ugly and frightening about the atmosphere."

After Kennedy's assassination President Lyndon B. Johnson asked Stevenson to remain at the U.N. Stevenson agreed, and during the next two years he defended American policy in Vietnam and the Dominican Republic before the increasingly unfriendly world body. In failing health, Stevenson suffered a fatal heart attack on a London street in July 1965. [See JOHNSON Volume]

[NNL]

For further information:
Kenneth S. Davis, *The Politics of Honor* (New York, 1967).

STEWART, POTTER

b. Jan. 23, 1915; Jackson, Mich.
Associate Justice, U.S. Supreme Court, 1958-   .

Born into a Cincinnati family long prominent in Ohio Republican politics, Stewart graduated from Yale University in 1937 and received a degree from Yale Law School in 1941. He moved from a Wall Street law practice to a leading Cincinnati firm in 1947. There he also served two terms as a city councilman and one as vice-mayor before President Dwight D. Eisenhower appointed him to the Sixth Circuit Court of Appeals in 1954.

Eisenhower named Stewart to the Supreme Court in October 1958. In his early years on the bench, Stewart was often considered a "swing" justice between the Court's liberal and conservative wings, casting the decisive vote particularly in civil liberties cases. He lost his pivotal position when a liberal majority developed on the Court in the early 1960s, but Stewart was still evaluated as a moderate justice, conservative on criminal rights questions, more liberal on race discrimination and free expression issues. [See EISENHOWER Volume]

Although Stewart was sensitive to First Amendment rights of free speech and association, he favored balancing individual rights against government needs. Thus he voted with the majority in a January 1961 decision to uphold a Chicago movie censorship ordinance and deny a claim that freedom of speech was an absolute right. In June 1961 he was part of a five-man majority that sustained federal laws requiring Communist action organizations to register with the Justice Department and making illegal active membership in a party advocating violent overthrow of the government.

While he opposed broad rulings that would prohibit government action in a specific area, Stewart supported more limited restraints on government power, especially to guarantee fair procedure. In two February 1961 cases Stewart's majority opinions upheld the power of the House Un-American Activities Committee to question individuals about their alleged prior membership in the Communist Party. Writing the opinion of the Court in cases decided in June 1961 and May 1962, however, Stewart overturned contempt-of-Congress convictions of witnesses who had refused to answer the Committee's questions because statutory and procedural requirements necessary for a valid conviction had not been met. Whether sustaining or invalidating government action, Stewart generally wrote narrowly based opinions limited to the facts of a case. His majority opinion in a December 1961 case, for example, voided a Florida loyalty oath law but only on the ground that this particular statute was unconstitutionally vague.

Stewart was the sole dissenter in three cases decided in June 1962 and June 1963 that held unconstitutional the use of a nondenominational prayer, the recitation of the Lord's Prayer and Bible-reading in public schools. Noncoercive, nondenominational religious exercises, Stewart argued, did not establish an official religion in violation of the First Amendment, and he suggested that prohibition of such practices denied the right to free exercise of religion without interference from government. Stewart also dissented in two May 1961 cases in which the majority sustained state laws ordering

Sunday closings of businesses against a challenge from Orthodox Jews, whose religion required them to close their stores on Saturdays. By forcing an individual to choose between his religion and economic gain, Stewart said, the state laws in this case violated the free exercise clause of the First Amendment.

Justice Stewart joined in several decisions expanding the rights of criminal defendants in the Kennedy years. In a unanimous decision Stewart wrote in March 1961 that the Fourth Amendment prohibited the use of evidence obtained by an electronic eavesdropping device that physically intruded into a defendant's home. His majority opinion in a June 1962 case held unconstitutional a California law that made drug addiction by itself, without any sale or possession of drugs, a crime. Stewart joined in a March 1963 decision requiring the states to supply free counsel to indigent defendants.

Stewart also concurred in a March 1962 Court ruling that federal courts could try legislative apportionment cases. In later cases, however, he dissented from the "one-man, one-vote" standard the majority established for congressional and state legislative districting. Stewart wrote the majority opinion in a February 1963 case reversing the breach of the peace convictions of civil rights demonstrators in South Carolina and upholding their rights to free speech, assembly and petition. During the Johnson years, however, he often voted to sustain state convictions of civil rights protesters, and he also dissented in several major criminal rights cases.

Even when they disagreed with his views, court observers praised Stewart for his clear, concise and direct opinions. Legal scholars have rated Stewart as a competent and fair-minded, if rather cautious jurist. [See JOHNSON, NIXON Volumes]

[CAB]

For further information:
Israel, Jerold H., "Potter Stewart" in Leon Friedman and Fred L. Israel, eds., *The Justices of the United States Supreme Court, 1789-1969* (New York, 1969), Vol. IV.
Barnett, Helaine M. and Kenneth Lewis, "Mr. Justice Potter Stewart," *New York University Law Review*, 40 (May, 1965), pp. 526-562.

STONE, I(SIDOR) F(EINSTEIN)
b. Dec. 24, 1907; Philadelphia, Pa.
Editor, Publisher, *I. F. Stone's Weekly*, 1953-67 *(Biweekly*, 1967-71).

Stone was raised in Haddonfield, N.J. While in high school he worked for the *Haddonfield Press* and the Camden (N.J.) *Courier-Post*. He left the University of Pennsylvania in 1927 during his junior year. A member of the Socialist Party, he worked for Norman Thomas's [*q.v.*] presidential campaign in 1928. From 1933 to 1952 Stone was associated with such liberal and left-wing publications as the *New York Post*, *The Nation*, *PM*, the *New York Star* and the *New York Daily Compass*. An opponent of American cold war policies, he supported Henry Wallace's 1948 Progressive Party presidential candidacy and in 1952 wrote *The Hidden History of the Korean War*, which questioned the prevailing view that North Korean aggression was responsible for initiating that conflict.

When the *Daily Compass* folded in 1952, Stone could not find a job because of his views. Using that newspaper's subscription list he began publishing *I. F. Stone's Weekly*, an independent newsletter, in January 1953. Among the early targets of the *Weekly* were Sen. Joseph R. McCarthy (R, Wisc.), the House Un-American Activities Committee and the practice of blacklisting radicals and alleged radicals. [See EISENHOWER Volume]

Describing himself as a democratic socialist, Stone was an independent radical who avoided affiliation with any organized political group and spoke only for himself. In his role as a journalist, he was also independent. His newsletter did not accept advertising. He did all research, reportorial and editorial work, and his wife handled the newsletter's business affairs. By 1963 his *Weekly* had a circulation of over 20,000.

Stone was best known for what his admirers believed was his iconoclastic skill in exposing the inconsistencies, mistakes and hypocrisy of public officials and his ability to detect the early signals of changes in government policies. Although he was based in Washington, his information did not come from personal contacts with highly placed sources, of which he had few, or from official briefings, from which he was often excluded. Stone's journalistic method was the diligent sifting and comparing of government publications, which were available to everyone but generally went unread.

During the early 1960s Stone, who did not endorse a presidential candidate in 1960, was disturbed by the efforts of the Kennedy Administration to combat revolutionary regimes and movements by military means. In April 1961 he warned that American support of the unsuccessful Bay of Pigs invasion and of the faltering effort of the Ngo Dinh Diem regime in South Vietnam to suppress the National Liberation Front demonstrated the Administration's failure to recognize that Communism could be fought successfully only by responding to the aspirations of the people of the world's poor nations.

Stone not only believed that efforts to suppress revolution abroad would fail but feared that they could lead to domestic repression. In April and May 1961 he noted the interest of the President and the military establishment in counterinsurgency operations to be carried out by such secret agencies as the Central Intelligence Agency. Stone observed that since such organizations functioned beyond the purview of the public, there was little to prevent them from attempting to destroy radical groups at home.

Stone felt that the Kennedy Administration recognized the danger of an unlimited nuclear arms race, but he found the President's initiatives to reduce U.S.-Soviet tensions wanting. In February 1962 he wrote that Kennedy was "racing so hard for peace that he had to increase the Eisenhower military budget by almost 25%." He also questioned the adequacy of the Administration's civil rights proposals of 1963. In September of that year he agreed with Bayard Rustin's [q.v.] contention that only a comprehensive plan to cope with technological unemployment could provide total emancipation for blacks. In an evaluation of the Kennedy Administration written in December 1963, Stone attributed the weaknesses of President Kennedy's programs to

a lack of daring. Fearing conservative reaction in Congress, Stone said, the Administration failed to press resolutely for anti-discrimination measures and peace initiatives. He concluded that in the last analysis, "Kennedy, when the tinsel was stripped away, was a conventional leader, no more than an enlightened conservative, cautious as an old man for all his youth, with a basic distrust of the people. . . ."

As opposition to the war in Vietnam mounted during the mid and late 1960s, Stone's *Weekly* became increasingly popular; by 1968 it had a circulation of 38,000. But he also incurred criticism when, after the 1967 Mideast war, he urged Israel to take a more conciliatory position towards the Arabs. In December 1971 Stone announced that he would cease publication of his newsletter at the end of the month. At the same time he became a contributing editor to the *New York Review of Books*, for which he had been writing occasionally since 1964. [See JOHNSON, NIXON Volumes]

[MLL]

For further information:
I. F. Stone, *In a Time of Torment* (New York, 1967).

SULLIVAN, WILLIAM H(EALY)
b. Oct. 12, 1922; Cranston, R.I.
Special Assistant to the Undersecretary of State for Political Affairs, March 1963-December 1964.

A career foreign service officer, William H. Sullivan spent most of his working life dealing with the Far East. During the postwar period he served in Bangkok, Calcutta and Tokyo. In 1952 he was sent to Rome and in 1955 to The Hague before resuming his Far Eastern assignments as officer-in-charge of Burma affairs for the Department of State in 1958. In 1960 Sullivan was appointed U.N. Adviser for the Bureau of Far Eastern Affairs.

While in the Bureau Sullivan was called to advise the State Department on American policy in Laos, where a civil war between American-supported Gen. Phoumi Nosovan and neutralist Prince Souvanna

Phouma threatened to bring about a Communist takeover of the country. Early in 1961 Sullivan tried to persuade the Department to accept a confederation of rightists and neutralists based on de facto regional control. His immediate superiors, however, continued to back the rightist Phoumi regime.

During the early months of the Kennedy Administration, the President decided to support a neutralist coalition government in Laos. When the Geneva Conference was convened in June 1961 to guarantee Laotian neutrality, Sullivan was named a member of the U.S. delegation. While at the conference he attracted the attention of Ambassador Averell Harriman [q.v.] who, bypassing 33 men with greater seniority, appointed Sullivan as his deputy. In this position Sullivan acted as liaison between Harriman and the National Security Council. In December 1961 Sullivan became acting head of the U.S. delegation when the Ambassador left to assume a State Department post in Washington.

During the opening months of 1962, Harriman sent Sullivan to Laos in an unsuccessful effort to persuade the intransigent Phoumi to accept a coalition government. On March 30 and 31 Sullivan made the U.S. government's first official contacts with the neutralist and Communist factions in a meeting designed to give mutual assurances of cooperation. After the formation of the neutralist government in June 1962, he continued to act as liaison between Laos and the U.S. government.

During the Johnson Administration Sullivan headed the Vietnam Working Group formed in February 1964 to plan the possible escalation of the Vietnam war. Following the Tonkin Gulf incident of August 1964, he opposed military pressure for intensive bombing of North Vietnam but accepted limited bombing. In December 1964 he was made ambassador to Laos, where Sullivan directed the U.S. secret war designed to prevent the North Vietnamese from using Laotian trials to resupply their troops in the South. Sullivan was apointed deputy assistant secretary of state for East Asia in 1969. [See JOHNSON Volume]

[EWS]

SULZBERGER, ARTHUR OCHS
b. Feb. 5, 1926; New York, N.Y.
President and Publisher, New York Times, 1963- .

The scion of the family that purchased the New York Times in 1896 and turned it into one of the world's most distinguished newspapers, Arthur Ochs Sulzberger served in the Marines during World War II, graduated from Columbia University in 1951 and began his career as a cub reporter with the Times in 1953. He joined the staff of the Milwaukee Journal in 1954 but was soon back with the Times as a reporter on the foreign news desk, then London correspondent and finally assistant to his father, Arthur Hays Sulzberger.

Sulzberger took over the newspaper in 1963 upon the death of his brother-in-law, Orville Dryfoos, who had been Times publisher since 1961. The young Sulzberger's career up to that time had been somewhat undistinguished, but upon assuming the role of Times publisher he demonstrated a talent for innovation, a methodical attention to detail, which he ascribed to his Marine Corps training, and a desire to dispel the paper's "gray lady" image. Sulzberger initiated a vast internal organizational shakeup by appointing Turner Catledge to the newly created post of executive editor, dispensing with the Times's faltering Western edition, appointing new chiefs to the Washington and New York bureaus and placing Pulitzer Prize-winning journalist A. M. Rosenthal in charge of the metropolitan news desk.

At the same time Sulzberger resisted President Kennedy's suggestion in October 1963 that controversial Times reporter David Halberstam [q.v.] be transferred from Vietnam to another assignment. Sulzberger told the President that Halberstam, whose critical reporting in Vietnam had disturbed the Administration, would remain at his post.

After the crippling newspaper strikes of 1963 and 1965, Sulzberger proposed a continuing series of talks with union leaders over the issue of automation. By 1966 the circulation of the Times had climbed to 800,000 for the weekday edition and

1,500,000 for the Sunday edition, and the *Times* had become one of only two morning newspapers published in New York City. While the *Times* operated on a slim yearly profit margin of $4 million, Sulzberger, at the expense of greater advertising revenues, continued a tradition of reprinting the complete texts of major political speeches, significant Supreme Court decisions and important congressional reports and resolutions. In 1964 the paper devoted 48 pages to publication of the Warren Commission Report on the assassination of President Kennedy. During his tenure Sulzberger also broadened coverage of religion, sports and womens' news.

[FHM]

For further reading:
Gay Talese, *The Kingdom and the Power* (New York, 1969).

SURREY, STANLEY S(TERLING)
b. Oct. 3, 1910; New York, N.Y.
Assistant Secretary of the Treasury for Tax Policy, February 1961-January 1969.

A graduate of Columbia Law School, Stanley Surrey worked for the National Recovery Administration and the National Labor Relations Board before entering the Treasury Department during World War II. From 1949 to 1961 he taught at Harvard Law School, where he established a reputation as a leading tax expert and a strong advocate of tax reform. After heading a pre-inaugural task force on tax policy for President-elect Kennedy, Surrey was appointed assistant secretary of the treasury in February 1961.

Because of his views on tax reform, particularly an article he wrote entitled, "The Congress and the Tax Lobbyist—How Special Tax Provisions Get Enacted," Surrey's nomination encountered difficulty at his confirmation hearings before the Senate Finance Committee. The Committee's chairman, Sen. Harry Flood Byrd (D, Va.) [q.v.], accused Surrey of not having "a very high opinion of Congress," and the Committee's conservative majority grilled

Surrey at length about his past proposals for sweeping tax revisions. Surrey was confirmed only after conservative Secretary of the Treasury C. Douglas Dillon [q.v.] promised that he, not Surrey, would have chief responsibility for tax policy.

Nevertheless, Surrey guided the preparatory staff work on the Kennedy tax program and inspired many of its reform proposals, although several of his previous recommendations, such as taxing the interest earned on government bonds, were not part of that program. Withholding taxes at the source of interest and dividend income was a long-standing proposal of Surrey's and a major element of Kennedy's 1961-62 tax reform package.

Withholding at the source was merely a change in the method of collection to curb tax evasion, but Surrey estimated that $600 million annually was lost to the Treasury because 9% of dividend income and 35% of interest income went unreported. Congress eliminated the withholding reform from the Revenue Act of 1962, however, following a massive lobbying campaign against it by savings and loan associations. Congress also rejected another reform favored by Surrey, the repeal of the $50 exemption and 4% credit that stockholders received on their dividend income. Surrey believed the exemption and credit were merely mechanisms "to reduce the impact of tax rates on certain middle and upper-bracket taxpayers."

The Administration sacrificed such reforms in 1962 in order to win passage of the 7% investment tax credit, which Surrey's pre-inaugural task force had advocated in January 1961. The credit was intended to spur modernization of plant and equipment, create jobs and speed economic growth.

Surrey led the Administration's fight against the so-called Keogh Plan to permit self-employed individuals to set up tax-sheltered retirement funds. Surrey testified in July 1961 that the plan would cost the Treasury $358 million annually and "create many inequities and unjustifiable differences in tax treatment." The measure passed the Congress in September 1962.

Long an advocate of combining tax reforms with an across-the-board reduction in tax rates, Surrey played an important role in convincing Secretary Dillon and President Kennedy to couple the 1963 request for $13.6 billion in tax cuts intended to stimulate the economy with $3.3 billion in tax reforms as well. The magazine *Nation's Business* called Surrey "the principal architect" of the tax cut-tax reform package. Limiting medical and charitable deductions, repealing the special exclusion and credit for dividend income and lengthening the holding period for capital gains were among the reforms put forth by the Administration to raise revenue and reduce the inequities of the tax system. As in 1962, however, the Administration ultimately sacrificed the reform part of the package in order to win approval from Congress for an $11 billion tax cut.

Surrey remained in his Treasury post throughout the Johnson Administration, following which he returned to teach at Harvard Law School. [See JOHNSON Volume]

[TO]

SWIDLER, JOSEPH C(HARLES)
b. Jan. 28, 1907; Chicago, Ill.
Chairman, Federal Power Commission, September 1961-February 1966.

A graduate of the University of Chicago Law School, Joseph Swidler left private law practice to join the legal staff of the Department of the Interior when President Franklin D. Roosevelt took office in 1933. The following year Swidler left to become an attorney for the newly formed Tennessee Valley Authority (TVA), a public power corporation created by Congress for the purposes of flood control and the generation of cheap hydroelectric power in the depressed Tennessee River basin. Appointed general counsel in 1945, Swidler remained with the TVA until 1957, when he returned to private law practice.

President Kennedy's nomination of Swidler to the Federal Power Commission (FPC) in January 1961 was greeted with apprehension by representatives of private power companies and the oil and gas industry. In hearings on his nomination before the Senate Commerce Committee in April,

Swidler stated that he did not favor a universal public power system. He said competition between public and private systems was best for the public, and he did not see "any likelihood of any great change in the balance." The Senate confirmed Swidler's appointment in June, and in September he was installed as FPC chairman.

In his study of federal regulatory agencies commissioned by President Kennedy, Dean James M. Landis [*q.v.*] of the Harvard Law School reported that the FPC was "an outstanding example . . . of breakdown in the administrative process." Beginning in November 1961 Swidler expedited the disposal of a large backlog of FPC rate regulation cases. By January 1963 the Commission reported that it had ordered refunds of $380 million to consumers since Swidler's taking office.

Industry spokesman displayed greater satisfaction with Swidler's tenure than had earlier been anticipated. *Business Week* lauded Swidler in September 1963 as a "model New Frontier regulator" who "leans toward negotiation and compromise." The magazine reported that power companies were "pleasantly surprised" to find Swidler more interested in "cheap kilowatts than in crusading for more public power." FPC Commissioner Howard V. Morgan [*q.v.*], however, criticized Swidler in January 1963 for being "soft" on private electrical utilities and too responsive to presidential pressure. Swidler vigorously defended his Commission's record against Morgan's charges, saying that he considered himself "a consumer's man second to none." Swidler left the FPC chairmanship in February 1966 to practice law in Washington, D.C.

[TO]

SYLVESTER, ARTHUR
b. Oct. 21, 1901; Montclair, N.J.
Assistant Secretary of Defense for Public Affairs, January 1961-January 1967.

Prior to becoming assistant secretary of defense for public affairs in January 1961, Arthur Sylvester was Washington reporter and bureau chief of the *Newark Evening News*.

As chief press officer Sylvester acted not only as liaison between the press and the military but also as Secretary of Defense Robert S. McNamara's [q.v.] personal spokesman. In this role Sylvester was often asked to publicize opinions McNamara was reluctant to express personally.

Sylvester's abrasive personality and his advocacy of government "management of the news" made him a center of controversy throughout the Kennedy years. His first major clash with the press came as a result of the Administration's handling of reporters during the Cuban missile crisis in October 1962. During the crisis Sylvester bore the brunt of accusations that the Administration deliberately lied to newsmen by denying that a military alert had been ordered or that emergency measures had been set in motion against Cuba. The press was particularly angered by an Oct. 24 White House memorandum suggesting guidelines on the type of news that should be kept from the public and an Oct. 27 order directing Pentagon officials to clear all press releases with Sylvester.

While admitting that the press had difficulty in covering the story, Sylvester claimed that the Administration had never deliberately lied to the press. However, Sylvester created a furor when, in an informal Oct. 30 interview with a *Washington Star* reporter, he allegedly maintained that "the generation of news by the government becomes one weapon in a strained situation; the results in my opinion justify the means." Despite requests from the White House that Sylvester release a letter explaining his choice of language and emphasizing his own and his Department's abhorrence of censorship, Sylvester continued to advance this opinion. The press secretary reiterated his views in a speech before the Deadline Club in New York on Dec. 6, arguing, "It's inherent in government's right . . . to lie to save itself when it's going up into nuclear war."

Because of the furor aroused by Sylvester's comments and press complaints that it had not been given the full missile crisis story, the House government information subcommittee opened hearings on the subject in March 1963. At the March 25 session Sylvester asserted that his "right to lie" remark had been a "shorthand answer" at a dinner he thought would be unreported. He maintained that the government did not have the right to lie to the American people but that it did have a right to try to mislead the enemy in time of crisis.

During the Johnson Administration Sylvester continued to be a central figure in the growing controversy over the Administration's "credibility gap" growing out of the Vietnam war. In an interview given reporters in Saigon on July 17, 1965, Sylvester allegedly stated that American newsmen should be "handmaidens" of the government.

Sylvester resigned from the Defense Department in January 1967 for personal reasons. [See JOHNSON Volume]

[EWS]

SYMINGTON, (WILLIAM) STUART
b. June 26, 1901; Amherst, Mass.
Democratic Senator, Mo., 1953-   .

Long a proponent of military preparedness, Stuart Symington was a major spokesman for the Defense Department and particularly for Air Force interests on Capitol Hill throughout the early 1960s. A descendant of a distinguished Southern family, Symington attended Yale University after serving in World War I. Following his graduation in 1923 he began a successful business career that earned him the reputation of being a "doctor of ailing corporations" because of his ability to redevelop foundering enterprises and to deal with labor problems.

During the Truman Administration Symington held important appointed posts in several federal agencies. From 1946 to 1950 he served as Secretary of the Air Force. Believing that the U.S. had to act from a position of military superiority against the expansionist policies of the Soviet Union, Symington became a leading proponent of increased defense spending. Symington particularly advocated the development of a large nuclear equipped Air Force as the cornerstone of a modern defense system. In 1950, shortly before the

Korean war, Symington resigned to protest a series of economy-minded armament reductions. [See TRUMAN Volume]

Symington was elected to the Senate from Missouri in 1952. While in the upper chamber he supported many domestic social welfare proposals but was primarily known as a "single issue man" devoted to protecting the interests of the Defense Department and the Air Force. He opposed Eisenhower Administration defense cuts and pushed for increased spending on missile development and satellite research in light of the Soviet superiority he believed existed in these fields. In 1960 Symington entered the campaign for the Democratic presidential nomination, running on a platform that attacked the defense policies of the Eisenhower Administration. He eventually threw his support behind the unsuccessful candidacy of Lyndon Johnson [q.v.] at the Los Angeles convention. [See EISENHOWER Volume]

In 1962 Symington was a member of the Special Preparedness Investigation Subcommittee probing charges that military education programs were "soft on Communism" and that military officers were being "muzzled" by White House and State Department officials. The Senator endorsed the subcommittee report that found troop information and education programs generally adequate but declared the operation of the speech review system capricious and criticized the practice of State Department review of military officers' statements before congressional committees. One year later Symington supported the development of the controversial TFX multi-service fighter/bomber and opposed hearings probing the granting of TFX contracts. Symington believed the investigation lowered the morale of the armed forces and was, therefore, "detrimental" to U.S. security.

During 1962 and 1963 Symington headed the Armed Services National Stockpile and Naval Petroleum Reserves Subcommittee's investigation of stockpiling practices during the Eisenhower Administration. Critics alleged that officials of that Administration had established stockpiling objectives far in excess of national require-

ments in order to aid specific industries. Some companies had also been permitted to defer the delivery of materials when a sharp increase in price made it more profitable to sell goods on the open market. After considerable partisan debate the Democrats on the subcommittee in September 1963 issued a draft report highly critical of stockpiling practices. The draft also recommended various reforms, including the reduction of surpluses and the provision that surpluses not be used to influence domestic prices, which were embodied in a bill that Symington submitted to the Senate in 1964. No action was taken on the measure.

Although an early supporter of the Vietnam war, Symington became a critic of the conflict after 1967. Believing that Congress had lost control of foreign policy and that this had led to the overextension of American defense and economic commitments throughout the world, Symington campaigned for greater congressional power over foreign policy in the early 1970s. [See JOHNSON, NIXON Volumes]

[EWS]

TALMADGE, HERMAN E(UGENE)
b. Aug. 9, 1913; McRae, Ga.
Democratic Senator, Ga., 1957-   .

Herman Talmadge was the son of Eugene Talmadge, a fiery white supremacist and anti-New Deal orator who was elected governor of Georgia four times in the 1930s and 1940s by appealing to the poor white farmers of the predominantly rural state. Herman Talmadge managed his father's gubernatorial campaigns of 1940 and 1946. When Eugene died a month after winning the 1946 election, Herman was chosen in a special poll to complete the term. He was reelected for a full four-year term in 1950.

Although less flamboyant than his father, the younger Talmadge also played strongly upon the racial fears of rural whites, asserting in 1952 that the black voter represented a threat "to our homes, our children, our institutions, our daily lives, our fortunes." Unlike his father, however, he made a serious effort to improve education and to attract industry to the state.

In 1956 Talmadge won a seat in the U.S. Senate by defeating longtime incumbent Walter F. George in the Democratic primary. Although his family name was associated with political demagoguery, Talmadge quickly gained a reputation among his fellow-senators as an intelligent and well-informed legislator. [See EISENHOWER Volume]

According to *Congressional Quarterly*, Talmadge was one of the nine leading Senate Democratic opponents of Administration bills during each year of John F. Kennedy's presidency and was the most consistent Southern Democratic supporter of the upper house's conservative coalition in 1963.

Talmadge opposed every Administration-sponsored civil rights measure during the early 1960s. In March 1962, during a debate over a bill to bar arbitrary use of literacy tests against blacks seeking to vote in federal elections, Talmadge asserted that Congress was "without constitutional power to prescribe qualifications for electors." During the summer of 1963 he denounced Secretary of Defense Robert S. McNamara's [*q.v.*] directive permitting base commanders to declare segregated civilian facilities off-limits, insisting that by law the civilian establishments outside of military bases were beyond the concern of the military.

Talmadge generally took positions favorable to the interests of private enterprise. In April 1961 he supported an amendment to exempt employees in cotton ginning, a major activity in Georgia, from the provisions of a minimum wage bill. In June 1962 Talmadge argued on the Senate floor for a Renegotiation Act amendment permitting defense contractors to appeal in circuit court the federal Renegotiation Board's rulings on excessive profits. As a member of the Senate Finance Committee, he opposed the Administration's efforts in 1962 to tighten expense account deductions for businesses.

Talmadge was widely respected in Congress as a skilled legislative craftsman, and in 1963 he and Sen. Hubert H. Humphrey (D, Minn.) [*q.v.*], members of the Agriculture and Forestry Committee, introduced a bill providing for abandonment of the complex cotton subsidy system in favor of a single price for U.S. cotton at approximately the world-market level. The bill was praised by the Administration as coming closer to its objectives than other proposed measures, and support for the bill cut across liberal-conservative lines.

Talmadge continued to vote against civil rights measures during the mid and late 1960s, but he became less vociferous in his opposition to integration. Initially supporting the war in Vietnam, in 1969 he questioned the purpose of fighting a war that the government, in his view, was not attempting to win. Two years later he urged the withdrawal of American troops from Indochina. In 1971 Talmadge became chairman of the Agriculture and Forestry Committee and two years later was appointed to the Senate Select Committee to Investigate Presidential Campaign Activities, popularly known as the Watergate Committee. [See JOHNSON, NIXON Volumes]

[MLL]

TAWES, J(OHN) MILLARD
b. April 8, 1894; Crisfield, Md.
Governor, Md., 1959-67.

Governor of Maryland during the turbulent 1960s, when racial clashes rocked that state, Tawes earned a reputation as a moderate on civil rights issues. Born and raised in Crisfield, Md., in the conservative Eastern Shore district of the state, Tawes began his business career in the lumbering and canning businesses founded and owned by his father. He entered politics in 1930, when he was elected clerk of the court of Somerset County. From 1938 to 1947 and again from 1950 to 1958 he served as state comptroller. In 1959 Tawes won the gubernatorial election by the largest vote margin in Maryland history.

During his administration Tawes successfully sponsored highway and auto safety legislation, banned slot machines, improved school facilities and teachers' salaries and backed measures approving Maryland's participation in the metropolitan Washington transit authority. However, his successive attempts at legislative reapportionment failed to satisfy the courts and were declared unconstitutional. On the national level Tawes supported the Kennedy Administration's depressed-area bill, which offered aid to the state's western Appalachia region.

In June 1963 the Eastern Shore community of Cambridge, Md., was the scene of racial clashes when local blacks attempted to integrate public accommodations. After rioting in the black district and an attempt by whites to invade the area, Tawes ordered the National Guard into Cambridge. In an effort to end tension he proposed that the Cambridge City Council adopt an ordinance against discrimination in public accommodations in return for a promise by black leaders not to conduct demonstrations for a year. His plan was rejected by the Cambridge Nonviolent Action Committee, which led the integration campaign.

Late in July Tawes appealed to all Maryland citizens to "appreciate the magnitude of the social revolution now underway" among blacks and warned that Maryland faced years of racial strife unless all citizens acted to "satisfy the legitimate pleas" of blacks for equality. Behind the scenes Tawes worked for a statewide public accommodations law. The statute, barring discrimination against blacks in hotels, motels and restaurants that did not serve liquor, was passed in May 1964. Tawes did not seek reelection in 1966. From 1969 to 1971 he served as secretary of the Maryland Department of Natural Resources.

[EWS]

TAYLOR, MAXWELL D(AVENPORT)
b. Aug. 26, 1901; Keytesville, Mo.
Military Representative of the President, July 1961-October 1962; Chairman of the Joint Chiefs of Staff, October 1962-June 1964.

Taylor graduated with the fourth highest average in the West Point class of 1922. Soon after Pearl Harbor, Taylor helped organize the 82nd Airborne Division, later commanding its artillery in the Sicilian and Italian campaigns. He was in command of the 101st Airborne by D-Day and parachuted with the division into Normandy, becoming the first American general to fight on French soil during the war. Following the war Taylor was superintendent of West Point for three years and then served in command and staff positions in Europe, the Far East and in Washington before being named Army Chief of Staff in 1955. As the Army's principal spokesman on defense strategy, Taylor vigorously opposed the Eisenhower Administration's reliance on massive nuclear retaliation, arguing that there was a continuing need for strong ground forces capable of fighting a conventional war. Taylor forcefully took his case to the public in his book *The Uncertain Trumpet*, published in 1959 after he retired from the Army. [See EISENHOWER Volume]

John Kennedy was impressed by *The Uncertain Trumpet* and used its arguments to support his own attacks on the Eisenhower Administration's defense policies during the 1960 presidential campaign. When the exile invasion of Cuba sponsored by the Central Intelligence Agency was crushed at the Bay of Pigs, Kennedy asked Taylor to lead an investigation of the CIA's role in the fiasco and to evaluate America's capability for conducting unconventional warfare. The central conclusion of the Taylor report was that the Defense Department, rather than the CIA, should be responsible for major paramilitary operations.

On June 26 Kennedy named Taylor to a newly created White House post as military representative of the President. The post was an interim appointment until there was an opportunity to name Taylor chairman of the Joint Chiefs of Staff. Kennedy was anxious to have a source of independent military advice from a professional detached from the inter-service rivalries of the Pentagon. In his new position, Taylor undertook a study for the President of psychological warfare and led a special committee on counterinsurgency.

Taylor's most important assignment was to lead a special mission to South Vietnam in the wake of major Communist victories in the autumn of 1961 to assess the military situation and recommend how the U.S. should respond. Although a general, Taylor was put in charge of the mission as a concession to those within the Administration who feared direct U.S. military involvement might be advocated by the mission's other leading figure, White House aide Walt W. Rostow [q.v.]. (Taylor was thought to be wary of committing U.S. troops to a land war in Asia.) The mission left Washington Oct. 15, arriving in Saigon Oct. 18. Taylor conferred with the South Vietnamese President Ngo Dinh Diem, South Vietnamese generals and U.S. military advisers and inspected South Vietnamese units in the field before leaving Oct. 25 for talks with Thai leaders in Bangkok. Taylor flew on to Manila Oct. 30, where he wrote his report for the President.

Although it was kept secret at the time, on his return to Washington Nov. 3 Taylor recommended—to the surprise of President Kennedy—sending some 8,000 U.S. combat troops to Vietnam. Taylor told Kennedy the troops were necessary to reassure Diem of the American commitment and to provide the South Vietnamese with a reserve force for emergencies. He acknowledged that it would be difficult to resist pressure for reinforcements once U.S. troops committed American prestige to the war and conceded the danger of backing into a major war, but he concluded U.S. ground troops were necessary to deter the Communists from escalating the conflict. Secretary of Defense Robert McNamara [q.v.] backed Taylor's recommendation. Resistance from the State Department, however, was strong. A compromise devised by McNamara emerged on Nov. 11: the U.S. would increase military aid, send more military advisers and helicopter pilots, and pressure Diem to carry out political reforms—all measures suggested in the Taylor-Rostow report. As a concession to Taylor's request for combat forces, the Pentagon was directed to prepare a plan for sending in troops on a contingency basis. The Administration's public position was that Taylor had recommended against the use of American combat troops. Nevertheless, the Taylor mission and the decisions made in late 1961, David Halberstam wrote in *The Best and the Brightest*, profoundly "changed and escalated the American commitment to Vietnam."

Taylor continued to advise the President on Laos, Vietnam, Berlin and other foreign policy crises during early 1962, until Kennedy appointed him July 20 to serve as chairman of the Joint Chiefs of Staff to replace Gen. Lyman L. Lemnitzer [q.v.], who was named commander of NATO forces in Europe. After denying in testimony before the Senate Armed Services Committee that his appointment signaled any American reluctance to use nuclear weapons in the defense of Europe, Taylor was approved unanimously by the Senate Aug. 8. Taylor returned to South Vietnam Sept. 10-13 to review the military situation. Meeting newsmen in Manila Sept. 19, he declared that "the Vietnamese are on the road to victory."

Taylor was a major participant in the crucial White House meetings during the Cuban missile crisis of October 1962, advocating a strong response to eliminate Soviet missiles from the island. Taylor also played an active role in the deployment of federal troops to protect James Meredith [q.v.] when he became the first Negro to openly register at the University of Mississippi in the fall of 1963.

During his term as chairman of the joint chiefs, Taylor loyally followed Administration policies in contrast to the other joint chiefs who were often at odds with President Kennedy's policies. He was the only member of the JCS to join the Administration in opposing the development of the RS-70 manned-bomber program. Taylor's support proved essential when the Administration sought Senate ratification of the nuclear test ban treaty with the Soviet Union. His testimony before the Preparedness Subcommittee of the Senate Armed Services Committee and the Senate Foreign Relations Committee on Aug. 14 and 15, 1963 that the treaty would not endanger U.S. security and his denial that the Pentagon had been dragooned into supporting the test ban effectively rebutted the arguments of the treaty's most vociferous opponents.

Reports that the Diem government's repression of the Buddhists was hampering the war effort prompted Kennedy to send Taylor and Defense Secretary McNamara on another mission to Vietnam in September 1963. On the surface, their joint report to the President Oct. 2 continued to express optimism about the military effort and predicted a victory over the Communists by 1965. McNamara, however, reportedly had begun to question Taylor's sanguine confidence that the political situation had not affected the war effort. As a result of Diem's inept handling of the Buddhist crisis, the Administration—with Taylor's concurrence—acquiesced in the military coup that overthrew the Diem regime at the beginning of November.

Taylor continued to serve as chairman of the joint chiefs after Kennedy's assassination until June 1964 when President Johnson appointed him ambassador to South Vietnam, a post he filled until July 1965. [See JOHNSON Volume]

[EWK]

For further information:
David Halberstam, *The Best and the Brightest* (New York, 1972)
"Maxwell Taylor," *Current Biography Yearbook, 1961* (New York, 1962), pp. 444-447.

TELLER, EDWARD

b. Jan. 15, 1908, Budapest, Hungary.
Associate Director, Lawrence Livermore Laboratory, Atomic Energy Commission, 1954-   .

After completing his doctorate in physical chemistry at the University of Leipzig in 1930, Teller studied with Niels Bohr, the distinguished Danish physicist. He left Germany when the Nazis came to power and became an American citizen in 1941. During World War II Teller worked on the Manhattan Project, which developed the atomic bomb, and from 1949 to 1951 he was an assistant director of the science laboratory at Los Alamos, N.M. During the 1950s he taught physics at the University of California. In 1954 he became an associate director of the Atomic Energy Commission's (AEC) Lawrence Livermore Laboratory in Livermore, Calif.

During the 1950s Teller became a leading scientific spokesman for the maintenance of U.S. atomic weapons superiority. He believed that American supremacy was the only means of countering what he viewed as an aggressive Soviet arms policy. Described by *Newsweek* as "the principal architect of the H-bomb," Teller was a lead-

ing advocate of that weapon's development. In the 1954 AEC security hearings, he testified against granting J. Robert Oppenheimer a security clearance, claiming that Oppenheimer's opposition to the H-bomb project had delayed its development. [See EISENHOWER Volume]

Teller had opposed the three-year moratorium on atomic testing that ended in September 1961 when the Soviet Union resumed atmospheric explosions, and he favored the renewed U.S. testing, which began later that month. Calling nuclear test ban negotiations "dangerous," he said they "have helped the Soviets" and "have impeded our own testing."

During the August 1963 Senate hearings on the nuclear test ban treaty, Teller was the most influential scientist to testify against ratification. His principal objection was to the ban's prohibition of atmospheric tests, which were necessary for the further development of anti-ballistic missiles (ABMs). Teller feared that the Soviets led in ABM production and that the treaty might enable them to increase that lead. Warning that current detection techniques would be ineffective for policing the agreement, Teller also believed that the treaty would inhibit the military's ability to respond in case of war since it stipulated that atomic weapons could be used only three months after repudiation of the agreement. "You will have given away the future safety of our country and increased the dangers of war," he said.

Teller's views were rejected by Gen. Maxwell Taylor [*q.v.*], John A. McCone [*q.v.*], Glenn Seaborg [*q.v.*] and other military and government officials who testified in support of the treaty. Taylor said that despite Soviet leads in multi-megaton bombs and anti-missile defenses, the treaty would make it difficult for the Soviet Union to reach the U.S. level of overall nuclear capability. President Kennedy rebutted many of Teller's objections in a news conference in late August and signed the treaty in October.

In addition to his call for atomic superiority, Teller believed that the threat of international Communism required an aggressive American stance in other areas. In

March 1962 he told a House Science and Astronautics Committee that U.S. security demanded control of the moon. He urged the establishment of a U.S. colony and the development of a nuclear reactor there. He was also a founding member of the Citizens Committee for a Free Cuba, a group formed in May 1963 that warned that "Castro-Communist infiltration of Latin America" threatened "democratic forces" throughout the hemisphere.

[MDB]

For further information:
Robert Gilpin, *American Scientists and Nuclear Weapons Policy* (Princeton, 1962).

TERRY, LUTHER L(EONIDAS)
b. Sept. 15, 1911; Red Level, Ala.
Surgeon General, April 1961-
September 1965.

Dr. Luther L. Terry, a medical researcher and specialist in hypertension, was named Surgeon General in the spring of 1961. The post was traditionally nonpolitical, but before his designation Terry gave assurances to Kennedy that he would not oppose the Administration's bill linking medical care for the aged to the Social Security system.

As head of the Public Health Service (PHS), the leading federal agency in the field, Terry's views commanded wide attention. Shortly after he assumed his new post, Terry became concerned with the hazards of radioactive fallout from aboveground nuclear testing. The Soviet Union had resumed testing in September 1961, and the U.S. followed suit in April 1962. PHS officials at first denied that there was any immediate danger from test-produced radiation, but a PHS report issued in October 1961 suggested that "the extra radiation caused by the Soviet tests will add to the risk of genetic effects in succeeding generations and possibly to the risk of health to some people in the United States."

In May 1962 Terry announced a stepped up PHS program to monitor the level of radioactive iodine-131 and strontium-90 in the U.S. milk supply. In June Terry received a report recommending that the U.S. embark immediately on a program to control radioactive contamination of the environment. Speaking before the American Medical Association that month, Terry argued that a health defense program was urgently needed not only to ensure survival but also victory in the event of a nuclear war. In August 1963 the U.S. and the Soviet Union signed a treaty prohibiting aboveground nuclear testing, and public concern about radiation hazards subsided.

As Surgeon General, Terry sought to advance widespread immunization against polio. He announced in August 1961 that an American firm had been licensed to manufacture the new Sabin oral polio vaccine. At the same time he stressed that vaccination with the older and somewhat less effective Salk vaccine should continue as it was "the only weapon we have today to provide protection against all three types of polio." A year later Terry reported that 13 adults were stricken with polio shortly after they had taken the Sabin Type III vaccine. Terry immediately warned against further use of Sabin Type III for adults and appointed a committee to study the drug's safety. The Sabine vaccine was eventually cleared for use.

Terry was a strong advocate of fluoridation, which he said was the safest and most effective method of protection against tooth decay. Despite strong criticism from the far right, he supported local government efforts to institute water fluoridation programs. Terry was also active in the movement for the mass innoculation of infants against measles and in March 1963 announced the PHS would license the manufacture of an anti-measles vaccine.

In the fall of 1962 Terry appointed a committee to study the effects of smoking on health. The report, released in January 1964, linked smoking to lung cancer, heart disease and various respiratory ailments. Cigarette manufacturers and some congressmen from tobacco-growing states argued that the findings were inaccurate or misleading because they were based on limited research. The report led to legislation requiring cigarette packages and advertisements to carry a warning against the dangers of smoking. In the fall of 1965 Terry left his post as Surgeon General to become vice president for medical affairs at the University of Pennsylvania. [See JOHNSON Volume]

[JLW]

THOMAS, ALBERT (LANGSTON)

b. April 12, 1898; Nacogdoches County, Tex.
d. Feb. 15, 1966; Washington, D.C.
Democratic Representative, Tex., 1937-66.

Thomas was first elected to Congress in 1936. His district included Houston, and he derived much of his electoral support from blacks, Mexican-Americans and the organized labor movement of that city. Thomas compiled a voting record in the House of Representatives that was consistently moderate to liberal, in contrast to the conservative positions of most of his fellow-Texans on Capitol Hill.

According to *Congressional Quarterly*, Thomas supported the Kennedy Administration on 89%, 83% and 80% of the key roll-call votes in 1961, 1962 and 1963, respectively. In each of those years he was among the nine Southern Democratic representatives who voted most consistently against the Southern Democrat-Republican conservative coalition.

Thomas was not widely known outside of Texas, but as the fourth-ranking member of the House Appropriations Committee he wielded considerable power in Congress. Despite his generally liberal record he often used his position on the Appropriations Committee to trim expenditures and increase congressional control over spending. In September 1961 he guided through the House an appropriations bill that, over Senate objections, required annual appropriations and thereby barred Treasury borrowing in advance of legislative funding for a number of social welfare programs.

Thomas's major source of power was his chairmanship of the Independent Offices Subcommittee of the Appropriations Committee. The subcommittee was in charge of funds for the Atomic Energy Commission, the National Aeronautics and Space Administration (NASA) and many other agencies. Thomas's most significant activity as chairman during the Kennedy presidency was his key role in NASA's decision of September 1961 to build its Manned Spacecraft Center near Houston. The location of the center was widely criticized because of its distance from NASA's rocket launching site at Cape Canaveral, Florida. But the center was expected to bring an industrial boom to the area in which it was situated, and, as head of the Independent Offices Subcommittee, Thomas could influence the selection of the site because he controlled NASA's funding. According to the authors of a history of the space program, *Journey into Tranquility*, NASA officials privately acknowledged, several years after the center was constructed, that the Congressman's views played a major role in bringing it to the Houston area.

Thomas was still in Congress when he died in February 1966. His wife won a special election the following month to fill his seat.

[MLL]

THOMAS, NORMAN (MATTOON)

b. Nov. 20, 1884; Marion, Ohio.
d. Dec. 19, 1968; Huntington, N.Y.
Peace and civil rights advocate.

Thomas studied at the Union Theological Seminary, where he was influenced by the writings of Dr. Walter Rauschenbusch, whose theology stressed the social responsibility of the Protestant churches. In 1911 Thomas received a bachelor of divinity degree and became pastor of the East Harlem Presbyterian Church in New York City. Five years later he joined the Fellowship of Reconciliation, a religious pacifist group. An opponent of American involvement in World War I, he assisted Roger N. Baldwin in founding the National Civil Liberties Bureau (later known as the American Civil Liberties Union) for the purpose of aiding conscientious objectors.

Thomas joined the Socialist Party in 1918 and during the same year abandoned his religious activity. During the 1920s he emerged as the Party's leader, succeeding Eugene V. Debs. Thomas headed the party's national ticket in every presidential election from 1928 through 1948. He received his greatest support in 1932, polling 844,000 votes. Fearing the anti-democratic consequences of international conflict in American domestic life, Thomas opposed U.S. entry into World War II. After Pearl Harbor he gave the war effort qualified support.

In 1950 Thomas urged the party to abandon its increasingly ineffectual electoral efforts. Although the Socialists fielded national tickets in 1952 and 1956, Thomas supported the Democratic candidacy of Adlai E. Stevenson in both elections. While believing in the moral superiority of the West over the Communist bloc, Thomas asserted in the 1950s that peaceful coexistence on the military level was necessary to avoid thermonuclear annihilation. In 1957 he was a founder of the Committee for a Sane Nuclear Policy (SANE). [See TRUMAN, EISENHOWER Volumes]

By 1960 Thomas was held in high regard by most liberals and even some conservatives. Part of the reason was the moderate character of his socialism. He had always favored the gradual development of a "cooperative commonwealth" within the framework of democratic constitutionalism, opposed violent revolution and rejected the doctrines of class conflict and the dictatorship of the proletariat. But the esteem in which Thomas was held also derived from belief in his personal integrity. Furthermore, the compassion for the weak and the moral concerns that formed the foundation of his views earned him wide admiration, if not agreement with his ideas.

Thomas had given up his Socialist Party posts by the early 1960s but remained the unofficial spokesman for the organization. However, the party had little influence in the 1960s, and Thomas's major activities during that period focused on the causes of peace and civil rights.

In 1960, the first presidential election year in which the Socialist Party did not field a national ticket, Thomas favored Stevenson for the Democratic nomination.

He supported the candidacy of Sen. John F. Kennedy only reluctantly, believing it did not offer a clear alternative to Republican policies.

During 1960 and 1961 he joined other national leaders of SANE in an effort to end Communist infiltration of the organization's New York City chapter. Thomas, who favored mutual arms control agreements but not unilateral American disarmament, believed that peace advocates should condemn Soviet as well as American militarism.

In 1962 Thomas was a founder of Turn Toward Peace, a league of peace and civic organizations dedicated to promoting initial American steps towards disarmament in the hope that such measures would elicit similar actions from the Soviet Union. During the same year Thomas criticized President Kennedy's response to the presence of Soviet missiles in Cuba, asserting that brinkmanship would eventually produce a thermonuclear war.

A longtime supporter of equal rights for blacks, Thomas testified in July 1963 before a House Judiciary subcommittee on behalf of President Kennedy's anti-discrimination proposals. Appearing as a spokesman for the Socialist Party, he said that the measures were "a step in the right direction. . . . But they do not go far enough." Fearing that automation would deprive unskilled blacks of jobs, he believed that civil rights legislation alone would be meaningless without government action to ensure full employment.

Favorably impressed by President Lyndon B. Johnson's [q.v.] civil rights and poverty programs and regarding Sen. Barry M. Goldwater (R, Ariz.) [q.v.] as a "prophet of war," Thomas supported the incumbent in the 1964 presidential race. But beginning in 1965 he was harshly critical of the Administration's Vietnam policies. He devoted his remaining years to working for the withdrawal of American forces from Indochina. In February 1967 it was revealed that the Institute for International Labor Research, with which Thomas had been affiliated, had received CIA funds. Thomas denied any knowledge of CIA financial support. In the fall of 1967 Thomas suffered a stroke; he died in a nursing home on Dec. 19, 1968. [See JOHNSON Volume]

[MLL]

For further information:
Harry Fleischman, *Norman Thomas—A Biography: 1884-1968* (New York, 1969).
Bernard K. Johnpoll, *Pacifist's Progress: Norman Thomas and the Decline of American Socialism* (Chicago, 1970).

THOMPSON, FRANK, JR.
b. July 16, 1918; Trenton, N.J.
Democratic Representative, N.J., 1955-

The son of a newspaperman and nephew of former New Jersey Democratic leader Crawford Jamieson, Thompson was elected to the state Assembly in 1949, the year after his admission to the bar, and to Congress as a self-styled "New Deal-Fair Deal Democrat of the Adlai Stevenson school" in 1954. Assigned to the Education and Labor Committee, Thompson was a principal sponsor of all major education acts over the next two decades. He also unsuccessfully attempted to include a cultural plank in the 1956 Democratic national platform. A strong advocate of government aid to the arts, he sponsored a 1958 House bill which provided funds for a cultural center in Washington. In 1959 Thompson co-founded the Democratic Study Group, which sought to develop a liberal legislative program and reform what it considered "antiquated and obstructive" House procedures, including the seniority system. In January 1959 Thompson sponsored a $1.1 billion educational appropriation bill drafted by the National Education Association. The Senate and House passed different versions of the bill in February and May 1960, respectively, but the House Rules Committee refused to authorize a House-Senate conference, and Congress adjourned in September 1960 without sending a bill to the President. Thompson's bill, which included a provision for federal grants to supplement teachers' salaries, became an issue during the 1960 presidential campaign. [See EISENHOWER Volume]

Described by the *New York Times* as a "politician of self-deprecating gregariousness," Thompson strongly supported John F. Kennedy's presidential candidacy and managed his national voter registration campaign in 1960. He introduced the new Administration's school aid proposal on Feb. 28, 1961. The bill included grants to the states of $2.3 billion over a three-year period for building new classrooms and supplementing teachers' salaries. The most contentious issue in the debate over the bill was whether parochial schools should share in any government assistance. Sensitive to any charges of favoritism towards the Catholic Church, Kennedy at first adamantly refused even to consider aid to any but public schools. However, in a press conference on March 8 the President indicated that special-purpose loans to Catholic schools to build classrooms and other facilities might be a debatable question. The next day Thompson suggested that a bill authorizing such loans to private schools could be passed separately. Despite this concession, which angered many congressional liberals, a coalition of Republicans, Southern Democrats and representatives from heavily Catholic areas failed to free the bill from the House Rules Committee in late August. After the vote Thompson commented that there was "very little use to try again until after the next presidential election."

In 1963 Thompson sponsored the Administration's national service corps bill, which was eventually incorporated into the 1964 Economic Opportunity Act. During the Johnson years Thompson introduced the bill that in September 1965 established the National Foundation on the Arts and Humanities. In 1966 he led the fight in the Education and Labor Committee to limit the power of Chairman Adam Clayton Powell, Jr., (D, N.Y.) [*q.v.*]. He was elected chairman of the House Administration Committee in June 1976. See JOHNSON, NIXON Volumes]

[DKR]

For further information:
Augusta E. Wilson, *Liberal Leader in the House: Frank Thompson, Jr.* (Washington, 1968).

THOMPSON, LLEWELLYN E., JR.
b. Aug. 24, 1904; Las Animas, Colo.
d. Feb. 2, 1972; Bethesda, Md.
Ambassador to the Soviet Union, April
1957-August 1962, January 1967-January
1969; Ambassador at Large and Special
Adviser on Soviet Affairs to the Secretary of State, August 1962-January
1967.

Following his graduation from the University of Colorado, Thompson entered the
foreign service in 1929. After initial assignments in Ceylon and Geneva, he specialized
in Soviet affairs, serving first as consul in
Moscow from 1940 to 1944 and then as
chief of the State Department's division of
Eastern European affairs before receiving
an appointment as deputy assistant secretary of state for European affairs in 1949. In
1952 Thompson was named U.S. high
commissioner for Austria. In that post he
helped negotiate the Italian-Yugoslavian
Trieste settlement and formulate the treaty
restoring Austria's independence. In April
1957 President Dwight D. Eisenhower
selected Thompson to succeed Charles E.
Bohlen [q.v.] as ambassador to Moscow. There he became a trusted acquaintance of many of the men in the Soviet
hierarchy. They respected Thompson not
only for his knowledge of the Russian language and culture but because he had
shared their suffering in wartime Moscow.
[See TRUMAN, EISENHOWER Volumes]

Thompson was retained at his Moscow
post during the first two years of the Kennedy Administration. During these years he
not only performed the daily functions of an
ambassador but became a trusted foreign
policy adviser to the President.

In February 1961 Thompson briefed
President Kennedy on Soviet-American
relations, which had deteriorated as a
result of the collapse of the proposed
Eisenhower-Khrushchev summit conference
in May 1960. At his briefing Thompson,
who believed it was extremely important
for the new President to get "the full flavor
of what he was up against in the Soviet
leader," favored Kennedy's proposal for a
face-to-face meeting with the Kremlin

leader. Returning to Moscow the Ambassador delivered a note from Kennedy to
Khrushchev suggesting a meeting in
Vienna. The result was the inconclusive
summit held in Vienna on June 3 and 4.

In April 1961 Kennedy asked Thompson's
advice on American strategy in the face of
the Kremlin's threat to sign a separate
peace treaty with East Germany and make
Berlin a "free city," theoretically independent of both Eastern and Western control.
In contrast to Dean Acheson [q.v.], who
thought that the Russian proposal revealed
a desire to test America's willingness to resist international challenges, Thompson,
along with former ambassador Averell Harriman [q.v.], believed that Khrushchev's
objectives were more limited. He felt that
the Soviet leader desired to improve the
Communist position in Eastern Europe
rather than achieve the worldwide political
humiliation of the U.S. that Acheson
feared. As evidence Thompson cited the
"free city" proposal, which he believed was
really intended as a means of accomplishing
Khrushchev's local aims and at the same
time saving face for the Western allies.
Thompson, therefore, opposed Acheson's
desire for military action and favored a policy of military buildup and diplomatic
negotiation to put America in the best possible bargaining position. Kennedy adopted
this position in July 1961.

Diplomatic negotiations over Berlin
broke down in the winter of 1961, and in
January and February 1962 Thompson initiated a series of four "probings" designed
to investigate the USSR's terms for reopen-
ing talks. The Kremlin, however, had decided to abandon its "free city" proposal,
and the question of negotiations over Berlin
was gradually dropped.

During the summer of 1961, while
Thompson was involved in discussions on
Berlin, he also advised President Kennedy
on nuclear disarmament policy. In June
1961 Khrushchev announced his refusal to
sign a nuclear test ban treaty and declared
his intention to resume testing. Thompson
suggested that the U.S. arrange a limited
ban outlawing tests in the atmosphere and
underwater rather than continue to press
for the total ban unacceptable to the Rus-

sians. On Sept. 3, 1961 this offer was formally presented to the Kremlin, which rejected it. However, a limited test ban treaty on these terms was eventually negotiated by the two countries in July 1963.

Thompson was appointed ambassador at large and special adviser to the State Department on Soviet affairs in August 1962. While in this post he was asked to serve as a member of the Executive Committee, the specially convened body of high-ranking officials gathered to advise Kennedy following the October 1962 discovery of Soviet offensive missiles in Cuba. During the discussions that followed that revelation, Thompson won the President's admiration for his accurate assessment of the situation. Thompson believed that the Russians were not so much concerned with Cuba or the missiles as with obtaining a bargaining position on other matters and thus would not risk military action.

At the initial Oct. 17 meeting of the Executive Committee, the President's advisers were divided on what steps should be taken. Some men, such as Charles Bohlen, hoped to gain the removal of the missiles through diplomatic channels; others, like Thompson, opposed this unilateral approach, believing that to inform the Soviets of our knowledge of the missiles and demand removal before some military action had been planned was to let the initiative pass to the Kremlin. Following the advice of the latter group, Kennedy announced a "quarantine" of Cuba on Oct. 23. Four days later, on Oct. 27, when Khrushchev suggested that the Kremlin would remove the missiles from Cuba if the U.S. would remove its missiles from Turkey, Thompson warned that the Russians would interpret the President's acceptance of the proposal as proof of weakness. Consequently, Kennedy ignored Khrushchev's letter and reiterated his demand for a halt to work on the Cuban missiles. On Oct. 28 Khrushchev agreed to disarm the weapons and remove them from Cuba.

In January 1967 Thompson returned as ambassador to Moscow, where he served until January 1969. As ambassador he un-successfully attempted to interest the Soviet Union in promoting peace negotiations in Vietnam. After his resignation he served as a foreign affairs consultant until his death on Feb. 2, 1972. [See JOHNSON Volume]

[EWS]

THURMOND, STROM
b. Dec. 5, 1902; Edgefield, S.C.
Democratic Senator, S.C., 1955-64;
Republican Senator, S.C., 1964-

The son of a South Carolina politician, Thurmond was elected to the state Senate in 1933 and five years later became a circuit court judge. He returned to the bench after serving in the Army during World War II and in 1946 was elected governor of South Carolina.

After the Democratic national convention of 1948 adopted a civil rights program, the breakaway States' Rights Party selected Thurmond to run for President. He denied being a white supremacist and stated that his opposition to anti-discrimination legislation stemmed from a belief that it represented unconstitutional federal interference in the affairs of the states. Thurmond carried South Carolina, Alabama, Mississippi and Louisiana, receiving 39 electoral votes.

In 1950 Thurmond ran unsuccessfully for the U.S. Senate. Four years later he won a Senate seat through a write-in vote, thereby becoming the first American to win a major office by that method.

Independent, irascible and sometimes vituperative, Thurmond was one of the leading opponents of anti-discrimination measures on Capitol Hill but always stood somewhat apart from his fellow-Southerners. In 1957, for example, he established a filibuster record by speaking for over 24 hours against a civil rights bill. Most Southern legislators, however, wanted the bill to pass because it did not contain effective enforcement provisions. Many of them regarded Thurmond's performance as self-serving flamboyance and kept their distance from him in succeeding years. [See TRUMAN, EISENHOWER Volumes]

During the early 1960s Thurmond opposed civil rights bills and social welfare legislation while favoring a militantly anti-Communst foreign policy and large defense appropriations. According to *Congressional Quarterly*, he was the most frequent Senate Democratic opponent of major Kennedy-backed measures in 1961, 1962 and 1963 and was the leading Southern Democratic senatorial supporter of the upper house's conservative coalition in 1961 and 1962.

Although a number of Southerners on Capitol Hill compiled voting records which approximated Thurmond's, he was one of the few to associate himself with the causes of ideological right-wing groups. In August 1961 Thurmond denounced what he called a campaign to "muzzle" military officers after Maj. Gen. Edwin A. Walker [*q.v.*], a John Birch Society member, had been reprimanded for allegedly indoctrinating his troops from a partisan, right-wing viewpoint. He demanded an investigation of the matter, which was conducted the following year by Sen. John Stennis (D, Miss.) [*q.v.*]. In March 1962 he joined Sens. Barry M. Goldwater (R, Ariz.) [*q.v.*] and John G. Tower (R, Tex.) [*q.v.*] and Rep. Donald Bruce (R, Ind.) as a speaker at a rally of the conservative Young Americans for Freedom.

In August 1961, one day after the Soviet Union announced that it would resume nuclear testing, Thurmond joined 12 other senators in urging that the United States do likewise. Two years later he opposed the nuclear test ban treaty. After Secretary of Defense Robert S. McNamara [*q.v.*] testified before the Senate Foreign Relations Committee that the treaty would increase America's nuclear superiority, Thurmond denounced McNamara on the Senate floor as a "confidence man." In November 1963 he opposed the nomination of Paul H. Nitze [*q.v.*] as Secretary of the Navy, alleging that Nitze, in a 1960 speech, had advocated that the United States turn over its military forces to such international organizations as the United Nations and the North Atlantic Treaty Organization.

In the spring of 1963 Thurmond, as a member of the Senate Armed Services Committee, advocated the appropriation of funds for the deployment of the extensive Nike-Zeus anti-missile system. The Committee voted 9-to-8 to appropriate the funds despite the opposition of the panel's chairman, Sen. Richard B. Russell (D, Ga.) [*q.v.*] and McNamara's request that the construction of an anti-missile system be postponed until the more advanced Nike-X was developed. On the Senate floor Thurmond argued that a potential "anti-missile gap" existed, but on Russell's motion the Committee's decision was reversed.

In May 1961 the Senate rejected a Thurmond amendment to an aid-to-education bill that would have prohibited the withholding of school aid funds from states or school districts maintaining segregated schools. During July 1963 he warned that the Kennedy Administration's civil rights bill would destroy property rights. The following month Thurmond denounced Bayard Rustin [*q.v.*], organizer of the civil rights March on Washington for Jobs and Freedom, charging, among other things, that Rustin was a former Communist and had been arrested for "sex perversion" and "vagrancy and lewdness."

Thurmond opposed national social legislation on the ground that it dangerously expanded federal power. In April 1961 he criticized an aid-to-dependent-children bill as "simply another insidious and deceptive welfare state proposal. . . ." Two years later he described a mass transit aid bill as a federal invasion of local responsibilities. During the summer of 1963 the Senate adopted an amendment offered by Thurmond to the national service corps bill that enabled governors to veto any program for their states.

Thurmond supported the presidential candidacy of Sen. Goldwater in 1964 and transferred his allegiance to the Republican Party during the campaign. In 1968 Thurmond backed Richard M. Nixon [*q.v.*] for the Republican presidential nomination and was credited with convincing most Southern delegates to the Republican national convention to back Nixon instead of Gov. Ronald Reagan of California. Many observers believed that the formulation of Nixon's "Southern strategy" initially stemmed from an agreement by the candidate to back Southern views on integration and other issues in exchange for the support of Thurmond and other Southern Republicans.

Thurmond maintained close ties with the Nixon Administration through presidential adviser Harry Dent and Defense Department general counsel J. Fred Buzhardt, both former aides of the Senator. A considerable number of other Thurmond associates and friends received posts in the Nixon Administration.

In the early 1970s Thurmond continued to vote against social welfare programs. However, in order to win support from South Carolina's growing black electorate, he began to actively seek federal housing and welfare funds for the state's minority population. [See JOHNSON, NIXON Volumes]

[MLL]

THURSTON, RAYMOND L(EROY)
b. Feb. 4, 1913; St. Louis, Mo.
Ambassador to Haiti, December 1961-November 1963.

After taking a Ph.D. from the University of Wisconsin, Thurston joined the Foreign Service in 1937. He served in a variety of posts in Europe, the Soviet Union, Canada, the Middle East and Washington. For a brief period in 1961 he was the alternate representative in the U.S. delegation to the North Atlantic Treaty Organization and then served as deputy director of the State Department's operations center. In November 1961 he was named ambassador to Haiti, his first post in Latin America.

During the Cuban missile crisis of October 1962, Thurston was successful in getting Haitian support of the U.S. "quarantine" against Cuba. Haiti made its harbor and airfield facilities available to the Americans. Yet, despite the strident anti-Communism of Haitian dictator Francois Duvalier, his extremely repressive regime in the poorest country in the hemisphere was not the type of government the Kennedy Administration wanted to encourage in Latin America. The Administration also felt that Duvalier might prove an unreliable ally.

In April 1963 Haitian police forcibly removed political refugees from the embassy of the Dominican Republic in Port-au-Prince. Noting the invasion of the embassy and charging that the Haitians had agreed to a secret economic assistance pact with Czechoslovakia in return for abetting Communist subversion in the Caribbean, the Dominicans threatened to invade Haiti. Duvalier declared martial law in May, and during the brutal repression that followed Thurston could secure the evacuation of U.S. citizens only by threatening to land U.S. Marines. In addition, Thurston protested police harassment of embassy personnel. On May 17 the U.S., along with other nations in the hemisphere, suspended diplomatic relations with Haiti, although Thurston was instructed to remain in Port-au-Prince. The U.S., Costa Rica, Venezuela and the Dominican Republic, believing that Duvalier would soon flee Haiti, planned to cooperate in supporting the formation of a democratic government. Duvalier, however, held on to his power, and in June the U.S. pragmatically resumed diplomatic relations. However, Haiti made it clear that it would not welcome the return of Thurston, who was then conferring with the State Department in Washington.

Thurston was formally replaced in November 1963. Between 1965 and 1969 he served as Ambassador to Somalia and then turned to teaching and college administration.

[JCH]

TOBIN, JAMES
b. March 5, 1918; Champaign, Ill.
Member, Council of Economic Advisers, January 1961-August 1962.

After serving with the Office of Price Administration during World War II, Tobin earned his Ph.D. in economics from Harvard. He joined the Yale faculty in 1950 and also became director of the Cowles Foundation for Research in Economics. Tobin soon won a prestigious reputation among his colleagues in the fields of econometrics and economic theory. When President-elect Kennedy offered him a post on the Council of Economic Advisers (CEA), Tobin cautioned, "Senator, I'm an ivory tower economist." Kennedy replied, "That's the best kind. I'm an ivory tower President." Tobin, like his CEA colleagues

Walter W. Heller [q.v.] and Kermit Gordon [q.v.], was an advocate of the Keynesian "new economics," which held that the federal government should pursue an aggressive fiscal and monetary policy in order to attain rapid growth and full employment.

Chairman Heller assigned to Tobin problems of debt management, econometric studies, forecasting, international finance and money and banking. While Heller labored to win over the Administration and the public to fiscal activism, Tobin advanced the "new economics" on the monetary front. In an article in *Challenge* magazine which appeared in January 1961, Tobin criticized the Federal Reserve's "tight" money policy during the Eisenhower Administration and expressed apprehension that its conservative Board of Governors might "resist and frustrate any effort by the Kennedy Administration to gear the federal budget and other instruments of economic policy to higher levels of employment and production." As a member of the CEA, Tobin argued for lower interest rates to make credit abundant and thus encourage investment by businesses and state and local governments.

The Federal Reserve, a bastion of fiscal orthodoxy under Chairman William McChesney Martin, Jr. [q.v.], moved only slowly in the direction favored by Tobin and other monetary expansionists. The Federal Reserve was more sensitive to the balance of payments problem than to the growth imperative of the Keynesians, and it feared that lower short-term rates would be an incentive to investors to shift into higher-yielding foreign assets. Monetary expansion, it also feared, would stimulate inflation and exacerbate the gold drain. It did hold long-term interest rates down during 1961, but it kept high the important short-term rates.

Tobin later recognized that "a really aggressive monetary policy was not in the cards because of the balance of payments." At the time Tobin had argued that the approach to problems like the payments deficit should rely less on domestic than on international solutions. He favored the centralization of monetary reserves, for example, in an expanded International Monetary Fund. Tobin attributed his general lack of success in this endeavor to the conservatism of the Treasury Department and the Federal Reserve. Furthermore, he believed that the "education of the President went more slowly on international trade and finance than on domestic macro-economics."

Tobin also spoke out on other areas of economic policy. In April 1961 he endorsed Sen. Paul Douglas's (D, Ill.) [q.v.] bill to require merchants and lenders to state all finance charges and annual rates on installment purchases. In October he warned against the inflationary potential of pay raises and said that wage increases should be limited to productivity gains. Tobin returned to Yale in August 1962 but remained actively involved in the formation of economic policy as a consultant to the CEA and as a public spokesman for liberal solutions to the problems of poverty and unemployment.

[TO]

For further information:
James Tobin, *National Economic Policy* (New Haven, 1966).
———, *The New Economics One Decade Older* (Princeton, 1974).

TOWER, JOHN G(OODWIN)
b. Sept. 29, 1925; Houston, Tex.
Republican Senator, Tex., 1961-   .

Tower was an assistant professor of political science at Midwestern University in Wichita Falls, Tex. from 1951 to 1960. In the 1950s he served on the Texas Republican Party's executive committee in the 23rd senatorial district, and in 1956 he was a delegate to the Republican National Convention.

In 1960 Tower ran for the U.S. Senate against Lyndon B. Johnson [q.v.], who was taking advantage of a special Texas law permitting him to run for the vice presidency and the Senate at the same time. Tower lost with 41% of the vote. In May 1961 he faced Democrat William Blakley in a special election to fill Johnson's vacant seat. Both candidates were conservatives. Tower's campaign was aided by support that he received from some of the members of the minority liberal faction of the state's Democratic Party. They felt that a Tower victory would cause Texas conservatives to rally to the Republican Party, leaving the Democratic machinery in liberal hands. Tower won the election with 444,813 ballots to Blakley's 436,815. Tower thereby became the first Republican U.S. senator from Texas since Reconstruction.

Tower was an ideological conservative who declined to modify his positions on what he regarded as fundamental issues; during his 1960 campaign he had criticized Johnson as "the great compromiser." In the Senate Tower quickly became identified as one of the leading and most articulate allies of Sen. Barry Goldwater (R, Ariz.) [q.v.]

In the area of foreign affairs, Tower favored a militantly anti-Communist stance; in a Senate speech of March 1962, he stated that Congress should declare that "victory over Communism is the aim and objective of United States foreign policy." Even before it became clear that Soviet missiles were being deployed in Cuba, Tower advocated action against the Castro regime. On Sept. 11, 1962 he denounced America's Cuban policy as "massive appeasement" and declared that the consensus of expert opinion was that Khrushchev "would not initiate a thermonuclear war to save Cuba for Communism."

Tower feared that a strong U.S. stance against Communism would be weakened by cooperation with the Soviet Union through either the United Nations or bilateral agreements. In April 1962 he said, "The theory that the U.N. has preserved and is preserving world peace is preposterous," warning that "we must not allow it to dictate our foreign policy." In the fall of 1963 he joined 18 other senators in voting against the limited nuclear test ban treaty.

In the area of domestic policy, Tower generally opposed Kennedy-sponsored programs for regulating the economy. In his 1962 book A Program for Conservatives, he stated that "the freer people are from government interference, the more progress they are likely to make." Tower denounced a 1962 Administration bill limiting the production of wheat and feed grains as "a gigantic step toward a planned economy in

the United States." During the same year he criticized a bill regulating the hours and pay of workers employed on projects done under federal contract or with federal aid, asserting that it "would impose a further mechanical and rigid uniformity inadequate to deal with the diverse conditions which exist in various sections of the country."

Tower also opposed Administration-supported social welfare programs, generally on the grounds that they dangerously expanded federal power and encroached upon individual rights. He often joined Sen. Goldwater, a fellow-member of the Labor and Public Welfare Committee, in issuing minority reports critical of such bills. In a joint report of July 1961, they attacked a bill for extending the National Defense Education Act because it went beyond the original purpose of improving education in defense-related areas and constituted "a giant step in the direction of federal control of our educational system." In September 1963 they criticized a medical training aid bill, contending that its provisions demonstrated that "the grand design of the advocates of huge central bureaucracy" included "a passionate desire and determination to strip from all subordinate levels of government and its people their just rights, duties and responsibilities."

Tower also rejected social welfare bills that, in his estimation, weakened traditional social institutions by transferring their functions to government agencies. In the spring of 1963 the Labor and Public Welfare Committee considered a youth employment bill, which provided for the establishment of a Youth Conservation Corps similar to the Civilian Conservation Corps of the 1930s. Led by Tower, the Committee's conservative minority stated that the provisions of the bill "consciously weaken the family relationship . . . a backbone of our free society" and "smack ominously of totalitarianism."

Tower was an enthusiastic supporter of Sen. Goldwater's drive for the 1964 Republican presidential nomination and was the chairman of the solidly pro-Goldwater Texas delegation to the Republican National Convention in San Francisco. He won reelection to the Senate in 1968 and 1972. [See JOHNSON, NIXON Volumes]

[MLL]

For further information:
Paul Casdorph, *A History of the Republican Party in Texas, 1865-1965* (Austin, 1965).

TRUDEAU, ARTHUR G(ILBERT)
b. July 5, 1902; Middlebury, Vt.
Chief, Army Research and Development Command, January 1958-April 1962.

A graduate of West Point with a master's degree in civil engineering from the University of California, Trudeau saw service in North Africa, Europe and the Pacific during World War II. He commanded the 7th Infantry Division in Korea for several months in 1953. As assistant chief of staff for intelligence from November 1953 to August 1955, Trudeau carried out a study of "brainwashing" of American troops in Korea which resulted in the issuance of the *Code of Conduct* for members of the U.S. armed forces.

In January 1958 Trudeau succeeded Lt. Gen. James M. Gavin [*q.v.*] as chief of research and development for the Army. Gavin, along with Army Chief of Staff Gen. Maxwell Taylor [*q.v.*], had enlisted the aid of scientists, engineers and computer specialists to develop new weapons systems. Trudeau was one of a number of more conservative generals who were critical of the growing influence of scientists in strategic military decisions. As head of the Army's research and development program, Trudeau began to reduce the authority of scientists within the Army by systematically denying them access to information, limiting their research to narrow questions and shelving their reports. The Operations Research Office, a nonprofit research organization at Johns Hopkins University under contract to study atomic, germ and gas warfare, was placed under such severe restrictions that in 1961 it ended its association with the Army.

Among the most active of military men on the lecture circuit—a newspaper once called him the "William Jennings Bryan of the Pentagon"—Trudeau consistently stressed the threat of Communism to the U.S. and its allies. During a 1960 visit to the Dugway, Utah, germ warfare proving grounds, he told reporters that "Russia could well be ahead of us in use of chemical and biological warfare" and issued an appeal for production of new weapons in those areas. On another occasion Trudeau asserted that the "Reds deliberately, fanatically, increasingly strive to destroy the shreds of domestic stability remaining as we enter the new frontiers of the 1960s."

During both the Eisenhower and Kennedy Administrations, mid-level officials in the Pentagon and State Department had routinely reviewed and in some cases censored the speeches made by military officers such as Trudeau. In the early 1960s this censorship became a national issue when a number of conservative congressmen charged President Kennedy and Secretary of Defense Robert S. McNamara [*q.v.*] with "muzzling" these officers. Chaired by Sen. John Stennis (D, Miss.) [*q.v.*], a special subcommittee of the Senate Armed Forces Committee began hearings on the issue in January 1962.

A number of conservative military officers were called to testify about the restrictions placed on their speech-making, but Trudeau proved a somewhat disappointing witness because he asserted that the review of his speeches was little different under Kennedy than under Eisenhower. His only objection was that he thought this review should be made by top policymaking officials at the Pentagon rather than by the anonymous junior officers who had been handling the procedure. When the Senate committee asked McNamara for the name of the officer who had revised a recent Trudeau speech, the Secretary of Defense invoked executive privilege, refused to make public the name of Trudeau's censor and accepted full responsibility for the review himself.

Trudeau resigned from the Army in April 1962 to become president of the Gulf Research and Development Company, where he served for the next six years.

[JLW]

TRUMAN, HARRY S
b. May 8, 1884; Lamar, Mo.
d. Dec. 26, 1972; Kansas City, Mo.
President of the United States, April 1945-January 1953.

Except for service in France as an artillery captain during World War I, Harry Truman spent his first 50 years in Missouri. He grew up in Independence, managed a farm near Grandview from 1906 to 1917 and after the war started a haberdashery business in Kansas City that failed in the depression of 1922. Backed by Tom Pendergast's powerful Democratic machine, Truman was elected judge of the Jackson County Court in 1922 and presiding judge in 1926. In these essentially administrative posts Truman carried out an extensive road-building program. He was elected to the U.S. Senate in 1934 on a platform endorsing the New Deal.

Truman first came to national attention during World War II when he chaired the "Truman Committee," which investigated abuses in the defense program. In 1944 he was chosen at the Democratic Convention to replace Vice President Henry A. Wallace as President Franklin D. Roosevelt's running mate. Elected in November, Truman became president upon Roosevelt's death in April 1945.

Truman took office at a pivotal point in world affairs: the replacement of the European-centered system of international politics with the global confrontation between two expanding superpowers, the United States and the Soviet Union. A vigorous anti-Communist, Truman initiated the postwar containment policy designed to halt Communist advances. The Marshall Plan and the North Atlantic Treaty Organization (NATO) were the twin pillars of this policy in the West. In the East Truman committed the United States in 1950 to the military defense of South Korea. The Korean War developed into a stalemate after the intervention of China and lasted for three years.

On the domestic front Truman fought to extend the New Deal with his own social welfare program. Despite some advances in social security, civil rights and housing, most of his Fair Deal was stymied by conservative congresses. A feisty campaigner, Truman won an upset reelection victory in 1948 against New York Gov. Thomas E. Dewey. Despite a sweeping "loyalty" program designed to root out Communists from the government, Truman spent much of his second term defending himself against charges by Sen. Joseph R. McCarthy (R, Wisc.) and other Republicans that his Administration was infiltrated by subversives. His popularity was diminished by these attacks and the Korean stalemate. Truman declined to run for reelection in 1952. [See TRUMAN Volume]

Returning to Independence in 1953, Truman issued public statements throughout the decade, usually attacking the Eisenhower Administration, defending his own record or supporting Democratic candidates. He backed Gov. Averell Harriman's [q.v.] unsuccessful candidacy for the Democratic presidential nomination in 1956. [See EISENHOWER Volume]

In May 1960 Truman endorsed Sen. Stuart Symington (D, Mo.) [q.v.] for the Democratic presidential nomination. But the former President resigned as a convention delegate on June 29 because, he said, the convention "was controlled in advance" by supporters of Sen. John F. Kennedy and delegates had "no opportunity for a democratic choice." After Kennedy's nomination Truman campaigned for him vigorously. In a speech in Texas, for example, he said that Kennedy's opponent, Vice President Richard M. Nixon [q.v.], had "never told the truth in his life." Truman told Nixon backers to "go to hell."

During the Kennedy Administration Truman publicly endorsed the President's policies. He defended Kennedy's resumption of atomic tests in September 1961, his fight against the steel price rise in April 1962, the U.N. loan bill in October 1962 and Kennedy's confrontation with Premier Nikita Khrushchev during the Cuban missile crisis. In August 1963 Truman supported the nuclear test ban treaty. However, he opposed Kennedy's proposed $11 billion tax cut in September.

Through 1961 and 1962 Truman engaged in extensive recorded conversations with author Merle Miller. A section of these transcripts was published in 1973 in Miller's *Plain Speaking: An Oral Biography of Harry S. Truman*. The book contains Truman's private opinions about several individuals prominent in politics during the 1960s. He characterized President Kennedy's father, Joseph P. Kennedy [q.v.], as a "crook" who "bought his son the nomination for the presidency." Truman disliked Robert F. Kennedy [q.v.] because he had "worked for old Joe McCarthy." Truman said that "the whole Kennedy family" was interested only in "getting the power. They don't care a hoot in hell about using it." Truman also called U.N. Ambassador Adlai Stevenson [q.v.] a "sissy" and Supreme Court Justice Tom C. Clark [q.v.] a "dumb son of a bitch." He stated that his appointment of Clark to the Court in 1949 was his worst mistake as president. Truman died on Dec. 26, 1972 at the age of 88. [See JOHNSON Volume]

[TO]

For further information:
Merle Miller, *Plain Speaking: An Oral Biography of Harry S. Truman* (New York, 1973).

UDALL, STEWART L(EE)

b. Jan. 31, 1920; St. Johns, Ariz.
Secretary of the Interior, January 1961-January 1969.

The grandson of a Mormon missionary and son of a justice of the Arizona Supreme Court, Stewart Udall belonged to one of the most successful political families in Arizona. Following Mormon missionary work in the East and Air Force service during World War II, he attended the University of Arizona and earned an LL.B. degree in 1948. Campaigning hard against a right-to-work law in 1954, Udall was elected to the U.S. House from Arizona's second district, which included all of the state except the city of Phoenix and its surrounding county.

In Congress he compiled a liberal record, became an energetic defender of conservation interests on the House Committee on Interior and Insular Affairs. He obtained more federal aid for his congressional dis-

trict than was won for any other in the country. A close associate of Sen. John F. Kennedy, Udall swung Arizona's votes from Sen. Lyndon B. Johnson (D, Tex.) [q.v.] to Kennedy at the 1960 Democratic National Convention. In December 1960 Kennedy named Udall as his Secretary of the Interior.

In his new post Udall headed a department of about 56,000 employes with a budget of nearly $900 million. It had jurisdiction over approximately a quarter of the U.S. land area and responsibility for conservation of water and mineral resources, protection of fish and wildlife, administration of national parks, historic sites and Indian reservations and reclamation of arid lands. Interior also held significant responsibility for construction of hydroelectric power systems.

Udall announced a new Administration policy on water and power, which broke sharply with the approach of the Eisenhower Administration. On the assumption that the nation's population and standard of living would continue to rise, he asserted that the federal government should assume the responsibility for ensuring that the people's energy needs would be met. "The Eisenhower Administration regarded public power as something of a necessary evil," asserted Udall. "We regard it as a necessary good; we're not—as they did—going to go out searching for ways to let private industry have access to hydroelectric sites and falling water at dams built with federal funds." The new Administration projected a series of integrated power pools so that widely separated power systems having complementary needs would share their energy through the building of long-distance, extra-high voltage lines. In addition, Udall wanted all new projects to have water available for multiple uses.

Among the Administration's more ambitious power proposals were three that aroused notable controversy. In December 1961 Udall proposed a West Coast power grid to feed power from the Pacific Northwest (the Bonneville System) through a 1,000-mile transmission line to the San Francisco and Los Angeles areas. Udall stated that the project, contingent upon congressional approval of funds, would send power back and forth along the coast to meet varying peak needs, enable the Northwest to sell annually $9-15 million worth of secondary surplus power and postpone the need for new steam plants in the arid Pacific Southwest. The plans called for the participation of federal and Pacific Coast public agencies, private utilities and Canada. Another 1961 proposal, which had also been recommended by the Eisenhower Administration, involved a 2,000 mile "backbone" transmission system for the giant Upper Colorado River Storage Project, consisting of 10 major lines to be built by the federal government. A third proposal was made by Udall in 1963 to harness the tidal power at Passamaquoddy Bay between Maine and Canada and the water power of the nearby St. Johns River.

All three proposals faced powerful opposition from private utility companies, which regarded them as a step toward "nationalization" of the U.S. power system through federal construction of ever-larger regional projects. The West Coast issue was not settled until 1964, when a combined federal-municipal-private system was authorized giving both public and private power in the Southwest and California direct access to the low-cost Bonneville System.

Although the Interior Department had been authorized by Congress to build all 10 transmission lines for the Upper Colorado River Storage Project, Udall pleased the private utility lobby when he announced in February 1962 that the Department had signed contracts with private utilities to build some of the transmission lines and to provide "wheeling" service to transmit power from the project to important Interior Department customers. Udall argued that these contracts would save the federal government money, but the American Public Power Association and the National Rural Electric Cooperative, advocates of public power, sharply attacked his decision. They claimed that federal power was better on principle and that there were insufficient assurances that the private companies would provide adequate and low-cost service.

The Passamaquoddy project was a revised version of a plan that had been judged un-

feasible. Republicans called the Udall plan a "billion dollar boondoggle," and private companies saw it as an attempt to bring federal power into northern New England for the first time. The project was subsequently shelved for further study.

The Kennedy-Udall policy on public lands continued a federal policy that had been evolving since the early part of the century. In effect, the federal government would retain most public lands in the West to develop or use as a public resource. Prospective buyers would have to prove that their intended uses were at least as valuable to the public welfare as the federal government's. Udall, in a February 1961 statement, indicated that, when sold, public lands would be offered at full value, every effort would be made to avoid selling to land speculators and marginal land would not be opened to agriculture. In addition, Udall ordered an 18-month moratorium on new Bureau of Land Management sales in order to discourage promoters and land speculators. These changes, however, did not apply to land sales under the mining laws or to federal, state and local government agencies.

Udall's position on the public lands, though part of a traditional Democratic preference for public ownership, also reflected a view of conservation that gathered an increasing number of adherents in the 1960s. Udall emphasized conservation so that the U.S. standard of living could be maintained or improved indefinitely, but, in addition, he stressed the need to maintain large areas in their natural state for their aesthetic and recreational values. Udall was himself an outdoorsman who believed that time spent in a natural environment "will renew the human spirit and sustain unborn generations. . . ." He favored creation of the National Wilderness System, finally enacted in 1964, and the expansion of wildlife refuge areas. Speaking in May 1961 Udall warned that the 1960s might prove the nation's "last chance" to save large blocs of land for park and wildlife use.

During the Kennedy Administration seashore national parks at Cape Cod, Point Reyes and Padre Island were added to the system. No previous administration in the postwar era had added such large areas to the National Park Service in so short a period of time. More significantly, the Cape Cod Seashore represented the first park-type unit in the system to be acquired largely through the purchase and condemnation of private land. Another important development was the April 1962 creation of a Bureau of Outdoor Recreation within the Interior Department by executive order.

In November 1963 Udall published *The Quiet Crisis*, a history of the exploitation of the American land and a defense of his conservation policies. Udall urged Americans to come into more contact with the wilderness and to treat the environment with greater care, even if that required some individual discomfort and inconvenience. The book was an influential contribution to the environmental movement of the 1960s.

Udall remained Secretary of the Interior until the end of the Johnson Administration. Under Lyndon Johnson environmental and "beautification" legislation was stressed as part of the Great Society's legislative program. In 1969 Udall became board chairman of the Overview Corporation and in 1970 began to write a syndicated column on the environment. [See JOHNSON Volume]

[JCH]

UNRUH, JESSE M(ARVIN)
b. Sept. 30, 1922; Newton, Kan.
Speaker, California State Assembly, 1961-69.

Jess Unruh's father, an illiterate sharecropper, was descended from German Mennonites. The drought of the 1930s forced the family to migrate to Texas, where Unruh, the youngest of five children, became the first member of his family to graduate from high school. After wartime service in the Naval Air Corps, he attended the University of Southern California, where the campus Communists appealed to his idealism and sense of class consciousness. In 1948, the year he received his B.A., Unruh rejected offers to join the Communist Party and campaigned for Rep.

Helen Gahagan Douglas (D, Calif.) and President Harry Truman [*q.v.*]. In 1950 and 1952 he unsuccessfully sought to represent Inglewood in Los Angeles County in the state Assembly. In 1954, a year of big Democratic gains throughout the state, Unruh finally won a seat.

As a young assemblyman Unruh was beset with attractive offers of money and favors from lobbyists. By his own admission Unruh accepted many offers, since money, he said, was "the mother's milk of politics." With money and a quickly acquired mastery of political skills, Unruh became one of the most powerful Democrats in the Assembly. He managed Edmund G. Brown Sr.'s [*q.v.*] successful gubernatorial campaign in 1958, which swept into office the first Democratic governor in 16 years and the first Democratic majority in the Assembly in 14 years. Unruh rose to the chairmanship of the influential Ways and Means Committee, where he was able to sponsor liberal legislation and channel surplus offers of campaign contributions to deserving liberal Democrats. He argued in favor of public funding of campaigns, but he felt that, until public funding was a reality, a united bloc of liberal legislators could most effectively counter the pernicious influence of the lobbyists. Such a group, Unruh believed, could gain more for the public interest and give up less when accepting the lobbyists' offers.

Unruh supported John F. Kennedy's presidential campaign before the decisive 1960 West Virginia primary victory. He later managed the Kennedy forces in Southern California and, after the inauguration, acted as the Administration's chief link to California politics. His close relationship with the Kennedy White House and his election as Speaker of the Assembly in September 1961 helped make Unruh, in the view of many political observers, the most influential politician in California and easily the most powerful state legislator in the country.

Called "Big Daddy" in the early 1960s because of his enormous weight, Unruh was likened by some conservative critics to the political bosses of the East. Nevertheless, he was credited with helping to make the

California Assembly into a model legislature. The Assembly became more professional, hired a well-paid and competent staff and offered university seminars for legislators. Unruh controlled committee assignments and had the power to approve the passage of all bills out of committee. To a greater extent than his counterparts in other states, Unruh initiated his own legislative program. Many political analysts assumed that he would succeed Gov. Brown in the executive mansion.

Unruh influenced Gov. Brown to favor increasingly more liberal positions, particularly in the areas of civil rights, labor and antipoverty legislation. Yet, Unruh's belief that the legislature should not be subordinate to the executive branch irritated Brown, who, according to Unruh, looked "upon our legitimate endeavors as a personal attack upon him. . . ." Unruh and Brown often sponsored rival candidates in primary elections and at party nominating conventions. Organized labor and the California Democratic Council, a liberal organization theoretically independent of the Party, usually sided with Brown in his disputes with Unruh. Labor found Unruh an unreliable supporter of its interests, while many liberals disliked Unruh's "boss" image and his tendency to moderate liberal programs because of political considerations.

According to political writer Lou Cannon, July 1963 marked a turning point in Unruh's career. Exploiting his power as Speaker he invoked an old rule to keep recalcitrant Republicans locked inside the Assembly chamber until they voted on the new state budget. A widespread negative reaction to the maneuver hurt Unruh's prestige in the state and lost him the confidence of the Kennedy Administration.

With the conservative trend in California politics in the mid-1960s and the election of conservative Republican Ronald Reagan, as governor in 1966, Unruh was forced to wield his diminished power more cautiously. In 1968 he became the first Democratic politician of national stature to endorse the presidential candidacy of Sen. Robert F. Kennedy (D, N.Y.) [q.v.], and at the end of March Unruh declared himself an opponent of President Lyndon Johnson's [q.v.] Vietnam policies. Because the Democrats lost their majority in the Assembly in the 1968 elections, Unruh was forced to step down as Speaker in January 1969. As leader of California's Democrats, he ran against the popular Ronald Reagan in the 1970 gubernatorial contest, relinquishing his Assembly seat in the process. Following a loss to Reagan, Unruh devoted himself to lecturing and teaching. [See JOHNSON Volume]

[JCH]

For further information:
Lou Cannon, *Ronnie and Jesse: A Political Odyssey* (Garden City, 1969).

VAN ALLEN, JAMES A(LFRED)
b. Sept. 7, 1914; Mount Pleasant, Iowa.
Physicist.

Van Allen received his doctorate in nuclear physics at the State University of Iowa in 1941. He served as a naval reserve commander in World War II and in 1946 became head of high altitude research at the Applied Physics Laboratory at Johns Hopkins University. He became a leading scientist and researcher in the fields of high altitude studies and rocket development and was an initiator of the International Geophysical Year (1957-58), dedicated to cooperative research in the various earth sciences. In 1951 he was appointed chairman of the physics department at Iowa State University, where he supervised the design of the Army's first earth satellites. Based on data collected by the satellites, Van Allen announced in 1958 the existence of two radiation bands 250 miles above the earth, which were named the Van Allen belts.

Van Allen was one of a group of leading scientists, including Wernher Von Braun [q.v.], who called upon the federal government to step up space exploration efforts. He was a member of the congressionally-chartered Space Science Board, which early in 1961 asked that "scientific exploration of the moon and planets should be clearly stated as the ultimate objective of the U.S. space program." This group influenced President Kennedy's decision, following the Soviet Union's first manned space flight in April 1961, to gear the National Aeronautics and Space Administration's activities toward a manned moon shot before 1970. Van Allen, on receiving the National Rocket Society's first research award in October 1961, warned that the U.S. space program was lagging because of a lack of competent scientists in crucial areas. He called for massive financial aid to universities for the training of students in those areas.

In November 1961 Van Allen criticized a widely read series of articles by Dr. Willard F. Libby entitled "You Can Survive an Atomic Attack." Dubious of the value of bomb shelters, Van Allen believed that atomic war would likely "mean the end of the civilization of both opponents."

While an adviser to governmental groups, Van Allen remained at the University of Iowa.

[MDB]

For further information:
John M. Logsdon, *The Decision to Go to the Moon: Project Apollo and the National Interest* (Cambridge, Mass., 1970).

VANCE, CYRUS R(OBERTS)

b. March 27, 1917; Clarksburg, W. Va.
General Counsel for the Department of Defense, January 1961-June 1962; Secretary of the Army, July 1962-January 1964.

After receiving his law degree from Yale in 1942, Vance served in the Navy before entering private law practice in New York. From 1957 to 1960, while practicing law, he also worked as special counsel to Senate committees investigating the satellite and missile programs. As legal adviser to the Senate Committee on Aeronautical and Space Sciences, Vance became a protege of Lyndon Johnson [q.v.], who recommended him for a high position in the Kennedy Administration. As a result Vance was appointed general counsel for the Department of Defense in January 1961.

In the Defense Department Vance developed a close working relationship with Secretary of Defense Robert S. McNamara [q.v.], who asked the lawyer to aid him in his plan to reorganize the Pentagon. Often acting on preliminary suggestions from McNamara, Vance and the Office of Organizational and Management Planning worked to restructure the Defense Department's bureaucracy. They recommended combining the offices of the assistant secretaries of defense for manpower, personnel, reserve and health and medical affairs into a single office of the assistant secretary of defense for manpower. They also advised assigning responsibility for the Defense Department's space research and development program to the Air Force and establishing a defense intelligence agency.

At the request of McNamara, who felt that the Army had become archaic, Vance and high Army officials developed new personnel and weapons policies designed to make that service more responsive to conditions of modern warfare. Their chief recommendations called for stressing the use of light weapons rather than heavy armor, increasing maneuverability and relying on helicopters to move troops quickly.

In July 1962 Vance was appointed secretary of the army upon the retirement of Elvis Stahr [q.v.], who could not work under the restrictions imposed by McNamara. As army secretary, Vance was one of the men who advised President Kennedy to send federal troops to the South during the violence that followed the October 1962 attempt to integrate the University of Mississippi and the May 1963 riots in Birmingham, Ala.

In January 1964 Vance replaced Roswell Gilpatric [q.v.] as deputy secretary of defense. He served until June 1967, when ill health forced him to retire from formal government service. During the Johnson years Vance served as a presidential adviser on Vietnam and as a "trouble shooter" for the President in Panama, the Dominican Republic, Cyprus, Korea and, during the racial riots, in Detroit and Washington, D.C. [See JOHNSON Volume]

[EWS]

VANDIVER, S(AMUEL) ERNEST
b. July 13, 1918; Canon, Ga.
Governor, Ga., 1959-63.

A lawyer by training, Vandiver was elected mayor of Lavonia, Ga., in 1946. In 1948 he managed the successful gubernatorial campaign of Herman Talmadge [q.v.], who appointed him adjutant general of Georgia. Elected lieutenant governor in 1954, Vandiver broke with Gov. Marvin Griffin over the issue of corruption in the state administration, asserting later, "The state of Georgia was buying rowboats that would not float. Some were wisely sent to parks without lakes." In 1958 he ran for governor as an anti-corruption candidate. Vandiver also stressed the race issue in his campaign, denouncing the Supreme Court's school integration decision as unconstitutional and declaring that "no, not one" Negro would enter the state's white schools. He easily won the Democratic nomination and faced only token general election opposition in the essentially one-party state. Reacting against what he regarded as the venal waste of the preceding administration, Vandiver attempted to reduce expenditures, and in 1962 he pressed the legislature to restirct the governor's control of the state's purse strings.

In 1959 Vandiver had proposed, and the legislature adopted, a law to shut down and deny state revenues to integrated schools. But in January 1961 Vandiver did not resist a federal court order that two blacks be admitted to the University of Georgia. In addition, he successfully urged the legislature to permit each community to decide whether or not to close desegregated schools. Explaining his altered position to state legislators, Vandiver said that unless there was accommodation to integration the race issue would, "like a cancerous growth . . . devour progress—consuming all in its path . . . stifling the economic growth of the state." In September 1962 he denounced Mississippi Gov. Ross Barnett [q.v.] for defying the school integration order of a federal court. During the same year Vandiver and the legislature attempted to preserve Georgia's rural-weighted county unit voting system by revising it, but a fed-

eral court ordered the total elimination of the system.

Prohibited by the state constitution from serving successive terms as governor, Vandiver left office in January 1963. In 1966 he planned to enter the Democratic gubernatorial primary, but dropped out of the race in May after suffering a heart attack.

[MLL]

VINSON, CARL
b. Nov. 18, 1883; Baldwin County, Ga.
Democratic Representative, Ga., 1914-65; Chairman, Armed Services Committee, 1949-53, 1955-65.

In 1902 Vinson received a law degree from Mercer University in Macon, Ga. After serving two terms in the Georgia House of Representatives, he was elected judge of the court of Baldwin County in 1912. Two years later Vinson won a race for a vacant seat in the U.S. House of Representatives. He became chairman of the House Naval Affairs Committee in 1931. During the 1930s Vinson advocated a substantial strengthening of the Navy, arguing that at all times it "must be strong enough to defend our possessions and to support our policies."

In 1947 the House's military committees were merged into the new Armed Services Committee. Two years later, after the Democrats had regained control of the House, Vinson became chairman of the new panel. The Georgia Congressman believed that peace depended upon a strong military posture, and in 1950 he attacked defense reductions proposed by Secretary of Defense Louis Johnson. During the Eisenhower Administration he opposed the doctrine of "massive retaliation" with its reliance on nuclear weapons and emphasized instead the importance of maintaining a strong conventional force capable of dealing with less than total war. He criticized those aspects of President Eisenhower's 1958 plan for the reorganization of the Pentagon that in his opinion, gave the Secretary of Defense excessive control over daily operational matters. [See TRUMAN, EISENHOWER Volumes]

Speaker Sam Rayburn (D, Tex.) [*q.v.*] described Vinson as the "best legislative technician in the House," and Vinson's political acumen earned him the nickname "Swamp Fox." He shunned publicity and was not well known to the general public, but as chairman of the Armed Services Committee he established himself as a crucial force in the shaping of military-related legislation. Almost all bills cleared by the Committee were approved by the House, and the great majority cleared the Senate to become law.

Vinson exercised firm control over the proceedings of the Committee. Rather than establishing regular subcommittees he divided the panel into three equal groups and determined which would receive each bill. This policy, Rowland Evans, Jr. wrote, "made him undisputed boss over such prestigious matters as who would introduce an important bill and get his name on it. . . ." Vinson also maintained complete control over the Committee's inspection and travel business, thereby determining which members would be sent on trips.

Vinson had great respect for the abilities of Robert S. McNamara [*q.v.*] and referred to him as "the greatest Secretary of Defense in history." But he strongly believed in preserving the specialized functions of the individual military services and opposed McNamara's propensity for transferring power from them to the Defense Department. In a March 1962 speech Vinson asserted that if the three services were merged into a single department "all military thinking [would] be directed toward one strategic concept."

Vinson regarded the Kennedy Administration's views on the production of manned bombers as an example of the danger of a one-concept strategy. The Administration, believing that the Pentagon's existing and planned stock of missiles represented the nation's major deterrent to the Soviet Union, planned to phase out manned bombers. But Vinson and Sen. Richard B. Russell (D, Ga.) [*q.v.*], his counterpart on the Senate Armed Services Committee, accepted the views of Gen. Curtis LeMay [*q.v.*] and other Air Force officers, who argued that bombers could perform many

missions that could not be accomplished by guided missiles. In 1961 Congress appropriated almost $800 million more for manned bombers than the Administration had requested, but McNamara announced that he would not spend the extra funds.

These developments set the stage for a controversy the following year over the RS-70 manned reconnaissance bomber. In March the House Armed Services Committee, under Vinson's direction, authorized $491 million for the RS-70 and offered an amendment ordering the Secretary of the Air Force to utilize the full amount. The panel issued a report explaining its action. Arguing that under the Constitution Congress possessed the authority to raise and support armies and to make the rules governing them, it challenged the right of the Administration to ignore congressional directives on defense spending. But later in the month President Kennedy met with Vinson in the White House Rose Garden and arranged a truce. McNamara agreed to reexamine the RX-70 program, and Vinson consented to withdraw the amendment. The Defense Secretary did not subsequently change his position on the RS-70.

Although Vinson was a foe of civil rights bills, he was known as a Southern loyalist who always backed Democratic national tickets and often supported liberal measures sponsored by Democratic presidents. In January 1961 he led a group of Southerners who voted with the Administration in its successful effort to enlarge Rep. Howard W. Smith's (D, Va.) [*q.v.*] Rules Committee for the purpose of eliminating the conservative majority on that panel. The following spring he agreed to support an Administration minimum wage bill if certain categories of workers were excluded from coverage. After a compromise was reached he helped to secure the votes needed for passage of the measure. According to *Congressional Quarterly*, Vinson supported Administration-backed bills on 62%, 67% and 62% of key House roll-call votes in 1961, 1962 and 1963, respectively.

In 1964 Vinson announced that he would not seek reelection. By that time he had surpassed the late Speaker Sam Rayburn's record for length of service in the House.

In October 1975 Vinson was hospitalized for treatment of circulatory problems. [See JOHNSON Volume]

[MLL]

For further information:
Rowland Evans, Jr., "The Sixth Sense of Carl Vinson," *The Reporter* (Jan. 4, 1962), pp. 25-30.

VOLPE, JOHN A(NTHONY)
b. Dec. 8, 1908; Wakefield, Mass.
Governor, Mass., 1961-63, 1967-69.

A successful Massachusetts building contractor, John Volpe was active in Republican state and national politics in the 1940s and 1950s. After service as his state's commissioner of public workers, Volpe was named by President Dwight Eisenhower as interim federal highway administrator for the years 1956 and 1957.

Volpe unsuccessfully sought his party's gubernatorial nomination in 1958 but won it two years later at a time when the issue of official corruption dominated Massachusetts politics. Disclosures of irregularities and corruption in the higway construction program of incumbent Democratic Gov. Foster Furcolo became a key issue in the campaign. Volpe won enough support from disgruntled Democrats and independent voters to defeat Commonwealth Secretary of State Joseph Ward by over 100,000 votes in the heavily Democratic state.

Once elected Volpe established a well funded State Crime Commission. The Commission soon reported: "Corruption permeates the state, from town government to the State House and involves politicians, businessmen, lawyers and ordinary citizens." Volpe proposed that the state General Court (legislature) enact a series of statutes to deal with the problem. These included a code of ethics for public officials, revision of the state constitution to allow four-year terms for governors and other elected officials and elimination of unnecessary political offices. However, because Volpe was the only Republican elected to statewide office in 1960 with both houses of the state legislature controlled by Democrats, few of the Governor's reforms were enacted during his two years in office.

In his 1962 campaign for reelection, Volpe faced Endicott Peabody [*q.v.*], a Protestant Democrat from a distinguished family who campaigned against the corruption of his own party. After an extremely close vote and recounts demanded by both candidates, Peabody was declared the winner by 3,000 votes.

Volpe won reelection to the Massachusetts governorship in 1966 and in early 1969 was appointed President Richard Nixon's first Secretary of Transportation. There he downgraded highway construction programs and began a cautious federal program to encourage urban mass transportation. [See JOHNSON, NIXON Volumes]

[NNL]

VON BRAUN, WERNHER
b. March 23, 1912; Wirsitz, Germany.
Director, Marshall Space Flight Center, National Aeronautics and Space Administration, January 1960-July 1972.

Von Braun was born into an aristocratic Prussian family and became obsessed with the idea of space travel at an early age. He began experimenting with rockets while an engineering student in Berlin and by 1932 was made chief of the German Army's secret rocket experimental station. Rocket development took a leap forward in 1936 when Hitler began to pour money into the program, and by 1938 Von Braun had developed the model for the V-2 missile used against the Allies in World War II. Von Braun joined the Nazi Party in 1940.

In 1945 he avoided capture by the Russians and arranged to surrender to American forces because he believed that the U.S. would be most likely to support his research. "The next time, I wanted to be on the winning side," he later said. He became director of the U.S. Army's Redstone Arsenal in 1950 and was joined by 117 scientists and engineers who had worked with him in Germany. He became a U.S. citizen in 1955.

In 1957 Von Braun proposed the creation of a national space agency to orbit men and space stations around the earth. The National Aeronautics and Space Administration (NASA) was formed in 1958, and Von Braun's group was transferred from the Army to NASA in 1959. Von Braun was credited with the development of the Jupiter-C launch vehicle, which was boosted by the Redstone rocket. The Redstone had launched the first U.S. earth satellite, Explorer 1, in early 1958. Von Braun also supervised the development of the much larger Saturn "super-boosters" later used in Project Apollo. In 1960 he was named to head NASA's Marshall Space Flight Center. [See EISENHOWER Volume]

A major justification for increasing NASA's budget in early 1961 was that rocket development could serve the military as well as the space program, a view Von Braun shared with NASA chief James E. Webb [q.v.] and Secretary of Defense Robert S. McNamara [q.v.]. However, in December 1961 it was decided that separate rockets would be developed by NASA, whose Saturn rockets used liquid fuel boosters, and the Air Force, whose Titan rockets used solid fuels.

Despite his belief in the need for an accelerated space program, Von Braun at first urged postponement of manned flights. He believed that the risks involved in such flights were still too great, and the first U.S. launching was therefore postponed until late April 1961. On April 14, however, America's presumed technological supremacy suffered a major blow when the Soviet Union became the first nation to put a man in space. The Bay of Pigs invasion failed a few days later. President Kennedy now looked to the space program to demonstrate American strength and will. Von Braun advised Kennedy that the U.S. currently lagged behind the Russians but that "we have an excellent chance of beating the Soviets to the first landing of a crew on the moon." He said he favored concentrating on "a few (the fewer the better) goals in the American space program as objectives of highest national priority. . . . Put all other elements on the back burner."

Von Braun led the NASA contingent that favored a moon landing from an earth orbit, but in June 1962 he became a convert to John C. Houboult's lunar orbit concept, which permitted the use of smaller booster rockets. This strategy was adopted later that year and was the method used in the first Apollo landing in 1969.

Von Braun's was one of NASA's most articulate public spokesmen. His books and articles on rocketry and space exploration helped to stimulate national interest in the space program during the 1950s and 1960s. He remained at his NASA post until 1972, when he left to become a corporate vice president at Fairchild Industries.

[MDB]

For further information:
Hugo Young, Bryan Silcock and Peter Dunn, *Journey to Tranquility: The Long Competitive Struggle to Reach the Moon* (Garden City, 1969).

WAGNER, ROBERT F(ERDINAND), JR.
b. April 20, 1910; New York, N.Y.
Mayor, New York, N.Y., 1954-65.

Robert F. Wagner, mayor of New York for 12 years, was deeply involved in politics from childhood. His father, Sen. Robert F. Wagner, Sr. (D, N.Y.), was a powerful figure in the liberal wing of the Democratic Party; the elder Wagner served in the Senate for 23 years, and his popularity was a crucial factor in the son's political advancement.

Wagner attended the Taft School and Yale University. After receiving an LL.B. from the Yale Law School in 1937, he was elected to the New York Assembly. He resigned his seat in 1941 to serve in the Air Corps in Europe. After the war, with the support of Tammany Hall, the regular New York City Democratic organization, Wagner advanced rapidly in politics. Under Mayor William O'Dwyer he served successively as city tax commissioner, commissioner of housing and buildings and chairman of the city planning commission. In 1949 Wagner was elected Manhattan Borough President. In August 1952 he was defeated in his bid for the Democratic senatorial nomination, but a year later he defeated incumbent Mayor Vincent Impellitteri for the mayoral nomination and swept on to an easy victory in November.

Wagner presided over New York during a period when thousands of poor blacks and Puerto Ricans were moving into the city as middle class whites were leaving for the suburbs. The presence of an increasingly large percentage of poor people was reflected in a rising crime rate, a growing drug problem and the deterioration of housing. Nonetheless, the period of the mid-1950s through the mid-1960s was one of relative prosperity for New York. A boom in the construction of luxury apartments and office buildings helped the city's tax base keep pace with the growth of costly social welfare programs.

In his first two terms Wagner won passage from the city council of the first legislation barring racial discrimination in the sale or rental of housing, and, by executive order, he gave city civil servants—with the exception of the police—the right to organize unions and enter into collective bargaining with the city. In 1960 New York thoroughly revised its zoning ordinances for the first time in 44 years. [See EISENHOWER Volume]

Wagner's authority, particularly in his first two terms, was limited by the presence of two powerful political figures, Carmine DeSapio [q.v.] and Robert Moses [q.v.]. DeSapio was the boss of Tammany Hall with whom Wagner had to deal on patronage matters. Robert Moses, the head of the Triborough Bridge and Tunnel Authority who held numerous other posts at the state and city level, was a dominating force in transportation, planning, housing and public works projects.

In seeking his third term as mayor in 1961, Wagner determined that he would have to break with the regular Democratic Party organization to retain the support of an increasingly powerful reform movement in Manhattan. Wagner denounced DeSapio, campaigned against "bossism" and defeated his Tammany opponent, Arthur Levitt, in the September mayoral primary. He then won an easy victory in the general election. When DeSapio was defeated in a contest for his district leadership post in Greenwich Village, Edward Costikyan, a Wagner man,

succeeded him as head of Tammany Hall.

During the early 1960s Wagner also increased his power relative to Robert Moses, who was coming under sustained attack for his management of the New York World's Fair and his advocacy of the unpopular Lower Manhattan Expressway project. Moses had resigned his post as head of the city's slum clearance program in 1959. Three years later Republican Gov. Nelson Rockefeller [q.v.] replaced him as chairman of the State Council of Parks and the State Power Authority. As Moses's power waned, Wagner's increased.

Wagner and Rockefeller exchanged criticism from time to time but nonetheless developed a useful working relationship. On several occasions Rockefeller helped Wagner extend his political influence, supporting, for example, 1961 revisions in New York City's charter to give the mayor's office increased authority in budgetary matters that previously had been the prerogative of the Board of Estimate. The Mayor also won greater control of street and sewer maintenance projects formerly under the authority of the borough presidents.

In national politics Wagner harbored vice presidential ambitions. He understood that a Kennedy-Wagner ticket was impossible since both were Catholic, and he therefore supported Sen. Lyndon B. Johnson (D, Tex.) [q.v.] for the 1960 Democratic presidential nomination. However, Wagner had no difficulty campaigning for Kennedy in the fall, and after the election he became a staunch supporter of the Administration's social welfare legislation. Following the ouster of DeSapio and his ally, Democratic State Party Chairman Michael J. Prendergast, the Kennedy Administration rewarded Wagner by temporarily channeling patronage through City Hall.

In the early 1960s the Wagner Administration attempted to streamline its inefficient housing and slum clearance programs. In 1960 a new housing and redevelopment board assumed responsibility for slum clearance and urban renewal projects which previously had been shared by four different agencies. In 1962 the state passed a law that permitted the city to take over and repair, at the expense of owners, apartment houses that were not properly maintained. A new department of relocation was established to aid in finding new quarters for families and businesses displaced by slum clearance projects. But at the close of his mayoralty, Wagner admitted that "red tape" in New York and Washington had slowed efforts to upgrade the city's housing stock.

Wagner maintained a close relationship with New York City labor leaders and as a result earned a reputation for skill in settling labor disputes. In April 1962 newly organized New York City teachers struck for higher salaries. The teachers agreed to end their one-day walkout when Gov. Rockefeller and Mayor Wagner announced that the state would make available to the city $13 million more than originally had been budgeted for the school system. Wagner also helped avert a teachers' strike in 1963 when he appointed a panel that successfully negotiated the union's first two-year contract. In March of the same year Wagner played a key role in ending a strike by typographers which had forced leading New York City newspapers to cease publication for 114 days.

Although Wagner felt obliged to try to head off teachers' strikes, he believed that the Board of Education rather than his office should assume responsibility for the management of public schools. In May 1961, however, a special state commission revealed that the New York City school board had grossly mismanaged funds for the repair and construction of schools. In August the state legislature, meeting in special session, passed legislation directing Wagner to name a new nine-member board. Wagner selected a distinguished group but continued to remain aloof from the problems that plagued the schools: increasing racial segregation, a rising school dropout rate and a teacher shortage.

The Wagner Administration attempted to combat juvenile delinquency through its support of a project to aid disadvantaged youth on the Lower East Side. Mobilization for Youth (MFY) was founded in 1961 with a $12.5 million grant from the City, the Federal government and the Ford Foundation. It was hailed as an exciting undertaking by President Kennedy and became a pilot project for the community action programs in slum areas that were later supported by the Johnson Administration's Office of Economic Opportunity. MFY, like other community action programs, was handicapped by internal dissension and mismanagement and, in the long run, did not fulfill the hopes of its founders.

During his last two years in office Wagner was called upon repeatedly to deal with increasing racial tension, including major riots which broke out in Harlem and the Bedford-Stuyvesant section of Brooklyn in the summer of 1964.

During his first year in office, 1954, Wagner had submitted a $1.5 billion expense budget for the City. By 1965 expense requests had climbed to the $3.8 billion level. Furthermore, in his final year, Wagner committed the city to borrowing at unprecedented levels to meet current expenses. He thereby established a precedent that contributed to the city's fiscal crisis of the mid-1970s. [See JOHNSON Volume]

Wagner was succeeded by Rep. John V. Lindsay (R, N.Y.) [q.v.]. He then returned to private life and practiced law in New York City.

[JLW]

WALKER, EDWIN A(NDERSON)

b. Nov. 10, 1909; Center Point, Tex.
Major General, U.S. Army, 1957-61.

A graduate of West Point, Walker began his military career as an artillery officer, later serving as a combat commander during World War II and in the Korean War. While in Korea Walker came to believe that the American failure to carry the war to mainland China was the result of a pro-Communist conspiracy in Washington.

In September 1957 Walker, then a major general and commander of the Arkansas Military District, was put in charge of the regular troops and the federalized National Guard sent to maintain order during the integration of Central High School in Little Rock, Ark. For Walker the use of federal troops to integrate a school was so distasteful that he offered to submit his resignation.

President Dwight D. Eisenhower, however, refused to accept it.

In 1959, the year Walker joined the right-wing John Birch Society, he was sent overseas to command the 13,000-man 24th Infantry Division in Augsburg, West Germany. In April 1961 Army Secretary Elvis J. Stahr, Jr. [q.v.] relieved Walker of his command pending an investigation of charges that he had been using his position to indoctrinate troops and their dependents with his right-wing political views. The investigation confirmed that in a speech to 200 members of his division and their families, Walker had declared that 60% of the press, along with Harry Truman [q.v.], Dean Acheson [q.v.] and Eleanor Roosevelt [q.v.], were "Communist influenced." Reports of this incident created a furor in the United States. The acting judge advocate of the Army, Major Gen. Robert H. McCaw, stated that Walker had violated the Hatch Act by "attempting to influence voting in the national election in favor of the ultra-conservative point of view. . . ."

Army Secretary Stahr admonished Walker for his conduct in June 1961. Walker resigned from the Army in November "to be free from the power of little men, who, in the name of my country, punish loyal service." Walker had now become a popular figure on the right. In April 1962 he appeared before a special Senate Armed Services Committee headed by Sen. John Stennis (D, Miss.) [q.v.], which was investigating charges that the Kennedy Administration was "muzzling" military officials to keep them from speaking out against Communism. According to Richard Dudman of the St. Louis Post Dispatch, Walker's rambling and incoherent testimony and his references to mysterious forces that were persecuting him effectively undermined his leadership role for the more sophisticated members of the right. National Review thought Walker's performance "pitiful," and its editor, William F. Buckley [q.v.] relegated him to "history's ashcan."

Walker entered the May 1962 Texas Democratic gubernatorial primary but finished last in a field of six.

Walker was arrested Oct. 1, 1962 in Oxford, Miss. for his participation in the riots resulting from the admission of James Meredith [q.v.] as the first Negro student at the University of Mississippi. Charges against Walker were later dropped, but he sued the Associated Press and the New Orleans Times-Picayune for libel because they described him as a leader of the riots. In October 1965 a Shreveport, La. jury awarded him $3 million in damages. In a unanimous decision in June 1966, the U.S. Supreme Court voided the judgment, declaring that the wire service and newspaper were protected by the First Amendment against libel suits by those who sought public attention.

After the death of President Kennedy, the Warren Commission revealed that the President's assassin, Lee Harvey Oswald [q.v.], had on April 10, 1963 shot at and barely missed General Walker at his home in Dallas.

[JLW]

WALKER, WYATT TEE

b. Aug. 15, 1929; Brockton, Mass.
Executive Director, Southern Christian Leadership Conference, 1960-64.

A Baptist minister who received his divinity degree from Virginia Union University, Walker was pastor of a Petersburg, Va., church and president of the NAACP in Virginia before joining the Southern Christian Leadership Conference (SCLC) as executive director in 1960. In that post Walker became one of the chief aides to SCLC President Martin Luther King [q.v.] with much of the responsibility for raising funds and for organizing SCLC direct action campaigns.

Walker joined the 1961 Freedom Rides, which challenged segregation in interstate transportation facilities, and was a member of the Freedom Rides Coordinating Committee organized in May. He was arrested twice during the rides—on May 25 in Montgomery, Ala., and on June 21 in Jackson, Miss.,—for entering the white section of Trailways bus terminals. Walker also helped direct an anti-segregation campaign in Albany, Ga., which began in November

1961 and which the SCLC joined in mid-December. The protests in Albany continued into 1962 and were intensified in July when King was jailed for violating a public assembly ordinance. Walker opened and ran an SCLC office in Albany and led many of the July demonstrations. Although the Albany movement was judged a failure by most observers, Walker later hailed it as "a mile-post in the early stage of the nonviolent revolution" and "a big beginning in the Deep South."

Walker played a key role in the planning and organization of the SCLC's desegregation drive in Birmingham, Ala., in the spring of 1963. With King and Ralph Abernathy [q.v.], Walker met with black leaders in the city to build unity and support for the campaign. Walker also did reconnaissance work in Birmingham before the demonstrations started to determine priority targets and map out routes for marches. Late in 1963 Walker also devised a direct action campaign to challenge segregation in public accommodations in Atlanta, Ga. His plans were adopted by the Negro Leadership Conference, an association of civil rights groups in the city, and were put into effect in January 1964.

Walker resigned as executive director of the SCLC in 1964 to become a vice president of Educational Heritage Inc., a new company created to publish a 24-volume series on the history and culture of black Americans. Working in New York City, Walker also became resident minister of the Canaan Baptist Church in Harlem. In 1966 Gov. Nelson Rockefeller [q.v.] appointed him a special assistant for urban affairs.

[CAB]

WALLACE, GEORGE C(ORLEY)
b. Aug. 25, 1919; Clio, Ala.
Governor, Ala., 1963-67.

Wallace was born and raised in southeastern Alabama and worked his way through the University of Alabama, receiving a law degree in 1942. He served as an assistant state attorney general in 1946 and in the state House of Representatives from 1947 to 1952. A protege of the state's neo-

populist governor, "Big Jim" Folson, Wallace established a liberal record in the legislature. He sponsored bills to provide scholarships to the dependents of deceased or disabled veterans, to increase old age pensions and to construct state vocational schools. Wallace then won election as judge of Alabama's third judicial circuit in 1952.

With other Southerners Wallace fought the adoption of a strong civil rights plank at the 1948 Democratic National Convention. As Alabama's delegate on the 1956 Democratic Convention Platform Committee, he helped secure a civil rights compromise acceptable to Southern Democrats. In 1958 Wallace entered the Democratic gubernatorial primary where he qualified for the runoff against state Attorney General John Patterson [q.v.]. During the campaign Patterson took a strong segregationist position, receiving the backing of the Ku Klux Klan. Wallace was considered the more moderate candidate, and he lost the June 3 runoff. According to his biographer, Marshall Frady, he said after his defeat that "John Patterson out-nigguhed me," but "I'm not goin' to be out-nigguhed again."

Wallace's term as circuit judge ended in January 1959. He spent the next three years campaigning for the 1962 gubernatorial elections. In his spring 1962 primary campaign, Wallace ran on a militant segregationist platform, promising to resist all efforts "of the federal courts, the Justice Department and the Civil Rights Commission to destroy our social and educational order." He was the front-runner in the May 1 Democratic primary and won the May 29 runoff primary with the largest popular vote ever received by a gubernatorial candidate in Alabama's history. In his January 1963 inaugural address, Wallace reasserted his segregationist stance. "I draw the line in the dust," he proclaimed, "and toss the gauntlet before the feet of tyranny, and I say: segregation now—segregation tomorrow—and segregation forever."

Wallace devoted much of his first year in office to vain attempts to prevent desegregation in Alabama. Shortly before a desegregation agreement was reached in Birmingham, where Martin Luther King [q.v.] led mass demonstrations in the spring of 1963, Wallace announced he would "not be a party to any. . .compromise on the issues of segregation." Rioting erupted in Birmingham on May 11 after the motel where King was staying and the home of King's brother were bombed. President Kennedy ordered federal troops to bases near Birmingham to be used in case more violence developed, and Wallace immediately filed a federal court suit challenging Kennedy's action and asking, among other things, that the 14th Amendment be held unconstitutional. The Supreme Court rejected his appeal in a *per curiam* opinion on May 27.

By 1963 Alabama was the only Southern state without any desegregated schools. During his campaign for governor, Wallace had promised to "resist any illegal federal court orders" for school desegregation "even to the point of standing at the schoolhouse door in person." He fulfilled the pledge on June 11, 1963 at the University of Alabama. On May 21 a federal district court had ordered the enrollment of two black students at the University's main campus in Tuscaloosa, and Wallace immediately announced he would "be present to bar the entrance of any Negro" who attempted to enroll. Hoping to avoid the violence that accompanied James Meredith's [q.v.] entry into the University of Mississippi in September 1962, the Justice Department secured a federal court injunction prohibiting Wallace from interfering with the students' enrollment and sent a team headed by Deputy Attorney General Nicholas Katzenbach [q.v.] to Tuscaloosa to help arrange for the peaceful entry of the students. President Kennedy placed nearby Army troops on alert and issued an executive proclamation ordering Wallace and all others to "cease and desist" from obstructing justice. Despite the court injunction, Wallace stood in the doorway of Foster Auditorium, the University's registration center, on June 11, blocking the entrance of the two students, Katzenbach and other Justice Department officials who accompanied them. Katzenbach read the President's proclamation and demanded that Wallace comply with the federal court orders.

Standing before a lectern, Wallace responded with his own proclamation, claiming that the federal government was usurping the state's authority to control its own school system. He was barring the doorway, he said, not "for defiance's sake, but for the purpose of raising basic and fundamental constitutional questions. My action is a call for strict adherence to the Constitution." Katzenbach withdrew, the two students were accompanied to their dormitory rooms. President Kennedy federalized the Alabama National Guard and ordered several units onto the campus. At a second confrontation late in the afternoon, the National Guard commander escorted the two students to the registration center where Wallace was again blocking the doorway. He told the Governor, "It is my sad duty to ask you to step aside, on order of the President of the United States." Wallace stepped aside. The two students registered, and two days later another black student enrolled at the University Center at Huntsville without incident.

Wallace again tried to forestall integration in the fall of 1963. Federal courts had ordered school desegregation at the elementary and secondary levels in Mobile, Tuskegee, Birmingham and Huntsville, and local authorities were prepared to comply when the schools opened in September. On Sept. 2, however, Wallace began eight days of defiance in which he issued executive orders delaying the opening of the schools and sent state troopers to physically keep them closed. On Sept. 9 Wallace opened the schools but used the troopers to keep blacks from entering them in three cities. On the same day all five federal district court judges in Alabama issued injunctions ordering Wallace and the state's forces not to interfere further with desegregation. Wallace replaced the state troopers with National Guardsmen, but on Sept. 10 Kennedy federalized the Guard and ordered all the troops back to their barracks. The black students finally entered the schools. Five days later a black church in Birmingham was bombed, killing four young girls. Wallace declared that the tragedy "saddened all Alabamians" and offered a $5000 reward for information leading to the arrest of the bombers. On Sept. 16, however, President Kennedy issued a statement saying it was "regrettable that public disparagement of law and order had encouraged violence which has fallen on the innocent." The remark was generally considered a reference to Wallace.

Aside from his efforts to prevent desegregation, Gov. Wallace built 14 new junior colleges and 15 new trade schools in the state, initiated another $100 million school construction program and expanded the state's free textbook system to include all 12 grades. He began the largest highway construction program in the state's history, introduced a clean water act, devised plans for new nursing homes and medical clinics, and encouraged greater industrialization in Alabama. However, his tax program was regressive, consisting of increased sales taxes and higher taxes on beer, cigarettes, gasoline and sports events. Organized labor criticized Wallace's administration, alleging that the state's highway patrolmen were union-busters and that the state's child labor laws were virtually worthless. Alabama had no minimum wage law, and the state ranked near the bottom of all states in welfare payments to dependent children. Although Wallace had promised to increase old age pensions to at least $100 per month, they rose only 36 cents during his term to $69.66 per month. Average unemployment compensation rose slightly to $38 per month.

Wallace's dramatic pose of defiance at the school-house door in June 1963 brought him nationwide publicity, and he began speaking throughout the country, especially on college campuses, shortly afterwards. In 1964 he entered three Democratic presidential primaries outside the South. Wallace won between 30% and 42% of the vote after campaigns in which he celebrated the workingman and attacked centralized government, the federal courts and the national news media. Unable to succeed himself as governor because of a provision in the state constitution, Wallace successfully promoted his wife Lurleen as his stand-in candidate for governor in 1966. In 1968 Wallace ran as an independent candidate for president and amassed 13.6% of the national vote. [JOHNSON Volume]

[CAB]

For further information:
Marshall Frady, *Wallace* (New York, 1968).

WALTER, FRANCIS E(UGENE)
b. May 26, 1894; Easton, Pa.
d. May 31, 1963; Washington, D.C.
Democratic Representative, Pa., 1933-63; Chairman, Committee on Un-American Activities, 1955-63.

After Walter graduated from Georgetown University Law School in 1919, he returned to Easton where he became a successful lawyer and businessman. He was appointed county solicitor in 1928 and four years later won election to the House of Representatives.

At first Walter was a supporter of the New Deal, especially its efforts to prevent floods and provide cheap hydroelectric power for his district. By the end of the 1930s, however, Walter had grown alarmed by what he considered the growing power of the government and the influence of organized labor. After the war Walter became identified with immigration affairs and control of internal—especially Communist—subversion. As chairman of the House Judiciary Subcommittee on Immigration Affairs, he was often described as the "Czar over immigration matters." While he involved the U.S. in international efforts to resettle Europeans made homeless by the war and in 1950 proposed a bill to eliminate all racial barriers to naturalization, his Immigration and Nationality Act of 1952, sometimes called the McCarran-Walter Act, set national quotas based on the 1920 census of the foreign born. Denounced by its opponents as "exclusionist," the bill eliminated the possibility of a large-scale immigration of Orientals.

The second-ranking Democrat on the House Un-American Activities Committee (HUAC) in 1949 and its chairman after 1955, Walter vigorously supported Committee investigations of individuals thought to be members of the Communist Party and co-authored a 1950 bill that required registration of Communists with the government and periodic reports on their activities. [See TRUMAN, EISENHOWER Volumes]

As chairman of the House Democratic caucus in 1961, Walter supported the bulk of President Kennedy's domestic economic and social legislation, but he was sometimes at odds with Kennedy on internal security and immigration matters. In March 1961 he opposed Kennedy's decision to terminate the interception of non-first class mail entering the U.S. from Communist countries, claiming that "poison will be poured into the veins of our society without restriction and without notice or warning of its nature." He introduced a bill to resume the program and create a "controller of foreign propaganda" in the Customs Service. The Administration argued that the existing control program yielded no intelligence information and impeded cultural exchange. Finally, Walter and the Administration agreed to a bill that required placing notices in post offices and alerting suspected recipients of Communist propaganda.

In his concern for refugee problems, Walter vigorously attacked Kennedy's appointment of Salvatore Bontempo [q.v.] and Michel Cieplinski as administrator and deputy administrator of the State Department's Bureau of Security and Consular Affairs. Walter characterized them as "totally unqualified political appointees" and, in addition, recommended that the Bureau be abolished. He wanted the official who handled passports, visas and immigration matters to be subject to Senate approval. Walter's pressure was successful. In December 1961 Bontempo resigned and was succeeded by Abba Schwartz, whom Walter had sponsored for the post. In June 1962 the President signed a bill that, although it did not abolish the Bureau, required Senate confirmation of the administrator.

As chairman of the Judiciary Subcommittee on Immigration and Nationality, Walter was the manager of a much-criticized bill passed in September 1961 which limited to one the number of appeals allowed for federal court review of alien deportation orders. In May 1962 Walter

backed Administration emergency measures to expedite the admission of political refugees into the U.S. and offer them economic aid. This measure permitted refugees from Communist China to enter the U.S. in disregard of the quota system. However, Walter successfully resisted demands favored by the Administration to overhaul the immigration laws, and he continued to favor the ethnic quota system set up by the McCarran-Walter Act.

In the early 1960s a handful of congressional liberals led by James Roosevelt (D, Calif.) and William Fitts Ryan (D, N.Y.) [q.v.] attacked HUAC as a threat to civil liberties. Liberal groups also sharply criticized Walter's Committee for making the film "Operation Abolition," a documentary that portrayed student demonstrations against HUAC in May 1960 as led by Communists. Six liberal congressmen voted against the $331,000 HUAC appropriation for 1961. Walter thought Roosevelt and other liberal critics failed to "comprehend, even remotely, the nature of Communism," and he relied upon reports by the FBI's J. Edgar Hoover [q.v.] to defend the Committee's activities.

Although pressure to abolish HUAC increased in the early 1960s, Walter successfully rejected a series of measures in 1963 that would have transferred HUAC functions to the Judiciary Committee. He thought that the atmosphere of the Judiciary Committee, headed by liberal Emanuel Celler (D, N.Y.) [q.v.], "is not conducive" to work against internal subversion. Walter also supported legislation, passed in September 1962, increasing internal security in the defense industry while providing appeal procedures to those denied employment on security grounds. Despite his fear of the internal Communist threat, Walter supported the Kennedy Administration policy of economic aid to Poland and Yugoslavia, claiming that aid to these countries had maximized cracks in the Communist bloc.

Early in 1963 Walter was hospitalized when it was discovered that he was suffering from leukemia. He died in Washington on May 31, 1963.

[JCH]

WARREN, EARL
b. March 19, 1891; Los Angeles, Calif.
d. July 9, 1974; Washington, D.C.
Chief Justice of the United States, September 1953-June 1969.

The son of Scandinavian immigrants, Warren worked his way through college and law school at the University of California, receiving his law degree in 1914. He began his public career in 1919, serving successively as deputy city attorney in Oakland, deputy district attorney of Alameda County, Calif., and for 13 years as county district attorney. Warren developed a reputation as a crusading, racket-busting prosecutor in these jobs and was elected state attorney general in 1938. He successfully ran for governor of California in 1944 and twice won reelection to that post. Warren was the Republican vice presidential candidate in 1948. He also made a bid for the Party's presidential nomination in 1952.

Warren's politics during these years in California were not easily categorized. He sometimes took positions that distressed liberals, such as strongly supporting the evacuation of Japanese-Americans from the West Coast during World War II. However, he became increasingly progressive during his years in public life. When Warren was named Chief Justice of the U.S. in September 1953, most observers expected him to be a moderate jurist with a cautious approach to the use of judicial power. [See TRUMAN, EISENHOWER Volumes]

Although no one could anticipate it at the time, Warren's appointment to the Supreme Court, as Archibald Cox later stated, "marked the beginning of an era of extraordinarily rapid development in our constitutional law," during which the Court broke new ground in a variety of fields. The first sign of this came on May 17, 1954, when Warren, speaking for a unanimous Court, delivered the opinion in *Brown* v. *Board of Education* that held racial segregation in public schools unconstitutional. The decision sparked the first major controversy over the Warren Court, helped launch a significant change in American race relations and also served as the base from which the Supreme Court went on to outlaw

all public discrimination during the 1960s.

Under Warren the Supreme Court also rewrote the law on the administration of criminal justice and extended its rulings to the states as well as the federal government. It also changed the operation of the political system by ordering legislative reapportionment on a "one-man, one-vote" basis, prohibited religious exercises in public schools, significantly broadened the rights of free speech and artistic expression and restricted the government's power to penalize individual beliefs and associations. Especially after a solid liberal majority emerged in the early 1960s, the Warren Court became synonymous with a libertarian variety of judicial activism, one with egalitarian ideas and devoted to the protection of individual rights and liberties.

Aside from the *Brown* decision Warren himself took a middle-of-the-road stance in his earliest years on the Court. By the late 1950s he had clearly aligned himself with such liberal justices as Hugo Black [*q.v.*] and William O. Douglas [*q.v.*]. With the exception of obscenity rulings, he supported every major change in constitutional law ultimately made by the Court.

During the Kennedy years, when the civil rights movement entered a new phase with widespread use of nonviolent protest, Warren delivered the Court's first ruling on sit-in demonstrations. In a December 1961 opinion he overturned the breach-of-the-peace convictions of 16 black protesters on the ground that there was no evidence to support the original charge. He again spoke for the Court in a May 1963 ruling that voided the convictions of civil rights demonstrators in six cases and concurred in similar rulings in June 1962 and February 1963. Warren also joined the majority in decisions that prohibited the exclusion of blacks from private restaurants situated on state-owned property and held invalid pupil-transfer plans designed to thwart school desegregation.

In a series of cases involving Communism, the Chief Justice repeatedly voted against the government. He dissented in June 1961 when a five-man majority sustained provisions in two federal antisubversive laws. Warren also opposed February

1961 rulings upholding the contempt of Congress convictions of individuals who refused to answer questions before the House Un-American Activities Committee. He joined with the majority to overturn similar convictions in June 1961, May 1962 and June 1963. Later Warren Court decisions further undermined the force of federal and state anti-subversive legislation and expanded the individual's freedom to hold and express dissident political views.

Warren's majority opinion in four May 1961 cases held that state "blue laws," prohibiting certain types of business on Sundays, did not violate the First Amendment. Although their origin was religious, Warren ruled that the laws had become secular in character and were designed to prevent overwork and unfair competition rather than to promote religious observance. In three cases decided in June 1962 and June 1963, Warren joined the majority to hold prayer and Bible-reading in public schools a violation of the First Amendment's guarantee of freedom of religion. The decisions resulted in a storm of criticism from certain congressmen and religious leaders and generated unsuccessful attempts to adopt a constitutional amendment restoring prayer to public schools.

In March 1962 Warren was part of a six-man majority that overturned a 1946 precedent and held that federal courts could try legislative apportionment cases. Two years later the Court went on to mandate a "one-man, one vote" standard of apportionment for congressional and state legislative districts. The cases resulted in reapportionment in nearly every state of the Union. In later years Warren labeled them the most significant action taken by the Court during his tenure.

The Court also advanced the rights of criminal defendants during the Kennedy years. In June 1961, with Warren in the majority, it held that illegally seized evidence could not be used in state courts. A unanimous Supreme Court also ruled that the Sixth Amendment's right to counsel applied to the states in June 1963. The Court placed limits on the use of evidence obtained by electronic eavesdropping in a March 1961 ruling and overturned a

California law making drug addiction a crime in June 1962.

In November 1963, at the urging of President Lyndon Johnson [q.v.], Warren accepted the chairmanship of a commission to investigate the assassination of John F. Kennedy. The Warren Commission's report of September 1964 concluded that Lee Harvey Oswald [q.v.] had killed President Kennedy and that he had acted alone. Widely acclaimed when it was first published, the report soon became a target of criticism for those who believed that Kennedy's assassination was the result of a conspiracy.

The Chief Justice's role in the Court's liberal departures has been debated. One skeptic, noting Warren's greater liberalism as a justice than when a politician, concluded it would be most accurate to say "that Warren has not formed the Court but rather that the Court has formed him." A larger number of observers, however, gave Warren great credit for supplying the leadership needed to carry forward the Court's constitutional changes. Warren was not the author of many of the opinions adopted by the Court or of the judicial philosophy underlying them, but his political and administrative skills were judged essential for achieving a new consensus and direction on the Court.

Whatever his actual role, the Chief Justice served as a symbol for the entire Court to both admirers and critics. Attacks on the Court for its desegregation, school prayer and criminal rights rulings often turned into attacks on Warren himself. For years the right-wing John Birch Society promoted a campaign to impeach Earl Warren. While the movement never made any real headway, Warren Court decisions did arouse significant public controversy and were issues in the 1964 and 1968 presidential campaigns.

Legal scholars generally supported the substantive results of major Warren Court rulings. Their strongest criticism was directed at the style of decision making employed by Warren and the other liberal justices. They were charged with concentrating too heavily on achieving their desired goals and, in the process, failing to support the Court's new departures with any rigorous and consistent legal reasoning. Warren's own concern for fairness over precedent or theory became legendary among Court-watchers. He was reported to have frequently interrupted counsel during oral argument to ask if particular actions had been fair. His opinions were criticized for being vague and moralistic and for ignoring history, precedent and conflicting legal approaches. Even the Court's strong supporters argued that such an approach left it open to charges that it subordinated law to the individual political preferences of the justices. They also feared that the Court was undermining its own prestige, authority and ability to command popular acceptance of its rulings by neglecting to explain and adequately justify new courses of decision.

Despite these criticisms Warren has been ranked as one of America's greatest chief justices, second only to John Marshall in the minds of many. His personal dedication to the ideal of equal justice for all Americans and to the protection of individual liberties has been widely praised. All observers agreed that the Court he presided over had an enormous impact on American law and life, giving support and impetus to significant social change. According to Leon Friedman, the Warren Court helped to "establish new goals for the nation, articulate a new moral sense for the people and, in effect, reorganize the political structure of the country itself."

During the Johnson Administration the Court continued to serve as a focal point of progressive reform and public controversy. It overturned federal laws limiting the rights of members of the Communist Party and handed down decisions on libel law that expanded freedom of the press and a citizen's right to criticize public officials. Warren himself delivered the Court's most controversial criminal rights ruling in the June 1966 *Miranda* case. This decision declared that a suspect in the hands of police authorities must be clearly informed of his right to remain silent and right to counsel prior to questioning. The justices sustained federal civil rights laws and prohibited racial discrimination in housing, but they be-

came increasingly divided in rulings concerning civil rights demonstrators. After 16 years on the bench, Warren retired in June 1969. He died in Washington on July 9, 1974. [See JOHNSON, NIXON Volumes]

[CAB]

For further information:
Alexander M. Bickel, *The Supreme Court and the Idea of Progress* (New York, 1970).
Archibald Cox, *The Warren Court* (Cambridge, Mass., 1968).
Philip Kurland, *Politics, the Constitution and the Warren Court* (Chicago, 1970).
Anthony Lewis, "Earl Warren," in Leon Friedman and Fred L. Israel, eds., *The Justices of the United States Supreme Court. 1789-1969* (New York, 1969), Vol. 4.
Richard H. Sayler, et al, eds., *The Warren Court: A Critical Analysis* (New York, 1969).

WATSON, THOMAS J(OHN), JR.
b. Jan. 8, 1914; Dayton, Ohio.
Chairman of the Board, International Business Machines Corporation, 1961-   .

Thomas Watson, Jr., was the son of the founder of International Business Machines Corp. (IBM), the international giant of the computer field. Watson graduated from Brown University in 1937 and the same year joined IBM as a salesman. After service in the Army Air Force during World War II, Watson returned to IBM, where he demonstrated managerial ability and a flair for salesmanship in a rapidly expanding organization whose principal source of profit was then in the field of office automation.

After rising quickly through the ranks at IBM, Watson was appointed president in 1952 and chairman of the board in 1961. The elder Watson had died in 1956, leaving a paternalistic and highly conformist stamp on the company inherited by his son. The younger Watson continued his father's policies and supervised IBM's changeover from mechanical to electronic computation during the 1950s.

Like many businessmen engaged in the management of technologically advanced industry during the early 1960s, Watson was a moderate liberal. A friend of John F.

Kennedy, he supported most of the President's policies and acted as a frequent liaison between the Administration and the business community. The President appointed Watson to several advisory panels. In February 1961 he was named a member of the Advisory Committee on Labor-Management Policy, and in March Watson was appointed to the 33-member National Advisory Council for the Peace Corps. Later that year he served on the Citizens Committee for International Development, a volunteer group formed to win public and congressional approval of President Kennedy's foreign aid program. The next year IBM and 37 other companies doing business with the Defense Department signed an agreement with the President's Committee on Equal Employment Opportunities to eliminate job discrimination against blacks.

During the early 1960s IBM increased its annual earnings by over $80 million—from $207 million in 1961 to $290 million in 1963. By the mid-1960s the company produced well over 70% of all computers in the world and had become a worldwide symbol of sophisticated American technology, management and planning.

As a result of IBM's domination of the computer field, the giant corporation faced several antitrust suits in the late 1960s and early 1970s, the largest of which was filed by the Justice Department in the closing days of the Johnson Administration. The suit asked for reorganization of IBM as well as separate pricing of computer hardware and software. Separate pricing was intended to stop IBM from selling or leasing a computer for a fixed fee that covered all costs. The highly complex litigation was still pending well into the 1970s.

In 1972 Watson became chairman of the executive committee of IBM. The next year the company was ranked as the sixth largest in the world, with sales of $8.3 billion. [See NIXON Volume]

[FHM]

For further information:
Robert Sobel, *The Age of Giant Corporations* (New York, 1972).

WEAVER, ROBERT C(LIFTON)
b. Dec. 29, 1907; Washington, D.C.
Administrator, Housing and Home Finance Agency, February 1961-January 1966.

Weaver, the highest ranking black in the Kennedy Administration, was raised in a middle-class, largely white suburb of Washington, D.C. Following his graduation from Dunbar High School in Washington, he went to Harvard University where he earned a B.A. in economics, cum laude, in 1929. During the New Deal and World War II, Weaver served on a number of commissions and agencies to ensure black participation in government-sponsored work and housing projects. Following the war Weaver worked briefly with the United Nations Relief and Rehabilitation Administration and lectured in economics and public affairs at Northwestern University, Columbia Teachers College and the New School for Social Research. From 1949 to 1955 he directed the awarding of fellowships for the John Hay Whitney Foundation.

In December 1955 New York Gov. W. Averell Harriman [q.v.] named Weaver state deputy rent commissioner. In this post, which he held for three years, Weaver earned a reputation for his expertise in city housing problems. In the latter half of 1960 Weaver served as head of the New York City Housing and Redevelopment Board.

In December 1960 President Kennedy announced that he would appoint Weaver administrator of the Housing and Home Finance Agency (HHFA). The appointment of a black to the high post proved controversial, particularly with Southern members of Congress who opposed Weaver's advocacy of integrated housing. Testifying before the Senate Banking and Currency Committee in January 1961, Weaver stated that he favored integrated housing but denied that he would order integration immediately in federal projects. "I don't think I could if I wanted, and I don't think I should if I could," he said. Sen. James O. Eastland (D, Miss.) [q.v.] suggested that Weaver had a "pro-Communist background." Despite such opposition Weaver's appointment was reported favorably from the Banking Committee and confirmed by the Senate in early 1961.

As head of the HHFA Weaver was responsible for management of federal housing, home finance, slum clearance and community development programs. These were of such importance, particularly to the welfare of the nation's cities, that President Kennedy urged that they be dealt with at the cabinet level. In March 1961 he proposed that Congress authorize creation of a new department of housing and urban affairs headed by Weaver.

The Kennedy proposal made no headway in Congress during 1961 because Southern Democrats opposed elevating Weaver to cabinet rank, conservative Republicans viewed the creation of a new cabinet department as a needless expansion of government and rural congressmen could see no benefit for their constituents. During 1962 Kennedy attempted to create the Department without explicit congressional sanction by using his authority under the 1949 Government Reorganization Act. This legislation gave the House or Senate 60 days to veto the Kennedy move by a simple majority vote. In February 1962 the House rejected the new Department, 264 to 150. It remained for the Johnson Administration to win approval of a cabinet-rank department.

Weaver was one of the architects of the Administration's omnibus housing bill, which became law in June 1961. The new law, the most important piece of housing legislation passed since 1949, authorized expenditure of up to $2 billion for construction of low-income public housing, farm dwellings and housing for the elderly. It increased funds available for the Federal National Mortgage Association for new low-interest home mortgages and authorized substantial low-interest loans to colleges, universities and hospitals for the construction of dormitories, dining halls and student centers. The measure won broad congressional approval because it promised to rejuvenate the depressed home building industry.

Weaver lobbied successfully on behalf of the 1962 Senior Citizens Housing Act and for the Johnson Administration's 1964 Housing Act. He was less successful in his efforts to win congressional subsidies for urban mass transit systems.

In January 1966 Weaver attained cabinet rank when named Secretary of the newly created Department of Housing and Urban Development. He continued to testify frequently before congressional committees on behalf of model cities, urban development and housing legislation. He also served as an adviser to President Johnson on civil rights matters. [See JOHNSON Volume]

At the end of the Johnson Administration, Weaver left government service to become president of Bernard M. Baruch College of the City of New York. In 1971 he returned to the classroom as a professor of public affairs at Hunter College of the City of New York. Weaver also served as a trustee of the Bowery Savings Bank and the Metropolitan Life Insurance Company.

[JLW]

WEBB, JAMES E(DWIN)

b. Oct. 7, 1906; Tally Ho, N.C.
Director, National Aeronautics and Space Administration, February 1961-October 1968.

The dominant themes in Webb's career before his appointment as director of the National Aeronautics and Space Administration (NASA) in 1961 were aviation and administration. He learned to fly in 1930 as a Marine Corps reservist. After active service in the early 1930s and during World War II, he retained his reserve commission and became a lieutenant colonel. In 1946 he was appointed director of the Bureau of the Budget and was undersecretary of the treasury from 1949 to 1952. Webb also served on President Harry S Truman's advisory committees on management and military assistance and was a deputy governor of both the International Bank for Reconstruction and Development and the International Monetary Fund. [See TRUMAN Volume]

From 1936 to 1943 Webb was an executive for the Sperry Gyroscope Corporation, which filled numerous military contracts for scientific equipment. When he left government service in 1952, he became Sen. Robert Kerr's (D, Okla.) [q.v.] assistant and a director of Kerr-McGee Oil Industries. During this period Webb was also a director of the McDonnell Aircraft Corporation, the Oak Ridge Institute for Nuclear Studies and banks in Topeka and Oklahoma City.

When Kerr succeeded Sen. Lyndon B. Johnson (D, Tex.) [q.v.] as chairman of the Senate Aeronautical and Space Committee in 1961, he recommended Webb for the top NASA position. Webb assumed the post in February 1961. He encouraged Kennedy to accelerate the cautious space policies of the Eisenhower years and worked with Secretary of Defense Robert S. McNamara [q.v.] to minimize rivalry for space appropriations between NASA and the Defense Department. Webb and McNamara agreed to speed up the development of rocket boosters required for manned flights and told Kennedy that such rockets could launch missiles as well as spacecraft. Kennedy remained skeptical about the huge sums that a more ambitious space program would involve until the Soviet Union made the first manned space flight in April 1961. This blow to American prestige was soon followed by the Bay of Pigs fiasco. With encouragement from Webb, Kennedy seized on space as the arena in which to demonstrate American power.

Scientists in NASA and on the President's Science Advisory Committee advised Kennedy that the U.S. had an excellent chance to be first with a man on the moon. However, several scientists, including Jerome Wiesner [q.v.], who headed the Advisory Committee, questioned the safety and scientific merit of manned flights. While assuring Wiesner that the program would proceed only if technologically sound, Webb joined McNamara in urging manned flights to increase America's international prestige. In a secret memo, which Kennedy received on May 8, they said, "It is man, not merely machines, in space, that captures the imagination of the world. . . . Major successes . . . lend national prestige even though the scientific, commercial or military value of the under-

taking may, by ordinary standards, be marginal or economically unjustified." On May 25 Kennedy announced his support for Project Apollo in a message to Congress, saying that "this nation should commit itself to achieving the goal, before this decade is out, of landing a man on the moon and returning him safely to earth."

Kennedy's proposal called for the rapid development of a lunar spacecraft and simultaneous work on both liquid and solid-fuel booster rockets. In addition, NASA was to supervise a related series of exploratory programs in space. These included unmanned probes to the moon and the nearby planets, a system of weather satellites and development of a Rover nuclear rocket. Congress enthusiastically supported the program and in July 1961 authorized appropriations of $1.671 billion for fiscal 1962, almost double NASA's budget for the previous year. In September 1961 Webb announced that the Apollo Command Center would be established in Houston. By the mid-1960s NASA was spending nearly $5 billion annually.

McNamara assigned all military space projects to the Air Force in March 1961 and in December of the same year ended the commitment to develop one rocket to fulfill both defense and space requirements. The Air Force was directed to develop the solid-fuel Titan 3, and NASA was assigned liquid-fuel boosters. In late 1962 Webb announced that NASA would attempt to land men on the moon through use of a lunar module or "bug." The two-man "bug" would descend to the lunar surface from an orbit around the moon rather than from an earth orbit or on direct flight from the earth itself. The effect of this decision was to enable NASA to put men on the moon without using the gigantic booster rockets once thought necessary.

To develop the Apollo program NASA let about 20,000 contracts and either directly or indirectly employed almost 400,000 workers. North American Aviation was awarded the prime Apollo contract in November 1961. Boeing built the Saturn booster, and Grumman was designated to build the sophisticated lunar "bug."

In his early appearances before Congress,

Webb had stressed that the Soviet Union was methodically working on its own program to land men on the moon. The Soviets, in fact, were not pursuing a moon flight program as aggressively as Webb believed. When Kennedy called for cooperation with the USSR toward a joint moon flight in September 1963, Congress rejected the proposal, although Webb and other NASA officials supported Kennedy. Arthur Schlesinger, Jr. [q.v.], later wrote that the President, concerned over possible Senate dilution of the 1963 nuclear test ban treaty, offered cooperation in space as proof of America's genuine desire for peace.

Although three American astronauts were killed in a controversial Apollo capsule fire in 1967, the U.S. successfully met Kennedy's original goal by landing an Apollo lunar module on the Sea of Tranquility on July 19, 1969, nine months after Webb resigned as NASA director.

[MDB]

For further information:
John M. Logsdon, *The Decision to Go the the Moon: Project Apollo and the National Interest* (Cambridge, Mass., 1970).
Hugo Young, Bryan Silcock, and Peter Dunn, *Journey to Tranquility: The Long Competitive Struggle to Reach the Moon* (Garden City, 1969).

WELCH, ROBERT H(ENRY) W(INBORNE)
b. Dec. 1, 1899; Chowan County, N.C.
Founder, John Birch Society, 1958- .

The son of a Baptist preacher, Welch graduated from the University of North Carolina in 1916. After attending the Naval Academy at Annapolis for one year and Harvard Law School for two years, he entered his family's candy business and became a successful sales manager. In 1941 Welch wrote *The Road to Salesmanship*, in which he contended that salesmen played a key role in stemming the tide of socialism by stimulating materialistic desires and acquisitive instincts.

During the early 1950s Welch became interested in the problem of Communist infiltration into American institutions, and in 1957 he left the vice presidency of the candy company to devote all of his time to anti-Communist work. In December 1958 he founded the John Birch Society (named after an American intelligence officer killed by the Chinese Communists in August 1945), which he directed from his hometown, Belmont, Mass. The major premise of the organization was that the Communist threat was represented not by Soviet military might but by the presence of traitors in America. He described the group as an educational society created for the purpose of alerting his countrymen to this internal threat.

The Birth Society first gained national attention under unfavorable circumstances in February 1961, when Sen. Milton R. Young (R, N.D.) [q.v.] revealed that Welch, in a privately printed book circulated in the 1950s (published in 1963 as *The Politician*), had denounced President Dwight D. Eisenhower [q.v.] as a "dedicated conscious agent of the Communist conspiracy. . . ." Welch asserted that the book represented only his personal view. But since the organization denounced Supreme Court Justice Earl Warren [q.v.] and many other widely respected figures as Communists and contended that the U.S. government was 40% to 60% Communist-controlled, the disavowal did little to mitigate the negative impression created by Sen. Young's revelation. Furthermore, since Welch exercised unquestioned control over the Society, with authority to remove members of its national council at will, it was difficult to separate his opinions from the official positions of the organization.

The Society, and particularly Welch's leadership, was criticized by much of the political right as well as by liberals. An editorial in the Feb. 13, 1962 issue of *National Review*, the most important magazine of American conservatism, asserted that Welch was harming the anti-Communist cause by failing to distinguish between "an active pro-Communist" and "an ineffectually anti-Communist liberal." Welch acknowledged that attacks such as these hampered the growth of the Society.

In 1964 Welch appointed John H. Rousselot [q.v.], an experienced public relations consultant, as the Society's national director of public relations. Rousselot had some success in creating a more moderate image for the Society, and its membership reached a peak of about 95,000 in the mid-1960s. But the resignations of key officers—including Rousselot—in 1966 and 1967 and the emergence of anti-Semitic tendencies within the organization in 1966, thwarted further growth. In the late 1960s and early 1970s, Welch articulated increasingly arcane conspiracy theories involving the Society of the Illuminati and international bankers, and the Society declined in strength. [See JOHNSON Volume]

[MLL]

For further information:
George Barrett, "Close-Up of the Birchers' 'Founder,'" The New York Times Magazine (May 14, 1961), p. 13+.
Chester Morrison, "The Man Behind the Birch Society," Look (Sept. 26, 1961), pp. 23-27.

WHITE, BYRON R(AYMOND)
b. June 8, 1917; Fort Collins, Colo.
Deputy Attorney General, January 1961-April 1962; U.S. Associate Justice, Supreme Court, 1957-62.

White grew up in Wellington, a small Colorado town near the Wyoming border. Class valedictorian when he graduated from the University of Colorado in 1938, "Whizzer" White was a football All-American in college and a Pittsburgh Steeler for the 1938 season. A Rhodes scholar at Oxford University in early 1939, White entered Yale Law School in October of that year and then played professional football for the Detroit Lions in 1940 and 1941. After service in the Navy in World War II, White completed his legal studies at Yale in November 1946 and served as law clerk to Supreme Court Chief Justice Fred Vinson during the Court's 1946-47 term. White then entered private practice, joining a prestigious Denver law firm.

A friend of John Kennedy's since 1939, White was an early supporter of Kennedy's bid for the 1960 Democratic presidential nomination. He led the Kennedy forces in Colorado, delivering 13½ of the state's 21 votes for Kennedy at the Democratic National Convention, and then headed a nationwide Citizens for Kennedy-Johnson organization during the 1960 campaign. Named Deputy Attorney General in January 1961, White assisted Attorney General Robert F. Kennedy [q.v.] in recruiting highly qualified attorneys for the Justice Department. Considered an able administrator, White supervised the Department's antitrust and civil rights suits and was in charge of evaluating candidates for federal judicial appointments.

On May 20, 1961 the freedom riders, civil rights demonstrators challenging segregated transportation, were assaulted by a mob in Montgomery, Ala. White personally commanded the more than 500 federal marshals ordered to Montgomery later that day by the Attorney General. He also conferred with Alabama Gov. John Patterson [q.v.] and the head of the Alabama National Guard during the crisis.

With the retirement of Associate Justice Charles Whittaker [q.v.], President Kennedy selected White as his first Supreme Court nominee on March 30, 1962. Confirmed by the Senate on April 11, White registered his first dissent in June in a case in which the Court majority overturned a California law that made drug addiction a crime. In the next Court term White surprised many observers who had expected this New Frontier Democrat to align himself with the Court's liberals. Instead Justice White usually voted with the conservative bloc in cases involving civil liberties and criminal rights. He dissented when the majority overturned a Virginia law barring the solicitation of legal business, which had been used to thwart litigation by the NAACP. He dissented in another case in which the majority placed limits on the powers of a Florida legislative committee investigating the NAACP. Justice White also voted to sustain federal laws providing for the revocation of the citizenship of Americans who left the country to avoid military service.

White remained a conservative on the issue of criminal rights during the Johnson years, dissenting for example from the Court's celebrated Miranda ruling in 1966.

He took a more liberal and activist position in certain race discrimination cases, however, and voted consistently in favor of the "one-man, one-vote" rule for reapportionment of legislative districts. [See JOHNSON, NIXON Volumes]

[CAB]

For further information:
Fred L. Israel, "Byron R. White," in Leon Friedman and Fred L. Israel, eds., *The Justices of the United States Supreme Court, 1789-1969* (New York, 1969), Vol. IV.

WHITE, THEODORE H(AROLD)
b. May 6, 1915; Boston, Mass.
Journalist.

After his graduation from Harvard in 1938, Theodore White became *Time* magazine's Far Eastern correspondent. One of the few journalists to predict that there would be a civil war in China and that the Communists would eventually win it, White was known as "the dean of the Chungking correspondents" during World War II. After a stint as senior editor of the liberal *New Republic*, White served as European correspondent for the Overseas News Agency and then for the *Reporter*. From his observations came the best-selling 1953 book *Fire in the Ashes*, a study of the postwar regeneration of Western Europe. In 1955 White joined *Collier's* as political affairs correspondent and covered the 1956 presidential election for the magazine. After the financial collapse of *Collier's*, he wrote two bestselling novels, *The Mountain Road* and *The View from the Fortieth Floor*.

In the fall of 1959 White began covering the seven most prominent Republican and Democratic presidential hopefuls. He followed the candidates closely during the course of the 1960 primaries, the convention proceedings and the general election campaign itself. White broke with journalistic tradition by gambling that a book-length, in-depth account of the campaign would find a wide readership several months after the results of the elections were known. *The Making of the President 1960*, subtitled "a narrative history of American politics in action," appeared in late 1961 and was an overnight best-seller. It won wide critical acclaim and stayed at the top of the *New York Times* bestseller list for more than a year.

White brought to the book the narrative skill and sociological and psychological insights of a novelist. The book detailed campaign strategy, offered glimpses into the inner workings of each candidate's organization and illustrated "the mood and the strains, the weariness, elation and uncertainty" of the candidates themselves. White focused particular attention on the Democratic candidate and applauded the Kennedy campaign organization's efficiency, toughness and energy. His sympathetic portrait of the Kennedys and their staff did much to enhance the Administration's prestige. After publication Kennedy expressed his admiration for the book, but according to historian Arthur M. Schlesinger, Jr. [*q.v.*], the President felt that the characters had been portrayed somewhat larger than life.

White continued to write best-selling *Making of the President* books after the 1964, 1968 and 1972 elections. His books drew increasingly less critical praise, however, in part because his narrative technique had influenced other journalists and was therefore no longer unique. In addition White's tendency to lionize political figures found less favor among American intellectuals during the more iconoclastic mood of the late 1960s and early 1970s.

[FHM]

For further information:
Theodore H. White, *The Making of the President 1960* (New York, 1961).

WHITTAKER, CHARLES E(VANS)
b. Feb. 22, 1901; Troy, Kan.
Associate Justice, U.S. Supreme Court, 1957-62.

Born on a Kansas farm, Whittaker moved to Kansas City, Mo., in 1920, where he worked as an office boy for a local law firm while attending the University of Kansas City Law School at night. He was admitted to the state bar in 1923 and received his law degree the next year. Joining the firm where he had been office boy, Whittaker eventually became one of the leading corporate attorneys in the Midwest. A conservative Republican but inactive and a close friend of President Eisenhower's brother Arthur, Whittaker was named a federal district court judge in Kansas City in 1954 with virtually unanimous support from local political and bar leaders. Two years later he was promoted to a judgeship on the Eighth Circuit Court of Appeals.

In March 1957 President Eisenhower nominated Whittaker as an associate justice of the Supreme Court. The Senate confirmed his appointment the same month. On the Court Whittaker generally aligned himself with justices such as Felix Frankfurter [q.v.], who advocated judicial self-restraint and deference to the legislature. Although Whittaker sometimes voted with the Court's "liberal bloc" in cases involving criminal rights, citizenship and the rights of aliens, he usually took what was considered a conservative position, voting to deny a claimed civil liberty or right and to uphold statutes against constitutional challenges. During his five-year Court tenure he voted with conservatives in 41 five-to-four decisions involving civil liberties. [See EISENHOWER Volume]

Whittaker wrote the opinion for a unanimous Court in a 1961 case holding that an uneducated and mentally ill defendant needed the assistance of counsel in a state prosecution for assault. He also delivered the majority opinion in a 6-3 decision the same year that overturned a federal conviction based on an illegal search by state police. Whittaker dissented, however, when the Court decided, 5-4, in Mapp v. Ohio (1961) that illegally seized evidence was inadmissible in state courts. He voted with a five-man majority in another 1961 case upholding a Chicago ordinance that barred public showing of movies without prior approval of city censors.

Whittaker voted with the majority in a series of 5-4 decisions in 1961 involving Communism. In two decisions handed down in February, he voted to uphold the investigative power of the House Un-American Activities Committee and to sustain the contempt of Congress convictions of witnesses who had refused to answer

Committee questions. Whittaker also voted in June to uphold the requirement in the 1950 Internal Security Act for Communist-action organizations to register with the government and the clause in the 1940 Smith Act that made it a crime to be an active member of a party advocating violent overthrow of the government.

On March 16, 1962 Whittaker entered the hospital suffering from exhaustion. He resigned from the Court on March 29, explaining that the "great volume and continuous stresses of the Court's work" had brought him to the "point of physical exhaustion" and that his doctors had warned him that staying on the Court would jeopardize his health. According to legal scholar Henry J. Abraham, Whittaker had not found genuine satisfaction on the Supreme Court and had been overwhelmed by both the volume and gravity of the Court's business.

On his retirement there was wide praise from his fellow justices and others for Whittaker's hard work on the Court and for his qualities of modesty, gentleness and sincerity. Court experts, however, did not rate his judicial performance highly. Whittaker had a narrow view of his role on the Court, wrote few opinions of consequence and was not considered significant as either a judicial thinker or a legal technician. He articulated no judicial philosophy, and in a 1970 survey of legal historians and scholars Whittaker was ranked as one of eight "failures" to serve on the Court since 1789. Whittaker retained his Supreme Court commission after he left the Court, but he resigned the commission in October 1965 to take a position on the legal staff of General Motors. In April 1966 he was appointed a consultant to the Senate Committee on Standards and Conduct to help work on code of senatorial ethics. He played an important role in the subsequent investigation of Sen. Thomas Dodd (D, Conn.) [q.v.] for improper use of campaign funds.

[CAB]

For further information:
Leon Friedman, "Charles Whittaker," in Leon Friedman and Fred L. Israel, eds., The Justices of the United States Supreme Court, 1789-1969 (New York, 1969), Vol. IV.

WIESNER, JEROME B(ERT)

b. May 30, 1915; Detroit, Mich.
Special Assistant to the President on Science and Technology, Chairman, President's Science Advisory Committee, February 1961-February 1964.

Wiesner received his masters degree in electrical engineering from the University of Michigan in 1937 and was appointed chief engineer of the acoustical and record laboratory of the Library of Congress in 1940. He worked on record preservation there and traveled with John and Alan Lomax recording folksongs in the field. He joined the radiation laboratory at the Massachusetts Institute of Technology in 1942 to work on radar development and in 1945-46 designed instrumentation at Los Alamos for the Bikini Island atom bomb tests. Wiesner accepted a teaching position at M.I.T. in 1946. There he conducted research on the transmission of radar signals around the curves of the earth and helped develop a "scatter" system for the reflection of high frequency waves. He was selected to head M.I.T.'s Center for Communications when it was established in 1958 and became a member of the Army Scientific Advisory Board in 1956. Wiesner joined the President's Science Advisory Committee (PSAC) in 1957.

During his 1960 presidential campaign Sen. John F. Kennedy named Wiesner to his academic advisory committee to counsel him on scientific issues during the campaign. Kennedy hoped this committee would help win him the support of liberal intellectuals. In February 1961 he appointed Wiesner his special assistant for science and technology and chairman of PSAC. One of Wiesner's first tasks was to set up an Ad Hoc Committee on Space to evaluate space programs under the National Aeronautics and Space Administration (NASA) and the Department of Defense. Advocating a more aggressive space program, the Committee criticized the duplication of research by NASA and the military and recommended greater coordination between the program's various functions. It criticized the program's emphasis on Project Mercury, calling manned flights an area where it was "unlikely that we shall be first." Wiesner favored the appointment of an experienced administrator to head NASA rather than a political or academic figure. His viewpoint prevailed when James E. Webb [q.v.] was selected in February 1961.

Following the Soviet Union's first manned space flight in April 1961, Kennedy became convinced of the importance of space exploration as an indication of the relative strength of each of the two major powers. Wiesner advised the President that while the Soviets held the lead in the earlier stages of space exploration, the U.S. had a better chance to be the first on the moon. He urged caution regarding the safety of manned flights and feared that concentrating scientific resources on the space program would produce distortions in scientific development. In May 1961, a few weeks after the failure of the Bay of Pigs invasion, Kennedy announced that the U.S. would attempt a manned moon landing by 1970. Wiesner later said he believed that Kennedy "felt some pressure to put something else in the foreground. . . . I think the Bay of Pigs put him in a mood to run harder than he might have."

Wiesner was also consulted on other areas of U.S.-Soviet policy. In November 1960 Kennedy sent him to Moscow as an unofficial emissary of the incoming Administration to negotiate the release of two American airmen whose jet had been shot down over the Barents Sea in July 1960. When the Soviet Union resumed atmospheric nuclear tests in September 1961, Wiesner opposed the resumption of American aboveground tests. He called the tests "not critical or even very important to our overall military posture." Nevertheless, Kennedy authorized resumption of atmospheric testing in March 1962. When the U.S. and the Soviet Union opened negotiations on a nuclear test ban treaty, the question of on-site test inspections was a stumbling block to an agreement. Nikita Khrushchev was at first adamantly opposed to any international inspections, but in December 1962 he indicated to Kennedy that he would consider three inspections a year. Kennedy then sent Wiesner and Arthur Dean [q.v.] to begin informal talks with the Soviets on a suspension of nuclear testing. Wiesner disagreed with Kennedy, maintaining that five inspections would be adequate, while Kennedy insisted on seven. When the test ban treaty was signed in August 1963, the issue was moot, since underground tests were left unrestricted.

Wiesner left his government posts in February 1964 but worked with Scientists and Engineers for Johnson-Humphrey in the November election. He was dean of science at M.I.T. from 1964 to 1966 and then served as provost until 1971 when he succeeded James R. Killian as M.I.T. president.

[MDB]

For further information:
John M. Logsdon, *The Decision to Go to the Moon: Project Apollo and the National Interest* (Cambridge, Mass., 1970).

WILEY, ALEXANDER
b. May 26, 1884; Chippewa Falls, Wisc.
d. Oct. 26, 1967; Philadelphia, Pa.
Republican Senator, Wisc., 1939-63.

Alexander Wiley returned to his home town of Chippewa Falls after receiving his law degree from the University of Michigan in 1907. For the next 32 years he was, according to his own description, "just a small-town banker, businessman, lawyer and operator of a dairy who became a typical American success." An active civic booster and a leader in the Kiwanis International, Wiley was labeled a "political Babbitt" by his opponents.

He was elected to the Senate in 1938 as a conservative Republican isolationist, but by 1943 Sen. Arthur Vandenberg (R, Mich.) had won him to the internationalist camp. On the Foreign Relations Committee from 1945 and as chairman during 1953-54, Wiley was an exponent of a bipartisan foreign policy and a supporter of major Administration initiatives in the Cold War era. Wiley's opposition to the Bricker Amendment, which would have limited the Executive's treaty-making powers, resulted in criticism from his Republican Wisconsin colleague, Sen. Joseph McCarthy and a vote of censure by the Wisconsin Republican organization. The state Party convention denied Wiley its endorsement in 1956 in favor of Glenn Davis, but Wiley went on to win the Republican primary and the election. [See TRUMAN, EISENHOWER Volumes]

At the outset of the Kennedy Administration, Wiley was the dean of Senate Republicans. He was the ranking Republican on the Aeronautical and Space Sciences, Judiciary and the Foreign Relations Committees. Wiley continued to couple a conservative posture on domestic issues with overall support for the Administration's foreign policy. *Congressional Quarterly* reported that in the 87th Congress Wiley supported the Kennedy Administration on 77% of foreign policy votes but on only 39% of its domestic legislative requests.

In April 1961 Wiley criticized Sen. Estes Kefauver's (D, Tenn.) [q.v.] probe of price-fixing in the electrical industry as "a publicity venture" prejudicial to pending damage suits against the firms. He voted for Kennedy's school-aid bill in May 1961 but opposed medicare in July 1962. Wiley prodded the Administration to pursue a more aggressive policy vis-a-vis Fidel Castro's Cuba, proposing in August 1962 that Cuba be blockaded by an inter-American "peace fleet" to keep it from receiving Communist military supplies. In November 1962 Wiley was defeated by Wisconsin's liberal Democratic governor, Gaylord Nelson [q.v.], in a senatorial race in which the 78-year-old Wiley's age was a campaign issue. Wiley died of a stroke on Oct. 26, 1967.

[TO]

WILKINS, ROY
b. Aug. 30, 1901; St. Louis, Mo.
Executive Secretary, NAACP, 1955-77.

Wilkins was raised by an aunt and uncle in an integrated neighborhood in St. Paul, Minn. In 1923, while working his way through the University of Minnesota, Wilkins became secretary of the local NAACP chapter. He left St. Paul the following year to become a reporter for the *Kansas City Call.* His leadership in local NAACP affairs persuaded the organization's national leadership to hire Wilkins in 1931 to work as an assistant secretary in its New York headquarters. Upon the death of NAACP executive secretary Walter White in 1955, Wilkins was unanimously elected as his successor.

As a U.S. senator, John F. Kennedy had been regarded by civil rights leaders, in Arthur M. Schlesinger's [*q.v.*] words, as a "sympathetic. . .but detached" friend of Negroes. Wilkins had provided Kennedy with a letter during his 1958 reelection campaign, endorsing his record as one of the best in the Senate. In his campaign for the presidency, Kennedy pledged executive action, particularly in the field of housing, to end discrimination "by a stroke of the president's pen." Executive actions were taken soon after his inauguration to end discrimination in federal employment, but they fell short of what civil rights leaders believed Kennedy had promised. There was no stroke of the pen ending discrimination in federally financed housing until Nov. 30, 1962. Wilkins and his colleagues were also disappointed in Kennedy's refusal to back civil rights legislation introduced by congressional liberals to fulfill the 1960 Democratic platform pledges. In July 1961 Wilkins led a delegation of NAACP officials to meet with the President and voice their dismay at "the absence of a clear call" from him for new legislation. Kennedy replied that existing civil rights legislation had not been fully utilized. Furthermore, he said, the Administration lacked the votes to pass significant legislation.

At the President's request, Wilkins submitted a 61-page memorandum in 1961 urging Kennedy to sign an across-the-board executive order—to govern "the whole executive branch of government"—barring employment discrimination throughout the federal government and in all state programs receiving federal aid. Federal expenditures in excess of $1.1 billion, the civil rights leader noted, continued to "require, support or condone" discrimination in 11 Southern states. Sensitive to the political repercussions of cutting off aid to state programs, President Kennedy never issued the sweeping order.

During 1961 the Administration pressed voting rights and school discrimination cases in the courts, used federal marshals to defend freedom riders in Alabama and successfully petitioned the Interstate Commerce Commission to order desegregation of facilities in interstate bus terminals. But the initiative Wilkins hoped for was missing. Addressing the annual meeting of the NAACP in January 1962, Wilkins praised Kennedy for "his personal role in civil rights" but declared his "disappointment with Mr. Kennedy's first year" because of his failure to issue the housing order and his strategy of "no legislative action on civil rights." When the Administration introduced a measure to bar the arbitrary use of literacy tests in January 1962, Wilkins testified for the bill but also complained that it was "inadequate" and only "a token offering." (Even this limited bill was killed by a Southern filibuster in the Senate.)

The rapid spread in early 1963 of the direct action movement and the repression it met in many Southern communities forced the Administration to revise the "no legislation" strategy. In June President Kennedy sent Congress a draft civil rights act aimed at ending discrimination in public accommodations, permitting federal initiation of school desegregation suits and eliminating racial bias in voter registration. Earlier in the month Wilkins, widely regarded as the most moderate of all the prominent civil rights leaders, had been arrested with the NAACP's Mississippi field secretary, Medgar Evers [*q.v.*], during a demonstration in Jackson. Evers was shot to death outside his home less than two weeks later.

Civil rights leaders feared that even the momentum generated by events in the South and the Administration's support might prove insufficient to overcome congressional resistance. The idea of a peaceful mass march on Washington began to win support as a dramatic protest against any congressional delay. Initially, Wilkins was skeptical about the march. But the competition from the more direct-action civil rights organizations, the abandonment of plans for civil disobedience by the march organizers and the threat of a Southern filibuster against the bill won him over. Reflecting the mood of militance among delegates to the NAACP's Chicago convention in early July, Wilkins endorsed the march. (One factor contributing to Wilkins's hesitation was the choice of Bayard Rustin [q.v.] to direct the march. He feared Rustin's radical past might discredit the demonstration in the eyes of moderates on Capitol Hill. As a compromise, A. Philip Randolph [q.v.] served as the director with Rustin acting as his deputy.) Addressing the throng of over 200,000 that assembled on Aug. 28 at the Lincoln Memorial, Wilkins demanded not only passage of the Kennedy bill but also the inclusion of a fair employment practices provision. (The legislation was eventually passed in 1964.)

Wilkins's and the NAACP's long preeminence in the struggle for equality was increasingly challenged during the early 1960s by more militant leaders and organizations. Dry and somewhat aloof in manner, Wilkins lacked the evangelical fervor of such Southern leaders as Martin Luther King [q.v.] and rejected the stridency of the student leaders. Under Wilkins's leadership, the NAACP continued to stress legislative and legal action, often being scorned for its moderation and ridiculed as part of the establishment by those seeking a revolutionary confrontation with white society. Despite these attacks, Wilkins remained the leader of the nation's largest and most active civil rights organization with some 500,000 members and 1,600 local chapters. By virtue of its size and stable leadership, the NAACP was a significant factor in the growth of the direct action movement. Wilkins, impatient with those who disparaged the NAACP, once remarked that the more militant organizations tended to garner "the publicity while the NAACP furnishes the manpower and pays the bills."

Wilkins continued to lead the NAACP during the tumultuous period of urban riots and escalating rhetoric after Kennedy's assassination, consistently repudiating the strategies and language of black nationalism and urging the complete integration of blacks into American society. [See JOHNSON, NIXON Volumes]

[EWK]

For further information:
Thomas R. Brooks, *The Walls Came Tumbling Down: A History of the Civil Rights Movement* (New York, 1974)

WILLIAMS, G(ERHARD) MENNEN
b. Feb. 23, 1911; Detroit, Mich.
Assistant Secretary of State for African Affairs, February 1961-March 1966.

The grandson of a men's soap manufacturer and the son of a pickle magnate, "Soapy" Williams graduated with honors from Princeton and the University of Michigan Law School. Beginning in 1937, Williams worked for Gov. Frank Murphy at Lansing and later at the Justice Department when Murphy served as United States Attorney General. In 1948 Williams formed a political alliance with Democratic liberals and the powerful United Auto Workers and won the first of six terms as governor of Michigan. Williams endorsed John F. Kennedy for the Democratic presidential nomination in June 1960, and he led a delegation to the Party's national convention which gave Kennedy 42½ of its 51 votes. [See TRUMAN, EISENHOWER Volumes]

Declining to seek reelection in 1960, Williams accepted Kennedy's offer in January 1961 to serve as assistant secretary of state for African affairs. Kennedy had rejected appointing Williams to a top cabinet position, and the Michigan politician agreed to a sub-cabinet designation with mixed feelings. However, sporting an emblematic green polka-dot bow tie, Williams soon brought his characteristic enthusiasm to the heretofore demoralized State Department African Bureau. For his prestige as a former governor and his outstanding civil rights record, Williams won the strong endorsement of African nations.

On his first African tour in February 1961, Williams called for a policy of "Africa for Africans" and offended European colonial powers and many white Africans, one of whom assaulted him during an August 1961 visit to Rhodesia. Kennedy defended Williams's "Africans" statement in a March 1961 press conference. The President supported his view that the Administration should adopt a "New Africa" foreign policy that generally favored the nationalist aspirations of new African countries.

The Congo [Zaire] crisis proved Williams's most important challenge during his service with the State Department. The

Congo had been torn by civil unrest since the new nation had received its independence from Belgium in June 1960. The mineral-rich Katanga province, which provided 60% of the national government's total revenue, seceded from the new state. Backed by important European mining insterests, Katanga province leader Moise Tshombe employed foreign white mercenary troops to fight the national Congolese army. Most of the new African states opposed Tshombe's action.

After much negotiation Williams, United States Ambassador Adlai E. Stevenson [q.v.] and State Department "New Africa" forces maneuvered a resolution on the Congo through the U.N. Security Council in February 1961. The resolution ordered the withdrawal of Belgian and white mercenary military personnel and called upon a U.N. peacekeeping force to use "force if necessary" to bring about a resolution of the civil war. In its attempt to end the Katangan secession, the U.N. force, financed largely by the U.S. government, soon engaged in sporadic warfare with Katangan forces. Despite the continued bloodshed, Tshombe refused to negotiate the issue of Katangan sovereignty. In late 1960 Katanga had established a New York public relations office which sought to win support from congressmen and journalists. Williams became increasingly frustrated by Tshombe's efforts to influence American public opinion, and in a December 1961 Detroit address, he critized the "horrendous lies of indiscriminate mayhem by United Nations troops" that he alleged Katanga's American supporters had spread. Immediately following his address, Undersecretary of State George C. McGhee ordered Williams to retract the word "lies" and asserted that Williams's address had not been "cleared at the highest levels of the [State] Department."

After McGhee's rebuke Williams paid greater attention to congressional opinion while continuing to work for a United Nations settlement of the Congolese conflict. In the summer of 1962 Williams and the "New Africa" group formulated a revised U.N. plan for the reunification of the Con-

go. The new proposal would have compelled the national government to share equally Katangan revenues with the province. If Katanga refused to accept the new proposal, the U.N. would have imposed an economic embargo against the secessionist state. McGhee, who was attempting to negotiate directly with Tshombe, urged caution, but Williams, having won the approval of some European powers, persuaded the Administration to announce its support of the plan on Aug. 25, 1962. Williams defended his policy stand in speeches that fall, warning that if the U.S. failed to support the Congolese government against Tshombe, it might seek the aid of the Soviet Union. Under pressure from the U.N., the Katanga leader agreed to the new unification plan in December 1962.

Williams's policymaking role all but ended after Kennedy's assassination. In April 1964 President Johnson designated Undersecretary of State W. Averell Harriman [q.v.] to be his chief adviser on Africa. Despite his loss of power, Williams waited until March 1966 to leave the State Department.

Williams's return to Michigan proved less than triumphant. Although he defeated Detroit Mayor Jerome P. Cavanagh [q.v.] for the senatorial nomination in the August 1966 primary, the once unbeatable governor lost to Sen. Robert P. Griffin (R, Mich.) [q.v.] by just under 300,000 votes in the general election. Johnson appointed Williams ambassador to the Philippines, where he served between May 1968 and March 1969. A second Michigan homecoming also proved disappointing, when the Michigan State University Board of Trustees rejected Willliams's nomination for the University presidency in October 1969. In November 1970, however, Williams won election to the state supreme court.

[JLB]

For further information:
Roger Hilsman, *To Move a Nation* (Garden City, 1967).
G. Mennen Williams, *Africa for Africans* (New York, 1969).

WILLIAMS, HARRISON A(RLINGTON), JR.

b. Dec. 10, 1919; Plainfield, N.J.
Democratic Senator, N.J., 1959- ;
Chairman, Labor and Public Welfare
Subcommittee on Migratory Labor,
1959-69.

Born and raised in Plainfield, N.J., Williams received his B.A. from Oberlin and his law degree from Columbia in 1948. After losing New Jersey state and municipal races in 1951 and 1952, Williams announced his candidacy for Congress following Rep. Clifford Case's (R, N.J.) [q.v.] resignation in August 1953. Informed by the Democratic National Committee that it was "against party policy to spend money in hopeless contests," Williams borrowed money to finance his campaign and in November 1953 defeated a conservative Republican to become the first Democratic congressman in the sixth district's 21-year history.

Williams lost his seat in the 1956 Eisenhower landslide but received important statewide exposure the next year as director of the Robert Meyner for Governor Clubs. In April 1958 Gov. Meyner designated Williams as the Democratic organization's senatorial candidate. Williams's November victory made him the first Democratic senator from New Jersey since 1936.

Williams supported Kennedy Administration social welfare programs and was floor manager of the Administration's urban mass transportation and national service corps proposals in 1963. He chaired the Labor and Public Welfare Subcommittee on Migratory Labor from its inception in 1959 and in February 1961 introduced an 11-bill package to aid farm workers. The measures proposed extension of the minimum wage to agricultural workers, stronger prohibitions against child labor on farms, federal registration of farm labor contractors and inclusion of agricultural employment under the National Labor Relations Act. He recommended the establishment of a presidential advisory council on migratory labor and increased federal appropriations for local

housing, education and health programs for farm laborers. The Senate passed five of Williams's bills in 1961, but the House failed to take action until September 1962, when it passed a Williams proposal appropriating $3 million to public and non-profit agencies for health services to domestic migrant workers. Kennedy signed the bill Sept. 25, 1962.

In 1963 the Senate again passed several of Williams's measures to aid migrant laborers, but none reached the House floor. Williams's bill requiring the annual registration of farm labor contractors became law in September 1964. Programs similar to his education, housing, day-care and sanitation proposals were incorporated into the Johnson Administration's Economic Opportunity Act and omnibus housing bill, which became law in 1964. During the Johnson years Williams strongly supported the Administration's Great Society programs and in 1967 became chairman of the Special Committee on Aging. Throughout the decade, as he later admitted, Williams undercut his effectiveness by heavy drinking. He reportedly gave up alcohol in 1968. [See JOHNSON Volume]

[DKR]

WILLIAMS, JOHN B(ELL)

b. Dec. 4, 1918; Raymond, Miss.
Democratic Representative, Miss.,
1947-68.

Consistently reelected to the U.S. House of Representatives with little or no opposition in the 1950s and 1960s, Williams was known as one of the leading opponents of civil rights measures on Capitol Hill. In December 1955 he and U.S. Sen. James O. Eastland (D, Miss.) [q.v.] recommended that the Southern states pass acts of nullification against the Supreme Court's school desegregation decision of the previous year. He refused to support Adlai E. Stevenson for president in 1956 because of the civil rights plank in the national Democratic Party's platform.

For the same reason Williams declined to endorse John F. Kennedy's presidential bid in 1960, and at the Democratic National

Convention in July he and Rep. William M. Colmer (D, Miss.) [*q.v.*] announced that they would back an independent slate of electors. During the Kennedy Administration Williams, as a member of the House's District of Columbia Committee, opposed Administration home rule bills for Washington, which had a large black population. He also denounced the integration of Washington's schools, asserting in January 1961 that "interracial strife will continue in the District schools . . . so long as those in power persist in their present practice of denying that ethnic differences do in fact exist." In October 1963 he played a leading role in the unsuccessful employment by Southerners of procedural tactics to block a bill extending the life of the U.S. Civil Rights Commission.

Williams opposed not only civil rights measures but also the entire spectrum of liberal legislation. During the three years of the Kennedy Administration, according to *Congressional Quarterly*, he never voted against the Southern Democrat-Republican conservative coalition. In August 1961 he offered an amendment to a foreign aid bill barring assistance to any nation which in the future voted for the admission of Communist China to the United Nations. It was rejected by a vote of 102 to 212. In September 1962 he initiated procedural delaying tactics that prevented liberals from circumventing the Rules Committee, chaired by conservative Rep. Howard Smith (D, Va.) [*q.v.*], and bringing Administration-backed mass transit and youth employment bills to the floor of the House.

In 1964 Williams backed Republican presidential candidate Sen. Barry M. Goldwater (R, Ariz.) [*q.v.*]. The Democratic House Caucus retaliated the following year by stripping Williams of his seniority. In 1967 Williams defeated racial moderates in the Democratic gubernatorial primary and the general election to win a four-year term as Mississippi's chief executive. [See JOHNSON Volume]

[MLL]

For further information:
Neal R. Peirce, *The Deep South States* of America (New York, 1972).

WILLIAMS, JOHN J(AMES)
b. May 17, 1904; Frankford, Del.
Republican Senator, Del., 1947-71.

As the senior senator from Delaware, John Williams gained a reputation as "the conscience of the Senate" for crusades against official corruption during his 24 years in the upper house. The owner of a chicken-feed business before entering national politics, Williams ran for the Senate in 1946 on a conservative platform advocating a reduction of government control over the economy. While in the Senate Williams voted against most domestic social welfare legislation and foreign aid measures. The Senator was a constant opponent of large-scale government spending and of measures that increased the powers of the executive branch. Williams was also one of the most consistent supporters of the conservative coalition of Southern Democrats and Republicans in the Senate.

Shortly after coming to the Senate, Williams became involved in investigations of corruption, a topic that would become his major political interest throughout his career. In 1947 he was on the committee that investigated defense spending. Four years later Williams opened a campaign against corruption in the Internal Revenue Service. Later in the decade he demanded an investigation of influence-peddling by presidential adviser Sherman Adams. [See TRUMAN, EISENHOWER Volumes]

During the Kennedy Administration Williams continued his one-man campaign against corruption. In 1961 he opposed the nomination of Julius Holmes to be ambassador to Iran because of the nominee's involvement in profitable sales of surplus tankers at the end of World War II. One year later he opposed the appointment of Matthew McCloskey [*q.v.*] as ambassador to Ireland because of his alleged involvement in government payoffs.

In February 1963 Williams attacked Rep. Adam Clayton Powell (D, N.Y.) [*q.v.*] for using taxpayers' money for private purposes, including frequent trips to Europe. In addition the Senator denounced the loose manner" in which government agencies including the Department of Health,

Education and Welfare and the Housing and Home Finance Agency, had been "shoveling the taxpayers' money" to Powell. He charged also that the Treasury Department had ignored Powell's tax delinquency. Powell called the charges "deliberate inaccuracies" and maintained that he had done nothing more than "just what every other" congressman and committee chairman had done. In reaction to Pwell's use of congressional funds for his travels, Williams unsuccessfully introduced a measure to limit the daily spending allowance granted to congressmen on trips abroad.

In 1963 Williams initiated a personal probe that led to the Senate investigation of Bobby Baker [q.v.], the secretary to the Senate majority. Williams retired in 1971. [See JOHNSON, NIXON Volumes]

[EWS]

WILSON, BOB (ROBERT) (CARLTON)

b. April 5, 1916; Calexico, Calif.
Republican Representative, Calif., 1953- ; Chairman, National Republican Congressional Committee, 1961-63.

Wilson worked for a San Diego public relations firm after World War II as an account executive for a number of right-wing Republicans. In 1952 he won a seat in the House of Representatives from San Diego, the U.S. Navy's West Coast headquarters and a major center for aerospace defense contractors. Wilson's constituents included many Navy personnel and aerospace employees, and his voting record reflected the district's conservative and pro-military sentiments. Appointed to the Armed Services Committee during his freshman term, he was able to channel many defense contracts and military installations into San Diego. Wilson served as campaign manager for Vice President Richard M. Nixon's [q.v.] reelection campaign in 1956 and as the scheduling director for Nixon's 1960 presidential bid.

Wilson was generally opposed to the policies of the Kennedy Administration in the early 1960s. According to Congressional Quarterly, he backed the Administration on only 32%, 33% and 30% of key House roll-call votes in 1961, 1962 and 1963, respectively.

In June 1961 Wilson became chairman of the National Republican Congressional Committee after former chairman Rep. William E. Miller (R, N.Y.) [q.v.] was named to head the Republican National Committee. The role of the Congressional Committee was to promote the election of Republicans to the House of Representatives, but when Wilson assumed the chairmanship it was little more than a clearing house for political contributions. Employing his public relations experience, Wilson not only enlarged the pool of funds available to candidates, from an average of about $1,000 per candidate to approximately $4,000 by the end of the decade, but also provided Republican nominees with a wide range of services.

In the 1962 congressional elections the Republicans scored only small gains. The following month Wilson charged that the Administration had manipulated the Cuban missile crisis to immediately precede the elections in order to favor Democratic candidates.

During the Johnson and Nixon years, Wilson continued his efforts to expand the work of the Republican Congressional Committee. His voting record remained conservative, and he supported the Vietnam policies of both Presidents. In 1966 Wilson assisted the political recovery of former Vice President Richard Nixon [q.v.] by allowing the Republican Congressional Committee to pay Nixon's expenses during a national campaign tour on behalf of the Party's congressional candidates. In 1972 Wilson was implicated in the events that allegedly linked International Telephone and Telegraph's [ITT] funding of the planned San Diego Republican National Convention with the out-of-court settlement of an antitrust suit against ITT. In March 1973 he resigned as chairman of the National Republican Congressional Committee at the request of the Administration after he had criticized the White House for monopolizing 1972 Republican campaign funds. [See NIXON Volume]

[MLL]

WILSON, DAGMAR
b. Jan. 25, 1916; New York, N.Y.
Founder, Women Strike for Peace.

The daughter of a foreign correspondent, Wilson was raised abroad. She attended a progressive school in London where, she later recalled, "We always seemed to be questioning the traditional ways of doing things." By 1961 Wilson was living in Washington, D.C., and working as an illustrator of children's books. In September 1961 she contacted friends in various cities to organize nationwide women's demonstrations in favor of disarmament and against Soviet nuclear bomb tests and proposals for an American resumption of tests. On Nov. 1 about 50,000 women turned out in 60 cities. Because of the success of the effort, Wilson and other organizers decided that the group, Women Strike for Peace (WSP), should be continued.

WSP was a loosely organized association that did not keep membership lists. Its supporters, most of whom were housewives, wrote to congressmen, picketed stores selling war toys, collected signatures for peace petitions, distributed leaflets at supermarkets, held discussion groups and demonstrated at the White House, the United Nations and other locations. They stressed the special concern of mothers in preventing nuclear annihilation.

In November 1961 Wilson sent letters calling for peace initiatives to the wives of President John F. Kennedy and Premier Nikita S. Khrushchev. The replies of the women, which restated their husbands' positions on disarmament, received extensive publicity. In April 1962 she went to Geneva and presented peace petitions to the 17-nation disarmament conference.

Some detractors of WSP contended that the group was more critical of the United States than of the Soviet Union, and they noted that Wilson opposed American insistence upon on-site inspection as a condition for a nuclear test ban treaty. While most critics of WSP attributed its position to political naivete, in December 1962 the House Un-American Activities Committee (HUAC) announced that it would investigate alleged Communist infiltration of the

organization. Wilson testified before the Committee on Dec. 13 and denied that WSP was Communist-controlled. However, she said that Communists, Nazis and fascists were welcome to enter the group because "unless everybody in the whole world joins us in this fight, then God help us."

In December 1964 Wilson refused to testify before a closed session of HUAC, which was investigating the admission of a Japanese pacifist into the United States in 1963 for a lecture tour with which WSP was associated. She was cited for contempt of Congress and was convicted by a federal district judge in April 1965. A U.S. Appeals Court overturned her conviction on a technicality in August 1966, and the Justice Department decided not to take the case to the Supreme Court.

In October 1967 Wilson was arrested during an anti-Vietnam war demonstration at the Pentagon. In subsequent years she continued to support the peace movement but withdrew from her leadership role in WSP.

[MLL]

Alvin Shuster, "Close-up of a 'Peace Striker,'" *The New York Times Magazine* (May 6, 1962), p. 32+.

WILSON, O(RLANDO) W(INFIELD)
b. May 15, 1900; Veblen, S.D.
Superintendent of Police, Chicago, 1960-67.

Wilson studied criminology at the University of California, Berkeley, under the distinguished criminologist, August Vollmer. After graduating with a B.A. in 1924, he served briefly as chief of police of Fullerton, Calif., and later worked as an investigator for the Pacific Finance Corporation. Upon Vollmer's recommendation Wilson was named head of the Wichita, Kan., police department in 1928. Wilson remained in Wichita until the summer of 1939, when he returned to Berkeley as Vollmer's successor. During World War II Wilson was a lieutenant colonel in the military police. After the war he was a public safety officer in charge of denazification activities in the American zone of Germany.

Wilson returned to his teaching duties at Berkeley in 1947 and remained there until 1960.

Wilson was called to Chicago under unusual circumstances. In January 1959 a professional thief confessed to the public defender that he had been a member of a burglary ring that included several Chicago policemen. The corruption scandal and the resulting public outcry seriously threatened Chicago Mayor Richard J. Daley's [q.v.] political standing. To placate public opinion the Mayor dismissed the head of the police force, who had not been linked to the scandal, and invited Wilson to Chicago to head a committee to choose a successor. After screening candidates for about a month, the committee in February 1960 invited Wilson himself to head the force. Wilson accepted but only after winning assurances from the Mayor that he would be given freedom to reform the department without political interference.

In appointing Wilson, Daley was widely credited with having successfully deflected attention from the police scandal while winning for himself a reputation as a reformer. Later that year Daley went on to play a key role in securing the nomination and election of Sen. John F. Kennedy as president.

Shortly after assuming office Wilson reduced the number of police districts from 38 to 21. By redrawing police district boundaries, which had formerly coincided with ward boundaries, Wilson helped break the control Democratic district leaders had exerted over police captains. Wilson also organized a special 100-man unit to investigate graft and corruption within the department. He hired more clerks and crossing-guards to free policemen for active patrol duty. He won substantial pay increases for policemen while opening up the civil service lists to advance those whose careers had been stymied by lack of political connections. Wilson won large appropriations for the purchase of new patrol cars and the development of a communications system that was regarded as one of the most sophisticated in the nation. During the early 1960s the news media pointed to Wilson's force as an example of how a police department could be reformed.

Civil rights leaders suggested that Wilson also had helped to curb police brutality directed against the city's black population. Chicago, however, did not escape serious racial disturbances. In August 1965 Wilson commanded Chicago policemen during the suppression of a riot on the city's predominently black West Side. National Guardsmen, called to the city at Wilson's request, were not needed in the streets. A year later Wilson met several times with Martin Luther King [q.v.] to help prevent violence during marches planned in Chicago's white neighborhoods to protest racial discrimination in housing.

In June 1967 Wilson resigned his post and was succeeded by James F. Conlisk, who was drawn from within the ranks of the Chicago Police Department.

[JLW]

For further information:
"O. W. Wilson," *Current Biography Yearbook, 1966* (New York, 1967), pp. 452-454.

WIRTZ, W(ILLIAM) WILLARD
b. March 14, 1912; DeKalb, Ill.
Undersecretary of Labor, January 1961-September 1962; Secretary of Labor, September 1962-January 1969.

Wirtz, a 1937 graduate of the Harvard Law School, taught law at the University of Iowa and Northwestern University. As a member of the War Labor Board from 1942 to 1945, he earned a reputation as an able mediator in labor disputes. After the war Wirtz served as a member of the National Wage Stabilization Board and then returned to teaching at Northwestern. In 1950 Illinois Gov. Adlai E. Stevenson [q.v.] appointed Wirtz to the Illinois Liquor Control Commission, and the two men thereafter became close associates. Wirtz was a key aide in Stevenson's 1956 presidential campaign.

In January 1961 Wirtz was named undersecretary of labor and 20 months later succeeded Arthur Goldberg [q.v.] as the Department's head. As Labor Secretary, Wirtz was personally involved in efforts to end the 114-day New York City newspaper strike, which began in November 1962. He also lent his offices to settling the longshoremen's walkouts that tied up East and West Coast ports during 1962 and 1963.

During his early months in office, Wirtz was most concerned with the threat of a nationwide rail strike. The Association of American Railroads had long demanded an end to "featherbedding" contract provisions that prevented management from firing some 35,000 fireman and other unnecessary train crew members. According to Theodore Sorensen [q.v.], the President's special counsel, Wirtz had "devoted night and day to the problem for months before he made his recommendations." In July 1963 he proposed a two-year strike moratorium during which the carriers and unions would continue negotiations. If they could not agree Assistant Labor Secretary James Reynolds would issue binding recommendations. The unions issued a statement that the Wirtz plan "was thinly disguised compulsory arbitration," which would be a "dangerous step toward totalitarianism."

On Aug. 28, 1963 Kennedy signed a compulsory arbitration bill to prevent a rail strike just six hours away. The resulting legislation established a board that ordered the elimination of 48,000 jobs over a period of several years. Union leaders were angry; early in 1964 planned strikes were blocked twice by court orders. Rail labor problems continued to smoulder, and in 1967 Congress was forced once more to pass legislation to halt a two-day rail strike.

Wirtz was a strong advocate of job retraining programs as a way of alleviating unemployment, and in 1963 he supported new amendments to the Manpower Development and Retraining Act passed a year earlier. The original legislation had been designed to retrain experienced workers who had lost jobs because of technological change. The amendments Wirtz proposed, and which Congress passed in July 1963, made provision for more extensive training, including remedial reading and writing courses for high school dropouts. The legislation also permitted the Secretary of Labor to establish experimental programs that were designed to assist the unemployed in relocating to find new jobs.

Wirtz also worked on behalf of major social legislation favored by organized labor, including federal aid to education, medicare and expanded social security measures. These were passed in 1964 and 1965.

During the Johnson years Wirtz attempted to end the dependence of American fruit and vegetable farmers on Mexican migrant labor, fought and lost in his bid to control a substantial portion of the poverty program and attempted to restrain organized labor in its demands for wage hikes during a time of rapidly mounting inflation. Despite his own increasingly strong opposition to the Vietnam war, Wirtz remained in the Johnson cabinet to its end. Thereafter, he practiced law in Washington, D.C. [See JOHNSON Volume]

[JLW]

WRIGHT, J(AMES) SKELLY
b. Jan. 14, 1911; New Orleans, La.
U.S. District Judge, 1949-62; U.S. Court of Appeals Judge, 1962- .

J. Skelly Wright graduated from Loyola University Law School in 1934. Following a year as a lecturer in English history at Loyola, Wright served as assistant U.S. attorney for New Orleans from 1937 to 1946 and as U.S. attorney for the eastern district of Louisiana from 1948 to 1949. In 1949 he became U.S. district judge for the eastern district of Louisiana, which included New Orleans.

In March 1962 Wright barred Tulane University from discriminating against Negro applicants and ordered the University to admit two black students. Wright ruled that Tulane was a "public institution" receiving a "very substantial state subsidy" and thus subject to the 14th Amendment's ban on discrimination.

One month later Wright invalidated Louisiana's pupil placement law and ordered the New Orleans public schools to accept blacks in the first six grades beginning with the fall term of 1962. He ruled that rather than being assigned to a school by the school board, a pupil could choose to attend either the Negro or white school nearest his or her home.

This decision was modified in May by Wright's successor, Frank Ellis [q.v.], who ruled that only the first grade had to be integrated that September. In December Ellis ruled that, because Tulane was a private institution, it could not be forced to admit blacks.

As U.S. Court of Appeals judge for the District of Columbia during the Johnson Administration, Wright continued to rule on important civil rights cases. In 1967 Wright, trying the case as a district judge, declared de facto segregation of blacks in the District of Columbia's public schools unconstitutional. The next year the Court of Appeals ruled in favor of renters in an opinion declaring that slum landlords had no legal right to evict tenants in retaliation for reporting housing code violations.

During the 1970s Wright handed down several important decisions dealing with the Alaska pipeline, military justice and nuclear reactors. Wright was a member of the court that, in 1973, ordered President Richard Nixon to turn over his Watergate tapes to the U.S. district court. [See JOHNSON, NIXON Volumes]

[EWS]

YARBOROUGH, RALPH W(EBSTER)
b. June 8, 1903; Chandler, Tex.
Democratic Senator, Tex., 1957-71.

Yarborough was admitted to the Texas bar and began his career as an attorney in 1927. Eleven years later he ran unsuccessfully for the office of state attorney general. In the 1950s Yarborough emerged as the leader of the minority liberal wing of the Texas Democratic Party. The liberal grouping was a coalition of intellectuals, trade unionists, blacks, Mexican-Americans and East Texas populists. Antagonistic to the powerful Texas business establishment, it opposed racial discrimination and Texas's extremely restrictive labor laws and supported social welfare measures to aid the poor.

Candidates of the dominant conservative faction defeated Yarborough in the gubernatorial primaries of 1952, 1954 and 1956 by approximately 145,000, 90,000 and 4,000 votes, respectively. His increasingly narrow defeats reflected the growing strength of the liberal segment of the party after World War II. Control of the national Democratic Party by liberal elements, the U.S. Supreme Court's 1944 ruling against the white primary and increased political participation by Mexican-Americans were major forces behind this trend.

In April 1957 Yarborough won a special election to fill a vacated U.S. Senate seat, and the following year he was elected to a full term in the Senate. Yarborough's victories, however, did not signify the defeat of the Party's conservative wing. Although the liberals went on to score some electoral successes in congressional and state legislative elections during the 1960s, they did not succeed in winning any additional statewide contests. [See EISENHOWER Volume]

In the Senate Yarborough joined his fellow-Texans on Capitol Hill in voting for oil depletion allowances and oil import quotas. But on most other issues he had a liberal voting record. According to the Congressional Quarterly, he generally opposed the Southern Democrat-Republican conservative coalition and supported major Kennedy Administration bills on 73% of the key votes in 1961 and on 69% of such votes in 1962 and 1963.

Yarborough voted for such social welfare programs as the Area Redevelopment Act of 1961, the minimum wage bill of the same year and the medicare program of 1962. Most striking in its contrast to the record of the majority of his fellow-Southerners was his support of civil rights measures. In 1961 he supported a bill to extend the life of the Civil Rights Commission for two years. In 1963 Yarborough voted to approve an Administration-supported constitutional amendment to bar the poll tax as a condition for voting in federal elections. He was the only senator from the five Southern states with a poll tax requirement to support the amendment.

In 1962 Yarborough was accused of improper involvement with Billy Sol Estes [q.v.]. Estes, a Texas promoter arrested for illegal business practices in March 1962 and subsequently convicted, had contributed more than $7,000 to Yarborough over a number of years. A former employe of the Agriculture Department alleged before a House subcommittee that Estes and Yarborough had met in September 1961 to discuss an investigation by the Department into the former's cotton allotment dealings. But in August 1962 the general counsel of the Agriculture Department testified that Yarborough had not asked for favoritism on Estes's behalf. The matter did not have a significant impact upon the Senator's political career.

In 1962 Texas liberals waged an intense campaign to gain control of the Texas Democratic Party. They chose Don Yarborough (no relation to the Senator) to run in the gubernatorial primary against John B. Connally [q.v.]. Connally was a close political associate of Vice President Lyndon Johnson [q.v.], who had been the leader of the conservative Texas Democrats since the mid-1950s. Heavily financed by the state's business interests, Connally narrowly defeated his opponent in the primary runoff and went on to win the election, thereby solidifying conservative control of the Party. The campaign left a bitter antagonism between Connally and the Senator. Most political observers believed that one of the purposes of President Kennedy's November 1963 trip to Texas, which ended with his assassination in Dallas, was to try to resolve the differences between the liberals and conservatives.

After Johnson succeeded to the presidency, he used his new position to attempt, with considerable success, to improve his chances of carrying Texas in 1964 by mending the factional rift. As a result of the truce that he arranged, Yarborough and Connally won easy reelection victories in 1964. In 1970, however, Lloyd Bentsen, a well-financed conservative, defeated Yarborough in the Democratic senatorial primary. [See JOHNSON Volume]

[MLL]

For further information:
O. Douglas Weeks, "Texas: Land of Conservative Expansiveness," in William C. Havard, ed., *The Changing Politics of the South* (Baton Rouge, 1972).

YARMOLINSKY, ADAM

b. Nov. 17, 1922; New York, N.Y.
Special Assistant to the Secretary of Defense, January 1961-September 1965.

Yarmolinsky was raised in New York City. His father, Avrahm Yarmolinsky, a distinguished scholar of Russian literature, was chief of the Slavonic division of the New York Public Library; his mother, Babette Deutsch, was a well-known poet and critic. A graduate of Fieldston, Harvard and Yale Law School, Yarmolinsky was a consultant to a number of private foundations. He served as public affairs editor for Doubleday and lectured at the American University of Yale Law Schools.

Shortly after the election of John F. Kennedy in 1960, Yarmolinsky joined a task force headed by Sargent Shriver [q.v.], Kennedy's brother-in-law, to screen candidates for posts in the new Administration. Yarmolinsky personally recommended Robert S. McNamara [q.v.] for Secretary of Defense, and shortly after his appointment in January 1961 McNamara named Yarmolinsky his special assistant. According to the journalist David Halberstam [q.v.], Yarmolinsky served as McNamara's liaison with the liberal community, defending Defense Department policies to those writers, columnists and academics who were often critical of the military.

While serving in the Defense Department in the summer of 1961, Yarmolinsky assumed temporary responsibility for the management of a $207 million national fallout shelter program. The Administration's goal, he said, was to provide shelter for all Americans. He predicted that by 1962 there would be fallout shelters for 25% of the population. However, despite its much heralded beginnings, the fallout shelter program was abandoned by the Administration within two years for lack of congressional funding.

Yarmolinsky was not among the more conspicuous members of the Kennedy Administration, but in April 1962 he came to public attention when former Maj. Gen. Edwin A. Walker [q.v.], in testimony before the Special Senate Preparedness Subcommittee, charged that Yarmolinsky, who

Walker believed had connections to the Communists, was in part responsible for ousting him from his command. McNamara defended Yarmolinsky, citing his record of "strong and active anti-Communism." Walker's remarks were widely dismissed as irresponsible, but they nonetheless marked the beginning of a right-wing attack on Yarmolinsky that ultimately limited his role in public life.

Yarmolinsky's standing among Southern congressmen was further eroded by his work on a White House commission, chaired by attorney Gerhard A. Gesell, which recommended that the Defense Department ban off-base discrimination against Negro servicemen. Southern congressmen charged that the Defense Department, in implementing the report, had exceeded its authority by forcing base commanders to integrate public facilities outside their jurisdiction.

Early in 1964 Yarmolinsky took temporary leave from the Defense Department to aid Sargent Shriver in shaping antipoverty legislation for the Johnson Administration. Yarmolinsky hoped that with the passage of the bill setting up the Office of Economic Opportunity (OEO) he could win appointment as its deputy director. However, a number of Southern congressmen informed the White House that they would vote for OEO only if Yarmolinsky were banned from the antipoverty programs. President Lyndon B. Johnson [q.v.] personally conceded the point, and in September 1964 Yarmolinsky returned to the Defense Department.

In September 1966 Yarmolinsky left the Defense Department and joined the faculty of Harvard University Law School. [See JOHNSON Volume]

[JLW]

YORTY, SAM(UEL WILLIAM)
b. Oct. 1, 1909; Lincoln, Neb.
Mayor, Los Angeles, Calif., 1961-73.

Raised in the tradition of Midwestern Democratic populism, Yorty arrived in Los Angeles following his high school graduation. During the Depression he was active in the Technocracy movement, which advocated government by scientists and engineers. He was also a supporter of the Townsend Plan, which proposed paying every citizen over 60 a $200-per-month pension. Yorty was elected as a Democrat to the state Assembly in 1936 and 1938, earning a reputation as an extreme liberal by sponsoring legislation in favor of organized labor, liberalized divorce, producer and consumer cooperatives and state-owned public utilities. At the same time he was responsible for establishing the nation's first un-American activities committee in the Assembly.

After losing a 1940 attempt to unseat isolationist Sen. Hiram Johnson (R, Calif.) on a platform advocating aid to the Allies, Yorty entered private law practice. He returned to the Assembly in 1949 and in 1950 and 1952 won election to the U.S. House of Representatives, where he championed California's oil and water claims and the interests of the Air Force. He left the House to run an unsuccessful senatorial campaign against Sen. Thomas Kuchel (R, Calif.) [q.v.] in 1954. Yorty's drift to the political right had estranged him from many influential members of the state Democratic Party. The refusal of the then powerful California Democratic Council (CDC) to nominate him for the U.S. Senate in 1956 made Yorty especially bitter against those whom he called "leftists." In the primary that followed he was humiliated by an overwhelming defeat.

An early supporter of Lyndon Johnson [q.v.], Yorty created a local sensation by endorsing Republican Richard Nixon [q.v.] over John F. Kennedy in the 1960 presidential contest, further alienating him from the Democratic state organization. During the campaign he issued a manifesto in which he accused Kennedy of trying to buy the election and claimed that Kennedy was inexperienced. According to Democratic Gov. Edmund G. "Pat" Brown [q.v.], Yorty's political enemy, the manifesto was also an unscrupulous attack on Kennedy's Catholicism.

Although Yorty's 1960 endorsement of Nixon cost him Party support in his 1961 Los Angeles mayoral campaign against incumbent Norris Poulson, his maverick reputation attracted many Republican voters. In addition, the April 1961 Bay of Pigs fiasco appeared to justify his criticism of Kennedy's inexperience. Yorty exploited television well as a campaign medium, made an appeal to the black and Mexican-American communities and sought to win support from housewives by making an issue of a city garbage ordinance. A Midwestern populist turned conservative, Yorty was representative of much of the Los Angeles electorate, and he narrowly upset Poulson in the May 1961 election.

Yorty's name received national exposure when, in an April 1962 speech before the Daughters of the American Revolution, Maj. Arch E. Roberts accused Yorty of having a "Communist background." Rep. Francis E. Walter (D, Pa.) [q.v.], chairman of the House Un-American Activities Committee, defended Yorty's conservative record, and the Army promptly suspended Roberts from military duty.

Despite Los Angeles's charter, which severely limited the mayor's authority, Yorty was successful in decreasing property taxes, attracting new industry and reviving the city's small downtown area, but he sustained considerable criticism for his handling of the 1965 Watts riots. Reelected mayor in 1965 and 1969, Yorty failed in his attempts to capture the Democratic nomination for governor in 1966 and 1970. Thomas Bradley, a black attorney and former police lieutenant, defeated Yorty in 1973 when the Mayor sought his fourth term. [See JOHNSON, NIXON Volumes]

[JCH]

For further information:
Ed Ainsworth, *Maverick Mayor: A Biography of Sam Yorty of Los Angeles* (Garden City, 1966).

YOST, CHARLES W(OODRUFF)
b. Nov. 6, 1907; Watertown, N.Y.
Deputy Ambassador to the U.N., February 1961-April 1966.

A career diplomat, Yost served in Bangkok, Vienna and Athens and as ambassador to Laos, Syria and Morocco before becoming deputy ambassador to the United Nations in February 1961.

At the U.N. Yost was overshadowed by Ambassador Adlai Stevenson [q.v.], who delivered most major policy statements and represented the U.S. in important debates. During his five years at the U.N., Yost was primarily the spokesman for the U.S. in Security Council matters that did not require the attention of the Ambassador. In 1961 Yost voiced the U.S. stand on three major questions: announcing the American refusal to admit Outer Mongolia to the U.N., appealing to France and Tunisia to end hostilities and presenting a resolution calling for international cooperation in the exploration of outer space. Two years later, in 1963, he urged the U.N. to press peace efforts in Yemen to prevent the fighting there from spreading to other Middle Eastern countries, announced U.S. approval of restoration of Hungary to full accredited status, voted for an embargo on arms shipments to South Africa and denounced the refusal of the Soviet Union to condemn Syria for the ambush of two Israeli farmers. In May 1964 he led the U.S. delegation in a debate on Cambodian charges of Communist aggression. There he defended the U.S. against Soviet charges of "criminal military aggression" against Cambodia. Yost said U.S. intervention in Southeast Asia had been prompted by a "large-scale, aggressive, Communist-armed assault, organized, directed, supported and supplied from outside South Vietnam."

After 1965 Yost continued as a representative to the Security Council in the delegation headed by Arthur Goldburg [q.v.]. That year he represented the U.S. in the Special Committee on Peace-Keeping Operations, where he indicated U.S. willingness to end its demand that U.N. voting rights be denied the USSR and other nations more than two years in arrears in their assessments for U.N. peace-keeping expenses. Yost also led the American delegation in the June 1965 Security Council discussion of the Dominican crisis. In that forum he termed the Soviet call for a debate on the issue an attempt to seek another "propaganda platform." In December he headed the delegation debating continued U.N. mediation of the Cyprus dispute.

Yost resigned from the U.N. delegation in April 1966 to become a senior fellow with the Council on Foreign Relations. In 1969 President Richard Nixon appointed him ambassador to the United Nations. [See NIXON Volume]

[EWS]

YOUNG, MILTON R.
b. Dec. 6, 1897; Berlin, N.D.
Republican Senator, N.D., 1945- .

A farmer and former state legislator, Young was first appointed to the Senate in 1945 to fill the vacancy left by the death of John Moses. Despite his long term of service and his position as secretary of the Senate Republican Conference Committee from 1946 to 1971, Young was virtually unknown outside of the Senate and North Dakota. Although he supported many civil rights measures, the Senator maintained a basically conservative position by voting against labor legislation and most foreign aid bills and public works projects, except those that benefited his state. From 1961 to 1963 he voted with the conservative coalition of Republicans and Southern Democrats about 80% of the time.

A conservative on most matters, Young was consistently liberal on agricultural legislation. Calling himself "a farmer first and a Republican second," Young's major concern was protecting the small farmers of North Dakota. During the early 1960s he successfully sponsored an amendment to the Minimum Wage Act of 1961 exempting small grain-elevator owners from the provisions of the statute. In 1962 Young was the only Republican to vote for the Administration's farm bill, which included provisions for strict control of wheat and feed grain production and for an expanded foreign sales program.

Although he had not supported the censure of Sen. Joseph McCarthy (R, Wisc.) in 1954, Young denounced the conservative John Birch Society in 1961 when it began making inroads among Republicans in North Dakota.

In the last half of the decade, the Senator, concerned by North Dakota's loss of population and low per-capita income, was instrumental in obtaining sizable military contracts for his state. Although his advanced age was frequently a campaign issue used against him by his opponents, Young was returned to the Senate in 1968 and 1974. [See JOHNSON, NIXON Volumes]

[EWS]

YOUNG, STEPHEN M(ARVIN)
b. May 4, 1890; Norwalk, Ohio.
Democratic Senator, Ohio, 1959-71.

The son of a farm county judge, Stephen M. Young took a law degree from Western Reserve University and then saw action in the 1916 Mexican campaign and both World Wars. Young first ran for public office as a Democrat in 1912, the year Woodrow Wilson captured the presidency. He twice won election to the state Assembly and served four terms as Ohio's U.S. Representative-at-Large, proving a strong supporter of liberal Democratic programs and of organized labor. Out of office, Young practiced criminal law in Cleveland. In 1958 Young scored a major political triumph by defeating Sen. John W. Bricker (R, Ohio), the state GOP's top vote-getter and the 1944 Republican vice presidential candidate. Upon taking office Young surprised his colleagues by becoming the first Senator to reveal his personal stock holdings and other assets. [See EISENHOWER Volume]

A freshman senator in his seventies, Young generally followed the lead of the Senate Democratic leadership and the Kennedy White House. According to Congressional Quarterly, he ranked seventh among senators in overall support of legislation supported by President Kennedy in 1961 and 1962. In April 1962 he defended the Administration's request for authorization to purchase $100 million in United Nations bonds, declaring the U.N. to be a vital instrument of American foreign policy that should not be allowed "to die or atrophy."

Young generally ranked as one of the Senate's more liberal members. In July 1961 he joined a small band of Democratic senators in voicing concern over the living conditions of Mexican farm laborers in the United States. Young also fought for reductions in the Civil Defense (CD) fallout shelter program; he secured a $207 million cut in CD appropriations in August 1961 but failed in similar initiatives in August 1962 and May 1963. By voice vote the Senate rejected a Young amendment to the 1963 foreign aid bill that would have ended all military assistance to Spain. Foreign Relations Committee Chairman J. William Fulbright (D, Ark.) [q.v.] was among those who defended the appropriation on the grounds that American air bases were still needed in Spain.

Much to the surprise of experienced political observers in Ohio, Young withstood strong primary and general election opposition in 1964 to win reelection. He maintained his liberal record and became an early opponent of an expanding American military involvement in South Vietnam. He declined to run for reelection in 1970. [See JOHNSON Volume]

[JLB]

YOUNG, WHITNEY M(OORE)

b. July 31, 1921; Lincoln Ridge, Ky.
d. March 11, 1971; Lagos, Nigeria.
Executive Director, National Urban League, August 1961-March 1971.

A graduate of Kentucky State College, Young received an M.A. in social work in 1947 from the University of Minnesota. He worked for the St. Paul Urban League from 1947 to 1950 and then served as executive secretary of the Omaha (Neb.) Urban League. Young was named dean of the School of Social Work at Atlanta University in 1954 and served as vice president of the NAACP in Georgia and as an adviser to the black students who organized the 1960 Atlanta sit-ins. In August 1961 Young was appointed executive director of the National Urban League, then a professional social work agency that provided a variety of social services for urban blacks. Throughout the 1960s the League remained one of the more conservative groups working for black rights, but the sophisticated and articulate Young broadened the League's programs and supplied it with more aggressive and outspoken leadership. He improved the planning and coordination between local branches and the national office early in his tenure, increased the League's funding, and expanded its staff. In 1963 he launched one of the League's most successful projects, the National Skills Bank, which collected job profiles on skilled blacks and placed them in positions in government and industry.

In line with the League's traditional social work interests, Young emphasized the economic and social needs of urban blacks in the early 1960s. At a September 1962 convention of the Southern Christian Leadership Conference, Young asserted that blacks had made little progress on the "meat, bread and potatoes issues" of integration and noted that the average black family's income was 54% of the average white family's income. At a June 1963 news conference Young presented his proposal for a "domestic Marshall Plan." Warning that racial incidents in the South were "mild in comparison with those on the verge of taking flame in the tinderbox of racial unrest in Northern cities," Young called for a massive aid program to close the economic, social and educational gaps between the races. Young's plan, which he said would indemnify blacks for past discrimination, proposed that $145 billion be spent on job training and apprenticeship programs, health programs and hospital construction, capitalization of cooperative business and industrial enterprises, programs for nursery children and working mothers, and scholarships, book-buying and tutorial programs. Young's widely publicized plan was one of several proposals for aid to the poor which contributed to the Johnson Administration's war on poverty legislation.

Young joined with the leaders of other civil rights organizations in July 1963 to form the Council for United Civil Rights Leadership. He was selected a co-chairman of the Council, which was designed to raise funds for civil rights work and to coordinate long-range planning and strategies among various rights organizations. Young also was a co-sponsor of the August 1963 March on Washington. After meeting with President Kennedy on the day of the march, Young addressed the crowd assembled at the Lincoln Memorial declaring, "Civil rights, which are God-given and constitutionally guaranteed, are not negotiable in 1963."

Young cooperated closely with the Johnson Administration in the planning and implementation of its antipoverty program. Skeptical of "black power" when the concept first captured national attention in 1966, Young eventually gave it a qualified endorsement. Young brought about a major reorientation within the Urban League in 1968, shifting its emphasis from social services to rehabilitation and institutional change in the black ghetto. [See JOHNSON, NIXON Volumes]

[CAB]

For further information:
Guichard Parris and Lester Brooks, *Blacks in the City: A History of the National Urban League* (Boston, 1971).

ZUCKERT, EUGENE M.
b. Nov. 9, 1911; New York, N.Y.
Secretary of the Air Force, January 1961-July 1965.

A graduate of the Yale Law School, Zuckert worked for the Securities and Exchange Commission during the late 1930s. He joined the faculty of the Harvard Business School in 1940 and was a key statistical consultant to the Army and Navy during the Second World War. Zuckert served as an assistant secretary of the Air Force from 1947 to 1952 and was on the board of the Atomic Energy Commission from 1952 to 1954. [See TRUMAN Volume]

In January 1961 Secretary of Defense Robert S. McNamara [q.v.] named Zuckert, his old colleague at the Harvard Business School, Secretary of the Air Force. Shortly after he assumed office Zuckert commissioned a study that revealed that McNamara, through his reorganization of the Pentagon, had stripped the Secretaries of the Army, Navy and Air Force of much

of their authority—especially their ability to oppose his decisions. "If they could not reconcile themselves to minor roles," wrote Pentagon reporter Clark Mollenhoff, "resignation was the only practical alternative." Zuckert, along with Navy Secretary John Connally [q.v.], eventually accepted the new situation which, Mollenhoff said, "made them subordinates to assistant secretaries of defense in many important matters."

Zuckert, however, did play an important role in the development of the controversial TFX (tactical fighter, experimental) airplane. In the summer of 1963 McNamara determined that the Air Force rather than the Navy should develop the TFX as a fighter plane suitable for both armed services. He ordered Zuckert to solicit bids for the plane, and eventually the choice was narrowed to competing designs offered by Boeing and General Dynamics. Zuckert, McNamara and Navy Secretary Fred Korth [q.v.] signed a memorandum on Nov. 21, 1963 awarding the contract to General Dynamics on the ground that its plane, with fewer technical innovations than Boeing's, would prove cheaper to manufacture. Moreover, the "commonality" rating of the General Dynamics aircraft—its adaptability to the needs of both the Air Force and the Navy—was 20% higher than Boeing's.

The decision angered a number of influential senators and congressmen, and in the summer of 1963 the Senate Permanent Investigations Subcommittee, under the chairmanship of Sen. John McClellan (D, Ark.) [q.v.], called Zuckert, Korth, McNamara and Deputy Secretary of Defense Roswell Gilpatric [q.v.] to explain how as civilians they could reject Boeing—the nearly unanimous choice of military officers.

In his testimony Zuckert argued that the military had been deceived by Boeing's promise of "extra performance" that depended on advanced and dubious technological developments, the cost of which Boeing had underestimated. Zuckert defended the "commonality" of the General Dynamics aircraft but was forced to admit that he had seriously underestimated the adaptability of Boeing's design. Neither

McNamara nor Zuckert was able to deny Comptroller General Joseph Campbell's allegations that the two men had relied on their own "rough judgment" rather than independent analysis in estimating costs.

Zuckert, along with Korth and Gilpatric, faced charges that they had been involved in business interests that should have disqualified them from making the TFX decision. The Senate subcommittee alleged that Zuckert favored General Dynamics because its chief subcontractor, Grumman Aviation, was located in Bethpage, Long Island in Zuckert's home state of New York. Zuckert dismissed the charge as "far fetched," pointing out that he had not lived in New York for many years.

General Dynamics eventually built the TFX, later designated the F-111, but the plane was plagued by mechanical problems, and its performance did not live up to expectations.

As Air Force Secretary in the early stages of American involvement in Vietnam, Zuckert authorized increased air support for ground troops. In May 1964 he was called before the House Armed Services Committee to answer charges that American planes in Vietnam were riddled with defects that had caused several crashes. Zuckert acknowledged that one or two crashes could be linked to mechanical failure but said most of the aircraft had performed well.

Early in 1964 Zuckert established a committee under ex-Army Chief of Staff Thomas D. White to investigate a scandal at the Air Force Academy in which 105 students were dismissed for cheating. In its report to House and Senate Armed Services Committees, the panel reported that one-third of the varsity football team had been involved in the scandal and recommended that the Academy de-emphasize intercollegiate football.

Zuckert resigned as Air Force Secretary in July 1965 and later served on the boards of several corporations, including Martin Marietta, an aircraft manufacturer.

[JLW]

Appendix

1960

JAN. 2—Sen. John F. Kennedy announces his candidacy for the Democratic presidential nomination.

JAN. 9—Vice President Richard M. Nixon announces his candidacy for the Republican presidential nomination.

FEB. 1—Civil rights demonstrators begin a sit-in movement to integrate public accommodations in Greensboro, N.C.

MARCH 8—Kennedy wins the New Hampshire Democratic primary with a record 42,969 votes.

APRIL 3—Daniel Bell's *The End of Ideology: On the Exhaustion of Political Ideas in the Fifties* is published.

APRIL 5—Kennedy wins the Wisconsin Democratic presidential primary by a four to three margin over Sen. Hubert H. Humphrey.

APRIL 8—The Senate invokes cloture, and, by a vote of 71-18, passes a civil rights bill that gives increased authority to the federal courts and Civil Rights Commission to prevent the intimidation of black voters in the South.

APRIL 26—Kennedy wins the Pennsylvania Democratic presidential primary by 49,838 votes.

MAY 5—An American U-2 spy plane is downed over the USSR.

MAY 10—Kennedy defeats Humphrey in the West Virginia Democratic primary by 77,305 votes. Humphrey withdraws from the presidential race.

MAY 16—The scheduled summit conference between President Dwight D. Eisenhower and Premier Nikita S. Khrushchev is canceled as a result of the U-2 incident.

JULY 13—Kennedy wins the Democratic presidential nomination on the first ballot at the Los Angeles convention. The vote is 806 for Kennedy, 409 for his chief rival Lyndon Johnson.
Johnson is chosen vice-presidential candidate at the following session.

JULY 25—Nixon easily wins the Republican presidential nomination on the first ballot in Chicago.

AUG. 9—The U.N. Security Council orders Katanga province to end its secession from the Congo.

SEPT. 26—Kennedy and Nixon hold the first of four televised debates between the presidential candidates.

NOV. 8—Kennedy defeats Nixon in the presidential election by 113,057 votes and receives 303 of the 537 electoral votes.

NOV. 17—The Central Intelligence Agency (CIA) briefs Kennedy on its involvement in training Cuban exiles in Guatemala to overthrow Fidel Castro.

NOV. 18—President Eisenhower orders U.S. naval units to patrol Central American waters to prevent Communist-led invasions of either Guatemala or Nicaragua.

1961

JAN. 3—The U.S. breaks diplomatic relations with Cuba.

Jan. 4—The Organization of American States votes to impose limited economic sanctions against the Dominican Republic.

JAN. 17—In his farewell address Eisenhower warns against the influence of a "military-industrial complex."

JAN. 20—Kennedy is inaugurated 35th President of the U.S.

JAN. 25—In his first presidential news conference, Kennedy supports the idea of a neutral Laos.

JAN. 28—Kennedy approves a Vietnam counter-insurgency plan that calls for government reform and military restructuring as the basis for expanded U.S. assistance.

JAN. 31—The House votes, 217-212, to expand the Rules Committee from 12 to 15 members.

FEB. 7—Kennedy orders a ban on most trade with Cuba.

FEB. 16—Kennedy warns of the risk of war if Belgium takes unilateral action in the Congo.

FEB. 20—In a special message to Congress, Kennedy asks for a five-year $5.625 billion program of federal aid to education.

MARCH 1—Kennedy establishes the Peace Corps by executive order.

MARCH 6—Kennedy issues an executive order establishing the Committee on Equal Employment Opportunity.

MARCH 13—Kennedy proposes that Latin America join the U.S. in an Alliance for Progress, a ten-year $20 billion program of economic and social development.

MARCH 21—Great Britain, the U.S. and the USSR resume their three-power nuclear test ban conference in Geneva.

MARCH 23—In a televised news conference Kennedy alerts the nation to Communist expansion in Laos and warns that a ceasefire must precede the start of negotiations to establish a neutral and independent nation.

MARCH 28—Kennedy announces the initiation of a program to rapidly increase U.S. military strength.

APRIL 12—Soviet cosmonaut Yuri Gagarin becomes the first man to orbit the earth.

APRIL 17—CIA-trained Cuban exiles begin the Bay of Pigs invasion.

APRIL 20—A Cuban government communique reports the defeat and capture of the invasion force.

APRIL 24—Kennedy accepts full responsibility for the Cuban invasion.

MAY 5—Kennedy signs a bill raising the minimum wage from $1 to $1.25 an hour.

MAY 5—Alan B. Shepard makes the first U.S. manned suborbital flight.

MAY 9-15—Vice President Lyndon B. Johnson visits Southeast Asia and recommends a "strong program of action" in Vietnam.

MAY 14—A freedom riders' bus is stoned and burned in Anniston, Ala.

MAY 21—Four hundred U.S. marshals are sent to Alabama after 20 people are hurt in racial violence stemming from the Freedom Rides.

MAY 25—Kennedy asks Congress for $1.8 billion to expand the space program and calls for a manned lunar landing by 1970.

MAY 31-JUNE 6—Kennedy meets with British and French leaders in Europe.

JUNE 3-4—Kennedy and Khrushchev hold an inconclusive summit meeting in Vienna.

JUNE 9—President Ngo Dinh Diem requests U.S. troops for training the South Vietnamese army.

JUNE 30—Kennedy signs a bill liberalizing Social Security benefits for 4.4 million persons.

JUNE 30—The President signs a compromise version of an Administration-backed omnibus housing bill that provides funds for urban renewal, community development and direct housing loans for the elderly. The bill also liberalizes loan requirements for the purchase of moderately-priced housing.

JULY 3—A Taft-Hartley injunction ends a 18-day maritime strike against U.S. flag ships.

JULY 5—Theodore White's *The Making of the President, 1960* is published.

JULY 25—Kennedy calls for $3.25 billion to meet commitments in the wake of the Berlin crisis and asks Congress for the power to increase the size of the armed forces by 217,000.

AUG. 13—East Germany seals its border with West Berlin to halt the flow of refugees to the West. Work begins on the Berlin wall.

AUG. 16—The U.S. and 19 other American countries adopt the Alliance for Progress charter at Punta del Este, Uruguay.

AUG. 18-21—Vice President Johnson visits Berlin to reaffirm the U.S. commitment there.

AUG. 30—The House votes, 242-170, against consideration of the Administration's school aid bill.

SEPT.-DEC.—East Germany hampers U.S. access to East Berlin.

SEPT. 1—The Soviet Union resumes atmospheric nuclear tests.

SEPT. 5—Kennedy announces that the U.S. will resume underground nuclear tests.

SEPT. 5—Following several mid-air hijackings Kennedy signs a bill making the crime of airplane hijacking punishable by death or imprisonment.

SEPT. 11—Congress approves a two-year extension of the Civil Rights Commission.

SEPT. 16—The U.S. backs U.N. military action in Katanga.

SEPT. 25—Kennedy delivers a "Proposal for General and Complete Disarmament in a Peaceful World" in his major foreign policy address to the U.N.

SEPT. 26—Kennedy signs a bill establishing the U.S. Arms Control and Disarmament Agency.

OCT. 1—South Vietnam requests a bilateral defense treaty with the U.S.

OCT. 4—An international group of protestors urging unilateral disarmament and an end to nuclear testing demonstrates in Moscow.

OCT. 27—U.S. and Soviet tanks confront each other at the Berlin border. They withdraw the next day.

NOV. 1—Fifty thousand demonstrators turn out in 60 cities for The Women Strike for Peace.

NOV. 3—After a trip to Vietnam Gen. Maxwell Taylor reports to Kennedy that prompt U.S. military, economic and political action can lead to victory without a U.S. takeover of the war.

NOV. 26—The "Thanksgiving Day Massacre" results in a major high-level reorganization of the State Department. Chester Bowles is replaced by George Ball as undersecretary of state.

DEC. 7—The U.S. begins its transport of U.N. troops to the Congo to end Katanga's secession.

DEC. 15—Kennedy renews the U.S. commitment to preserve the independence of Vietnam and pledges American assistance to its defense effort.

DEC. 15-17—Kennedy makes a triumphant goodwill tour to Puerto Rico, Venezuela and Colombia.

DEC. 20—The *New York Times* reports that 2,000 U.S. uniformed troops and specialists are stationed in Vietnam.

1962

JAN. 2—The U.S. begins a series of diplomatic "probes" of Moscow regarding Berlin.

JAN. 6—The U.S. resumes diplomatic ties with the Dominican Republic after a 14-month suspension.

JAN. 12—The directors of the Pennsylvania and New York Central railroads approve a merger of the two lines.

JAN. 16—The U.S. and Common Market agree to mutual tariff reductions.

JAN. 21—The House votes down, 264-150, an Administration plan to create an Urban Affairs and Housing Department.

JAN. 23—The Senate Armed Services Committee's Preparedness Investigating Subcommittee begins a probe of military "muzzling."

JAN. 29—The U.S., the USSR and Great Britain nuclear test ban conference at Geneva adjourns after a three-year period. Talks remain deadlocked over a system of international control.

FEB. 3—Kennedy orders an almost complete end to U.S. trade with Cuba.

FEB. 8—The Defense Department announces the creation of a Military Assistance Command in Vietnam.

FEB. 14—Kennedy announces that U.S. troops in Vietnam are instructed to use weapons for defensive purposes.

FEB. 20—John Glenn becomes the first American to orbit the earth.

FEB. 26—The Supreme Court holds that no state can require racial segregation of interstate or intrastate transportaion.

MARCH 1—In the biggest antitrust case in U.S. history, a federal district court orders E. I. DuPont de Nemours & Co. to divest itself of 63 million shares of General Motors stock.

MARCH 2—Kennedy announces his decision to resume atmospheric nuclear tests.

MARCH 14—The 17-nation U.N. disarmament conference opens in Geneva.

MARCH 18—In a message to Krushchev Kennedy proposes the joint exploration of outer space.

MARCH 19—Michael Harrington's *The Other America: Poverty in the United States* is published.

MARCH 22—The U.S. begins its first involvement in the Vietnam Strategic Hamlet (rural pacification) Program.

MARCH 26—The Supreme Court holds that the distribution of seats in state legislatures is subject to the constitutional scrutiny of the federal courts.

MARCH 29—The FBI arrests Billy Sol Estes on fraud charges.

MARCH 31—The United Steelworkers Union and U.S. Steel Corp. formally ratify a pact providing for a 10¢-an-hour fringe benefit increase. The agreement is the most modest contract improvement since 1942.

APRIL 3—The Defense Department orders the integration of all military reserve units except the National Guard.

APRIL 10—The U.S. Steel Corporation announces a $6-per-ton steel price increase; other steel companies follow.

APRIL 11—A Taft-Hartley injunction ends the 27-day West Coast shipping strike.

APRIL 13—Reacting to Administration pressure, the major steel companies rescind their price increases.

APRIL 25—The U.S. opens a nuclear test series in the air over the Pacific.

MAY 9—The Senate votes, 43-53, to reject cloture on a bill outlawing literacy tests in federal elections.

MAY 15—Kennedy sends 5,000 Marines and 50 jet fighters to Thailand in response to Communist expansion in Laos.

MAY 24—Scott Carpenter becomes the second American to orbit the earth.

MAY 25—The AFL-CIO announces a drive for a 35-hour week to reduce unemployment.

MAY 28—Shares on the New York Stock Exchange lose $20.8 billion in the biggest one-day drop in prices since Oct. 29, 1929.

JUNE—Students for a Democratic Society (SDS) adopts the "Port Huron Statement" in its second annual convention, held at Port Huron, Mich.

JUNE 25—The Supreme Court outlaws an official New York State school prayer.

JULY 10—Telstar relays live pictures from the U.S. to Europe.

JULY 17—The Senate votes, 52-48, to table a compromise medicare plan.

JULY 23—Fourteen nations sign the Geneva Accords guaranteeing the neutrality of Laos.

JULY 25—Kennedy approves a Puerto Rican plebiscite on the political status of the island.

JULY 27—The Justice Department requires the General Electric Company to pay $7.5 million in damages for price fixing.

JULY-AUG.—Martin Luther King, Jr., leads a series of unsuccessful demonstrations in Albany, Ga., for the integration of public facilities.

AUG. 6—Marchers opposed to nuclear tests bring petitions to the American and Soviet U.N. missions.

AUG. 14—The Senate, 63-27, invokes cloture for the first time since 1927. The move ends a liberal filibuster against the President's communications satellite bill.

AUG. 27—Congress approves a constitutional amendment barring poll tax requirements for voting in federal elections.

SEPT. 14—Kennedy signs a $900 million public works bill.

SEPT. 24—The House grants Kennedy's request for special limited power to call up to 150,000 reservists for one year and to extend active duty tours without declaring a state of emergency.

SEPT. 28—A U.S. court of appeals finds Gov. Ross R. Barnett guilty of civil contempt for attempting to block the integration of the University of Mississippi.

OCT. 1—Three thousand troops quell Mississippi rioting and arrest 200 as James Meredith enrolls at the University of Mississippi.

OCT. 2—The U.S. bars its ports to all ships carrying cargoes to Cuba.

OCT. 2—Kennedy signs a bill authorizing a $100 million U.N. loan.

OCT. 10—Kennedy signs the first major improvement in food and drug laws since

1938, protecting individuals against untested and ineffective drugs.

OCT. 11—Kennedy signs the Trade Expansion Act that reduces tariffs and gives the President greater discretionary power in making trade agreements.

OCT. 14—U.S. intelligence receives the first photographic evidence of Soviet offensive missiles in Cuba.

OCT. 16—Kennedy signs a tax revision bill that provides for a 7% tax credit for businesses. However, the measure does not fulfill his request for withholding income taxes on dividends and interest.

OCT. 16—Excom, the President's specially chosen bipartisan advisory committee, convenes on the Cuban missile crisis.

OCT. 22—Kennedy announces a "quarantine" of Cuba to force the removal of Soviet missiles.

OCT. 28—Khrushchev agrees to dismantle the Soviet missiles in Cuba and withdraw Russian weapons under U.N. supervision.

NOV. 3-10—The U.S. supplies emergency military aid to India in its border war with Communist China.

NOV. 6—The Democrats increase their Senate majority by four but lose six House seats in the mid-term election. Republicans capture governorships in Pennsylvania, Ohio and Michigan. Richard Nixon loses his California gubernatorial race by 500,000 votes to Edmund G. Brown. Edward Kennedy wins a Massachusetts Senate seat.

NOV. 20—The U.S. lifts its naval blockade of Cuba.

NOV. 20—Kennedy signs an executive order barring racial discrimination in housing built or purchased with federal funds.

NOV. 24—The Pentagon awards General Dynamics the F-111 (TFX) fighter/bomber contract.

DEC. 8—The International Typographers Union begins a 114-day strike against New York City newspapers.

DEC. 14—In a speech to the Economics Club, Kennedy declares a need for an "across-the-board" cut in personal and corporate income taxes.

DEC. 21—Kennedy and Prime Minister Harold Macmillian sign the Nassau Pact granting Great Britain Polaris missiles and pledging the commitment of American and British atomic weapons to a multilateral NATO nuclear force.

DEC. 23—The Cuban government begins the release of prisoners captured in the 1961 Bay of Pigs invasion.

DEC. 31—The U.S. cancels the joint U.S.-Great Britain Skybolt missile project.

1963

JAN.—U.N. troops reunify the Congo.

JAN. 24—Kennedy proposes a $13.6 billion tax cut over a three-year period.

JAN. 26—The Senate Permanent Investigations Subcommittee begins a probe of the TFX contract award.

FEB. 21—Kennedy proposes a hospital insurance plan to be financed through Social Security.

FEB. 24—A Senate panel reports that annual American aid to South Vietnam is $400 million and that 12,000 Americans are stationed there "on dangerous assignment."

FEB. 28—Kennedy sends a civil rights message to Congress that stresses the need to ensure Negroes the right to vote.

MARCH 15—Kennedy signs $435 million Manpower and Development Act.

MARCH 18—The Supreme Court holds that states must supply free counsel for all indigents facing serious criminal charges.

MARCH 19—In a San Jose, Costa Rica, meeting Kennedy and six Latin American presidents pledge resistance to Soviet aggression in the Western Hemisphere.

MARCH 21—A commission headed by retired Gen. Lucius Clay recommends reductions in the U.S. foreign aid program.

MARCH 28—A federal jury convicts Billy Sol Estes of mail fraud and conspiracy.

MARCH 31—The 114-day New York City newspaper strike is settled.

APRIL 1—A federal grand jury indicts the U.S. Steel Corporation and six other steel manufacturers for price fixing.

APRIL 2—Led by Martin Luther King, the Southern Christian Leadership Conference begins an integration campaign in Birmingham, Ala.

APRIL 9—Wheeling Steel Corporation announces a $6-a-ton price increase. Other major steel companies follow suit. The Administration takes no action.

APRIL 10—The atomic submarine *Thresher* is lost with 129 crewmen aboard.

APRIL 20—A U.S.-supported 80-day general strike begins in British Guiana and leads to the fall of the Jagan government.

APRIL 22—Twenty-two units of the 7th Fleet are sent to the Gulf of Siam as a "precautionary" measure during fighting in Laos.

MAY 2-7—Major civil rights demonstrations

take place in Birmingham, Ala. Police assaults and arrests lead to black riots.

MAY 9—Birmingham leaders announce an agreement calling for the phased integration of business facilities and the establishment of a permanent biracial committee.

MAY 11—Kennedy and Prime Minister Lester Pearson announce a joint defense agreement. Canada agrees to accept nuclear warheads for missiles located in its territory.

MAY 12—Kennedy dispatches federal troops to bases near Birmingham, Ala., when riots break out there.

MAY 20—The Supreme Court rules that state and local governments cannot interfere with peaceful sit-in demonstrations for racial integration in public places of business.

MAY 21—In a referendum, wheat farmers reject a mandatory acreage control plan.

MAY 27—The Supreme Court prohibits an "indefinite delay" in the desegration of public schools.

MAY 31—Jackson, Miss., police arrest 600 black children involved in an integration demonstration.

JUNE 3—The Supreme Court rules that desegregation plans permitting pupils to transfer out of schools where their race is a minority are unconstitutional.

JUNE 10—Kennedy signs a bill requiring employers subject to the Fair Standards Act to pay equal wages for equal work, regardless of the sex of the workers.

JUNE 10—Kennedy delivers a major policy address at American University that calls for a reexamination of Cold War attitudes as a necessary prelude to world peace and announces new test ban negotiations in Moscow.

JUNE 11—The first blacks enroll at the

University of Alabama over the protest of Gov. George C. Wallace.

JUNE 12—Civil rights workers picket New York City construction sites to protest racial discrimination in hiring.

JUNE 12—Mississippi NAACP field secretary Medgar W. Evers is murdered following mass demonstrations in Jackson, Miss.

JUNE 17—The Supreme Court prohibits the use of the Lord's Prayer and Bible reading in public schools.

JUNE 19—Kennedy asks Congress to enact extensive civil rights legislation to give all citizens equal opportunity in employment, public accommodations, voting and education.

JUNE 26—On a visit to West Berlin Kennedy delivers his "Ich bin ein Berliner" address that promises continued support of that city.

JULY 8—The U.S. bans virtually all financial transactions with Cuba in a move toward economic isolation of that country.

JULY 12—Modified martial law is imposed in Cambridge, Md., after racial strife.

JULY 15—The U.S., Great Britain and the USSR open disarmament talks in Moscow.

JULY 16—The Federal Reserve Board increases the discount rate from 3% to 3½%

JULY 18—The U.S. and Mexico agree on a settlement of the disputed El Chamizal border area between El Paso, Tex., and Ciudad Juarez, Chihuahua.

JULY 18-19—The U.S. suspends relations and aid to Peru following a military coup.

JULY 25—The U.S., the USSR and Great Britain initial a test ban treaty in Moscow that prohibits nuclear testing in the atmosphere, space and underwater.

AUG. 2—The U.S. cuts off all economic assistance to Haiti to show its disapproval of the dictatorial government of Francois Duvalier.

AUG. 21—The South Vietnam government attacks Buddhist pagodas.

AUG. 24—Vietnam Ambassador Henry Cabot Lodge receives a State Department cable stating that the U.S. can no longer tolerate Ngo Dinh Nhu's influence in President Ngo Dinh Diem's regime.

AUG. 28—Kennedy signs a compulsory arbitration bill blocking a threatened railroad strike.

AUG. 28—Over 200,000 participate in the March on Washington and hear King deliver his "I Have a Dream" speech.

AUG. 30—The Washington-Moscow hot line is made operational.

SEPT. 10—Kennedy federalizes the Alabama National Guard to prevent its use against the desegration of public schools.

SEPT. 15—A bomb blast in a Birmingham, Ala., church kills four black girls.

SEPT. 24—The Senate, 80-19, ratifies the partial nuclear test ban treaty.

SEPT. 25—Following a successful military coup against President Juan Bosch, the U.S. suspends diplomatic relations and economic aid to the Dominican Republic.

OCT. 7—Bobby Baker resigns as secretary to the Senate majority after being charged with using his position for personal financial gain.

OCT. 9—Kennedy approves a $250 million wheat sale to the USSR.

OCT. 10—Kennedy signs a bill controlling possibly hazardous drugs such as thalidomide.

OCT. 22—Chicago civil rights forces stage a one-day "Freedom Day" boycott of public schools in which about 225,000 pupils stay home to protest de facto segregation in that city.

NOV. 1—South Vietnamese generals stage a successful coup. Diem and Nhu are assassinated.

NOV. 16—Through personal intervention with the Soviet authorities, Kennedy obtains the release of Prof. Frederick Barghoorn, who had been imprisoned in Russia on espionage charges.

NOV. 22—Kennedy is assassinated in Dallas, Tex., by Lee Harvey Oswald. Lyndon Johnson is sworn in as the 36th President.

NOV. 24—Jack Ruby kills Oswald in Dallas. The incident is seen live on TV.

NOV. 26—In a railroad work-rules dispute, a government arbitration board calls for the elimination of 40,000 jobs.

NOV. 27—Johnson asks Congress for the "earliest possible passage" of a civil rights program.

NOV. 29—The Warren Commission is set up to investigate the assassination of Kennedy.

Alabama

Lister Hill (D) 1938-69
John J. Sparkman (D) 1946-

Alaska

E. L. Bartlett (D) 1959-69
Ernest Gruening (D) 1959-69

Arizona

Carl Hayden (D) 1927-69
Barry M. Goldwater (R) 1953-65; 1969-

Arkansas

J. William Fulbright (D) 1945-75
John L. McClellan (D) 1943-

California

Clair Engle (D) 1959-64
Thomas H. Kuchel (R) 1953-69

Colorado

John A. Carroll (D) 1957-63
Gordon Allott (R) 1955-73
Peter Dominick (R) 1963-75

Connecticut

Thomas J. Dodd (D) 1959-71
Abraham A. Ribicoff (D) 1963-
Prescott Bush (R) 1952-63

Delaware

J. Caleb Boggs (R) 1961-73
John J. Williams (R) 1947-71

Florida

Spessard L. Holland (D) 1946-71
George P. Smathers (D) 1951-69

Georgia

Richard B. Russell (D) 1933-71
Herman E. Talmadge (D) 1957-

Hawaii

Oren E. Long (D) 1959-63
Daniel K. Inouye (D) 1963-
Hiram Fong (R) 1959-

Idaho

Frank Church (D) 1957-
Henry C. Dworshak (R) 1949-62
Len B. Jordan (R) 1962-73

Illinois

Paul H. Douglas (D) 1949-67
Everett M. Dirksen (R) 1951-69

Indiana

Birch Bayh (D) 1963-
Vance Hartke (D) 1959-
Homer E. Capehart (R) 1945-63

Iowa

Bourke B. Hickenlooper (R) 1945-69
Jack Miller (R) 1961-73

Kansas

Frank Carlson (R) 1950-69
James B. Pearson (R) 1962-
Andrew F. Schoeppel (R) 1949-62

Kentucky

John Sherman Cooper (R) 1956-75
Thruston B. Morton (R) 1957-69

Louisiana

Allen J. Ellender (D) 1937-72
Russell B. Long (D) 1948-

Maine

Edmund S. Muskie (D) 1959-
Margaret Chase Smith (R) 1949-73

Maryland

Daniel B. Brewster (D) 1963-69
J. Glenn Beall (R) 1953-65
John Marshall Butler (R) 1951-63

Massachusetts

Edward M. Kennedy (D) 1963-
Benjamin A. Smith, II (D) 1960-63
Leverett Saltonstall (R) 1945-67

Michigan

Philip A. Hart (D) 1959-
Pat V. McNamara (D) 1955-66

Minnesota

Hubert H. Humphrey (D) 1949-65; 1970-
Eugene J. McCarthy (D) 1959-71

Mississippi

James O. Eastland (D) 1943-
John Stennis (D) 1947-

Missouri

Edward V. Long (D) 1960-69
Stuart Symington (D) 1953-

Montana

Mike Mansfield (D) 1953-
Lee Metcalf (D) 1961-

Nebraska

Carl T. Curtis (R) 1955-
Roman Hruska (R) 1954-

Nevada

Alan Bible (D) 1954-
Howard W. Cannon (D) 1959-

New Hampshire

Thomas J. McIntyre (D) 1963-
H. Styles Bridges (R) 1937-61
Perkins Bass (R) 1961-63
Norris Cotton (R) 1954-75

New Jersey

Harrison A. Williams (D) 1959-
Clifford P. Chase (R) 1955-

New Mexico

Clinton P. Anderson (D) 1949-73
Dennis Chavez (D) 1935-62
Edwin L. Mechem (R) 1962-65

New York

Jacob K. Javits (R) 1957-
Kenneth B. Keating (R) 1959-65

North Carolina

Sam J. Ervin (D) 1954-75
B. Everett Jordan (D) 1958-73

North Dakota

Quentin Burdick (D) 1959-
Milton R. Young (R) 1945-

Ohio

Frank J. Lausche (D) 1957-69
Stephen M. Young (D) 1959-71

Oklahoma

J. Howard Edmondson (D) 1963-65
Robert S. Kerr (D) 1949-63
A. S. Mike Monroney (D) 1951-69

Oregon

Maurine P. Neuburger (D) 1960-67
Wayne Morse (R) 1945-52; (Ind.) 1952-55; (D)
1955-69

Pennsylvania

Joseph S. Clark (D) 1957-69
Hugh Scott (R) 1959-

Rhode Island

John O. Pastore (D) 1950-
Clairborne Pell (D) 1961-

South Carolina

Olin D. Johnston (D) 1945-65
Strom Thurmond (D) 1955-64; (R) 1964-

South Dakota

George McGovern (D) 1963-
Joseph Bottum (R) 1963
Francis Case (R) 1951-1962
Karl E. Mundt (R) 1948-73

Tennessee

Albert Gore (D) 1953-71
Estes Kefauver (D) 1949-63

Texas

Ralph W. Yarborough (D) 1957-71
John G. Tower (R) 1961-

Utah

Frank E. Moss (D) 1959-
Wallace F. Bennett (R) 1951-75

Vermont

George D. Aiken (R) 1941-75
Winston L. Prouty (R) 1959-71

Virginia

Harry Flood Byrd (D) 1933-65
A. Willis Robertson (D) 1946-67

Washington

Henry M. Jackson (D) 1953-
Warren G. Magnuson (D) 1944-

West Virginia

Robert C. Byrd (D) 1959-
Jennings Randolph (D) 1958-

Wisconsin

Gaylord Nelson (D) 1963-
William Proxmire (D) 1957-
Alexander Wiley (R) 1939-1963

Wyoming

J. J. Hickey (D) 1961-62
Gale W. McGee (D) 1959-
Milward L. Simpson (R) 1962-67

HOUSE

Alabama

George Andrews (D) 1944-73
Frank W. Boyki (D) 1935-63
Carl Elliott (D) 1949-65
George M. Grant (D) 1938-65
George Huddleston, Jr. (D) 1955
Robert E. Jones (D) 1947-
Albert Rains (D) 1945-65
Kenneth A. Roberts (D) 1951-65
Armistead I. Selden, Jr. (D) 1953

Alaska

Ralph Rivers (D) 1959-67

Arizona

George F. Senner (D) 1963-67
Morris K. Udall (D) 1961-
Stewart L. Udall (D) 1955-61
John J. Rhodes (R) 1953-

Arkansas

Dale Alford (D) 1959-63
E. C. Gathings (D) 1939-69
Oren Harris (D) 1941-66
Wilbur D. Mills (D) 1939-
W. F. Norrell (D) 1939-61
James W. Trimble (D) 1945-67

California

George E. Brown, Jr. (D) 1963-
Everett G. Burkhalter (D) 1963-65
Ronald B. Cameron (D) 1963-67
Jeffrey Cohelan (D) 1959-71
James C. Corman (D) 1961-
Clyde D. Doyle (D) 1949-63
Don Edwards (D) 1963-
Harlan D. Hagen (D) 1953-67
Richard T. Hanna (D) 1963-75
Augustus F. Hawkins (D) 1963-
Chet Holifield (D) 1943-75
Harold T. Johnson (D) 1959-
Cecil R. King (D) 1942-69
Robert L. Leggett (D) 1963-
John J. McFall (D) 1957-
Clem Miller (D) 1959-62
George P. Miller (D) 1945-
John E. Moss (D) 1953-
James Roosevelt (D) 1955-65
Edward R. Roybal (D) 1963-
D. S. Saund (D) 1957-63
John F. Shelley (D) 1949-64
Harry R. Sheppard (D) 1937-65
B. F. Sisk (D) 1955-
Lionel Van Deerlin (D) 1963-
Charles H. Wilson (D) 1963-
John F. Baldwin (R) 1955-66
Alphonzo Bell (R) 1961-
Don H. Clausen (R) 1963-
Charles S. Gubser (R) 1953-75
Edgar W. Hiestand (R) 1953-63
Craig Hosmer (R) 1953-75
Lenard P. Lipscomb (R) 1953-70
William S. Mailliard (R) 1953-74
Gordon L. McDonough (R) 1945-63
Pat Minor Martin (R) 1963-65
John H. Rousselot (R) 1961-63; 1971-
H. Allen Smith (R) 1957-73
Burt L. Talcott (R) 1963-
Charles M. Teague (R) 1955-
James B. Utt (R) 1953-70
Bob Wilson (R) 1953-
J. Arthur Younger (R) 1953-67

Colorado

Wayne N. Aspinall (D) 1949-73
Bryon G. Rogers (D) 1951-71
Donald G. Brotzman (R) 1963-65; 1967-75
J. Edgar Chenoweth (R) 1941-49; 1951-65
Peter H. Dominick (R) 1961-63

Connecticut

Emilio Q. Daddario (D) 1959-71

Robert N. Giaimo (D) 1959-
Bernard F. Grabowski (D) 1963-67
Frank Kowalski (D) 1959-63
John S. Monagan (D) 1959-73
William L. St. Onge (D) 1963-71
Horace Seely-Brown (R) 1961-63
Abner W. Sibal (R) 1961-65

Delaware

Harris B. McDowell, Jr. (D) 1955-57; 1959-67

Florida

Charles E. Bennett (D) 1949
Dante B. Fascell (D) 1955
Don Fuqua (D) 1963-
Sam M. Gibbons (D) 1963-
James A. Haley (D) 1953-
A. Sydney Herlong, Jr. (D) 1949-69
D. R. (Billy) Matthews (D) 1953-67
Claude Pepper (D) 1963-
Paul G. Rogers (D) 1955-
Robert L. F. Sikes (D) 1945-
William C. Cramer (R) 1955-71
Edward J. Gurney (R) 1963-69

Georgia

Iris F. Blitch (D) 1955-63
James C. Davis (D) 1947-63
John W. Davis (D) 1961-75
John J. Flynt (D) 1954-
E. L. Forrester (D) 1951-65
G. Elliot Hagan (D) 1961-73
Phil M. Landrum (D) 1953-
John L. Pilcher (D) 1953-65
Robert Stephens (D) 1961-
J. Russell Tuten (D) 1963-67
Carl Vinson (D) 1914-65
Charles L. Weltner (D) 1963-67

Hawaii

Thomas P. Gill (D) 1963-65
Daniel K. Inouye (D) 1959-63
Spark M. Matsunaga (D) 1963-

Idaho

Ralph R. Harding (D) 1961-65
Gracie Pfost (D) 1953-63
Compton I. White (D) 1963-67

Illinois

William L. Dawson (D) 1943-70
Edward R. Finnegan (D) 1961-65
Kenneth J. Gray (D) 1955-75
John C. Kluczynski (D) 1951-75
Roland V. Libonati (D) 1957-65
Peter F. Mack, Jr. (D) 1949-63
William T. Murphy (D) 1959-71
Thomas J. O'Brien (D) 1933-37; 1943-64
Barratt O'Hara (D) 1949-51; 1953-69
Melvin Price (D) 1945-
Roman O. Pucinski (D) 1959-73
Dan Rostenkowski (D) 1959-
George E. Shipley (D) 1959-
Sidney R. Yates (D) 1949-63
John B. Anderson (R) 1961-
Leslie C. Arends (R) 1935-75
Robert B. Chiperfield (R) 1939-63
Marguerite Stitt Church (R) 1951-63
Harold R. Collier (R) 1957-75
Edward J. Derwinski (R) 1959-
Paul Findley (R) 1961-
Elmer J. Hoffman (R) 1959-65
Robert McClory (R) 1963-
Noah M. Mason (R) 1937-63
Robert H. Michel (R) 1957-
Charlotte T. Reid (R) 1963-71
Donald Rumsfeld (R) 1963-69
William L. Springer (R) 1951-73

Indiana

John Brademas (D) 1959-
Winfield K. Denton (D) 1949-53; 1955-66
Ray J. Madden (D) 1943-
J. Edward Roush (D) 1959-69
E. Ross Adair (R) 1951-71
William G. Bray (R) 1951-75
Donald C. Bruce (R) 1961-65
Charles A. Halleck (R) 1935-69
Ralph Harvey (R) 1947-59; 1961-66
Richard L. Roudebush (R) 1961-71
Earl Wilson (R) 1941-59; 1961-65

Iowa

Merwin Coad (D) 1957-63
Neal Smith (D) 1959-
James E. Bromwell (R) 1961-65
H. R. Gross (R) 1949-75
Charles B. Hoeven (R) 1943-65
Ben F. Jensen (R) 1939-65
John Kyl (R) 1959-65; 1967-73
Fred Schwengel (R) 1955-65; 1967-73

Kansas

J. Floyd Breeding (D) 1957-63
William H. Avery (R) 1955-65
Robert Dole (R) 1961-69
Robert F. Ellsworth (R) 1961-67
Walter L. McVey (R) 1961-63
Garner Shriver (R) 1961-
Joe Skubitz (R) 1963-
Larry Winn, Jr. (R) 1967-

Kentucky

Frank W. Burke (D) 1959-63
Frank Chelf (D) 1945-67
William H. Natcher (D) 1953-
Carl D. Perkins (D) 1949-
Brent Spence (D) 1931-63
Frank A. Stubblefield (D) 1959-75
John C. Watts (D) 1951-71
Eugene Siler (R) 1955-65
M. G. (Gene) Snyder (R) 1963-65; 1967-

Louisiana

Hale Boggs (D) 1941-43; 1947-72
Overton Brooks (D) 1937-61
F. Edward Hebert (D) 1941-
Gillis W. Long (D) 1963-
Harold B. McSween (D) 1959-63
James H. Morrison (D) 1943-67
Otto E. Passman (D) 1947-
T. Ashton Thompson (D) 1953-65
Joe D. Waggoner, Jr. (D) 1961-
Edwin Willis (D) 1949-69

Maine

Peter A. Garland (R) 1961-63
Clifford G. McIntire (R) 1951-65
Stanley R. Tupper (R) 1961-67

Maryland

Daniel B. Brewster (D) 1959-63
George H. Fallon (D) 1945-71
Samuel N. Friedel (D) 1953-71
Edward A. Garmatz (D) 1947-73
Thomas F. Johnson (D) 1959-63
Richard Lankford (D) 1955-65
Clarence D. Long (D) 1963-
Carlton R. Sickles (D) 1963-67
Charles McC. Mathias, Jr. (R) 1961-69
Rogers C. B. Morton (R) 1963-70

Massachusetts

Edward P. Boland (D) 1953-
James A. Burke (D) 1959-
Harold D. Donohue (D) 1947-75
Thomas J. Lane (D) 1941-63
Torbert H. Macdonald (D) 1955-75
John W. McCormack (D) 1928-71
Thomas P. O'Neill, Jr. (D) 1953-
Philip J. Philbin (D) 1943-71
William H. Bates (R) 1950-69
Silvio O. Conte (R) 1959-
Thomas B. Curtis (R) 1953-63
Hastings Keith (R) 1959-73
Joseph W. Martin, Jr. (R) 1925-67
F. Bradford Morse (R) 1961-72

Michigan

Charles C. Diggs, Jr. (D) 1955-
John D. Dingell (D) 1955-63
Martha A. Griffiths (D) 1955-75
John Lesinski (D) 1951-65
Thaddeus M. Machrowicz (D) 1951-61
Lucien N. Nedzi (D) 1961-
James G. O'Hara (D) 1959-
Louis C. Rabaut (D) 1949-61
Harold M. Ryan (D) 1962-65
Neil Staebler (D) 1963-65
John B. Bennett (R) 1943-45; 1947-64
William S. Bromfield (R) 1957-
Elford A. Cederberg (R) 1953-
Charles F. Chamberlain (R) 1957-75
Gerald R. Ford (R) 1949-73
Robert P. Griffin (R) 1957-66
James Harvey (R) 1961-74
Clare E. Hoffman (R) 1935-63
Edward Hutchinson (R) 1963-
August E. Johansen (R) 1955-65
Victor A. Knox (R) 1953-65
George Meader (R) 1951-65

Minnesota

John A. Blatnik (D) 1947-75
Donald M. Fraser (D) 1963-
Joseph E. Karth (D) 1959-
Fred Marshall (D) 1949-63
Alec G. Olson (D) 1963-67
H. Carl Andersen (R) 1939-63
Walter H. Judd (R) 1943-63
Odin Langen (R) 1959-71
Clark MacGregor (R) 1961-71
Ancher Nelsen (R) 1959-75
Albert H. Quie (R) 1958-

Mississippi

Thomas G. Abernethy (D) 1943-73
William M. Colmer (D) 1933-73
Frank E. Smith (D) 1951-63
Jamie L. Whitten (D) 1941-
John Bell Williams (D) 1947-68
Arthur Winstead (D) 1943-65

Missouri

Richard Bolling (D) 1949-
Clarence Cannon (D) 1923-64
W. R. Hull, Jr. (D) 1955-73
Richard H. Ichord (D) 1961-
Paul C. Jones (D) 1948-69
Frank M. Karsten (D) 1947-69
Morgan M. Moulder (D) 1949-63
William J. Randall (D) 1959-
Leonor Kretzer Sullivan (D) 1953-
Thomas B. Curtis (R) 1951-69
Durward G. Hall (R) 1961-73

Montana

Arnold Olsen (D) 1961-71
James F. Battin (R) 1961-69

Nebraska

Ralph F. Beermann (R) 1961-65
Glenn Cunningham (R) 1957-71
David T. Martin (R) 1961-75
Phil Weaver (R) 1955-63

Nevada

Walter S. Baring (D) 1949-53; 1957-73

New Hamshire

Perkins Bass (R) 1955-63
James C. Cleveland (R) 1963-
Chester E. Merrow (R) 1943-63
Louis C. Wyman (R) 1963-65; 1967-75

New Jersey

Hugh J. Addonizio (D) 1949-62
Dominick V. Daniels (D) 1959-
Cornelius E. Gallagher (D) 1959-73
Charles S. Joelson (D) 1961-69
Joseph G. Minish (D) 1963-
Edward J. Patten (D) 1963-

Peter W. Rodino (D) 1949-
Frank Thompson, Jr. (D) 1955-
James C. Auchincloss (R) 1943-65
William T. Cahill (R) 1959-69
Florence P. Dwyer (R) 1957-73
Peter Frelinghuysen, Jr. (R) 1953-75
Milton W. Glenn (R) 1957-65
Frank C. Osmers, Jr. (R) 1939-43; 1951-65
George M. Wallhauser (R) 1959-65
William B. Widnall (R) 1950-75

New Mexico

Joseph M. Montoya (D) 1957-65
Thomas G. Morris (D) 1959-69

New York

Joseph P. Addabbo (D) 1961-
Victor L. Anfuso (D) 1955-63
Charles A. Buckley (D) 1935-65
Hugh L. Carey (D) 1961-75
Emanuel Celler (D) 1923-73
James J. Delaney (D) 1949-
Thaddeus J. Dulski (D) 1959-75
Leonard Farbstein (D) 1957-71
Jacob H. Gilbert (D) 1960-71
James C. Healey (D) 1956-65
Lester Holtzman (D) 1953-61
Edna F. Kelly (D) 1949-69
Eugene J. Keogh (D) 1937-67
Abraham J. Multer (D) 1947-68
John M. Murphy (D) 1963-
Leo W. O'Brien (D) 1952-66
Otis G. Pike (D) 1961-
Adam C. Powell (D) 1945-67; 1969-71
John J. Rooney (D) 1944-75
Benjamin S. Rosenthal (D) 1961-
William Fitts Ryan (D) 1961-72
Alfred E. Santangelo (D) 1957-63
Samuel S. Stratton (D) 1959-
Herbert Zelenko (D) 1955-63
Robert R. Barry (R) 1959-65
Frank S. Becker (R) 1953-65
Steven B. Derounian (R) 1953-65
Edwin B. Dooley (R) 1957-63
Paul A. Fino (R) 1953-69
Charles E. Goodell (R) 1959-68
James R. Grover, Jr. (R) 1963-75
Seymour Halpern (R) 1959-73
Frank J. Horton (R) 1963-
Clarence Kilburn (R) 1940-65
Carleton J. King (R) 1961-75
John V. Lindsay (R) 1959-65
William E. Miller (R) 1951-65
Harold C. Ostertag (R) 1951-65
John R. Pillion (R) 1953-65

Alexander Pirnie (R) 1959-73
John H. Ray (R) 1953-63
Ogden R. Reid (R) 1963-72; (D) 1972-75
R. Walter Riehlman (R) 1947-65
Howard W. Robison (R) 1958-75
Katharine St. George (R) 1947-65
John Taber (R) 1923-63
Jessica McC. Weis (R) 1959-63
J. Ernest Wharton (R) 1951-65
John W. Wydler (R) 1963-

North Carolina

Hugh Alexander (D) 1953-63
Herbert C. Bonner (D) 1940-65
Harold D. Cooley (D) 1934-66
L. H. Fountain (D) 1953-
David N. Henderson (D) 1961-
A. Paul Kitchin (D) 1957-63
Horace R. Kornegay (D) 1961-69
Alton Lennon (D) 1957-73
Ralph J. Scott (D) 1957-67
Roy A. Taylor (D) 1960-
Basil L. Whitener (D) 1957-69
James T. Broyhill (R) 1963-
Charles R. Jonas (R) 1953-73

North Dakota

Hjalmar C. Nygaard (R) 1961-63
Don L. Short (R) 1959-65

Ohio

Thomas L. Ashley (D) 1955-
Robert E. Cook (D) 1959-63
Michael A. Feighan (D) 1943-71
Wayne L. Hays (D) 1949-
Michael J. Kirwan (D) 1937-70
Walter H. Moeller (D) 1959-63
Robert T. Secrest (D) 1949-54; 1963-66
Charles A. Vanik (D) 1955-
Homer E. Abele (R) 1963-65
John M. Ashbrook (R) 1961-
William J. Ayres (R) 1951-71
Jackson E. Betts (R) 1951-73
Frances P. Bolton (R) 1940-69
Oliver P. Bolton (R) 1953-55; 1963-65
Frank T. Bow (R) 1951-72
Clarence J. Brown (R) 1939-65
Donald D. Clancy (R) 1961-
Samuel L. Devine (R) 1959-
William J. Harsha (R) 1961-
Delbert L. Latta (R) 1959-
William M. McCulloch (R) 1947-73
William E. Minshall (R) 1955-75

Tom V. Moorehead (R) 1961-63
Charles A. Mosher (R) 1961-
Carl W. Rich (R) 1963-65
Paul F. Schenck (R) 1951-65
Gordon H. Scherer (R) 1953-63
Robert Taft, Jr. (R) 1963-65; 1967-71

Oklahoma

Carl Albert (D) 1957-
Ed Edmondson (D) 1953-73
John Jarman (D) 1951-
Tom Steed (D) 1949-
Victor Wickersham (D) 1941-47; 1949-57; 1961-65
Page Belcher (R) 1951-73

Oregon

Robert B. Duncan (D) 1963-67
Edith Green (D) 1955-75
Al Ullman (D) 1957-
Edwin R. Durno (R) 1961-63
Walter Norblad (R) 1946-64

Pennsylvania

William A. Barrett (D) 1945-47; 1949-
James A. Byrne (D) 1953-73
Frank M. Clark (D) 1955-
John H. Dent (D) 1958-
Daniel J. Flood (D) 1954-
Kathryn E. Granahan (D) 1956-63
William J. Green, Jr. (D) 1949-63
Elmer Holland (D) 1942-43; 1956-68
William S. Moorhead (D) 1959-
Thomas E. Morgan (D) 1945-
Robert N. C. Nix (D) 1958-
George M. Rhodes (D) 1949-69
Herman Toll (D) 1959-66
Francis E. Walter (D) 1933-63
Robert J. Corbett (R) 1939-41; 1945-71
Willard S. Curtin (R) 1957-67
Paul B. Dague (R) 1947-67
Ivor D. Fenton (R) 1939-63
James G. Fulton (R) 1945-71
Leon H. Gavin (R) 1943-63
George A. Goodling (R) 1961-65; 1967-75
Carroll D. Kearns (R) 1947-63
John C. Kunkel (R) 1961-61
Joseph M. McDade (R) 1963-
William H. Milliken (R) 1959-65
Walter M. Mumma (R) 1951-61
John P. Saylor (R) 1949-73
Herman T. Schneebeli (R) 1960-
Richard S. Schweiker (R) 1961-69

William W. Scranton (R) 1961-63
James E. Van Zandt (R) 1947-63
James D. Weaver (R) 1963-65
J. Irving Whalley (R) 1960-73

Rhode Island

John E. Fogarty (D) 1941-67
Fernand J. St. Germain (D) 1961-

South Carolina

Robert T. Ashmore (D) 1953-69
W. J. Bryan Dorn (D) 1947-49; 1951-75
Robert W. Hemphill (D) 1957-64
John L. McMillan (D) 1939-73
John J. Riley (D) 1951-62
L. Mendel Rivers (D) 1941-70
Albert W. Watson (D) 1963-65; (R) 1965-71

South Dakota

E. Y. Berry (R) 1951-71
Ben Reifel (R) 1961-71

Tennessee

Ross Bass (D) 1955-64
Clifford Davis (D) 1940-65
Robert A. Everett (D) 1958-69
Joe L. Evins (D) 1947-
James B. Frazier, Jr. (D) 1949-63
Richard H. Fulton (D) 1963-
J. Carlton Loser (D) 1957-63
Tom Murray (D) 1943-66
Howard H. Baker (R) 1951-64
William E. Brock, III (R) 1963-71
James H. Quillen (R) 1963-
B. Carroll Reece (R) 1951-61

Texas

Lindley Beckworth (D) 1939-53; 1957-67
Jack Brooks (D) 1953-
Omar Burleson (D) 1947-73
Bob Casey (D) 1959-
John Dowdy (D) 1952-72
O. C. Fisher (D) 1943-75
Henry B. Gonzalez (D) 1961-
Frank Ikard (D) 1951-61
Paul J. Kilday (D) 1939-61
Joe M. Kilgore (D) 1955-65
George H. Mahon (D) 1935-
Wright Patman (D) 1929-76
W. R. Poage (D) 1937-

Joe Pool (D) 1963-68
Graham Purcell (D) 1962-73
Sam Rayburn (D) 1913-61
Ray Roberts (D) 1962-
Walter Rogers (D) 1951-67
J. T. Rutherford (D) 1955-63
Olin E. Teague (D) 1946-
Albert Thomas (D) 1937-66
Clark W. Thompson (D) 1933-35; 1947-66
Homer Thornberry (D) 1949-63
James C. Wright (D) 1955-
John Young (D) 1957-
Bruce Alger (R) 1955-65
Ed Foreman (R) 1963-65; 1969-71 (New Mexico)

Utah

David S. King (D) 1959-63
M. Blaine Peterson (D) 1961-63
Laurence J. Burton (R) 1963-71
Sherman P. Lloyd (R) 1963-73

Vermont

Robert T. Stafford (R) 1961-71

Virginia

Watkins M. Abbitt (D) 1948-73
Thomas N. Downing (D) 1959-
J Vaughan Gary (D) 1945-65
Porter J. Hardy (D) 1947-69
Burr P. Harrison (D) 1946-63
W. Pat Jennings (D) 1955-67
John O. Marsh, Jr. (D) 1963-71
Howard W. Smith (D) 1921-67
William M. Tuck (D) 1953-69
Joel T. Broyhill (R) 1953-75
Richard H. Poff (R) 1953-72

Washington

Julia Butler Hansen (D) 1960-75
Don Magnuson (D) 1953-63
Walt Horan (R) 1943-65
Catherine May (R) 1959-71
Thomas M. Pelly (R) 1953-73
William Stinson (R) 1963-65
Thomas M. Tollefson (R) 1947
Jack Westland (R) 1953-65

West Virginia

M. Bailey (D 1949-63
Ken Hechler (D) 1959-
Elizabeth Kee (D) 1951-65
John M. Slack, Jr. (D) 1959-
Harley O. Staggers (D) 1949-
Arch A. Moore, Jr. (R) 1957-69

Wisconsin

Lester R. Johnson (D) 1953-65
Robert W. Kastenmeier (D) 1959-
Henry S. Reuss (D) 1955-
Clement J. Zablocki (D) 1949-
John W. Byrnes (R) 1945-73
Melvin R. Laird (R) 1953-69
Alvin E. O'Konski (R) 1943-73
Henry C. Schadeberg (R) 1961-65; 1967-71
Vernon W. Thomson (R) 1961-75
William K. Van Pelt (R) 1951-65

Wyoming

William Henry Harrison (R) 1951-55; 1961-65; 1967-69

SUPREME COURT

Earl Warren, Chief Justice 1953-69
Hugo L. Black 1937-71
William J. Brennan 1956-75
Tom C. Clark 1949-67
William O. Douglas 1939-75
Felix Frankfurter 1939-62

Arthur J. Goldberg 1962-65
John Marshall Harlan 1955-71
Potter Stewart 1958-
Byron R. White 1962-
Charles E. Whittaker 1957-61

EXECUTIVE DEPARTMENTS

Department of Agriculture

Secretary of Agriculture
Orville L. Freeman, 1961-69

Undersecretary
Charles S. Murphy, 1961-65

Deputy Undersecretary
J. L. Sundquist, 1963-65

Assistant Secretary—Federal-States Relations
Frank J. Welch, 1961-62
John A. Baker, 1962-69
Reorganized as Rural Development and Conservation, 1963

Assistant Secretary—Marketing and Foreign Agriculture
John P. Duncan, Jr., 1961-63
Reorganized under Marketing and Stabilization, 1963
George L. Mehren, 1963-68

Assistant Secretary—Agriculture Stabilization
James T. Ralph, 1961-63
Reorganized under Marketing and Stabilization, and International Affairs 1963 (See above.)

Assistant Secretary—International Affairs
Roland R. Renne, 1963-64

Assistant Secretary for Department Administration
Joseph M. Robertson, 1961-

Department of Commerce

Secretary of Commerce
Luther H. Hodges, 1961-64

Undersecretary
Edward Gudeman, 1961-63
Franklin D. Roosevelt, Jr., 1963-65

Undersecretary for Transportation
Clarence D. Martin, Jr., 1961-65

Deputy Undersecretary for Transportation
Frank Barton, 1961-64
E. Grosvenor Plowman, 1963-64

Assistant for Administration and Public Affairs
William Ruder, 1961-62
Herbert W. Klotz, 1962-65

Assistant Secretary for International Affairs
Rowland Burnstan, 1961-62
Jack N. Behrman, 1962
Reorganized under Domestic and International Business, 1962

Assistant Secretary for Domestic Affairs
Hickman Price, Jr., 1961-62
Reorganized under Domestic and International Business, 1962

Assistant Secretary for Science and Technology
J. Herbert Holloman, 1962-67

Assistant Secretary for Economic Affairs
Richard H. Holton, 1963-65

Assistant Secretary for Domestic and International Business
Jack N. Behrman, 1962-64

Department of Defense

Secretary of Defense
Robert S. McNamara, 1961-68

Deputy Secretary of Defense
Roswell L. Gilpatric, 1961-64

Secretary of the Air Force
Eugene M. Zuckert, 1961-65

Secretary of the Army
Elvis J. Stahr, 1961-62
Cyrus R. Vance, 1962-64

Secretary of the Navy
John B. Connally, 1961
Fred Korth, 1961-63
Paul H. Nitze, 1963-67

Assistant Secretary
John H. Rubel, 1961-63
Eugene C. Fubini, 1963-65

Assistant Secretary (Comptroller)
Charles J. Hitch, 1961-65

Assistant Secretary (Installations and Logistics)
Thomas D. Morris, 1961-64

Assistant Secretary (International Security)
Paul H. Nitze, 1961-63
William P. Bundy, 1963-64

Assistant Secretary (Manpower)
Carlisle P. Runge, 1961-62
Norman S. Paul, 1962-65

Assistant Secretary (Public Affairs)
Arthur Sylvester, 1961-66

Department of Health, Education and Welfare

Secretary of Health, Education and Welfare
Abraham A Ribicoff, 1961-62
Anthony J. Celebrezze, 1962-65

Undersecretary
Ivan A. Nestingen, 1961-65

Assistant Secretary for Legislation
Wilbur J. Cohen, 1961-65

Assistant Secretary
James M. Quigley, 1961-66

Administrative Assistant secretary
Rufus E. Miles, Jr., 1961-65

Department of the Interior

Secretary of the Interior
Stewart L. Udall, 1961-69

Undersecretary
James K. Carr, 1961-64

Assistant Secretary—Fish and Wildlife
Frank P. Briggs, 1961-65

Assistant Secretary—Mineral Resources
John M. Kelly, 1961-65

Assistant Secretary—Public Land Management
John A. Carver, Jr., 1961-64

Assistant Secretary—Water and Power Development
Kenneth Holum, 1961-69

Administrative Assistant Secretary
D. Otis Beasly, 1952-65

Department of Justice

Attorney General
Robert F. Kennedy, 1961-64

Deputy Attorney General
Byron R. White, 1961-62
Nicholas deB. Katzenbach, 1962-64

Solicitor General
Archibald Cox, 1961-65

Assistant Attorney General/Antitrust Division
Lee Loevinger, 1961-63
William H. Orrick, Jr., 1963-65

Assistant Attorney General/Civil Division
William H. Orrick, Jr., 1961-62
John W. Douglas, 1963-66

Assistant Attorney General/Criminal Division
Herbert J. Miller, Jr., 1961-65

Assistant Attorney General/Internal Security Division
J. Walter Yeagley, 1959-70

Assistant Attorney General/Lands Division
Ramsey Clark, 1961-65

Assistant Attorney General/Tax Division
Louis Falk Oberdorfer, 1961-65

Assistant Attorney General/Civil Rights Division
Burke Marshall, 1961-65

Assistant Attorney General/Office of Legal Counsel
Nicholas deB. Katzenbach, 1961-62
Norbert A. Schlei, 1962-66

Department of Labor

Secretary of Labor
   Arthur M. Goldberg, 1961-62
   W. Willard Wirtz, 1962-69

Undersecretary
   W. Willard Wirtz, 1961-62
   John F. Henning, 1962-67

Deputy Undersecretary
   Millard Cass, 1955-71

Assistant Secretary for Labor-Management
Relations
   James J. Reynolds, 1961-67

Assistant Secretary for Employment and
Manpower
   Jerry R. Holleman, 1961-62

Assistant Secretary for International Labor
Affairs
   George C. Lodge, 1961
   George L. P. Weaver, 1961-69

Assistant Secretary for Labor Standards
   Esther Peterson, 1961-69

Assistant Secretary for Policy Planning and
Research
   Daniel P. Moynihan, 1963-65

Post Office Department

Post Master General
   J. Edward Day, 1961-63
   John A. Gronouski, 1963-65

Deputy Post Master General
   H. W. Brawley, 1961-62
   Sidney Bishop, 1963-64

Assistant Post Master General/Bureau of
Operations
   Frederick C. Belen, 1961-64

Assistant Post Master General/Bureau of
Transportation
   William J. Hartigan, 1961-62
   F. E. Batrus, (acting) 1962-63
   William J. Hartigan, 1963-67

Assistant Post Master General/Bureau of

Finance
   Ralph W. Nicholson, 1961-69

Assistant Post Master General/Bureau of
Facilities
   Robert J. Burkhardt, Jr., 1961-62
   Sidney W. Bishop, 1962-64

Assistant Post Master General/Bureau of
Personnel
   Richard James Murphy, 1961-69

State Department

Secretary of State
   Dean Rusk, 1961-69

Undersecretary
   Chester Bowles, 1961
   George W. Ball, 1961-66

Undersecretary for Economic Affairs
   George W. Ball, 1961

Undersecretary for Political Affairs
   George C. McGhee, 1961-63
   W. Averell Harriman, 1963-65

Deputy Undersecretary for Administration
   Roger W. Jones, 1961-62
   William H. Orrick, 1962-63
   William J. Crockett, 1963-67

Deputy Undersecretary for Political Affairs
   U. Alexis Johnson, 1961-64

Assistant Secretary for Public Affairs
   Roger W. Tubby, 1961-62
   Robert J. Manning, 1962-64

Assistant Secretary for Congressional Rela-
tions
   Brooks Hays, 1961
   Frederick G. Dutton, 1961-64

Assistant Secretary for Inter-American Af-
fairs
   Wymberley deR. Coerr, (acting) 1961
   Edwin M. Martin, 1961-63

Assistant Secretary for European Affairs
   Foy D. Kohler, 1961-62
   William R. Tyler, 1962-65

Assistant Secretary for Far Eastern Affairs
  Walter P. McConaughy, 1961
  Averell Harriman, 1961-63
  Roger Hilsman, Jr., 1963-64

Assistant Secretary for Near Eastern and
  South Asian Affairs
  Phillips Talbot, 1961-65

Assistant Secretary for African Affairs
  G. Mennen Williams, 1961-66

Assistant Secretary for International Organization Affairs
  Harlan Cleveland, 1961-65

Assistant Secretary for Administration
  William J. Crockett, 1961-62
  Dwight J. Porter, 1963-65

Assistant Secretary for Educational and Cul-
  tural Affairs
  Philip H. Coombs, 1961-62
  Lucius D. Battle, 1962-64

Assistant Secretary for Economic Affairs

G. Griffith Johnson, Jr., 1962-65

Department of the Treasury

Secretary of the Treasury
  Douglas Dillon, 1961-65

Undersecretary
  Henry H. Fowler, 1961-64

Undersecretary for Monetary Affairs
  Robert V. Roosa, 1961-64

Deputy Undersecretary for Monetary Affairs
  J. Dewey Daane, 1961-63

Assistant Secretaries
  A. Gilmore Flues, 1961
  John M. Leddy, 1961-62
  Stanley Surrey, 1961-69
  James A. Reed, 1961-65
  John C. Bullitt, 1963-64
  Robert A. Wallace, 1963-69

REGULATORY COMMISSIONS
AND INDEPENDENT AGENCIES

Atomic Energy Commission

John S. Graham, 1957-62
Dr. Leland J. Haworth, 1961-63
John A. McCone, 1958-61; Chairman,
  1958-61
Loren K. Olson, 1960-62
John Palfrey, 1962-66
James T. Ramey, 1962-73
Glenn T. Seaborg, 1961-71; Chairman,
  1961-71
Gerald F. Tape, 1963-69
Robert E. Wilson, 1960-64

Civil Aeronautics Board

Alan S. Boyd, 1959-65; Chairman, 1961-65
Whitney Gillilland, 1959-
Chan Gurney, 1951-65; Chairman, 1954.

G. Joseph Minetti, 1956-74
Robert T. Murphy, 1961-

Federal Communications Commission

Robert T. Bartley, 1952-72
Kenneth A. Cox, 1963-70
T. A. M. Craven, 1956-63
John S. Cross, 1958-62
Frederick W. Ford, 1957-65; Chairman,
  1960-61
E. William Henry, 1962-66; Chairman,
  1963-66
Rosel H. Hyde, 1946-1969; Chairman,
  1953-54, 1966-69
Robert E. Lee, 1953-
Lee Loevinger, 1963-68
Newton N. Minow, 1961-63; Chairman,
  1961-63

Federal Power Commission

David S. Black, 1963-66
Arthur Kline, 1956-61
Jerome K. Kuy Kendall, 1953-61; Chairman, 1953-61
Howard Morgan, 1961-63
Lawrence J. O'Connor, Jr., 1962-71
Charles R. Ross, 1961-68
Frederick Stueck, 1954-61
Paul A. Sweeny, 1960-61
Joseph C. Swidler, 1961-65; Chairman, 1961-65
Harold C. Woodward, 1962-64

Federal Reserve Board

C. Canby Balderston, 1954-66
J. Dewey Daane, 1963-
G. H. King, Jr., 1959-63
William McC. Martin, Jr., 1951-70; Chairman, 1951-70
A. L. Mills, Jr., 1952-65
George W. Mitchell, 1961-
J. L. Robertson, 1952-73
Charles N. Shepardson, 1955-67
M. S. Szymczak, 1945-61

Federal Trade Commission

Sigurd Anderson, 1955-64
Paul Rand Dixon, 1961- ; Chairman, 1961-
Philip Elman, 1961-70
A. Leon Higginbotham, 1962-64
William C. Kern, 1955-62
Earl W. Kintner, 1959-61; Chairman, 1959-61
A. Everette MacIntyre, 1961-73
Edward K. Mills, Jr., 1960-61
Robert T. Secrest, 1954-61

Securities and Exchange Commission

William L. Gary, 1961-64
Manuel F. Cohen, 1961-69; Chairman, 1964-69
J. Allen Frear, 1961-63
Edward N. Gadsby, 1957-61; Chairman, 1957-61
Earl Freeman Hastings, 1956-61
Jack M. Whitney, 1961-64
Byron D. Woodside, 1960-67

GOVERNORS

Alabama

John Patterson (D) 1959-63
George C. Wallace (D) 1963-67

Alaska

William A. Egan (D) 1959-67

Arizona

Paul Fannin (R) 1959-65

Arkansas

Orval E. Faubus (D) 1955-67

California

Edmund G. Brown (D) 1959-67

Colorado

Stephen L. McNichols (D) 1959-63
John A. Love (R) 1963-75

Connecticut

Abramah A. Ribicoff (D) 1959-61
John N. Dempsey (D) 1961-71

Delaware

Elbert N. Carvel (D) 1961-65

Florida

C. Farris Bryant (D) 1961-65

Georgia

Ernest Vandiver (D) 1959-63
Carl E. Sanders (D) 1963-67

Hawaii

William F. Quinn (R) 1959-63
John A. Burns (D) 1963-74

Idaho

Robert E. Smylie (D) 1955-67

Illinois

Otto Kerner (D) 1961-68

Indiana

Matthew E. Welsh (D) 1961-65

Iowa

Norman A. Erbe (R) 1961-63
Harold E. Hughes (D) 1963-69

Kansas

John Anderson (R) 1961-65

Kentucky

Bert T. Combs (D) 1959-63
Edward T. Breathitt (D) 1963-67

Louisiana

Jimmie H. Davis (D) 1960-64

Maine

John H. Reed (R) 1960-67

Maryland

J. Millard Tawes (D) 1959-67

Massachusetts

John A. Volpe (R) 1961-63; 1965-69
Endicott Peabody (D) 1963-65

Michigan

John B. Swainson (D) 1961-63
George W. Romney (R) 1963-69

Minnesota

Elmer L. Andersen (R) 1961-63
Karl F. Rovaag (D) 1963-67

Mississippi

Ross R. Barnett (D) 1960-64

Missouri

John M. Dalton (D) 1961-65

Montana

Donald G. Nutter (R) 1961-62
Tim M. Babcock (R) 1962-69

Nebraska

Frank B. Morrison (D) 1961-67

Nevada

Grant Sawyer (D) 1959-67

New Hampshire

Wesley Powell (R) 1959-63
John W. King (D) 1963-69

New Jersey

Robert B. Meyner (D) 1954-62
Richard J. Hughes (D) 1962-70

New Mexico

Edwin L. Mechem (R) 1961-63
Jack M. Campbell (D) 1963-67

New York

Nelson A. Rockefeller (R) 1959-73

North Dakota

William L. Guy (D) 1961-73

Ohio

Michael V. DiSalle (D) 1959-63
James A. Rhodes (R) 1963-71

Oklahoma

J. Howard Edmondson (D) 1959-63
Henry Bellmon (R) 1963-67

Oregon

Mark O. Hatfield (R) 1959-67

Pennsylvania

David L. Lawrence (D) 1959-63
William W. Scranton (R) 1963-67

Rhode Island

John A. Notte, Jr. (D) 1961-63
John H. Chafee (R) 1963-69

South Carolina

Ernest F. Hollings (D) 1959-63
Donald S. Russell (D) 1963-65

South Dakota

Archie M. Gubbrud (R) 1961-65

Tennessee

Buford Ellington (D) 1959-63
Frank G. Clement (D) 1963-67

Texas

Price Daniel (D) 1957-63
John B. Connally, Jr. (D) 1963-69

Utah

George Dewey Clyde (R) 1957-65

Vermont

Ray Keyser (R) 1961-63
Philip H. Hoff (D) 1963-69

Virginia

J. Lindsay Almond, Jr. (D) 1958-62
Albertis S. Harrison (D) 1962-66

Washington

Albert D. Rosellini (D) 1957-65

West Virginia

W. W. Barron (D) 1961-65

Wisconsin

Gaylord A. Nelson (D) 1959-63
John W. Reynolds (D) 1963-65

Wyoming

J. J. Hickey (D) 1961
Jack Gage (D) 1961-63
Clifford P. Hansen (R) 1963-67

BIBLIOGRAPHY

THE KENNEDY ERA

Most historians have judged the early 1960s as the start of a new era in postwar American history. Several important surveys of the decade have already appeared. Among the most scholarly and thoughtful are Jim F. Heath, *Decade of Disillusionment: The Kennedy-Johnson Years* (Bloomington, 1975) and David Burner, Robert Marcus and Thomas West, *A Giant's Strength: America in the 1960s* (New York, 1971). William O'Neill, *Coming Apart: An Informal History of America in the 1960s* (New York, 1971) is a lively and iconoclastic book-length essay. An excellent conservative intellectual history is Ronald Berman, *America in the Sixties, an Intellectual History* (New York, 1968). Two good anthologies are Ronald Lora, ed., *America in the '60s, Cultural Authorities in Transition* (New York, 1974) and Edward Quinn and Paul J. Dolan, eds., *The Sense of the Sixties* (New York, 1968). Two recent surveys of the postwar era devote full chapters to the early 1960s. Robert A. Divine, *Since 1945: Politics and Diplomacy in Recent American History* (New York, 1975) offers a conventional interpretation of the period. Lawrence S. Wittner, *Cold War America: From Hiroshima to Watergate* (New York, 1975) provides a left-wing critique. The Facts on File *Yearbooks* contain a wealth of information indexed for easy reference.

THE PRESIDENCY AND THE ADMINISTRATION

National politics during the early 1960s has been well recorded, with most attention focused on the politics and personalities of the Kennedy Administration itself. Theodore White, *The Making of the President 1960* (New York, 1961) wrote the classic account of the election. Two essential works for a study of the Administration were written by Kennedy aides shortly after the assassination. Arthur Schlesinger, Jr., *A Thousand Days* (New York, 1965) and Theodore Sorenson, *Kennedy* (New York, 1965) are thorough, lively and sympathetic histories of a fallen chief and his policymaking inner circle. Far more critical are Henry Fairlie, *The Kennedy Promise* (New York, 1973) and Richard J. Walton, *Cold War and Counterrevolution* (New York, 1972). An analytic and scholarly study of Kennedy's leadership is Lewis J. Paper, *The Promise and the Performance* (New York, 1975). An early, hence incomplete, bibliography is James T. Crown, *The Kennedy Literature* (New York, 1968).

Other Works

Alsop, Stewart, *The Center* (New York, 1968).

Anderson, Patrick, *The President's Men* (New York, 1968).

Bradlee, Benjamin, *Conversations with Kennedy* (New York, 1975).

Cochen, Bert, *Adlai Stevenson* (New York, 1969).

David, Paul T., ed., *The Presidential Election and Transition, 1960-1961* (New York, 1961).

Donald, Aida Di Pace, ed., *John F. Kennedy and the New Frontier* (New York, 1966).

Fuchs, Lawrence H., *John F. Kennedy and American Catholicism* (New York, 1967).

Kearns, Doris, *Lyndon Johnson and the American Dream* (New York, 1976).

Key, V. O., *The Responsible Electorate: Rationality in Presidential Voting, 1936-1960* (Cambridge, Mass., 1966).

Lasky, Victor, *JFK: The Man and the Myth* (New York, 1963).

Leiserson, Avery, ed., *The American South in the 1960s* (New York, 1964).

Liston, Robert, *Sargent Shriver: A Candid Portrait* (New York, 1964).

Lodge, Henry Cabot, *The Storm Has Many Eyes* (New York, 1973).

Lubell, Samuel, *The Future of American Politics* (New York, 1965).

Manchester, William, *The Death of a President* (New York, 1967).

Mazo, Earl, and Stephen Hess, *Nixon: A Political Portrait* (New York, 1968).

Miles, Rufus, *The Department of Health, Education and Welfare* (New York, 1974).

Neustadt, Richard E., "Kennedy in the Presidency: a Premature Appraisal," *Political Science Quarterly*, LXXIX (September 1964).

O'Donnell, Kenneth P., and David F. Powers, *"Johnny We Hardly Knew Ye": Memories of John F. Kennedy* (New York, 1972).

Novak, Robert D., *The Agony of the GOP 1964* (New York, 1965).

O'Brien, Lawrence F., *No Final Victories* (New York, 1968).

Parmet, Herbert S., *The Democrats, the Years after FDR* (New York, 1976).

———, *Eisenhower and the American Crusades* (New York, 1972).

Pollard, James E., *The Presidents and the Press: Truman to Johnson* (Washington, 1964).

Rowe, Robert, *The Bobby Baker Story* (New York, 1967).

Salinger, Pierre, *With Kennedy* (New York, 1966).

Sevareid, Eric, ed., *Candidates 1960* (New York, 1959).

Sorenson, Theodore, *The Kennedy Legacy* (New York, 1969).

———, "The Election of 1960" in Arthur M. Schlesinger, Jr., ed., *History of American Presidential Elections, 1789-1968*, (New York, 1971) Vol. IV.

Simons, Louise Fitz, *The Kennedy Doctrine* (New York, 1972).

Thomas, Norman C., *Education in National Politics* (New York, 1975).

Ungar, Sanford, J., *FBI: An Uncensored Look Behind the Walls* (Boston, 1976).

Whalen, Richard, *The Founding Father* (New York, 1964). Joseph Kennedy.

Wicker, Tom, *JFK and LBJ: The Influence of Personality Upon Politics* (New York, 1968).

———, *Kennedy without Tears* (New York, 1964).

Wills, Garry, *Nixon Agonistes: The Crisis of the Self-Made Man* (New York, 1969).

The Assassination

Epstein, Edward Jay, *Inquest: The Warren Commission* (New York, 1966).

Lane, Mark, *Rush to Judgment* (New York, 1966).

Manchester, William, *The Death of a President* (New York, 1967).

Meagher, Sylvia, *Accessories after the Fact: The Warren Commission, the Authorities and the Report* (Indianapolis, 1967).

President's Commission on the Assassination of President John F. Kennedy, *Report* (Washington, 1964).

Scott, Peter Dale, Paul L. Hoen, and Russell Stetler, eds., *The Assassinations; Dallas and Beyond* (New York, 1976).

CONGRESS

The annual *Congressional Quarterly Almanac* (Washington, 1945-   ) is an essential tool for examining the operation of Congress on a year-by-year basis. It describes the content of major bills and traces their legislative history in both chambers. Important committee investigations are also examined. Roll call votes, studies of voting patterns and membership lists of committees and subcommittees are among its other features.

Scholarly works on the organization of Congress that are pertinent to the Kennedy years include John D. Lees, *Committee System of the United States Congress* (New York, 1967); Kenneth Kofmehl, *Professional Staffs of Congress* (n.p., 1962); Randolph B. Ripley, *Majority Party Leadership in Congress* (Boston, 1969) and *Party Leaders in the House of Representatives* (Washington, 1967). The structure and procedures of Congress in the early and mid 1960s are criticized as undemocratic and inefficient in Rep. Richard W. Bolling, *House Out of Order* (New York, 1966) and Sen. Joseph S. Clark, *The Senate Establishment* (New York, 1963) and *Congress: The Sapless Branch* (New York, 1967). *The Case Against Congress* (New York, 1968), by Drew Pearson and Jack Anderson, is in the muckraking genre.

Douglass Cater, *Power in Washington* (New York, 1964) describes the role of Congress in the context of the network of power centers in Washington. For the relationship between Kennedy and Congress see: James L. Sundquist, *Politics and Policy: The Eisenhower, Kennedy and Johnson Years* (Washington, 1968) and Tom Wicker's insightful *JFK and LBJ: The Influence of Personality on Politics* (New York, 1969). Both deal with the relative failure of Kennedy's domestic programs. See also, Abraham Holtzman, *Legislative Liaison: Executive Leadership in Congress* (Chicago, 1970) and Carroll Kilpatrick, "The Kennedy Style and Congress," *Virginia Quarterly Review* (Winter, 1963). James MacGregor Burns, *The Deadlock of Democracy: Four-Party Politics in America* (Englewood Cliffs, 1963) attributes Kennedy's legislative difficulties to the dominance of the conservative wings of the Democratic and Republican Parties over their liberal factions.

Books dealing with Congress's handling of specific Kennedy Administration programs include Joseph M. Becker, et al, *Programs to Aid the Unemployed in the 1960s* (Kalamazoo, 1965); Sam Levitan, *Federal Aid to Depressed Areas* (Baltimore, 1964); Don Hadwiger, *Pressures and Protests: The Kennedy Farm Program and the Wheat Referendum of 1963* (San Francisco, 1965); Richard Harris, *The Real Voice* (New York, 1964) and *A Sacred Trust* (New York, 1966) on the 1962 drug bill and medicare respectively. Also see Eugene Eidenberg and Roy D. Morey, *An Act of Congress: The Legislative Process and the Making of Education Policy* (New York, 1969).

Other Works

Anson, Robert Sam, *McGovern: A Biography* (New York, 1972).

Burns, James MacGregor, *Edward Kennedy and the Camelot Legacy* (New York, 1976).

Chamberlain, Hope, *A Minority of Members: Women in the U.S. Congress* (New York, 1973).

Coffin, Tristram, *Senator Fulbright: Portrait of a Public Philosopher* (New York, 1966).

Collins, Frederic W., "How to be a Leader Without Leading," *The New York Times Magazine* (July 30, 1961). Sen. Mike Mansfield.

Douglas, Paul H., *In the Fullness of Time* (New York, 1972).

Eisele, Albert, *Almost to the Presidency* (Blue Earth, Minn., 1972). Sens. Hubert H. Humphrey and Eugene J. McCarthy.

Evans, Rowland, Jr., "Louisiana's Passman: The Scourge of Foreign Aid," *Harper's* (January 1962).

———, "The Sixth Sense of Carl Vinson," *The Reporter* (Jan. 4, 1962).

Gore, Albert, *Let the Glory Out* (New York, 1972).

Gorman, Joseph B., *Estes Kefauver* (New York, 1971).

Greenfield, Meg, "The Man Who Leads the Southern Senators," *The Reporter* (May 21, 1964). Sen. Richard B. Russell.

Gruening, Ernest H., *Many Battles* (New York, 1973).

Johnson, Haynes, and Bernard M. Gwertzman, *Fulbright: The Dissenter* (Garden City, 1968).

Kay, Hubert, "The Warrior from Patman's Switch," *Fortune* (April, 1965). Rep. Wright Patman.

Lippman, Theo, Jr., *Senator Ted Kennedy* (New York, 1976).

McNeil, Neil, *Dirksen: Portrait of a Public Man* (New York, 1970).

Nevin, David, *Muskie of Maine* (New York, 1972).

Ognibene, Peter J., *Scoop: The Life and Politics of Henry M. Jackson* (New York, 1975).

Powell, Adam Clayton, *Adam by Adam* (New York, 1971).

Scheele, Henry Z., *Charlie Halleck* (New York, 1966).

Smith, A. Robert, *The Tiger in the Senate: The Biography of Wayne Morse* (Garden City, 1962).

Smith, Margaret Chase, *Declaration of Conscience* (New York, 1972).

Steinberg, Alfred, *Sam Rayburn* (New York, 1973).

Sykes, Jay G., *Proxmire* (Washington, 1972).

terHorst, J. F., *Gerald Ford* (New York, 1974).

Viorst, Milton, "Could this Jew be President?," *Esquire* (April 1966). Sen. Jacob K. Javits.

Wilkinson, J. Harvie III, *Harry Byrd and the Changing Face of Virginia Politics, 1945-1966* (Charlottesville, 1968).

Wilson, Augusta E., *Liberal Leader in the House: Frank Thompson, Jr.* (Washington, 1968).

Committee Studies

Ralph Nader Congress Project,

———, *The Commerce Committees: A Study of the House and Senate Commerce Committees*, David Price, director (New York, 1975).

———, *The Environment Committees: A Study of the House and Senate Interior, Agriculture, and Science Committees* (New York, 1975).

———, *The Judiciary Committees: A Study of the House and Senate Judiciary Committees*, Peter Schuck, director (New York, 1975).

———, *The Money Committees: A Study of the House Banking and Currency Committee and the Senate Banking, Housing and Urban Affairs Committee*, Lester Salamon, director (New York, 1975).

———, *The Revenue Committees: A Study of the House Ways and Means and Senate Finance Committees and the House and Senate Appropriations Committees*, Richard Spohn and Charles McCollum, directors (New York, 1975).

———, *Ruling Congress: A Study of How the House and Senate Rules Govern the Legislative Process*, Ted Siff and Alan Weil, directors (New York, 1975).

STATE AND LOCAL GOVERNMENT

The most thorough and recent state political studies have been made by Neal R. Peirce. Writing in the tradition of John Gunther, he produced *The Megastates* (New York, 1972) and followed it up with five regional surveys covering a majority of the American states. (See below.) Others who have produced excellent regional studies are Robert Sherrill, *Gothic Politics in the Deep South* (New York, 1968) and John H. Fenton, *Midwest Politics* (New York, 1966). Kevin P. Phillips, *Emerging Republican Majority* (Garden City, 1969) contains good studies of state voting behavior in the 1960s.

Urban problems and politics won great attention in the 1960s. Two classic elite studies by important political scientists are Robert E. Dahl, *Who Governs: Democracy and Power in an American City* (New York, 1961) and Edward C. Banfield, *Big City Politics: a Comparative Guide to the Political Systems of Nine American Cities* (New York, 1965). A close examination of labor's impact on the politics of three major cities is found in J. David Greenstone, *Labor in American Politics* (Chicago, 1969). One of the most important urban studies of the 1960s is Jane Jacobs, *The Death and Life of Great American Cities* (New York, 1969), an attack on massive urban renewal and superhighway projects that destroyed sound old city neighborhoods. In this tradition see: Mike Royko, *Boss: Richard J. Daley of Chicago* (New York, 1971) and Robert Caro, *The Power Broker: Robert Moses and the Fall of New York* (New York, 1974).

Other Works

Ainsworth, Ed, *Maverick Mayor: A Biography of Sam Yorty of Los Angeles* (Garden City, 1966).

Bartley, Numan V., *From Thurmond to Wallace: Political Tendencies in Georgia, 1948-1968* (Baltimore, 1968).

Cannon, Lou, *Ronnie and Jesse: A Political Odyssey* (Garden City, 1969).

Casdorph, Paul, *A History of the Republican Party in Texas, 1865-1965* (Austin, 1965).

Caudill, Harry M., *Night Comes to the Cumberlands: A Biography of a Depressed Area* (Boston, 1963).

Clark, Thomas D., *Kentucky: Land of Contrast* (New York, 1968).

Coffman, Tom, *Catch A Wave: A Case Study of Hawaii's New Politics* (Honolulu, 1973).

Cooke, Edward F., and Edward G. Janosik, *Pennsylvania Politics* (New York, 1965).

Conot, Robert, *American Odyssey* (New York, 1974). Detroit.

Connery, Robert H., and Gerald Benjamin, ed., *Governing New York State: The Rockefeller Years* (New York, 1974).

Costikyan, Edward N., *Behind Closed Doors, Politics in the Public Interest* (New York, 1966).

Crouch, Winston W., et al, *California Government and Politics* (Englewood Cliffs, 1967).

Delmatier, Royce D., and C. McIntosh, *The Rumble of California Politics, 1848-1970* (New York, 1970).

Douglas, Marjory Stoneman, *Florida, the Long Frontier* (New York, 1967).

Frady, Marshall, *Wallace* (New York, 1971). George Wallace.

Heard, Alexander, ed., *State Legislatures in American Politics* (Englewood Cliffs, 1966).

Hill, Gladwin, *Dancing Bear: An Inside Look at California Politics* (Cleveland, 1968).

Hoover, Edgar M., and Raymond Vernon, *Anotomy of a Metropolis* (New York, 1962).

Gray, Francine du Plessix, *Hawaii: The Sugar-Coated Fortress* (New York, 1972).

Havard, William C., ed., *Politics of the Contemporary South* (Baton Rouge, 1972).

Jacobs, Jane, *The Economy of Cities* (New York, 1969).

Jonas, Frank H., ed., *Politics in the American West* (Salt Lake City, 1969).

Key, V. O., *American State Politics* (New York, 1966).

Litt, Edgar, *The Political Cultures of Massachusetts* (Cambridge, Mass., 1965).

Lord, Walter, *The Past That Would Not Die* (New York, 1965). On the integration crisis at the University of Mississippi.

Lowe, Jeanne, *Cities in a Race with Time: Progress and Poverty in America's Growing Cities* (New York, 1967).

McWilliams, Cary, ed., *The California Revolution* (New York, 1968).

Meyerson, Martin, and Edward C. Banfield, *Politics, Planning and the Public Interest: The Case of Public Housing in Chicago* (Glencoe, 1964).

Mitau, G. Theodore, *Politics in Minnesota* (Minneapolis, 1970).

Mollenhoff, Clark, *George Romney: A Mormon in Politics* (New York, 1968).

Morgan, Neil, *Westward Tilt: The American West Today* (New York, 1961).

Moscow, Warren, *The Last of the Big-Time Bosses: The Life and Times of Carmine DeSapio and the Decline and Fall of Tammany Hall* (New York, 1971).

Moses, Robert, *Public Works: A Dangerous Trade* (New York, 1970).

Nevins, Allan, *Herbert H. Lehman and His Era* (New York, 1963).

Ostrander, Gilman M., *Nevada: The Great Rotten Borough 1895-1964* (New York, 1966).

Peirce, Neal R., *The Border South States* (New York, 1975).

————, *The Deep South States* (New York, 1974).

————, *The Great Plains States* (New York, 1973).

————, *The Mountain States* (New York, 1972).

————, *The Pacific States* (New York, 1974).

Petshak, Kirk, *The Challenge of Urban Reform: Policies and Programs in Philadelphia* (Philadelphia, 1973).

Phelan, James, and Robert Pozen, *The Company State, Ralph Nader's Study Group Report on DuPont in Delaware* (New York, 1973).

Phillips, Herbert L., *Big Wayward Girl: An Informal Political History of California* (Garden City, 1968).

Ravitch, Diane, *The Great School Wars, New York City, 1805-1973: A History of the Public Schools as Battlefield of Social Change* (New York, 1974).

Reichley, James, *States in Crisis* (New York, 1964).

Silver, James W., *Mississippi: The Closed Society* (New York, 1964).

Sindler, Allen P., ed., *Change in the Contemporary South* (Durham, 1963).

Talbot, Allan R., *The Mayor's Game: Richard Lee of New Haven and the Politics of Change* (New York, 1967).

Turner, Wallace, *The Mormon Establishment* (Boston, 1966).

Watters, Pat, and Reese Cleghorn, *Climbing Jacobs Ladder: The Arrival of Negroes in Southern Politics* (New York, 1967).

FOREIGN AFFAIRS

Among the vast number of works written on Kennedy's foreign policy, three are particularly useful overviews of the period. Richard Walton, *Cold War and Counterrevolution: The Foreign Policy of John F. Kennedy* (New York, 1972) is critical of the Administration, seeing its policies as a continuation of Cold War attitudes. Roger Hilsman, *To Move a Nation: The Politics of Foreign Policy in the Administration of John F. Kennedy* (Garden City, 1967) is an excellent favorable account that concentrates primarily on those topics of which Hilsman, as undersecretary of state, had personal knowledge—Southeast Asia, the Congo and Cuba. Walt W. Rostow, *The Diffusion of Power: An Essay in Recent History* (New York, 1972) is a favorable analysis of both the Kennedy and Johnson Administrations that has come under sharp attack by revisionist historians. Arthur Schlesinger, Jr., *A Thousand Days* (Boston, 1965) also contains valuable information on foreign affairs.

Several major crises highlighted the Kennedy years. For a discussion of the Soviet-American confrontation over Berlin see Jack M. Schick, *The Berlin Crisis, 1958-1962* (Philadelphia, 1971). The Administration's abortive 1961 Bay of Pigs invasion is discussed by Haynes Johnson, *The Bay of Pigs: The Leaders Story* (New York, 1964) and Karl E. Mayer and Tad Szulc, *The Cuban Invasion: The Chance of a Disaster* (New York, 1962). Graham Allison, *The Essence of Decision: Explaining the Cuban Missile Crisis* (Boston, 1971) examines the process of policy formulation during the Cuban missile crisis in October 1962. Also valuable is Robert F. Kennedy, *Thirteen Days: A Memoir of the Missile Crisis* (New York, 1969), a personal account by one of the President's closest advisers.

Kennedy's attempts to negotiate a test ban treaty with the Soviet Union are discussed by Arthur Dean, U.S. representative to the test ban talks, in *Test Ban and Disarmament: The Path of Negotiation* (New York, 1966). Also valuable as a study of the political events leading to the signing and ratification of the treaty is Mary Milling Lepper, *Foreign Policy Formulation: A Case Study of the Nuclear Test Ban Treaty of 1963* (Columbus, 1971). For a useful chronology of events surrounding the negotiations see Lester Sobel, *Disarmament and Nuclear Tests, 1960-1963* (New York, 1964).

U.S. attempts to deal with problems in the Congo during the early 1960s are examined in detail by Stephen Weissman, *American Policy in the Congo, 1960-1964* (Ithaca, 1974). American relations with Latin America focused on the Alliance for Progress, which is analyzed in Jerome Levinson and Juan de Oris, *The Alliance That Lost Its Way: A Critical Report on the Alliance for Progress* (Chicago, 1970).

U.S. problems with its allies are examined carefully by Henry A. Kissinger, *The. Troubled Partnership: A Reappraisal of the Atlantic Alliance* (New York, 1965) and by Richard Neustadt, *Alliance Politics* (New York, 1970). An excellent description and analysis of U.S. relations with its closest ally, Great Britain, is David Nunnerly, *President Kennedy and Britain* (New York, 1972).

A large body of literature traces the growing U.S. commitment in Vietnam. Most useful is David Halberstam, *The Best and the Brightest* (New York, 1972), an opinionated study that focuses on the role of American leaders in the struggle. *The Pentagon Papers* are invaluable in tracing U.S. involvement in Southeast Asia but are often difficult to use because of their poor organization. For a readable account based on *The Pentagon Papers* see Ralph Stavins, et al, *Washington Plans an Aggressive War* (New York, 1971), which attacks American leadership during this period. An excellent chronology of the events in Southeast Asia is John Galloway, *The Kennedys and Vietnam* (New York, 1971).

General Works

Attwood, William, *The Reds and the Blacks* (New York, 1967). Guinea.

Barnet, Richard J., *Intervention and Revolution* (New York, 1968).

Bohlen, Charles E., *The Transformation of American Foreign Policy* (New York, 1969).

Bowles, Chester, *Promises to Keep* (New York, 1971).

Brown, Seyom, *The Faces of Power: Consistency and Change in United States Foreign Policy from Truman to Johnson* (New York, 1968).

Bundy, McGeorge, "The Presidency and the Peace," *Foreign Affairs* (April, 1964).

Carey, Robert O., *The Peace Corps* (New York, 1970).

Cochen, Bert, *Adlai Stevenson* (New York, 1969).

Davis, Kenneth Sydney, *The Politics of Honor* (New York, 1967). Adlai Stevenson.

Destler, I. M., *Presidents, Bureaucrats, and Foreign Policy: The Politics of Or-ganizational Reform* (Princeton, 1972).

Draper, Theodore, *Abuse of Power* (New York, 1967).

Emerson, Rupert, *Africa and United States Policy* (Englewood Cliffs, 1967).

Fairlie, Henry, "A Cheer for American Imperialism," *The New York Times Magazine,* (July 11, 1965).

Feis, Herbert, *Foreign Aid and Foreign Policy* (New York, 1964).

——, *The Arrogance of Power* (New York, 1967).

——, *Old Myths and New Realities* (New York, 1964).

Fulbright, J. William, *Prospects for the West* (Cambridge, Mass., 1963).

Galbraith, John Kenneth, *Ambassador's Journal: A Personal Account of the Kennedy Years* (Boston, 1969).

Halle, Louis J., *The Cold War as History* (New York, 1967).

Hance, William A., ed., *Southern Africa and the United States* (New York, 1968).

Hartley, Anthony, "John Kennedy's Foreign Policy," *Foreign Policy* (Fall, 1971).

Hatch, Alden, *The Lodges of Massachusetts* (New York, 1973).

Hodgson, Godfrey, "The Establishment," *Foreign Policy* (Spring, 1973).

Horowitz, David, *The Free World Colossus* (New York, 1965).

Johnson, Haynes and Bernard M. Gwertzman, *Fulbright: The Dissenter* (New York, 1968).

Johnson, Richard A., *The Administration of United States Foreign Policy* (Austin, 1971).

Kateb, George, "Kennedy as Statesman," *Commentary* (June, 1966).

Kennan, George F., *Memoirs: 1960-1963* (Boston, 1972).

Kolko, Gabriel, *Roots of American Foreign Policy* (Boston, 1969).

Leuchtenburg, William, "President Kennedy and the End of the Postwar World," *The American Review* (Winter 1963).

Miller, William, *Henry Cabot Lodge* (New York, 1967).

Radosh, Ronald, *American Labor and United States Foreign Policy* (New York, 1970).

Rostow, Walt W., *View From the Seventh Floor* (New York, 1964).

Shriver, Sargent, *Point of the Lance* (New York, 1964).

Terchek, Ronald J., *The Making of the Test Ban Treaty* (The Hague, 1970).

Walton, Richard J., *The Remnants of Power: The Tragic Last Years of Adlai Stevenson* (New York, 1968).

Williams, G. Mennen, *Africa for the Africans* (Grand Rapids, 1969).

Windmiller, Marshall, *The Peace Corps and Pax Americana* (Washington, 1970).

Asia

Barnet, Richard J., *Roots of War* (New York, 1972). Origins of Vietnam War.

Bator, Victor, *Vietnam: A Diplomatic Tragedy: The Origins of the United States Involvement* (Dobbs Ferry, 1965).

Chomsky, Noam, *American Power and the New Mandarins* (New York, 1967). Vietnam.

Critchfield, Richard, *The Long Charade:* *Political Subversions in the Vietnam War* (New York, 1968).

Dommen, Arthur J., *Conflict in Laos* (New York, 1971).

Fall, Bernard B., and Roger Smith, eds., *Anatomy of a Crisis: The Laotian Crisis of 1960-1961* (Garden City, 1969).

Fitzgerald, Frances, *Fire in the Lake: The Vietnamese and the Americans in Vietnam* (Boston, 1972).

Gettleman, Marvin E. and Susan, and Kaplan, Lawrence and Carol, *Conflict in Indochina* (New York, 1970).

Goldstein, Martin, *American Policy Toward Laos* (Rutherford, 1973).

Halberstam, David, *The Making of a Quagmire* (New York, 1964).

Hurley, Robert Michael, "President John F. Kennedy and Vietnam, 1961-1963," unpublished doctoral dissertation, University of Hawaii, 1970.

Kahin, George M., and John W. Lewis, *The United States in Vietnam* (New York, 1967).

Lacouture, Jean, *Vietnam: Between Two Truces* (New York, 1966).

Lansdale, Edward G., *In the Midst of Wars: An American's Mission to Southeast Asia* (New York, 1972).

Shaplen, Robert, *The Lost Revolution: The U.S. in Vietnam, 1946-1966* (New York, 1966).

Steele, A. T., *The American People and China* (New York, 1966).

Stevenson, Charles A., *The End of Nowhere, American Policy Toward Laos Since 1954* (Boston, 1972).

Toye, Hugh, *Laos: Buffer State or Battle Ground* (New York, 1968).

Europe and the Cold War

Burns, Eedson L. M., *A Seat at the Table* (Toronto, 1972). Nuclear test ban discussions.

Dean, Arthur, *Test Ban and Disarmament: The Path of Negotiation* (New York, 1966).

Harriman, W. Averell, *America and Russia in a Changing World* (Garden City, 1971).

Jacobson, Harold D., *Diplomats, Scientists*

and Politicians (Ann Arbor, 1966). Nuclear policy.

LaFeber, Walter, America, Russia, and The Cold War, 1945-1971 (New York, 1967).

Moulton, Harland B., From Superiority to Parity: The United States and the Strategic Arms Race, 1961-1971 (Westport, 1972).

Newhouse, John, De Gaulle and the Anglo-Saxons (New York, 1970).

Planck, Charles R., The Changing Status of German Reunification in Western Diplomacy, 1955-1966 (Baltimore, 1967).

Slusser, Robert M., The Berlin Crisis of 1961 (Baltimore, 1973).

Tatu, Michel, Power in the Kremlin: From Krushchev to Kosygin (New York, 1969).

Whiteside, Henry O., "Kennedy and the Kremlin: Soviet-American Relations, 1961-1963," unpublished doctoral dissertation, Stanford University, 1969.

Latin America

Abel, Elie, The Missile Crisis (New York, 1966).

Berle, Adolf A., Jr., Latin America: Diplomacy and Reality (New York, 1962).

Bonsal, Philip W., Cuba, Castro and the United States (Pittsburgh, 1971).

Burr, Robert N., Our Troubled Hemisphere: Perspectives on United States-Latin American Relations (Washington, 1967).

Chayes, Abram, The Cuban Missile Crisis: International Crises and the Rule of Law (New York, 1973).

Crane, Robert, "The Cuban Missile Crisis: A Strategic Analysis of American and Soviet Policy," Orbis (Winter, 1963).

Dewart, Leslie, "The Cuban Missile Crisis Revisited," Studies on the Left (Spring, 1965).

Fall, Bernard B., Anatomy of a Crisis (Garden City, 1969).

George, Alexander, "The Cuban Missile Crisis, 1962," in Alexander George, et al, The Limits of Coercive Democracy (Boston, 1971).

Larson, David L., ed., The "Cuban Crisis" of 1962 (Boston, 1963).

Levinson, Jerome, and Juan de Onis, The

Alliance that Lost its Way: A Critical Report on the Alliance for Progress (Chicago, 1970).

Lewis, Gordon K., Puerto Rico: Freedom and Power in the Caribbean (New York, 1963).

Lowenthal, Abraham P., "Alliance Rhetoric Versus Latin America Reality," Foreign Affairs (April, 1970).

Martin, John Bartlow, Overtaken by Events: The Dominican Crisis from the Fall of Trujillo to the Civil War (Garden City, 1966).

Mezerik, A. G., Cuba and the United States (New York, 1963).

McClellan, Grant S., ed., U.S. Policy in Latin America (New York, 1963).

Morrison, DeLesseps S., Latin American Mission: An Adventure in Hemisphere Diplomacy (New York, 1965).

Rogers, William D., The Twilight Struggle: The Alliance for Progress and the Politics of Development in Latin America (New York, 1967).

Thomas, Hugh, Cuba: The Pursuit of Freedom (New York, 1971).

Walton, Richard J., The United States and Latin America (New York, 1972).

Wells, Henry, The Modernization of Puerto Rico: A Political Study of Changing Values and Institutions (Cambridge, Mass., 1969).

Williams, William Appleman, The United States, Cuba, and Castro (New York, 1962).

The Central Intelligence Agency

Agee, Philip, Inside the Company: CIA Diary (New York, 1975).

Berman, Jerry J., and Morton H. Halperin, eds., The Abuses of the Intelligence Agencies (Washington, 1975).

Dulles, Allen W., The Craft of Intelligence (New York, 1963).

Marchetti, Victor, and John D. Marks, The CIA and the Cult of Intelligence (New York, 1974).

U.S. Commission on CIA Activities within the United States, Report to the President by the Commission on CIA Activities within the United States (Washington, 1975).

U.S. Senate, Select Committee on Intelligence Activities, *Alleged Assassination Plots Involving Foreign Leaders* (Washington, 1975).

————, *Intelligence Activities and the Rights of Americans* (Washington, 1976).

Wise, David, and Thomas B. Ross, *The Invisible Government* (New York, 1964).

DEFENSE

During the Kennedy years the Pentagon was dominated by the presence of Robert S. McNamara. The definitive work on McNamara is yet to be written, but Henry Trewhitt, *McNamara: His Ordeal in the Pentagon* (New York, 1971) is a useful and readable study. Of more limited interest are William F. Kaufmann, *The McNamara Strategy* (New York, 1964) and James F. Roherty, *Decisions of Robert S. McNamara* (New York, 1964). In *Congress and the Nation: 1945-1964* (Washington, 1965), the staff of the *Congressional Quarterly* has compiled a good detailed summary of McNamara's policies under Kennedy.

A number of useful works are devoted to specific controversies involving the Defense Department. The best study of the TFX controversy is Robert J. Art, *The TFX Decision: McNamara and the Military* (Boston, 1968). The "missile gap" was an important campaign issue in 1960 and is dealt with in Edgar Bottome, *The Missile Gap: A Study of the Formation of Military and Political Policy* (Rutherford, 1971). For reasons of economy and efficiency, McNamara ordered the Army, Navy and Air Force to cooperate in the research, development and procurement of new weapons. This policy created tensions within the Pentagon and is the subject of a study by Demetrios Caraley, *The Politics of Military Unification: A Study of Conflict and the Policy Process* (New York, 1966). Martha Derthick, in *The National Guard in Politics* (Cambridge, Mass., 1971), explains why McNamara was unable to merge the National Guard with the Reserves.

In his 1961 farewell address President Dwight D. Eisenhower warned against the growth of the "military-industrial complex . . . the conjunction of an immense military establishment and a large arms industry." The dangers of the "military-industrial complex" became the theme of a vast literature critical of the Pentagon. A good starting point in this area is Marcus G. Raskin, "The Kennedy Hawks Assume Power from the Eisenhower Vultures," in Leonard S. Rodberg and Derek Shearer, eds., *The Pentagon Watchers: Students Report on the National Security* (New York, 1970). Seymour Melman, a Columbia University engineering professor, became a conspicuous critic of defense spending. His study, *Our Depleted Society* (New York, 1965), was an important contribution to the literature. Other indictments of the Pentagon include Tristram Coffin, *The Armed Society: Militarism in Modern America* (Baltimore, 1964); Seymour Hersh, *Chemical and Biological Warfare* (Garden City, 1969); and Clark R. Mollenhoff, *The Pentagon* (New York, 1967).

Other Works

Borklund, C. W., *The Department of Defense* (New York, 1968).

————, *Men of the Pentagon: From Forrestal to McNamara* (New York, 1966).

Davis, Vincent, *The Admirals Lobby* (Chapel Hill, 1967).

Fitzgerald, Frances, *Fire in the Lake* (Boston, 1972).

Gilpin, Robert, *American Scientists and Nuclear Weapons Policy* (Princeton, 1962).

Glines, Carroll, V., Jr., *The Compact History of the United States Air Force* (New York, 1973).

Hammond, Paul Y., *Organizing for Defense: The American Military Establishment in the Twentieth Century* (Princeton, 1961).

Huntington, Samuel P., *The Common Defense: Strategic Programs in National Politics* (New York, 1961).

Landsdale, Edward G., *In the Midst of Wars: An American's Mission to Southeast Asia* (New York, 1972).

LeMay, Curtis E., with MacKinlay Kantor, *Mission with LeMay: My Story* (New York, 1965).

Lowe, George E., *The Age of Deterrence* (Boston, 1964).

Lyons, Gene, *Schools for Strategy: Education and Research in National Security Affairs* (New York, 1965).

McCahill, William P., *The Marine Corps Reserve: A History* (Washington, 1966).

Moulton, Harland B., *From Superiority to Parity: The United States and the Strategic Arms Race, 1961-71* (Westport, 1973).

Schwarz, Urs, *American Strategy: A New Perspective* (Garden City, 1966).

Schwiebert, Ernest G., *A History of Air Force Ballistic Missiles* (New York, 1965).

Smith, Bruce L. R., *The Rand Corporation: Case Study of A Nonprofit Advisory Agency* (Cambridge, Mass., 1966).

Taylor, Maxwell G., *Swords and Plowshares* (New York, 1972).

Twining, Nathan F., *Neither Liberty nor Safety: A Hard Look at U.S. Military Policy and Strategy* (New York, 1966).

Weigley, Russell F., *History of the United States Army* (New York, 1967).

Yarmolinsky, Adam, *The Military Establishment: Its Impact on American Society* (New York, 1971).

SPACE

Kennedy's commitment to a manned lunar landing by 1970 was greeted with a general enthusiasm reflected in Jay Holmes, *America on the Moon: the Enterprise of the Sixties* (Philadelphia, 1962) and Richard S. Lewis, *Appointment on the Moon* (New York, 1968). John M. Logsdon, *The Decision to Go to the Moon: Project Apollo and the National Interest* (Cambridge, Mass., 1970) is a detailed examination of the early internal politics of NASA and Kennedy's decision to assign a high priority to the space program. The technical risks imposed by Kennedy's timetable are described in Hugo Young, Bryan Silcock and Peter Dunn, *Journey to Tranquility: The Long Competitive Struggle to Reach the Moon* (Garden City, 1969), which also disputes the social and scientific value of the costly project.

Other Works

Emme, Eugene M., ed., *The History of Rocket Technology: Essays on Research, Development and Utility* (Detroit, 1964).

Etzioni, Amitai, *The Moondoggle* (New York, 1964).

Green, Constance McLaughlin, and Milton Lomask, *Vanguard: A History* (Washington, 1971).

Hayes, E. Nelson, *Trackers of the Skies* (Cambridge, Mass., 1968).

Kennan, Erland, and Edmund H. Harvey Jr., *Mission to the Moon: A Critical Examination of NASA and the Space Program* (New York, 1969).

Shelton, William, *American Space Exploration: The First Decade* (Boston, 1967).

Schwiebert, Ernest G., et al, *A History of the U.S. Air Force Ballistic Missiles* (New York, 1965).

Sobel, Lester A., *Space: From Sputnik to Gemini* (New York, 1965).

Swenson, Loyd S., Jr., et al, *The New Ocean: A History of Project Mercury* (Washington, 1966).

Van Dyke, Vernon, *Pride and Power: The Rationale of the Space Program* (Urbana, 1964).

BUSINESS, LABOR AND ECONOMIC POLICY

The literature on national economic policy during the Kennedy Administration is not as ample as that dealing with foreign affairs or the military. Hobart Rowen, *The Free Enterprisers: Kennedy, Johnson and the Business Community* (New York, 1964) is an incisive and readable account by an economic journalist. Rowen emphasizes the conservative nature of Kennedy policy and strongly disputes characterizations of Kennedy as "anti-business." *The Economics of the Kennedy Years* (New York, 1964), by Seymour E. Harris, is an analysis by a prominent liberal economist who worked in the Treasury Department as an adviser to C. Douglas Dillon. Walter W. Heller, *New Dimensions of Political Economy* (New York, 1966) and James Tobin, *National Economic Policy* (New Haven, 1966) are important discussions of the Keynesian approach by key members of the Kennedy economic policymaking team. *Economics on a New Frontier* (Belmont, 1968), by E. Ray Canterbery, is a valuable study by an economist of Kennedy-Johnson economic policy. It is one of the few overviews of Democratic economic policy of the 1960s. Jim F. Heath, *John F. Kennedy and the Business Community* (Chicago, 1969) is a brief, scholarly study, limited in intent but containing useful references and bibliography.

Other Works

Aubrey, Henry C., *The Dollar in World Affairs* (New York, 1964).

Baldwin, David A., *Economic Development and American Foreign Policy, 1943-1962* (Chicago, 1966).

Barber, Richard J., *The Politics of Research* (Washington, 1966).

Bauer, Raymond A., Ithiel de Sola Pool and Lewis A. Dexter, *American Business and Public Policy: The Politics of Foreign Trade* (New York, 1963).

Benoit, Emile, and Kenneth Boulding, eds., *Disarmament and the Economy* (New York, 1963).

Berle, Adolf A., Jr., *The American Economic Republic* (New York, 1963).

Blough, Roger, *The Washington Embrace of Business* (New York, 1976).

———, "My Side of the Steel Price Story," *Look*, (Jan. 29, 1963).

Bolton, Roger E., *Defense Purchases and Regional Growth* (Washington, 1966).

Cary, William L., *Politics and the Regulatory Agencies* (New York, 1967).

Cheit, Earl F., ed., *The Business Establishment* (New York, 1964).

Cherington, Paul W., and Ralph L. Gillen, *The Business Representative in Washington* (Washington, 1962).

Coffin, Frank M., *Witness for Aid* (Boston, 1964).

Cormier, Frank, and William J. Eaton, *Reuther* (Englewood Cliffs, 1970).

Deaken, James, *The Lobbyists* (Washington, 1966).

Dillon, Conley H., *The Area Redevelopment Administration* (College Park, 1964).

Flash, Edward S., Jr., *Economic Advice and Presidential Leadership* (New York, 1965).

Galbraith, John Kenneth, *The New Industrial State* (New York, 1967).

Galligan, David J., *Politics and the Businessman* (New York, 1964).

Gerber, Albert B., *Bashful Billionaire* (New

York, 1967). Howard Hughes.

Goulden, Joseph C., *Meany: The Unchallenged Strongman of American Labor* (New York, 1972).

Hall, Burton H., ed., *Autocracy and Insurgency in Organized Labor* (New Brunswick, 1972).

Harris, Seymour, *The Economics of Political Parties* (New York, 1962).

Herling, John, *Right to Challenge: People and Power in the Steelworkers Union* (New York, 1972).

Hoopes, Roy, *The Steel Crisis* (New York, 1963).

James, Ralph C. and Estelle, *James Hoffa and the Teamsters: A Study of Union Power* (Princeton, 1965).

Kaplan, A. D. H., *Big Enterprise in a Competitive System* (Washington, 1964).

Kutz, Meyer, *Rockefeller Power* (New York, 1974).

Larrowe, Charles P., *Harry Bridges, The Rise and Fall of Radical Labor in the United States* (New York, 1972).

Levitan, Sar A., *Federal Aid to Depressed Areas* (Baltimore, 1964).

Lewis, Wilfred, Jr., *Federal Fiscal Policy in the Postwar Recessions* (Washington, 1962).

McConnell, Grant, *Private Power and American Democracy* (New York, 1966).

————. *Steel and the Presidency—1962* (New York, 1963).

McDonald, David J., *Union Man* (New York, 1969).

McGuiness, Kenneth C., *The New Frontier NLRB* (Washington, 1963).

Metzger, Stanley D., *Trade Agreements and the Kennedy Round* (Fairfax, 1964).

Monsen, R. Joseph, Jr., *Modern American Capitalism: Ideologies and Issues* (Boston, 1963).

Nossiter, Bernard, *The Mythmakers* (Boston, 1964).

Reagan, Michael, *The Managed Economy* (New York, 1963).

Sampson, Anthony, *The Sovereign State of ITT* (New York, 1973).

Sobel, Robert, *The Age of Giant Corporations* (New York, 1972).

Stern, Philip M., *The Great Treasury Raid* (New York, 1964).

Triffin, Robert, *Gold and the Dollar Crisis* (New Haven, 1961).

Whittemore, L. H., *The Man Who Ran the Subways: The Story of Mike Quill* (New York, 1968).

Widick, B. J., *Labor Today* (New York, 1964).

White, Lawrence J., *The Automobile Industry since 1945* (Cambridge, Mass., 1971).

CIVIL RIGHTS

Elizabeth W. Miller, *The Negro in America* (Cambridge, Mass., 1970) is a topically organized bibliography. James M. McPherson, et al, *Blacks in America* (Garden City, 1971) contains bibliographic essays on the periods of black history, including a chapter on the 1954-1970 era. Victor Navasky, *Kennedy Justice* (New York, 1971) is a critical study of Robert Kennedy as Attorney General and contains considerable information on civil rights. The Justice Department's own point of view is provided in Burke Marshall, *Federalism and Civil Rights* (New York, 1964). *The Warren Court* (Cambridge, Mass., 1968), by Archibald Cox, includes a good discussion of the Supreme Court's decisions in civil rights cases of the 1960s. Another scholarly evaluation of the court focusing on the individual high court judges is found in Leon Friedman and Fred L. Israel, eds., *The Justices of the United States Supreme Court, 1789-1969* (New York, 1969).

David Lewis, *King: A Critical Biography* (New York, 1970) is the best biography of Martin Luther King. Thomas R. Brooks, *Walls Come Tumbling Down: A History of the Civil Rights Movement, 1940-1970* (Englewood Cliffs, 1974) is a useful survey of the recent era. Howard Zinn, *SNCC, the New Abolitionists* (Boston,

1965) and August Meier and Elliott Rudwick, *CORE: A Study in the Civil Rights Movement, 1942-1968* (New York, 1973) examine two of the most important movement organizations in the early 1960s. Lester A. Sobel, *Civil Rights, 1960-1966* (New York, 1967) is a good chronology of important events in the civil rights movement.

Other Works

Anderson, Jervis, *A. Philip Randolph* (New York, 1973).

Baldwin, James, *The Fire Next Time* (New York, 1963).

Black, Earl, *Southern Governors and Civil Rights* (Cambridge, Mass., 1976).

Bland, Randall, W., *Private Pressure on Public Law: The Legal Career of Justice Thurgood Marshall* (Port Washington, 1973).

Brauer, Carl M., "The Kennedy Administration and Civil Rights," unpublished Ph.D. dissertation, Harvard University, 1973.

Dulles, Foster Rhea, *The Civil Rights Commission: 1957-1965* (East Lansing, 1968).

Forman, James, *The Making of Black Revolutionaries* (New York, 1972).

Lewis, Anthony, et al, *Portrait of a Decade: The Second American Revolution* (New York, 1964).

Lincoln, C. Eric., *The Black Muslims in America* (Boston, 1961).

Lord, Walter, *The Past That Would Not Die* (New York, 1975). On the integration crisis at the University of Mississippi.

Malcolm X and Alex Haley, *Autobiography of Malcolm X* (New York, 1965).

Muse, Benjamin, *The American Negro Revolution: From Non-Violence to Black Power, 1963-1967* (Bloomington, 1968).

Muse, Benjamin, *Ten Years of Prelude: The Story of Integration Since the Supreme Court's 1964 Decision* (New York, 1964).

Parris, Guichard, and Lester Brooks, *Blacks in the City: A History of the National Urban League* (Boston, 1971).

Parsons, Talcott, and Kenneth B. Clark, eds., *The Negro American* (Boston, 1966).

Peck, James, *Freedom Ride* (New York, 1962).

Rustin, Bayard, *Down the Line* (New York, 1971).

Silverman, Charles, *Crisis in Black and White* (New York, 1964).

Warren, Robert Penn, *Who Speaks for the Negro?* (New York, 1966).

Wolk, Allan, *The Presidency and Black Civil Rights: Eisenhower to Nixon* (Rutherford, 1971).

SOCIAL MOVEMENTS AND POLITICAL THOUGHT

Two good studies of the relationship between American intellectuals and politics in the early 1960s are Ronald Berman, *America in the 60's, an Intellectual History* (New York, 1968) and Irwin Unger, *The Movement: A History of the American New Left, 1959-1972* (New York, 1974). The best history of an early new left organization is Kirkpatrick Sale, *SDS* (New York, 1973). The John Birch Society and other right-wing organizations are critically examined in Benjamin R. Epstein and Arnold Forster, *Danger on the Right* (New York, 1964). Daniel Bell, ed., *The Radical Right* (Garden City, 1963) contains essays offering historical, sociological and psychological explanations for the appearance of new forms of ultra-conservative thought in the early 1960s.

Other Works

Bacciocco, Edward J., Jr., *The New Left in America: Reform to Revolution, 1956-1970* (Stanford, 1974).

Bell, Daniel, *The End of Ideology* (New York, 1961).

Bottomore, T. B., *Critics of Society, Radical Thought in North America* (New York, 1966).

Clecak, Peter, *Radical Paradoxes: Dilemmas of the American Left, 1945-1970* (New York, 1974).

Diggins, John P., *Up from Communism, Conservative Odysseys in American Intellectual History* (New York, 1975).

Friedan, Betty, *The Feminine Mystique* (New York, 1963).

Harrington, Michael, *Fragments of the Century: A Social Autobiography* (New York, 1973).

Harrington, Michael, *The Other America* (New York, 1962).

Hentoff, Nat, *Peace Agitator: The Story of A. J. Muste* (New York, 1963).

Hofstadter, Richard, *The Paranoid Style in American Politics and other Essays* (New York, 1965).

Goodman, Paul, *Growing Up Absurd: Problems of Youth in the Organized System* (New York, 1960).

———, *Utopian Essays and Practical Proposals* (New York, 1964).

Jacobs, Paul, and Saul Landau, *The New Radicals* (New York, 1966).

Kerr, Clark, *The Uses of the University* (Cambridge, Mass., 1963).

Lasch, Christopher, *The Agony of the American Left* (New York, 1969).

———, *The New Radicalism in America, 1889-1963: The Intellectual as a Social Type* (New York, 1965).

Newfield, Jack, *A Prophetic Minority* (New York, 1966).

O'Brien, James Putnam, "The Development of a New Left in the United States, 1960-1965," unpublished doctoral dissertation, University of Wisconsin, 1971.

Podhoretz, Norman, *Making It* (New York, 1968).

———, ed., *The Commentary Reader* (New York, 1966).

Thayer, George, *The Farther Shores of Politics* (New York, 1967).

Stone, I. F., *In a Time of Torment* (New York, 1967).

MEDIA

The best study of the most influential newspaper of the 1960s is Gay Talese's investigation of the *New York Times: The Kingdom and the Power* (New York, 1966). W. A. Swanberg has written an equally critical account of *Luce and his Empire* (New York, 1972). An excellent history of television in the 1960s is Erik Barnouw, *The Image Empire* (New York, 1970). Newton Minow, *Equal Time* (New York, 1965) is an account of government broadcast policy during the Kennedy years.

Other Works

Arlen, Michael J., *The Living Room War* (New York, 1969).

Aronson, James, *The Press and the Cold War* (Indianapolis, 1970).

Barnouw, Erik, *The Golden Web: A History of Broadcasting in the United States* (New York, 1968).

Brown, Les, *Television: The Business Behind the Box* (New York, 1971).

Bliss, Edward, Jr., ed., *In Search of Light: The Broadcasts of Edward R. Murrow, 1938-1961* (New York, 1967).

Boorstin, Daniel J., *The Image: A Guide to Pseudo-Events in America* (New York, 1961).

Cash, Kevin, *Who the hell is William Loeb?* (Manchester, 1975).

Catledge, Turner, *My Life and the Times* (New York, 1971).

Lippmann, Walter, *Conversations with Walter Lippmann* (New York, 1960).

Crouse, Timothy, *The Boys on the Bus* (New York, 1972).

Epstein, Edward Jay, *News from Nowhere: Television and the News* (New York, 1973).

Fixx, James F., ed., *The Mass Media and Politics* (New York, 1972).

Hilliard, Robert L., *Understanding Television: An Introduction to Broadcasting* (New York, 1964).

Kendrick, Alexander, *Prime Time: The Life of Edward R. Murrow* (Boston, 1969).

Krock, Arthur, *Sixty Years on the Firing Line* (New York, 1968).

Lawrence, Bill, *Six Presidents, Too Many Wars* (New York, 1971).

Markmann, Charles Lam, *The Buckleys* (New York, 1973).

Metz, Robert, *CBS: Reflections in a Bloodshot Eye* (New York, 1970).

Michie, Allan A., *Voices Through the Iron Curtain: The Radio Free Europe Story* (New York, 1963).

Pilat, Oliver, *Drew Pearson* (New York, 1973).

Roberts, Chalmers M., *First Rough Draft: A Journalist's Journal of Our Times* (New York, 1973).

CAREER INDEX

The following is a list of individuals profiled in the Kennedy years according to their most important public activity. In some cases names appear under two or more categories.

House of Representatives

Albert, Carl (D, Okla.)
Alger, Bruce (R, Tex.)
Arends, Leslie C. (R, Ill.)
Aspinall, Wayne N. (D, Colo.)
Boggs, Hale (D, La.)
Bolling, Richard W. (D, Mo.)
Bonner, Herbert C. (D, N.C.)
Boykin, Frank W. (D, Ala.)
Brown, Clarence (R, Ohio)
Buckley, Charles A. (D, N.Y.)
Byrnes, John W. (R, Wisc.)
Cannon, Clarence (D, Mo.)
Celler, Emanuel (D, N.Y.)
Colmer, William M. (D, Miss.)
Cooley, Harold D. (D, N.C.)
Curtis, Thomas B. (R, Mo.)
Dawson, William L. (D, Ill.)
Delaney, James J. (D, N.Y.)
Findley, Paul (R, Ill.)
Ford, Gerald R., Jr. (R, Mich.)
Frelinghuysen, Peter, Jr. (R, N.J.)
Gonzales, Henry (D, Tex.)
Goodell, Charles E. (R, N.Y.)
Green, Edith (D, Ore.)

Green, William J., Jr. (D, Pa.)
Gross, H. R. (R, Iowa)
Halleck, Charles A. (R, Ind.)
Harris, Oren (D, Ark.)
Hebert, F. Edward (D, La.)
Holifield, Chet (D, Calif.)
Jennings, W. Pat (D, Va.)
Johnson, Thomas F. (D, Md.)
Judd, Walter H. (R, Minn.)
Keogh, Eugene J. (D, N.Y.)
King, Cecil (D, Calif.)
Laird, Melvin (R, Wisc.)
Landrum, Phil M. (D, Ga.)
Lindsay, John V. (R, N.Y.)
McCormack, John W. (D, Mass.)
McCulloch, William (R, Ohio)
McMillan, John C. (D, S.C.)
Mahon, George H. (D, Tex.)
Mathias, Charles (R, Md.)
Miller, George P. (D, Calif.)
Miller, William E. (R, N.Y.)
Mills, Wilbur D. (D, Ark.)
Morgan, Thomas E. (D, Pa.)
Moss, John E. (D, Calif.)
Mundt, Karl E. (R, N.D.)
Passman, Otto E. (D, La.)

Patman, Wright (D, Tex.)
Powell, Adam Clayton, Jr., (D, N.Y.)
Rayburn, Samuel T. (D, Tex.)
Reuss, Henry S. (D, Wisc.)
Rhodes, John (R, Ariz.)
Rooney, John J. (D, N.Y.)
Rousselot, John H. (D, Calif.)
Ryan, William F. (D, N.Y.)
Sikes, Robert L. F. (D, Fla.)
Smith, Howard W. (D, Va.)
Thomas, Albert (D, Tex.)
Thompson, Frank, Jr. (D, N.J.)
Vinson, Carl (D, Ga.)
Walters, Francis E. (D, Pa.)
Wiley, Alexander (R, Wisc.)
Williams, John B. (D, Miss.)
Wilson, Robert C. (R, Calif.)

Senate

Aiken, George D. (R, Vt.)
Allott, Gordon L. (R, Colo.)
Anderson, Clinton P. (D, N.M.)
Bartlett, Edward L. (D, Alaska)
Bayh, Birch E., Jr. (D, Ind.)
Bennett, Wallace F. (R, Utah)
Bible, Alan D. (D, Nev.)
Bridges, Styles (R, N.H.)
Burdick, Quentin (D, N.D.)
Bush, Prescott (R, Conn.)
Byrd, Harry F. (D, Va.)
Byrd, Robert C. (D, W. Va.)
Cannon, Howard W. (D, Nev.)
Capehart, Homer E. (R, Ind.)
Carroll, John A. (D, Colo.)
Case, Clifford P., Jr. (R, N.J.)
Case, Francis H. (R, S.D.)
Church, Frank (D, Ida.)
Clark, Joseph, Jr. (D, Pa.)
Cooper, John S. (D, Ky.)
Cotton, Norris (R, N.H.)
Curtis, Carl T. (R, Neb.)
Dirksen, Everett M. (R, Ill.)
Dodd, Thomas C. (D, Conn.)
Dominick, Peter H. (R, Colo.)
Douglas, Paul H. (D, Ill.)
Eastland, James O. (D, Miss.)
Ellender, Allen J. (D, La.)
Engle, Clair (R, Calif.)
Ervin, Sam J., Jr. (D, N.C.)
Fong, Hiram (R, Hawaii)
Fulbright, J. William (D, Ark.)
Goldwater, Barry M. (R, Ariz.)
Gore, Albert A. (D, Tenn.)
Gruening, Ernest (D, Alaska)

Hart, Philip A. (D, Mich.)
Hartke, Vance (D, Ind.)
Hayden, Carl (D, Ariz.)
Hickenlooper, Bourke B. (R, Iowa)
Hill, Lister (D, Ala.)
Holland, Spessard L. (D, Fla.)
Hruska, Roman L. (R, Neb.)
Humphrey, Hubert H. (D, Minn.)
Jackson, Henry M. (D, Wash.)
Javits, Jacob K. (R, N.Y.)
Johnston, Olin D. (D, S.C.)
Jordan, B. Everett (D, N.C.)
Keating, Kenneth B. (R, N.Y.)
Kefauver, Estes (D, Tenn.)
Kennedy, Edward M. (D, Mass.)
Kerr, Robert S. (D, Okla.)
Kuchel, Thomas W. (R, Calif.)
Lausche, Frank J., (D, Ohio)
Long, Edward V. (D, Mo.)
Long, Oren E. (D, Hawaii)
Long, Russell B. (D, La.)
McCarthy, Eugene J. (D, Minn.)
McClellan, John J. (D, Ark.)
McGee, Gale W. (D, Wyo.)
McGovern, George S. (D, S.D.)
McIntyre, Thomas J. (D, N.H.)
McNamara, Patrick V. (D, Mich.)
Magnuson, Warren G. (D, Wash.)
Mansfield, Mike (D, Mont.)
Metcalf, Lee (D, Mont.)
Monroney, A. S. (D, Okla.)
Morse, Wayne L. (D, Ore.)
Morton, Thruston B. (R, Ky.)
Moss, Frank E. (D, Utah)
Muskie, Edmund S. (D, Me.)
Nelson, Gaylord (D, Wisc.)
Neuberger, Maurine B. (D, Ore.)
Pastore, John O. (D, R.I.)
Pell, Claiborne (D, R.I.)
Proxmire, William (D, Wisc.)
Randolph, Jennings (D, W. Va.)
Robertson, A. Willis (D, Va.)
Russell, Richard B. (D, Ga.)
Saltonstall, Leverett (R, Mass.)
Scott, Hugh D., Jr. (R, Pa.)
Smathers, George A. (D, Fla.)
Smith, Margaret Chase (R, Me.)
Sparkman, John J. (D, Ala.)
Stennis, John (D, Miss.)
Symington, Stuart, III (D, Mo.)
Talmadge, Herman E. (D, Ga.)
Thurmond, Strom (D, S.C.)
Tower, John G. (R, Tex.)
Williams, Harrison A., Jr. (D, N.J.)
Williams, John J. (R, Del.)
Yarborough, Ralph (D, Tex.)
Young, Milton R. (R, N.D.)
Young, Stephen M. (D, Ohio)

Greenberg, Jack
Harrington, Michael
Henry, Aaron E.
Hill, Herbert
King, Martin Luther, Jr.
Lewis, John
Malcolm X
Moses, Robert Parris
Meredith, James
Mitchell, Clarence
Muste, A. J.
Randolph, A. Philip
Richardson, Gloria
Rustin, Bayard
Shuttlesworth, Fred
Thomas, Norman
Walker, Wyatt
Wilkins, Roy
Wilson, Dagmar
Young, Whitney M., Jr.

Journalists, Academics, Churchmen

Alsop, Joseph
Alsop, Stewart
Arendt, Hannah
Barghoorn, Frederick C.
Bell, Daniel
Blake, Eugene C.
Brinkley, David
Buckley, William F., Jr.
Burns, James M.
Cousins, Norman
Cronkite, Walter
Eisenhower, Milton S.
Goldmann, Nahum
Goodman, Paul
Graham, Billy
Graham, Philip
Halberstam, David
Harrington, Michael
Hesburgh, Theodore M.
Hughes, A. Stuart
Huntley, Chet
Hutchins, Robert
Jacobs, Jane
Kahn, Herman

Kerr, Clark
Keyserling, Leon
Lippmann, Walter
Loeb, William
Luce, Henry
Mailer, Norman
Mills, C. Wright
Neustadt, Richard
Niebuhr, Reinhold
Pauling, Linus C.
Pearson, Drew
Pike, James A.
Podhoretz, Norman
Reston, James
Samuelson, Paul E.
Scali, John
Spellman, Francis Cardinal
Stone, I. F.
Sulzberger, Arthur Ochs
White, Theodore

National Politics, Organizations and Issues

Annis, Edward R.
Bailey, John M.
Baker, Robert G.
Brower, David
Clifford, Clark
Eisenhower, Dwight D.
Estes, Billie Sol
Hall, Gus
Harris, Louis
Humphrey, George M.
Kennedy, Joseph, Sr.
Larson, Leonard W.
McCloskey, Matthew
Nixon, Richard M.
Oswald, Lee Harvey
Patton, James
Rauh, Joseph, Jr.
Rockwell, George Lincoln
Schwarz, Fred C.
Shuman, Charles B.
Sinatra, Frank
Truman, Harry S
Welch, Robert H. W., Jr.

Index

A

GO Tell it On the Mountain (book)—19

GOULART, President Joao—190, 353

GRAHAM, Billy—Profile 193

GRAHAM, Philip—Profile 193-194

GREAT Britain—See UNITED Kingdom

GREATHOUSE, Pat—428

GREECE—83, 354, 444

GREEN, Rep. Edith—Profile 194-195

GREEN, Sen. Theodore—407

GREEN, Rep. William—Profile 195; 119, 299

GREENBERG, Jack—Profile 195-196; 355

GREENSBORO, N.C.—149

GREENWOOD, Miss.—157

GRIFFIN, Marvin—460

GRIFFIN, Rep. Robert—155, 185

GRISSOM, Virgil—178

GROMYKO, Andrei—21

GROSS, Rep. Harold—Profile 196

GROWING Up Absurd: Problems of Youth in the Organized System (book)—186, 410

GRUENING, Sen. Ernest—Profile 196-197; 310

GRUMMAN Corp.—532, 555

GUEVARA, Ernesto "Che"—187-188

GUN Control—125

H

HACKER, Andrew—245

HAGGERTY, Cornelius—Profile 198

HAITI—506

HALABY, Najeeb—Profile 198-199

HALBERSTAM, David—Profile 199-200; 9, 490

HALL, Gus—Profile 200-201

HALL, Joseph—218

HALL, Paul—Profile 201-202

HALLECK, Rep. Charles—Profile 202-203; 120, 155, 347, 429

HAMILTON, Fowler—Profile 204-205; 27

HAMMARSKJOLD, Dag—59, 99

HANE, Arthur—42

HANNA Co., M.A.—144, 239

HANSBERRY, Lorraine—19

HARKINS, Gen. Paul—Profile 205-206; 329

HARLAN, Justice John Marshall—Profile 206-208

HARRIMAN, Averell—Profile 208-210; and Forrestal 158; and Laos 54; Wm. Miller scores 358; and nuclear test ban treaty talks 112-113, 153, 160, 261, 272, 290, 338; and W. Sullivan 490; and Vietnam 21, 158-159, 225, 308

HARRINGTON, Michael—Profile 210-211; 245, 410

HARRIS, Louis—Profile 211-212

HARRIS, Rep. Oren—Profile 212-213; 367

HART, Sen. Philip—Profile 213-214

HARTKE, Sen. Vance—Profile 214

HARTSDALE, William—7

HARVEY, James—57

HATFIELD, Gov. Mark—Profile 214-215

HAYA de la Torre, Victor Raul—309

HAYDEN, Sen. Carl—Profile 215-216; 71

HAYDEN, Tom—360

HEAD Start, Project—185

HEALTH, Education and Welfare, Dept. of—1961 appropriations bill 6; Celebrezze appointed Secretary 79-80; Cohen appointed assistant secretary 91; and Kefauver drug bill 262-263; McMurrin appointed Commissioner of Education 332-333; Patton and 404; Proxmire opposes fund increase for 416; Ribicoff appointed Secretary of 270, 430-431; John J. Williams scores 543-544

HEALTH and Safety Legislation—13, 24; See also DRUGS, MEDICINE

HEBERT, Rep. F. Edward—Profile 216-217; 335, 408; 410

HELLER, Walter—Profile 217-219; and balance of payments 117; and economic policy 273, 350; and economic policy taskforce 459, 460; fiscal policy 116-118; 1962 legislative program 27; monetary policy 117-118; and steel price hike 180

HELLS River Canyon—83

HELMS, Richard—Profile 219-220; 111

HELSTEIN, Ralph—427

HENRY, Aaron—Profile 220-221; 375

HERTER, Christian—38

HESBURGH, Rev. Theodore—Profile 221-222

HICKENLOOPER, Sen. Bourke—Profile 222; 190, 347, 368, 369

HIGHER Education Facilities Act—91, 280

HIGH Point, N.C.—149

HIESTAND, Rep. Edgar—448

HILL, David I.—397-398

HILL, Herbert—Profile 222-224; 133

HILL, Sen. Lister—Profile 224-225

HILL, Ralph—18

HILSMAN, Roger—Profile 225-226; and Cuban missile crisis 463; on Diem regime 61, 158; and 1963 Vietnam Buddhist crisis 21, 210, 308; in State Department 44, 450, 452

HIROSHIMA Day Committee—381

HITCH, Charles—Profile 226-227; 335

HODGES, Luther—Profile 227-228; 100

HOEVEN, Rep. Charles—155, 185, 203

HOFFA, James—Profile 228-230; 276, 310; 417

HOLIFIELD, Rep. Chet—Profile 230

HOLLAND, Sen. Spessard—Profile 230-231

HOLLEMAN, Jerry R.—146; 223

HOLLIDAY, Raymond M.—237

HOLLINGS, Gov. Ernest—Profile 231-232; 255

HOLMES, Julius—543

HONOLULU, Hawaii—329

HOOVER, J. Edgar—Profile 232-235; 271, 276, 441; 526

HORNE, Lena—19

HOSTY, James—396

HOUBOULT, John C.—519

HOUSE of Representatives—and Federal Communications Commission reorganization 363; delays manpower development and training bill 179, votes expansion of the Rules Committee 249, 393, 476; Social Security increase 68, 361; acts on 1963 tax cut 362; passes Trade Expansion Act 362; and Administration welfare program 361.

Committees—Agriculture Committee 98, 152; Appropriations Committee 71, 432, 500; Appropriations Committee, Foreign Operations Subcommittee 155, 398-399, 429; Appropriations Committee, Independent Offices Subcommittee 500; Appropriations Committee, Subcommittee on the Departments of State, Justice and Commerce 440-441; Armed Services Committee 14, 216-217, 410, 517; Banking and Currency Committee 401, 425, 462; District of Columbia Committee 110, 331-332, 350, 543; Education and Labor Committee 79-80, 185, 365, 411, 412; Education and Labor Committee, Subcommittee on Integration in Federally Assisted Education 430; Foreign Affairs Committee 166, 368; Government Operations Committee 110; Interior and Insular Affairs Committee 15-16; Interstate and Foreign Commerce Committee 76, 212-213; Judiciary Committee: Celler and 81, Lindsay and 305, civil rights legislation 326, 350, 359, 365, 501; Judiciary Committee, Immigration and Nationality Subcommittee 526;

I

J

N

Y

Z